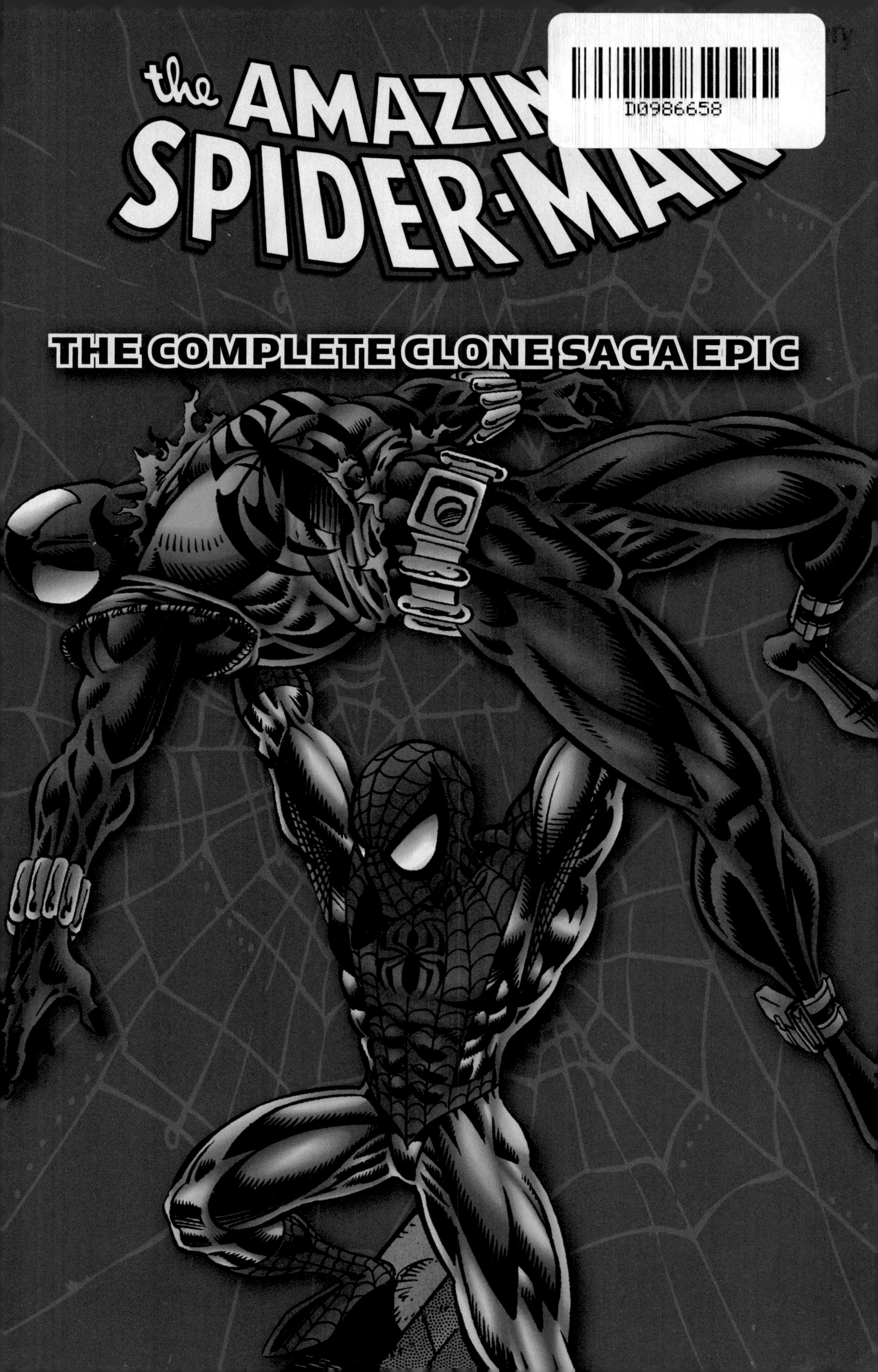
the AMAZIN
SPIDER-MAN
THE COMPLETE CLONE SAGA EPIC

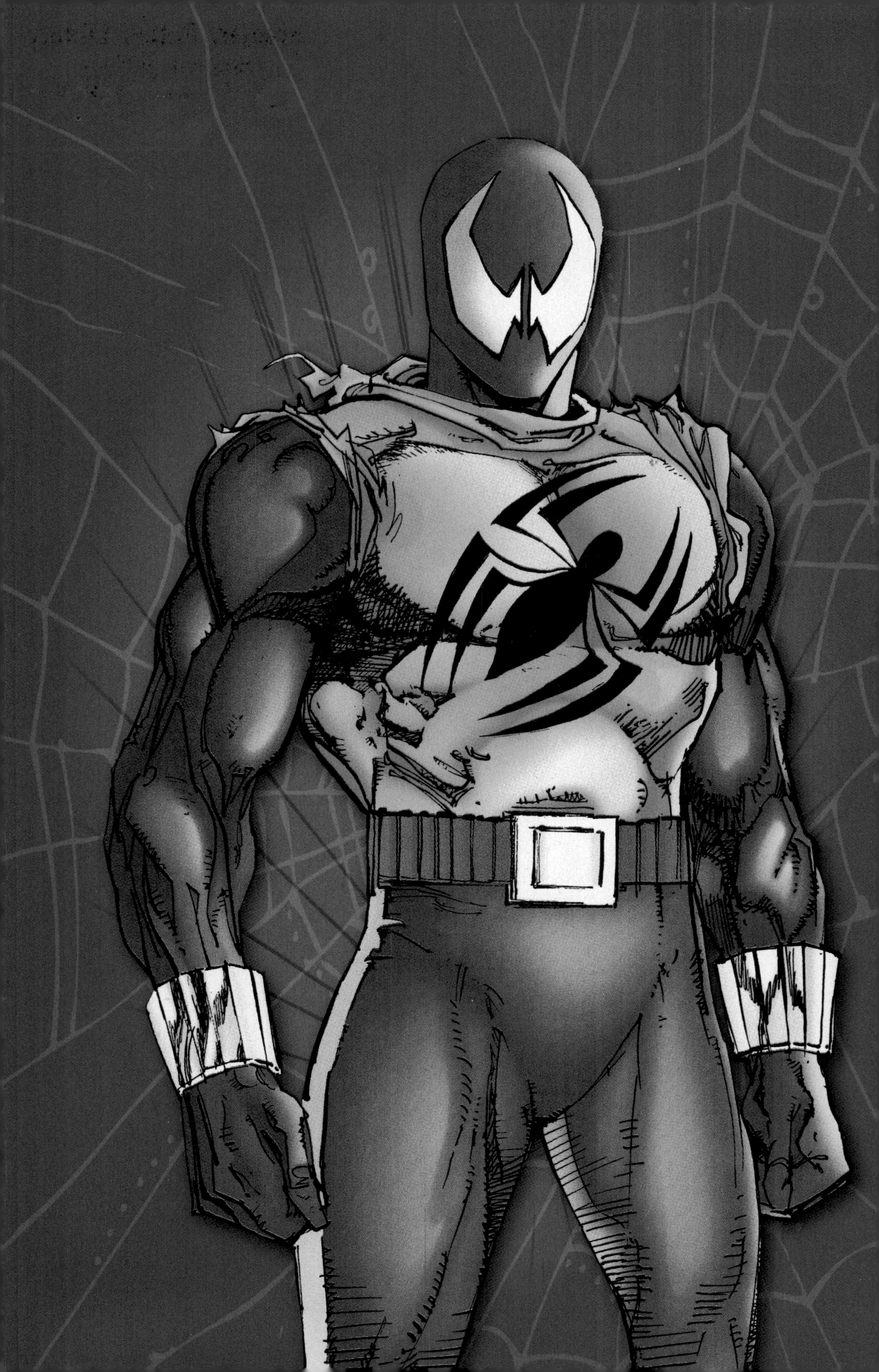

the AMAZING SPIDER-MAN

THE COMPLETE CLONE SAGA EPIC
BOOK 5

WRITERS
Tom DeFalco, J.M. DeMatteis,
Todd DeZago, Terry Kavanagh, Mike
Lackey, Howard Mackie, Tom Peyer,
Evan Skolnick & Mark Waid

PENCILERS
Claude St. Aubin, Pat Broderick,
Roy Burdine, Sal Buscema,
Steven Butler, Phil Gosier, Gil Kane,
Ken Lashley, Shawn McManus,
Angel Medina, Darick Robertson,
Roger Robinson, Tod Smith, Kevin West
& Patrick Zircher

INKERS
Greg Adams, Sal Buscema,
Ralph Cabrera, Tom Christopher,
Hector Collazo, Saleem Crawford,
Randy Emberlin, Chris Ivy,
Larry Mahlstedt, Shawn McManus,
Al Milgrom, John Nyberg, Tom Palmer,
Andrew Pepoy, Matt Robertson,
Vince Russell & Bill Sienkiewicz

COLORISTS
John Kalisz, Malibu, Clem Robins,
Joe Rosas, Bob Sharen, Tom Smith,
Kevin Tinsley & Chia Chi Wang

LETTERERS
John Costanza, Steve Dutro,
Chris Eliopoulos, Loretta Krol, Ken
Lopez, James Novak, Bill Oakley/N.J.Q.,
Clem Robins and Richard Starkings &
Comicraft

EDITORS
Tom Brevoort, Bob Budiansky, Eric Fein
& Danny Fingeroth

WITH THANKS TO
Scott Lobdell

Front Cover Artists: Sal Buscema & Bill Sienkiewicz
Front Cover Colorist: Chris Sotomayor

Collection Editor: Mike O'Sullivan
Editorial Assistants: James Emmett & Joe Hochstein
Assistant Editors: Nelson Ribeiro & Alex Starbuck
Editors, Special Projects: Mark D. Beazley & Jennifer Grünwald
Senior Editor, Special Projects: Jeff Youngquist
Senior Vice President of Sales: David Gabriel
Research: Jeph York
Production: Ryan Devall & ColorTek
Book Designer: Arlene So

Editor In Chief: Joe Quesada
Publisher: Dan Buckley
Executive Producer: Alan Fine

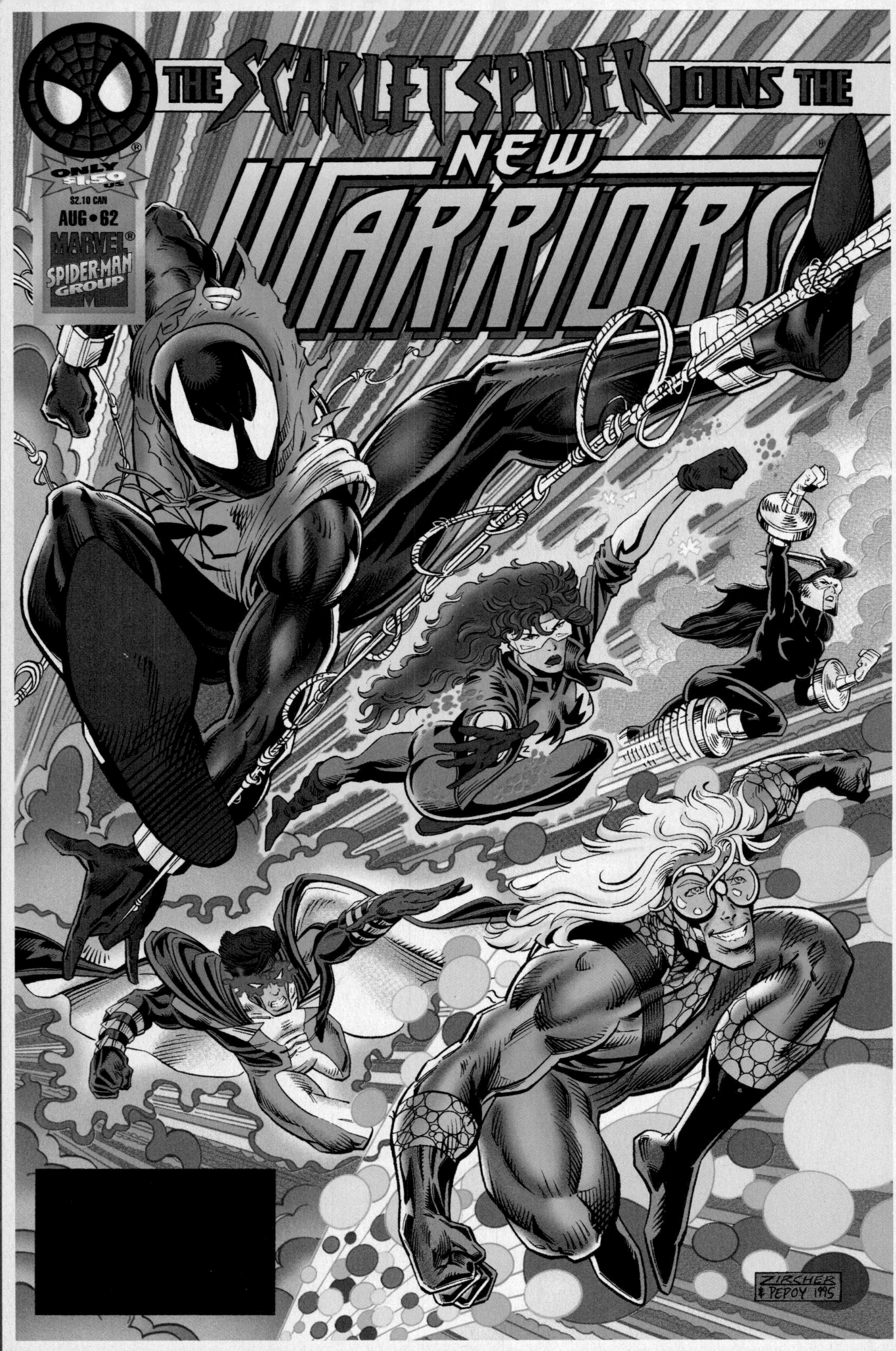
THE SCARLET SPIDER JOINS THE
NEW WARRIORS
ONLY $1.50 US
$2.10 CAN
AUG • 62
MARVEL
SPIDER-MAN GROUP
ZIRCHER & PEPOY 1995

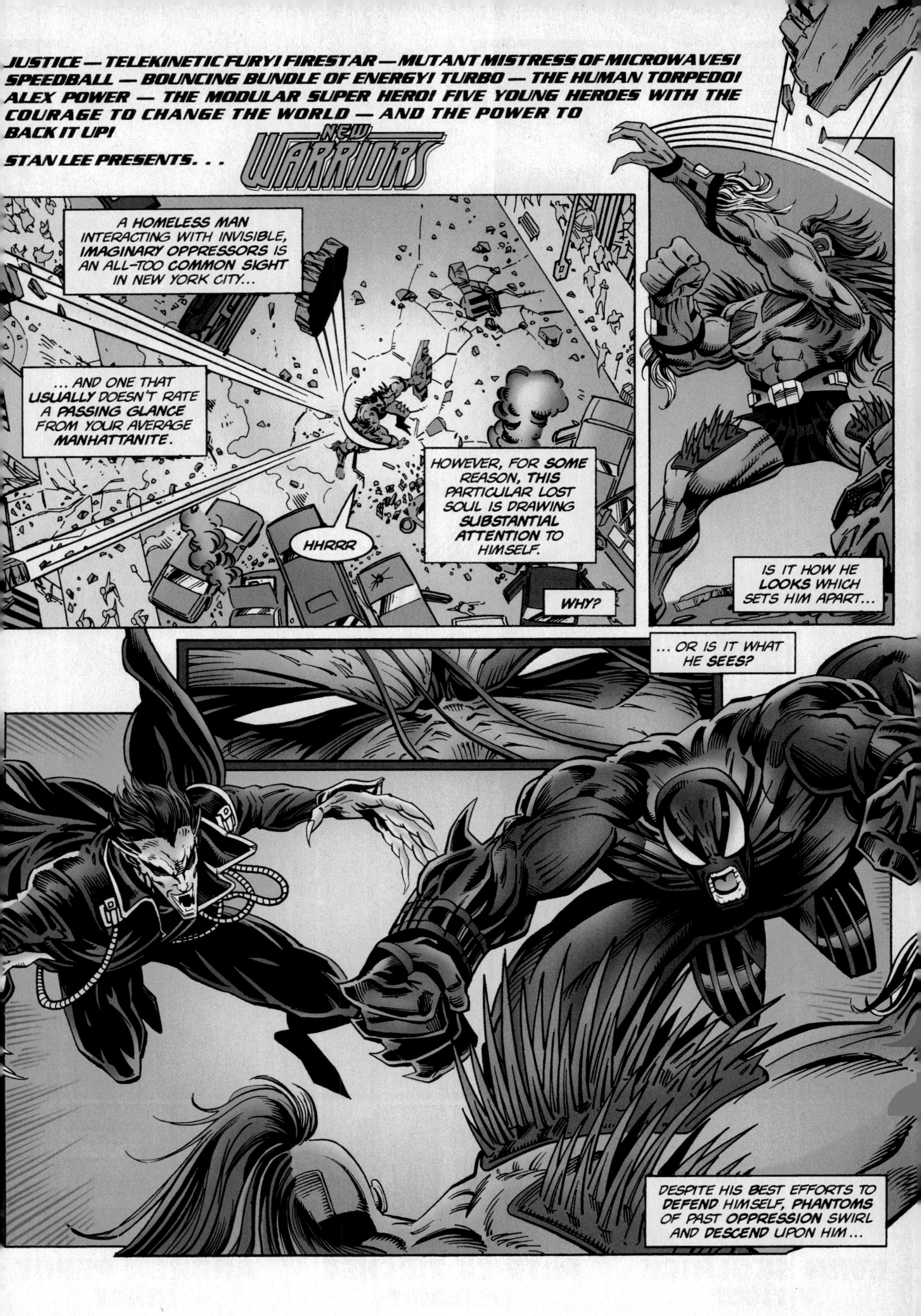

JUSTICE — TELEKINETIC FURY! FIRESTAR — MUTANT MISTRESS OF MICROWAVES! SPEEDBALL — BOUNCING BUNDLE OF ENERGY! TURBO — THE HUMAN TORPEDO! ALEX POWER — THE MODULAR SUPER HERO! FIVE YOUNG HEROES WITH THE COURAGE TO CHANGE THE WORLD — AND THE POWER TO BACK IT UP!
STAN LEE PRESENTS. . .
NEW WARRIORS
A HOMELESS MAN INTERACTING WITH INVISIBLE, IMAGINARY OPPRESSORS IS AN ALL-TOO COMMON SIGHT IN NEW YORK CITY...
... AND ONE THAT USUALLY DOESN'T RATE A PASSING GLANCE FROM YOUR AVERAGE MANHATTANITE.
HHRRR
HOWEVER, FOR SOME REASON, THIS PARTICULAR LOST SOUL IS DRAWING SUBSTANTIAL ATTENTION TO HIMSELF.
WHY?
IS IT HOW HE LOOKS WHICH SETS HIM APART...
... OR IS IT WHAT HE SEES?
DESPITE HIS BEST EFFORTS TO DEFEND HIMSELF, PHANTOMS OF PAST OPPRESSION SWIRL AND DESCEND UPON HIM...

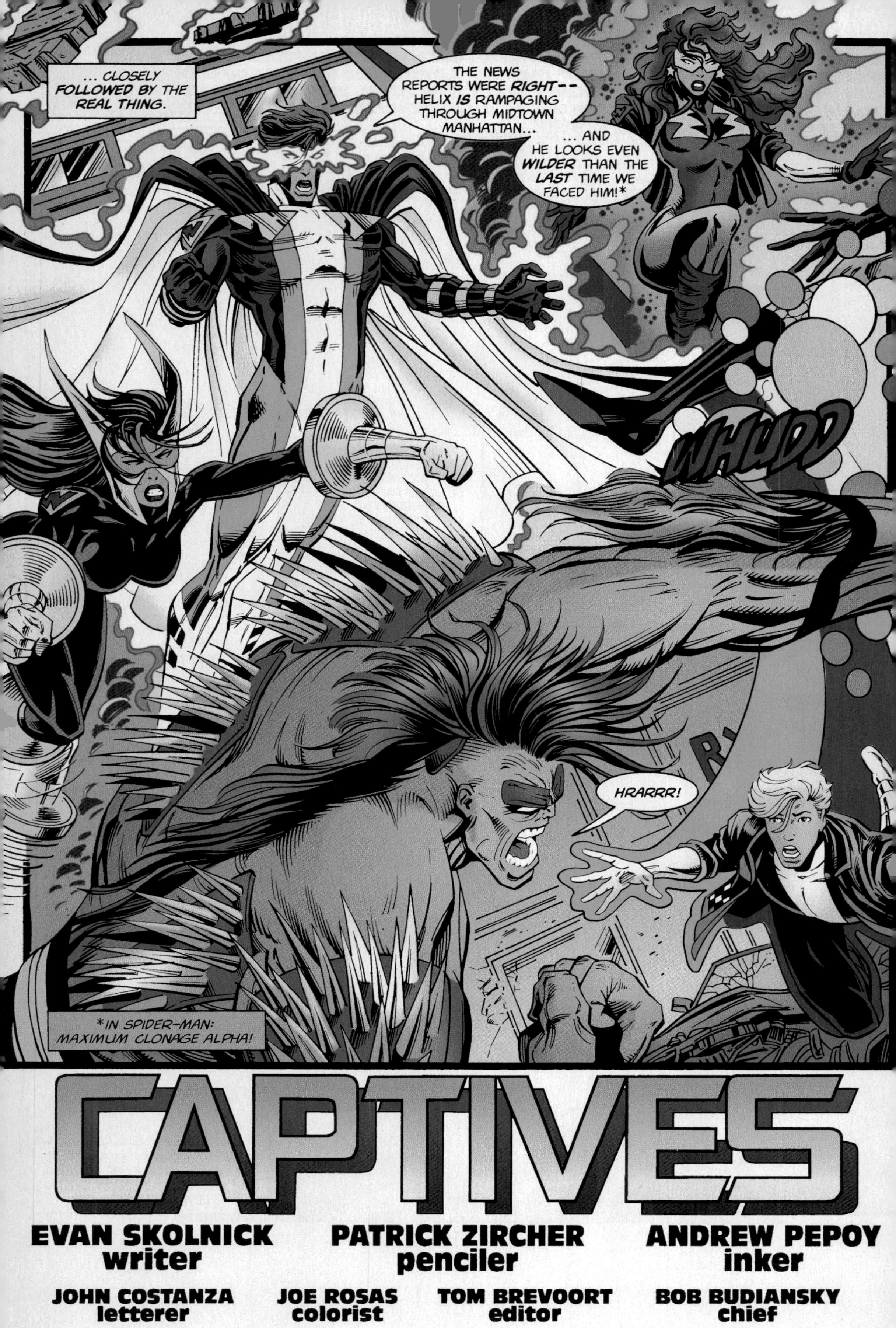
... CLOSELY FOLLOWED BY THE REAL THING.
THE NEWS REPORTS WERE RIGHT-- HELIX IS RAMPAGING THROUGH MIDTOWN MANHATTAN...
... AND HE LOOKS EVEN WILDER THAN THE LAST TIME WE FACED HIM!*
WHUDD
HRARRR!
*IN SPIDER-MAN: MAXIMUM CLONAGE ALPHA!

CAPTIVES

EVAN SKOLNICK writer
PATRICK ZIRCHER penciler
ANDREW PEPOY inker
JOHN COSTANZA letterer
JOE ROSAS colorist
TOM BREVOORT editor
BOB BUDIANSKY chief

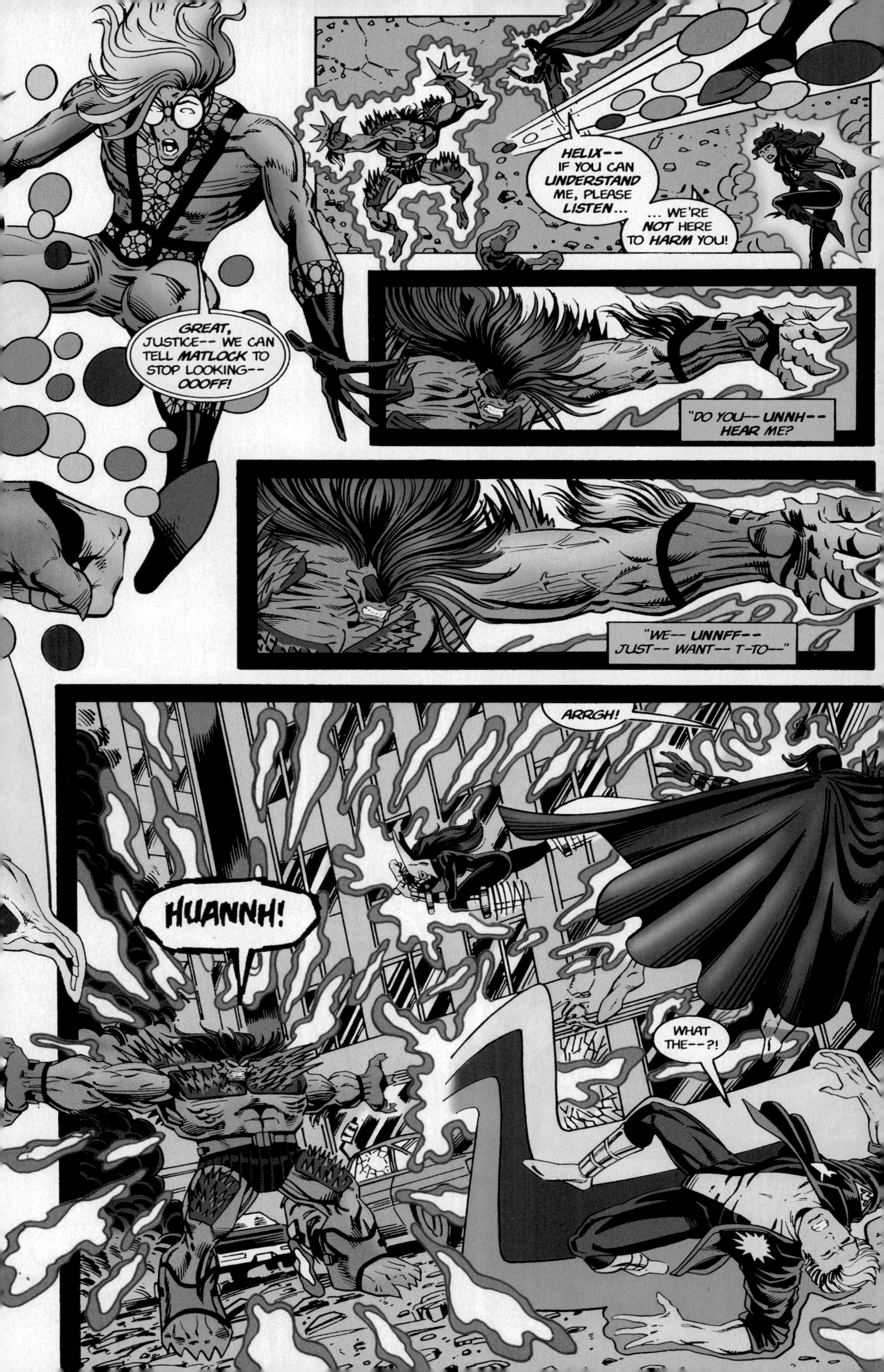
HELIX-- IF YOU CAN UNDERSTAND ME, PLEASE LISTEN...
... WE'RE NOT HERE TO HARM YOU!
GREAT, JUSTICE-- WE CAN TELL MATLOCK TO STOP LOOKING-- OOOFF!
"DO YOU-- UNNH-- HEAR ME?
"WE-- UNNFF-- JUST-- WANT-- T-TO--"
ARRGH!
HUANNH!
WHAT THE--?!

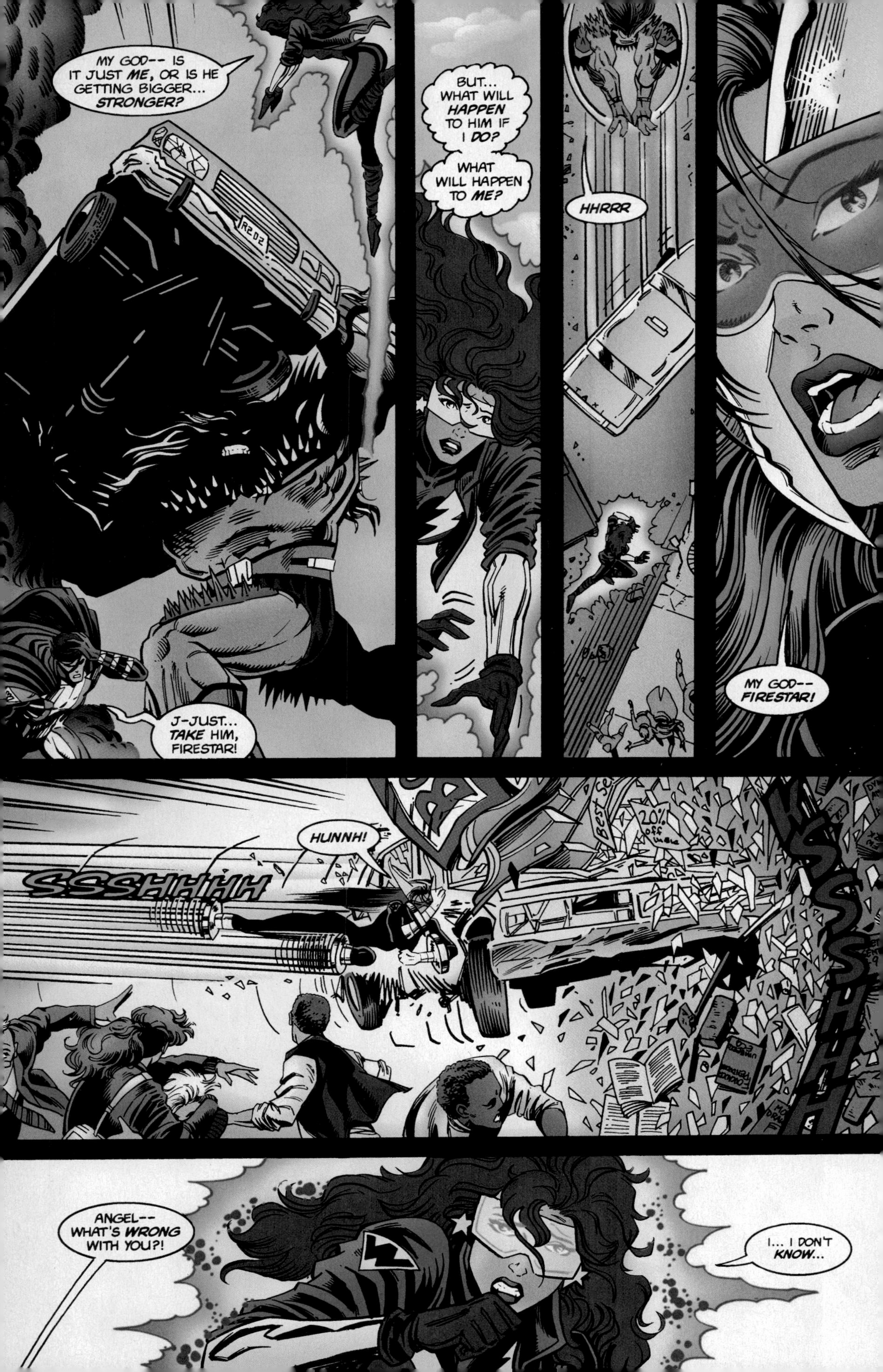

MY GOD-- IS IT JUST ME, OR IS HE GETTING BIGGER... STRONGER?
J-JUST... TAKE HIM, FIRESTAR!
BUT... WHAT WILL HAPPEN TO HIM IF I DO?
WHAT WILL HAPPEN TO ME?
HHRRR
MY GOD-- FIRESTAR!
SSSHHHH
HUNNH!
20% off
ANGEL-- WHAT'S WRONG WITH YOU?!
I... I DON'T KNOW...

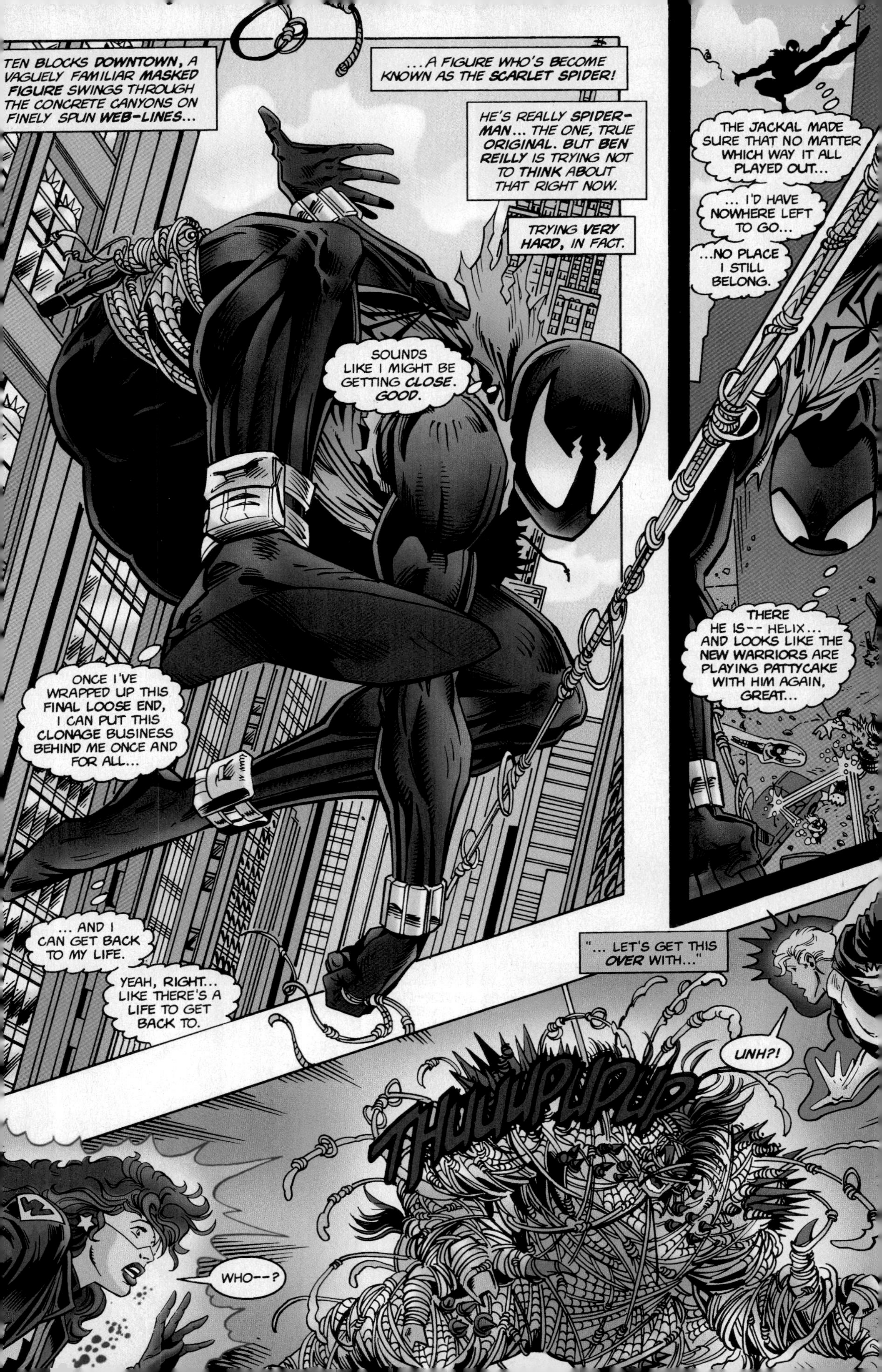
TEN BLOCKS DOWNTOWN, A VAGUELY FAMILIAR MASKED FIGURE SWINGS THROUGH THE CONCRETE CANYONS ON FINELY SPUN WEB-LINES...
...A FIGURE WHO'S BECOME KNOWN AS THE SCARLET SPIDER!
HE'S REALLY SPIDER-MAN... THE ONE, TRUE ORIGINAL. BUT BEN REILLY IS TRYING NOT TO THINK ABOUT THAT RIGHT NOW.
TRYING VERY HARD, IN FACT.
SOUNDS LIKE I MIGHT BE GETTING CLOSE. GOOD.
ONCE I'VE WRAPPED UP THIS FINAL LOOSE END, I CAN PUT THIS CLONAGE BUSINESS BEHIND ME ONCE AND FOR ALL...
... AND I CAN GET BACK TO MY LIFE.
YEAH, RIGHT... LIKE THERE'S A LIFE TO GET BACK TO.
THE JACKAL MADE SURE THAT NO MATTER WHICH WAY IT ALL PLAYED OUT...
... I'D HAVE NOWHERE LEFT TO GO...
...NO PLACE I STILL BELONG.
THERE HE IS-- HELIX... AND LOOKS LIKE THE NEW WARRIORS ARE PLAYING PATTYCAKE WITH HIM AGAIN. GREAT...
"... LET'S GET THIS OVER WITH..."
UNH?!
THUUUPUPUP
WHO--?

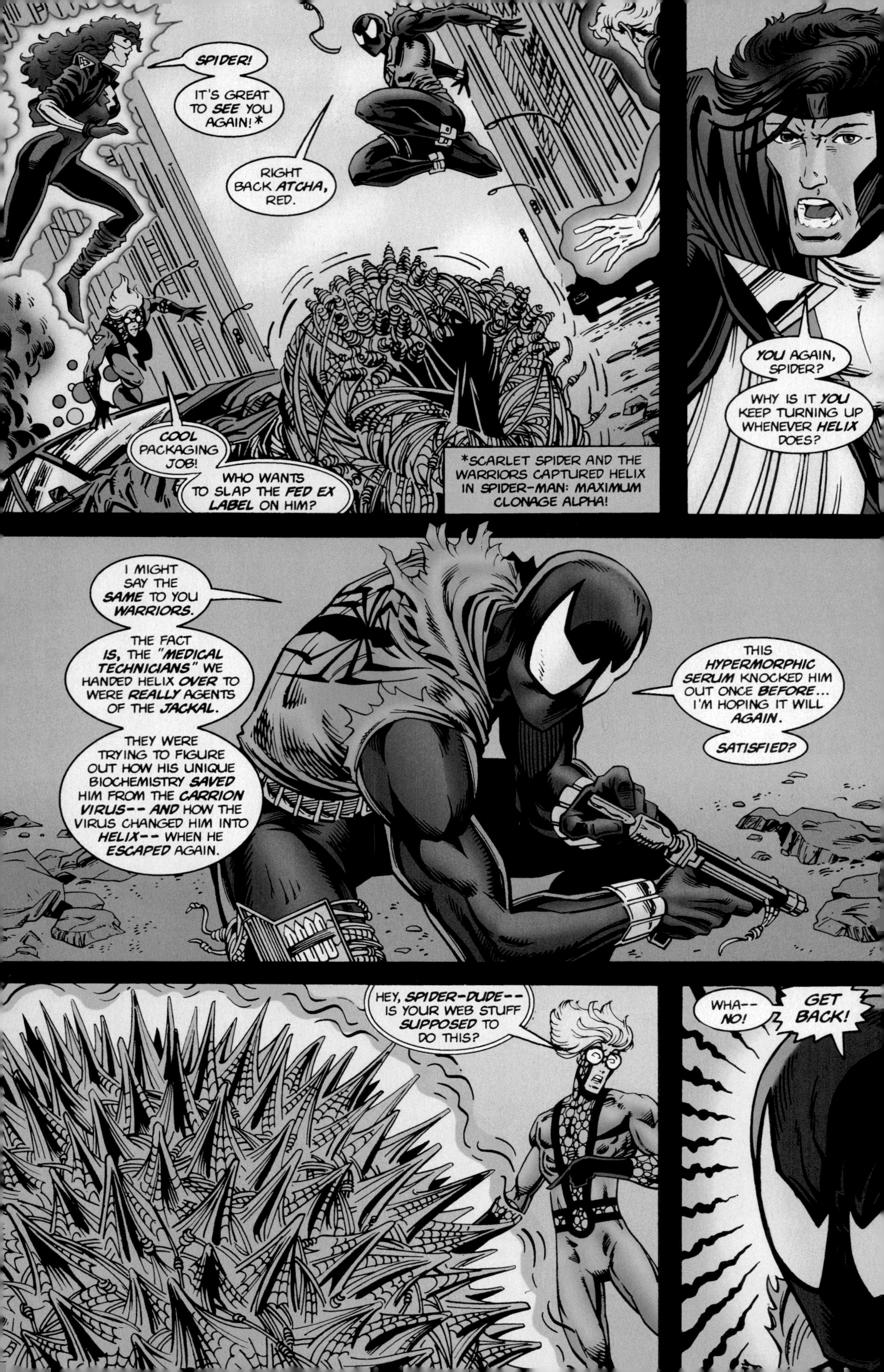

SPIDER!
IT'S GREAT TO SEE YOU AGAIN!*
RIGHT BACK ATCHA, RED.
COOL PACKAGING JOB!
WHO WANTS TO SLAP THE FED EX LABEL ON HIM?
*SCARLET SPIDER AND THE WARRIORS CAPTURED HELIX IN SPIDER-MAN: MAXIMUM CLONAGE ALPHA!
YOU AGAIN, SPIDER?
WHY IS IT YOU KEEP TURNING UP WHENEVER HELIX DOES?
I MIGHT SAY THE SAME TO YOU WARRIORS.
THE FACT IS, THE "MEDICAL TECHNICIANS" WE HANDED HELIX OVER TO WERE REALLY AGENTS OF THE JACKAL.
THEY WERE TRYING TO FIGURE OUT HOW HIS UNIQUE BIOCHEMISTRY SAVED HIM FROM THE CARRION VIRUS-- AND HOW THE VIRUS CHANGED HIM INTO HELIX-- WHEN HE ESCAPED AGAIN.
THIS HYPERMORPHIC SERUM KNOCKED HIM OUT ONCE BEFORE... I'M HOPING IT WILL AGAIN.
SATISFIED?
HEY, SPIDER-DUDE-- IS YOUR WEB STUFF SUPPOSED TO DO THIS?
WHA-- NO!
GET BACK!

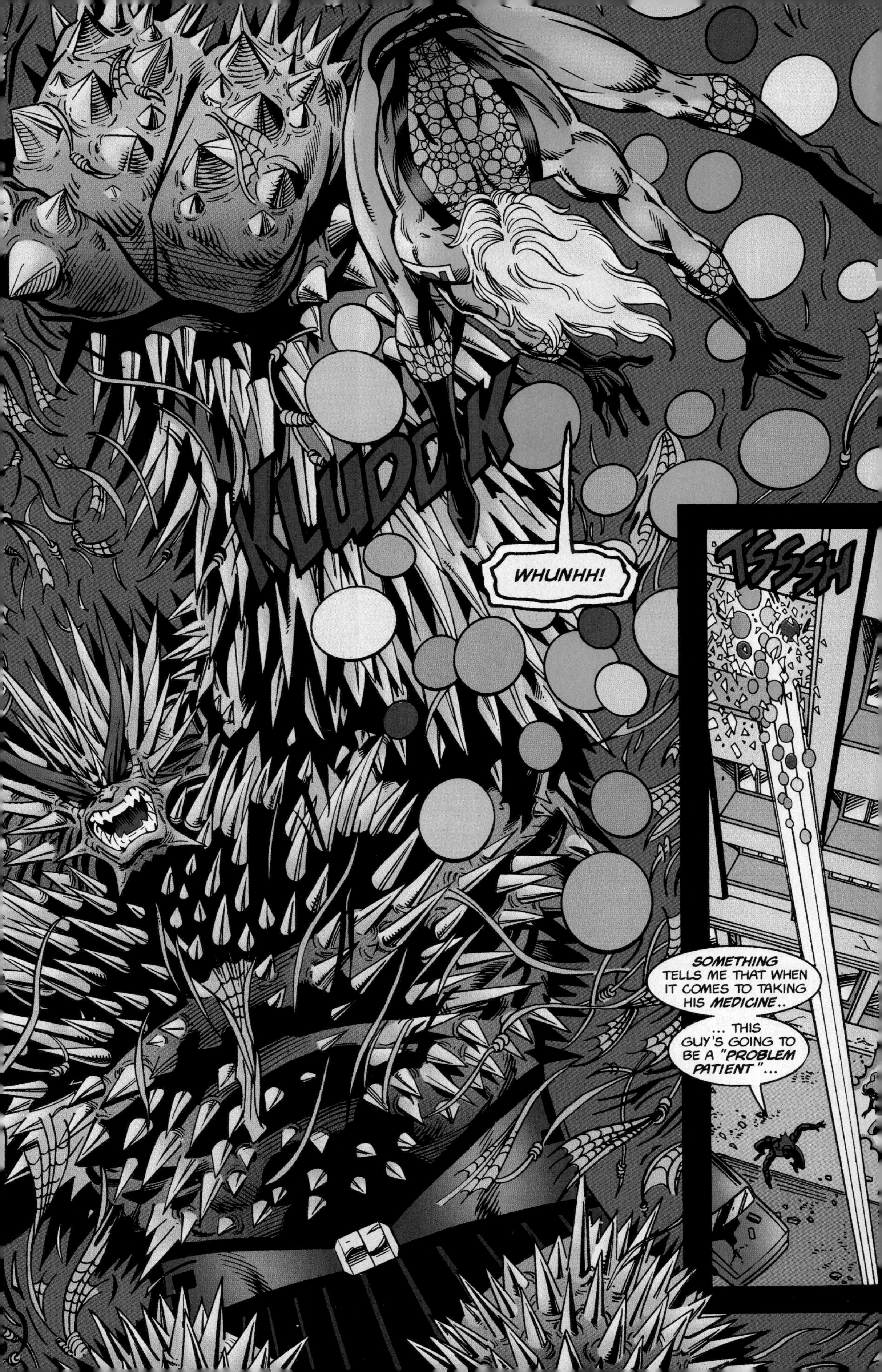
KLUDDK
WHUNHH!
TSSSH
SOMETHING TELLS ME THAT WHEN IT COMES TO TAKING HIS MEDICINE..
... THIS GUY'S GOING TO BE A "PROBLEM PATIENT"...

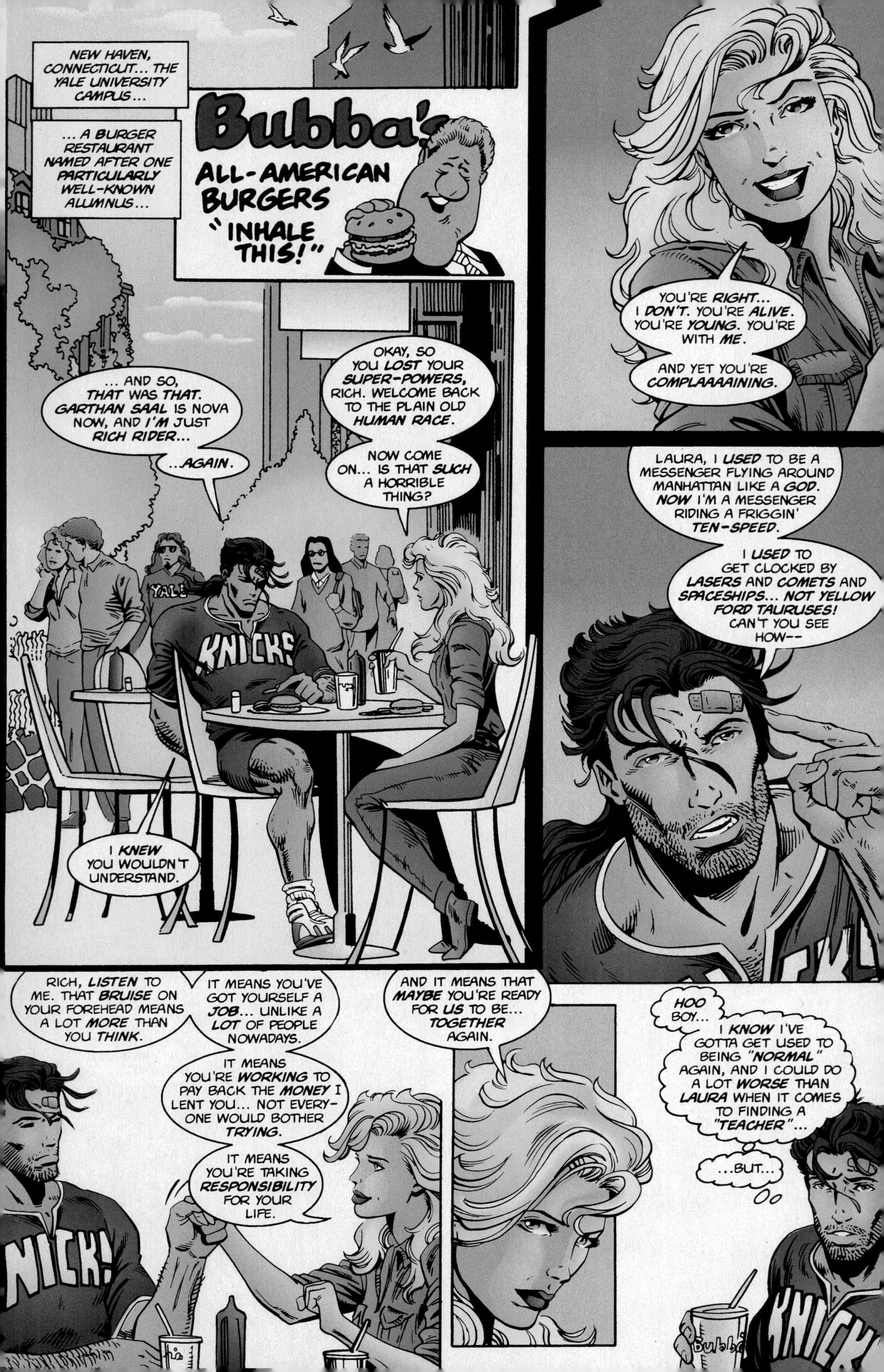
NEW HAVEN, CONNECTICUT... THE YALE UNIVERSITY CAMPUS...
...A BURGER RESTAURANT NAMED AFTER ONE PARTICULARLY WELL-KNOWN ALUMNUS...
Bubba's ALL-AMERICAN BURGERS "INHALE THIS!"
...AND SO, THAT WAS THAT. GARTHAN SAAL IS NOVA NOW, AND I'M JUST RICH RIDER...
...AGAIN.
OKAY, SO YOU LOST YOUR SUPER-POWERS, RICH. WELCOME BACK TO THE PLAIN OLD HUMAN RACE.
NOW COME ON... IS THAT SUCH A HORRIBLE THING?
YALE
KNICKS
I KNEW YOU WOULDN'T UNDERSTAND.
YOU'RE RIGHT... I DON'T. YOU'RE ALIVE. YOU'RE YOUNG. YOU'RE WITH ME.
AND YET YOU'RE COMPLAAAAINING.
LAURA, I USED TO BE A MESSENGER FLYING AROUND MANHATTAN LIKE A GOD. NOW I'M A MESSENGER RIDING A FRIGGIN' TEN-SPEED.
I USED TO GET CLOCKED BY LASERS AND COMETS AND SPACESHIPS... NOT YELLOW FORD TAURUSES! CAN'T YOU SEE HOW--
RICH, LISTEN TO ME. THAT BRUISE ON YOUR FOREHEAD MEANS A LOT MORE THAN YOU THINK.
IT MEANS YOU'VE GOT YOURSELF A JOB... UNLIKE A LOT OF PEOPLE NOWADAYS.
IT MEANS YOU'RE WORKING TO PAY BACK THE MONEY I LENT YOU... NOT EVERY-ONE WOULD BOTHER TRYING.
IT MEANS YOU'RE TAKING RESPONSIBILITY FOR YOUR LIFE.
AND IT MEANS THAT MAYBE YOU'RE READY FOR US TO BE... TOGETHER AGAIN.
HOO BOY...
I KNOW I'VE GOTTA GET USED TO BEING "NORMAL" AGAIN, AND I COULD DO A LOT WORSE THAN LAURA WHEN IT COMES TO FINDING A "TEACHER"...
...BUT...

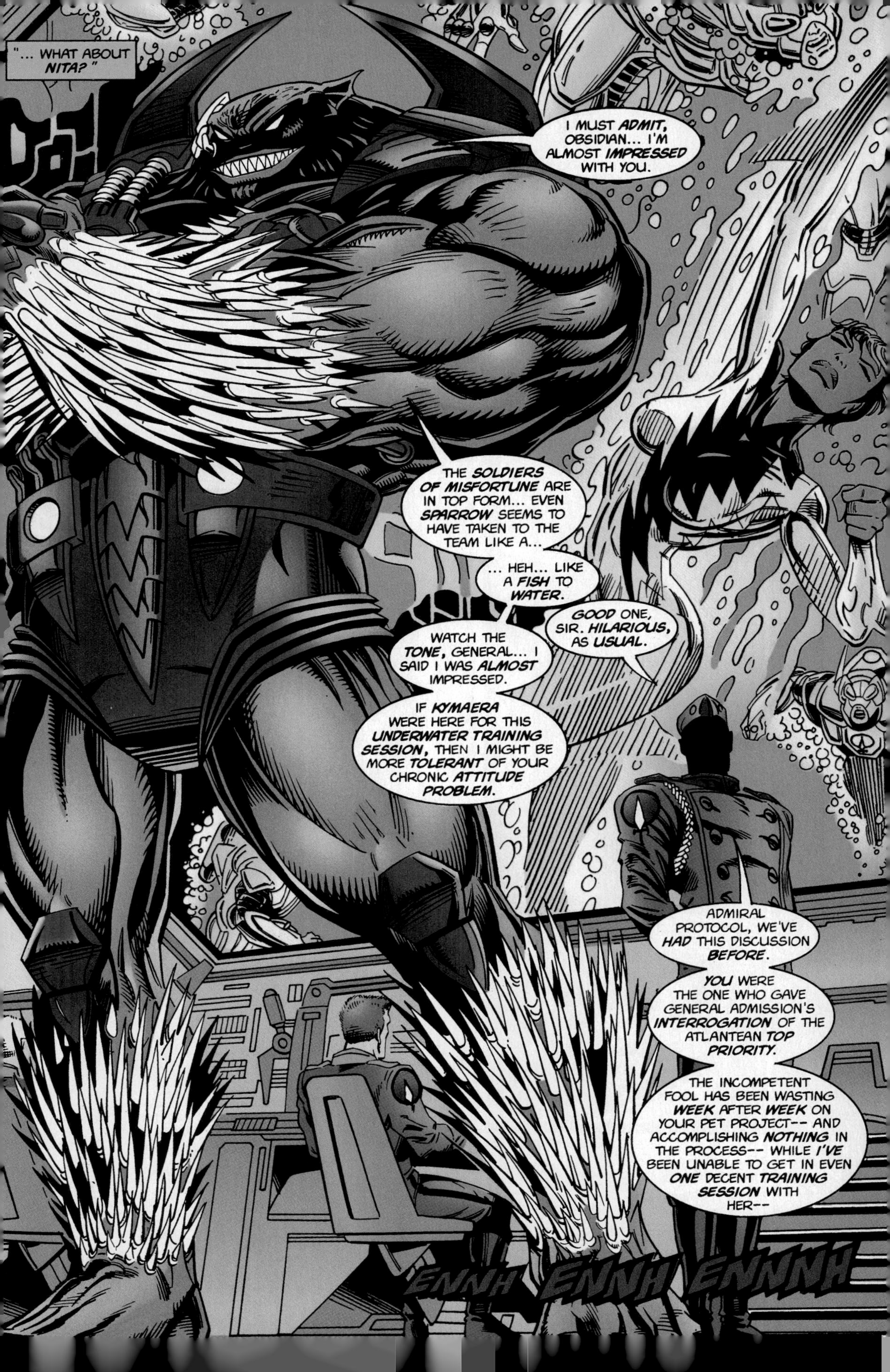
"... WHAT ABOUT NITA?"
I MUST ADMIT, OBSIDIAN... I'M ALMOST IMPRESSED WITH YOU.
THE SOLDIERS OF MISFORTUNE ARE IN TOP FORM... EVEN SPARROW SEEMS TO HAVE TAKEN TO THE TEAM LIKE A...
... HEH... LIKE A FISH TO WATER.
GOOD ONE, SIR. HILARIOUS, AS USUAL.
WATCH THE TONE, GENERAL... I SAID I WAS ALMOST IMPRESSED.
IF KYMAERA WERE HERE FOR THIS UNDERWATER TRAINING SESSION, THEN I MIGHT BE MORE TOLERANT OF YOUR CHRONIC ATTITUDE PROBLEM.
ADMIRAL PROTOCOL, WE'VE HAD THIS DISCUSSION BEFORE.
YOU WERE THE ONE WHO GAVE GENERAL ADMISSION'S INTERROGATION OF THE ATLANTEAN TOP PRIORITY.
THE INCOMPETENT FOOL HAS BEEN WASTING WEEK AFTER WEEK ON YOUR PET PROJECT-- AND ACCOMPLISHING NOTHING IN THE PROCESS-- WHILE I'VE BEEN UNABLE TO GET IN EVEN ONE DECENT TRAINING SESSION WITH HER--
ENNH ENNH ENNNH

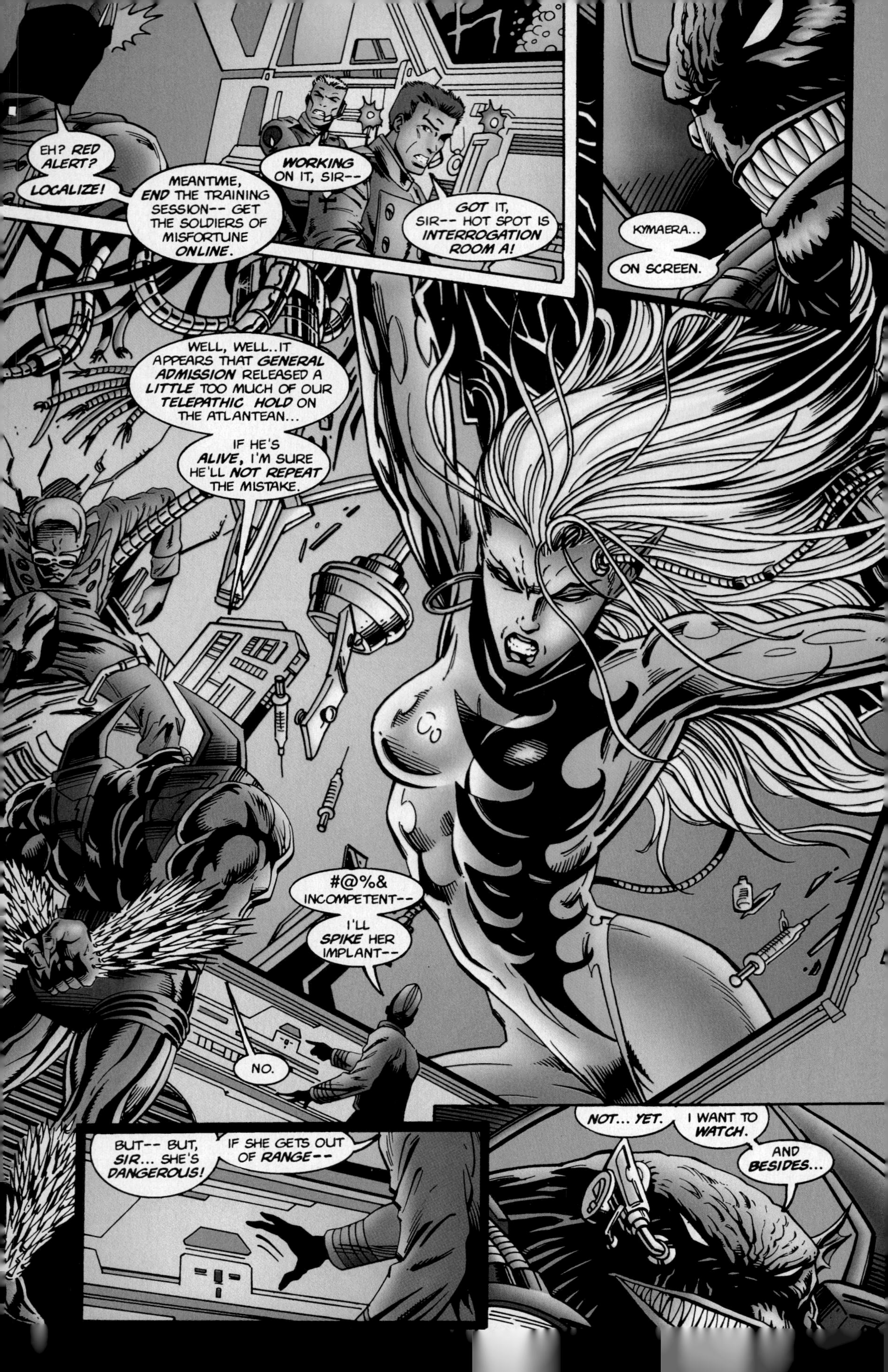
EH? RED ALERT?
LOCALIZE!
MEANTIME, END THE TRAINING SESSION-- GET THE SOLDIERS OF MISFORTUNE ONLINE.
WORKING ON IT, SIR--
GOT IT, SIR-- HOT SPOT IS INTERROGATION ROOM A!
KYMAERA...
ON SCREEN.
WELL, WELL..IT APPEARS THAT GENERAL ADMISSION RELEASED A LITTLE TOO MUCH OF OUR TELEPATHIC HOLD ON THE ATLANTEAN...
IF HE'S ALIVE, I'M SURE HE'LL NOT REPEAT THE MISTAKE.
#@%& INCOMPETENT--
I'LL SPIKE HER IMPLANT--
NO.
NOT... YET.
I WANT TO WATCH.
AND BESIDES...
BUT-- BUT, SIR... SHE'S DANGEROUS!
IF SHE GETS OUT OF RANGE--

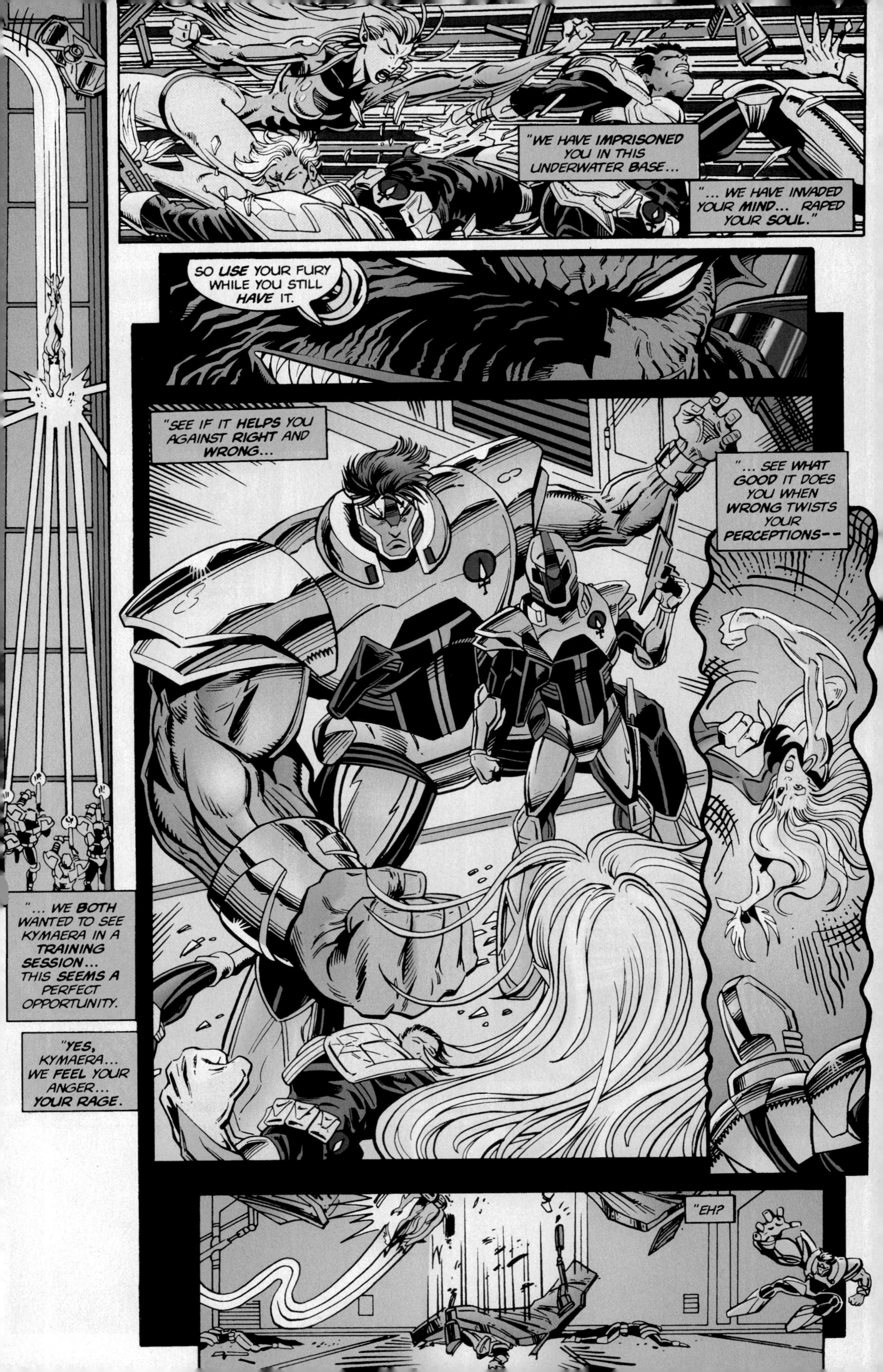
"WE HAVE IMPRISONED YOU IN THIS UNDERWATER BASE...
"... WE HAVE INVADED YOUR MIND... RAPED YOUR SOUL."
SO USE YOUR FURY WHILE YOU STILL HAVE IT.
"SEE IF IT HELPS YOU AGAINST RIGHT AND WRONG...
"... SEE WHAT GOOD IT DOES YOU WHEN WRONG TWISTS YOUR PERCEPTIONS--
"... WE BOTH WANTED TO SEE KYMAERA IN A TRAINING SESSION... THIS SEEMS A PERFECT OPPORTUNITY.
"YES, KYMAERA... WE FEEL YOUR ANGER... YOUR RAGE.
"EH?

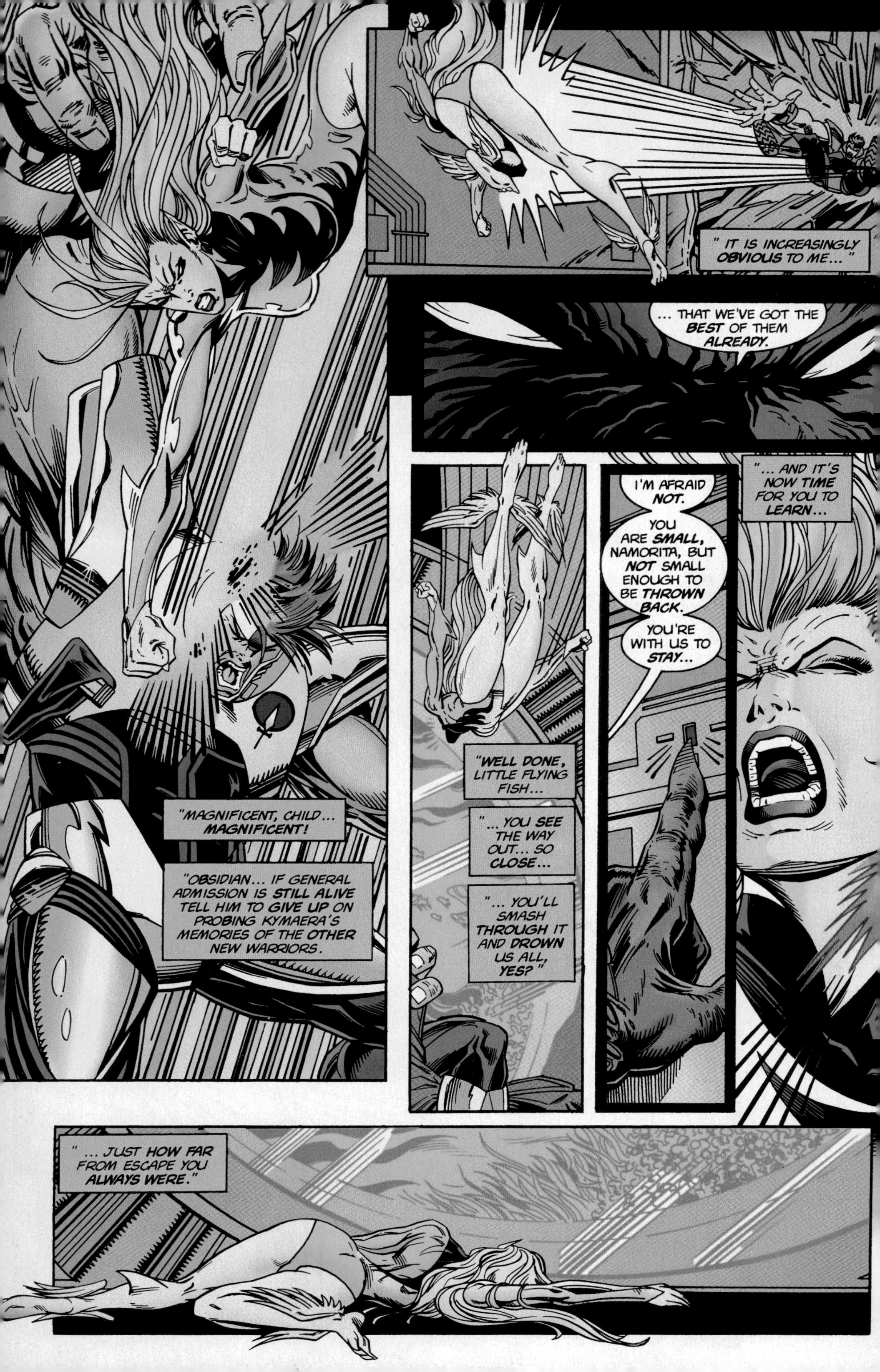
"IT IS INCREASINGLY OBVIOUS TO ME..."
... THAT WE'VE GOT THE BEST OF THEM ALREADY.
"MAGNIFICENT, CHILD... MAGNIFICENT!
"OBSIDIAN... IF GENERAL ADMISSION IS STILL ALIVE TELL HIM TO GIVE UP ON PROBING KYMAERA'S MEMORIES OF THE OTHER NEW WARRIORS.
"WELL DONE, LITTLE FLYING FISH...
"... YOU SEE THE WAY OUT... SO CLOSE...
"... YOU'LL SMASH THROUGH IT AND DROWN US ALL, YES?"
I'M AFRAID NOT.
YOU ARE SMALL, NAMORITA, BUT NOT SMALL ENOUGH TO BE THROWN BACK.
YOU'RE WITH US TO STAY...
"... AND IT'S NOW TIME FOR YOU TO LEARN...
"... JUST HOW FAR FROM ESCAPE YOU ALWAYS WERE."

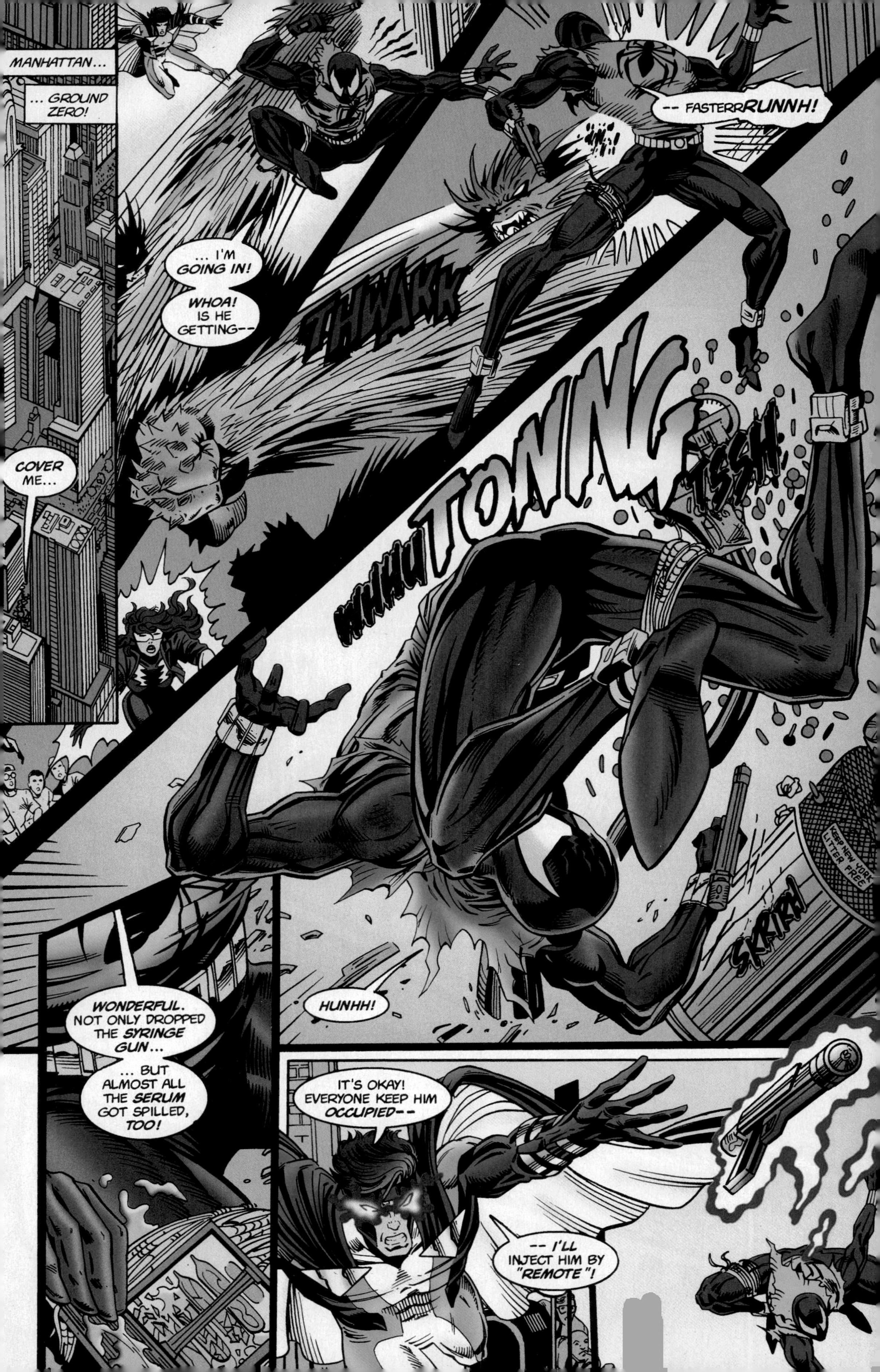

MANHATTAN...
... GROUND ZERO!
COVER ME...
... I'M GOING IN!
WHOA! IS HE GETTING--
-- FASTERRRUNNH!
THWAKK
WHHHUTONNG
TSSSH
SKRIHH
KEEP NEW YORK LITTER FREE
HUNHH!
WONDERFUL. NOT ONLY DROPPED THE SYRINGE GUN...
... BUT ALMOST ALL THE SERUM GOT SPILLED, TOO!
IT'S OKAY! EVERYONE KEEP HIM OCCUPIED--
-- I'LL INJECT HIM BY "REMOTE"!

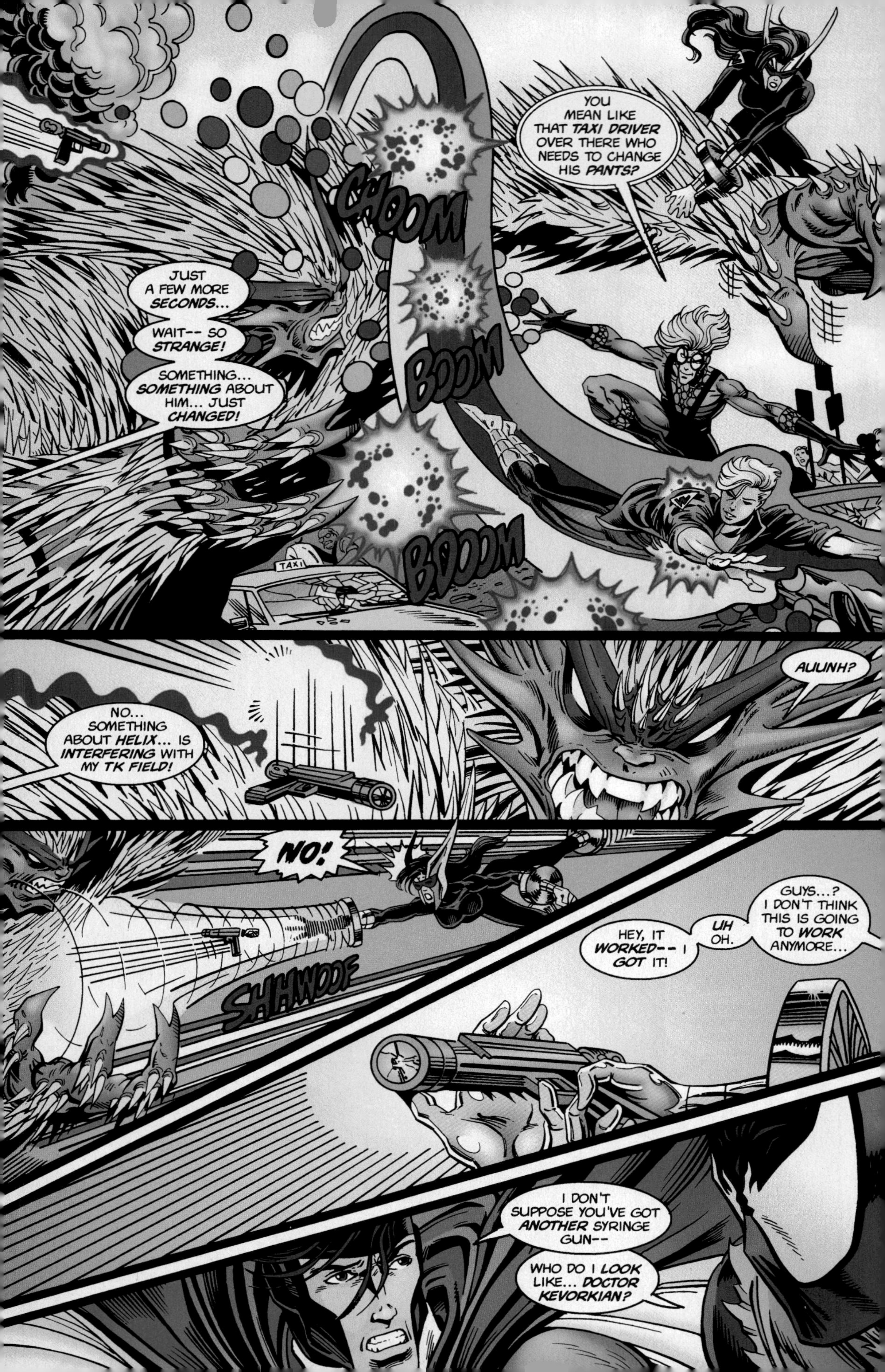
YOU MEAN LIKE THAT TAXI DRIVER OVER THERE WHO NEEDS TO CHANGE HIS PANTS?
JUST A FEW MORE SECONDS...
WAIT-- SO STRANGE!
SOMETHING... SOMETHING ABOUT HIM... JUST CHANGED!
CHOOM
BOOM
BOOOM
TAXI
NO... SOMETHING ABOUT HELIX... IS INTERFERING WITH MY TK FIELD!
AUUNH?
NO!
SHHWOOF
HEY, IT WORKED-- I GOT IT!
UH OH.
GUYS...? I DON'T THINK THIS IS GOING TO WORK ANYMORE...
I DON'T SUPPOSE YOU'VE GOT ANOTHER SYRINGE GUN--
WHO DO I LOOK LIKE... DOCTOR KEVORKIAN?

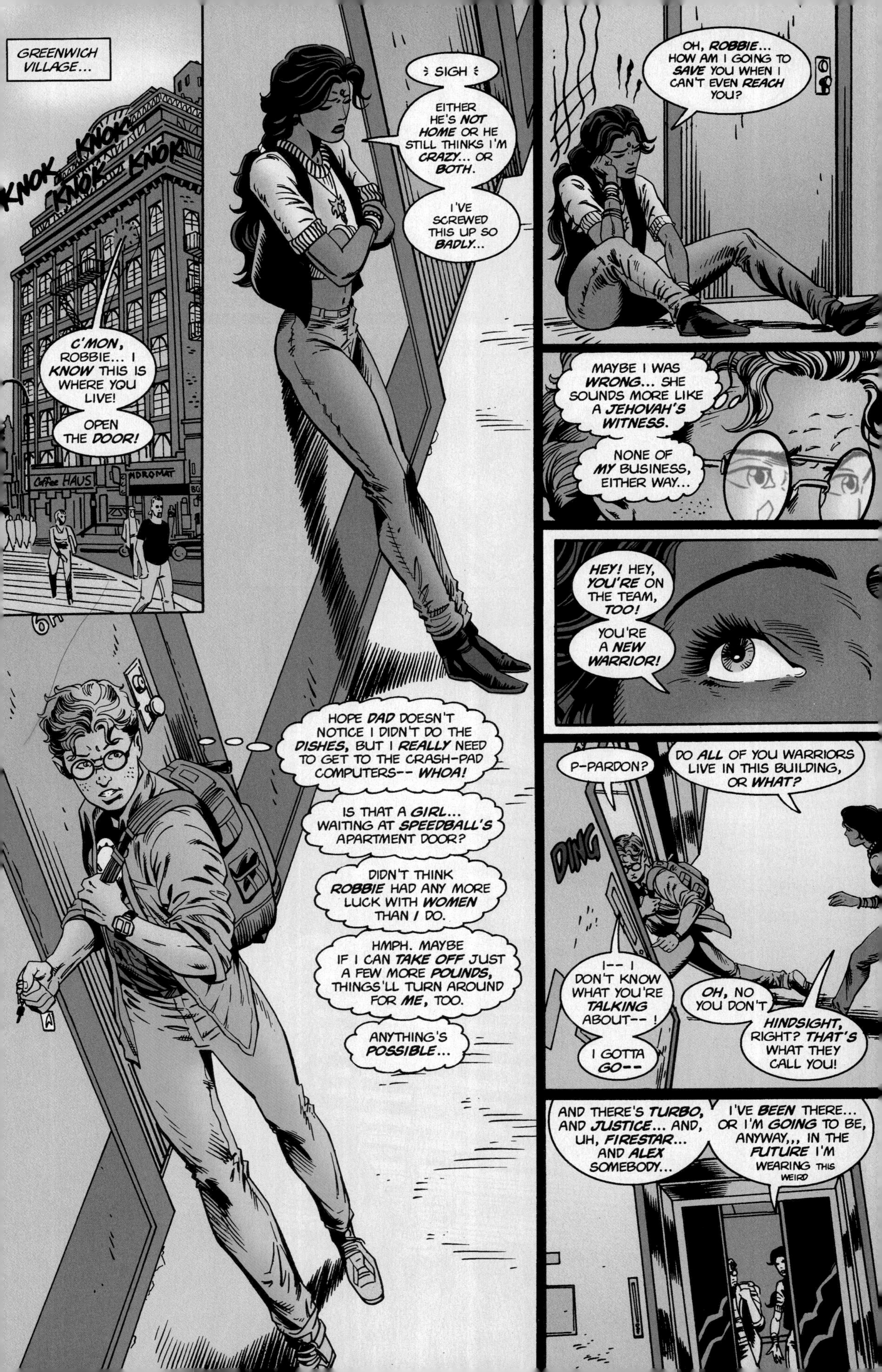
GREENWICH VILLAGE...
KNOK KNOK KNOK KNOK
C'MON, ROBBIE... I KNOW THIS IS WHERE YOU LIVE!
OPEN THE DOOR!
Coffee HAUS
NDROMAT
⁑ SIGH ⁑
EITHER HE'S NOT HOME OR HE STILL THINKS I'M CRAZY... OR BOTH.
I'VE SCREWED THIS UP SO BADLY...
HOPE DAD DOESN'T NOTICE I DIDN'T DO THE DISHES, BUT I REALLY NEED TO GET TO THE CRASH-PAD COMPUTERS-- WHOA!
IS THAT A GIRL... WAITING AT SPEEDBALL'S APARTMENT DOOR?
DIDN'T THINK ROBBIE HAD ANY MORE LUCK WITH WOMEN THAN I DO.
HMPH. MAYBE IF I CAN TAKE OFF JUST A FEW MORE POUNDS, THINGS'LL TURN AROUND FOR ME, TOO.
ANYTHING'S POSSIBLE...
OH, ROBBIE... HOW AM I GOING TO SAVE YOU WHEN I CAN'T EVEN REACH YOU?
MAYBE I WAS WRONG... SHE SOUNDS MORE LIKE A JEHOVAH'S WITNESS.
NONE OF MY BUSINESS, EITHER WAY...
HEY! HEY, YOU'RE ON THE TEAM, TOO!
YOU'RE A NEW WARRIOR!
P-PARDON?
DO ALL OF YOU WARRIORS LIVE IN THIS BUILDING, OR WHAT?
DING
I-- I DON'T KNOW WHAT YOU'RE TALKING ABOUT-- !
I GOTTA GO--
OH, NO YOU DON'T.
HINDSIGHT, RIGHT? THAT'S WHAT THEY CALL YOU!
AND THERE'S TURBO, AND JUSTICE... AND, UH, FIRESTAR... AND ALEX SOMEBODY...
I'VE BEEN THERE... OR I'M GOING TO BE, ANYWAY,,, IN THE FUTURE I'M WEARING THIS WEIRD

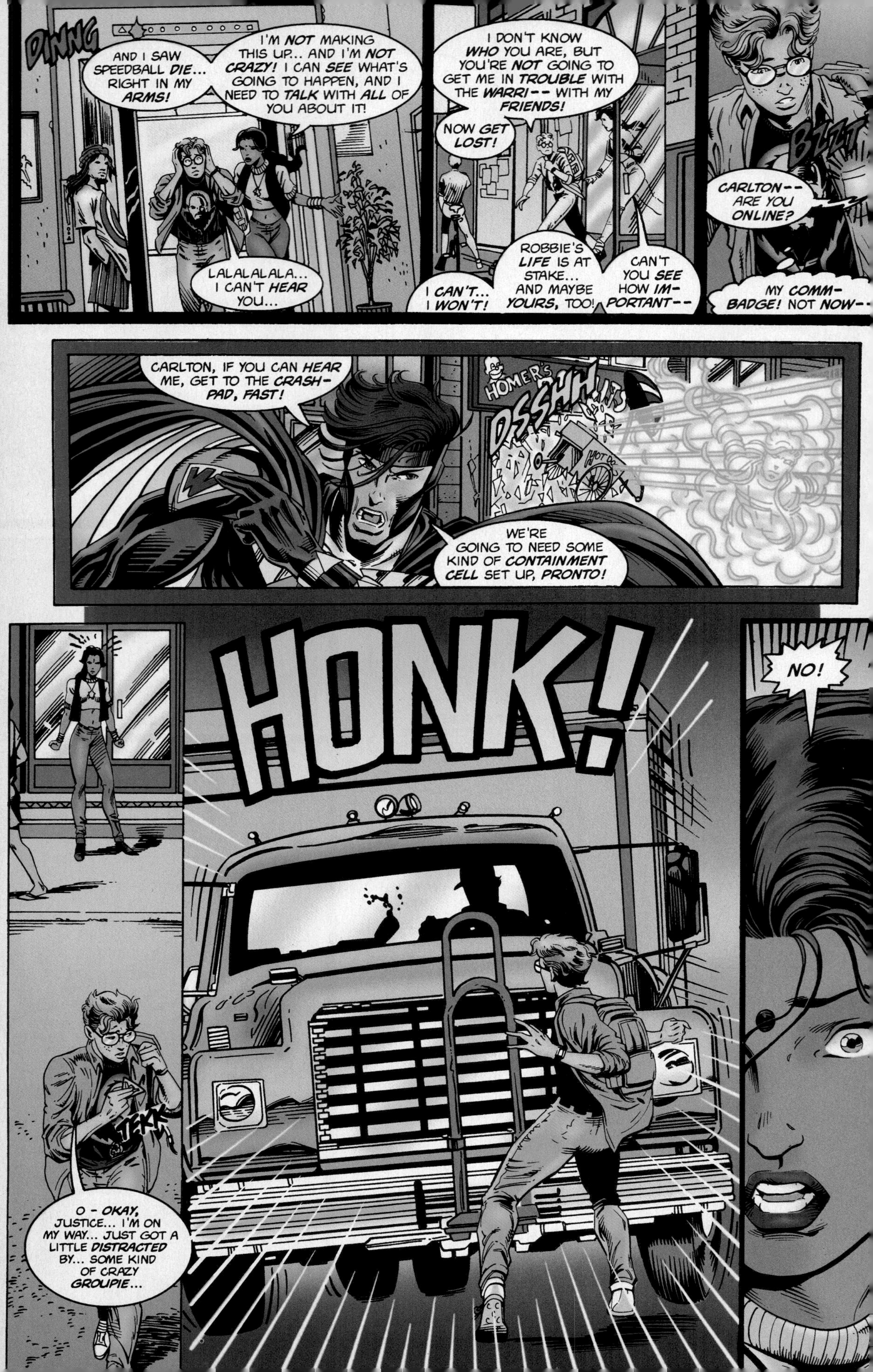
DINNG
AND I SAW SPEEDBALL DIE... RIGHT IN MY ARMS!
I'M NOT MAKING THIS UP... AND I'M NOT CRAZY! I CAN SEE WHAT'S GOING TO HAPPEN, AND I NEED TO TALK WITH ALL OF YOU ABOUT IT!
LALALALALA... I CAN'T HEAR YOU...
I DON'T KNOW WHO YOU ARE, BUT YOU'RE NOT GOING TO GET ME IN TROUBLE WITH THE WARRI-- WITH MY FRIENDS!
NOW GET LOST!
I CAN'T... I WON'T!
ROBBIE'S LIFE IS AT STAKE... AND MAYBE YOURS, TOO!
CAN'T YOU SEE HOW IM-PORTANT--
BZZZT
CARLTON-- ARE YOU ONLINE?
MY COMM-BADGE! NOT NOW--
CARLTON, IF YOU CAN HEAR ME, GET TO THE CRASH-PAD, FAST!
HOMER'S
DSSHH!!
WE'RE GOING TO NEED SOME KIND OF CONTAINMENT CELL SET UP, PRONTO!
HONK!
NO!
TEKK
O-OKAY, JUSTICE... I'M ON MY WAY... JUST GOT A LITTLE DISTRACTED BY... SOME KIND OF CRAZY GROUPIE...

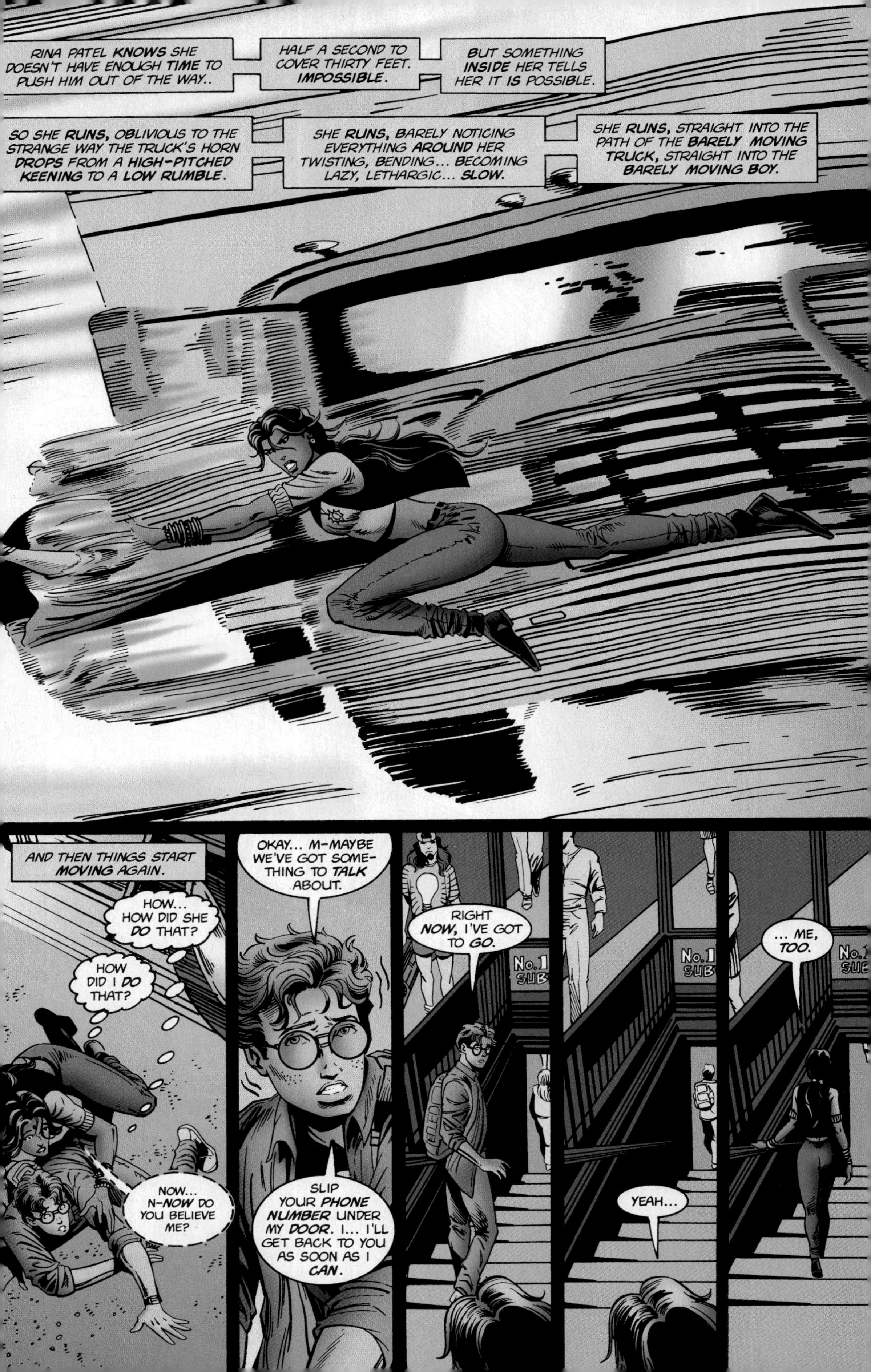
RINA PATEL KNOWS SHE DOESN'T HAVE ENOUGH TIME TO PUSH HIM OUT OF THE WAY..
HALF A SECOND TO COVER THIRTY FEET. IMPOSSIBLE.
BUT SOMETHING INSIDE HER TELLS HER IT IS POSSIBLE.
SO SHE RUNS, OBLIVIOUS TO THE STRANGE WAY THE TRUCK'S HORN DROPS FROM A HIGH-PITCHED KEENING TO A LOW RUMBLE.
SHE RUNS, BARELY NOTICING EVERYTHING AROUND HER TWISTING, BENDING... BECOMING LAZY, LETHARGIC... SLOW.
SHE RUNS, STRAIGHT INTO THE PATH OF THE BARELY MOVING TRUCK, STRAIGHT INTO THE BARELY MOVING BOY.
AND THEN THINGS START MOVING AGAIN.
HOW... HOW DID SHE DO THAT?
HOW DID I DO THAT?
NOW... N-NOW DO YOU BELIEVE ME?
OKAY... M-MAYBE WE'VE GOT SOMETHING TO TALK ABOUT.
SLIP YOUR PHONE NUMBER UNDER MY DOOR. I... I'LL GET BACK TO YOU AS SOON AS I CAN.
RIGHT NOW, I'VE GOT TO GO.
YEAH...
... ME, TOO.

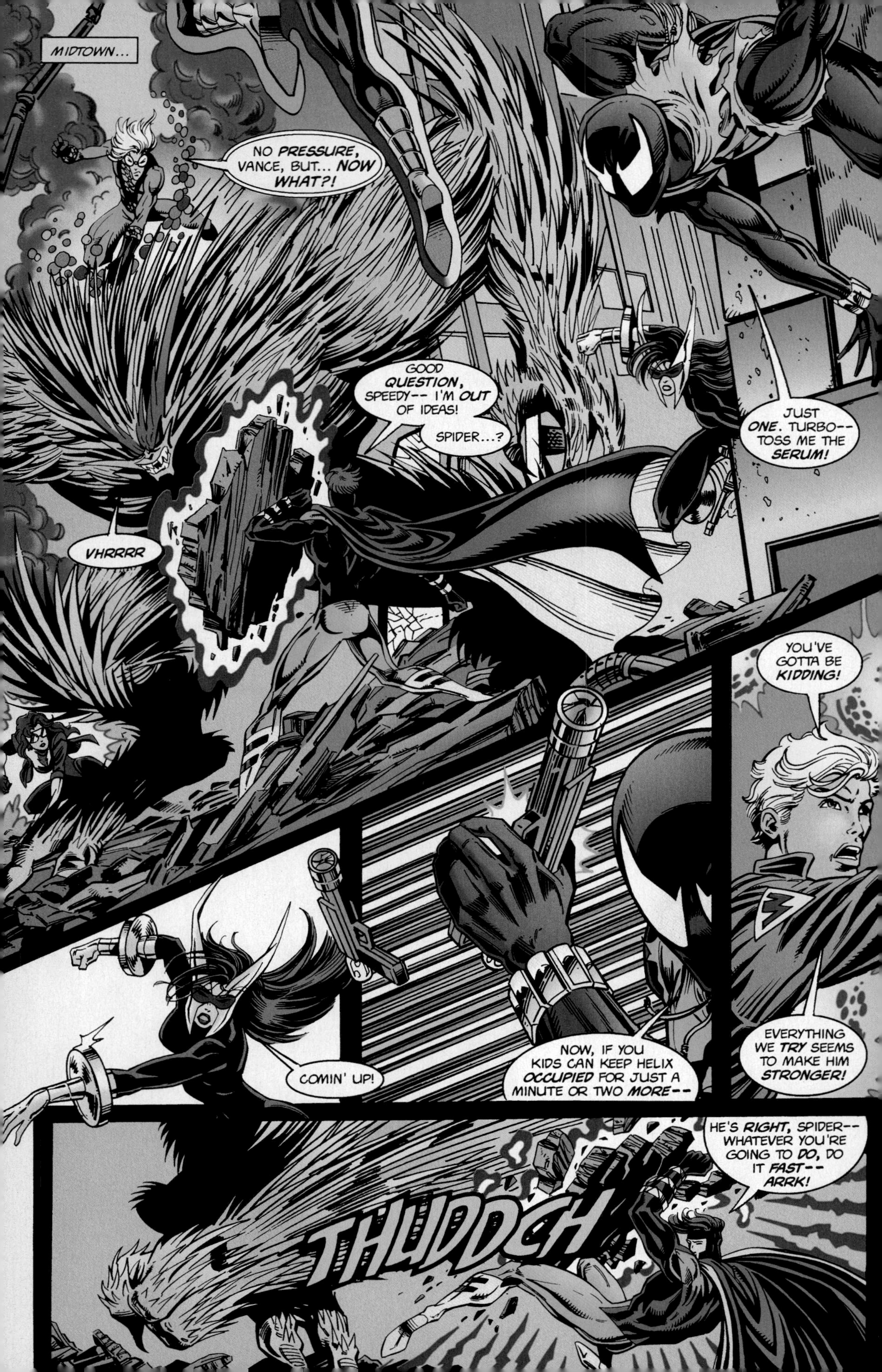
MIDTOWN...
NO PRESSURE, VANCE, BUT... NOW WHAT?!
GOOD QUESTION, SPEEDY-- I'M OUT OF IDEAS!
SPIDER...?
JUST ONE. TURBO-- TOSS ME THE SERUM!
VHRRRR
YOU'VE GOTTA BE KIDDING!
COMIN' UP!
NOW, IF YOU KIDS CAN KEEP HELIX OCCUPIED FOR JUST A MINUTE OR TWO MORE--
EVERYTHING WE TRY SEEMS TO MAKE HIM STRONGER!
HE'S RIGHT, SPIDER-- WHATEVER YOU'RE GOING TO DO, DO IT FAST-- ARRK!
THUDDCH

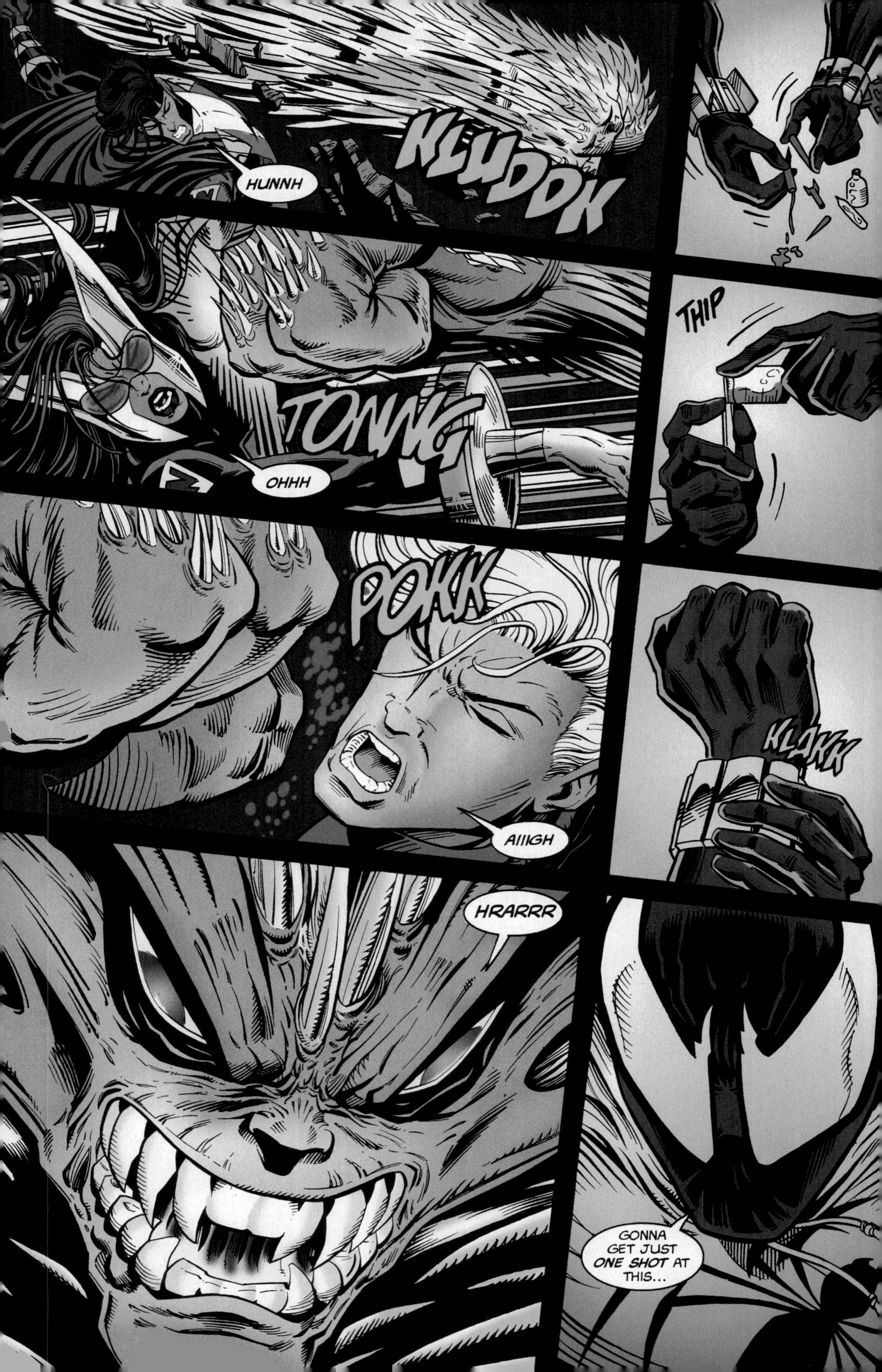
KLUDDK
HUNNH
TONNG
OHHH
POKK
AIIIGH
HRARRR
THIP
KLAKK
GONNA GET JUST ONE SHOT AT THIS...

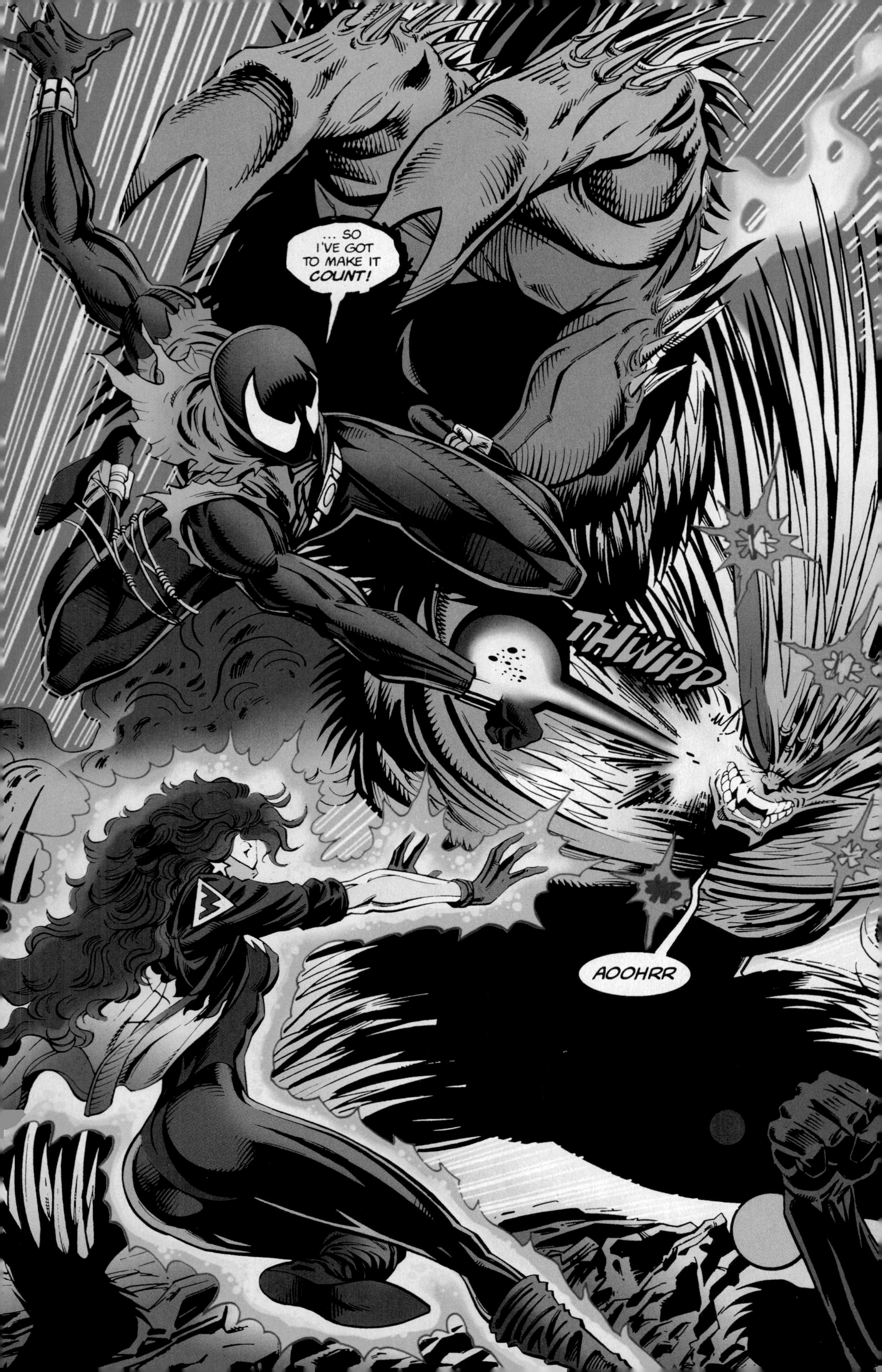
... SO I'VE GOT TO MAKE IT COUNT!
THWIPP
AOOHRR

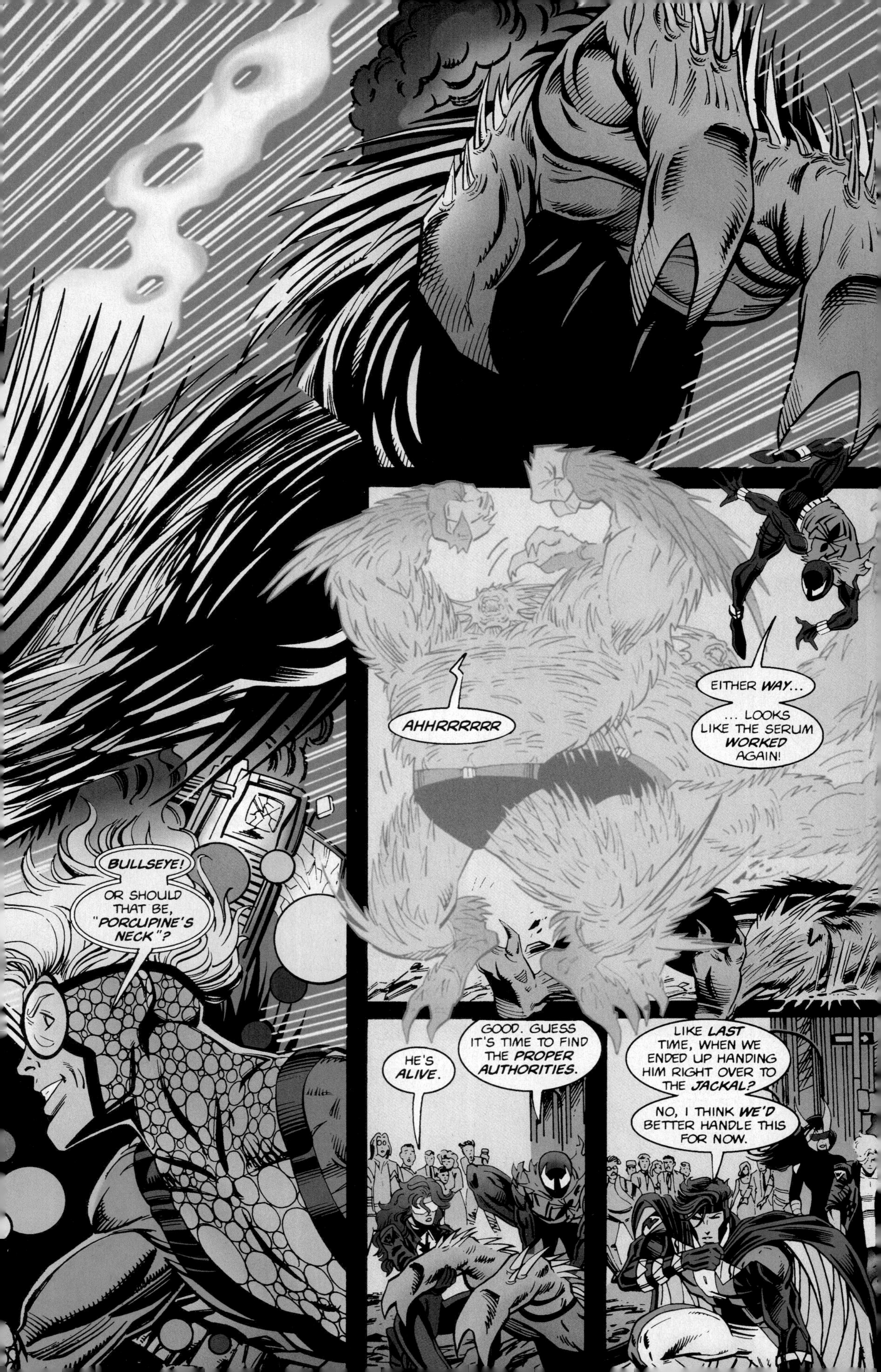
AHHRRRRRR
EITHER WAY...
... LOOKS LIKE THE SERUM WORKED AGAIN!
BULLSEYE!
OR SHOULD THAT BE, "PORCUPINE'S NECK"?
HE'S ALIVE.
GOOD. GUESS IT'S TIME TO FIND THE PROPER AUTHORITIES.
LIKE LAST TIME, WHEN WE ENDED UP HANDING HIM RIGHT OVER TO THE JACKAL?
NO, I THINK WE'D BETTER HANDLE THIS FOR NOW.

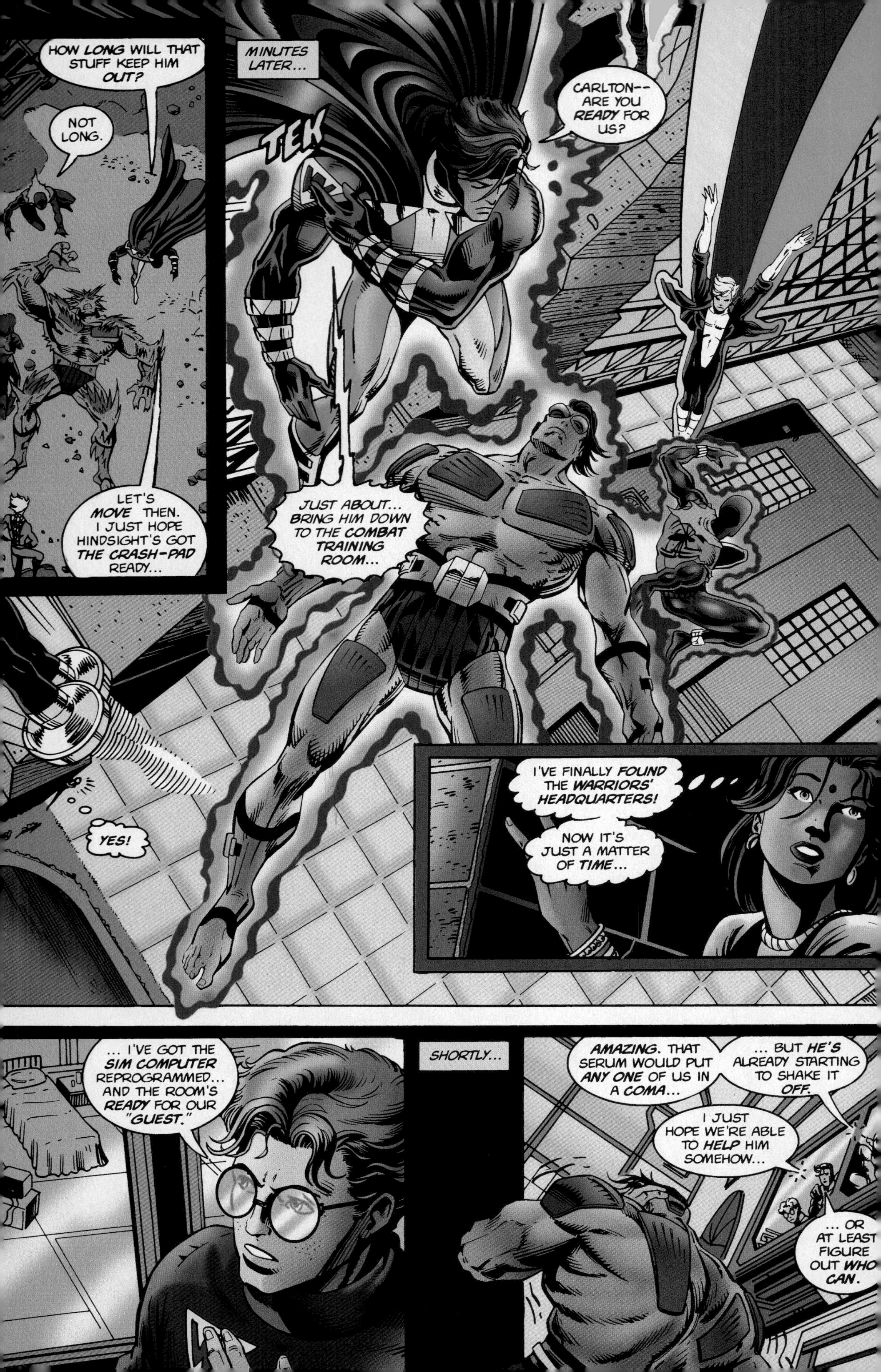
HOW LONG WILL THAT STUFF KEEP HIM OUT?
NOT LONG.
LET'S MOVE THEN. I JUST HOPE HINDSIGHT'S GOT THE CRASH-PAD READY...
MINUTES LATER...
TEK
CARLTON-- ARE YOU READY FOR US?
JUST ABOUT... BRING HIM DOWN TO THE COMBAT TRAINING ROOM...
YES!
I'VE FINALLY FOUND THE WARRIORS' HEADQUARTERS!
NOW IT'S JUST A MATTER OF TIME...
... I'VE GOT THE SIM COMPUTER REPROGRAMMED... AND THE ROOM'S READY FOR OUR "GUEST."
SHORTLY...
AMAZING. THAT SERUM WOULD PUT ANY ONE OF US IN A COMA...
... BUT HE'S ALREADY STARTING TO SHAKE IT OFF.
I JUST HOPE WE'RE ABLE TO HELP HIM SOMEHOW...
... OR AT LEAST FIGURE OUT WHO CAN.

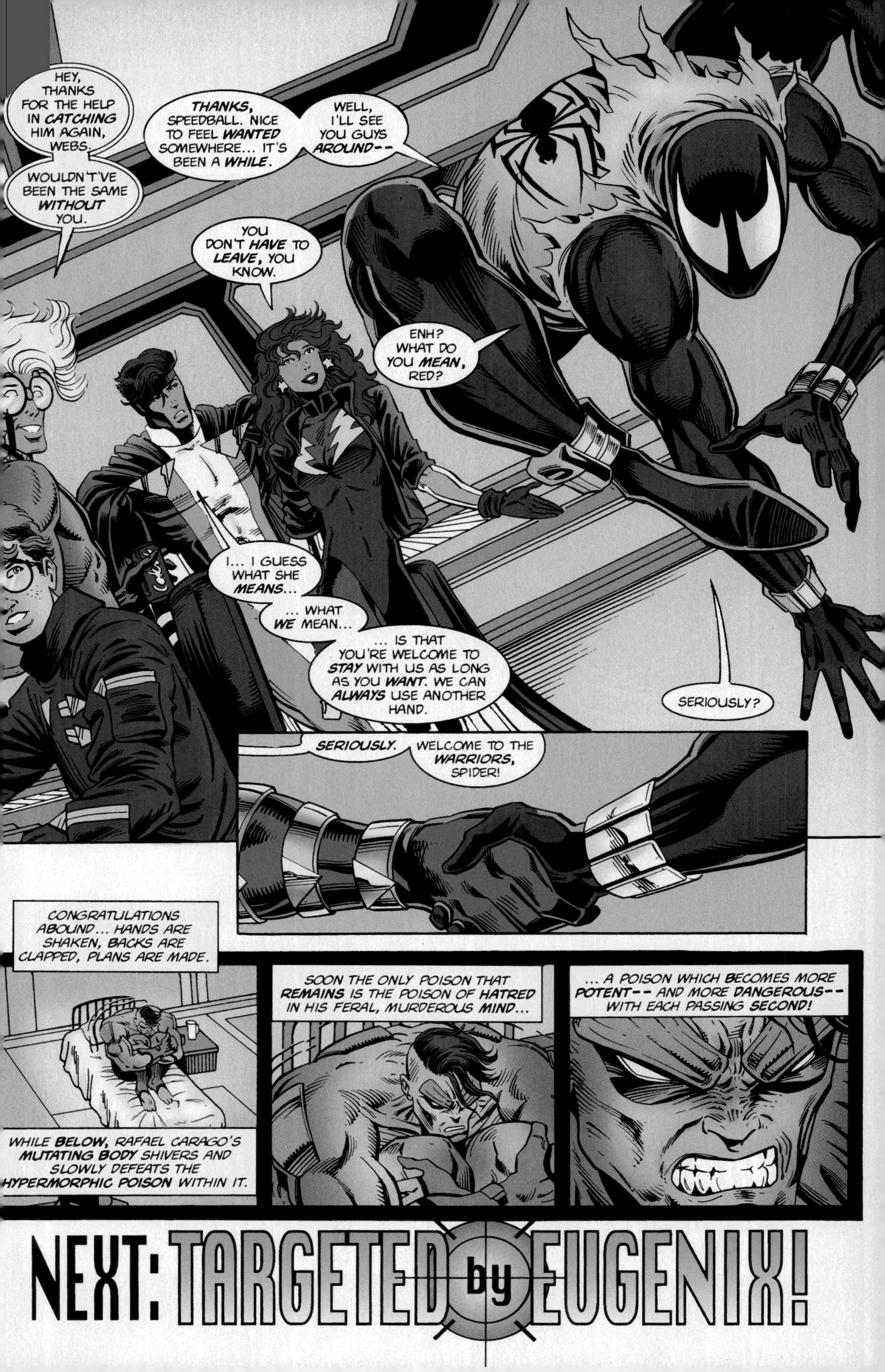

HEY, THANKS FOR THE HELP IN CATCHING HIM AGAIN, WEBS.
WOULDN'T'VE BEEN THE SAME WITHOUT YOU.
THANKS, SPEEDBALL. NICE TO FEEL WANTED SOMEWHERE... IT'S BEEN A WHILE.
WELL, I'LL SEE YOU GUYS AROUND--
YOU DON'T HAVE TO LEAVE, YOU KNOW.
ENH? WHAT DO YOU MEAN, RED?
I... I GUESS WHAT SHE MEANS...
... WHAT WE MEAN...
... IS THAT YOU'RE WELCOME TO STAY WITH US AS LONG AS YOU WANT. WE CAN ALWAYS USE ANOTHER HAND.
SERIOUSLY?
SERIOUSLY.
WELCOME TO THE WARRIORS, SPIDER!
CONGRATULATIONS ABOUND... HANDS ARE SHAKEN, BACKS ARE CLAPPED, PLANS ARE MADE.
WHILE BELOW, RAFAEL CARAGO'S MUTATING BODY SHIVERS AND SLOWLY DEFEATS THE HYPERMORPHIC POISON WITHIN IT.
SOON THE ONLY POISON THAT REMAINS IS THE POISON OF HATRED IN HIS FERAL, MURDEROUS MIND...
... A POISON WHICH BECOMES MORE POTENT-- AND MORE DANGEROUS-- WITH EACH PASSING SECOND!
NEXT: TARGETED by EUGENIX!

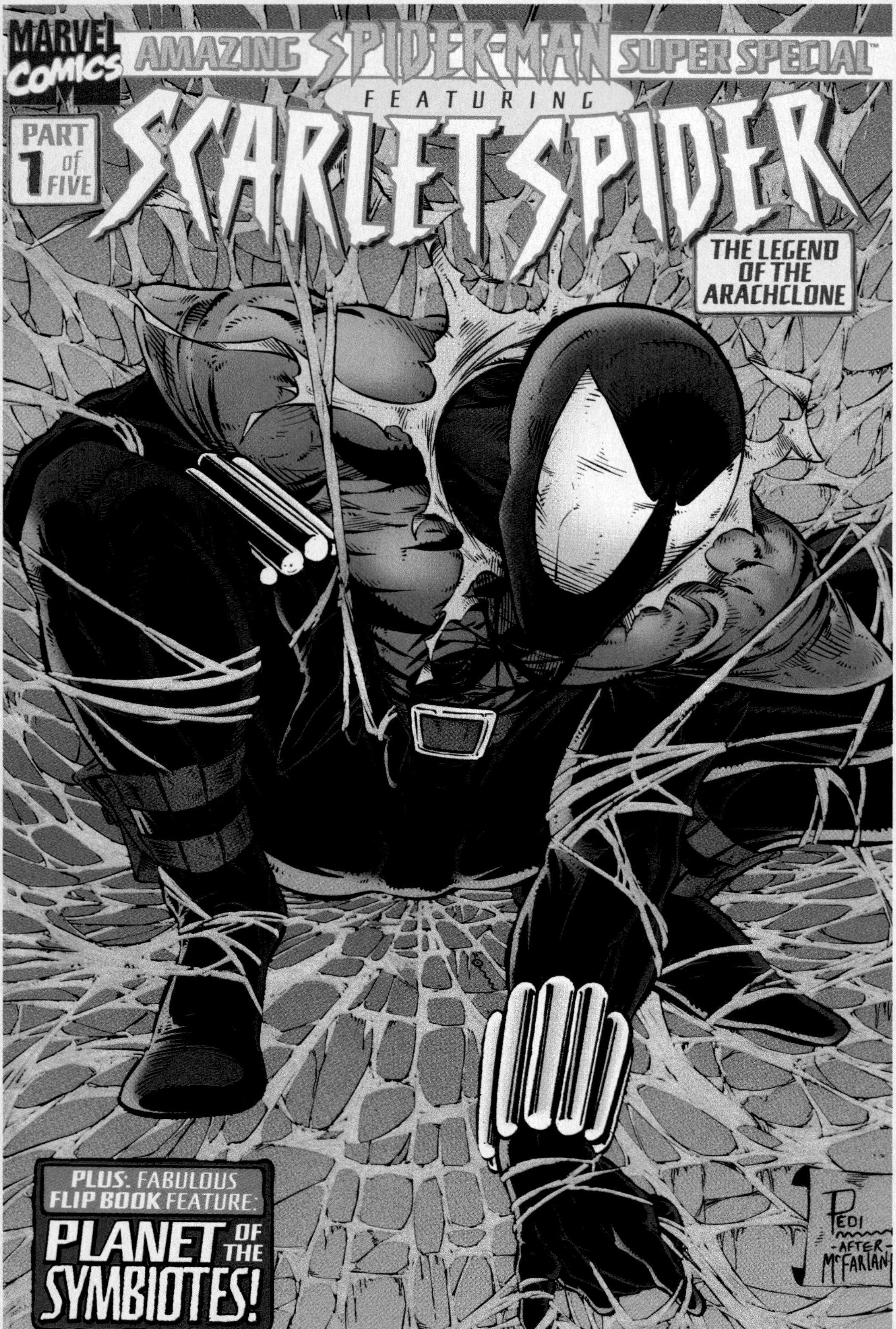

MARVEL COMICS
AMAZING SPIDER-MAN SUPER SPECIAL™
FEATURING
SCARLET SPIDER
PART 1 of FIVE
THE LEGEND OF THE ARACHCLONE
PLUS: FABULOUS FLIP BOOK FEATURE:
PLANET OF THE SYMBIOTES!
PEDI -AFTER- McFARLANE

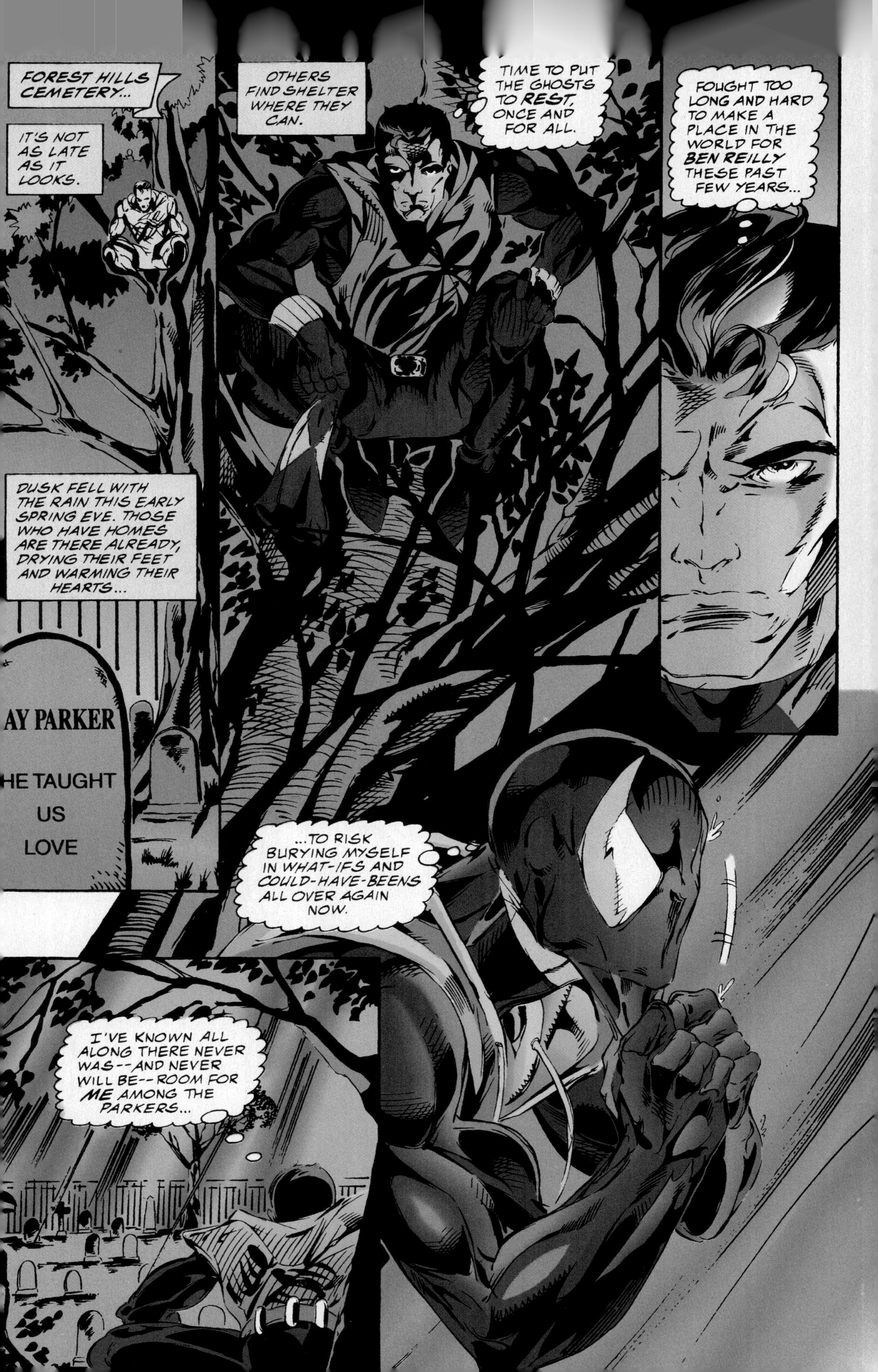

FOREST HILLS CEMETERY...
IT'S NOT AS LATE AS IT LOOKS.
DUSK FELL WITH THE RAIN THIS EARLY SPRING EVE. THOSE WHO HAVE HOMES ARE THERE ALREADY, DRYING THEIR FEET AND WARMING THEIR HEARTS...
AY PARKER
HE TAUGHT
US
LOVE
OTHERS FIND SHELTER WHERE THEY CAN.
TIME TO PUT THE GHOSTS TO REST, ONCE AND FOR ALL.
FOUGHT TOO LONG AND HARD TO MAKE A PLACE IN THE WORLD FOR BEN REILLY THESE PAST FEW YEARS...
...TO RISK BURYING MYSELF IN WHAT-IFS AND COULD-HAVE-BEENS ALL OVER AGAIN NOW.
I'VE KNOWN ALL ALONG THERE NEVER WAS--AND NEVER WILL BE--ROOM FOR ME AMONG THE PARKERS...

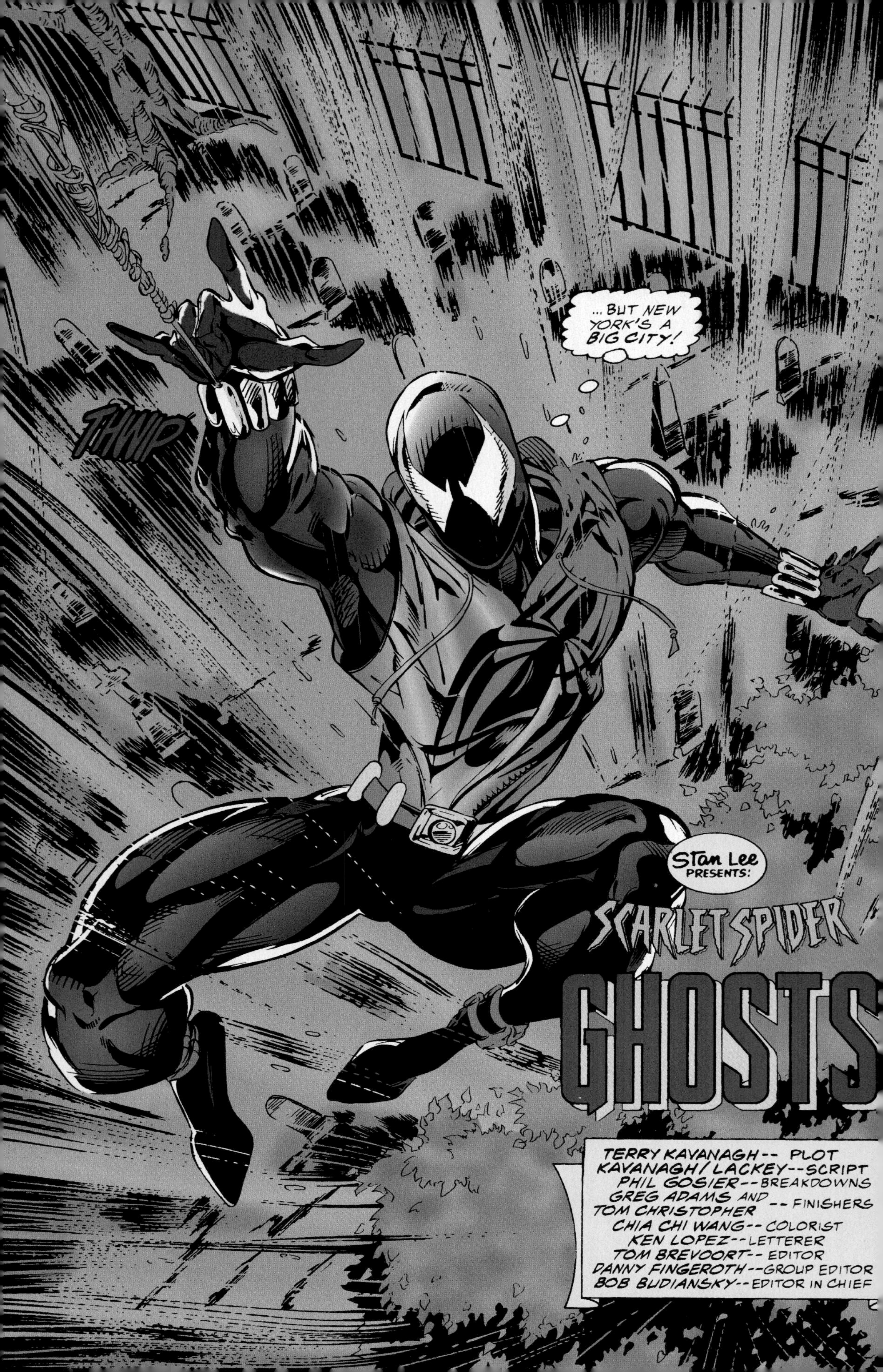
THWIP
...BUT NEW YORK'S A BIG CITY!
STAN LEE PRESENTS:
SCARLET SPIDER
GHOSTS
TERRY KAVANAGH-- PLOT
KAVANAGH/ LACKEY--SCRIPT
PHIL GOSIER--BREAKDOWNS
GREG ADAMS AND TOM CHRISTOPHER -- FINISHERS
CHIA CHI WANG--COLORIST
KEN LOPEZ--LETTERER
TOM BREVOORT-- EDITOR
DANNY FINGEROTH--GROUP EDITOR
BOB BUDIANSKY--EDITOR IN CHIEF

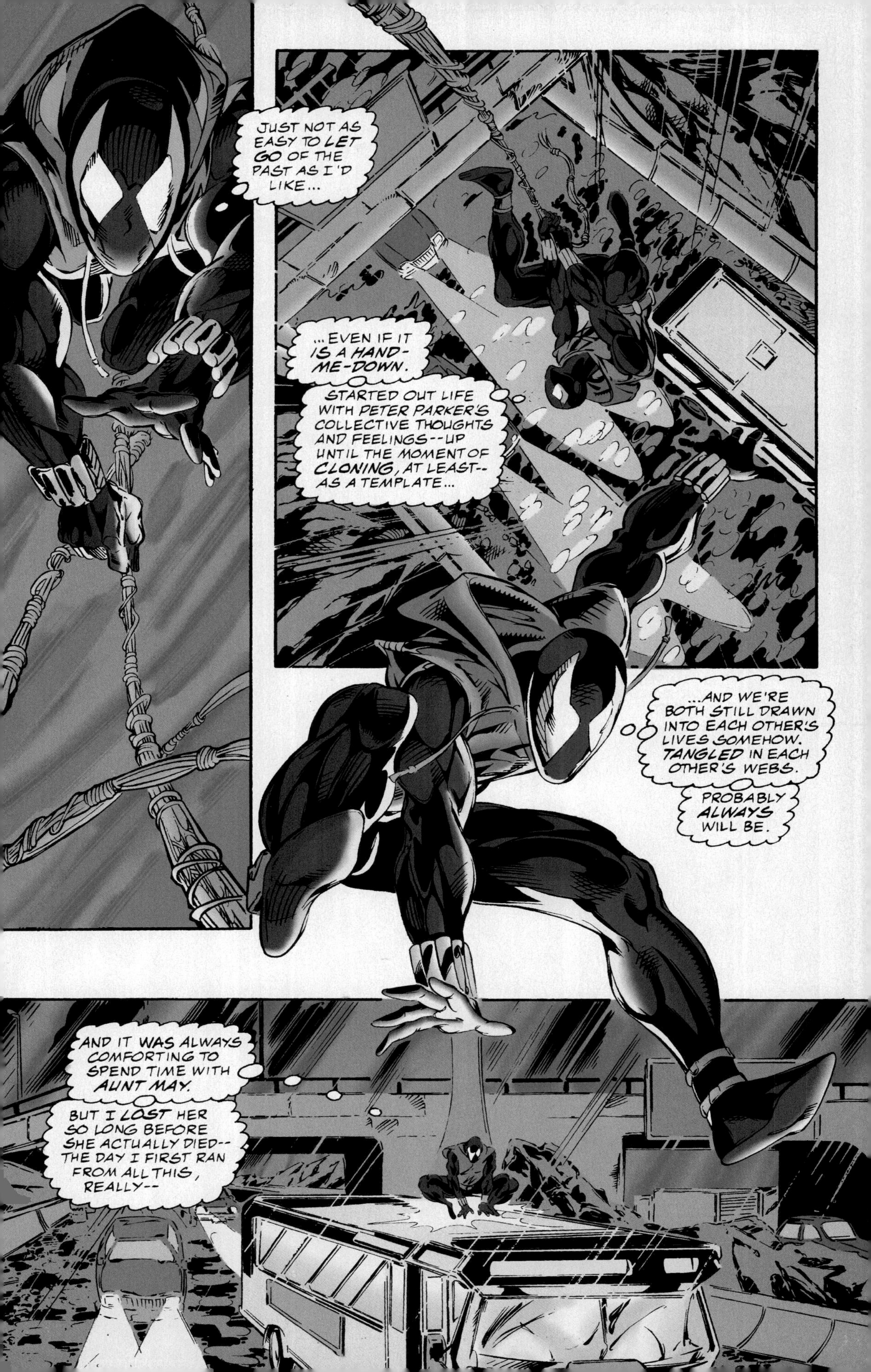
JUST NOT AS EASY TO LET GO OF THE PAST AS I'D LIKE...
...EVEN IF IT IS A HAND-ME-DOWN.
STARTED OUT LIFE WITH PETER PARKER'S COLLECTIVE THOUGHTS AND FEELINGS--UP UNTIL THE MOMENT OF CLONING, AT LEAST--AS A TEMPLATE...
...AND WE'RE BOTH STILL DRAWN INTO EACH OTHER'S LIVES SOMEHOW. TANGLED IN EACH OTHER'S WEBS.
PROBABLY ALWAYS WILL BE.
AND IT WAS ALWAYS COMFORTING TO SPEND TIME WITH AUNT MAY.
BUT I LOST HER SO LONG BEFORE SHE ACTUALLY DIED--THE DAY I FIRST RAN FROM ALL THIS, REALLY--

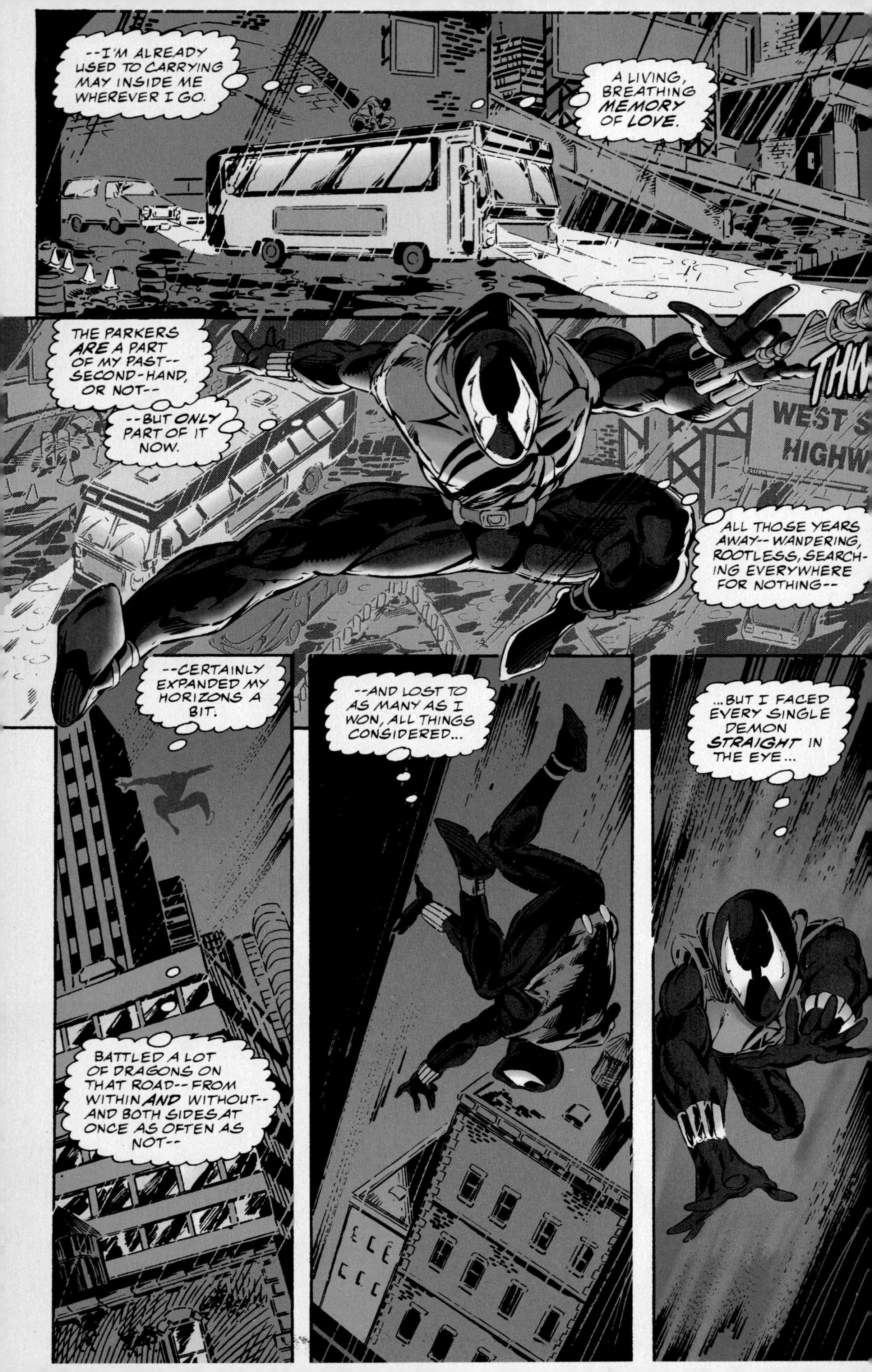
--I'M ALREADY USED TO CARRYING MAY INSIDE ME WHEREVER I GO.
A LIVING, BREATHING MEMORY OF LOVE.
THE PARKERS ARE A PART OF MY PAST-- SECOND-HAND, OR NOT--
--BUT ONLY PART OF IT NOW.
THW
WEST S
HIGHW
ALL THOSE YEARS AWAY-- WANDERING, ROOTLESS, SEARCHING EVERYWHERE FOR NOTHING--
--CERTAINLY EXPANDED MY HORIZONS A BIT.
BATTLED A LOT OF DRAGONS ON THAT ROAD-- FROM WITHIN AND WITHOUT-- AND BOTH SIDES AT ONCE AS OFTEN AS NOT--
--AND LOST TO AS MANY AS I WON, ALL THINGS CONSIDERED...
...BUT I FACED EVERY SINGLE DEMON STRAIGHT IN THE EYE...

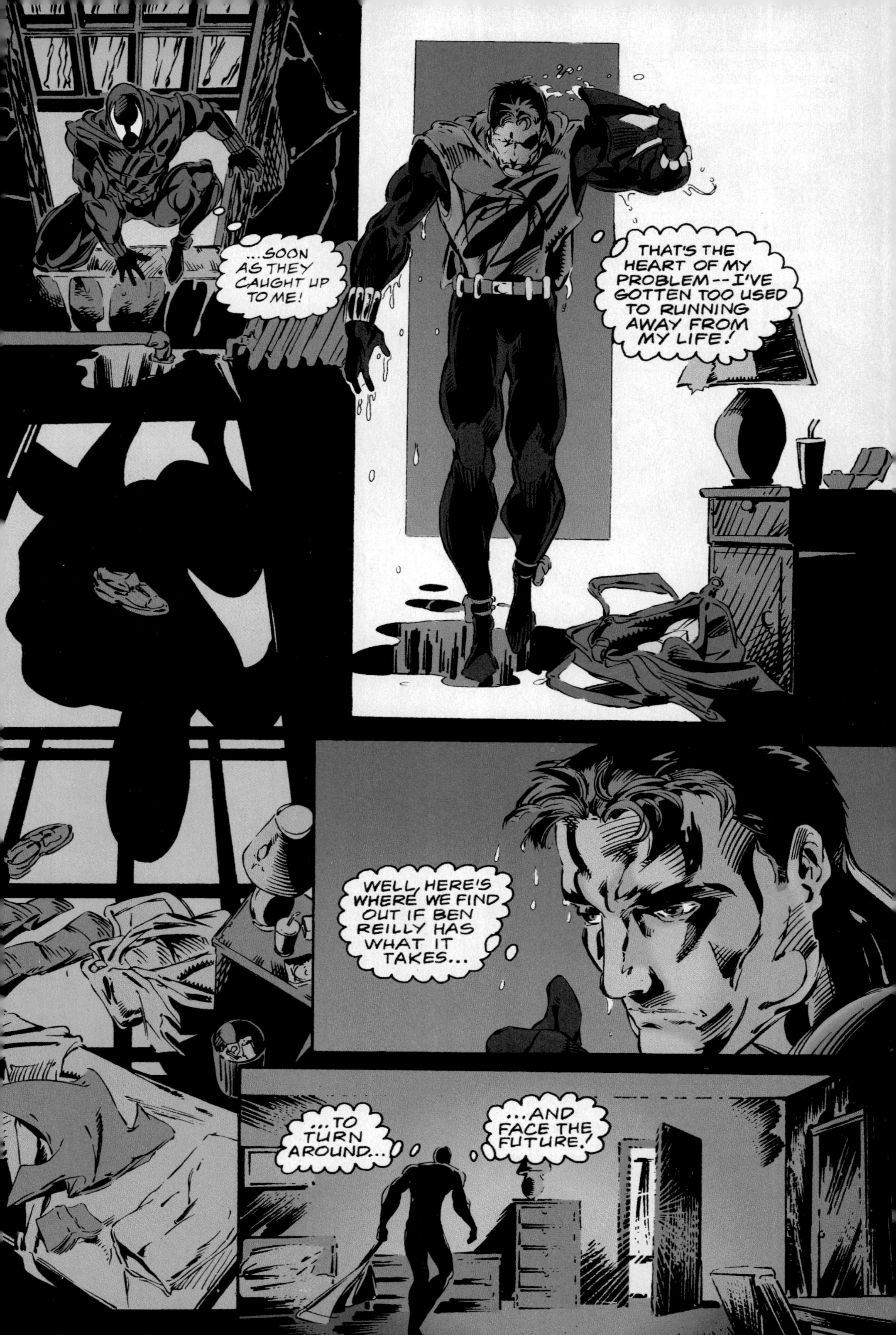
...SOON AS THEY CAUGHT UP TO ME!
THAT'S THE HEART OF MY PROBLEM--I'VE GOTTEN TOO USED TO RUNNING AWAY FROM MY LIFE!
WELL, HERE'S WHERE WE FIND OUT IF BEN REILLY HAS WHAT IT TAKES...
...TO TURN AROUND...
...AND FACE THE FUTURE!

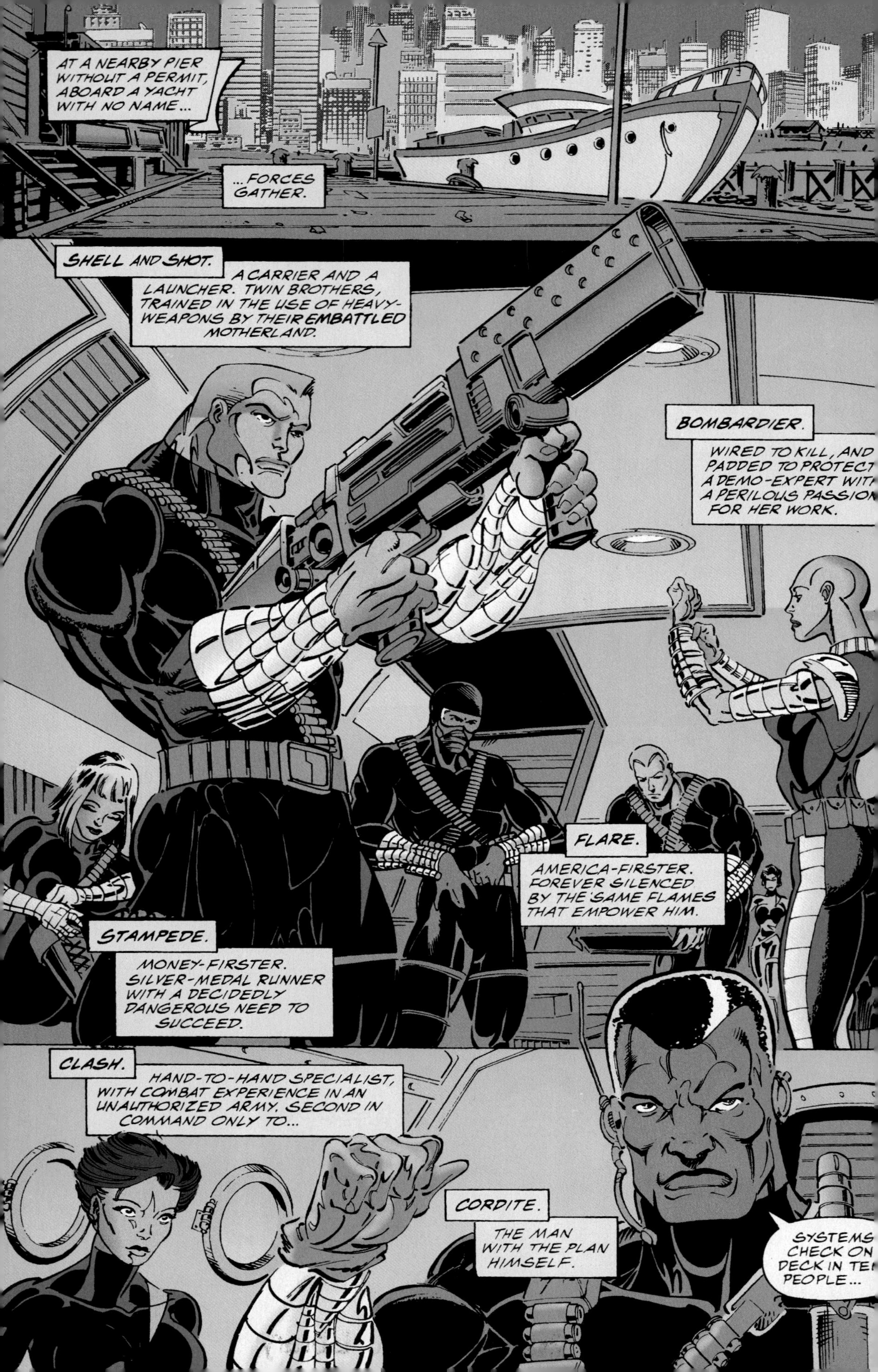
AT A NEARBY PIER WITHOUT A PERMIT, ABOARD A YACHT WITH NO NAME...
...FORCES GATHER.
SHELL AND SHOT.
A CARRIER AND A LAUNCHER. TWIN BROTHERS, TRAINED IN THE USE OF HEAVY-WEAPONS BY THEIR EMBATTLED MOTHERLAND.
BOMBARDIER.
WIRED TO KILL, AND PADDED TO PROTECT. A DEMO-EXPERT WITH A PERILOUS PASSION FOR HER WORK.
FLARE.
AMERICA-FIRSTER. FOREVER SILENCED BY THE SAME FLAMES THAT EMPOWER HIM.
STAMPEDE.
MONEY-FIRSTER. SILVER-MEDAL RUNNER WITH A DECIDEDLY DANGEROUS NEED TO SUCCEED.
CLASH.
HAND-TO-HAND SPECIALIST, WITH COMBAT EXPERIENCE IN AN UNAUTHORIZED ARMY. SECOND IN COMMAND ONLY TO...
CORDITE.
THE MAN WITH THE PLAN HIMSELF.
SYSTEMS CHECK ON DECK IN TE PEOPLE...

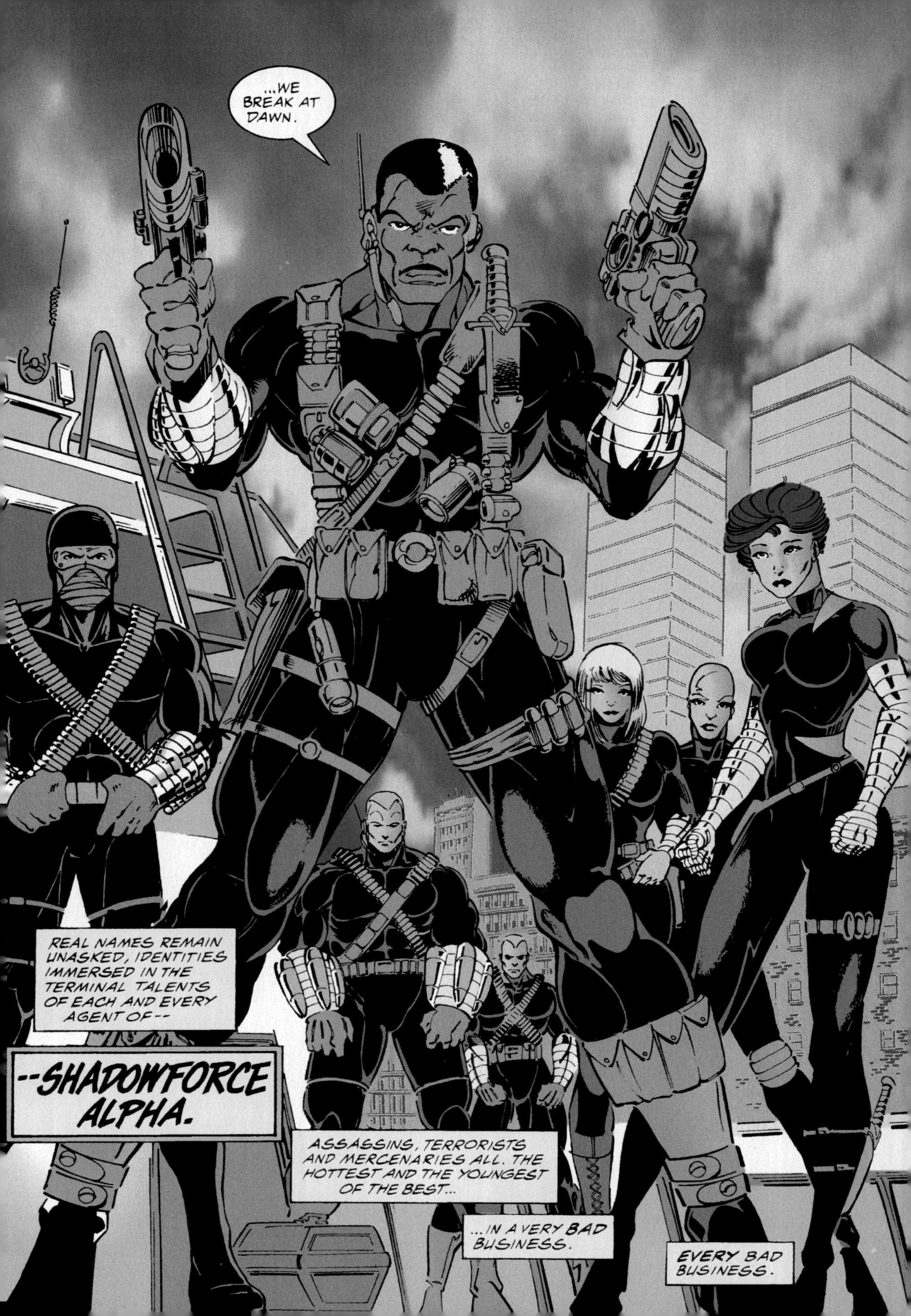
...WE BREAK AT DAWN.
REAL NAMES REMAIN UNASKED, IDENTITIES IMMERSED IN THE TERMINAL TALENTS OF EACH AND EVERY AGENT OF--
--SHADOWFORCE ALPHA.
ASSASSINS, TERRORISTS AND MERCENARIES ALL. THE HOTTEST AND THE YOUNGEST OF THE BEST...
...IN A VERY BAD BUSINESS.
EVERY BAD BUSINESS.

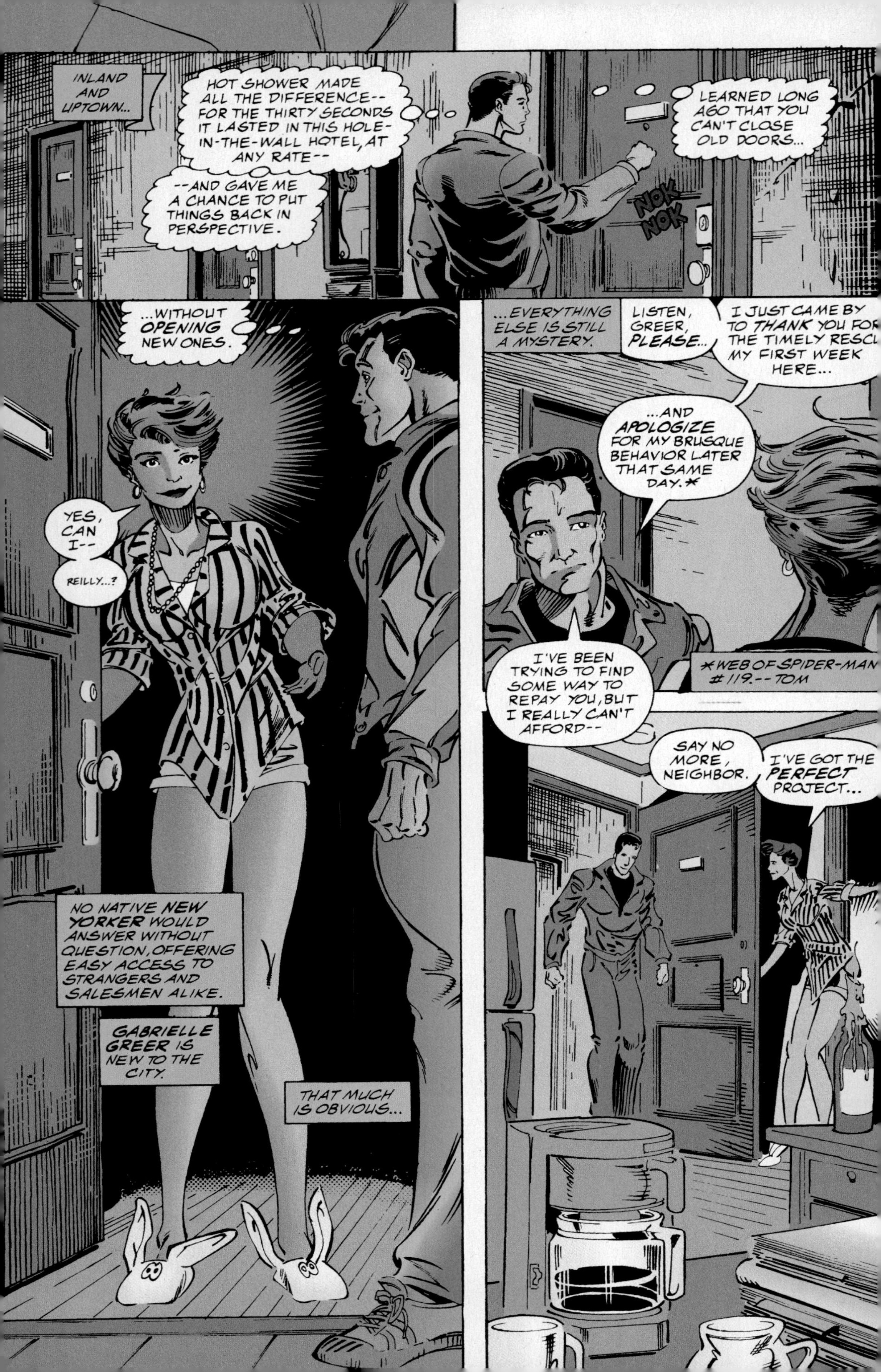
INLAND AND UPTOWN...
HOT SHOWER MADE ALL THE DIFFERENCE-- FOR THE THIRTY SECONDS IT LASTED IN THIS HOLE-IN-THE-WALL HOTEL, AT ANY RATE--
--AND GAVE ME A CHANCE TO PUT THINGS BACK IN PERSPECTIVE.
LEARNED LONG AGO THAT YOU CAN'T CLOSE OLD DOORS...
NOK NOK
...WITHOUT OPENING NEW ONES.
YES, CAN I--
REILLY...?
NO NATIVE NEW YORKER WOULD ANSWER WITHOUT QUESTION, OFFERING EASY ACCESS TO STRANGERS AND SALESMEN ALIKE.
GABRIELLE GREER IS NEW TO THE CITY.
THAT MUCH IS OBVIOUS...
...EVERYTHING ELSE IS STILL A MYSTERY.
LISTEN, GREER, PLEASE...
I JUST CAME BY TO THANK YOU FOR THE TIMELY RESCU MY FIRST WEEK HERE...
...AND APOLOGIZE FOR MY BRUSQUE BEHAVIOR LATER THAT SAME DAY.*
I'VE BEEN TRYING TO FIND SOME WAY TO REPAY YOU, BUT I REALLY CAN'T AFFORD--
*WEB OF SPIDER-MAN #119.--TOM
SAY NO MORE, NEIGHBOR.
I'VE GOT THE PERFECT PROJECT...

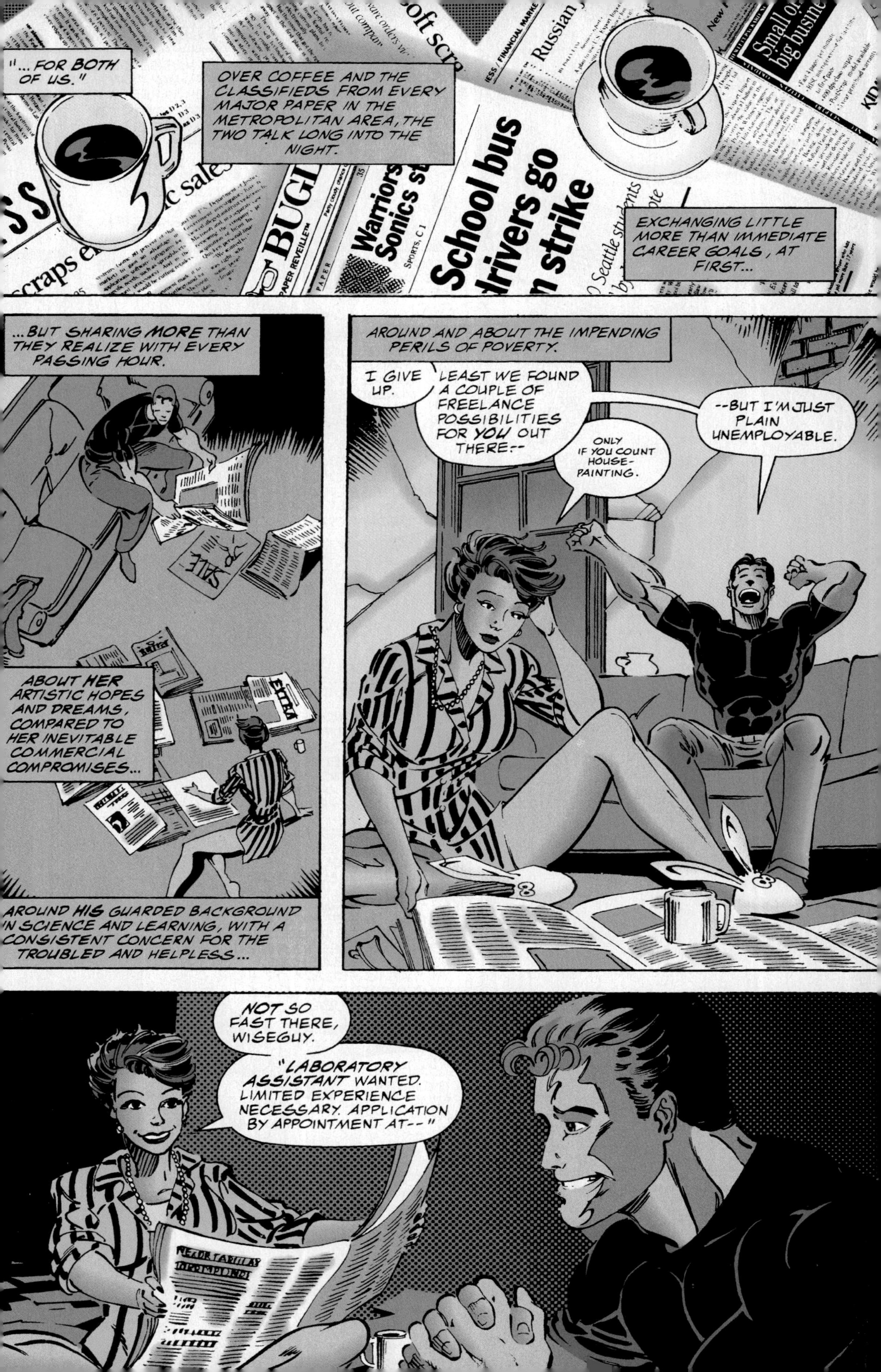
"...FOR BOTH OF US."
OVER COFFEE AND THE CLASSIFIEDS FROM EVERY MAJOR PAPER IN THE METROPOLITAN AREA, THE TWO TALK LONG INTO THE NIGHT.
School bus drivers go on strike
Warriors Sonics
EXCHANGING LITTLE MORE THAN IMMEDIATE CAREER GOALS, AT FIRST...
...BUT SHARING MORE THAN THEY REALIZE WITH EVERY PASSING HOUR.
SALE
ABOUT HER ARTISTIC HOPES AND DREAMS, COMPARED TO HER INEVITABLE COMMERCIAL COMPROMISES...
AROUND HIS GUARDED BACKGROUND IN SCIENCE AND LEARNING, WITH A CONSISTENT CONCERN FOR THE TROUBLED AND HELPLESS...
AROUND AND ABOUT THE IMPENDING PERILS OF POVERTY.
I GIVE UP.
LEAST WE FOUND A COUPLE OF FREELANCE POSSIBILITIES FOR YOU OUT THERE:--
--BUT I'M JUST PLAIN UNEMPLOYABLE.
ONLY IF YOU COUNT HOUSE-PAINTING.
NOT SO FAST THERE, WISEGUY.
"LABORATORY ASSISTANT WANTED. LIMITED EXPERIENCE NECESSARY. APPLICATION BY APPOINTMENT AT--"

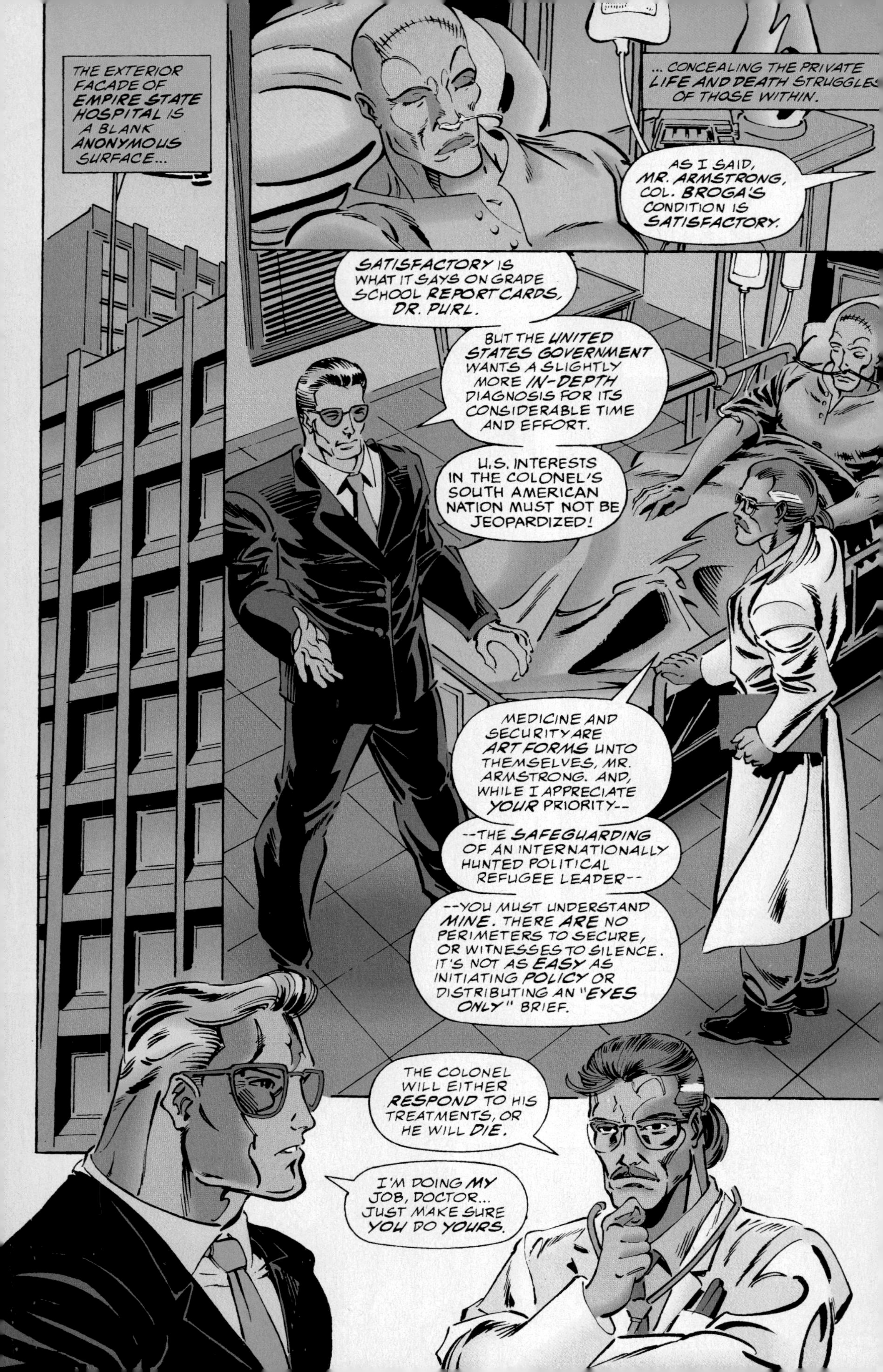

THE EXTERIOR FACADE OF EMPIRE STATE HOSPITAL IS A BLANK ANONYMOUS SURFACE...
...CONCEALING THE PRIVATE LIFE AND DEATH STRUGGLES OF THOSE WITHIN.
AS I SAID, MR. ARMSTRONG, COL. BROGA'S CONDITION IS SATISFACTORY.
SATISFACTORY IS WHAT IT SAYS ON GRADE SCHOOL REPORT CARDS, DR. PURL.
BUT THE UNITED STATES GOVERNMENT WANTS A SLIGHTLY MORE IN-DEPTH DIAGNOSIS FOR ITS CONSIDERABLE TIME AND EFFORT.
U.S. INTERESTS IN THE COLONEL'S SOUTH AMERICAN NATION MUST NOT BE JEOPARDIZED!
MEDICINE AND SECURITY ARE ART FORMS UNTO THEMSELVES, MR. ARMSTRONG. AND, WHILE I APPRECIATE YOUR PRIORITY--
--THE SAFEGUARDING OF AN INTERNATIONALLY HUNTED POLITICAL REFUGEE LEADER--
--YOU MUST UNDERSTAND MINE. THERE ARE NO PERIMETERS TO SECURE, OR WITNESSES TO SILENCE. IT'S NOT AS EASY AS INITIATING POLICY OR DISTRIBUTING AN "EYES ONLY" BRIEF.
THE COLONEL WILL EITHER RESPOND TO HIS TREATMENTS, OR HE WILL DIE.
I'M DOING MY JOB, DOCTOR... JUST MAKE SURE YOU DO YOURS.

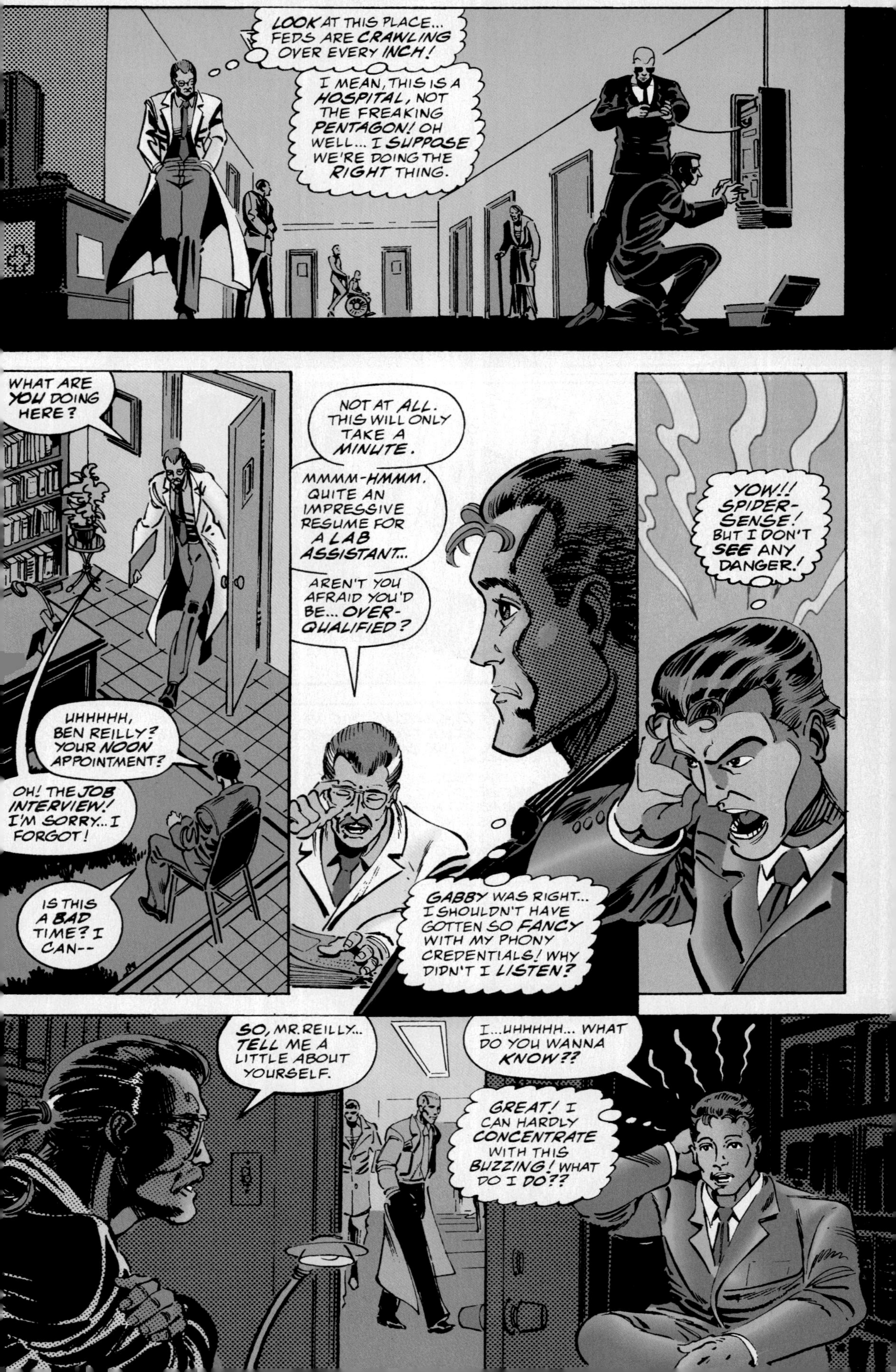

LOOK AT THIS PLACE... FEDS ARE CRAWLING OVER EVERY INCH!
I MEAN, THIS IS A HOSPITAL, NOT THE FREAKING PENTAGON! OH WELL... I SUPPOSE WE'RE DOING THE RIGHT THING.
WHAT ARE YOU DOING HERE?
UHHHHH, BEN REILLY? YOUR NOON APPOINTMENT?
OH! THE JOB INTERVIEW! I'M SORRY... I FORGOT!
IS THIS A BAD TIME? I CAN--
NOT AT ALL. THIS WILL ONLY TAKE A MINUTE.
MMMM-HMMM. QUITE AN IMPRESSIVE RESUME FOR A LAB ASSISTANT...
AREN'T YOU AFRAID YOU'D BE... OVER-QUALIFIED?
GABBY WAS RIGHT... I SHOULDN'T HAVE GOTTEN SO FANCY WITH MY PHONY CREDENTIALS! WHY DIDN'T I LISTEN?
YOW!! SPIDER-SENSE! BUT I DON'T SEE ANY DANGER!
SO, MR. REILLY.. TELL ME A LITTLE ABOUT YOURSELF.
I...UHHHHH... WHAT DO YOU WANNA KNOW??
GREAT! I CAN HARDLY CONCENTRATE WITH THIS BUZZING! WHAT DO I DO??

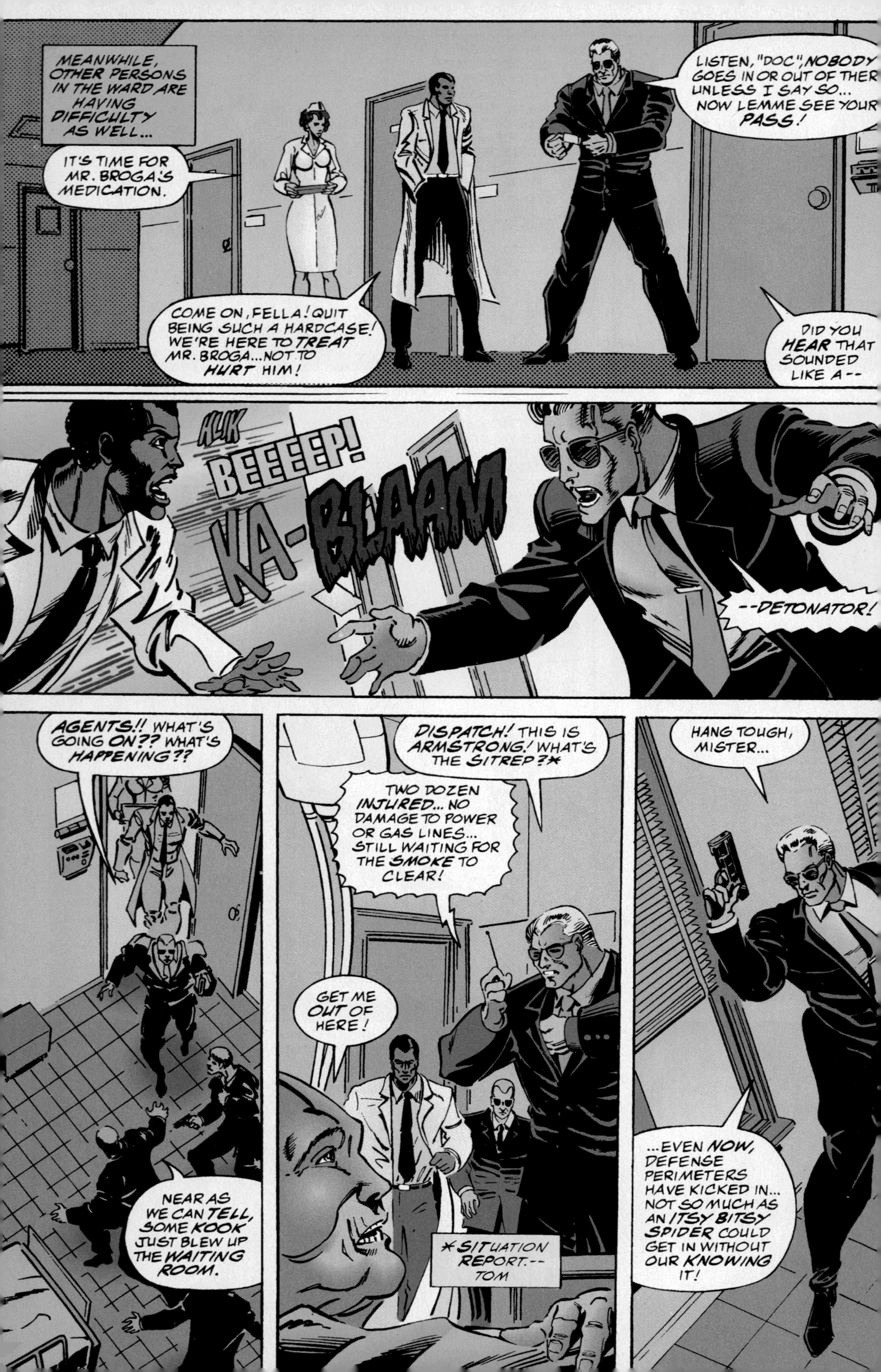
MEANWHILE, OTHER PERSONS IN THE WARD ARE HAVING DIFFICULTY AS WELL...
IT'S TIME FOR MR. BROGA'S MEDICATION.
LISTEN, "DOC", NOBODY GOES IN OR OUT OF THERE UNLESS I SAY SO... NOW LEMME SEE YOUR PASS!
COME ON, FELLA! QUIT BEING SUCH A HARDCASE! WE'RE HERE TO TREAT MR. BROGA...NOT TO HURT HIM!
DID YOU HEAR THAT SOUNDED LIKE A --
KLIK
BEEEEP!
KA-BLAAM
--DETONATOR!
AGENTS!! WHAT'S GOING ON?? WHAT'S HAPPENING??
NEAR AS WE CAN TELL, SOME KOOK JUST BLEW UP THE WAITING ROOM.
DISPATCH! THIS IS ARMSTRONG! WHAT'S THE SITREP?*
TWO DOZEN INJURED... NO DAMAGE TO POWER OR GAS LINES... STILL WAITING FOR THE SMOKE TO CLEAR!
GET ME OUT OF HERE!
*SITUATION REPORT.-- TOM
HANG TOUGH, MISTER...
...EVEN NOW, DEFENSE PERIMETERS HAVE KICKED IN... NOT SO MUCH AS AN ITSY BITSY SPIDER COULD GET IN WITHOUT OUR KNOWING IT!

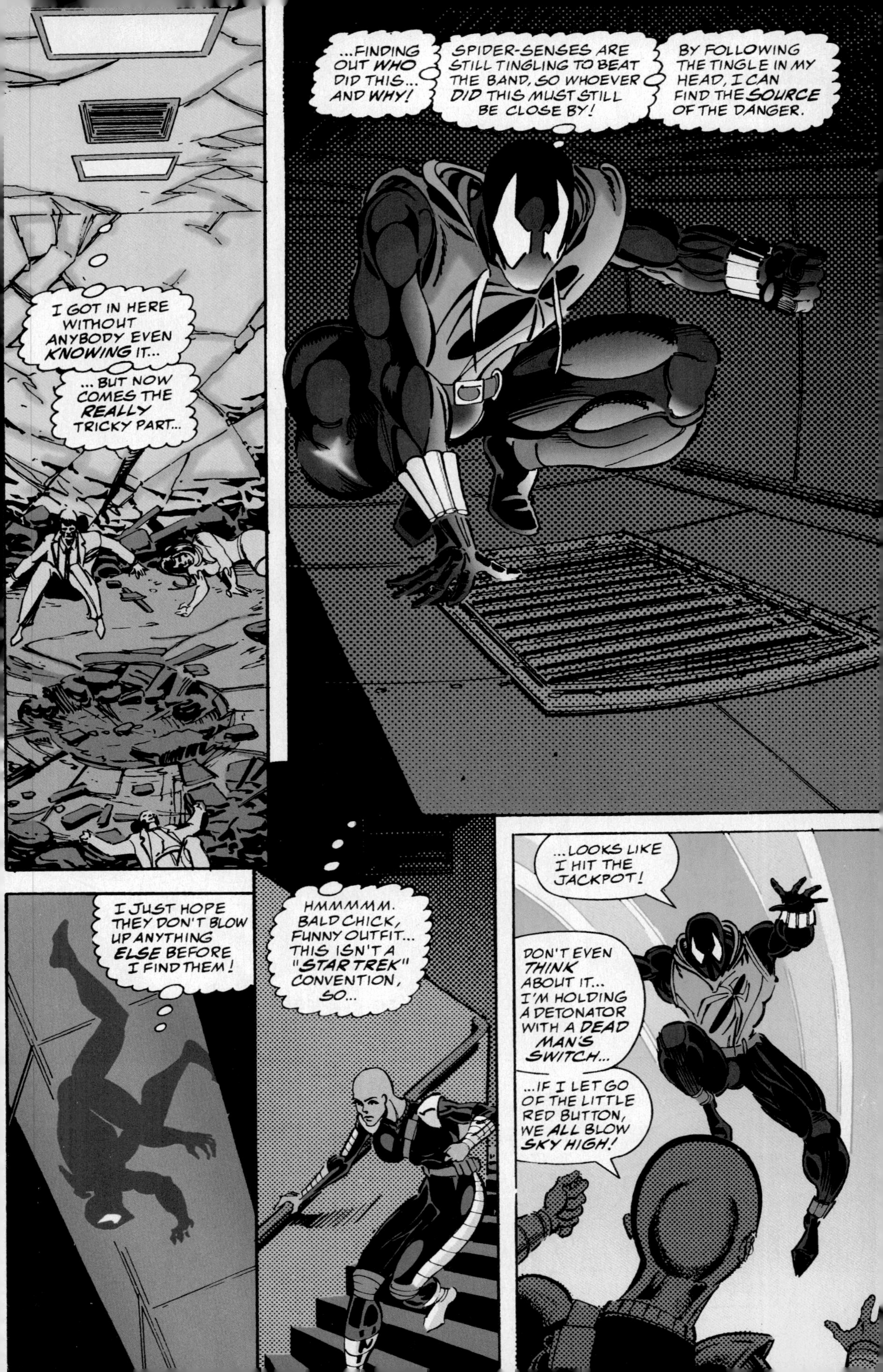
I GOT IN HERE WITHOUT ANYBODY EVEN KNOWING IT...
... BUT NOW COMES THE REALLY TRICKY PART...
...FINDING OUT WHO DID THIS... AND WHY!
SPIDER-SENSES ARE STILL TINGLING TO BEAT THE BAND, SO WHOEVER DID THIS MUST STILL BE CLOSE BY!
BY FOLLOWING THE TINGLE IN MY HEAD, I CAN FIND THE SOURCE OF THE DANGER.
I JUST HOPE THEY DON'T BLOW UP ANYTHING ELSE BEFORE I FIND THEM!
HMMMMM. BALD CHICK, FUNNY OUTFIT... THIS ISN'T A "STAR TREK" CONVENTION, SO...
...LOOKS LIKE I HIT THE JACKPOT!
DON'T EVEN THINK ABOUT IT... I'M HOLDING A DETONATOR WITH A DEAD MAN'S SWITCH...
...IF I LET GO OF THE LITTLE RED BUTTON, WE ALL BLOW SKY HIGH!

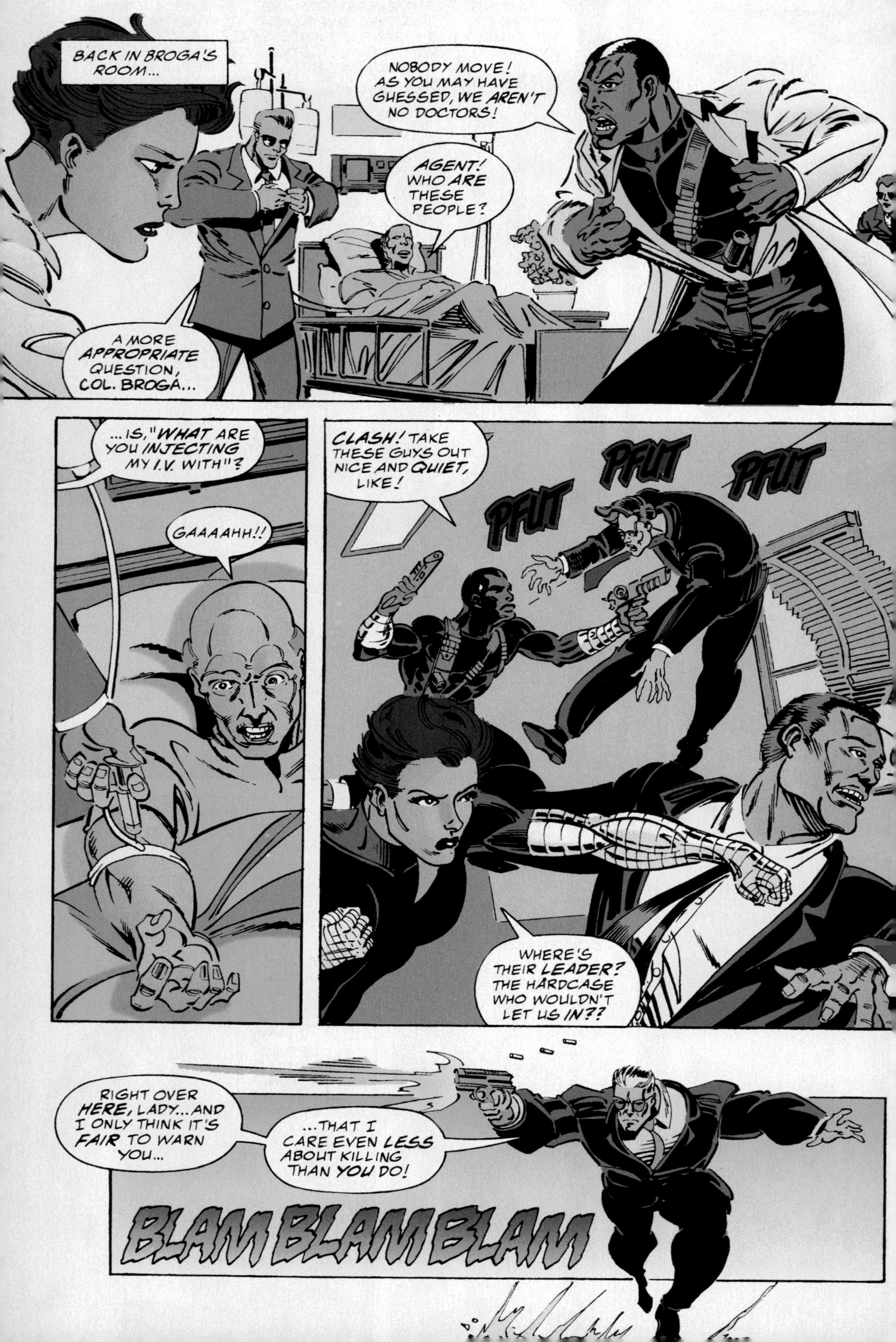
BACK IN BROGA'S ROOM...
NOBODY MOVE! AS YOU MAY HAVE GUESSED, WE AREN'T NO DOCTORS!
AGENT! WHO ARE THESE PEOPLE?
A MORE APPROPRIATE QUESTION, COL. BROGA...
...IS, "WHAT ARE YOU INJECTING MY I.V. WITH"?
GAAAAHH!!
CLASH! TAKE THESE GUYS OUT NICE AND QUIET, LIKE!
PFUT
PFUT
PFUT
WHERE'S THEIR LEADER? THE HARDCASE WHO WOULDN'T LET US IN??
RIGHT OVER HERE, LADY... AND I ONLY THINK IT'S FAIR TO WARN YOU...
...THAT I CARE EVEN LESS ABOUT KILLING THAN YOU DO!
BLAM BLAM BLAM

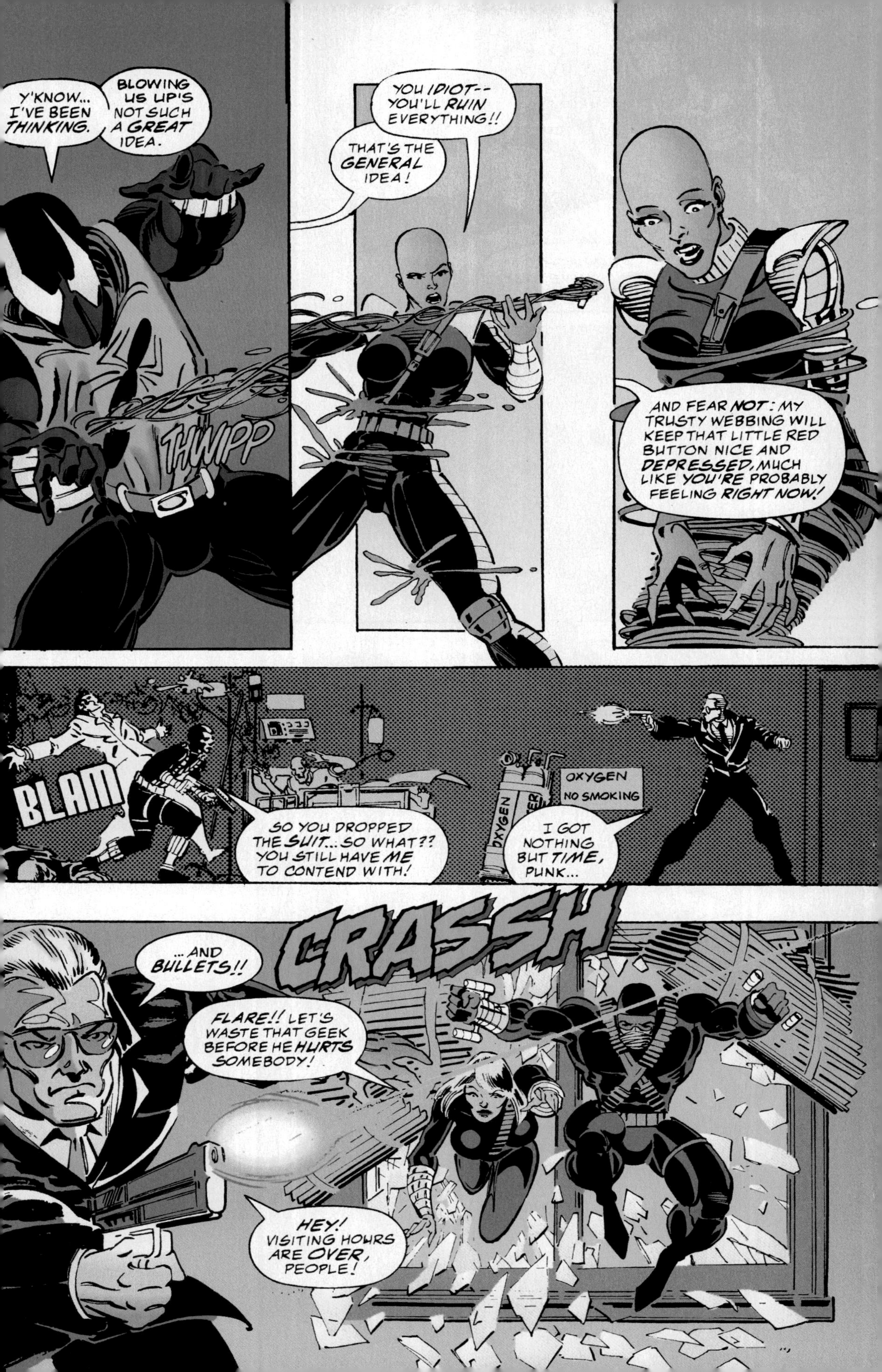
Y'KNOW... I'VE BEEN THINKING.
BLOWING US UP'S NOT SUCH A GREAT IDEA.
YOU IDIOT-- YOU'LL RUIN EVERYTHING!!
THAT'S THE GENERAL IDEA!
THWIPP
AND FEAR NOT: MY TRUSTY WEBBING WILL KEEP THAT LITTLE RED BUTTON NICE AND DEPRESSED, MUCH LIKE YOU'RE PROBABLY FEELING RIGHT NOW!
BLAM
OXYGEN
NO SMOKING
OXYGEN
SO YOU DROPPED THE SUIT... SO WHAT?? YOU STILL HAVE ME TO CONTEND WITH!
I GOT NOTHING BUT TIME, PUNK...
CRASSH
...AND BULLETS!!
FLARE!! LET'S WASTE THAT GEEK BEFORE HE HURTS SOMEBODY!
HEY! VISITING HOURS ARE OVER, PEOPLE!

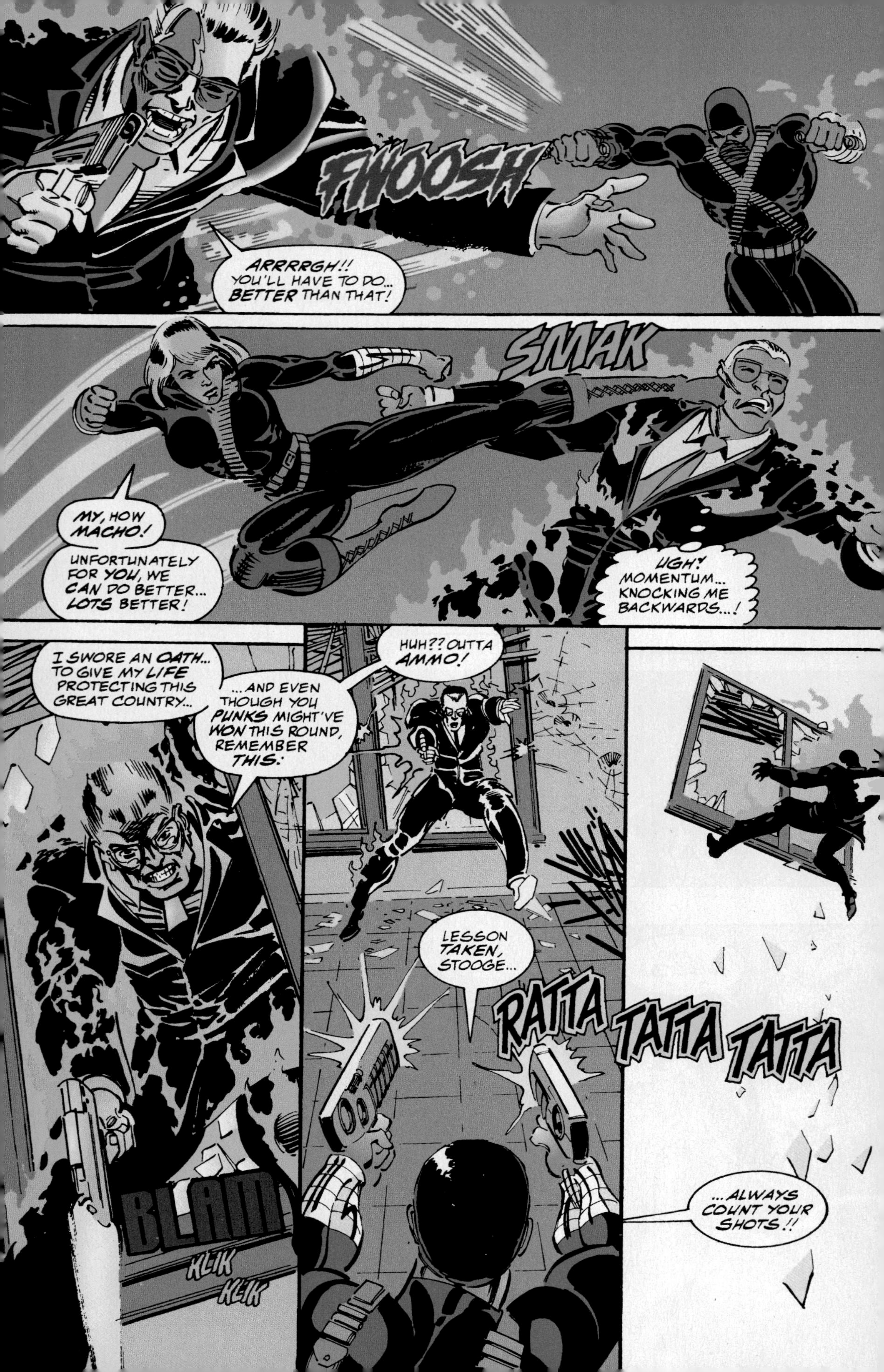
FWOOSH
ARRRRGH!! YOU'LL HAVE TO DO... BETTER THAN THAT!
SMAK
MY, HOW MACHO!
UNFORTUNATELY FOR YOU, WE CAN DO BETTER... LOTS BETTER!
UGH! MOMENTUM... KNOCKING ME BACKWARDS...!
I SWORE AN OATH... TO GIVE MY LIFE PROTECTING THIS GREAT COUNTRY...
...AND EVEN THOUGH YOU PUNKS MIGHT'VE WON THIS ROUND, REMEMBER THIS:
BLAM
KLIK
KLIK
HUH?? OUTTA AMMO!
LESSON TAKEN, STOOGE...
RATTA TATTA TATTA
...ALWAYS COUNT YOUR SHOTS!!

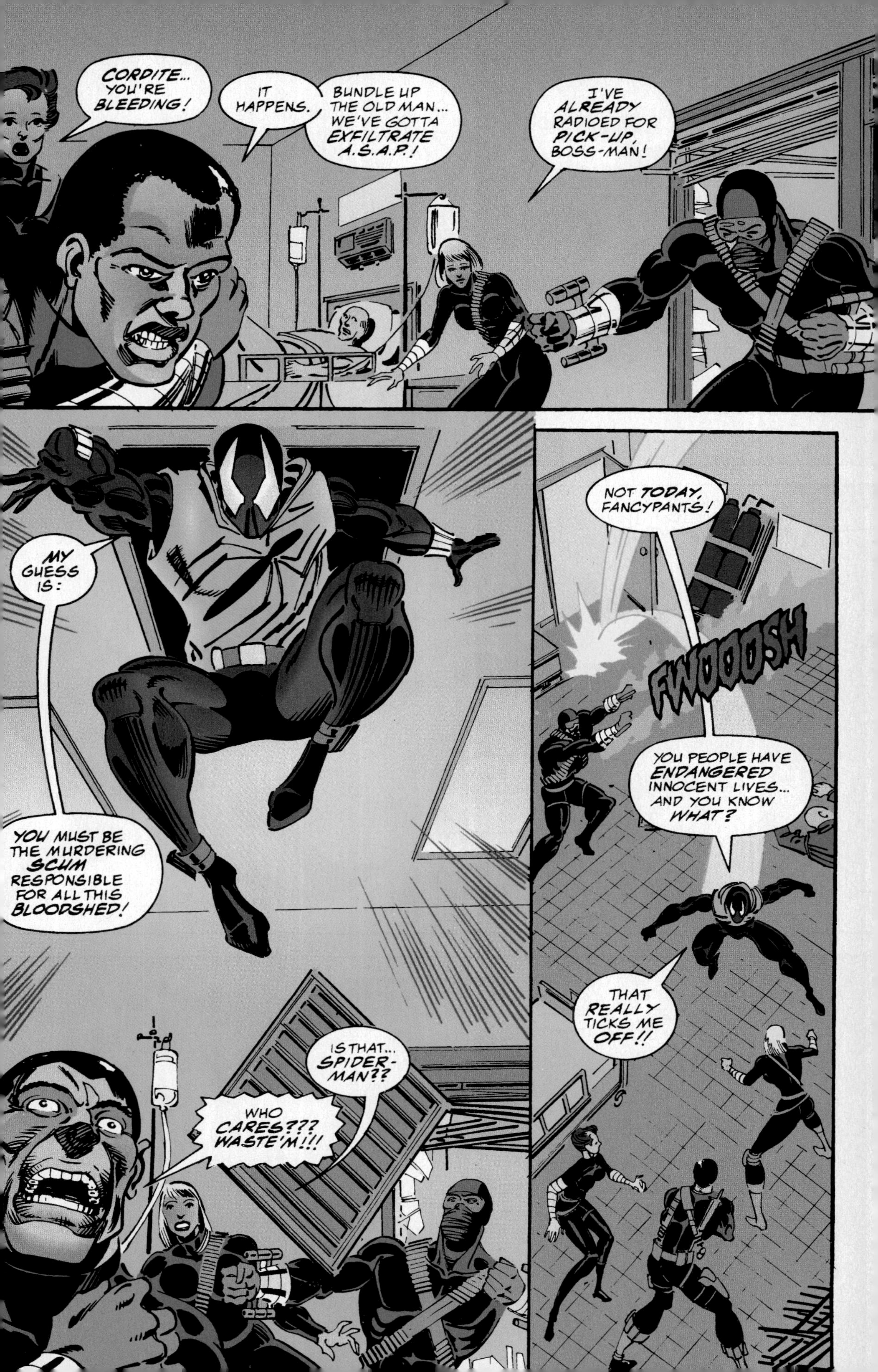
CORDITE... YOU'RE BLEEDING!
IT HAPPENS.
BUNDLE UP THE OLD MAN... WE'VE GOTTA EXFILTRATE A.S.A.P.!
I'VE ALREADY RADIOED FOR PICK-UP, BOSS-MAN!
MY GUESS IS:
YOU MUST BE THE MURDERING SCUM RESPONSIBLE FOR ALL THIS BLOODSHED!
IS THAT... SPIDER-MAN??
WHO CARES??? WASTE'M!!!
NOT TODAY, FANCYPANTS!
FWOOOSH
YOU PEOPLE HAVE ENDANGERED INNOCENT LIVES... AND YOU KNOW WHAT?
THAT REALLY TICKS ME OFF!!

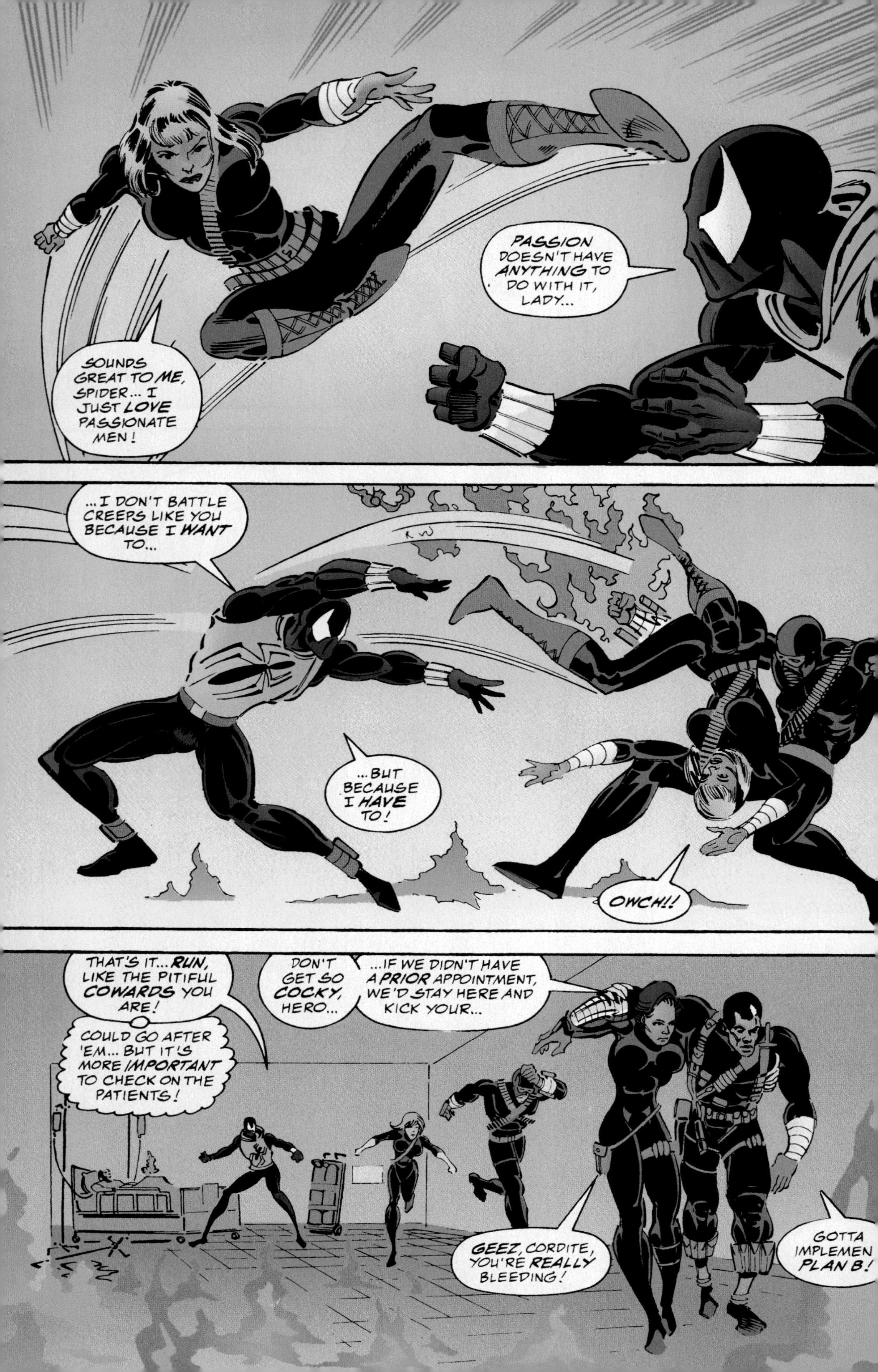
PASSION DOESN'T HAVE ANYTHING TO DO WITH IT, LADY...
SOUNDS GREAT TO ME, SPIDER... I JUST LOVE PASSIONATE MEN!
...I DON'T BATTLE CREEPS LIKE YOU BECAUSE I WANT TO...
...BUT BECAUSE I HAVE TO!
OWCH!!
THAT'S IT... RUN, LIKE THE PITIFUL COWARDS YOU ARE!
COULD GO AFTER 'EM... BUT IT'S MORE IMPORTANT TO CHECK ON THE PATIENTS!
DON'T GET SO COCKY, HERO...
...IF WE DIDN'T HAVE A PRIOR APPOINTMENT, WE'D STAY HERE AND KICK YOUR...
GEEZ, CORDITE, YOU'RE REALLY BLEEDING!
GOTTA IMPLEMEN PLAN B!

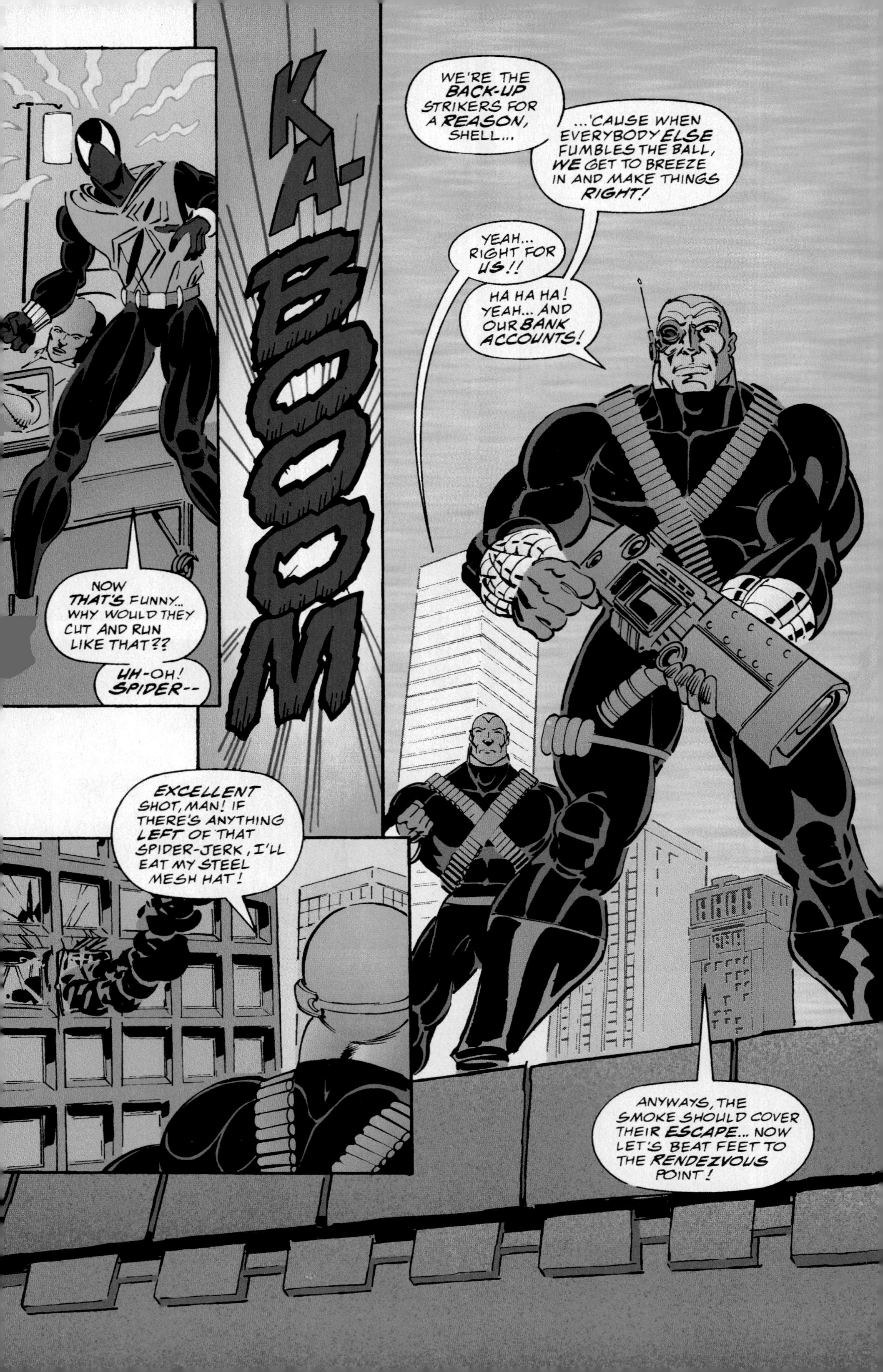
NOW THAT'S FUNNY... WHY WOULD THEY CUT AND RUN LIKE THAT??
UH-OH! SPIDER--
KA-BOOOOM
WE'RE THE BACK-UP STRIKERS FOR A REASON, SHELL...
...'CAUSE WHEN EVERYBODY ELSE FUMBLES THE BALL, WE GET TO BREEZE IN AND MAKE THINGS RIGHT!
YEAH... RIGHT FOR US!!
HA HA HA! YEAH... AND OUR BANK ACCOUNTS!
EXCELLENT SHOT, MAN! IF THERE'S ANYTHING LEFT OF THAT SPIDER-JERK, I'LL EAT MY STEEL MESH HAT!
ANYWAYS, THE SMOKE SHOULD COVER THEIR ESCAPE... NOW LET'S BEAT FEET TO THE RENDEZVOUS POINT!

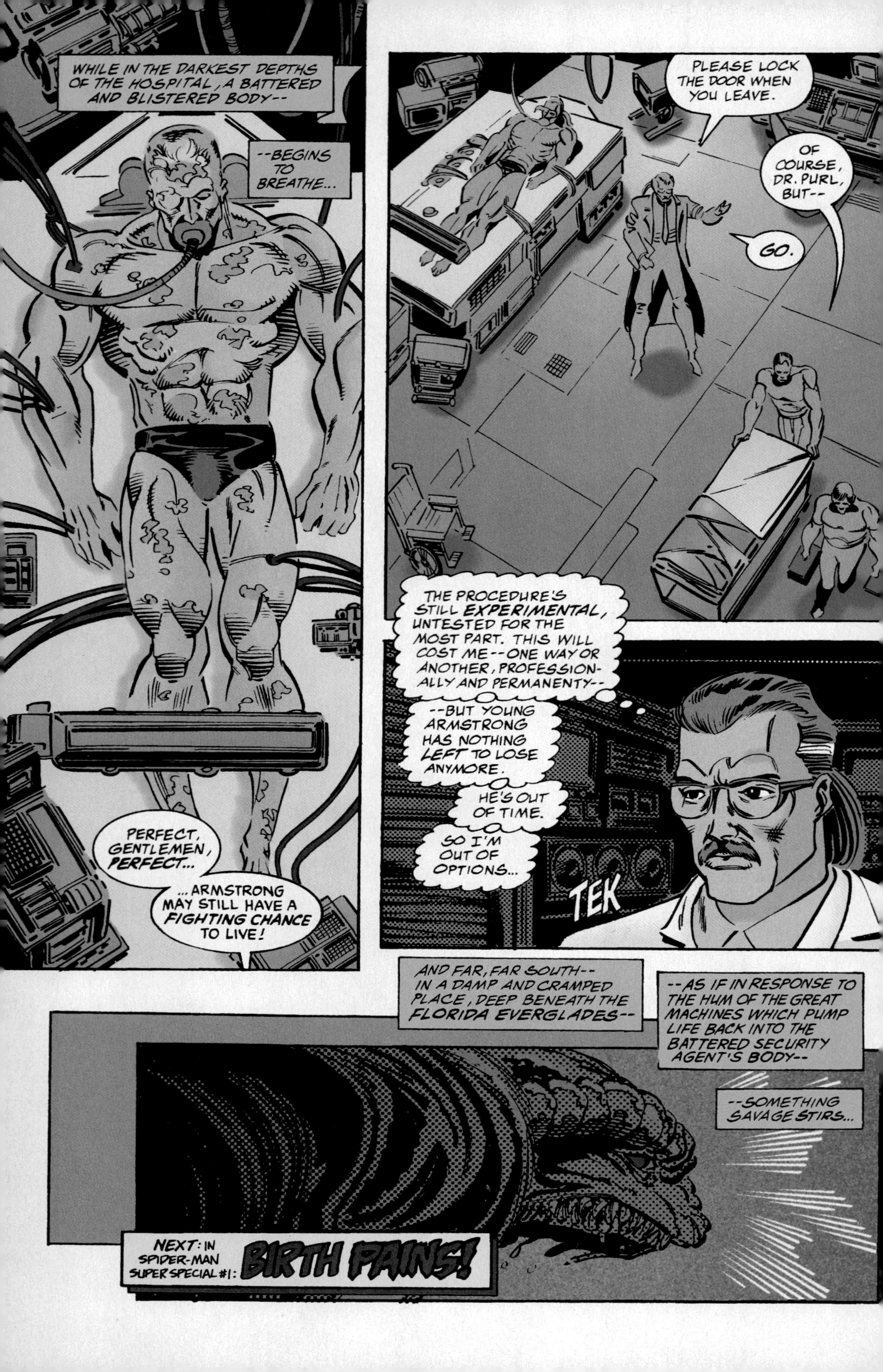
WHILE IN THE DARKEST DEPTHS OF THE HOSPITAL, A BATTERED AND BLISTERED BODY--
--BEGINS TO BREATHE...
PERFECT, GENTLEMEN, PERFECT...
...ARMSTRONG MAY STILL HAVE A FIGHTING CHANCE TO LIVE!
PLEASE LOCK THE DOOR WHEN YOU LEAVE.
OF COURSE, DR. PURL, BUT--
GO.
THE PROCEDURE'S STILL EXPERIMENTAL, UNTESTED FOR THE MOST PART. THIS WILL COST ME--ONE WAY OR ANOTHER, PROFESSIONALLY AND PERMANENTY--
--BUT YOUNG ARMSTRONG HAS NOTHING LEFT TO LOSE ANYMORE.
HE'S OUT OF TIME.
SO I'M OUT OF OPTIONS...
TEK
AND FAR, FAR SOUTH-- IN A DAMP AND CRAMPED PLACE, DEEP BENEATH THE FLORIDA EVERGLADES--
--AS IF IN RESPONSE TO THE HUM OF THE GREAT MACHINES WHICH PUMP LIFE BACK INTO THE BATTERED SECURITY AGENT'S BODY--
--SOMETHING SAVAGE STIRS...
NEXT: IN SPIDER-MAN SUPER SPECIAL #1: BIRTH PAINS!

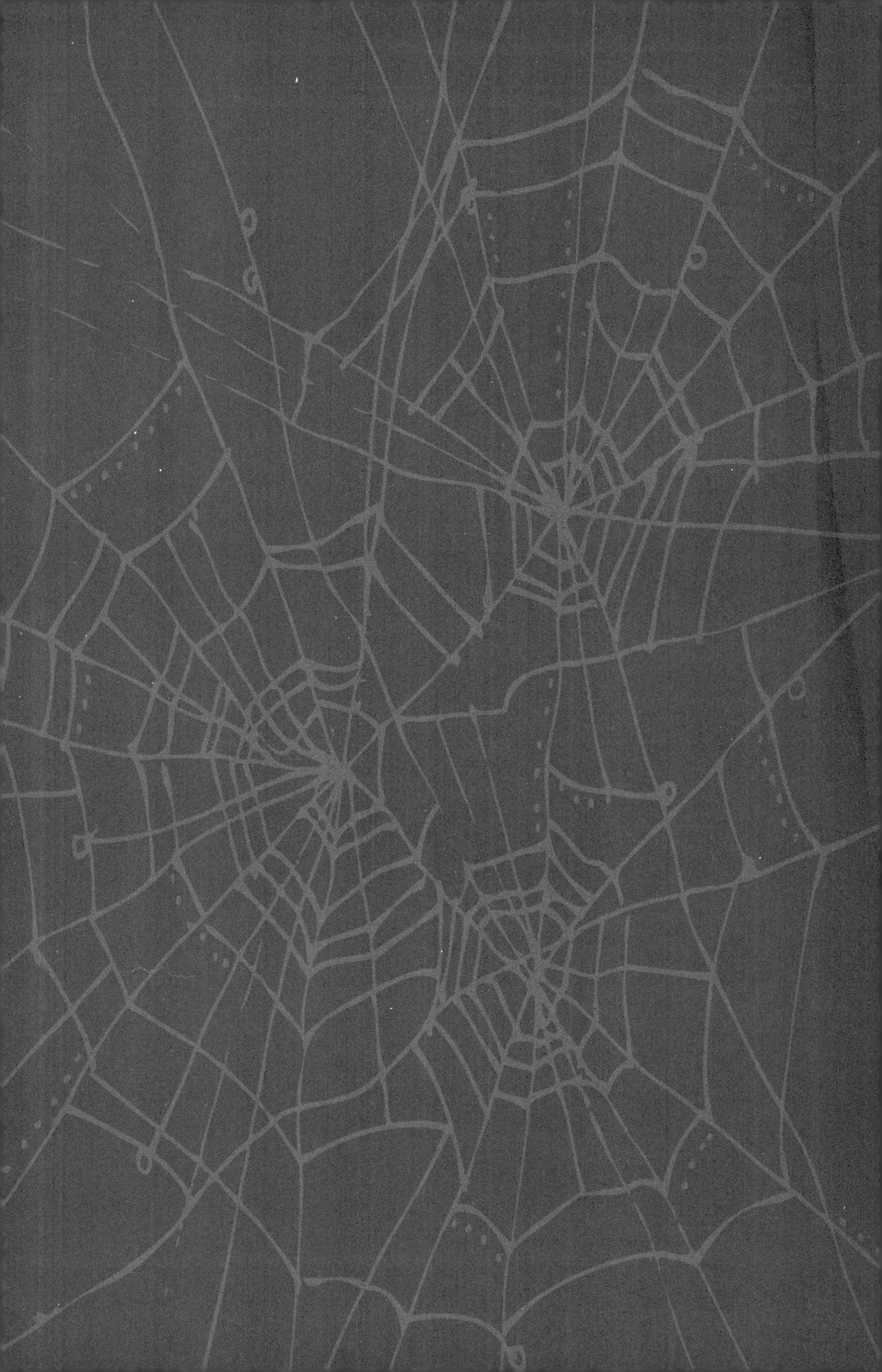

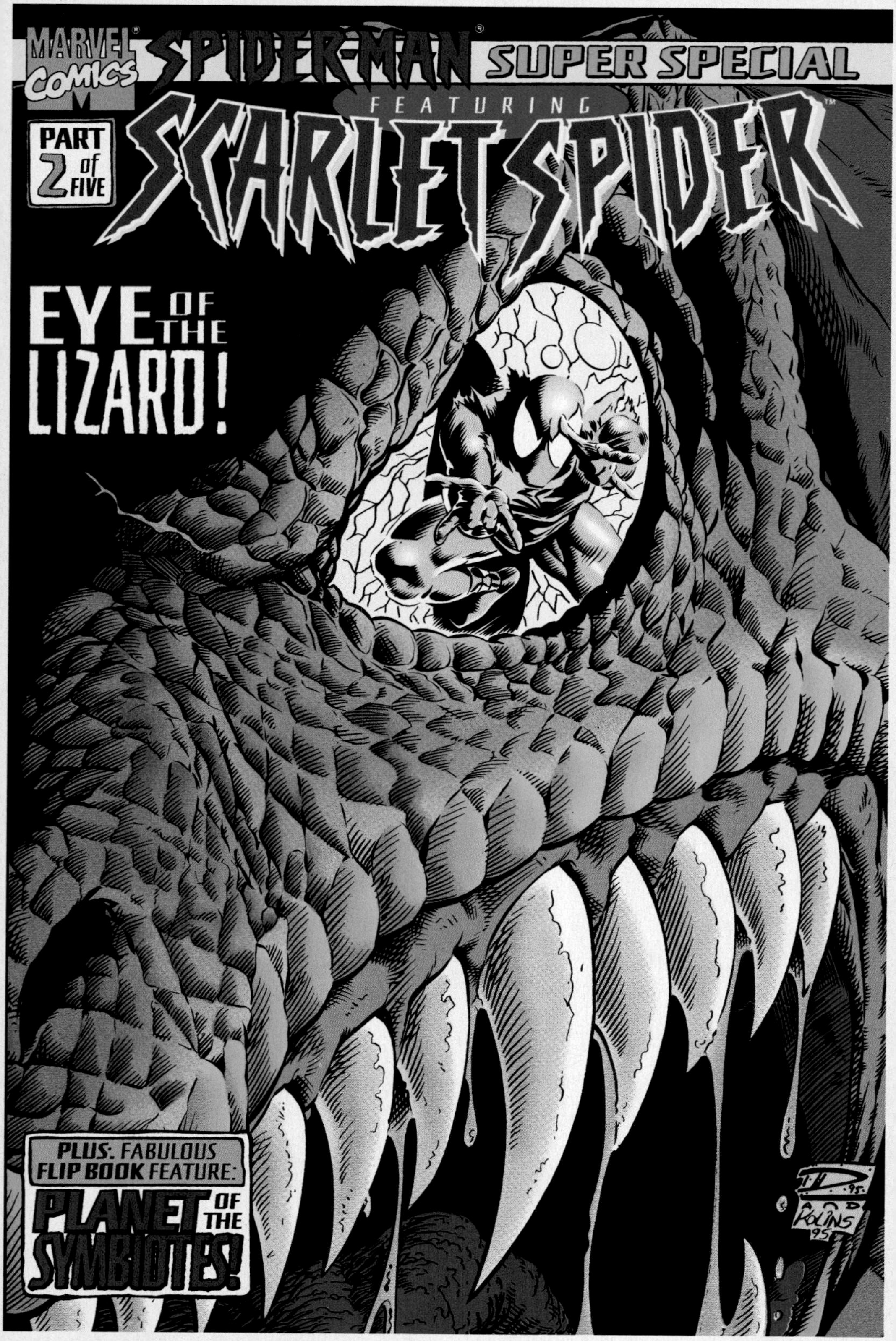
MARVEL COMICS
SPIDER-MAN
SUPER SPECIAL
FEATURING
SCARLET SPIDER
PART 2 of FIVE
EYE OF THE LIZARD!
PLUS: FABULOUS FLIP BOOK FEATURE:
PLANET OF THE SYMBIOTES!

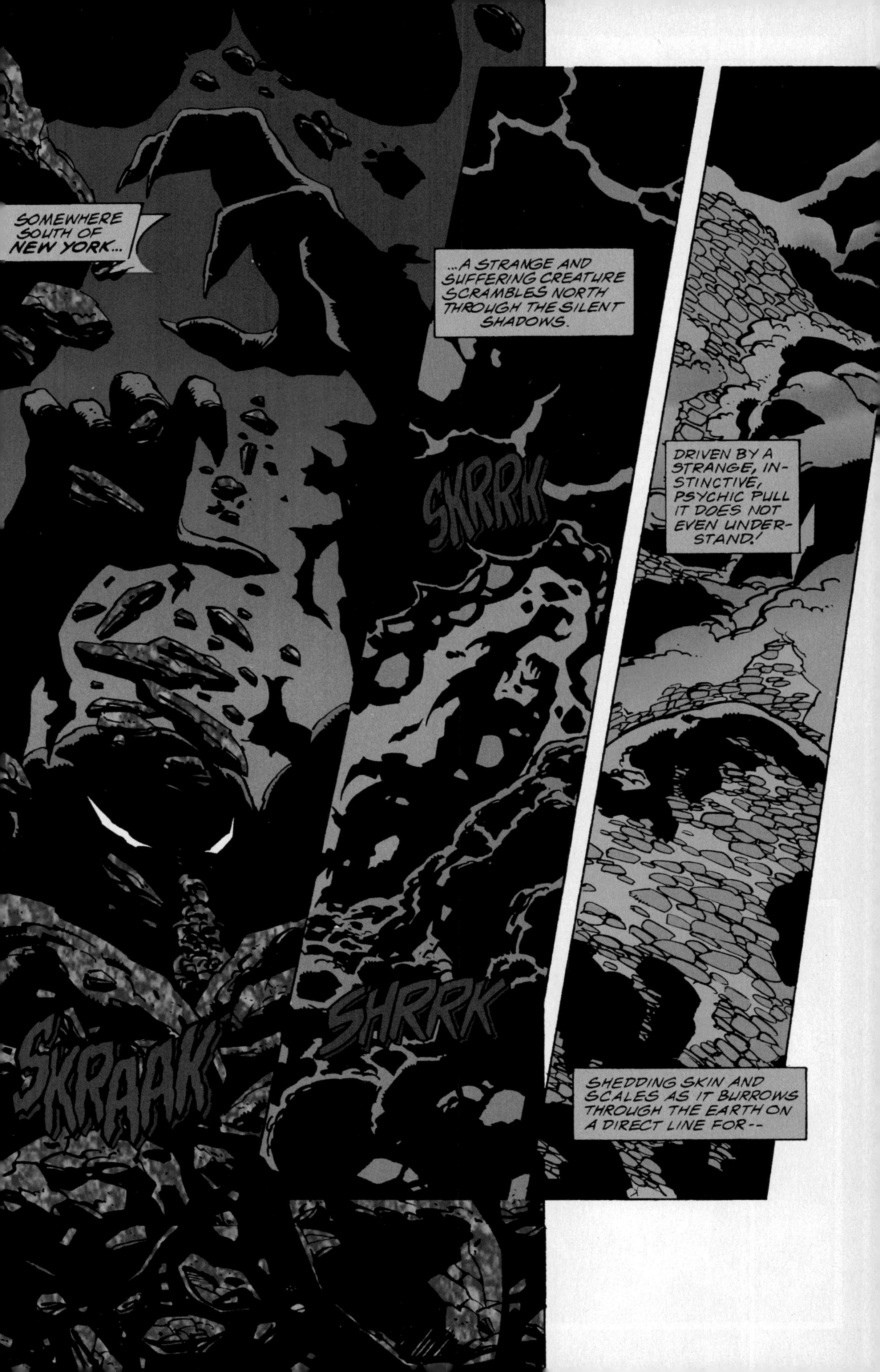
SOMEWHERE SOUTH OF NEW YORK...
...A STRANGE AND SUFFERING CREATURE SCRAMBLES NORTH THROUGH THE SILENT SHADOWS.
SKRAAK
SHRRK
SHRRK
DRIVEN BY A STRANGE, INSTINCTIVE, PSYCHIC PULL IT DOES NOT EVEN UNDERSTAND!
SHEDDING SKIN AND SCALES AS IT BURROWS THROUGH THE EARTH ON A DIRECT LINE FOR--

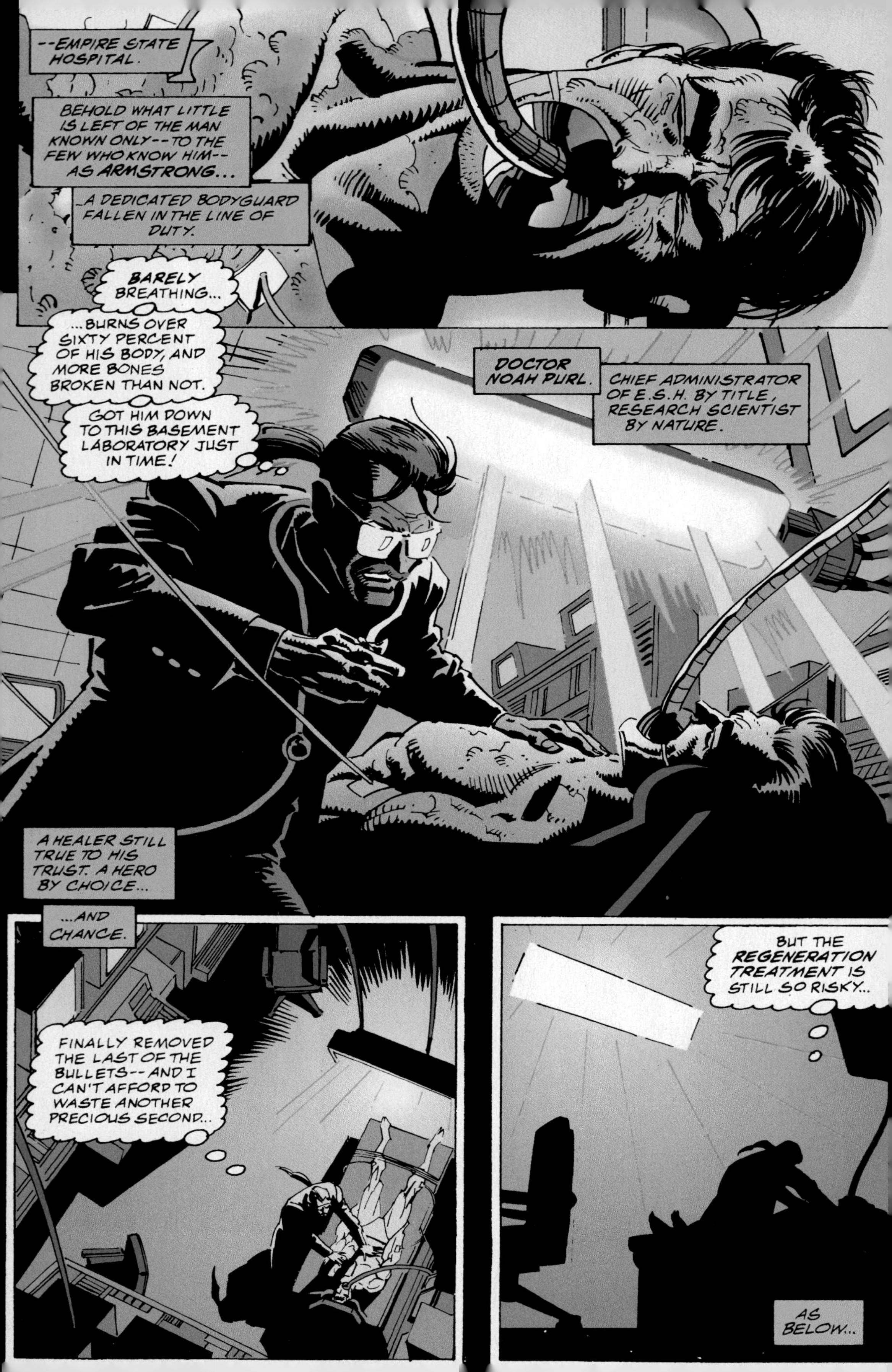
--EMPIRE STATE HOSPITAL.
BEHOLD WHAT LITTLE IS LEFT OF THE MAN KNOWN ONLY--TO THE FEW WHO KNOW HIM--AS ARMSTRONG...
...A DEDICATED BODYGUARD FALLEN IN THE LINE OF DUTY.
BARELY BREATHING...
...BURNS OVER SIXTY PERCENT OF HIS BODY, AND MORE BONES BROKEN THAN NOT.
GOT HIM DOWN TO THIS BASEMENT LABORATORY JUST IN TIME!
DOCTOR NOAH PURL.
CHIEF ADMINISTRATOR OF E.S.H. BY TITLE, RESEARCH SCIENTIST BY NATURE.
A HEALER STILL TRUE TO HIS TRUST. A HERO BY CHOICE...
...AND CHANCE.
FINALLY REMOVED THE LAST OF THE BULLETS--AND I CAN'T AFFORD TO WASTE ANOTHER PRECIOUS SECOND...
BUT THE REGENERATION TREATMENT IS STILL SO RISKY...
AS BELOW...

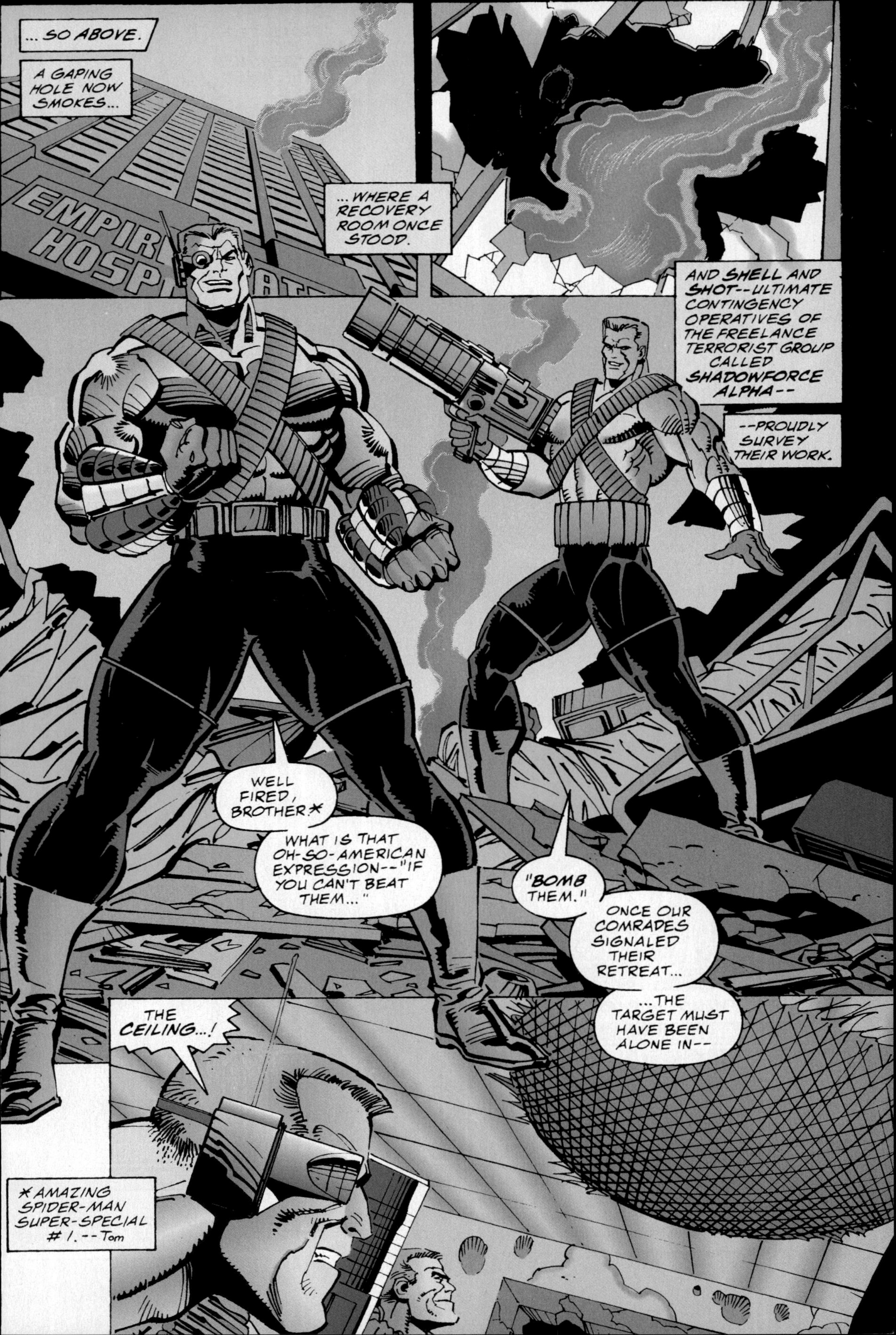
... SO ABOVE.
A GAPING HOLE NOW SMOKES...
EMPIRE HOSPITAL
...WHERE A RECOVERY ROOM ONCE STOOD.
AND SHELL AND SHOT--ULTIMATE CONTINGENCY OPERATIVES OF THE FREELANCE TERRORIST GROUP CALLED SHADOWFORCE ALPHA--
--PROUDLY SURVEY THEIR WORK.
WELL FIRED, BROTHER.*
WHAT IS THAT OH-SO-AMERICAN EXPRESSION--"IF YOU CAN'T BEAT THEM..."
"BOMB THEM."
ONCE OUR COMRADES SIGNALED THEIR RETREAT...
...THE TARGET MUST HAVE BEEN ALONE IN--
THE CEILING...!
*AMAZING SPIDER-MAN SUPER-SPECIAL # 1. --Tom

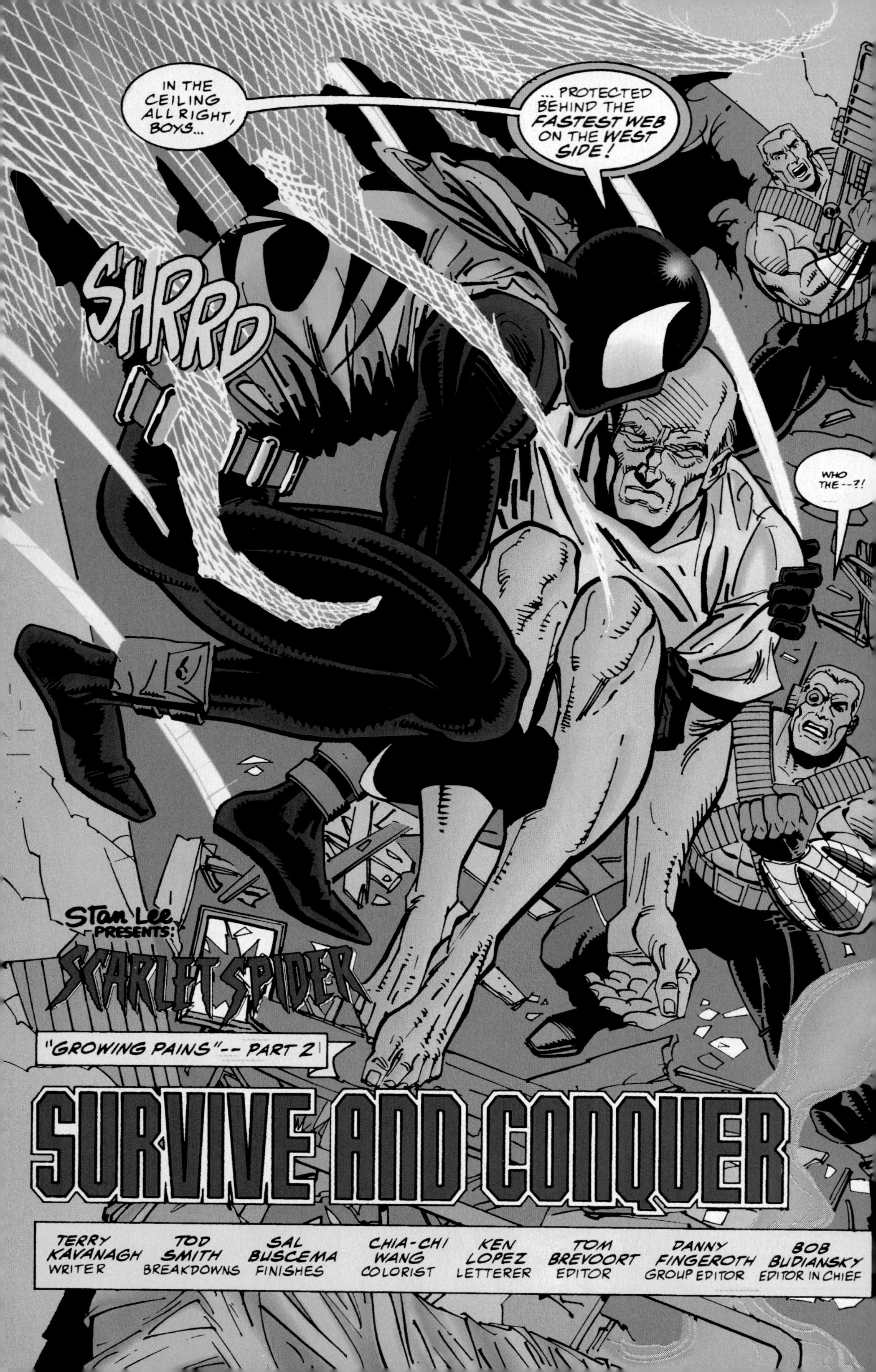
IN THE CEILING ALL RIGHT, BOYS...
... PROTECTED BEHIND THE FASTEST WEB ON THE WEST SIDE!
SHRRD
WHO THE--?!
STAN LEE PRESENTS:
SCARLET SPIDER
"GROWING PAINS"-- PART 2
SURVIVE AND CONQUER
TERRY KAVANAGH WRITER
TOD SMITH BREAKDOWNS
SAL BUSCEMA FINISHES
CHIA-CHI WANG COLORIST
KEN LOPEZ LETTERER
TOM BREVOORT EDITOR
DANNY FINGEROTH GROUP EDITOR
BOB BUDIANSKY EDITOR IN CHIEF

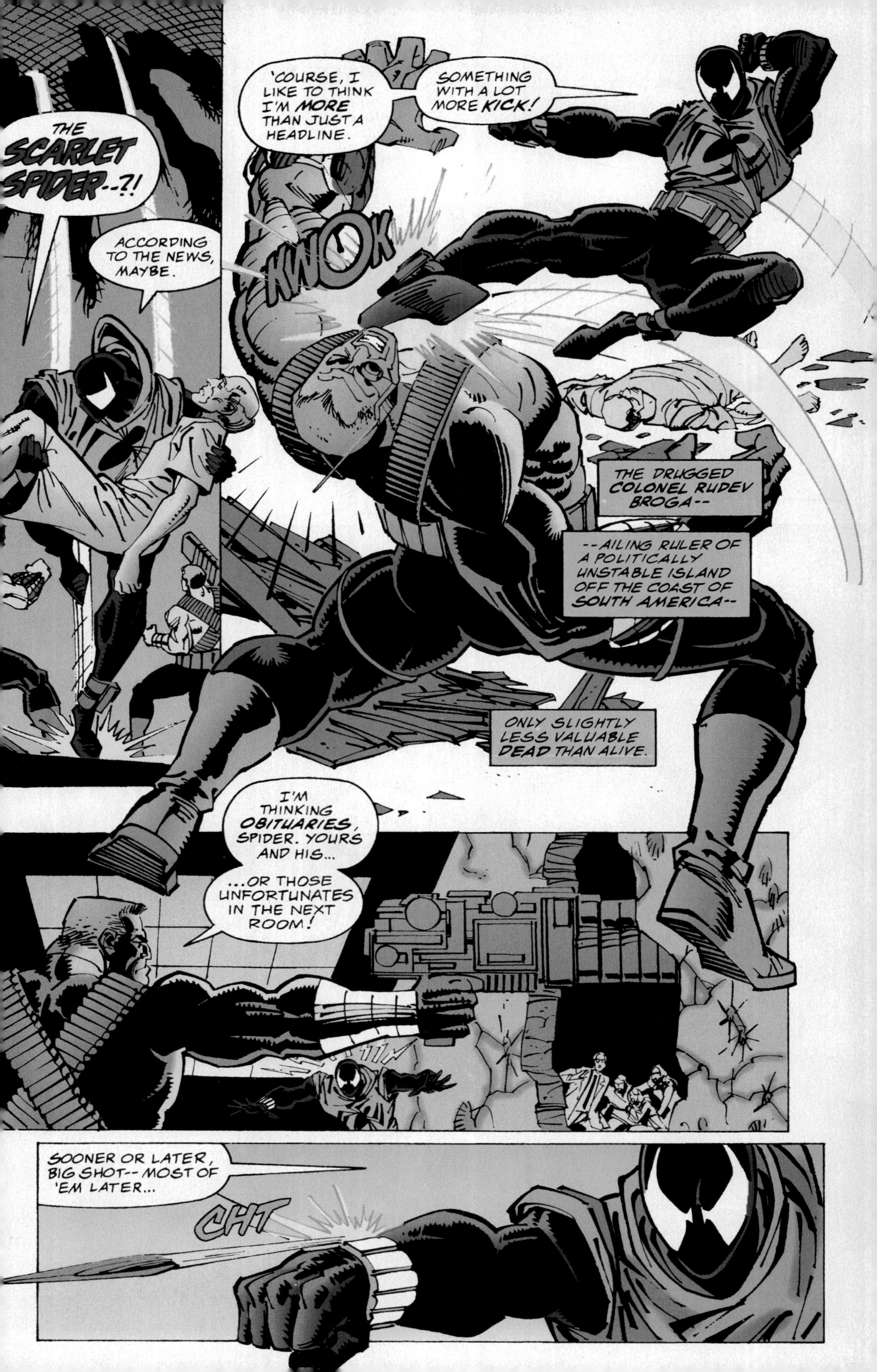
THE SCARLET SPIDER--?!
ACCORDING TO THE NEWS, MAYBE.
'COURSE, I LIKE TO THINK I'M MORE THAN JUST A HEADLINE.
SOMETHING WITH A LOT MORE KICK!
KWOK
THE DRUGGED COLONEL RUDEV BROGA--
--AILING RULER OF A POLITICALLY UNSTABLE ISLAND OFF THE COAST OF SOUTH AMERICA--
ONLY SLIGHTLY LESS VALUABLE DEAD THAN ALIVE.
I'M THINKING OBITUARIES, SPIDER. YOURS AND HIS...
...OR THOSE UNFORTUNATES IN THE NEXT ROOM!
SOONER OR LATER, BIG SHOT-- MOST OF 'EM LATER...
CHT

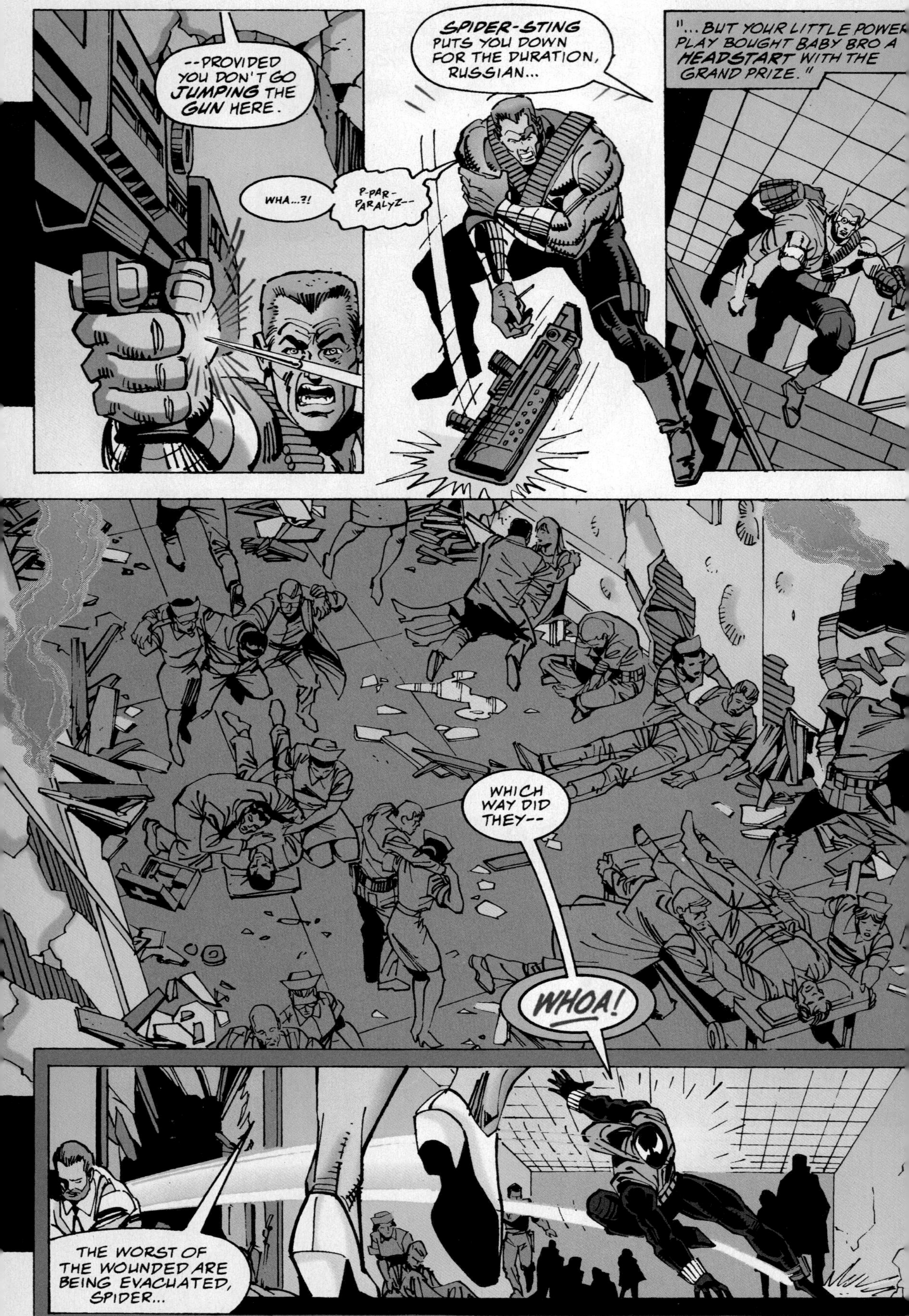
--PROVIDED YOU DON'T GO JUMPING THE GUN HERE.
WHA...?!
P-PAR-PARALYZ--
SPIDER-STING PUTS YOU DOWN FOR THE DURATION, RUSSIAN...
"...BUT YOUR LITTLE POWER PLAY BOUGHT BABY BRO A HEADSTART WITH THE GRAND PRIZE."
WHICH WAY DID THEY--
WHOA!
THE WORST OF THE WOUNDED ARE BEING EVACUATED, SPIDER...

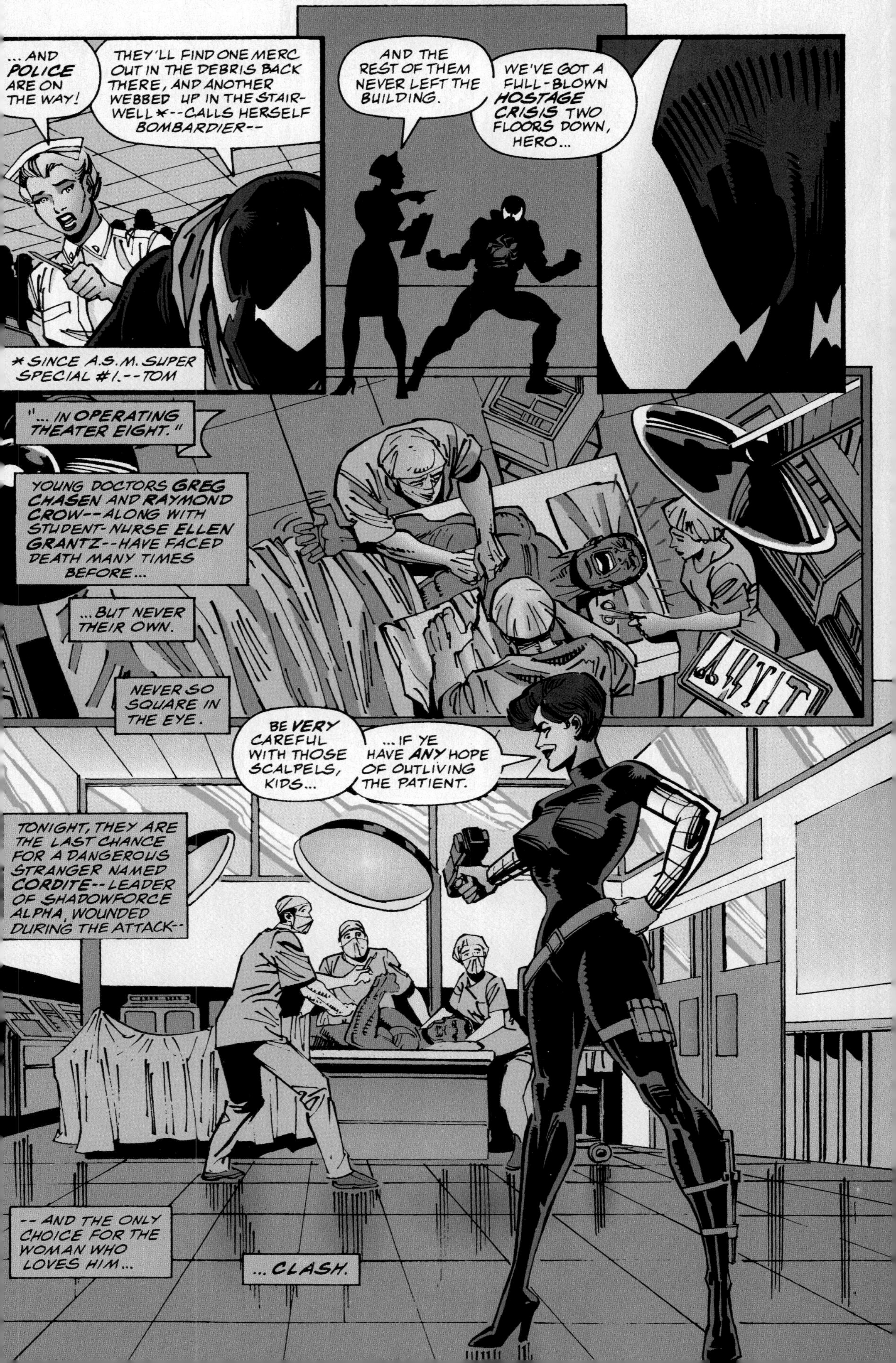

...AND POLICE ARE ON THE WAY!
THEY'LL FIND ONE MERC OUT IN THE DEBRIS BACK THERE, AND ANOTHER WEBBED UP IN THE STAIRWELL*--CALLS HERSELF BOMBARDIER--
*SINCE A.S.M. SUPER SPECIAL #1.--TOM
AND THE REST OF THEM NEVER LEFT THE BUILDING.
WE'VE GOT A FULL-BLOWN HOSTAGE CRISIS TWO FLOORS DOWN, HERO...
"...IN OPERATING THEATER EIGHT."
YOUNG DOCTORS GREG CHASEN AND RAYMOND CROW--ALONG WITH STUDENT-NURSE ELLEN GRANTZ--HAVE FACED DEATH MANY TIMES BEFORE...
...BUT NEVER THEIR OWN.
NEVER SO SQUARE IN THE EYE.
BE VERY CAREFUL WITH THOSE SCALPELS, KIDS...
...IF YE HAVE ANY HOPE OF OUTLIVING THE PATIENT.
TONIGHT, THEY ARE THE LAST CHANCE FOR A DANGEROUS STRANGER NAMED CORDITE--LEADER OF SHADOWFORCE ALPHA, WOUNDED DURING THE ATTACK--
--AND THE ONLY CHOICE FOR THE WOMAN WHO LOVES HIM...
...CLASH.

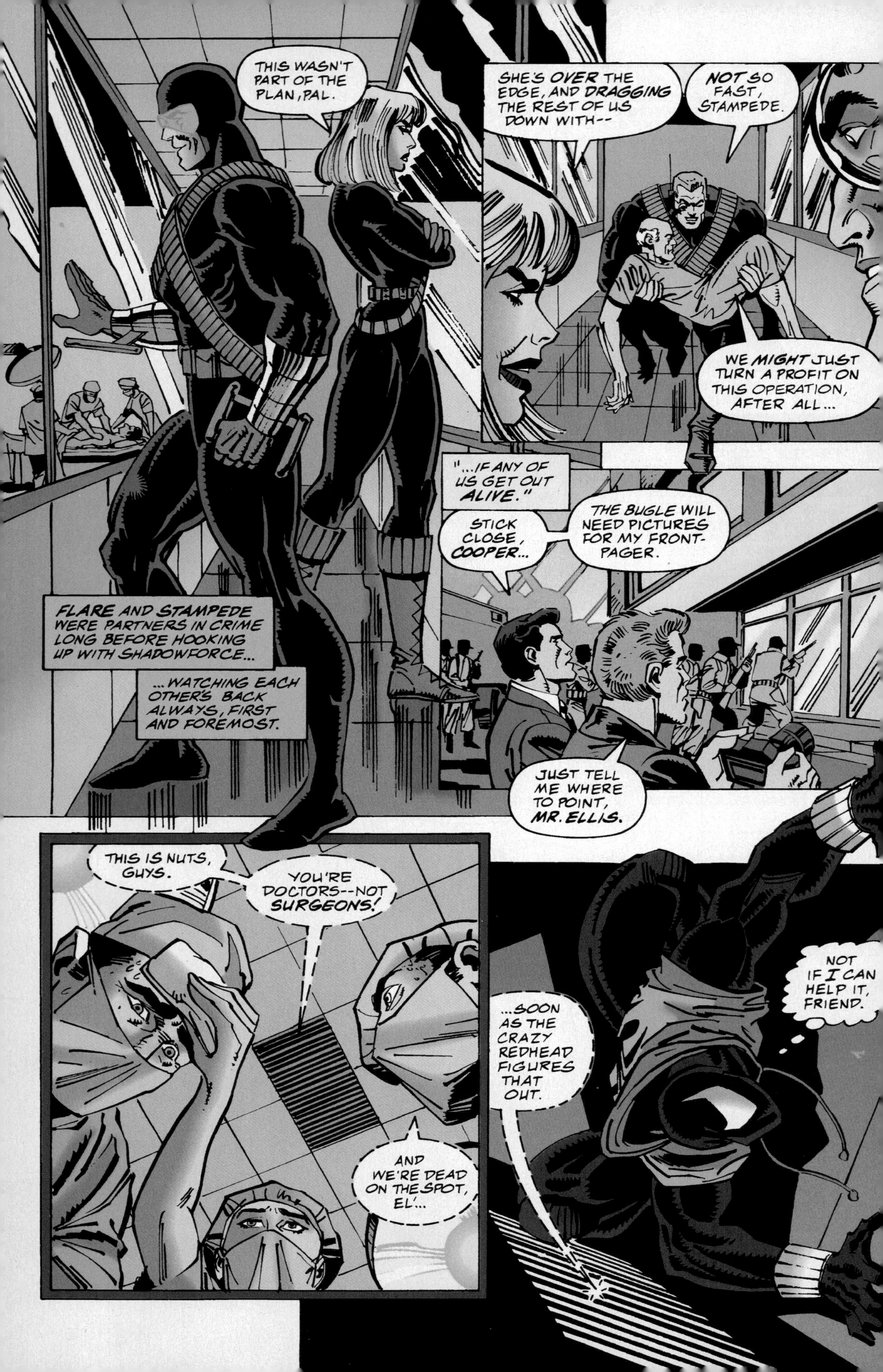
THIS WASN'T PART OF THE PLAN, PAL.
FLARE AND STAMPEDE WERE PARTNERS IN CRIME LONG BEFORE HOOKING UP WITH SHADOWFORCE...
...WATCHING EACH OTHER'S BACK ALWAYS, FIRST AND FOREMOST.
SHE'S OVER THE EDGE, AND DRAGGING THE REST OF US DOWN WITH--
NOT SO FAST, STAMPEDE.
WE MIGHT JUST TURN A PROFIT ON THIS OPERATION, AFTER ALL...
"...IF ANY OF US GET OUT ALIVE."
STICK CLOSE, COOPER...
THE BUGLE WILL NEED PICTURES FOR MY FRONT-PAGER.
JUST TELL ME WHERE TO POINT, MR. ELLIS.
THIS IS NUTS, GUYS.
YOU'RE DOCTORS--NOT SURGEONS!
AND WE'RE DEAD ON THE SPOT, EL'...
...SOON AS THE CRAZY REDHEAD FIGURES THAT OUT.
NOT IF I CAN HELP IT, FRIEND.

WHILE IN DR. PURL'S BASEMENT LABORATORY...

... A STRANGE GREEN GLOW-- REFLECTIONS OF AN EERIE EMERALD RADIATION-- CONSUMES ALL WITHIN.

AND IN THE HOSPITAL LOBBY...

SQUADS BLUE AND GOLD, *SECURE* THE PERIMETERS!

SILVER FOLLOWS ME INTO THE ZONE, AND I WANT BLACK *PREPPED* TO DEFUSE--

--ON MY MARK...

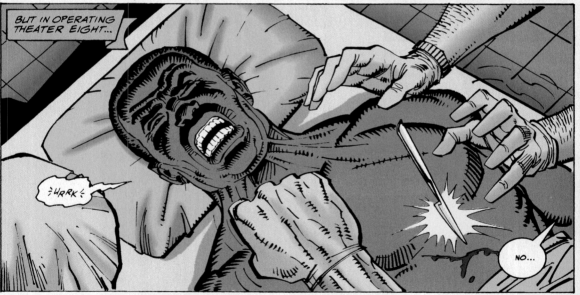

BUT IN OPERATING THEATER EIGHT...

~URRK~

NO...

MISTAKE, DOCTOR. YOUR *LAST*...

CHK

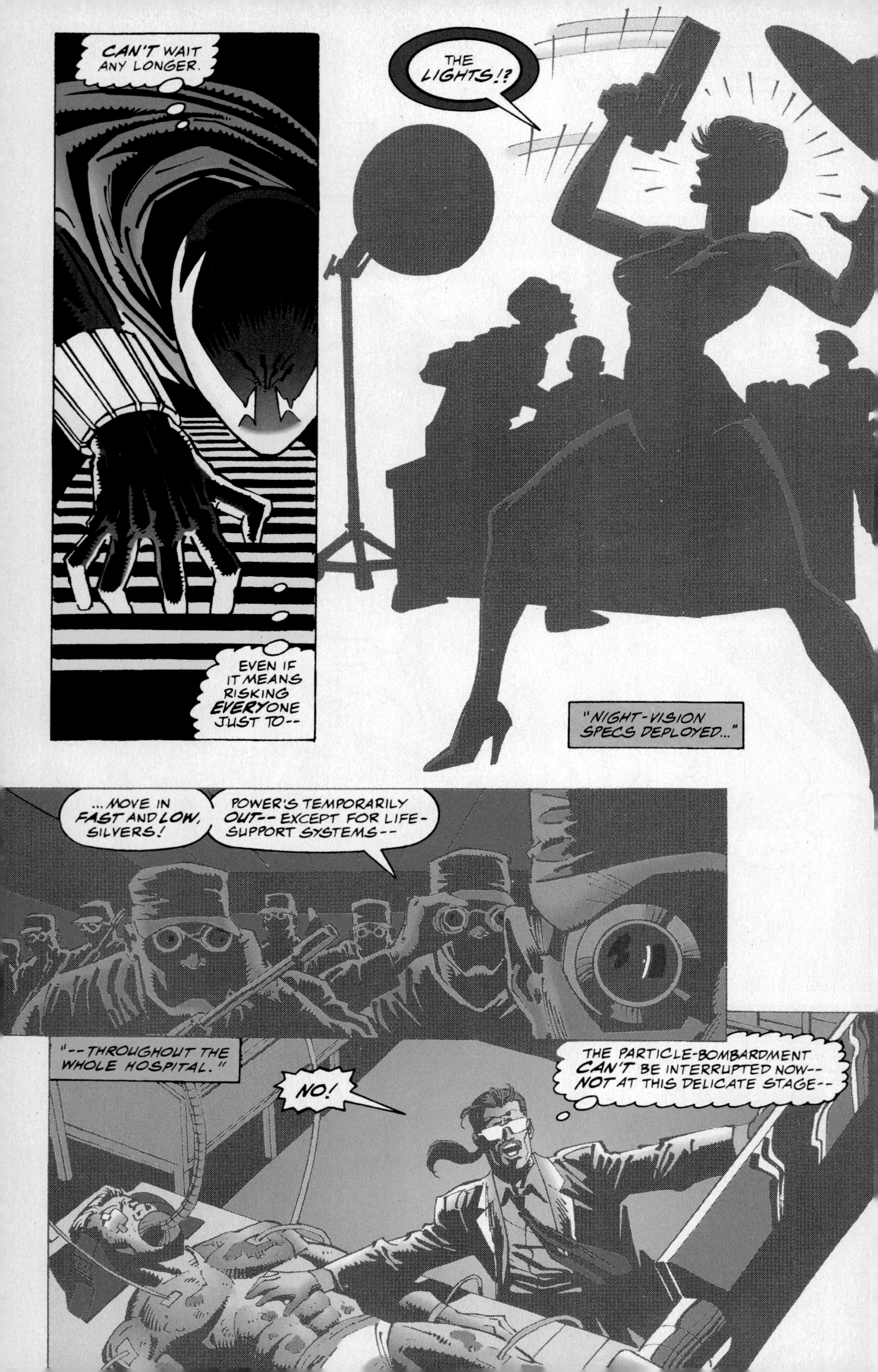

CAN'T WAIT ANY LONGER.
EVEN IF IT MEANS RISKING EVERYONE JUST TO--
THE LIGHTS!?
"NIGHT-VISION SPECS DEPLOYED..."
...MOVE IN FAST AND LOW, SILVERS!
POWER'S TEMPORARILY OUT-- EXCEPT FOR LIFE-SUPPORT SYSTEMS--
"--THROUGHOUT THE WHOLE HOSPITAL."
NO!
THE PARTICLE-BOMBARDMENT CAN'T BE INTERRUPTED NOW-- NOT AT THIS DELICATE STAGE--

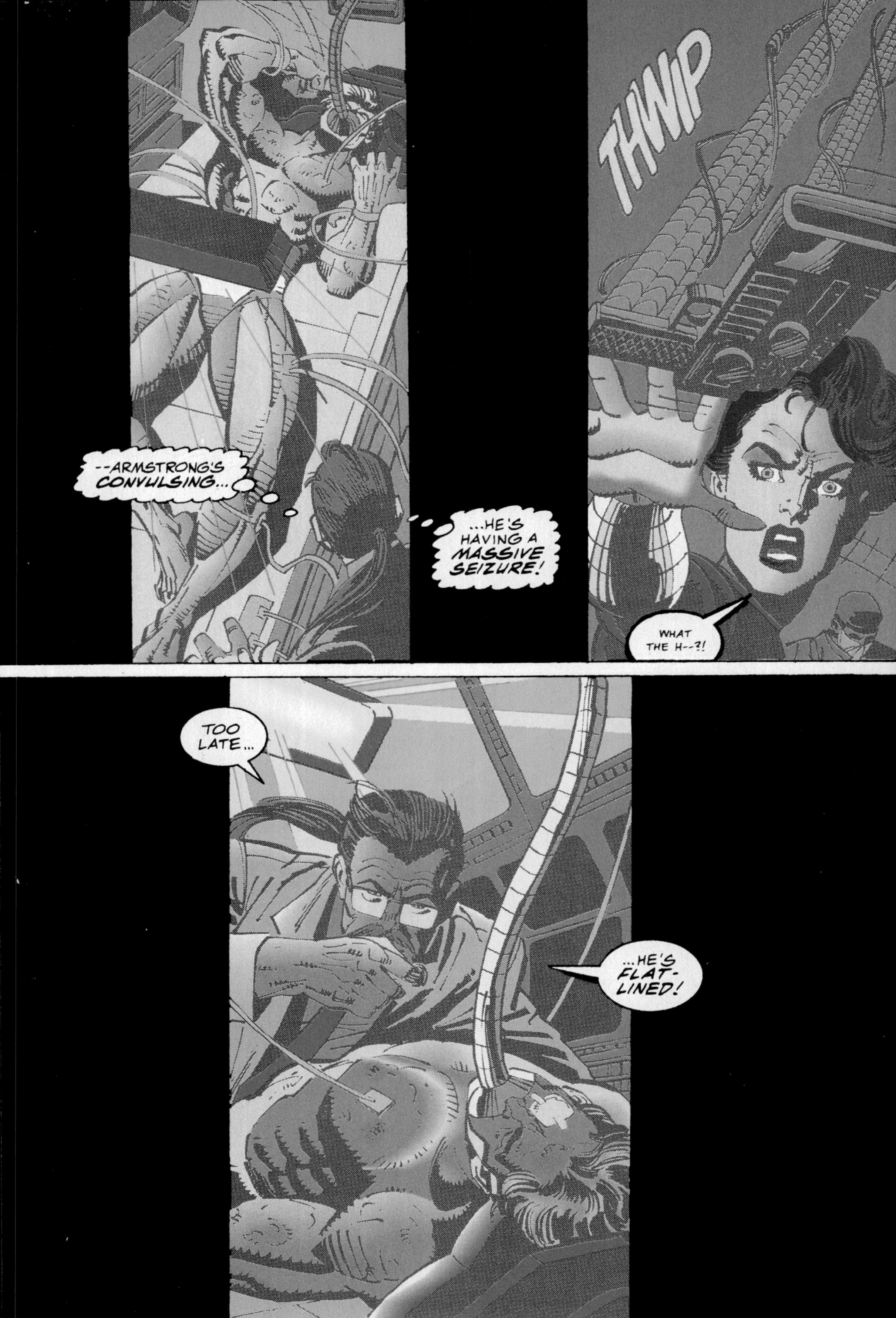
--ARMSTRONG'S CONVULSING...
...HE'S HAVING A MASSIVE SEIZURE!
THWIP
WHAT THE H--?!
TOO LATE...
...HE'S FLAT-LINED!

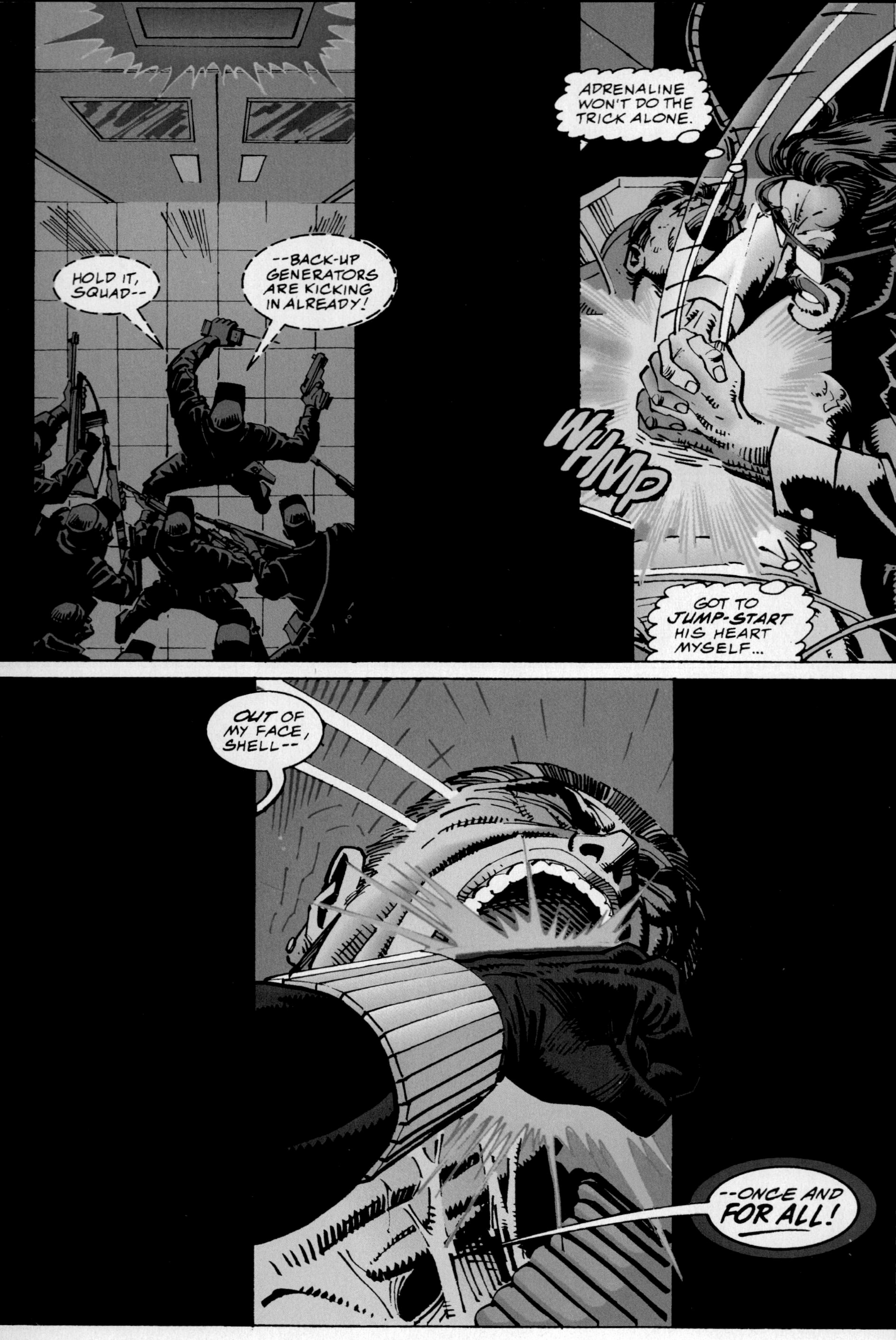
HOLD IT, SQUAD--
--BACK-UP GENERATORS ARE KICKING IN ALREADY!
ADRENALINE WON'T DO THE TRICK ALONE.
WHMP
GOT TO JUMP-START HIS HEART MYSELF...
OUT OF MY FACE, SHELL--
--ONCE AND FOR ALL!

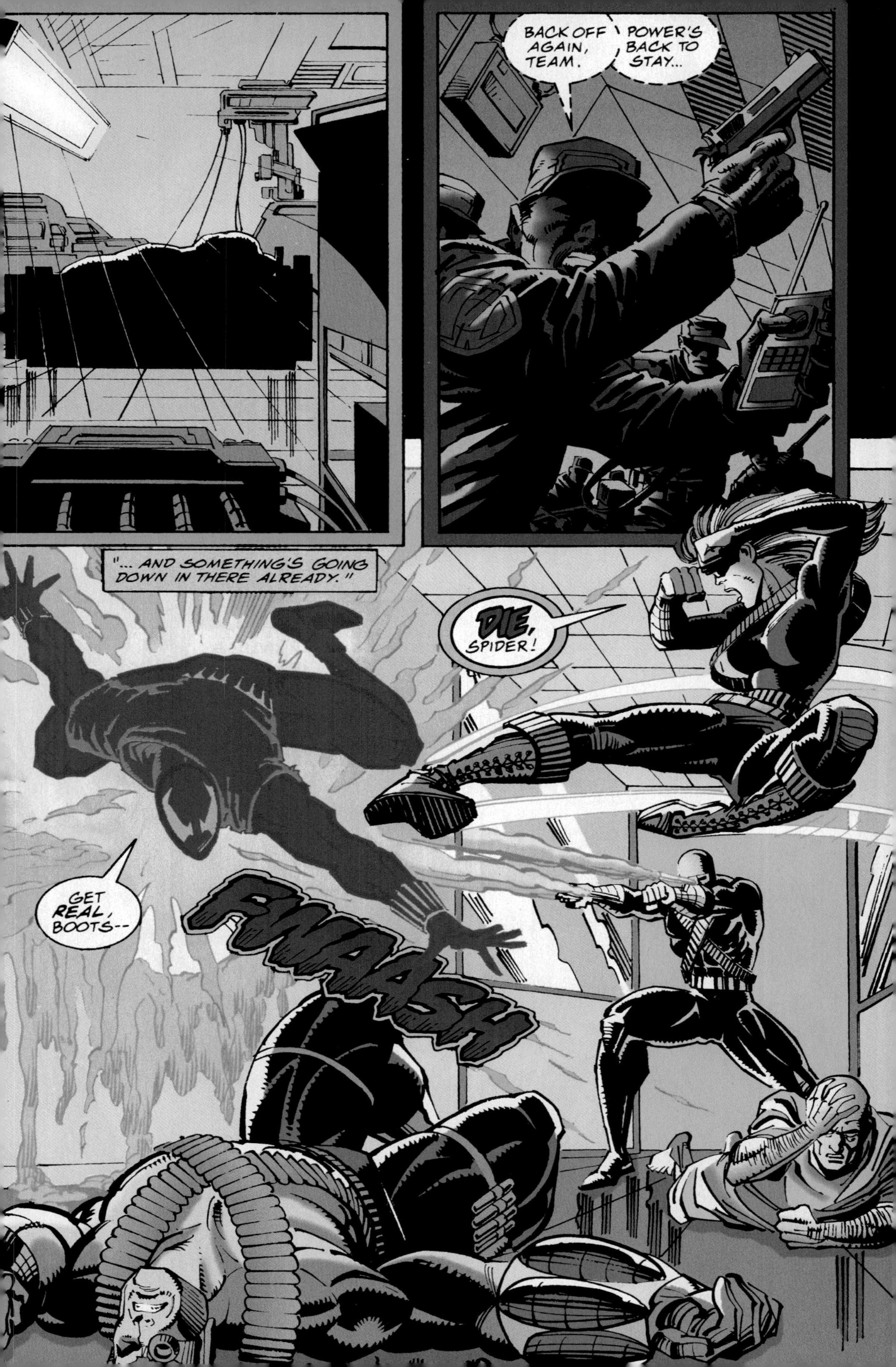
BACK OFF AGAIN, TEAM.
POWER'S BACK TO STAY...
"... AND SOMETHING'S GOING DOWN IN THERE ALREADY."
DIE, SPIDER!
GET REAL, BOOTS--
FWAASH

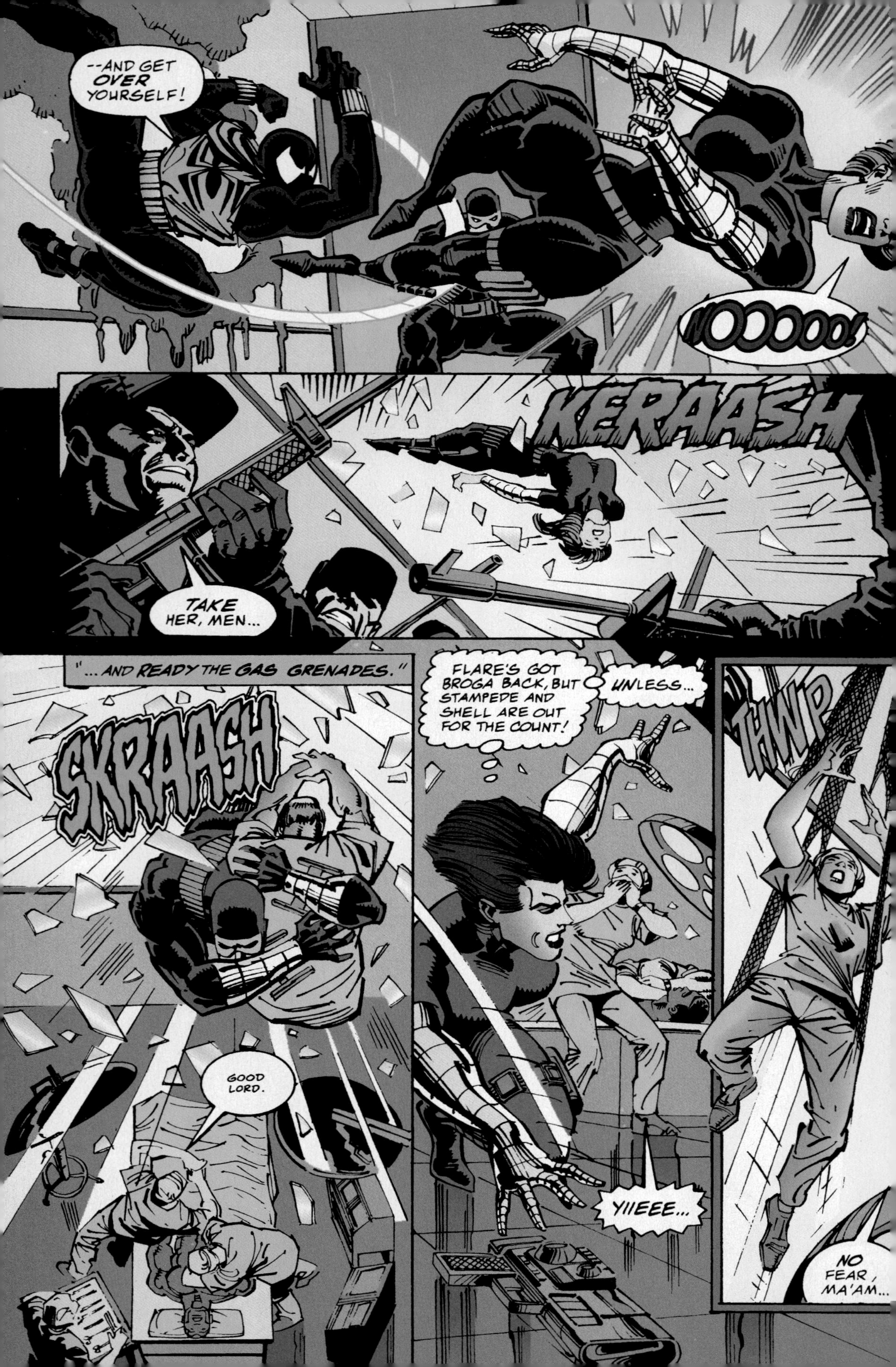
--AND GET OVER YOURSELF!
NOOOOO!
KERAASH
TAKE HER, MEN...
"...AND READY THE GAS GRENADES."
SKRAASH
GOOD LORD.
FLARE'S GOT BROGA BACK, BUT STAMPEDE AND SHELL ARE OUT FOR THE COUNT!
UNLESS...
YIIEEE...
THWP
NO FEAR, MA'AM...

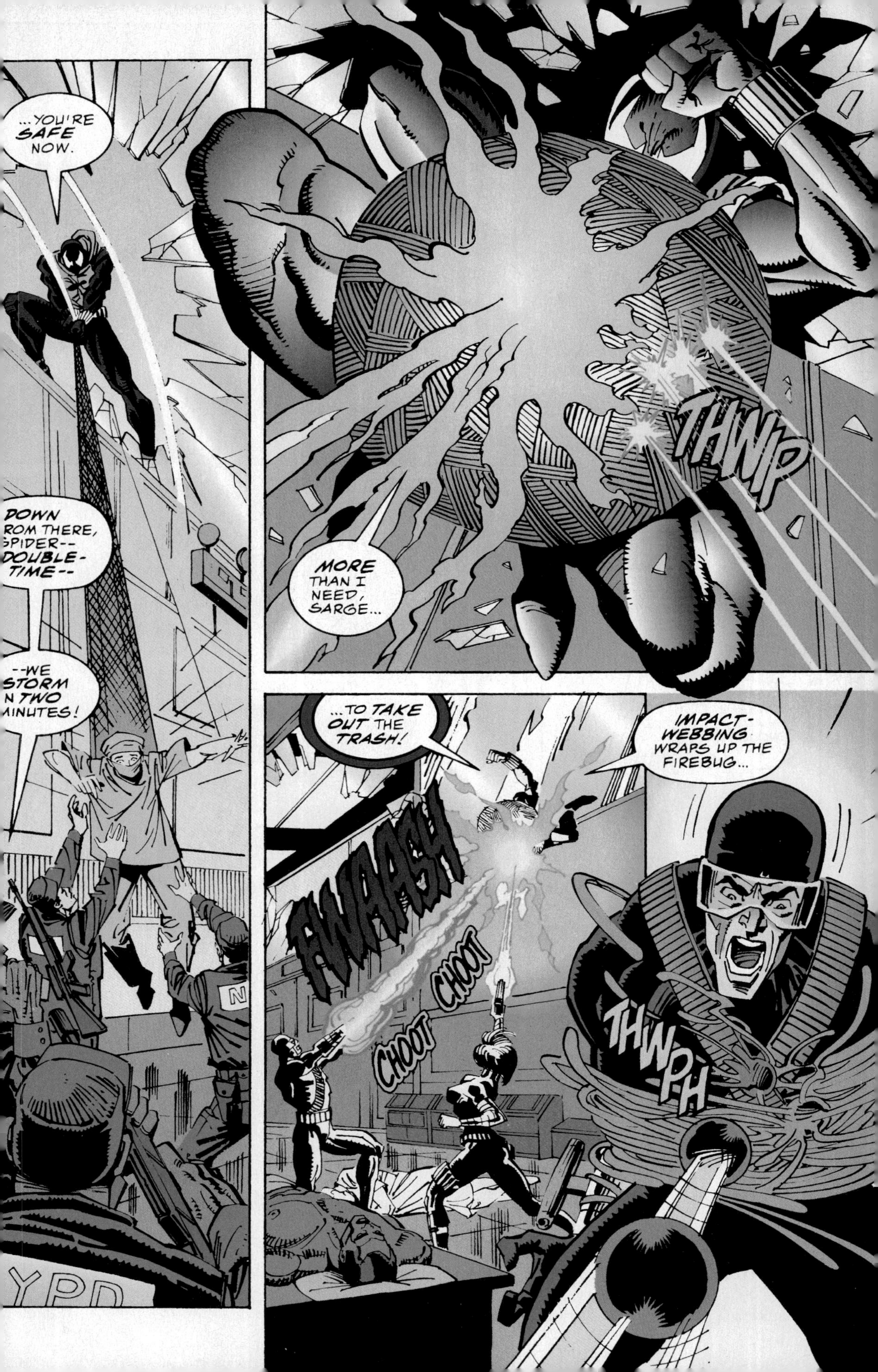
...YOU'RE SAFE NOW.
DOWN ROM THERE, SPIDER-- DOUBLE-TIME--
--WE STORM N TWO MINUTES!
MORE THAN I NEED, SARGE...
THWIP
...TO TAKE OUT THE TRASH!
IMPACT-WEBBING WRAPS UP THE FIREBUG...
FWAASH
CHOOT
CHOOT
THWPH
YPD

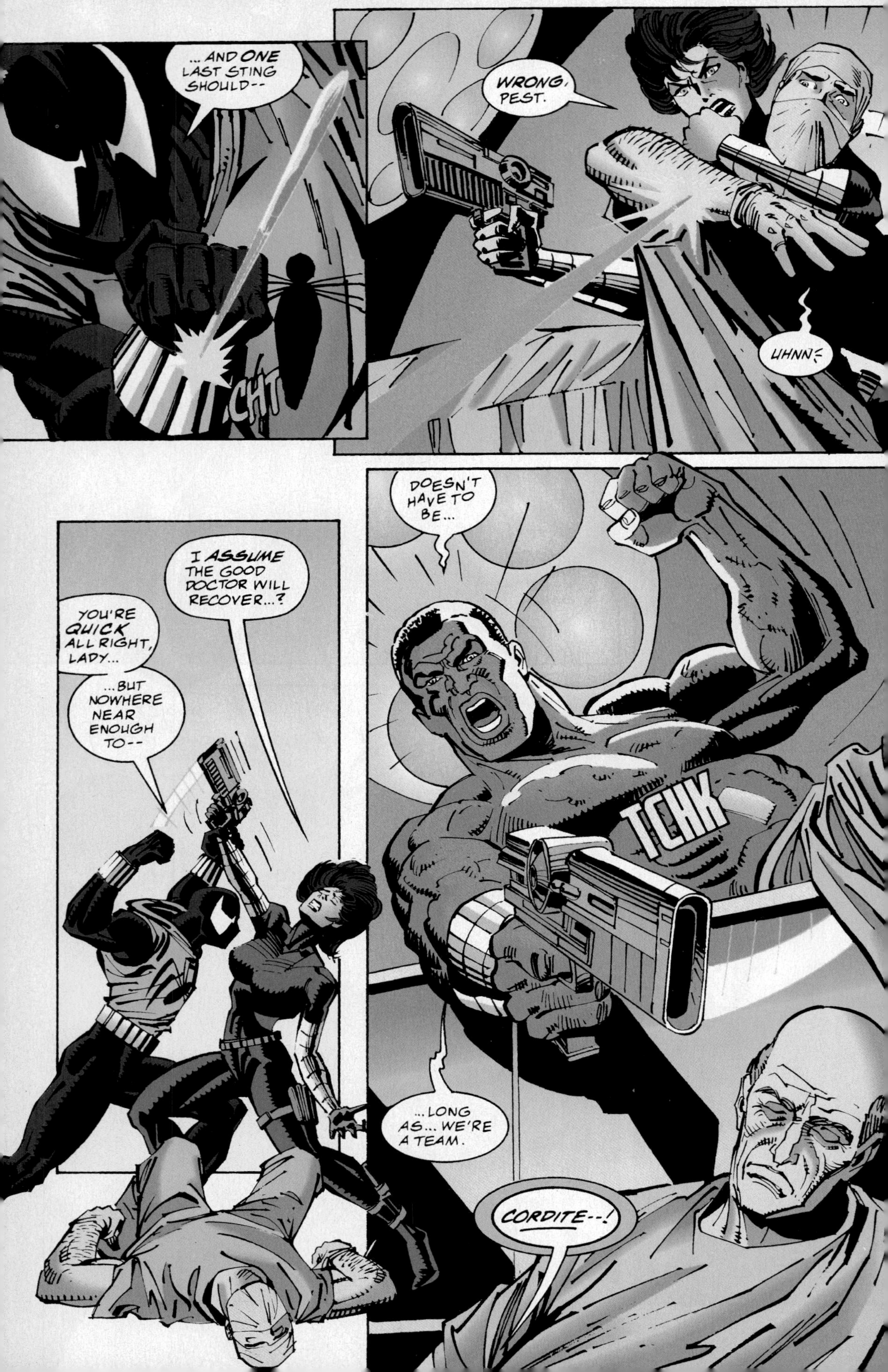
...AND ONE LAST STING SHOULD--
CHT
WRONG, PEST.
UHNN!
I ASSUME THE GOOD DOCTOR WILL RECOVER...?
YOU'RE QUICK ALL RIGHT, LADY...
...BUT NOWHERE NEAR ENOUGH TO--
DOESN'T HAVE TO BE...
TCHK
...LONG AS... WE'RE A TEAM.
CORDITE--!

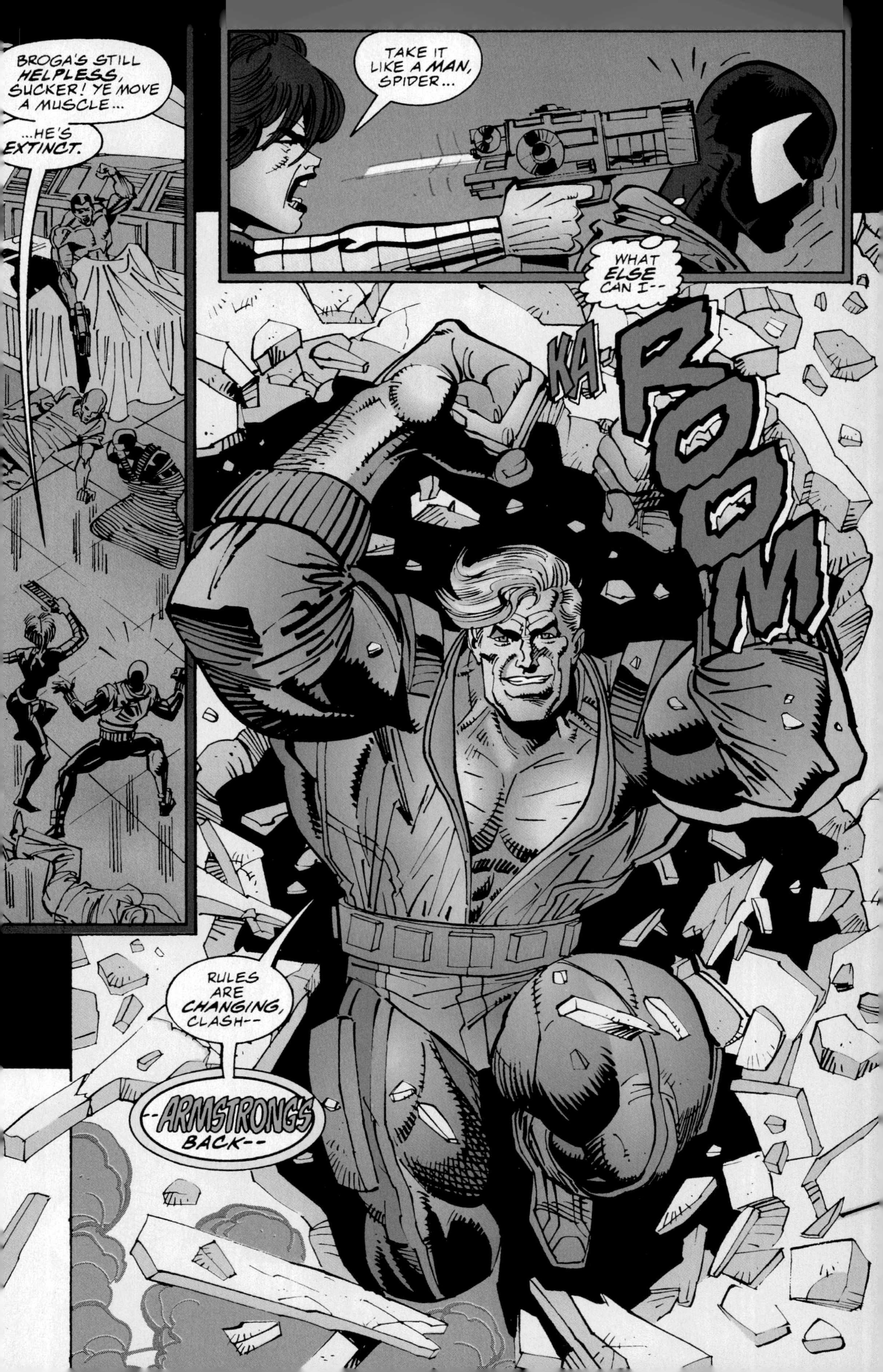
BROGA'S STILL HELPLESS, SUCKER! YE MOVE A MUSCLE...
...HE'S EXTINCT.
TAKE IT LIKE A MAN, SPIDER...
WHAT ELSE CAN I--
KA-ROOM
RULES ARE CHANGING, CLASH--
--ARMSTRONG'S BACK--

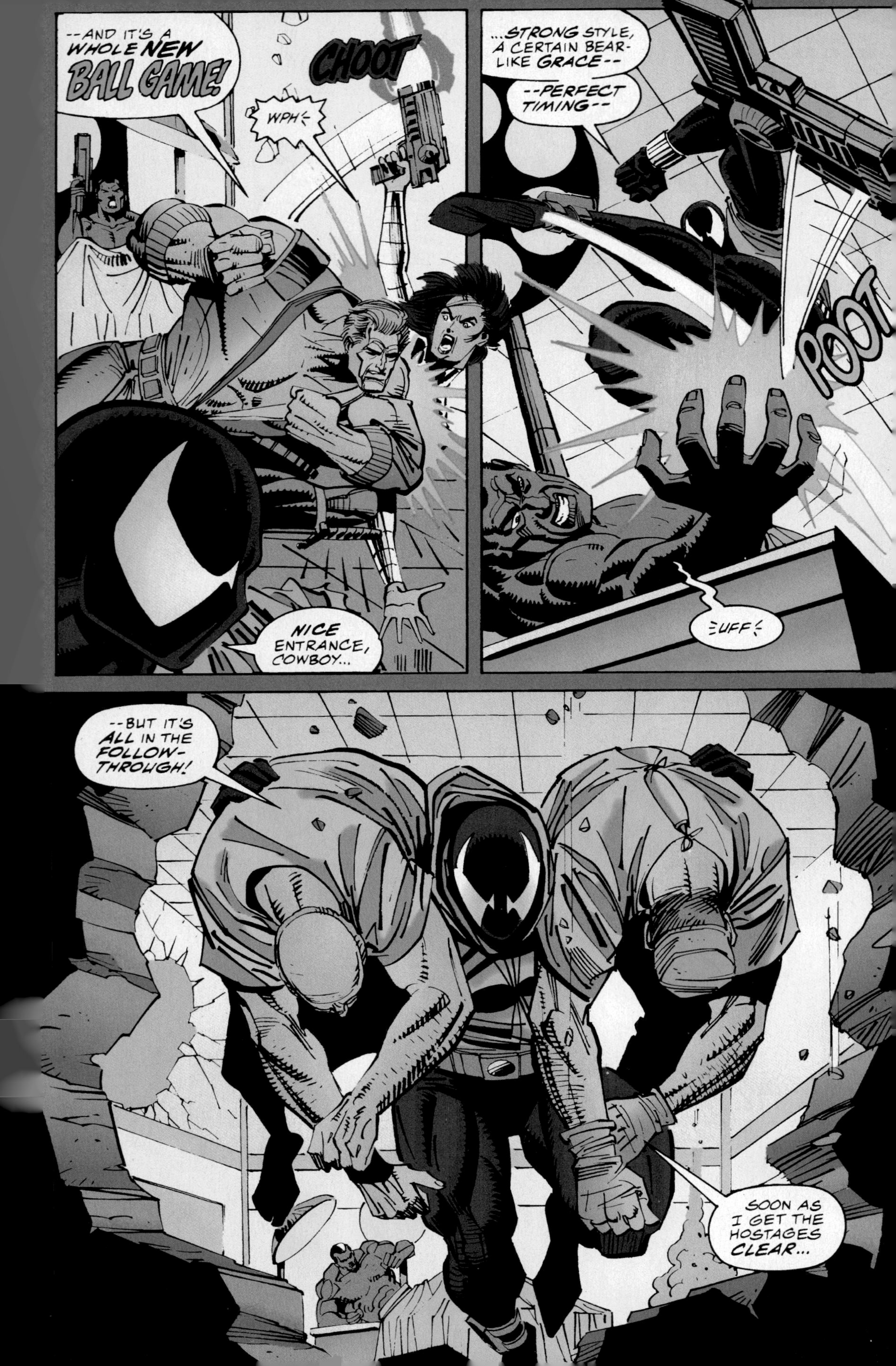

--AND IT'S A WHOLE NEW BALL GAME!
CHOOT
WPH
NICE ENTRANCE, COWBOY...
...STRONG STYLE, A CERTAIN BEAR-LIKE GRACE--
--PERFECT TIMING--
POOT
UFF
--BUT IT'S ALL IN THE FOLLOW-THROUGH!
SOON AS I GET THE HOSTAGES CLEAR...

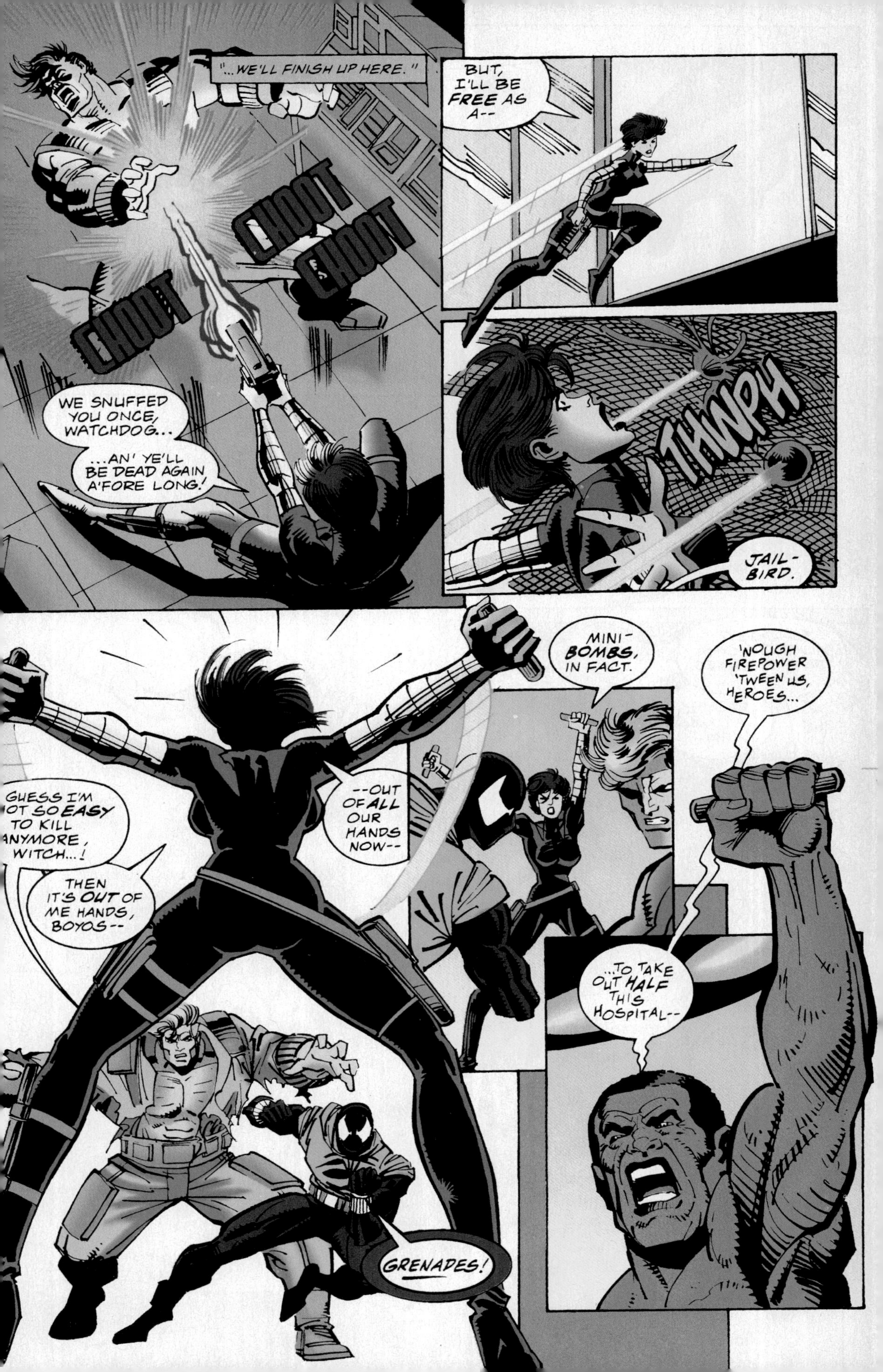
"...WE'LL FINISH UP HERE."
CHOOT
CHOOT
CHOOT
CHOOT
WE SNUFFED YOU ONCE, WATCHDOG...
...AN' YE'LL BE DEAD AGAIN A'FORE LONG!
BUT, I'LL BE FREE AS A--
THWPH
JAIL-BIRD.
GUESS I'M OT SO EASY TO KILL ANYMORE, WITCH...!
THEN IT'S OUT OF ME HANDS, BOYOS--
--OUT OF ALL OUR HANDS NOW--
MINI-BOMBS, IN FACT.
'NOUGH FIREPOWER 'TWEEN US, HEROES...
...TO TAKE OUT HALF THIS HOSPITAL--
GRENADES!

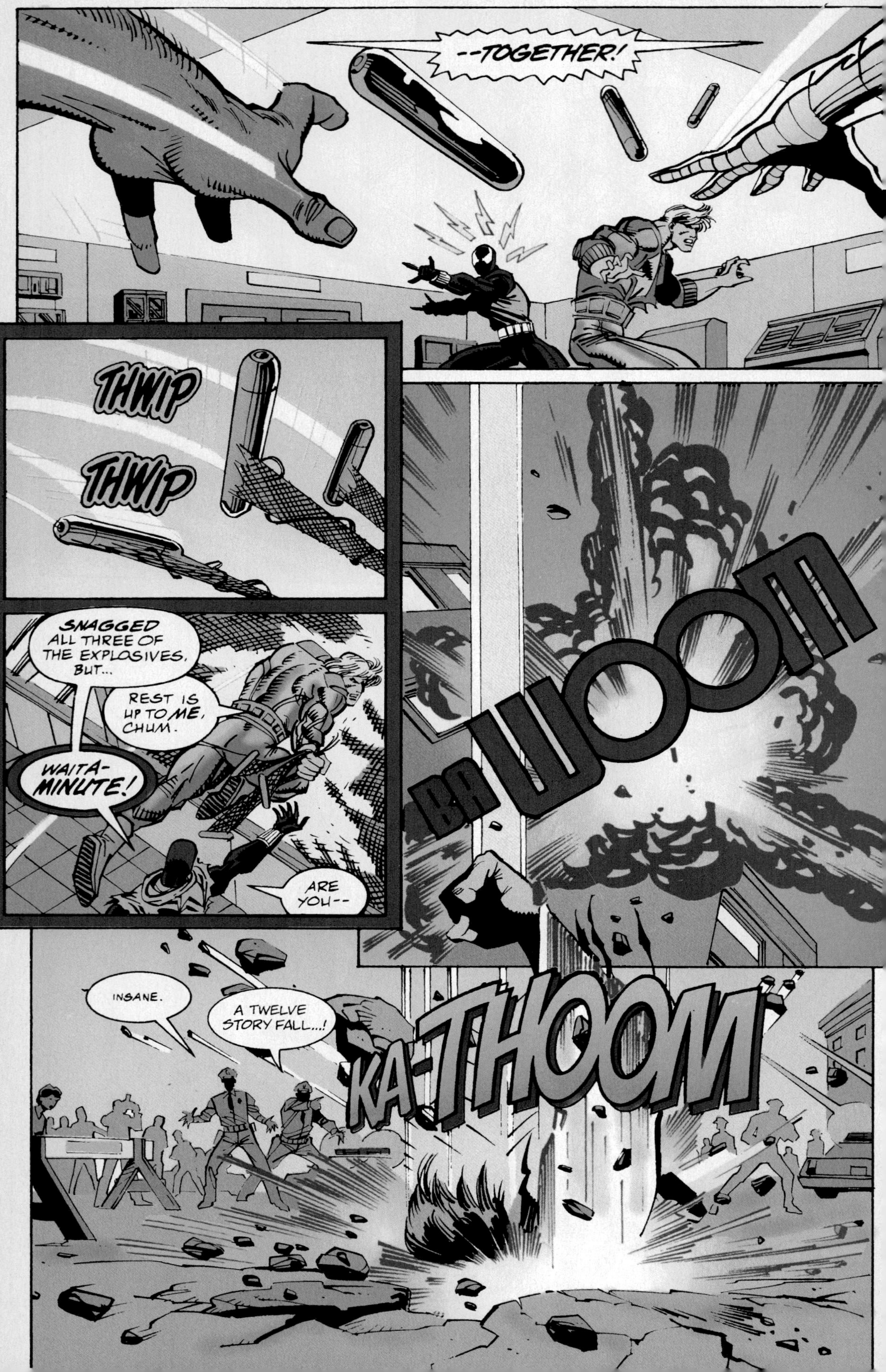
--TOGETHER!
THWIP
THWIP
SNAGGED ALL THREE OF THE EXPLOSIVES, BUT...
REST IS UP TO ME, CHUM.
WAITA-MINUTE!
ARE YOU--
BRWOOM
INSANE.
A TWELVE STORY FALL...!
KA-THOOM

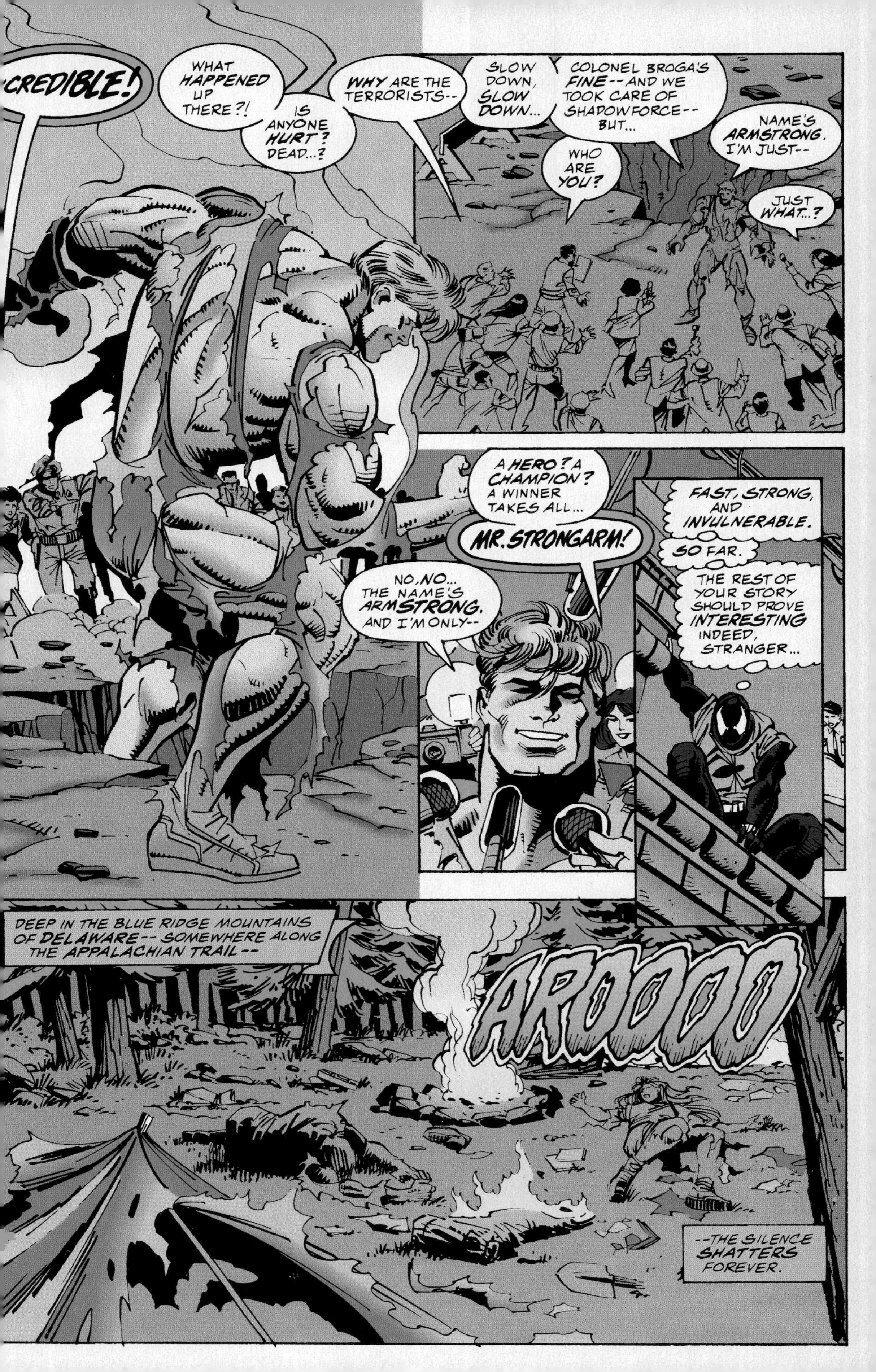

...CREDIBLE!
WHAT HAPPENED UP THERE?!
IS ANYONE HURT? DEAD...?
WHY ARE THE TERRORISTS--
SLOW DOWN, SLOW DOWN...
COLONEL BROGA'S FINE--AND WE TOOK CARE OF SHADOWFORCE--BUT...
WHO ARE YOU?
NAME'S ARMSTRONG. I'M JUST--
JUST WHAT...?
A HERO? A CHAMPION? A WINNER TAKES ALL...
MR. STRONGARM!
NO, NO... THE NAME'S ARMSTRONG. AND I'M ONLY--
FAST, STRONG, AND INVULNERABLE.
SO FAR.
THE REST OF YOUR STORY SHOULD PROVE INTERESTING INDEED, STRANGER...
DEEP IN THE BLUE RIDGE MOUNTAINS OF DELAWARE--SOMEWHERE ALONG THE APPALACHIAN TRAIL--
AROOOO
--THE SILENCE SHATTERS FOREVER.

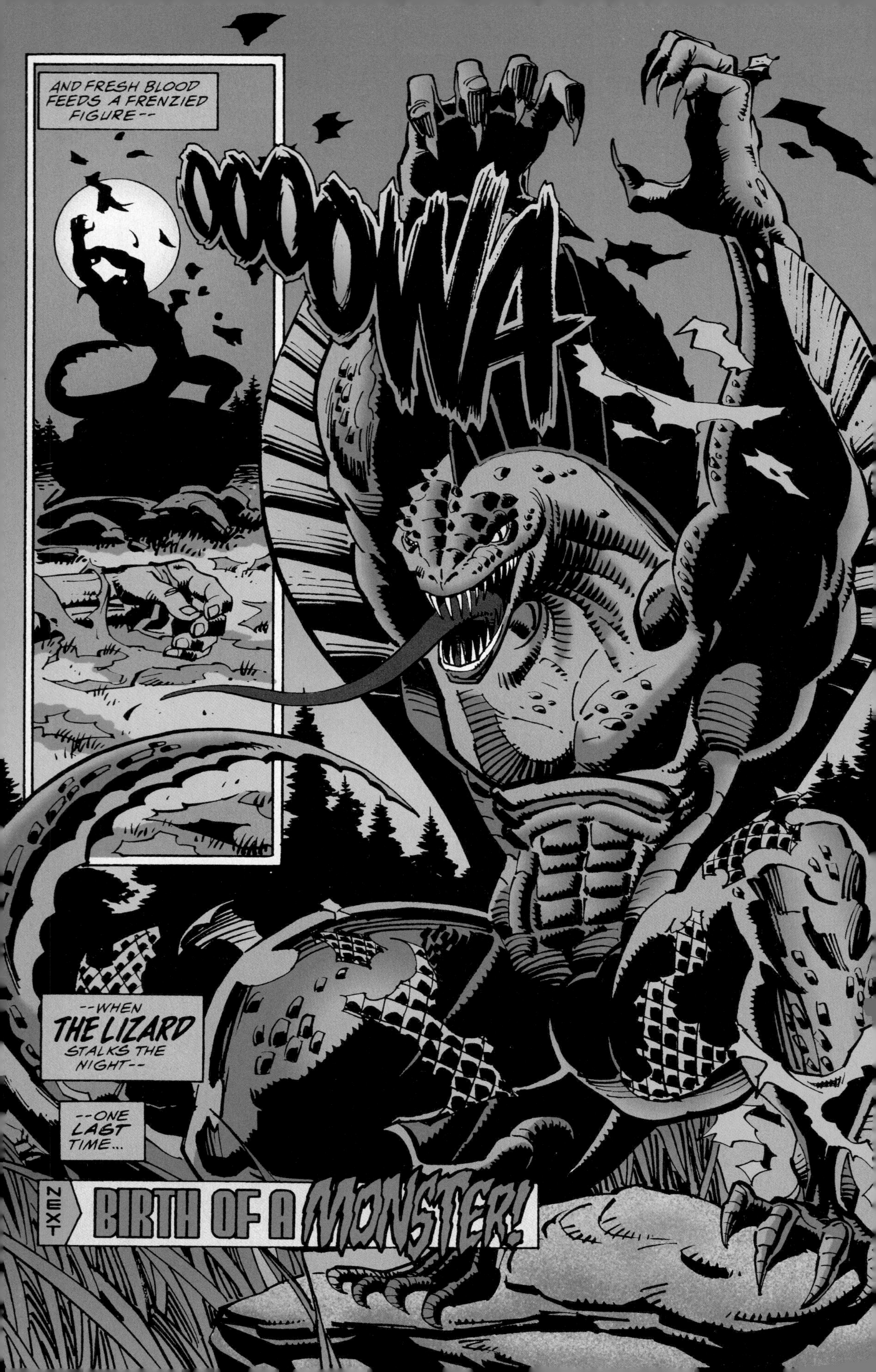
AND FRESH BLOOD FEEDS A FRENZIED FIGURE--
OOOOOWA
--WHEN THE LIZARD STALKS THE NIGHT--
--ONE LAST TIME...
NEXT BIRTH OF A MONSTER!

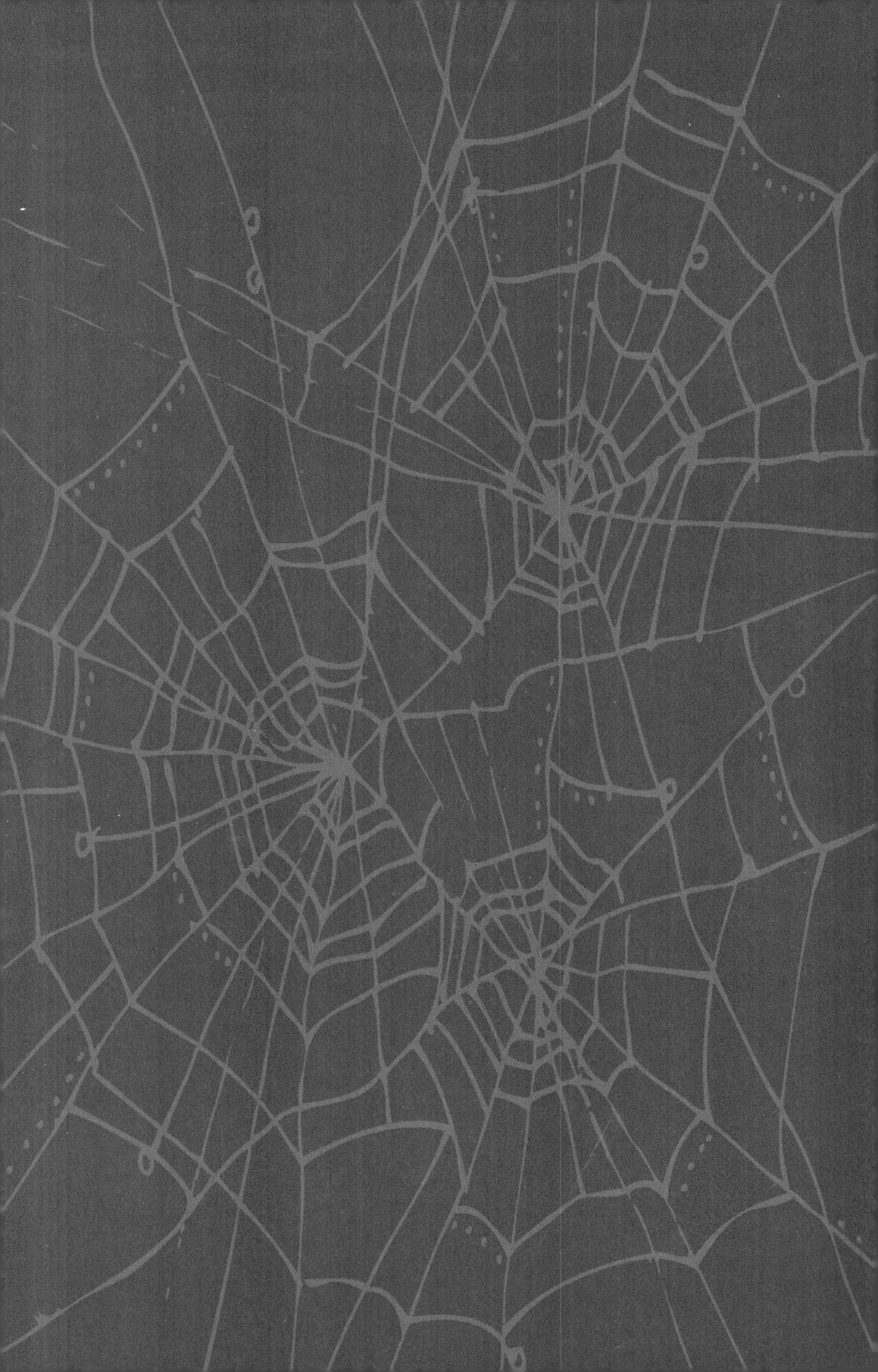

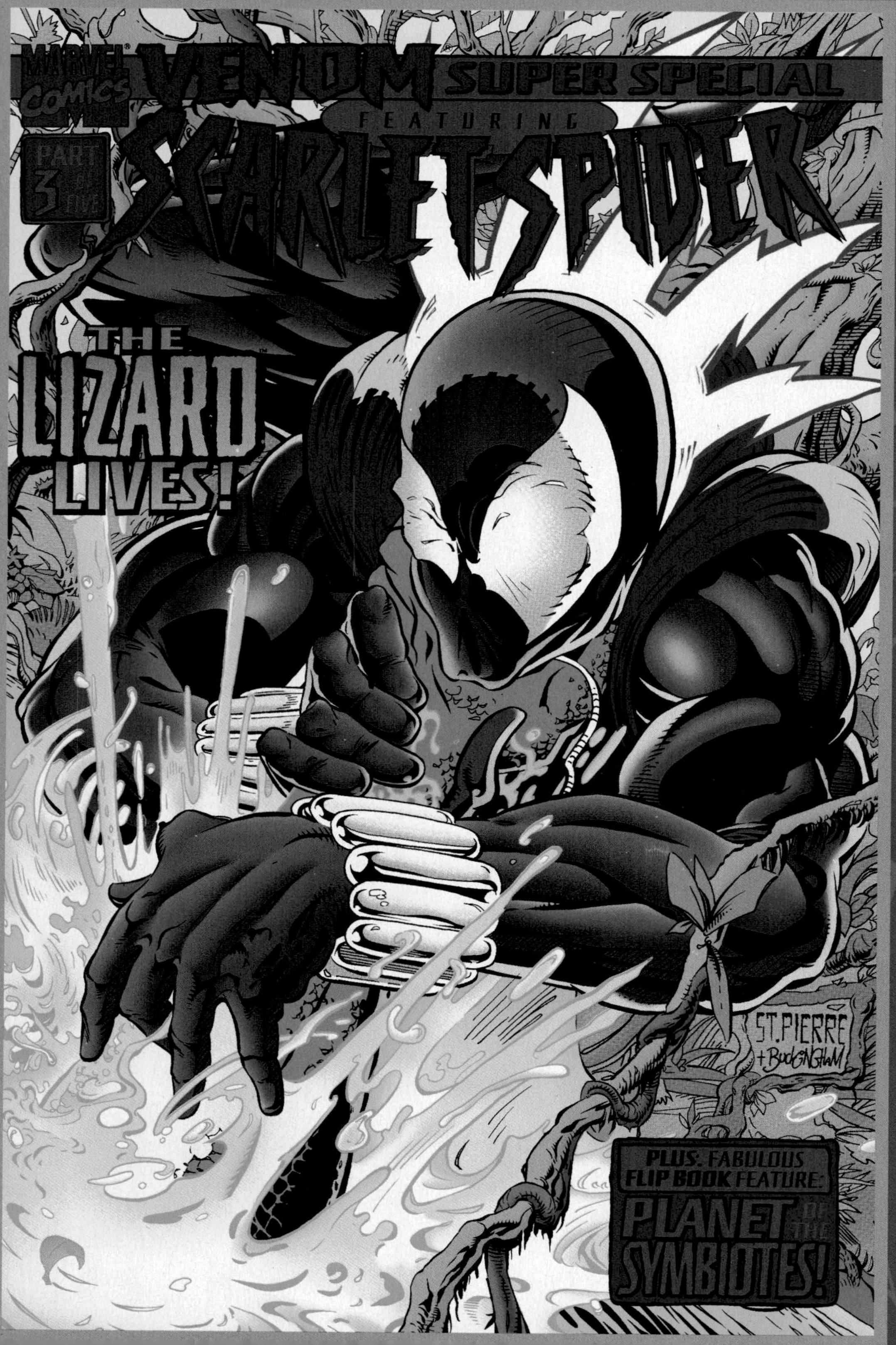
MARVEL COMICS
VENOM SUPER SPECIAL
FEATURING
SCARLET SPIDER
PART 3 OF FIVE
THE LIZARD LIVES!
ST. PIERRE + BUCKINGHAM
PLUS: FABULOUS FLIP BOOK FEATURE:
PLANET OF THE SYMBIOTES!

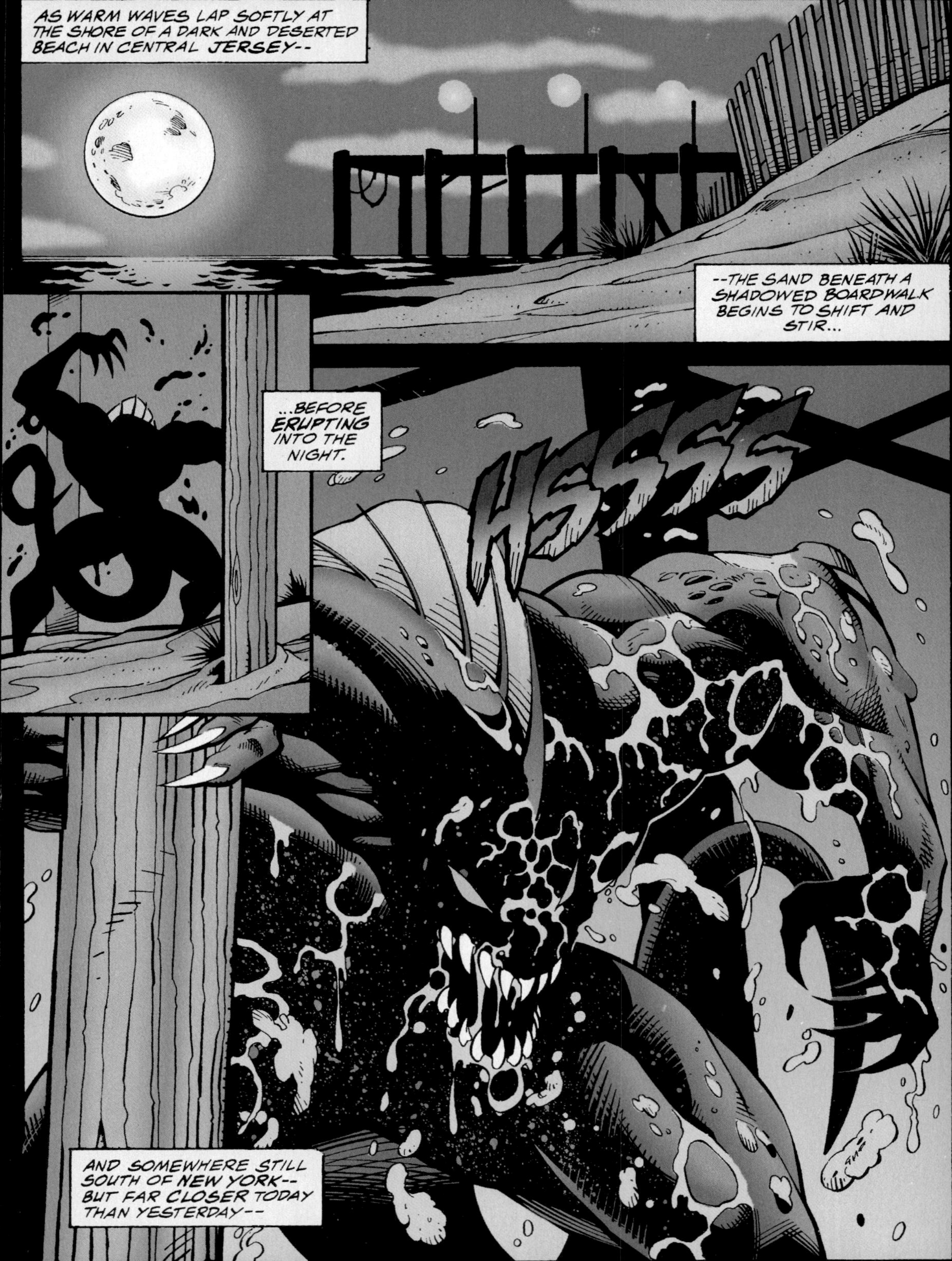
AS WARM WAVES LAP SOFTLY AT THE SHORE OF A DARK AND DESERTED BEACH IN CENTRAL JERSEY--
--THE SAND BENEATH A SHADOWED BOARDWALK BEGINS TO SHIFT AND STIR...
...BEFORE ERUPTING INTO THE NIGHT.
HSSSS
AND SOMEWHERE STILL SOUTH OF NEW YORK-- BUT FAR CLOSER TODAY THAN YESTERDAY--

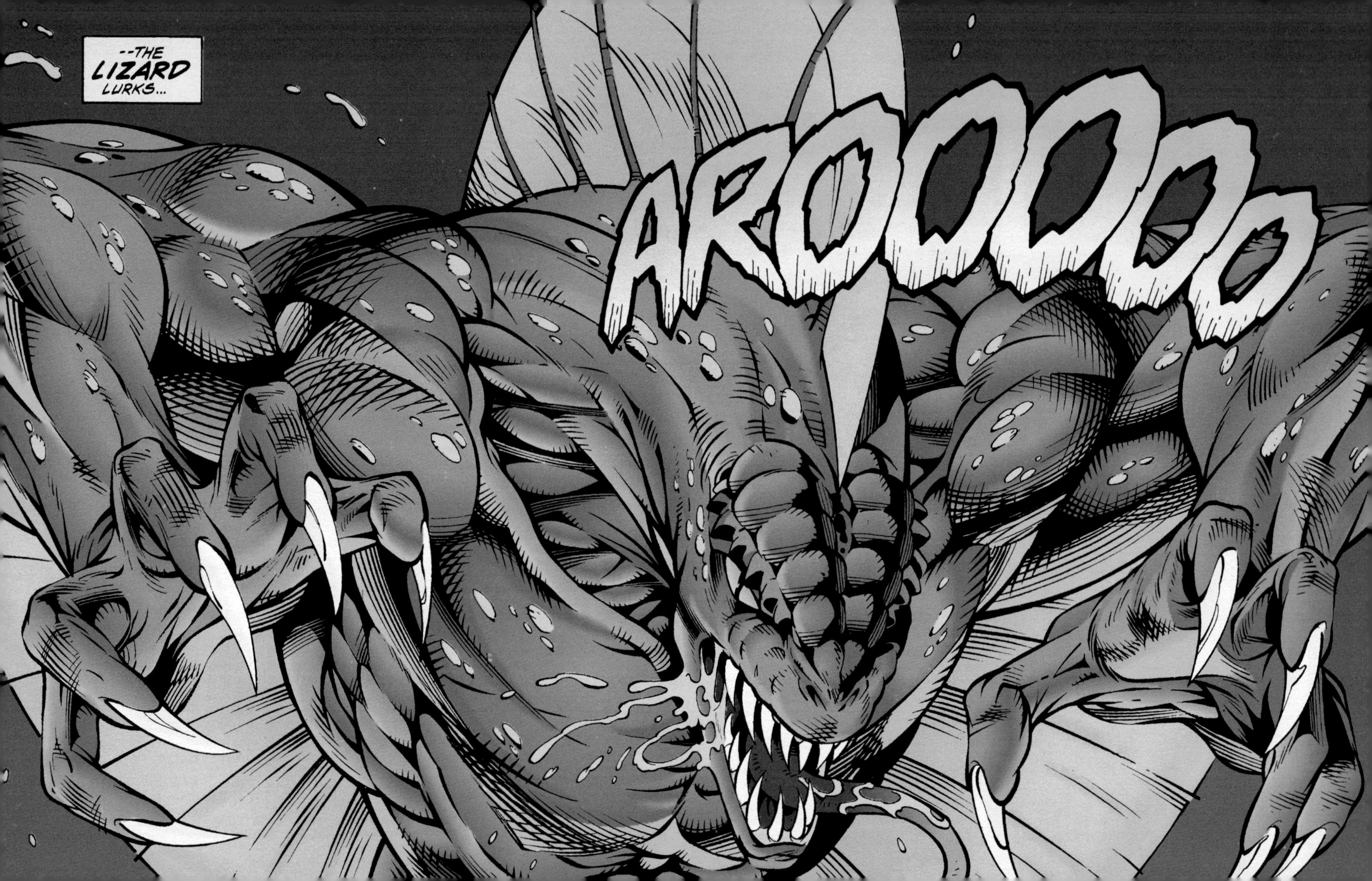
--THE LIZARD LURKS...
AROOOOOO

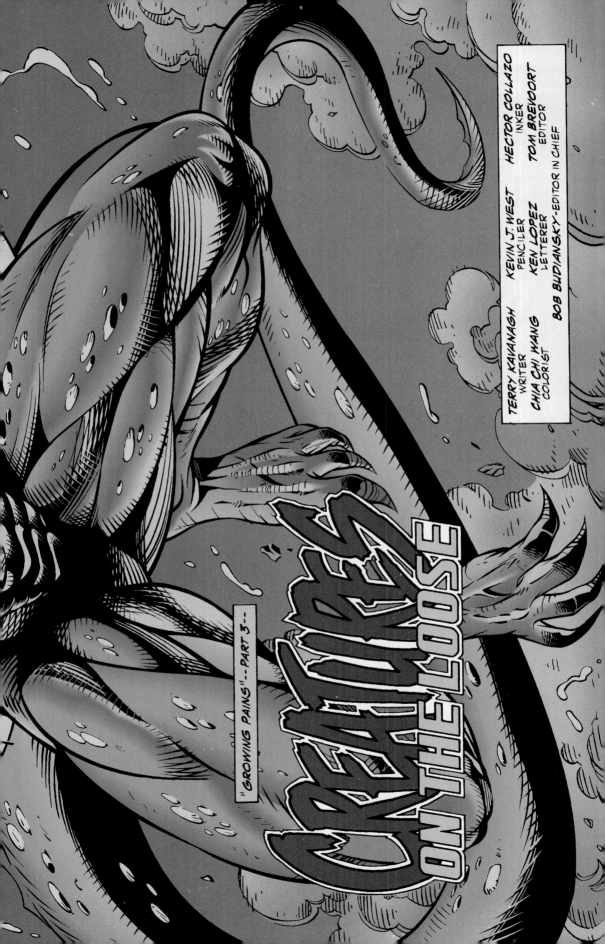

TERRY KAVANAGH
WRITER

CHIA CHI WANG
COLORIST

KEVIN J. WEST
PENCILER

KEN LOPEZ
LETTERER

HECTOR COLLAZO
INKER

TOM BREVOORT
EDITOR

BOB BUDIANSKY–EDITOR IN CHIEF

"GROWING PAINS"--PART 3--

CREATURES ON THE LOOSE

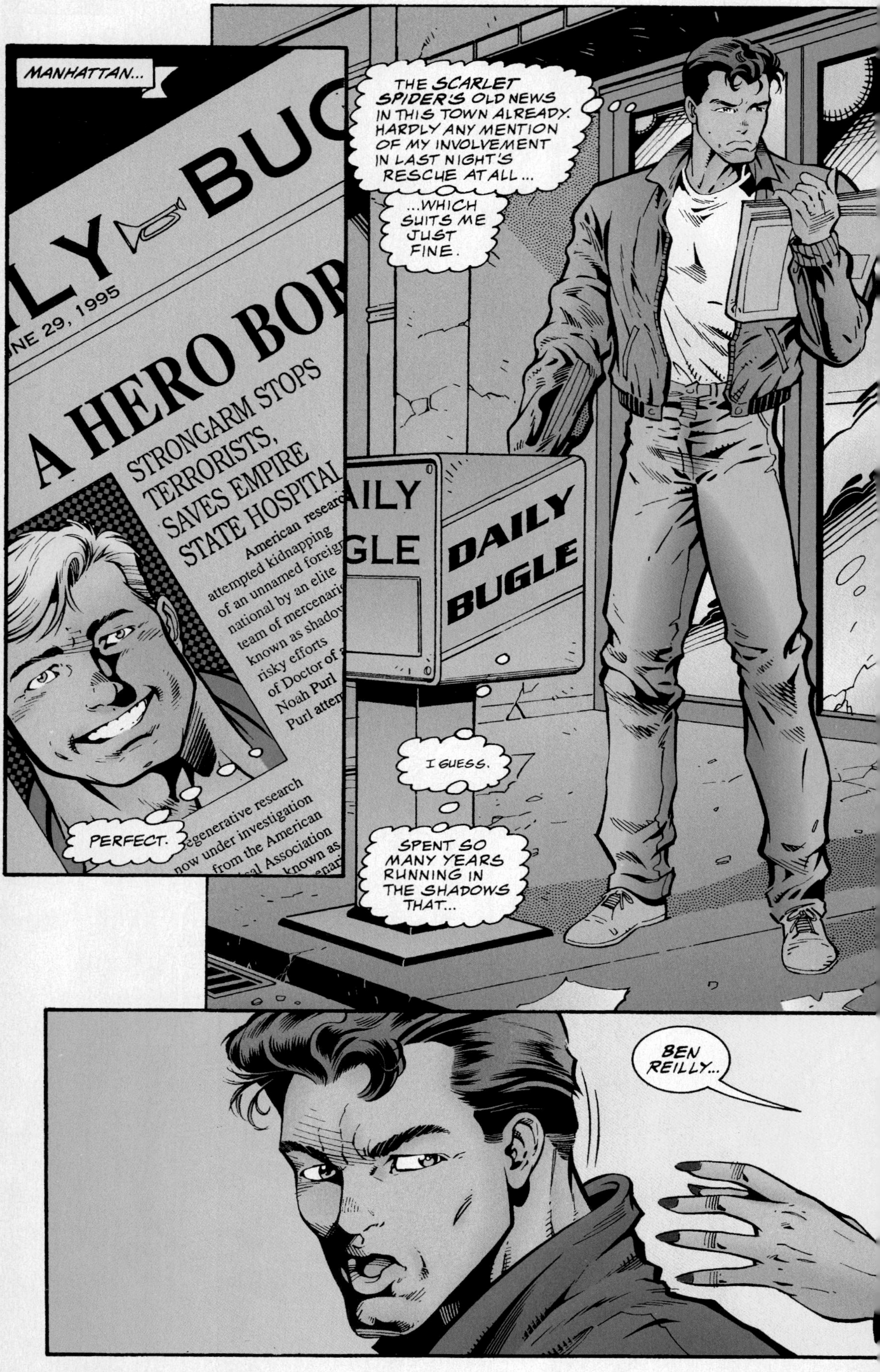

MANHATTAN...
STRONGARM STOPS
TERRORISTS,
SAVES EMPIRE
THE SCARLET SPIDER'S OLD NEWS IN THIS TOWN ALREADY. HARDLY ANY MENTION OF MY INVOLVEMENT IN LAST NIGHT'S RESCUE AT ALL...
...WHICH SUITS ME JUST FINE.
DAILY BUGLE
PERFECT.
I GUESS.
SPENT SO MANY YEARS RUNNING IN THE SHADOWS THAT...
BEN REILLY...

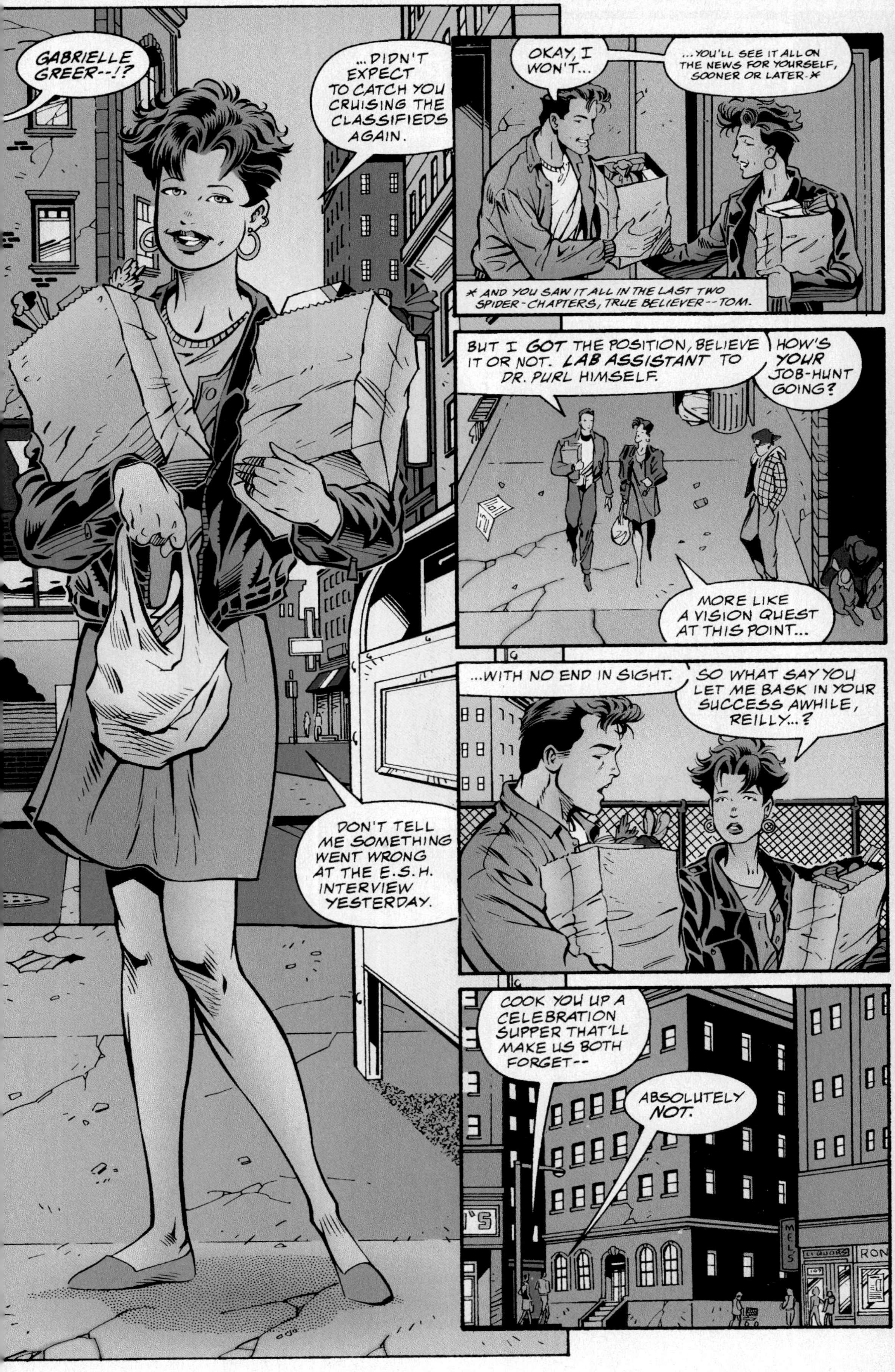
GABRIELLE GREER--!?
...DIDN'T EXPECT TO CATCH YOU CRUISING THE CLASSIFIEDS AGAIN.
DON'T TELL ME SOMETHING WENT WRONG AT THE E.S.H. INTERVIEW YESTERDAY.
OKAY, I WON'T...
...YOU'LL SEE IT ALL ON THE NEWS FOR YOURSELF, SOONER OR LATER.*
* AND YOU SAW IT ALL IN THE LAST TWO SPIDER-CHAPTERS, TRUE BELIEVER--TOM.
BUT I GOT THE POSITION, BELIEVE IT OR NOT. LAB ASSISTANT TO DR. PURL HIMSELF.
HOW'S YOUR JOB-HUNT GOING?
MORE LIKE A VISION QUEST AT THIS POINT...
...WITH NO END IN SIGHT.
SO WHAT SAY YOU LET ME BASK IN YOUR SUCCESS AWHILE, REILLY...?
COOK YOU UP A CELEBRATION SUPPER THAT'LL MAKE US BOTH FORGET--
ABSOLUTELY NOT.
MEL'S
LIQUORS
RON

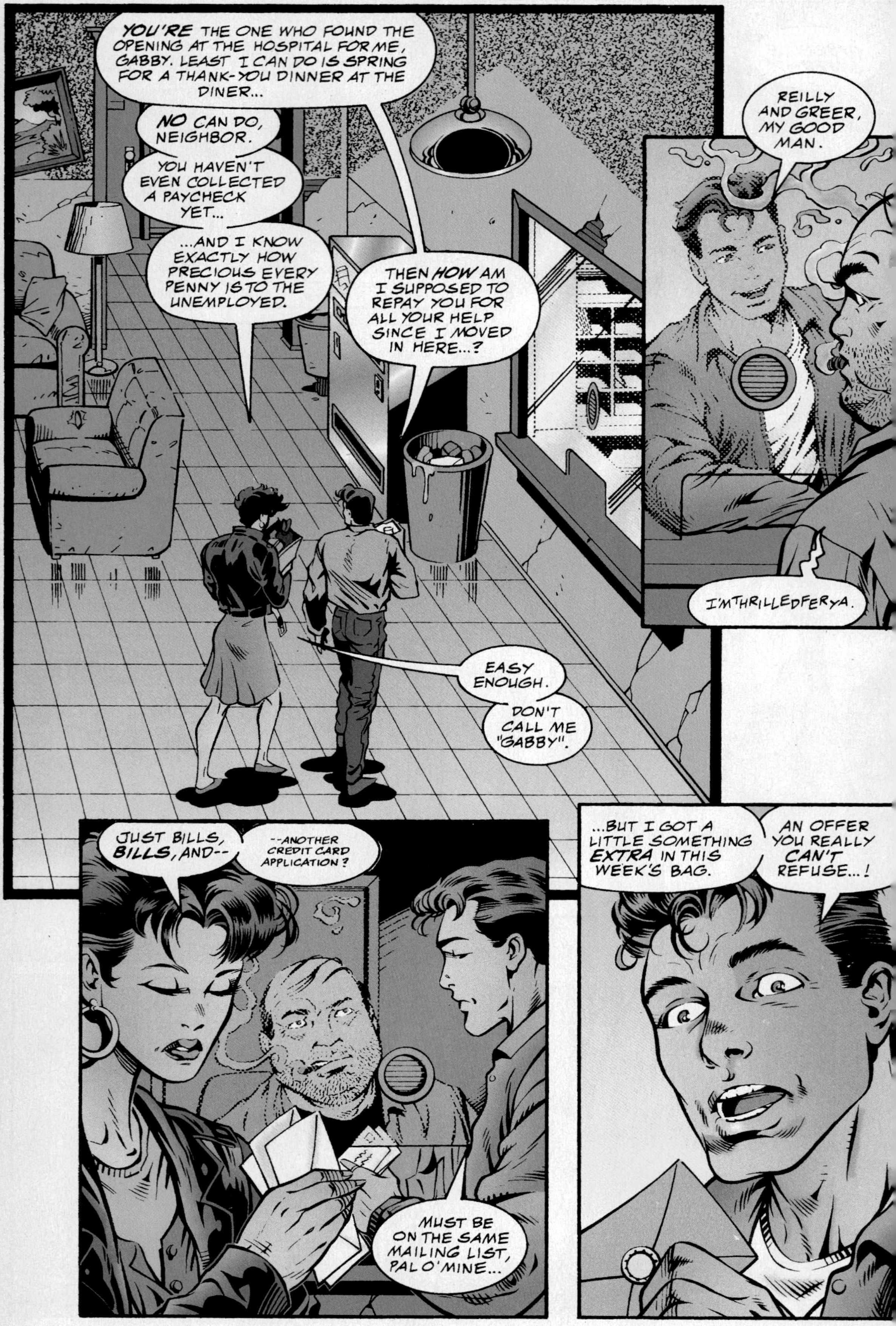
YOU'RE THE ONE WHO FOUND THE OPENING AT THE HOSPITAL FOR ME, GABBY. LEAST I CAN DO IS SPRING FOR A THANK-YOU DINNER AT THE DINER...
NO CAN DO, NEIGHBOR.
YOU HAVEN'T EVEN COLLECTED A PAYCHECK YET...
...AND I KNOW EXACTLY HOW PRECIOUS EVERY PENNY IS TO THE UNEMPLOYED.
THEN HOW AM I SUPPOSED TO REPAY YOU FOR ALL YOUR HELP SINCE I MOVED IN HERE...?
EASY ENOUGH.
DON'T CALL ME "GABBY".
REILLY AND GREER, MY GOOD MAN.
I'MTHRILLEDFERYA.
JUST BILLS, BILLS, AND--
--ANOTHER CREDIT CARD APPLICATION?
MUST BE ON THE SAME MAILING LIST, PAL O'MINE...
...BUT I GOT A LITTLE SOMETHING EXTRA IN THIS WEEK'S BAG.
AN OFFER YOU REALLY CAN'T REFUSE...!

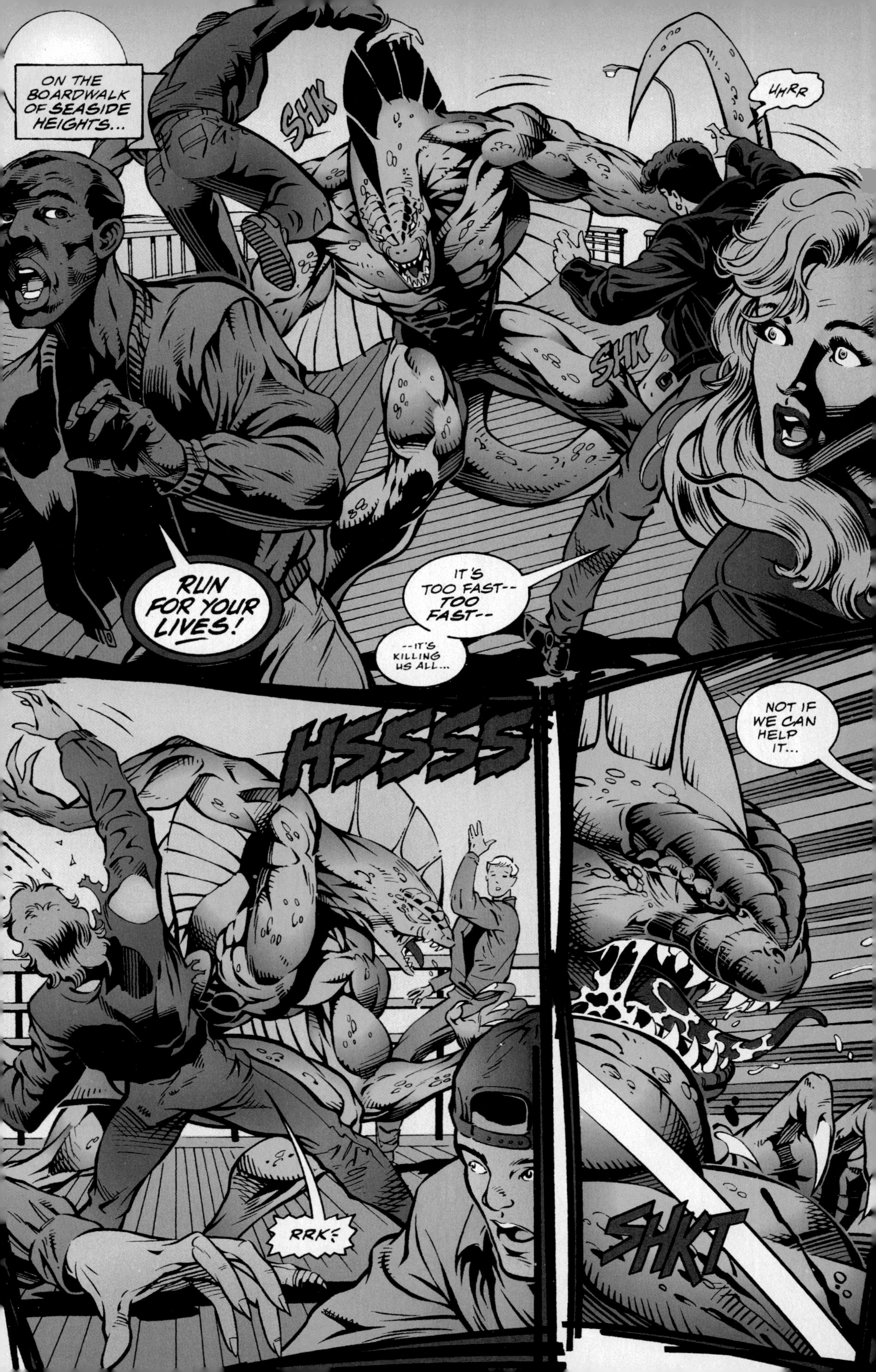

ON THE BOARDWALK OF SEASIDE HEIGHTS...
SHK
UHRR
SHK
RUN FOR YOUR LIVES!
IT'S TOO FAST-- TOO FAST--
--IT'S KILLING US ALL...
HSSSSS
NOT IF WE CAN HELP IT...
RRK!
SHKT

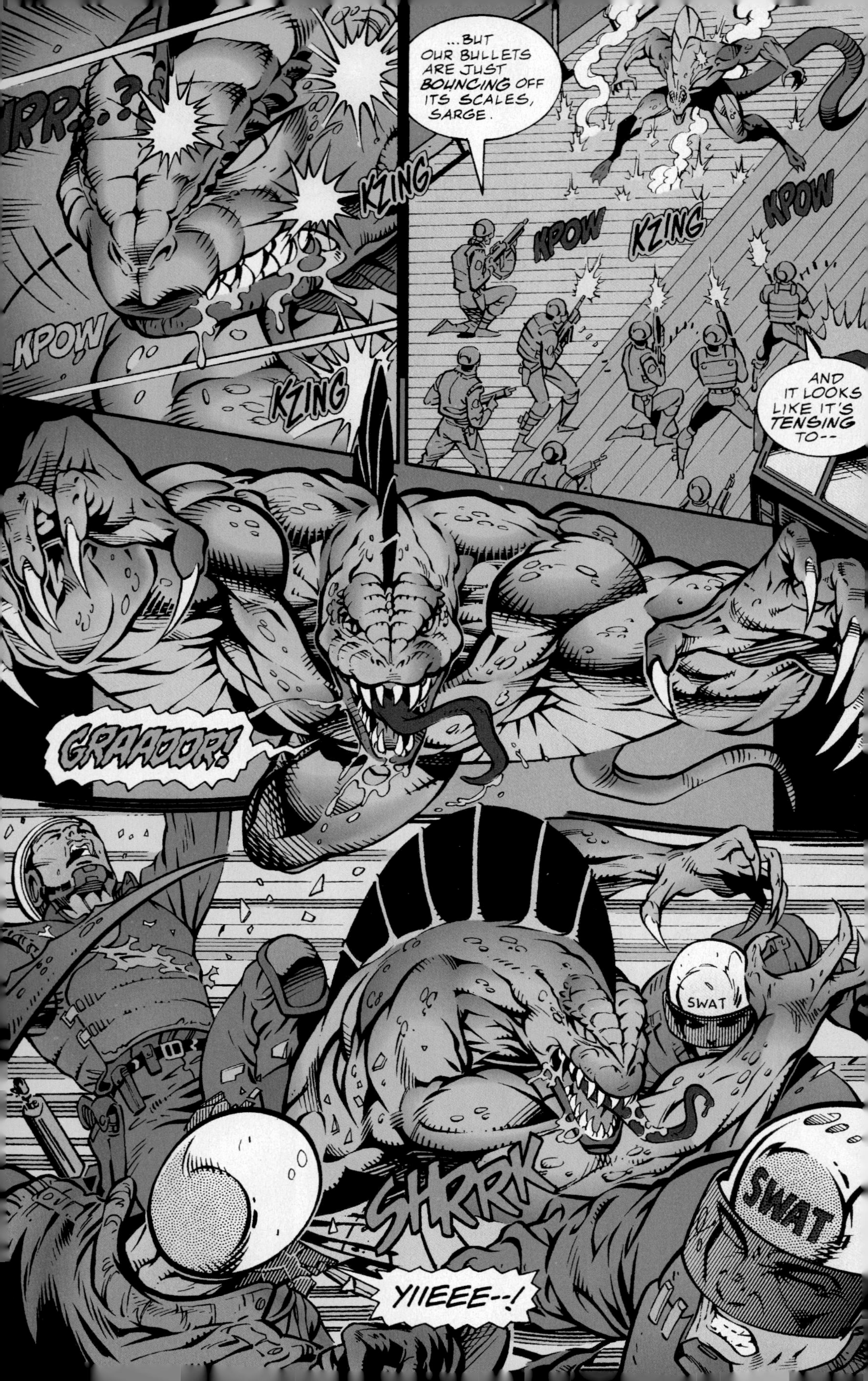

RRR...?
KZING
KPOW
KZING
...BUT OUR BULLETS ARE JUST BOUNCING OFF ITS SCALES, SARGE.
KPOW
KZING
KPOW
AND IT LOOKS LIKE IT'S TENSING TO--
GRAAOOR!
SWAT
SHRRK
SWAT
YIIEEE--!

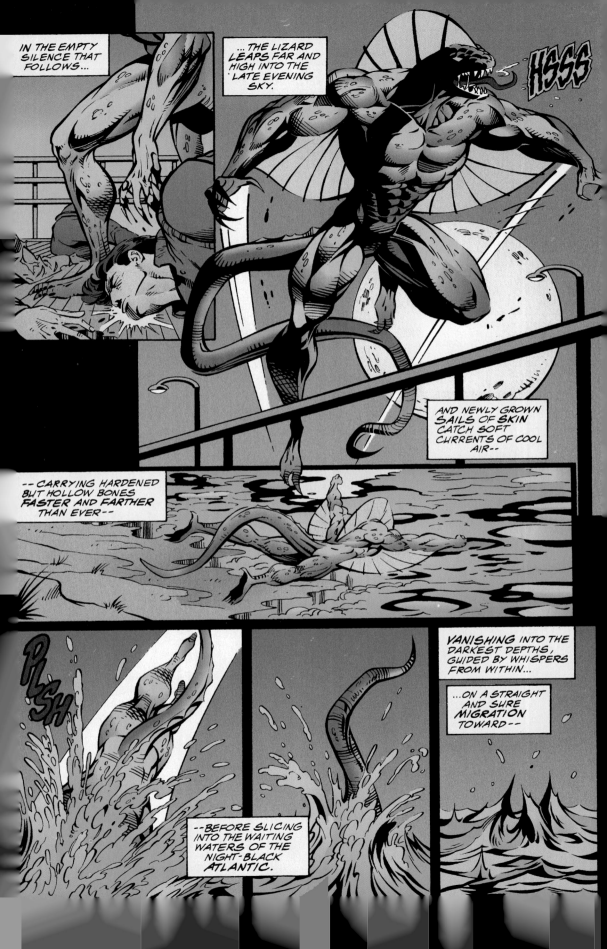

IN THE EMPTY SILENCE THAT FOLLOWS...

...THE LIZARD LEAPS FAR AND HIGH INTO THE LATE EVENING SKY.

HSSS

AND NEWLY GROWN SAILS OF SKIN CATCH SOFT CURRENTS OF COOL AIR--

-- CARRYING HARDENED BUT HOLLOW BONES FASTER AND FARTHER THAN EVER--

VANISHING INTO THE DARKEST DEPTHS, GUIDED BY WHISPERS FROM WITHIN...

...ON A STRAIGHT AND SURE MIGRATION TOWARD--

PLSH

--BEFORE SLICING INTO THE WAITING WATERS OF THE NIGHT-BLACK ATLANTIC.

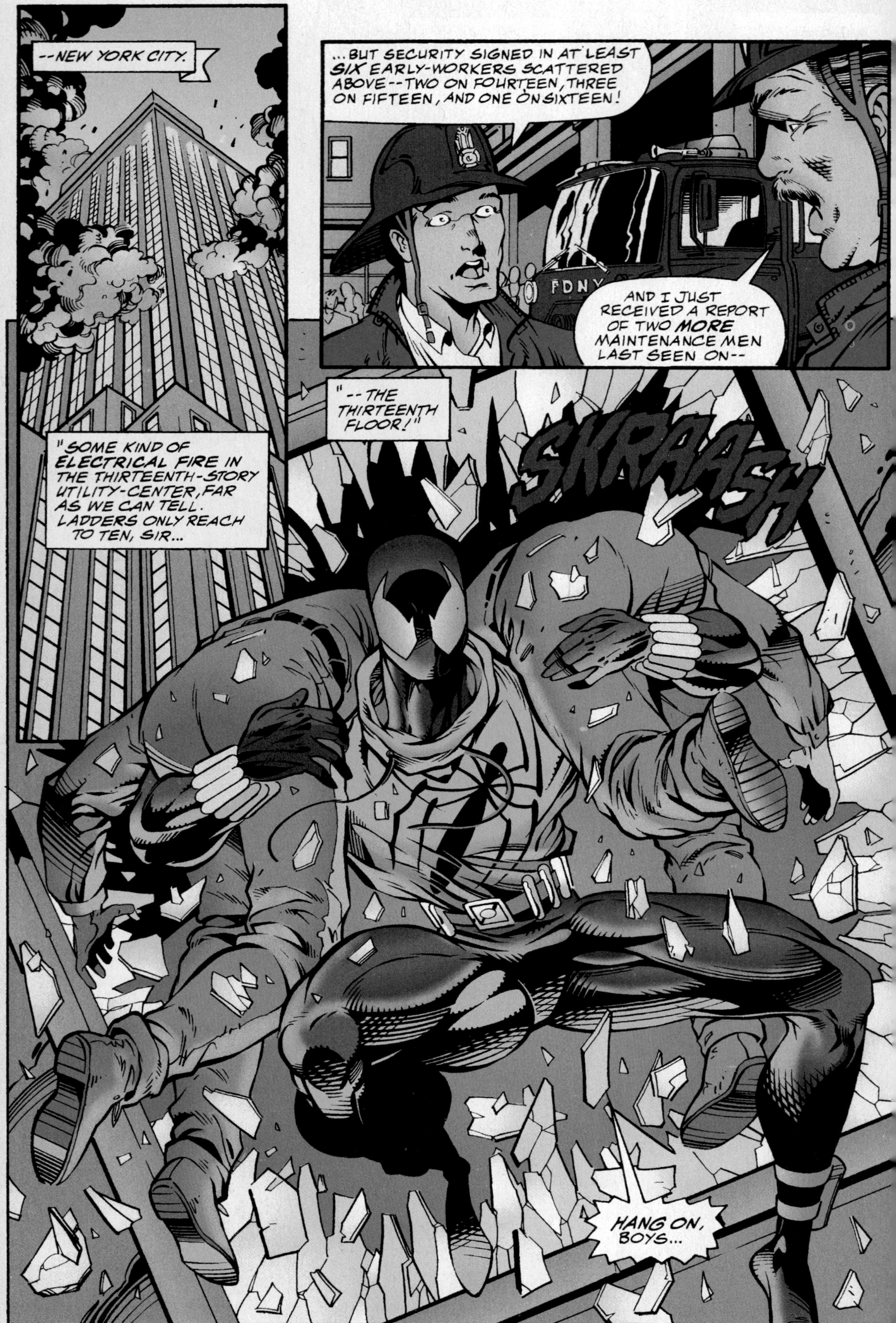
--NEW YORK CITY.
"SOME KIND OF ELECTRICAL FIRE IN THE THIRTEENTH-STORY UTILITY-CENTER, FAR AS WE CAN TELL. LADDERS ONLY REACH TO TEN, SIR...
...BUT SECURITY SIGNED IN AT LEAST SIX EARLY-WORKERS SCATTERED ABOVE--TWO ON FOURTEEN, THREE ON FIFTEEN, AND ONE ON SIXTEEN!
FDNY
AND I JUST RECEIVED A REPORT OF TWO MORE MAINTENANCE MEN LAST SEEN ON--
"--THE THIRTEENTH FLOOR!"
SKRAASH
HANG ON, BOYS...

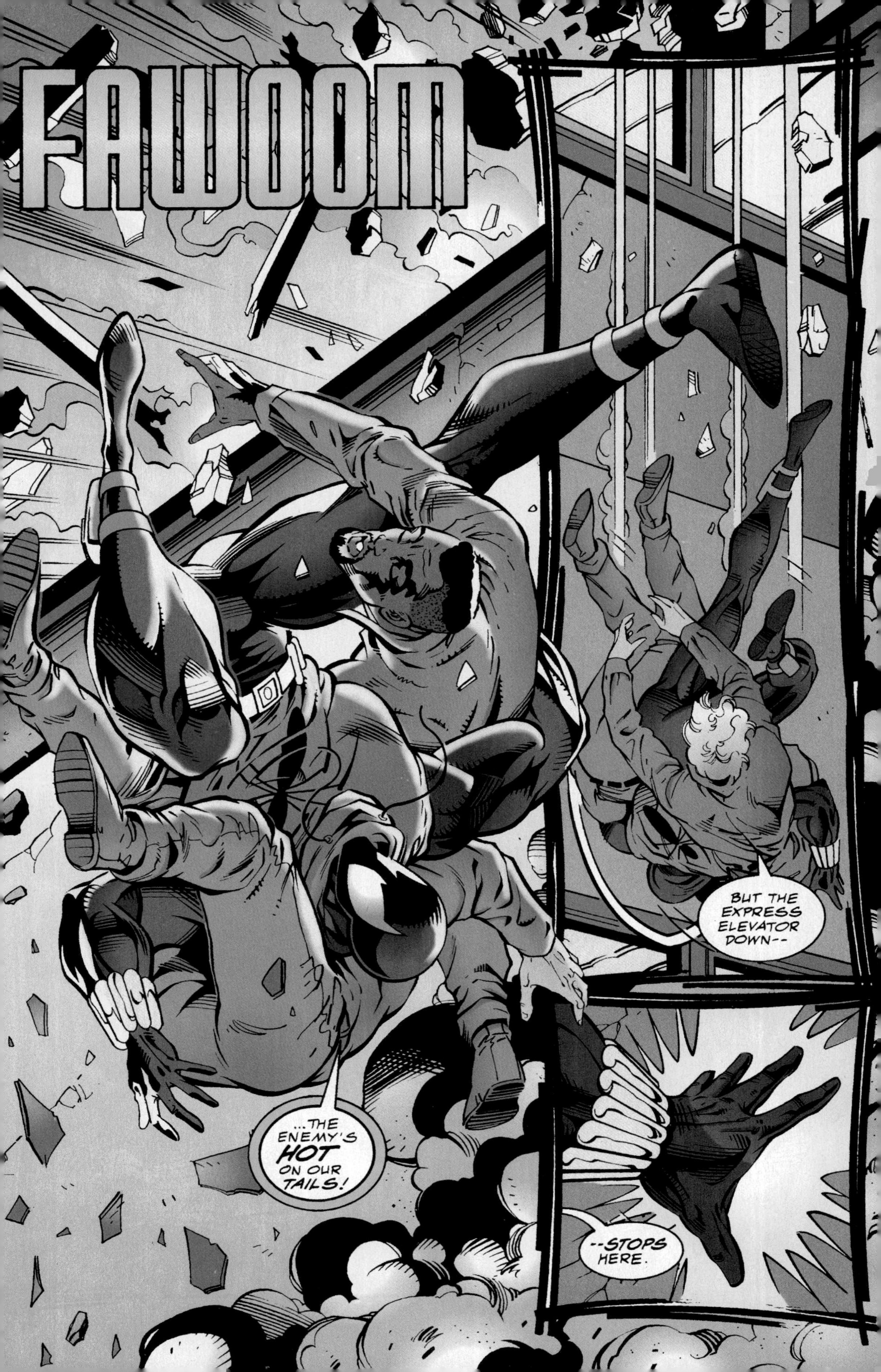
FAWOOM
...THE ENEMY'S HOT ON OUR TAILS!
BUT THE EXPRESS ELEVATOR DOWN--
--STOPS HERE.

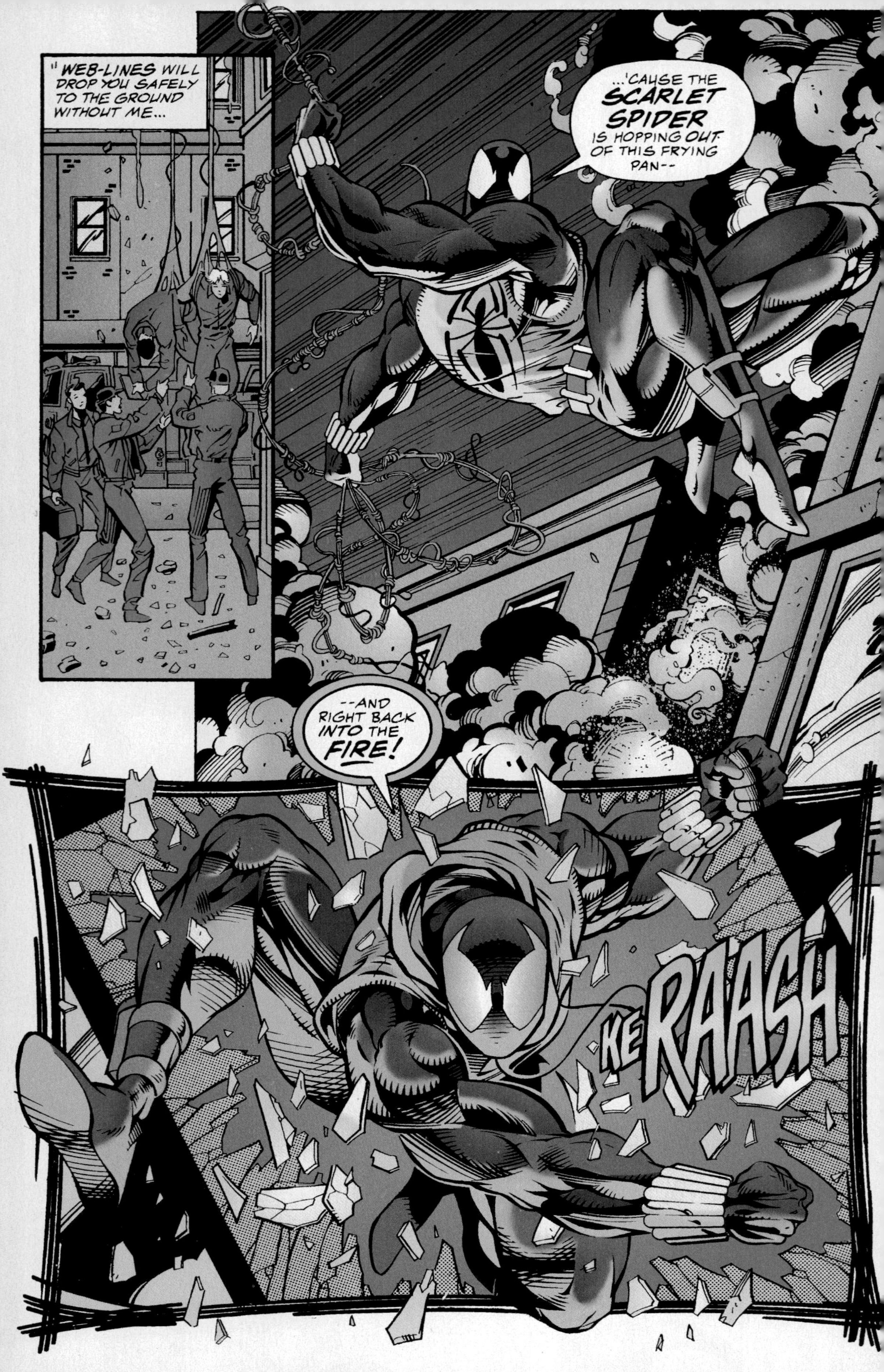
"WEB-LINES WILL DROP YOU SAFELY TO THE GROUND WITHOUT ME...
...'CAUSE THE SCARLET SPIDER IS HOPPING OUT OF THIS FRYING PAN--
--AND RIGHT BACK INTO THE FIRE!
KERAASH

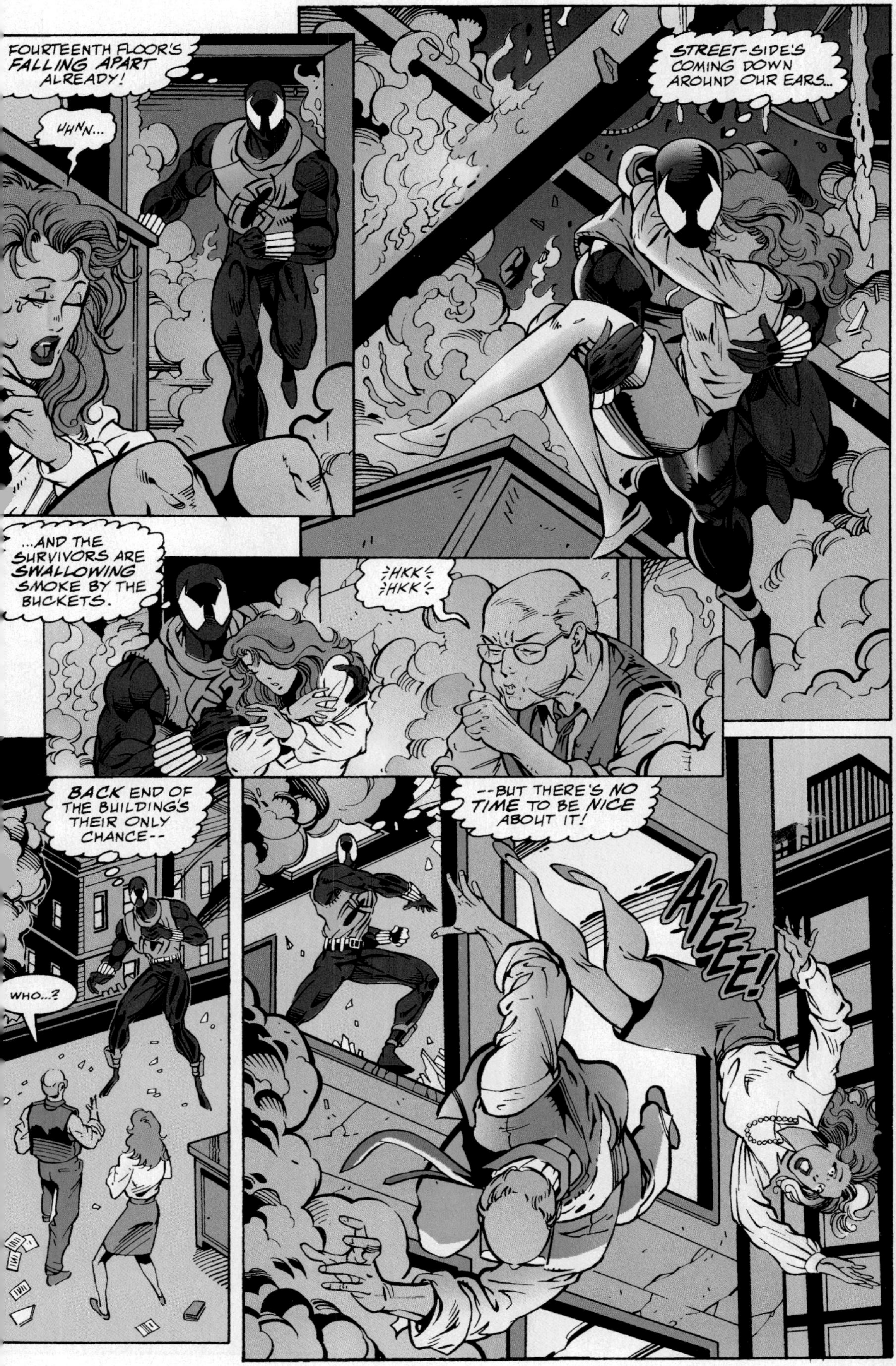
FOURTEENTH FLOOR'S FALLING APART ALREADY!
UHNN...
STREET-SIDE'S COMING DOWN AROUND OUR EARS...
...AND THE SURVIVORS ARE SWALLOWING SMOKE BY THE BUCKETS.
HKK HKK
BACK END OF THE BUILDING'S THEIR ONLY CHANCE--
WHO...?
--BUT THERE'S NO TIME TO BE NICE ABOUT IT!
AIEEE!

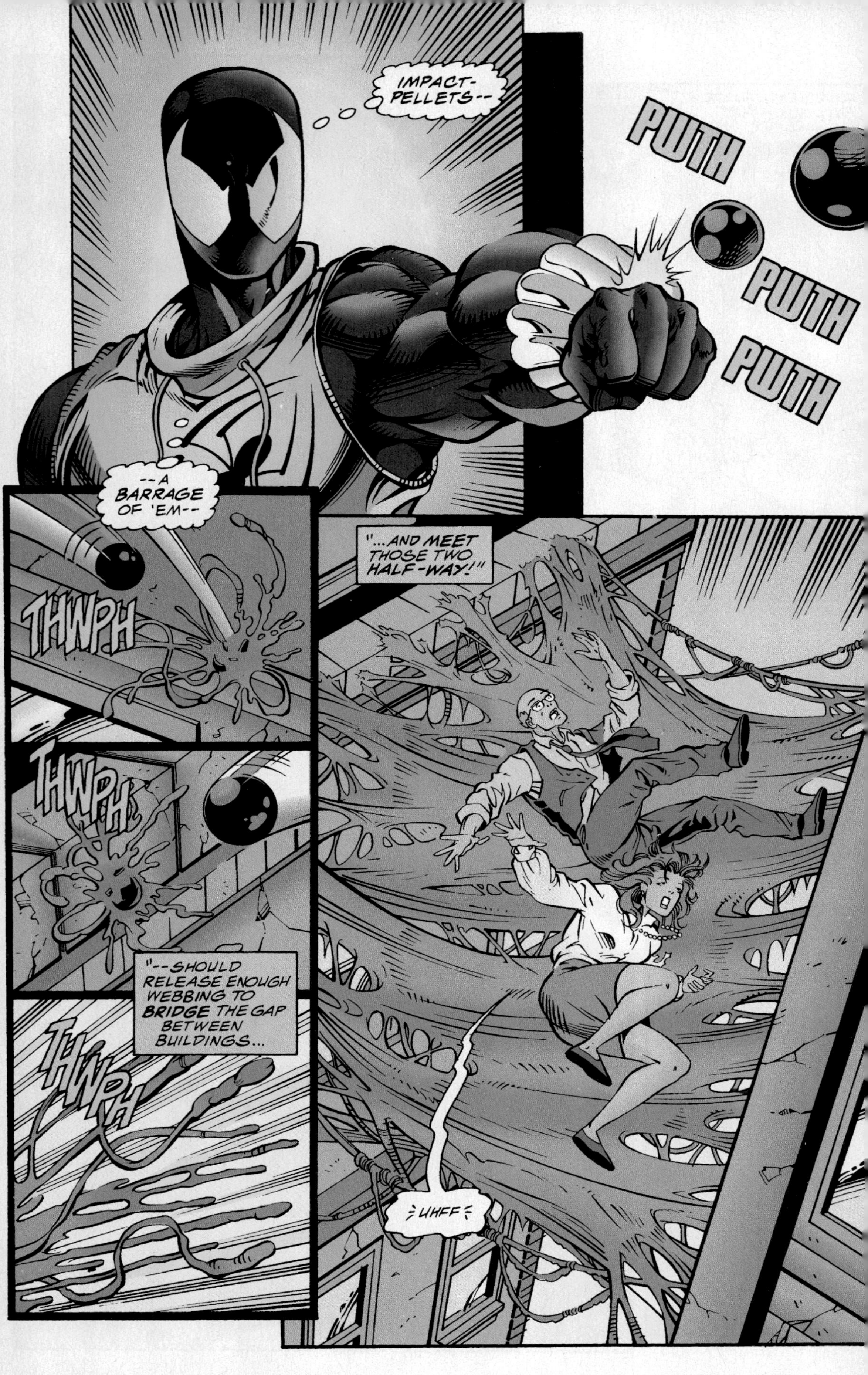
IMPACT-PELLETS--
PWTH
PWTH
PWTH
--A BARRAGE OF 'EM--
THWPH
THWPH
"--SHOULD RELEASE ENOUGH WEBBING TO BRIDGE THE GAP BETWEEN BUILDINGS...
THWPH
"...AND MEET THOSE TWO HALF-WAY!"
UHFF

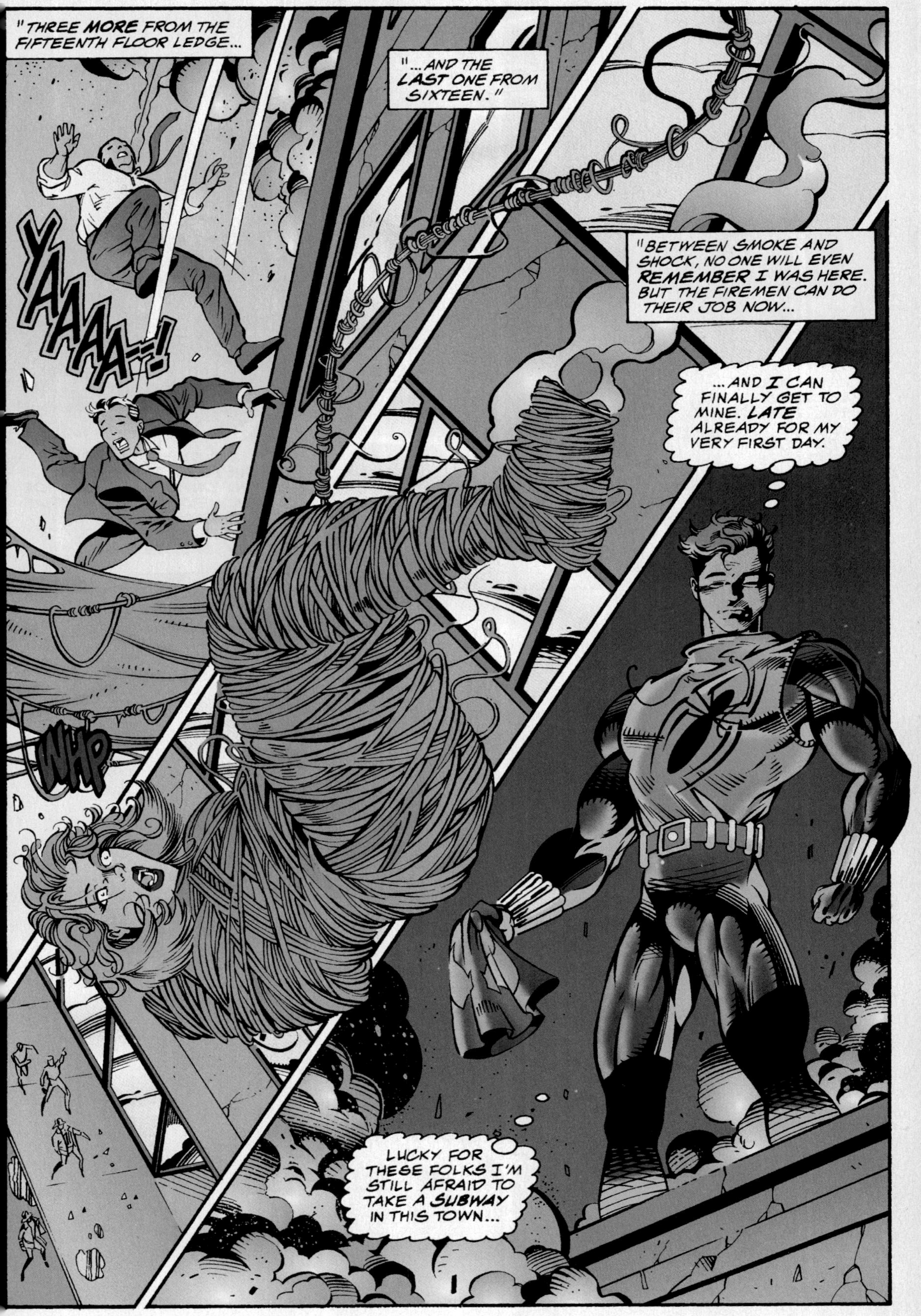
"THREE MORE FROM THE FIFTEENTH FLOOR LEDGE...
YAAAAA--!
"...AND THE LAST ONE FROM SIXTEEN."
"BETWEEN SMOKE AND SHOCK, NO ONE WILL EVEN REMEMBER I WAS HERE. BUT THE FIREMEN CAN DO THEIR JOB NOW...
...AND I CAN FINALLY GET TO MINE. LATE ALREADY FOR MY VERY FIRST DAY.
WHP
LUCKY FOR THESE FOLKS I'M STILL AFRAID TO TAKE A SUBWAY IN THIS TOWN...

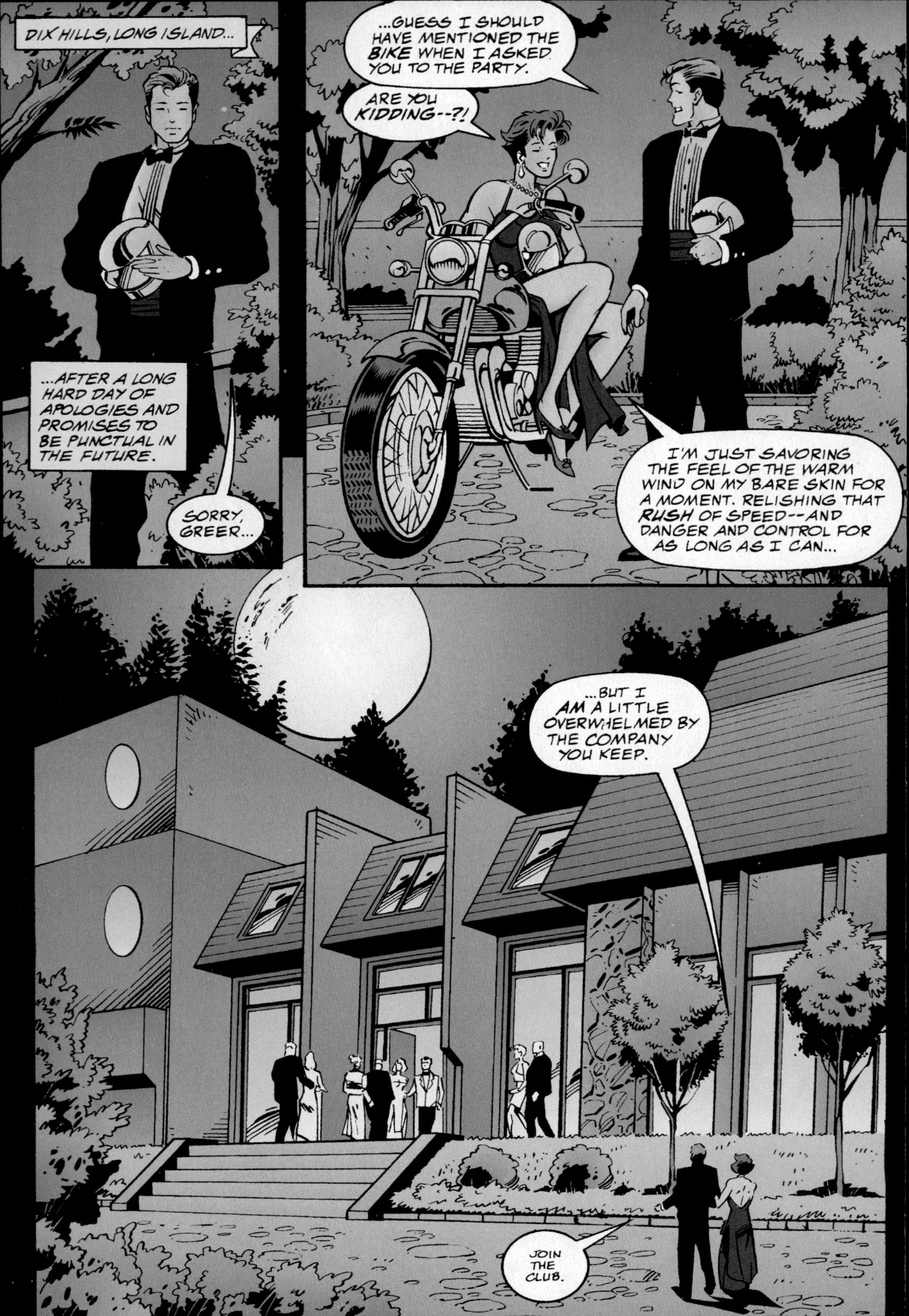
DIX HILLS, LONG ISLAND...
...AFTER A LONG HARD DAY OF APOLOGIES AND PROMISES TO BE PUNCTUAL IN THE FUTURE.
SORRY, GREER...
...GUESS I SHOULD HAVE MENTIONED THE BIKE WHEN I ASKED YOU TO THE PARTY.
ARE YOU KIDDING--?!
I'M JUST SAVORING THE FEEL OF THE WARM WIND ON MY BARE SKIN FOR A MOMENT. RELISHING THAT RUSH OF SPEED--AND DANGER AND CONTROL FOR AS LONG AS I CAN...
...BUT I AM A LITTLE OVERWHELMED BY THE COMPANY YOU KEEP.
JOIN THE CLUB.

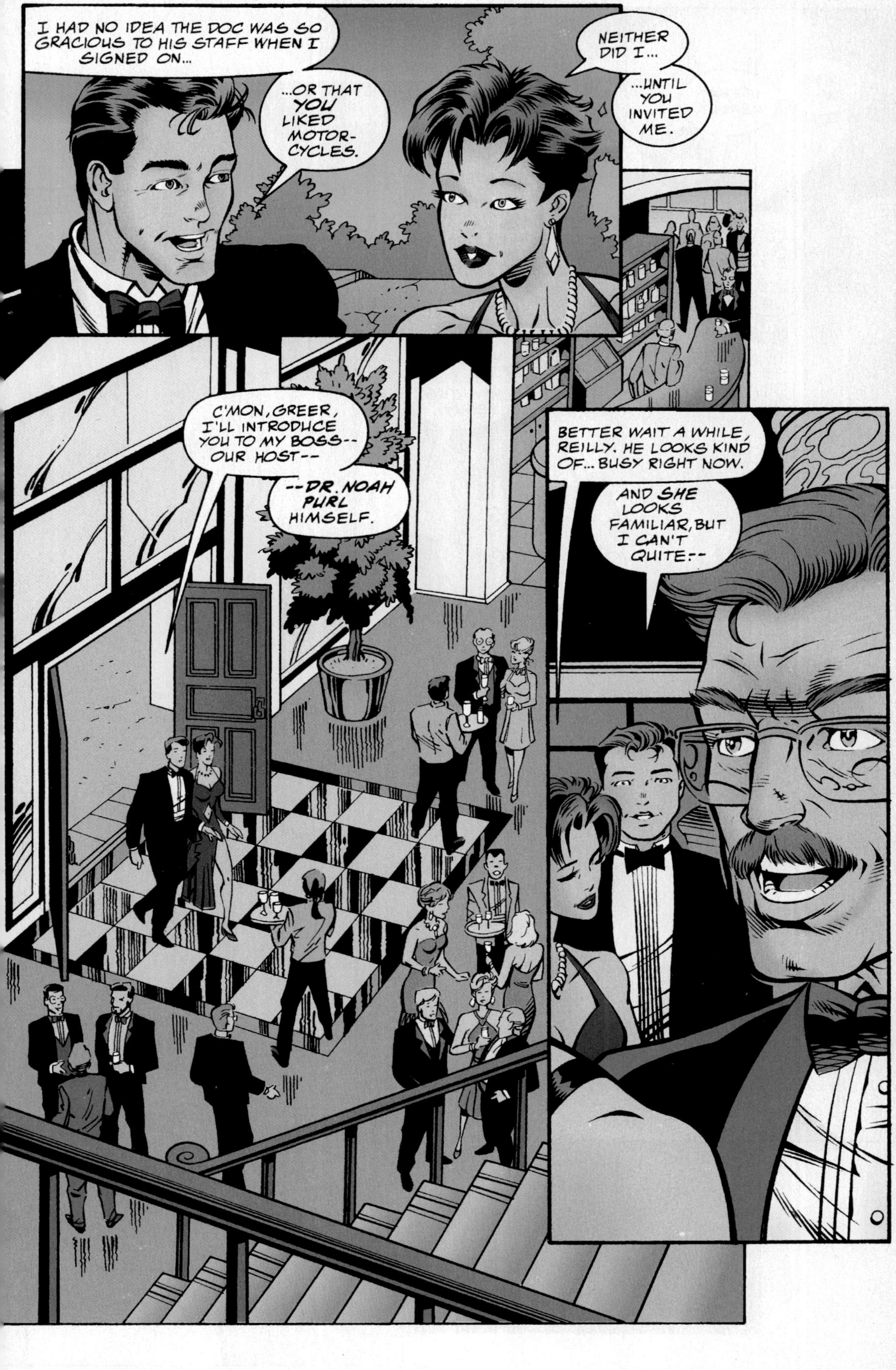
I HAD NO IDEA THE DOC WAS SO GRACIOUS TO HIS STAFF WHEN I SIGNED ON...
...OR THAT YOU LIKED MOTOR-CYCLES.
NEITHER DID I...
...UNTIL YOU INVITED ME.
C'MON, GREER, I'LL INTRODUCE YOU TO MY BOSS-- OUR HOST--
--DR. NOAH PURL HIMSELF.
BETTER WAIT A WHILE, REILLY. HE LOOKS KIND OF... BUSY RIGHT NOW.
AND SHE LOOKS FAMILIAR, BUT I CAN'T QUITE:--

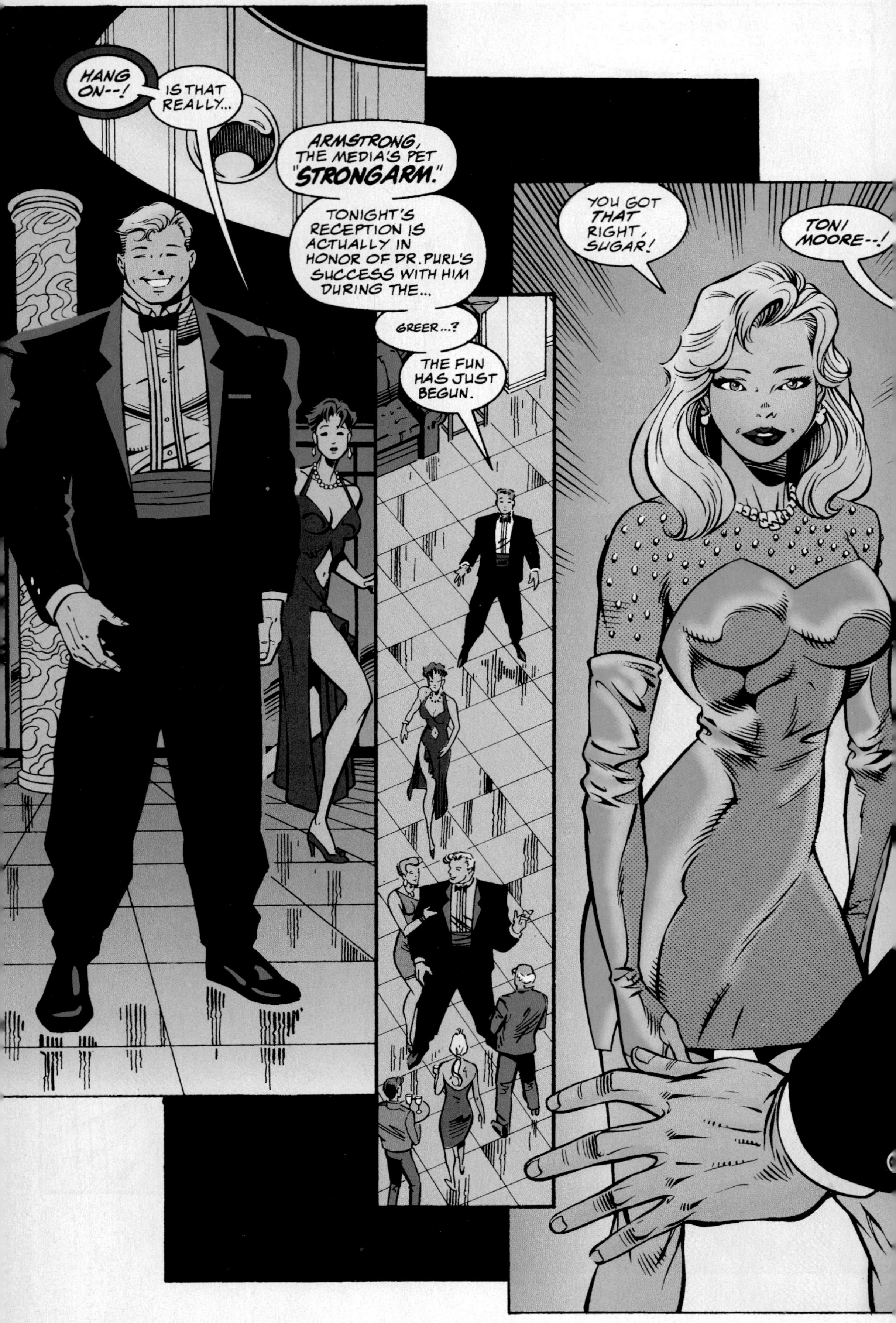

HANG ON--!
IS THAT REALLY...
ARMSTRONG, THE MEDIA'S PET "STRONGARM."
TONIGHT'S RECEPTION IS ACTUALLY IN HONOR OF DR. PURL'S SUCCESS WITH HIM DURING THE...
GREER...?
THE FUN HAS JUST BEGUN.
YOU GOT THAT RIGHT, SUGAR!
TONI MOORE--!

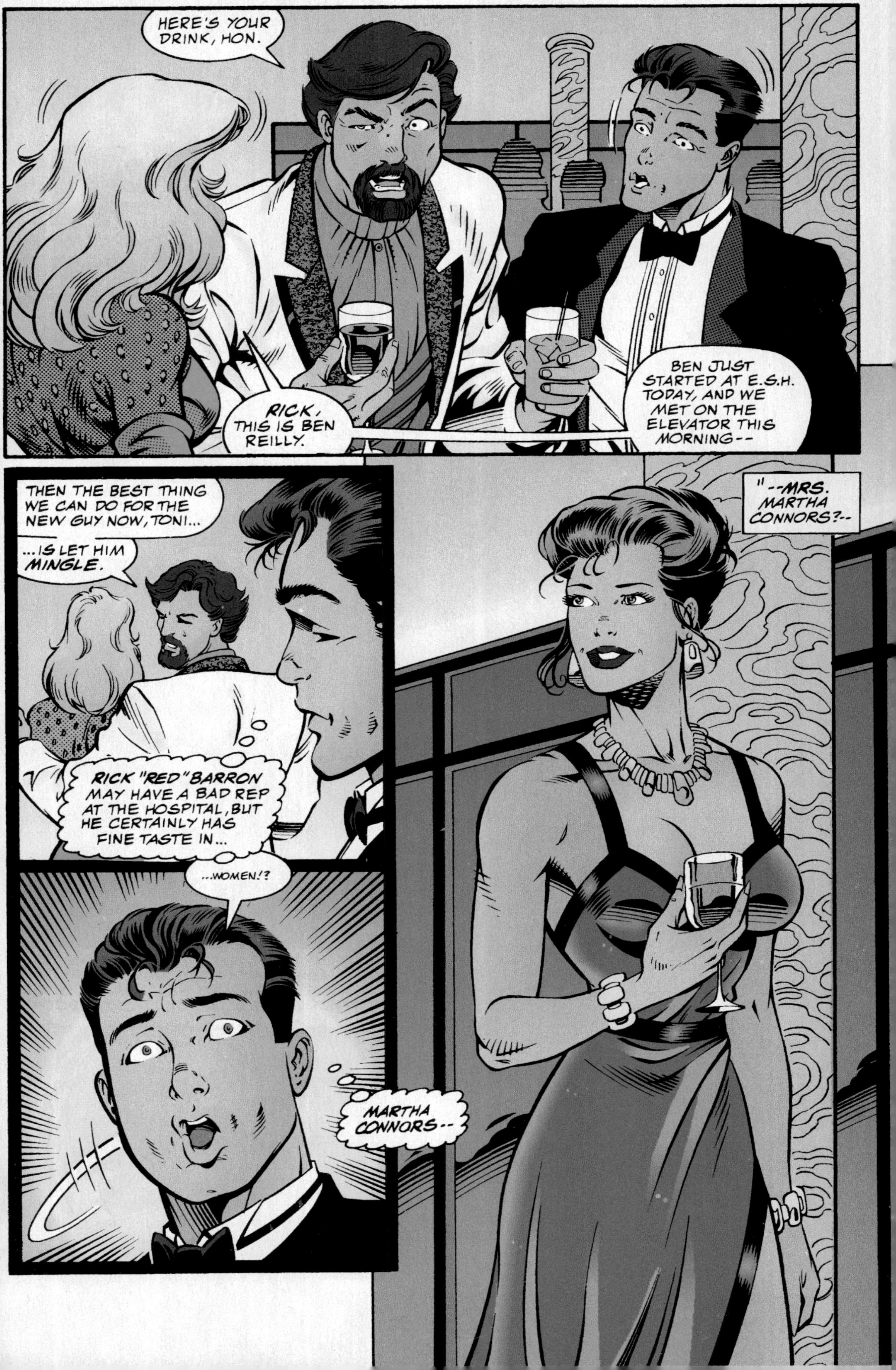
HERE'S YOUR DRINK, HON.
RICK, THIS IS BEN REILLY.
BEN JUST STARTED AT E.S.H. TODAY, AND WE MET ON THE ELEVATOR THIS MORNING--
THEN THE BEST THING WE CAN DO FOR THE NEW GUY NOW, TONI...
...IS LET HIM MINGLE.
RICK "RED" BARRON MAY HAVE A BAD REP AT THE HOSPITAL, BUT HE CERTAINLY HAS FINE TASTE IN...
...WOMEN!?
MARTHA CONNORS--
"--MRS. MARTHA CONNORS?--

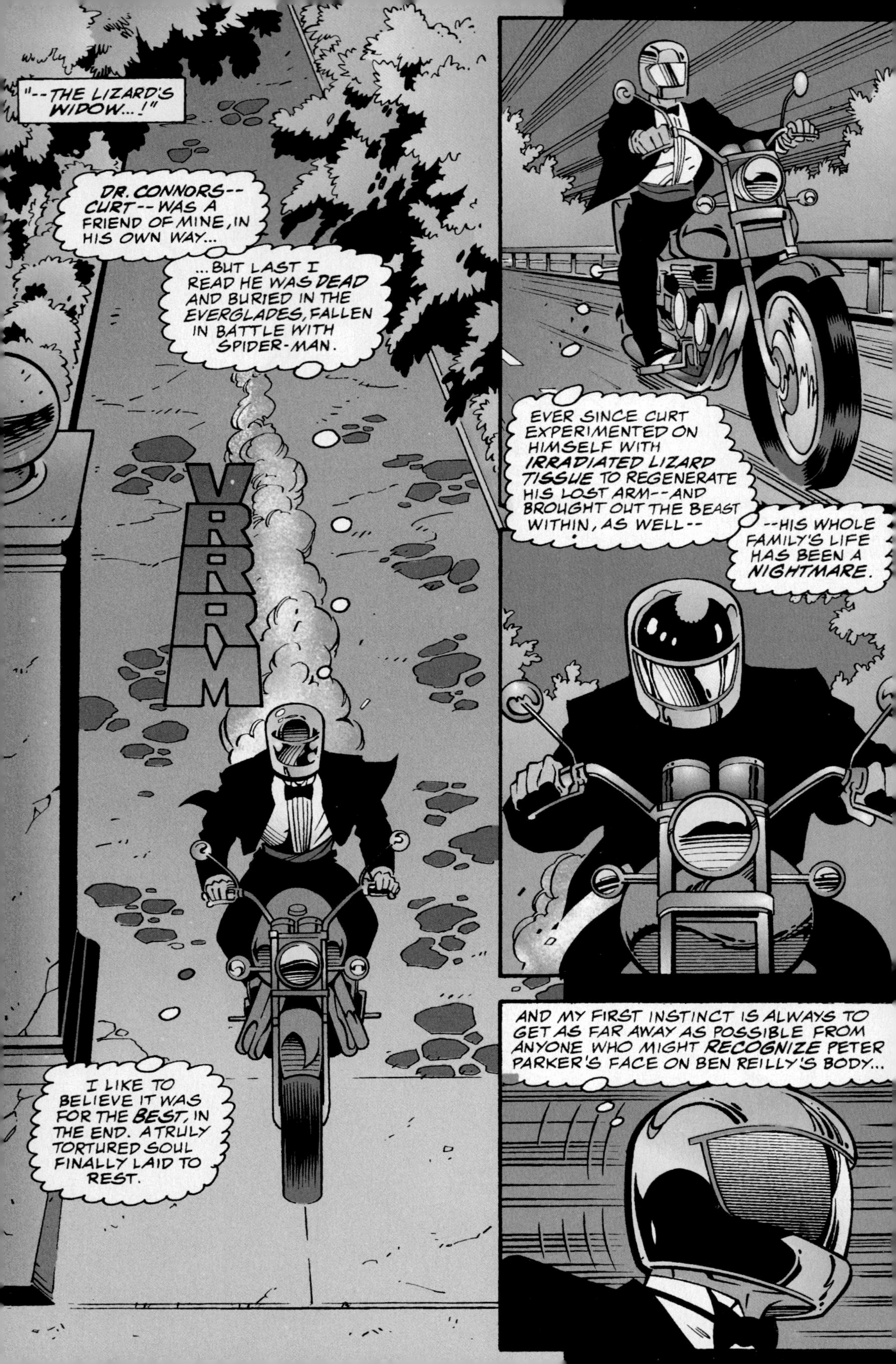
"--THE LIZARD'S WIDOW...!"
DR. CONNORS-- CURT--WAS A FRIEND OF MINE, IN HIS OWN WAY...
...BUT LAST I READ HE WAS DEAD AND BURIED IN THE EVERGLADES, FALLEN IN BATTLE WITH SPIDER-MAN.
VRRRM
I LIKE TO BELIEVE IT WAS FOR THE BEST, IN THE END. A TRULY TORTURED SOUL FINALLY LAID TO REST.
EVER SINCE CURT EXPERIMENTED ON HIMSELF WITH IRRADIATED LIZARD TISSUE TO REGENERATE HIS LOST ARM--AND BROUGHT OUT THE BEAST WITHIN, AS WELL--
--HIS WHOLE FAMILY'S LIFE HAS BEEN A NIGHTMARE.
AND MY FIRST INSTINCT IS ALWAYS TO GET AS FAR AWAY AS POSSIBLE FROM ANYONE WHO MIGHT RECOGNIZE PETER PARKER'S FACE ON BEN REILLY'S BODY...

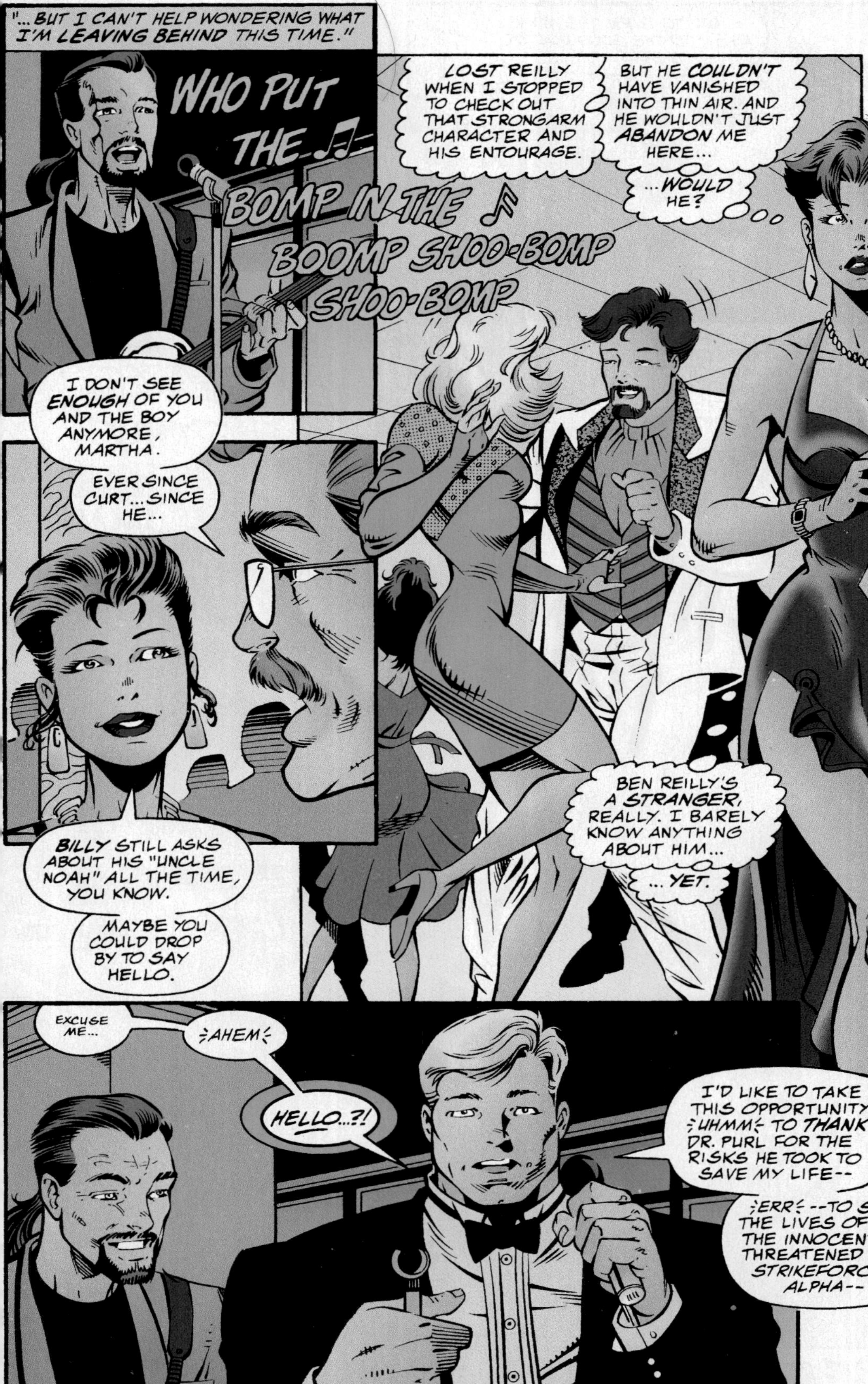
"...BUT I CAN'T HELP WONDERING WHAT I'M LEAVING BEHIND THIS TIME."
WHO PUT THE ♫ BOMP IN THE ♪ BOOMP SHOO-BOMP SHOO-BOMP
LOST REILLY WHEN I STOPPED TO CHECK OUT THAT STRONGARM CHARACTER AND HIS ENTOURAGE.
BUT HE COULDN'T HAVE VANISHED INTO THIN AIR. AND HE WOULDN'T JUST ABANDON ME HERE...
...WOULD HE?
I DON'T SEE ENOUGH OF YOU AND THE BOY ANYMORE, MARTHA.
EVER SINCE CURT... SINCE HE...
BILLY STILL ASKS ABOUT HIS "UNCLE NOAH" ALL THE TIME, YOU KNOW.
MAYBE YOU COULD DROP BY TO SAY HELLO.
BEN REILLY'S A STRANGER, REALLY. I BARELY KNOW ANYTHING ABOUT HIM...
...YET.
EXCUSE ME...
AHEM
HELLO...?!
I'D LIKE TO TAKE THIS OPPORTUNITY UHMM TO THANK DR. PURL FOR THE RISKS HE TOOK TO SAVE MY LIFE--
ERR --TO SAVE THE LIVES OF ALL THE INNOCENTS THREATENED BY STRIKEFORCE ALPHA--

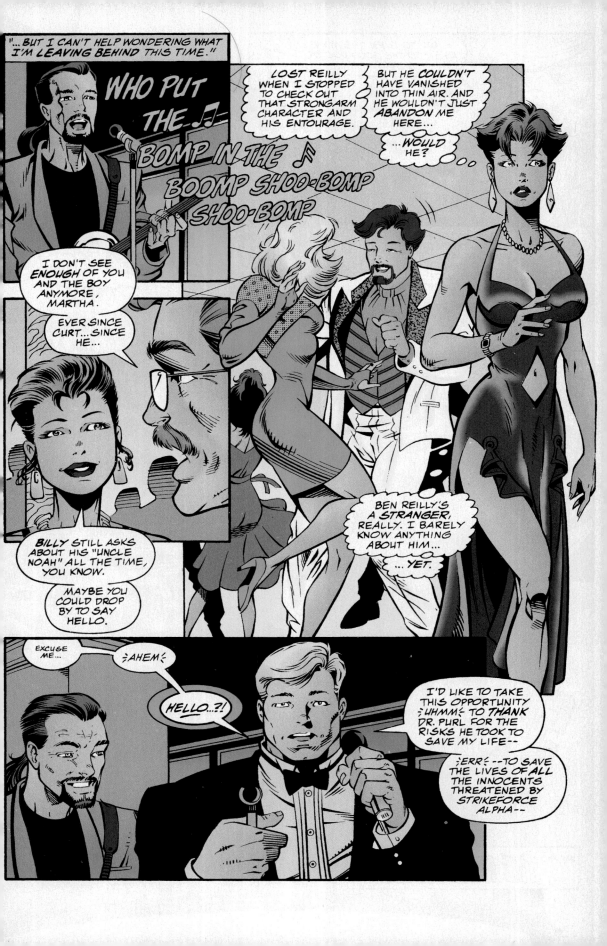

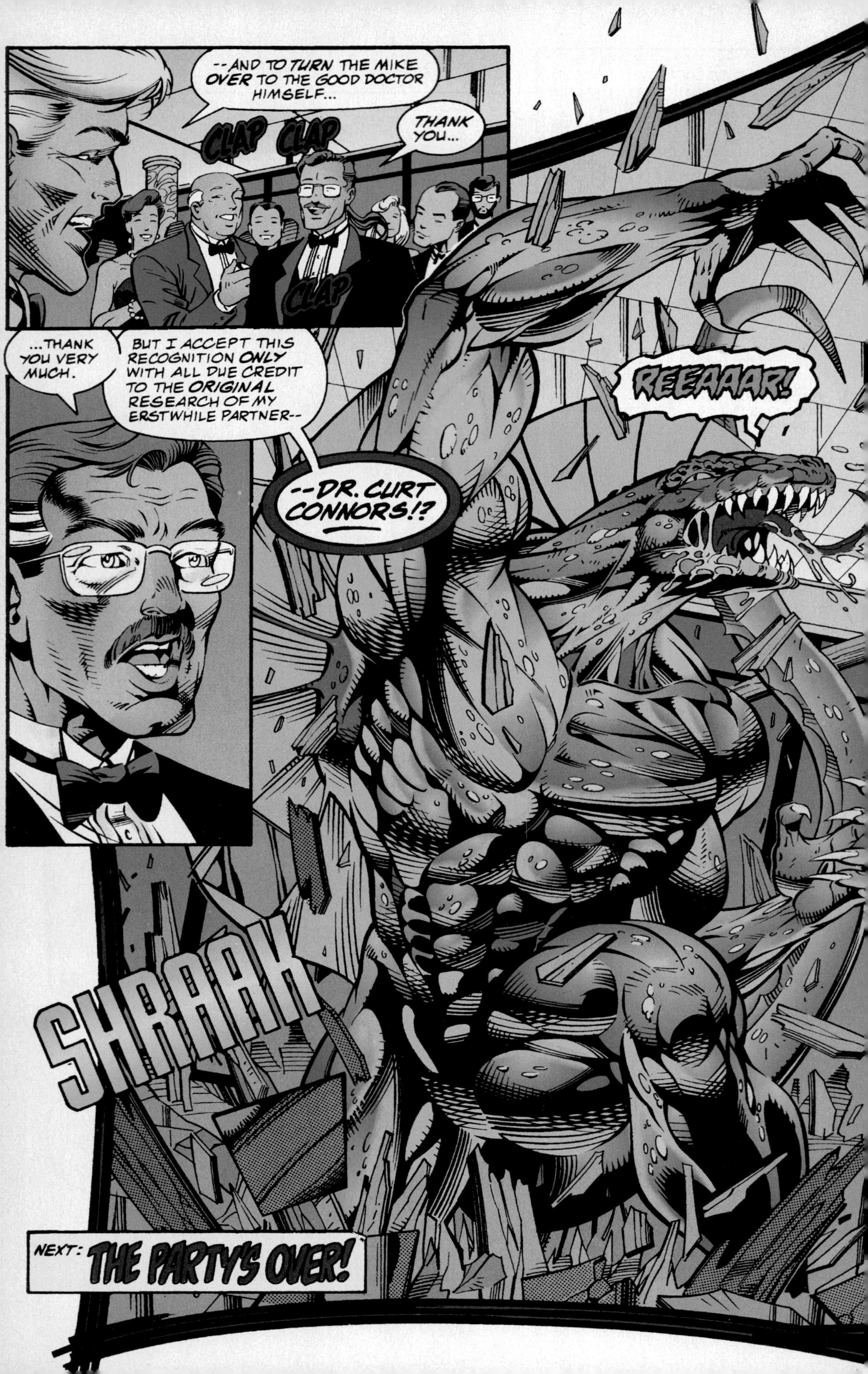
--AND TO TURN THE MIKE OVER TO THE GOOD DOCTOR HIMSELF...
CLAP CLAP
THANK YOU...
CLAP
...THANK YOU VERY MUCH.
BUT I ACCEPT THIS RECOGNITION ONLY WITH ALL DUE CREDIT TO THE ORIGINAL RESEARCH OF MY ERSTWHILE PARTNER--
--DR. CURT CONNORS!?
REEAAAR!
SHRAAK
NEXT: THE PARTY'S OVER!

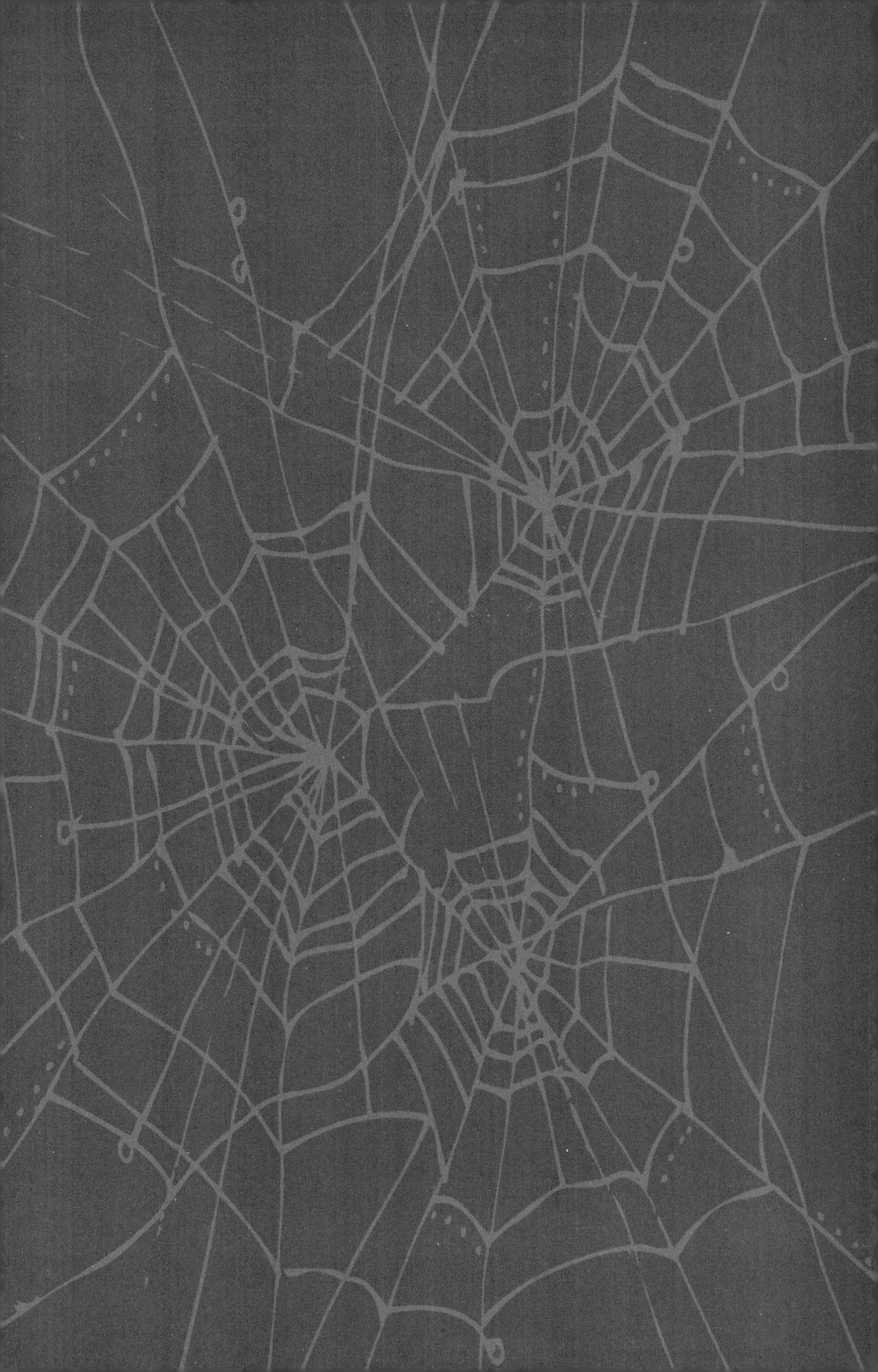

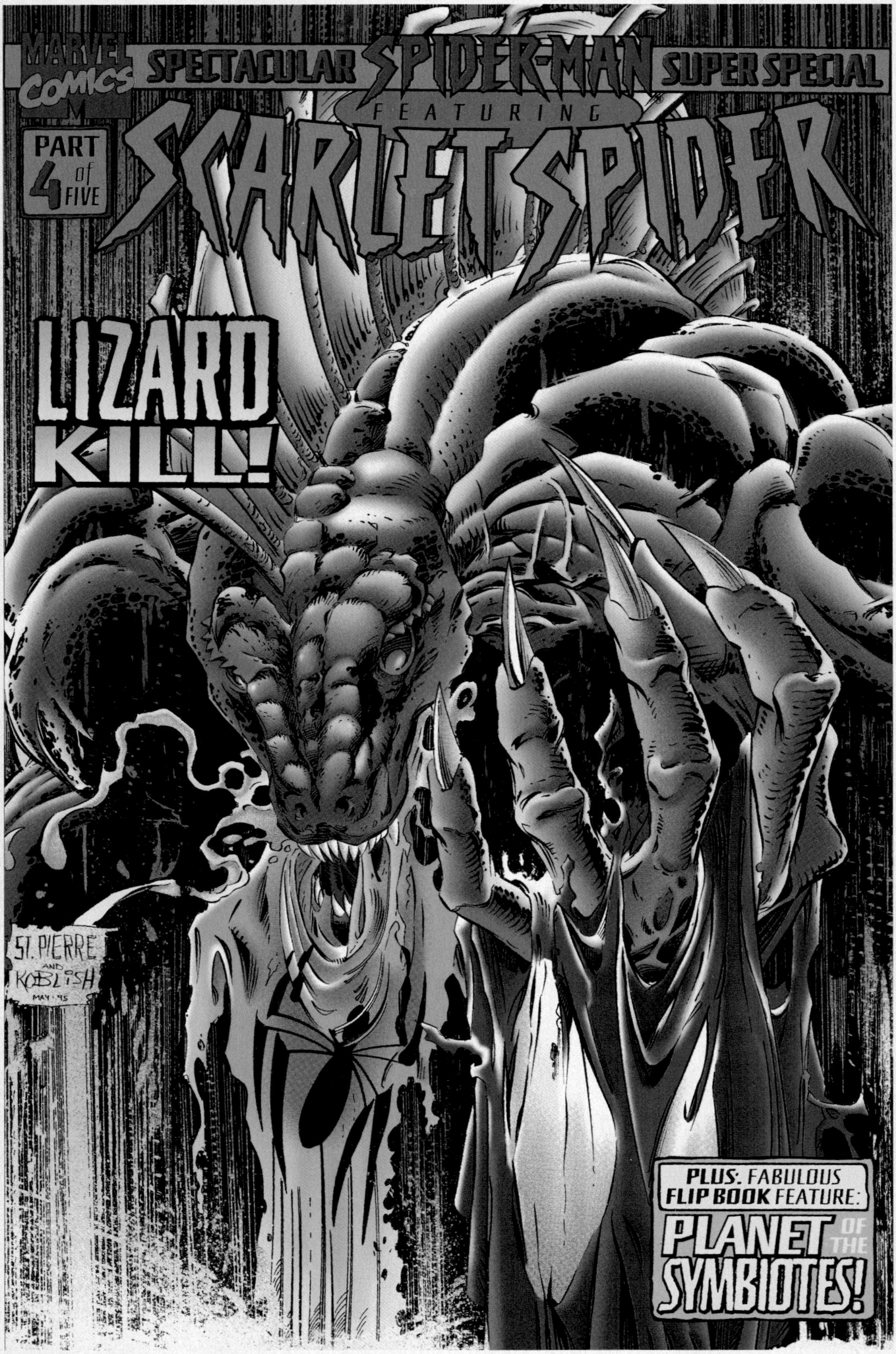

MARVEL COMICS
SPECTACULAR SPIDER-MAN SUPER SPECIAL
FEATURING
SCARLET SPIDER
PART 4 of FIVE
LIZARD KILL!
ST. PIERRE AND KOBLISH MAY '95
PLUS: FABULOUS FLIP BOOK FEATURE:
PLANET OF THE SYMBIOTES!

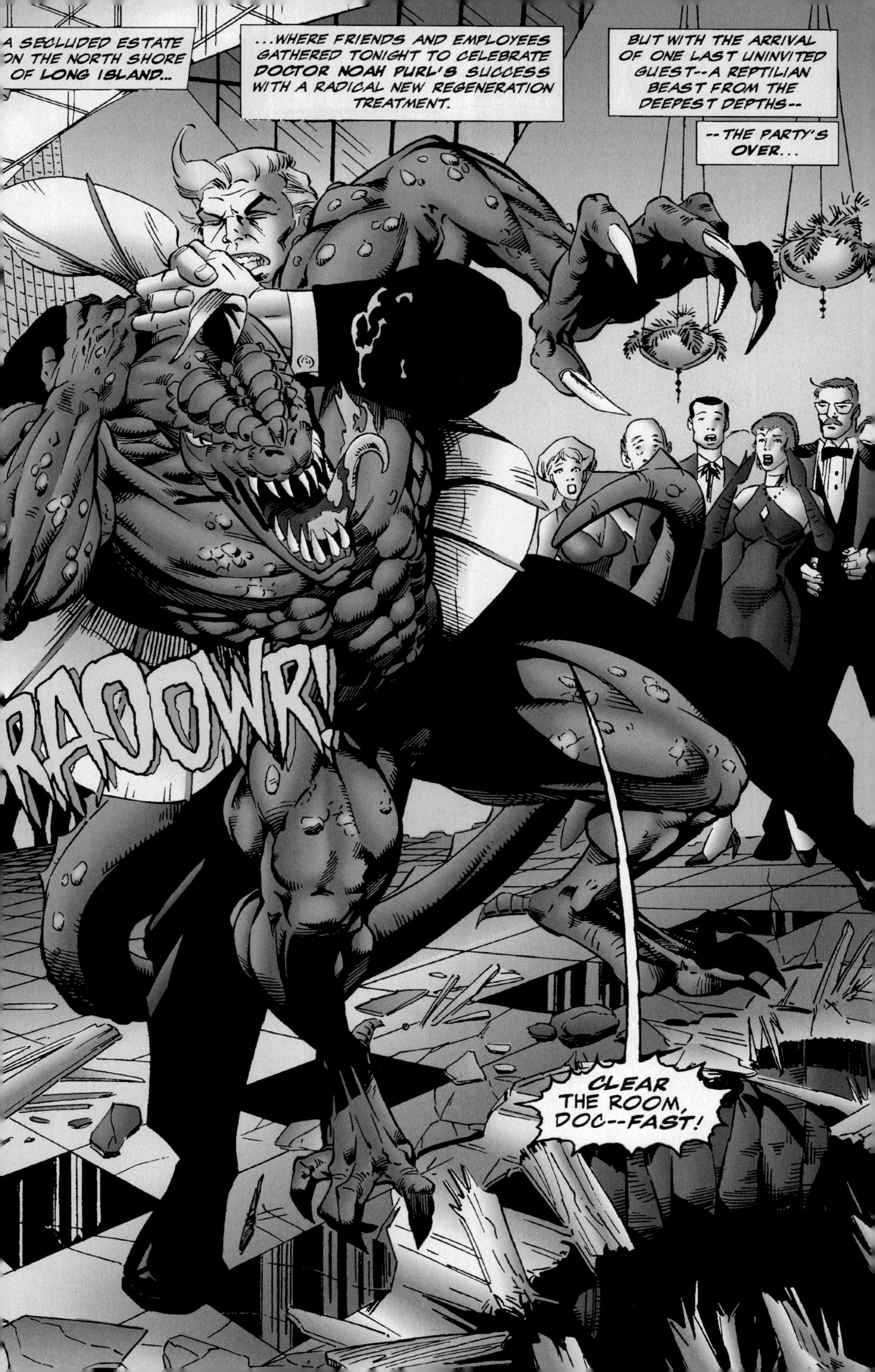
A SECLUDED ESTATE ON THE NORTH SHORE OF LONG ISLAND...
...WHERE FRIENDS AND EMPLOYEES GATHERED TONIGHT TO CELEBRATE DOCTOR NOAH PURL'S SUCCESS WITH A RADICAL NEW REGENERATION TREATMENT.
BUT WITH THE ARRIVAL OF ONE LAST UNINVITED GUEST--A REPTILIAN BEAST FROM THE DEEPEST DEPTHS--
--THE PARTY'S OVER...
RAOOWR!
CLEAR THE ROOM, DOC--FAST!

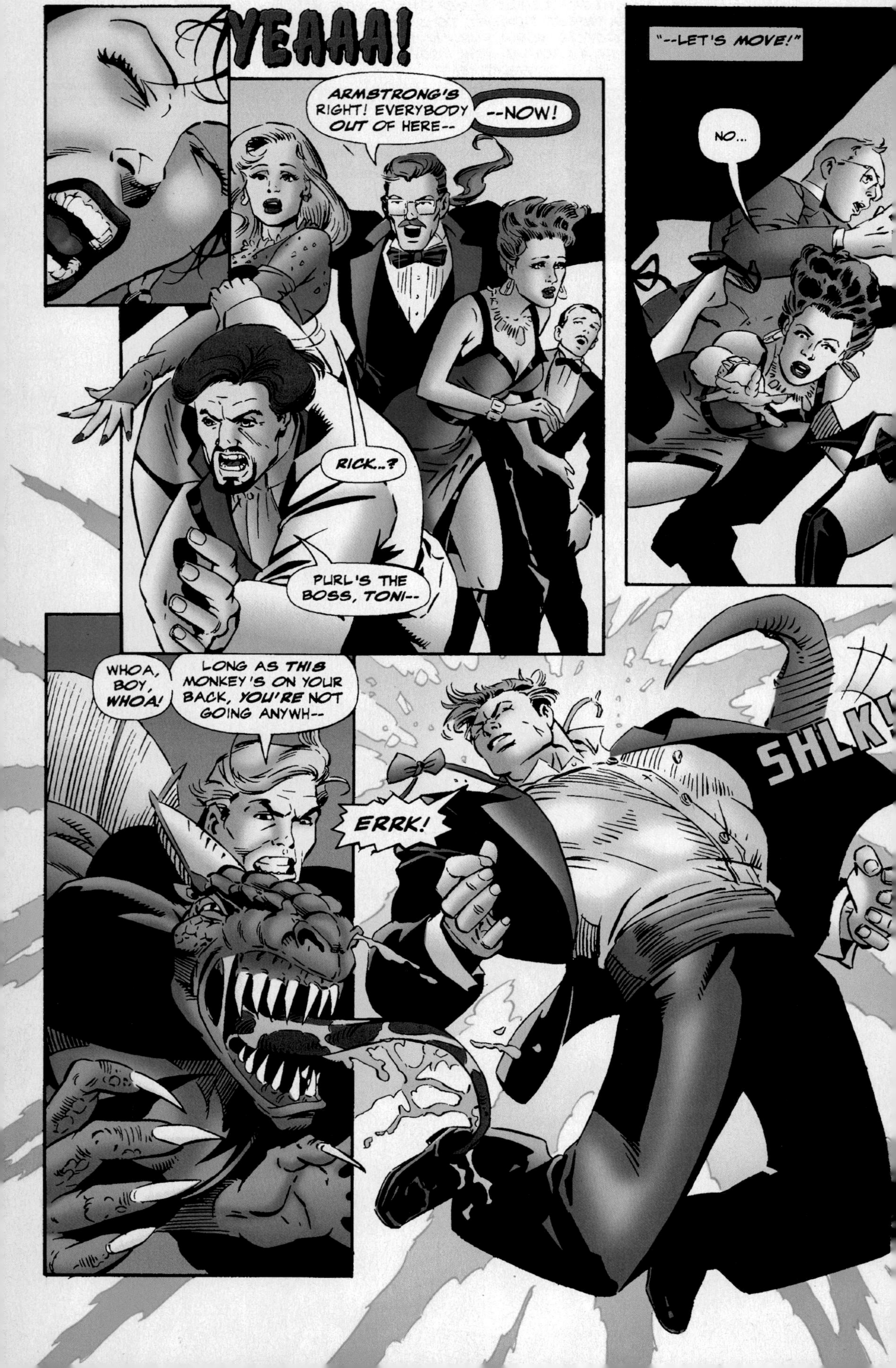
YEAAA!
ARMSTRONG'S RIGHT! EVERYBODY OUT OF HERE--
--NOW!
RICK..?
PURL'S THE BOSS, TONI--
"--LET'S MOVE!"
NO...
WHOA, BOY, WHOA!
LONG AS THIS MONKEY'S ON YOUR BACK, YOU'RE NOT GOING ANYWH--
ERRK!
SHLK!

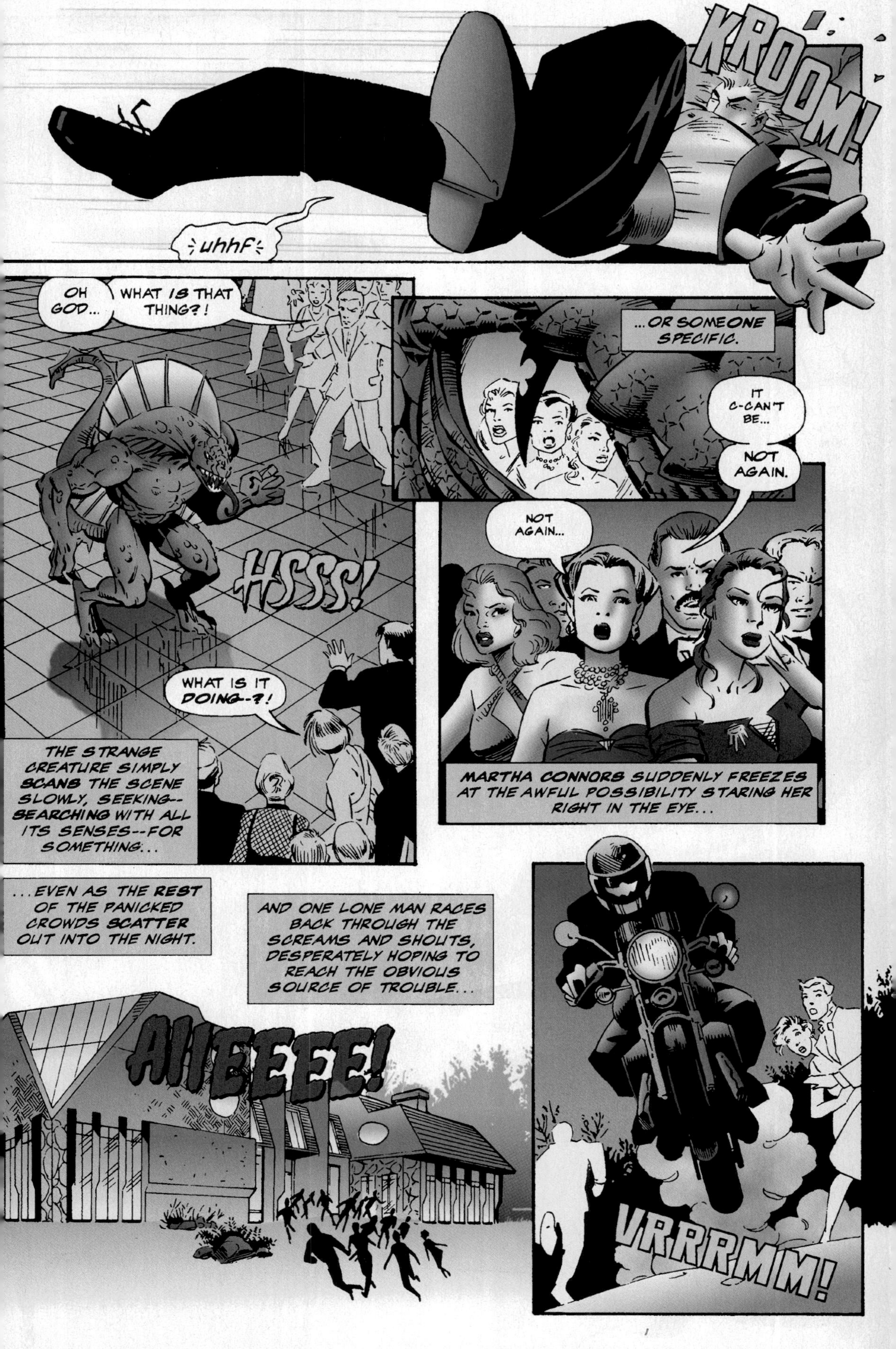
KROOM!
uhhf
OH GOD...
WHAT IS THAT THING?!
HSSS!
WHAT IS IT DOING--?!
THE STRANGE CREATURE SIMPLY SCANS THE SCENE SLOWLY, SEEKING--SEARCHING WITH ALL ITS SENSES--FOR SOMETHING...
...OR SOMEONE SPECIFIC.
IT C-CAN'T BE...
NOT AGAIN.
NOT AGAIN...
MARTHA CONNORS SUDDENLY FREEZES AT THE AWFUL POSSIBILITY STARING HER RIGHT IN THE EYE...
...EVEN AS THE REST OF THE PANICKED CROWDS SCATTER OUT INTO THE NIGHT.
AIIEEEE!
AND ONE LONE MAN RACES BACK THROUGH THE SCREAMS AND SHOUTS, DESPERATELY HOPING TO REACH THE OBVIOUS SOURCE OF TROUBLE...
VRRRRMM!

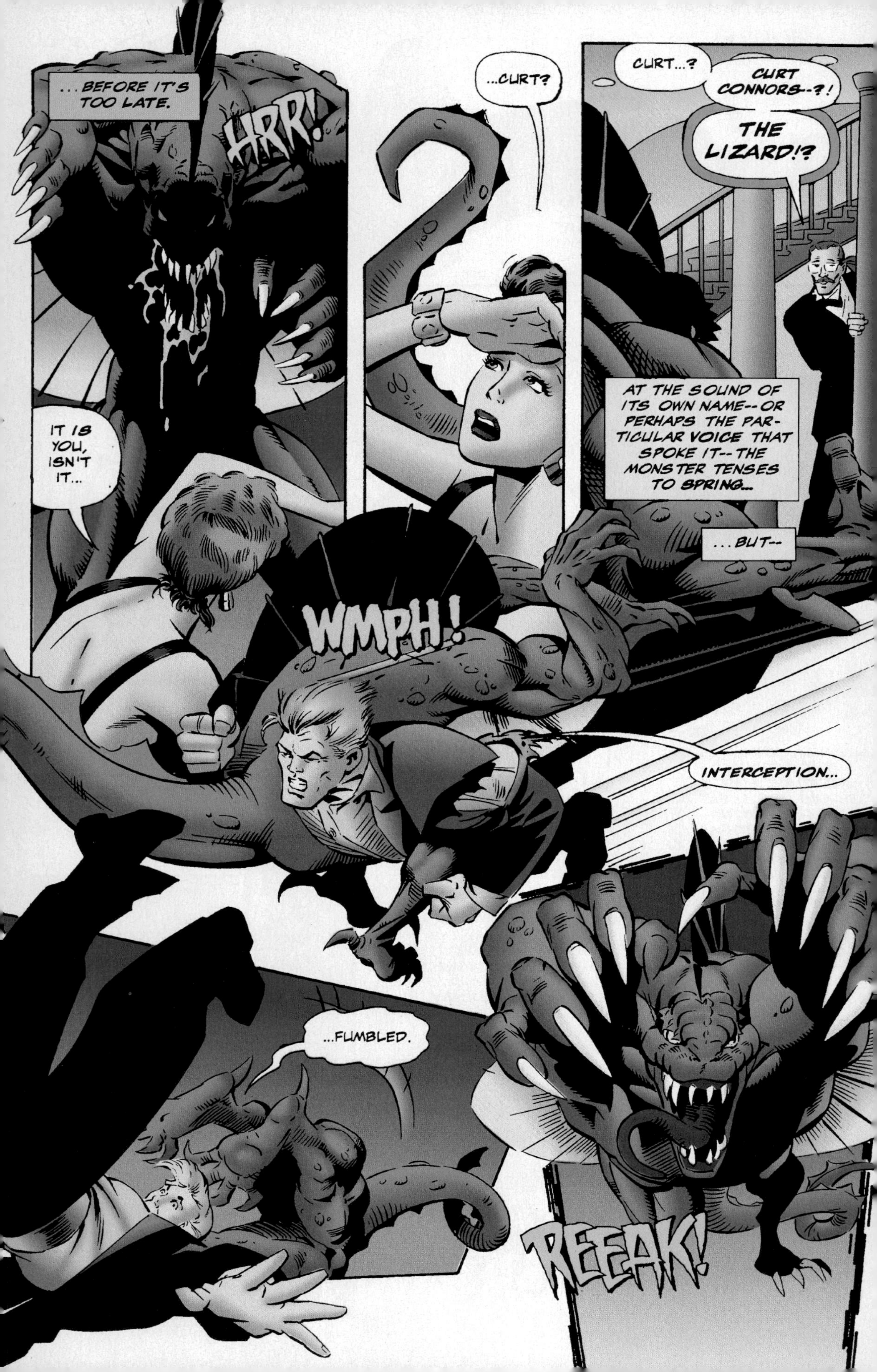
...BEFORE IT'S TOO LATE.
HRR!
IT IS YOU, ISN'T IT...
...CURT?
CURT...?
CURT CONNORS--?!
THE LIZARD!?
AT THE SOUND OF ITS OWN NAME--OR PERHAPS THE PARTICULAR VOICE THAT SPOKE IT--THE MONSTER TENSES TO SPRING...
...BUT--
WMPH!
INTERCEPTION...
...FUMBLED.
REEEAK!

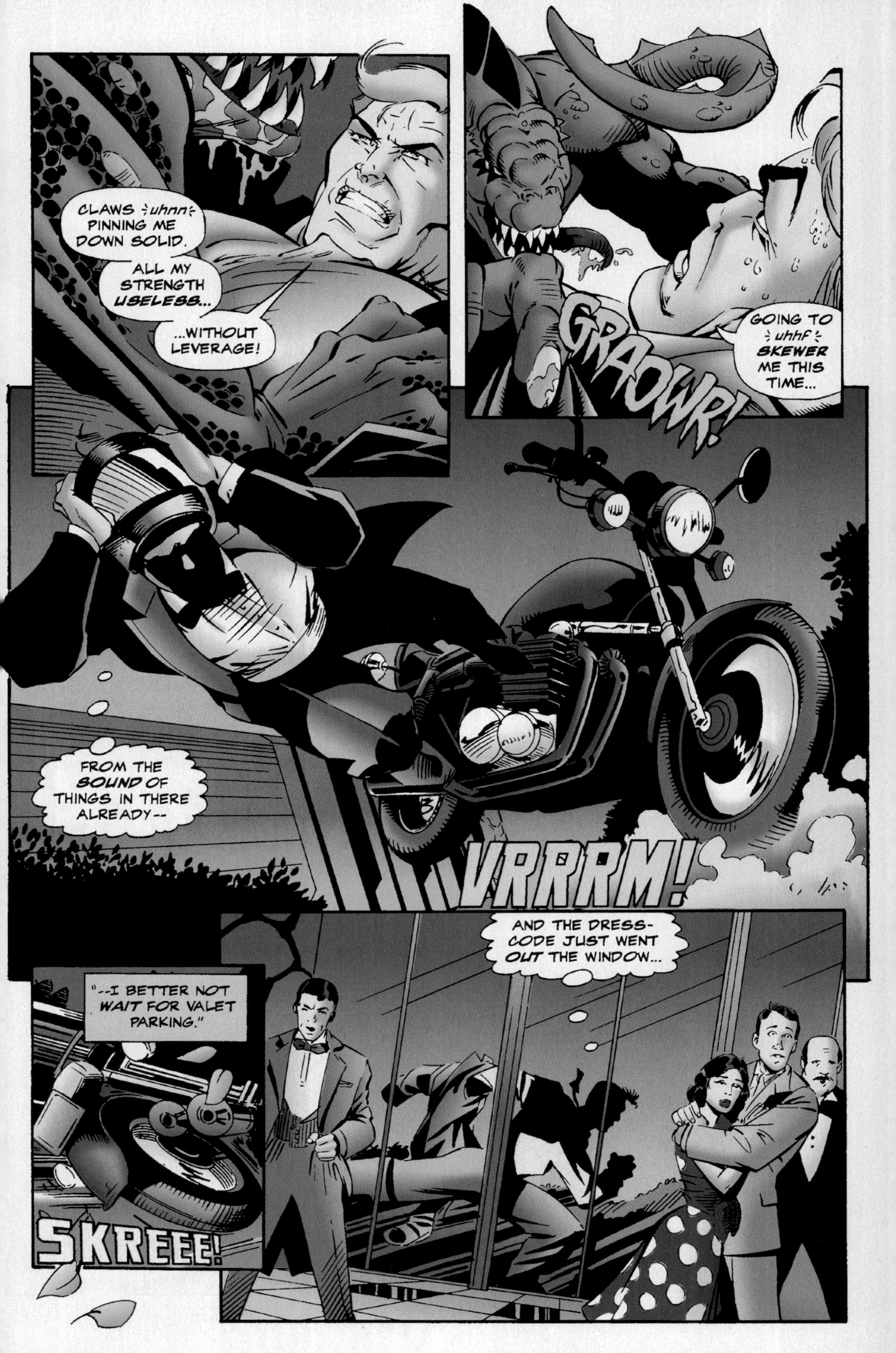
CLAWS ⁝uhnn⁝ PINNING ME DOWN SOLID.
ALL MY STRENGTH USELESS...
...WITHOUT LEVERAGE!
GRAOWR!
GOING TO ⁝uhhf⁝ SKEWER ME THIS TIME...
FROM THE SOUND OF THINGS IN THERE ALREADY--
VRRRM!
"--I BETTER NOT WAIT FOR VALET PARKING."
SKREEE!
AND THE DRESS-CODE JUST WENT OUT THE WINDOW...

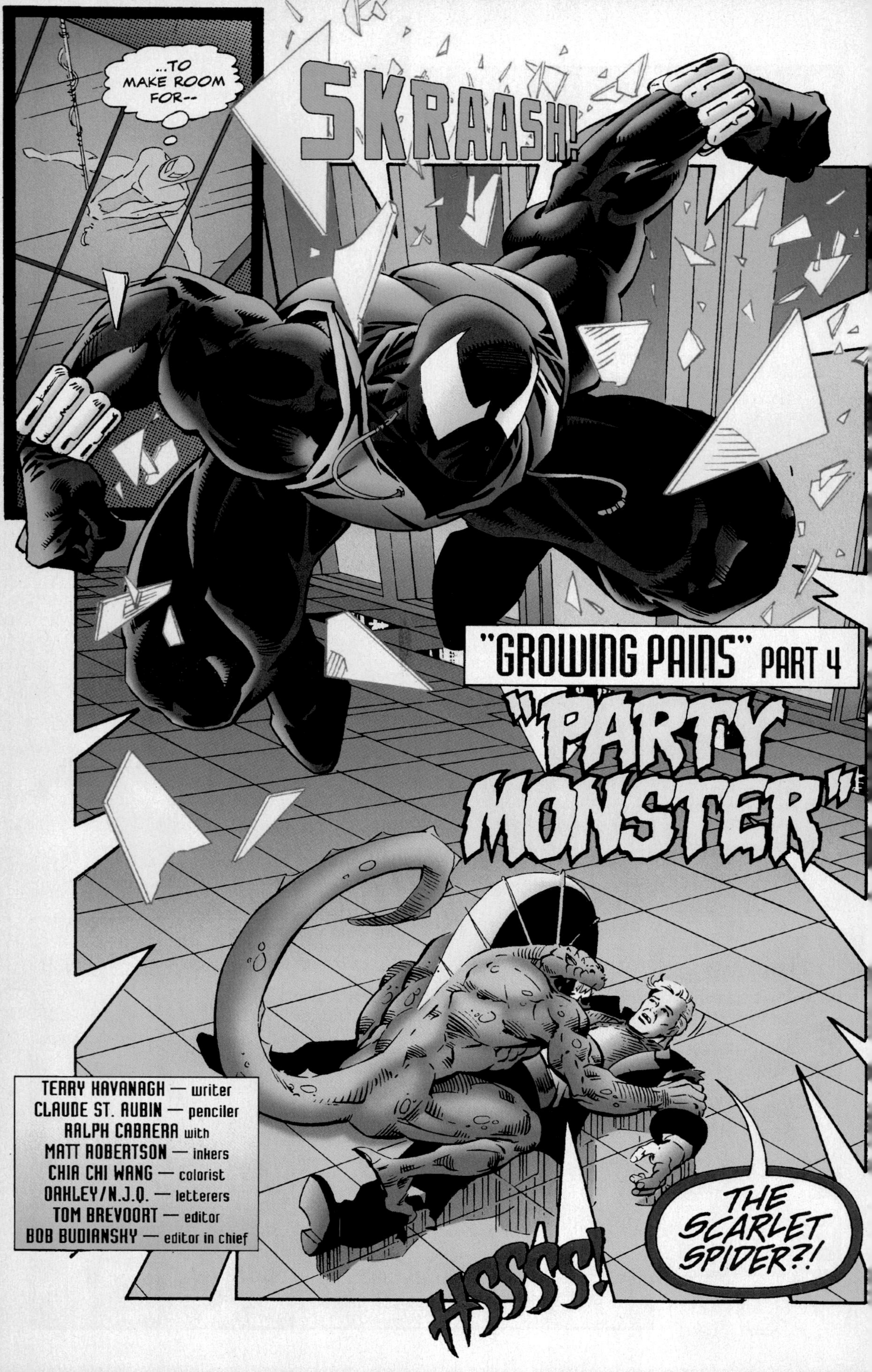
...TO MAKE ROOM FOR--
SKRAASH!
"GROWING PAINS" PART 4
"PARTY MONSTER"
TERRY KAVANAGH — writer
CLAUDE ST. AUBIN — penciler
RALPH CABRERA with
MATT ROBERTSON — inkers
CHIA CHI WANG — colorist
OAKLEY/N.J.Q. — letterers
TOM BREVOORT — editor
BOB BUDIANSKY — editor in chief
HSSSSS!
THE SCARLET SPIDER?!

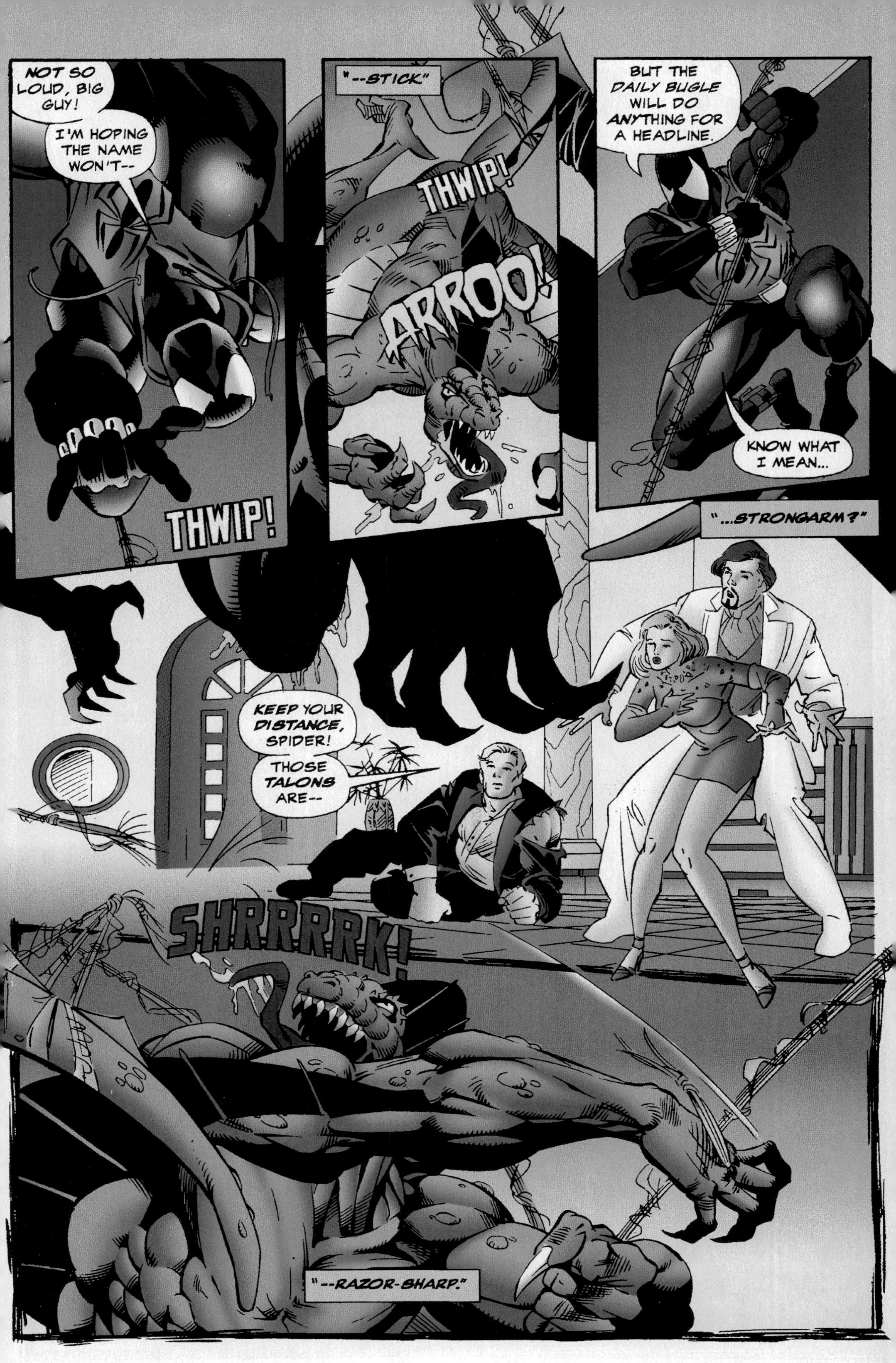
NOT SO LOUD, BIG GUY!
I'M HOPING THE NAME WON'T--
THWIP!
"--STICK"
THWIP!
ARROO!
BUT THE DAILY BUGLE WILL DO ANYTHING FOR A HEADLINE.
KNOW WHAT I MEAN...
"...STRONGARM?"
KEEP YOUR DISTANCE, SPIDER!
THOSE TALONS ARE--
SHRRRRK!
"--RAZOR-SHARP."

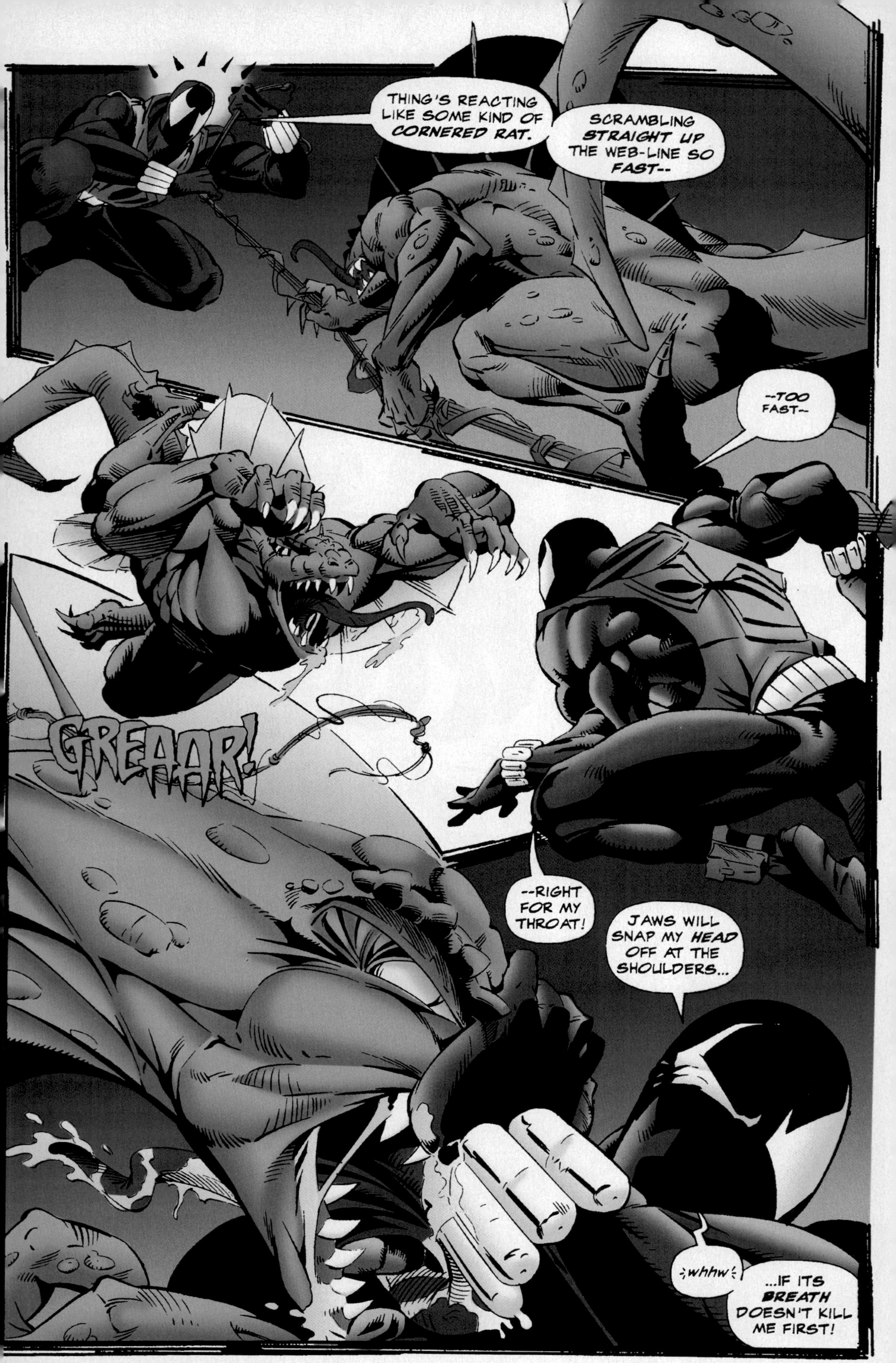
THING'S REACTING LIKE SOME KIND OF CORNERED RAT.
SCRAMBLING STRAIGHT UP THE WEB-LINE SO FAST--
--TOO FAST--
GREAAR!
--RIGHT FOR MY THROAT!
JAWS WILL SNAP MY HEAD OFF AT THE SHOULDERS...
whhw
...IF ITS BREATH DOESN'T KILL ME FIRST!

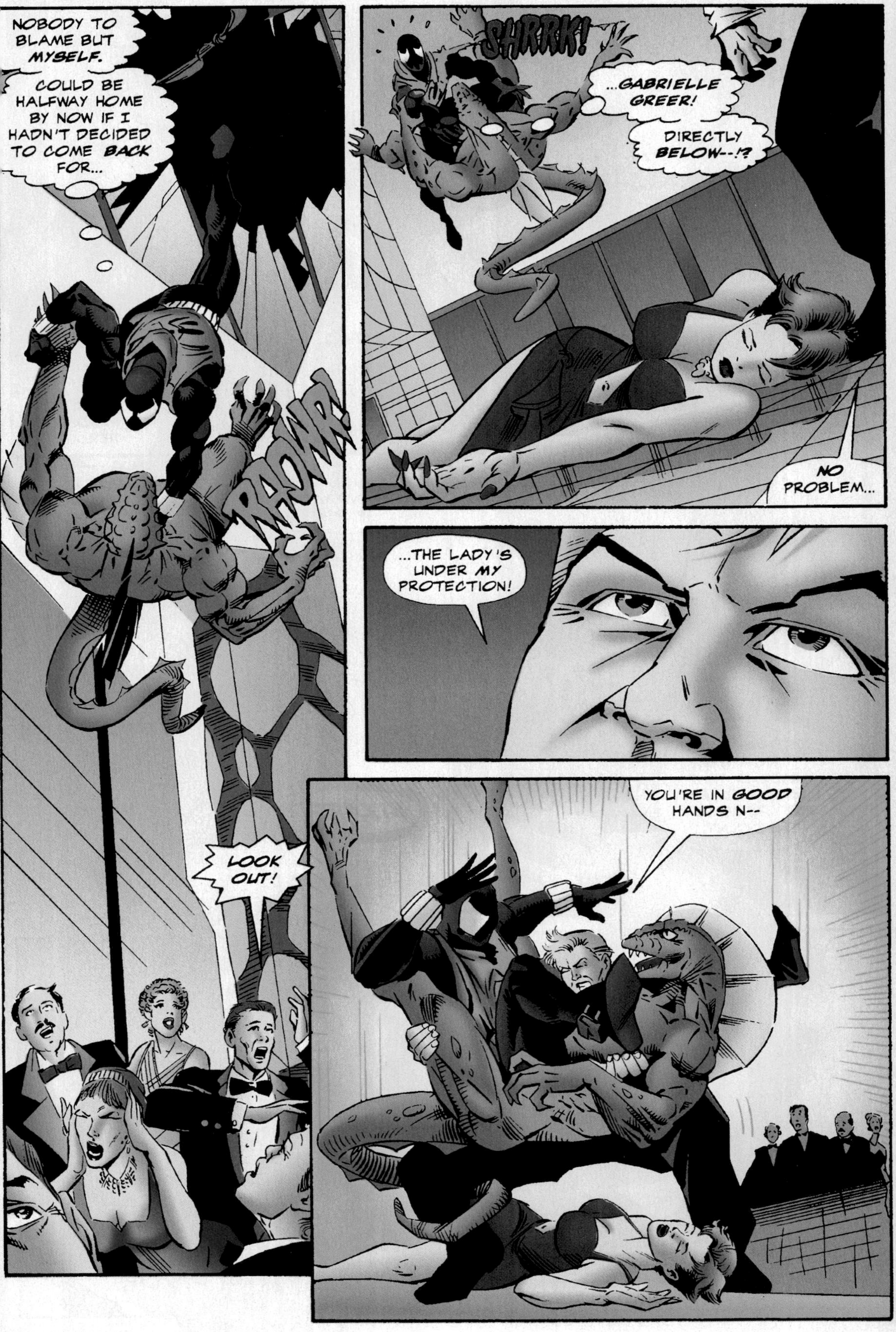
NOBODY TO BLAME BUT *MYSELF.*
COULD BE HALFWAY HOME BY NOW IF I HADN'T DECIDED TO COME *BACK* FOR...
RAOWR!
SHRRK!
...GABRIELLE GREER!
DIRECTLY BELOW--!?
NO PROBLEM...
...THE LADY'S UNDER *MY* PROTECTION!
LOOK OUT!
YOU'RE IN *GOOD* HANDS N--

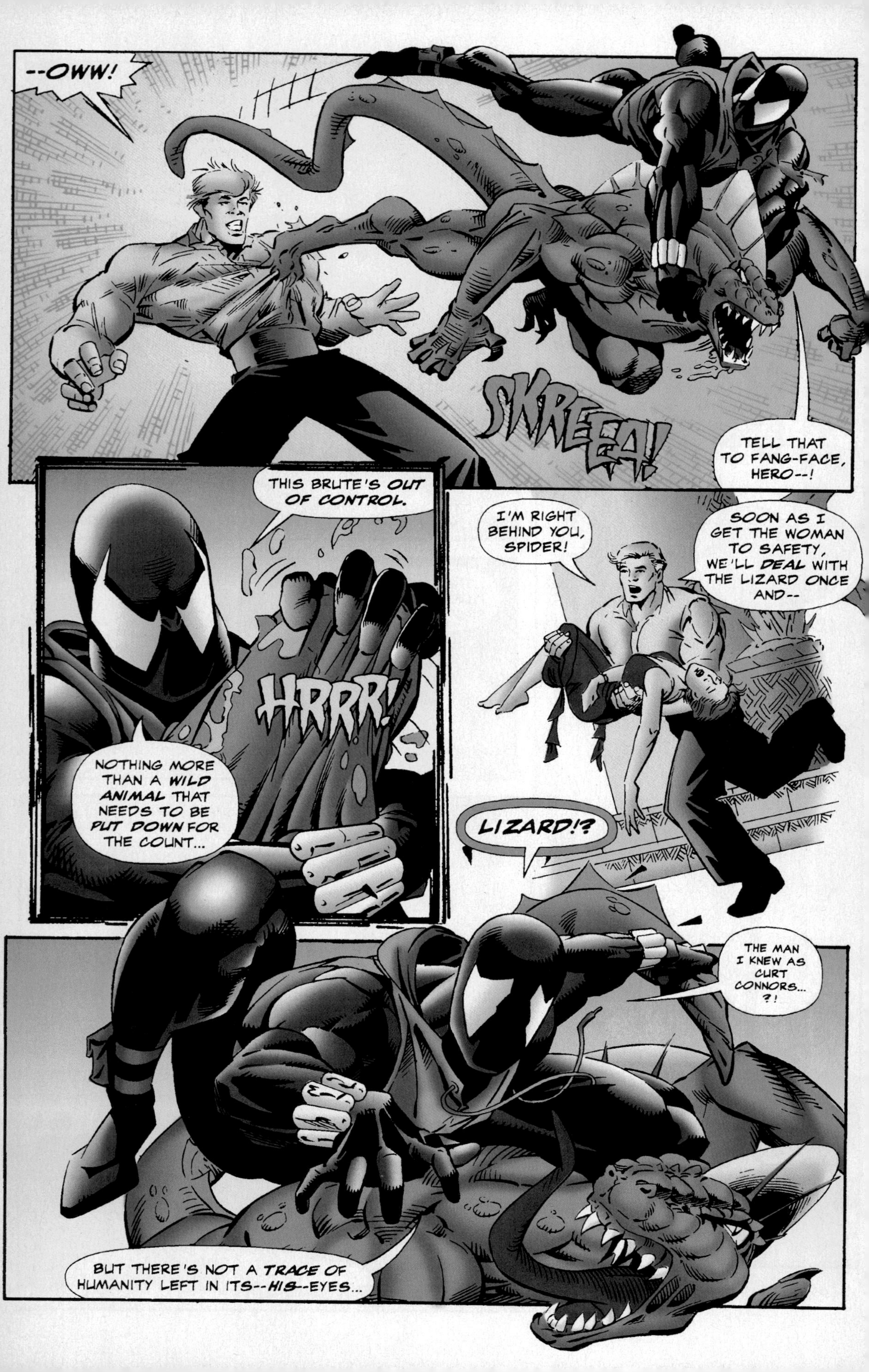
--OWW!
SKREEEA!
TELL THAT TO FANG-FACE, HERO--!
THIS BRUTE'S OUT OF CONTROL.
HRRR!
NOTHING MORE THAN A WILD ANIMAL THAT NEEDS TO BE PUT DOWN FOR THE COUNT...
I'M RIGHT BEHIND YOU, SPIDER!
SOON AS I GET THE WOMAN TO SAFETY, WE'LL DEAL WITH THE LIZARD ONCE AND--
LIZARD!?
THE MAN I KNEW AS CURT CONNORS...?!
BUT THERE'S NOT A TRACE OF HUMANITY LEFT IN ITS--HIS--EYES...

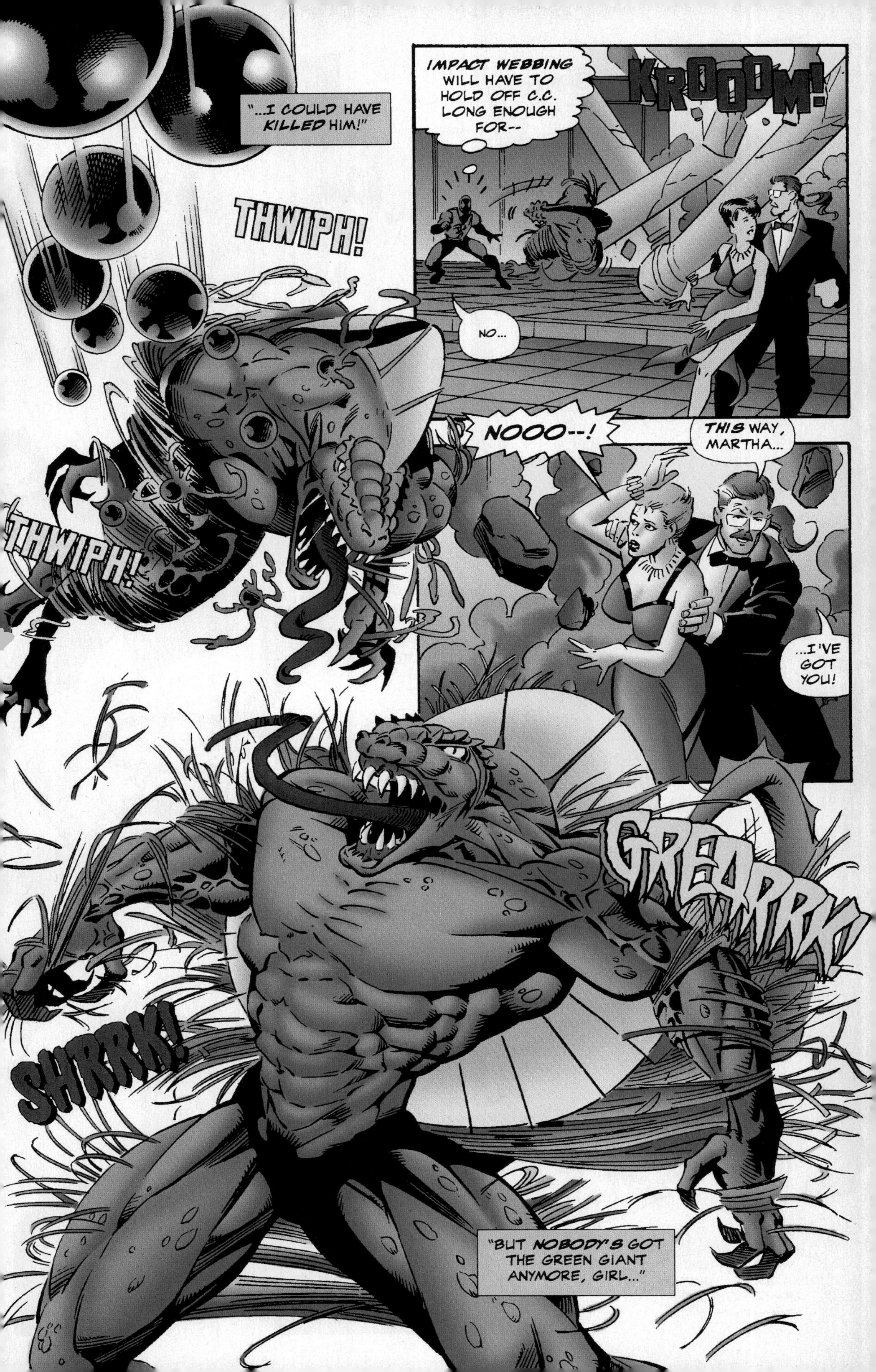"...I COULD HAVE KILLED HIM!"
THWIPH!
THWIPH!
IMPACT WEBBING WILL HAVE TO HOLD OFF C.C. LONG ENOUGH FOR--
KROOOM!
NO...
NOOO--!
THIS WAY, MARTHA...
...I'VE GOT YOU!
GREARRK!
SHRRK!
"BUT NOBODY'S GOT THE GREEN GIANT ANYMORE, GIRL..."

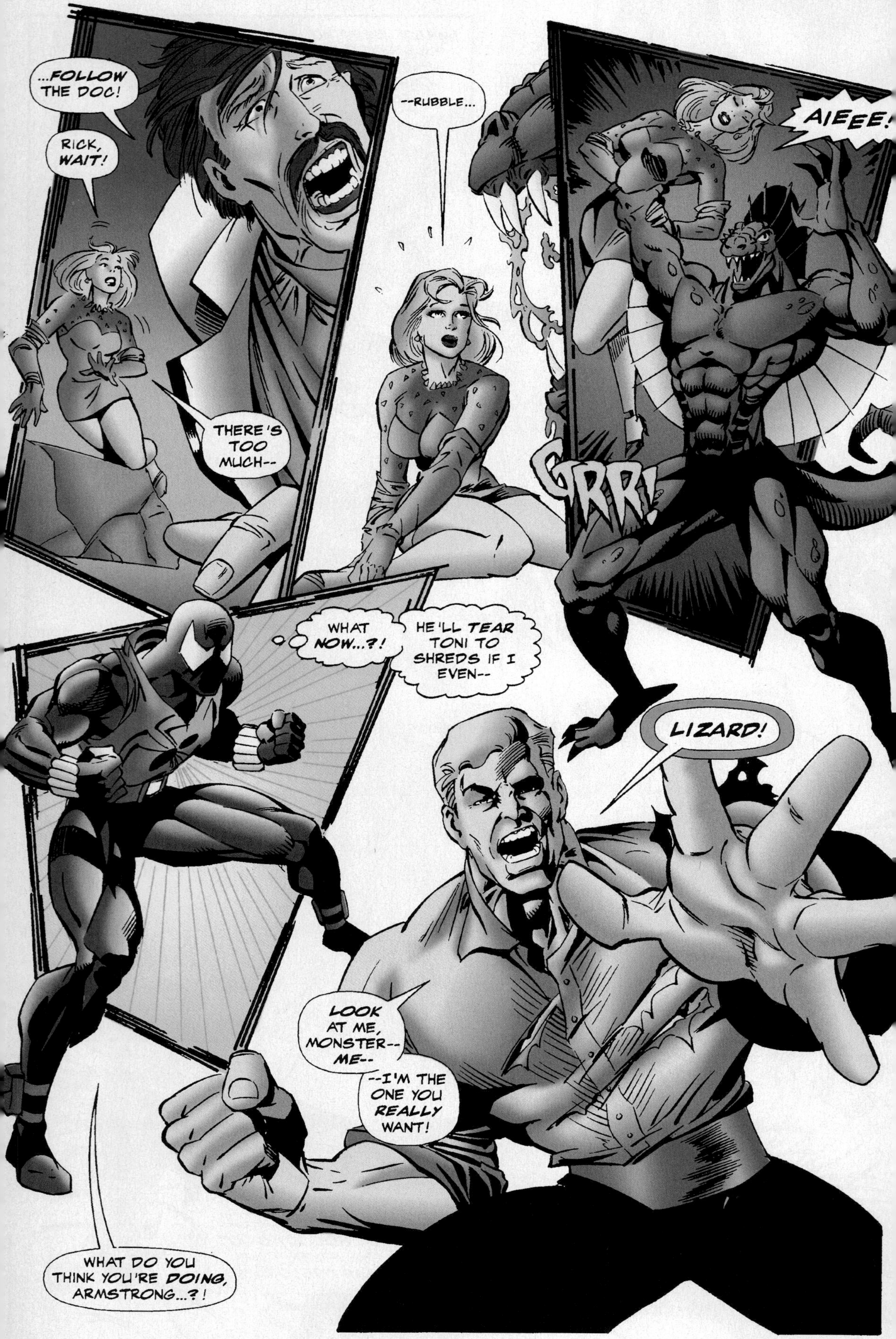
...FOLLOW THE DOC!
RICK, WAIT!
THERE'S TOO MUCH--
--RUBBLE...
AIEEE!
GRRR!
WHAT NOW...?!
HE'LL TEAR TONI TO SHREDS IF I EVEN--
LIZARD!
LOOK AT ME, MONSTER-- ME--
--I'M THE ONE YOU REALLY WANT!
WHAT DO YOU THINK YOU'RE DOING, ARMSTRONG...?!

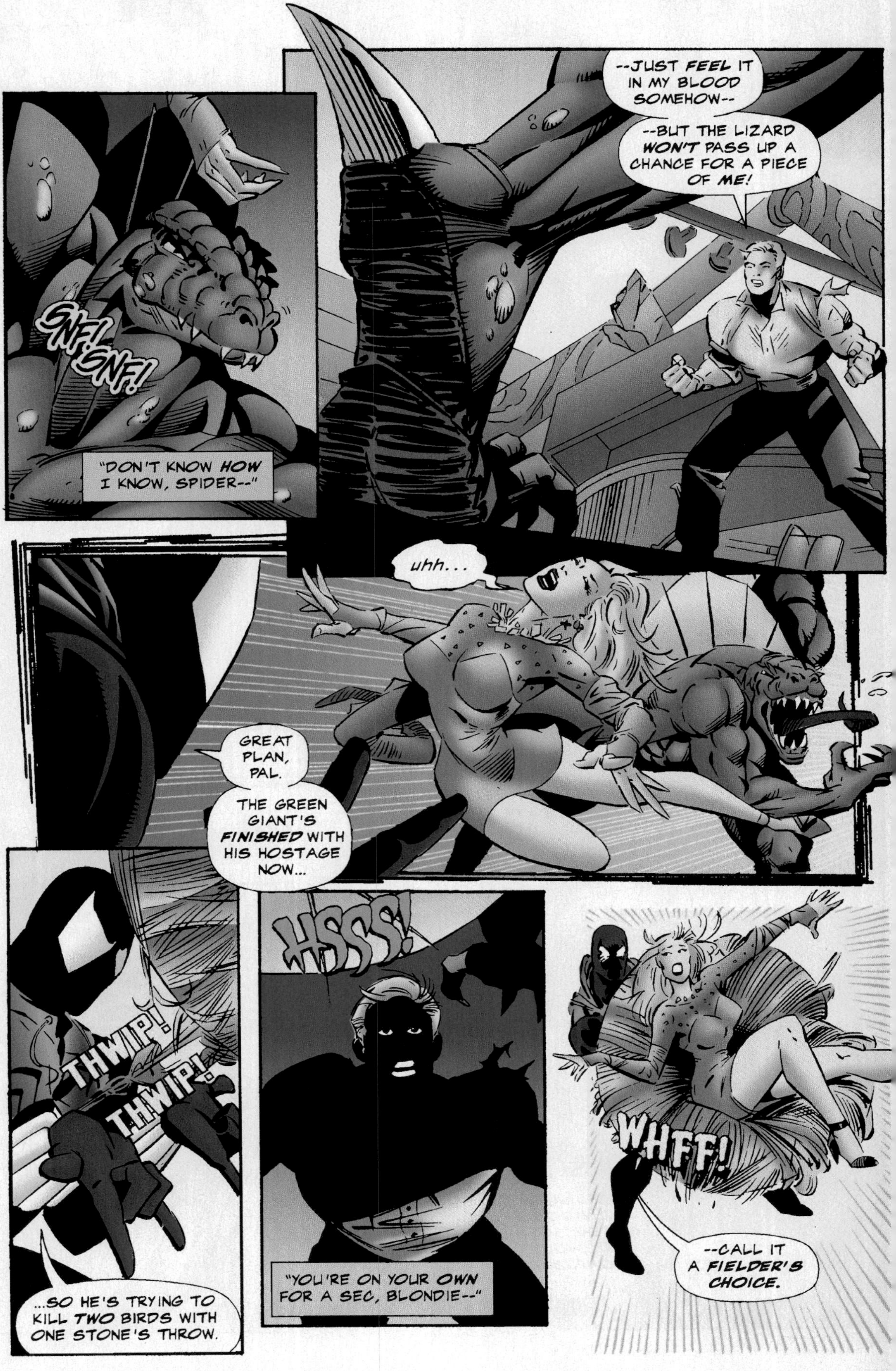

SNF! SNF!
"DON'T KNOW HOW I KNOW, SPIDER--"
--JUST FEEL IT IN MY BLOOD SOMEHOW--
--BUT THE LIZARD WON'T PASS UP A CHANCE FOR A PIECE OF ME!
uhh...
GREAT PLAN, PAL.
THE GREEN GIANT'S FINISHED WITH HIS HOSTAGE NOW...
THWIP! THWIP!
...SO HE'S TRYING TO KILL TWO BIRDS WITH ONE STONE'S THROW.
HSSS!
"YOU'RE ON YOUR OWN FOR A SEC, BLONDIE--"
WHFF!
--CALL IT A FIELDER'S CHOICE.

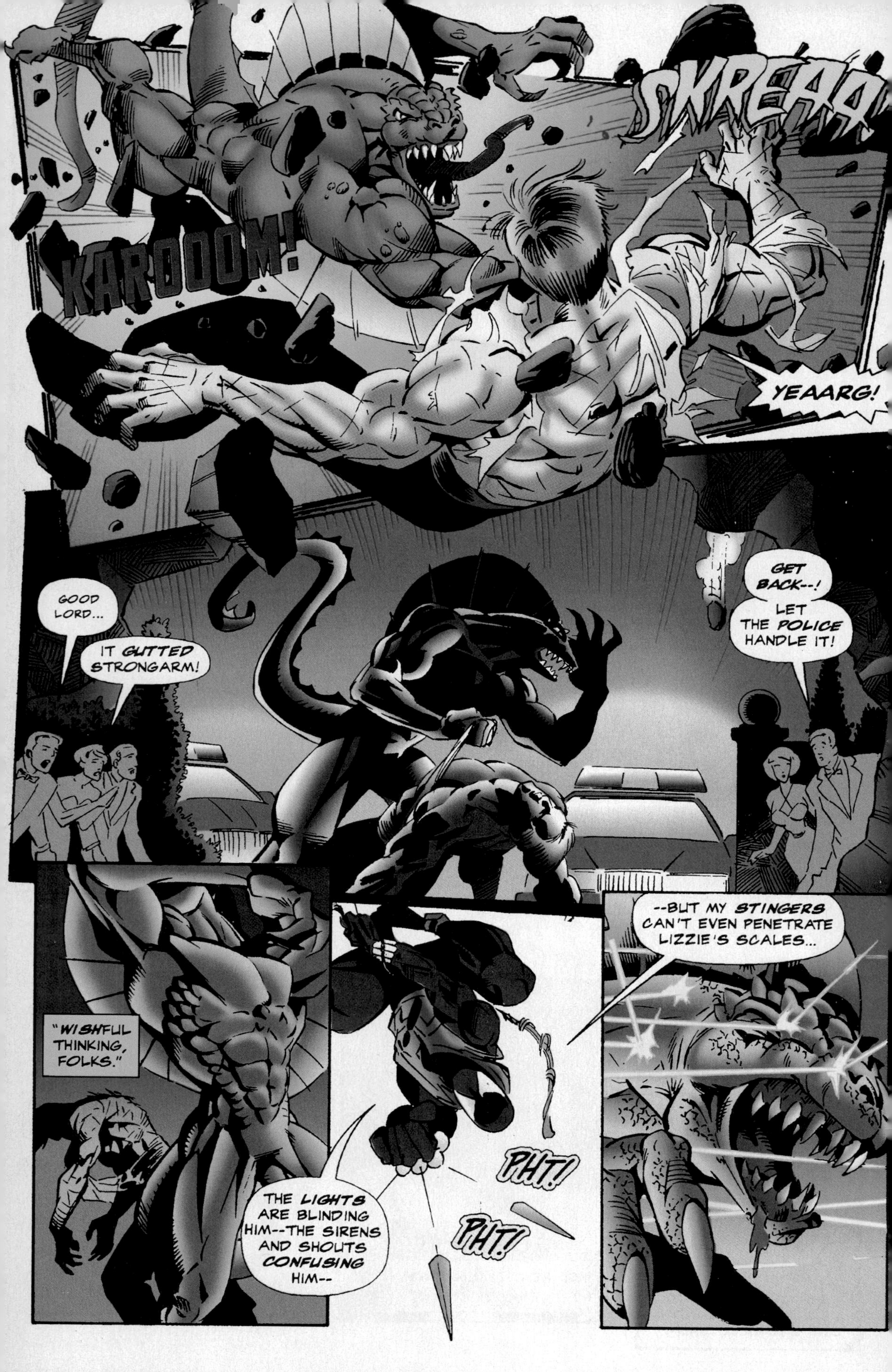
SKREAA
KAROOOM!
YEAARG!
GOOD LORD...
IT GUTTED STRONGARM!
GET BACK--! LET THE POLICE HANDLE IT!
"WISHFUL THINKING, FOLKS."
THE LIGHTS ARE BLINDING HIM--THE SIRENS AND SHOUTS CONFUSING HIM--
PHT!
PHT!
--BUT MY STINGERS CAN'T EVEN PENETRATE LIZZIE'S SCALES...

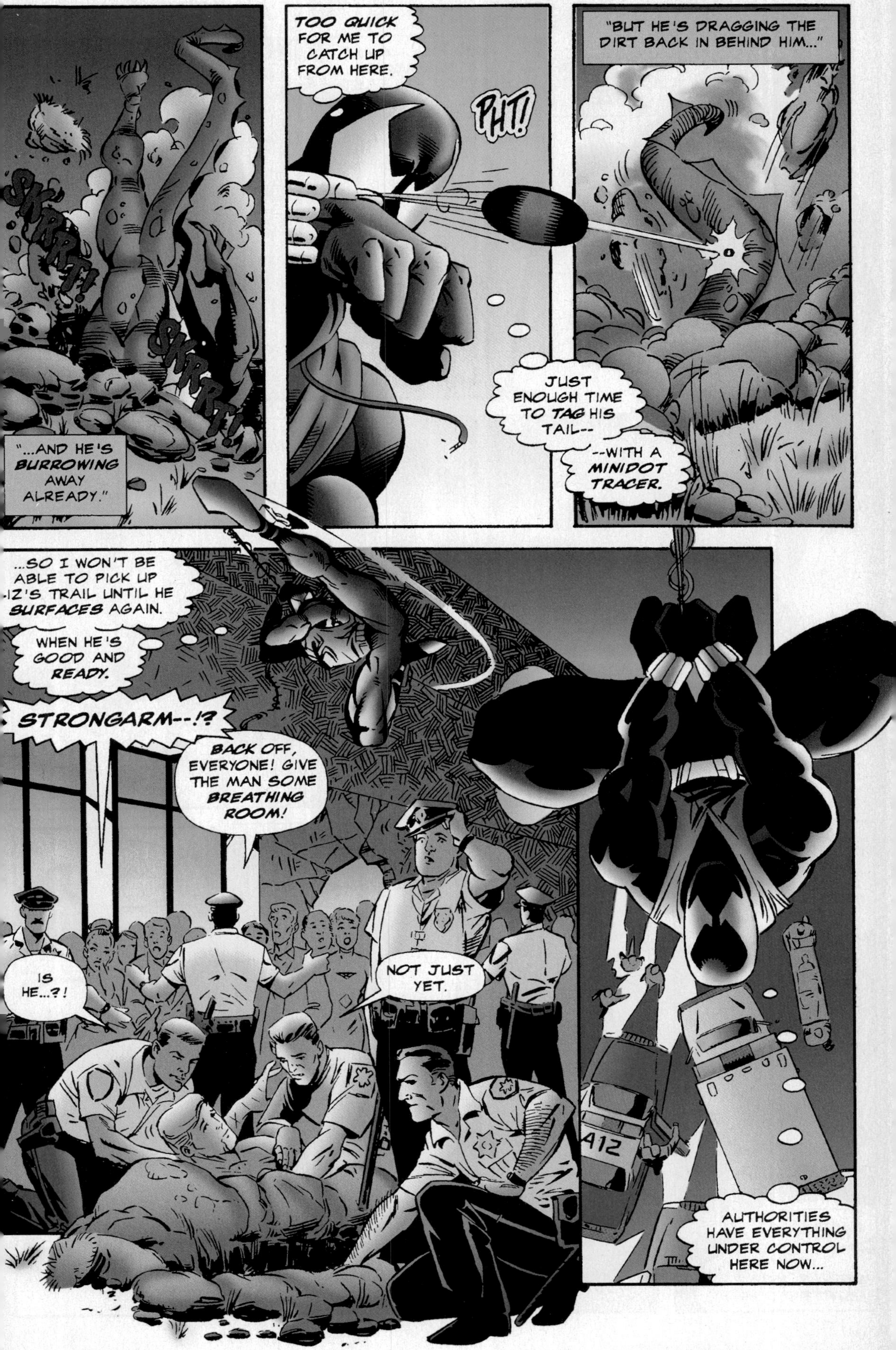
SKRRRT!
SKRRRT!
"...AND HE'S BURROWING AWAY ALREADY."
TOO QUICK FOR ME TO CATCH UP FROM HERE.
PHT!
"BUT HE'S DRAGGING THE DIRT BACK IN BEHIND HIM..."
JUST ENOUGH TIME TO TAG HIS TAIL--
--WITH A MINIDOT TRACER.
...SO I WON'T BE ABLE TO PICK UP -IZ'S TRAIL UNTIL HE SURFACES AGAIN.
WHEN HE'S GOOD AND READY.
STRONGARM--!?
BACK OFF, EVERYONE! GIVE THE MAN SOME BREATHING ROOM!
IS HE...?!
NOT JUST YET.
412
AUTHORITIES HAVE EVERYTHING UNDER CONTROL HERE NOW...

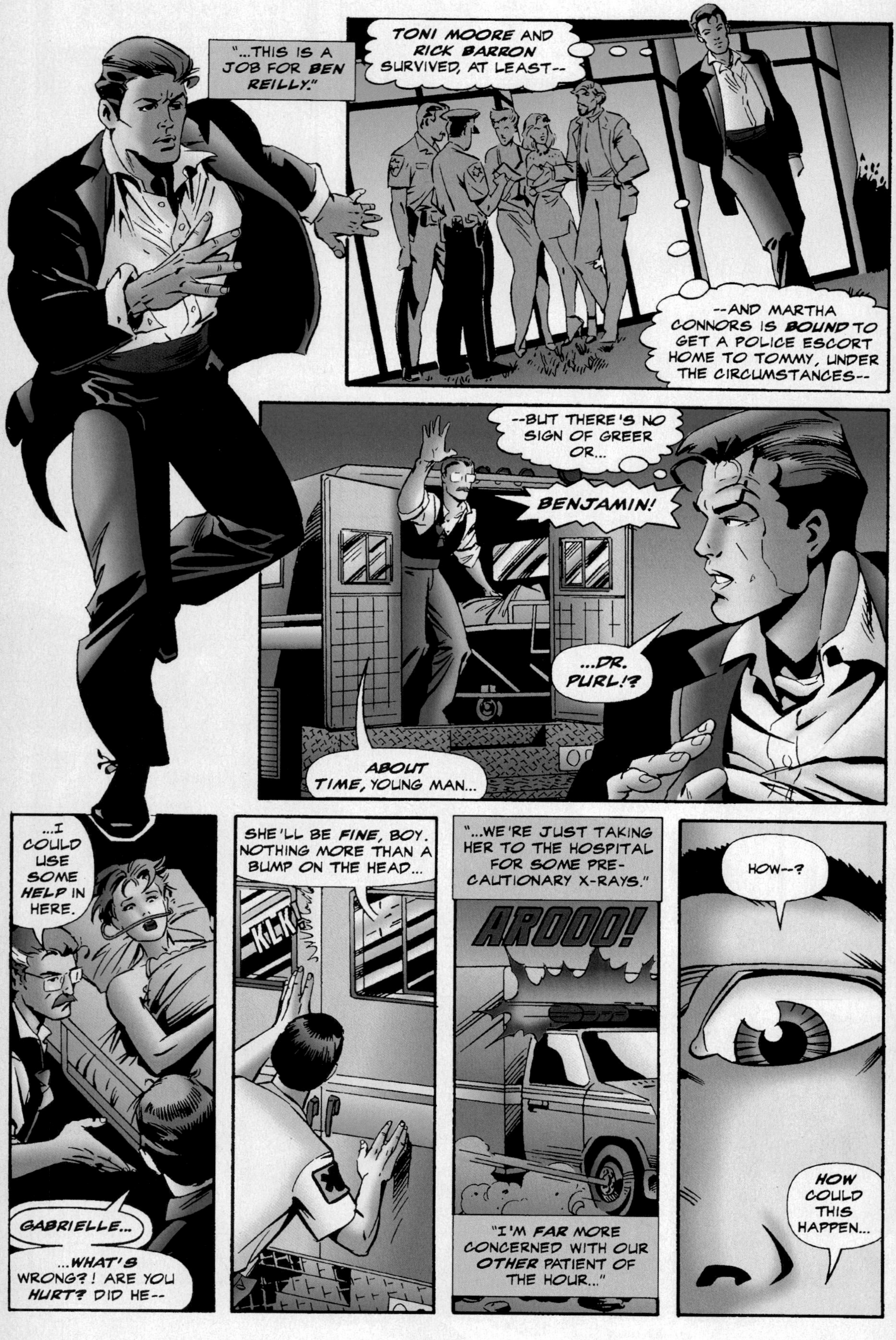
"...THIS IS A JOB FOR BEN REILLY."
TONI MOORE AND RICK BARRON SURVIVED, AT LEAST--
--AND MARTHA CONNORS IS BOUND TO GET A POLICE ESCORT HOME TO TOMMY, UNDER THE CIRCUMSTANCES--
--BUT THERE'S NO SIGN OF GREER OR...
BENJAMIN!
...DR. PURL!?
ABOUT TIME, YOUNG MAN...
...I COULD USE SOME HELP IN HERE.
GABRIELLE...
...WHAT'S WRONG?! ARE YOU HURT? DID HE--
SHE'LL BE FINE, BOY. NOTHING MORE THAN A BUMP ON THE HEAD...
"...WE'RE JUST TAKING HER TO THE HOSPITAL FOR SOME PRE-CAUTIONARY X-RAYS."
AROOO!
"I'M FAR MORE CONCERNED WITH OUR OTHER PATIENT OF THE HOUR..."
HOW--?
HOW COULD THIS HAPPEN...

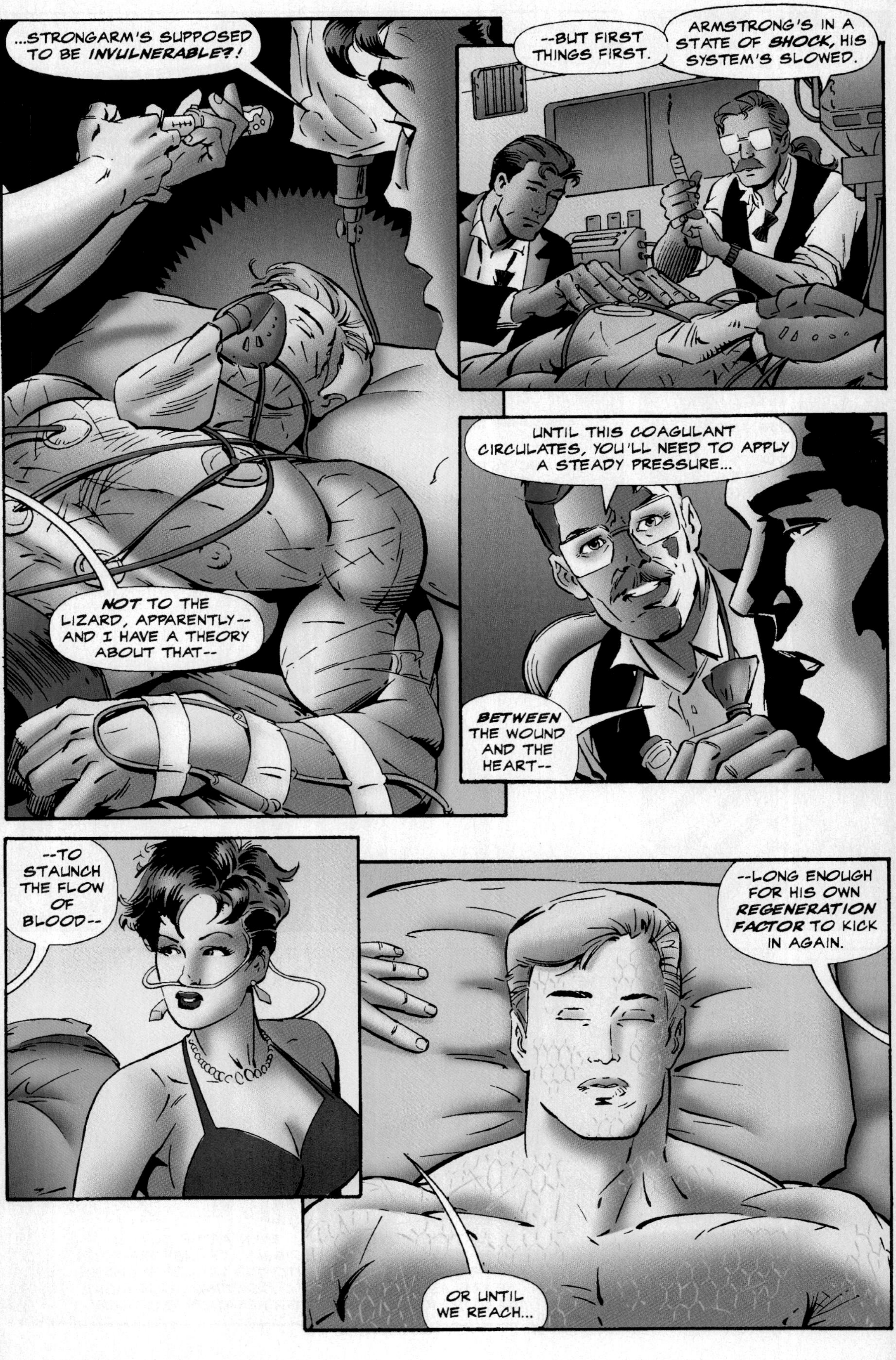
...STRONGARM'S SUPPOSED TO BE INVULNERABLE?!
NOT TO THE LIZARD, APPARENTLY-- AND I HAVE A THEORY ABOUT THAT--
--BUT FIRST THINGS FIRST.
ARMSTRONG'S IN A STATE OF SHOCK, HIS SYSTEM'S SLOWED.
UNTIL THIS COAGULANT CIRCULATES, YOU'LL NEED TO APPLY A STEADY PRESSURE...
BETWEEN THE WOUND AND THE HEART--
--TO STAUNCH THE FLOW OF BLOOD--
--LONG ENOUGH FOR HIS OWN REGENERATION FACTOR TO KICK IN AGAIN.
OR UNTIL WE REACH...

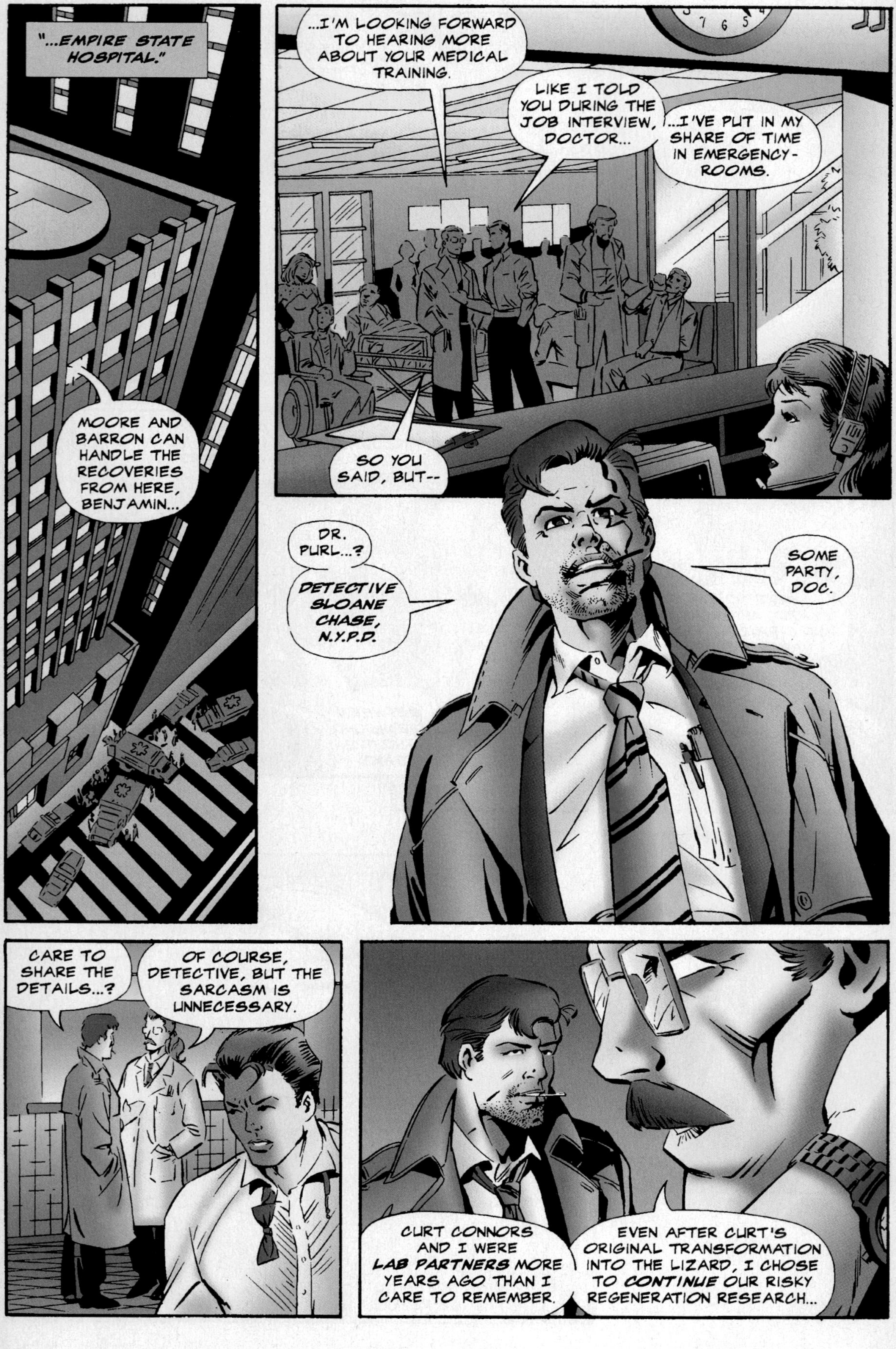
"...EMPIRE STATE HOSPITAL."
MOORE AND BARRON CAN HANDLE THE RECOVERIES FROM HERE, BENJAMIN...
...I'M LOOKING FORWARD TO HEARING MORE ABOUT YOUR MEDICAL TRAINING.
LIKE I TOLD YOU DURING THE JOB INTERVIEW, DOCTOR...
...I'VE PUT IN MY SHARE OF TIME IN EMERGENCY-ROOMS.
SO YOU SAID, BUT--
DR. PURL...?
DETECTIVE SLOANE CHASE, N.Y.P.D.
SOME PARTY, DOC.
CARE TO SHARE THE DETAILS...?
OF COURSE, DETECTIVE, BUT THE SARCASM IS UNNECESSARY.
CURT CONNORS AND I WERE LAB PARTNERS MORE YEARS AGO THAN I CARE TO REMEMBER.
EVEN AFTER CURT'S ORIGINAL TRANSFORMATION INTO THE LIZARD, I CHOSE TO CONTINUE OUR RISKY REGENERATION RESEARCH...

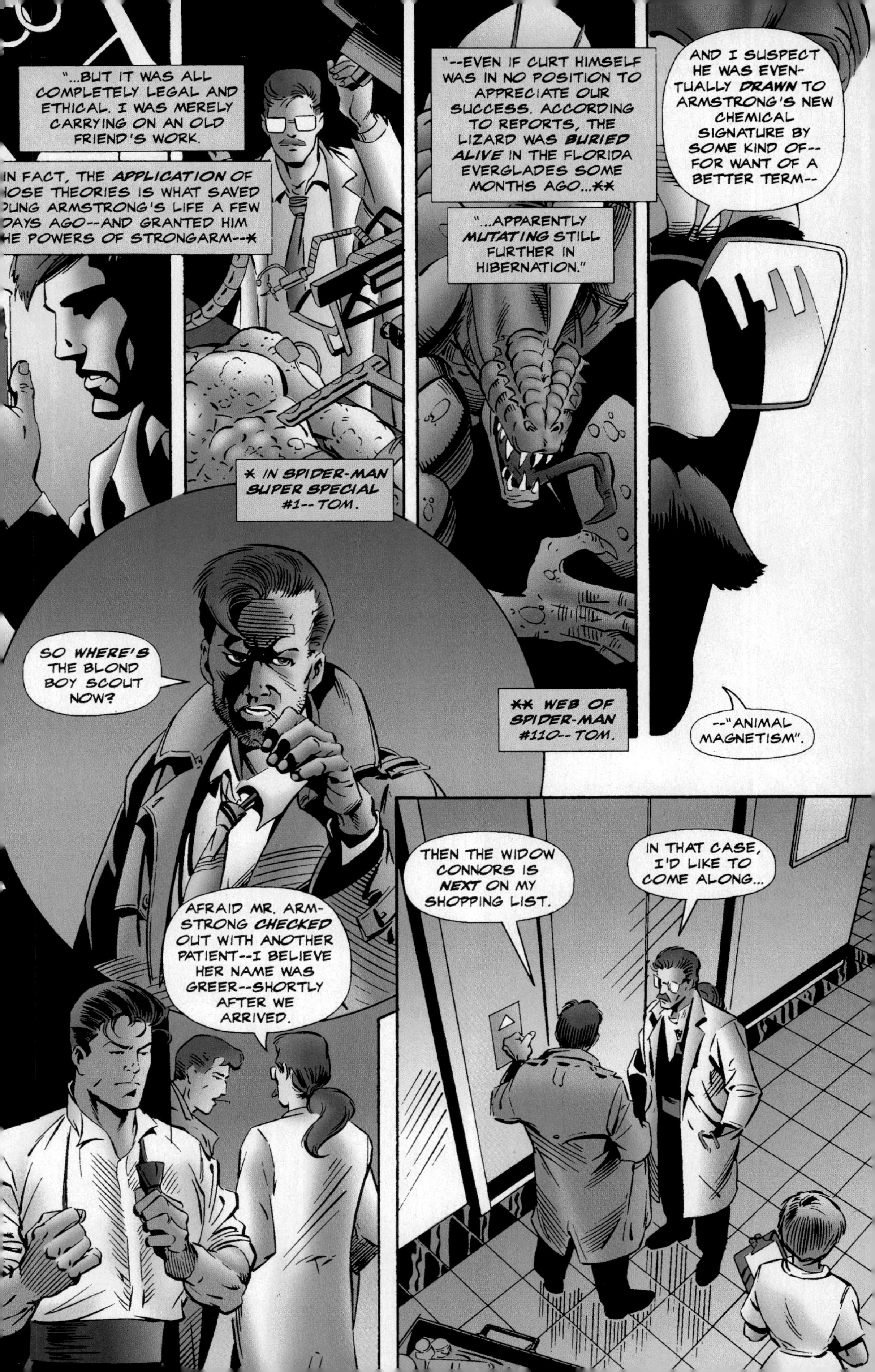
"...BUT IT WAS ALL COMPLETELY LEGAL AND ETHICAL. I WAS MERELY CARRYING ON AN OLD FRIEND'S WORK.
IN FACT, THE APPLICATION OF HOSE THEORIES IS WHAT SAVED OUNG ARMSTRONG'S LIFE A FEW DAYS AGO--AND GRANTED HIM HE POWERS OF STRONGARM--*
* IN SPIDER-MAN SUPER SPECIAL #1--TOM.
"--EVEN IF CURT HIMSELF WAS IN NO POSITION TO APPRECIATE OUR SUCCESS. ACCORDING TO REPORTS, THE LIZARD WAS BURIED ALIVE IN THE FLORIDA EVERGLADES SOME MONTHS AGO...**
"...APPARENTLY MUTATING STILL FURTHER IN HIBERNATION."
** WEB OF SPIDER-MAN #110--TOM.
AND I SUSPECT HE WAS EVEN-TUALLY DRAWN TO ARMSTRONG'S NEW CHEMICAL SIGNATURE BY SOME KIND OF--FOR WANT OF A BETTER TERM--
--"ANIMAL MAGNETISM".
SO WHERE'S THE BLOND BOY SCOUT NOW?
AFRAID MR. ARM-STRONG CHECKED OUT WITH ANOTHER PATIENT--I BELIEVE HER NAME WAS GREER--SHORTLY AFTER WE ARRIVED.
THEN THE WIDOW CONNORS IS NEXT ON MY SHOPPING LIST.
IN THAT CASE, I'D LIKE TO COME ALONG...

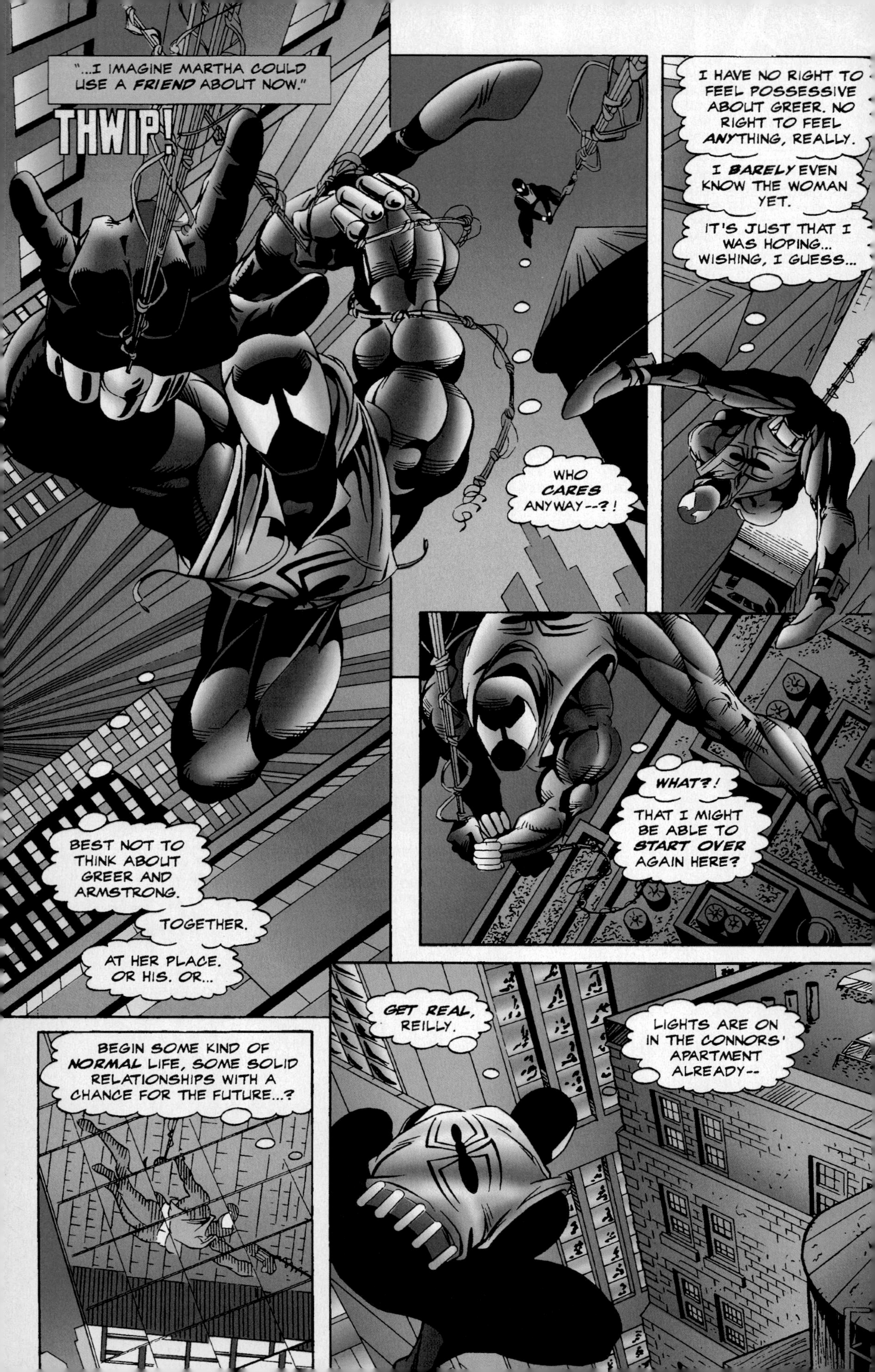
"...I IMAGINE MARTHA COULD USE A *FRIEND* ABOUT NOW."
THWIP!
WHO *CARES* ANYWAY--?!
I HAVE NO RIGHT TO FEEL POSSESSIVE ABOUT GREER. NO RIGHT TO FEEL *ANY*THING, REALLY.
I *BARELY* EVEN KNOW THE WOMAN YET.
IT'S JUST THAT I WAS HOPING... WISHING, I GUESS...
BEST NOT TO THINK ABOUT GREER AND ARMSTRONG.
TOGETHER.
AT HER PLACE. OR HIS. OR...
WHAT?!
THAT I MIGHT BE ABLE TO *START OVER* AGAIN HERE?
BEGIN SOME KIND OF *NORMAL* LIFE, SOME SOLID RELATIONSHIPS WITH A CHANCE FOR THE FUTURE...?
GET REAL, REILLY.
LIGHTS ARE ON IN THE CONNORS' APARTMENT ALREADY--

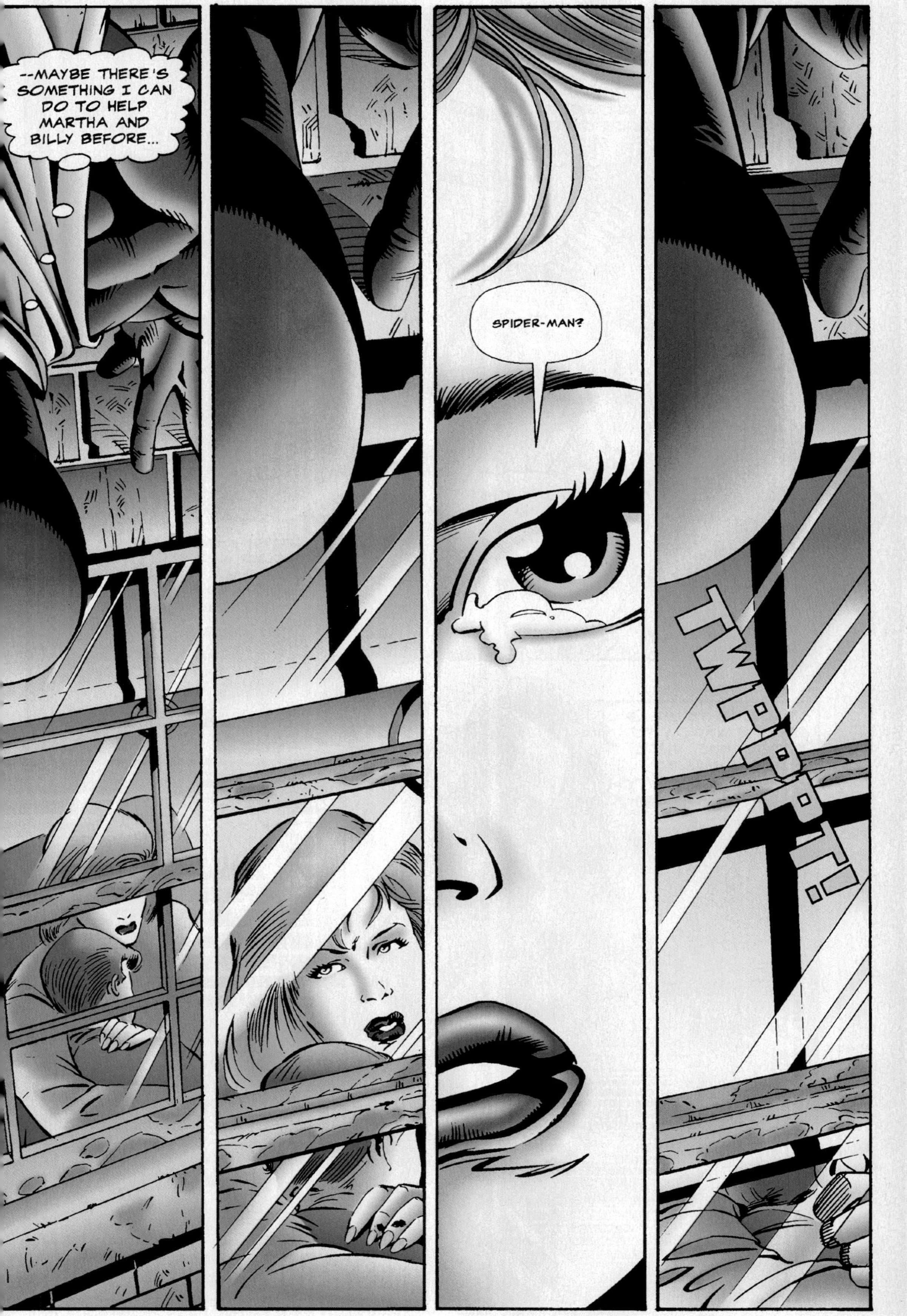
--MAYBE THERE'S SOMETHING I CAN DO TO HELP MARTHA AND BILLY BEFORE...
SPIDER-MAN?
TWIPPPT!

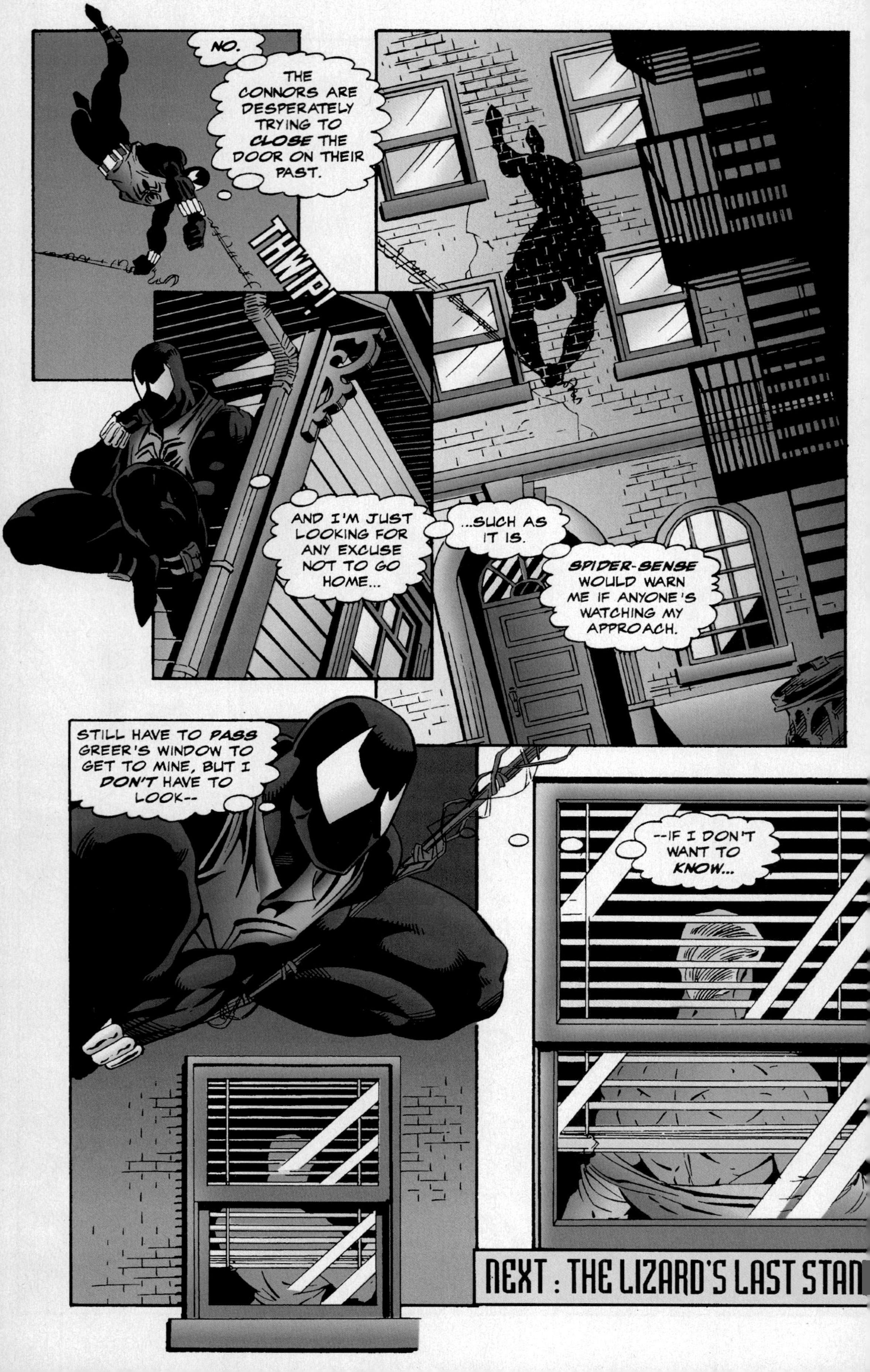

NO.
THE CONNORS ARE DESPERATELY TRYING TO CLOSE THE DOOR ON THEIR PAST.
THWIP!
AND I'M JUST LOOKING FOR ANY EXCUSE NOT TO GO HOME...
...SUCH AS IT IS.
SPIDER-SENSE WOULD WARN ME IF ANYONE'S WATCHING MY APPROACH.
STILL HAVE TO PASS GREER'S WINDOW TO GET TO MINE, BUT I DON'T HAVE TO LOOK--
--IF I DON'T WANT TO KNOW...
NEXT : THE LIZARD'S LAST STAN

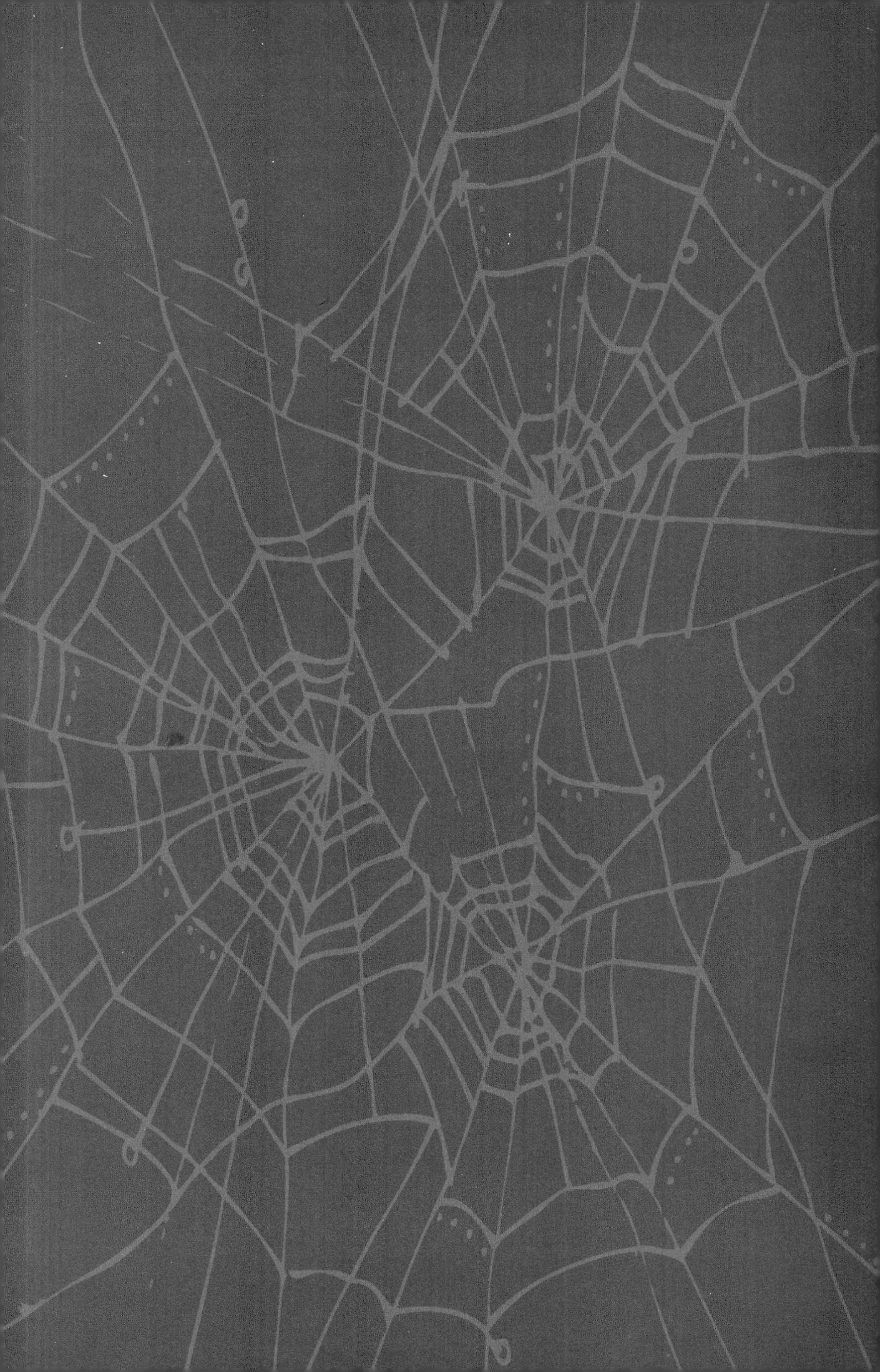

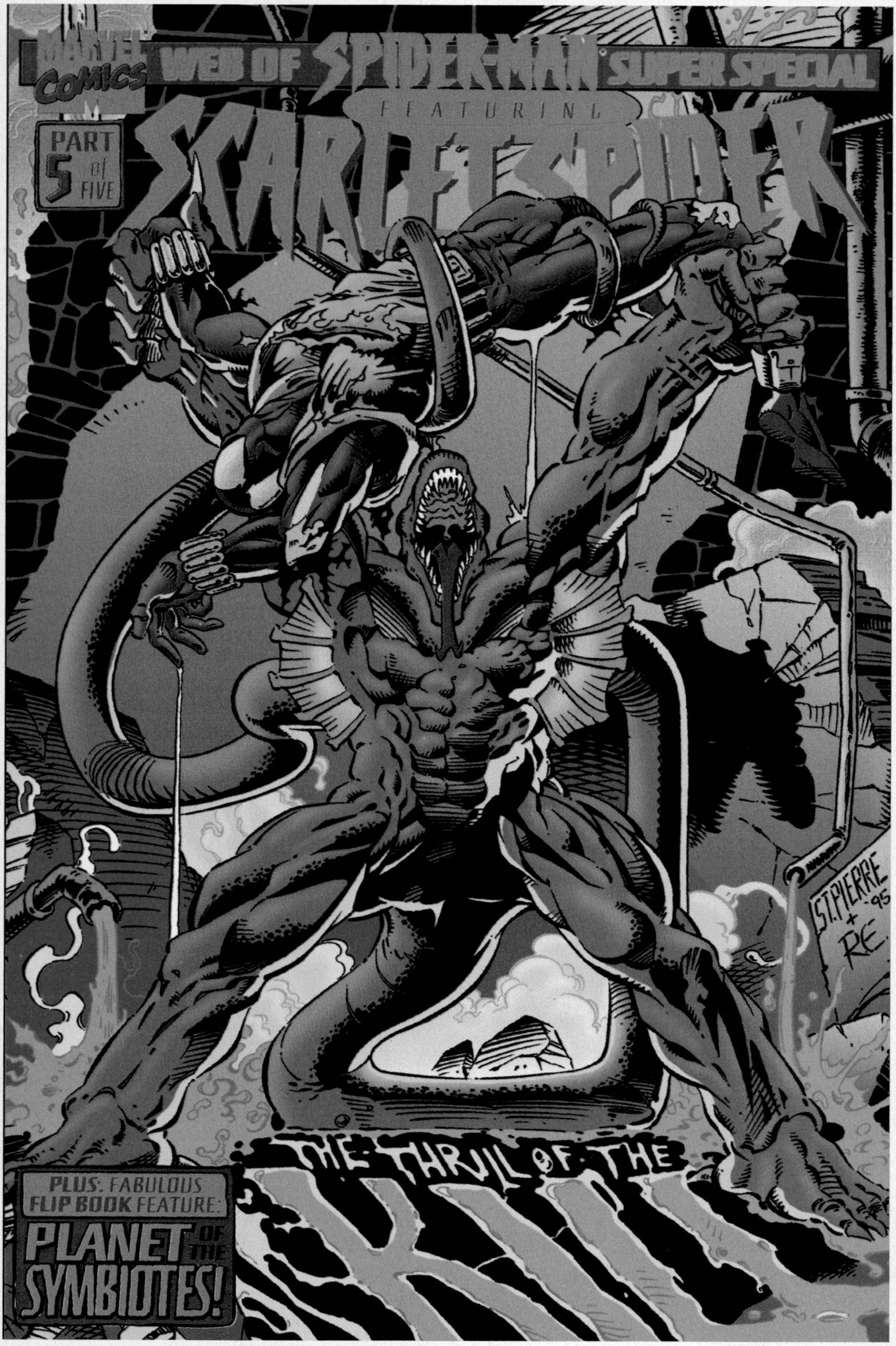
MARVEL COMICS
WEB OF SPIDER-MAN SUPER SPECIAL
FEATURING
SCARLET SPIDER
PART 5 of FIVE
ST. PIERRE '95 + RE
THE THRILL OF THE
PLUS: FABULOUS FLIP BOOK FEATURE:
PLANET OF THE SYMBIOTES!

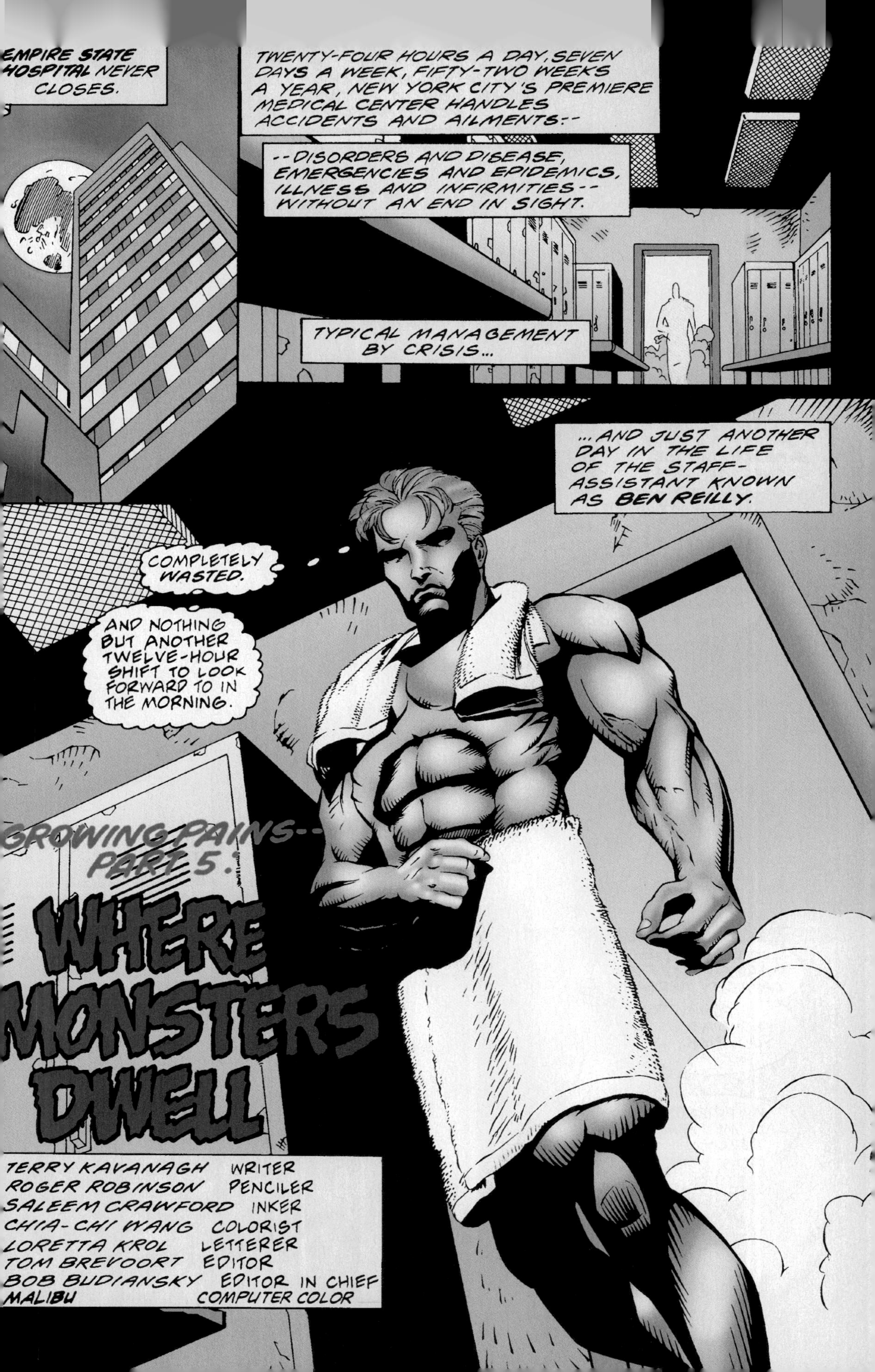
EMPIRE STATE HOSPITAL NEVER CLOSES.
TWENTY-FOUR HOURS A DAY, SEVEN DAYS A WEEK, FIFTY-TWO WEEKS A YEAR, NEW YORK CITY'S PREMIERE MEDICAL CENTER HANDLES ACCIDENTS AND AILMENTS:--
--DISORDERS AND DISEASE, EMERGENCIES AND EPIDEMICS, ILLNESS AND INFIRMITIES-- WITHOUT AN END IN SIGHT.
TYPICAL MANAGEMENT BY CRISIS...
...AND JUST ANOTHER DAY IN THE LIFE OF THE STAFF-ASSISTANT KNOWN AS BEN REILLY.
COMPLETELY WASTED.
AND NOTHING BUT ANOTHER TWELVE-HOUR SHIFT TO LOOK FORWARD TO IN THE MORNING.
GROWING PAINS-- PART 5:
WHERE MONSTERS DWELL
TERRY KAVANAGH WRITER
ROGER ROBINSON PENCILER
SALEEM CRAWFORD INKER
CHIA-CHI WANG COLORIST
LORETTA KROL LETTERER
TOM BREVOORT EDITOR
BOB BUDIANSKY EDITOR IN CHIEF
MALIBU COMPUTER COLOR

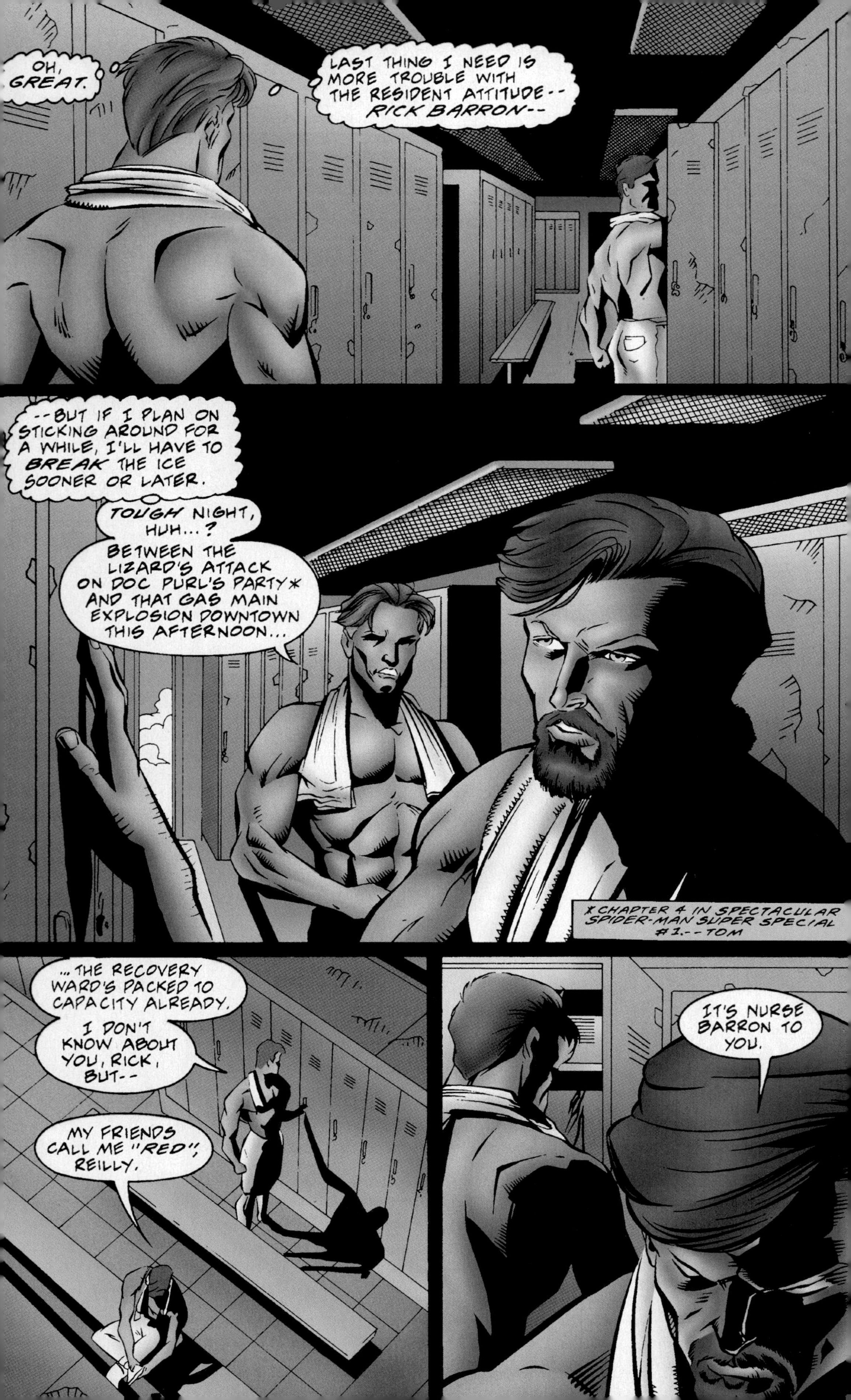
OH, GREAT.
LAST THING I NEED IS MORE TROUBLE WITH THE RESIDENT ATTITUDE-- RICK BARRON--
--BUT IF I PLAN ON STICKING AROUND FOR A WHILE, I'LL HAVE TO BREAK THE ICE SOONER OR LATER.
TOUGH NIGHT, HUH...?
BETWEEN THE LIZARD'S ATTACK ON DOC PURL'S PARTY* AND THAT GAS MAIN EXPLOSION DOWNTOWN THIS AFTERNOON...
*CHAPTER 4 IN SPECTACULAR SPIDER-MAN SUPER SPECIAL #1.--TOM
...THE RECOVERY WARD'S PACKED TO CAPACITY ALREADY.
I DON'T KNOW ABOUT YOU, RICK, BUT--
MY FRIENDS CALL ME "RED", REILLY.
IT'S NURSE BARRON TO YOU.

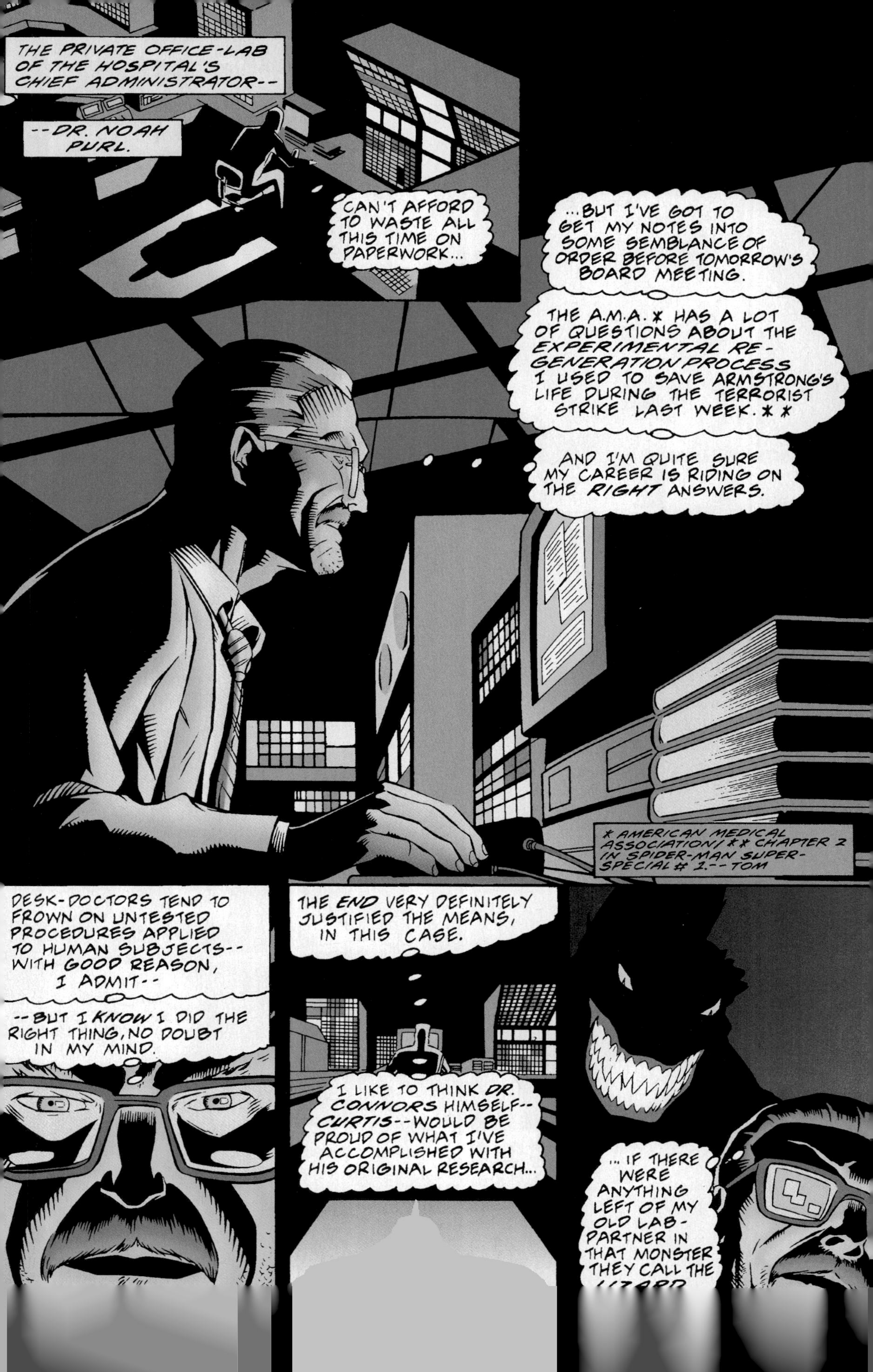
THE PRIVATE OFFICE-LAB OF THE HOSPITAL'S CHIEF ADMINISTRATOR--
--DR. NOAH PURL.
CAN'T AFFORD TO WASTE ALL THIS TIME ON PAPERWORK...
...BUT I'VE GOT TO GET MY NOTES INTO SOME SEMBLANCE OF ORDER BEFORE TOMORROW'S BOARD MEETING.
THE A.M.A. * HAS A LOT OF QUESTIONS ABOUT THE EXPERIMENTAL RE-GENERATION PROCESS I USED TO SAVE ARMSTRONG'S LIFE DURING THE TERRORIST STRIKE LAST WEEK. * *
AND I'M QUITE SURE MY CAREER IS RIDING ON THE RIGHT ANSWERS.
* AMERICAN MEDICAL ASSOCIATION / * * CHAPTER 2 IN SPIDER-MAN SUPER-SPECIAL # 1.--TOM
DESK-DOCTORS TEND TO FROWN ON UNTESTED PROCEDURES APPLIED TO HUMAN SUBJECTS--WITH GOOD REASON, I ADMIT--
--BUT I KNOW I DID THE RIGHT THING, NO DOUBT IN MY MIND.
THE END VERY DEFINITELY JUSTIFIED THE MEANS, IN THIS CASE.
I LIKE TO THINK DR. CONNORS HIMSELF--CURTIS--WOULD BE PROUD OF WHAT I'VE ACCOMPLISHED WITH HIS ORIGINAL RESEARCH...
...IF THERE WERE ANYTHING LEFT OF MY OLD LAB-PARTNER IN THAT MONSTER THEY CALL THE

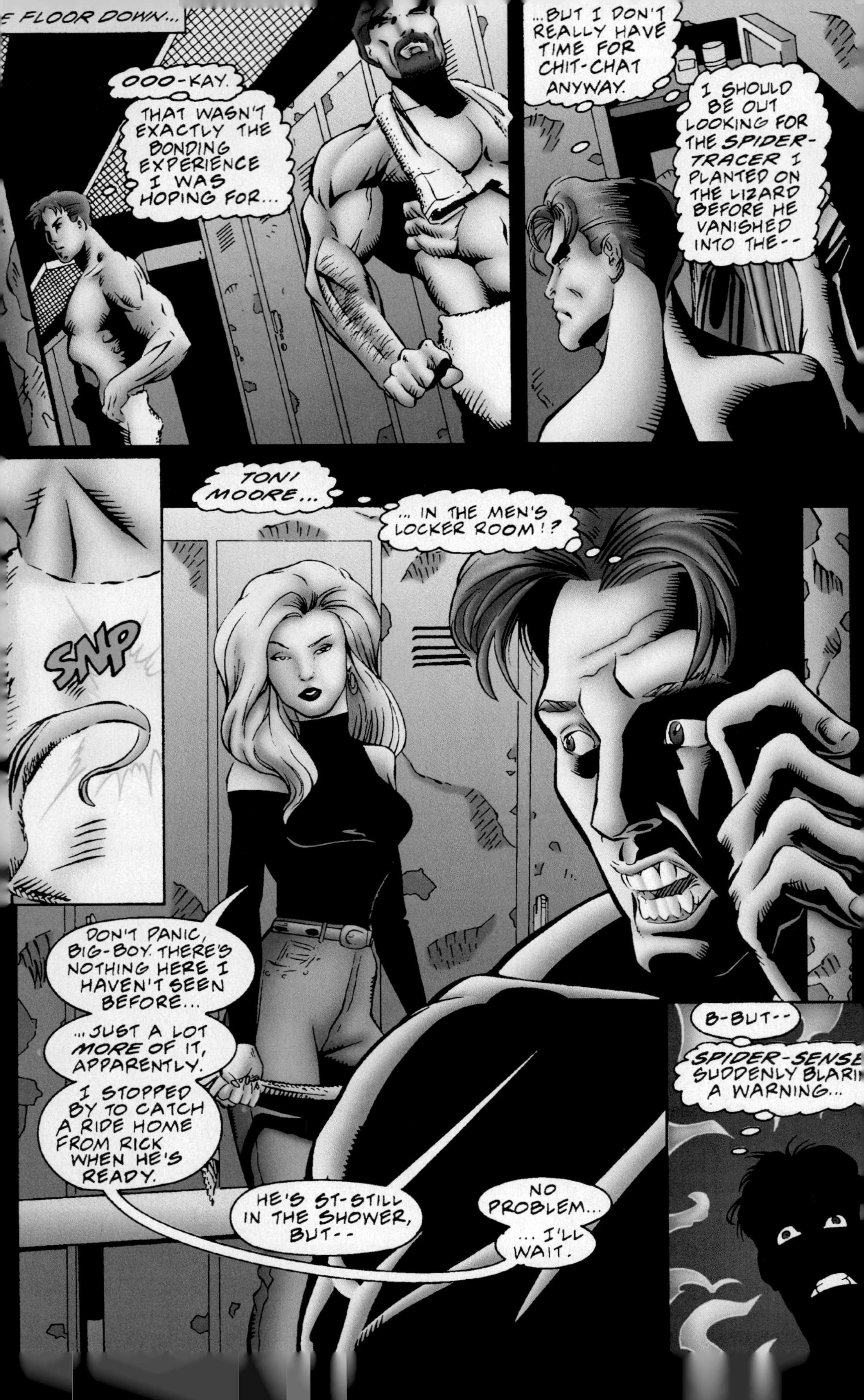

...E FLOOR DOWN...
OOO-KAY.
THAT WASN'T EXACTLY THE BONDING EXPERIENCE I WAS HOPING FOR...
...BUT I DON'T REALLY HAVE TIME FOR CHIT-CHAT ANYWAY.
I SHOULD BE OUT LOOKING FOR THE SPIDER-TRACER I PLANTED ON THE LIZARD BEFORE HE VANISHED INTO THE--
SNP
TONI MOORE...
...IN THE MEN'S LOCKER ROOM!?
DON'T PANIC, BIG-BOY. THERE'S NOTHING HERE I HAVEN'T SEEN BEFORE...
...JUST A LOT MORE OF IT, APPARENTLY.
I STOPPED BY TO CATCH A RIDE HOME FROM RICK WHEN HE'S READY.
HE'S ST-STILL IN THE SHOWER, BUT--
NO PROBLEM...
...I'LL WAIT.
B-BUT--
SPIDER-SENSE SUDDENLY BLARI... A WARNING...

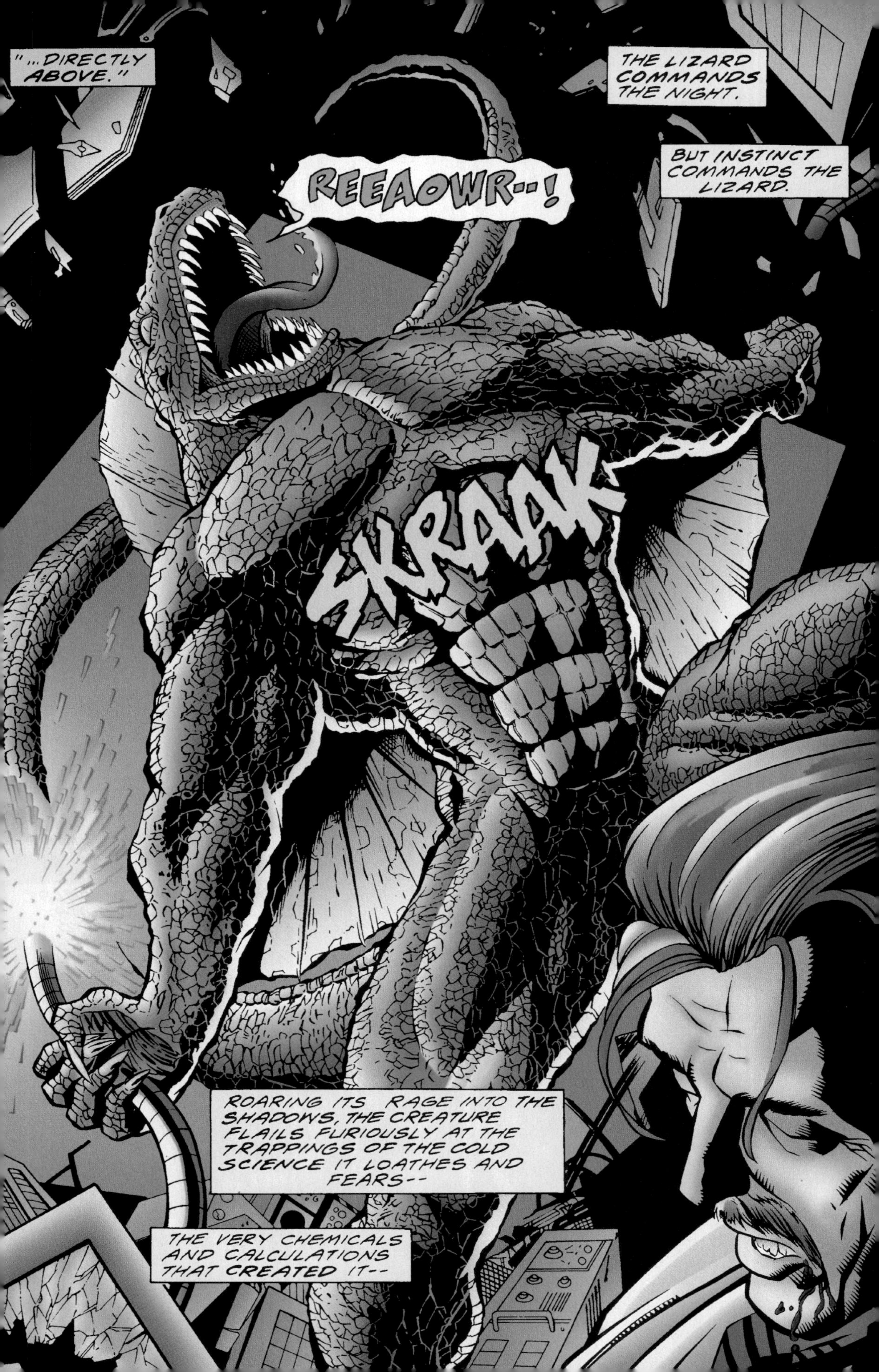
"...DIRECTLY ABOVE."
THE LIZARD COMMANDS THE NIGHT.
BUT INSTINCT COMMANDS THE LIZARD.
REEAOWR--!
SKRAAK
ROARING ITS RAGE INTO THE SHADOWS, THE CREATURE FLAILS FURIOUSLY AT THE TRAPPINGS OF THE COLD SCIENCE IT LOATHES AND FEARS--
THE VERY CHEMICALS AND CALCULATIONS THAT CREATED IT--

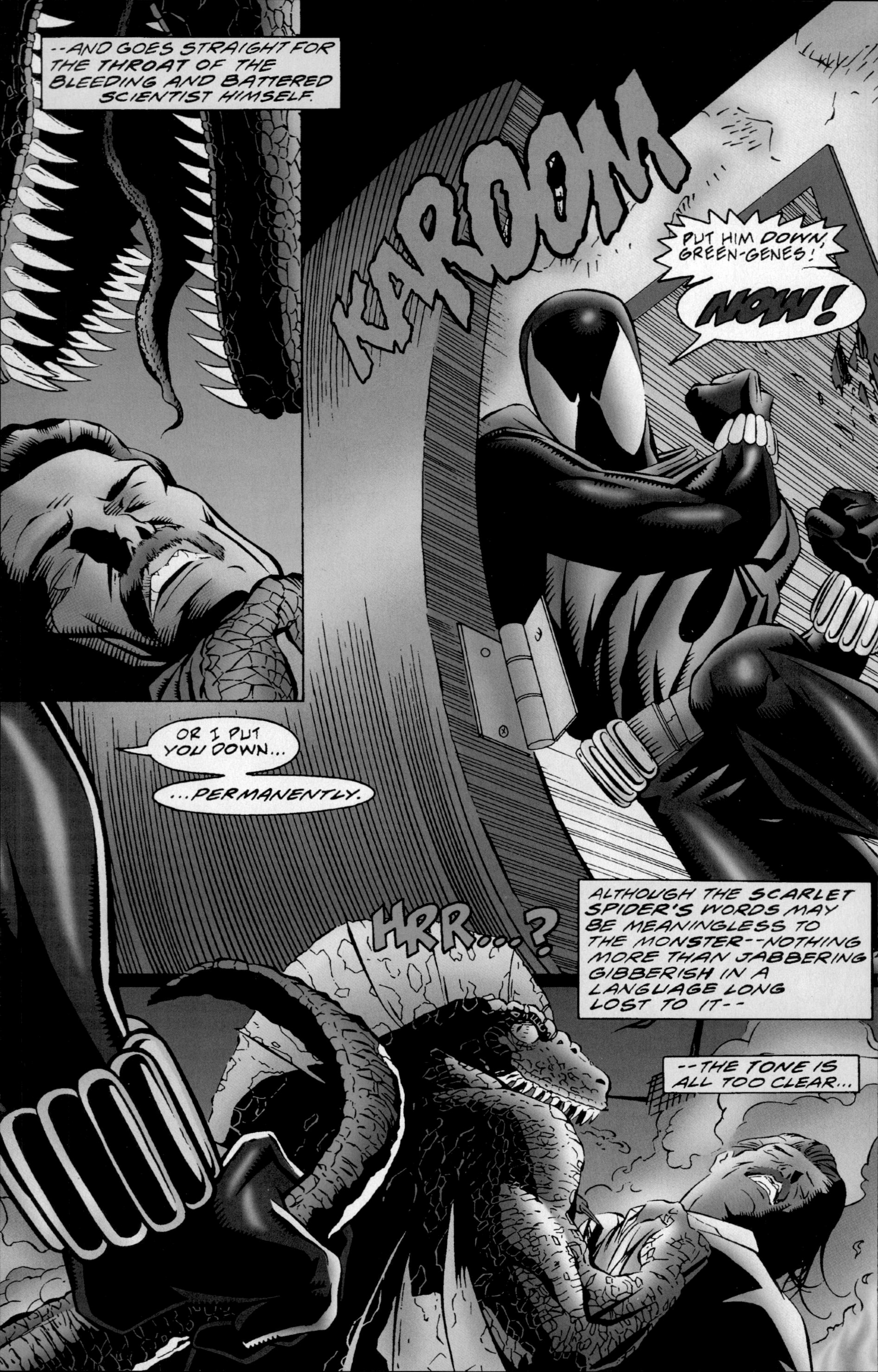
--AND GOES STRAIGHT FOR THE THROAT OF THE BLEEDING AND BATTERED SCIENTIST HIMSELF.
KAROOM
PUT HIM DOWN, GREEN-GENES!
NOW!
OR I PUT YOU DOWN...
...PERMANENTLY.
HRR...?
ALTHOUGH THE SCARLET SPIDER'S WORDS MAY BE MEANINGLESS TO THE MONSTER--NOTHING MORE THAN JABBERING GIBBERISH IN A LANGUAGE LONG LOST TO IT--
--THE TONE IS ALL TOO CLEAR...

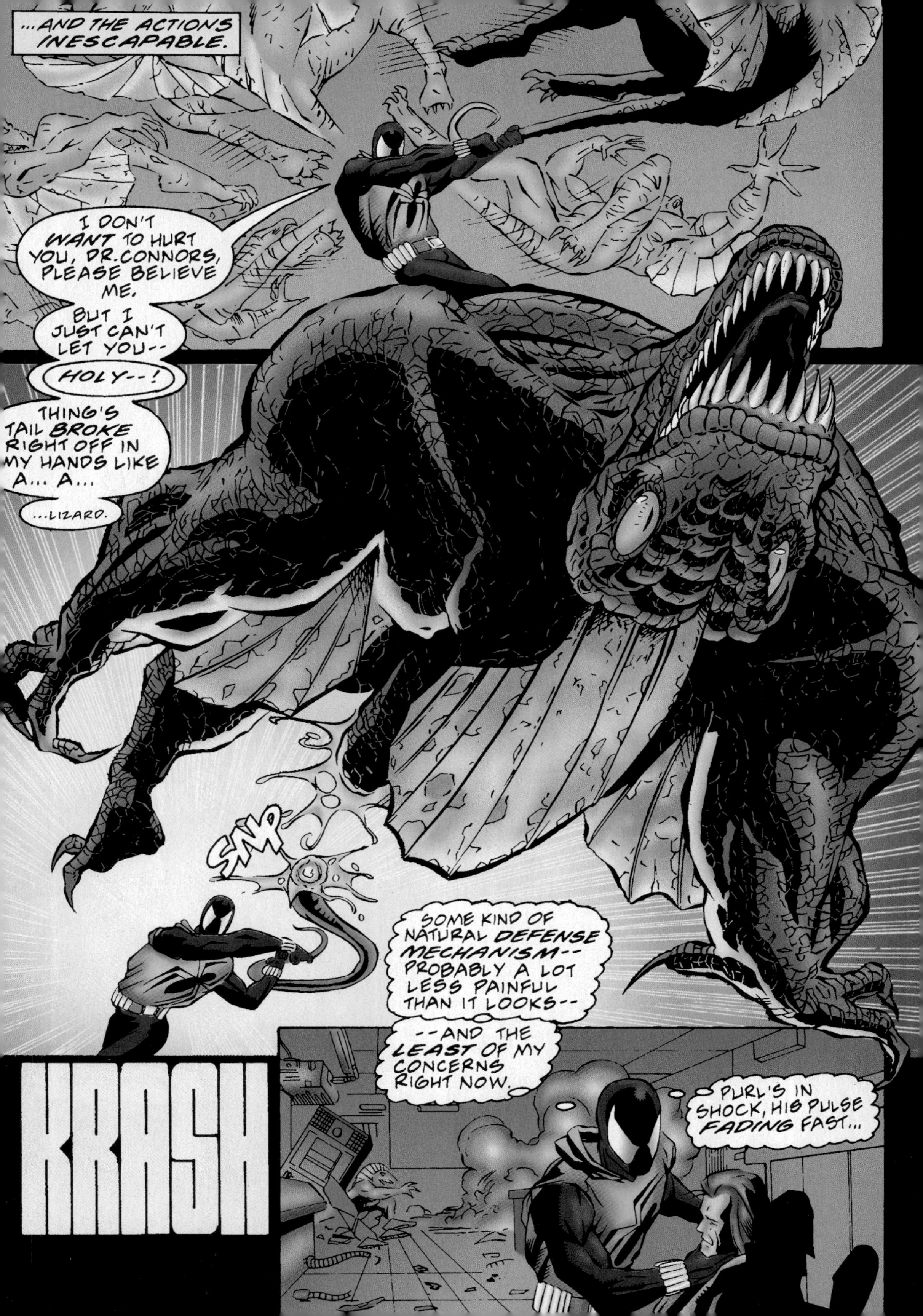
...AND THE ACTIONS INESCAPABLE.
I DON'T WANT TO HURT YOU, DR. CONNORS, PLEASE BELIEVE ME.
BUT I JUST CAN'T LET YOU--
HOLY--!
THING'S TAIL BROKE RIGHT OFF IN MY HANDS LIKE A... A...
...LIZARD.
SNAP
SOME KIND OF NATURAL DEFENSE MECHANISM-- PROBABLY A LOT LESS PAINFUL THAN IT LOOKS--
--AND THE LEAST OF MY CONCERNS RIGHT NOW.
KRASH
PURL'S IN SHOCK, HIS PULSE FADING FAST...

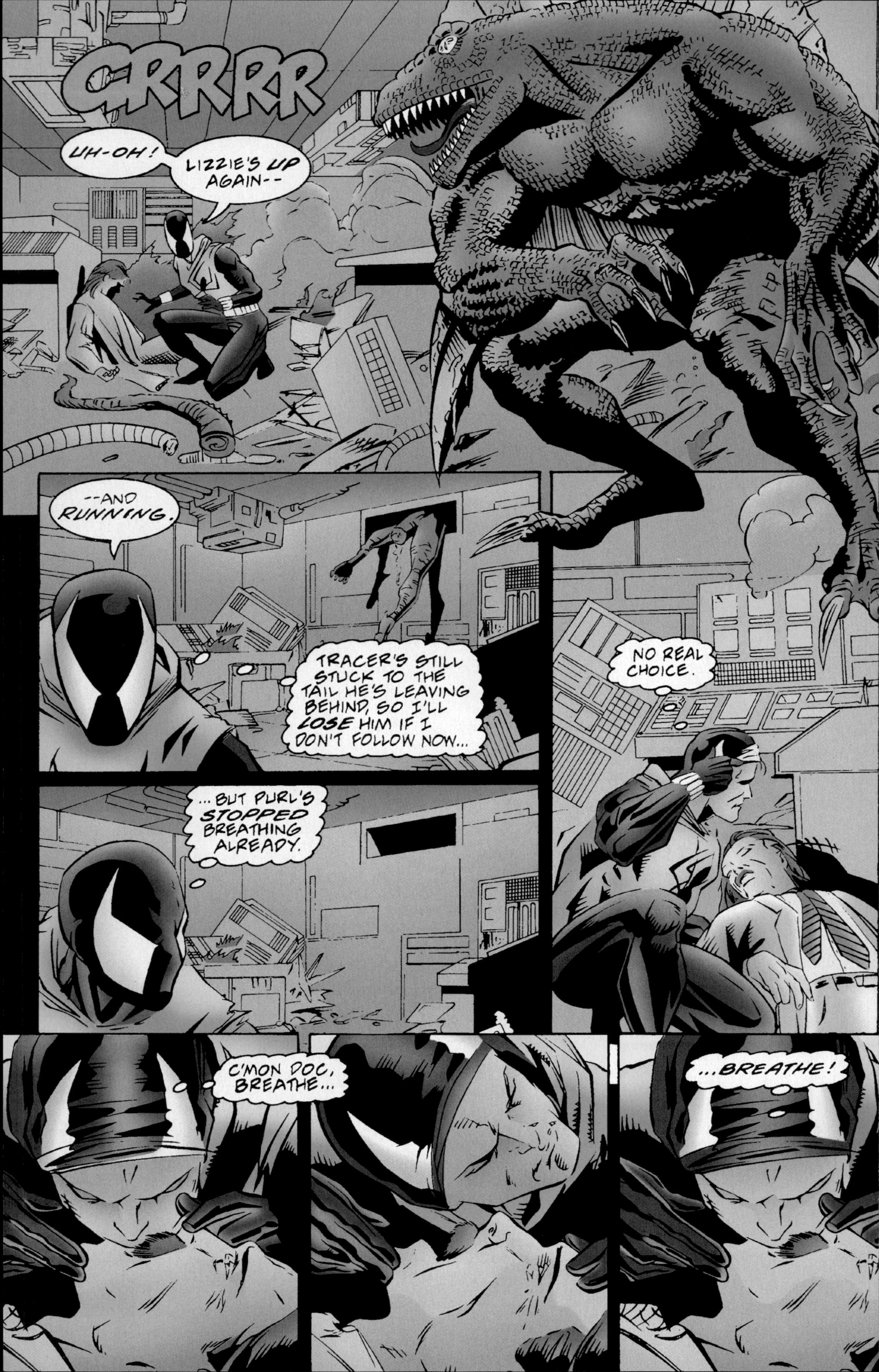
GRRRR
UH-OH!
LIZZIE'S UP AGAIN--
--AND RUNNING.
TRACER'S STILL STUCK TO THE TAIL HE'S LEAVING BEHIND, SO I'LL LOSE HIM IF I DON'T FOLLOW NOW...
...BUT PURL'S STOPPED BREATHING ALREADY.
NO REAL CHOICE.
C'MON DOC, BREATHE...
...BREATHE!

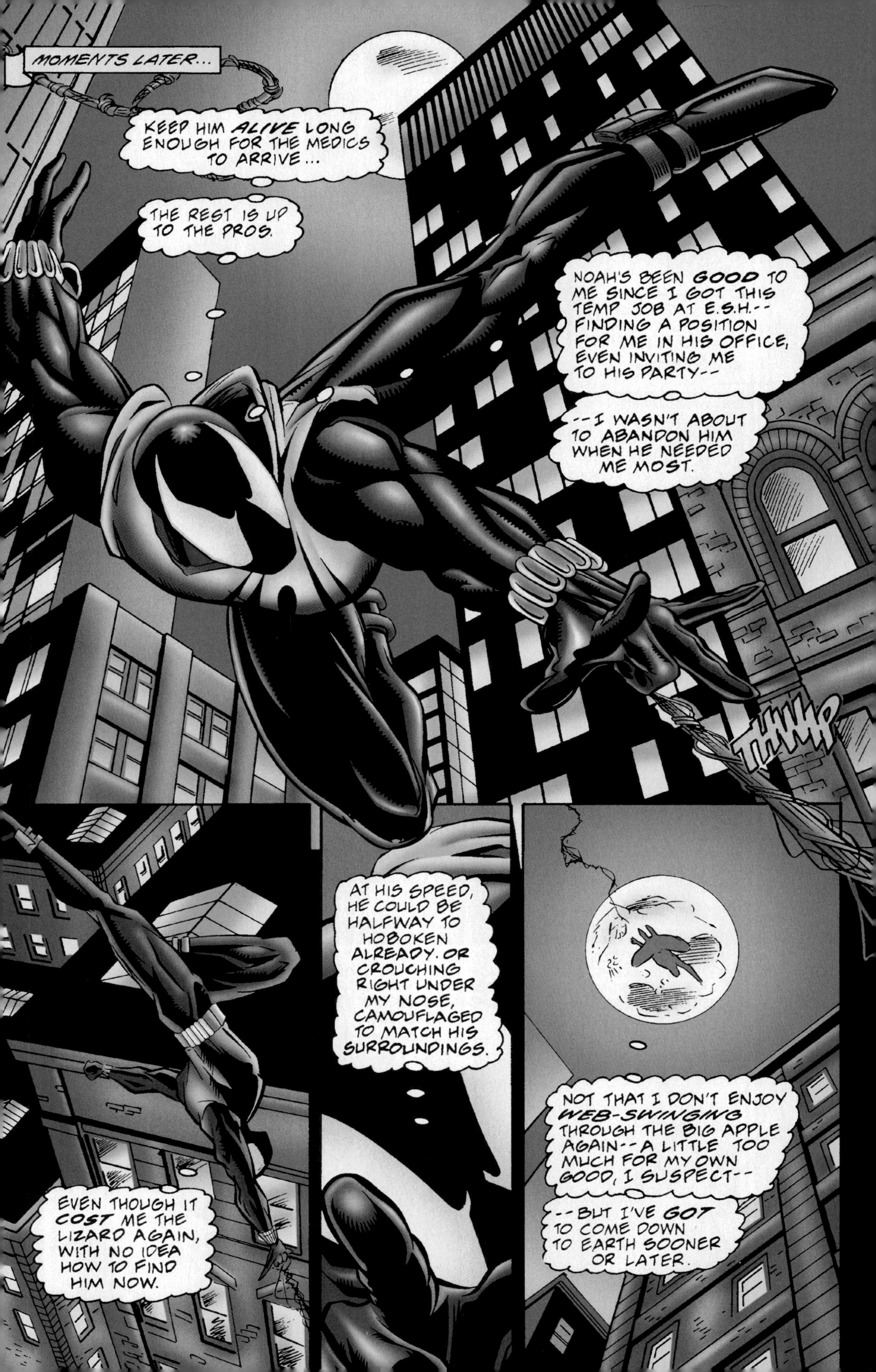
MOMENTS LATER...
KEEP HIM ALIVE LONG ENOUGH FOR THE MEDICS TO ARRIVE...
THE REST IS UP TO THE PROS.
NOAH'S BEEN GOOD TO ME SINCE I GOT THIS TEMP JOB AT E.S.H.-- FINDING A POSITION FOR ME IN HIS OFFICE, EVEN INVITING ME TO HIS PARTY--
--I WASN'T ABOUT TO ABANDON HIM WHEN HE NEEDED ME MOST.
THWIP
EVEN THOUGH IT COST ME THE LIZARD AGAIN, WITH NO IDEA HOW TO FIND HIM NOW.
AT HIS SPEED, HE COULD BE HALFWAY TO HOBOKEN ALREADY. OR CROUCHING RIGHT UNDER MY NOSE, CAMOUFLAGED TO MATCH HIS SURROUNDINGS.
NOT THAT I DON'T ENJOY WEB-SWINGING THROUGH THE BIG APPLE AGAIN--A LITTLE TOO MUCH FOR MY OWN GOOD, I SUSPECT--
--BUT I'VE GOT TO COME DOWN TO EARTH SOONER OR LATER.

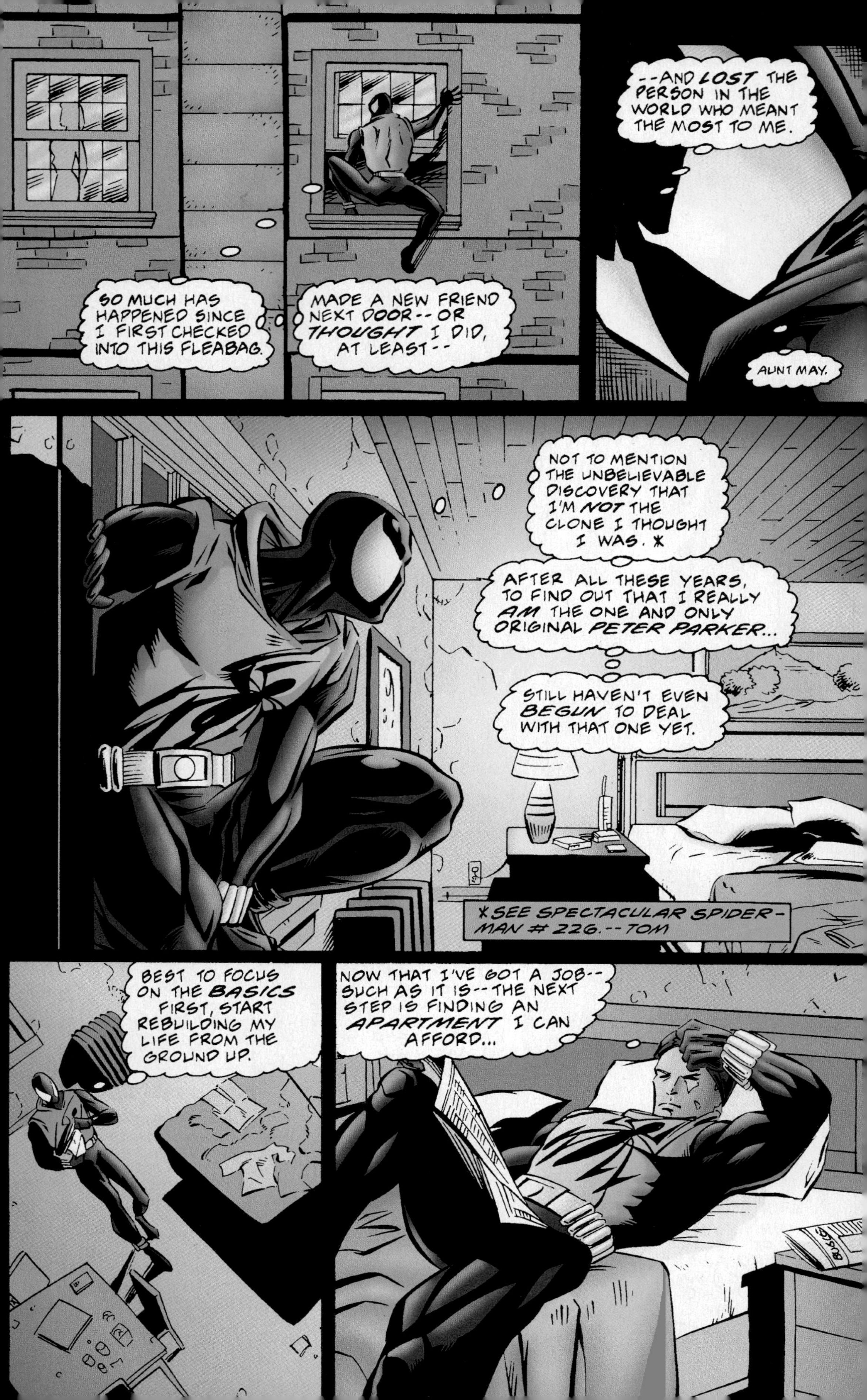
SO MUCH HAS HAPPENED SINCE I FIRST CHECKED INTO THIS FLEABAG.
MADE A NEW FRIEND NEXT DOOR--OR THOUGHT I DID, AT LEAST--
--AND LOST THE PERSON IN THE WORLD WHO MEANT THE MOST TO ME.
AUNT MAY.
NOT TO MENTION THE UNBELIEVABLE DISCOVERY THAT I'M NOT THE CLONE I THOUGHT I WAS. *
AFTER ALL THESE YEARS, TO FIND OUT THAT I REALLY AM THE ONE AND ONLY ORIGINAL PETER PARKER...
STILL HAVEN'T EVEN BEGUN TO DEAL WITH THAT ONE YET.
*SEE SPECTACULAR SPIDER-MAN # 226.--TOM
BEST TO FOCUS ON THE BASICS FIRST, START REBUILDING MY LIFE FROM THE GROUND UP.
NOW THAT I'VE GOT A JOB--SUCH AS IT IS--THE NEXT STEP IS FINDING AN APARTMENT I CAN AFFORD...

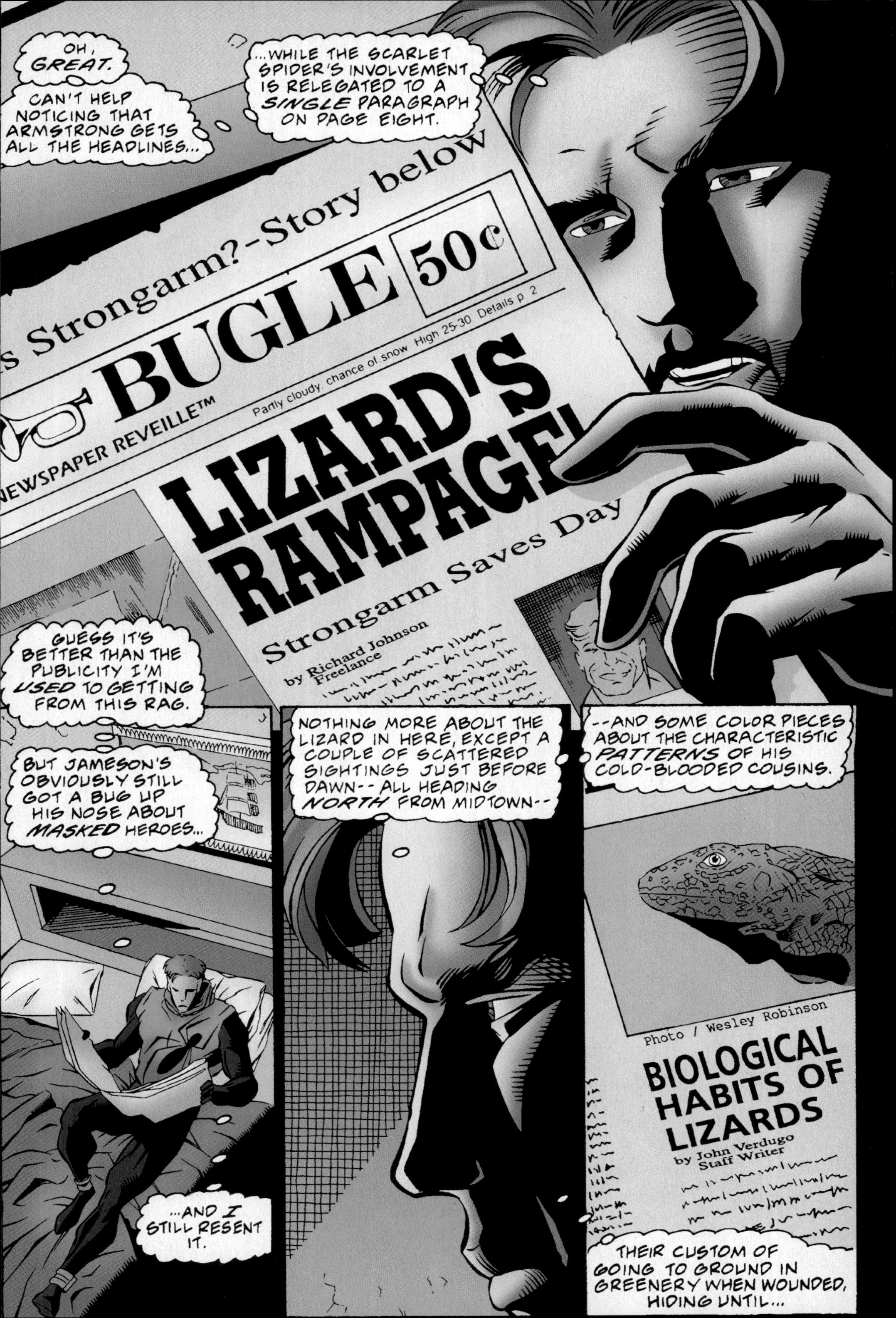

OH, GREAT.
CAN'T HELP NOTICING THAT ARMSTRONG GETS ALL THE HEADLINES...
...WHILE THE SCARLET SPIDER'S INVOLVEMENT IS RELEGATED TO A SINGLE PARAGRAPH ON PAGE EIGHT.
...s Strongarm?-Story below
BUGLE
50¢
NEWSPAPER REVEILLE™
Partly cloudy, chance of snow High 25-30 Details p. 2
LIZARD'S RAMPAGE!
Strongarm Saves Day
by Richard Johnson
Freelance
GUESS IT'S BETTER THAN THE PUBLICITY I'M USED TO GETTING FROM THIS RAG.
BUT JAMESON'S OBVIOUSLY STILL GOT A BUG UP HIS NOSE ABOUT MASKED HEROES...
...AND I STILL RESENT IT.
NOTHING MORE ABOUT THE LIZARD IN HERE, EXCEPT A COUPLE OF SCATTERED SIGHTINGS JUST BEFORE DAWN--ALL HEADING NORTH FROM MIDTOWN--
--AND SOME COLOR PIECES ABOUT THE CHARACTERISTIC PATTERNS OF HIS COLD-BLOODED COUSINS.
Photo / Wesley Robinson
BIOLOGICAL HABITS OF LIZARDS
by John Verdugo
Staff Writer
THEIR CUSTOM OF GOING TO GROUND IN GREENERY WHEN WOUNDED, HIDING UNTIL...

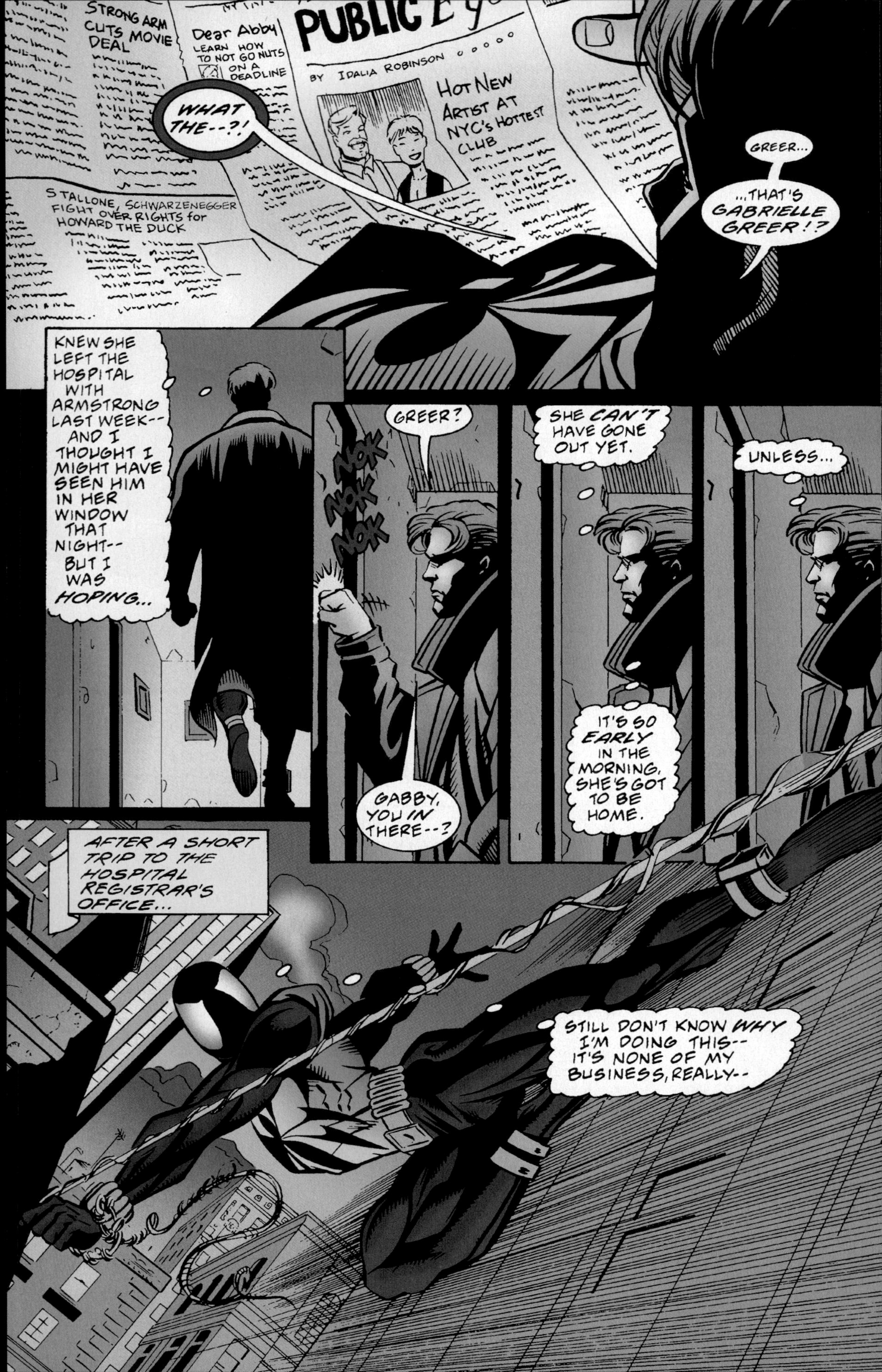
STRONG ARM CUTS MOVIE DEAL
Dear Abby
LEARN HOW TO NOT GO NUTS ON A DEADLINE
PUBLIC
BY IDALIA ROBINSON
HOT NEW ARTIST AT NYC's HOTTEST CLUB
STALLONE, SCHWARZENEGGER FIGHT OVER RIGHTS for HOWARD THE DUCK
WHAT THE--?!
GREER...
...THAT'S GABRIELLE GREER!?
KNEW SHE LEFT THE HOSPITAL WITH ARMSTRONG LAST WEEK-- AND I THOUGHT I MIGHT HAVE SEEN HIM IN HER WINDOW THAT NIGHT-- BUT I WAS HOPING...
GREER?
NOK NOK NOK
GABBY, YOU IN THERE--?
SHE CAN'T HAVE GONE OUT YET.
IT'S SO EARLY IN THE MORNING, SHE'S GOT TO BE HOME.
UNLESS...
AFTER A SHORT TRIP TO THE HOSPITAL REGISTRAR'S OFFICE...
STILL DON'T KNOW WHY I'M DOING THIS-- IT'S NONE OF MY BUSINESS, REALLY--

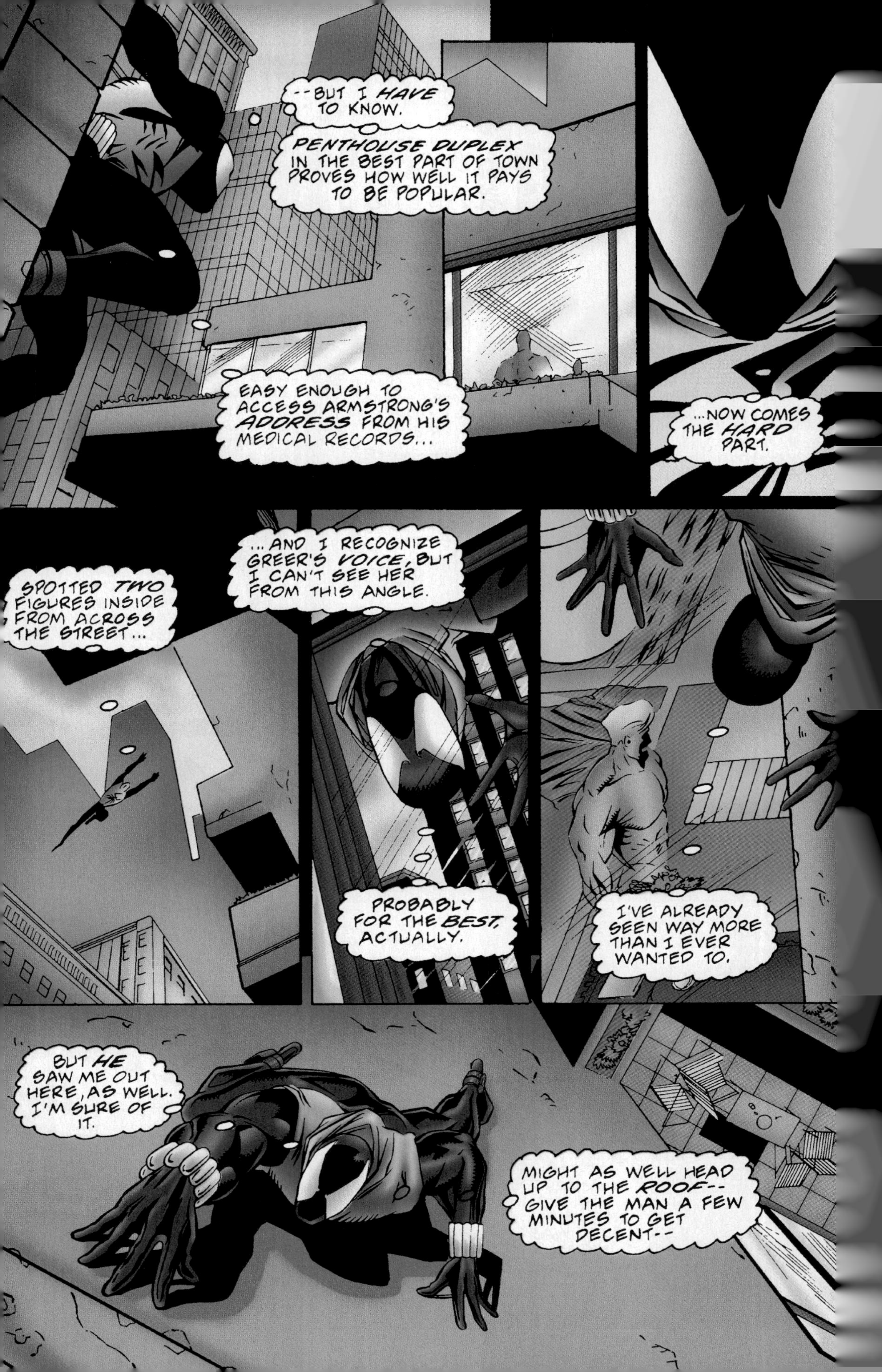
--BUT I HAVE TO KNOW.
PENTHOUSE DUPLEX IN THE BEST PART OF TOWN PROVES HOW WELL IT PAYS TO BE POPULAR.
EASY ENOUGH TO ACCESS ARMSTRONG'S ADDRESS FROM HIS MEDICAL RECORDS...
...NOW COMES THE HARD PART.
SPOTTED TWO FIGURES INSIDE FROM ACROSS THE STREET...
...AND I RECOGNIZE GREER'S VOICE, BUT I CAN'T SEE HER FROM THIS ANGLE.
PROBABLY FOR THE BEST, ACTUALLY.
I'VE ALREADY SEEN WAY MORE THAN I EVER WANTED TO.
BUT HE SAW ME OUT HERE, AS WELL. I'M SURE OF IT.
MIGHT AS WELL HEAD UP TO THE ROOF-- GIVE THE MAN A FEW MINUTES TO GET DECENT--

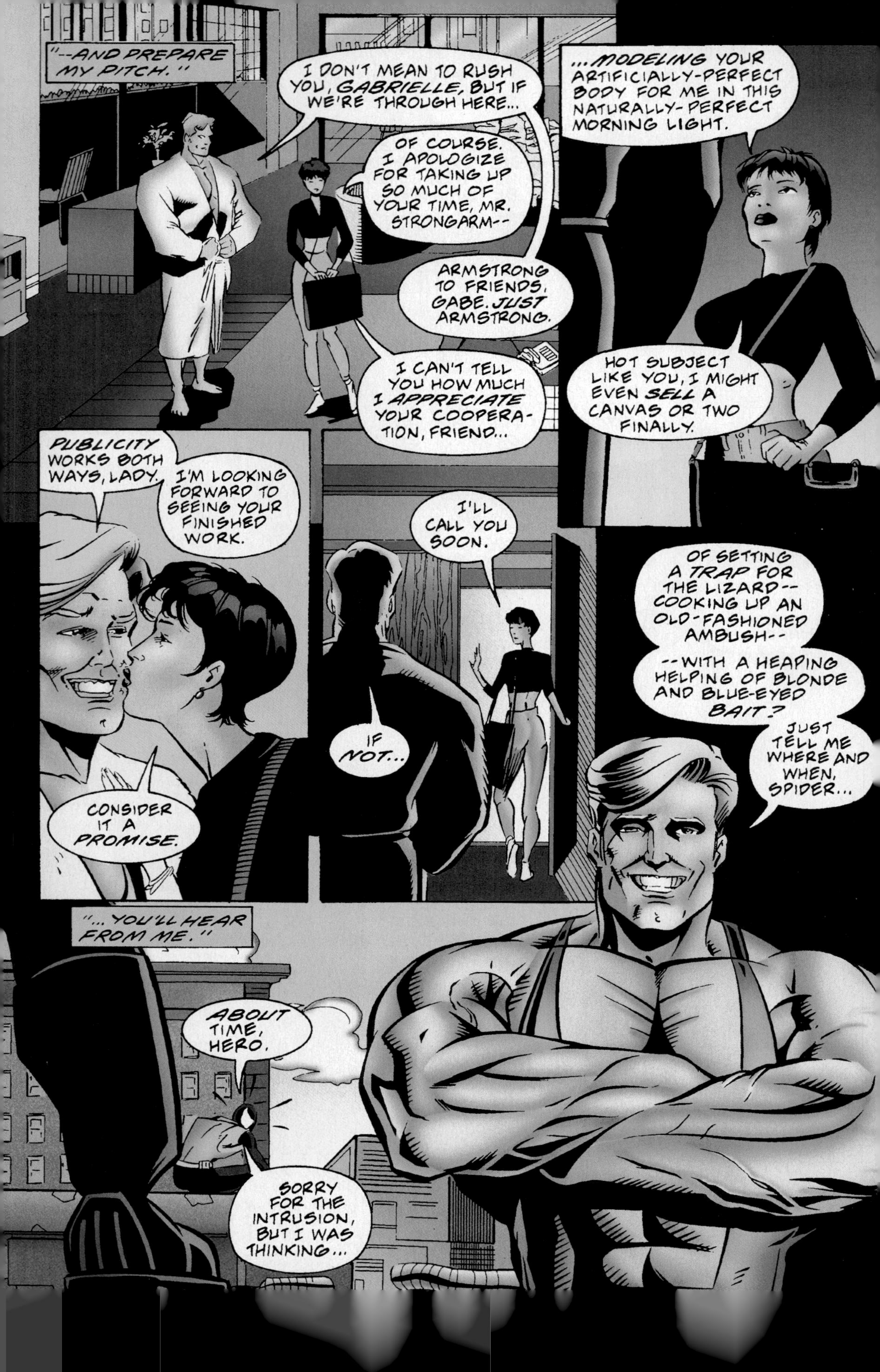
"--AND PREPARE MY PITCH."
I DON'T MEAN TO RUSH YOU, GABRIELLE, BUT IF WE'RE THROUGH HERE...
OF COURSE. I APOLOGIZE FOR TAKING UP SO MUCH OF YOUR TIME, MR. STRONGARM--
ARMSTRONG TO FRIENDS, GABE. JUST ARMSTRONG.
I CAN'T TELL YOU HOW MUCH I APPRECIATE YOUR COOPERATION, FRIEND...
...MODELING YOUR ARTIFICIALLY-PERFECT BODY FOR ME IN THIS NATURALLY-PERFECT MORNING LIGHT.
HOT SUBJECT LIKE YOU, I MIGHT EVEN SELL A CANVAS OR TWO FINALLY.
PUBLICITY WORKS BOTH WAYS, LADY.
I'M LOOKING FORWARD TO SEEING YOUR FINISHED WORK.
CONSIDER IT A PROMISE.
I'LL CALL YOU SOON.
IF NOT...
"...YOU'LL HEAR FROM ME."
ABOUT TIME, HERO.
SORRY FOR THE INTRUSION, BUT I WAS THINKING...
OF SETTING A TRAP FOR THE LIZARD--COOKING UP AN OLD-FASHIONED AMBUSH--
--WITH A HEAPING HELPING OF BLONDE AND BLUE-EYED BAIT?
JUST TELL ME WHERE AND WHEN, SPIDER...

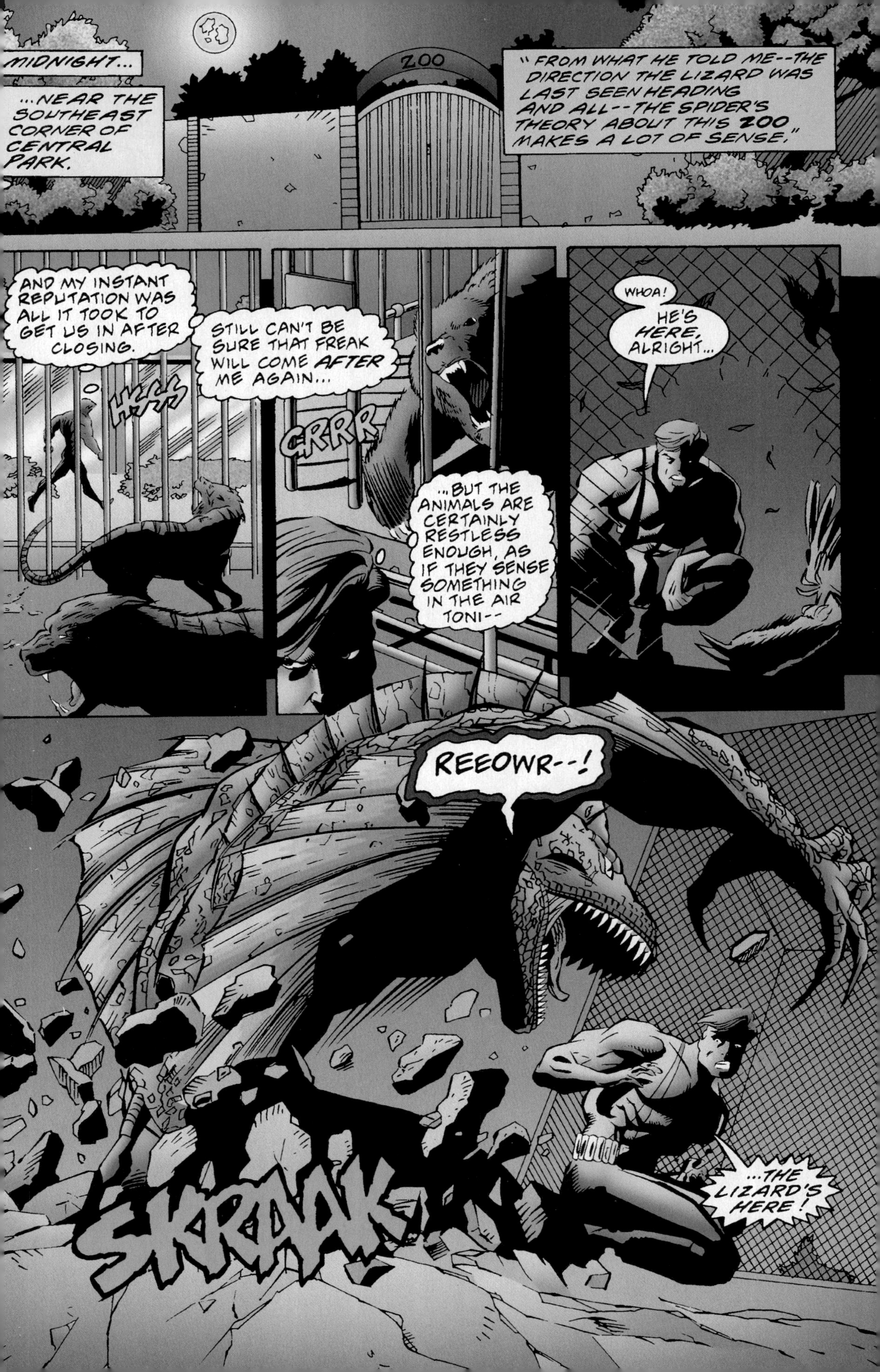
ZOO
MIDNIGHT...
...NEAR THE SOUTHEAST CORNER OF CENTRAL PARK.
"FROM WHAT HE TOLD ME--THE DIRECTION THE LIZARD WAS LAST SEEN HEADING AND ALL--THE SPIDER'S THEORY ABOUT THIS ZOO MAKES A LOT OF SENSE."
AND MY INSTANT REPUTATION WAS ALL IT TOOK TO GET US IN AFTER CLOSING.
HSSS
STILL CAN'T BE SURE THAT FREAK WILL COME AFTER ME AGAIN...
GRRR
...BUT THE ANIMALS ARE CERTAINLY RESTLESS ENOUGH, AS IF THEY SENSE SOMETHING IN THE AIR TONI--
WHOA!
HE'S HERE, ALRIGHT...
REEOWR--!
SKRAAK
...THE LIZARD'S HERE!

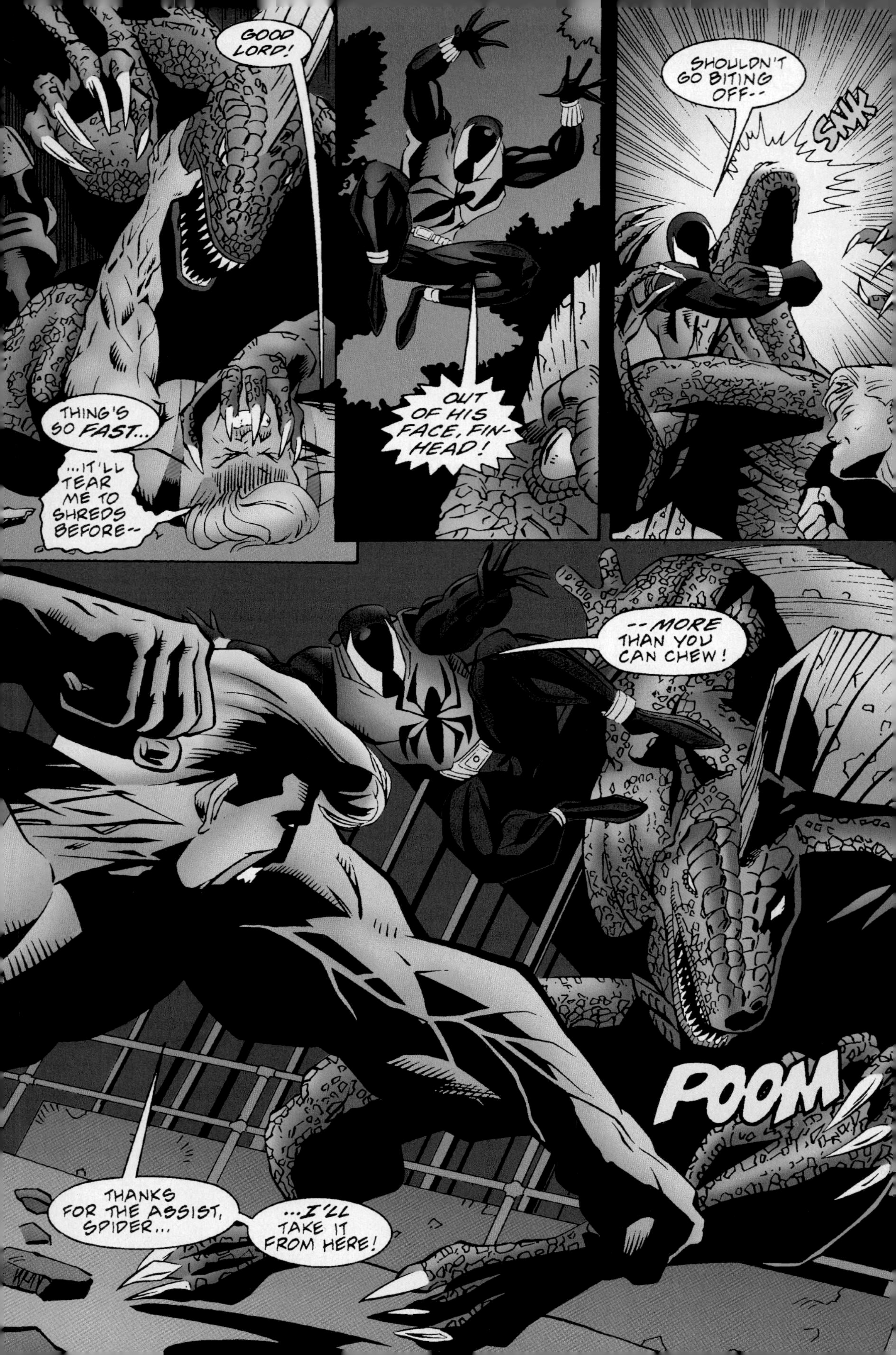
GOOD LORD!
THING'S SO FAST...
...IT'LL TEAR ME TO SHREDS BEFORE--
OUT OF HIS FACE, FIN-HEAD!
SHOULDN'T GO BITING OFF--
SNIK
--MORE THAN YOU CAN CHEW!
POOM
THANKS FOR THE ASSIST, SPIDER...
...I'LL TAKE IT FROM HERE!

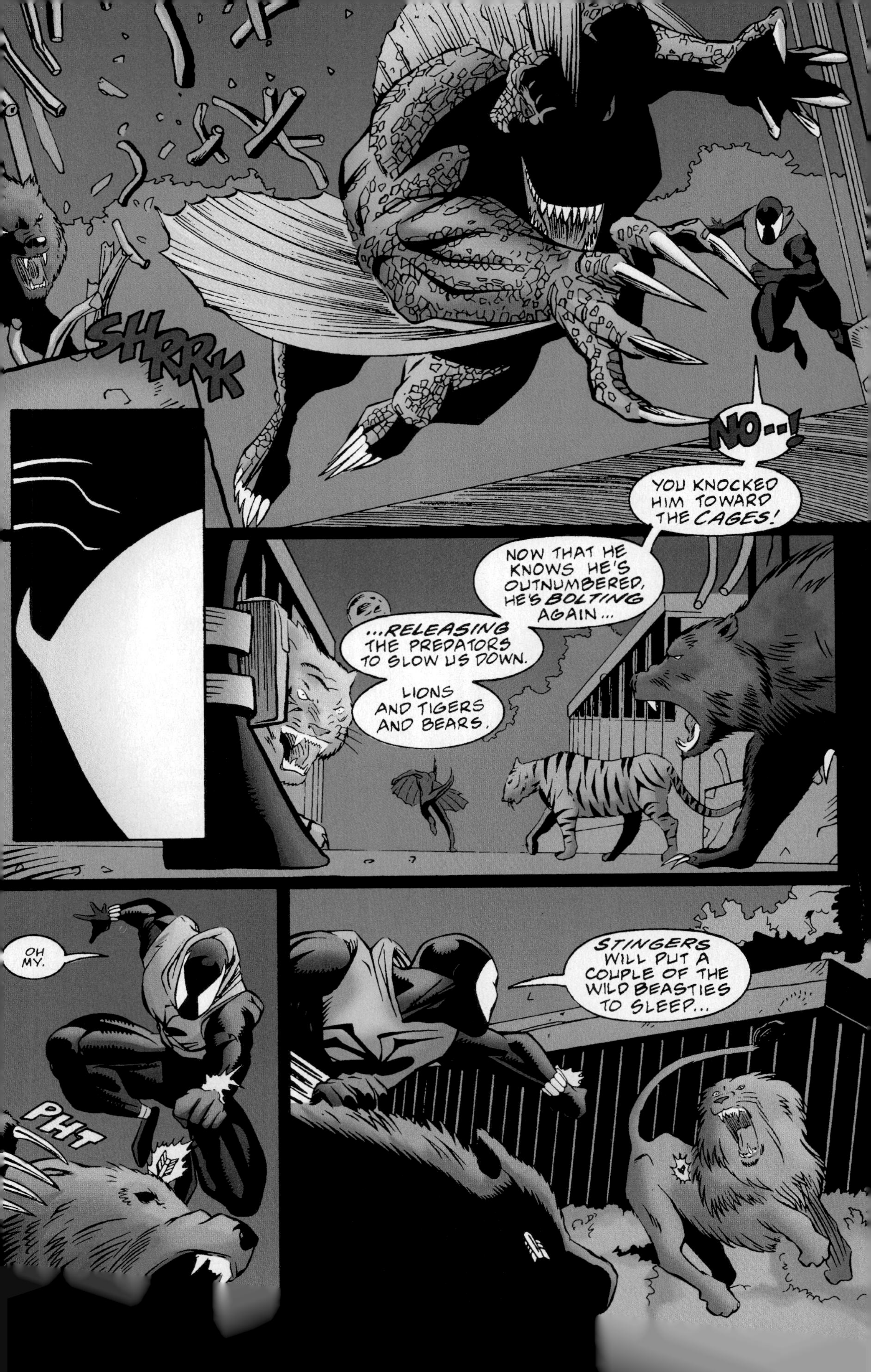
SHRRK
NO--!
YOU KNOCKED HIM TOWARD THE CAGES!
NOW THAT HE KNOWS HE'S OUTNUMBERED, HE'S BOLTING AGAIN...
...RELEASING THE PREDATORS TO SLOW US DOWN.
LIONS AND TIGERS AND BEARS.
OH MY.
PHT
STINGERS WILL PUT A COUPLE OF THE WILD BEASTIES TO SLEEP...

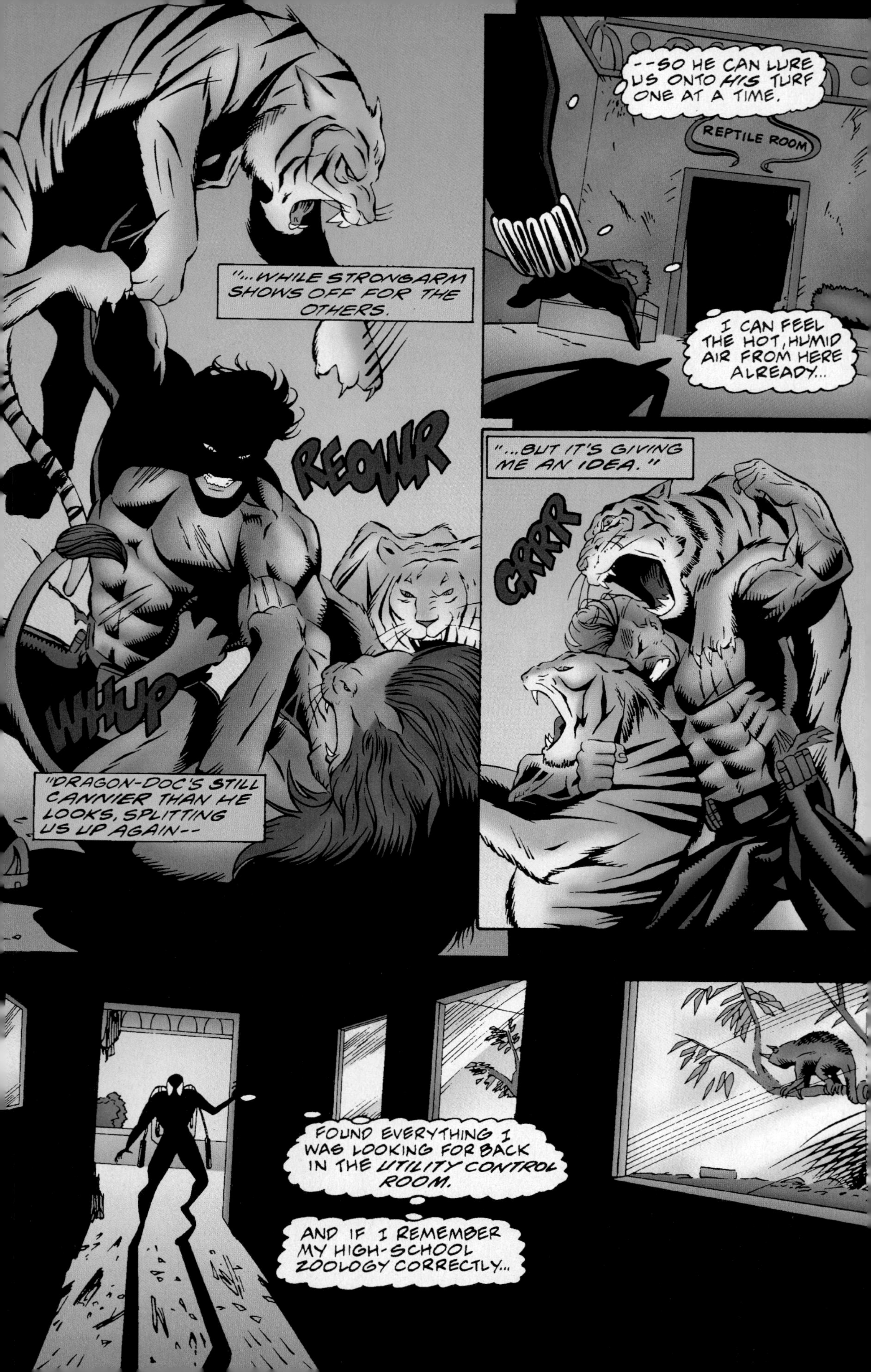
"...WHILE STRONGARM SHOWS OFF FOR THE OTHERS.
REOWR
WHUP
"DRAGON-DOC'S STILL CANNIER THAN HE LOOKS, SPLITTING US UP AGAIN--
--SO HE CAN LURE US ONTO HIS TURF ONE AT A TIME.
REPTILE ROOM
I CAN FEEL THE HOT, HUMID AIR FROM HERE ALREADY...
"...BUT IT'S GIVING ME AN IDEA."
GRRR
FOUND EVERYTHING I WAS LOOKING FOR BACK IN THE UTILITY CONTROL ROOM.
AND IF I REMEMBER MY HIGH-SCHOOL ZOOLOGY CORRECTLY...

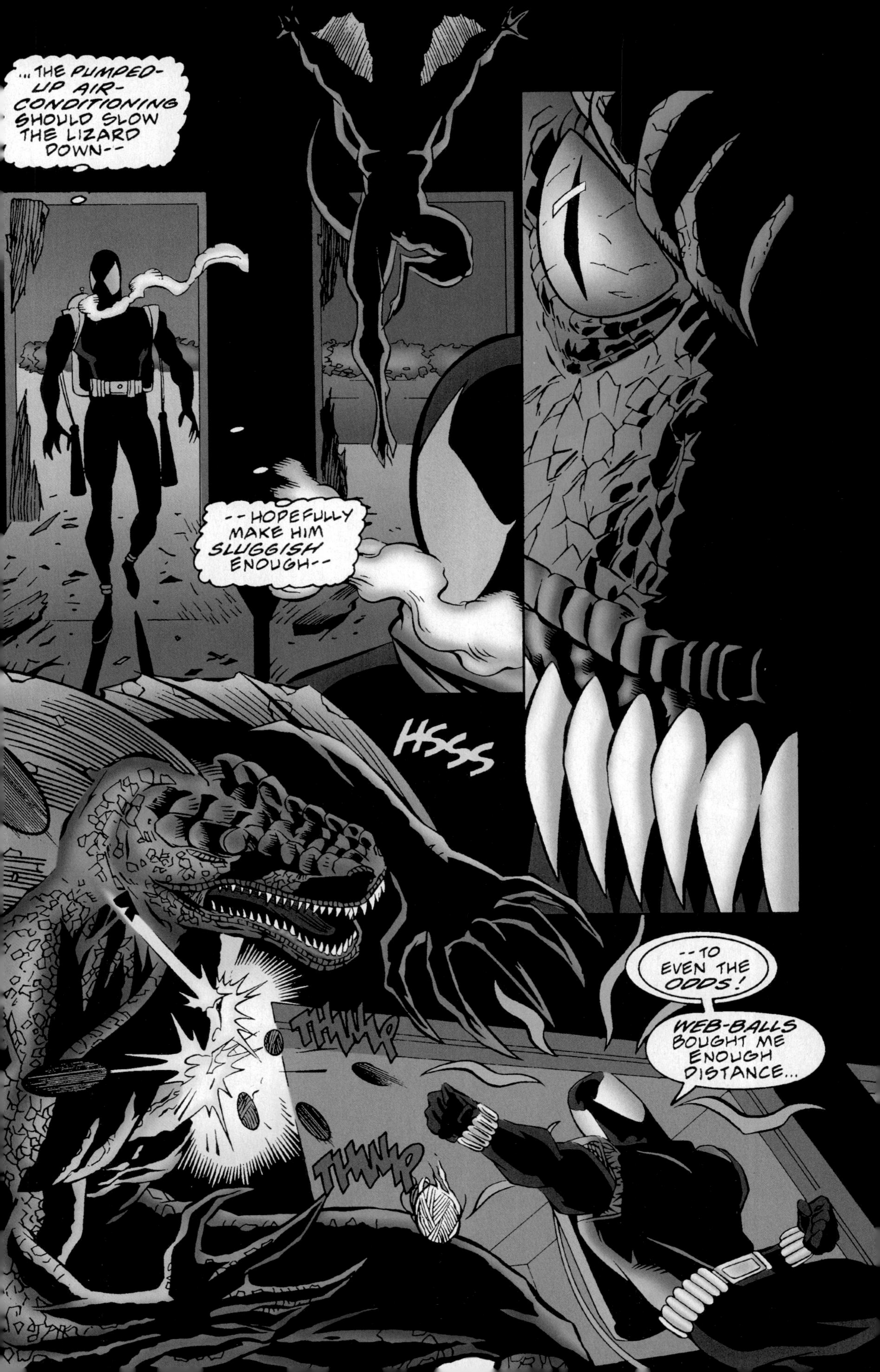
...THE PUMPED-UP AIR-CONDITIONING SHOULD SLOW THE LIZARD DOWN--
--HOPEFULLY MAKE HIM SLUGGISH ENOUGH--
HSSSS
--TO EVEN THE ODDS!
WEB-BALLS BOUGHT ME ENOUGH DISTANCE...
THWP
THWP

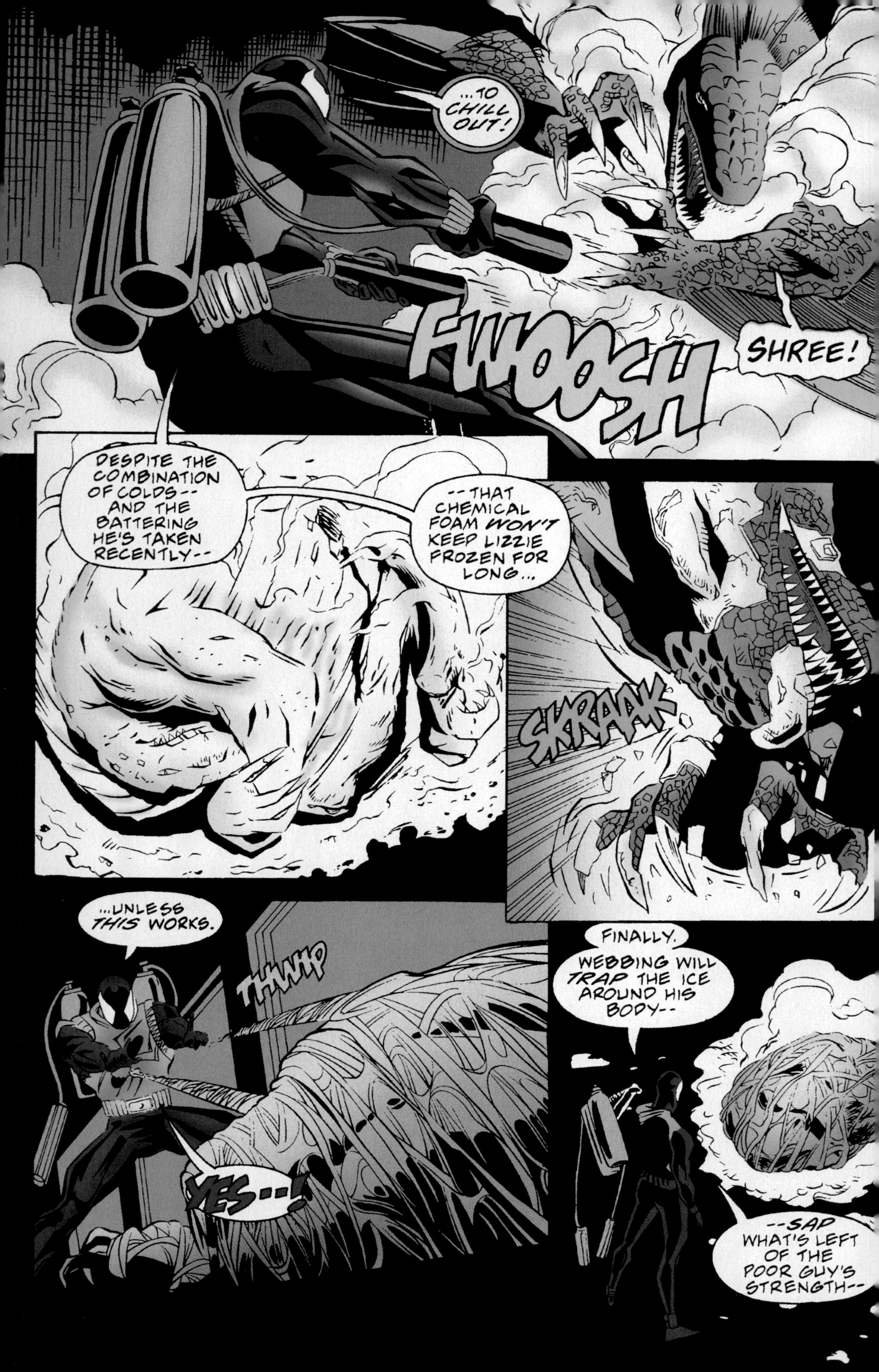
...TO CHILL OUT!
FWOOSH
SHREE!
DESPITE THE COMBINATION OF COLDS-- AND THE BATTERING HE'S TAKEN RECENTLY--
--THAT CHEMICAL FOAM WON'T KEEP LIZZIE FROZEN FOR LONG...
SKRAAK
...UNLESS THIS WORKS.
THWHP
YES--!
FINALLY.
WEBBING WILL TRAP THE ICE AROUND HIS BODY--
--SAP WHAT'S LEFT OF THE POOR GUY'S STRENGTH--

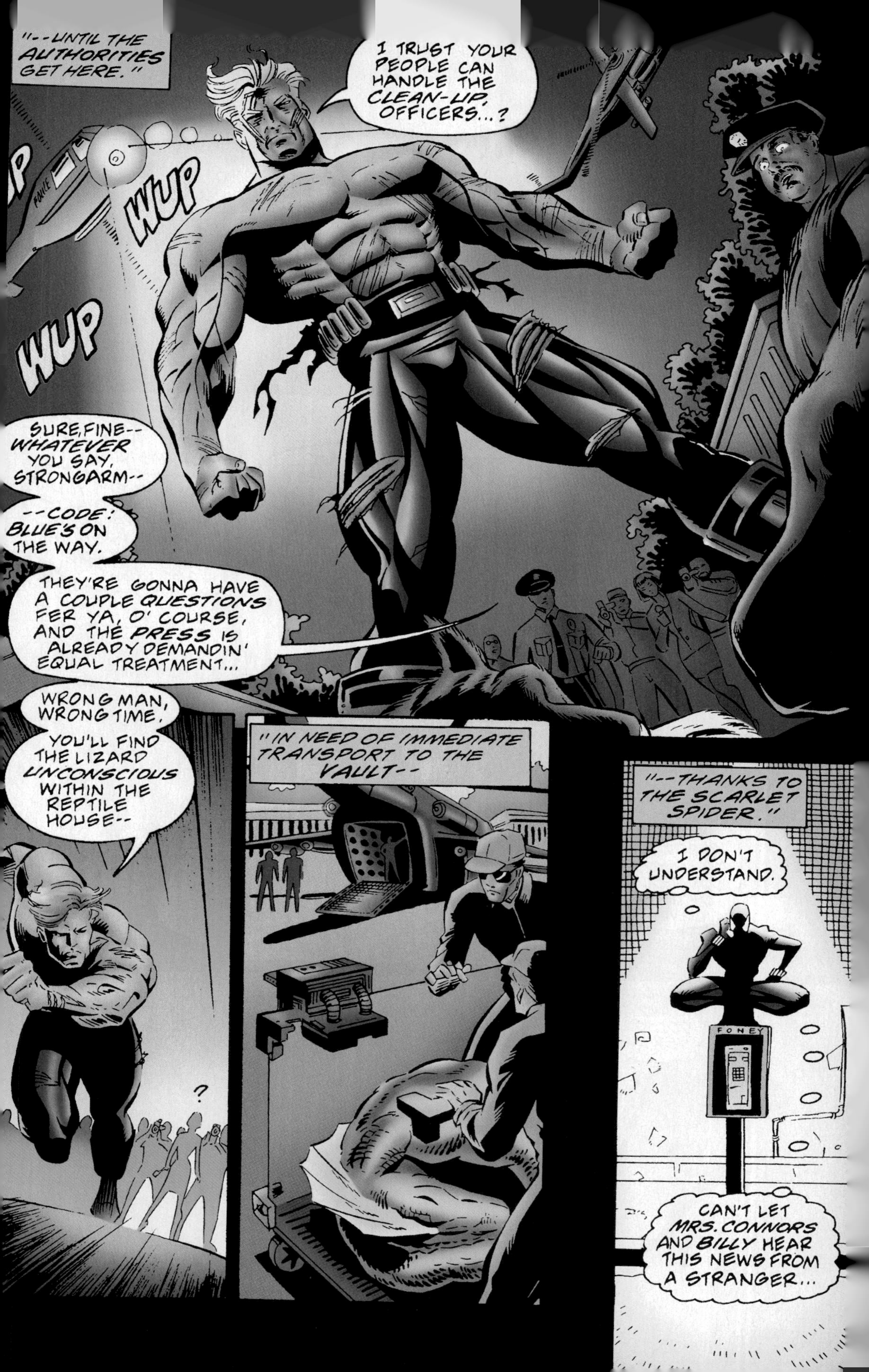
"--UNTIL THE AUTHORITIES GET HERE."
I TRUST YOUR PEOPLE CAN HANDLE THE CLEAN-UP, OFFICERS...?
WUP
WUP
SURE, FINE-- WHATEVER YOU SAY, STRONGARM--
--CODE: BLUE'S ON THE WAY.
THEY'RE GONNA HAVE A COUPLE QUESTIONS FER YA, O' COURSE, AND THE PRESS IS ALREADY DEMANDIN' EQUAL TREATMENT...
WRONG MAN, WRONG TIME.
YOU'LL FIND THE LIZARD UNCONSCIOUS WITHIN THE REPTILE HOUSE--
?
"IN NEED OF IMMEDIATE TRANSPORT TO THE VAULT--
"--THANKS TO THE SCARLET SPIDER."
I DON'T UNDERSTAND.
FONEY
CAN'T LET MRS. CONNORS AND BILLY HEAR THIS NEWS FROM A STRANGER...

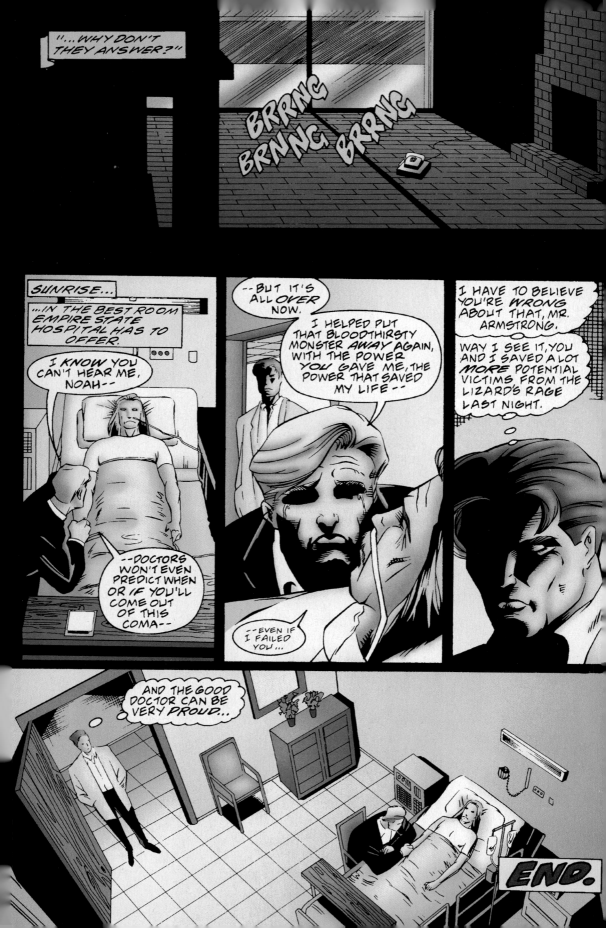

"...WHY DON'T THEY ANSWER?"

BRRNG BRRNG BRRNG

SUNRISE...

...IN THE BEST ROOM EMPIRE STATE HOSPITAL HAS TO OFFER.

I KNOW YOU CAN'T HEAR ME, NOAH--

--DOCTORS WON'T EVEN PREDICT WHEN OR IF YOU'LL COME OUT OF THIS COMA--

--BUT IT'S ALL OVER NOW.

I HELPED PUT THAT BLOODTHIRSTY MONSTER AWAY AGAIN, WITH THE POWER YOU GAVE ME, THE POWER THAT SAVED MY LIFE --

--EVEN IF I FAILED YOU...

I HAVE TO BELIEVE YOU'RE WRONG ABOUT THAT, MR. ARMSTRONG.

WAY I SEE IT, YOU AND I SAVED A LOT MORE POTENTIAL VICTIMS FROM THE LIZARD'S RAGE LAST NIGHT.

AND THE GOOD DOCTOR CAN BE VERY PROUD...

END.

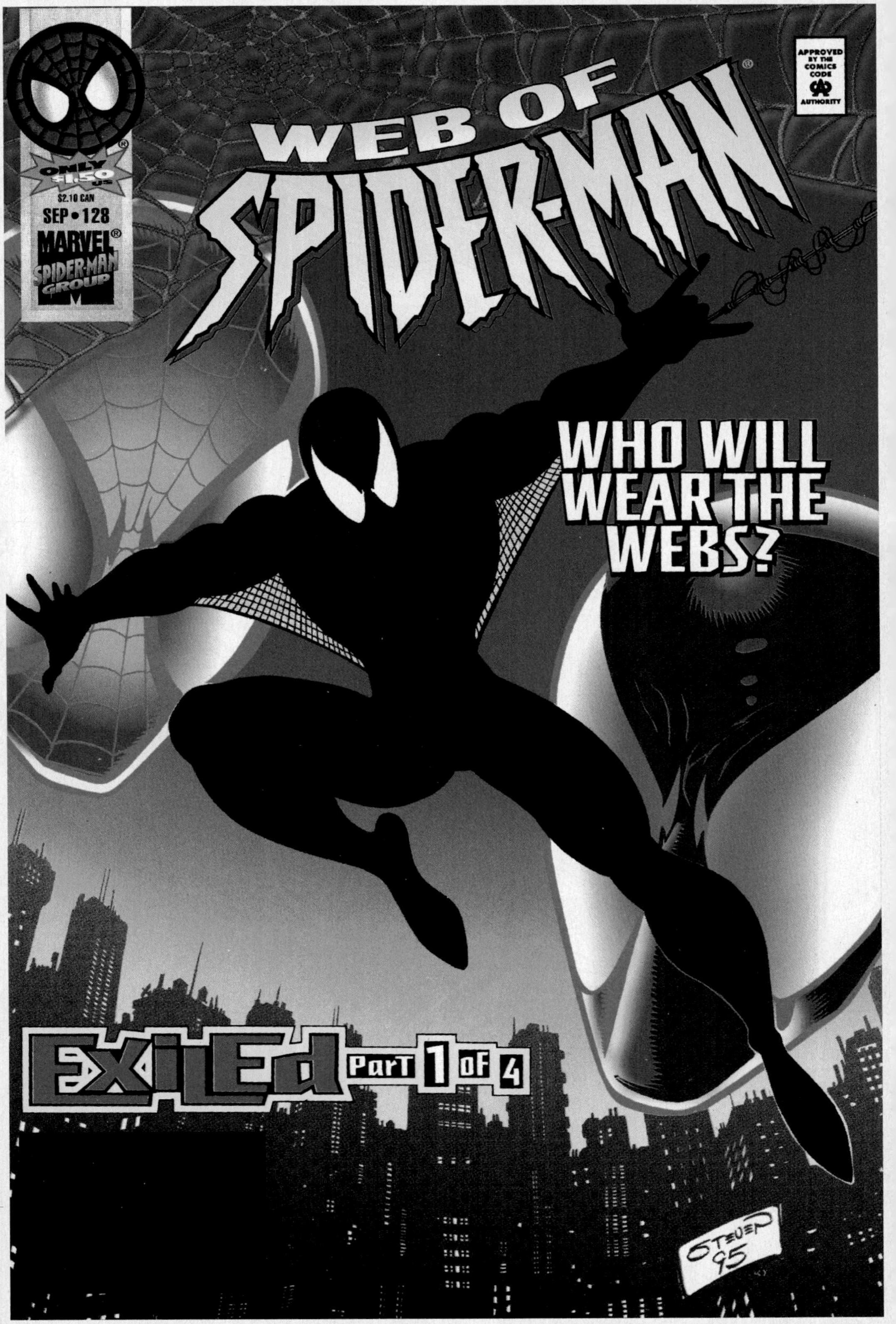

ONLY $1.50 US
$2.10 CAN
SEP • 128
MARVEL
SPIDER-MAN GROUP
APPROVED BY THE COMICS CODE AUTHORITY
WEB OF SPIDER-MAN
WHO WILL WEAR THE WEBS?
EXILED PART 1 OF 4

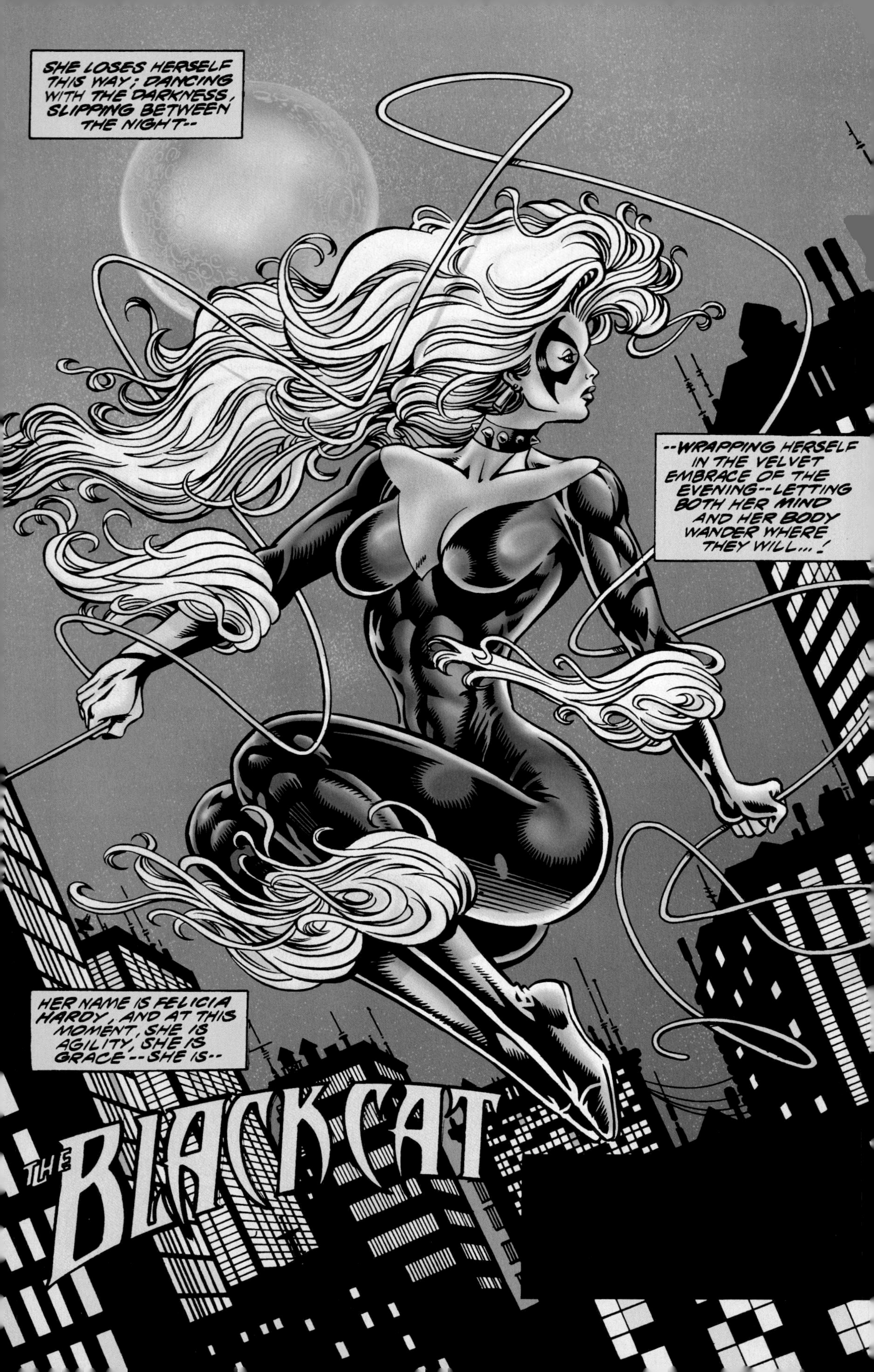
SHE LOSES HERSELF THIS WAY; DANCING WITH THE DARKNESS, SLIPPING BETWEEN THE NIGHT--
--WRAPPING HERSELF IN THE VELVET EMBRACE OF THE EVENING--LETTING BOTH HER MIND AND HER BODY WANDER WHERE THEY WILL...!
HER NAME IS FELICIA HARDY, AND AT THIS MOMENT, SHE IS AGILITY, SHE IS GRACE--SHE IS--
THE BLACK CAT

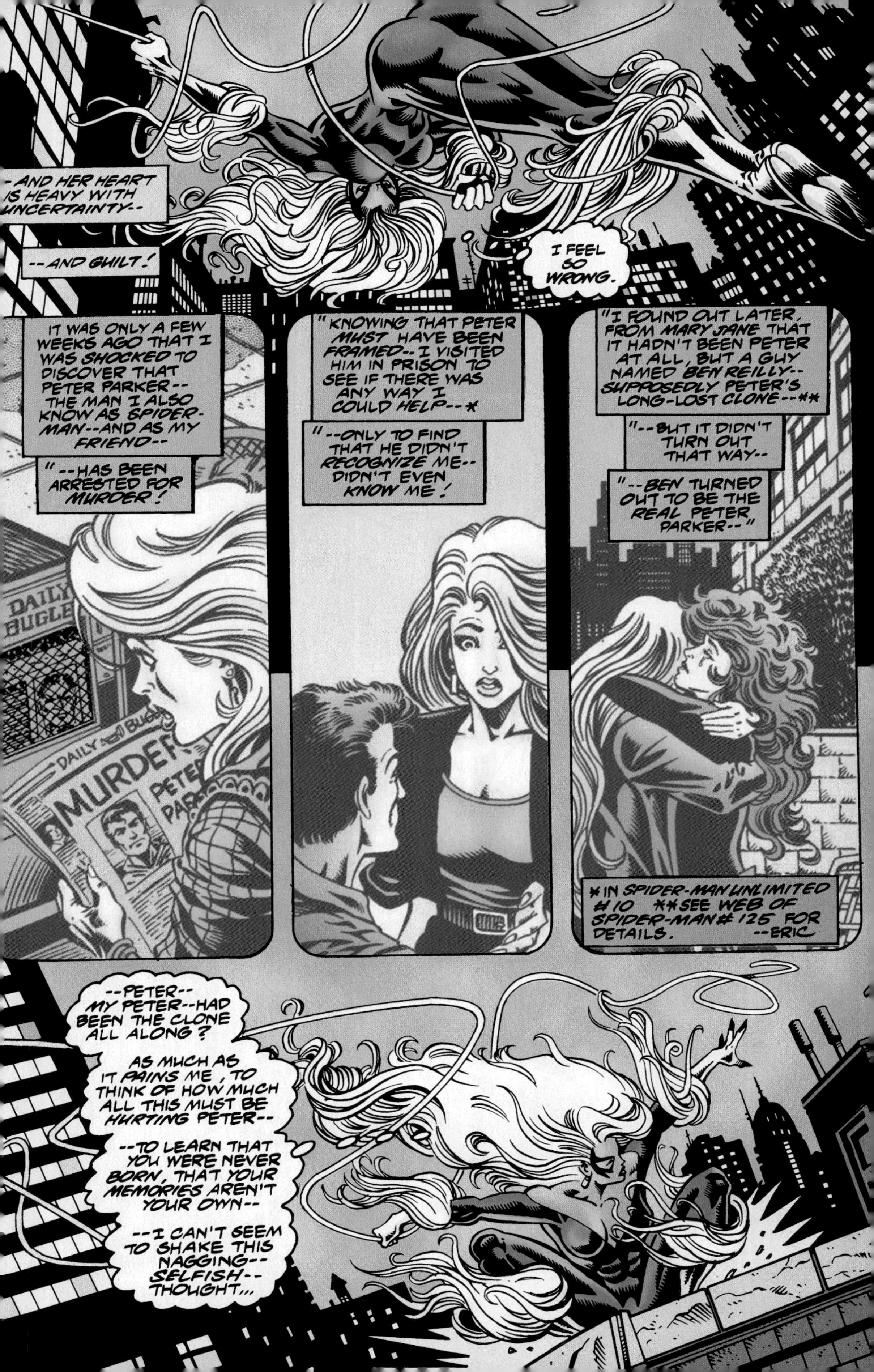

--AND HER HEART IS HEAVY WITH UNCERTAINTY--
--AND GUILT!
I FEEL SO WRONG.
IT WAS ONLY A FEW WEEKS AGO THAT I WAS SHOCKED TO DISCOVER THAT PETER PARKER--THE MAN I ALSO KNOW AS SPIDER-MAN--AND AS MY FRIEND--
"--HAS BEEN ARRESTED FOR MURDER!
DAILY BUGLE
DAILY BUGLE
MURDER
PETER PARKER
"KNOWING THAT PETER MUST HAVE BEEN FRAMED--I VISITED HIM IN PRISON TO SEE IF THERE WAS ANY WAY I COULD HELP--*
"--ONLY TO FIND THAT HE DIDN'T RECOGNIZE ME--DIDN'T EVEN KNOW ME!
"I FOUND OUT LATER, FROM MARY JANE THAT IT HADN'T BEEN PETER AT ALL, BUT A GUY NAMED BEN REILLY--SUPPOSEDLY PETER'S LONG-LOST CLONE--**
"--BUT IT DIDN'T TURN OUT THAT WAY--
"--BEN TURNED OUT TO BE THE REAL PETER PARKER--"
*IN SPIDER-MAN UNLIMITED #10 **SEE WEB OF SPIDER-MAN #125 FOR DETAILS. --ERIC
--PETER--MY PETER--HAD BEEN THE CLONE ALL ALONG?
AS MUCH AS IT PAINS ME, TO THINK OF HOW MUCH ALL THIS MUST BE HURTING PETER--
--TO LEARN THAT YOU WERE NEVER BORN, THAT YOUR MEMORIES AREN'T YOUR OWN--
--I CAN'T SEEM TO SHAKE THIS NAGGING--SELFISH--THOUGHT...

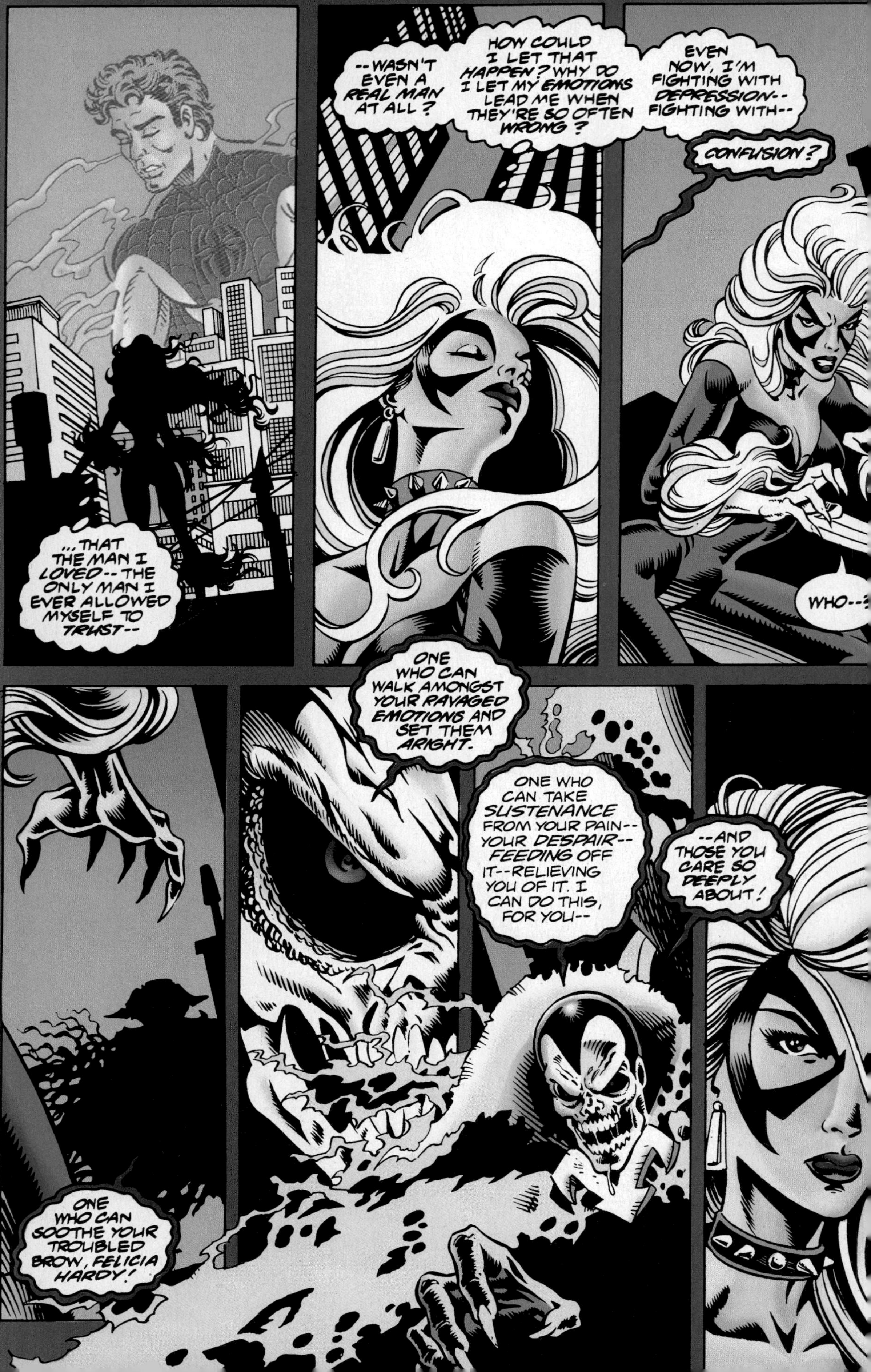
...THAT THE MAN I LOVED-- THE ONLY MAN I EVER ALLOWED MYSELF TO TRUST--
--WASN'T EVEN A REAL MAN AT ALL?
HOW COULD I LET THAT HAPPEN? WHY DO I LET MY EMOTIONS LEAD ME WHEN THEY'RE SO OFTEN WRONG?
EVEN NOW, I'M FIGHTING WITH DEPRESSION-- FIGHTING WITH--
CONFUSION?
WHO--?
ONE WHO CAN SOOTHE THE YOUR TROUBLED BROW, FELICIA HARDY!
ONE WHO CAN WALK AMONGST YOUR RAVAGED EMOTIONS AND SET THEM ARIGHT.
ONE WHO CAN TAKE SUSTENANCE FROM YOUR PAIN-- YOUR DESPAIR-- FEEDING OFF IT--RELIEVING YOU OF IT. I CAN DO THIS, FOR YOU--
--AND THOSE YOU CARE SO DEEPLY ABOUT!

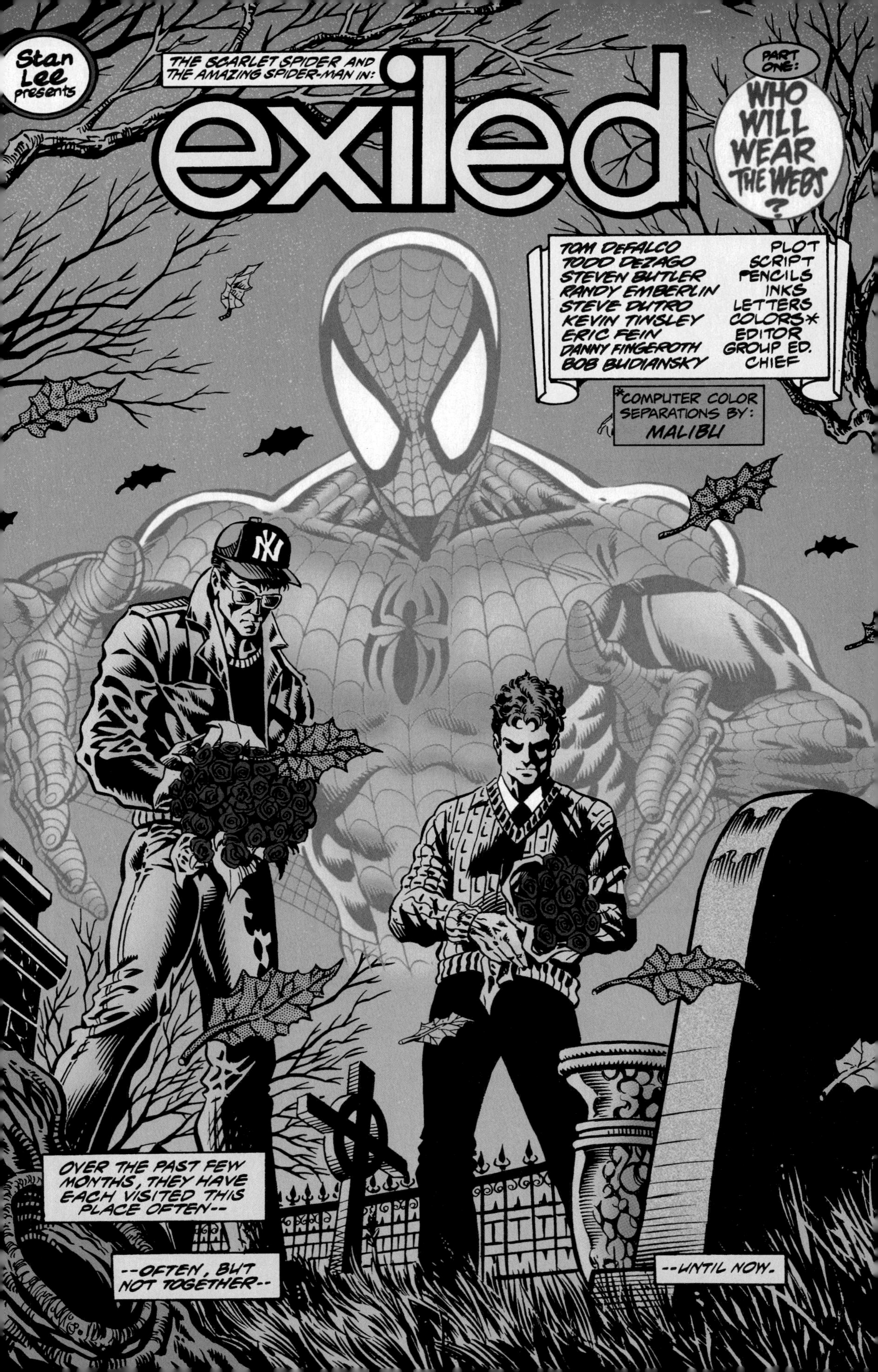
Stan Lee presents
THE SCARLET SPIDER AND THE AMAZING SPIDER-MAN IN:
exiled
PART ONE:
WHO WILL WEAR THE WEBS?
TOM DEFALCO PLOT
TODD DEZAGO SCRIPT
STEVEN BUTLER PENCILS
RANDY EMBERLIN INKS
STEVE DUTRO LETTERS
KEVIN TINSLEY COLORS*
ERIC FEIN EDITOR
DANNY FINGEROTH GROUP ED.
BOB BUDIANSKY CHIEF
*COMPUTER COLOR SEPARATIONS BY: MALIBU
OVER THE PAST FEW MONTHS, THEY HAVE EACH VISITED THIS PLACE OFTEN--
--OFTEN, BUT NOT TOGETHER--
--UNTIL NOW.

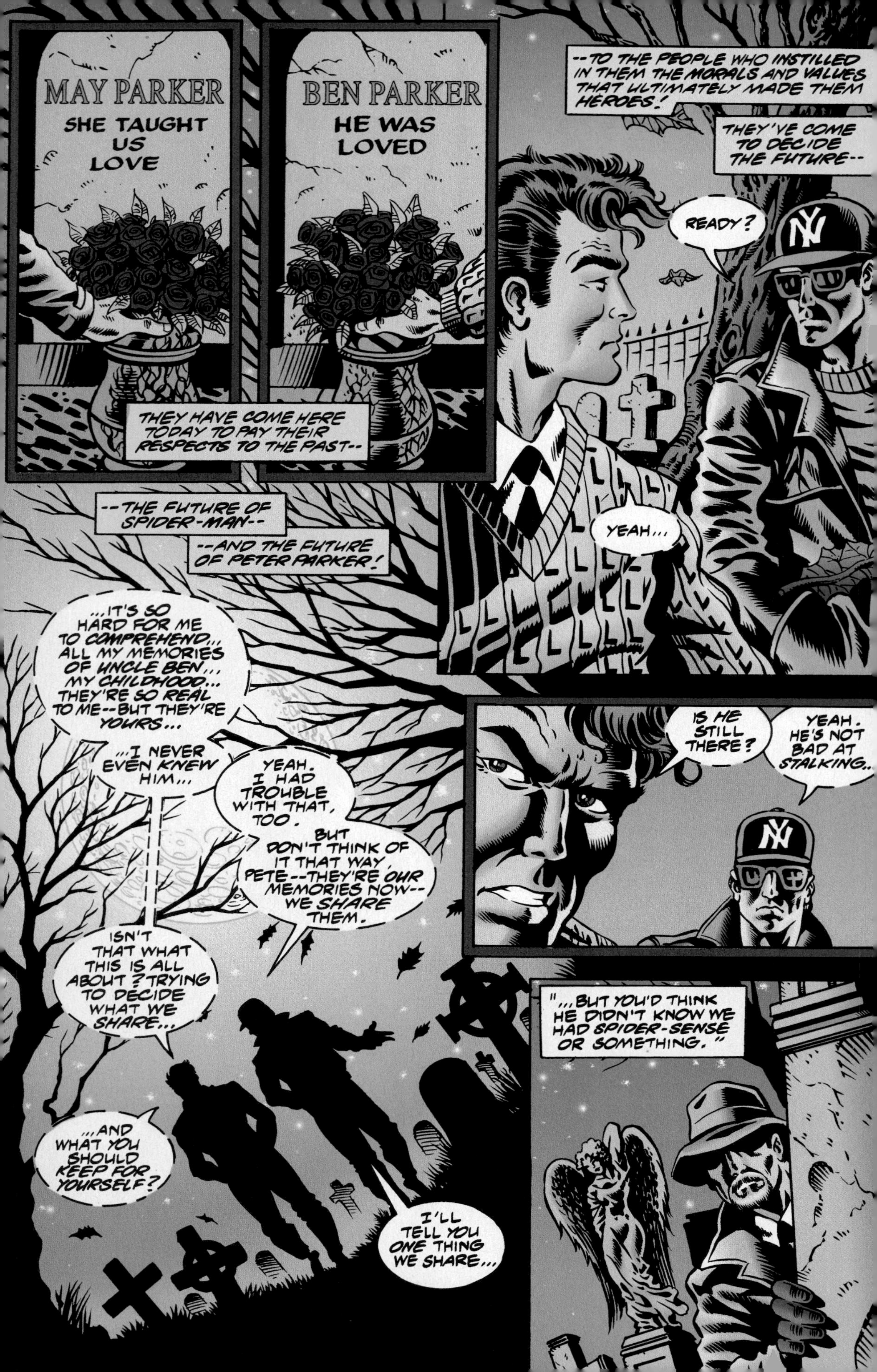
MAY PARKER
SHE TAUGHT US LOVE
BEN PARKER
HE WAS LOVED
THEY HAVE COME HERE TODAY TO PAY THEIR RESPECTS TO THE PAST--
--TO THE PEOPLE WHO INSTILLED IN THEM THE MORALS AND VALUES THAT ULTIMATELY MADE THEM HEROES!
THEY'VE COME TO DECIDE THE FUTURE--
READY?
YEAH...
--THE FUTURE OF SPIDER-MAN--
--AND THE FUTURE OF PETER PARKER!
...IT'S SO HARD FOR ME TO COMPREHEND... ALL MY MEMORIES OF UNCLE BEN... MY CHILDHOOD... THEY'RE SO REAL TO ME--BUT THEY'RE YOURS...
...I NEVER EVEN KNEW HIM...
YEAH. I HAD TROUBLE WITH THAT, TOO.
BUT DON'T THINK OF IT THAT WAY, PETE--THEY'RE OUR MEMORIES NOW--WE SHARE THEM.
ISN'T THAT WHAT THIS IS ALL ABOUT? TRYING TO DECIDE WHAT WE SHARE...
...AND WHAT YOU SHOULD KEEP FOR YOURSELF?
I'LL TELL YOU ONE THING WE SHARE...
IS HE STILL THERE?
YEAH. HE'S NOT BAD AT STALKING..
"...BUT YOU'D THINK HE DIDN'T KNOW WE HAD SPIDER-SENSE OR SOMETHING."

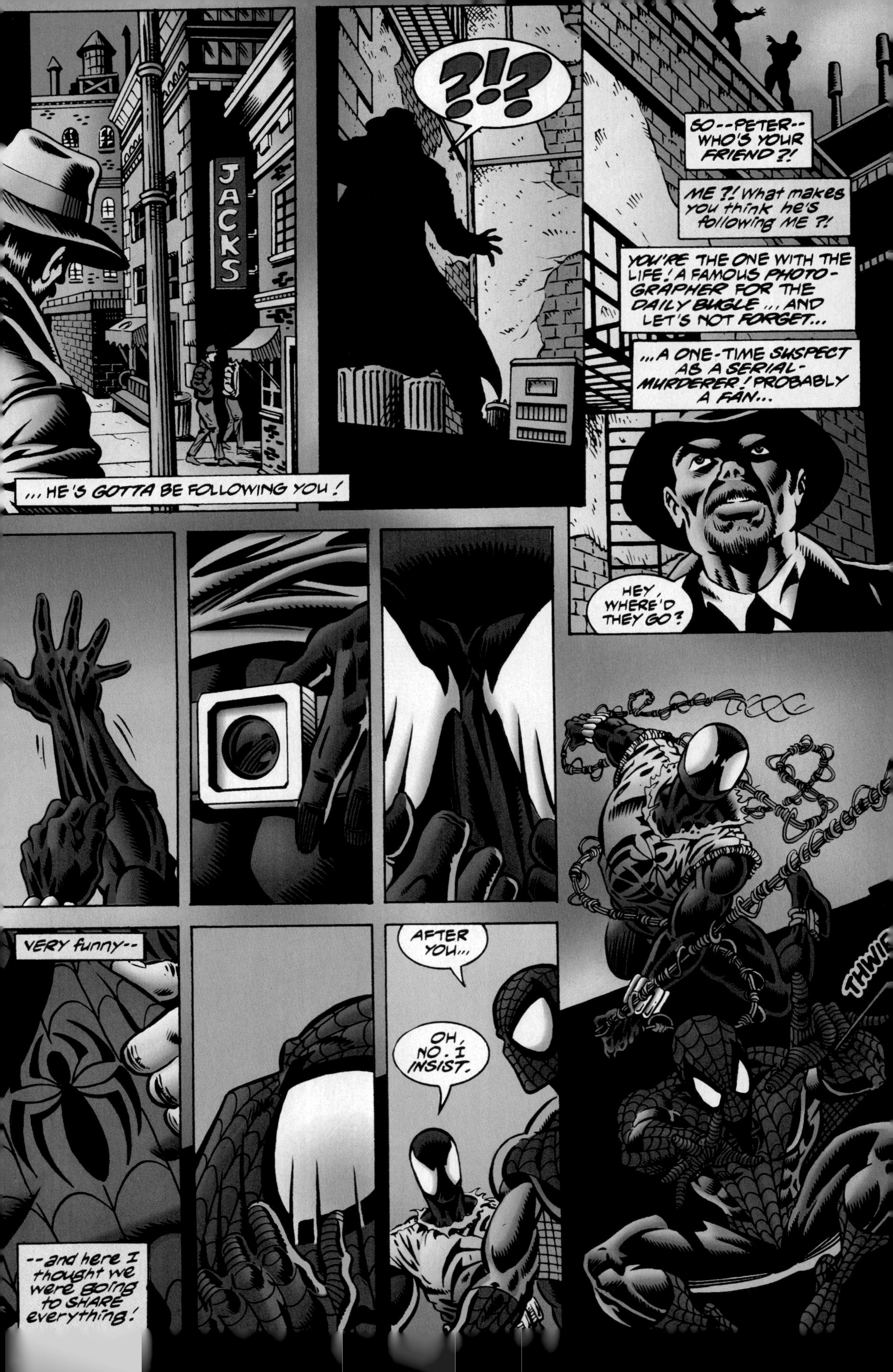

...HE'S GOTTA BE FOLLOWING YOU!
?!?
SO--PETER--WHO'S YOUR FRIEND?!
ME?! What makes you think he's following ME?!
YOU'RE THE ONE WITH THE LIFE! A FAMOUS PHOTOGRAPHER FOR THE DAILY BUGLE... AND LET'S NOT FORGET...
...A ONE-TIME SUSPECT AS A SERIAL-MURDERER! PROBABLY A FAN...
HEY, WHERE'D THEY GO?
VERY funny--
--and here I thought we were going to SHARE everything!
AFTER YOU...
OH, NO. I INSIST.

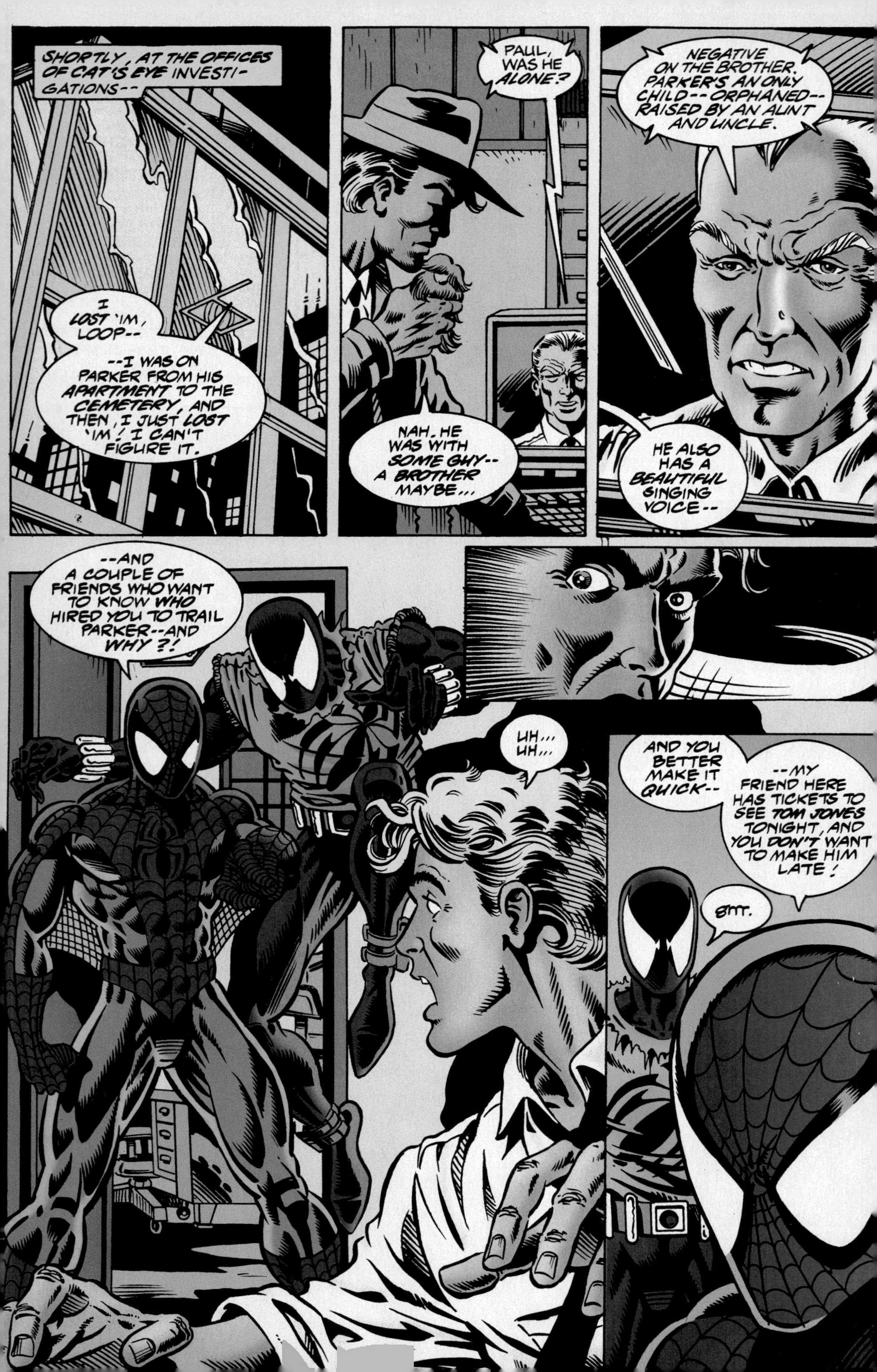
SHORTLY, AT THE OFFICES OF CAT'S EYE INVESTIGATIONS--
I LOST 'IM, LOOP--
--I WAS ON PARKER FROM HIS APARTMENT TO THE CEMETERY, AND THEN, I JUST LOST 'IM! I CAN'T FIGURE IT.
PAUL, WAS HE ALONE?
NAH. HE WAS WITH SOME GUY-- A BROTHER MAYBE...
NEGATIVE ON THE BROTHER. PARKER'S AN ONLY CHILD--ORPHANED--RAISED BY AN AUNT AND UNCLE.
HE ALSO HAS A BEAUTIFUL SINGING VOICE--
--AND A COUPLE OF FRIENDS WHO WANT TO KNOW WHO HIRED YOU TO TRAIL PARKER--AND WHY?!
UH... UH...
AND YOU BETTER MAKE IT QUICK--
--MY FRIEND HERE HAS TICKETS TO SEE TOM JONES TONIGHT, AND YOU DON'T WANT TO MAKE HIM LATE!
SNRT.

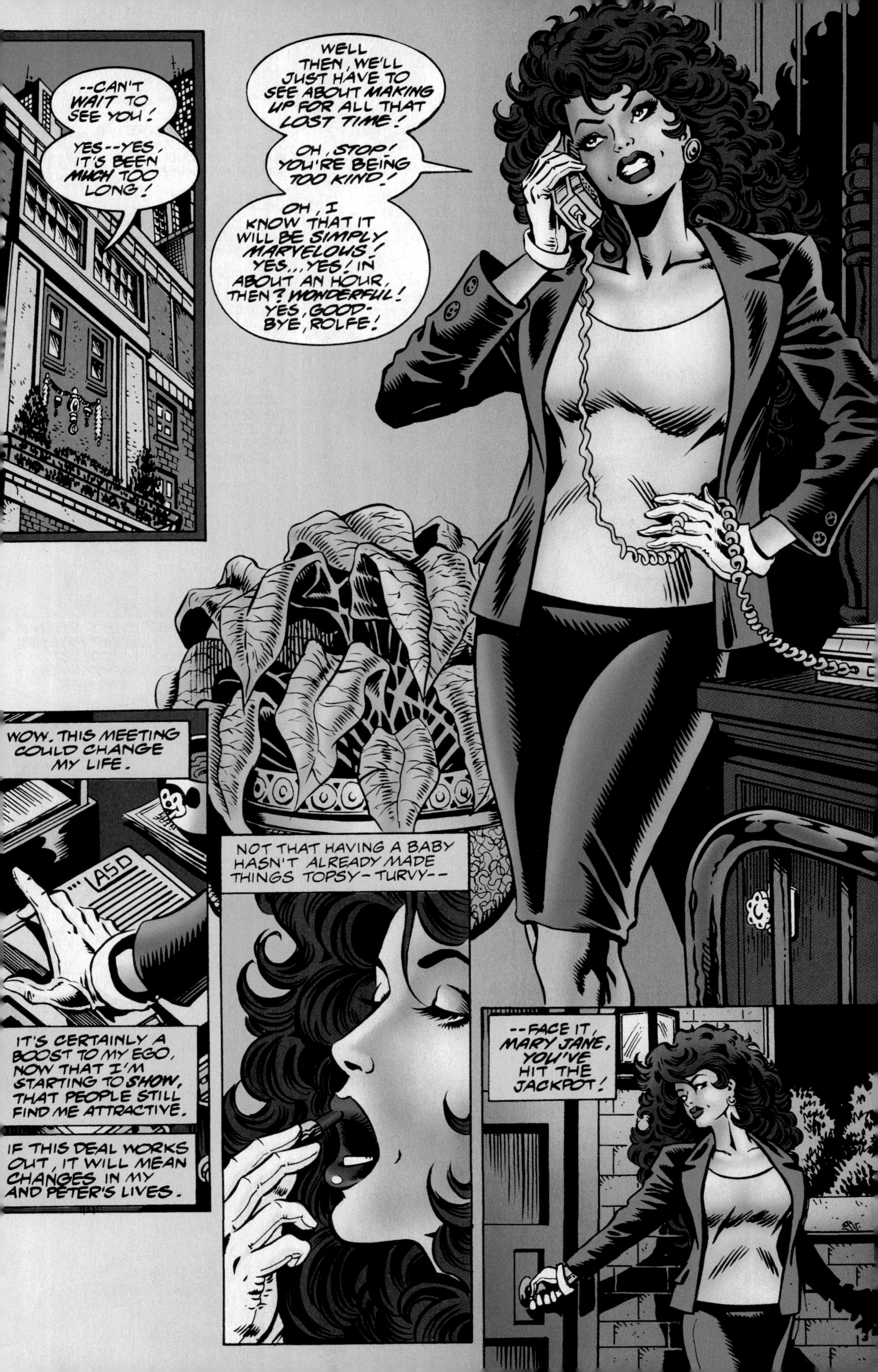

--CAN'T WAIT TO SEE YOU!
YES--YES, IT'S BEEN MUCH TOO LONG!
WELL THEN, WE'LL JUST HAVE TO SEE ABOUT MAKING UP FOR ALL THAT LOST TIME!
OH, STOP! YOU'RE BEING TOO KIND!
OH, I KNOW THAT IT WILL BE SIMPLY MARVELOUS! YES... YES! IN ABOUT AN HOUR, THEN? WONDERFUL! YES, GOOD-BYE, ROLFE!
WOW. THIS MEETING COULD CHANGE MY LIFE.
IT'S CERTAINLY A BOOST TO MY EGO, NOW THAT I'M STARTING TO SHOW, THAT PEOPLE STILL FIND ME ATTRACTIVE.
IF THIS DEAL WORKS OUT, IT WILL MEAN CHANGES IN MY AND PETER'S LIVES.
NOT THAT HAVING A BABY HASN'T ALREADY MADE THINGS TOPSY-TURVY--
--FACE IT, MARY JANE, YOU'VE HIT THE JACKPOT!

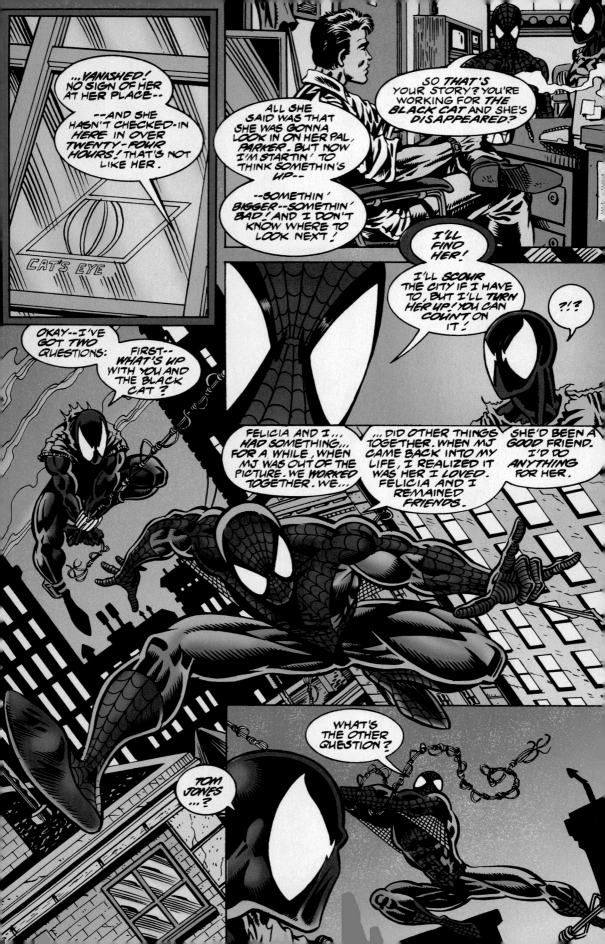

...VANISHED! NO SIGN OF HER AT HER PLACE--

--AND SHE HASN'T CHECKED-IN HERE IN OVER TWENTY-FOUR HOURS! THAT'S NOT LIKE HER.

CAT'S EYE

ALL SHE SAID WAS THAT SHE WAS GONNA LOOK IN ON HER PAL, PARKER. BUT NOW I'M STARTIN' TO THINK SOMETHIN'S UP--

--SOMETHIN' BIGGER--SOMETHIN' BAD! AND I DON'T KNOW WHERE TO LOOK NEXT!

SO THAT'S YOUR STORY? YOU'RE WORKING FOR THE BLACK CAT AND SHE'S DISAPPEARED?

I'LL FIND HER!

I'LL SCOUR THE CITY IF I HAVE TO, BUT I'LL TURN HER UP! YOU CAN COUNT ON IT!

?!?

OKAY--I'VE GOT TWO QUESTIONS: FIRST-- WHAT'S UP WITH YOU AND THE BLACK CAT?

FELICIA AND I... HAD SOMETHING... FOR A WHILE, WHEN MJ WAS OUT OF THE PICTURE. WE WORKED TOGETHER. WE...

...DID OTHER THINGS TOGETHER. WHEN MJ CAME BACK INTO MY LIFE, I REALIZED IT WAS HER I LOVED. FELICIA AND I REMAINED FRIENDS.

SHE'D BEEN A GOOD FRIEND. I'D DO ANYTHING FOR HER.

WHAT'S THE OTHER QUESTION?

TOM JONES ...?

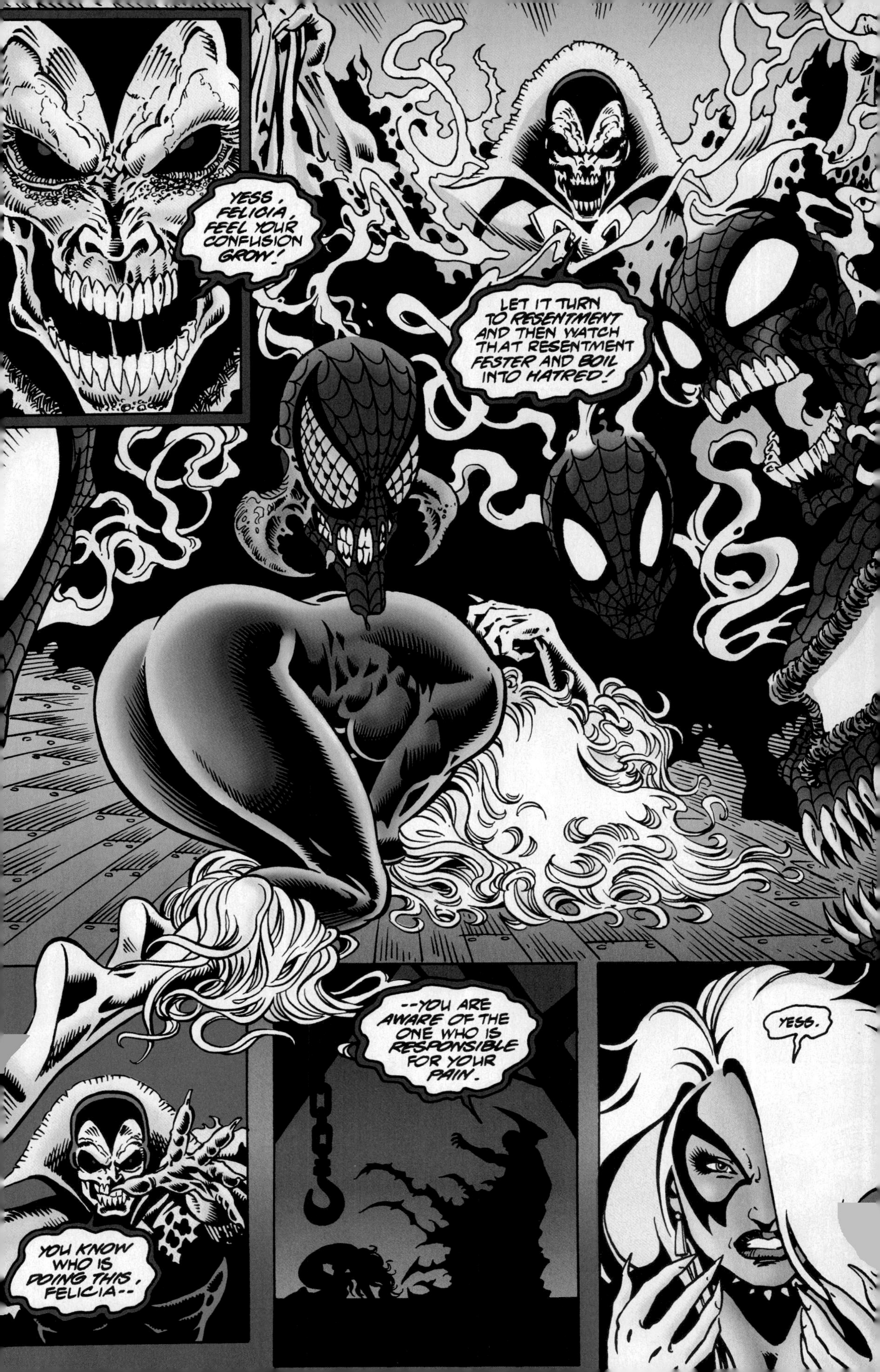
YESS, FELICIA, FEEL YOUR CONFUSION GROW!
LET IT TURN TO RESENTMENT AND THEN WATCH THAT RESENTMENT FESTER AND BOIL INTO HATRED!
YOU KNOW WHO IS DOING THIS, FELICIA--
--YOU ARE AWARE OF THE ONE WHO IS RESPONSIBLE FOR YOUR PAIN.
YESS.

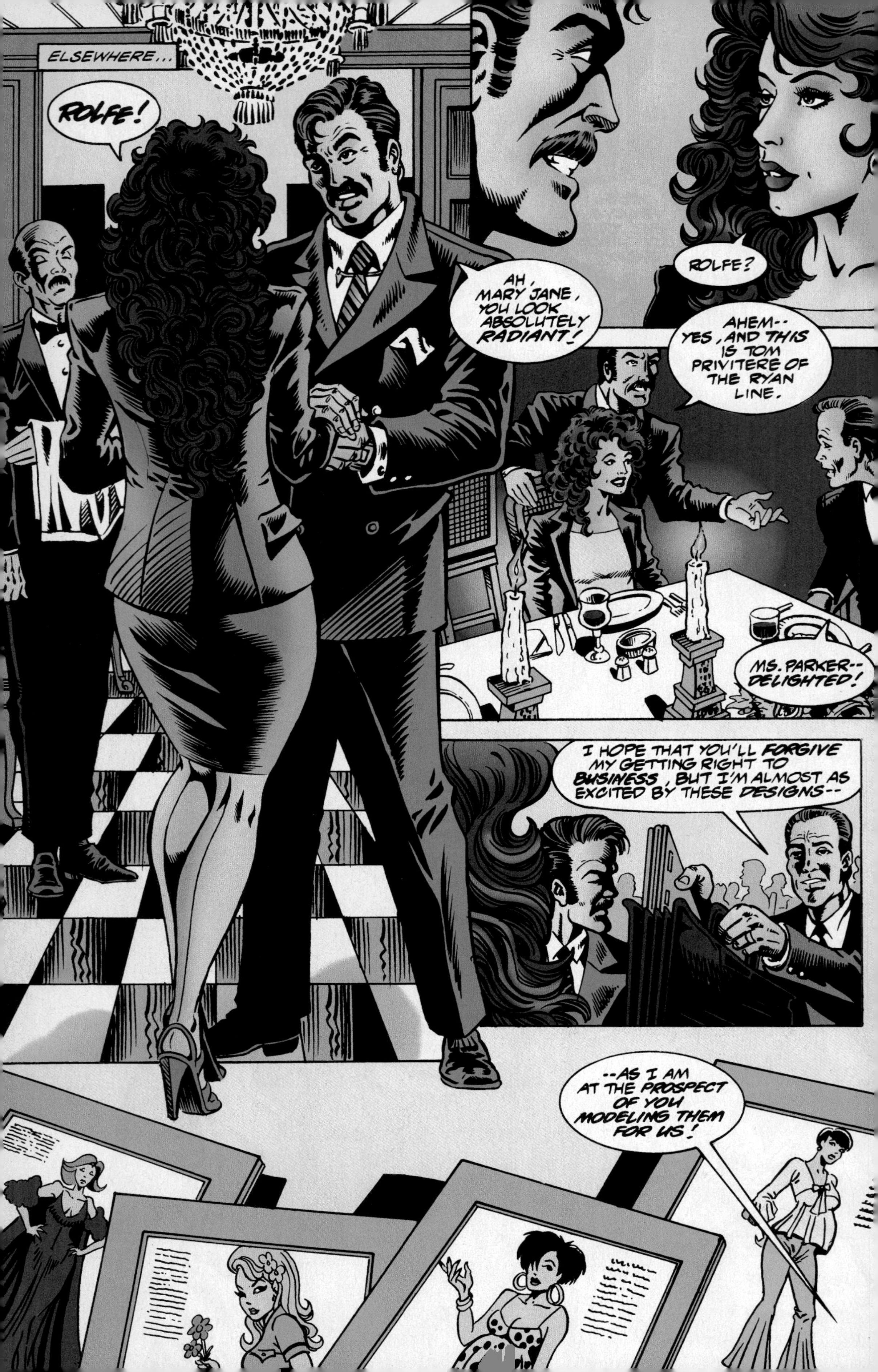
ELSEWHERE...
ROLFE!
AH, MARY JANE, YOU LOOK ABSOLUTELY RADIANT!
ROLFE?
AHEM-- YES, AND THIS IS TOM PRIVITERE OF THE RYAN LINE.
MS. PARKER-- DELIGHTED!
I HOPE THAT YOU'LL FORGIVE MY GETTING RIGHT TO BUSINESS, BUT I'M ALMOST AS EXCITED BY THESE DESIGNS--
--AS I AM AT THE PROSPECT OF YOU MODELING THEM FOR US!

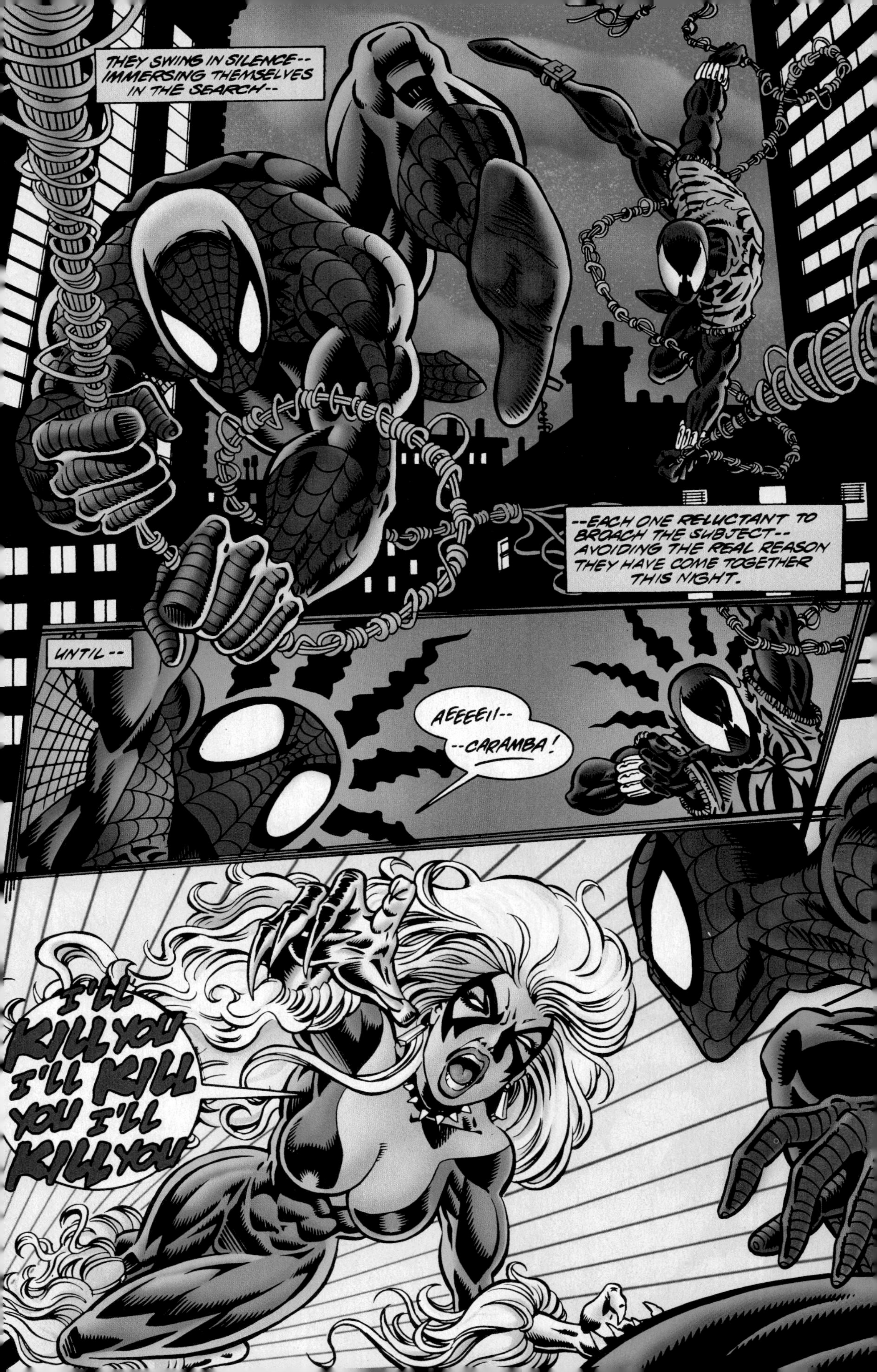
THEY SWING IN SILENCE-- IMMERSING THEMSELVES IN THE SEARCH--
--EACH ONE RELUCTANT TO BROACH THE SUBJECT-- AVOIDING THE REAL REASON THEY HAVE COME TOGETHER THIS NIGHT.
UNTIL--
AEEEEII--
--CARAMBA!
I'LL KILL YOU I'LL KILL YOU I'LL KILL YOU

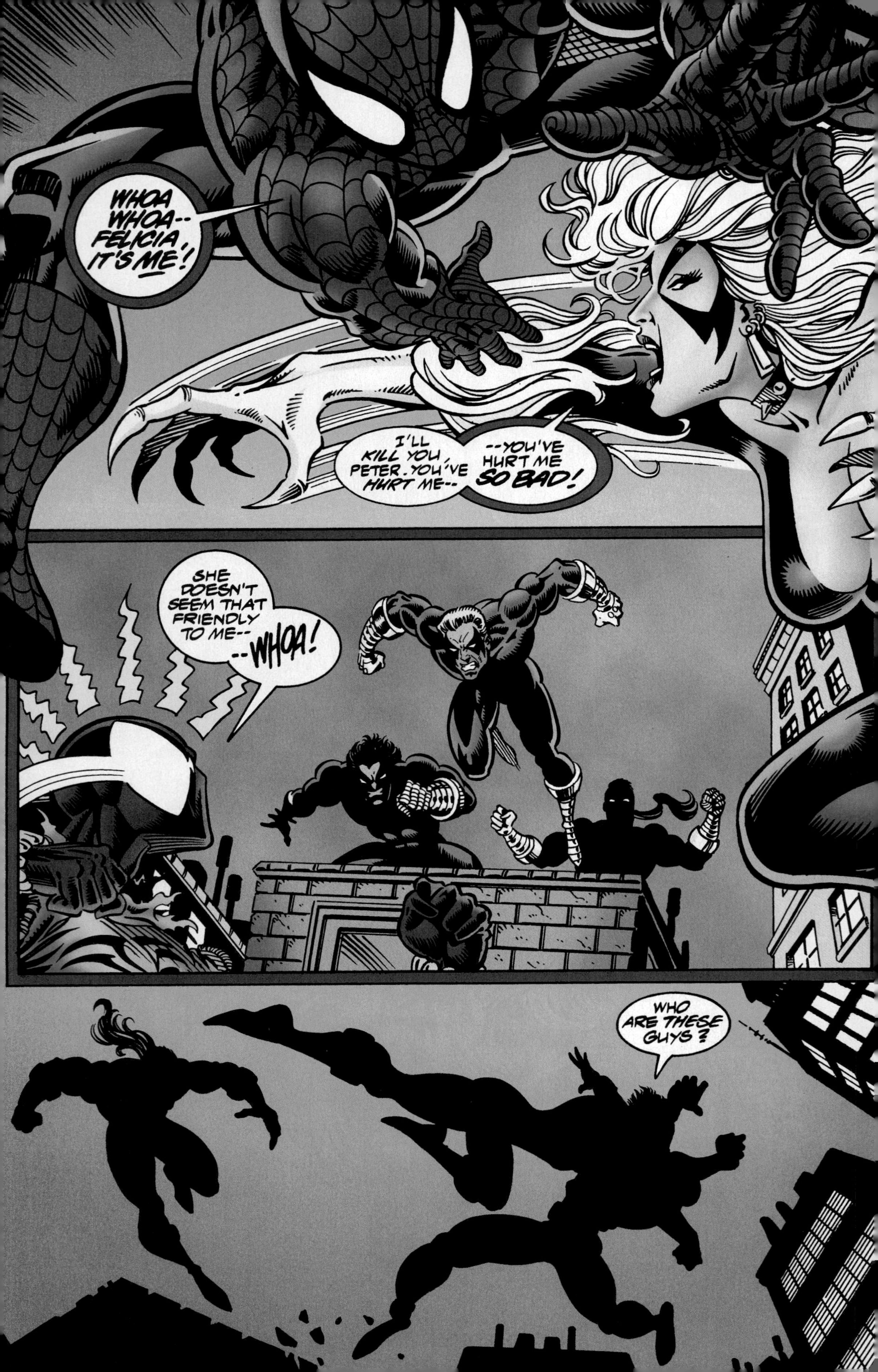
WHOA WHOA-- FELICIA, IT'S ME!
I'LL KILL YOU, PETER. YOU'VE HURT ME--
--YOU'VE HURT ME SO BAD!
SHE DOESN'T SEEM THAT FRIENDLY TO ME--
--WHOA!
WHO ARE THESE GUYS?

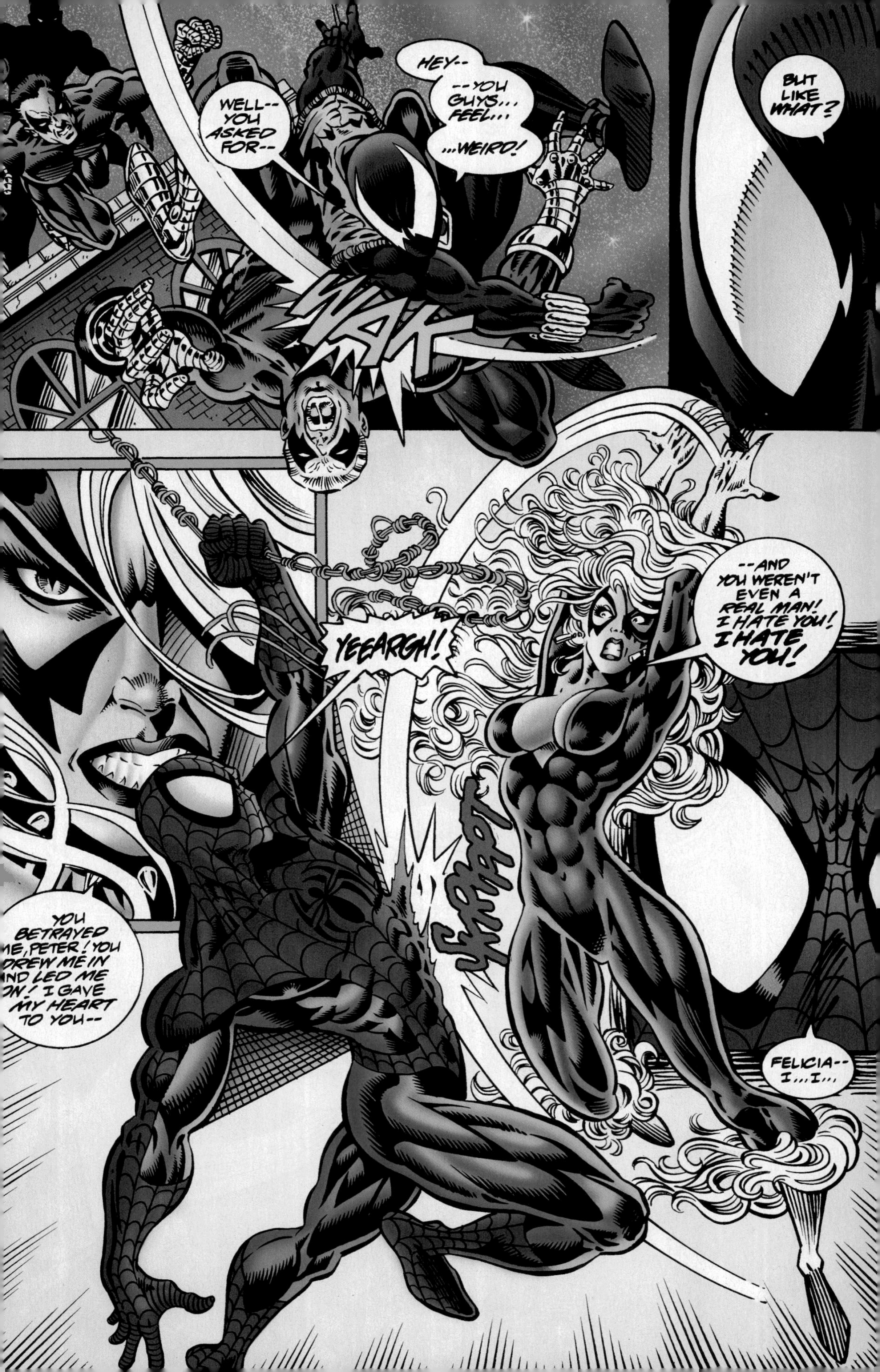
WELL-- YOU ASKED FOR--
HEY--
--YOU GUYS... FEEL...
...WEIRD!
WAK
BUT LIKE WHAT?
YEEARGH!
--AND YOU WEREN'T EVEN A REAL MAN! I HATE YOU! I HATE YOU!
YOU BETRAYED ME, PETER! YOU DREW ME IN AND LED ME ON! I GAVE MY HEART TO YOU--
FELICIA-- I... I...

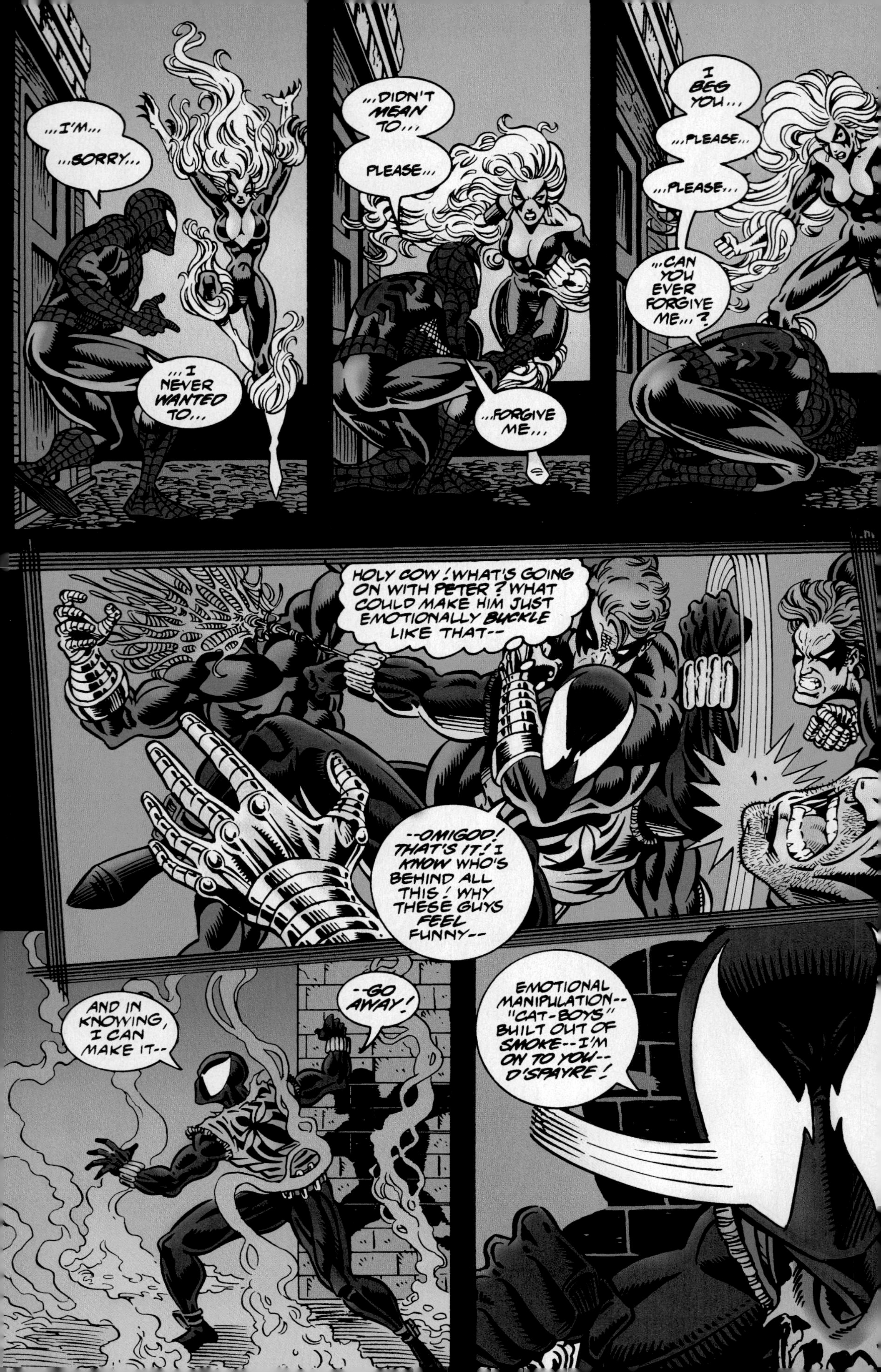
...I'M...
...SORRY...
...I NEVER WANTED TO...
...DIDN'T MEAN TO...
PLEASE...
...FORGIVE ME...
I BEG YOU...
...PLEASE...
...PLEASE...
...CAN YOU EVER FORGIVE ME...?
HOLY COW! WHAT'S GOING ON WITH PETER? WHAT COULD MAKE HIM JUST EMOTIONALLY BUCKLE LIKE THAT--
--OMIGOD! THAT'S IT! I KNOW WHO'S BEHIND ALL THIS! WHY THESE GUYS FEEL FUNNY--
AND IN KNOWING, I CAN MAKE IT--
--GO AWAY!
EMOTIONAL MANIPULATION-- "CAT-BOYS" BUILT OUT OF SMOKE--I'M ON TO YOU-- D'SPAYRE!

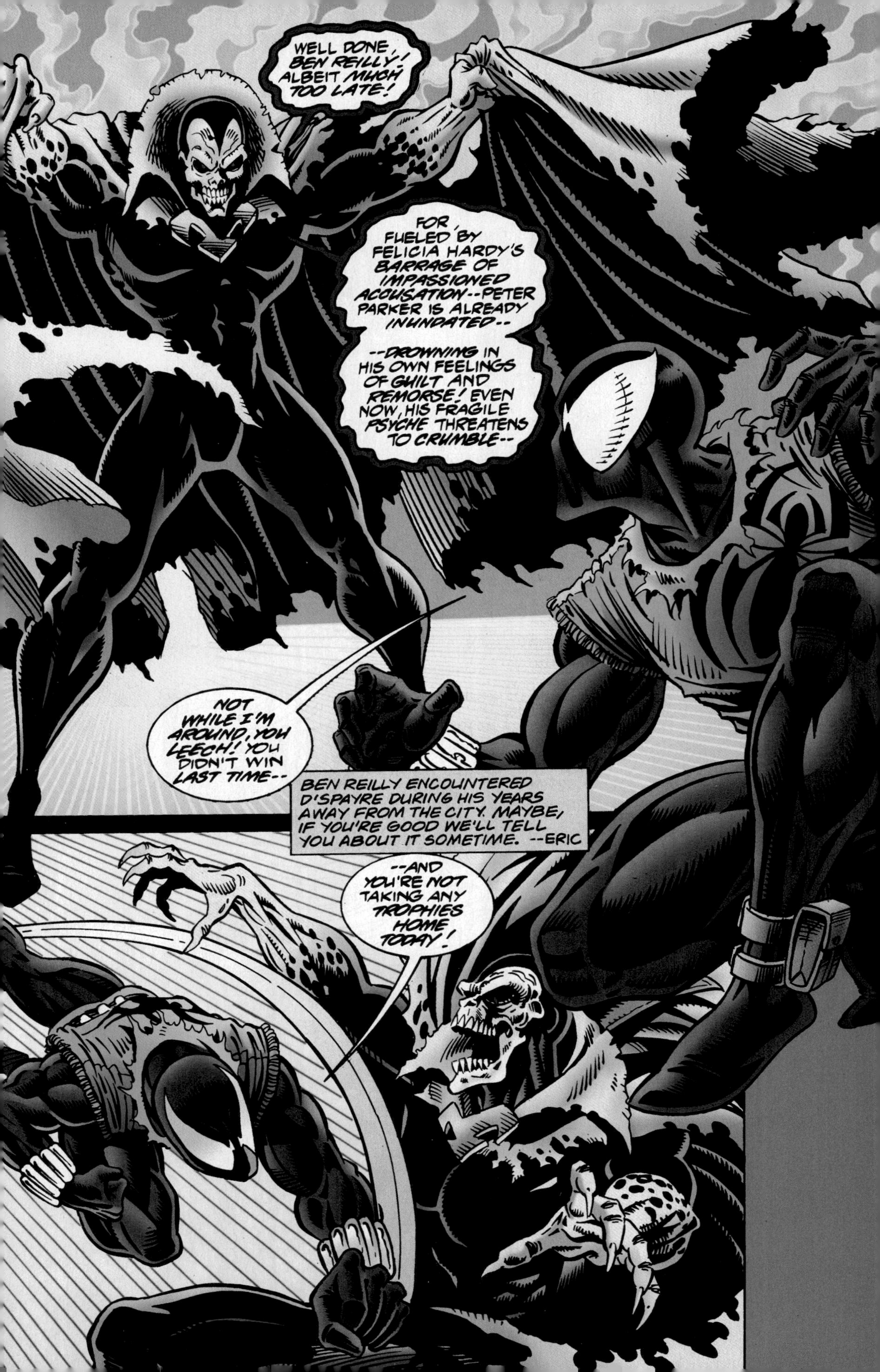
WELL DONE, BEN REILLY! ALBEIT MUCH TOO LATE!
FOR, FUELED BY FELICIA HARDY'S BARRAGE OF IMPASSIONED ACCUSATION--PETER PARKER IS ALREADY INUNDATED--
--DROWNING IN HIS OWN FEELINGS OF GUILT AND REMORSE! EVEN NOW, HIS FRAGILE PSYCHE THREATENS TO CRUMBLE--
NOT WHILE I'M AROUND, YOU LEECH! YOU DIDN'T WIN LAST TIME--
BEN REILLY ENCOUNTERED D'SPAYRE DURING HIS YEARS AWAY FROM THE CITY. MAYBE, IF YOU'RE GOOD WE'LL TELL YOU ABOUT IT SOMETIME. --ERIC
--AND YOU'RE NOT TAKING ANY TROPHIES HOME TODAY!

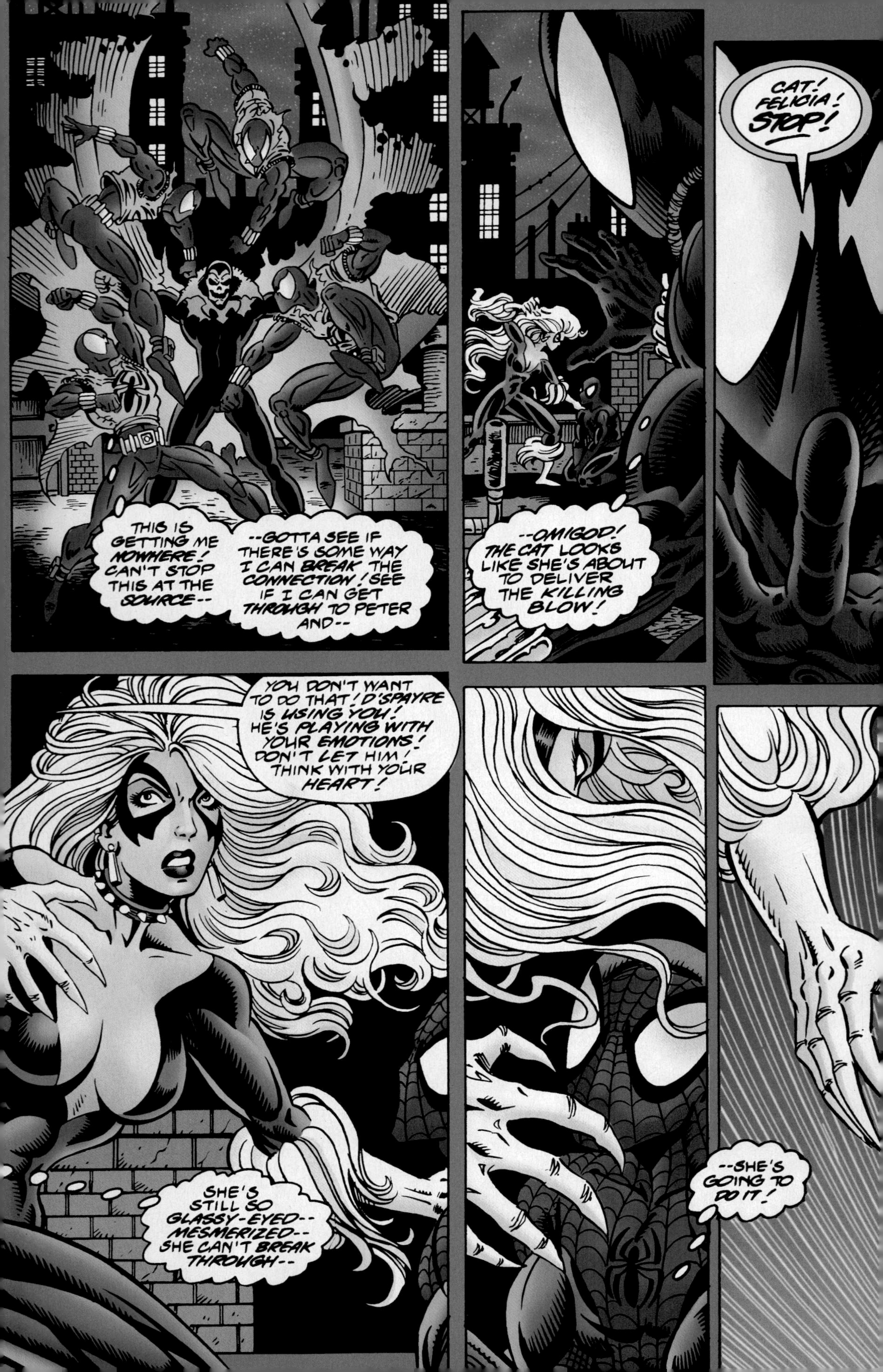
THIS IS GETTING ME NOWHERE! CAN'T STOP THIS AT THE SOURCE--
--GOTTA SEE IF THERE'S SOME WAY I CAN BREAK THE CONNECTION! SEE IF I CAN GET THROUGH TO PETER AND--
--OMIGOD! THE CAT LOOKS LIKE SHE'S ABOUT TO DELIVER THE KILLING BLOW!
CAT! FELICIA! STOP!
YOU DON'T WANT TO DO THAT! D'SPAYRE IS USING YOU! HE'S PLAYING WITH YOUR EMOTIONS! DON'T LET HIM! THINK WITH YOUR HEART!
SHE'S STILL SO GLASSY-EYED-- MESMERIZED-- SHE CAN'T BREAK THROUGH--
--SHE'S GOING TO DO IT!

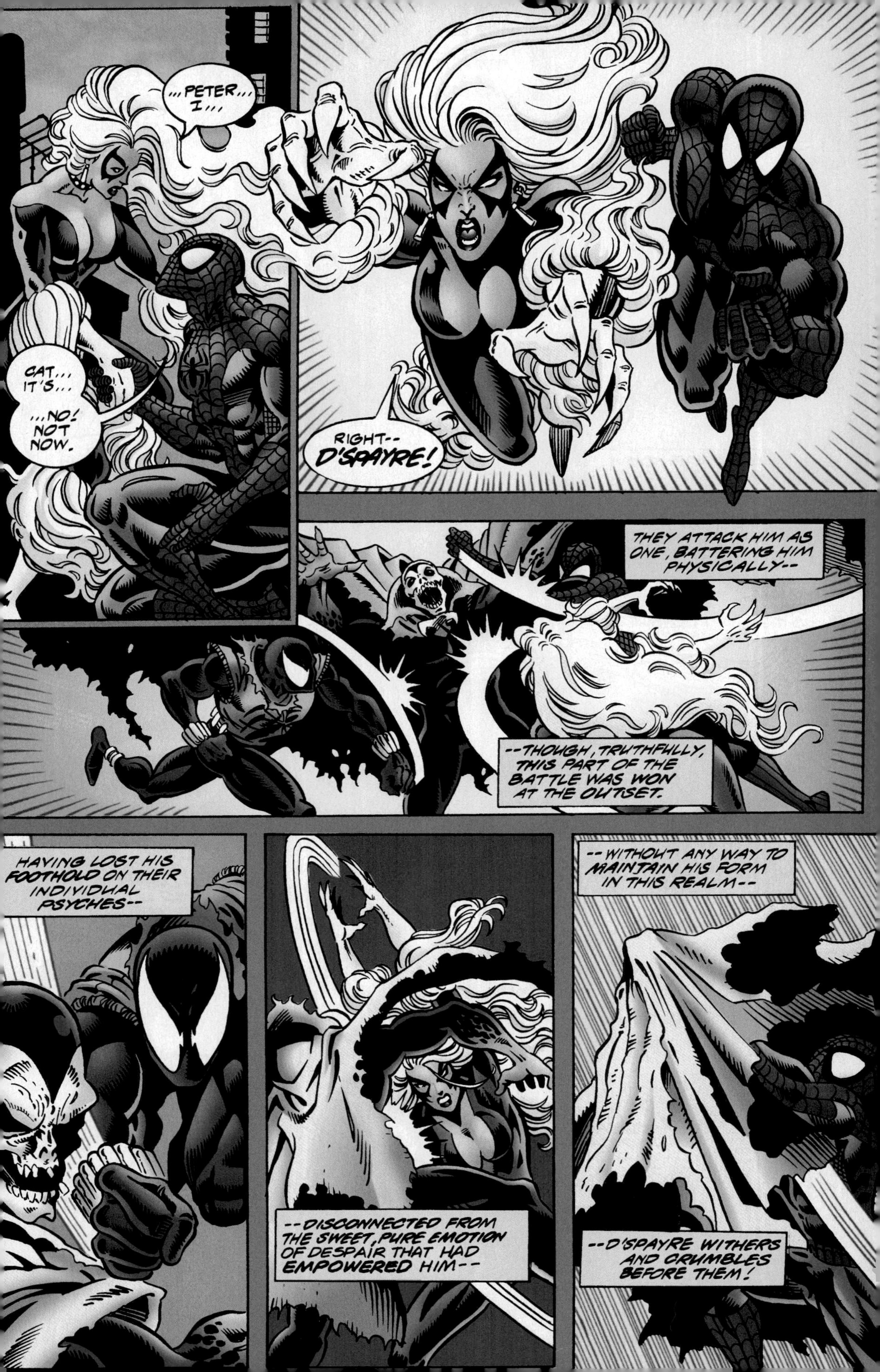
...PETER... I...
CAT... IT'S...
...NO! NOT NOW.
RIGHT-- D'SPAYRE!
THEY ATTACK HIM AS ONE, BATTERING HIM PHYSICALLY--
--THOUGH, TRUTHFULLY, THIS PART OF THE BATTLE WAS WON AT THE OUTSET.
HAVING LOST HIS FOOTHOLD ON THEIR INDIVIDUAL PSYCHES--
--DISCONNECTED FROM THE SWEET, PURE EMOTION OF DESPAIR THAT HAD EMPOWERED HIM--
--WITHOUT ANY WAY TO MAINTAIN HIS FORM IN THIS REALM--
--D'SPAYRE WITHERS AND CRUMBLES BEFORE THEM!

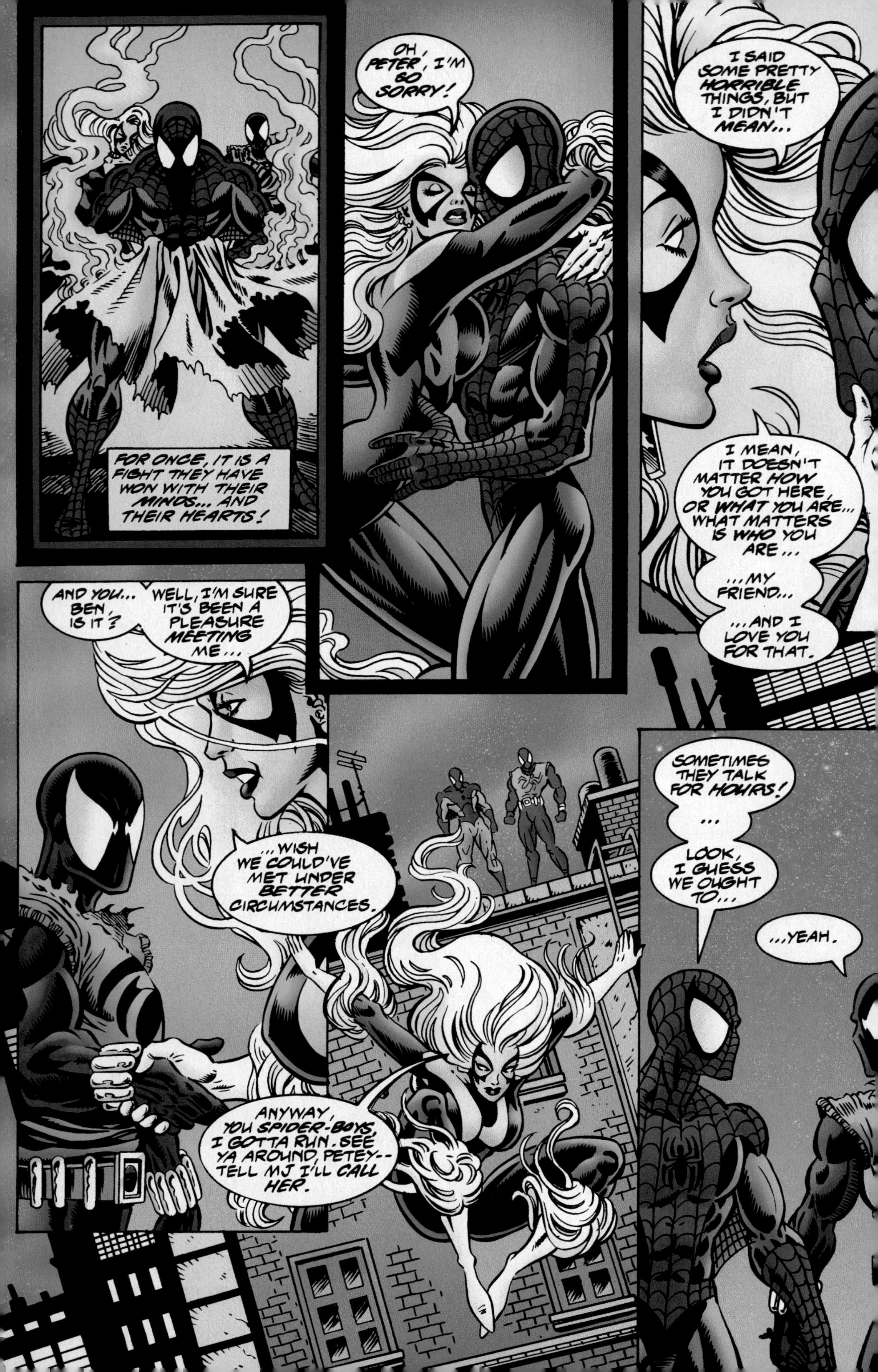
FOR ONCE, IT IS A FIGHT THEY HAVE WON WITH THEIR MINDS... AND THEIR HEARTS!
OH, PETER, I'M SO SORRY!
I SAID SOME PRETTY HORRIBLE THINGS, BUT I DIDN'T MEAN...
I MEAN, IT DOESN'T MATTER HOW YOU GOT HERE, OR WHAT YOU ARE... WHAT MATTERS IS WHO YOU ARE...
...MY FRIEND...
...AND I LOVE YOU FOR THAT.
AND YOU... BEN, IS IT?
WELL, I'M SURE IT'S BEEN A PLEASURE MEETING ME...
...WISH WE COULD'VE MET UNDER BETTER CIRCUMSTANCES.
ANYWAY, YOU SPIDER-BOYS, I GOTTA RUN. SEE YA AROUND, PETEY-- TELL MJ I'LL CALL HER.
SOMETIMES THEY TALK FOR HOURS!
...
LOOK, I GUESS WE OUGHT TO...
...YEAH.

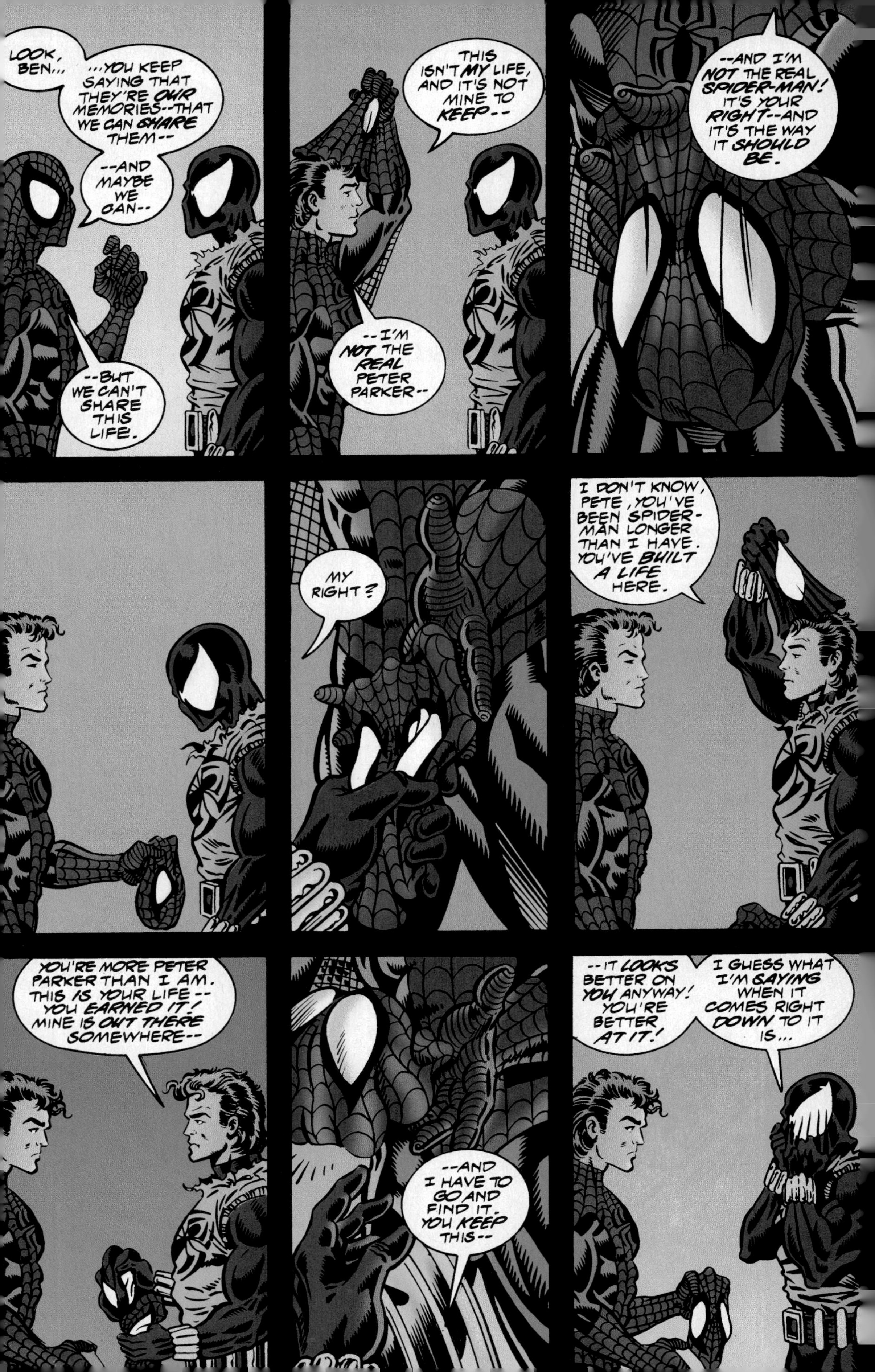
LOOK, BEN...
...YOU KEEP SAYING THAT THEY'RE OUR MEMORIES--THAT WE CAN SHARE THEM--
--AND MAYBE WE CAN--
--BUT WE CAN'T SHARE THIS LIFE.
THIS ISN'T MY LIFE, AND IT'S NOT MINE TO KEEP--
--I'M NOT THE REAL PETER PARKER--
--AND I'M NOT THE REAL SPIDER-MAN! IT'S YOUR RIGHT--AND IT'S THE WAY IT SHOULD BE.
MY RIGHT?
I DON'T KNOW, PETE, YOU'VE BEEN SPIDER-MAN LONGER THAN I HAVE. YOU'VE BUILT A LIFE HERE.
YOU'RE MORE PETER PARKER THAN I AM. THIS IS YOUR LIFE--YOU EARNED IT! MINE IS OUT THERE SOMEWHERE--
--AND I HAVE TO GO AND FIND IT. YOU KEEP THIS--
I GUESS WHAT I'M SAYING WHEN IT COMES RIGHT DOWN TO IT IS...
--IT LOOKS BETTER ON YOU ANYWAY! YOU'RE BETTER AT IT!

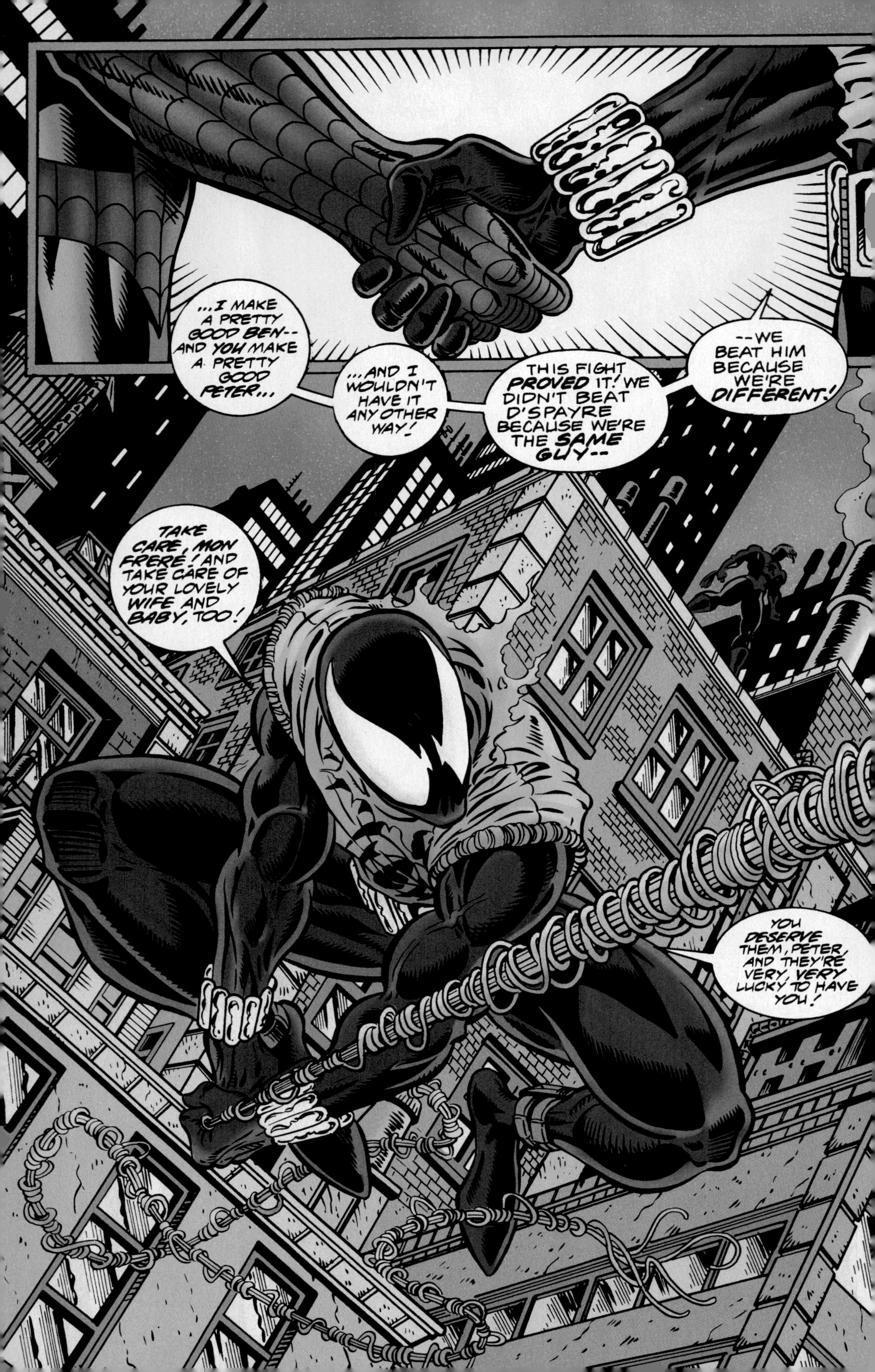
...I MAKE A PRETTY GOOD BEN--AND YOU MAKE A PRETTY GOOD PETER...
...AND I WOULDN'T HAVE IT ANY OTHER WAY!
THIS FIGHT PROVED IT! WE DIDN'T BEAT D'SPAYRE BECAUSE WE'RE THE SAME GUY--
--WE BEAT HIM BECAUSE WE'RE DIFFERENT!
TAKE CARE, MON FRERÉ! AND TAKE CARE OF YOUR LOVELY WIFE AND BABY, TOO!
YOU DESERVE THEM, PETER, AND THEY'RE VERY, VERY LUCKY TO HAVE YOU!

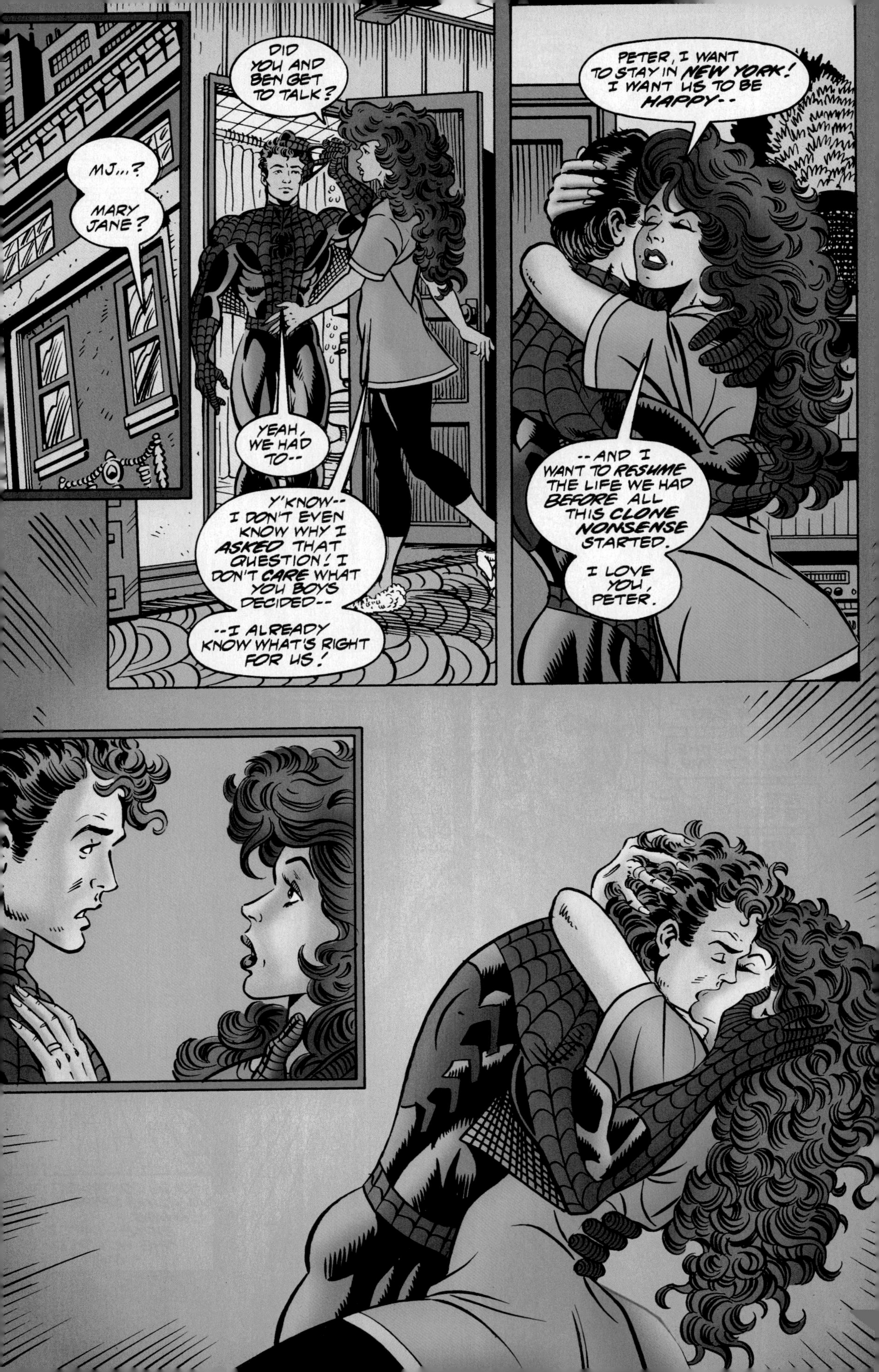
MJ...?
MARY JANE?
DID YOU AND BEN GET TO TALK?
YEAH, WE HAD TO--
Y'KNOW-- I DON'T EVEN KNOW WHY I ASKED THAT QUESTION! I DON'T CARE WHAT YOU BOYS DECIDED--
--I ALREADY KNOW WHAT'S RIGHT FOR US!
PETER, I WANT TO STAY IN NEW YORK! I WANT US TO BE HAPPY--
--AND I WANT TO RESUME THE LIFE WE HAD BEFORE ALL THIS CLONE NONSENSE STARTED.
I LOVE YOU, PETER.

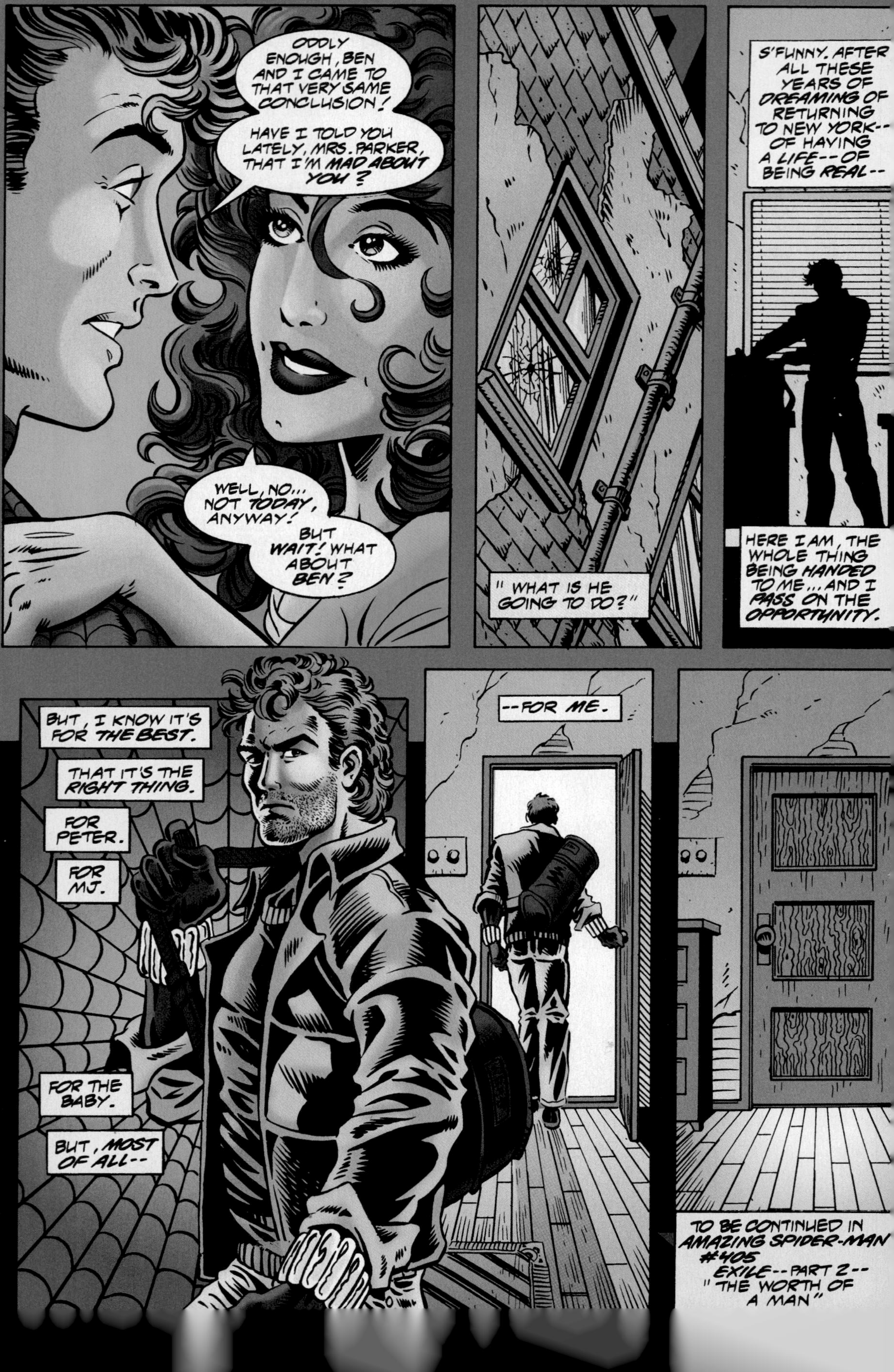
ODDLY ENOUGH, BEN AND I CAME TO THAT VERY SAME CONCLUSION!
HAVE I TOLD YOU LATELY, MRS. PARKER, THAT I'M MAD ABOUT YOU?
WELL, NO... NOT TODAY, ANYWAY!
BUT WAIT! WHAT ABOUT BEN?
"WHAT IS HE GOING TO DO?"
S'FUNNY. AFTER ALL THESE YEARS OF DREAMING OF RETURNING TO NEW YORK-- OF HAVING A LIFE-- OF BEING REAL--
HERE I AM, THE WHOLE THING BEING HANDED TO ME... AND I PASS ON THE OPPORTUNITY.
BUT, I KNOW IT'S FOR THE BEST.
THAT IT'S THE RIGHT THING.
FOR PETER.
FOR MJ.
FOR THE BABY.
BUT, MOST OF ALL--
--FOR ME.
TO BE CONTINUED IN AMAZING SPIDER-MAN #405
EXILE--PART 2-- "THE WORTH OF A MAN"

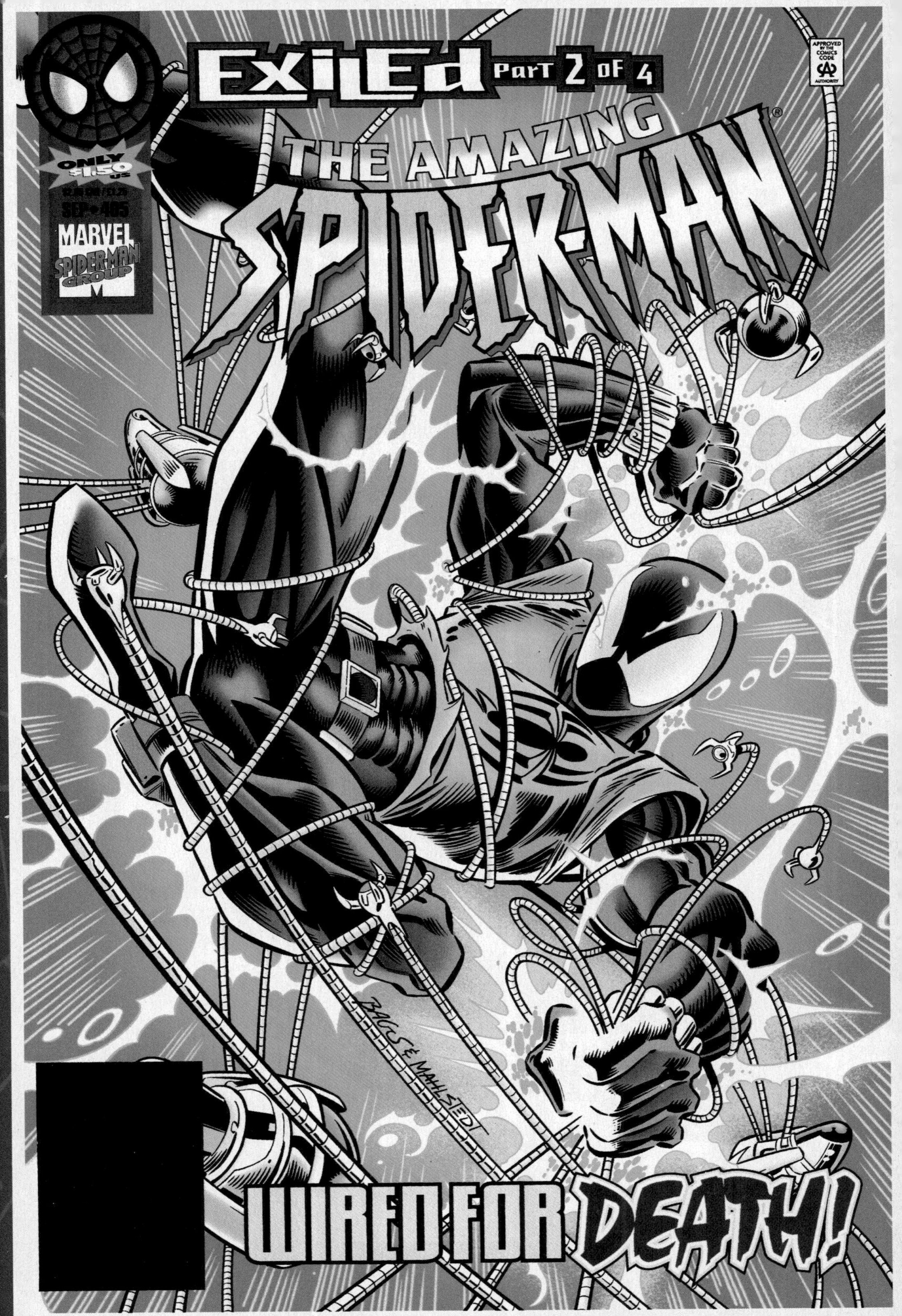
ExiLEd PART 2 OF 4
THE AMAZING
SPIDER-MAN
ONLY $1.50 US
SEP 405
MARVEL
SPIDER-MAN GROUP
APPROVED BY THE COMICS CODE AUTHORITY
BAGS & MAHLSTEDT
WIRED FOR DEATH!

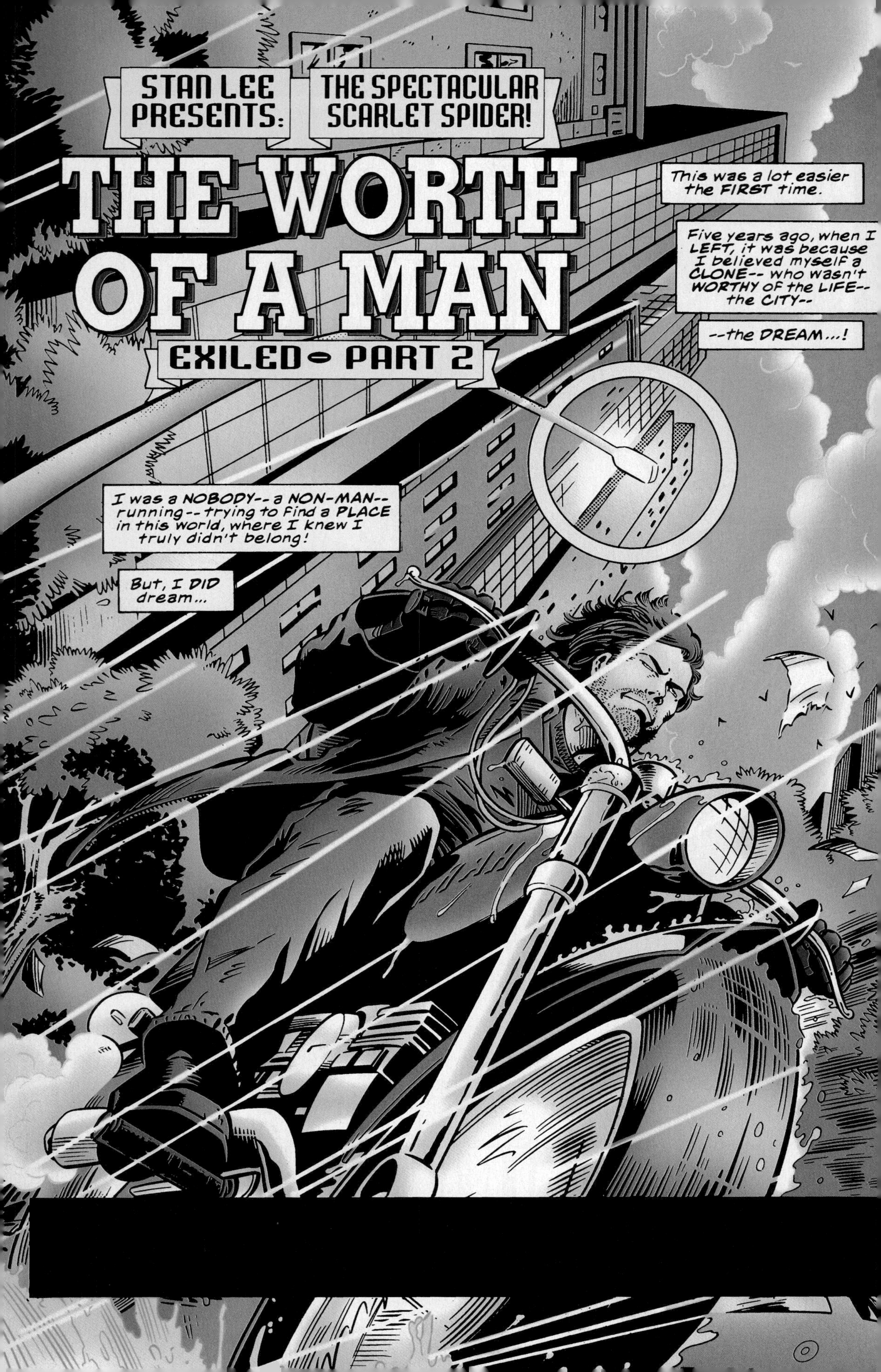
STAN LEE PRESENTS:
THE SPECTACULAR SCARLET SPIDER!
THE WORTH OF A MAN
EXILED - PART 2
This was a lot easier the FIRST time.
Five years ago, when I LEFT, it was because I believed myself a CLONE-- who wasn't WORTHY of the LIFE-- the CITY--
--the DREAM...!
I was a NOBODY-- a NON-MAN-- running-- trying to find a PLACE in this world, where I knew I truly didn't belong!
But, I DID dream...
[redacted]

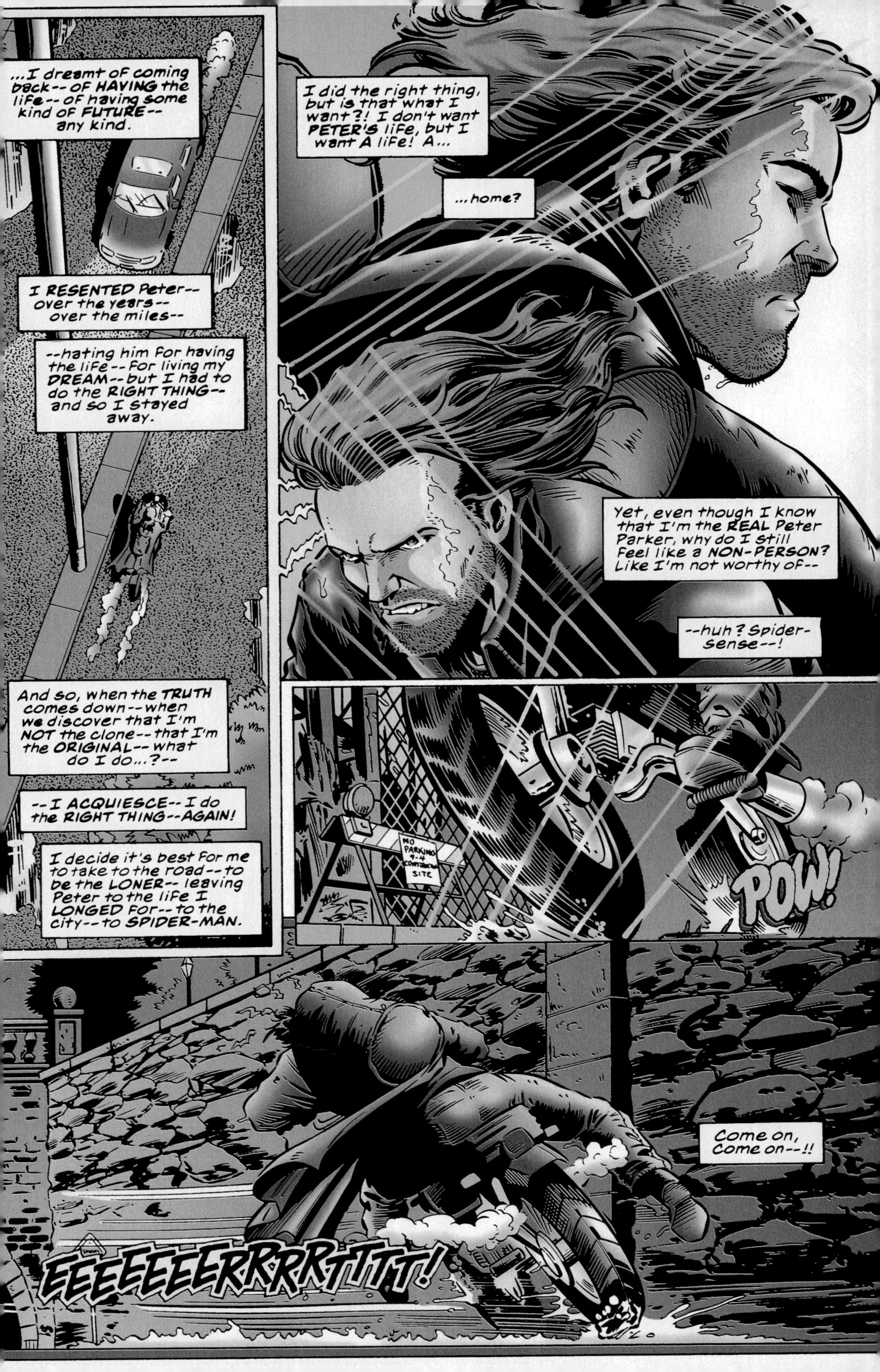
...I dreamt of coming back--of HAVING the life--of having some kind of FUTURE--any kind.
I RESENTED Peter--over the years--over the miles--
--hating him for having the life--for living my DREAM--but I had to do the RIGHT THING--and so I stayed away.
And so, when the TRUTH comes down--when we discover that I'm NOT the clone--that I'm the ORIGINAL--what do I do...?--
--I ACQUIESCE--I do the RIGHT THING--AGAIN!
I decide it's best for me to take to the road--to be the LONER--leaving Peter to the life I LONGED for--to the city--to SPIDER-MAN.
I did the right thing, but is that what I want?! I don't want PETER'S life, but I want A life! A...
...home?
Yet, even though I know that I'm the REAL Peter Parker, why do I still feel like a NON-PERSON? Like I'm not worthy of--
--huh? Spider-sense--!
NO PARKING 9-4 CONSTRUCTION SITE
POW!
Come on, Come on--!!
EEEEEEEERRRRTTTT!

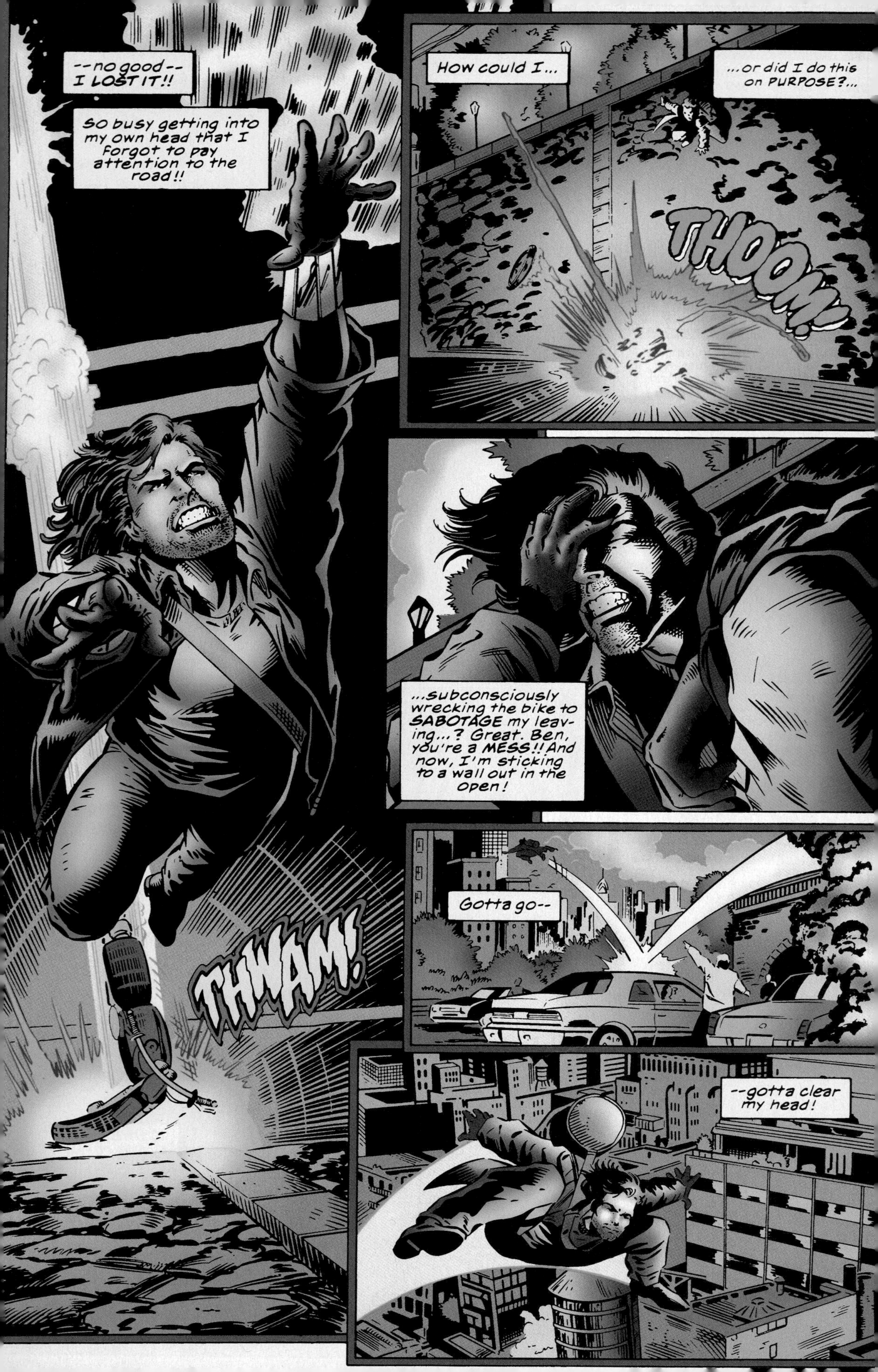
--no good--
I LOST IT!!
So busy getting into my own head that I forgot to pay attention to the road!!
How could I...
...or did I do this on PURPOSE?...
THOOM!
...subconsciously wrecking the bike to SABOTAGE my leaving...? Great. Ben, you're a MESS!! And now, I'm sticking to a wall out in the open!
THWAM!
Gotta go--
--gotta clear my head!

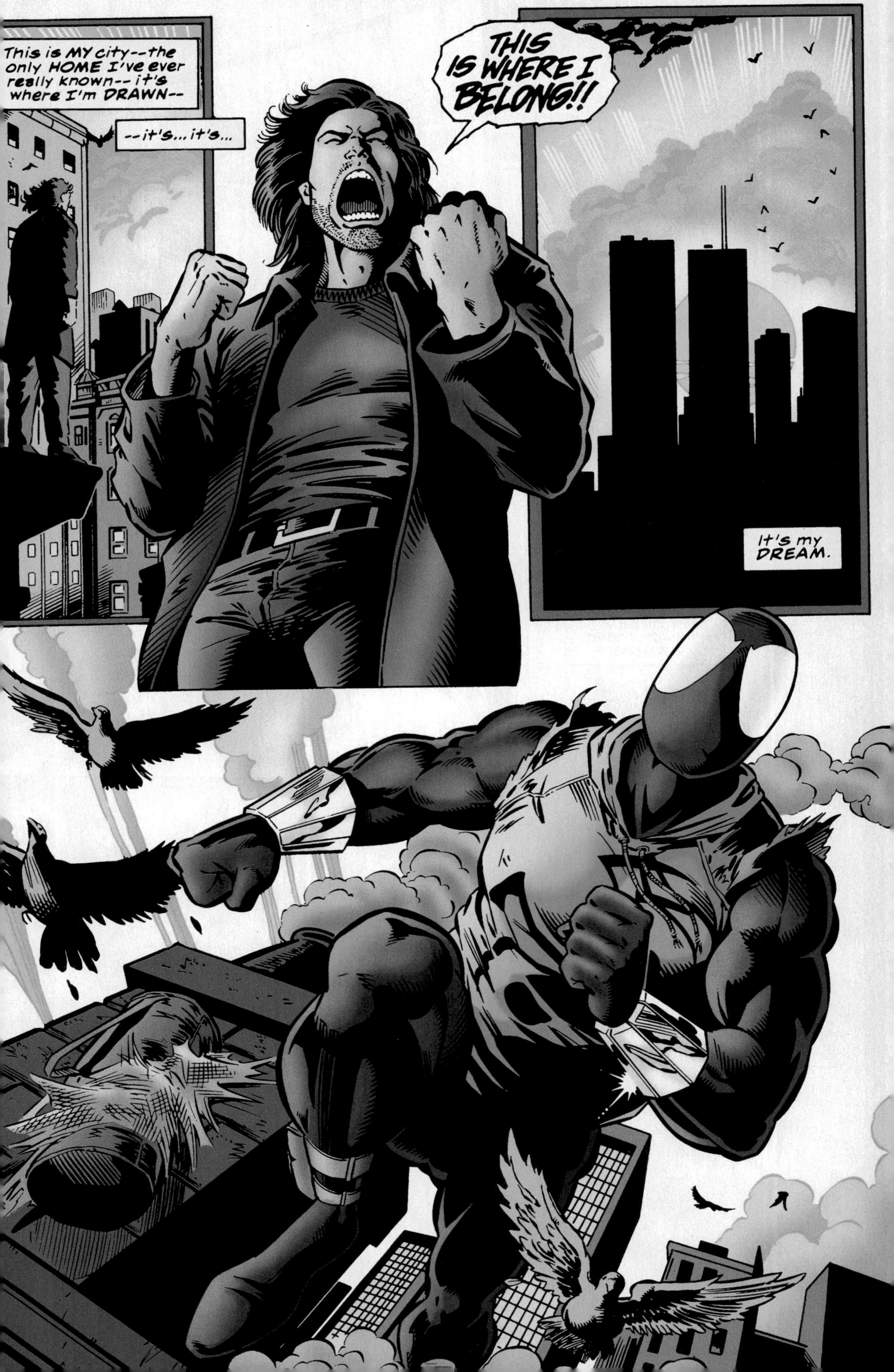
This is MY city--the only HOME I've ever really known--it's where I'm DRAWN--
--it's...it's...
THIS IS WHERE I BELONG!!
It's my DREAM.

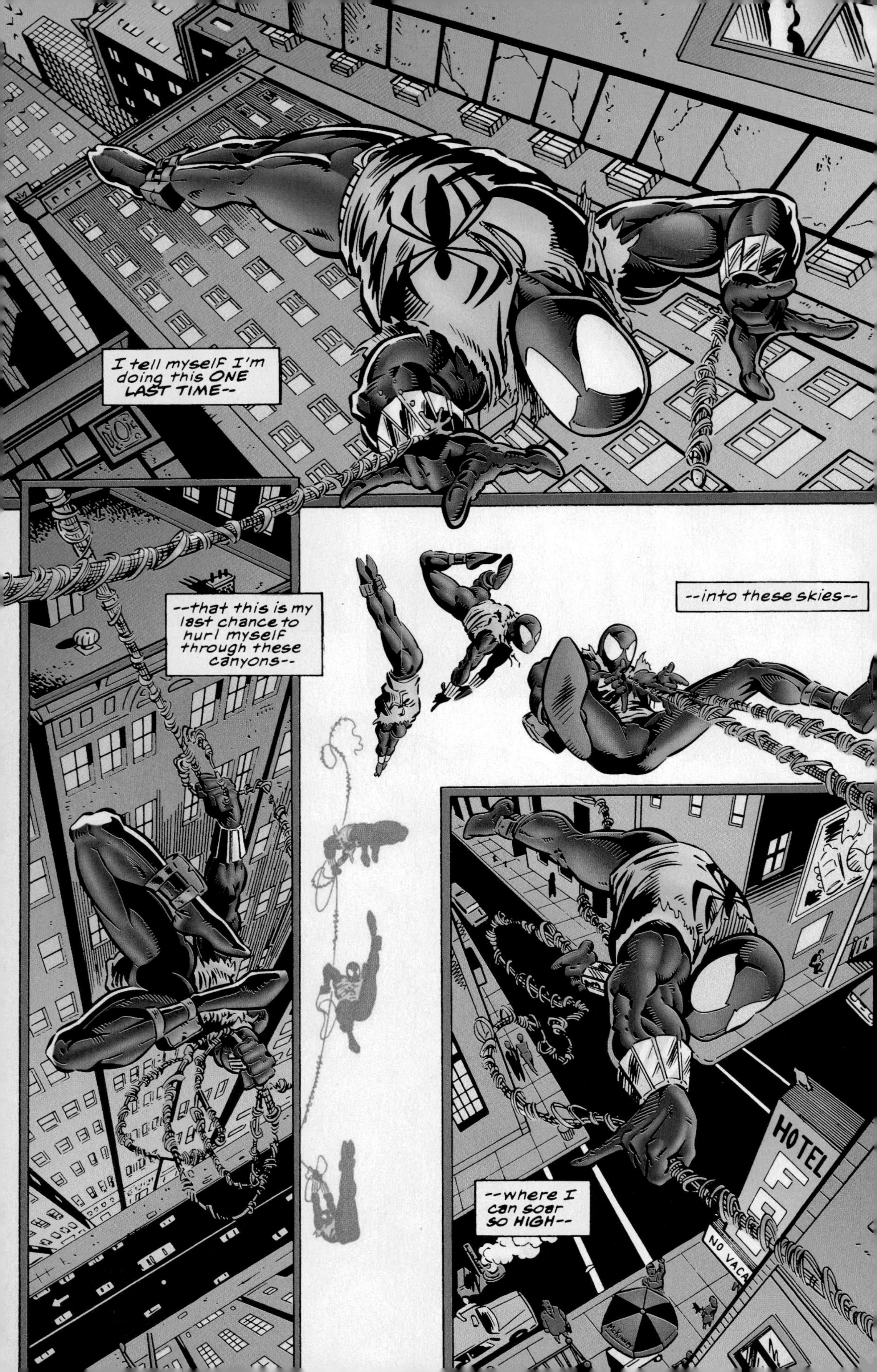

I tell myself I'm doing this ONE LAST TIME--
--that this is my last chance to hurl myself through these canyons--
--into these skies--
--where I can soar SO HIGH--
HOTEL
NO VACA

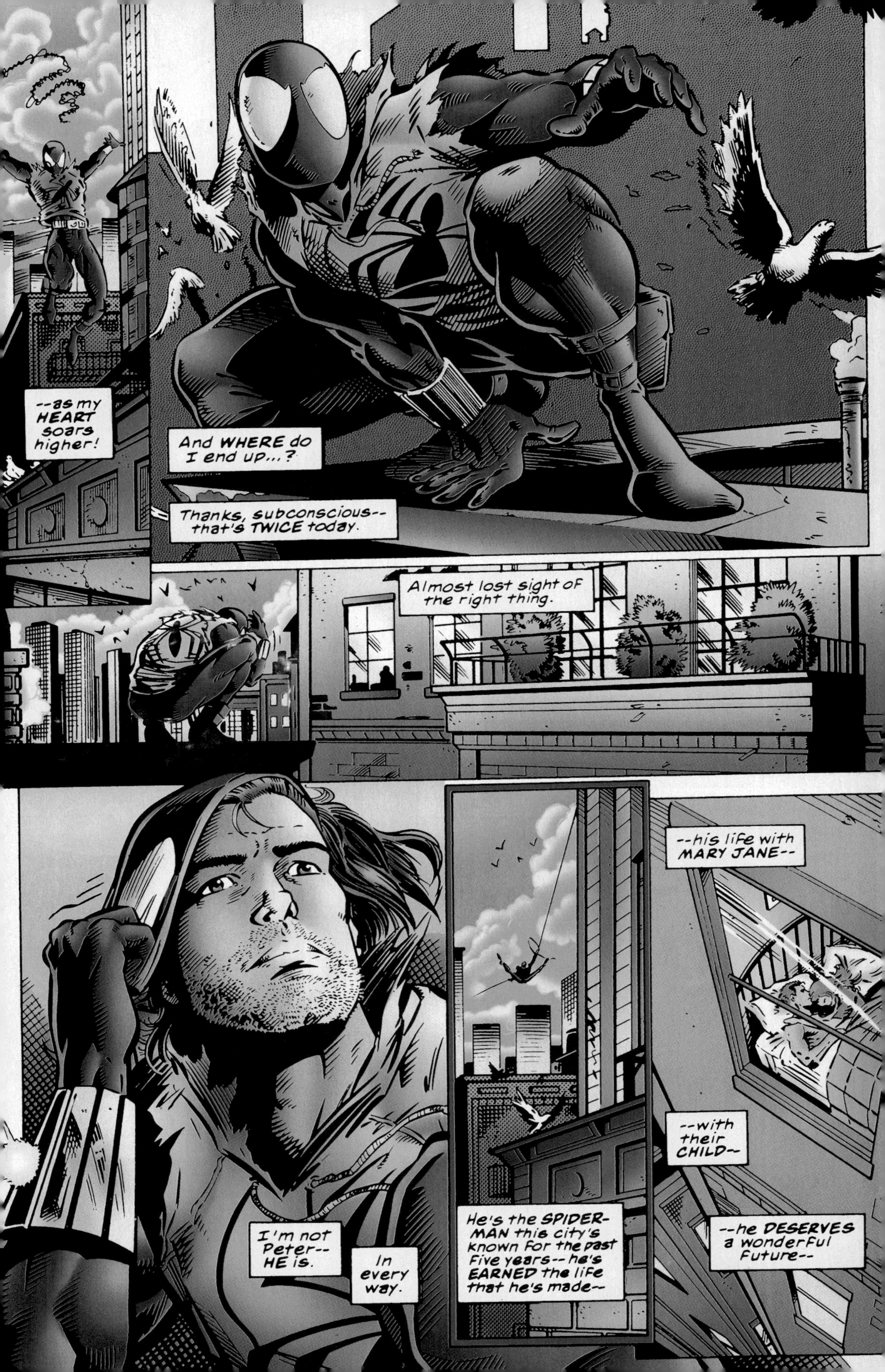
--as my HEART soars higher!
And WHERE do I end up...?
Thanks, subconscious--that's TWICE today.
Almost lost sight of the right thing.
I'm not Peter--HE is.
In every way.
He's the SPIDER-MAN this city's known for the past five years--he's EARNED the life that he's made--
--his life with MARY JANE--
--with their CHILD--
--he DESERVES a wonderful future--

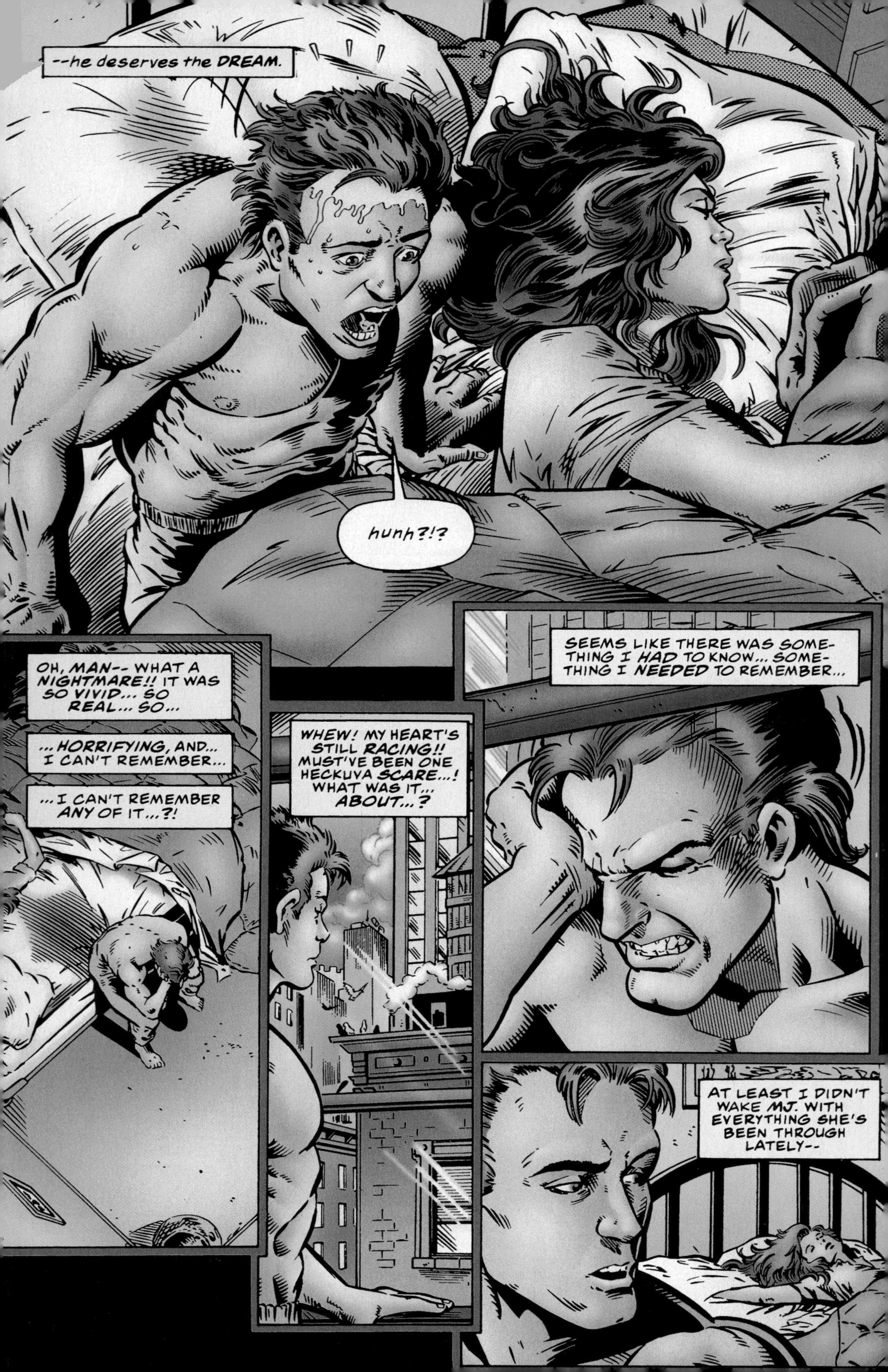
--he deserves the DREAM.
hunh?!?
OH, MAN-- WHAT A NIGHTMARE!! IT WAS SO VIVID... SO REAL... SO...
...HORRIFYING, AND... I CAN'T REMEMBER...
...I CAN'T REMEMBER ANY OF IT...?!
WHEW! MY HEART'S STILL RACING!! MUST'VE BEEN ONE HECKUVA SCARE...! WHAT WAS IT... ABOUT...?
SEEMS LIKE THERE WAS SOMETHING I HAD TO KNOW... SOMETHING I NEEDED TO REMEMBER...
AT LEAST I DIDN'T WAKE MJ. WITH EVERYTHING SHE'S BEEN THROUGH LATELY--

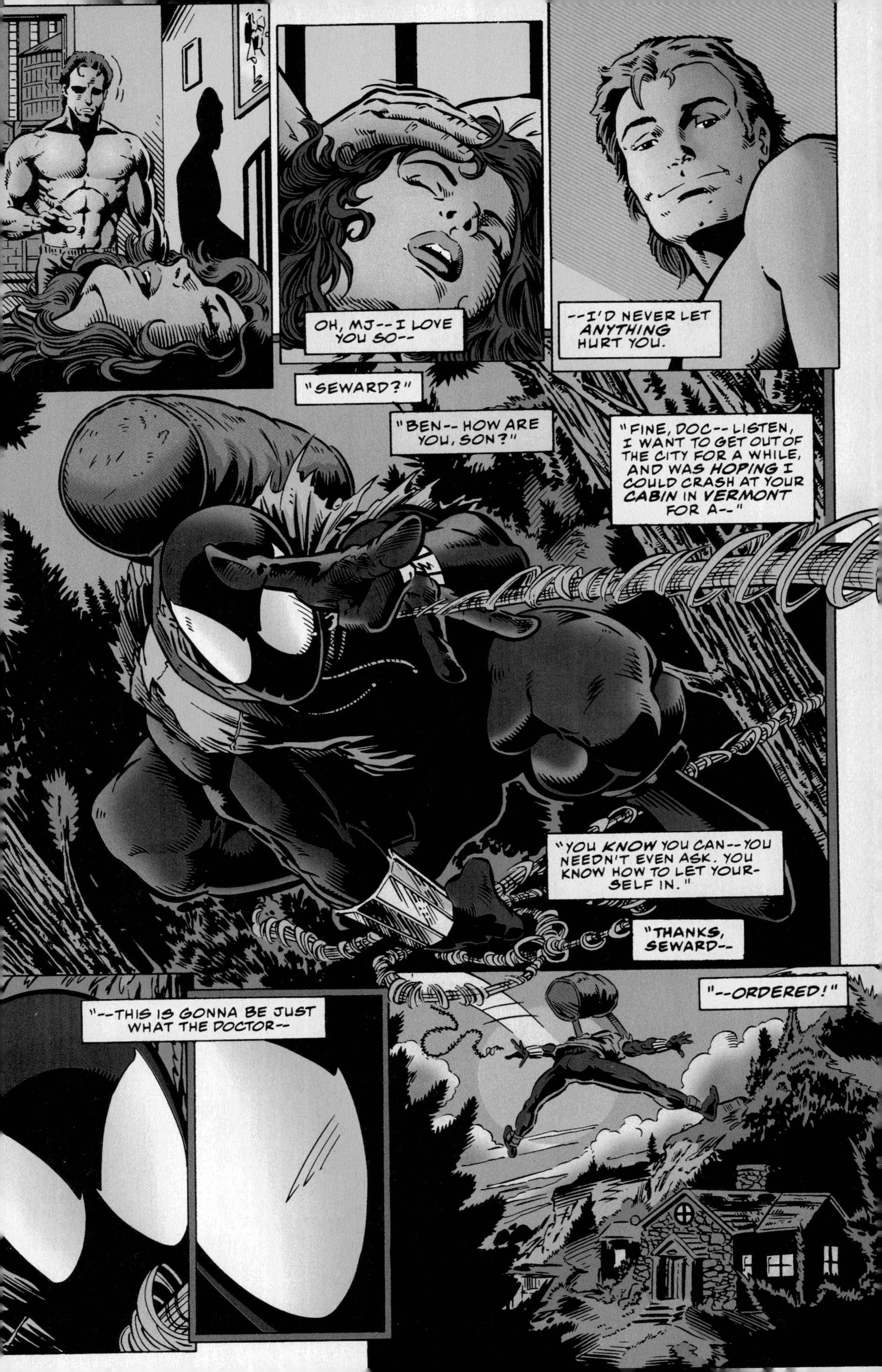
OH, MJ--I LOVE YOU SO--
--I'D NEVER LET ANYTHING HURT YOU.
"SEWARD?"
"BEN--HOW ARE YOU, SON?"
"FINE, DOC--LISTEN, I WANT TO GET OUT OF THE CITY FOR A WHILE, AND WAS HOPING I COULD CRASH AT YOUR CABIN IN VERMONT FOR A--"
"YOU KNOW YOU CAN--YOU NEEDN'T EVEN ASK. YOU KNOW HOW TO LET YOURSELF IN."
"THANKS, SEWARD--
"--THIS IS GONNA BE JUST WHAT THE DOCTOR--
"--ORDERED!"

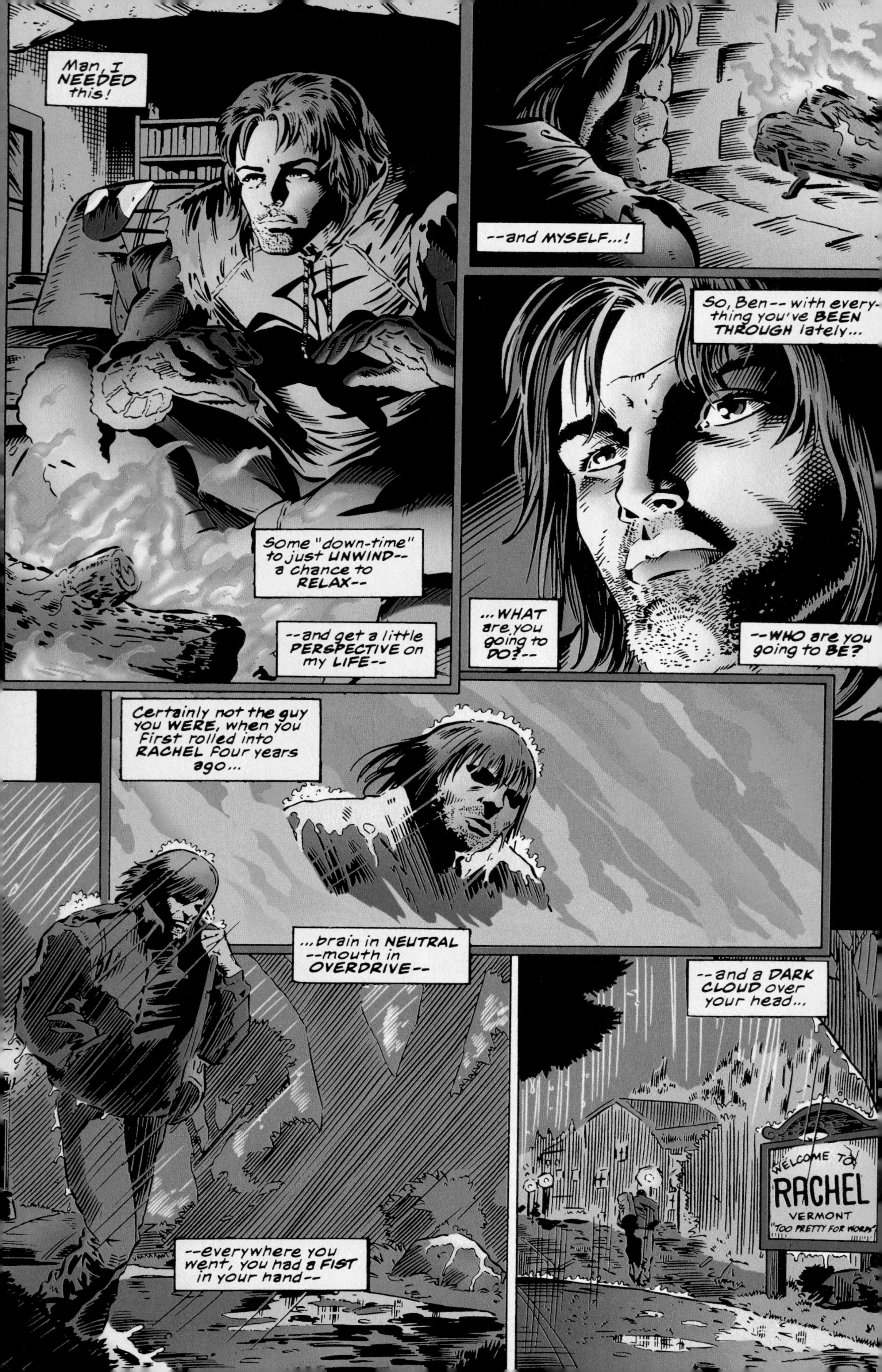
Man, I NEEDED this!
Some "down-time" to just UNWIND-- a chance to RELAX--
--and get a little PERSPECTIVE on my LIFE--
--and MYSELF...!
So, Ben-- with everything you've BEEN THROUGH lately...
...WHAT are you going to DO?--
--WHO are you going to BE?
Certainly not the guy you WERE, when you first rolled into RACHEL four years ago...
...brain in NEUTRAL --mouth in OVERDRIVE--
--everywhere you went, you had a FIST in your hand--
--and a DARK CLOUD over your head...
WELCOME TO
RACHEL
VERMONT
"TOO PRETTY FOR WORDS"

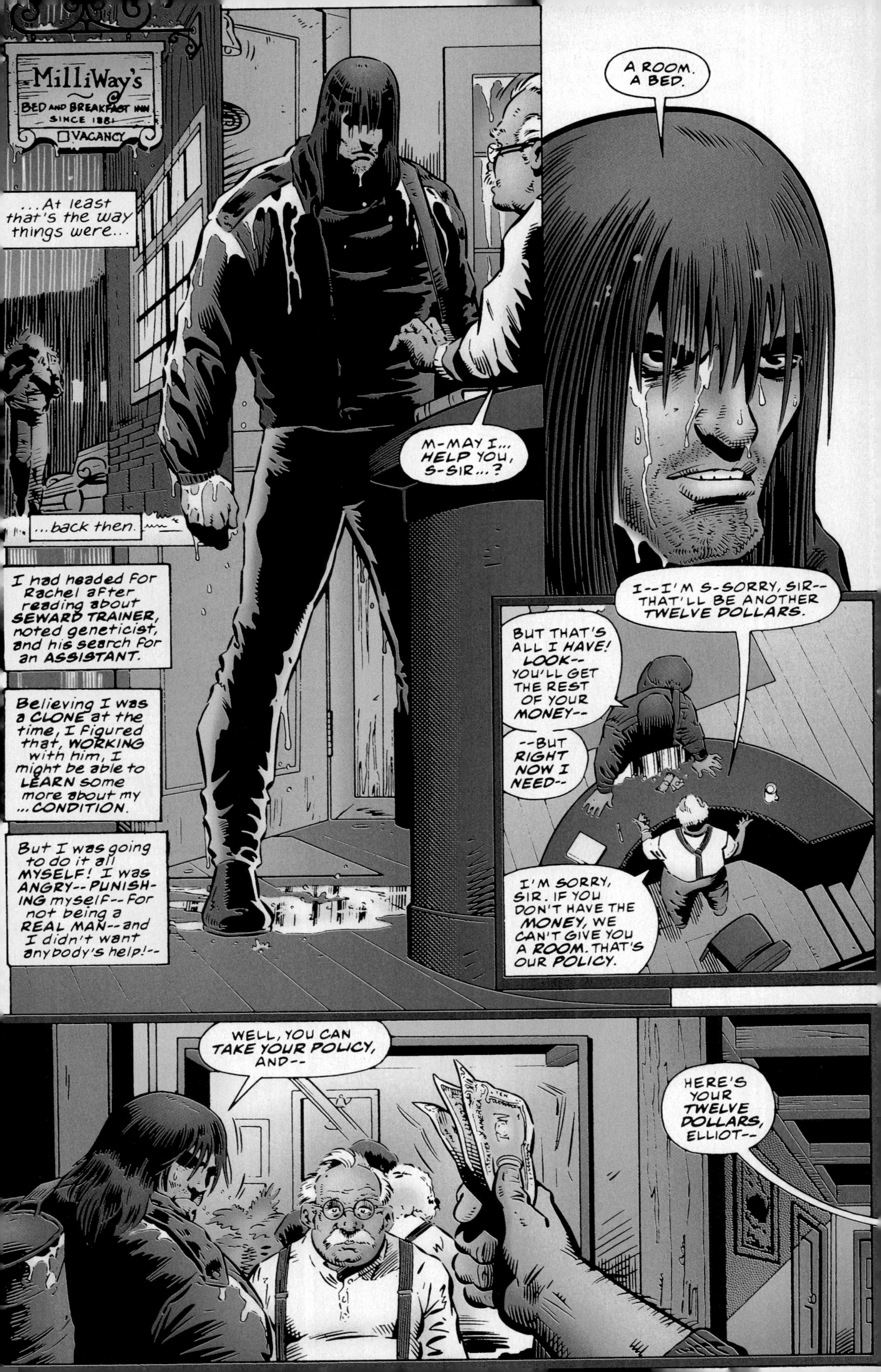
MilliWay's
BED AND BREAKFAST INN
SINCE 1881
VACANCY
...At least that's the way things were...
...back then.
M-MAY I... HELP YOU, S-SIR...?
A ROOM. A BED.
I had headed for Rachel after reading about SEWARD TRAINER, noted geneticist, and his search for an ASSISTANT.
Believing I was a CLONE at the time, I figured that, WORKING with him, I might be able to LEARN some more about my ...CONDITION.
But I was going to do it all MYSELF! I was ANGRY--PUNISHING myself--for not being a REAL MAN--and I didn't want anybody's help!--
I--I'M S-SORRY, SIR--THAT'LL BE ANOTHER TWELVE DOLLARS.
BUT THAT'S ALL I HAVE! LOOK--YOU'LL GET THE REST OF YOUR MONEY--
--BUT RIGHT NOW I NEED--
I'M SORRY, SIR. IF YOU DON'T HAVE THE MONEY, WE CAN'T GIVE YOU A ROOM. THAT'S OUR POLICY.
WELL, YOU CAN TAKE YOUR POLICY, AND--
HERE'S YOUR TWELVE DOLLARS, ELLIOT--

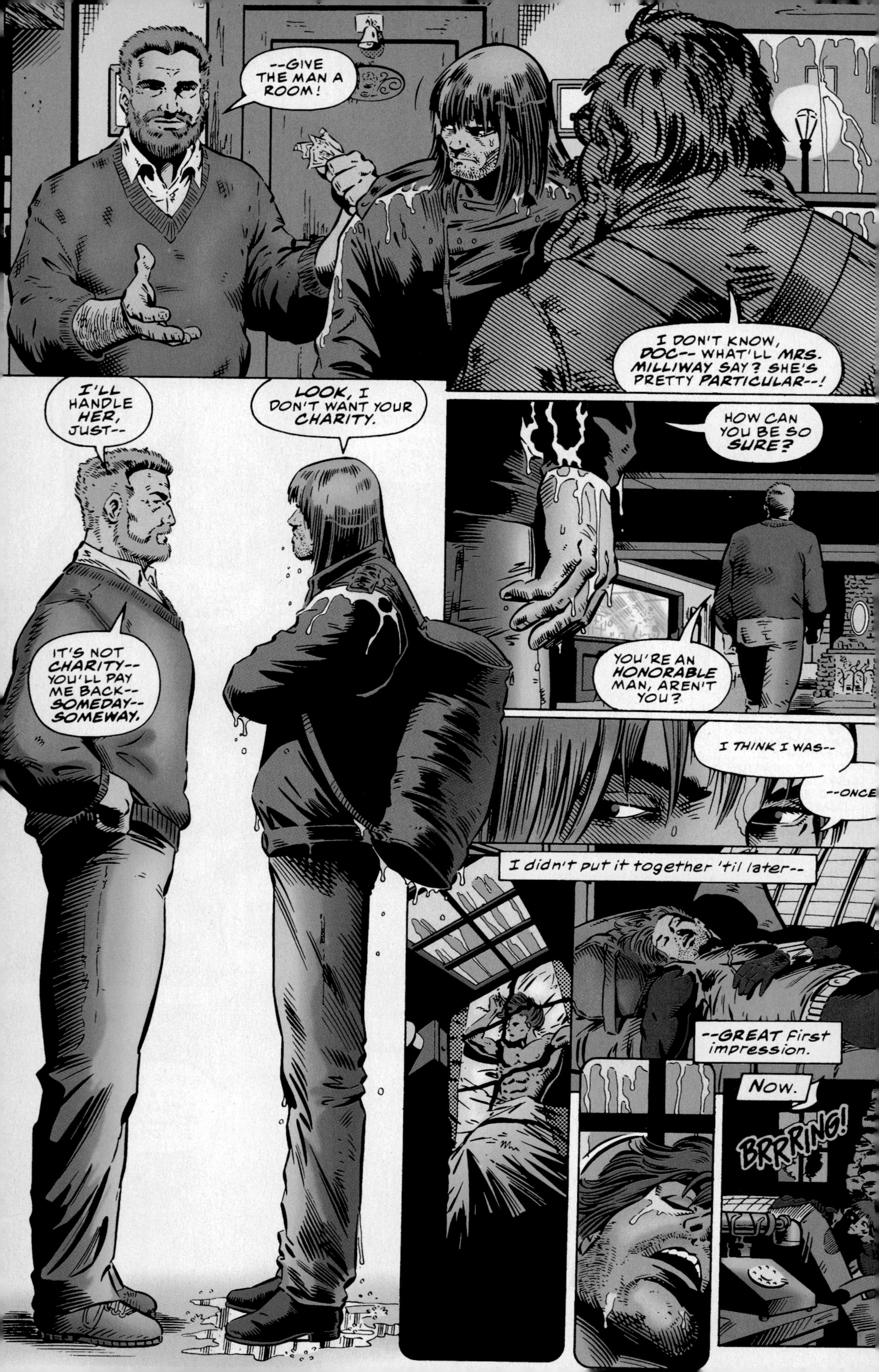
--GIVE THE MAN A ROOM!
I DON'T KNOW, DOC-- WHAT'LL MRS. MILLIWAY SAY? SHE'S PRETTY PARTICULAR--!
I'LL HANDLE HER, JUST--
LOOK, I DON'T WANT YOUR CHARITY.
IT'S NOT CHARITY-- YOU'LL PAY ME BACK-- SOMEDAY-- SOMEWAY.
HOW CAN YOU BE SO SURE?
YOU'RE AN HONORABLE MAN, AREN'T YOU?
I THINK I WAS--
--ONCE
I didn't put it together 'til later--
--GREAT first impression.
Now.
BRRRING!

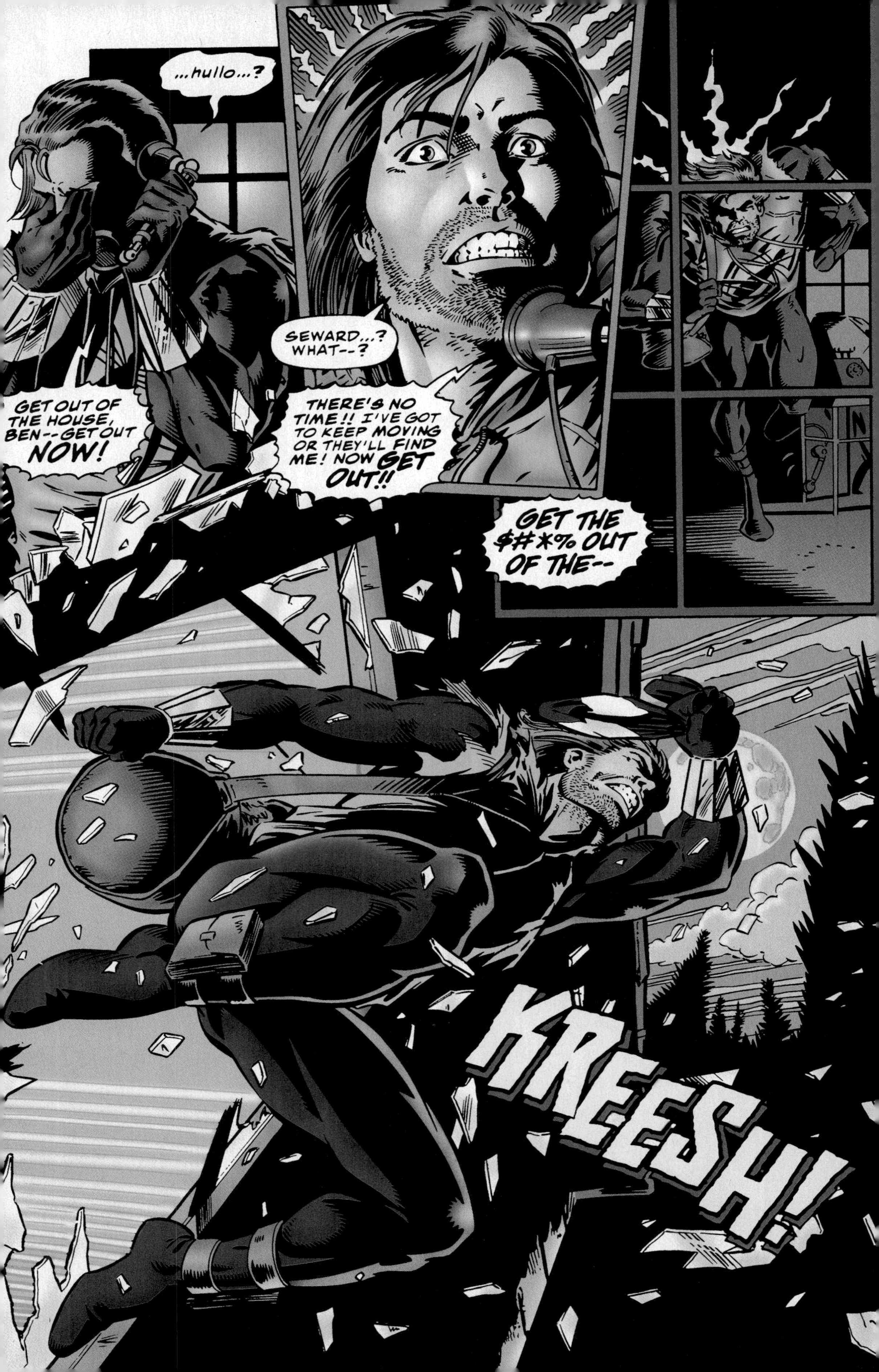

...hullo...?
SEWARD...? WHAT--?
GET OUT OF THE HOUSE, BEN--GET OUT NOW!
THERE'S NO TIME!! I'VE GOT TO KEEP MOVING OR THEY'LL FIND ME! NOW GET OUT!!
GET THE $#*% OUT OF THE--
KREESH!!

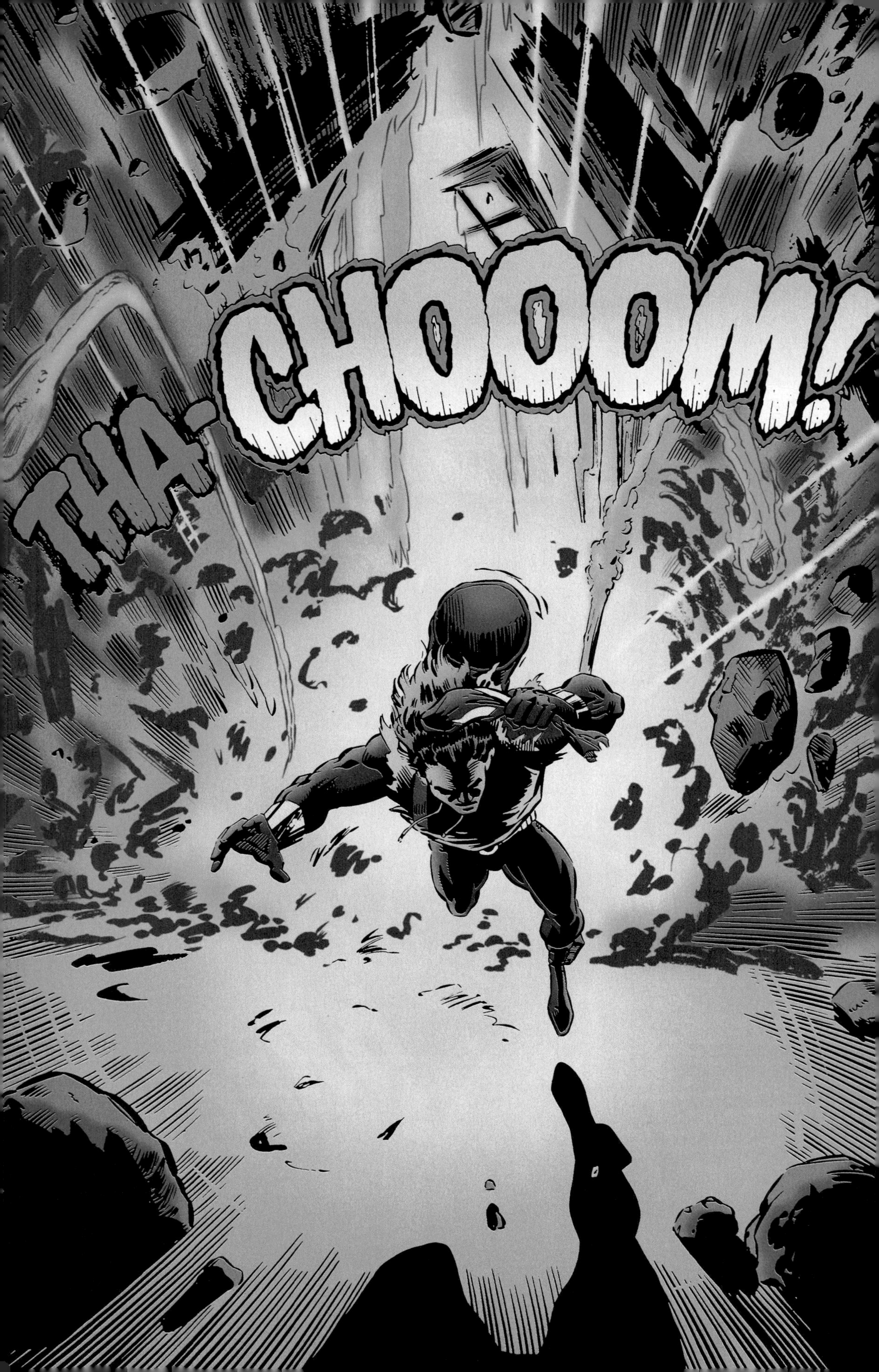
THA-CHOOOM!

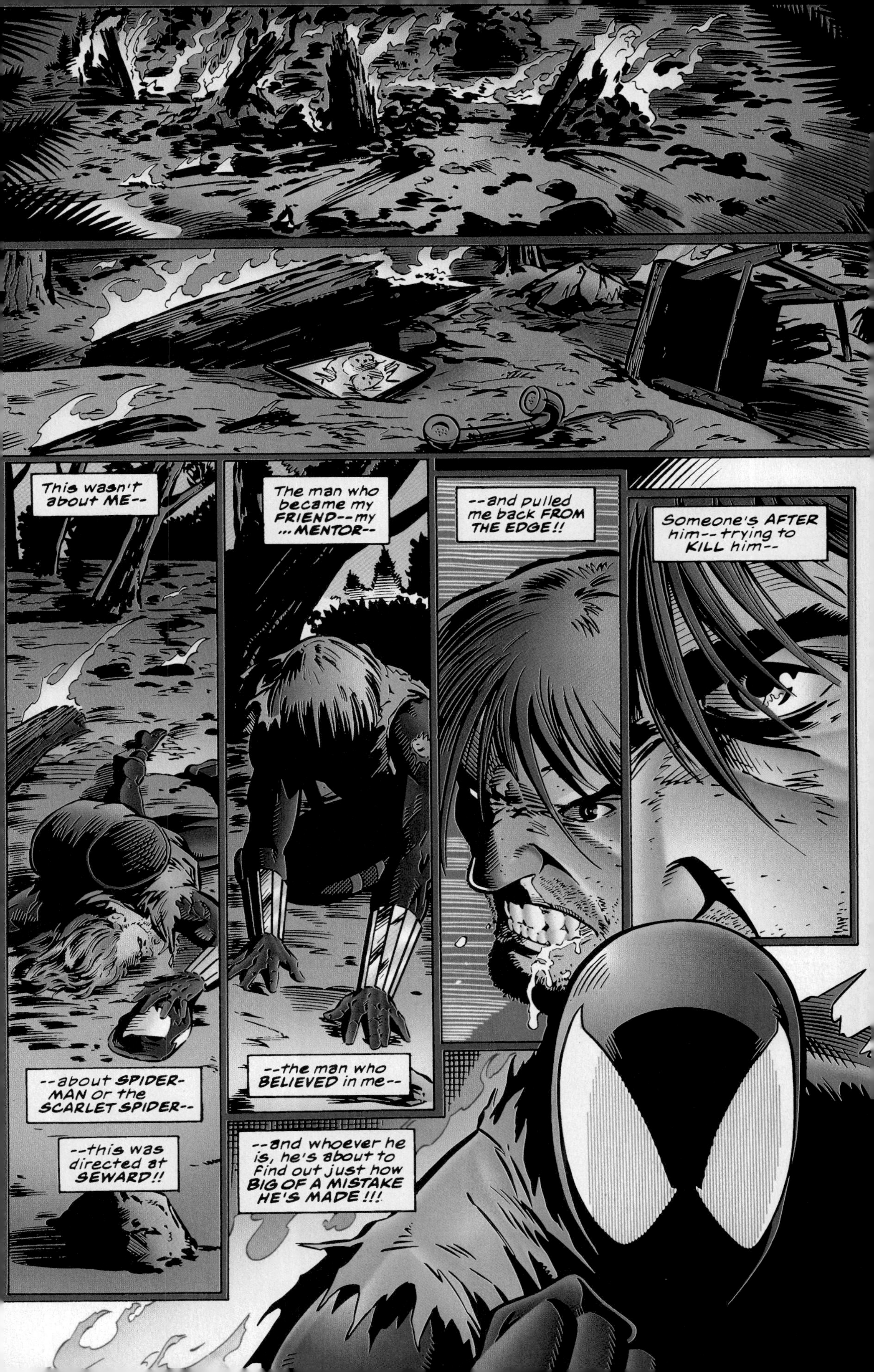
This wasn't about ME--
--about SPIDER-MAN or the SCARLET SPIDER--
--this was directed at SEWARD!!
The man who became my FRIEND--my ...MENTOR--
--the man who BELIEVED in me--
--and pulled me back FROM THE EDGE!!
Someone's AFTER him--trying to KILL him--
--and whoever he is, he's about to find out just how BIG OF A MISTAKE HE'S MADE!!!

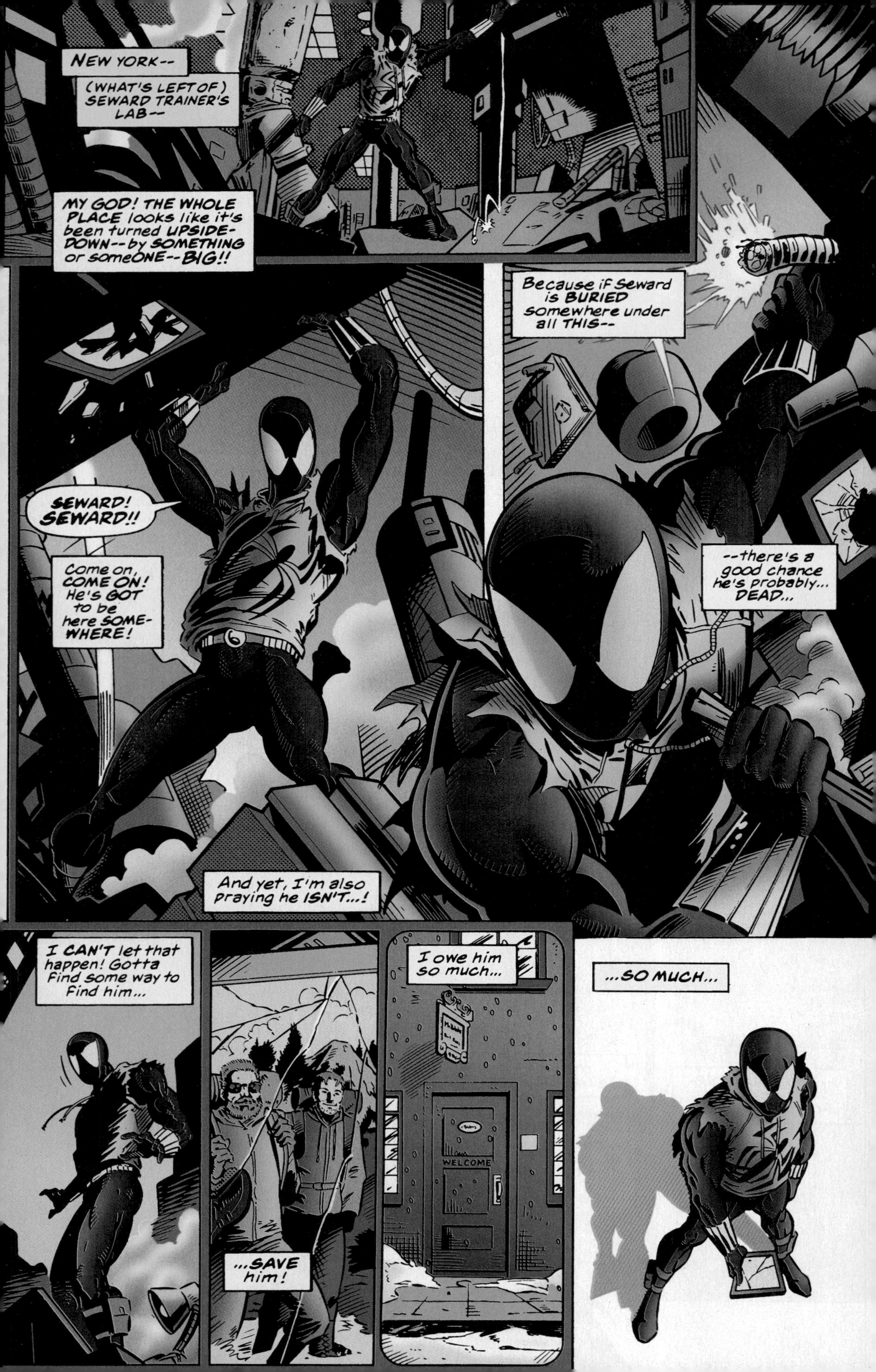
NEW YORK--
(WHAT'S LEFT OF) SEWARD TRAINER'S LAB--
MY GOD! THE WHOLE PLACE looks like it's been turned UPSIDE-DOWN--by SOMETHING or someONE--BIG!!
SEWARD! SEWARD!!
Come on, COME ON! He's GOT to be here SOME-WHERE!
Because if Seward is BURIED somewhere under all THIS--
--there's a good chance he's probably... DEAD...
And yet, I'm also praying he ISN'T...!
I CAN'T let that happen! Gotta find some way to find him...
...SAVE him!
I owe him so much...
WELCOME
...SO MUCH...

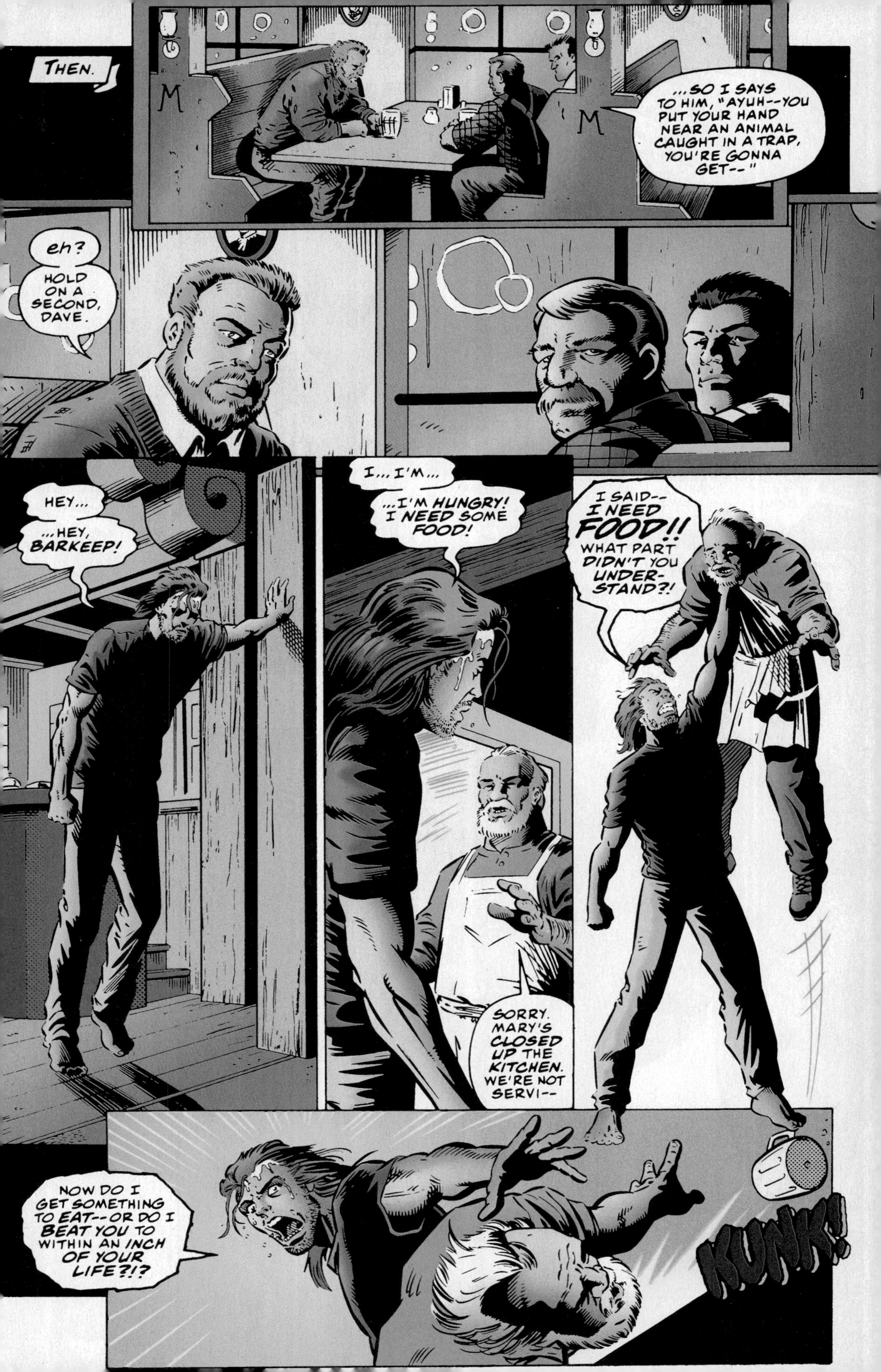

THEN.
...SO I SAYS TO HIM, "AYUH--YOU PUT YOUR HAND NEAR AN ANIMAL CAUGHT IN A TRAP, YOU'RE GONNA GET--"
eh?
HOLD ON A SECOND, DAVE.
HEY...
...HEY, BARKEEP!
I... I'M...
...I'M HUNGRY! I NEED SOME FOOD!
SORRY. MARY'S CLOSED UP THE KITCHEN. WE'RE NOT SERVI--
I SAID-- I NEED FOOD!! WHAT PART DIDN'T YOU UNDER-STAND?!
NOW DO I GET SOMETHING TO EAT--OR DO I BEAT YOU TO WITHIN AN INCH OF YOUR LIFE?!?
KUNK!

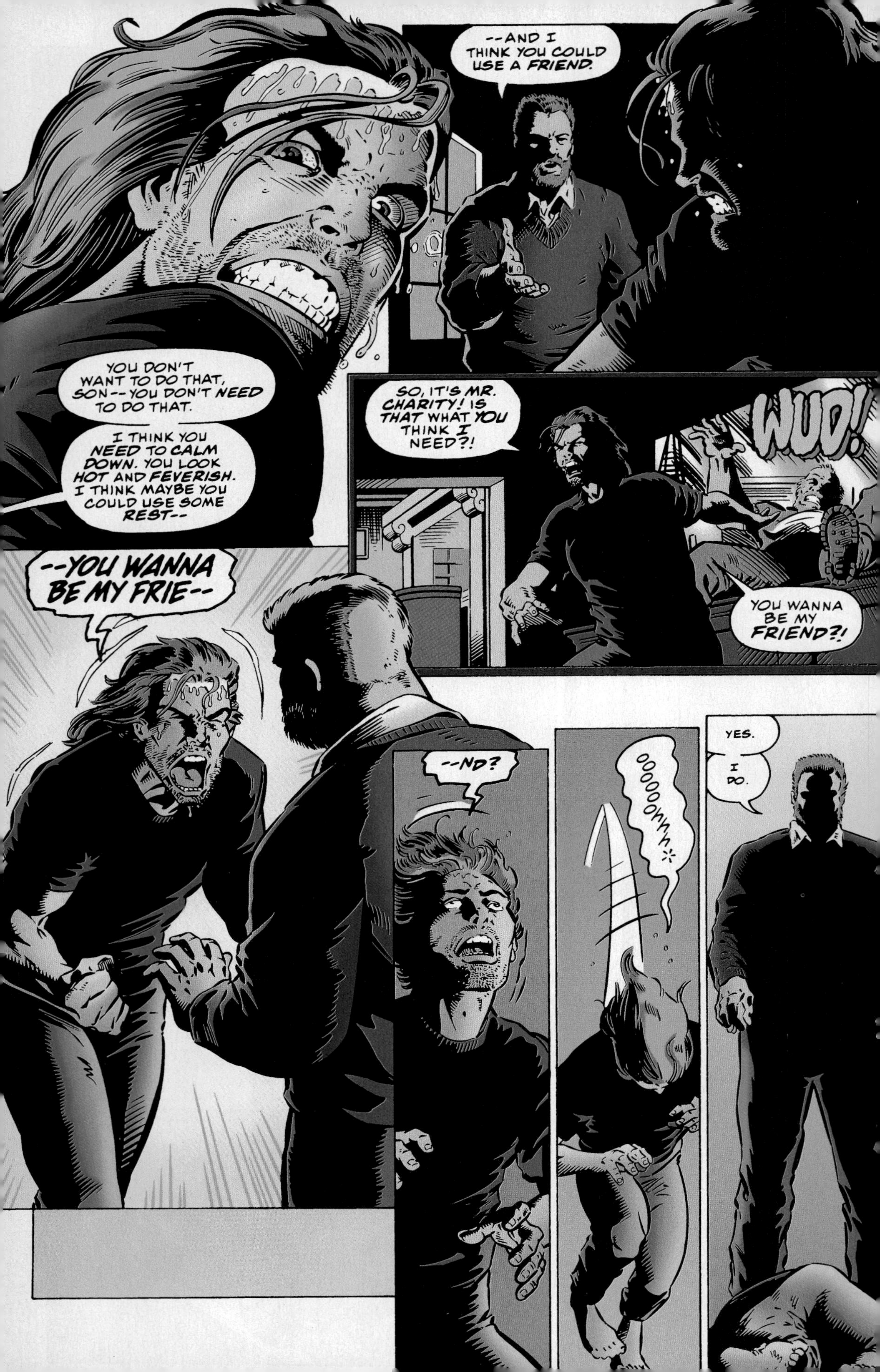
--AND I THINK YOU COULD USE A FRIEND.
YOU DON'T WANT TO DO THAT, SON--YOU DON'T NEED TO DO THAT.
I THINK YOU NEED TO CALM DOWN. YOU LOOK HOT AND FEVERISH. I THINK MAYBE YOU COULD USE SOME REST--
SO, IT'S MR. CHARITY! IS THAT WHAT YOU THINK I NEED?!
WUD!
YOU WANNA BE MY FRIEND?!
--YOU WANNA BE MY FRIE--
--ND?
OOOOOOHHH!*
YES.
I DO.

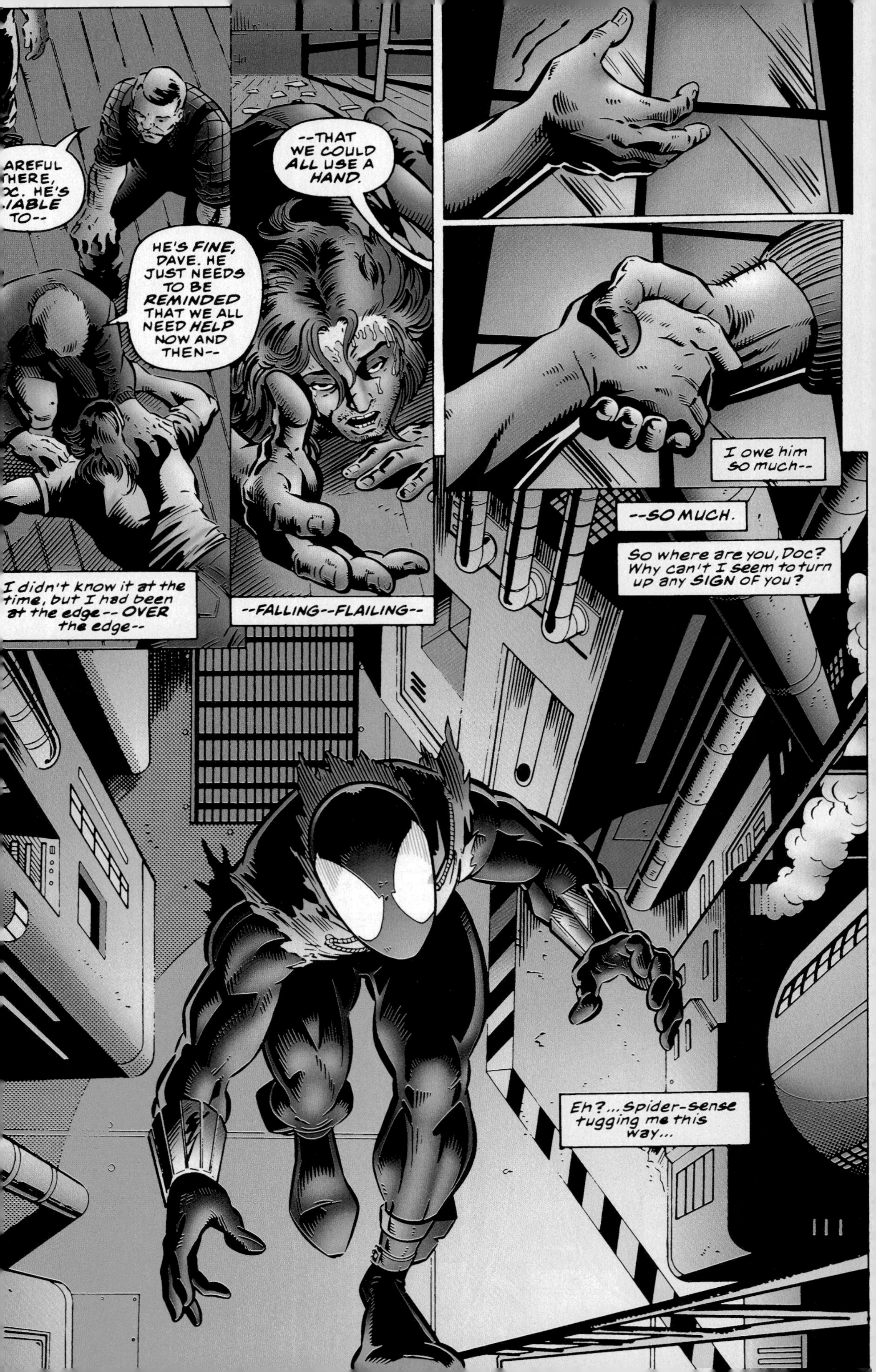

AREFUL THERE, OC. HE'S IABLE TO--
HE'S FINE, DAVE. HE JUST NEEDS TO BE REMINDED THAT WE ALL NEED HELP NOW AND THEN--
--THAT WE COULD ALL USE A HAND.
I didn't know it at the time, but I had been at the edge--OVER the edge--
--FALLING--FLAILING--
I owe him so much--
--SO MUCH.
So where are you, Doc? Why can't I seem to turn up any SIGN of you?
Eh?... Spider-sense tugging me this way...

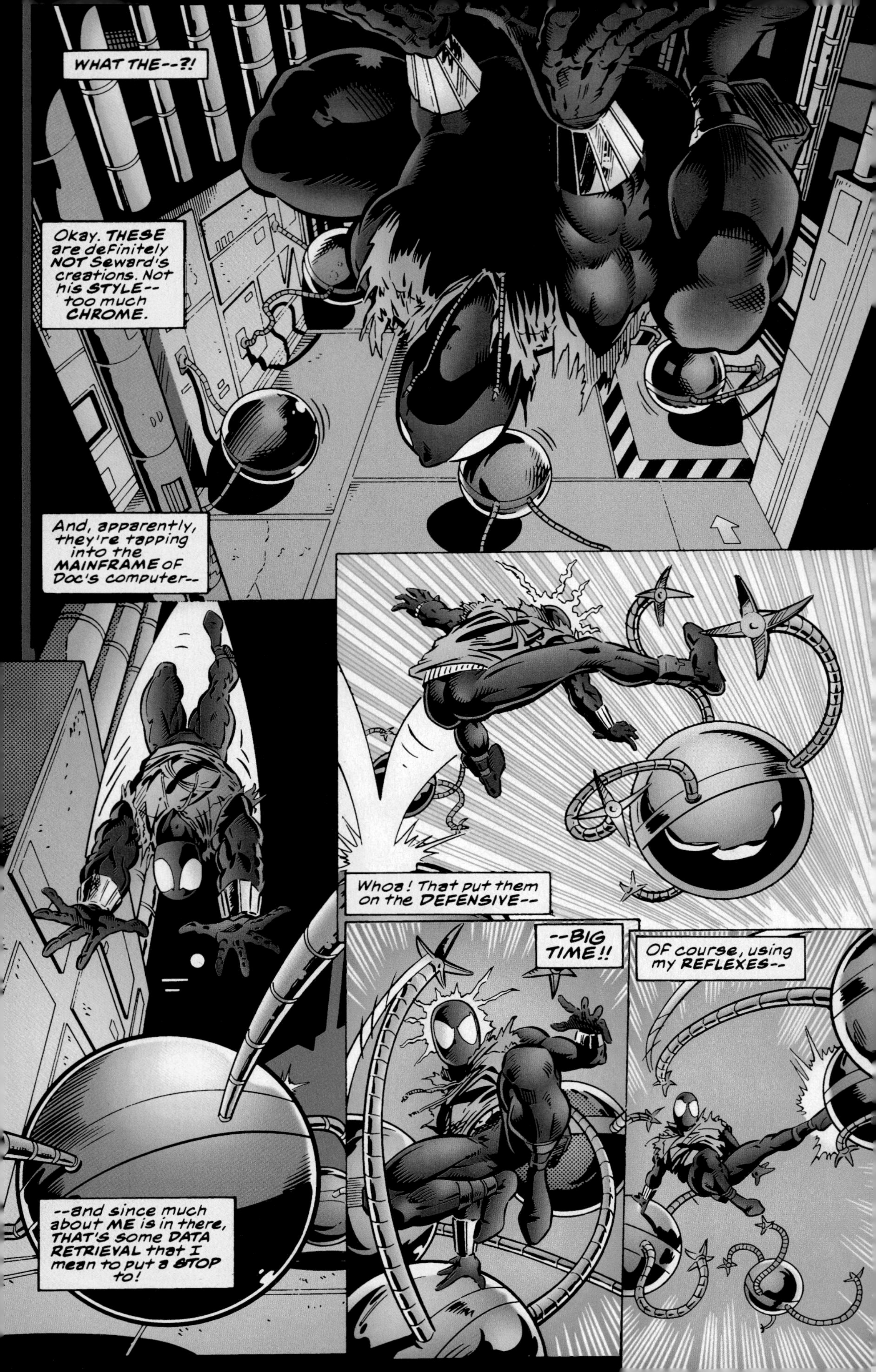
WHAT THE--?!
Okay. THESE are definitely NOT Seward's creations. Not his STYLE-- too much CHROME.
And, apparently, they're tapping into the MAINFRAME OF Doc's computer--
--and since much about ME is in there, THAT'S some DATA RETRIEVAL that I mean to put a STOP to!
Whoa! That put them on the DEFENSIVE--
--BIG TIME!!
OF course, using my REFLEXES--

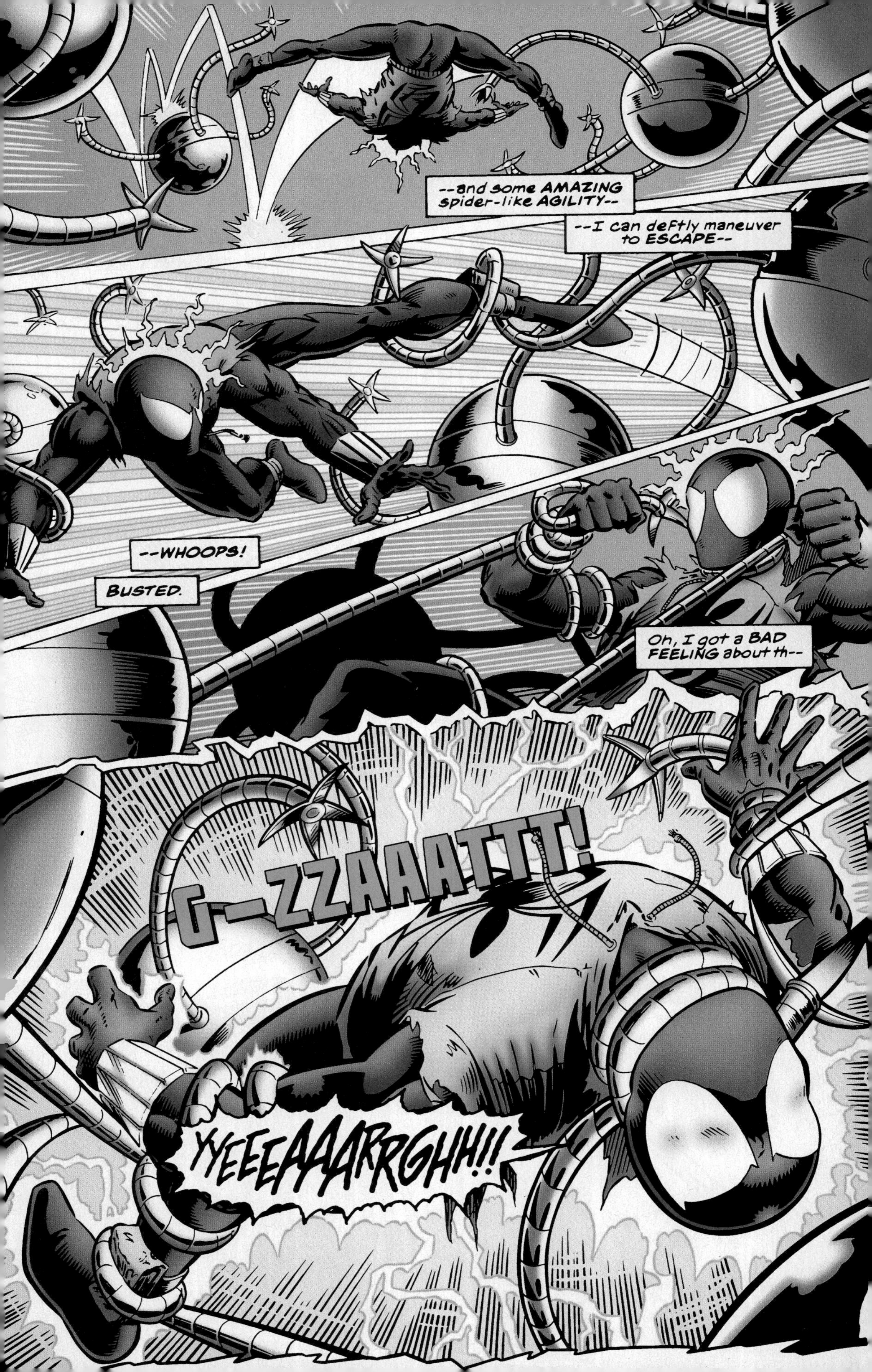
--and some AMAZING spider-like AGILITY--
--I can deftly maneuver to ESCAPE--
--WHOOPS!
BUSTED.
Oh, I got a BAD FEELING about th--
G--ZZAAATTT!
YYEEEAAARRGHH!!

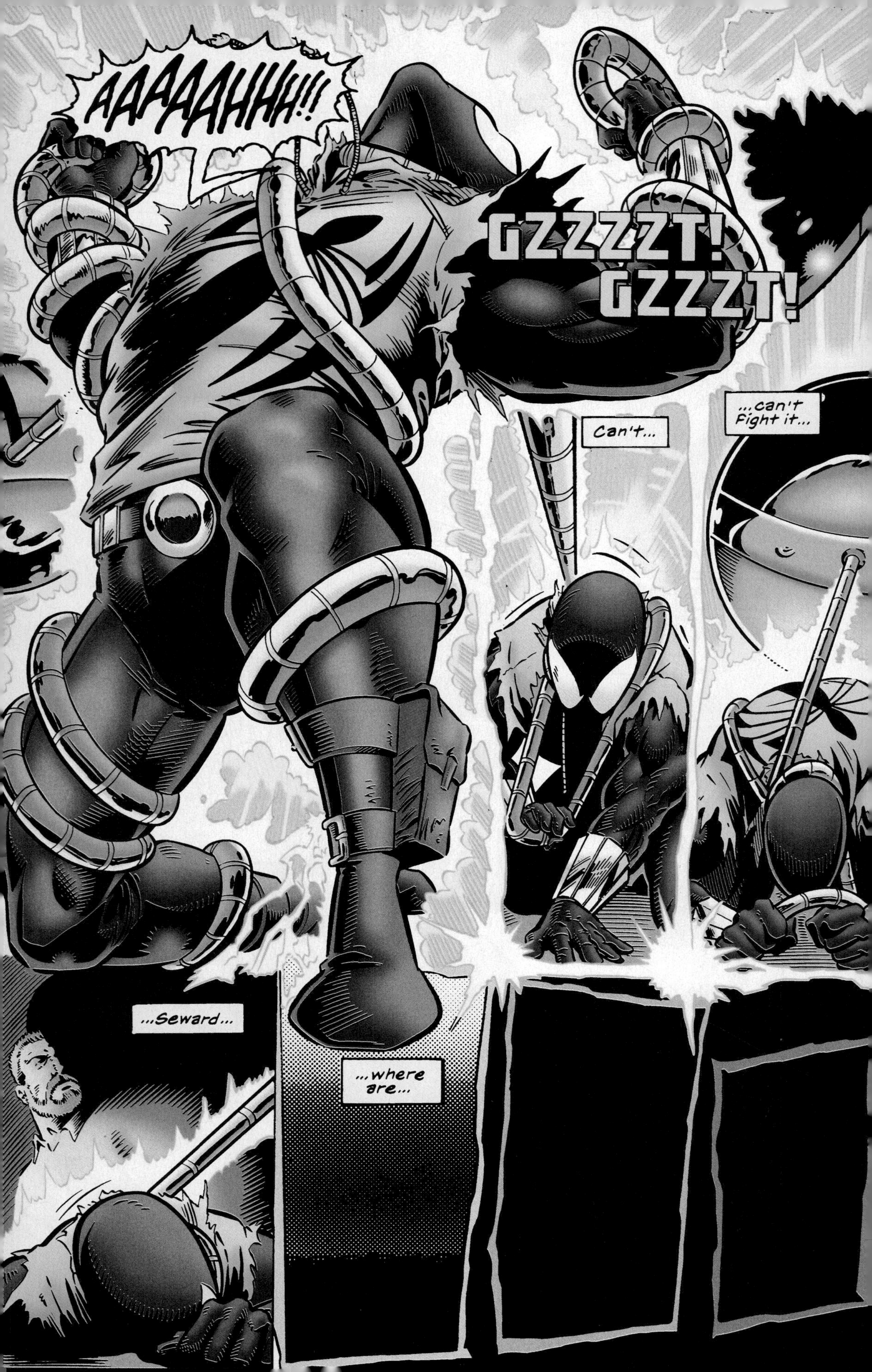
AAAAAHHH!!!
GZZZZT! GZZZT!
Can't...
...can't fight it...
...Seward...
...where are...

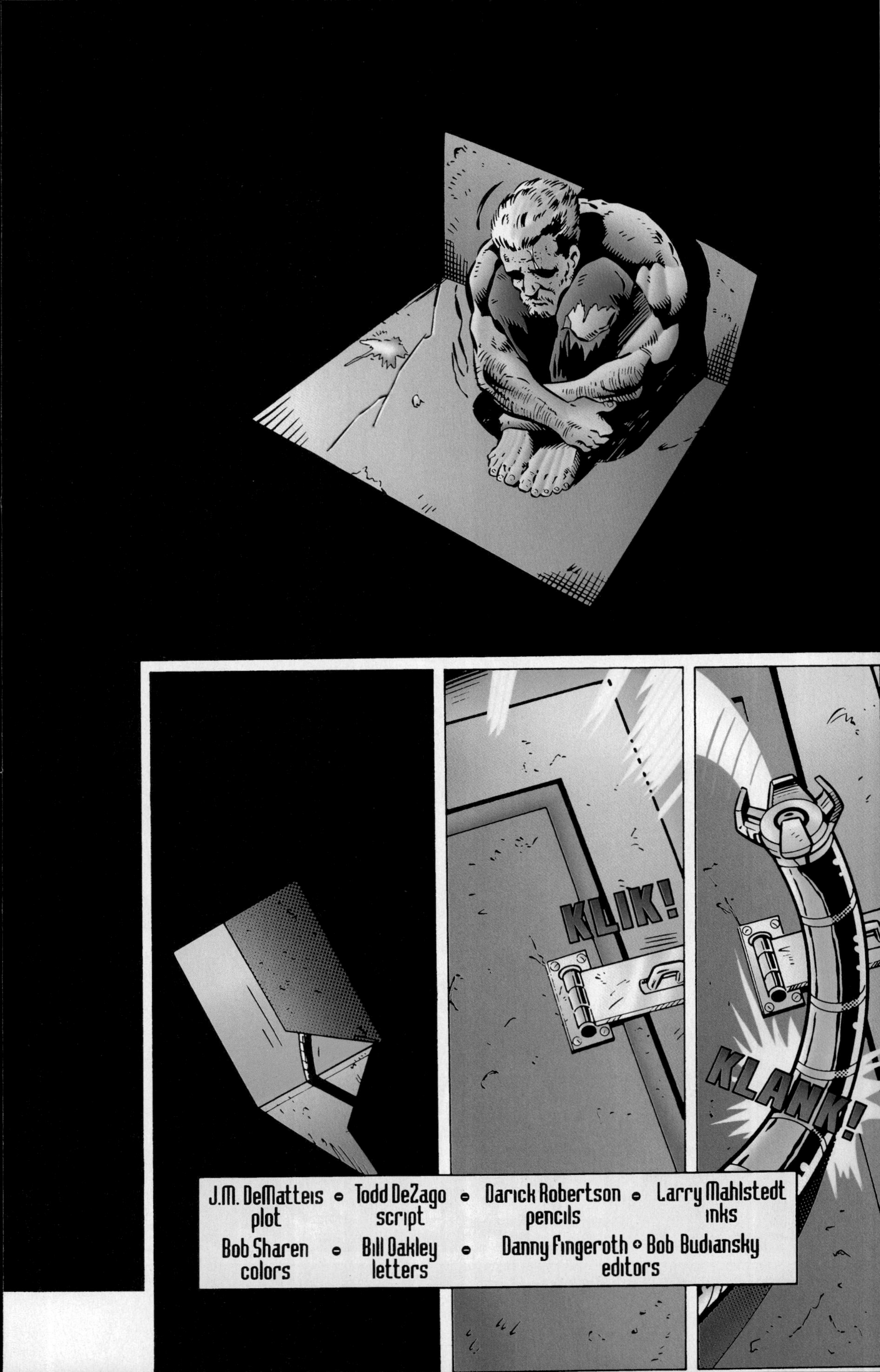
KLIK!
KLANK!
J.M. DeMatteis • Todd DeZago • Darick Robertson • Larry Mahlstedt
plot • script • pencils • inks
Bob Sharen • Bill Oakley • Danny Fingeroth • Bob Budiansky
colors • letters • editors

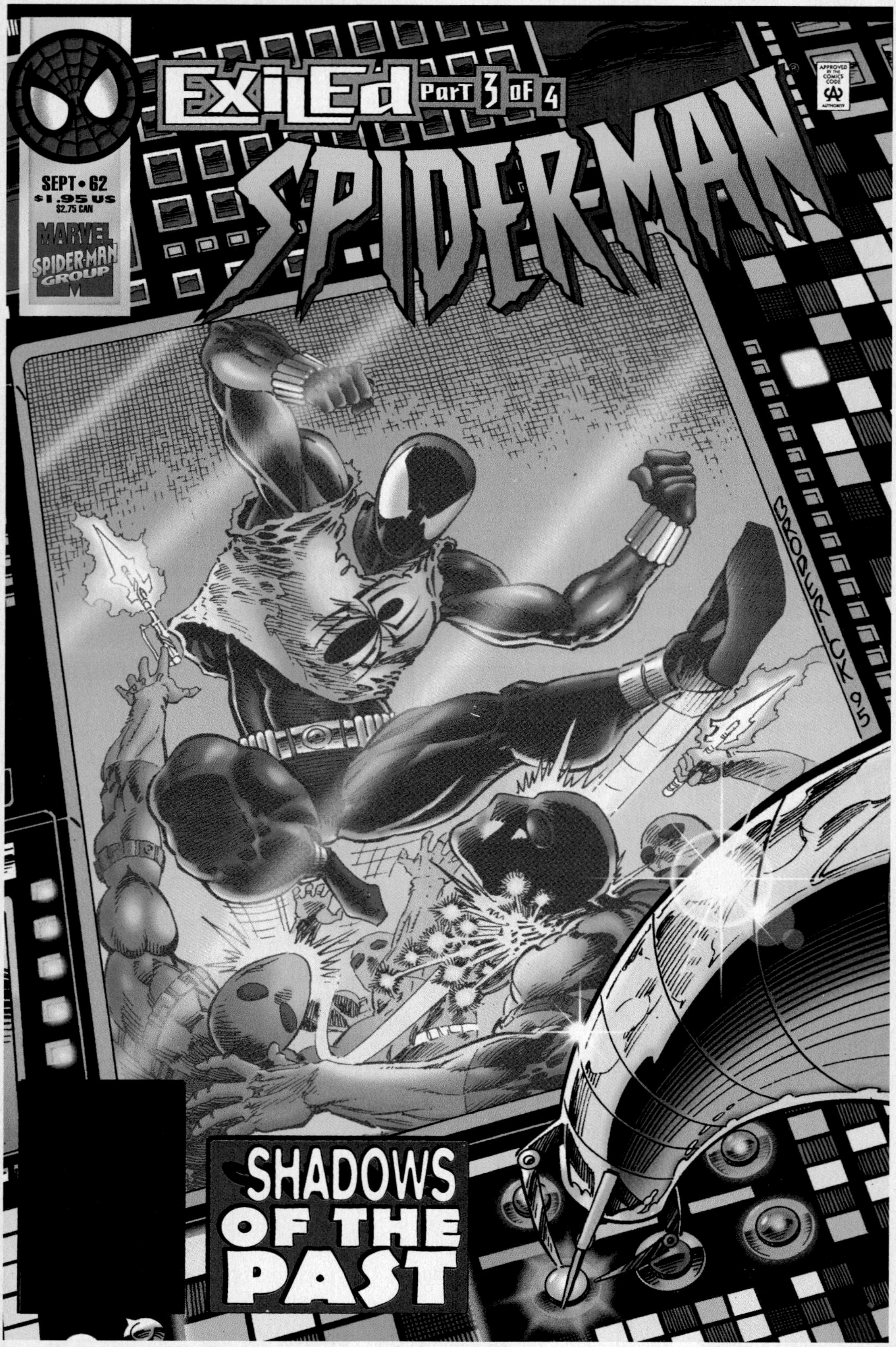

ExiLEd PART 3 OF 4
SPIDER-MAN
SEPT • 62
$1.95 US
$2.75 CAN
MARVEL
SPIDER-MAN GROUP
APPROVED BY THE COMICS CODE AUTHORITY
SHADOWS OF THE PAST

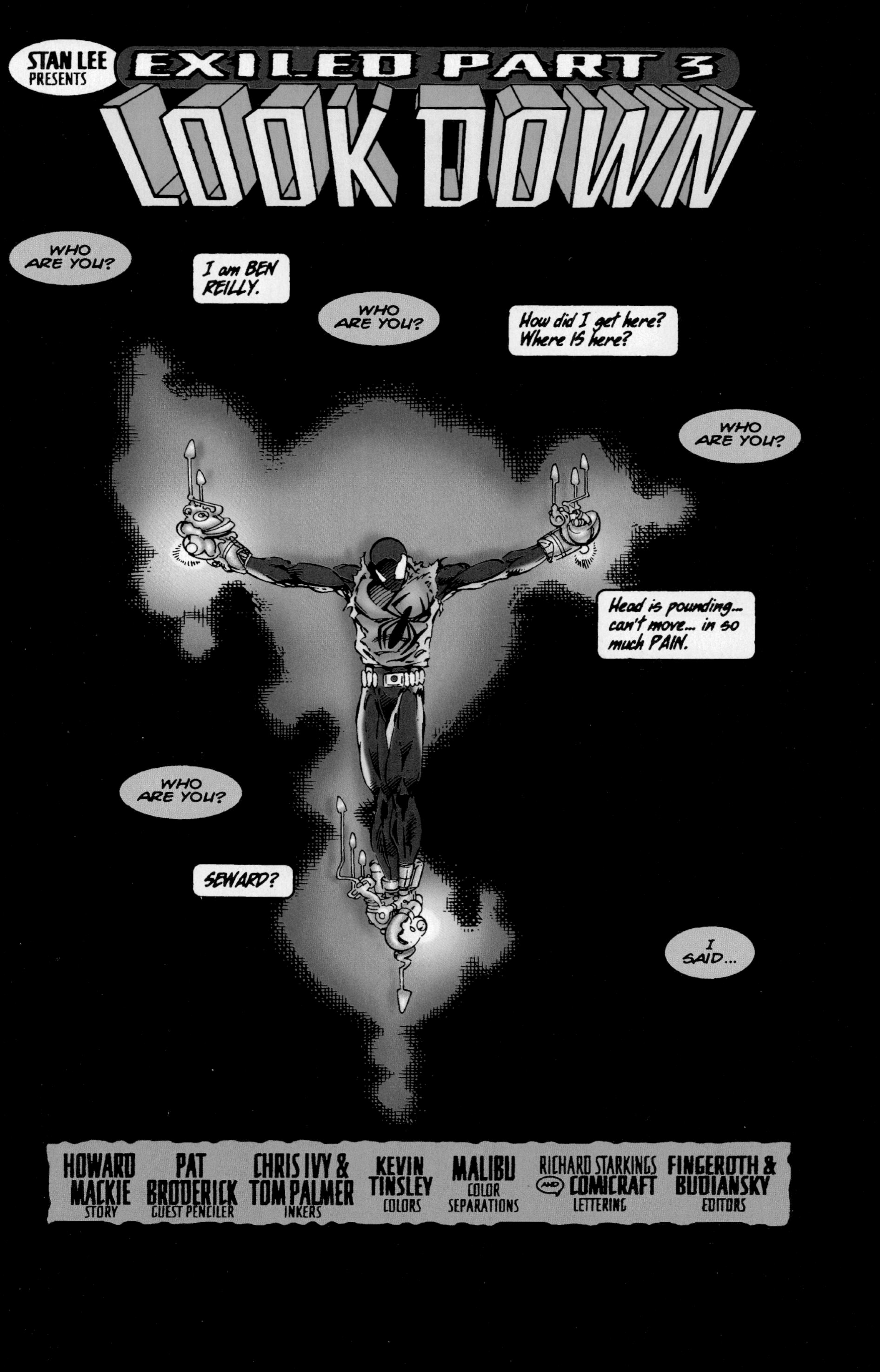
STAN LEE PRESENTS
EXILED PART 3
LOOK DOWN
WHO ARE YOU?
I am BEN REILLY.
WHO ARE YOU?
How did I get here? Where IS here?
WHO ARE YOU?
Head is pounding... can't move... in so much PAIN.
WHO ARE YOU?
SEWARD?
I SAID...
HOWARD MACKIE STORY
PAT BRODERICK GUEST PENCILER
CHRIS IVY & TOM PALMER INKERS
KEVIN TINSLEY COLORS
MALIBU COLOR SEPARATIONS
RICHARD STARKINGS AND COMICRAFT LETTERING
FINGEROTH & BUDIANSKY EDITORS

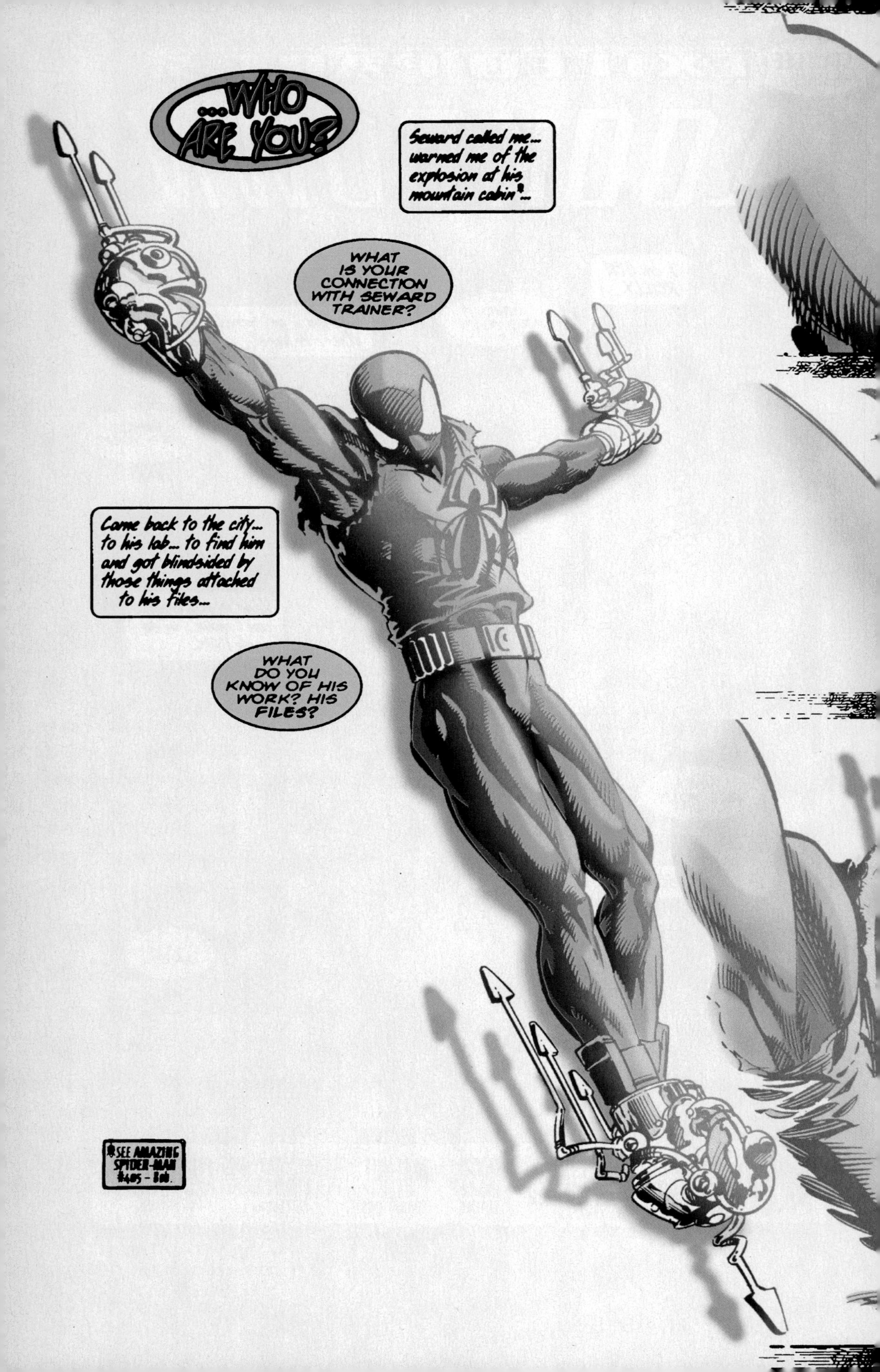
...WHO ARE YOU?
Seward called me... warned me of the explosion at his mountain cabin*...
WHAT IS YOUR CONNECTION WITH SEWARD TRAINER?
Came back to the city... to his lab... to find him and got blindsided by those things attached to his files...
WHAT DO YOU KNOW OF HIS WORK? HIS FILES?
*SEE AMAZING SPIDER-MAN #405 - Bob.

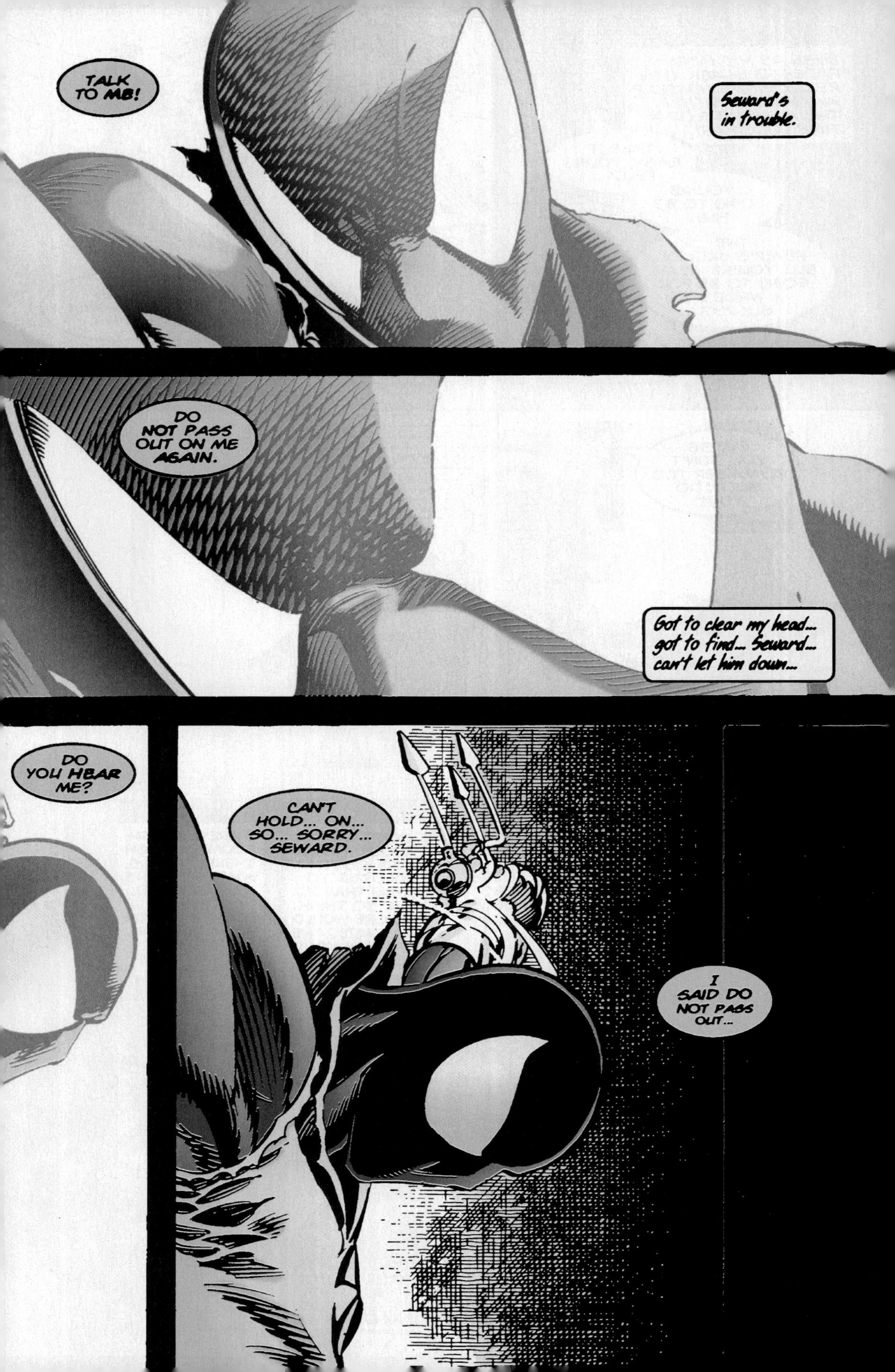
TALK TO ME!
Seward's in trouble.
DO NOT PASS OUT ON ME AGAIN.
Got to clear my head... got to find... Seward... can't let him down...
DO YOU HEAR ME?
CAN'T HOLD... ON... SO... SORRY... SEWARD.
I SAID DO NOT PASS OUT...

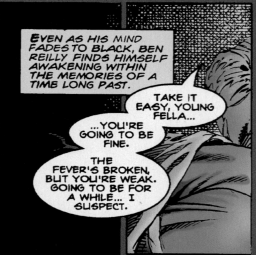

EVEN AS HIS MIND FADES TO BLACK, BEN REILLY FINDS HIMSELF AWAKENING WITHIN THE MEMORIES OF A TIME LONG PAST.

TAKE IT EASY, YOUNG FELLA...

...YOU'RE GOING TO BE FINE.

THE FEVER'S BROKEN, BUT YOU'RE WEAK. GOING TO BE FOR A WHILE... I SUSPECT.

WHERE AM I? HOW..? WHO..?

GUESS YOU DON'T REMEMBER TOO MUCH, DO YOU?

YOU'RE IN VERMONT... THIS IS MY PLACE... AND MY NAME IS SEWARD TRAINER.

OH, YEAH...

I'M SORRY ABOUT THE WAY I ACTED AT THE INN. IF THERE ARE ANY DAMAGES...

DON'T WORRY ABOUT IT. YOU WERE SICK, LAD. CLOSER TO DYING THAN I'D LIKE TO THINK. ANYONE WOULD HAVE ACTED THE SAME IN YOUR CONDITION.*

* FOR COMPLETE DETAILS OF SEWARD AND BEN'S MEETING, SEE AMAZING SPIDER-MAN #405 — Bob.

THERE'S A BATHROOM THROUGH THERE. TOWELS, SOAP, SCISSORS, A RAZOR AND SOME OLD CLOTHES OF MINE YOU CAN WEAR... IF YOU WANT THEM. IT'S UP TO YOU.

THANK...

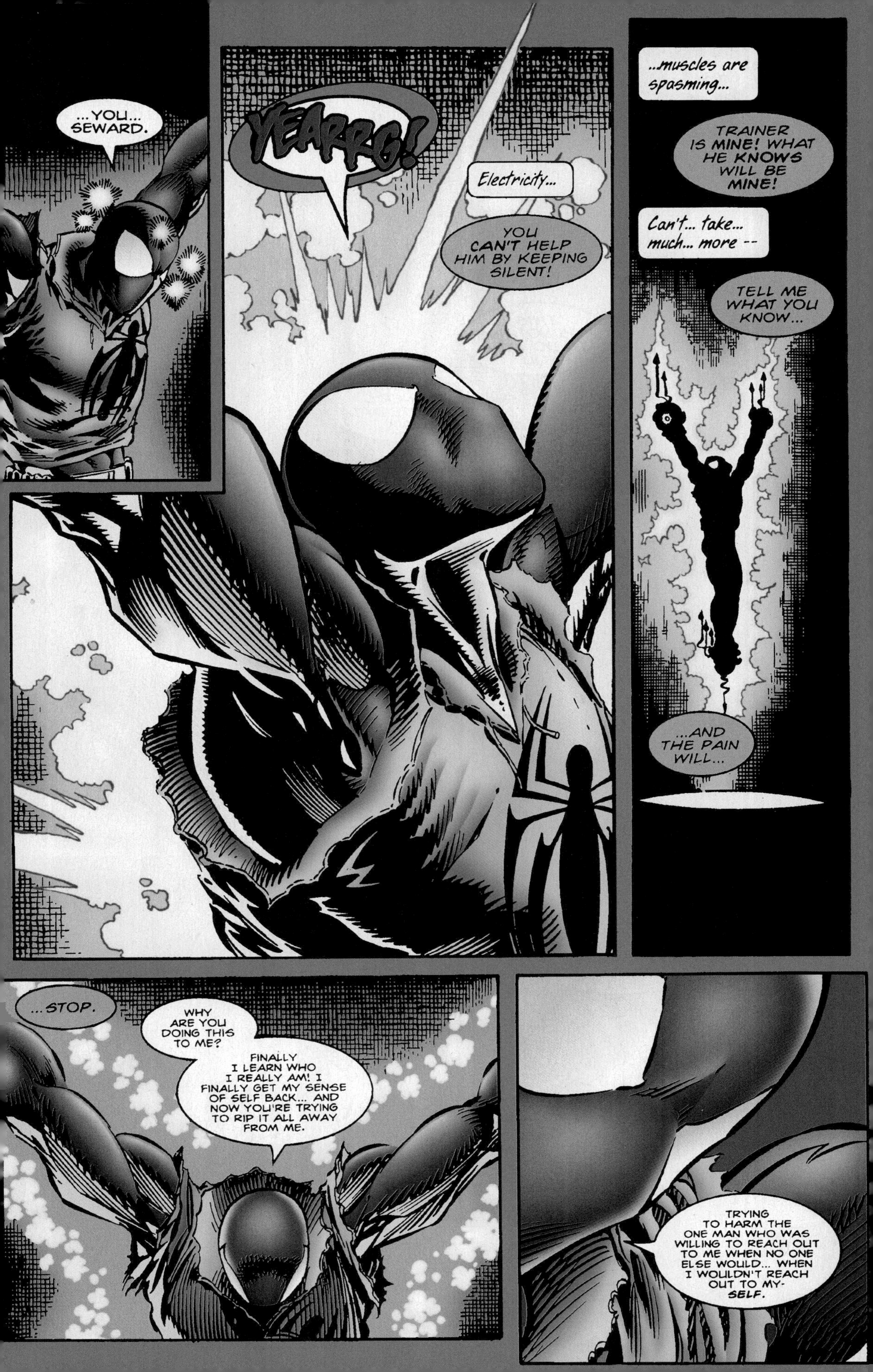
...YOU... SEWARD.
YEARRG!
Electricity...
YOU CAN'T HELP HIM BY KEEPING SILENT!
...muscles are spasming...
TRAINER IS MINE! WHAT HE KNOWS WILL BE MINE!
Can't... take... much... more --
TELL ME WHAT YOU KNOW...
...AND THE PAIN WILL...
...STOP.
WHY ARE YOU DOING THIS TO ME?
FINALLY I LEARN WHO I REALLY AM! I FINALLY GET MY SENSE OF SELF BACK... AND NOW YOU'RE TRYING TO RIP IT ALL AWAY FROM ME.
TRYING TO HARM THE ONE MAN WHO WAS WILLING TO REACH OUT TO ME WHEN NO ONE ELSE WOULD... WHEN I WOULDN'T REACH OUT TO MY-SELF.

WHY?

THIS HAS NOTHING TO DO WITH YOU.

I WANT TRAINER'S COMPLETE DATA BANK.

DON'T YOU PASS ON ME AGAIN. SLEEP WHEN YOU CAN S-- NOW LOC--

DOES THE GENTLEMAN LOOK FAMILIAR?

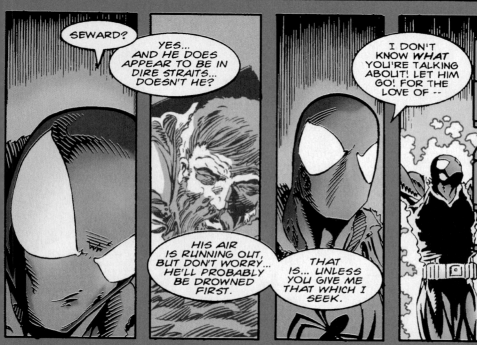

SEWARD?

YES... AND HE DOES APPEAR TO BE IN DIRE STRAITS... DOESN'T HE?

HIS AIR IS RUNNING OUT, BUT DON'T WORRY... HE'LL PROBABLY BE DROWNED FIRST.

I DON'T KNOW WHAT YOU'RE TALKING ABOUT! LET HIM GO! FOR THE LOVE OF --

THAT IS... UNLESS YOU GIVE ME THAT WHICH I SEEK.

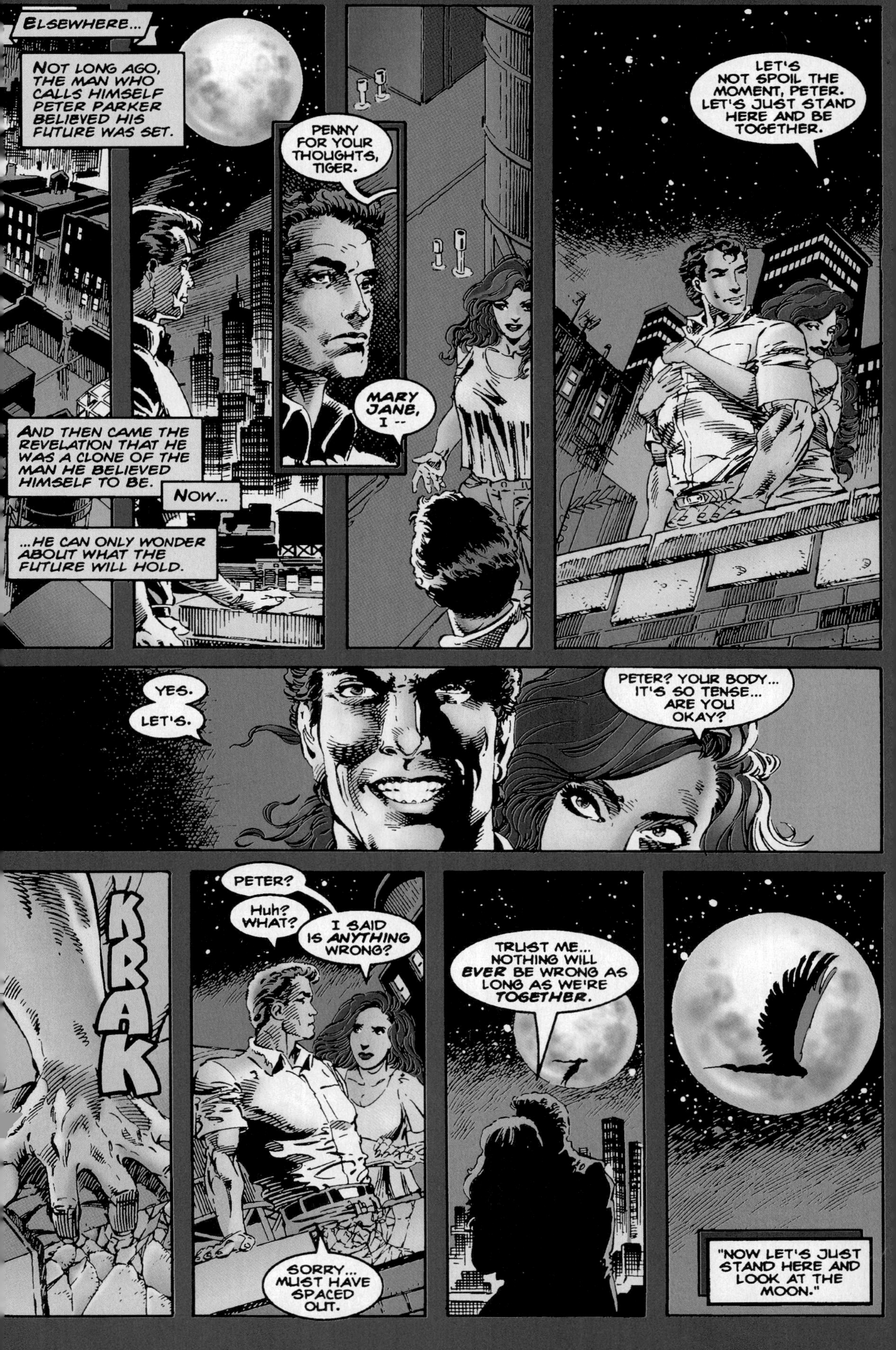
ELSEWHERE...
NOT LONG AGO, THE MAN WHO CALLS HIMSELF PETER PARKER BELIEVED HIS FUTURE WAS SET.
AND THEN CAME THE REVELATION THAT HE WAS A CLONE OF THE MAN HE BELIEVED HIMSELF TO BE.
NOW...
...HE CAN ONLY WONDER ABOUT WHAT THE FUTURE WILL HOLD.
PENNY FOR YOUR THOUGHTS, TIGER.
MARY JANE, I --
LET'S NOT SPOIL THE MOMENT, PETER. LET'S JUST STAND HERE AND BE TOGETHER.
YES.
LET'S.
PETER? YOUR BODY... IT'S SO TENSE... ARE YOU OKAY?
KRAK
PETER?
Huh? WHAT?
I SAID IS ANYTHING WRONG?
SORRY... MUST HAVE SPACED OUT.
TRUST ME... NOTHING WILL EVER BE WRONG AS LONG AS WE'RE TOGETHER.
"NOW LET'S JUST STAND HERE AND LOOK AT THE MOON."

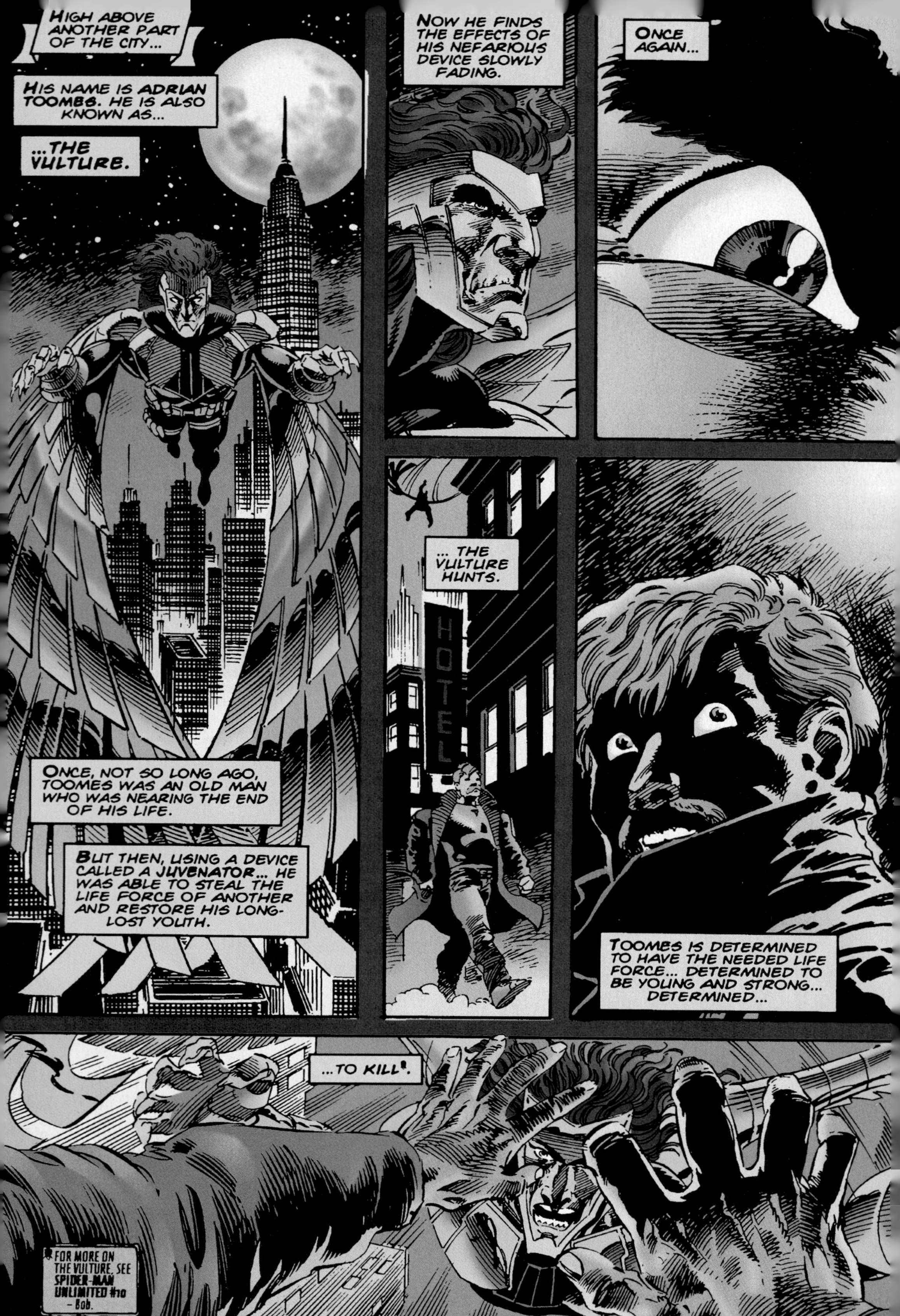
HIGH ABOVE ANOTHER PART OF THE CITY...
HIS NAME IS ADRIAN TOOMBS. HE IS ALSO KNOWN AS...
...THE VULTURE.
ONCE, NOT SO LONG AGO, TOOMES WAS AN OLD MAN WHO WAS NEARING THE END OF HIS LIFE.
BUT THEN, USING A DEVICE CALLED A JUVENATOR... HE WAS ABLE TO STEAL THE LIFE FORCE OF ANOTHER AND RESTORE HIS LONG-LOST YOUTH.
NOW HE FINDS THE EFFECTS OF HIS NEFARIOUS DEVICE SLOWLY FADING.
ONCE AGAIN...
... THE VULTURE HUNTS.
HOTEL
TOOMES IS DETERMINED TO HAVE THE NEEDED LIFE FORCE... DETERMINED TO BE YOUNG AND STRONG... DETERMINED...
...TO KILL*.
*FOR MORE ON THE VULTURE, SEE SPIDER-MAN UNLIMITED #10 – Bob.

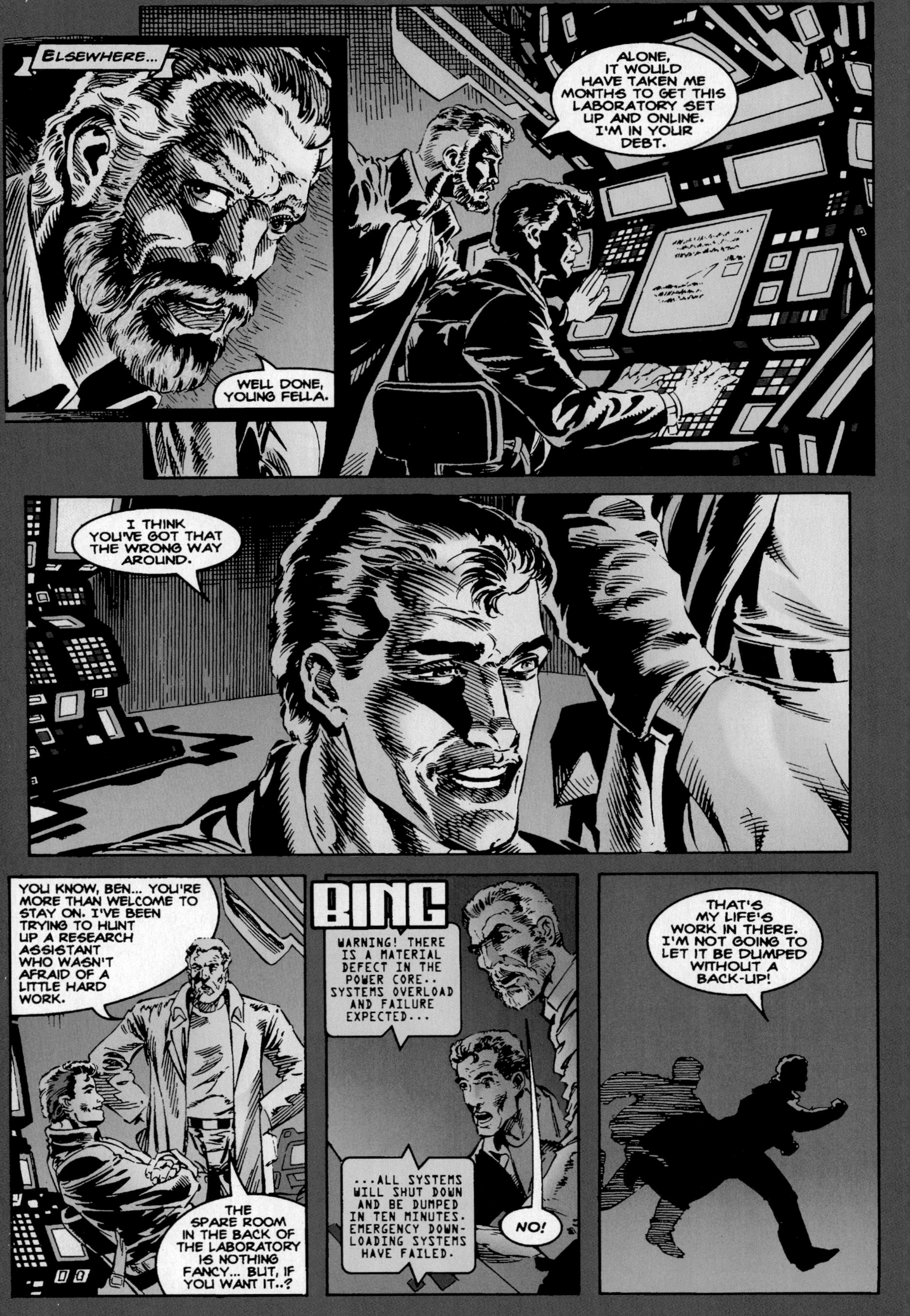
Elsewhere...
Well done, young fella.
Alone, it would have taken me months to get this laboratory set up and online. I'm in your debt.
I think you've got that the wrong way around.
You know, Ben... you're more than welcome to stay on. I've been trying to hunt up a research assistant who wasn't afraid of a little hard work.
The spare room in the back of the laboratory is nothing fancy... but, if you want it..?
BING
WARNING! THERE IS A MATERIAL DEFECT IN THE POWER CORE.. SYSTEMS OVERLOAD AND FAILURE EXPECTED...
...ALL SYSTEMS WILL SHUT DOWN AND BE DUMPED IN TEN MINUTES. EMERGENCY DOWN-LOADING SYSTEMS HAVE FAILED.
No!
That's my life's work in there. I'm not going to let it be dumped without a back-up!

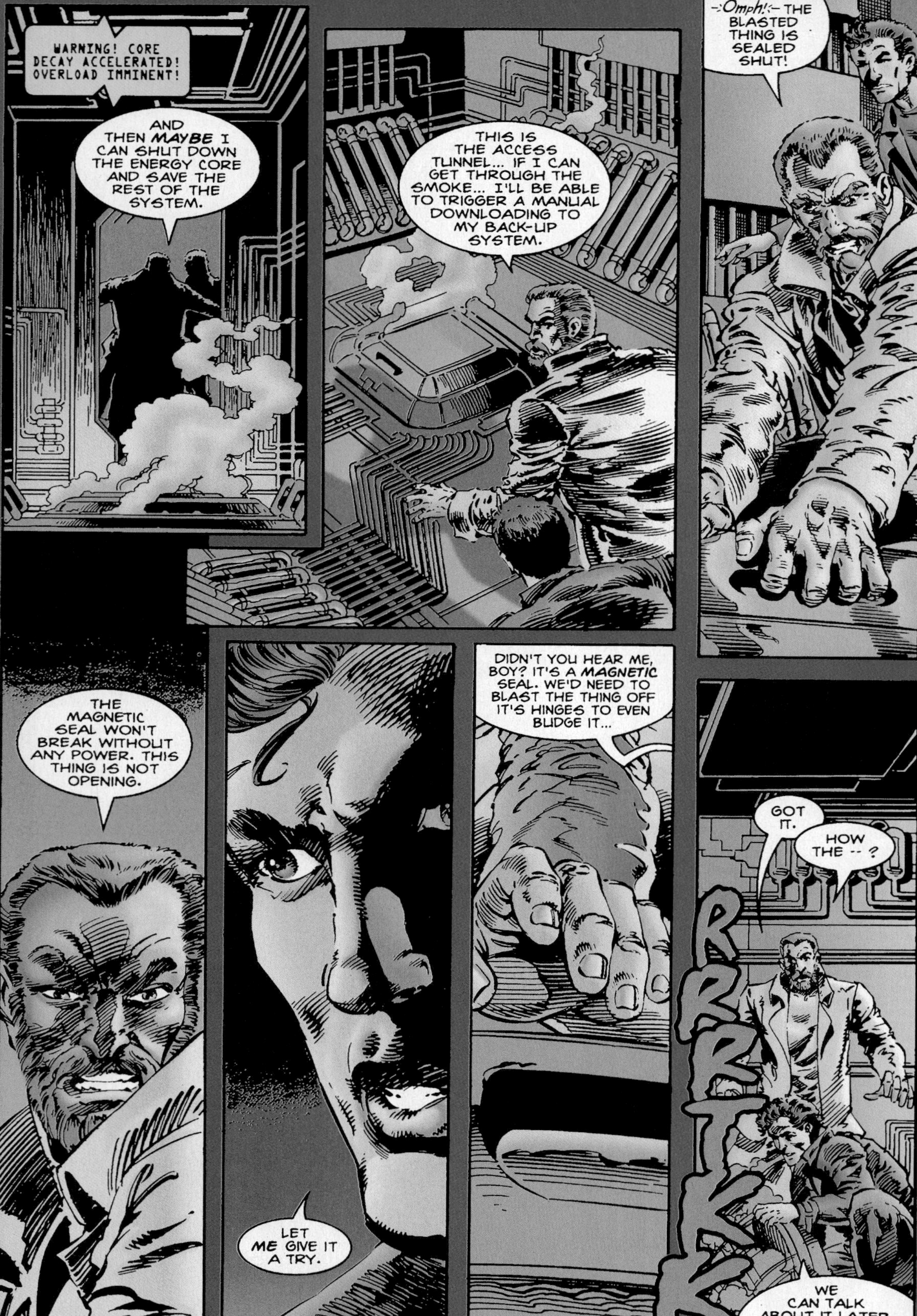
WARNING! CORE DECAY ACCELERATED! OVERLOAD IMMINENT!
AND THEN MAYBE I CAN SHUT DOWN THE ENERGY CORE AND SAVE THE REST OF THE SYSTEM.
THIS IS THE ACCESS TUNNEL... IF I CAN GET THROUGH THE SMOKE... I'LL BE ABLE TO TRIGGER A MANUAL DOWNLOADING TO MY BACK-UP SYSTEM.
-Omph!- THE BLASTED THING IS SEALED SHUT!
THE MAGNETIC SEAL WON'T BREAK WITHOUT ANY POWER. THIS THING IS NOT OPENING.
LET ME GIVE IT A TRY.
DIDN'T YOU HEAR ME, BOY? IT'S A MAGNETIC SEAL. WE'D NEED TO BLAST THE THING OFF IT'S HINGES TO EVEN BUDGE IT...
GOT IT.
HOW THE -- ?
RRRK
WE CAN TALK ABOUT IT LATER. RIGHT NOW, WE'VE GOT WORK TO DO.

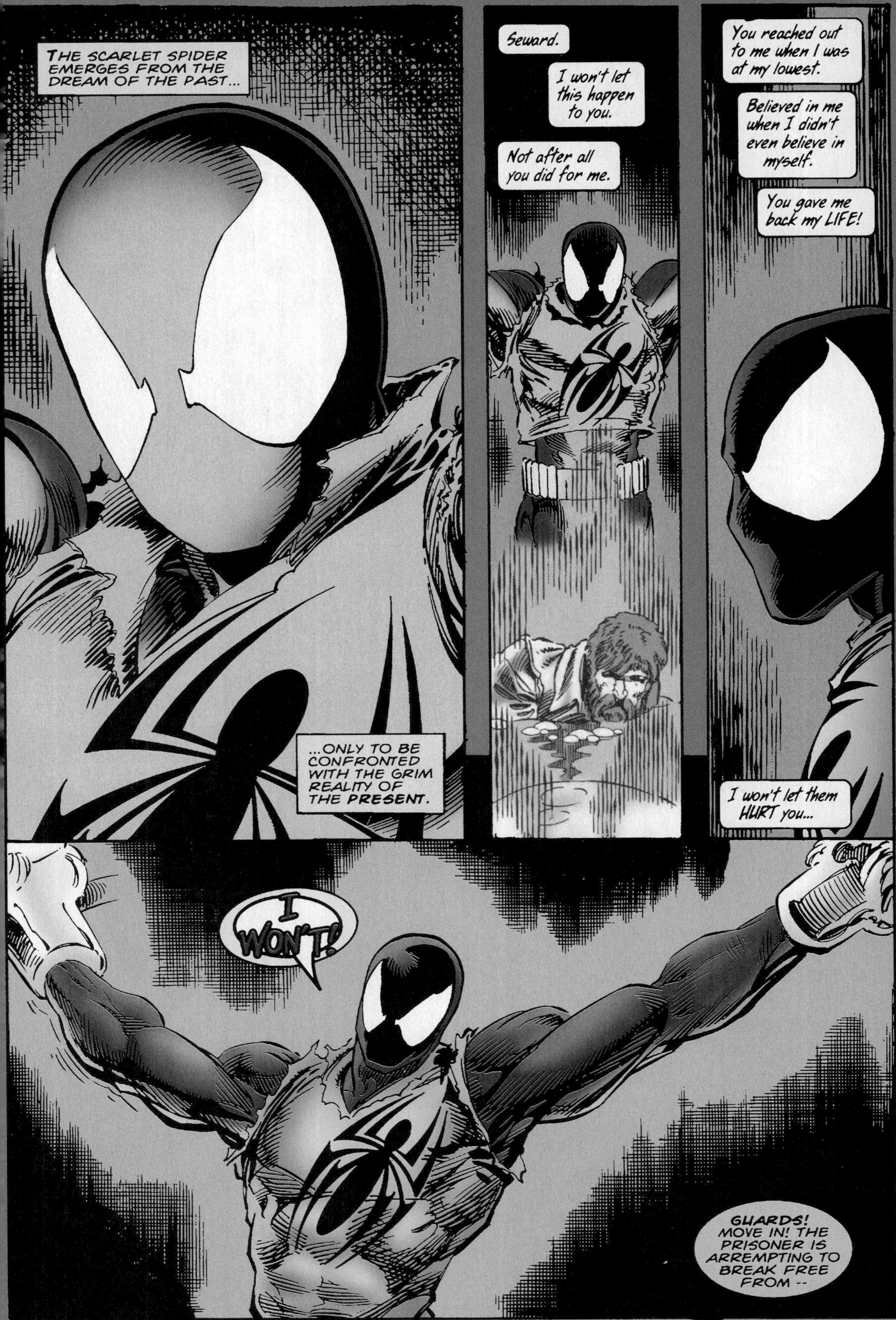

THE SCARLET SPIDER EMERGES FROM THE DREAM OF THE PAST...
...ONLY TO BE CONFRONTED WITH THE GRIM REALITY OF THE PRESENT.
Seward.
I won't let this happen to you.
Not after all you did for me.
You reached out to me when I was at my lowest.
Believed in me when I didn't even believe in myself.
You gave me back my LIFE!
I won't let them HURT you...
I WON'T!
GUARDS! MOVE IN! THE PRISONER IS ARREMPTING TO BREAK FREE FROM --

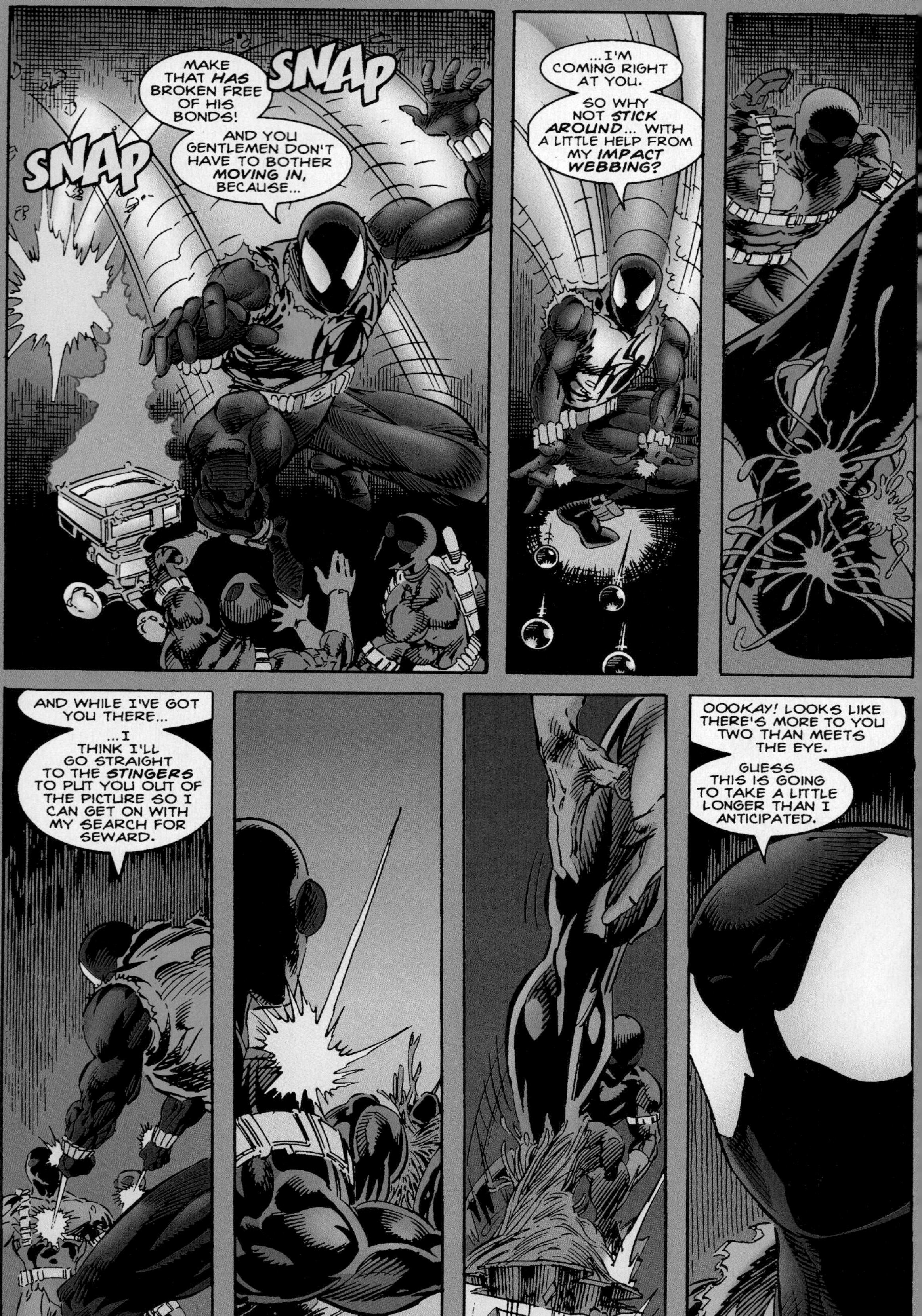
SNAP
MAKE THAT HAS BROKEN FREE OF HIS BONDS!
AND YOU GENTLEMEN DON'T HAVE TO BOTHER MOVING IN, BECAUSE...
SNAP
...I'M COMING RIGHT AT YOU.
SO WHY NOT STICK AROUND... WITH A LITTLE HELP FROM MY IMPACT WEBBING?
AND WHILE I'VE GOT YOU THERE...
...I THINK I'LL GO STRAIGHT TO THE STINGERS TO PUT YOU OUT OF THE PICTURE SO I CAN GET ON WITH MY SEARCH FOR SEWARD.
OOOKAY! LOOKS LIKE THERE'S MORE TO YOU TWO THAN MEETS THE EYE.
GUESS THIS IS GOING TO TAKE A LITTLE LONGER THAN I ANTICIPATED.

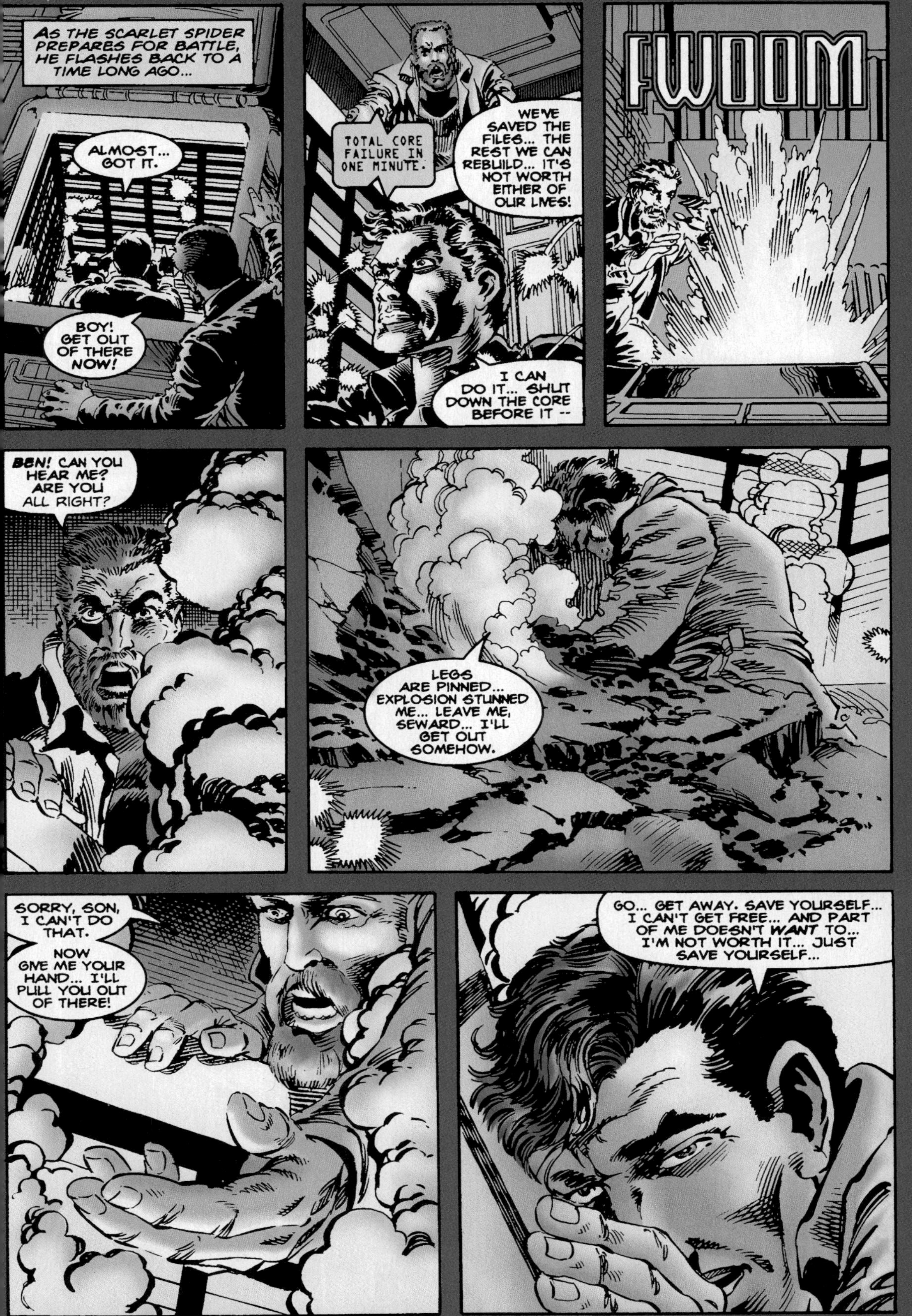
AS THE SCARLET SPIDER PREPARES FOR BATTLE, HE FLASHES BACK TO A TIME LONG AGO...
ALMOST... GOT IT.
BOY! GET OUT OF THERE NOW!
TOTAL CORE FAILURE IN ONE MINUTE.
WE'VE SAVED THE FILES... THE REST WE CAN REBUILD... IT'S NOT WORTH EITHER OF OUR LIVES!
I CAN DO IT... SHUT DOWN THE CORE BEFORE IT --
FWOOM
BEN! CAN YOU HEAR ME? ARE YOU ALL RIGHT?
LEGS ARE PINNED... EXPLOSION STUNNED ME... LEAVE ME, SEWARD... I'LL GET OUT SOMEHOW.
SORRY, SON, I CAN'T DO THAT.
NOW GIVE ME YOUR HAND... I'LL PULL YOU OUT OF THERE!
GO... GET AWAY. SAVE YOURSELF... I CAN'T GET FREE... AND PART OF ME DOESN'T WANT TO... I'M NOT WORTH IT... JUST SAVE YOURSELF...

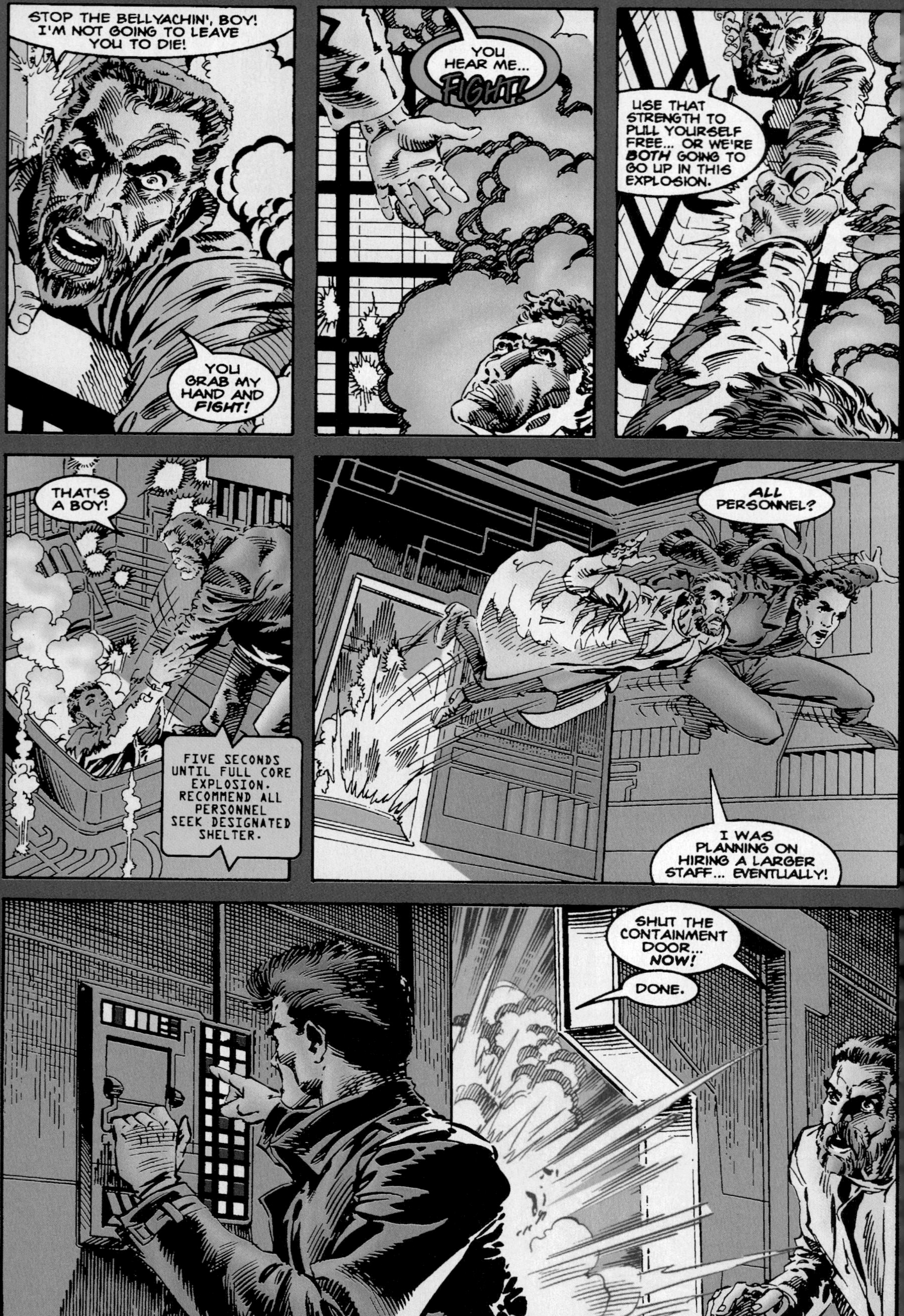
STOP THE BELLYACHIN', BOY! I'M NOT GOING TO LEAVE YOU TO DIE!
YOU GRAB MY HAND AND FIGHT!
YOU HEAR ME... FIGHT!
USE THAT STRENGTH TO PULL YOURSELF FREE... OR WE'RE BOTH GOING TO GO UP IN THIS EXPLOSION.
THAT'S A BOY!
FIVE SECONDS UNTIL FULL CORE EXPLOSION. RECOMMEND ALL PERSONNEL SEEK DESIGNATED SHELTER.
ALL PERSONNEL?
I WAS PLANNING ON HIRING A LARGER STAFF... EVENTUALLY!
SHUT THE CONTAINMENT DOOR... NOW!
DONE.

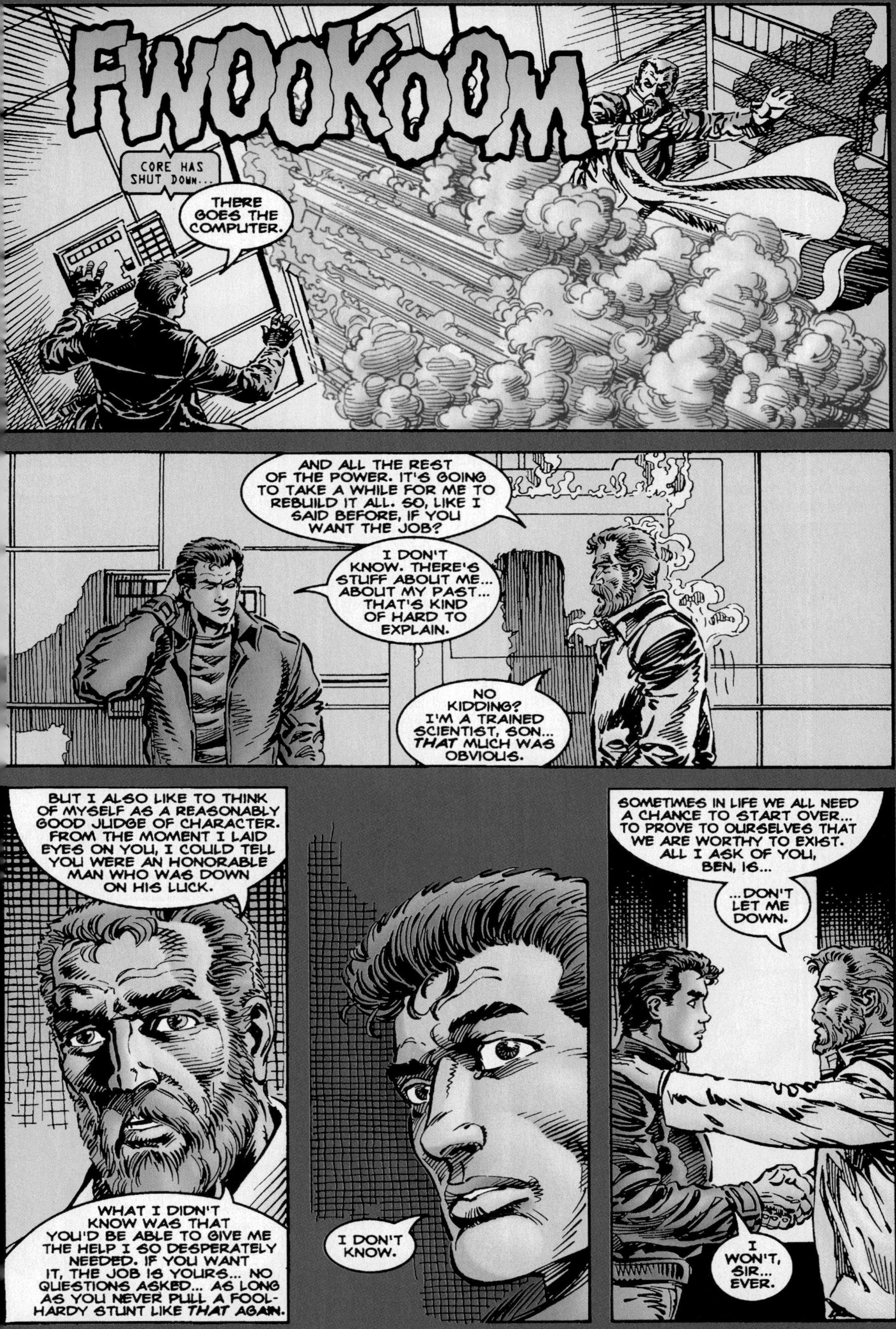
FWOOKOOM
CORE HAS SHUT DOWN...
THERE GOES THE COMPUTER.
AND ALL THE REST OF THE POWER. IT'S GOING TO TAKE A WHILE FOR ME TO REBUILD IT ALL. SO, LIKE I SAID BEFORE, IF YOU WANT THE JOB?
I DON'T KNOW. THERE'S STUFF ABOUT ME... ABOUT MY PAST... THAT'S KIND OF HARD TO EXPLAIN.
NO KIDDING? I'M A TRAINED SCIENTIST, SON... THAT MUCH WAS OBVIOUS.
BUT I ALSO LIKE TO THINK OF MYSELF AS A REASONABLY GOOD JUDGE OF CHARACTER. FROM THE MOMENT I LAID EYES ON YOU, I COULD TELL YOU WERE AN HONORABLE MAN WHO WAS DOWN ON HIS LUCK.
WHAT I DIDN'T KNOW WAS THAT YOU'D BE ABLE TO GIVE ME THE HELP I SO DESPERATELY NEEDED. IF YOU WANT IT, THE JOB IS YOURS... NO QUESTIONS ASKED... AS LONG AS YOU NEVER PULL A FOOL-HARDY STUNT LIKE THAT AGAIN.
I DON'T KNOW.
SOMETIMES IN LIFE WE ALL NEED A CHANCE TO START OVER... TO PROVE TO OURSELVES THAT WE ARE WORTHY TO EXIST. ALL I ASK OF YOU, BEN, IS...
...DON'T LET ME DOWN.
I WON'T, SIR... EVER.

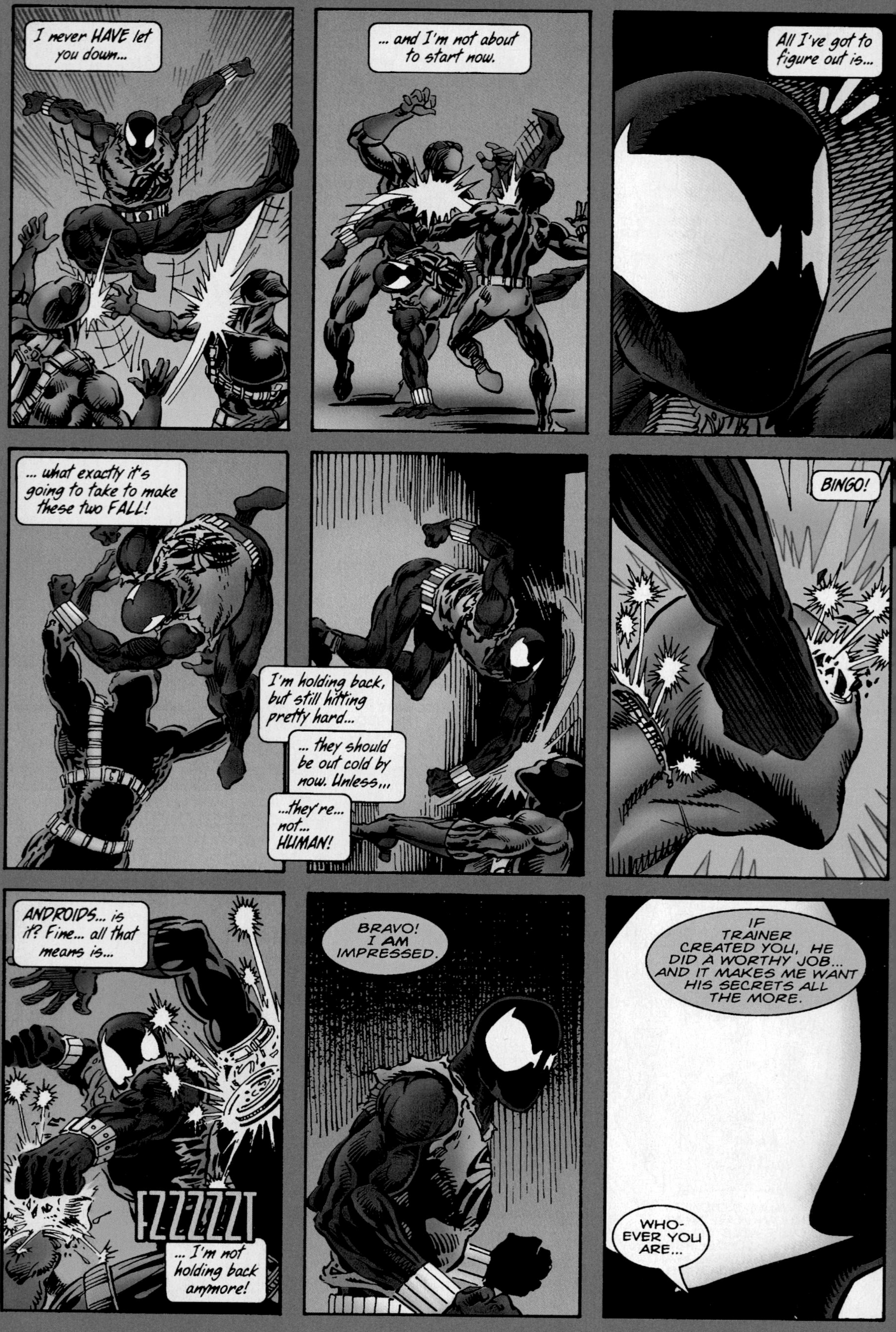
I never HAVE let you down...
... and I'm not about to start now.
All I've got to figure out is...
... what exactly it's going to take to make these two FALL!
I'm holding back, but still hitting pretty hard...
... they should be out cold by now. Unless...
...they're... not... HUMAN!
BINGO!
ANDROIDS... is it? Fine... all that means is...
FZZZZZT
... I'm not holding back anymore!
BRAVO! I AM IMPRESSED.
IF TRAINER CREATED YOU, HE DID A WORTHY JOB... AND IT MAKES ME WANT HIS SECRETS ALL THE MORE.
WHO-EVER YOU ARE...

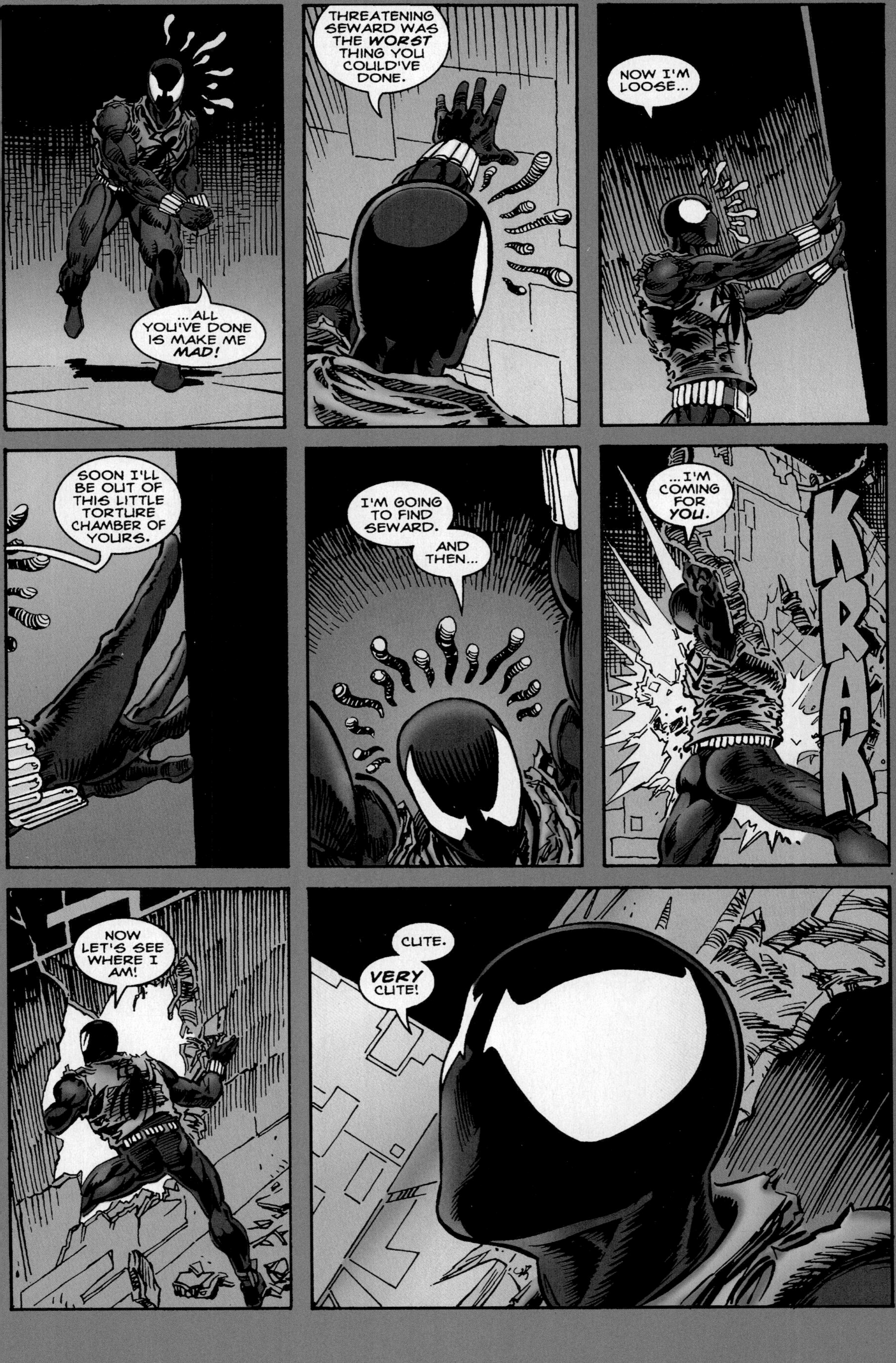
...ALL YOU'VE DONE IS MAKE ME MAD!
THREATENING SEWARD WAS THE WORST THING YOU COULD'VE DONE.
NOW I'M LOOSE...
SOON I'LL BE OUT OF THIS LITTLE TORTURE CHAMBER OF YOURS.
I'M GOING TO FIND SEWARD.
AND THEN...
...I'M COMING FOR YOU.
KRAK
NOW LET'S SEE WHERE I AM!
CUTE.
VERY CUTE!

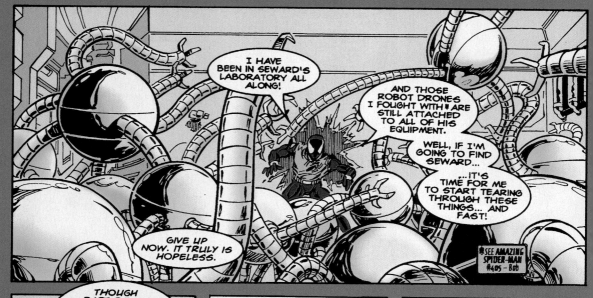

I HAVE BEEN IN SEWARD'S LABORATORY ALL ALONG!

AND THOSE ROBOT DRONES I FOUGHT WITH * ARE STILL ATTACHED TO ALL OF HIS EQUIPMENT.

WELL, IF I'M GOING TO FIND SEWARD...

...IT'S TIME FOR ME TO START TEARING THROUGH THESE THINGS... AND FAST!

NOW. GIVE UP NOW. IT TRULY IS HOPELESS.

*SEE AMAZING SPIDER-MAN #405 - Bob

THOUGH PART OF ME REALLY HOPES YOU'LL TRY. I'D LOVE TO SEE YOU IN ACTION AGAINST SUCH OVERWHELMING ODDS.

DON'T COUNT ME OUT, MISTER? MISS? YOU REALLY HAVE TO WORK ON THE SOUND QUALITY OF YOUR VOICE PROJECTOR.

IT'S TIME FOR THIS GAME OF YOURS TO COME TO AN END.

FIRST THINGS FIRST. THIS FLOATING CAMERA SEEMS TO BE YOUR EYES AND EARS, SO...

...I'D LIKE TO SAY IT'S BEEN A PLEASURE, BUT...

...IT HASN'T.

GOOD-BYYYE! I'M THROUGH PERFORMING FOR YOU! ZZZt

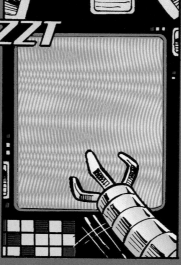

WE'LL SEE ABOUT THAT!

KTASH!

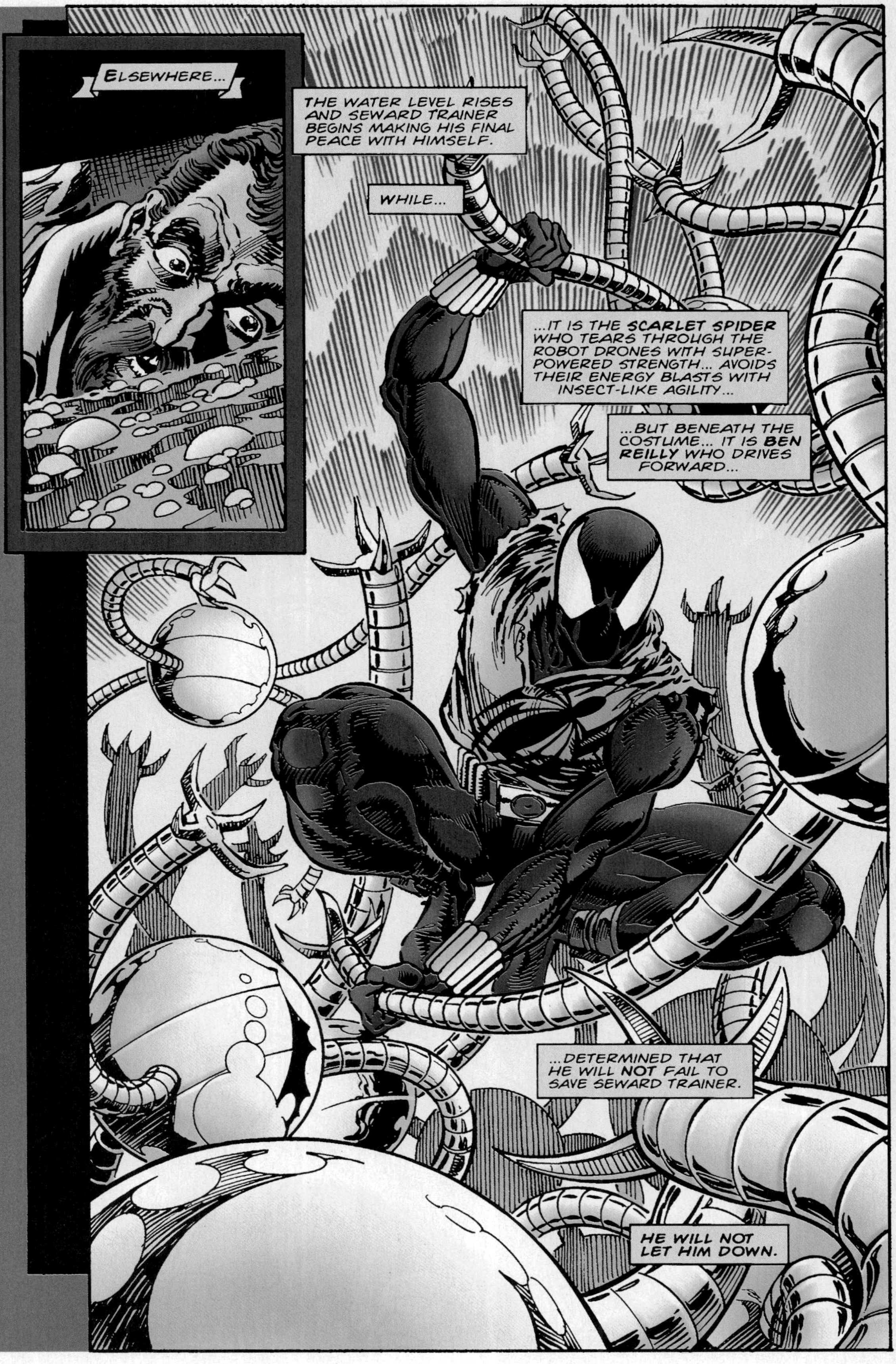
ELSEWHERE...
THE WATER LEVEL RISES AND SEWARD TRAINER BEGINS MAKING HIS FINAL PEACE WITH HIMSELF.
WHILE...
...IT IS THE SCARLET SPIDER WHO TEARS THROUGH THE ROBOT DRONES WITH SUPER-POWERED STRENGTH... AVOIDS THEIR ENERGY BLASTS WITH INSECT-LIKE AGILITY...
...BUT BENEATH THE COSTUME... IT IS BEN REILLY WHO DRIVES FORWARD...
...DETERMINED THAT HE WILL NOT FAIL TO SAVE SEWARD TRAINER.
HE WILL NOT LET HIM DOWN.

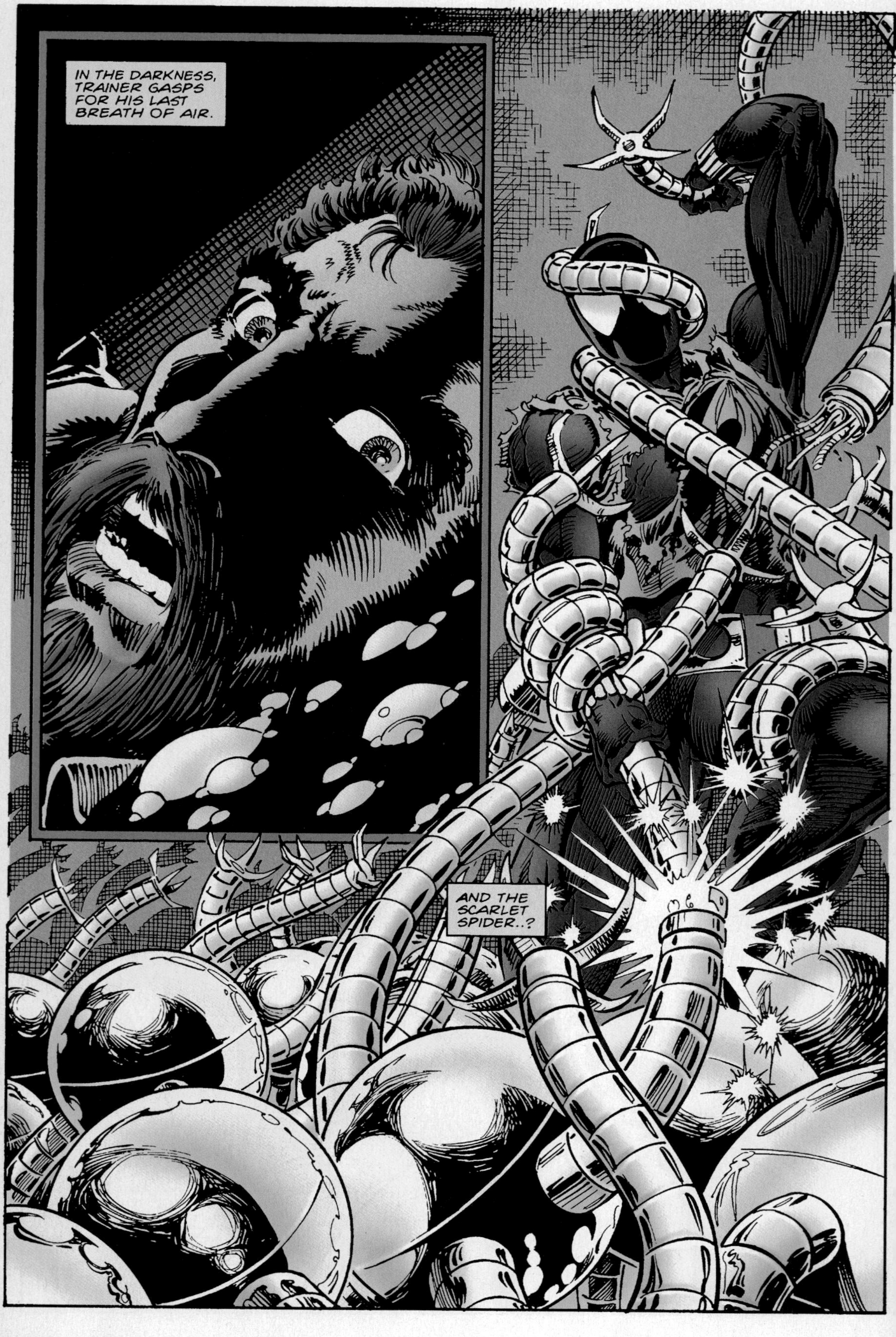
IN THE DARKNESS, TRAINER GASPS FOR HIS LAST BREATH OF AIR.
AND THE SCARLET SPIDER..?

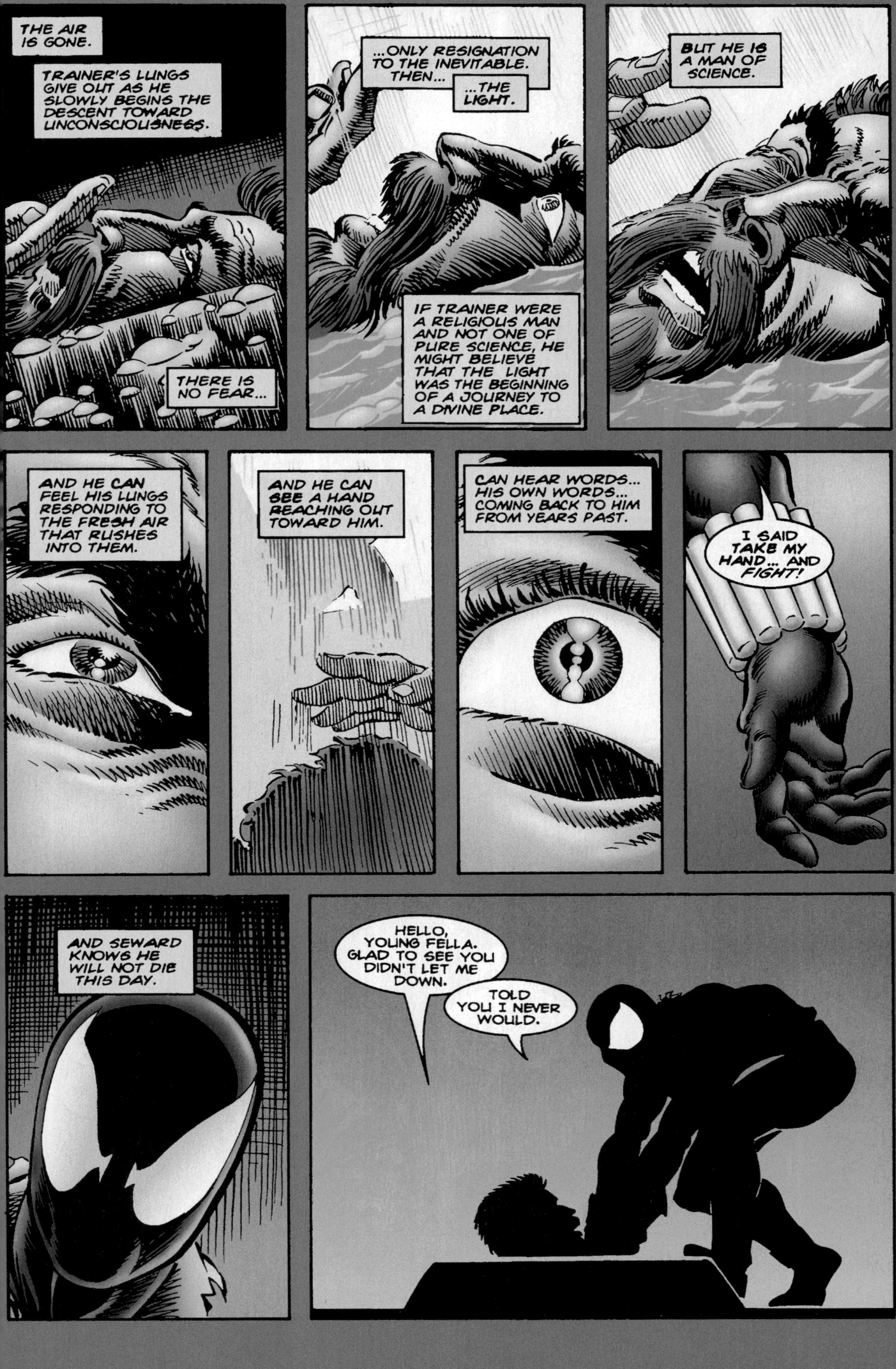
THE AIR IS GONE.
TRAINER'S LUNGS GIVE OUT AS HE SLOWLY BEGINS THE DESCENT TOWARD UNCONSCIOUSNESS.
THERE IS NO FEAR...
...ONLY RESIGNATION TO THE INEVITABLE. THEN...
...THE LIGHT.
IF TRAINER WERE A RELIGIOUS MAN AND NOT ONE OF PURE SCIENCE, HE MIGHT BELIEVE THAT THE LIGHT WAS THE BEGINNING OF A JOURNEY TO A DIVINE PLACE.
BUT HE IS A MAN OF SCIENCE.
AND HE CAN FEEL HIS LUNGS RESPONDING TO THE FRESH AIR THAT RUSHES INTO THEM.
AND HE CAN SEE A HAND REACHING OUT TOWARD HIM.
CAN HEAR WORDS... HIS OWN WORDS... COMING BACK TO HIM FROM YEARS PAST.
I SAID TAKE MY HAND... AND FIGHT!
AND SEWARD KNOWS HE WILL NOT DIE THIS DAY.
HELLO, YOUNG FELLA. GLAD TO SEE YOU DIDN'T LET ME DOWN.
TOLD YOU I NEVER WOULD.

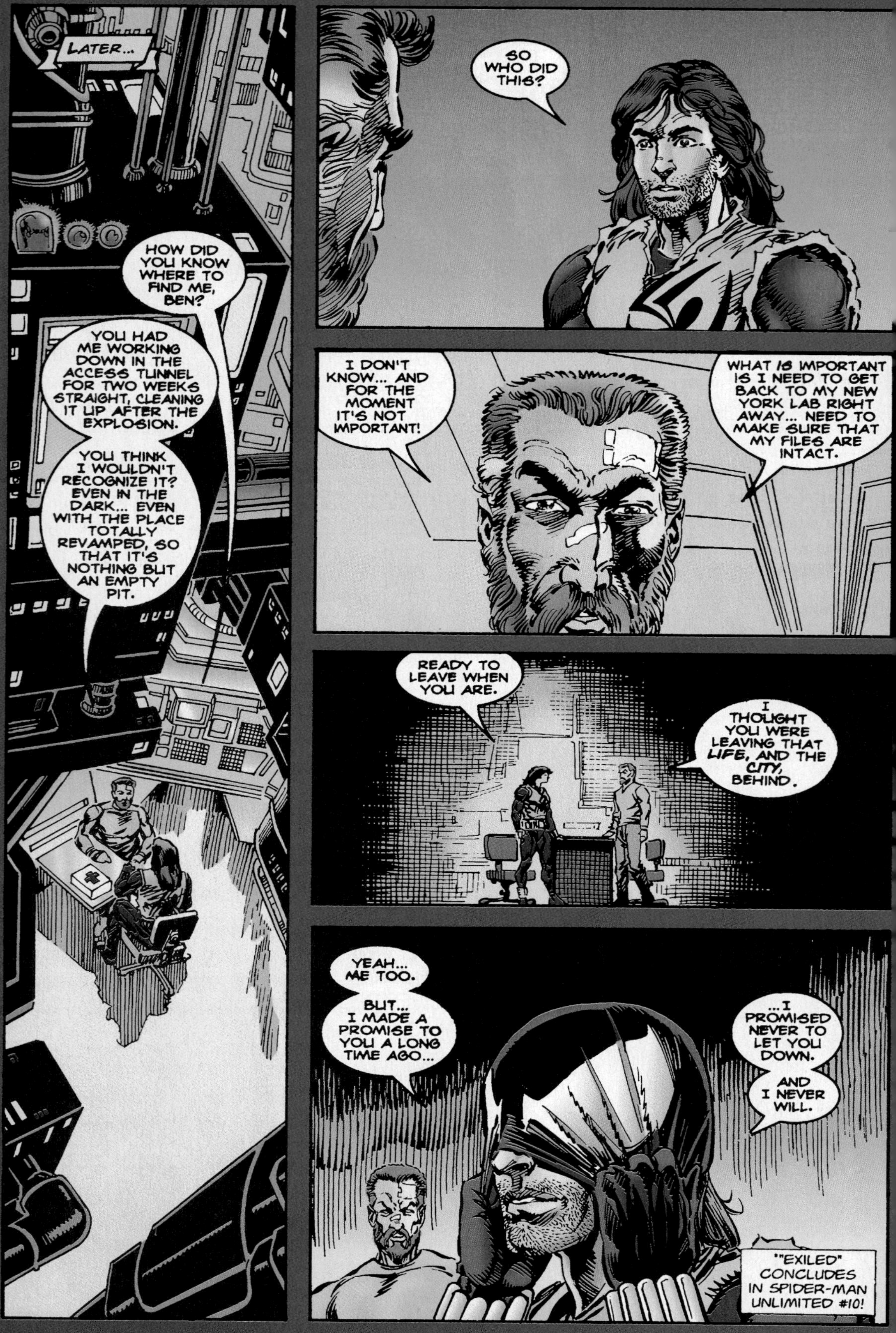
LATER...
HOW DID YOU KNOW WHERE TO FIND ME, BEN?
YOU HAD ME WORKING DOWN IN THE ACCESS TUNNEL FOR TWO WEEKS STRAIGHT, CLEANING IT UP AFTER THE EXPLOSION.
YOU THINK I WOULDN'T RECOGNIZE IT? EVEN IN THE DARK... EVEN WITH THE PLACE TOTALLY REVAMPED, SO THAT IT'S NOTHING BUT AN EMPTY PIT.
SO WHO DID THIS?
I DON'T KNOW... AND FOR THE MOMENT IT'S NOT IMPORTANT!
WHAT IS IMPORTANT IS I NEED TO GET BACK TO MY NEW YORK LAB RIGHT AWAY... NEED TO MAKE SURE THAT MY FILES ARE INTACT.
READY TO LEAVE WHEN YOU ARE.
I THOUGHT YOU WERE LEAVING THAT LIFE, AND THE CITY, BEHIND.
YEAH... ME TOO.
BUT... I MADE A PROMISE TO YOU A LONG TIME AGO...
...I PROMISED NEVER TO LET YOU DOWN.
AND I NEVER WILL.
"EXILED" CONCLUDES IN SPIDER-MAN UNLIMITED #10!

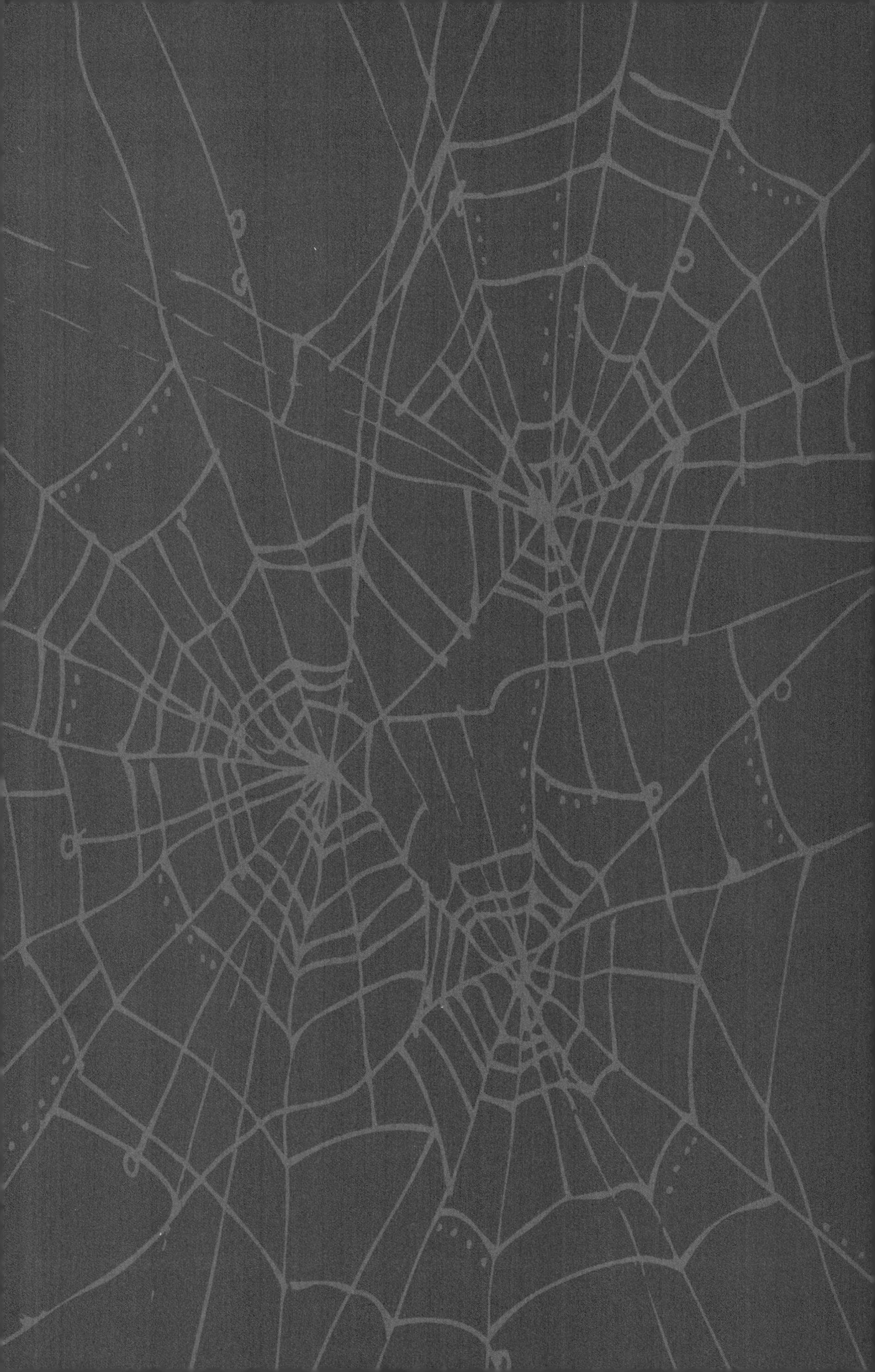

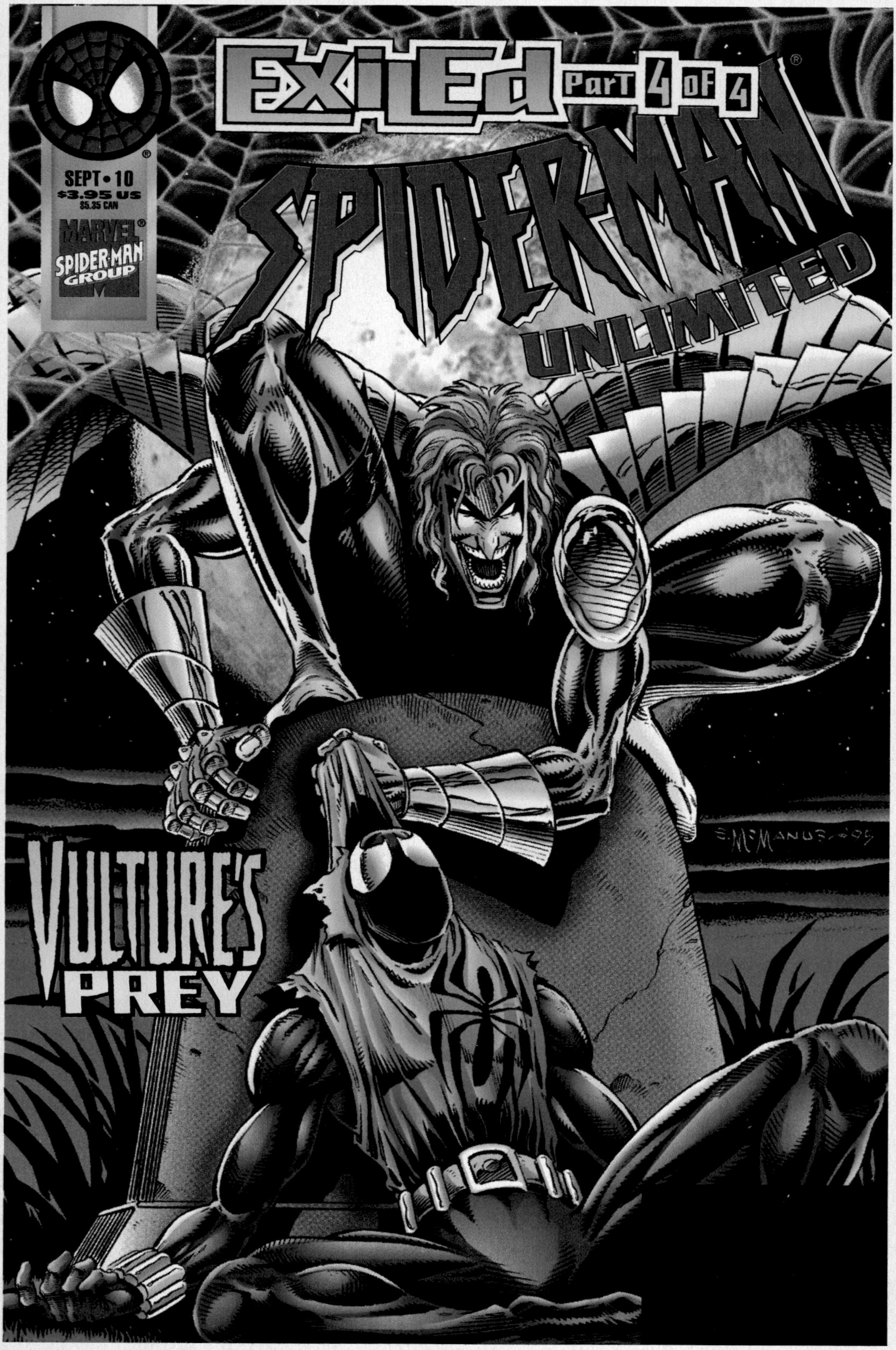
EXILED PART 4 OF 4
SPIDER-MAN UNLIMITED
SEPT • 10
$3.95 US
$5.35 CAN
MARVEL
SPIDER-MAN GROUP
VULTURE'S PREY

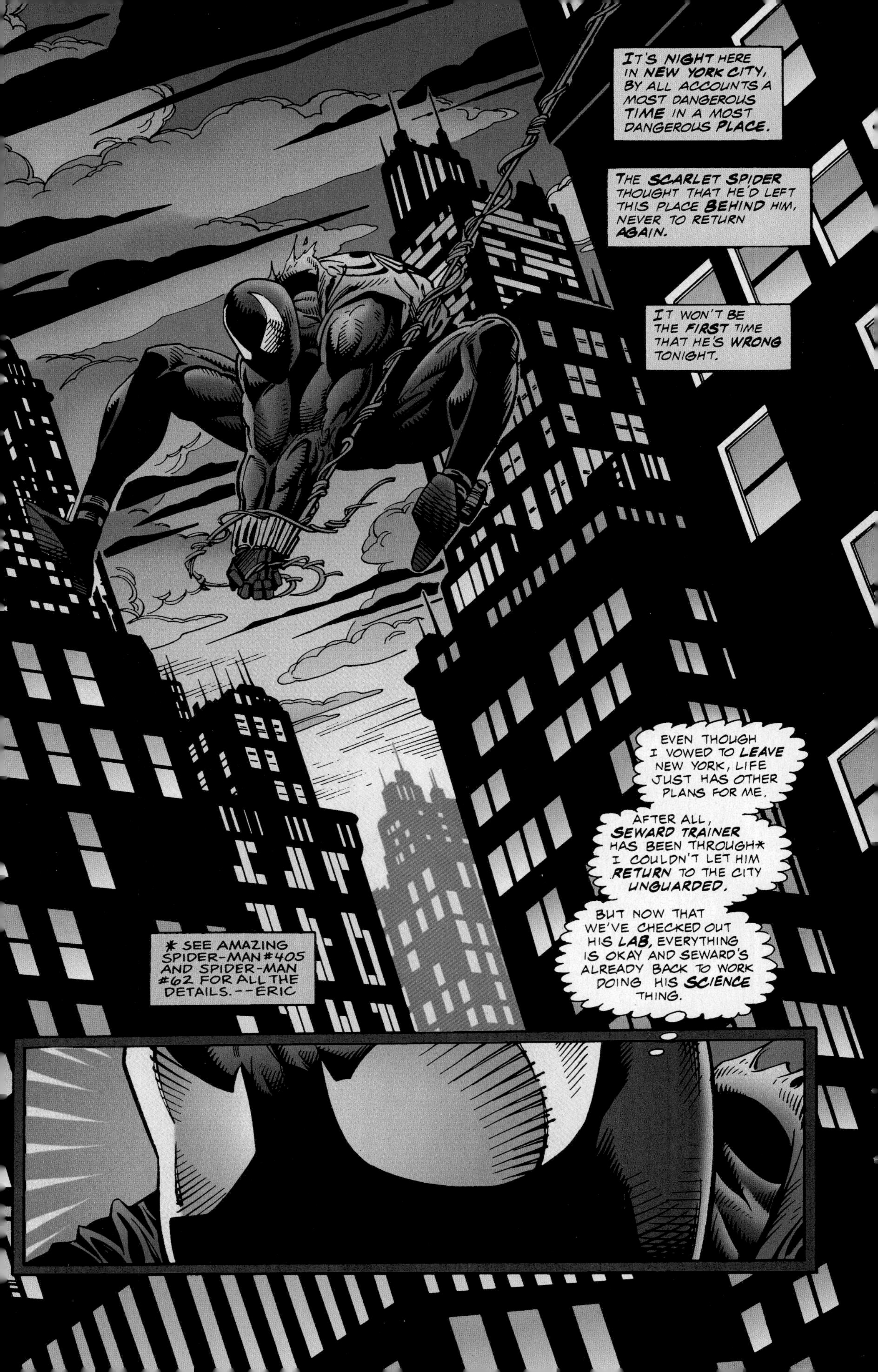
IT'S NIGHT HERE IN NEW YORK CITY, BY ALL ACCOUNTS A MOST DANGEROUS TIME IN A MOST DANGEROUS PLACE.
THE SCARLET SPIDER THOUGHT THAT HE'D LEFT THIS PLACE BEHIND HIM, NEVER TO RETURN AGAIN.
IT WON'T BE THE FIRST TIME THAT HE'S WRONG TONIGHT.
EVEN THOUGH I VOWED TO LEAVE NEW YORK, LIFE JUST HAS OTHER PLANS FOR ME.
AFTER ALL SEWARD TRAINER HAS BEEN THROUGH* I COULDN'T LET HIM RETURN TO THE CITY UNGUARDED.
BUT NOW THAT WE'VE CHECKED OUT HIS LAB, EVERYTHING IS OKAY AND SEWARD'S ALREADY BACK TO WORK DOING HIS SCIENCE THING.
* SEE AMAZING SPIDER-MAN #405 AND SPIDER-MAN #62 FOR ALL THE DETAILS.--ERIC

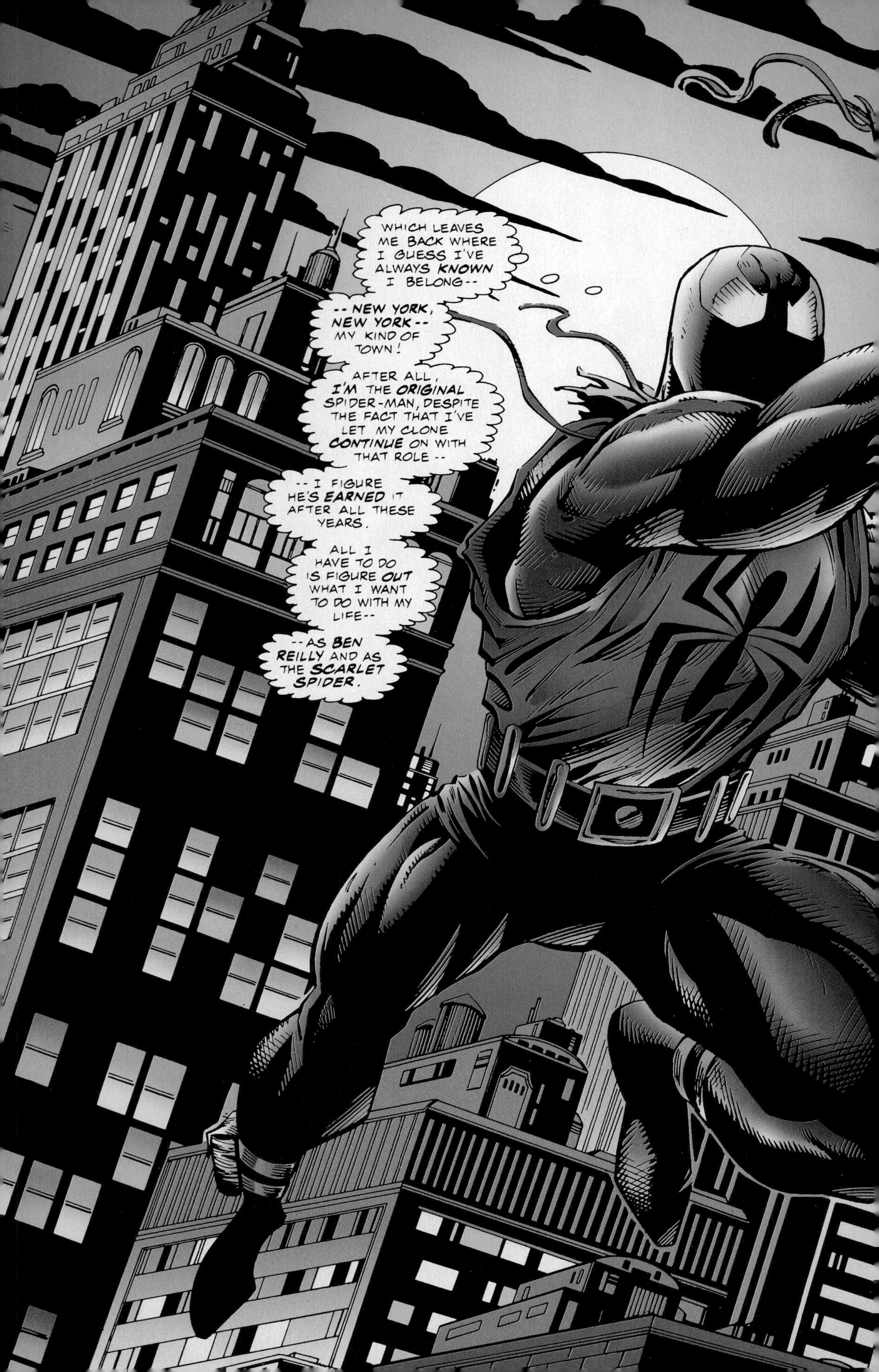
WHICH LEAVES ME BACK WHERE I GUESS I'VE ALWAYS KNOWN I BELONG--
--NEW YORK, NEW YORK-- MY KIND OF TOWN!
AFTER ALL, I'M THE ORIGINAL SPIDER-MAN, DESPITE THE FACT THAT I'VE LET MY CLONE CONTINUE ON WITH THAT ROLE--
--I FIGURE HE'S EARNED IT AFTER ALL THESE YEARS.
ALL I HAVE TO DO IS FIGURE OUT WHAT I WANT TO DO WITH MY LIFE--
--AS BEN REILLY AND AS THE SCARLET SPIDER.

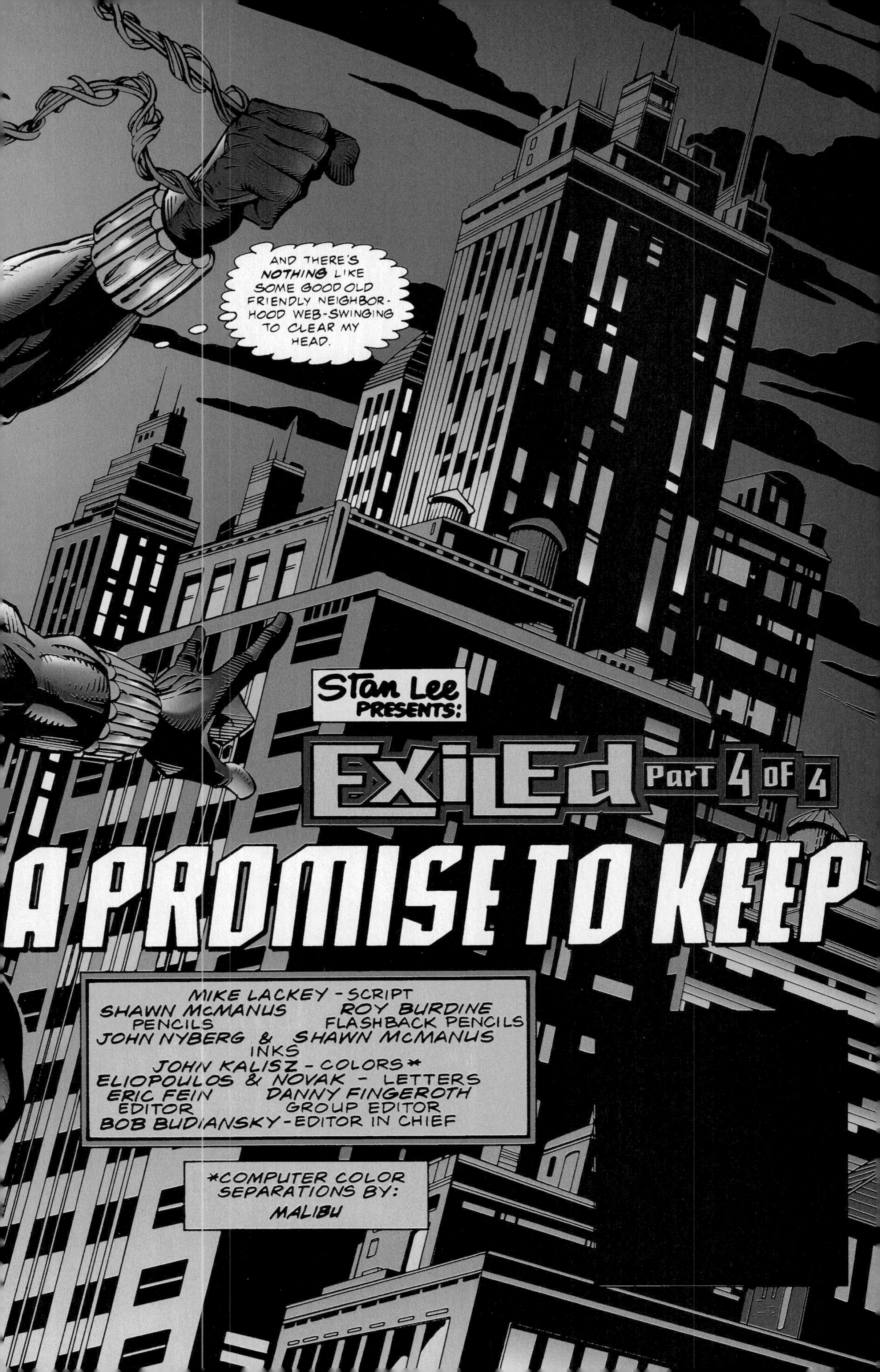

AND THERE'S NOTHING LIKE SOME GOOD OLD FRIENDLY NEIGHBOR-HOOD WEB-SWINGING TO CLEAR MY HEAD.
STAN LEE PRESENTS:
EXILED PART 4 OF 4
A PROMISE TO KEEP
MIKE LACKEY - SCRIPT
SHAWN McMANUS PENCILS
ROY BURDINE FLASHBACK PENCILS
JOHN NYBERG & SHAWN McMANUS INKS
JOHN KALISZ - COLORS*
ELIOPOULOS & NOVAK - LETTERS
ERIC FEIN EDITOR
DANNY FINGEROTH GROUP EDITOR
BOB BUDIANSKY - EDITOR IN CHIEF
*COMPUTER COLOR SEPARATIONS BY: MALIBU

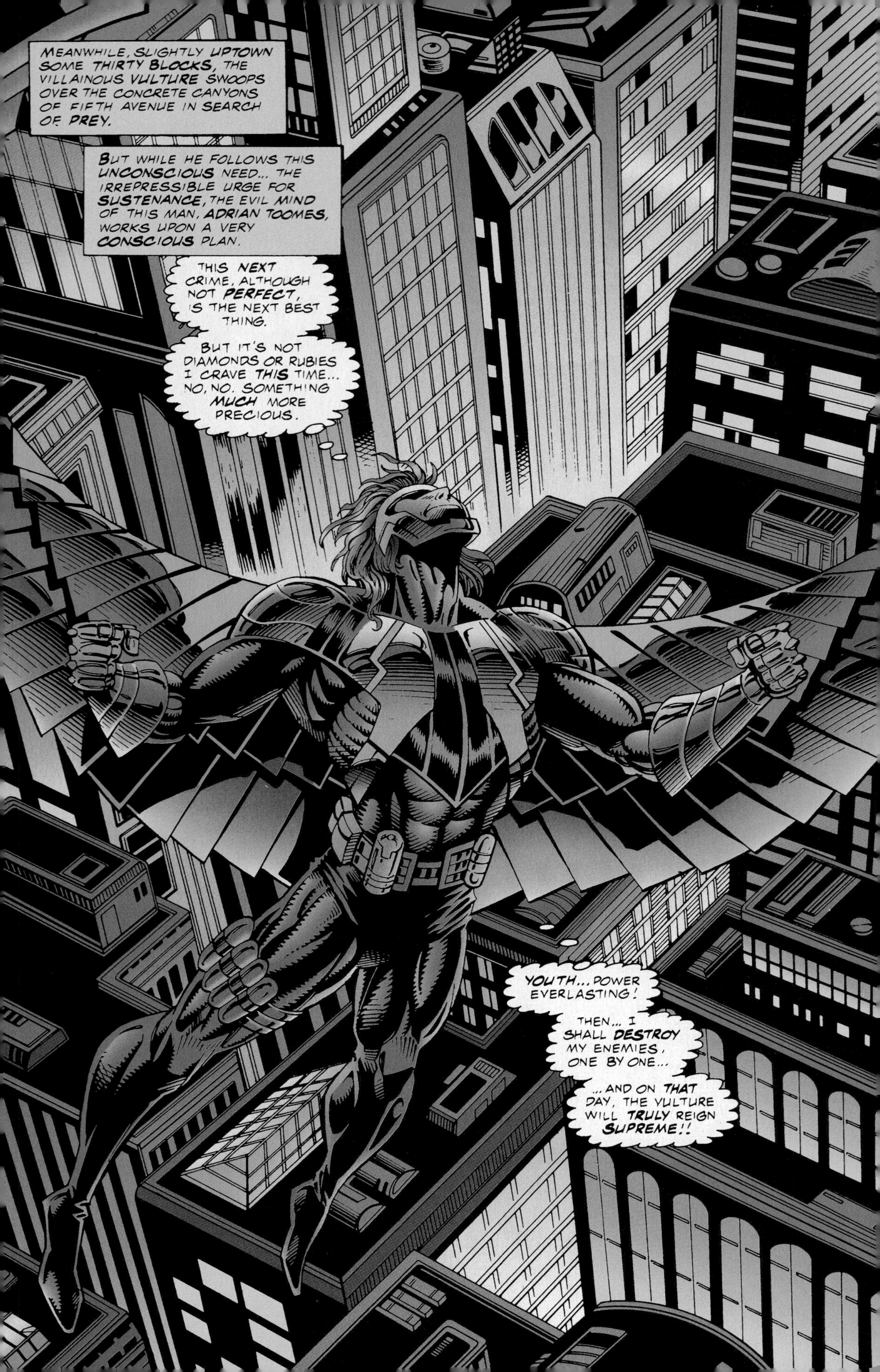
MEANWHILE, SLIGHTLY UPTOWN SOME THIRTY BLOCKS, THE VILLAINOUS VULTURE SWOOPS OVER THE CONCRETE CANYONS OF FIFTH AVENUE IN SEARCH OF PREY.
BUT WHILE HE FOLLOWS THIS UNCONSCIOUS NEED... THE IRREPRESSIBLE URGE FOR SUSTENANCE, THE EVIL MIND OF THIS MAN, ADRIAN TOOMES, WORKS UPON A VERY CONSCIOUS PLAN.
THIS NEXT CRIME, ALTHOUGH NOT PERFECT, IS THE NEXT BEST THING.
BUT IT'S NOT DIAMONDS OR RUBIES I CRAVE THIS TIME... NO, NO. SOMETHING MUCH MORE PRECIOUS.
YOUTH... POWER EVERLASTING!
THEN... I SHALL DESTROY MY ENEMIES, ONE BY ONE...
...AND ON THAT DAY, THE VULTURE WILL TRULY REIGN SUPREME!!

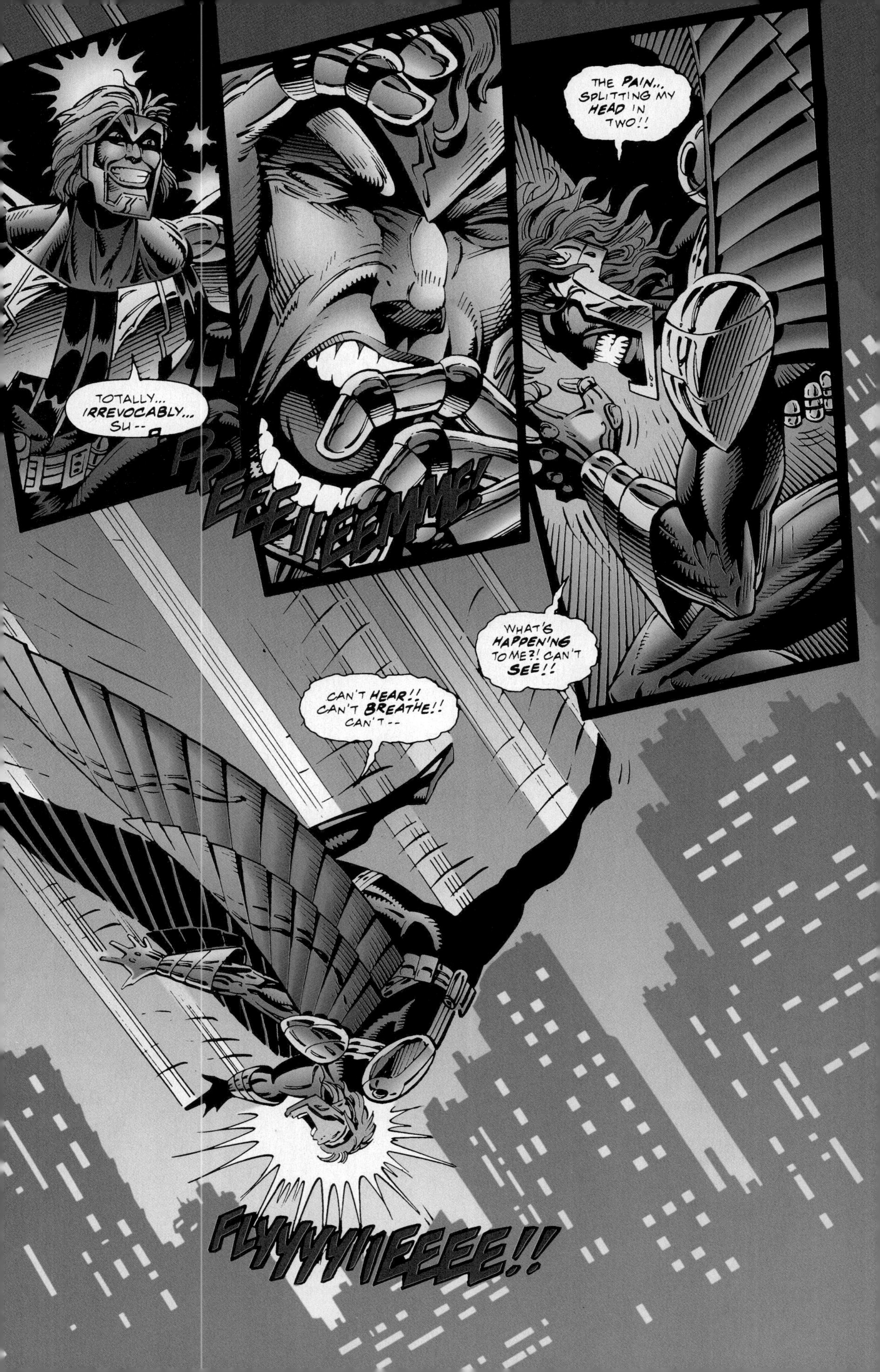

TOTALLY... IRREVOCABLY... SU--
PREEEIIEEMME!
THE PAIN... SPLITTING MY HEAD IN TWO!!
WHAT'S HAPPENING TO ME?! CAN'T SEE!!
CAN'T HEAR!! CAN'T BREATHE!! CAN'T--
FLYYYYIIEEEE!!

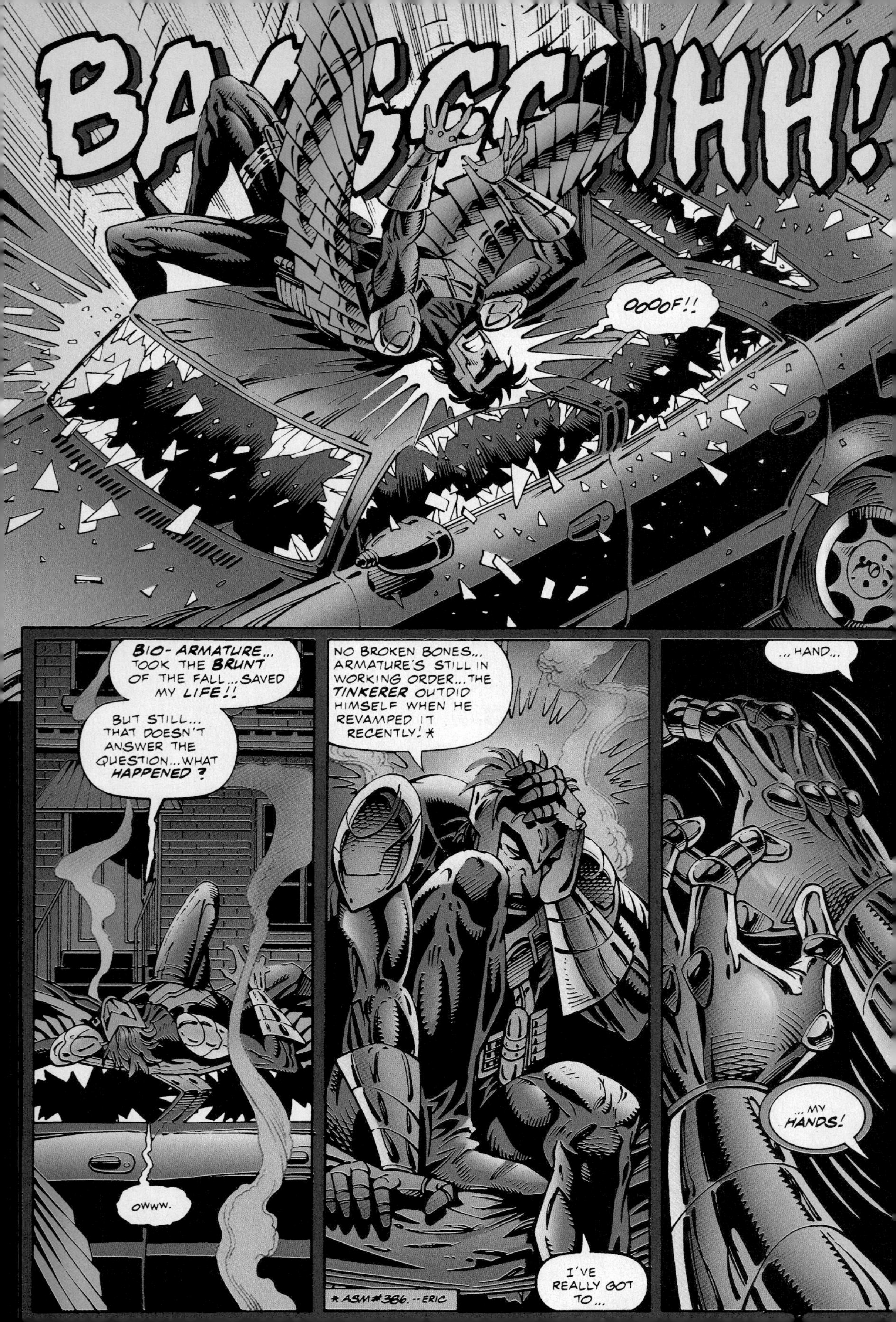
BAKGGUHH!
OOOOF!!
BIO-ARMATURE... TOOK THE BRUNT OF THE FALL...SAVED MY LIFE!!
BUT STILL... THAT DOESN'T ANSWER THE QUESTION...WHAT HAPPENED?
OWWW.
NO BROKEN BONES... ARMATURE'S STILL IN WORKING ORDER...THE TINKERER OUTDID HIMSELF WHEN HE REVAMPED IT RECENTLY! *
I'VE REALLY GOT TO...
* ASM #386. --ERIC
...HAND...
...MY HANDS!

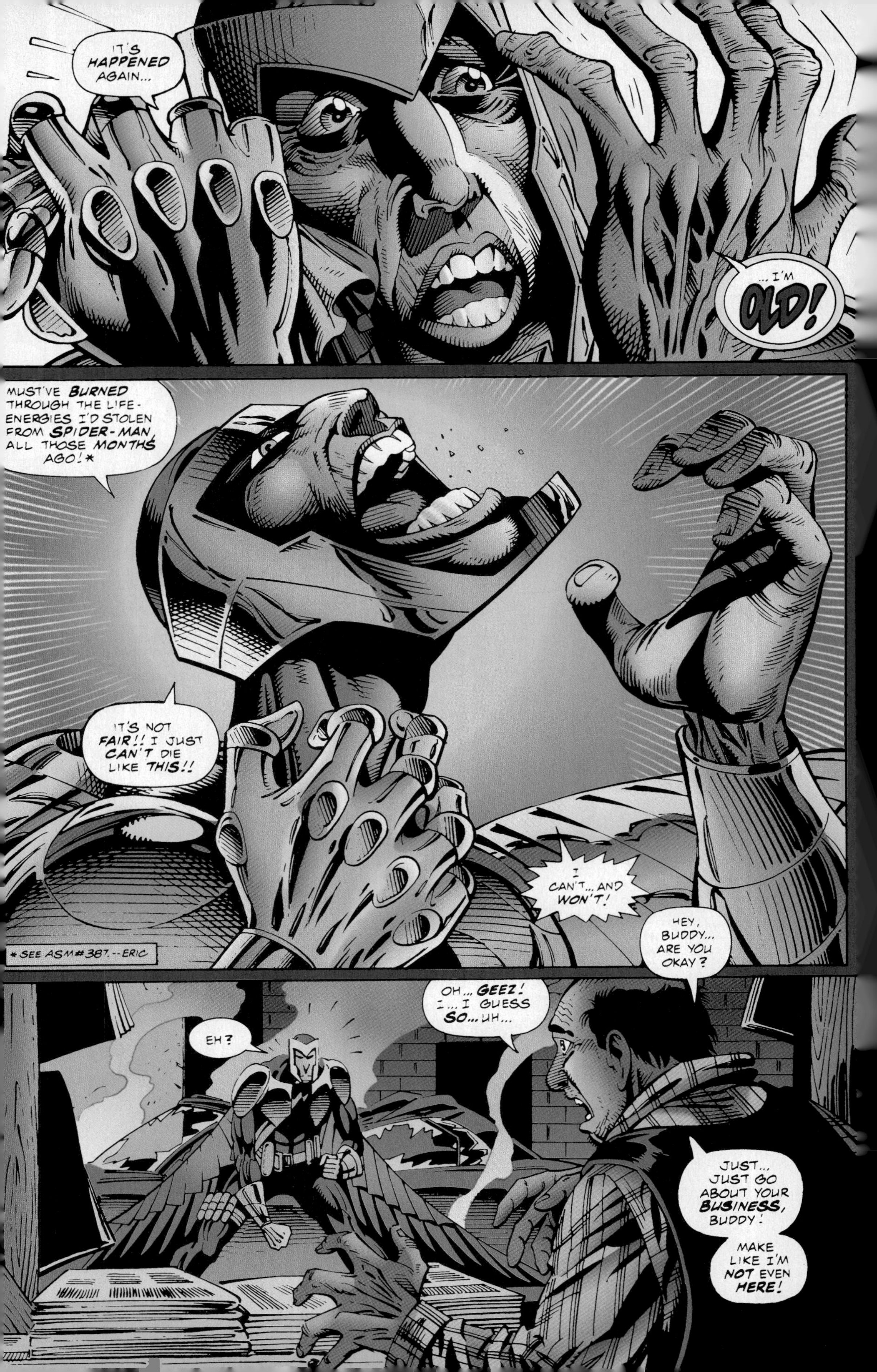
IT'S HAPPENED AGAIN...
...I'M OLD!
MUST'VE BURNED THROUGH THE LIFE-ENERGIES I'D STOLEN FROM SPIDER-MAN ALL THOSE MONTHS AGO!*
IT'S NOT FAIR!! I JUST CAN'T DIE LIKE THIS!!
I CAN'T... AND WON'T!
*SEE ASM #387. --ERIC
HEY, BUDDY... ARE YOU OKAY?
EH?
OH... GEEZ! I... I GUESS SO... UH...
JUST... JUST GO ABOUT YOUR BUSINESS, BUDDY!
MAKE LIKE I'M NOT EVEN HERE!

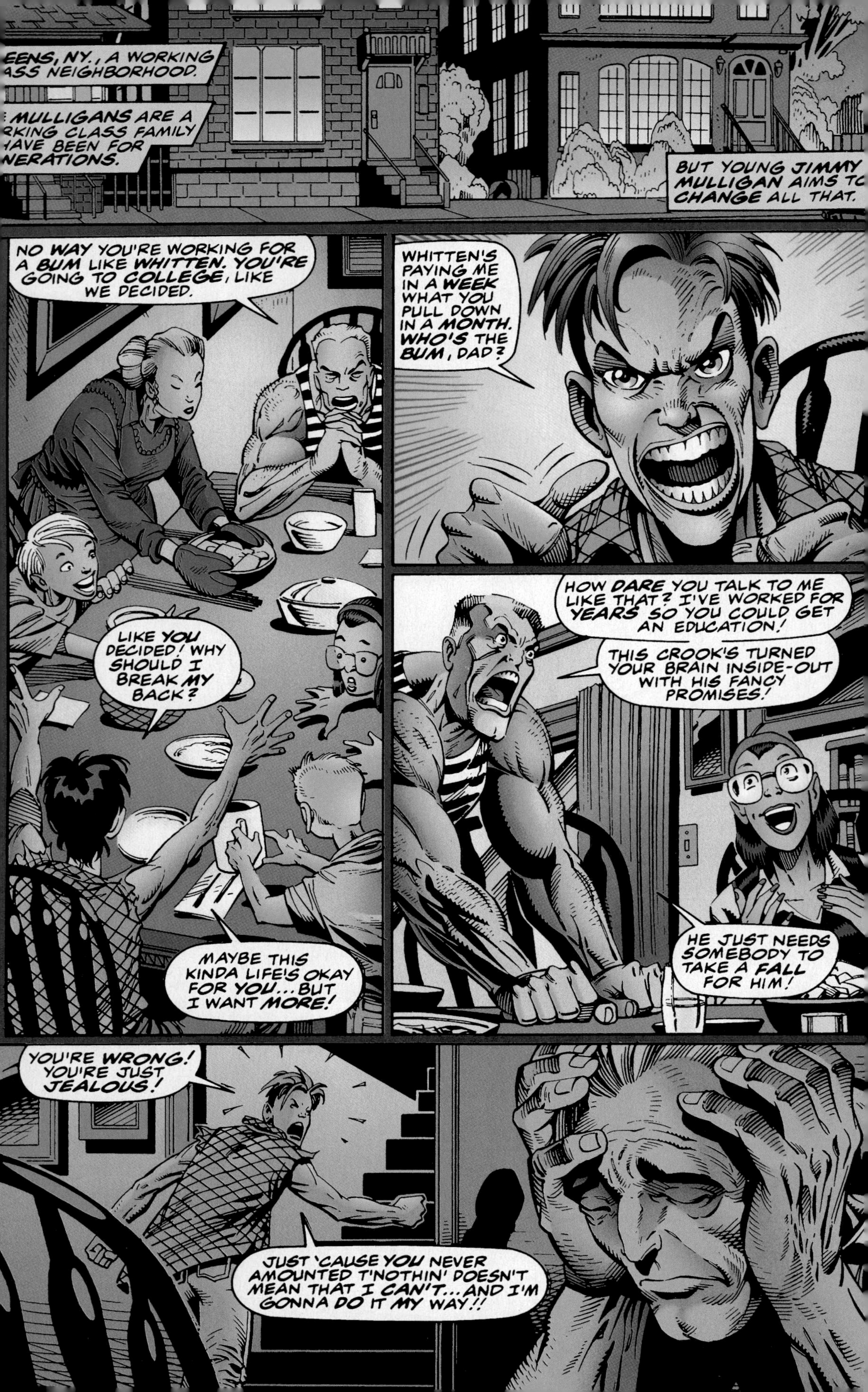
EENS, NY., A WORKING ASS NEIGHBORHOOD.
E MULLIGANS ARE A RKING CLASS FAMILY HAVE BEEN FOR NERATIONS.
BUT YOUNG JIMMY MULLIGAN AIMS TO CHANGE ALL THAT.
NO WAY YOU'RE WORKING FOR A BUM LIKE WHITTEN. YOU'RE GOING TO COLLEGE, LIKE WE DECIDED.
LIKE YOU DECIDED! WHY SHOULD I BREAK MY BACK?
MAYBE THIS KINDA LIFE'S OKAY FOR YOU... BUT I WANT MORE!
WHITTEN'S PAYING ME IN A WEEK WHAT YOU PULL DOWN IN A MONTH. WHO'S THE BUM, DAD?
HOW DARE YOU TALK TO ME LIKE THAT? I'VE WORKED FOR YEARS SO YOU COULD GET AN EDUCATION!
THIS CROOK'S TURNED YOUR BRAIN INSIDE-OUT WITH HIS FANCY PROMISES!
HE JUST NEEDS SOMEBODY TO TAKE A FALL FOR HIM!
YOU'RE WRONG! YOU'RE JUST JEALOUS!
JUST 'CAUSE YOU NEVER AMOUNTED T'NOTHIN' DOESN'T MEAN THAT I CAN'T... AND I'M GONNA DO IT MY WAY!!

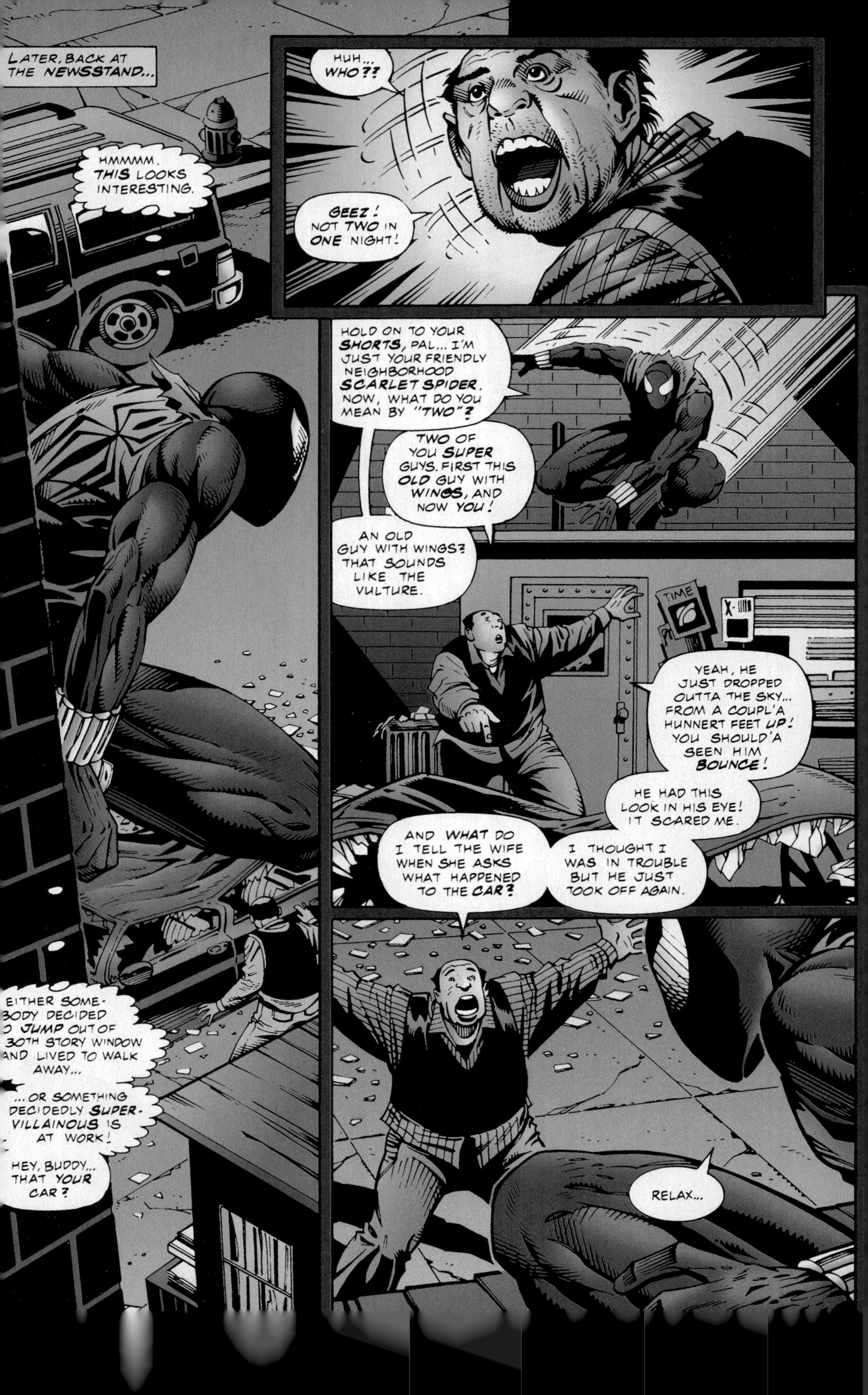
LATER, BACK AT THE NEWSSTAND...
HMMMM. THIS LOOKS INTERESTING.
HUH... WHO??
GEEZ! NOT TWO IN ONE NIGHT!
HOLD ON TO YOUR SHORTS, PAL... I'M JUST YOUR FRIENDLY NEIGHBORHOOD SCARLET SPIDER. NOW, WHAT DO YOU MEAN BY "TWO"?
TWO OF YOU SUPER GUYS. FIRST THIS OLD GUY WITH WINGS, AND NOW YOU!
AN OLD GUY WITH WINGS? THAT SOUNDS LIKE THE VULTURE.
YEAH, HE JUST DROPPED OUTTA THE SKY... FROM A COUPL'A HUNNERT FEET UP! YOU SHOULD'A SEEN HIM BOUNCE!
HE HAD THIS LOOK IN HIS EYE! IT SCARED ME.
I THOUGHT I WAS IN TROUBLE BUT HE JUST TOOK OFF AGAIN.
AND WHAT DO I TELL THE WIFE WHEN SHE ASKS WHAT HAPPENED TO THE CAR?
EITHER SOME-BODY DECIDED TO JUMP OUT OF A 30TH STORY WINDOW AND LIVED TO WALK AWAY...
...OR SOMETHING DECIDEDLY SUPER-VILLAINOUS IS AT WORK!
HEY, BUDDY... THAT YOUR CAR?
RELAX...

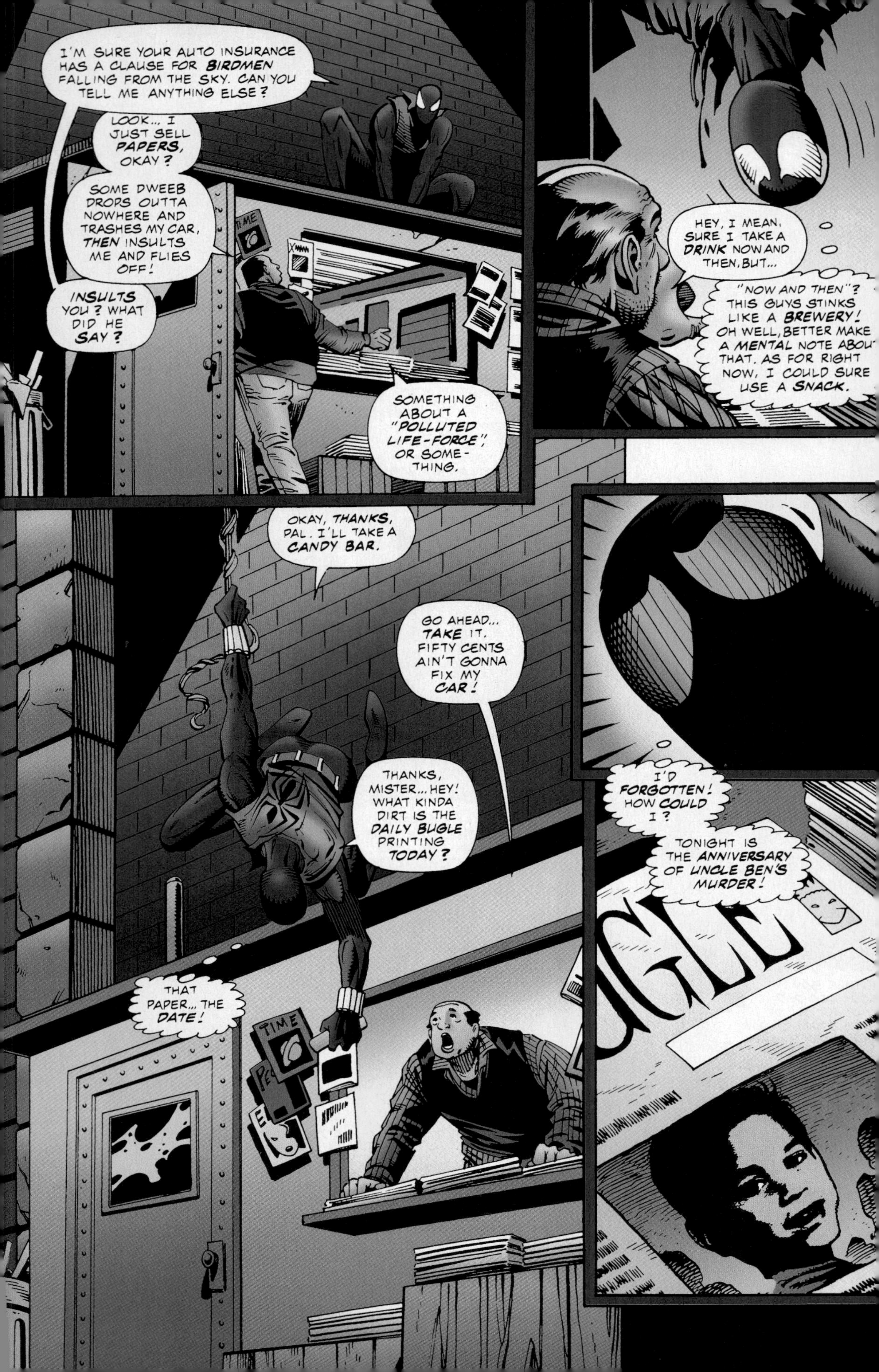
I'M SURE YOUR AUTO INSURANCE HAS A CLAUSE FOR BIRDMEN FALLING FROM THE SKY. CAN YOU TELL ME ANYTHING ELSE?
LOOK... I JUST SELL PAPERS, OKAY?
SOME DWEEB DROPS OUTTA NOWHERE AND TRASHES MY CAR, THEN INSULTS ME AND FLIES OFF!
INSULTS YOU? WHAT DID HE SAY?
SOMETHING ABOUT A "POLLUTED LIFE-FORCE", OR SOME-THING.
HEY, I MEAN, SURE I TAKE A DRINK NOW AND THEN, BUT...
"NOW AND THEN"? THIS GUYS STINKS LIKE A BREWERY! OH WELL, BETTER MAKE A MENTAL NOTE ABOUT THAT. AS FOR RIGHT NOW, I COULD SURE USE A SNACK.
OKAY, THANKS, PAL. I'LL TAKE A CANDY BAR.
GO AHEAD... TAKE IT. FIFTY CENTS AIN'T GONNA FIX MY CAR!
THANKS, MISTER... HEY! WHAT KINDA DIRT IS THE DAILY BUGLE PRINTING TODAY?
THAT PAPER... THE DATE!
I'D FORGOTTEN! HOW COULD I?
TONIGHT IS THE ANNIVERSARY OF UNCLE BEN'S MURDER!
TIME

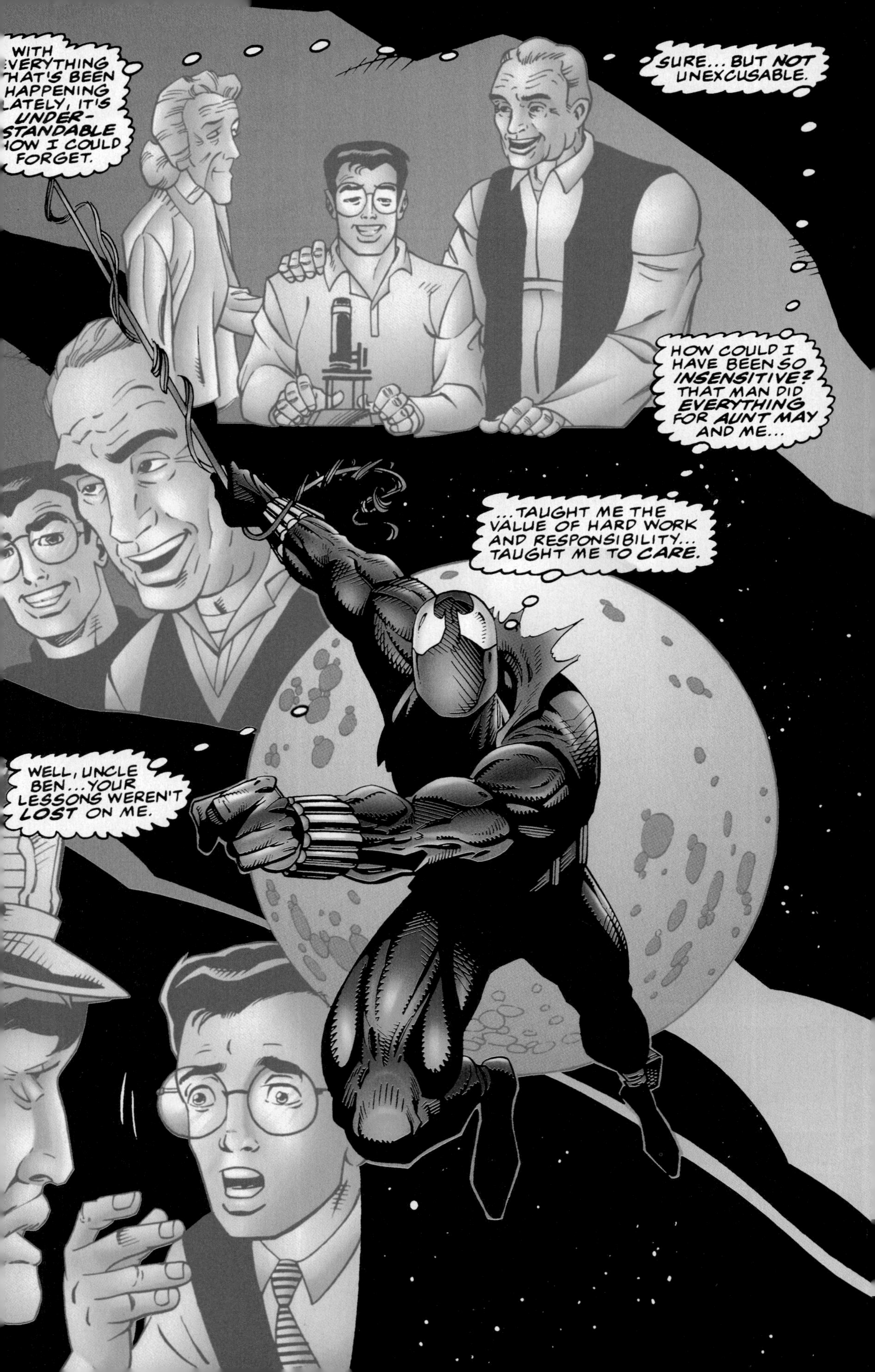

WITH EVERYTHING THAT'S BEEN HAPPENING LATELY, IT'S UNDER-STANDABLE HOW I COULD FORGET.
SURE... BUT NOT UNEXCUSABLE.
HOW COULD I HAVE BEEN SO INSENSITIVE? THAT MAN DID EVERYTHING FOR AUNT MAY AND ME...
...TAUGHT ME THE VALUE OF HARD WORK AND RESPONSIBILITY... TAUGHT ME TO CARE.
WELL, UNCLE BEN... YOUR LESSONS WEREN'T LOST ON ME.

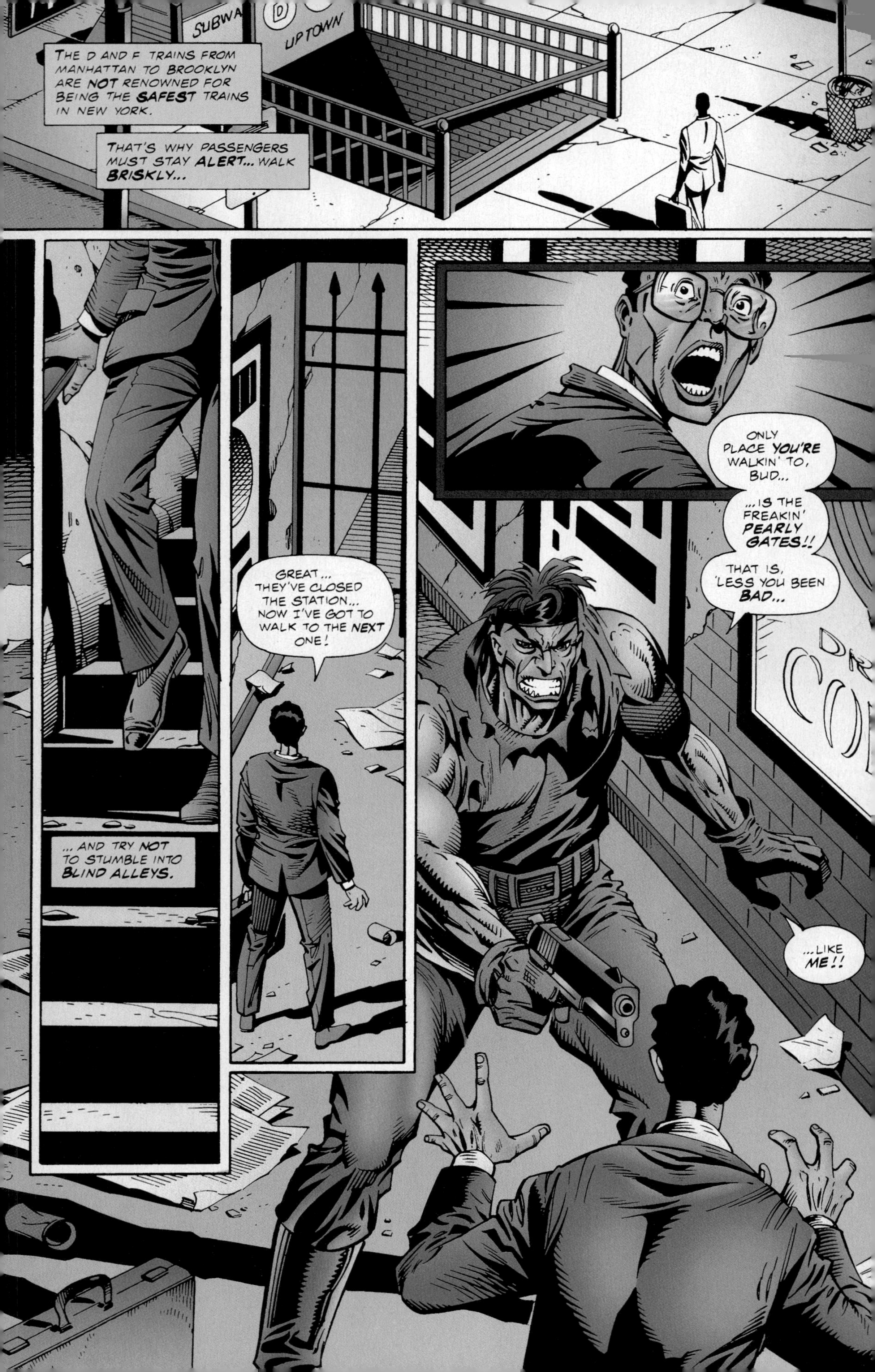
SUBWA
UPTOWN
THE D AND F TRAINS FROM MANHATTAN TO BROOKLYN ARE NOT RENOWNED FOR BEING THE SAFEST TRAINS IN NEW YORK.
THAT'S WHY PASSENGERS MUST STAY ALERT... WALK BRISKLY...
...AND TRY NOT TO STUMBLE INTO BLIND ALLEYS.
GREAT... THEY'VE CLOSED THE STATION... NOW I'VE GOT TO WALK TO THE NEXT ONE!
ONLY PLACE YOU'RE WALKIN' TO, BUD...
...IS THE FREAKIN' PEARLY GATES!!
THAT IS, 'LESS YOU BEEN BAD...
...LIKE ME!!

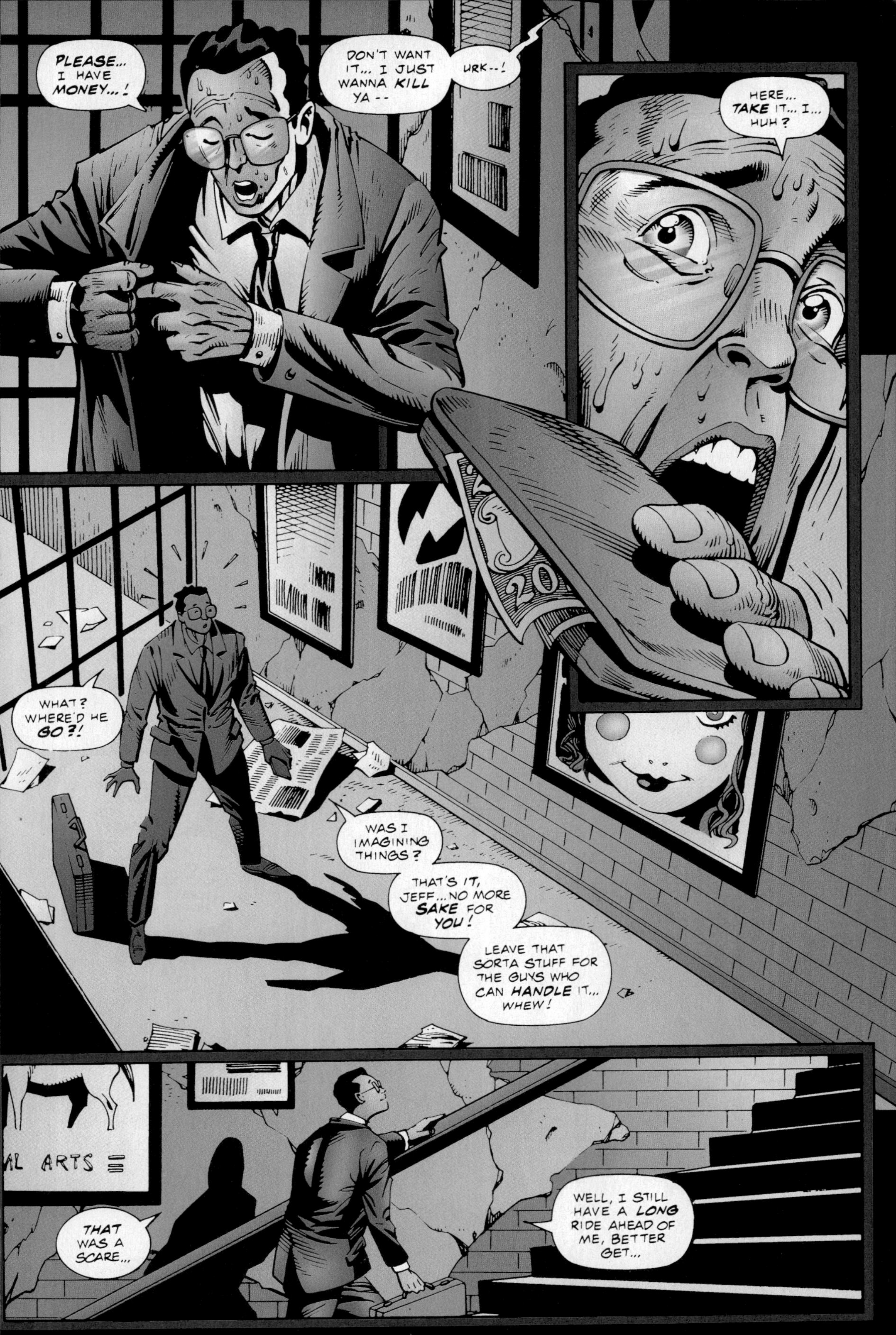
PLEASE... I HAVE MONEY...!
DON'T WANT IT... I JUST WANNA KILL YA --
URK--!
HERE... TAKE IT... I... HUH?
WHAT? WHERE'D HE GO?!
WAS I IMAGINING THINGS?
THAT'S IT, JEFF... NO MORE SAKE FOR YOU!
LEAVE THAT SORTA STUFF FOR THE GUYS WHO CAN HANDLE IT... WHEW!
AL ARTS
THAT WAS A SCARE...
WELL, I STILL HAVE A LONG RIDE AHEAD OF ME, BETTER GET...

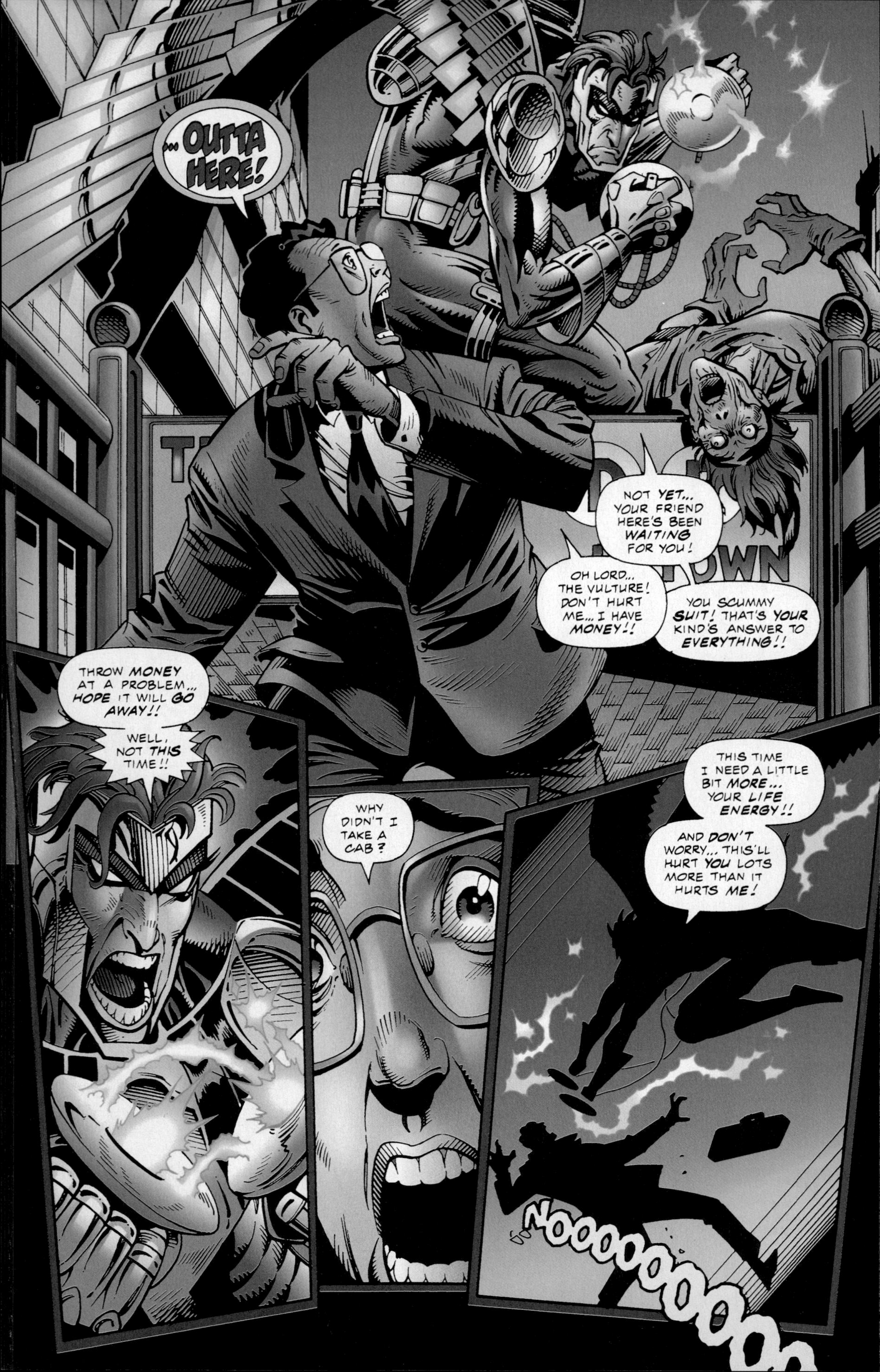

...OUTTA HERE!
NOT YET... YOUR FRIEND HERE'S BEEN WAITING FOR YOU!
OH LORD... THE VULTURE! DON'T HURT ME... I HAVE MONEY!!
YOU SCUMMY SUIT! THAT'S YOUR KIND'S ANSWER TO EVERYTHING!!
THROW MONEY AT A PROBLEM... HOPE IT WILL GO AWAY!!
WELL, NOT THIS TIME!!
WHY DIDN'T I TAKE A CAB?
THIS TIME I NEED A LITTLE BIT MORE... YOUR LIFE ENERGY!!
AND DON'T WORRY... THIS'LL HURT YOU LOTS MORE THAN IT HURTS ME!
NOOOOOOOOOOO

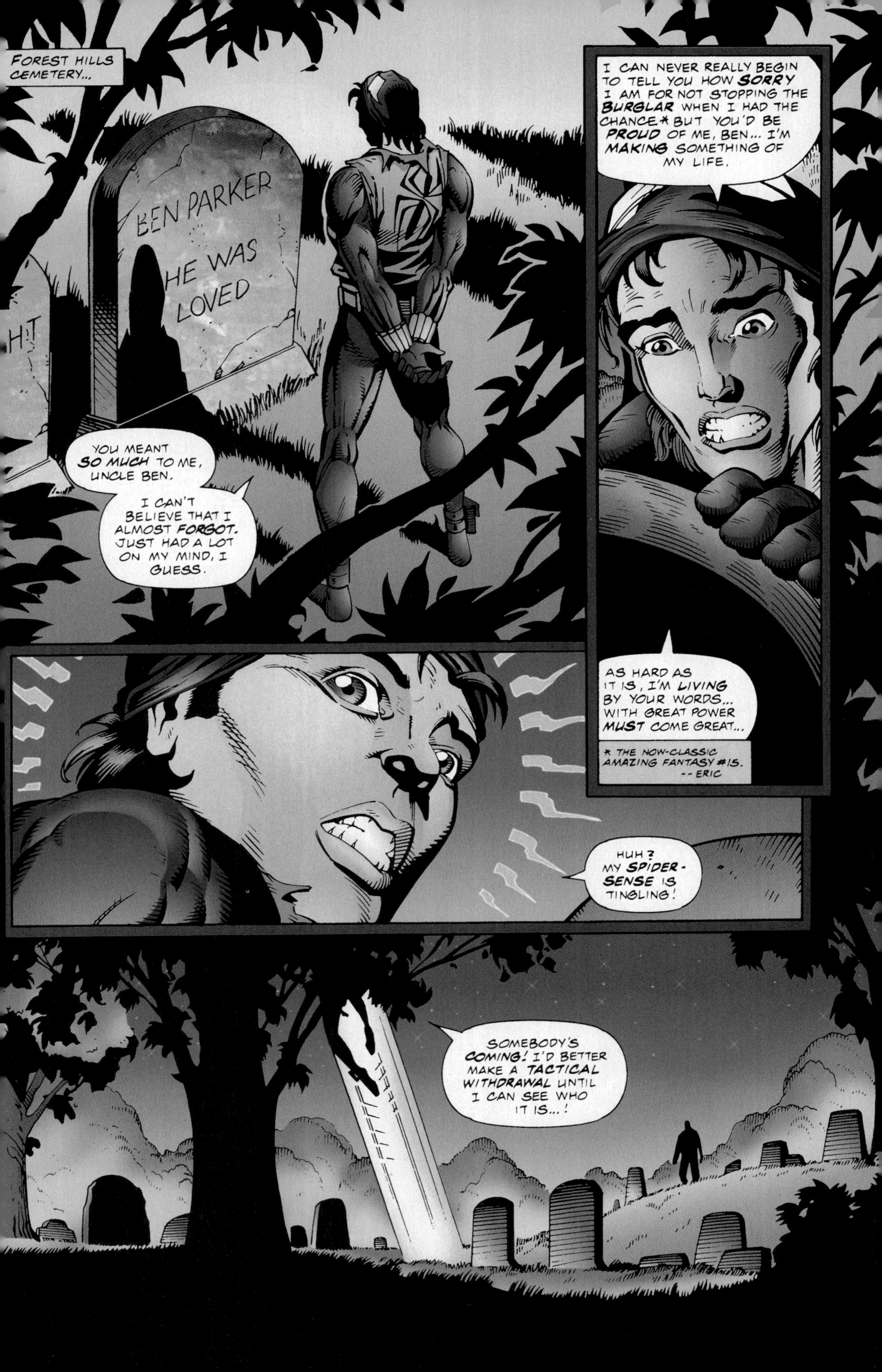
FOREST HILLS CEMETERY...
BEN PARKER
HE WAS LOVED
YOU MEANT SO MUCH TO ME, UNCLE BEN.
I CAN'T BELIEVE THAT I ALMOST FORGOT. JUST HAD A LOT ON MY MIND, I GUESS.
I CAN NEVER REALLY BEGIN TO TELL YOU HOW SORRY I AM FOR NOT STOPPING THE BURGLAR WHEN I HAD THE CHANCE.* BUT YOU'D BE PROUD OF ME, BEN... I'M MAKING SOMETHING OF MY LIFE.
AS HARD AS IT IS, I'M LIVING BY YOUR WORDS... WITH GREAT POWER MUST COME GREAT...
* THE NOW-CLASSIC AMAZING FANTASY #15. --ERIC
HUH? MY SPIDER-SENSE IS TINGLING!
SOMEBODY'S COMING! I'D BETTER MAKE A TACTICAL WITHDRAWAL UNTIL I CAN SEE WHO IT IS...!

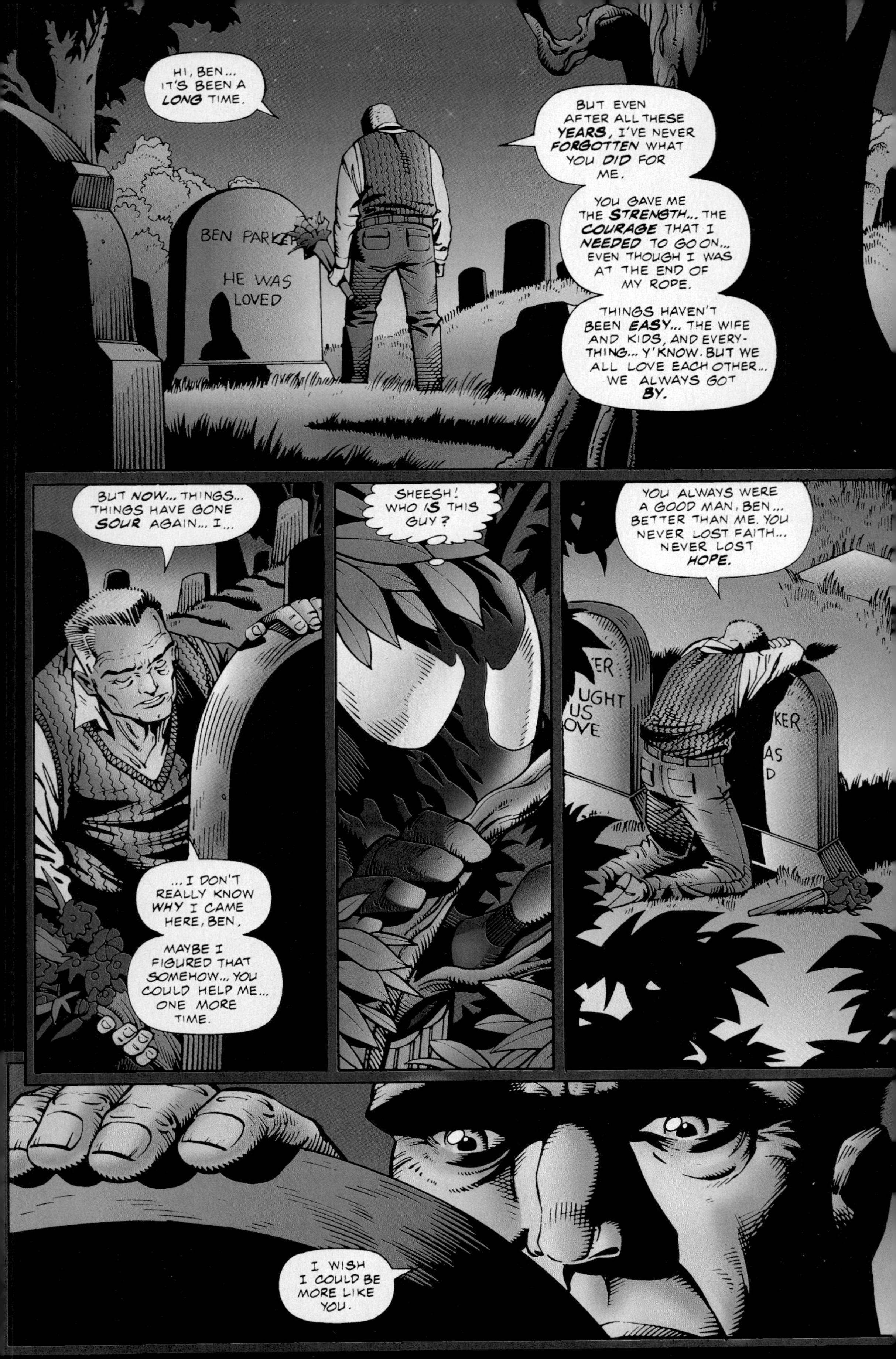
HI, BEN... IT'S BEEN A LONG TIME.
BUT EVEN AFTER ALL THESE YEARS, I'VE NEVER FORGOTTEN WHAT YOU DID FOR ME.
YOU GAVE ME THE STRENGTH... THE COURAGE THAT I NEEDED TO GO ON... EVEN THOUGH I WAS AT THE END OF MY ROPE.
THINGS HAVEN'T BEEN EASY... THE WIFE AND KIDS, AND EVERY-THING... Y'KNOW. BUT WE ALL LOVE EACH OTHER... WE ALWAYS GOT BY.
BEN PARKER
HE WAS LOVED
BUT NOW... THINGS... THINGS HAVE GONE SOUR AGAIN... I...
...I DON'T REALLY KNOW WHY I CAME HERE, BEN.
MAYBE I FIGURED THAT SOMEHOW... YOU COULD HELP ME... ONE MORE TIME.
SHEESH! WHO IS THIS GUY?
YOU ALWAYS WERE A GOOD MAN, BEN... BETTER THAN ME. YOU NEVER LOST FAITH... NEVER LOST HOPE.
I WISH I COULD BE MORE LIKE YOU.

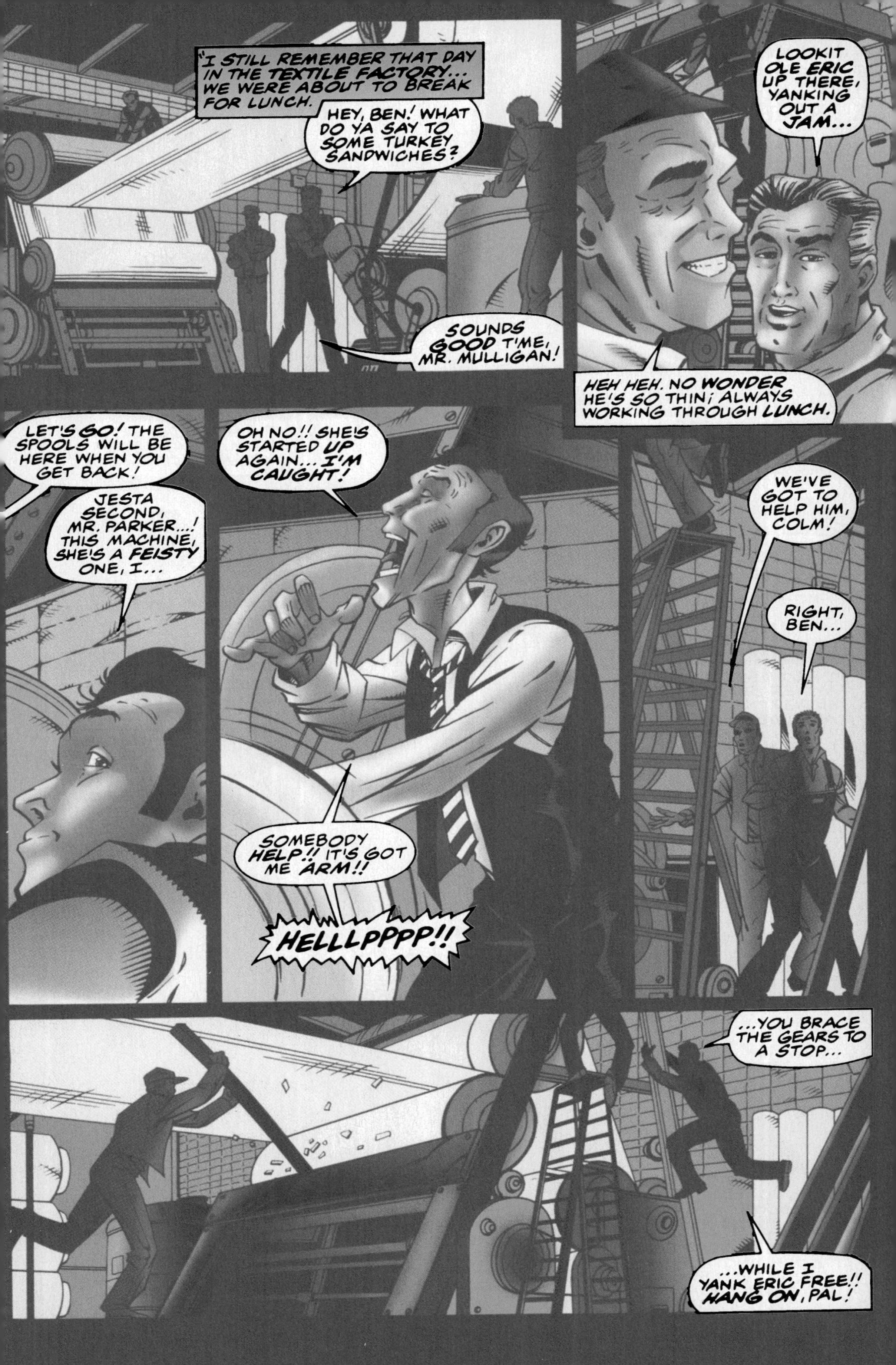
"I STILL REMEMBER THAT DAY IN THE TEXTILE FACTORY... WE WERE ABOUT TO BREAK FOR LUNCH.
HEY, BEN! WHAT DO YA SAY TO SOME TURKEY SANDWICHES?
SOUNDS GOOD TIME, MR. MULLIGAN!
LOOKIT OLE ERIC UP THERE, YANKING OUT A JAM...
HEH HEH. NO WONDER HE'S SO THIN; ALWAYS WORKING THROUGH LUNCH.
LET'S GO! THE SPOOLS WILL BE HERE WHEN YOU GET BACK!
JESTA SECOND, MR. PARKER...! THIS MACHINE, SHE'S A FEISTY ONE, I...
OH NO!! SHE'S STARTED UP AGAIN... I'M CAUGHT!
SOMEBODY HELP!! IT'S GOT ME ARM!!
HELLLPPPP!!
WE'VE GOT TO HELP HIM, COLM!
RIGHT, BEN...
...YOU BRACE THE GEARS TO A STOP...
...WHILE I YANK ERIC FREE!! HANG ON, PAL!

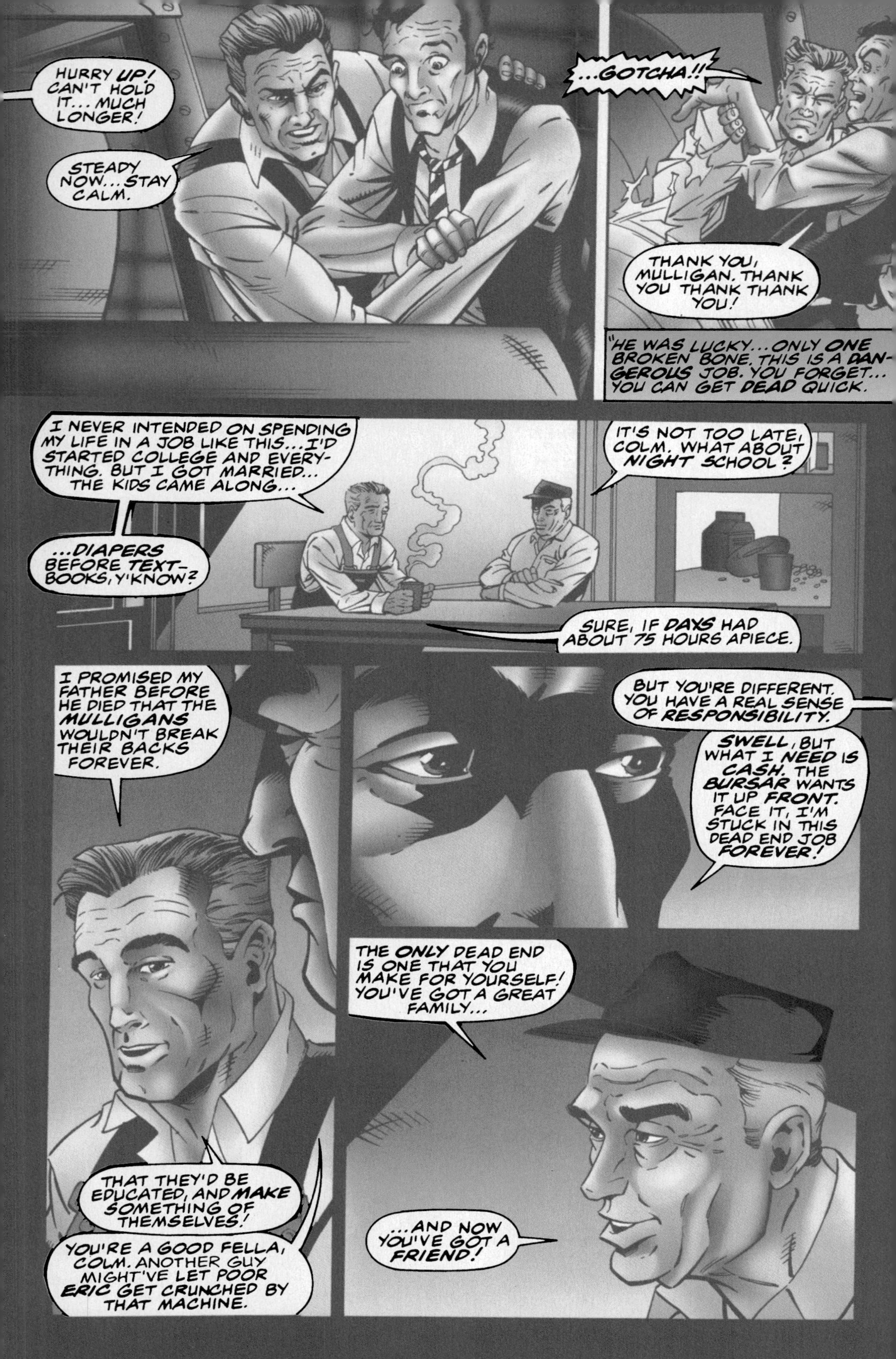

HURRY UP! CAN'T HOLD IT... MUCH LONGER!
STEADY NOW... STAY CALM.
...GOTCHA!!
THANK YOU, MULLIGAN. THANK YOU THANK THANK YOU!
"HE WAS LUCKY... ONLY ONE BROKEN BONE. THIS IS A DANGEROUS JOB. YOU FORGET... YOU CAN GET DEAD QUICK.
I NEVER INTENDED ON SPENDING MY LIFE IN A JOB LIKE THIS... I'D STARTED COLLEGE AND EVERYTHING. BUT I GOT MARRIED... THE KIDS CAME ALONG...
...DIAPERS BEFORE TEXTBOOKS, Y'KNOW?
IT'S NOT TOO LATE, COLM. WHAT ABOUT NIGHT SCHOOL?
SURE, IF DAYS HAD ABOUT 75 HOURS APIECE.
I PROMISED MY FATHER BEFORE HE DIED THAT THE MULLIGANS WOULDN'T BREAK THEIR BACKS FOREVER.
BUT YOU'RE DIFFERENT. YOU HAVE A REAL SENSE OF RESPONSIBILITY.
SWELL, BUT WHAT I NEED IS CASH. THE BURSAR WANTS IT UP FRONT. FACE IT, I'M STUCK IN THIS DEAD END JOB FOREVER!
THE ONLY DEAD END IS ONE THAT YOU MAKE FOR YOURSELF! YOU'VE GOT A GREAT FAMILY...
THAT THEY'D BE EDUCATED, AND MAKE SOMETHING OF THEMSELVES!
YOU'RE A GOOD FELLA, COLM. ANOTHER GUY MIGHT'VE LET POOR ERIC GET CRUNCHED BY THAT MACHINE.
...AND NOW YOU'VE GOT A FRIEND!

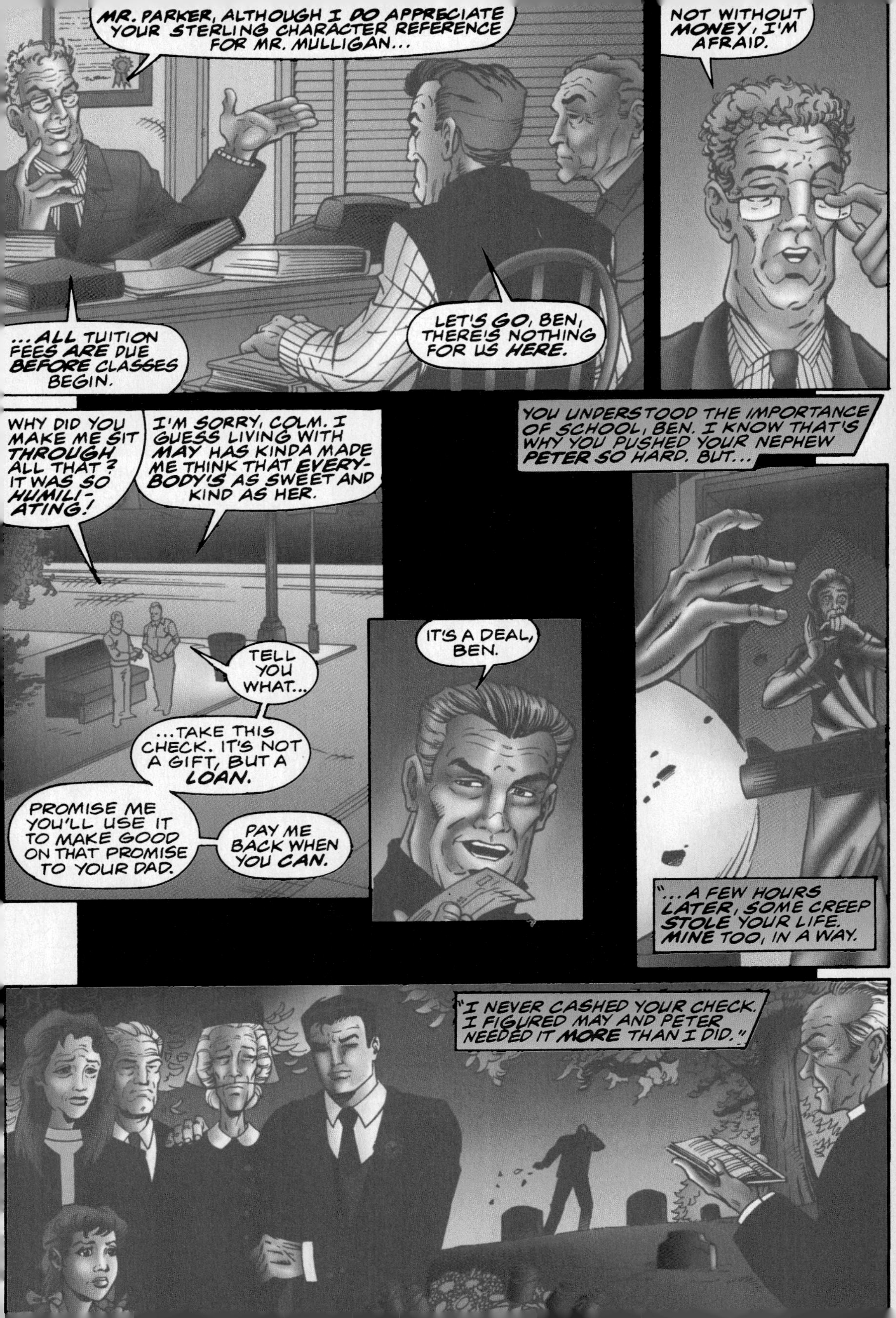
MR. PARKER, ALTHOUGH I DO APPRECIATE YOUR STERLING CHARACTER REFERENCE FOR MR. MULLIGAN...
...ALL TUITION FEES ARE DUE BEFORE CLASSES BEGIN.
LET'S GO, BEN, THERE'S NOTHING FOR US HERE.
NOT WITHOUT MONEY, I'M AFRAID.
WHY DID YOU MAKE ME SIT THROUGH ALL THAT? IT WAS SO HUMILIATING!
I'M SORRY, COLM. I GUESS LIVING WITH MAY HAS KINDA MADE ME THINK THAT EVERYBODY'S AS SWEET AND KIND AS HER.
TELL YOU WHAT...
...TAKE THIS CHECK. IT'S NOT A GIFT, BUT A LOAN.
PROMISE ME YOU'LL USE IT TO MAKE GOOD ON THAT PROMISE TO YOUR DAD.
PAY ME BACK WHEN YOU CAN.
IT'S A DEAL, BEN.
YOU UNDERSTOOD THE IMPORTANCE OF SCHOOL, BEN. I KNOW THAT'S WHY YOU PUSHED YOUR NEPHEW PETER SO HARD. BUT...
"...A FEW HOURS LATER, SOME CREEP STOLE YOUR LIFE. MINE TOO, IN A WAY.
"I NEVER CASHED YOUR CHECK. I FIGURED MAY AND PETER NEEDED IT MORE THAN I DID."

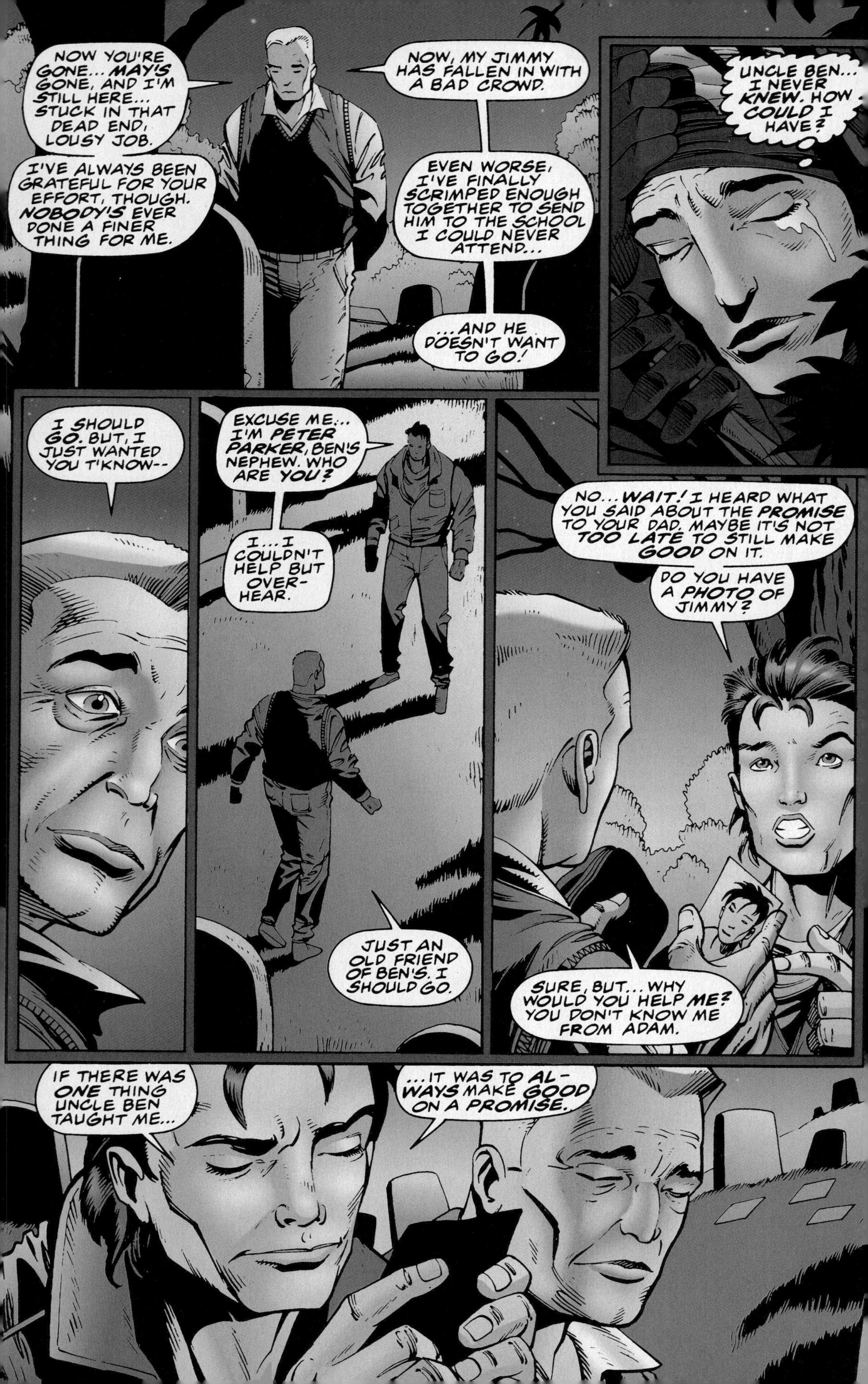
NOW YOU'RE GONE... MAY'S GONE, AND I'M STILL HERE... STUCK IN THAT DEAD END, LOUSY JOB.
I'VE ALWAYS BEEN GRATEFUL FOR YOUR EFFORT, THOUGH. NOBODY'S EVER DONE A FINER THING FOR ME.
NOW, MY JIMMY HAS FALLEN IN WITH A BAD CROWD.
EVEN WORSE, I'VE FINALLY SCRIMPED ENOUGH TOGETHER TO SEND HIM TO THE SCHOOL I COULD NEVER ATTEND...
...AND HE DOESN'T WANT TO GO!
UNCLE BEN... I NEVER KNEW. HOW COULD I HAVE?
I SHOULD GO. BUT, I JUST WANTED YOU T'KNOW--
EXCUSE ME... I'M PETER PARKER, BEN'S NEPHEW. WHO ARE YOU?
I... I COULDN'T HELP BUT OVER-HEAR.
JUST AN OLD FRIEND OF BEN'S. I SHOULD GO.
NO... WAIT! I HEARD WHAT YOU SAID ABOUT THE PROMISE TO YOUR DAD. MAYBE IT'S NOT TOO LATE TO STILL MAKE GOOD ON IT.
DO YOU HAVE A PHOTO OF JIMMY?
SURE, BUT... WHY WOULD YOU HELP ME? YOU DON'T KNOW ME FROM ADAM.
IF THERE WAS ONE THING UNCLE BEN TAUGHT ME...
...IT WAS TO AL-WAYS MAKE GOOD ON A PROMISE.

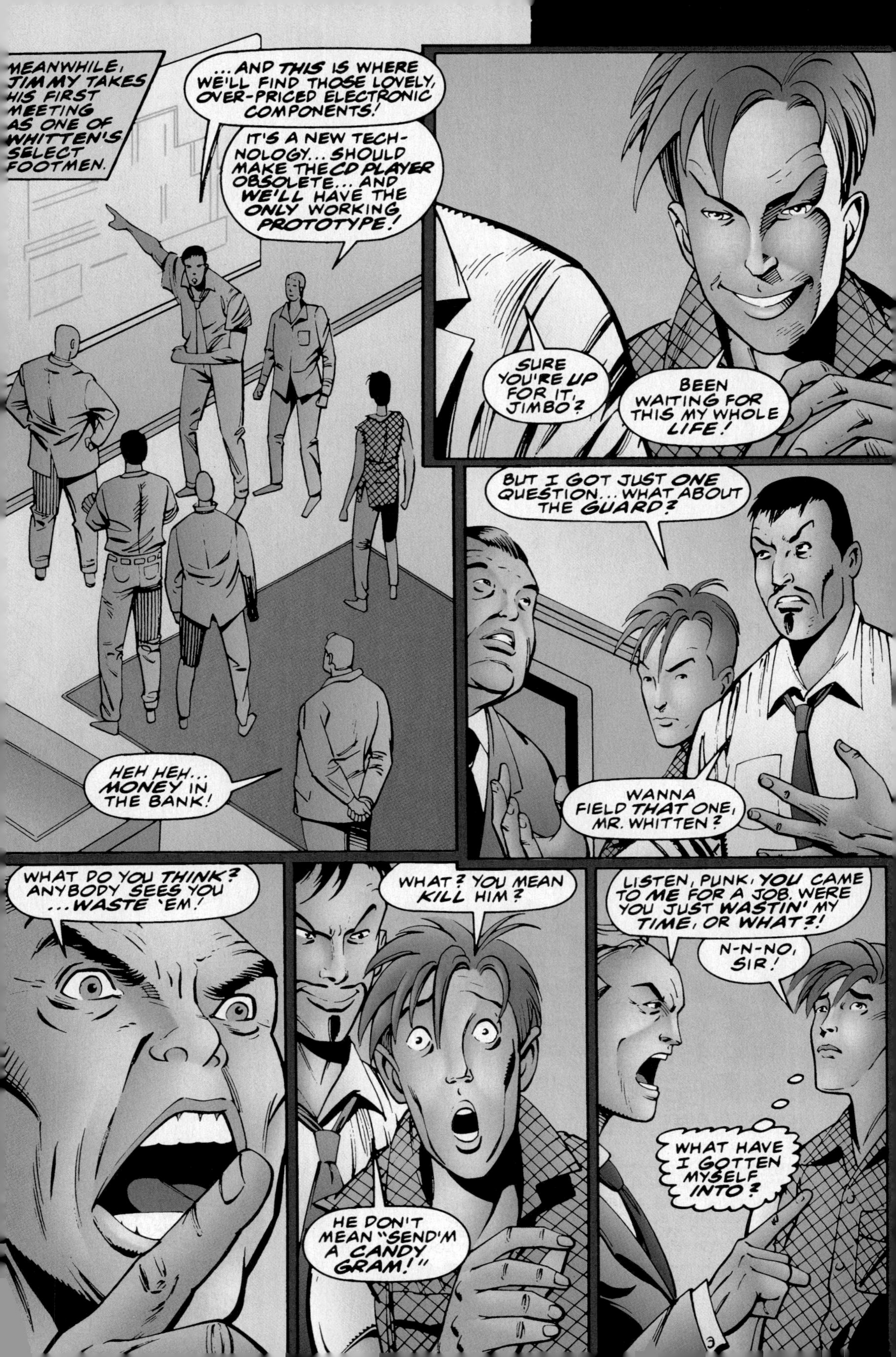
MEANWHILE, JIMMY TAKES HIS FIRST MEETING AS ONE OF WHITTEN'S SELECT FOOTMEN.
...AND THIS IS WHERE WE'LL FIND THOSE LOVELY, OVER-PRICED ELECTRONIC COMPONENTS!
IT'S A NEW TECHNOLOGY... SHOULD MAKE THE CD PLAYER OBSOLETE... AND WE'LL HAVE THE ONLY WORKING PROTOTYPE!
HEH HEH... MONEY IN THE BANK!
SURE YOU'RE UP FOR IT, JIMBO?
BEEN WAITING FOR THIS MY WHOLE LIFE!
BUT I GOT JUST ONE QUESTION... WHAT ABOUT THE GUARD?
WANNA FIELD THAT ONE, MR. WHITTEN?
WHAT DO YOU THINK? ANYBODY SEES YOU ...WASTE 'EM!
WHAT? YOU MEAN KILL HIM?
HE DON'T MEAN "SEND'M A CANDY GRAM!"
LISTEN, PUNK, YOU CAME TO ME FOR A JOB. WERE YOU JUST WASTIN' MY TIME, OR WHAT?!
N-N-NO, SIR!
WHAT HAVE I GOTTEN MYSELF INTO?

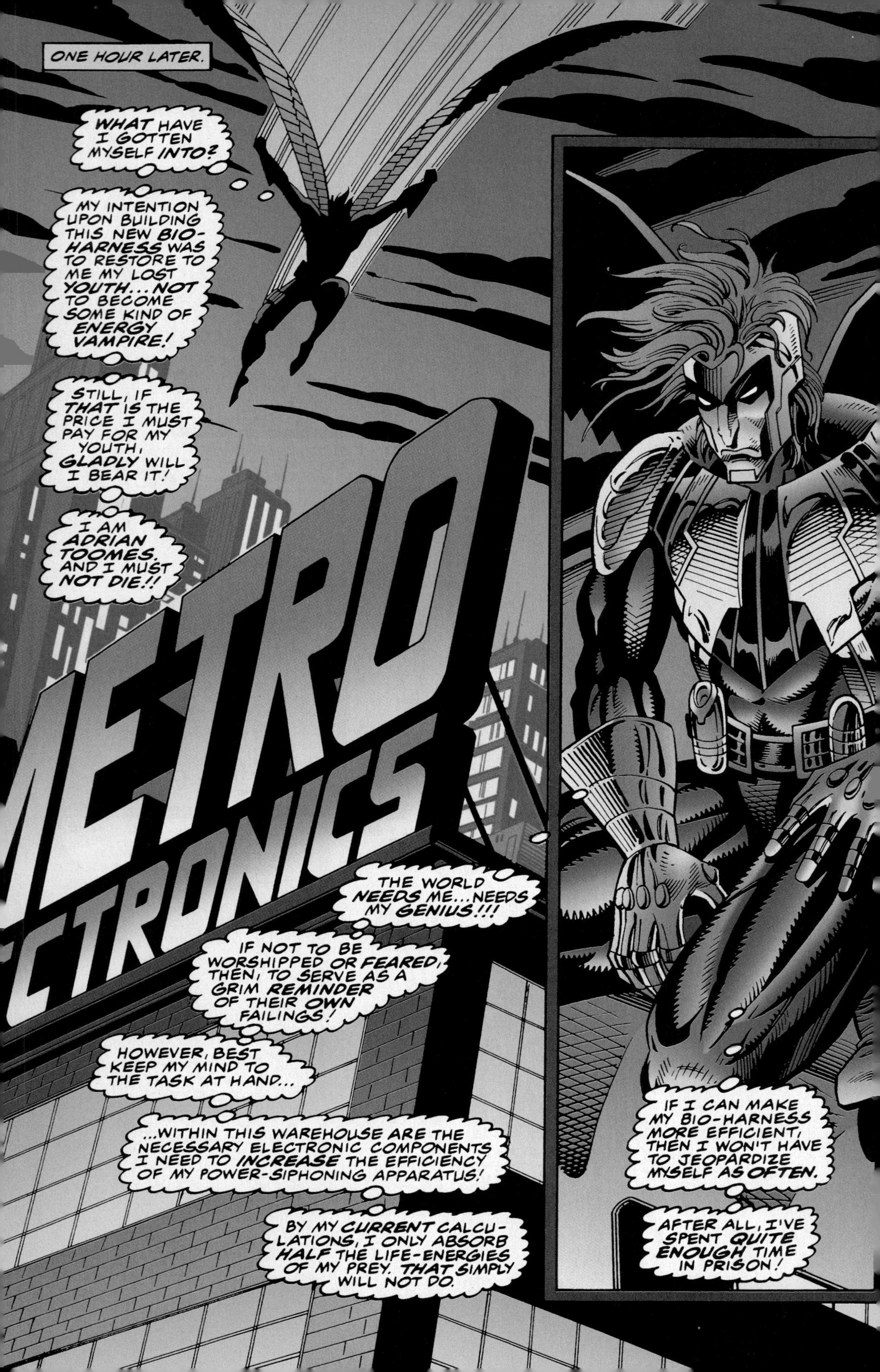
ONE HOUR LATER.
WHAT HAVE I GOTTEN MYSELF INTO?
MY INTENTION UPON BUILDING THIS NEW BIO-HARNESS WAS TO RESTORE TO ME MY LOST YOUTH...NOT TO BECOME SOME KIND OF ENERGY VAMPIRE!
STILL, IF THAT IS THE PRICE I MUST PAY FOR MY YOUTH, GLADLY WILL I BEAR IT!
I AM ADRIAN TOOMES. AND I MUST NOT DIE!!
METRO
CTRONICS
THE WORLD NEEDS ME...NEEDS MY GENIUS!!!
IF NOT TO BE WORSHIPPED OR FEARED, THEN, TO SERVE AS A GRIM REMINDER OF THEIR OWN FAILINGS!
HOWEVER, BEST KEEP MY MIND TO THE TASK AT HAND...
...WITHIN THIS WAREHOUSE ARE THE NECESSARY ELECTRONIC COMPONENTS I NEED TO INCREASE THE EFFICIENCY OF MY POWER-SIPHONING APPARATUS!
BY MY CURRENT CALCULATIONS, I ONLY ABSORB HALF THE LIFE-ENERGIES OF MY PREY. THAT SIMPLY WILL NOT DO.
IF I CAN MAKE MY BIO-HARNESS MORE EFFICIENT, THEN I WON'T HAVE TO JEOPARDIZE MYSELF AS OFTEN.
AFTER ALL, I'VE SPENT QUITE ENOUGH TIME IN PRISON!

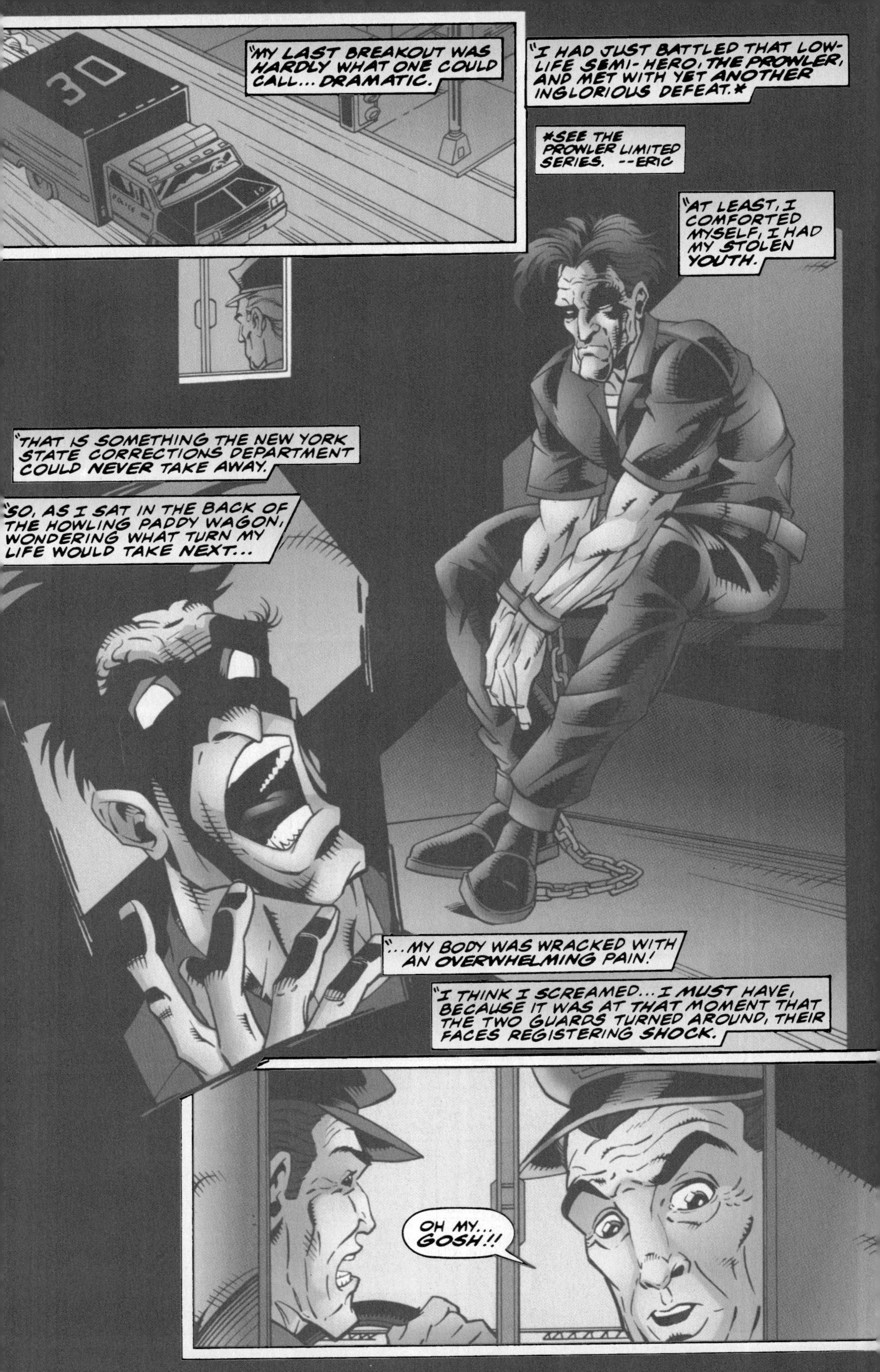
"MY LAST BREAKOUT WAS HARDLY WHAT ONE COULD CALL... DRAMATIC.
30
"I HAD JUST BATTLED THAT LOW-LIFE SEMI-HERO, THE PROWLER, AND MET WITH YET ANOTHER INGLORIOUS DEFEAT.*
*SEE THE PROWLER LIMITED SERIES. --ERIC
"AT LEAST, I COMFORTED MYSELF, I HAD MY STOLEN YOUTH.
"THAT IS SOMETHING THE NEW YORK STATE CORRECTIONS DEPARTMENT COULD NEVER TAKE AWAY.
"SO, AS I SAT IN THE BACK OF THE HOWLING PADDY WAGON, WONDERING WHAT TURN MY LIFE WOULD TAKE NEXT...
"...MY BODY WAS WRACKED WITH AN OVERWHELMING PAIN!
"I THINK I SCREAMED... I MUST HAVE, BECAUSE IT WAS AT THAT MOMENT THAT THE TWO GUARDS TURNED AROUND, THEIR FACES REGISTERING SHOCK.
OH MY... GOSH!!

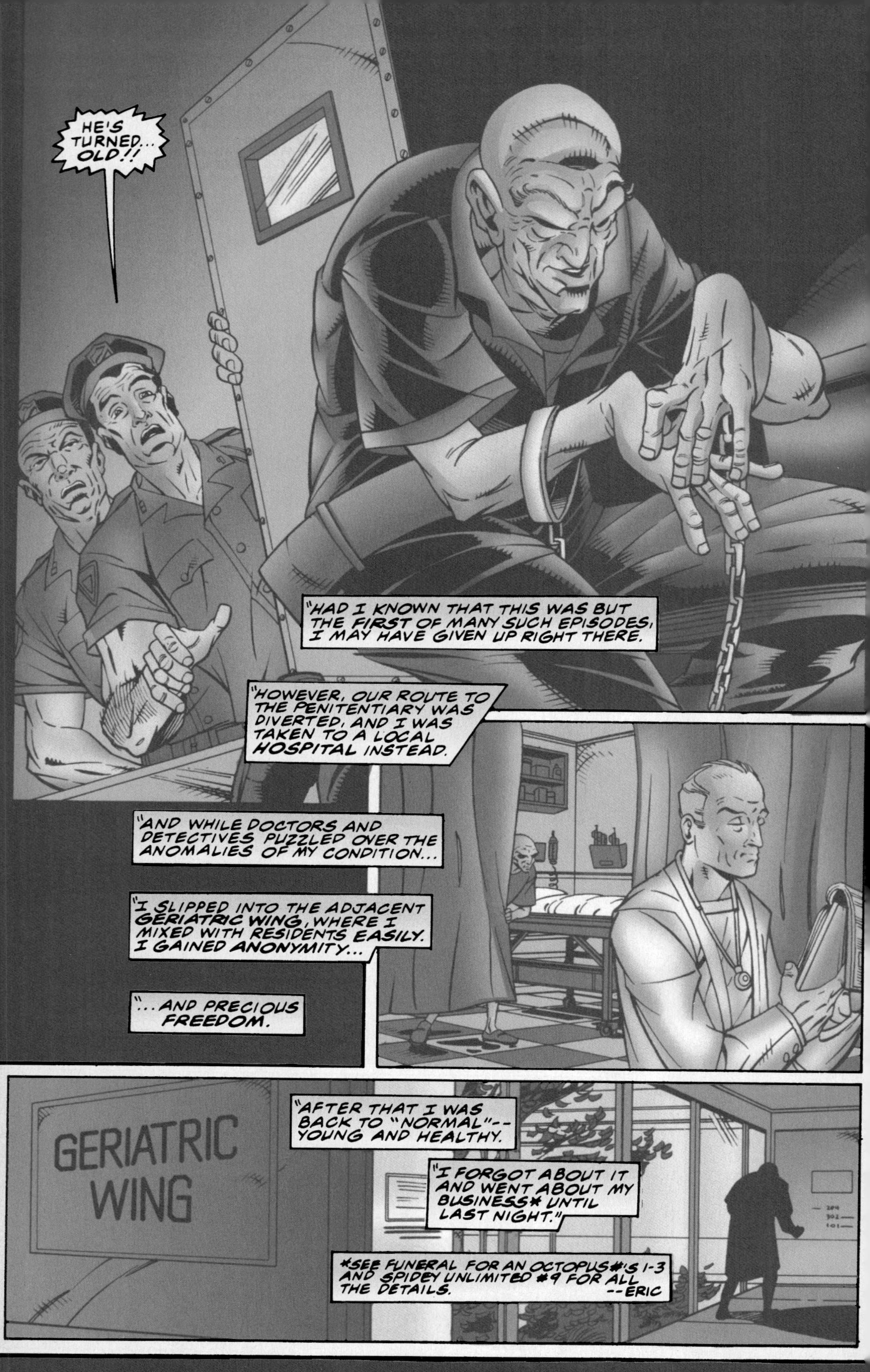
HE'S TURNED... OLD!!
"HAD I KNOWN THAT THIS WAS BUT THE FIRST OF MANY SUCH EPISODES, I MAY HAVE GIVEN UP RIGHT THERE.
"HOWEVER, OUR ROUTE TO THE PENITENTIARY WAS DIVERTED, AND I WAS TAKEN TO A LOCAL HOSPITAL INSTEAD.
"AND WHILE DOCTORS AND DETECTIVES PUZZLED OVER THE ANOMALIES OF MY CONDITION...
"I SLIPPED INTO THE ADJACENT GERIATRIC WING, WHERE I MIXED WITH RESIDENTS EASILY. I GAINED ANONYMITY...
"...AND PRECIOUS FREEDOM.
GERIATRIC WING
"AFTER THAT I WAS BACK TO "NORMAL"-- YOUNG AND HEALTHY.
"I FORGOT ABOUT IT AND WENT ABOUT MY BUSINESS* UNTIL LAST NIGHT."
*SEE FUNERAL FOR AN OCTOPUS #'S 1-3 AND SPIDEY UNLIMITED #9 FOR ALL THE DETAILS. --ERIC

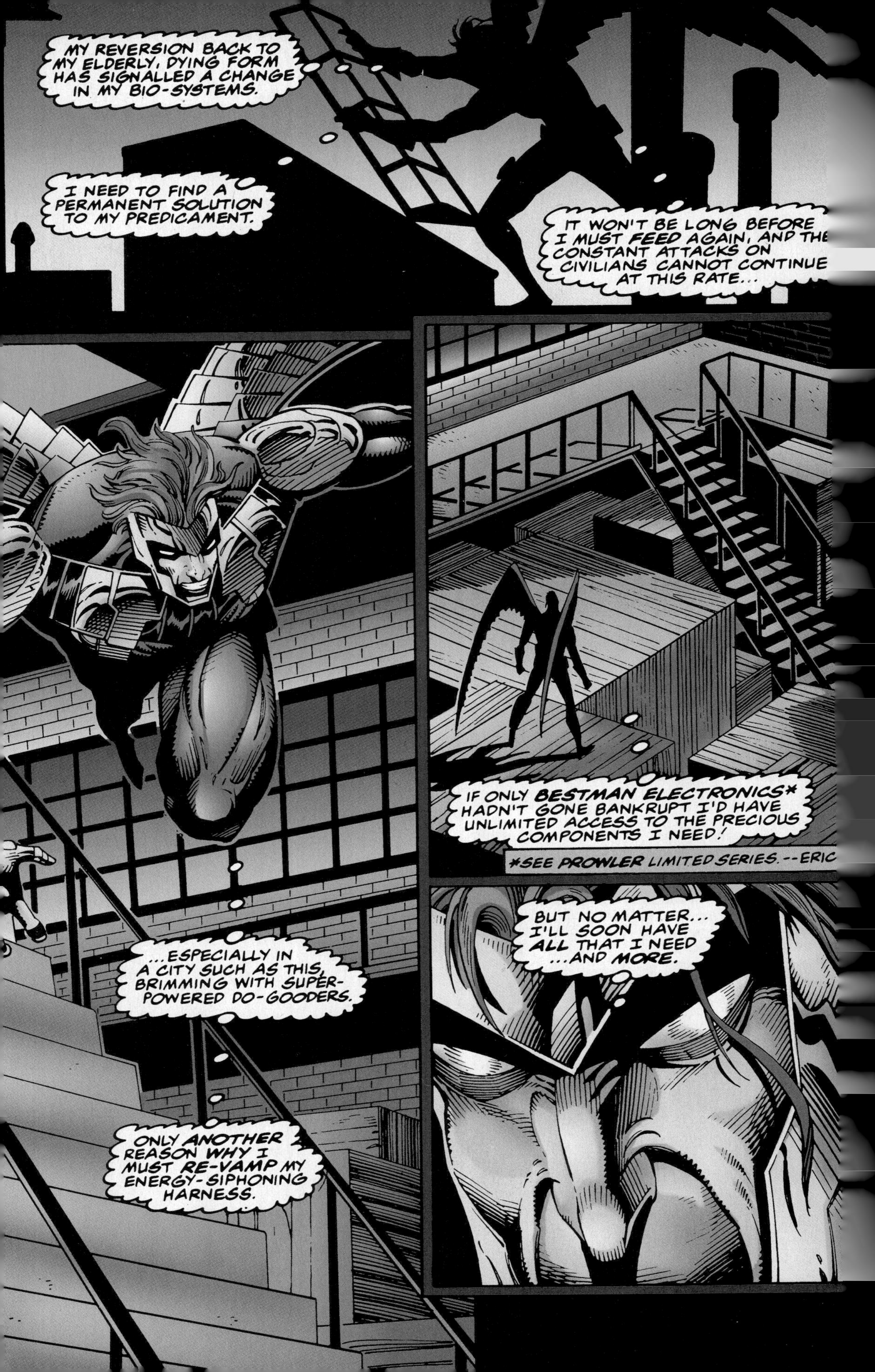

MY REVERSION BACK TO MY ELDERLY, DYING FORM HAS SIGNALLED A CHANGE IN MY BIO-SYSTEMS.
I NEED TO FIND A PERMANENT SOLUTION TO MY PREDICAMENT.
IT WON'T BE LONG BEFORE I MUST FEED AGAIN, AND THE CONSTANT ATTACKS ON CIVILIANS CANNOT CONTINUE AT THIS RATE...
...ESPECIALLY IN A CITY SUCH AS THIS, BRIMMING WITH SUPER-POWERED DO-GOODERS.
ONLY ANOTHER REASON WHY I MUST RE-VAMP MY ENERGY-SIPHONING HARNESS.
IF ONLY BESTMAN ELECTRONICS* HADN'T GONE BANKRUPT I'D HAVE UNLIMITED ACCESS TO THE PRECIOUS COMPONENTS I NEED!
*SEE PROWLER LIMITED SERIES. --ERIC
BUT NO MATTER... I'LL SOON HAVE ALL THAT I NEED ...AND MORE.

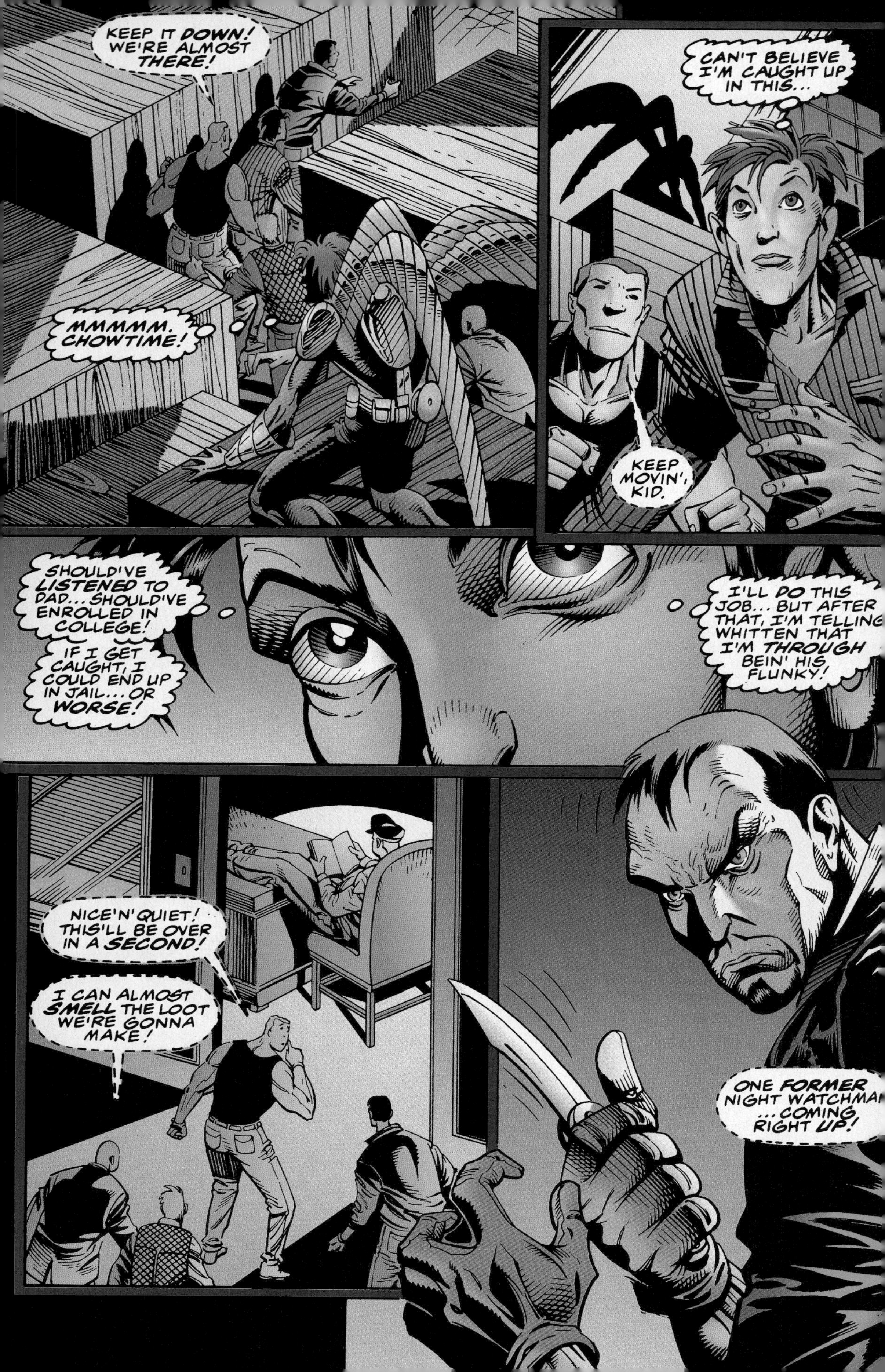
KEEP IT DOWN! WE'RE ALMOST THERE!
MMMMMM. CHOWTIME!
CAN'T BELIEVE I'M CAUGHT UP IN THIS...
KEEP MOVIN', KID.
SHOULD'VE LISTENED TO DAD... SHOULD'VE ENROLLED IN COLLEGE!
IF I GET CAUGHT, I COULD END UP IN JAIL... OR WORSE!
I'LL DO THIS JOB... BUT AFTER THAT, I'M TELLING WHITTEN THAT I'M THROUGH BEIN' HIS FLUNKY!
NICE'N' QUIET! THIS'LL BE OVER IN A SECOND!
I CAN ALMOST SMELL THE LOOT WE'RE GONNA MAKE!
ONE FORMER NIGHT WATCHMAN ...COMING RIGHT UP!

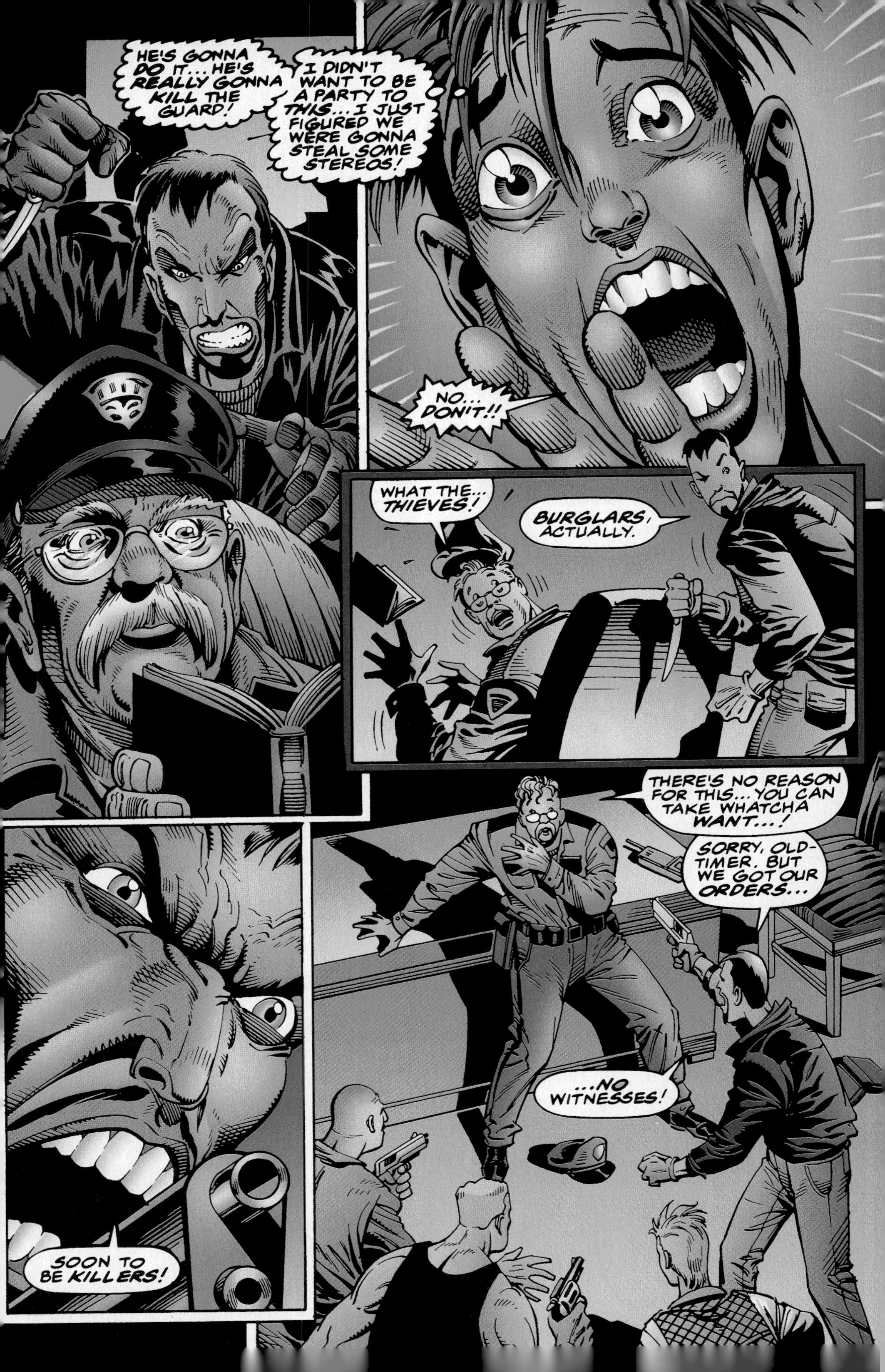
HE'S GONNA DO IT... HE'S REALLY GONNA KILL THE GUARD!
I DIDN'T WANT TO BE A PARTY TO THIS... I JUST FIGURED WE WERE GONNA STEAL SOME STEREOS!
NO... DON'T!!
WHAT THE... THIEVES!
BURGLARS, ACTUALLY.
SOON TO BE KILLERS!
THERE'S NO REASON FOR THIS... YOU CAN TAKE WHATCHA WANT...!
SORRY, OLD-TIMER, BUT WE GOT OUR ORDERS...
...NO WITNESSES!

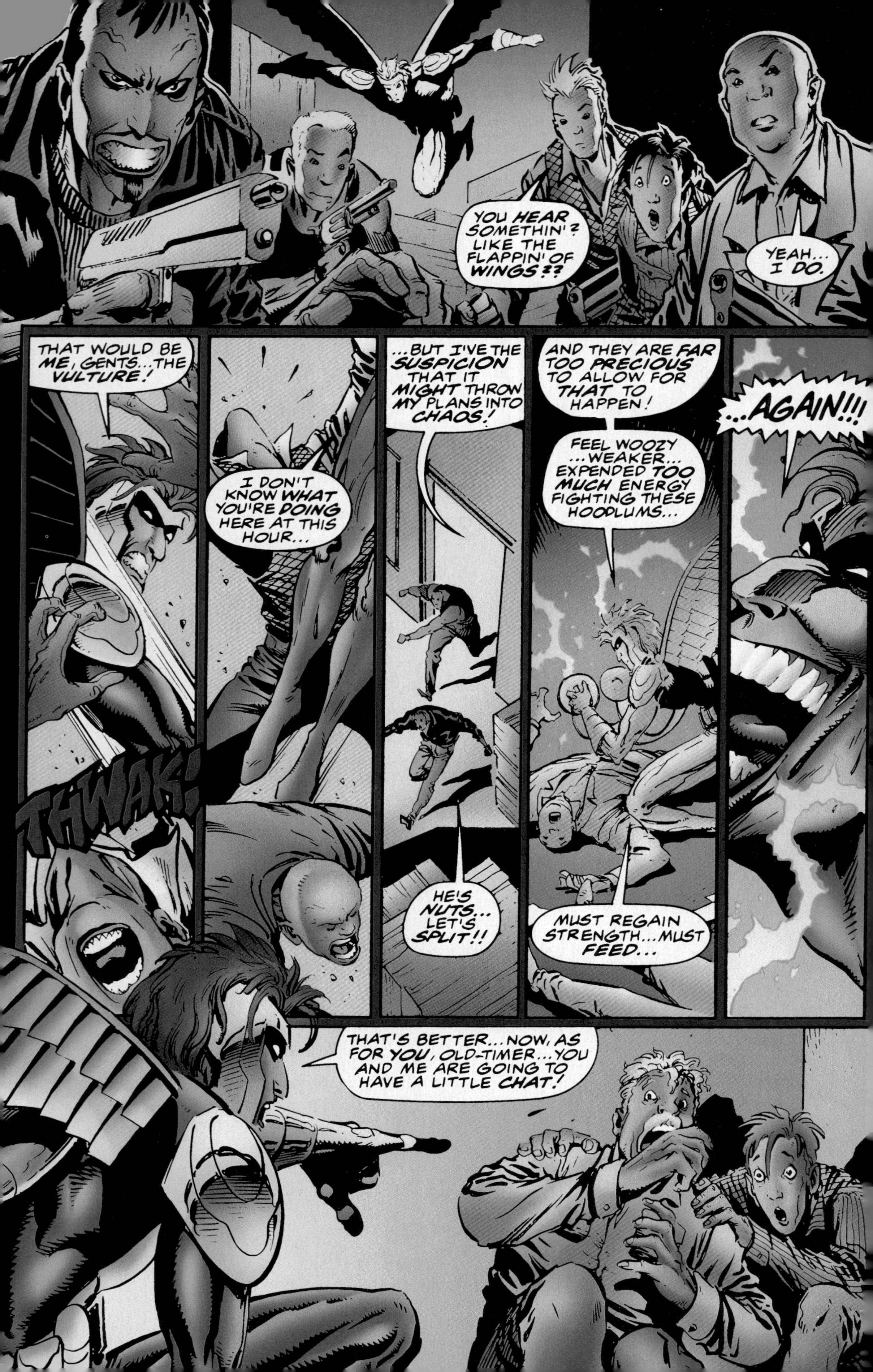

YOU HEAR SOMETHIN'? LIKE THE FLAPPIN' OF WINGS??
YEAH... I DO.
THAT WOULD BE ME, GENTS... THE VULTURE!
THWAK!
I DON'T KNOW WHAT YOU'RE DOING HERE AT THIS HOUR...
...BUT I'VE THE SUSPICION THAT IT MIGHT THROW MY PLANS INTO CHAOS!
HE'S NUTS... LET'S SPLIT!!
AND THEY ARE FAR TOO PRECIOUS TO ALLOW FOR THAT TO HAPPEN!
FEEL WOOZY ...WEAKER... EXPENDED TOO MUCH ENERGY FIGHTING THESE HOODLUMS...
MUST REGAIN STRENGTH...MUST FEED...
...AGAIN!!!
THAT'S BETTER...NOW, AS FOR YOU, OLD-TIMER...YOU AND ME ARE GOING TO HAVE A LITTLE CHAT!

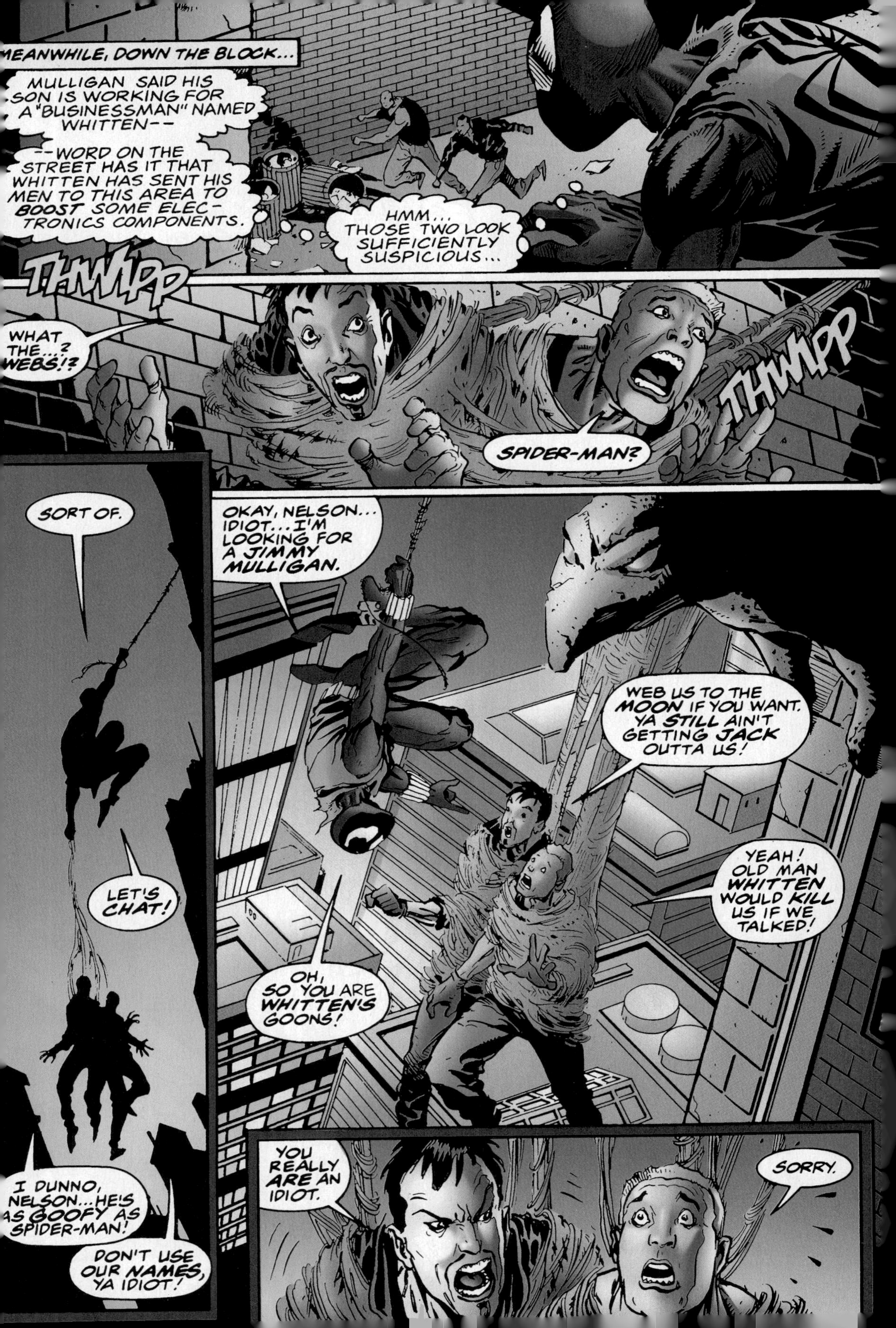
MEANWHILE, DOWN THE BLOCK...
MULLIGAN SAID HIS SON IS WORKING FOR A "BUSINESSMAN" NAMED WHITTEN--
--WORD ON THE STREET HAS IT THAT WHITTEN HAS SENT HIS MEN TO THIS AREA TO BOOST SOME ELECTRONICS COMPONENTS.
HMM... THOSE TWO LOOK SUFFICIENTLY SUSPICIOUS...
THWIPP
WHAT THE...? WEBS!?
THWIPP
SPIDER-MAN?
SORT OF.
LET'S CHAT!
OKAY, NELSON... IDIOT... I'M LOOKING FOR A JIMMY MULLIGAN.
WEB US TO THE MOON IF YOU WANT. YA STILL AIN'T GETTING JACK OUTTA US!
YEAH! OLD MAN WHITTEN WOULD KILL US IF WE TALKED!
OH, SO YOU ARE WHITTEN'S GOONS!
I DUNNO, NELSON... HE'S AS GOOFY AS SPIDER-MAN!
DON'T USE OUR NAMES, YA IDIOT!
YOU REALLY ARE AN IDIOT.
SORRY.

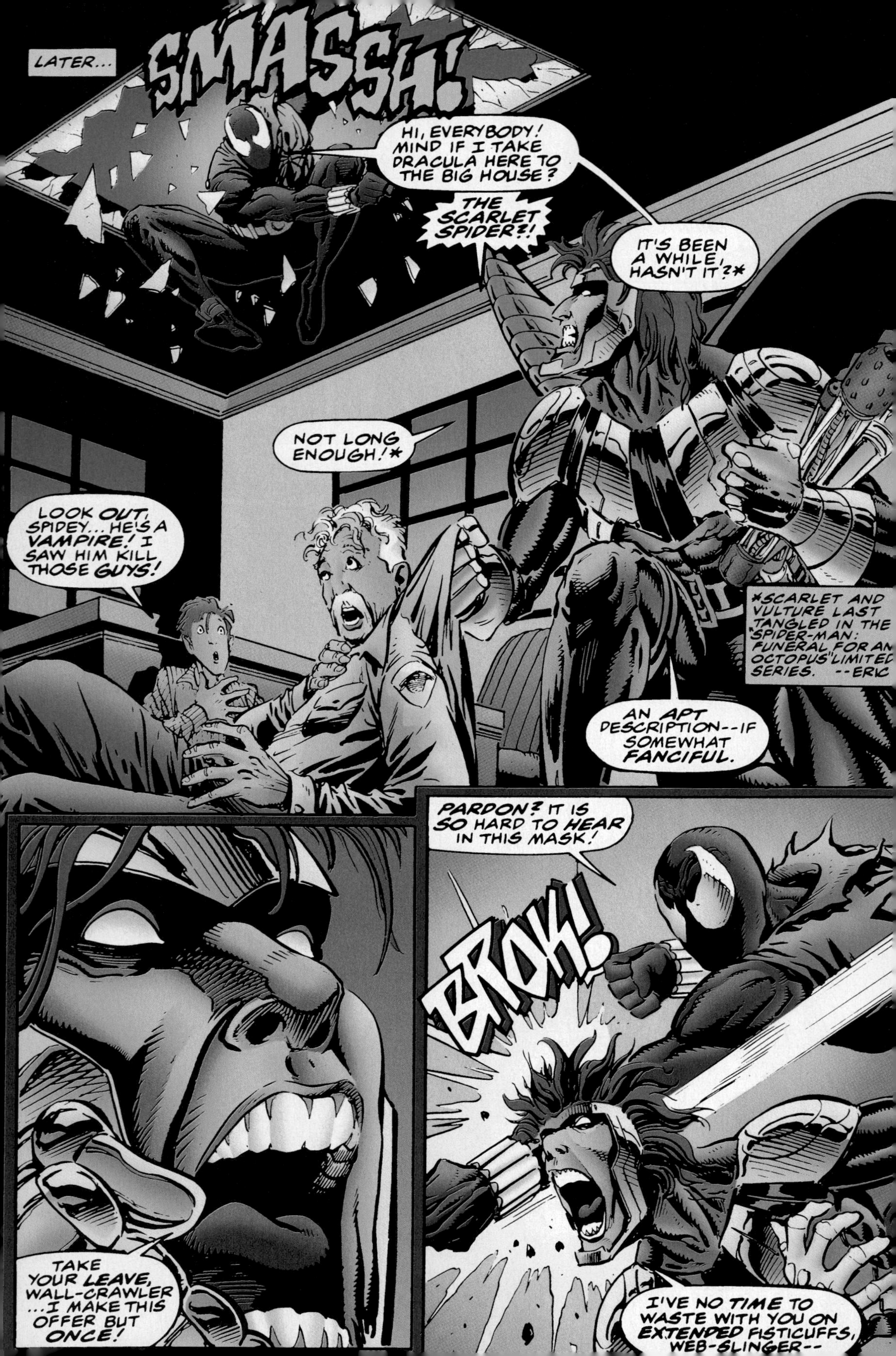
LATER...
SMASSH!
HI, EVERYBODY! MIND IF I TAKE DRACULA HERE TO THE BIG HOUSE?
THE SCARLET SPIDER?!
IT'S BEEN A WHILE, HASN'T IT?*
NOT LONG ENOUGH!*
LOOK OUT, SPIDEY... HE'S A VAMPIRE! I SAW HIM KILL THOSE GUYS!
AN APT DESCRIPTION--IF SOMEWHAT FANCIFUL.
*SCARLET AND VULTURE LAST TANGLED IN THE "SPIDER-MAN: FUNERAL FOR AN OCTOPUS" LIMITED SERIES. --ERIC
TAKE YOUR LEAVE, WALL-CRAWLER ...I MAKE THIS OFFER BUT ONCE!
PARDON? IT IS SO HARD TO HEAR IN THIS MASK!
BROK!
I'VE NO TIME TO WASTE WITH YOU ON EXTENDED FISTICUFFS, WEB-SLINGER--

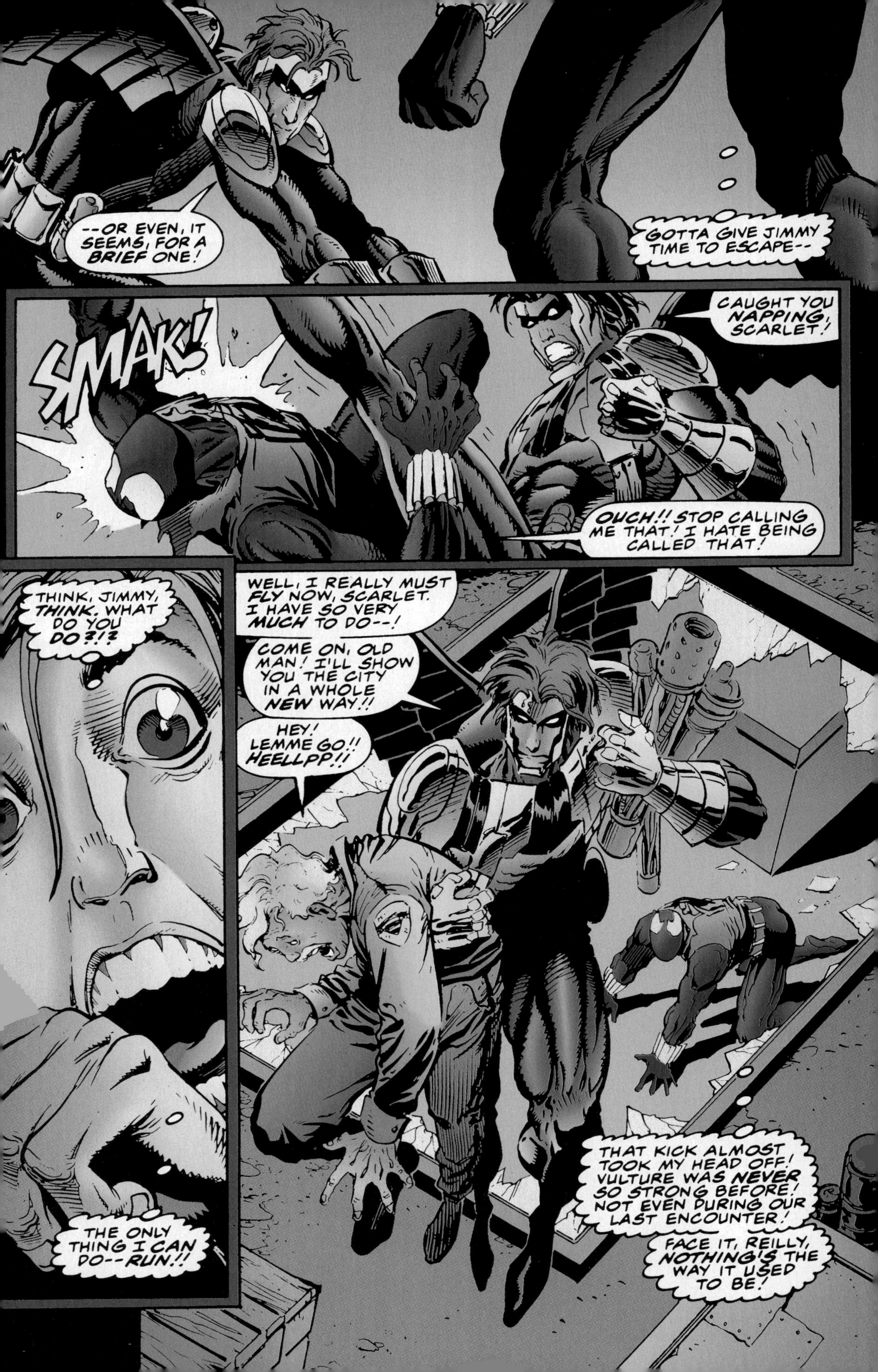
--OR EVEN, IT SEEMS, FOR A BRIEF ONE!
GOTTA GIVE JIMMY TIME TO ESCAPE--
SMAK!
CAUGHT YOU NAPPING, SCARLET!
OUCH!! STOP CALLING ME THAT! I HATE BEING CALLED THAT!
THINK, JIMMY, THINK. WHAT DO YOU DO?!?
THE ONLY THING I CAN DO--RUN!!
WELL, I REALLY MUST FLY NOW, SCARLET. I HAVE SO VERY MUCH TO DO--!
COME ON, OLD MAN! I'LL SHOW YOU THE CITY IN A WHOLE NEW WAY!!
HEY! LEMME GO!! HEELLPP!!
THAT KICK ALMOST TOOK MY HEAD OFF! VULTURE WAS NEVER SO STRONG BEFORE! NOT EVEN DURING OUR LAST ENCOUNTER!
FACE IT, REILLY, NOTHING'S THE WAY IT USED TO BE!

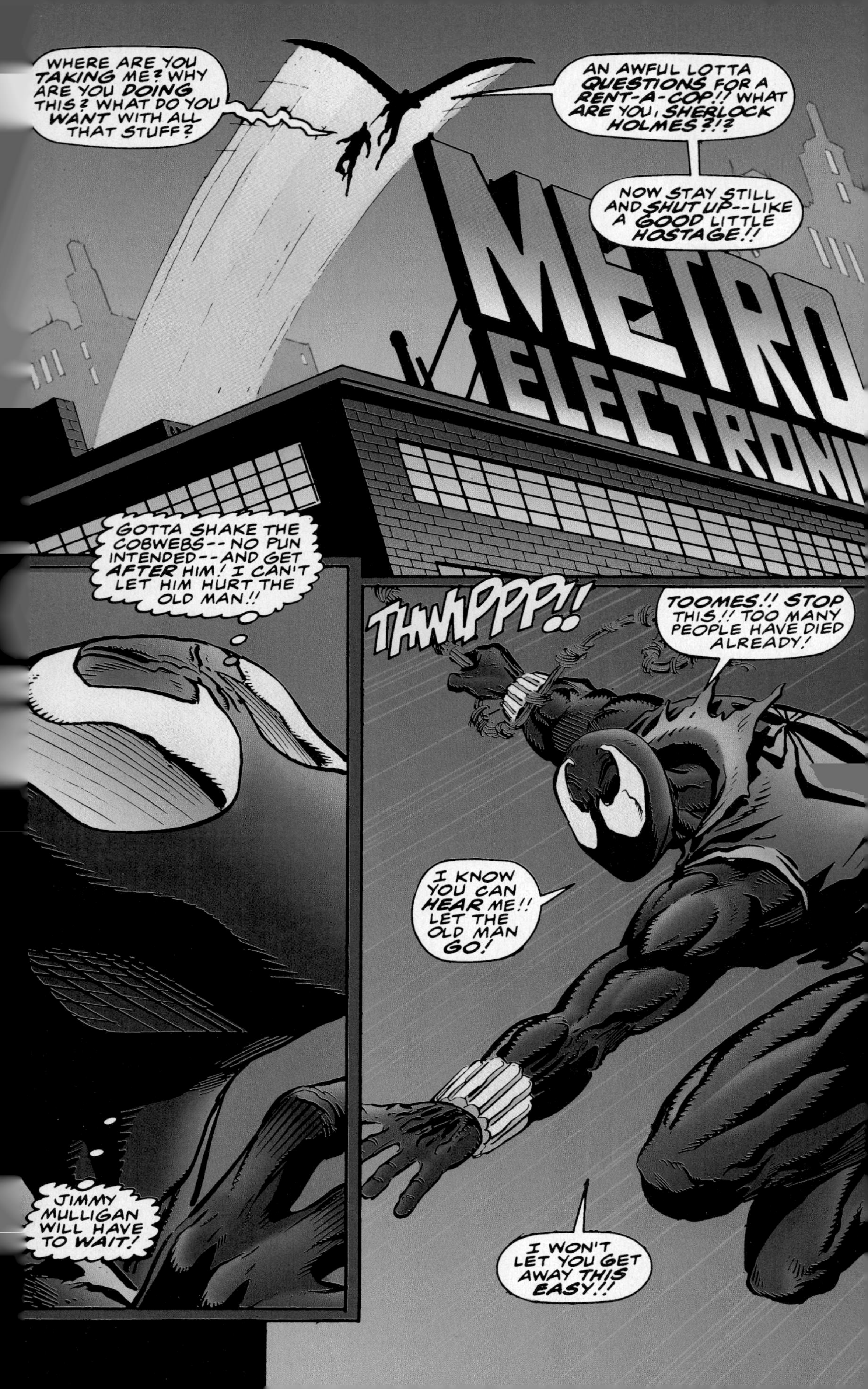

WHERE ARE YOU TAKING ME? WHY ARE YOU DOING THIS? WHAT DO YOU WANT WITH ALL THAT STUFF?
AN AWFUL LOTTA QUESTIONS FOR A RENT-A-COP!! WHAT ARE YOU, SHERLOCK HOLMES?!?
NOW STAY STILL AND SHUT UP--LIKE A GOOD LITTLE HOSTAGE!!
METRO ELECTRONI
GOTTA SHAKE THE COBWEBS-- NO PUN INTENDED--AND GET AFTER HIM! I CAN'T LET HIM HURT THE OLD MAN!!
JIMMY MULLIGAN WILL HAVE TO WAIT!
THWIPPP!!
TOOMES!! STOP THIS!! TOO MANY PEOPLE HAVE DIED ALREADY!
I KNOW YOU CAN HEAR ME!! LET THE OLD MAN GO!
I WON'T LET YOU GET AWAY THIS EASY!!

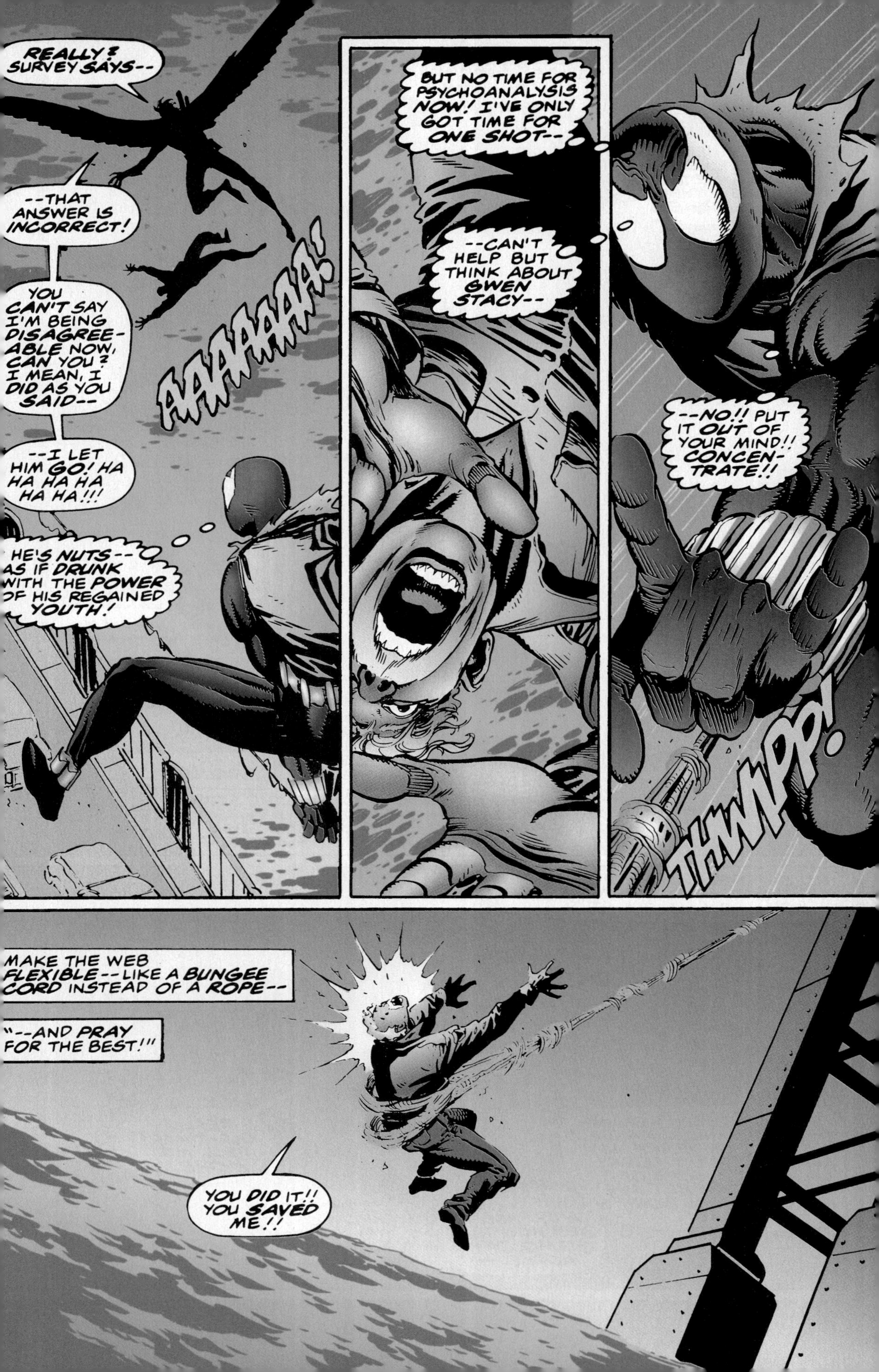
REALLY? SURVEY SAYS--
--THAT ANSWER IS INCORRECT!
YOU CAN'T SAY I'M BEING DISAGREE-ABLE NOW, CAN YOU? I MEAN, I DID AS YOU SAID--
--I LET HIM GO! HA HA HA HA HA HA!!!
AAAAAAA!
HE'S NUTS-- AS IF DRUNK WITH THE POWER OF HIS REGAINED YOUTH!
BUT NO TIME FOR PSYCHOANALYSIS NOW! I'VE ONLY GOT TIME FOR ONE SHOT--
--CAN'T HELP BUT THINK ABOUT GWEN STACY--
--NO!! PUT IT OUT OF YOUR MIND!! CONCEN-TRATE!!
THWIPP!
MAKE THE WEB FLEXIBLE--LIKE A BUNGEE CORD INSTEAD OF A ROPE--
"--AND PRAY FOR THE BEST!"
YOU DID IT!! YOU SAVED ME!!

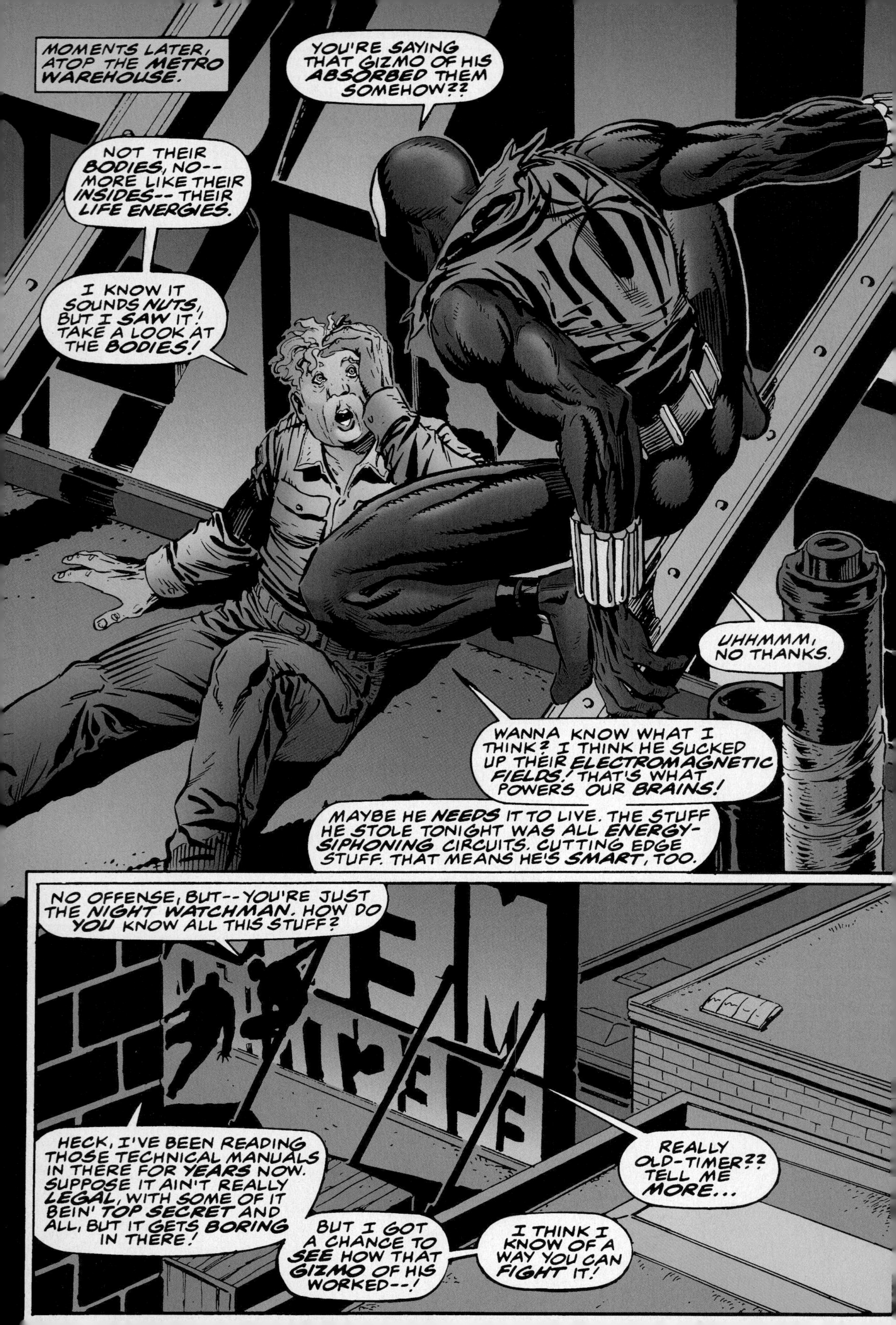
MOMENTS LATER, ATOP THE METRO WAREHOUSE.
YOU'RE SAYING THAT GIZMO OF HIS ABSORBED THEM SOMEHOW??
NOT THEIR BODIES, NO-- MORE LIKE THEIR INSIDES-- THEIR LIFE ENERGIES.
I KNOW IT SOUNDS NUTS, BUT I SAW IT! TAKE A LOOK AT THE BODIES!
UHHMMM, NO THANKS.
WANNA KNOW WHAT I THINK? I THINK HE SUCKED UP THEIR ELECTROMAGNETIC FIELDS! THAT'S WHAT POWERS OUR BRAINS!
MAYBE HE NEEDS IT TO LIVE. THE STUFF HE STOLE TONIGHT WAS ALL ENERGY-SIPHONING CIRCUITS. CUTTING EDGE STUFF. THAT MEANS HE'S SMART, TOO.
NO OFFENSE, BUT--YOU'RE JUST THE NIGHT WATCHMAN. HOW DO YOU KNOW ALL THIS STUFF?
HECK, I'VE BEEN READING THOSE TECHNICAL MANUALS IN THERE FOR YEARS NOW. SUPPOSE IT AIN'T REALLY LEGAL, WITH SOME OF IT BEIN' TOP SECRET AND ALL, BUT IT GETS BORING IN THERE!
BUT I GOT A CHANCE TO SEE HOW THAT GIZMO OF HIS WORKED--!
I THINK I KNOW OF A WAY YOU CAN FIGHT IT!
REALLY OLD-TIMER?? TELL ME MORE...

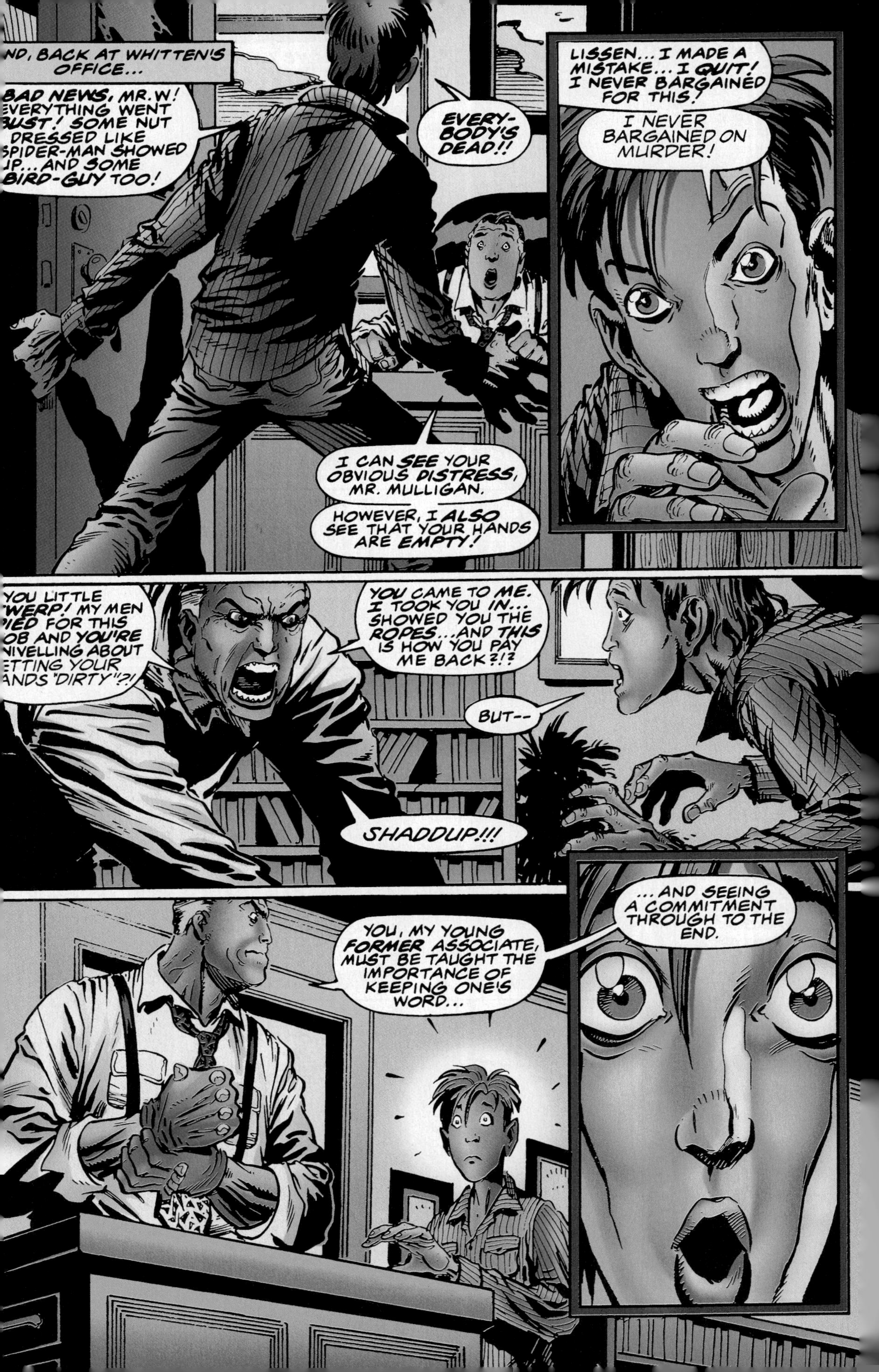
ND, BACK AT WHITTEN'S OFFICE...
BAD NEWS, MR. W! EVERYTHING WENT BUST! SOME NUT DRESSED LIKE SPIDER-MAN SHOWED UP... AND SOME BIRD-GUY TOO!
EVERY-BODY'S DEAD!!
LISSEN... I MADE A MISTAKE... I QUIT! I NEVER BARGAINED FOR THIS!
I NEVER BARGAINED ON MURDER!
I CAN SEE YOUR OBVIOUS DISTRESS, MR. MULLIGAN.
HOWEVER, I ALSO SEE THAT YOUR HANDS ARE EMPTY!
YOU LITTLE TWERP! MY MEN DIED FOR THIS JOB AND YOU'RE SNIVELLING ABOUT GETTING YOUR HANDS "DIRTY"?!
YOU CAME TO ME. I TOOK YOU IN... SHOWED YOU THE ROPES... AND THIS IS HOW YOU PAY ME BACK?!?
BUT--
SHADDUP!!!
YOU, MY YOUNG FORMER ASSOCIATE, MUST BE TAUGHT THE IMPORTANCE OF KEEPING ONE'S WORD...
...AND SEEING A COMMITMENT THROUGH TO THE END.

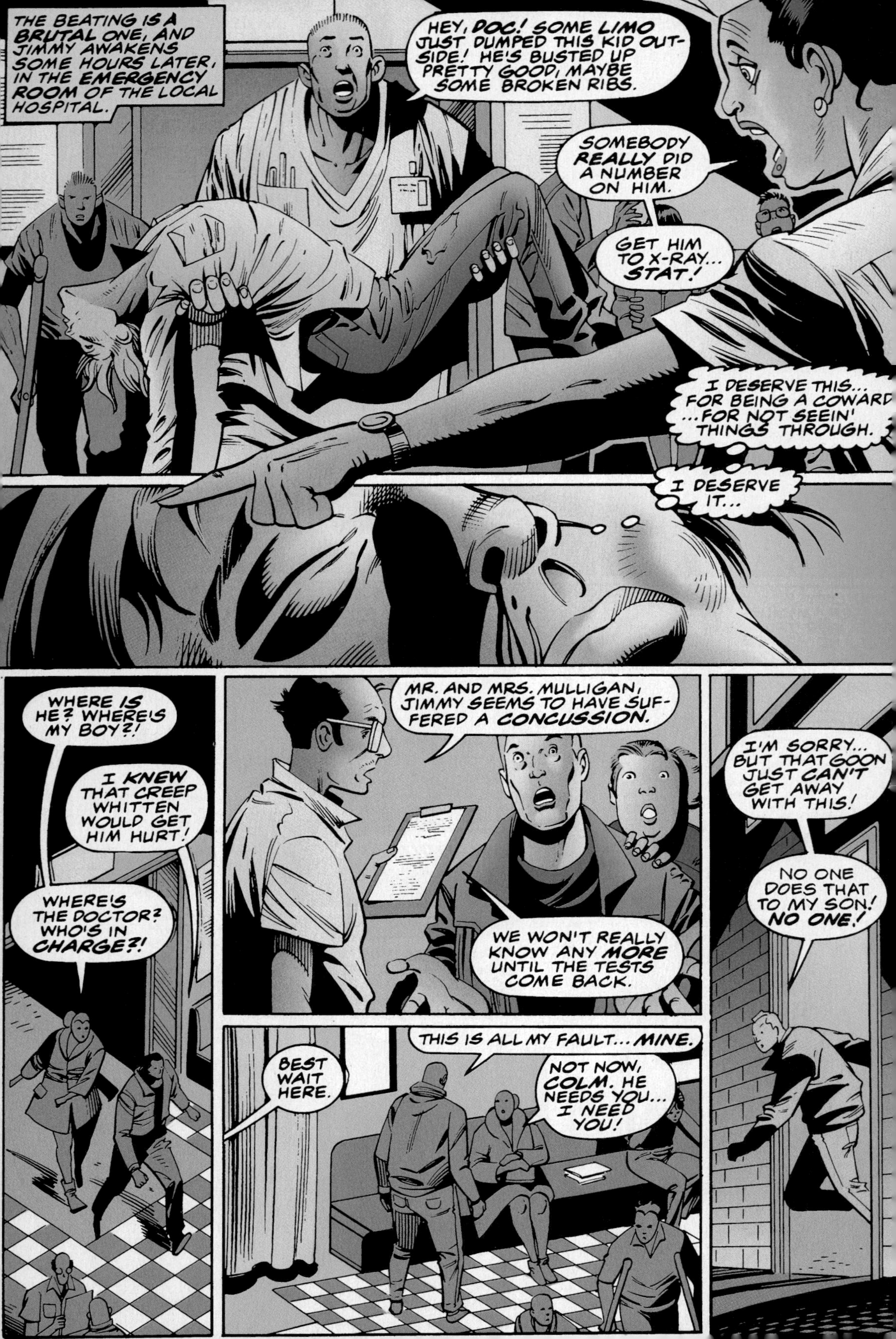
THE BEATING IS A BRUTAL ONE, AND JIMMY AWAKENS SOME HOURS LATER, IN THE EMERGENCY ROOM OF THE LOCAL HOSPITAL.
HEY, DOC! SOME LIMO JUST DUMPED THIS KID OUTSIDE! HE'S BUSTED UP PRETTY GOOD, MAYBE SOME BROKEN RIBS.
SOMEBODY REALLY DID A NUMBER ON HIM.
GET HIM TO X-RAY... STAT!
I DESERVE THIS... FOR BEING A COWARD ...FOR NOT SEEIN' THINGS THROUGH.
I DESERVE IT...
WHERE IS HE? WHERE'S MY BOY?!
I KNEW THAT CREEP WHITTEN WOULD GET HIM HURT!
WHERE'S THE DOCTOR? WHO'S IN CHARGE?!
MR. AND MRS. MULLIGAN, JIMMY SEEMS TO HAVE SUFFERED A CONCUSSION.
WE WON'T REALLY KNOW ANY MORE UNTIL THE TESTS COME BACK.
THIS IS ALL MY FAULT... MINE.
BEST WAIT HERE.
NOT NOW, COLM. HE NEEDS YOU... I NEED YOU!
I'M SORRY... BUT THAT GOON JUST CAN'T GET AWAY WITH THIS!
NO ONE DOES THAT TO MY SON! NO ONE!

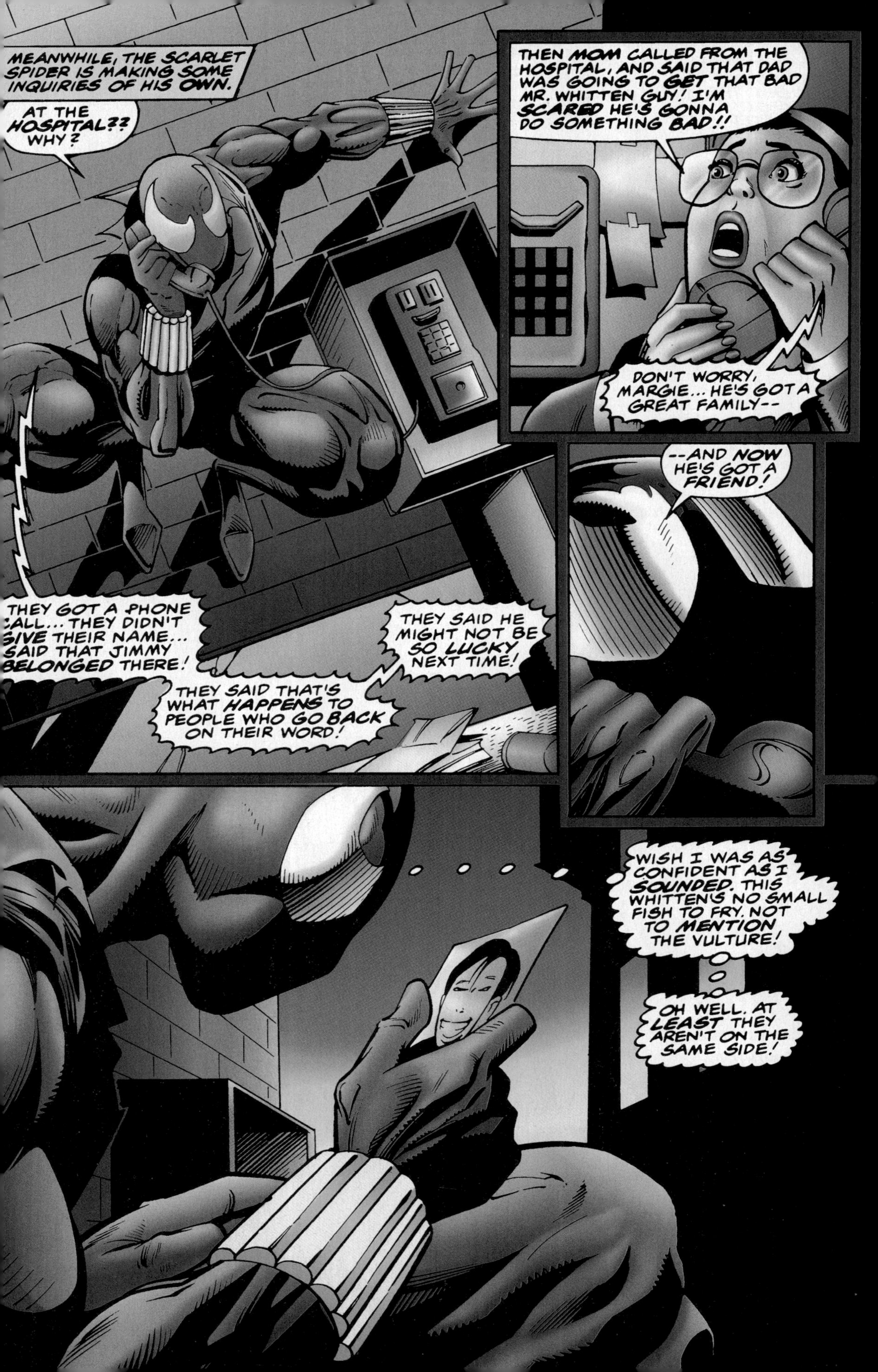
MEANWHILE, THE SCARLET SPIDER IS MAKING SOME INQUIRIES OF HIS OWN.
AT THE HOSPITAL?? WHY?
THEN MOM CALLED FROM THE HOSPITAL, AND SAID THAT DAD WAS GOING TO GET THAT BAD MR. WHITTEN GUY! I'M SCARED HE'S GONNA DO SOMETHING BAD!!
THEY GOT A PHONE CALL... THEY DIDN'T GIVE THEIR NAME... SAID THAT JIMMY BELONGED THERE!
THEY SAID THAT'S WHAT HAPPENS TO PEOPLE WHO GO BACK ON THEIR WORD!
THEY SAID HE MIGHT NOT BE SO LUCKY NEXT TIME!
DON'T WORRY, MARGIE... HE'S GOT A GREAT FAMILY--
--AND NOW HE'S GOT A FRIEND!
WISH I WAS AS CONFIDENT AS I SOUNDED. THIS WHITTEN'S NO SMALL FISH TO FRY. NOT TO MENTION THE VULTURE!
OH WELL. AT LEAST THEY AREN'T ON THE SAME SIDE!

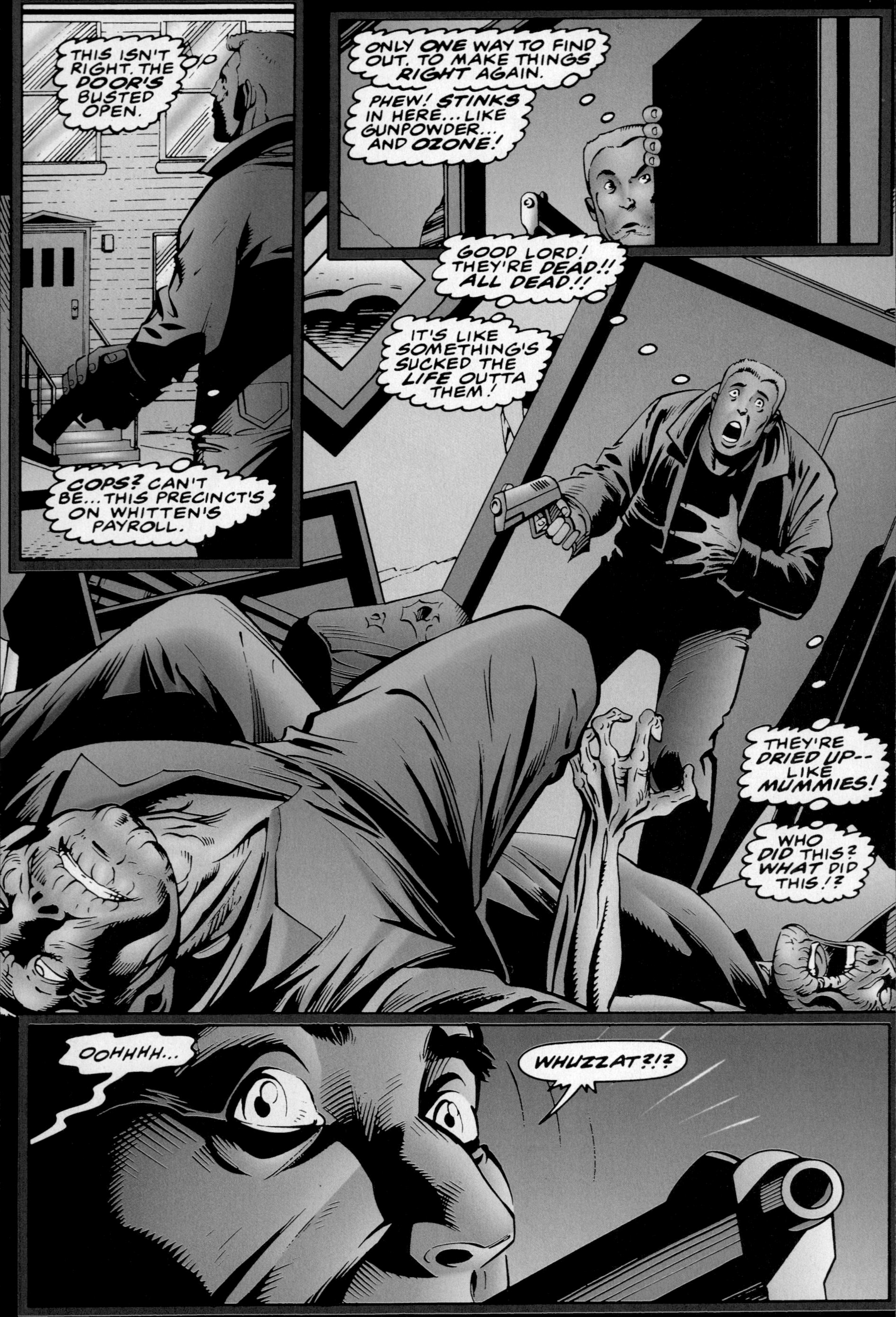
THIS ISN'T RIGHT. THE DOOR'S BUSTED OPEN.
COPS? CAN'T BE... THIS PRECINCT'S ON WHITTEN'S PAYROLL.
ONLY ONE WAY TO FIND OUT. TO MAKE THINGS RIGHT AGAIN.
PHEW! STINKS IN HERE... LIKE GUNPOWDER... AND OZONE!
GOOD LORD! THEY'RE DEAD!! ALL DEAD!!
IT'S LIKE SOMETHING'S SUCKED THE LIFE OUTTA THEM!
THEY'RE DRIED UP-- LIKE MUMMIES!
WHO DID THIS? WHAT DID THIS!?
OOHHHH...
WHUZZAT?!?

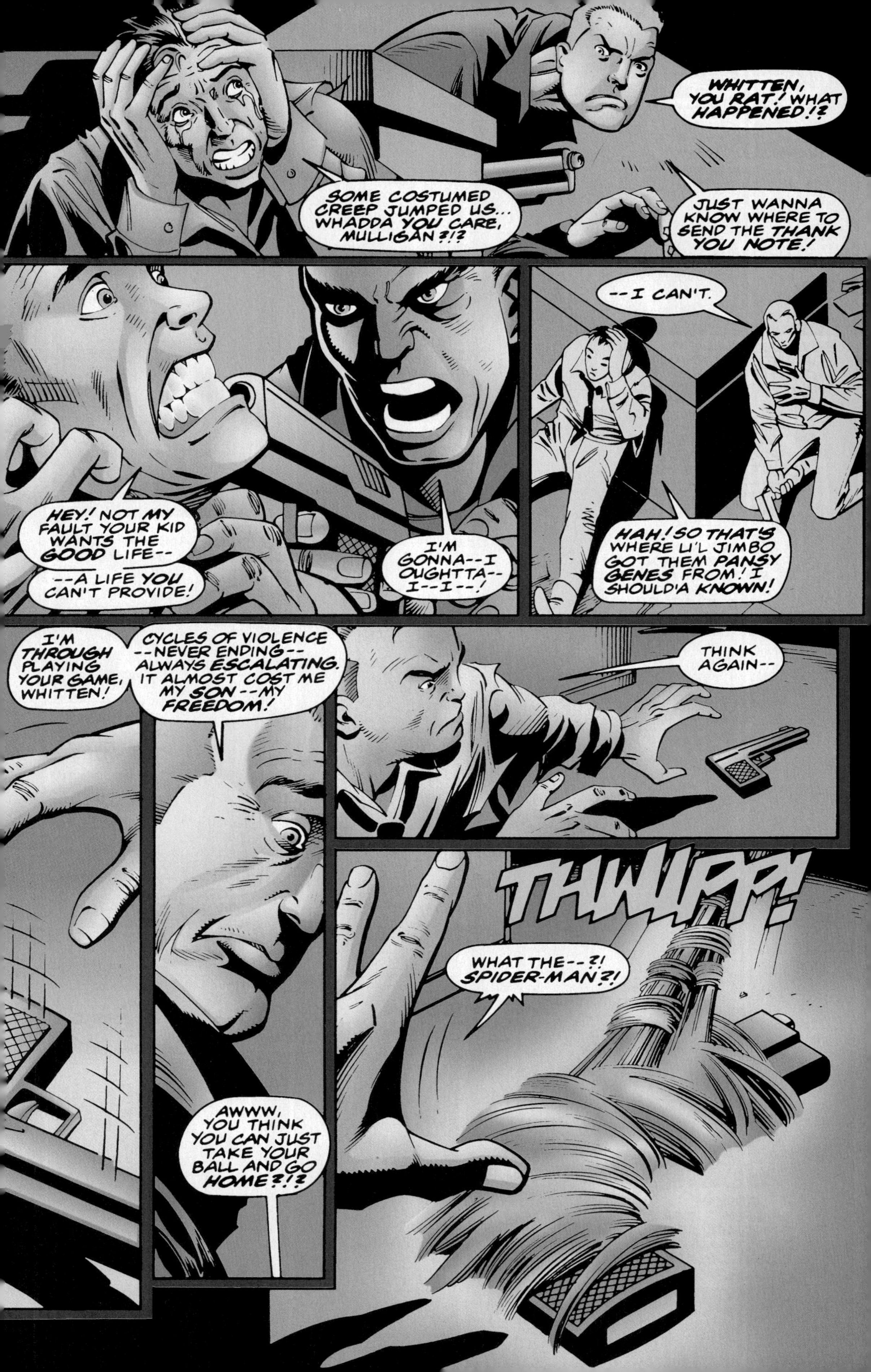
WHITTEN, YOU RAT! WHAT HAPPENED!?
SOME COSTUMED CREEP JUMPED US... WHADDA YOU CARE, MULLIGAN?!?
JUST WANNA KNOW WHERE TO SEND THE THANK YOU NOTE!
HEY! NOT MY FAULT YOUR KID WANTS THE GOOD LIFE--
--A LIFE YOU CAN'T PROVIDE!
I'M GONNA--I OUGHTTA-- I--I--!
--I CAN'T.
HAH! SO THAT'S WHERE LI'L JIMBO GOT THEM PANSY GENES FROM! I SHOULD'A KNOWN!
I'M THROUGH PLAYING YOUR GAME, WHITTEN!
CYCLES OF VIOLENCE --NEVER ENDING-- ALWAYS ESCALATING. IT ALMOST COST ME MY SON--MY FREEDOM!
AWWW, YOU THINK YOU CAN JUST TAKE YOUR BALL AND GO HOME?!?
THINK AGAIN--
THWIPP!
WHAT THE--?! SPIDER-MAN?!

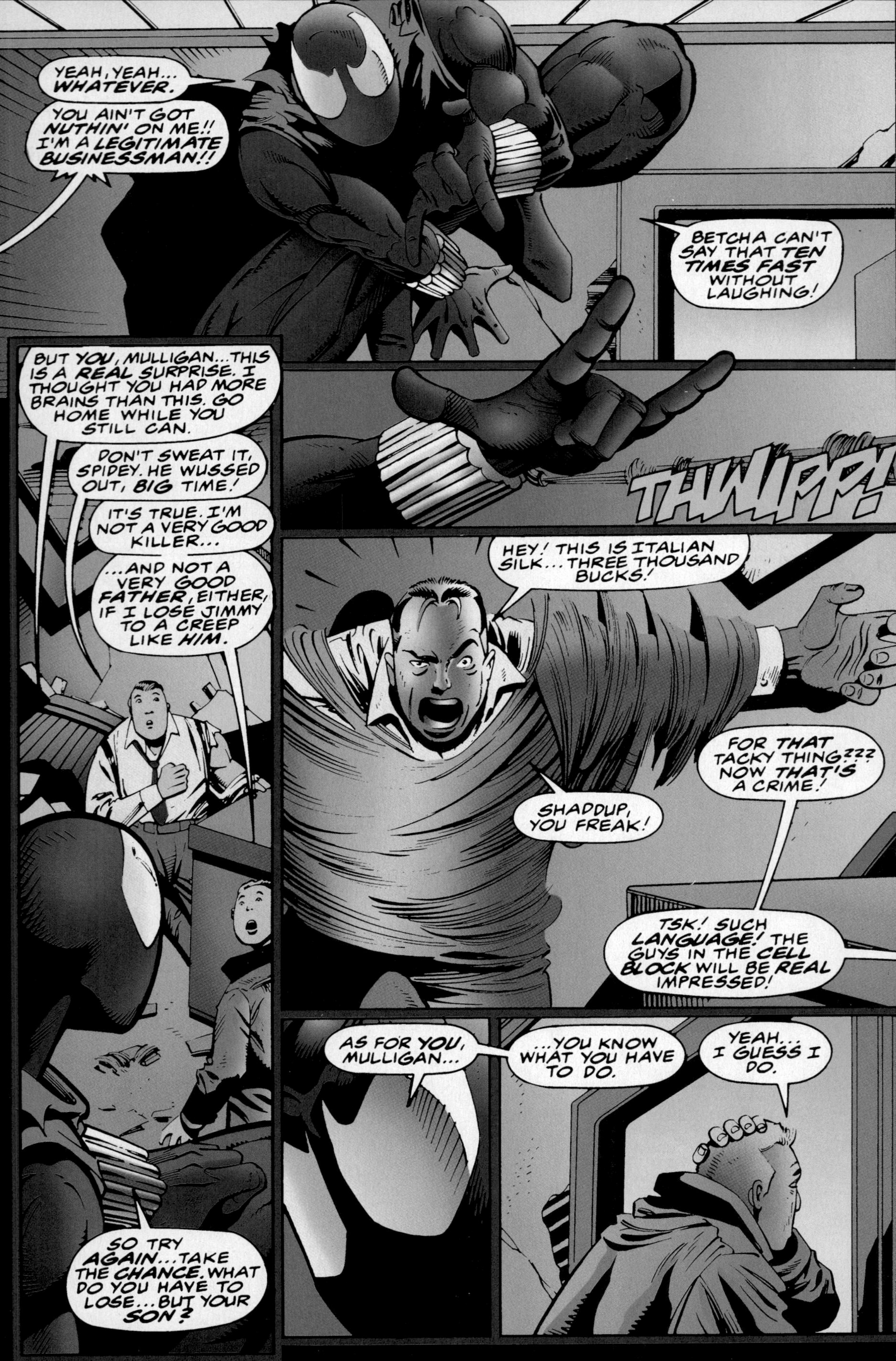
YEAH, YEAH... WHATEVER.
YOU AIN'T GOT NUTHIN' ON ME!! I'M A LEGITIMATE BUSINESSMAN!!
BETCHA CAN'T SAY THAT TEN TIMES FAST WITHOUT LAUGHING!
BUT YOU, MULLIGAN... THIS IS A REAL SURPRISE. I THOUGHT YOU HAD MORE BRAINS THAN THIS. GO HOME WHILE YOU STILL CAN.
DON'T SWEAT IT, SPIDEY. HE WUSSED OUT, BIG TIME!
IT'S TRUE. I'M NOT A VERY GOOD KILLER...
...AND NOT A VERY GOOD FATHER, EITHER, IF I LOSE JIMMY TO A CREEP LIKE HIM.
SO TRY AGAIN... TAKE THE CHANCE. WHAT DO YOU HAVE TO LOSE... BUT YOUR SON?
THWIPP!
HEY! THIS IS ITALIAN SILK... THREE THOUSAND BUCKS!
FOR THAT TACKY THING??? NOW THAT'S A CRIME!
SHADDUP, YOU FREAK!
TSK! SUCH LANGUAGE! THE GUYS IN THE CELL BLOCK WILL BE REAL IMPRESSED!
AS FOR YOU, MULLIGAN...
...YOU KNOW WHAT YOU HAVE TO DO.
YEAH... I GUESS I DO.

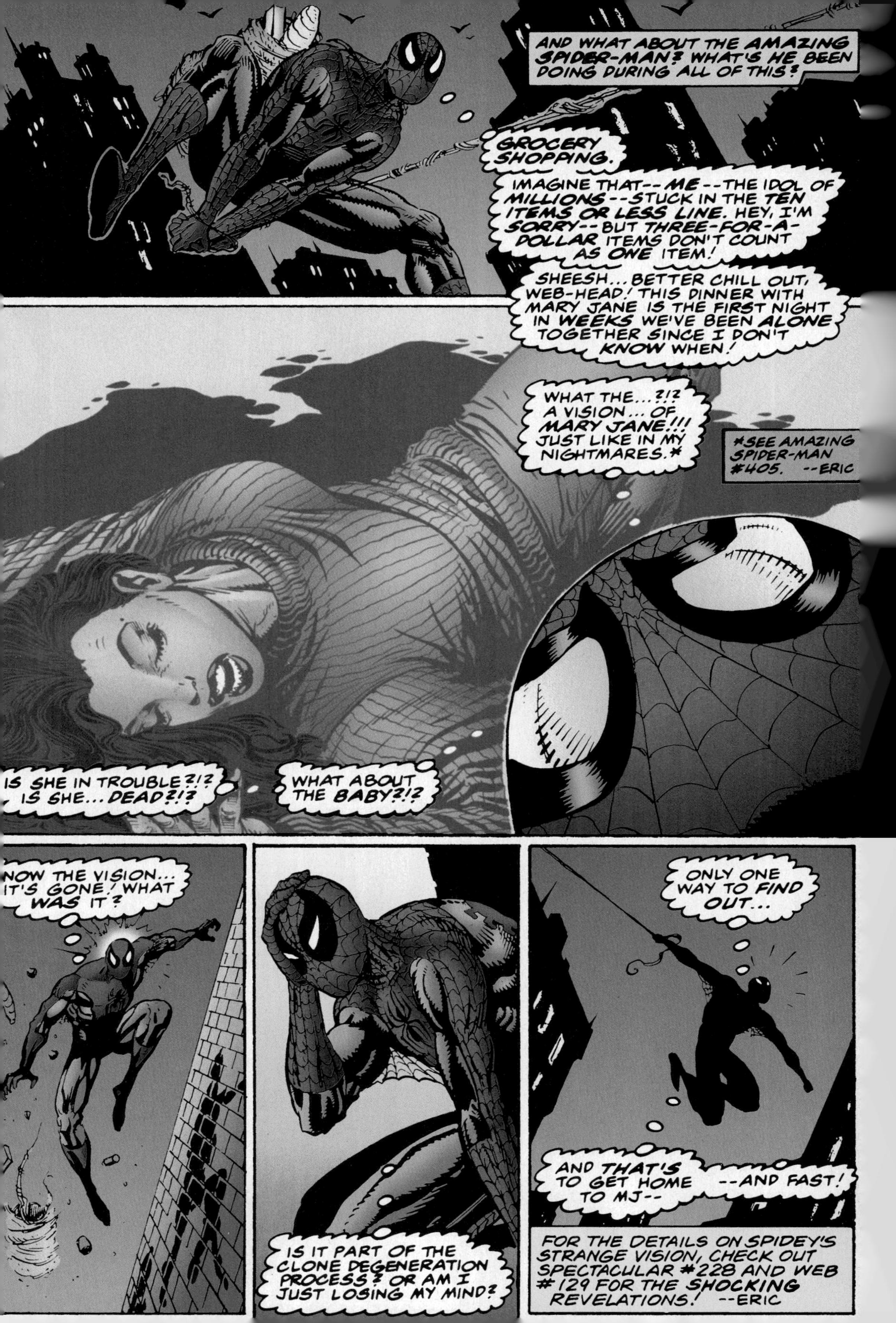
AND WHAT ABOUT THE AMAZING SPIDER-MAN? WHAT'S HE BEEN DOING DURING ALL OF THIS?
GROCERY SHOPPING.
IMAGINE THAT--ME--THE IDOL OF MILLIONS--STUCK IN THE TEN ITEMS OR LESS LINE. HEY, I'M SORRY--BUT THREE-FOR-A-DOLLAR ITEMS DON'T COUNT AS ONE ITEM!
SHEESH... BETTER CHILL OUT, WEB-HEAD! THIS DINNER WITH MARY JANE IS THE FIRST NIGHT IN WEEKS WE'VE BEEN ALONE TOGETHER SINCE I DON'T KNOW WHEN!
WHAT THE...?!? A VISION... OF MARY JANE!!! JUST LIKE IN MY NIGHTMARES.*
*SEE AMAZING SPIDER-MAN #405. --ERIC
IS SHE IN TROUBLE?!? IS SHE... DEAD?!?
WHAT ABOUT THE BABY?!?
NOW THE VISION... IT'S GONE! WHAT WAS IT?
IS IT PART OF THE CLONE DEGENERATION PROCESS? OR AM I JUST LOSING MY MIND?
ONLY ONE WAY TO FIND OUT...
AND THAT'S TO GET HOME TO MJ--
--AND FAST!
FOR THE DETAILS ON SPIDEY'S STRANGE VISION, CHECK OUT SPECTACULAR #228 AND WEB #129 FOR THE SHOCKING REVELATIONS! --ERIC

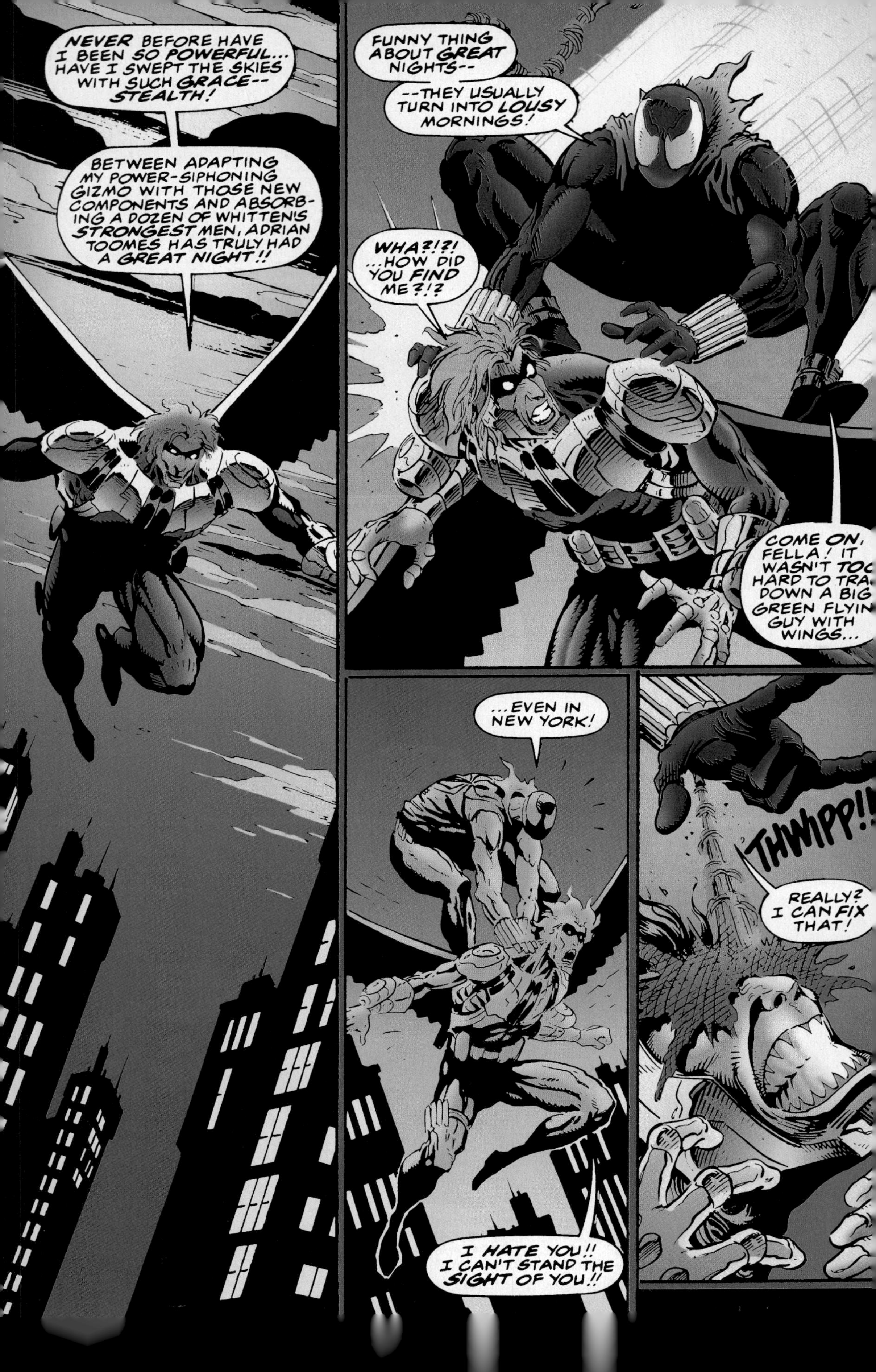
NEVER BEFORE HAVE I BEEN SO POWERFUL... HAVE I SWEPT THE SKIES WITH SUCH GRACE-- STEALTH!
BETWEEN ADAPTING MY POWER-SIPHONING GIZMO WITH THOSE NEW COMPONENTS AND ABSORBING A DOZEN OF WHITTEN'S STRONGEST MEN, ADRIAN TOOMES HAS TRULY HAD A GREAT NIGHT!!
FUNNY THING ABOUT GREAT NIGHTS--
--THEY USUALLY TURN INTO LOUSY MORNINGS!
WHA?!?! ...HOW DID YOU FIND ME?!?
COME ON, FELLA! IT WASN'T TOO HARD TO TRA DOWN A BIG GREEN FLYIN GUY WITH WINGS...
...EVEN IN NEW YORK!
I HATE YOU!! I CAN'T STAND THE SIGHT OF YOU!!
THWIPP!!
REALLY? I CAN FIX THAT!

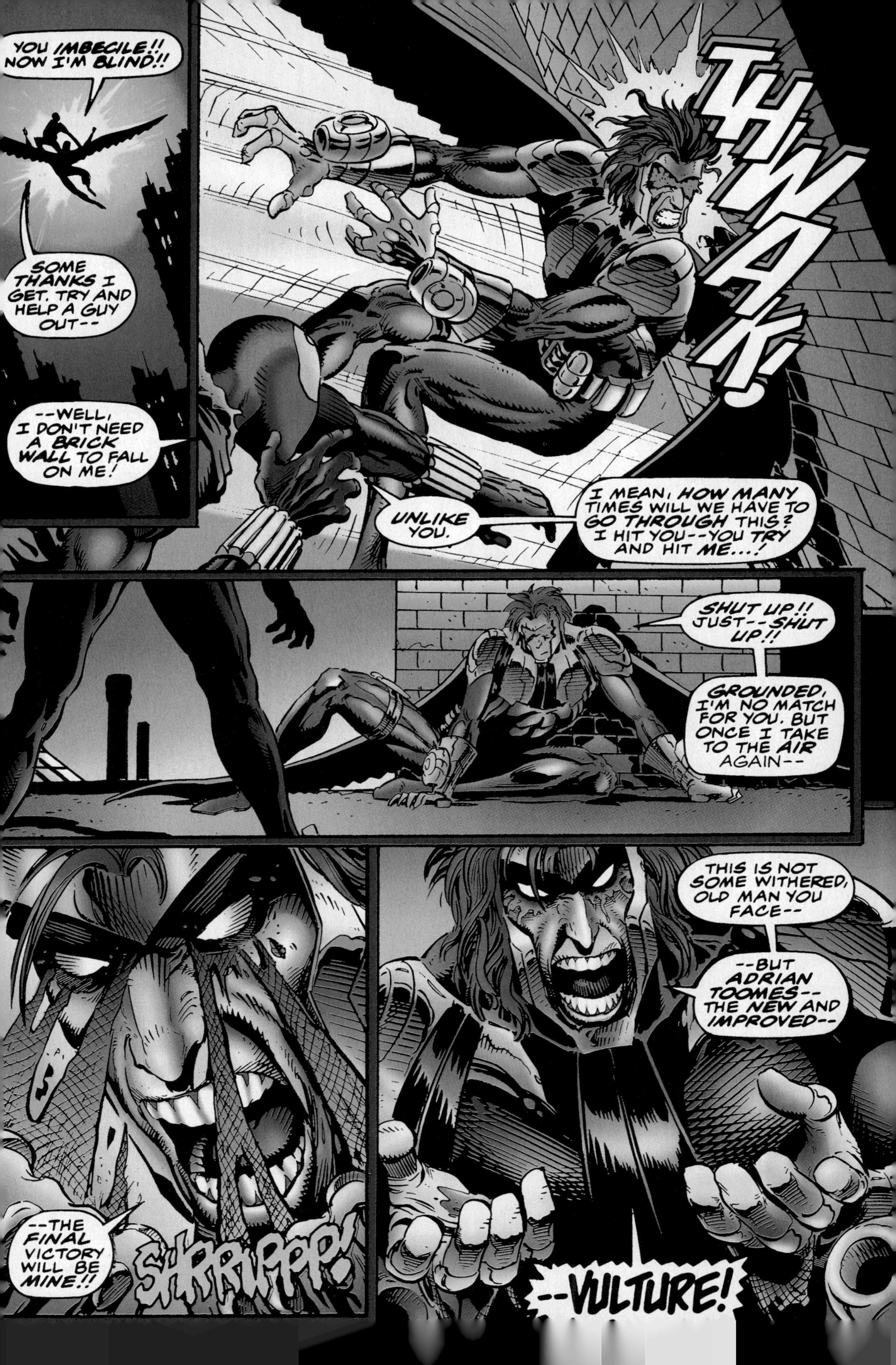
YOU IMBECILE!! NOW I'M BLIND!!
SOME THANKS I GET. TRY AND HELP A GUY OUT--
--WELL, I DON'T NEED A BRICK WALL TO FALL ON ME!
THWAK!
I MEAN, HOW MANY TIMES WILL WE HAVE TO GO THROUGH THIS? I HIT YOU--YOU TRY AND HIT ME...!
UNLIKE YOU.
SHUT UP!! JUST--SHUT UP!!
GROUNDED, I'M NO MATCH FOR YOU. BUT ONCE I TAKE TO THE AIR AGAIN--
--THE FINAL VICTORY WILL BE MINE!!
SHRRIPPP!
THIS IS NOT SOME WITHERED, OLD MAN YOU FACE--
--BUT ADRIAN TOOMES--THE NEW AND IMPROVED--
--VULTURE!

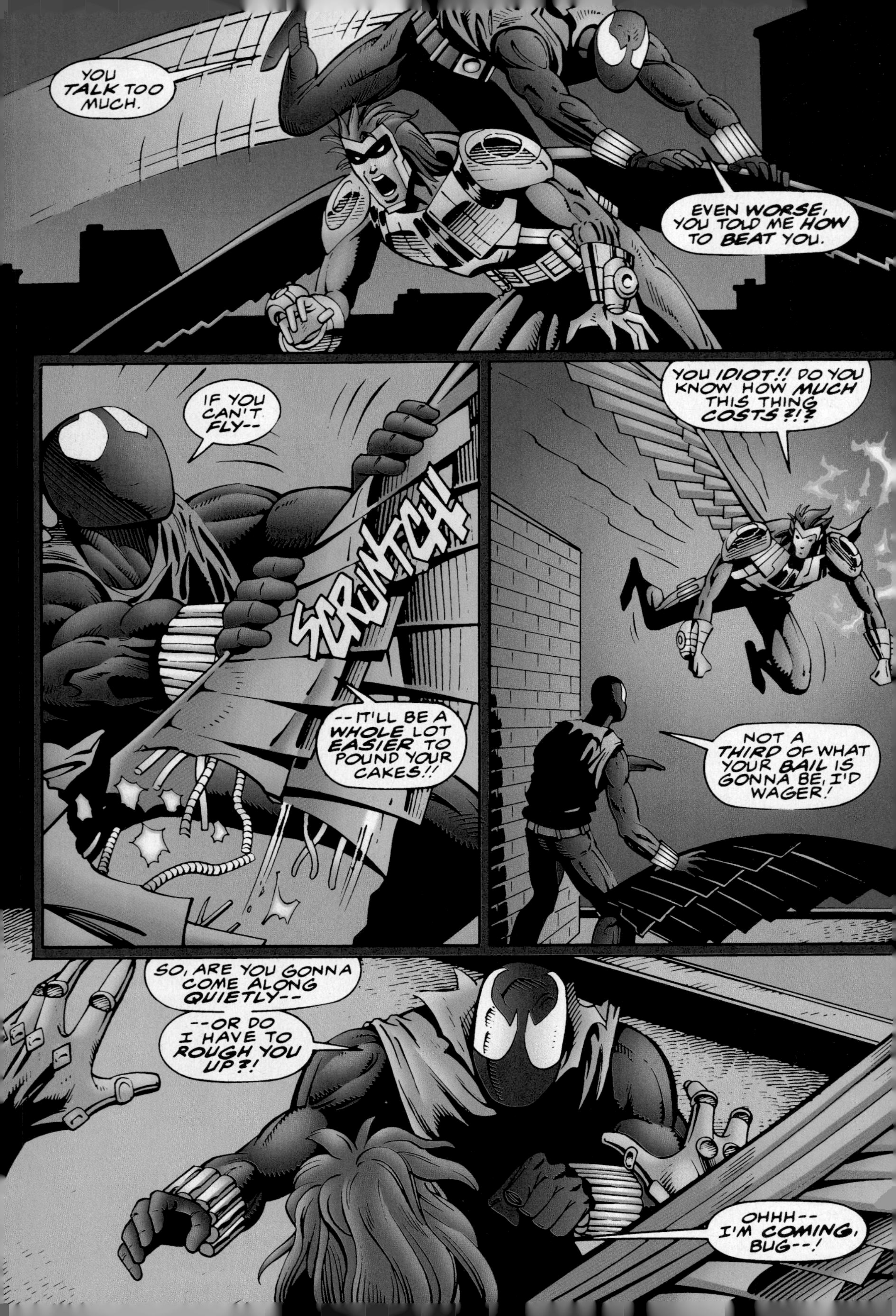
YOU TALK TOO MUCH.
EVEN WORSE, YOU TOLD ME HOW TO BEAT YOU.
IF YOU CAN'T FLY--
SCRUNTCH!
--IT'LL BE A WHOLE LOT EASIER TO POUND YOUR CAKES!!
YOU IDIOT!! DO YOU KNOW HOW MUCH THIS THING COSTS?!?
NOT A THIRD OF WHAT YOUR BAIL IS GONNA BE, I'D WAGER!
SO, ARE YOU GONNA COME ALONG QUIETLY--
--OR DO I HAVE TO ROUGH YOU UP?!
OHHH-- I'M COMING, BUG--!

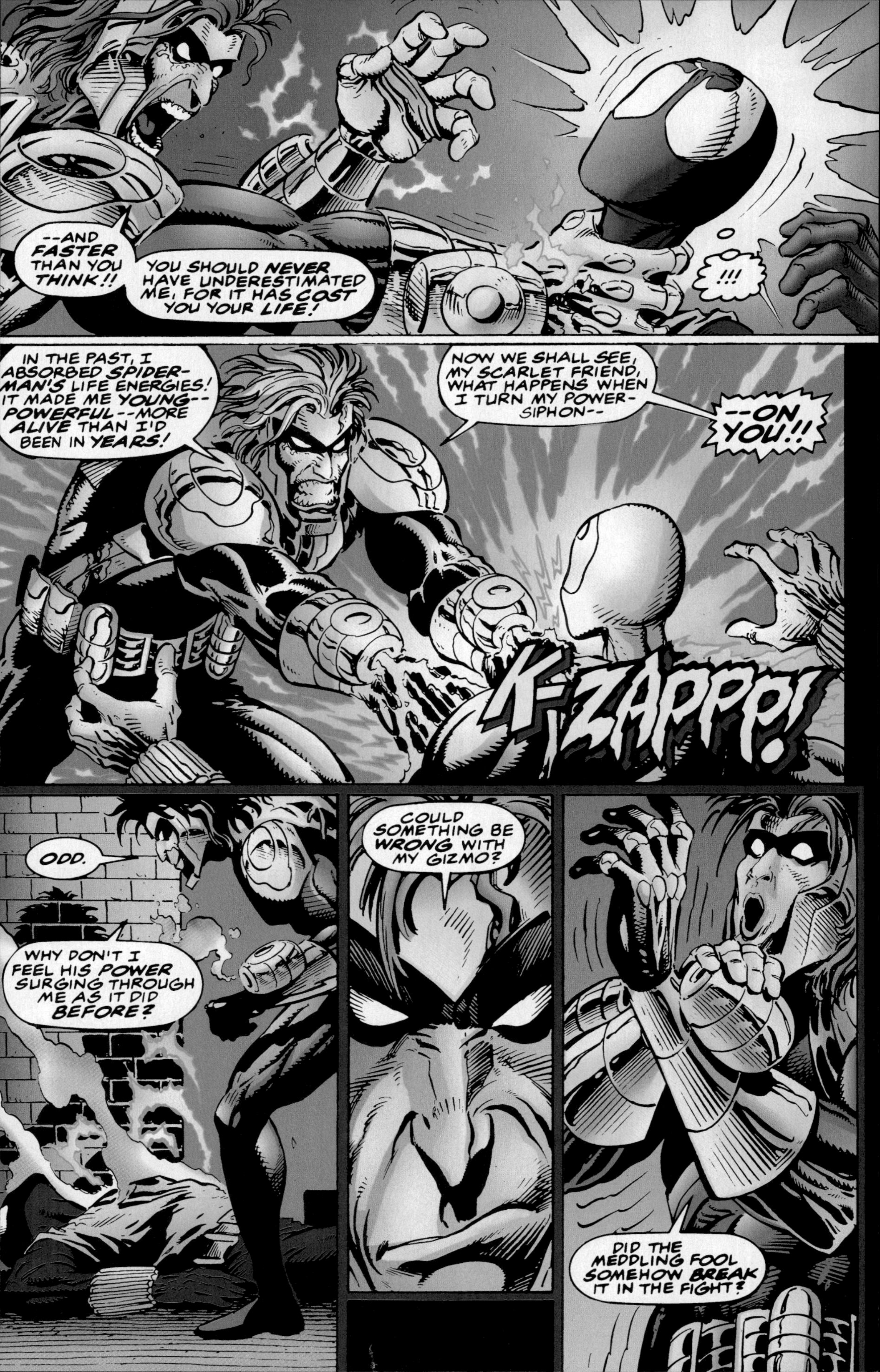
--AND FASTER THAN YOU THINK!!
YOU SHOULD NEVER HAVE UNDERESTIMATED ME, FOR IT HAS COST YOU YOUR LIFE!
!!!
IN THE PAST, I ABSORBED SPIDER-MAN'S LIFE ENERGIES! IT MADE ME YOUNG-- POWERFUL--MORE ALIVE THAN I'D BEEN IN YEARS!
NOW WE SHALL SEE, MY SCARLET FRIEND, WHAT HAPPENS WHEN I TURN MY POWER-SIPHON--
--ON YOU!!
K-ZAPPP!
ODD.
WHY DON'T I FEEL HIS POWER SURGING THROUGH ME AS IT DID BEFORE?
COULD SOMETHING BE WRONG WITH MY GIZMO?
DID THE MEDDLING FOOL SOMEHOW BREAK IT IN THE FIGHT?

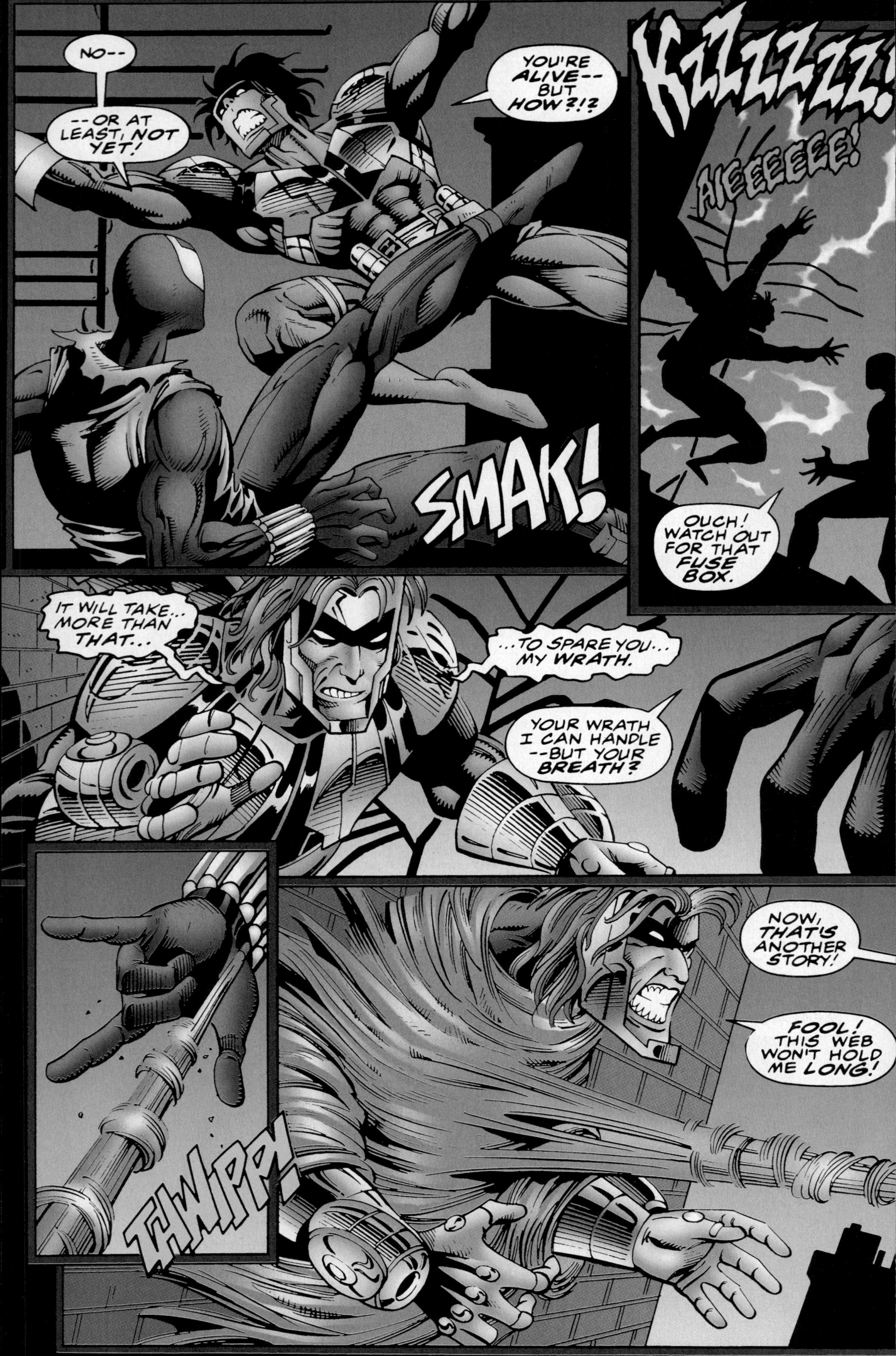
NO--
--OR AT LEAST, NOT YET!
YOU'RE ALIVE-- BUT HOW?!?
SMAK!
KZZZZZZZ!
AIEEEEEE!
OUCH! WATCH OUT FOR THAT FUSE BOX.
IT WILL TAKE... MORE THAN THAT...
...TO SPARE YOU... MY WRATH.
YOUR WRATH I CAN HANDLE --BUT YOUR BREATH?
THWIPP!
NOW, THAT'S ANOTHER STORY!
FOOL! THIS WEB WON'T HOLD ME LONG!

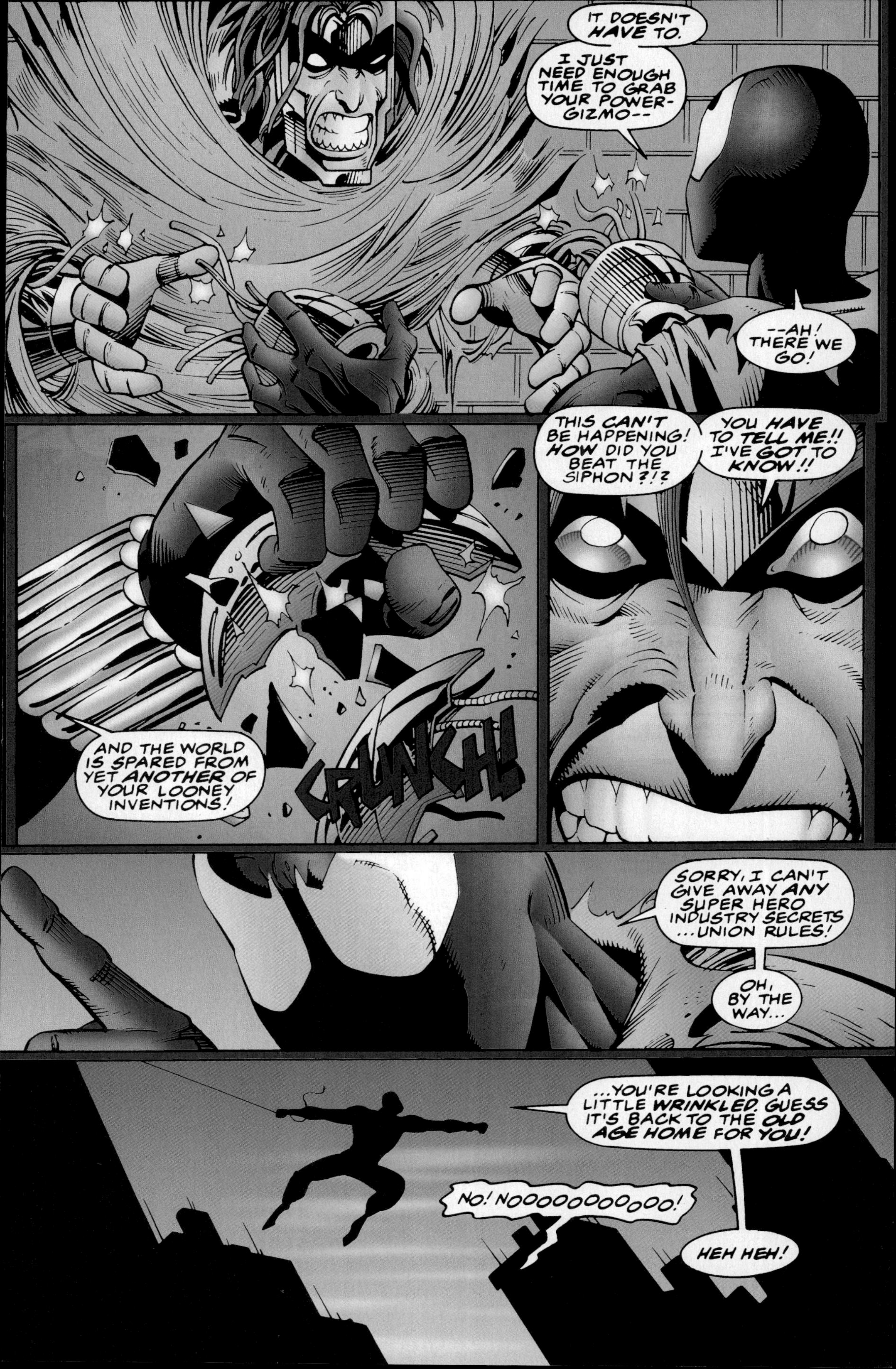

IT DOESN'T HAVE TO.
I JUST NEED ENOUGH TIME TO GRAB YOUR POWER-GIZMO--
--AH! THERE WE GO!
AND THE WORLD IS SPARED FROM YET ANOTHER OF YOUR LOONEY INVENTIONS!
CRUNCH!
THIS CAN'T BE HAPPENING! HOW DID YOU BEAT THE SIPHON?!?
YOU HAVE TO TELL ME!! I'VE GOT TO KNOW!!
SORRY, I CAN'T GIVE AWAY ANY SUPER HERO INDUSTRY SECRETS ...UNION RULES!
OH, BY THE WAY...
...YOU'RE LOOKING A LITTLE WRINKLED. GUESS IT'S BACK TO THE OLD AGE HOME FOR YOU!
NO! NOOOOOOOOOOO!
HEH HEH!

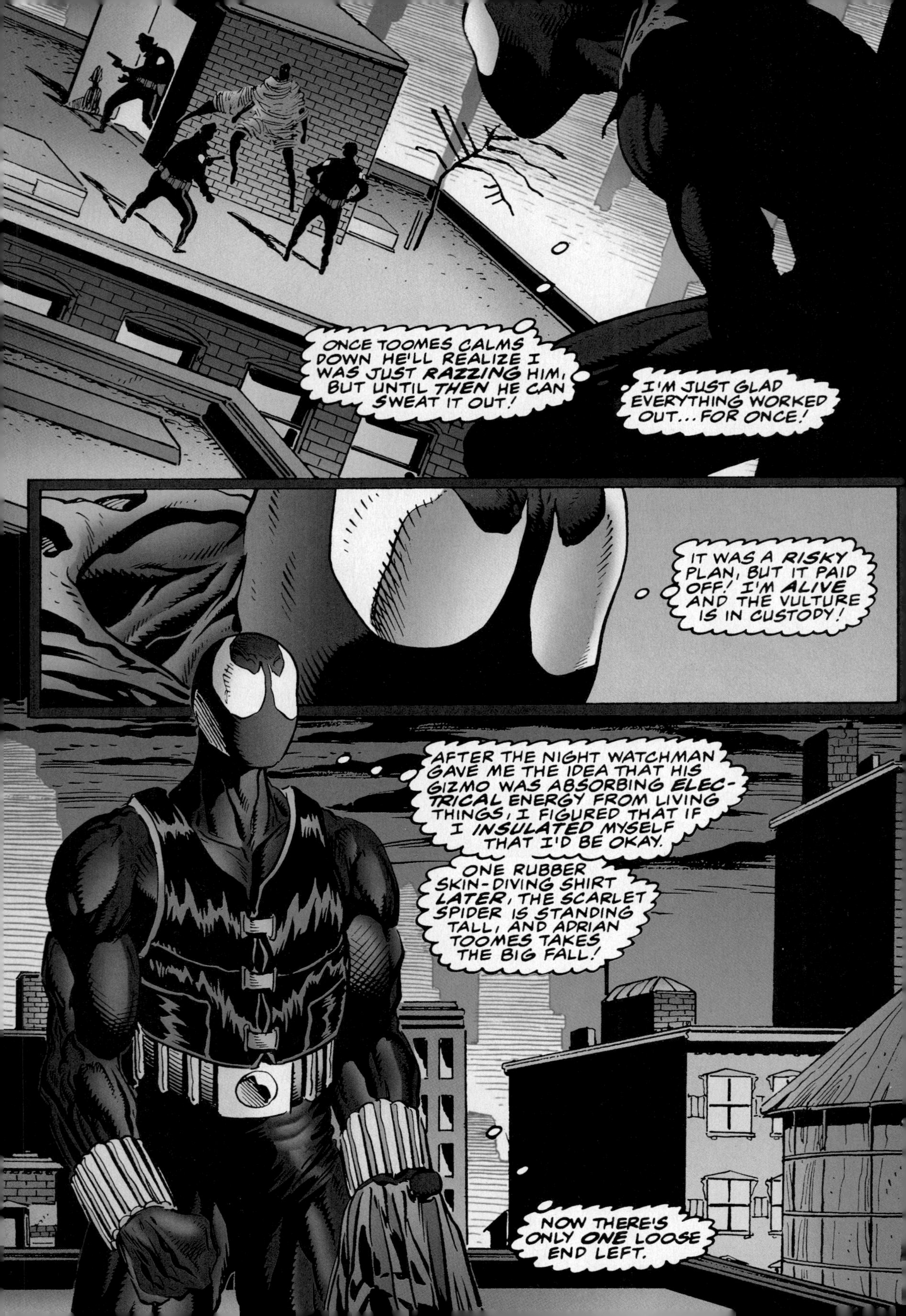
ONCE TOOMES CALMS DOWN HE'LL REALIZE I WAS JUST RAZZING HIM, BUT UNTIL THEN HE CAN SWEAT IT OUT!
I'M JUST GLAD EVERYTHING WORKED OUT... FOR ONCE!
IT WAS A RISKY PLAN, BUT IT PAID OFF! I'M ALIVE AND THE VULTURE IS IN CUSTODY!
AFTER THE NIGHT WATCHMAN GAVE ME THE IDEA THAT HIS GIZMO WAS ABSORBING ELEC-TRICAL ENERGY FROM LIVING THINGS, I FIGURED THAT IF I INSULATED MYSELF THAT I'D BE OKAY.
ONE RUBBER SKIN-DIVING SHIRT LATER, THE SCARLET SPIDER IS STANDING TALL, AND ADRIAN TOOMES TAKES THE BIG FALL!
NOW THERE'S ONLY ONE LOOSE END LEFT.

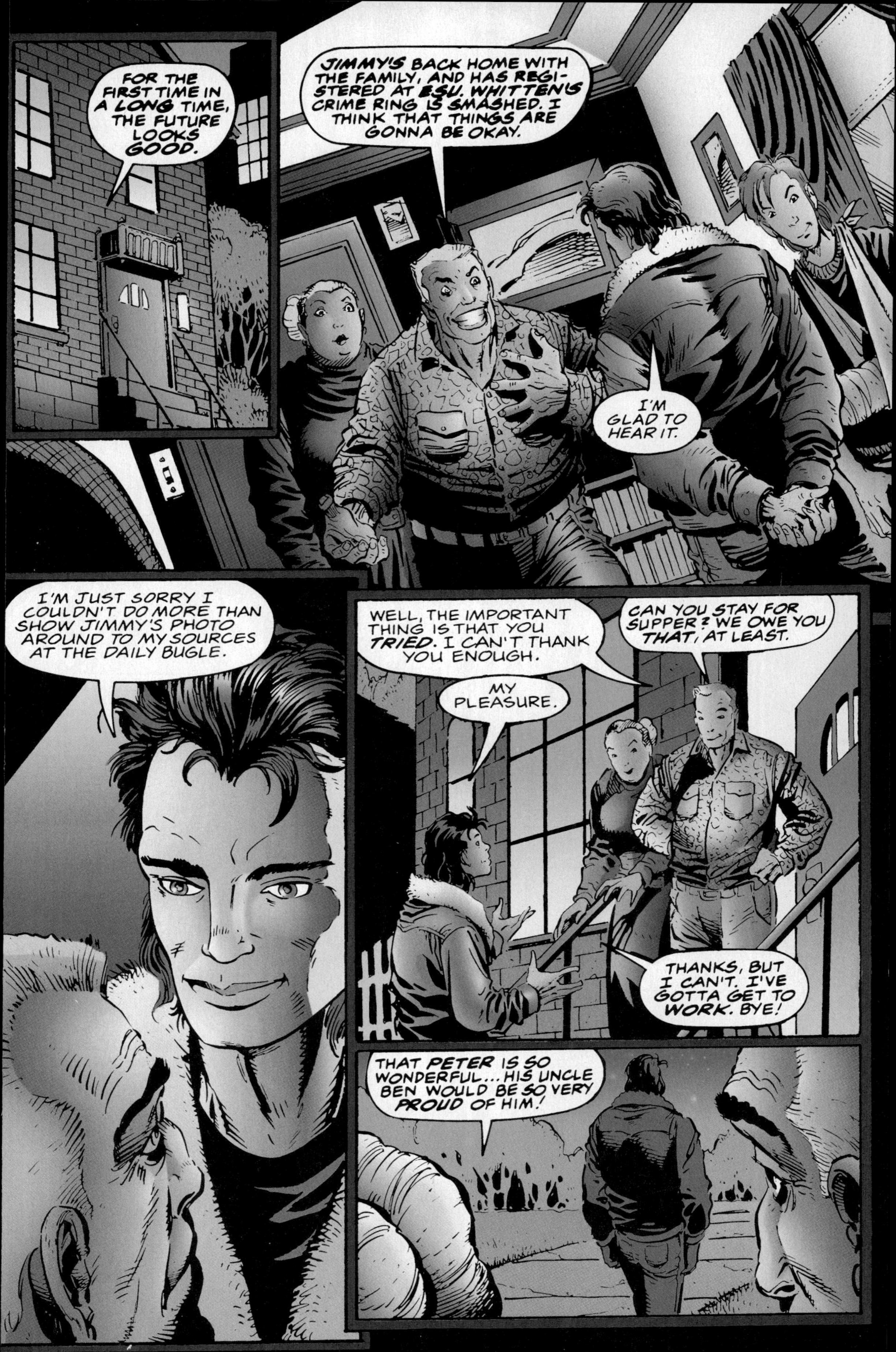
FOR THE FIRST TIME IN A LONG TIME, THE FUTURE LOOKS GOOD.
JIMMY'S BACK HOME WITH THE FAMILY, AND HAS REGISTERED AT ESU. WHITTEN'S CRIME RING IS SMASHED. I THINK THAT THINGS ARE GONNA BE OKAY.
I'M GLAD TO HEAR IT.
I'M JUST SORRY I COULDN'T DO MORE THAN SHOW JIMMY'S PHOTO AROUND TO MY SOURCES AT THE DAILY BUGLE.
WELL, THE IMPORTANT THING IS THAT YOU TRIED. I CAN'T THANK YOU ENOUGH.
MY PLEASURE.
CAN YOU STAY FOR SUPPER? WE OWE YOU THAT, AT LEAST.
THANKS, BUT I CAN'T. I'VE GOTTA GET TO WORK. BYE!
THAT PETER IS SO WONDERFUL... HIS UNCLE BEN WOULD BE SO VERY PROUD OF HIM!

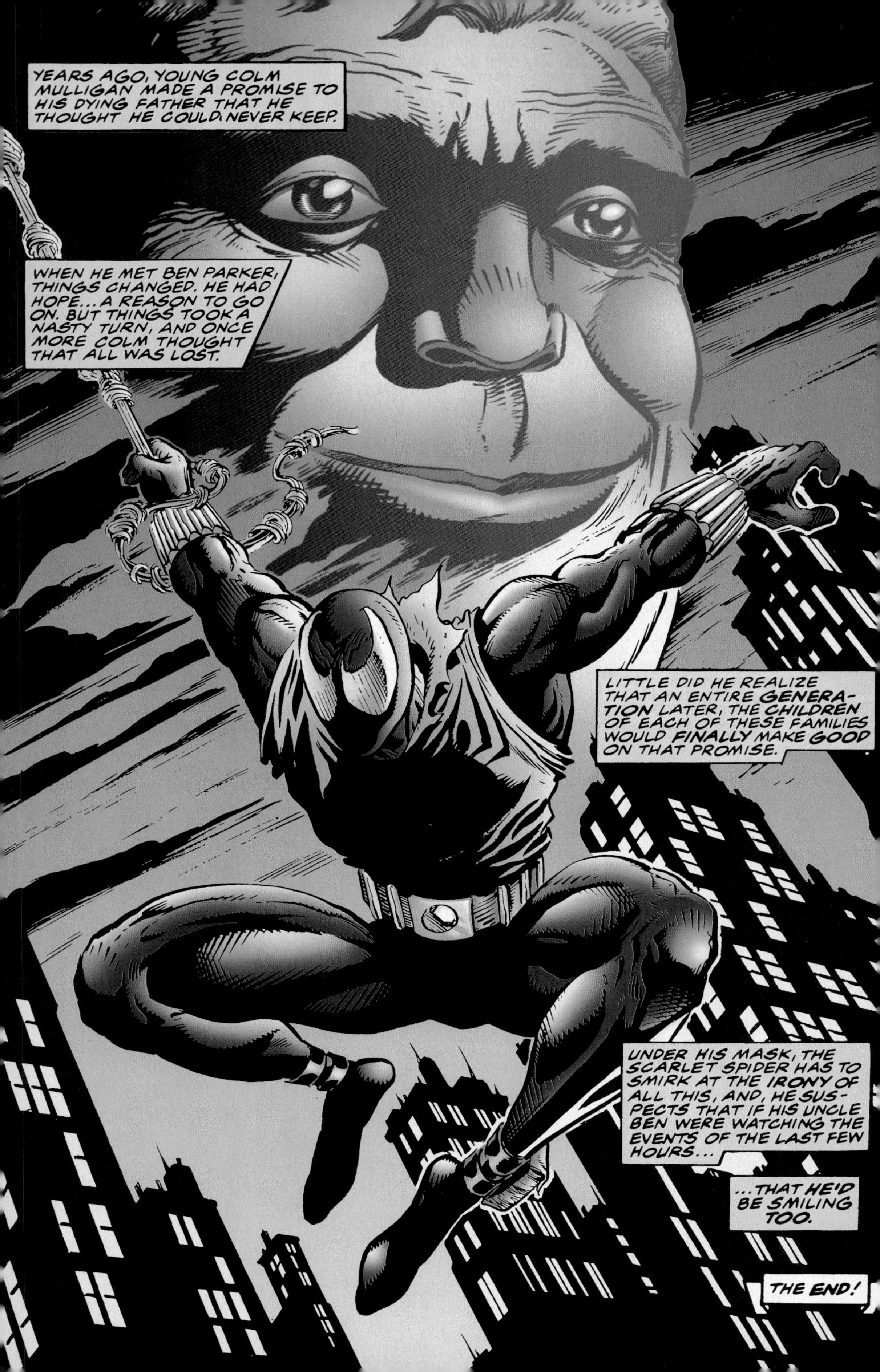
YEARS AGO, YOUNG COLM MULLIGAN MADE A PROMISE TO HIS DYING FATHER THAT HE THOUGHT HE COULD NEVER KEEP.
WHEN HE MET BEN PARKER, THINGS CHANGED. HE HAD HOPE... A REASON TO GO ON. BUT THINGS TOOK A NASTY TURN, AND ONCE MORE COLM THOUGHT THAT ALL WAS LOST.
LITTLE DID HE REALIZE THAT AN ENTIRE GENERATION LATER, THE CHILDREN OF EACH OF THESE FAMILIES WOULD FINALLY MAKE GOOD ON THAT PROMISE.
UNDER HIS MASK, THE SCARLET SPIDER HAS TO SMIRK AT THE IRONY OF ALL THIS, AND, HE SUSPECTS THAT IF HIS UNCLE BEN WERE WATCHING THE EVENTS OF THE LAST FEW HOURS...
...THAT HE'D BE SMILING TOO.
THE END!

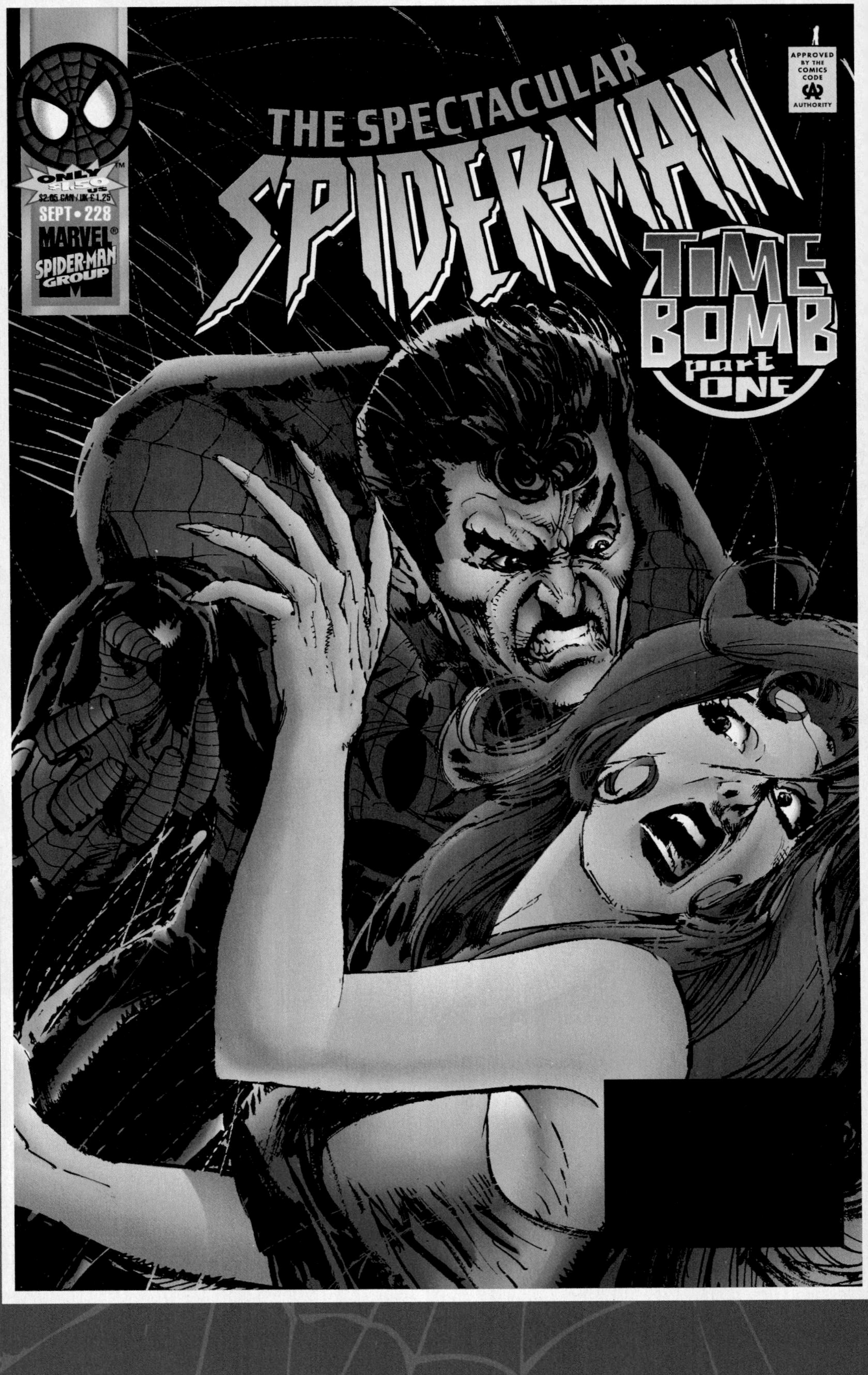

APPROVED BY THE COMICS CODE AUTHORITY
THE SPECTACULAR
SPIDER-MAN
ONLY $1.50 US
$2.05 CAN / UK £ 1.25
SEPT • 228
MARVEL
SPIDER-MAN GROUP
TIME BOMB part ONE

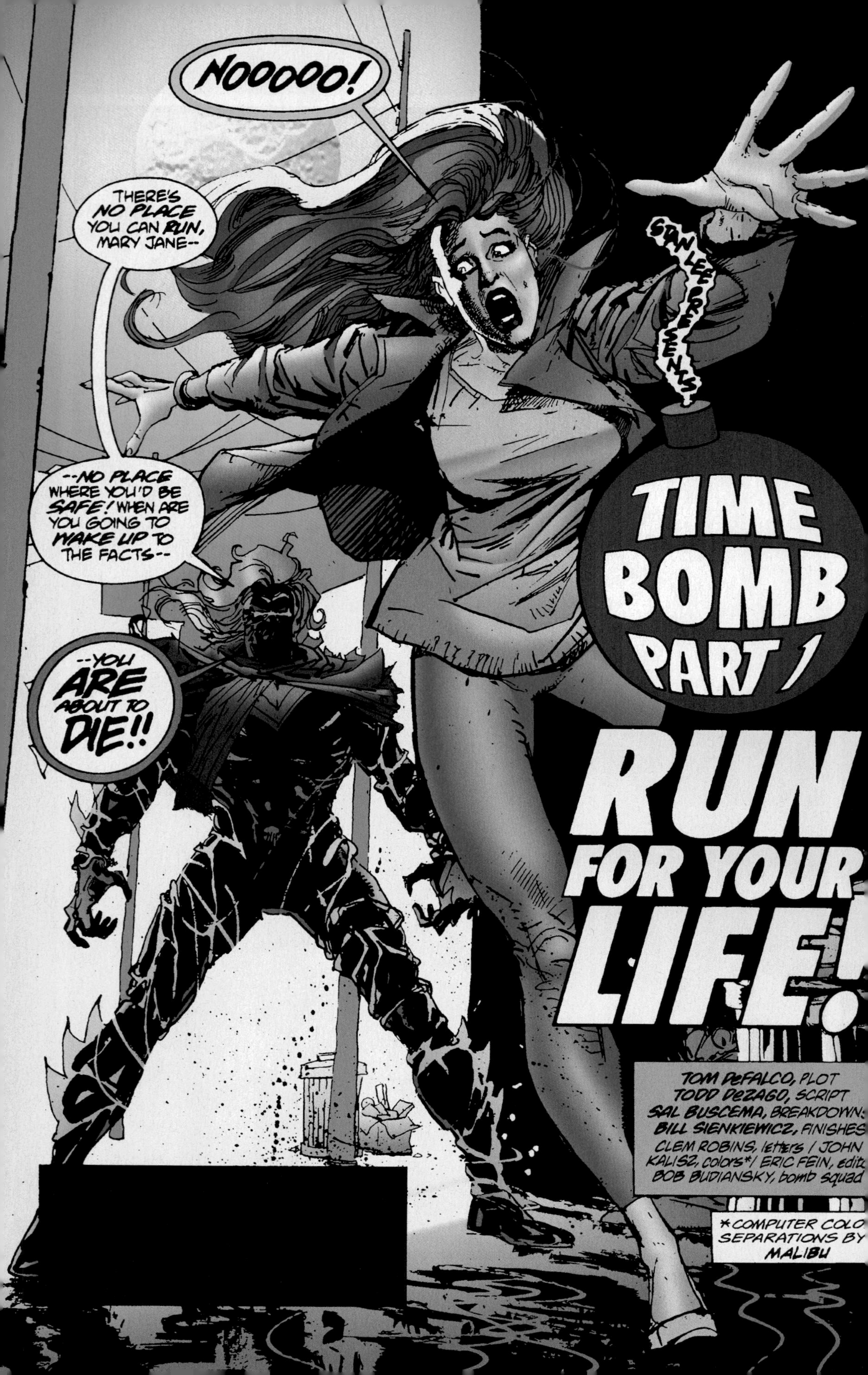
NOOOOO!
THERE'S NO PLACE YOU CAN RUN, MARY JANE--
--NO PLACE WHERE YOU'D BE SAFE! WHEN ARE YOU GOING TO WAKE UP TO THE FACTS--
--YOU ARE ABOUT TO DIE!!
STAN LEE PRESENTS
TIME BOMB PART 1
RUN FOR YOUR LIFE!
TOM DeFALCO, PLOT
TODD DeZAGO, SCRIPT
SAL BUSCEMA, BREAKDOWN
BILL SIENKIEWICZ, FINISHES
CLEM ROBINS, letters / JOHN KALISZ, colors*/ ERIC FEIN, edit
BOB BUDIANSKY, bomb squad
*COMPUTER COLO SEPARATIONS BY MALIBU
[redacted]

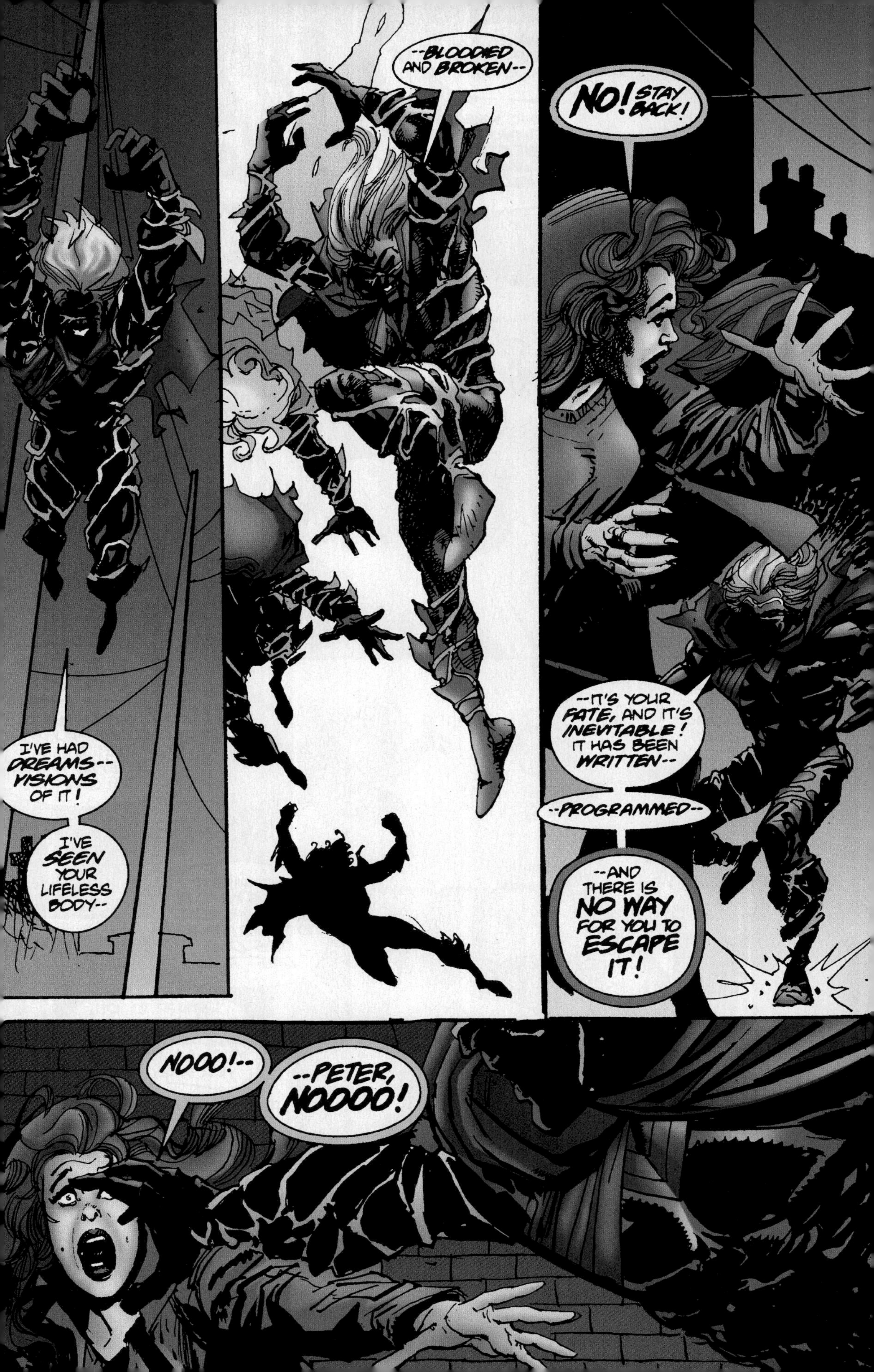
I'VE HAD DREAMS-- VISIONS OF IT!
I'VE SEEN YOUR LIFELESS BODY--
--BLOODIED AND BROKEN--
NO! STAY BACK!
--IT'S YOUR FATE, AND IT'S INEVITABLE! IT HAS BEEN WRITTEN--
--PROGRAMMED--
--AND THERE IS NO WAY FOR YOU TO ESCAPE IT!
NOOO!--
--PETER, NOOOO!

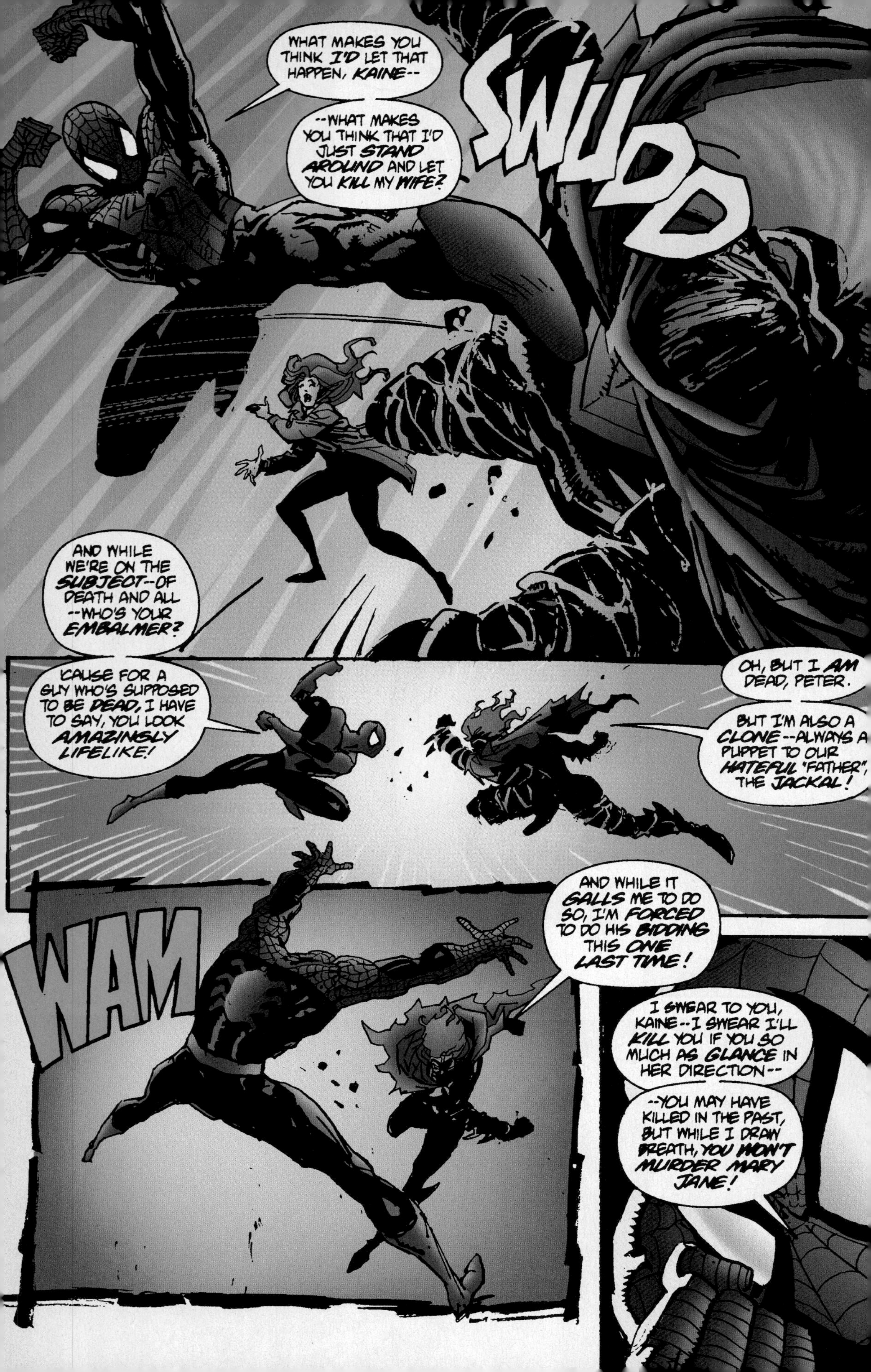
WHAT MAKES YOU THINK I'D LET THAT HAPPEN, KAINE--
--WHAT MAKES YOU THINK THAT I'D JUST STAND AROUND AND LET YOU KILL MY WIFE?
SWUDD
AND WHILE WE'RE ON THE SUBJECT--OF DEATH AND ALL --WHO'S YOUR EMBALMER?
'CAUSE FOR A GUY WHO'S SUPPOSED TO BE DEAD, I HAVE TO SAY, YOU LOOK AMAZINGLY LIFELIKE!
OH, BUT I AM DEAD, PETER.
BUT I'M ALSO A CLONE--ALWAYS A PUPPET TO OUR HATEFUL "FATHER", THE JACKAL!
WAM
AND WHILE IT GALLS ME TO DO SO, I'M FORCED TO DO HIS BIDDING THIS ONE LAST TIME!
I SWEAR TO YOU, KAINE--I SWEAR I'LL KILL YOU IF YOU SO MUCH AS GLANCE IN HER DIRECTION--
--YOU MAY HAVE KILLED IN THE PAST, BUT WHILE I DRAW BREATH, YOU WON'T MURDER MARY JANE!

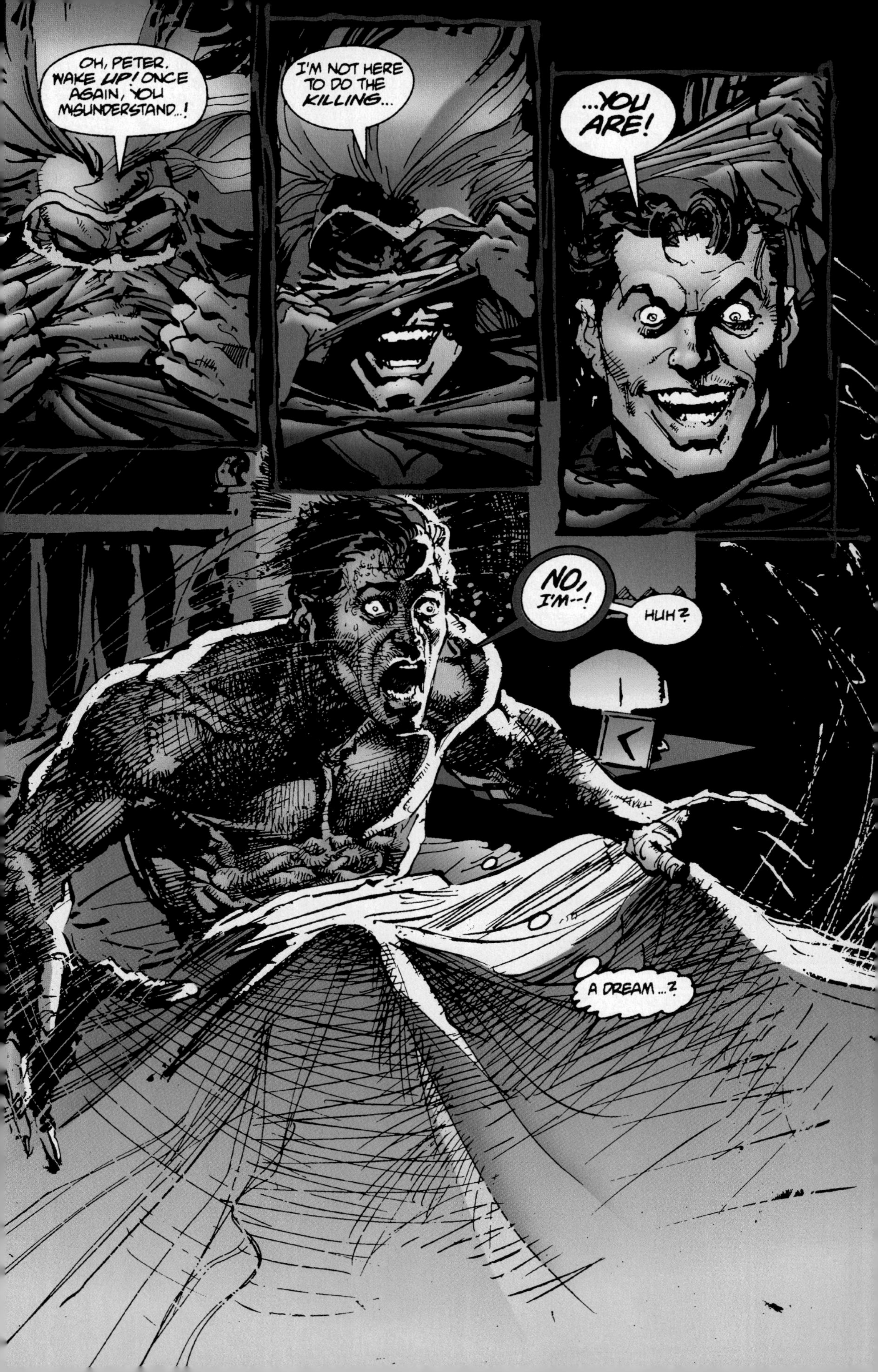
OH, PETER. WAKE UP! ONCE AGAIN, YOU MISUNDERSTAND...!
I'M NOT HERE TO DO THE KILLING...
...YOU ARE!
NO, I'M--!
HUH?
A DREAM...?

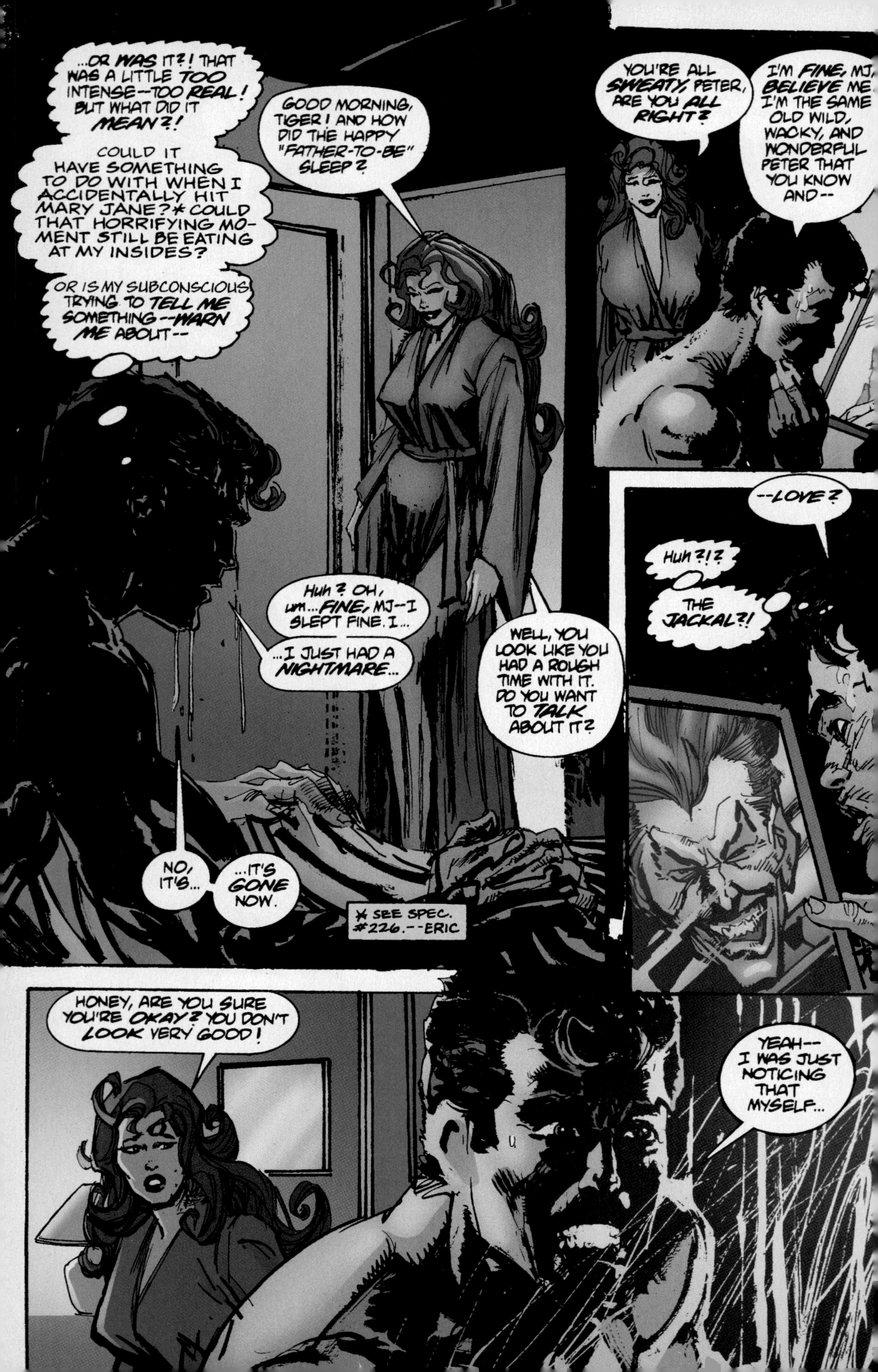

...OR WAS IT?! THAT WAS A LITTLE TOO INTENSE--TOO REAL! BUT WHAT DID IT MEAN?!
COULD IT HAVE SOMETHING TO DO WITH WHEN I ACCIDENTALLY HIT MARY JANE?* COULD THAT HORRIFYING MOMENT STILL BE EATING AT MY INSIDES?
OR IS MY SUBCONSCIOUS TRYING TO TELL ME SOMETHING--WARN ME ABOUT--
GOOD MORNING, TIGER! AND HOW DID THE HAPPY "FATHER-TO-BE" SLEEP?
Huh? OH, um...FINE, MJ--I SLEPT FINE. I...
...I JUST HAD A NIGHTMARE...
WELL, YOU LOOK LIKE YOU HAD A ROUGH TIME WITH IT. DO YOU WANT TO TALK ABOUT IT?
NO, IT'S...
...IT'S GONE NOW.
* SEE SPEC. #226.--ERIC
YOU'RE ALL SWEATY, PETER, ARE YOU ALL RIGHT?
I'M FINE, MJ, BELIEVE ME. I'M THE SAME OLD WILD, WACKY, AND WONDERFUL PETER THAT YOU KNOW AND--
--LOVE?
Huh?!?
THE JACKAL?!
HONEY, ARE YOU SURE YOU'RE OKAY? YOU DON'T LOOK VERY GOOD!
YEAH-- I WAS JUST NOTICING THAT MYSELF...

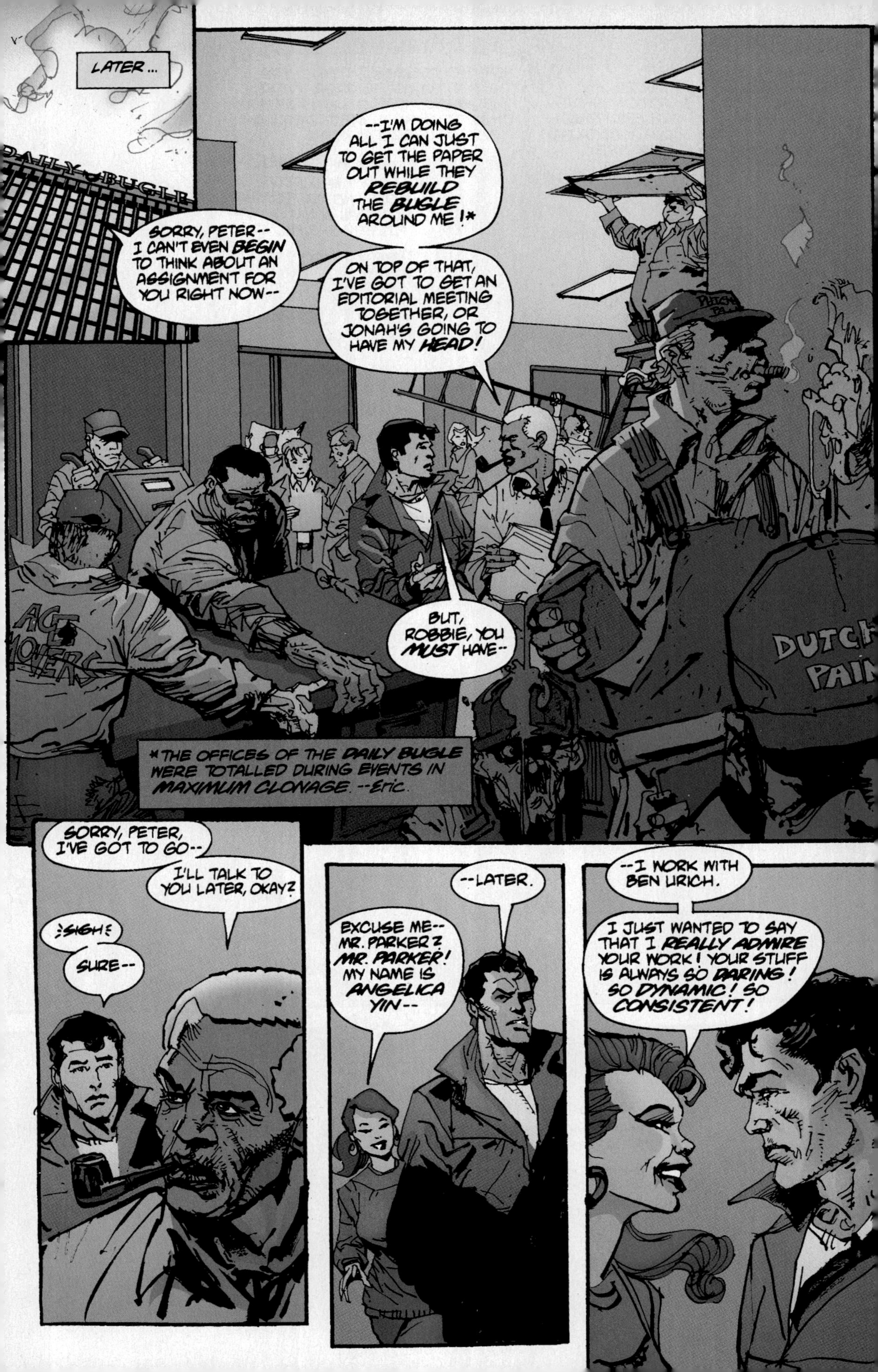
LATER...
DAILY BUGLE
SORRY, PETER-- I CAN'T EVEN BEGIN TO THINK ABOUT AN ASSIGNMENT FOR YOU RIGHT NOW--
--I'M DOING ALL I CAN JUST TO GET THE PAPER OUT WHILE THEY REBUILD THE BUGLE AROUND ME!*
ON TOP OF THAT, I'VE GOT TO GET AN EDITORIAL MEETING TOGETHER, OR JONAH'S GOING TO HAVE MY HEAD!
BUT, ROBBIE, YOU MUST HAVE--
ACE MOVERS
DUTCH PAIN
*THE OFFICES OF THE DAILY BUGLE WERE TOTALLED DURING EVENTS IN MAXIMUM CLONAGE. --Eric.
SORRY, PETER, I'VE GOT TO GO--
I'LL TALK TO YOU LATER, OKAY?
SIGH
SURE--
--LATER.
EXCUSE ME-- MR. PARKER? MR. PARKER! MY NAME IS ANGELICA YIN--
--I WORK WITH BEN URICH.
I JUST WANTED TO SAY THAT I REALLY ADMIRE YOUR WORK! YOUR STUFF IS ALWAYS SO DARING! SO DYNAMIC! SO CONSISTENT!

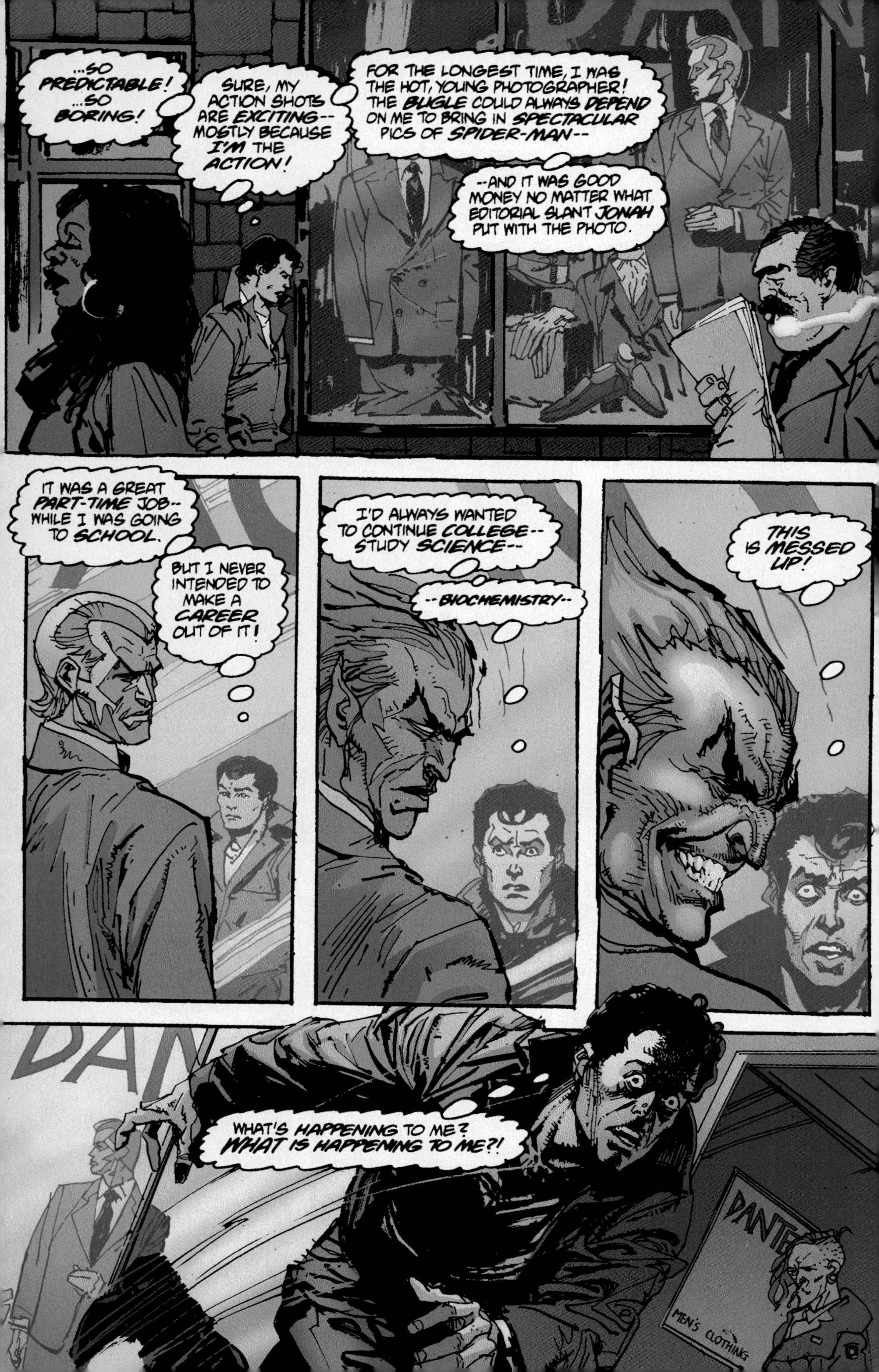
...SO PREDICTABLE! ...SO BORING!
SURE, MY ACTION SHOTS ARE EXCITING-- MOSTLY BECAUSE I'M THE ACTION!
FOR THE LONGEST TIME, I WAS THE HOT, YOUNG PHOTOGRAPHER! THE BUGLE COULD ALWAYS DEPEND ON ME TO BRING IN SPECTACULAR PICS OF SPIDER-MAN--
--AND IT WAS GOOD MONEY NO MATTER WHAT EDITORIAL SLANT JONAH PUT WITH THE PHOTO.
IT WAS A GREAT PART-TIME JOB-- WHILE I WAS GOING TO SCHOOL.
BUT I NEVER INTENDED TO MAKE A CAREER OUT OF IT!
I'D ALWAYS WANTED TO CONTINUE COLLEGE-- STUDY SCIENCE--
--BIOCHEMISTRY--
THIS IS MESSED UP!
WHAT'S HAPPENING TO ME? WHAT IS HAPPENING TO ME?!
DANTE
MEN'S CLOTHING

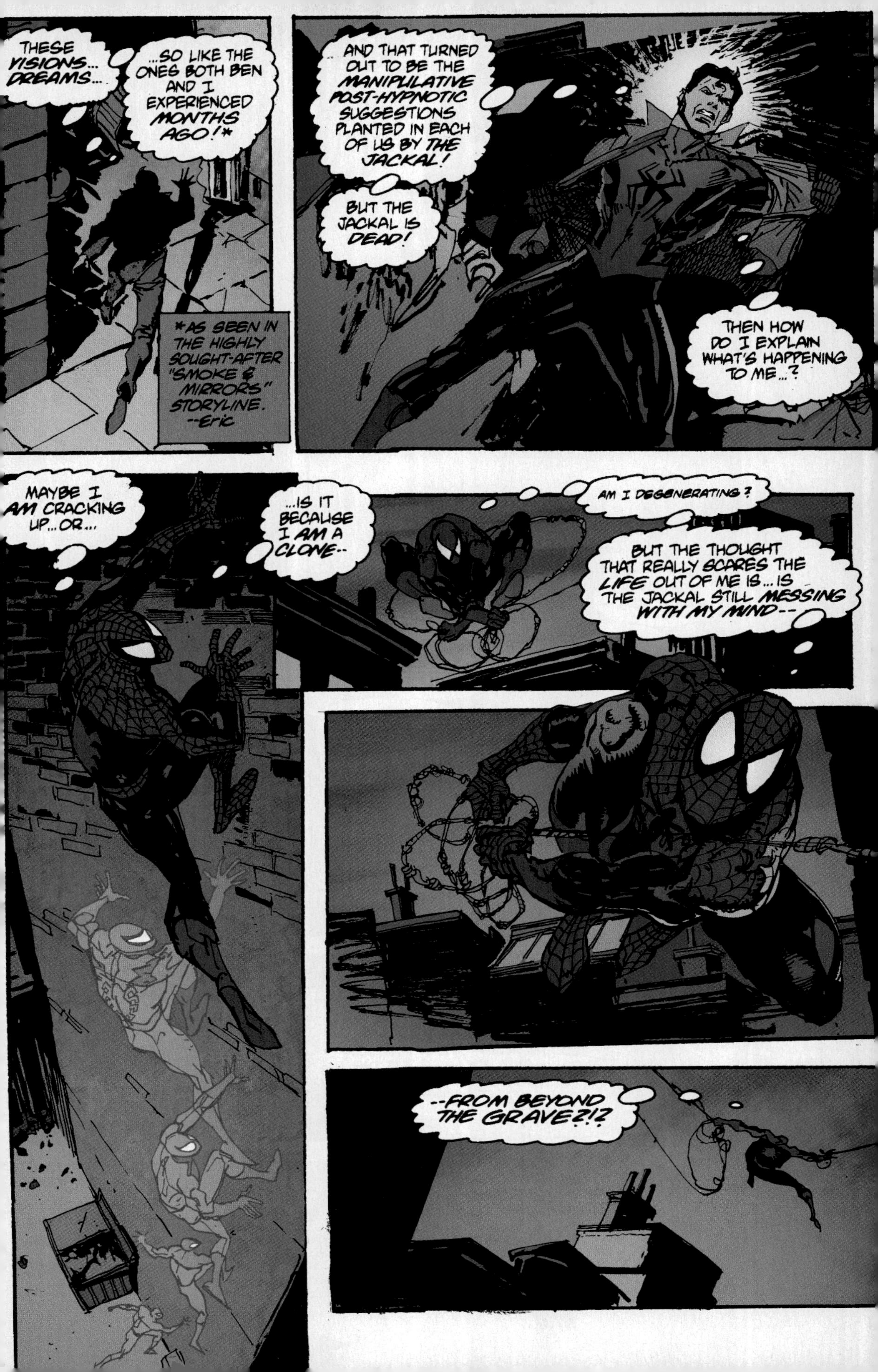
THESE VISIONS... DREAMS...
...SO LIKE THE ONES BOTH BEN AND I EXPERIENCED MONTHS AGO!*
*AS SEEN IN THE HIGHLY SOUGHT-AFTER "SMOKE & MIRRORS" STORYLINE. --Eric
AND THAT TURNED OUT TO BE THE MANIPULATIVE POST-HYPNOTIC SUGGESTIONS PLANTED IN EACH OF US BY THE JACKAL!
BUT THE JACKAL IS DEAD!
THEN HOW DO I EXPLAIN WHAT'S HAPPENING TO ME...?
MAYBE I AM CRACKING UP...OR...
...IS IT BECAUSE I AM A CLONE--
AM I DEGENERATING?
BUT THE THOUGHT THAT REALLY SCARES THE LIFE OUT OF ME IS... IS THE JACKAL STILL MESSING WITH MY MIND--
--FROM BEYOND THE GRAVE?!?

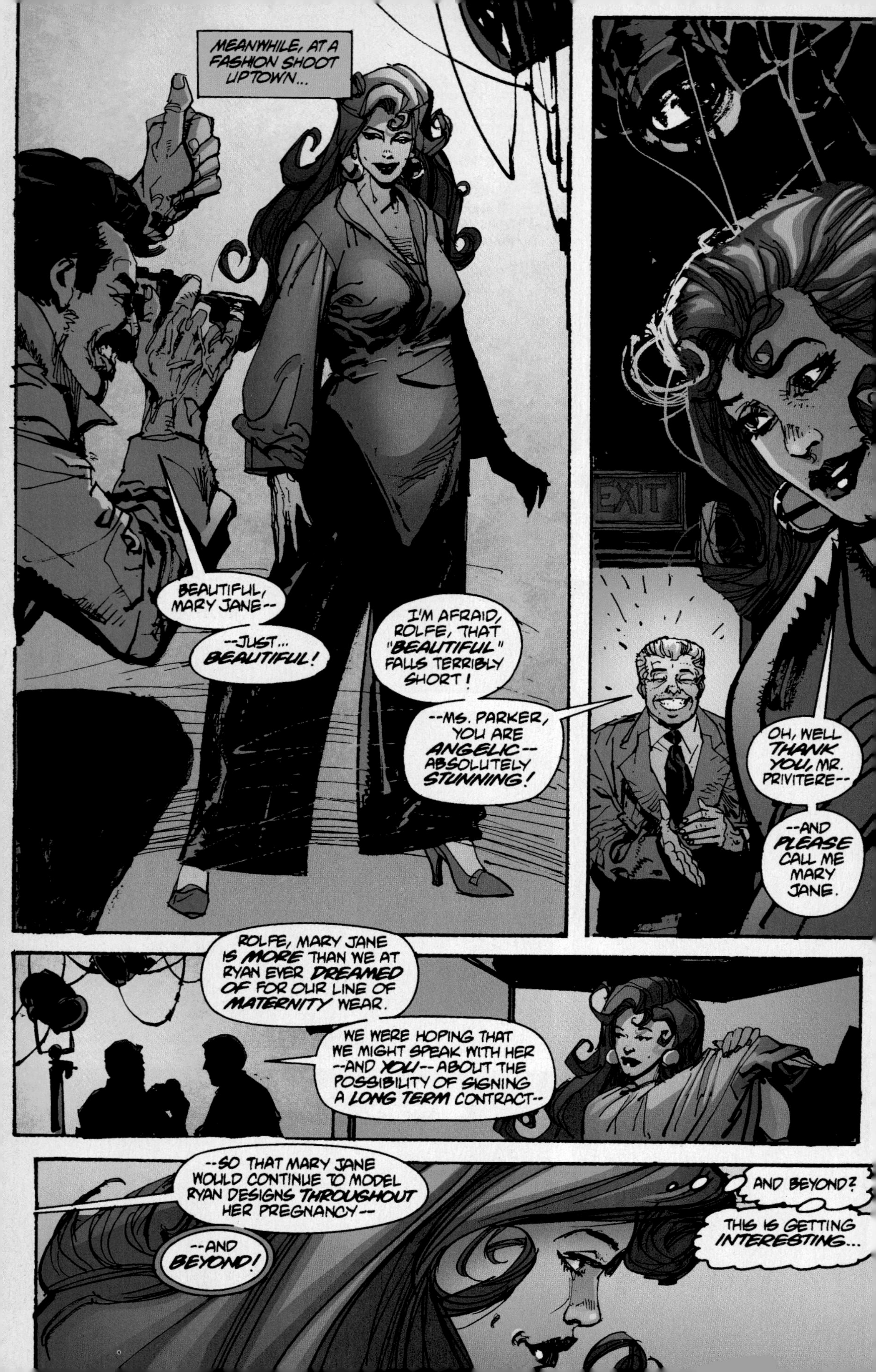
MEANWHILE, AT A FASHION SHOOT UPTOWN...
BEAUTIFUL, MARY JANE--
--JUST... BEAUTIFUL!
I'M AFRAID, ROLFE, THAT "BEAUTIFUL" FALLS TERRIBLY SHORT!
--MS. PARKER, YOU ARE ANGELIC--ABSOLUTELY STUNNING!
EXIT
OH, WELL THANK YOU, MR. PRIVITERE--
--AND PLEASE CALL ME MARY JANE.
ROLFE, MARY JANE IS MORE THAN WE AT RYAN EVER DREAMED OF FOR OUR LINE OF MATERNITY WEAR.
WE WERE HOPING THAT WE MIGHT SPEAK WITH HER --AND YOU-- ABOUT THE POSSIBILITY OF SIGNING A LONG TERM CONTRACT--
--SO THAT MARY JANE WOULD CONTINUE TO MODEL RYAN DESIGNS THROUGHOUT HER PREGNANCY--
--AND BEYOND!
AND BEYOND?
THIS IS GETTING INTERESTING...

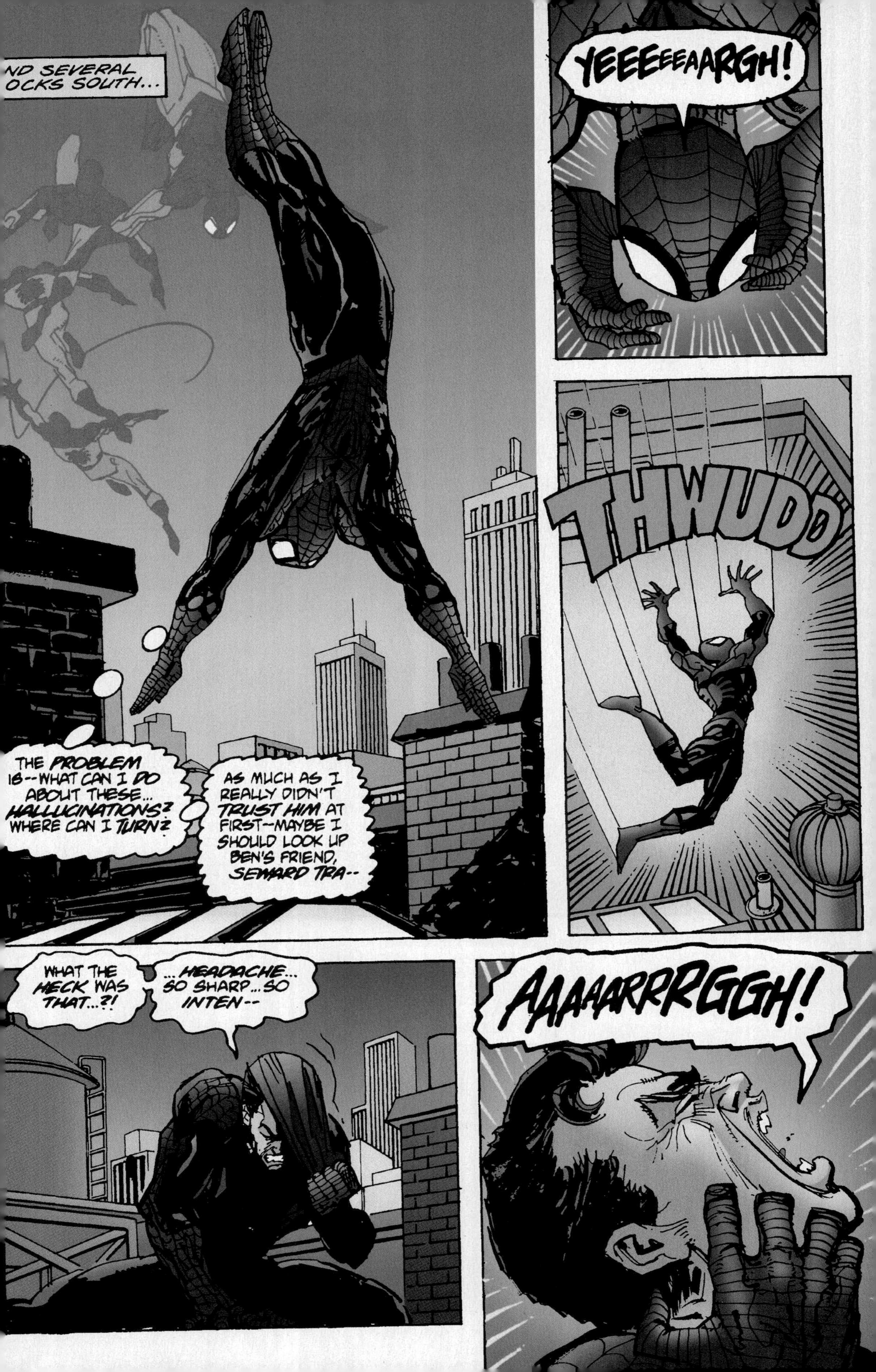

ND SEVERAL OCKS SOUTH...
THE PROBLEM IS--WHAT CAN I DO ABOUT THESE... HALLUCINATIONS? WHERE CAN I TURN?
AS MUCH AS I REALLY DIDN'T TRUST HIM AT FIRST--MAYBE I SHOULD LOOK UP BEN'S FRIEND, SEWARD TRA--
YEEEEEAARGH!
THWUDD
WHAT THE HECK WAS THAT...?!
...HEADACHE... SO SHARP...SO INTEN--
AAAAARRRGGH!

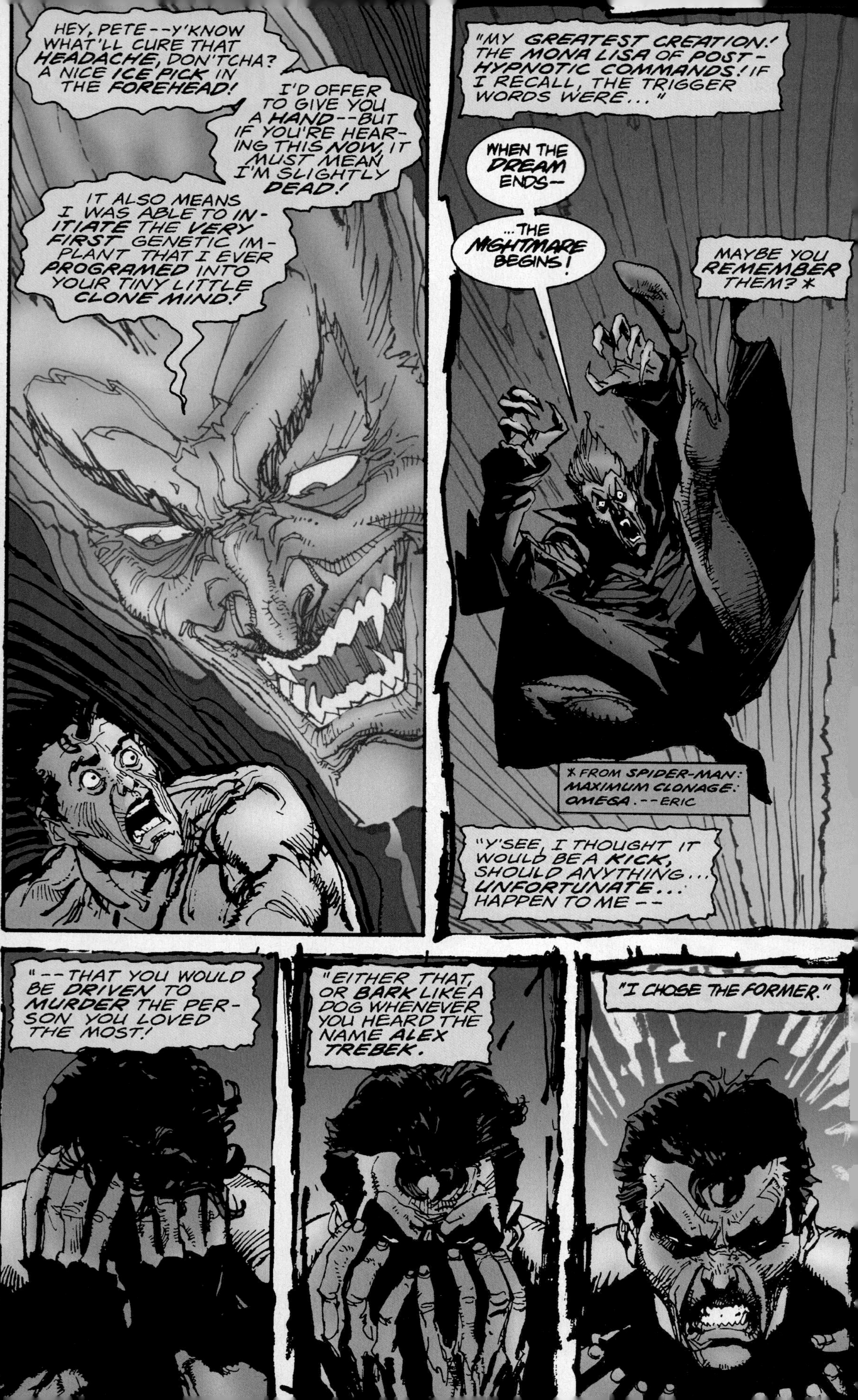
HEY, PETE--Y'KNOW WHAT'LL CURE THAT HEADACHE, DON'TCHA? A NICE ICE PICK IN THE FOREHEAD!
I'D OFFER TO GIVE YOU A HAND--BUT IF YOU'RE HEARING THIS NOW, IT MUST MEAN I'M SLIGHTLY DEAD!
IT ALSO MEANS I WAS ABLE TO INITIATE THE VERY FIRST GENETIC IMPLANT THAT I EVER PROGRAMED INTO YOUR TINY LITTLE CLONE MIND!
"MY GREATEST CREATION! THE MONA LISA OF POST-HYPNOTIC COMMANDS! IF I RECALL, THE TRIGGER WORDS WERE..."
WHEN THE DREAM ENDS--
...THE NIGHTMARE BEGINS!
MAYBE YOU REMEMBER THEM? *
* FROM SPIDER-MAN: MAXIMUM CLONAGE: OMEGA.--ERIC
"Y'SEE, I THOUGHT IT WOULD BE A KICK, SHOULD ANYTHING... UNFORTUNATE... HAPPEN TO ME--
"--THAT YOU WOULD BE DRIVEN TO MURDER THE PERSON YOU LOVED THE MOST!
"EITHER THAT, OR BARK LIKE A DOG WHENEVER YOU HEARD THE NAME ALEX TREBEK.
"I CHOSE THE FORMER."

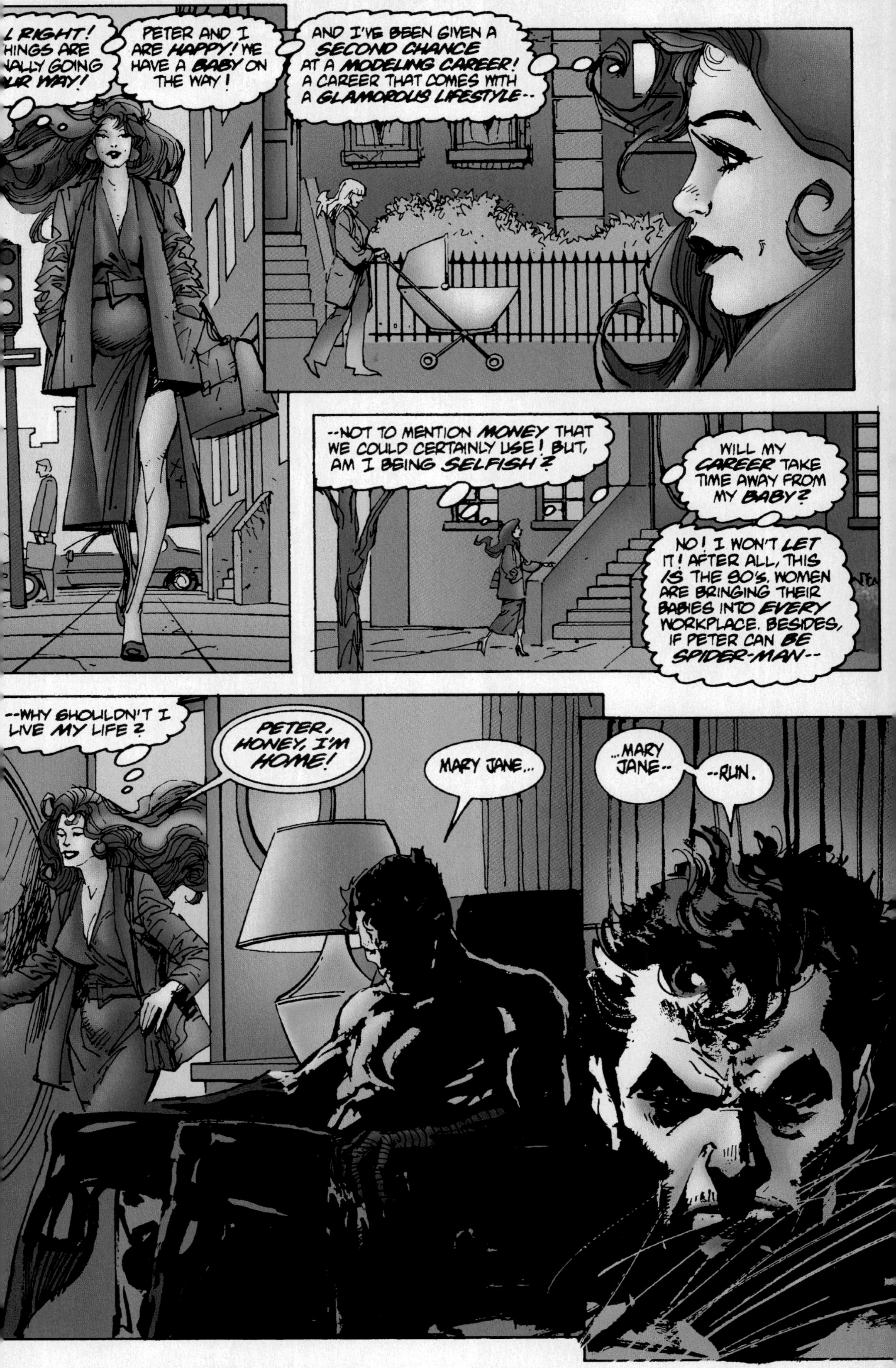
L RIGHT! HINGS ARE NALLY GOING UR WAY!
PETER AND I ARE HAPPY! WE HAVE A BABY ON THE WAY!
AND I'VE BEEN GIVEN A SECOND CHANCE AT A MODELING CAREER! A CAREER THAT COMES WITH A GLAMOROUS LIFESTYLE--
--NOT TO MENTION MONEY THAT WE COULD CERTAINLY USE! BUT, AM I BEING SELFISH?
WILL MY CAREER TAKE TIME AWAY FROM MY BABY?
NO! I WON'T LET IT! AFTER ALL, THIS IS THE 90'S. WOMEN ARE BRINGING THEIR BABIES INTO EVERY WORKPLACE. BESIDES, IF PETER CAN BE SPIDER-MAN--
--WHY SHOULDN'T I LIVE MY LIFE?
PETER, HONEY, I'M HOME!
MARY JANE...
...MARY JANE--
--RUN.

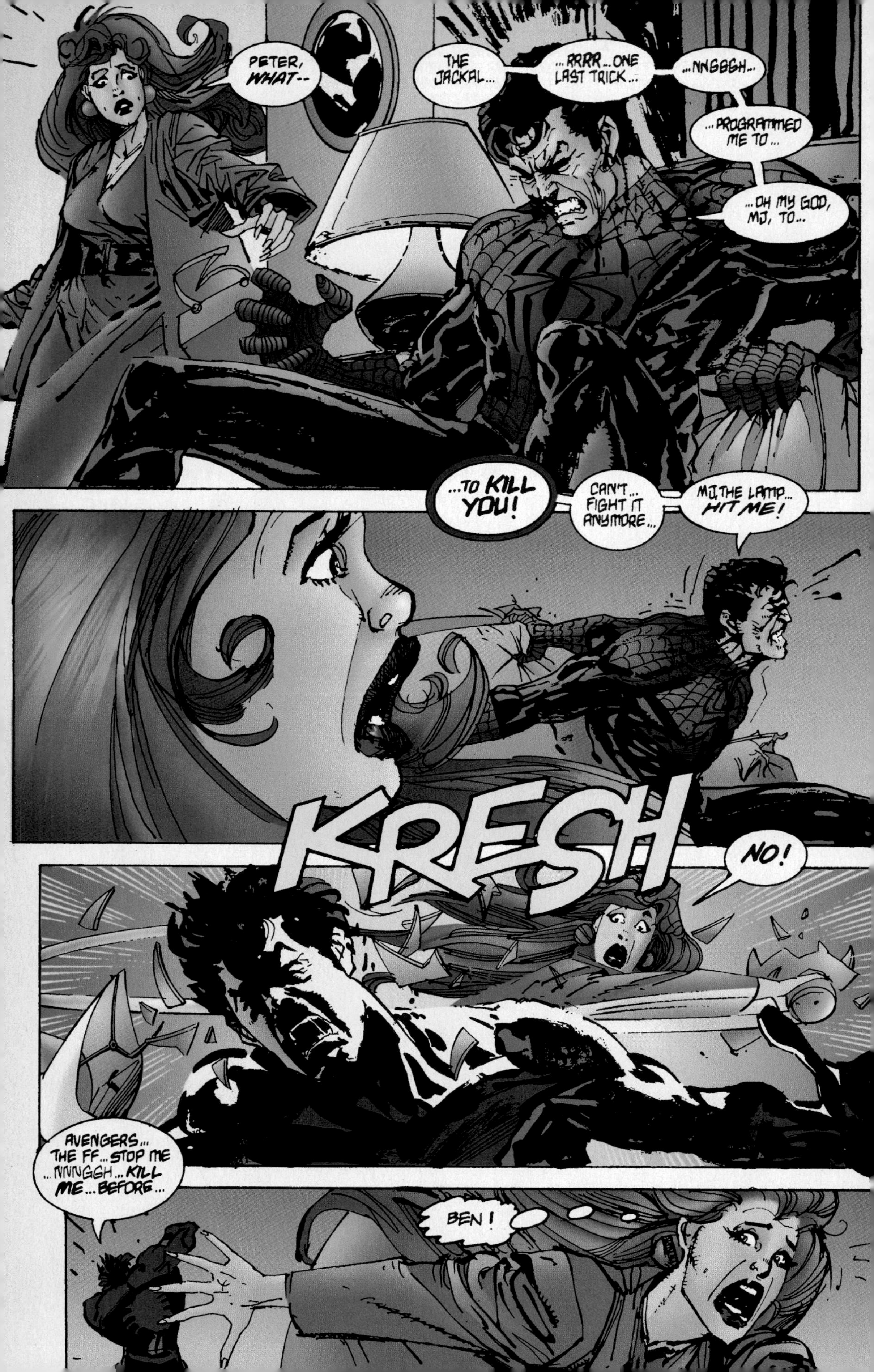
PETER, WHAT--
THE JACKAL...
...RRRR...ONE LAST TRICK...
...NNGGGH...
...PROGRAMMED ME TO...
...OH MY GOD, MJ, TO...
...TO KILL YOU!
CAN'T... FIGHT IT ANYMORE...
MJ, THE LAMP... HIT ME!
KRESH
NO!
AVENGERS... THE FF...STOP ME ...NNNGGH...KILL ME...BEFORE...
BEN!

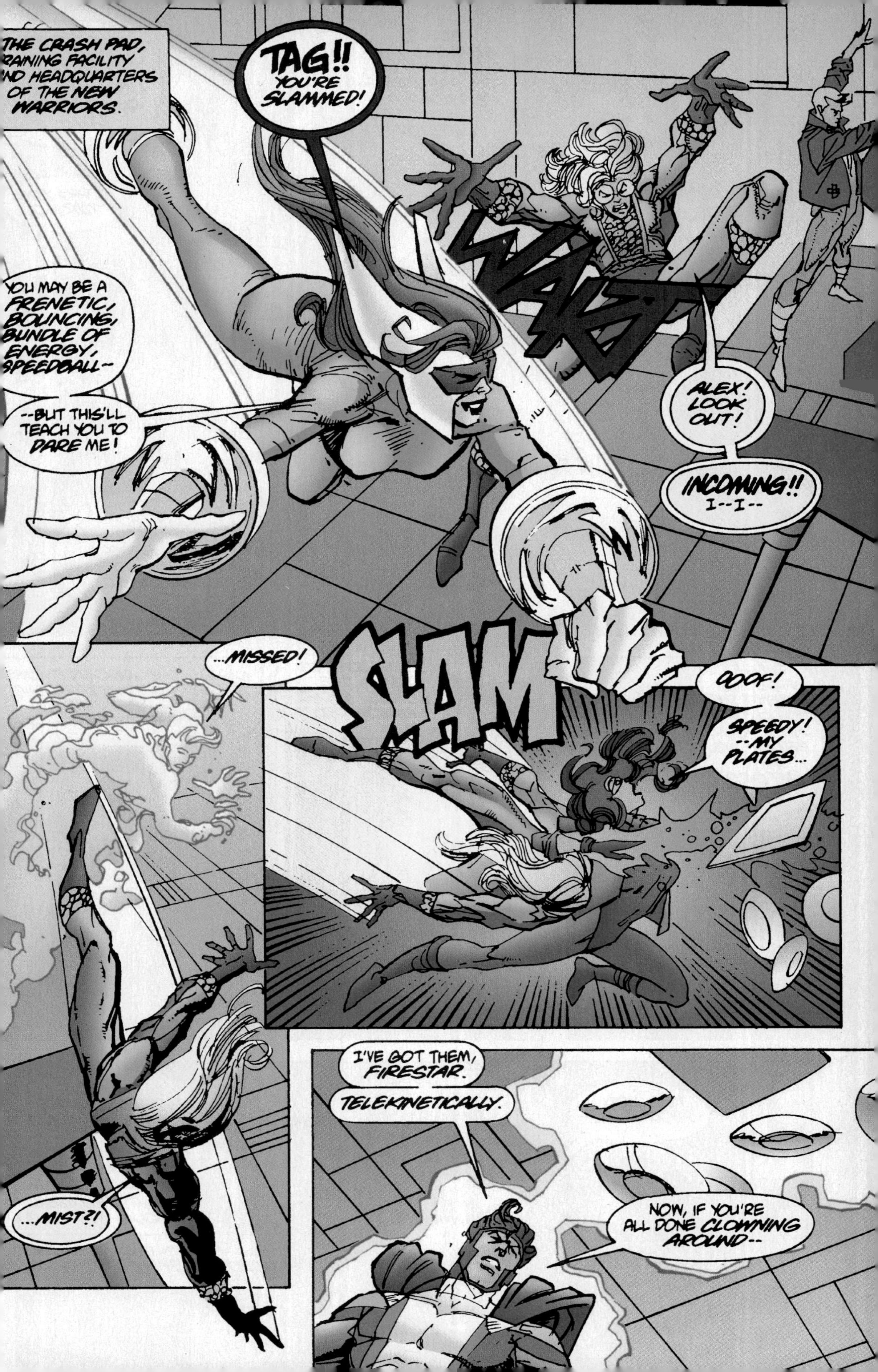
THE CRASH PAD, TRAINING FACILITY AND HEADQUARTERS OF THE NEW WARRIORS.
TAG!! YOU'RE SLAMMED!
WAKT
YOU MAY BE A FRENETIC, BOUNCING, BUNDLE OF ENERGY, SPEEDBALL--
--BUT THIS'LL TEACH YOU TO DARE ME!
ALEX! LOOK OUT!
INCOMING!! I--I--
SLAM
...MISSED!
OOOF!
SPEEDY! --MY PLATES...
...MIST?!
I'VE GOT THEM, FIRESTAR.
TELEKINETICALLY.
NOW, IF YOU'RE ALL DONE CLOWNING AROUND--

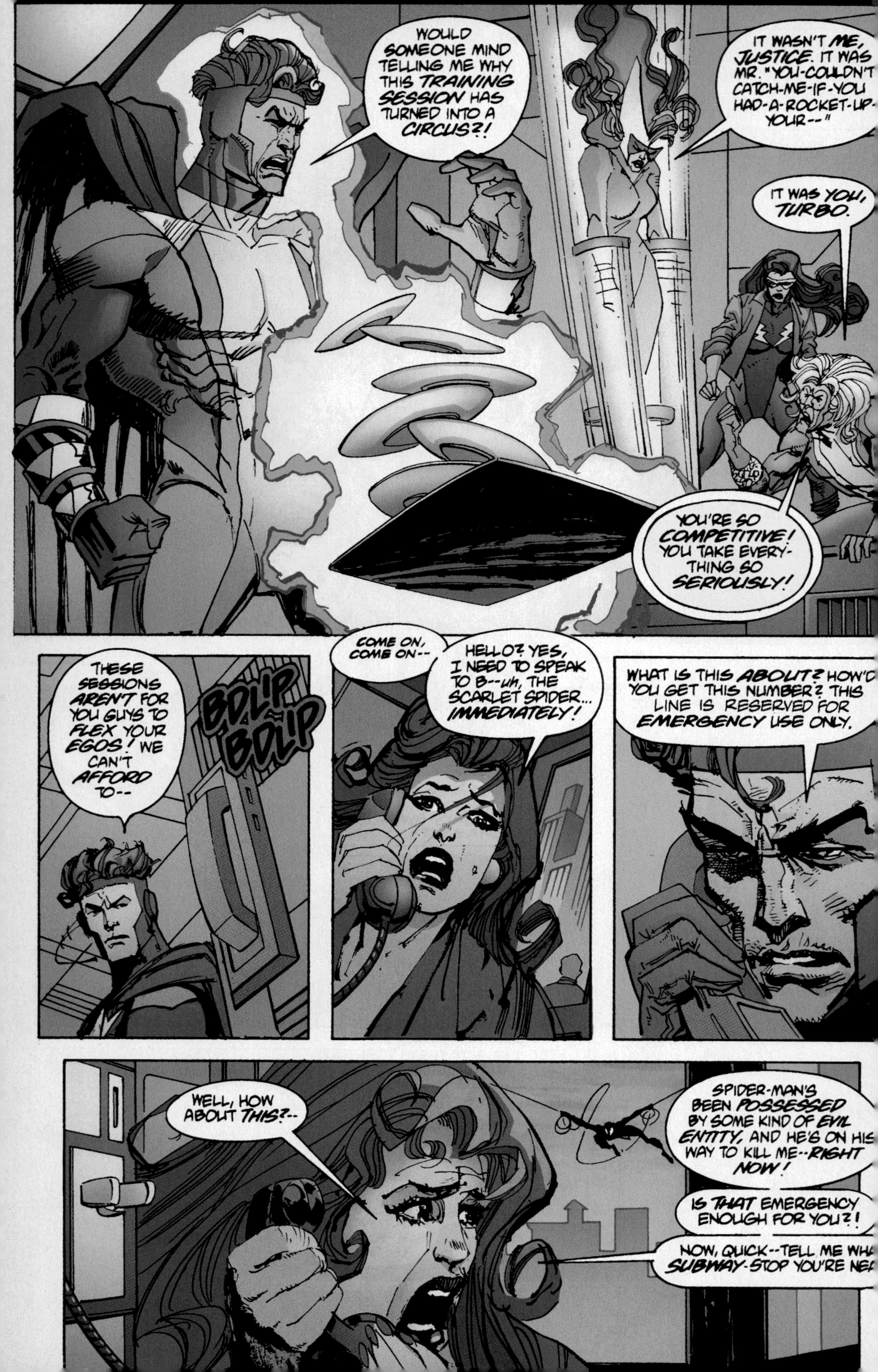
WOULD SOMEONE MIND TELLING ME WHY THIS TRAINING SESSION HAS TURNED INTO A CIRCUS?!
IT WASN'T ME, JUSTICE. IT WAS MR. "YOU-COULDN'T CATCH-ME-IF-YOU HAD-A-ROCKET-UP-YOUR--"
IT WAS YOU, TURBO.
YOU'RE SO COMPETITIVE! YOU TAKE EVERY-THING SO SERIOUSLY!
THESE SESSIONS AREN'T FOR YOU GUYS TO FLEX YOUR EGOS! WE CAN'T AFFORD TO--
BDLIP BDLIP
COME ON, COME ON--
HELLO? YES, I NEED TO SPEAK TO B--uh, THE SCARLET SPIDER... IMMEDIATELY!
WHAT IS THIS ABOUT? HOW'D YOU GET THIS NUMBER? THIS LINE IS RESERVED FOR EMERGENCY USE ONLY.
WELL, HOW ABOUT THIS?--
SPIDER-MAN'S BEEN POSSESSED BY SOME KIND OF EVIL ENTITY, AND HE'S ON HIS WAY TO KILL ME--RIGHT NOW!
IS THAT EMERGENCY ENOUGH FOR YOU?!
NOW, QUICK--TELL ME WHA SUBWAY-STOP YOU'RE NEA

...CAN'T...FIGHT THE JACKAL'S PROGRAMMING...

...PLEASE...

...PLEASE... SOMEBODY STOP ME!

HOLD THE DOOR! HOLD THE DOOR!

I'M IN...I'M IN. I GOT AWAY...FOR NOW! BUT I'VE GOT TO BE READY...WHAT DO I DO NEXT?!

SHUMMMMM

AAARRGH!

I...MISSED HER! I LOST HER!

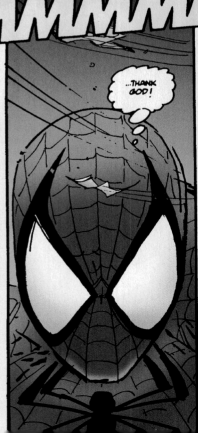

...THANK GOD!

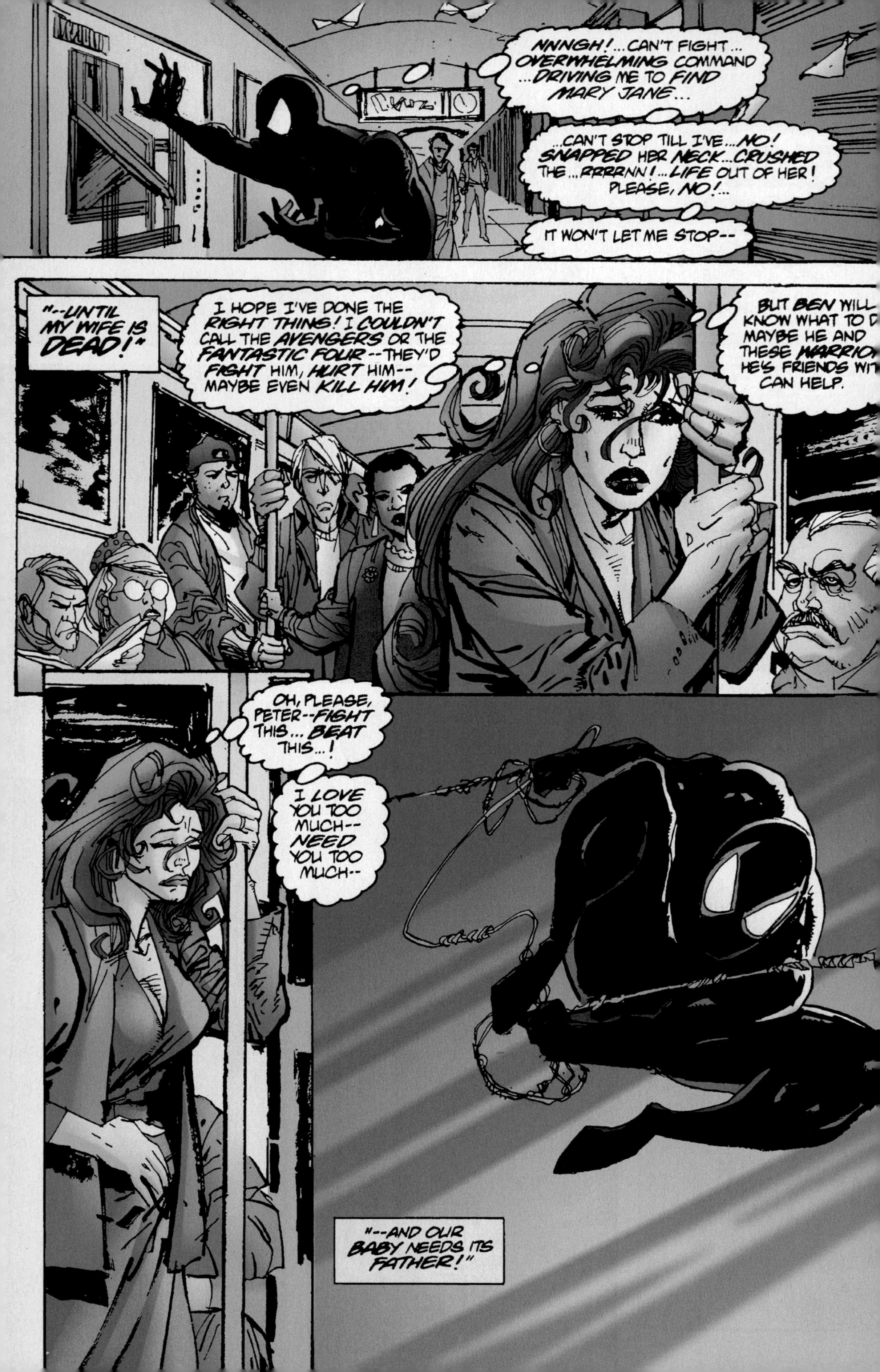
NNNGH!... CAN'T FIGHT... OVERWHELMING COMMAND ...DRIVING ME TO FIND MARY JANE...
...CAN'T STOP TILL I'VE... NO! SNAPPED HER NECK... CRUSHED THE... RRRRNN!... LIFE OUT OF HER! PLEASE, NO!...
IT WON'T LET ME STOP--
"--UNTIL MY WIFE IS DEAD!"
I HOPE I'VE DONE THE RIGHT THING! I COULDN'T CALL THE AVENGERS OR THE FANTASTIC FOUR--THEY'D FIGHT HIM, HURT HIM--MAYBE EVEN KILL HIM!
BUT BEN WILL KNOW WHAT TO D MAYBE HE AND THESE WARRIO HE'S FRIENDS WIT CAN HELP.
OH, PLEASE, PETER--FIGHT THIS... BEAT THIS...!
I LOVE YOU TOO MUCH--NEED YOU TOO MUCH--
"--AND OUR BABY NEEDS ITS FATHER!"

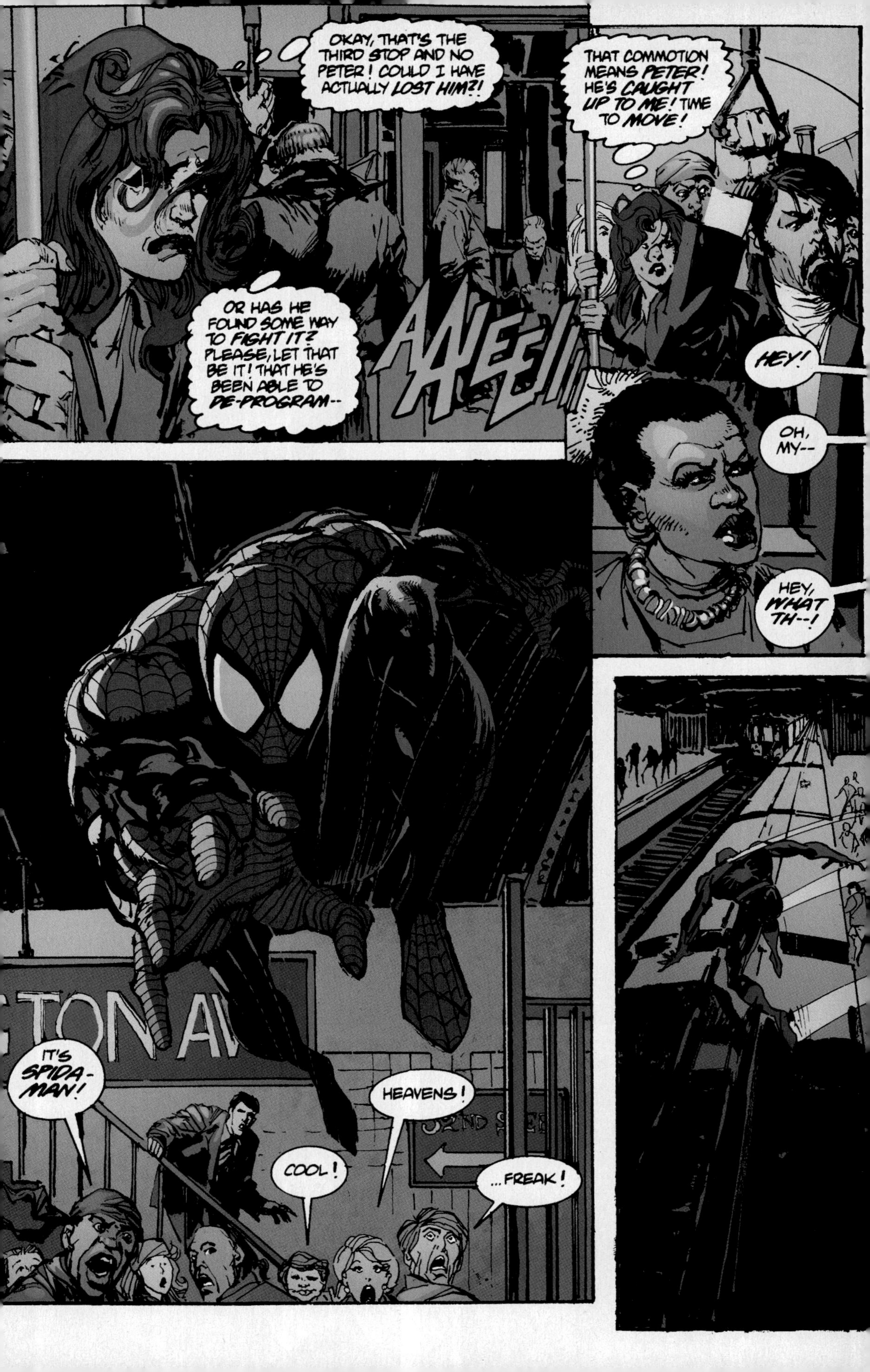
OKAY, THAT'S THE THIRD STOP AND NO PETER! COULD I HAVE ACTUALLY LOST HIM?!
OR HAS HE FOUND SOME WAY TO FIGHT IT? PLEASE, LET THAT BE IT! THAT HE'S BEEN ABLE TO DE-PROGRAM--
AAEEE!!!
THAT COMMOTION MEANS PETER! HE'S CAUGHT UP TO ME! TIME TO MOVE!
HEY!
OH, MY--
HEY, WHAT TH--!
TON AV
IT'S SPIDA-MAN!
HEAVENS!
COOL!
...FREAK!
52ND ST

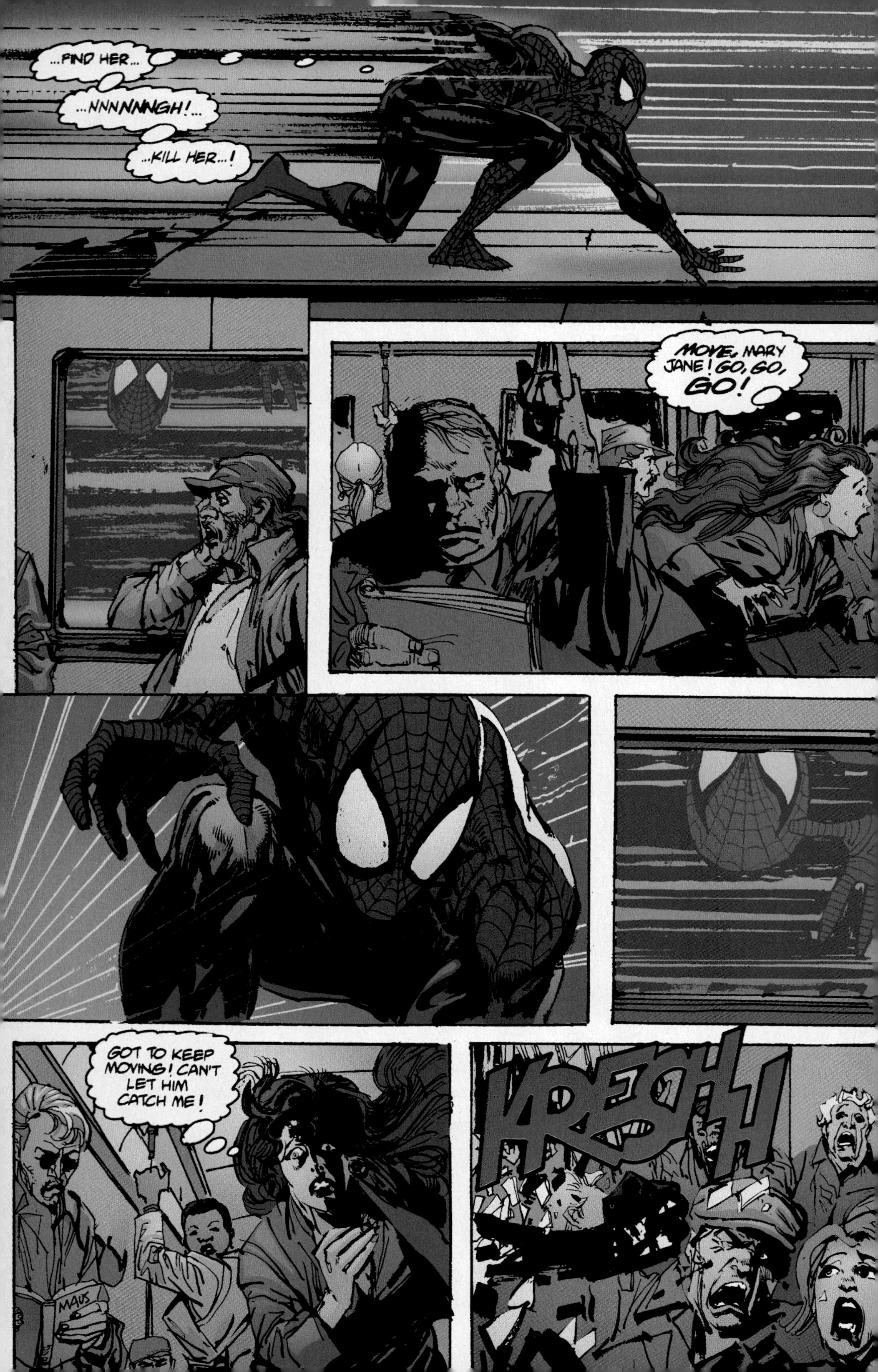

...FIND HER...
...NNNNNNGH!...
...KILL HER...!
MOVE, MARY JANE! GO, GO, GO!
GOT TO KEEP MOVING! CAN'T LET HIM CATCH ME!
MAUS
KRESH

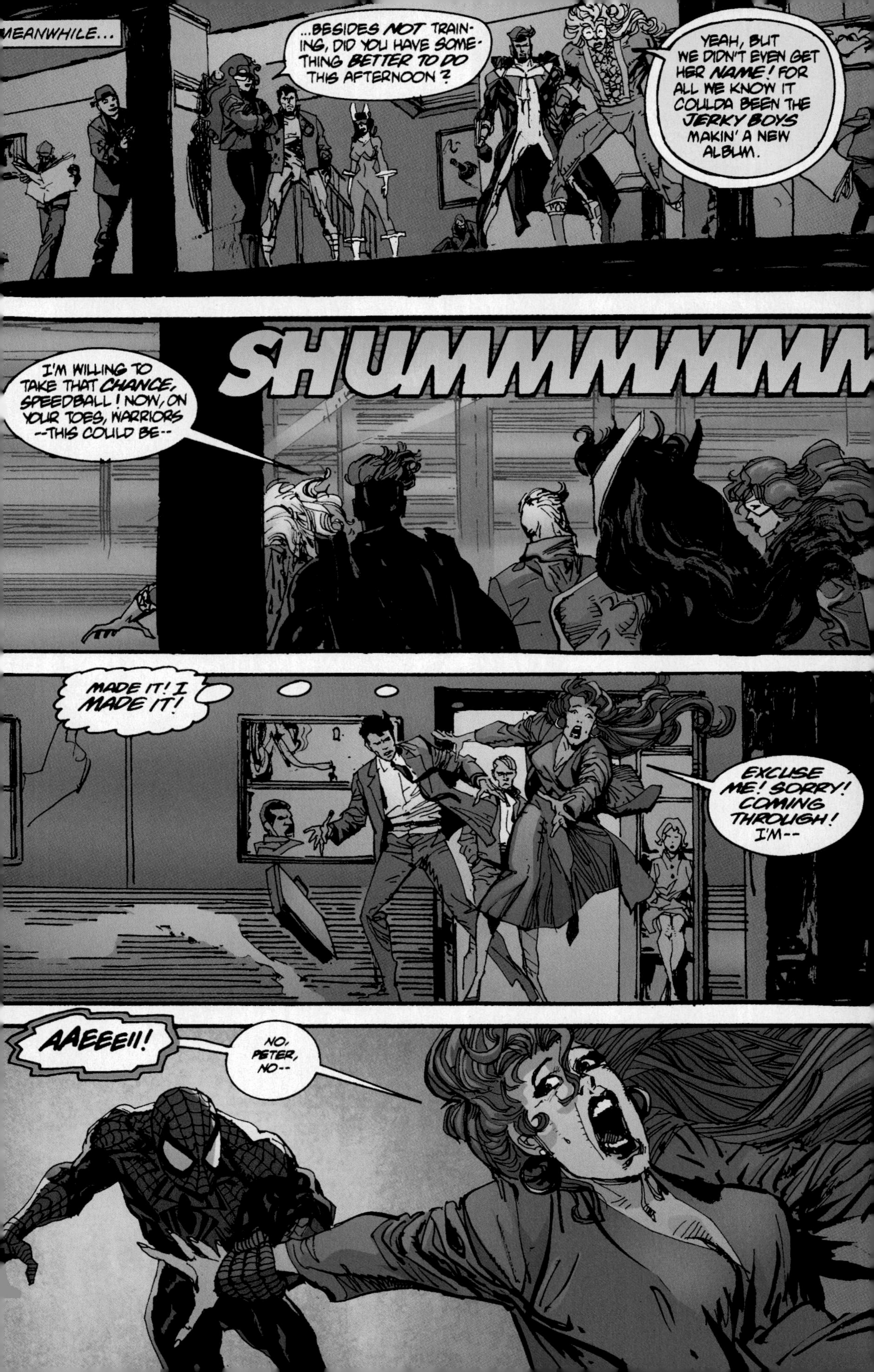
MEANWHILE...
...BESIDES NOT TRAINING, DID YOU HAVE SOMETHING BETTER TO DO THIS AFTERNOON?
YEAH, BUT WE DIDN'T EVEN GET HER NAME! FOR ALL WE KNOW IT COULDA BEEN THE JERKY BOYS MAKIN' A NEW ALBUM.
SHUMMMMMM
I'M WILLING TO TAKE THAT CHANCE, SPEEDBALL! NOW, ON YOUR TOES, WARRIORS --THIS COULD BE--
MADE IT! I MADE IT!
EXCUSE ME! SORRY! COMING THROUGH! I'M--
AAEEEII!
NO, PETER, NO--

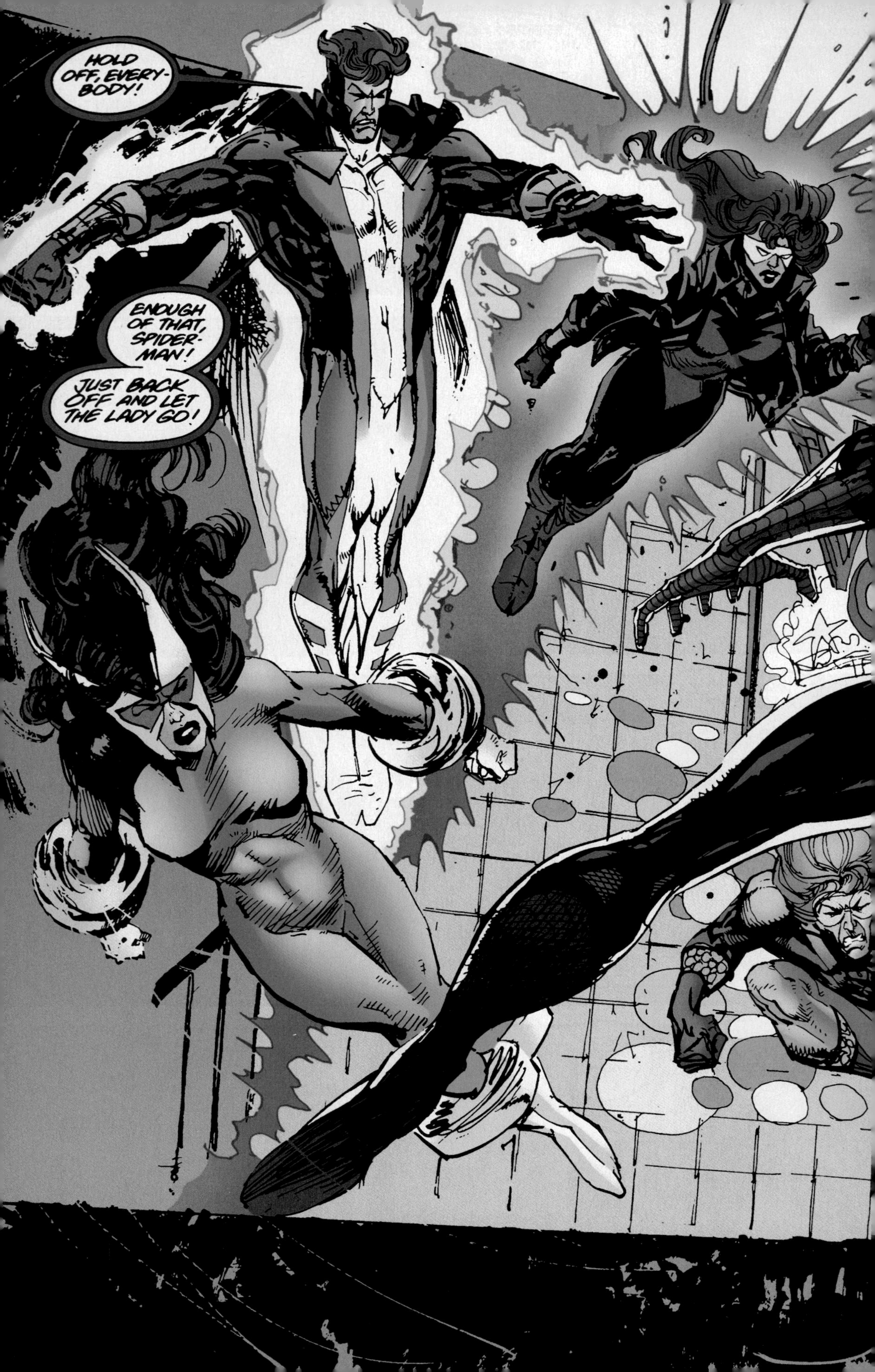
HOLD OFF, EVERY-BODY!
ENOUGH OF THAT, SPIDER-MAN!
JUST BACK OFF AND LET THE LADY GO!

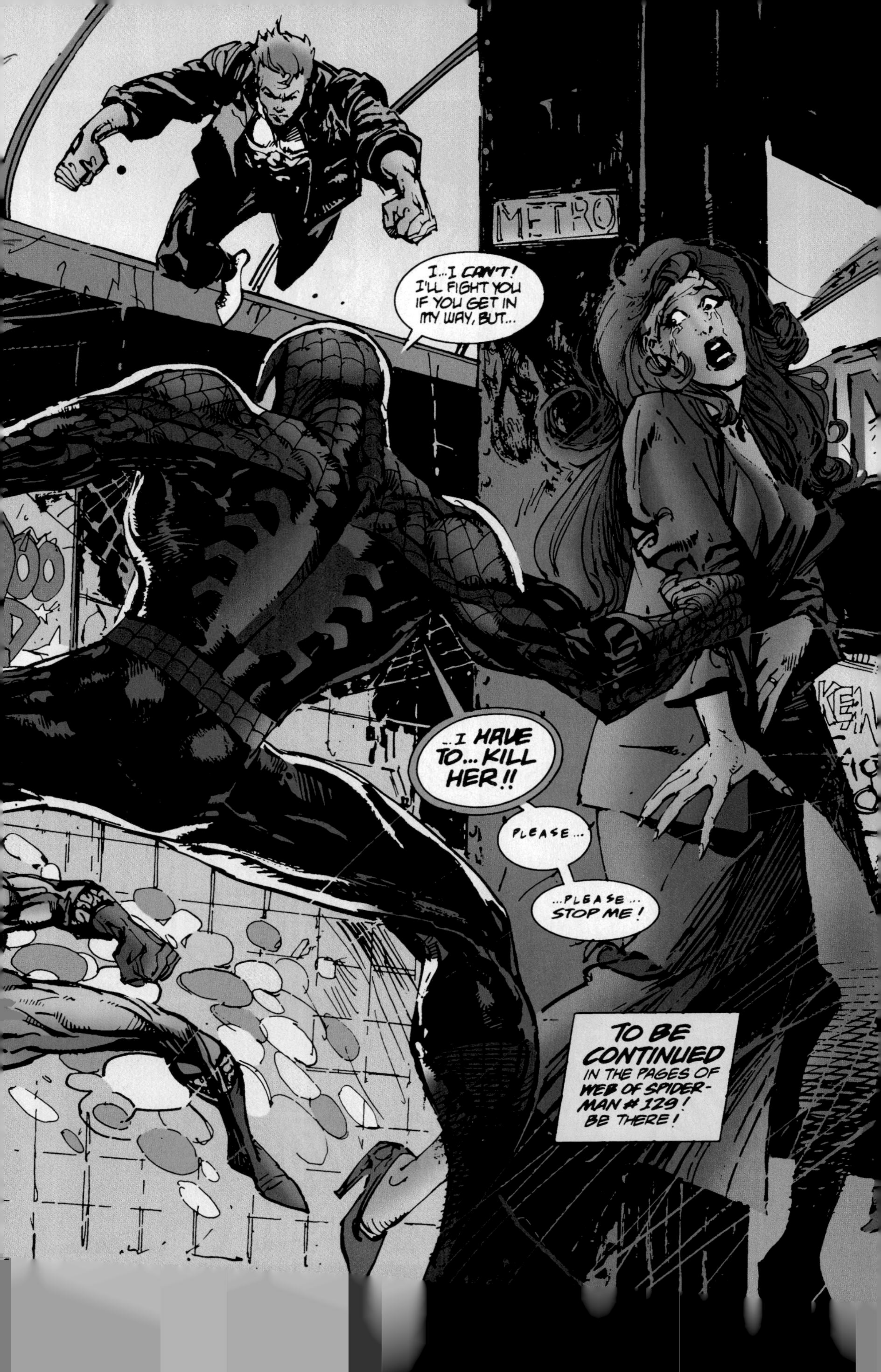

METRO
I...I CAN'T! I'LL FIGHT YOU IF YOU GET IN MY WAY, BUT...
...I HAVE TO... KILL HER!!
PLEASE...
...PLEASE... STOP ME!
TO BE CONTINUED IN THE PAGES OF WEB OF SPIDER-MAN #129! BE THERE!

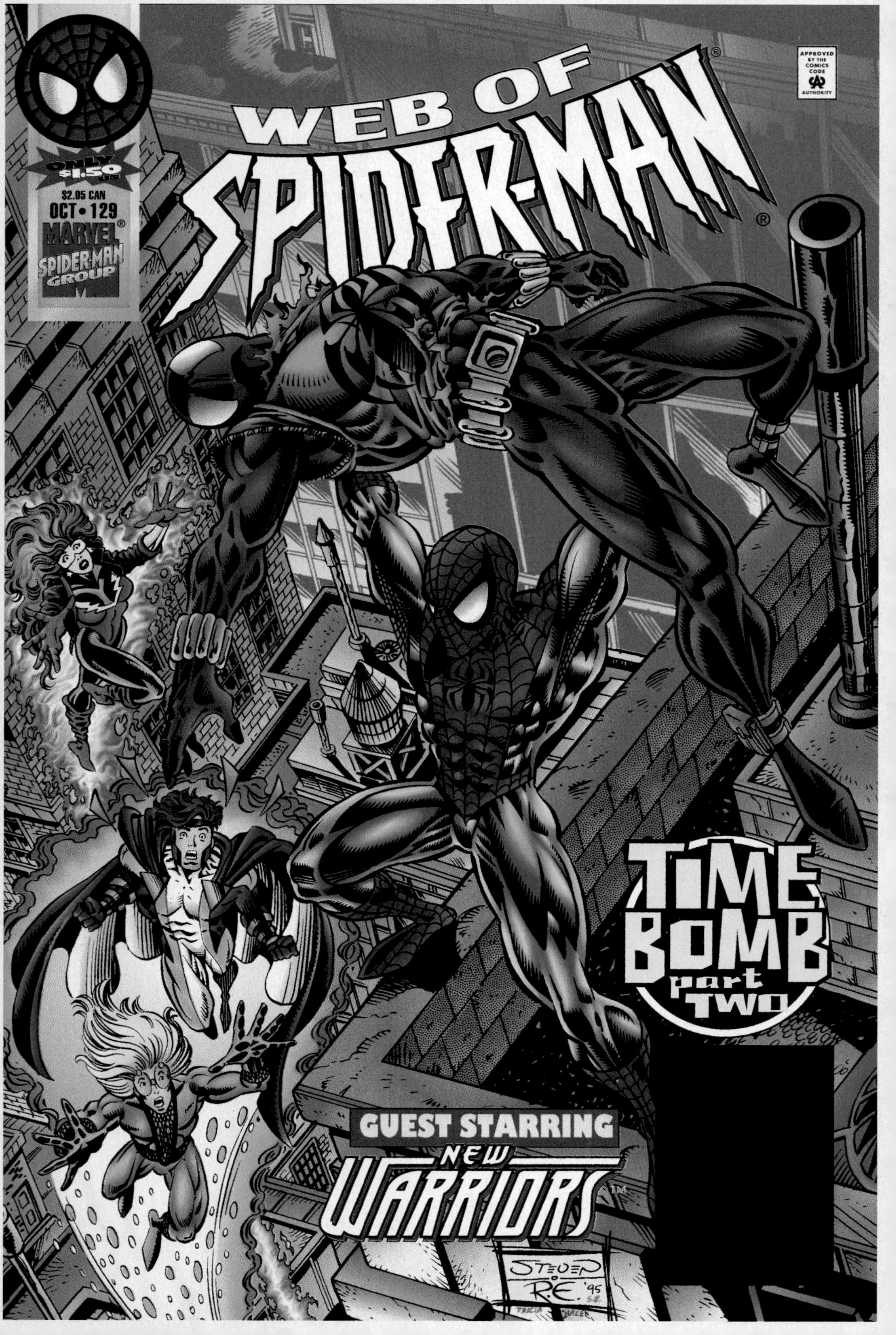
WEB OF
SPIDER-MAN
ONLY $1.50 US
$2.05 CAN
OCT • 129
MARVEL
SPIDER-MAN GROUP
APPROVED BY THE COMICS CODE AUTHORITY
TIME BOMB part TWO
GUEST STARRING
NEW WARRIORS

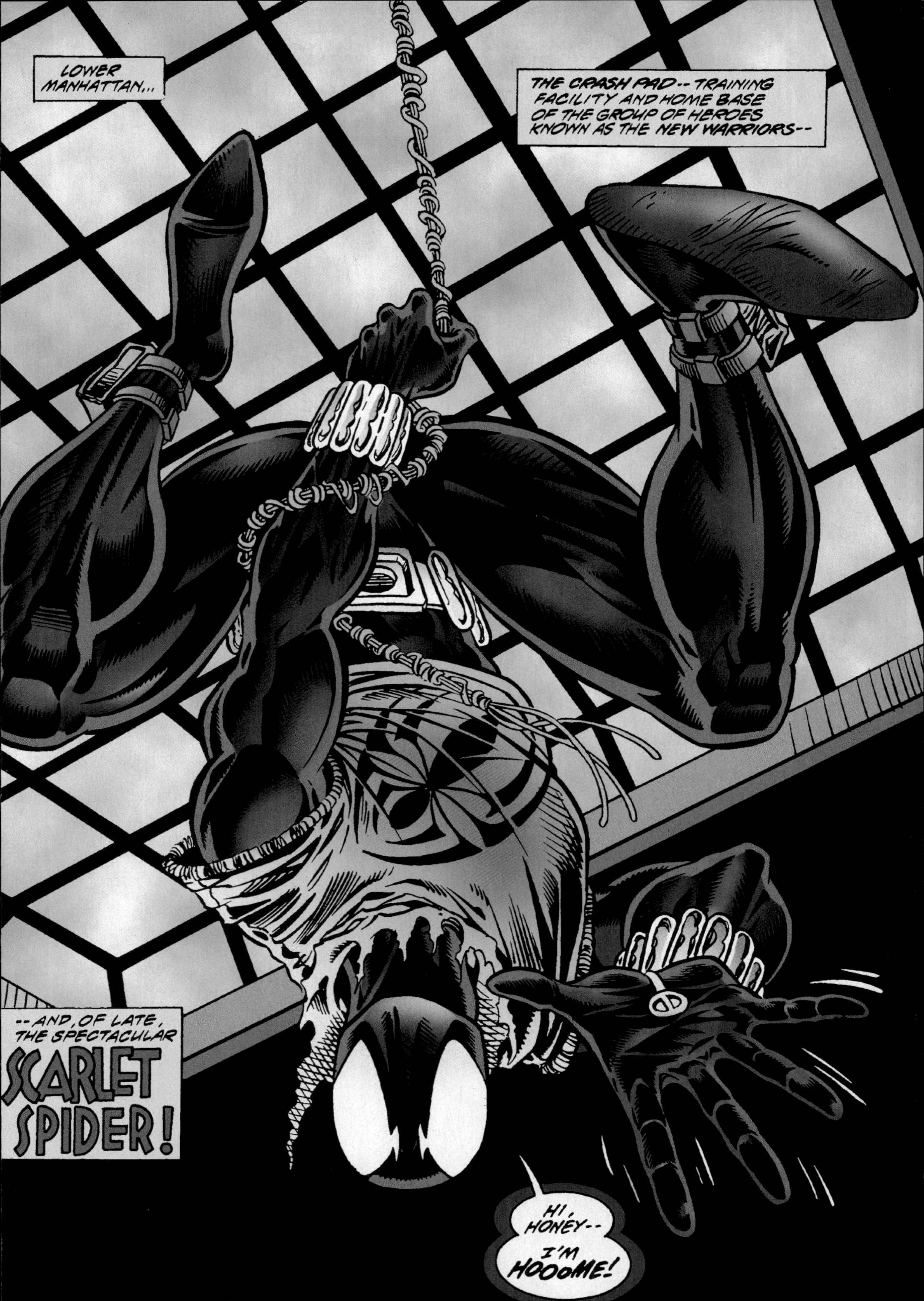
LOWER MANHATTAN...
THE CRASH PAD-- TRAINING FACILITY AND HOME BASE OF THE GROUP OF HEROES KNOWN AS THE NEW WARRIORS--
--AND, OF LATE, THE SPECTACULAR
SCARLET SPIDER!
HI, HONEY-- I'M HOOOME!

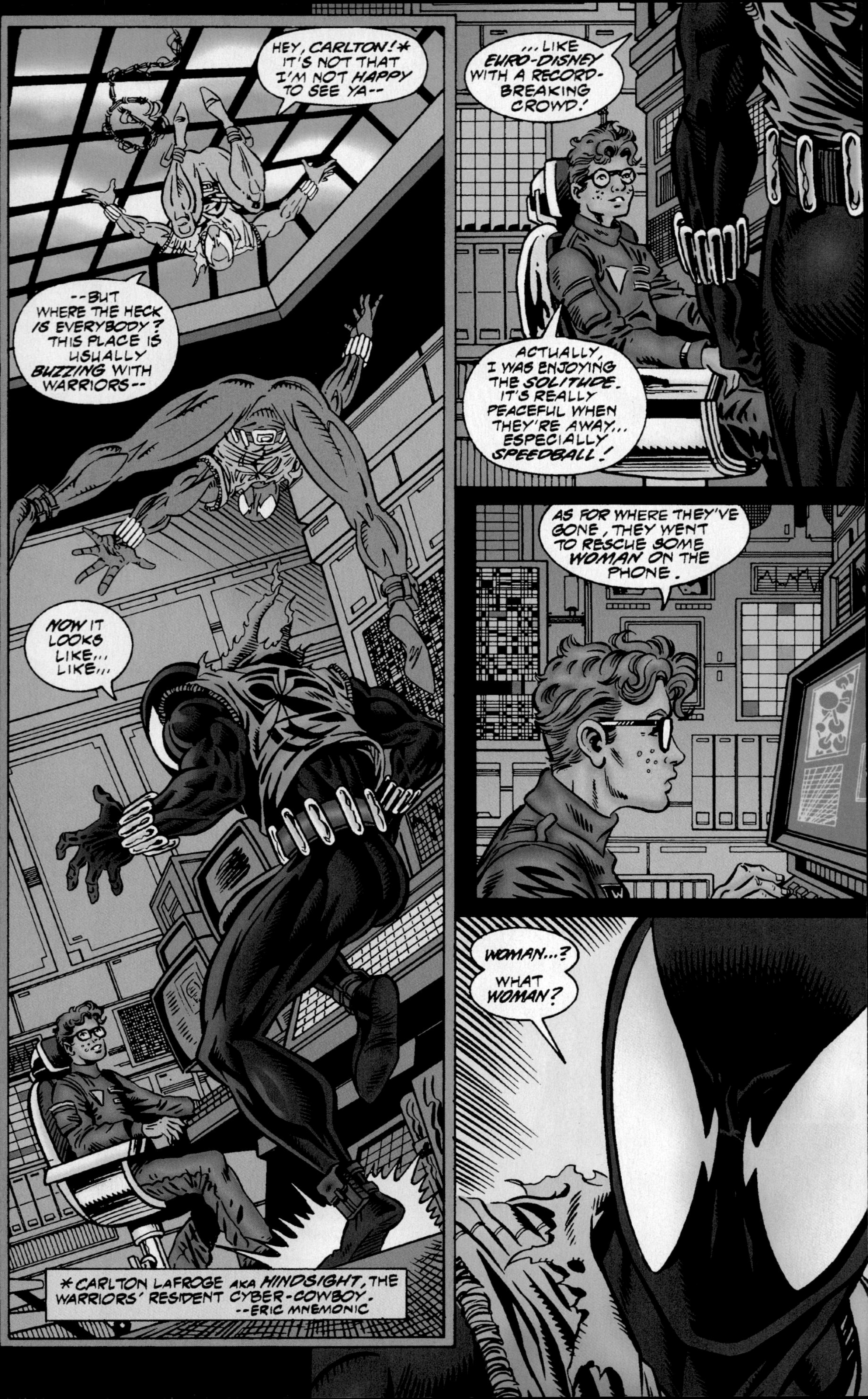
HEY, CARLTON!* IT'S NOT THAT I'M NOT HAPPY TO SEE YA--
--BUT WHERE THE HECK IS EVERYBODY? THIS PLACE IS USUALLY BUZZING WITH WARRIORS--
NOW IT LOOKS LIKE... LIKE...
*CARLTON LAFROGE AKA HINDSIGHT, THE WARRIORS' RESIDENT CYBER-COWBOY. --ERIC MNEMONIC
...LIKE EURO-DISNEY WITH A RECORD-BREAKING CROWD!
ACTUALLY, I WAS ENJOYING THE SOLITUDE. IT'S REALLY PEACEFUL WHEN THEY'RE AWAY... ESPECIALLY SPEEDBALL!
AS FOR WHERE THEY'VE GONE, THEY WENT TO RESCUE SOME WOMAN ON THE PHONE.
WOMAN...? WHAT WOMAN?

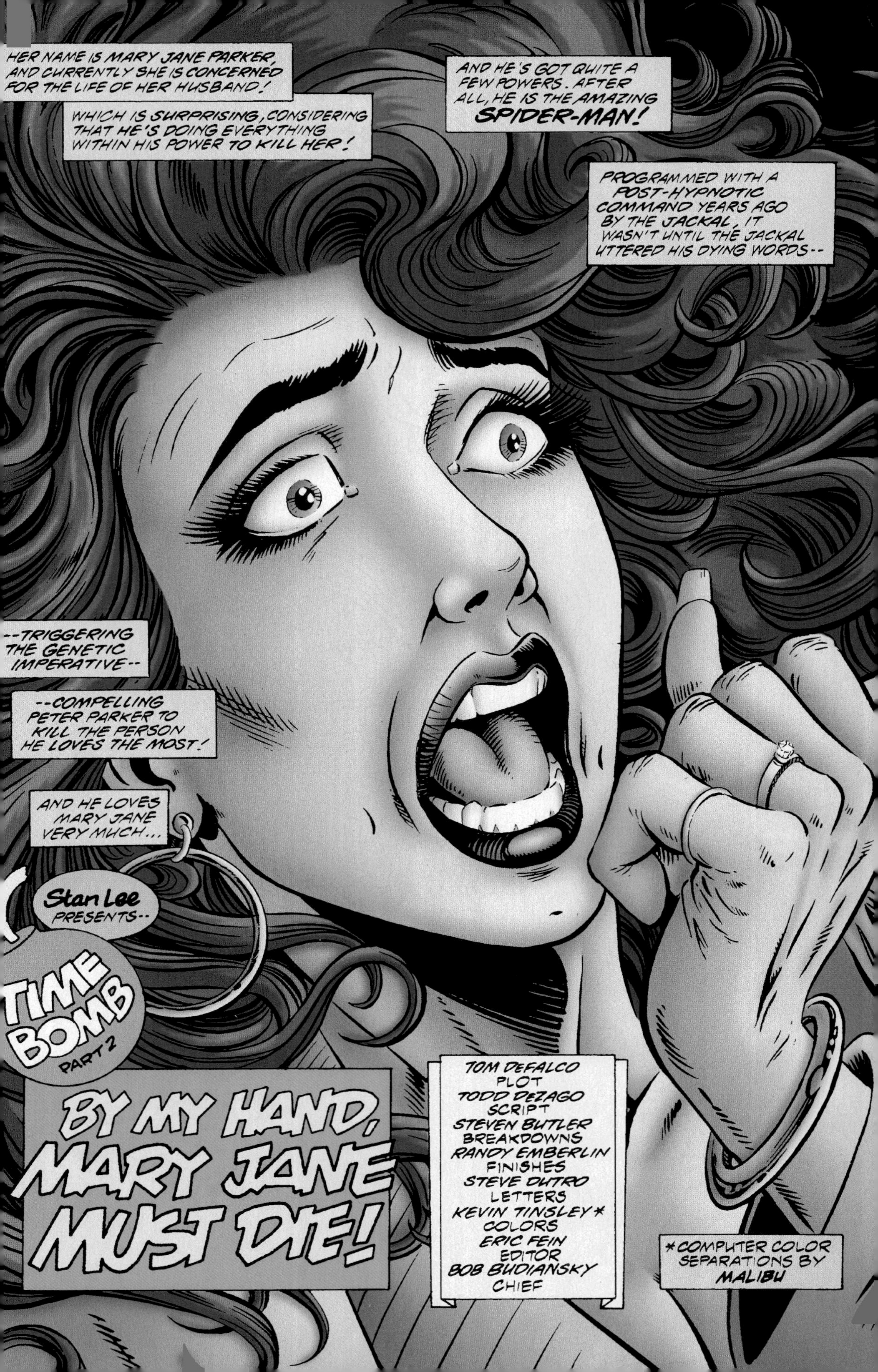
HER NAME IS MARY JANE PARKER, AND CURRENTLY SHE IS CONCERNED FOR THE LIFE OF HER HUSBAND!
WHICH IS SURPRISING, CONSIDERING THAT HE'S DOING EVERYTHING WITHIN HIS POWER TO KILL HER!
AND HE'S GOT QUITE A FEW POWERS. AFTER ALL, HE IS THE AMAZING SPIDER-MAN!
PROGRAMMED WITH A POST-HYPNOTIC COMMAND YEARS AGO BY THE JACKAL, IT WASN'T UNTIL THE JACKAL UTTERED HIS DYING WORDS--
--TRIGGERING THE GENETIC IMPERATIVE--
--COMPELLING PETER PARKER TO KILL THE PERSON HE LOVES THE MOST!
AND HE LOVES MARY JANE VERY MUCH...
Stan Lee PRESENTS--
TIME BOMB PART 2
BY MY HAND, MARY JANE MUST DIE!
TOM DEFALCO PLOT
TODD DEZAGO SCRIPT
STEVEN BUTLER BREAKDOWNS
RANDY EMBERLIN FINISHES
STEVE DUTRO LETTERS
KEVIN TINSLEY* COLORS
ERIC FEIN EDITOR
BOB BUDIANSKY CHIEF
*COMPUTER COLOR SEPARATIONS BY MALIBU

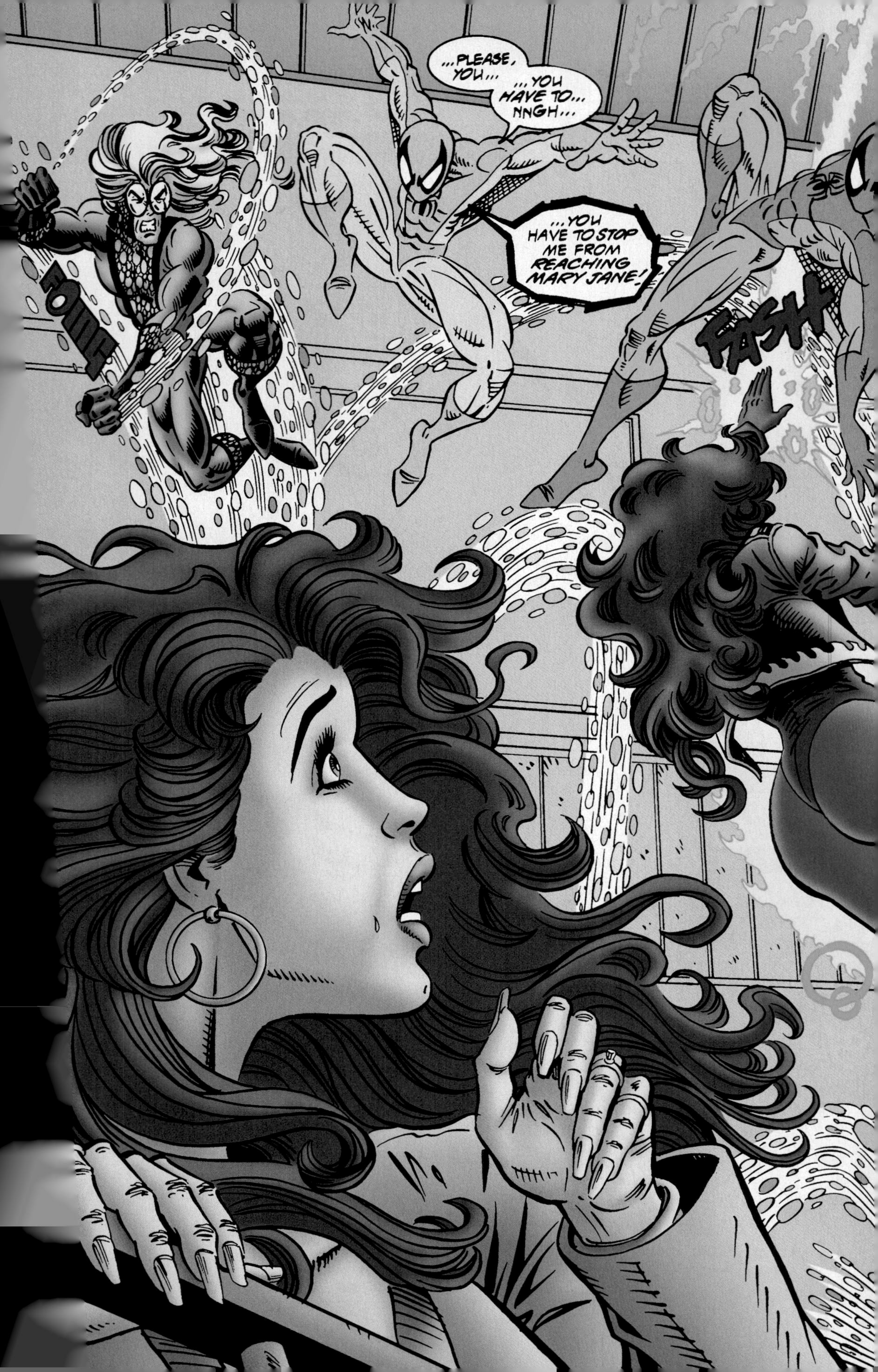
...PLEASE, YOU...
...YOU HAVE TO... NNGH...
...YOU HAVE TO STOP ME FROM REACHING MARY JANE!
FASH

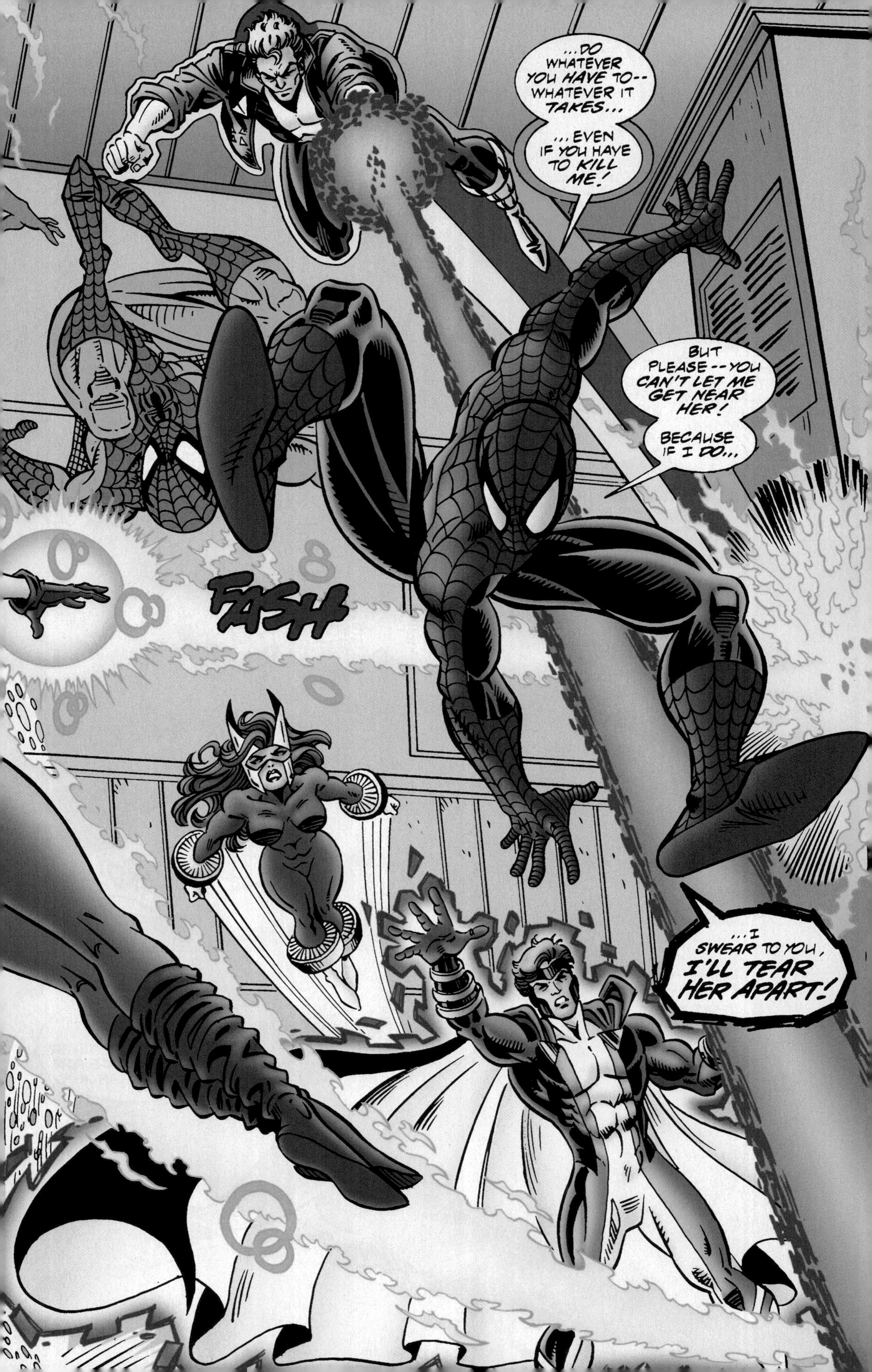
...DO WHATEVER YOU HAVE TO-- WHATEVER IT TAKES...
...EVEN IF YOU HAVE TO KILL ME!
BUT PLEASE--YOU CAN'T LET ME GET NEAR HER!
BECAUSE IF I DO...
FASH
...I SWEAR TO YOU, I'LL TEAR HER APART!

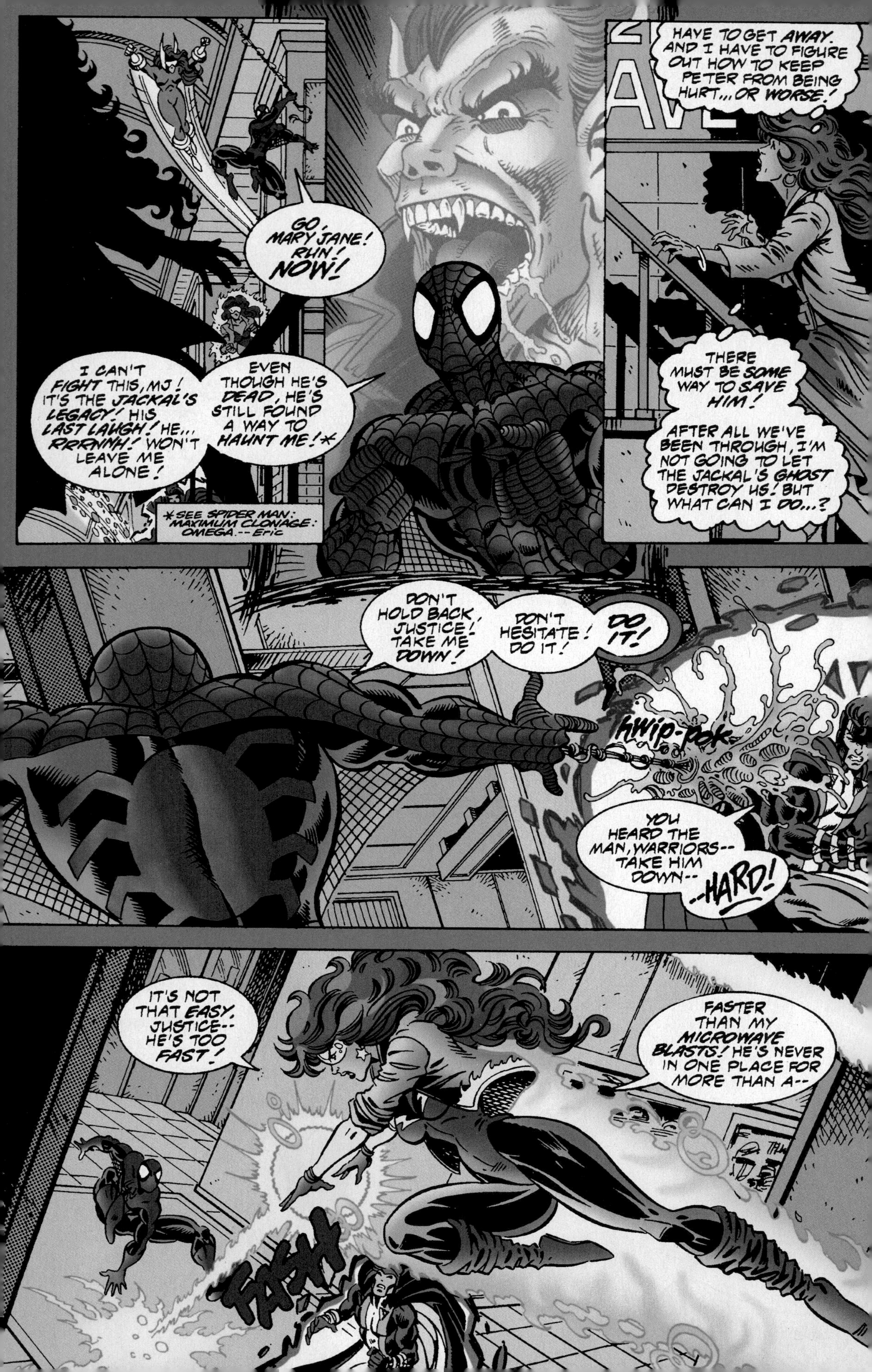
HAVE TO GET AWAY. AND I HAVE TO FIGURE OUT HOW TO KEEP PETER FROM BEING HURT... OR WORSE!
GO, MARY JANE! RUN! NOW!
I CAN'T FIGHT THIS, MJ! IT'S THE JACKAL'S LEGACY! HIS LAST LAUGH! HE... RRRNNH! WON'T LEAVE ME ALONE!
EVEN THOUGH HE'S DEAD, HE'S STILL FOUND A WAY TO HAUNT ME!*
*SEE SPIDER MAN: MAXIMUM CLONAGE: OMEGA.--Eric
THERE MUST BE SOME WAY TO SAVE HIM!
AFTER ALL WE'VE BEEN THROUGH, I'M NOT GOING TO LET THE JACKAL'S GHOST DESTROY US! BUT WHAT CAN I DO...?
DON'T HOLD BACK, JUSTICE! TAKE ME DOWN!
DON'T HESITATE! DO IT!
DO IT!
HWIP-POK
YOU HEARD THE MAN, WARRIORS-- TAKE HIM DOWN--
--HARD!
IT'S NOT THAT EASY, JUSTICE-- HE'S TOO FAST!
FASTER THAN MY MICROWAVE BLASTS! HE'S NEVER IN ONE PLACE FOR MORE THAN A--
FASH

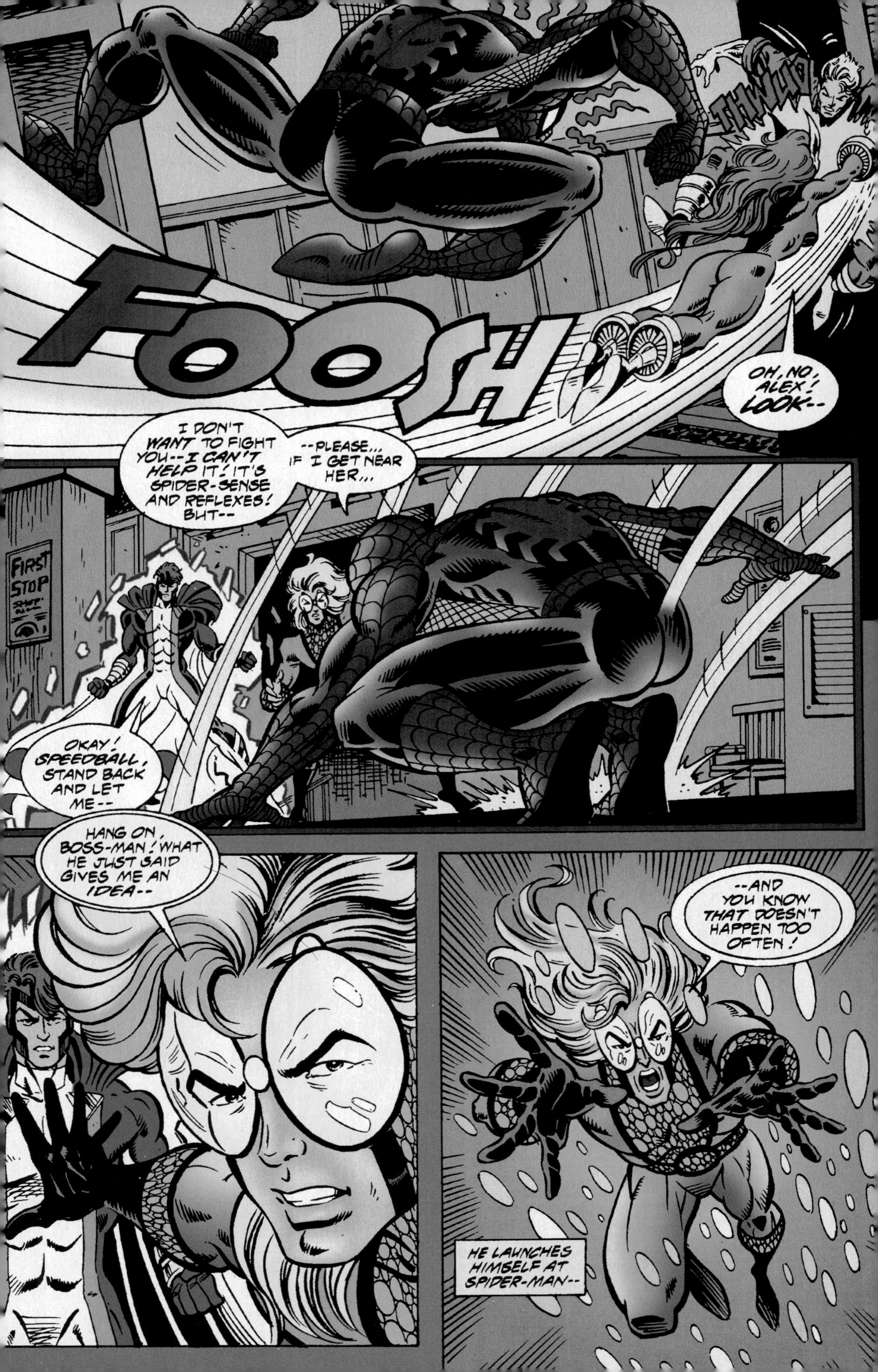
THWUD!
FOOSH
OH, NO! ALEX! LOOK--
I DON'T WANT TO FIGHT YOU--I CAN'T HELP IT! IT'S SPIDER-SENSE AND REFLEXES! BUT--
--PLEASE... IF I GET NEAR HER...
FIRST STOP
OKAY! SPEEDBALL, STAND BACK AND LET ME--
HANG ON, BOSS-MAN! WHAT HE JUST SAID GIVES ME AN IDEA--
--AND YOU KNOW THAT DOESN'T HAPPEN TOO OFTEN!
HE LAUNCHES HIMSELF AT SPIDER-MAN--

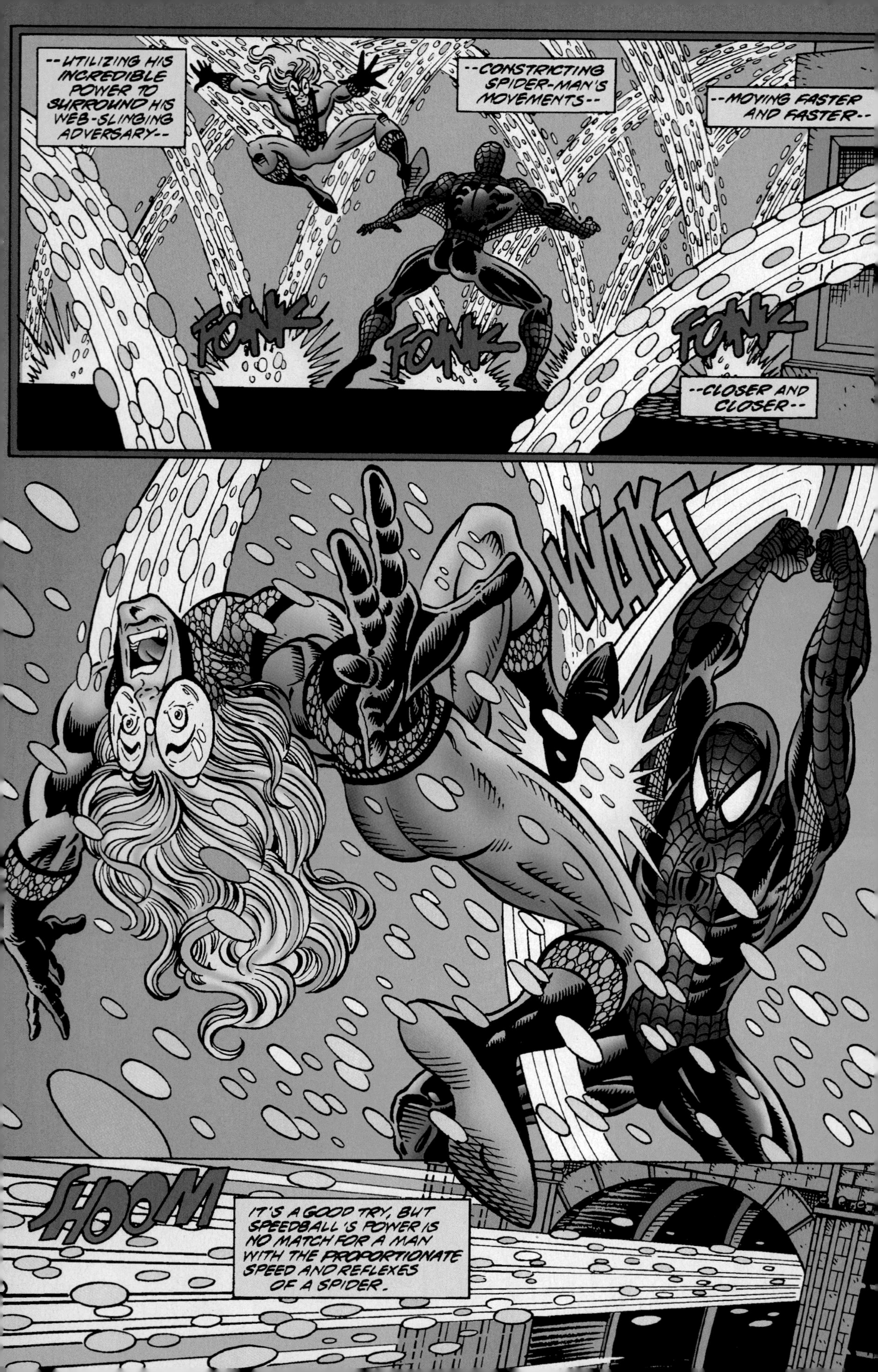
--UTILIZING HIS INCREDIBLE POWER TO SURROUND HIS WEB-SLINGING ADVERSARY--
--CONSTRICTING SPIDER-MAN'S MOVEMENTS--
--MOVING FASTER AND FASTER--
FONK
FONK
FONK
--CLOSER AND CLOSER--
WAKT
SHOOM
IT'S A GOOD TRY, BUT SPEEDBALL'S POWER IS NO MATCH FOR A MAN WITH THE PROPORTIONATE SPEED AND REFLEXES OF A SPIDER.

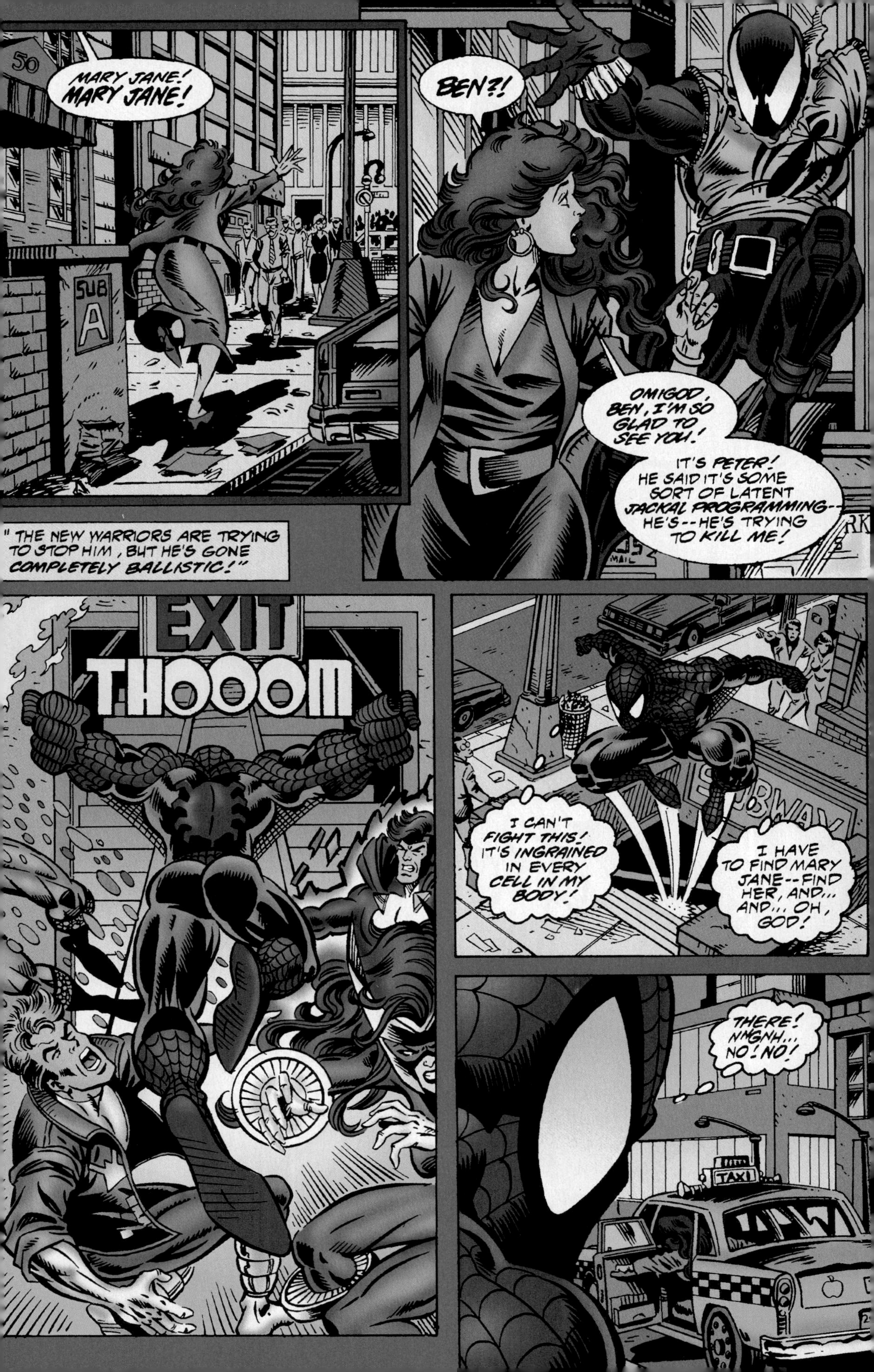
MARY JANE! MARY JANE!
BEN?!
OMIGOD, BEN, I'M SO GLAD TO SEE YOU!
IT'S PETER! HE SAID IT'S SOME SORT OF LATENT JACKAL PROGRAMMING-- HE'S--HE'S TRYING TO KILL ME!
"THE NEW WARRIORS ARE TRYING TO STOP HIM, BUT HE'S GONE COMPLETELY BALLISTIC!"
EXIT
THOOOM
I CAN'T FIGHT THIS! IT'S INGRAINED IN EVERY CELL IN MY BODY!
I HAVE TO FIND MARY JANE--FIND HER, AND... AND... OH, GOD!
THERE! NNGNH... NO! NO!
TAXI

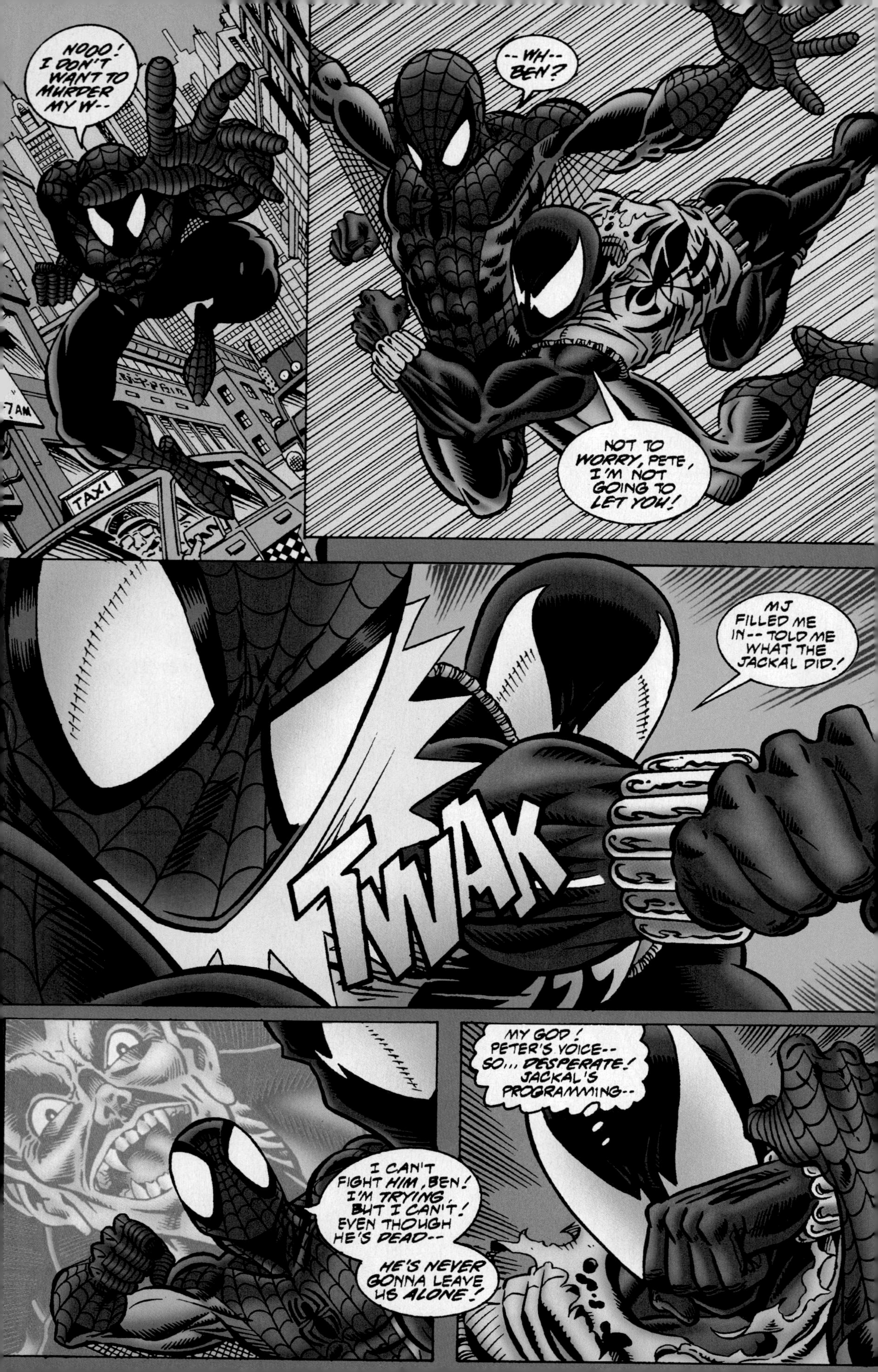
NOOO! I DON'T WANT TO MURDER MY W--
TAXI
7AM
--WH-- BEN?
NOT TO WORRY, PETE, I'M NOT GOING TO LET YOU!
MJ FILLED ME IN-- TOLD ME WHAT THE JACKAL DID!
TWAK
I CAN'T FIGHT HIM, BEN! I'M TRYING, BUT I CAN'T! EVEN THOUGH HE'S DEAD--
HE'S NEVER GONNA LEAVE US ALONE!
MY GOD! PETER'S VOICE-- SO... DESPERATE! JACKAL'S PROGRAMMING--

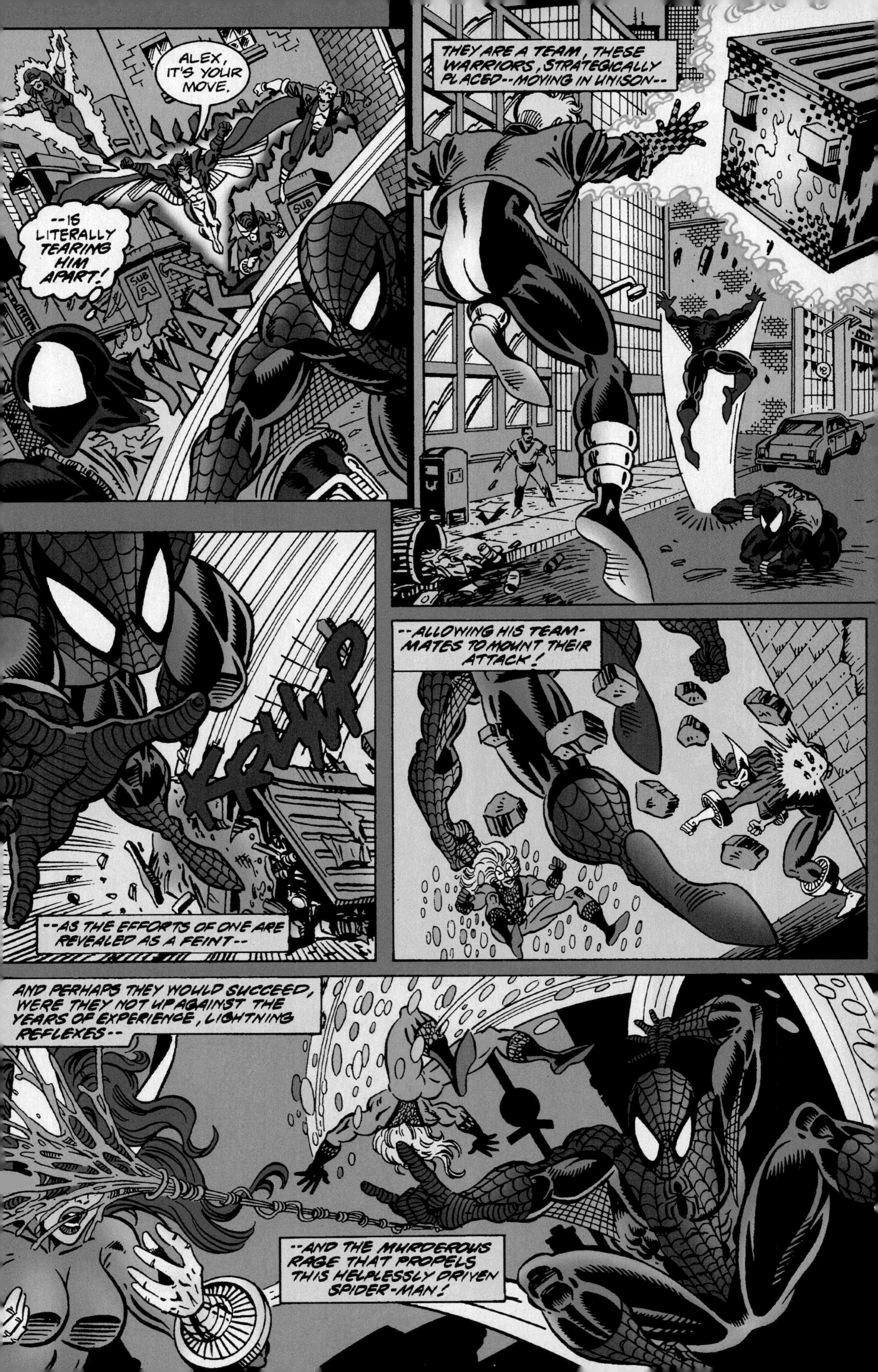
ALEX, IT'S YOUR MOVE.
--IS LITERALLY TEARING HIM APART!
THEY ARE A TEAM, THESE WARRIORS, STRATEGICALLY PLACED--MOVING IN UNISON--
--AS THE EFFORTS OF ONE ARE REVEALED AS A FEINT--
--ALLOWING HIS TEAM-MATES TO MOUNT THEIR ATTACK!
AND PERHAPS THEY WOULD SUCCEED, WERE THEY NOT UP AGAINST THE YEARS OF EXPERIENCE, LIGHTNING REFLEXES--
--AND THE MURDEROUS RAGE THAT PROPELS THIS HELPLESSLY DRIVEN SPIDER-MAN!

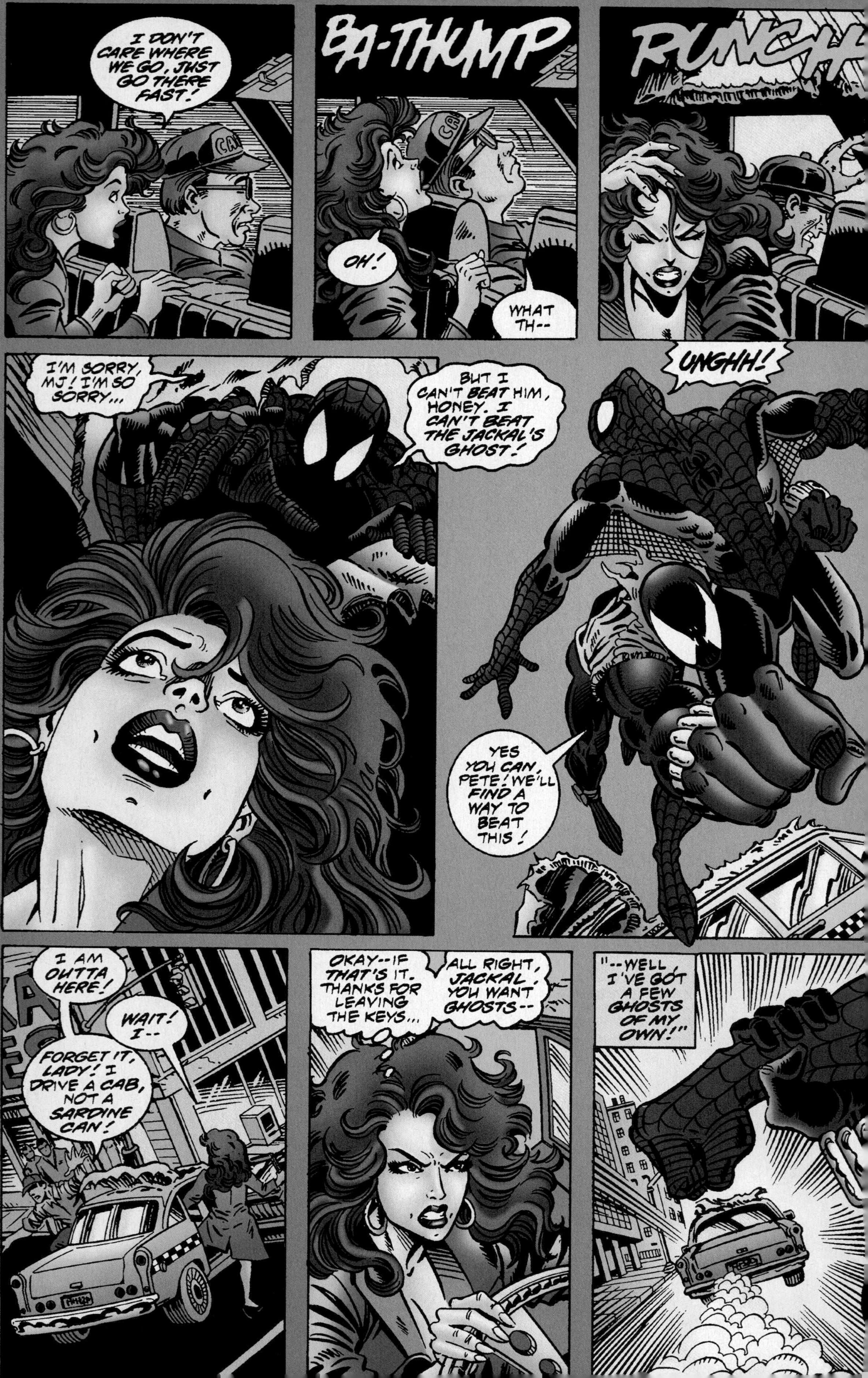
I DON'T CARE WHERE WE GO, JUST GO THERE FAST!
BA-THUMP
OH!
WHAT TH--
RUNCH
UNGHH!
I'M SORRY, MJ! I'M SO SORRY...
BUT I CAN'T BEAT HIM, HONEY. I CAN'T BEAT THE JACKAL'S GHOST!
YES YOU CAN, PETE! WE'LL FIND A WAY TO BEAT THIS!
I AM OUTTA HERE!
WAIT! I--
FORGET IT, LADY! I DRIVE A CAB, NOT A SARDINE CAN!
OKAY--IF THAT'S IT. THANKS FOR LEAVING THE KEYS...
ALL RIGHT, JACKAL. YOU WANT GHOSTS--
"--WELL, I'VE GOT A FEW GHOSTS OF MY OWN!"

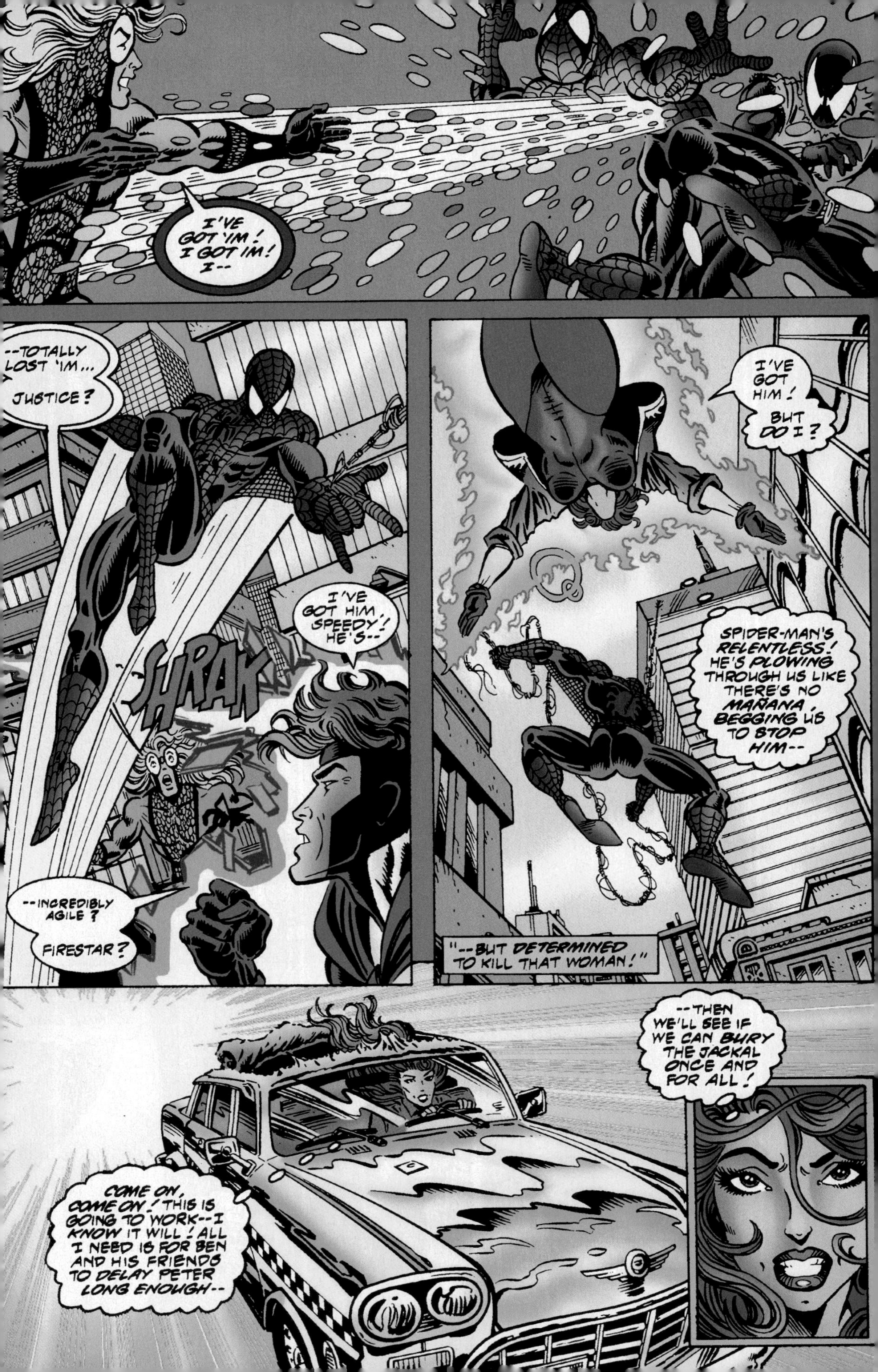
I'VE GOT 'IM! I GOT IM! I--
--TOTALLY LOST 'IM...
JUSTICE?
I'VE GOT HIM SPEEDY! HE'S--
SHRAK
--INCREDIBLY AGILE?
FIRESTAR?
I'VE GOT HIM! BUT DO I?
SPIDER-MAN'S RELENTLESS! HE'S PLOWING THROUGH US LIKE THERE'S NO MAÑANA, BEGGING US TO STOP HIM--
"--BUT DETERMINED TO KILL THAT WOMAN!"
COME ON, COME ON! THIS IS GOING TO WORK--I KNOW IT WILL! ALL I NEED IS FOR BEN AND HIS FRIENDS TO DELAY PETER LONG ENOUGH--
--THEN WE'LL SEE IF WE CAN BURY THE JACKAL ONCE AND FOR ALL!

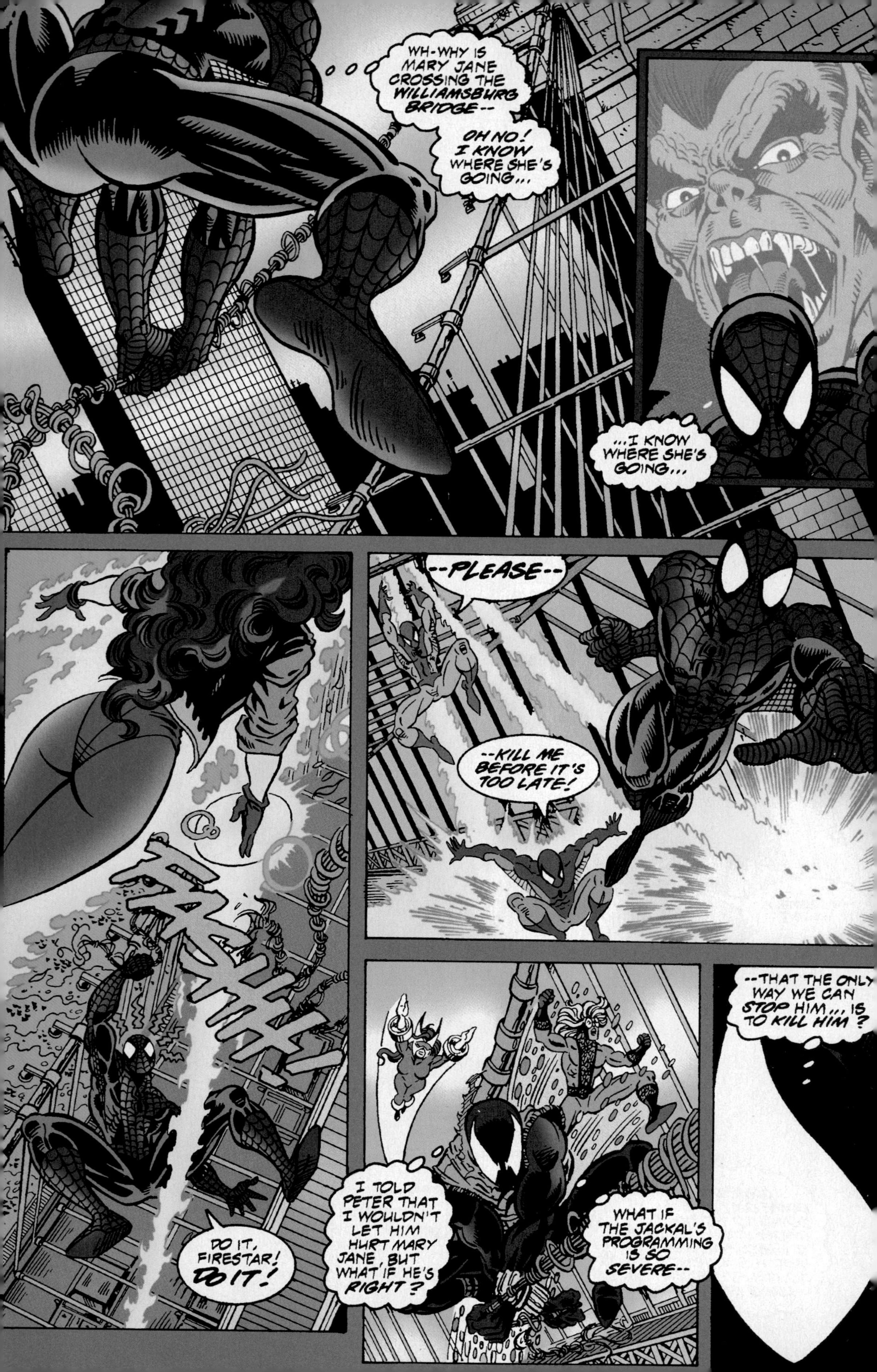
WH-WHY IS MARY JANE CROSSING THE WILLIAMSBURG BRIDGE--
OH NO! I KNOW WHERE SHE'S GOING...
...I KNOW WHERE SHE'S GOING...
--PLEASE--
--KILL ME BEFORE IT'S TOO LATE!
DO IT, FIRESTAR! DO IT!
I TOLD PETER THAT I WOULDN'T LET HIM HURT MARY JANE, BUT WHAT IF HE'S RIGHT?
WHAT IF THE JACKAL'S PROGRAMMING IS SO SEVERE--
--THAT THE ONLY WAY WE CAN STOP HIM... IS TO KILL HIM?

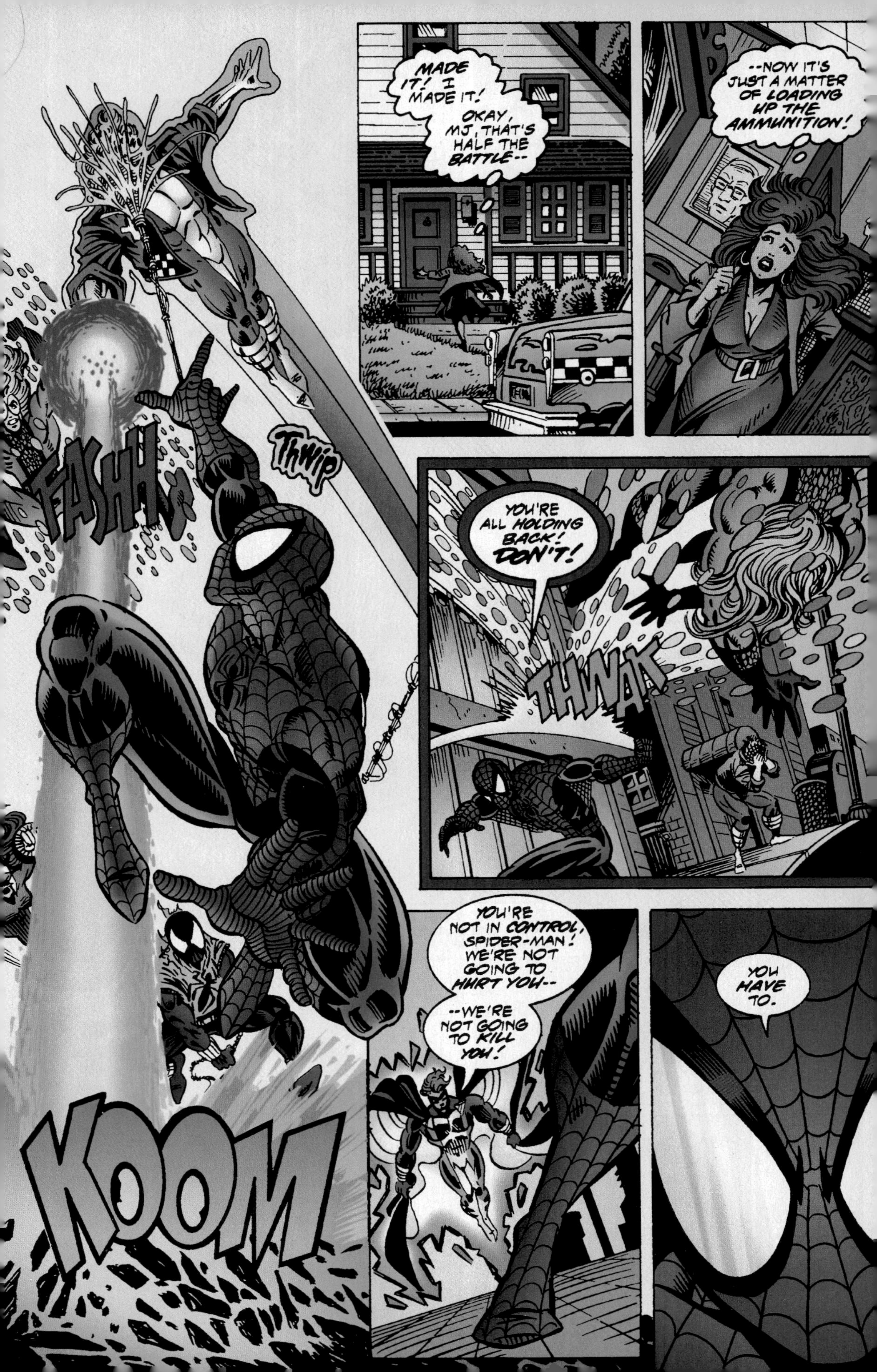
FASHH
THWIP
KOOM
MADE IT! I MADE IT!
OKAY, MJ, THAT'S HALF THE BATTLE--
--NOW IT'S JUST A MATTER OF LOADING UP THE AMMUNITION!
YOU'RE ALL HOLDING BACK! DON'T!
THWAK
YOU'RE NOT IN CONTROL, SPIDER-MAN! WE'RE NOT GOING TO HURT YOU--
--WE'RE NOT GOING TO KILL YOU!
YOU HAVE TO.

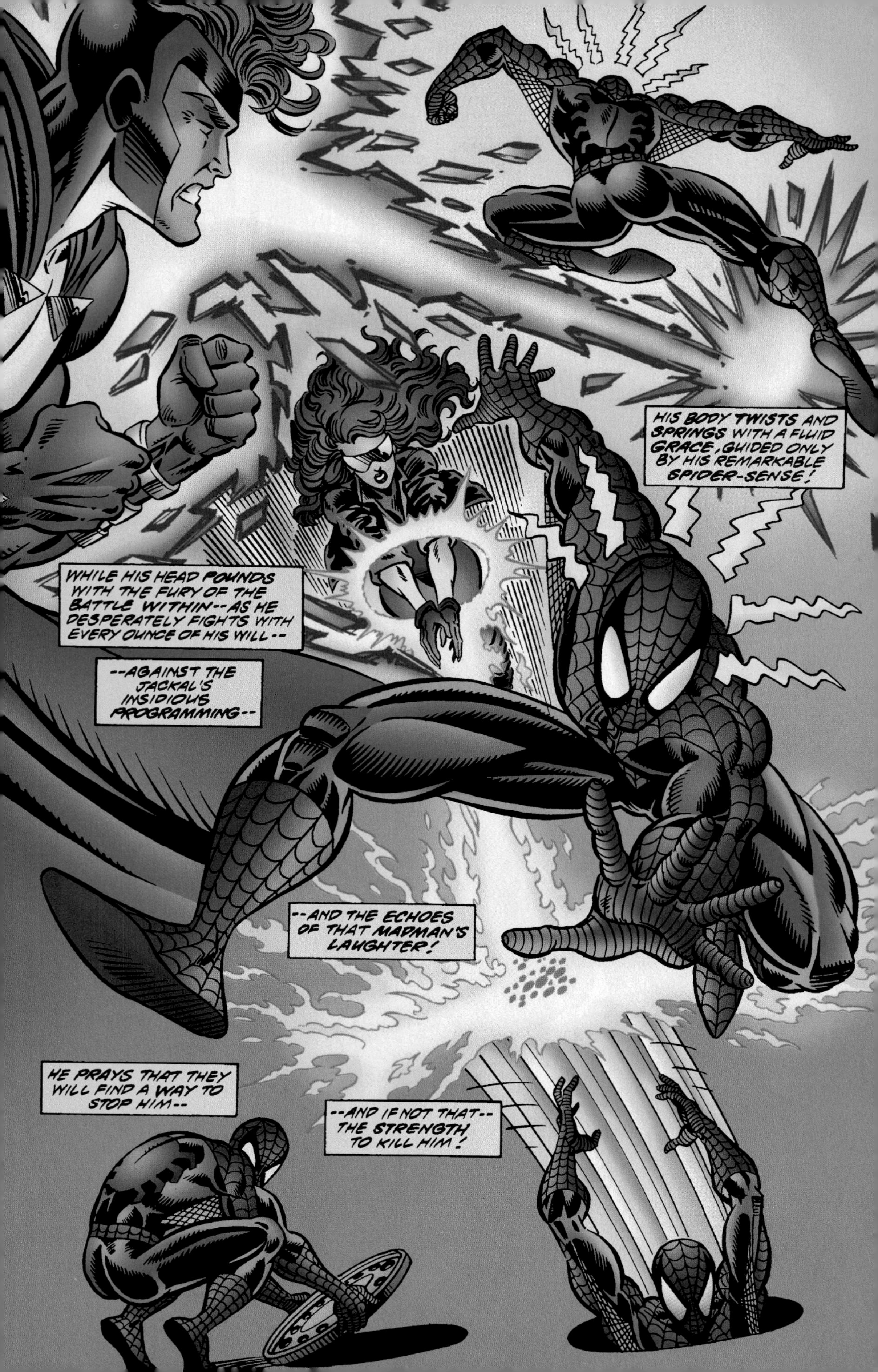
HIS BODY TWISTS AND SPRINGS WITH A FLUID GRACE, GUIDED ONLY BY HIS REMARKABLE SPIDER-SENSE!
WHILE HIS HEAD POUNDS WITH THE FURY OF THE BATTLE WITHIN--AS HE DESPERATELY FIGHTS WITH EVERY OUNCE OF HIS WILL--
--AGAINST THE JACKAL'S INSIDIOUS PROGRAMMING--
--AND THE ECHOES OF THAT MADMAN'S LAUGHTER!
HE PRAYS THAT THEY WILL FIND A WAY TO STOP HIM--
--AND IF NOT THAT--THE STRENGTH TO KILL HIM!

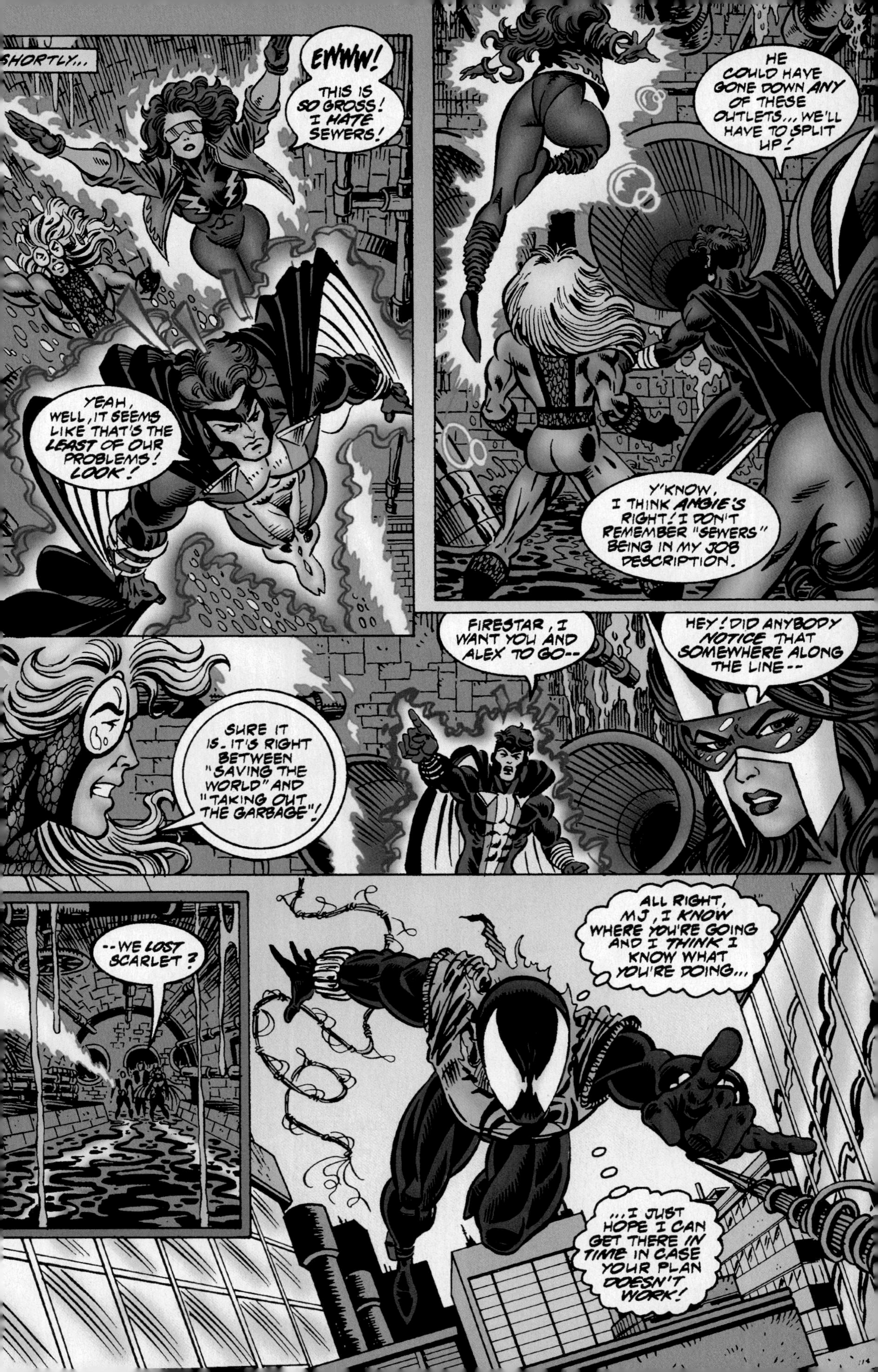
SHORTLY...
EWWW!
THIS IS SO GROSS! I HATE SEWERS!
YEAH, WELL, IT SEEMS LIKE THAT'S THE LEAST OF OUR PROBLEMS! LOOK!
HE COULD HAVE GONE DOWN ANY OF THESE OUTLETS... WE'LL HAVE TO SPLIT UP!
Y'KNOW, I THINK ANGIE'S RIGHT! I DON'T REMEMBER "SEWERS" BEING IN MY JOB DESCRIPTION.
SURE IT IS. IT'S RIGHT BETWEEN "SAVING THE WORLD" AND "TAKING OUT THE GARBAGE"!
FIRESTAR, I WANT YOU AND ALEX TO GO--
HEY! DID ANYBODY NOTICE THAT SOMEWHERE ALONG THE LINE--
--WE LOST SCARLET?
ALL RIGHT, MJ, I KNOW WHERE YOU'RE GOING AND I THINK I KNOW WHAT YOU'RE DOING...
...I JUST HOPE I CAN GET THERE IN TIME IN CASE YOUR PLAN DOESN'T WORK!

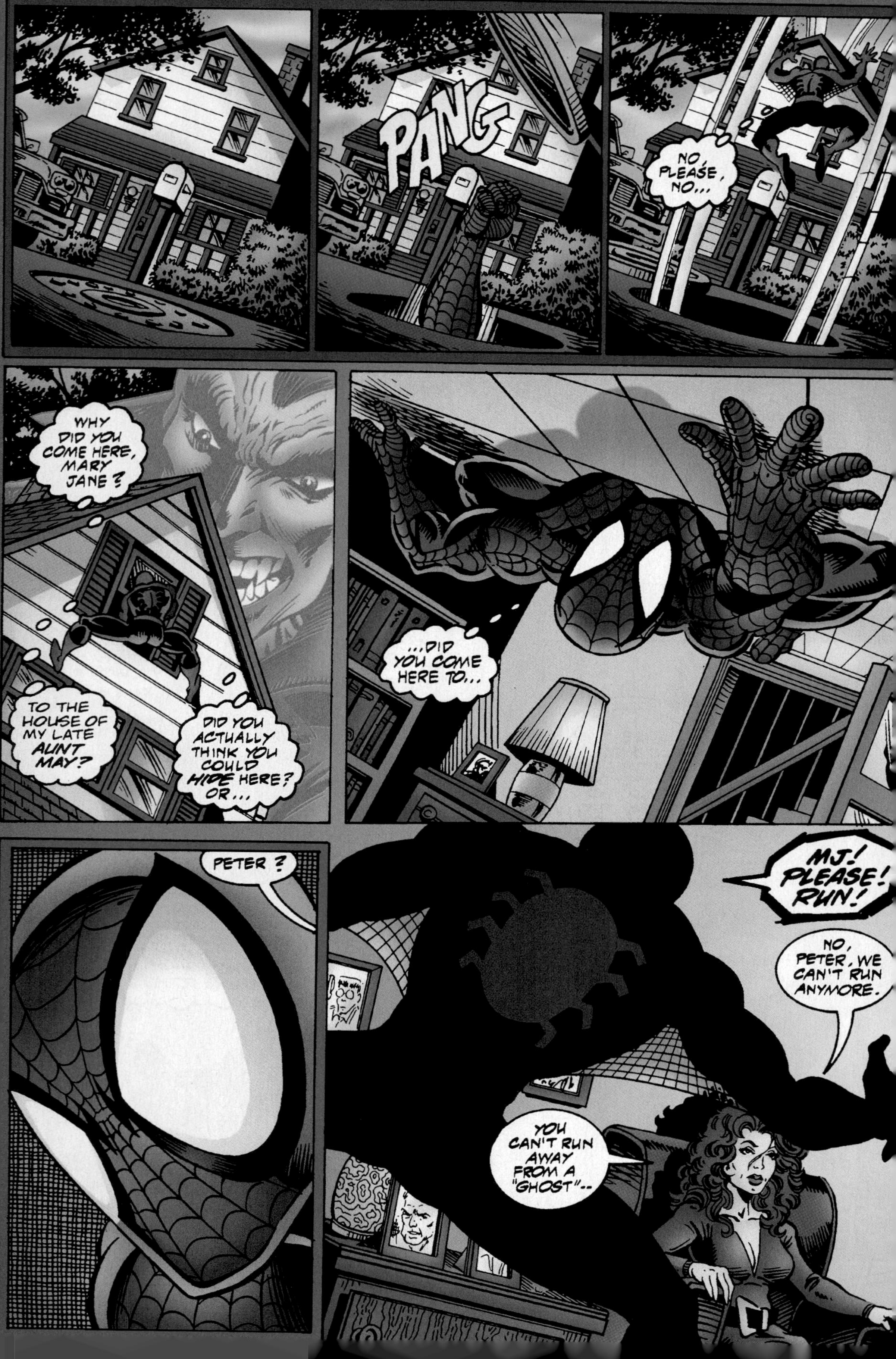
PANG
NO, PLEASE, NO...
WHY DID YOU COME HERE, MARY JANE?
TO THE HOUSE OF MY LATE AUNT MAY?
DID YOU ACTUALLY THINK YOU COULD HIDE HERE? OR...
...DID YOU COME HERE TO...
PETER?
MJ! PLEASE! RUN!
NO, PETER, WE CAN'T RUN ANYMORE.
YOU CAN'T RUN AWAY FROM A "GHOST"..

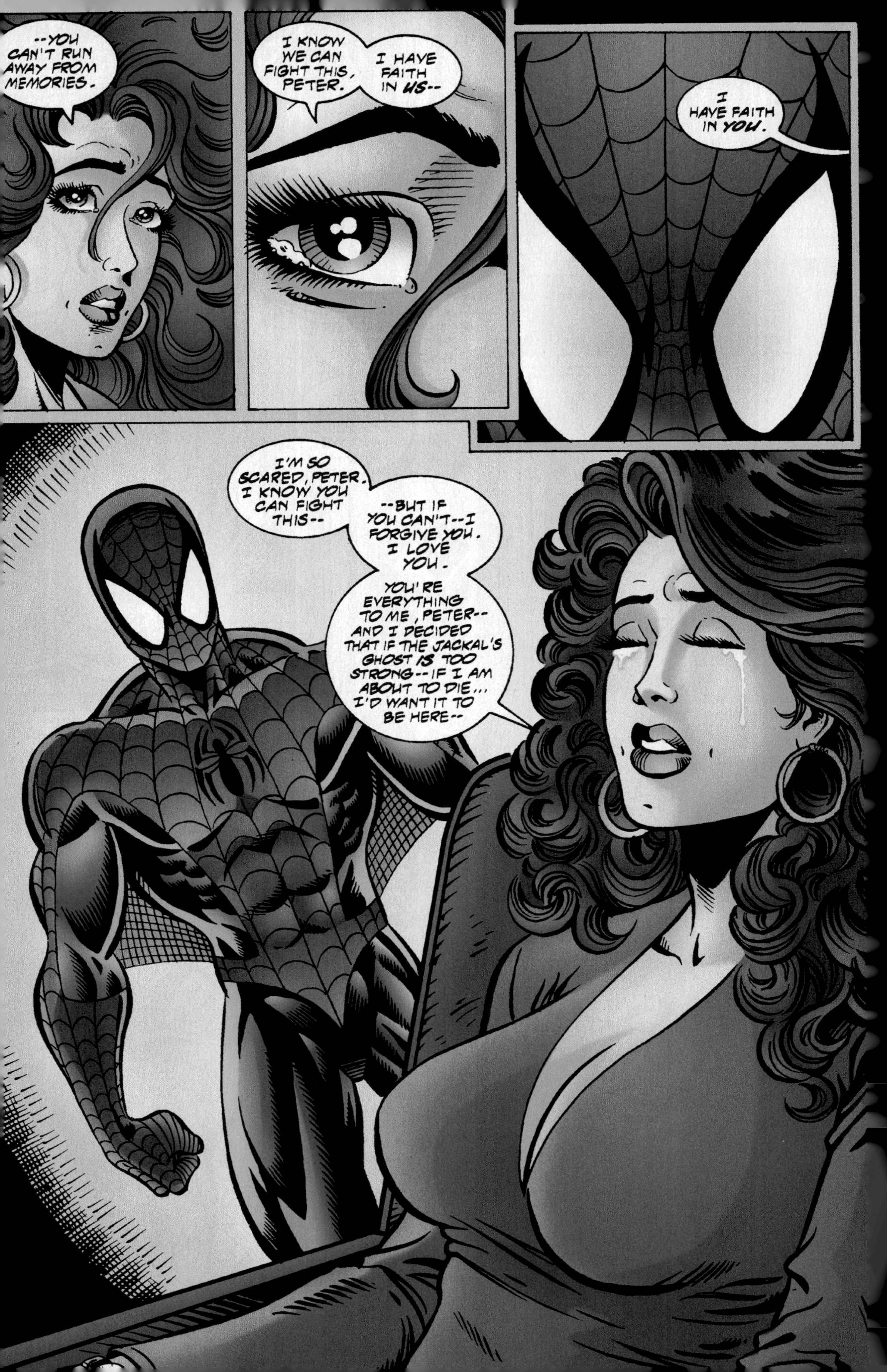
--YOU CAN'T RUN AWAY FROM MEMORIES.
I KNOW WE CAN FIGHT THIS, PETER.
I HAVE FAITH IN US--
I HAVE FAITH IN YOU.
I'M SO SCARED, PETER. I KNOW YOU CAN FIGHT THIS--
--BUT IF YOU CAN'T--I FORGIVE YOU. I LOVE YOU.
YOU'RE EVERYTHING TO ME, PETER--AND I DECIDED THAT IF THE JACKAL'S GHOST IS TOO STRONG--IF I AM ABOUT TO DIE... I'D WANT IT TO BE HERE--

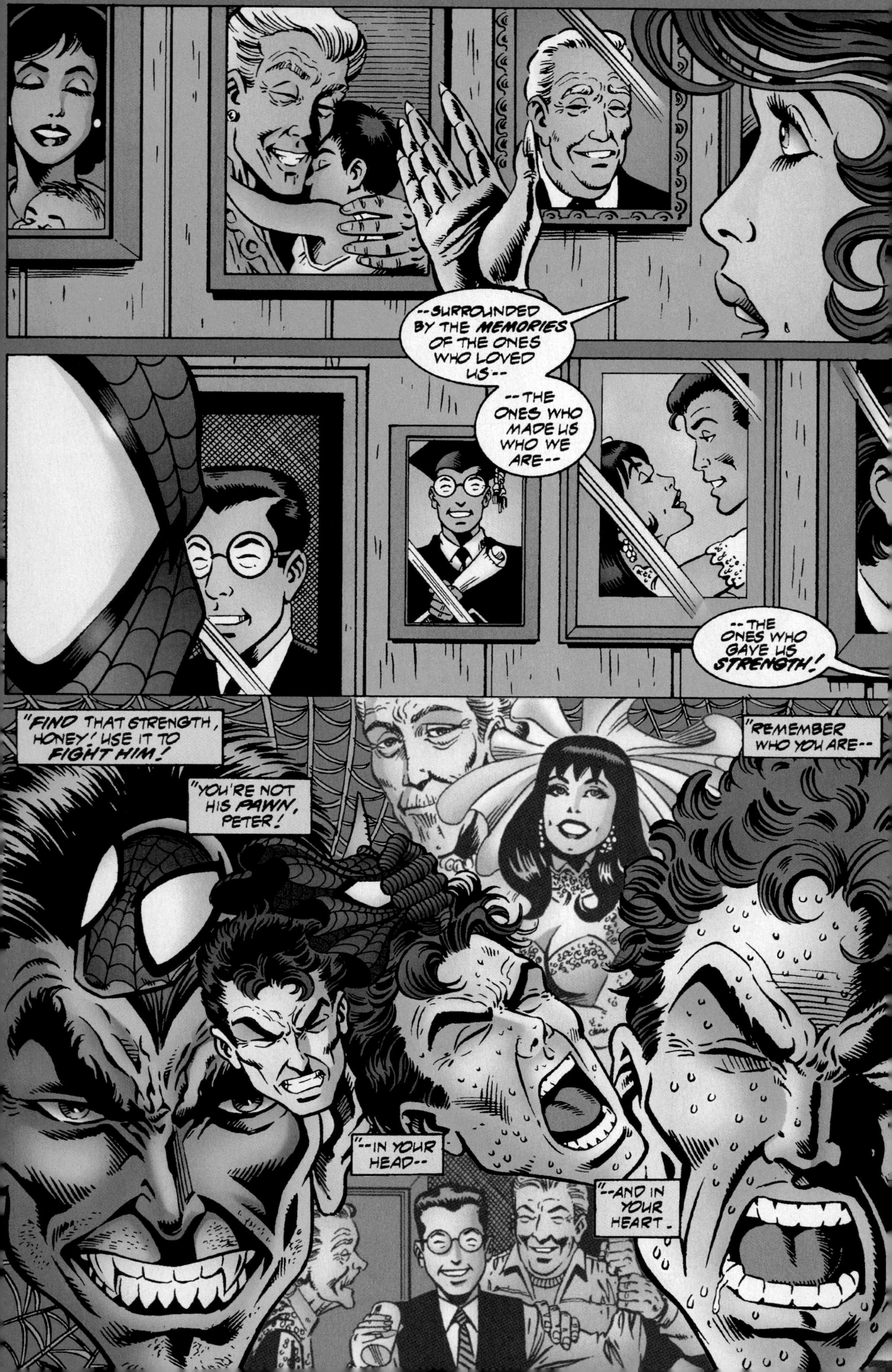

--SURROUNDED BY THE MEMORIES OF THE ONES WHO LOVED US--
--THE ONES WHO MADE US WHO WE ARE--
--THE ONES WHO GAVE US STRENGTH!
"FIND THAT STRENGTH, HONEY! USE IT TO FIGHT HIM!
"YOU'RE NOT HIS PAWN, PETER!
"REMEMBER WHO YOU ARE--
"--IN YOUR HEAD--
"--AND IN YOUR HEART.

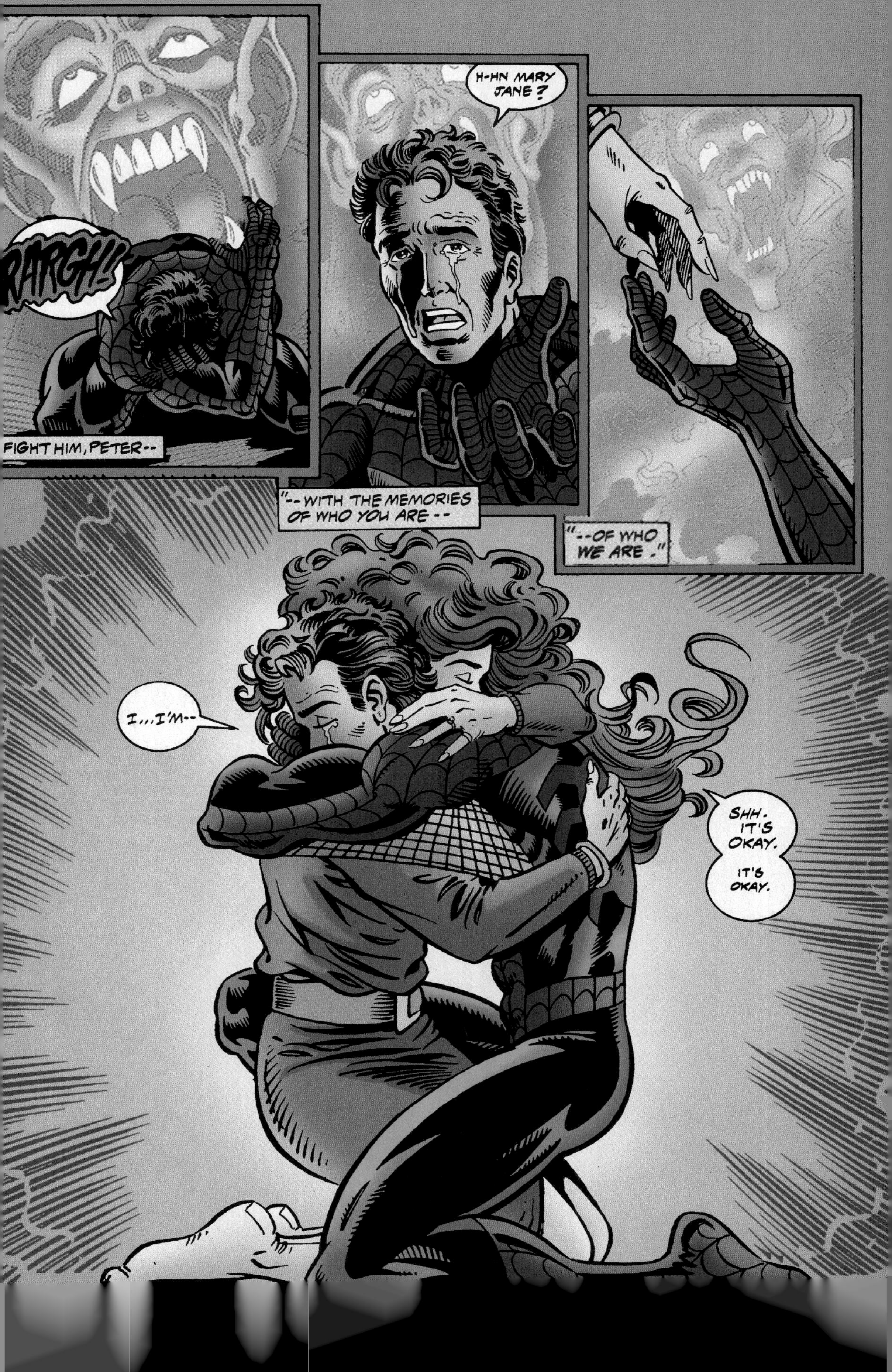
RARGH!!
FIGHT HIM, PETER--
H-HN MARY JANE?
"--WITH THE MEMORIES OF WHO YOU ARE--
"--OF WHO WE ARE."
I...I'M--
SHH. IT'S OKAY.
IT'S OKAY.

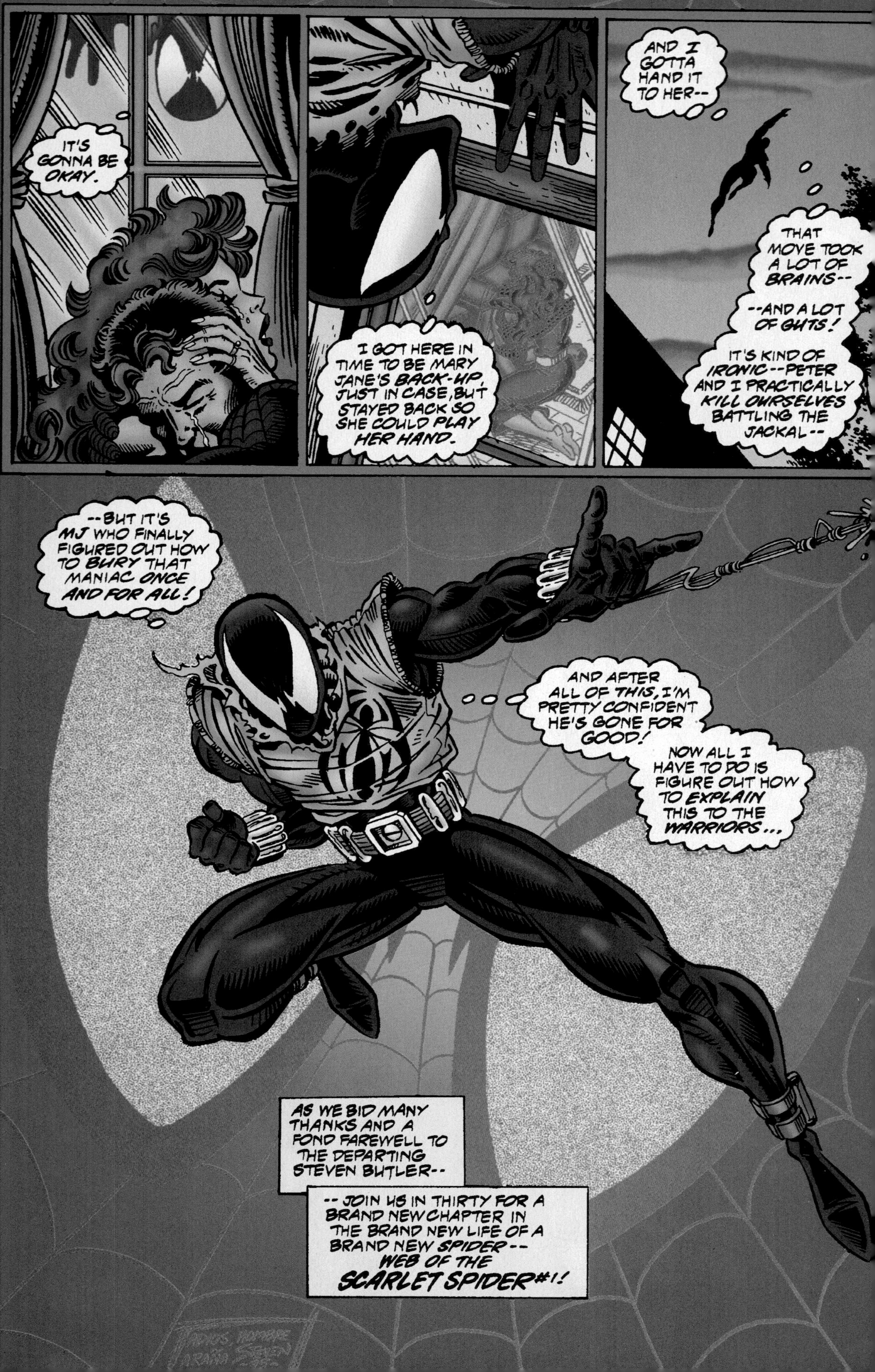
IT'S GONNA BE OKAY.
I GOT HERE IN TIME TO BE MARY JANE'S BACK-UP, JUST IN CASE, BUT STAYED BACK SO SHE COULD PLAY HER HAND.
AND I GOTTA HAND IT TO HER--
THAT MOVE TOOK A LOT OF BRAINS--
--AND A LOT OF GUTS!
IT'S KIND OF IRONIC--PETER AND I PRACTICALLY KILL OURSELVES BATTLING THE JACKAL--
--BUT IT'S MJ WHO FINALLY FIGURED OUT HOW TO BURY THAT MANIAC ONCE AND FOR ALL!
AND AFTER ALL OF THIS, I'M PRETTY CONFIDENT HE'S GONE FOR GOOD!
NOW ALL I HAVE TO DO IS FIGURE OUT HOW TO EXPLAIN THIS TO THE WARRIORS...
AS WE BID MANY THANKS AND A FOND FAREWELL TO THE DEPARTING STEVEN BUTLER--
--JOIN US IN THIRTY FOR A BRAND NEW CHAPTER IN THE BRAND NEW LIFE OF A BRAND NEW SPIDER-- WEB OF THE SCARLET SPIDER #1!

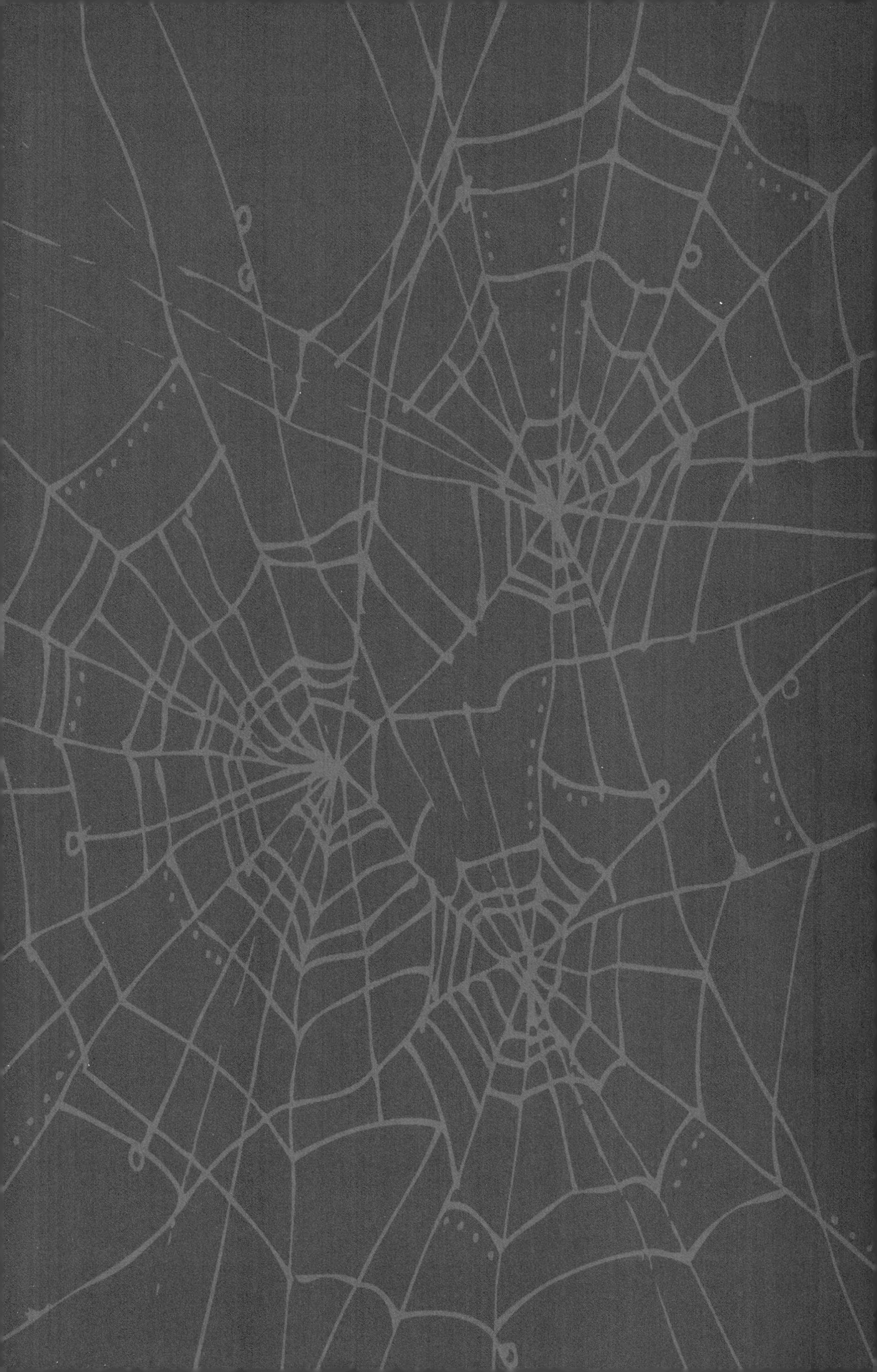

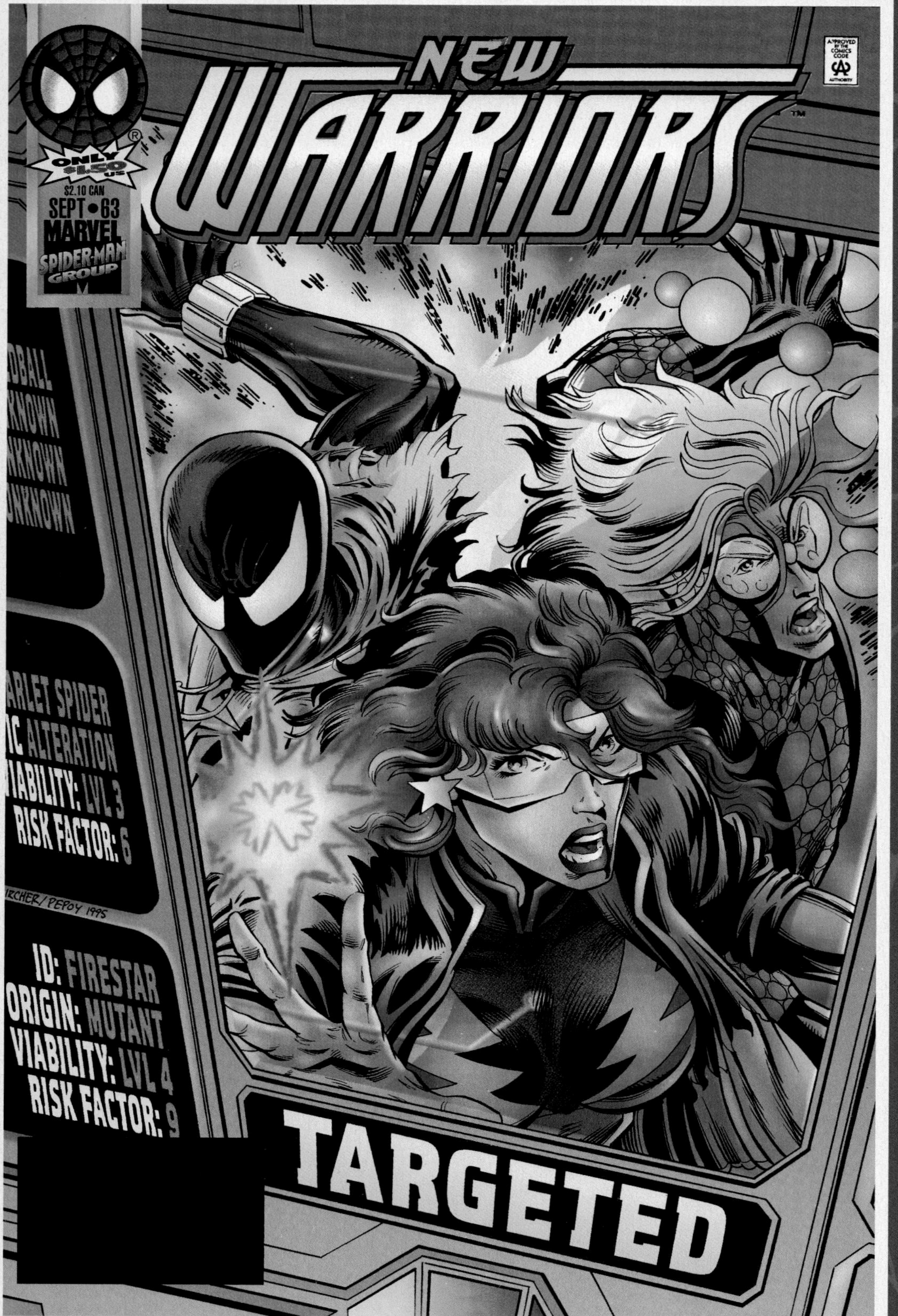

NEW WARRIORS
ONLY $1.50 US
$2.10 CAN
SEPT • 63
MARVEL
SPIDER-MAN GROUP
APPROVED BY THE COMICS CODE AUTHORITY
RISK FACTOR: 6
ID: FIRESTAR
ORIGIN: MUTANT
VIABILITY: LVL 4
RISK FACTOR: 9
TARGETED

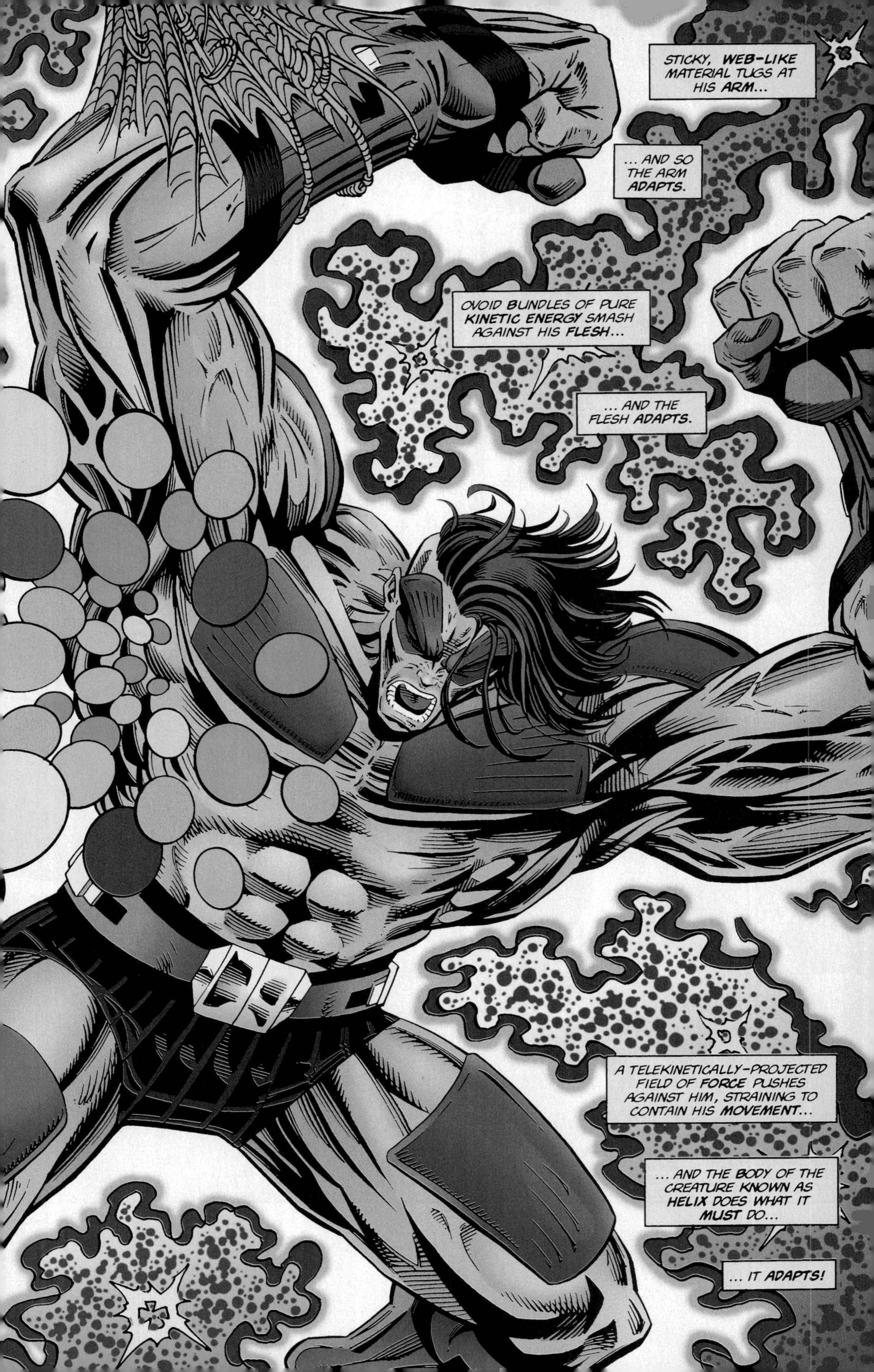
STICKY, WEB-LIKE MATERIAL TUGS AT HIS ARM...
... AND SO THE ARM ADAPTS.
OVOID BUNDLES OF PURE KINETIC ENERGY SMASH AGAINST HIS FLESH...
... AND THE FLESH ADAPTS.
A TELEKINETICALLY-PROJECTED FIELD OF FORCE PUSHES AGAINST HIM, STRAINING TO CONTAIN HIS MOVEMENT...
... AND THE BODY OF THE CREATURE KNOWN AS HELIX DOES WHAT IT MUST DO...
... IT ADAPTS!

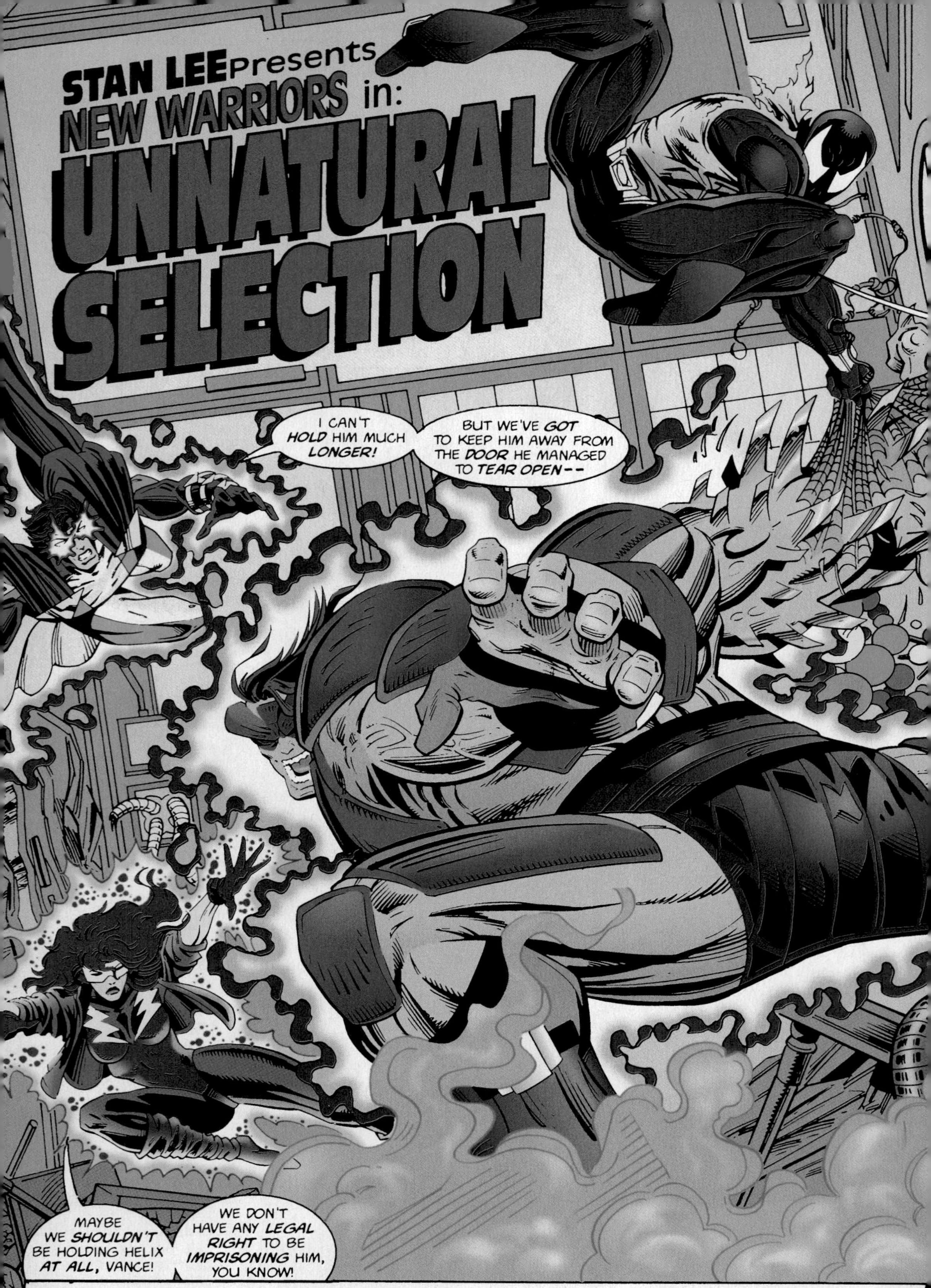
STAN LEE Presents
NEW WARRIORS in:
UNNATURAL SELECTION
I CAN'T HOLD HIM MUCH LONGER!
BUT WE'VE GOT TO KEEP HIM AWAY FROM THE DOOR HE MANAGED TO TEAR OPEN--
MAYBE WE SHOULDN'T BE HOLDING HELIX AT ALL, VANCE!
WE DON'T HAVE ANY LEGAL RIGHT TO BE IMPRISONING HIM, YOU KNOW!

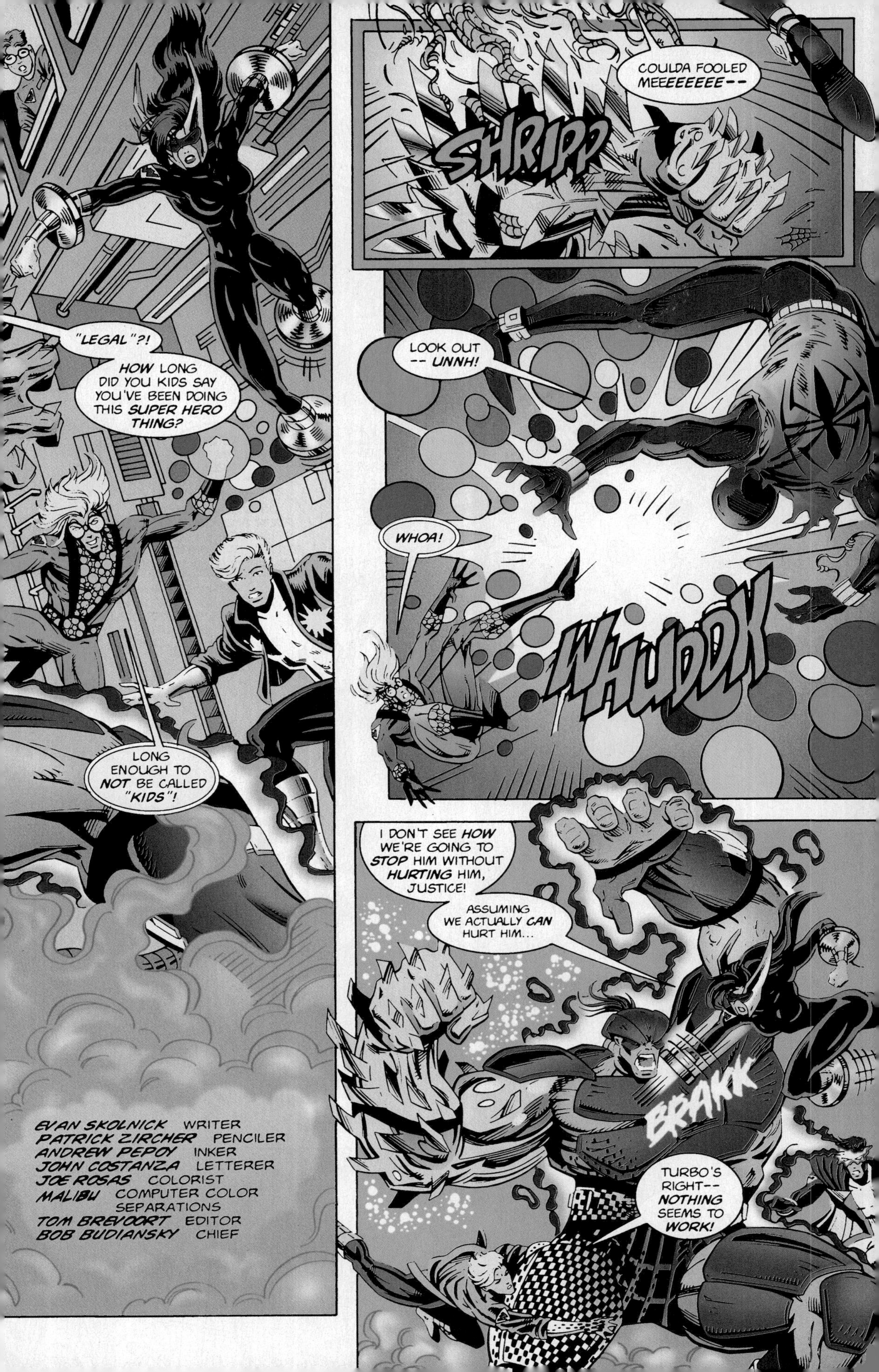

"LEGAL"?!
HOW LONG DID YOU KIDS SAY YOU'VE BEEN DOING THIS SUPER HERO THING?
LONG ENOUGH TO NOT BE CALLED "KIDS"!
EVAN SKOLNICK WRITER
PATRICK ZIRCHER PENCILER
ANDREW PEPOY INKER
JOHN COSTANZA LETTERER
JOE ROSAS COLORIST
MALIBU COMPUTER COLOR SEPARATIONS
TOM BREVOORT EDITOR
BOB BUDIANSKY CHIEF
COULDA FOOLED MEEEEEEE--
SHRIPP
LOOK OUT -- UNNH!
WHOA!
WHUDDK
I DON'T SEE HOW WE'RE GOING TO STOP HIM WITHOUT HURTING HIM, JUSTICE!
ASSUMING WE ACTUALLY CAN HURT HIM...
BRAKK
TURBO'S RIGHT-- NOTHING SEEMS TO WORK!

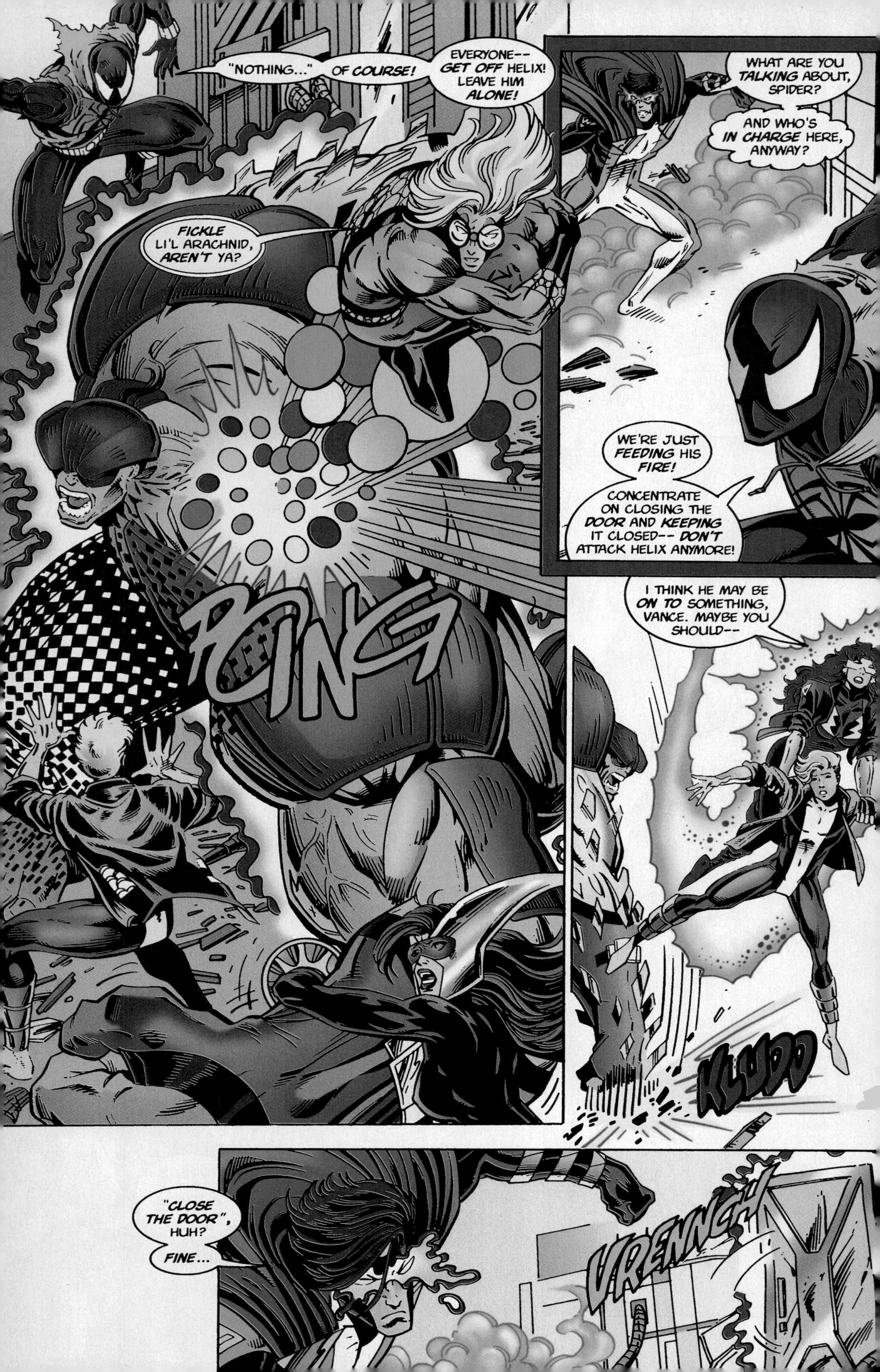

"NOTHING..." OF COURSE!
EVERYONE-- GET OFF HELIX! LEAVE HIM ALONE!
FICKLE LI'L ARACHNID, AREN'T YA?
PING
WHAT ARE YOU TALKING ABOUT, SPIDER?
AND WHO'S IN CHARGE HERE, ANYWAY?
WE'RE JUST FEEDING HIS FIRE!
CONCENTRATE ON CLOSING THE DOOR AND KEEPING IT CLOSED-- DON'T ATTACK HELIX ANYMORE!
I THINK HE MAY BE ON TO SOMETHING, VANCE. MAYBE YOU SHOULD--
KLUDD
"CLOSE THE DOOR", HUH?
FINE...
VRENNCH

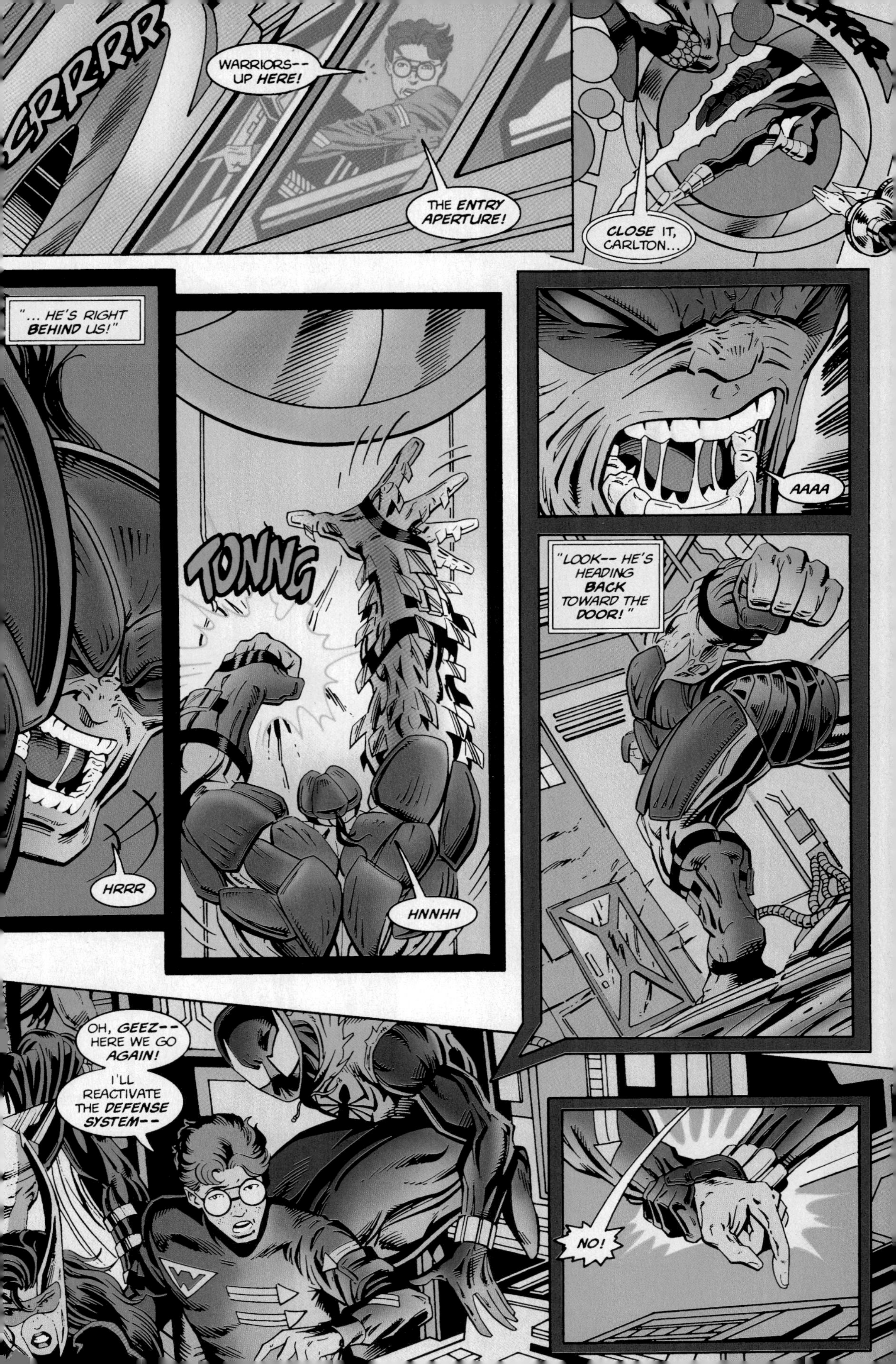
SCRRRR
WARRIORS-- UP HERE!
THE ENTRY APERTURE!
CLOSE IT, CARLTON...
"... HE'S RIGHT BEHIND US!"
HRRR
TONNG
HNNHH
AAAA
"LOOK-- HE'S HEADING BACK TOWARD THE DOOR!"
OH, GEEZ-- HERE WE GO AGAIN!
I'LL REACTIVATE THE DEFENSE SYSTEM--
NO!

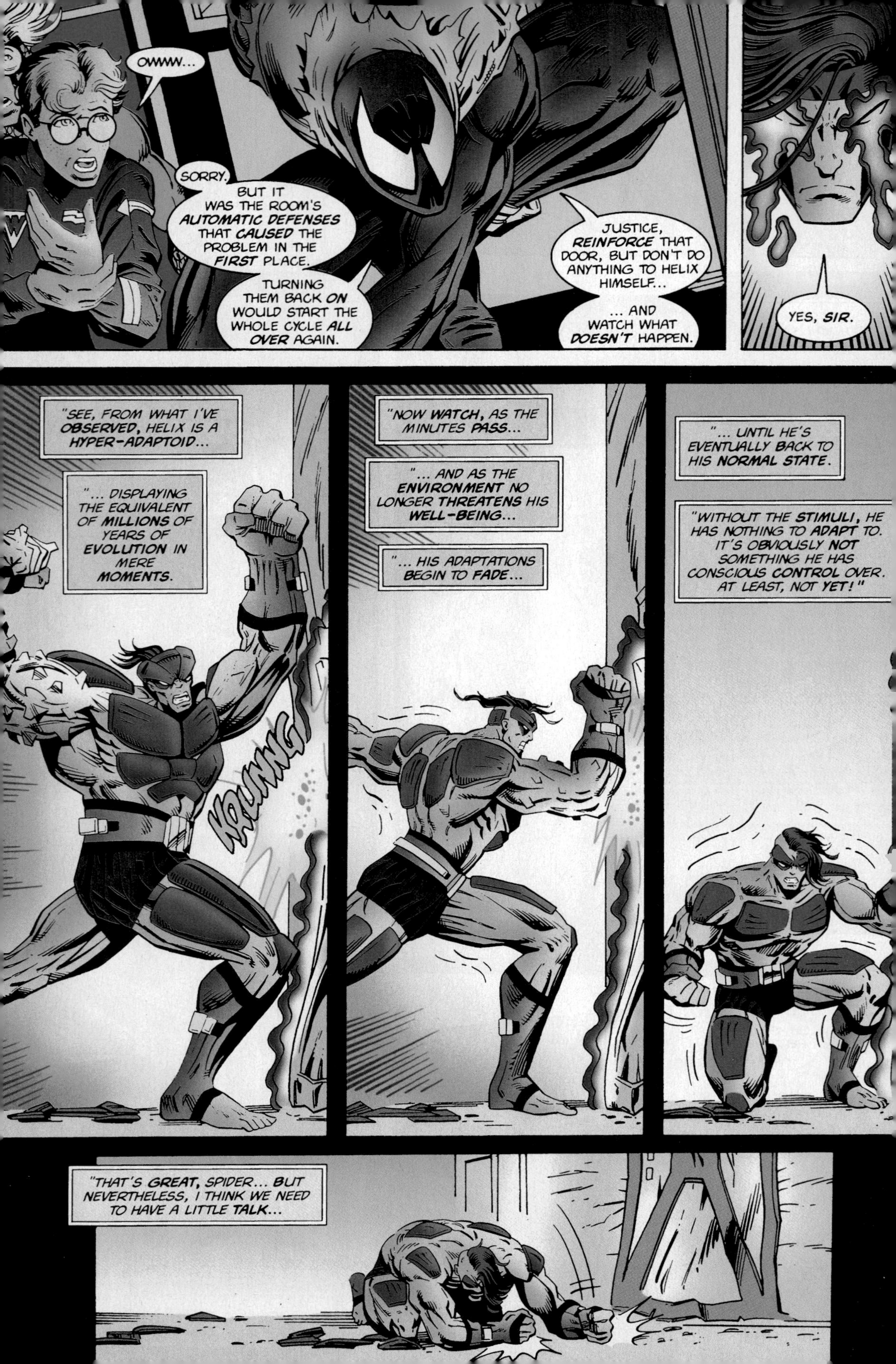
OWWW...
SORRY.
BUT IT WAS THE ROOM'S AUTOMATIC DEFENSES THAT CAUSED THE PROBLEM IN THE FIRST PLACE.
TURNING THEM BACK ON WOULD START THE WHOLE CYCLE ALL OVER AGAIN.
JUSTICE, REINFORCE THAT DOOR, BUT DON'T DO ANYTHING TO HELIX HIMSELF...
... AND WATCH WHAT DOESN'T HAPPEN.
YES, SIR.
"SEE, FROM WHAT I'VE OBSERVED, HELIX IS A HYPER-ADAPTOID...
"... DISPLAYING THE EQUIVALENT OF MILLIONS OF YEARS OF EVOLUTION IN MERE MOMENTS.
KRUNNG
"NOW WATCH, AS THE MINUTES PASS...
"... AND AS THE ENVIRONMENT NO LONGER THREATENS HIS WELL-BEING...
"... HIS ADAPTATIONS BEGIN TO FADE...
"... UNTIL HE'S EVENTUALLY BACK TO HIS NORMAL STATE.
"WITHOUT THE STIMULI, HE HAS NOTHING TO ADAPT TO. IT'S OBVIOUSLY NOT SOMETHING HE HAS CONSCIOUS CONTROL OVER. AT LEAST, NOT YET!"
"THAT'S GREAT, SPIDER... BUT NEVERTHELESS, I THINK WE NEED TO HAVE A LITTLE TALK...

-- SO **NEXT** TIME, I'D APPRECIATE YOUR **NOT** SUDDENLY **TAKING CONTROL** OF THE SITUATION WITHOUT AT LEAST RUNNING THE PLAN BY **ME** FIRST.

YOU'RE ON A **TEAM NOW***, AND WE NEED YOU TO BE A **TEAM PLAYER.**

STILL, IT'S A GOOD THING YOU FIGURED IT **OUT.** DO YOU HAVE A **SCIENTIFIC** BACKGROUND?

I **UNDERSTAND**, JUSTICE... AND I'M **SORRY.** I DIDN'T MEAN TO **UNDERMINE** YOUR AUTHORITY.

BUT IF WE HAD **KEPT FIGHTING** FELIX, HE WOULD HAVE SOON EVOLVED TO THE POINT THAT HE BECAME TOO MUCH FOR **ALL** OF US...

... AND HE WOULD HAVE **GOTTEN AWAY.**

I'M NOT SAYING YOU DID THE **WRONG** THING, SPIDER... JUST THE WRONG **WAY.**

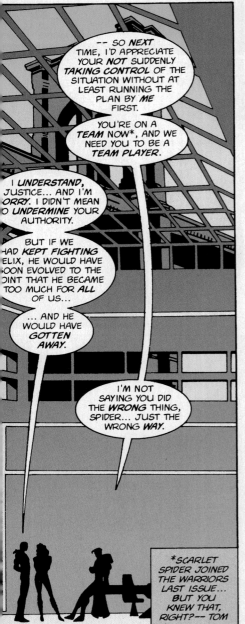

*SCARLET SPIDER JOINED THE WARRIORS LAST ISSUE... BUT YOU **KNEW** THAT, RIGHT?-- TOM

FRESH, GORGEOUS, FULL OF **LIFE...**

... AH, ANGEL, YOU REMIND ME OF **ANOTHER** YOUNG RED-HEAD I ONCE KNEW...

... A **LIFETIME** AGO.

I... I'VE BEEN KNOWN TO DABBLE **HERE** AND **THERE,** FIRESTAR.

WHERE, EXACTLY? YOU KNOW, YOU'VE BEEN ON THE TEAM FOR ALMOST A **WEEK** NOW, AND YOU **STILL** HAVEN'T EVEN SHOWN US YOUR **FACE,** OR TOLD US YOUR **REAL** NAME.

WE'RE NOT BIG INTO **SECRETS** AROUND HERE, "SCARLET"...

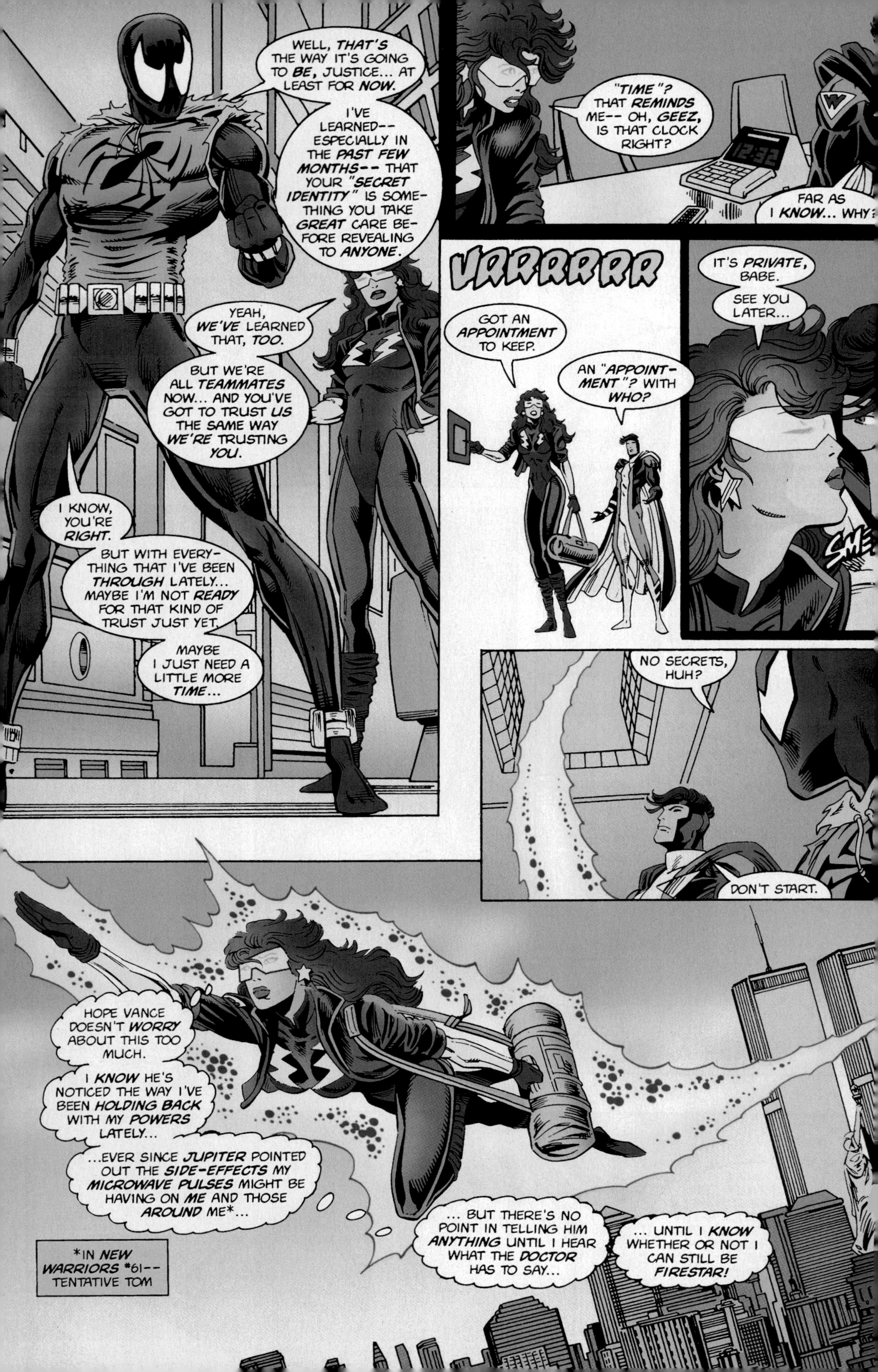
WELL, THAT'S THE WAY IT'S GOING TO BE, JUSTICE... AT LEAST FOR NOW.
I'VE LEARNED-- ESPECIALLY IN THE PAST FEW MONTHS-- THAT YOUR "SECRET IDENTITY" IS SOMETHING YOU TAKE GREAT CARE BEFORE REVEALING TO ANYONE.
YEAH, WE'VE LEARNED THAT, TOO.
BUT WE'RE ALL TEAMMATES NOW... AND YOU'VE GOT TO TRUST US THE SAME WAY WE'RE TRUSTING YOU.
I KNOW, YOU'RE RIGHT.
BUT WITH EVERYTHING THAT I'VE BEEN THROUGH LATELY... MAYBE I'M NOT READY FOR THAT KIND OF TRUST JUST YET.
MAYBE I JUST NEED A LITTLE MORE TIME...
"TIME"? THAT REMINDS ME-- OH, GEEZ, IS THAT CLOCK RIGHT?
12:32
FAR AS I KNOW... WHY?
VRRRRRR
GOT AN APPOINTMENT TO KEEP.
AN "APPOINTMENT"? WITH WHO?
IT'S PRIVATE, BABE.
SEE YOU LATER...
NO SECRETS, HUH?
DON'T START.
HOPE VANCE DOESN'T WORRY ABOUT THIS TOO MUCH.
I KNOW HE'S NOTICED THE WAY I'VE BEEN HOLDING BACK WITH MY POWERS LATELY...
...EVER SINCE JUPITER POINTED OUT THE SIDE-EFFECTS MY MICROWAVE PULSES MIGHT BE HAVING ON ME AND THOSE AROUND ME*...
... BUT THERE'S NO POINT IN TELLING HIM ANYTHING UNTIL I HEAR WHAT THE DOCTOR HAS TO SAY...
... UNTIL I KNOW WHETHER OR NOT I CAN STILL BE FIRESTAR!
*IN NEW WARRIORS #61-- TENTATIVE TOM

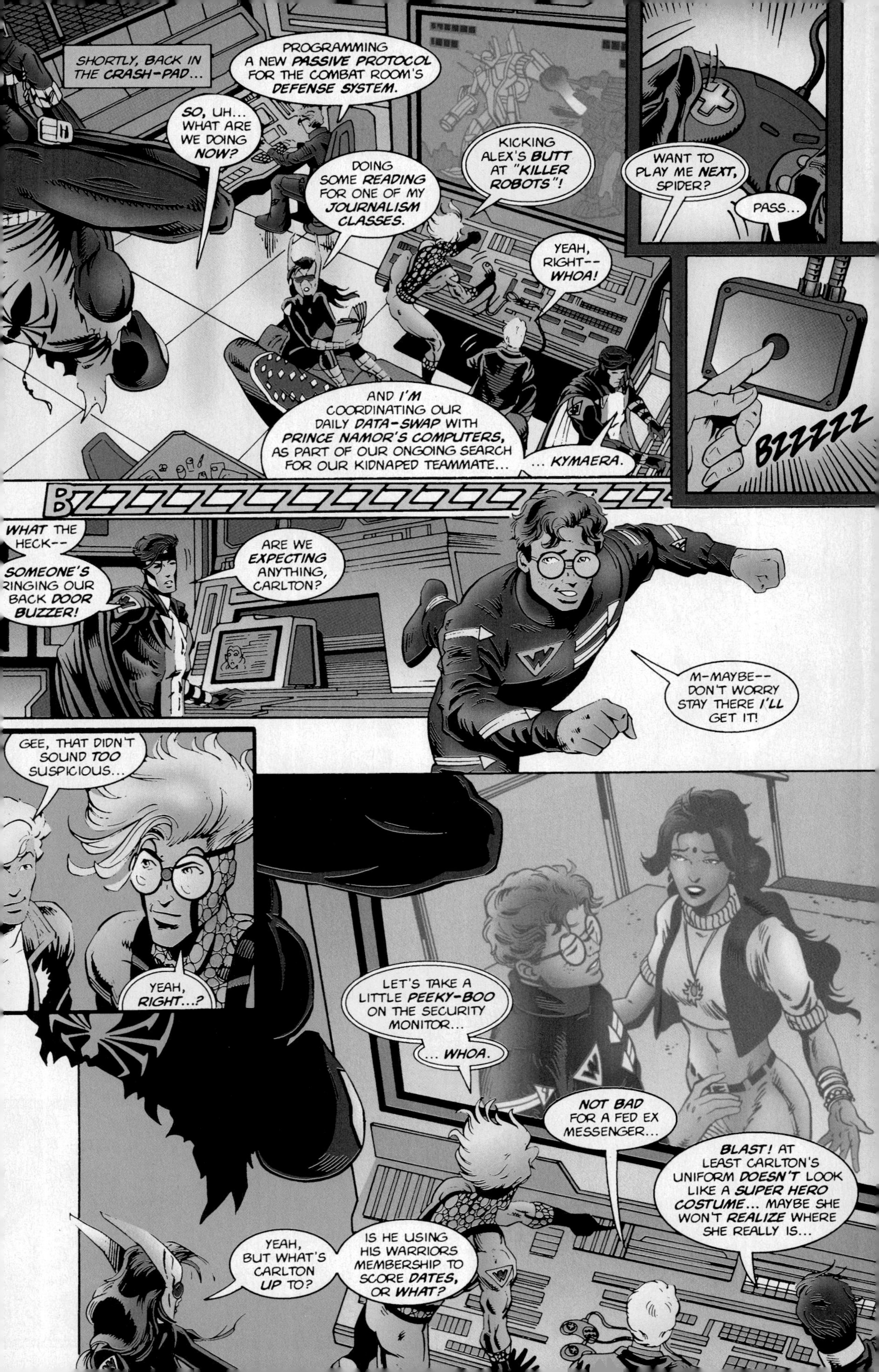

SHORTLY, BACK IN THE CRASH-PAD...
SO, UH... WHAT ARE WE DOING NOW?
PROGRAMMING A NEW PASSIVE PROTOCOL FOR THE COMBAT ROOM'S DEFENSE SYSTEM.
DOING SOME READING FOR ONE OF MY JOURNALISM CLASSES.
KICKING ALEX'S BUTT AT "KILLER ROBOTS"!
YEAH, RIGHT-- WHOA!
AND I'M COORDINATING OUR DAILY DATA-SWAP WITH PRINCE NAMOR'S COMPUTERS, AS PART OF OUR ONGOING SEARCH FOR OUR KIDNAPED TEAMMATE...
... KYMAERA.
WANT TO PLAY ME NEXT, SPIDER?
PASS...
BZZZZZ
BZZZZZZZZZZZZZZZZZ
WHAT THE HECK--
SOMEONE'S RINGING OUR BACK DOOR BUZZER!
ARE WE EXPECTING ANYTHING, CARLTON?
M-MAYBE-- DON'T WORRY STAY THERE I'LL GET IT!
GEE, THAT DIDN'T SOUND TOO SUSPICIOUS...
YEAH, RIGHT...?
LET'S TAKE A LITTLE PEEKY-BOO ON THE SECURITY MONITOR...
... WHOA.
NOT BAD FOR A FED EX MESSENGER...
BLAST! AT LEAST CARLTON'S UNIFORM DOESN'T LOOK LIKE A SUPER HERO COSTUME... MAYBE SHE WON'T REALIZE WHERE SHE REALLY IS...
YEAH, BUT WHAT'S CARLTON UP TO?
IS HE USING HIS WARRIORS MEMBERSHIP TO SCORE DATES, OR WHAT?

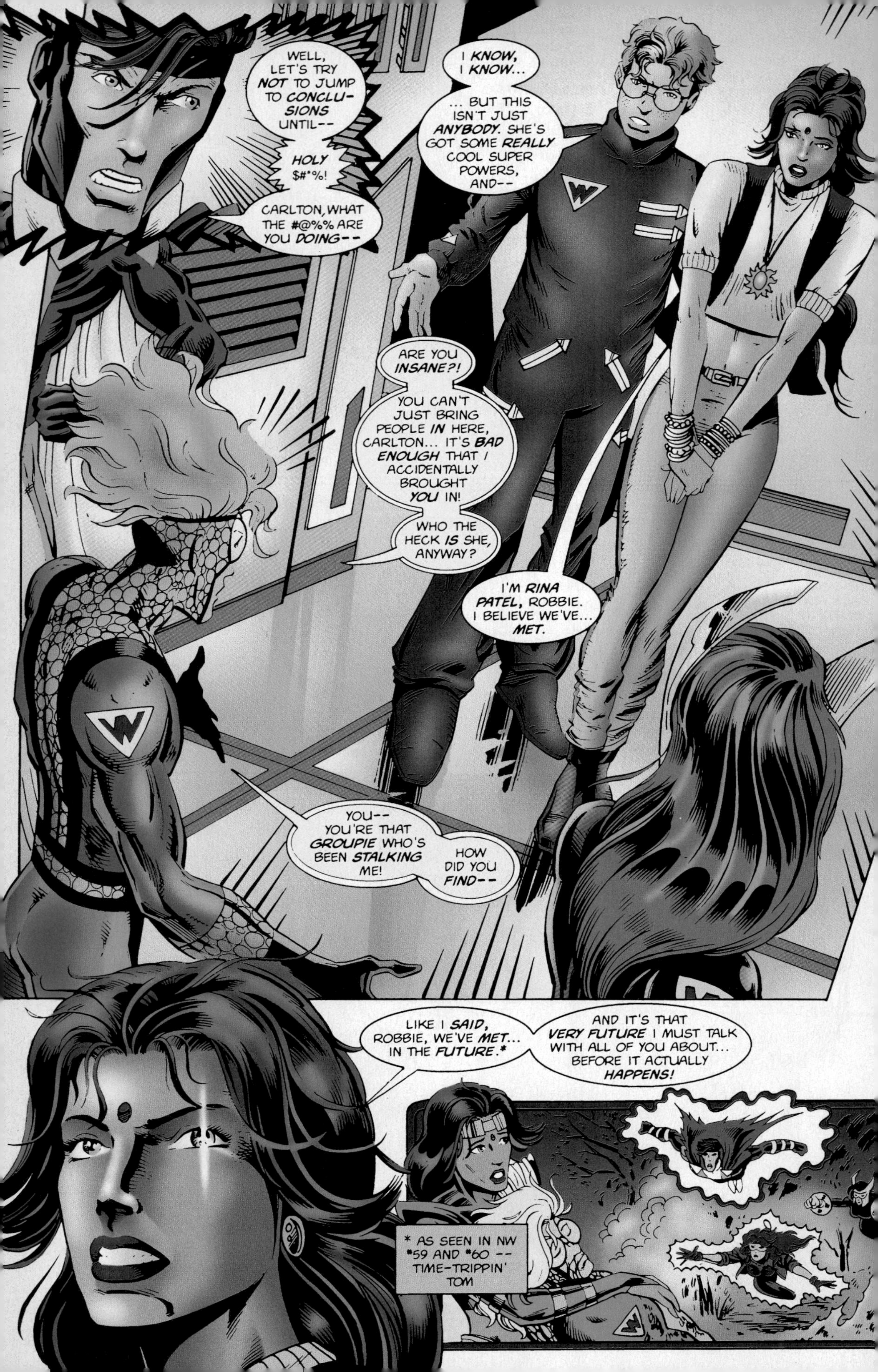
WELL, LET'S TRY NOT TO JUMP TO CONCLUSIONS UNTIL--
HOLY $#*%!
CARLTON, WHAT THE #@%% ARE YOU DOING--
I KNOW, I KNOW...
... BUT THIS ISN'T JUST ANYBODY. SHE'S GOT SOME REALLY COOL SUPER POWERS, AND--
ARE YOU INSANE?!
YOU CAN'T JUST BRING PEOPLE IN HERE, CARLTON... IT'S BAD ENOUGH THAT I ACCIDENTALLY BROUGHT YOU IN!
WHO THE HECK IS SHE, ANYWAY?
I'M RINA PATEL, ROBBIE. I BELIEVE WE'VE... MET.
YOU-- YOU'RE THAT GROUPIE WHO'S BEEN STALKING ME!
HOW DID YOU FIND--
LIKE I SAID, ROBBIE, WE'VE MET... IN THE FUTURE.*
AND IT'S THAT VERY FUTURE I MUST TALK WITH ALL OF YOU ABOUT... BEFORE IT ACTUALLY HAPPENS!
* AS SEEN IN NW #59 AND #60 -- TIME-TRIPPIN' TOM

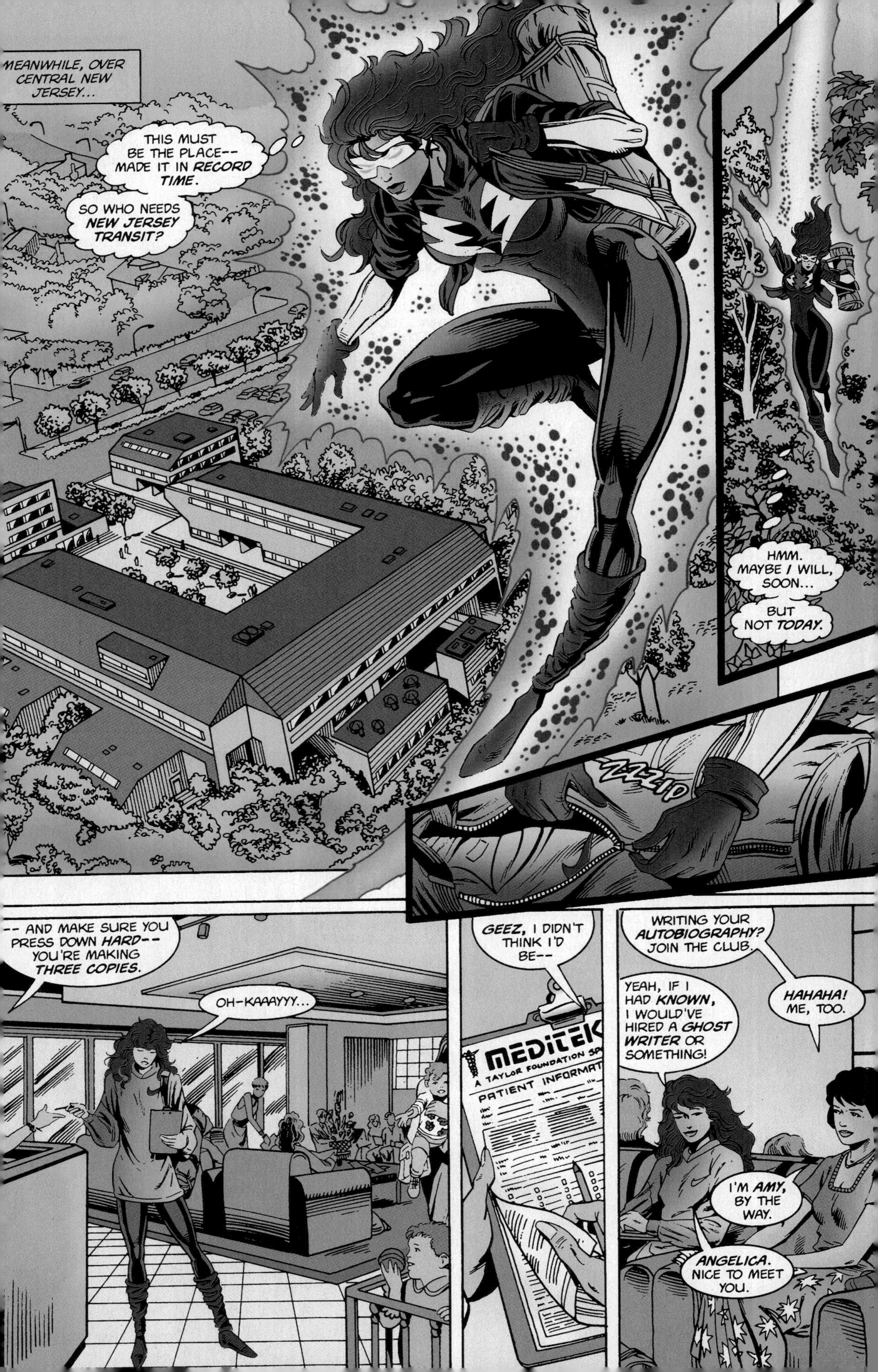
MEANWHILE, OVER CENTRAL NEW JERSEY...
THIS MUST BE THE PLACE-- MADE IT IN RECORD TIME.
SO WHO NEEDS NEW JERSEY TRANSIT?
HMM. MAYBE I WILL, SOON...
BUT NOT TODAY.
ZZZIP
-- AND MAKE SURE YOU PRESS DOWN HARD-- YOU'RE MAKING THREE COPIES.
OH-KAAAYYY...
GEEZ, I DIDN'T THINK I'D BE--
MEDITEK
A TAYLOR FOUNDATION
PATIENT INFORMAT
WRITING YOUR AUTOBIOGRAPHY? JOIN THE CLUB.
YEAH, IF I HAD KNOWN, I WOULD'VE HIRED A GHOST WRITER OR SOMETHING!
HAHAHA! ME, TOO.
I'M AMY, BY THE WAY.
ANGELICA. NICE TO MEET YOU.

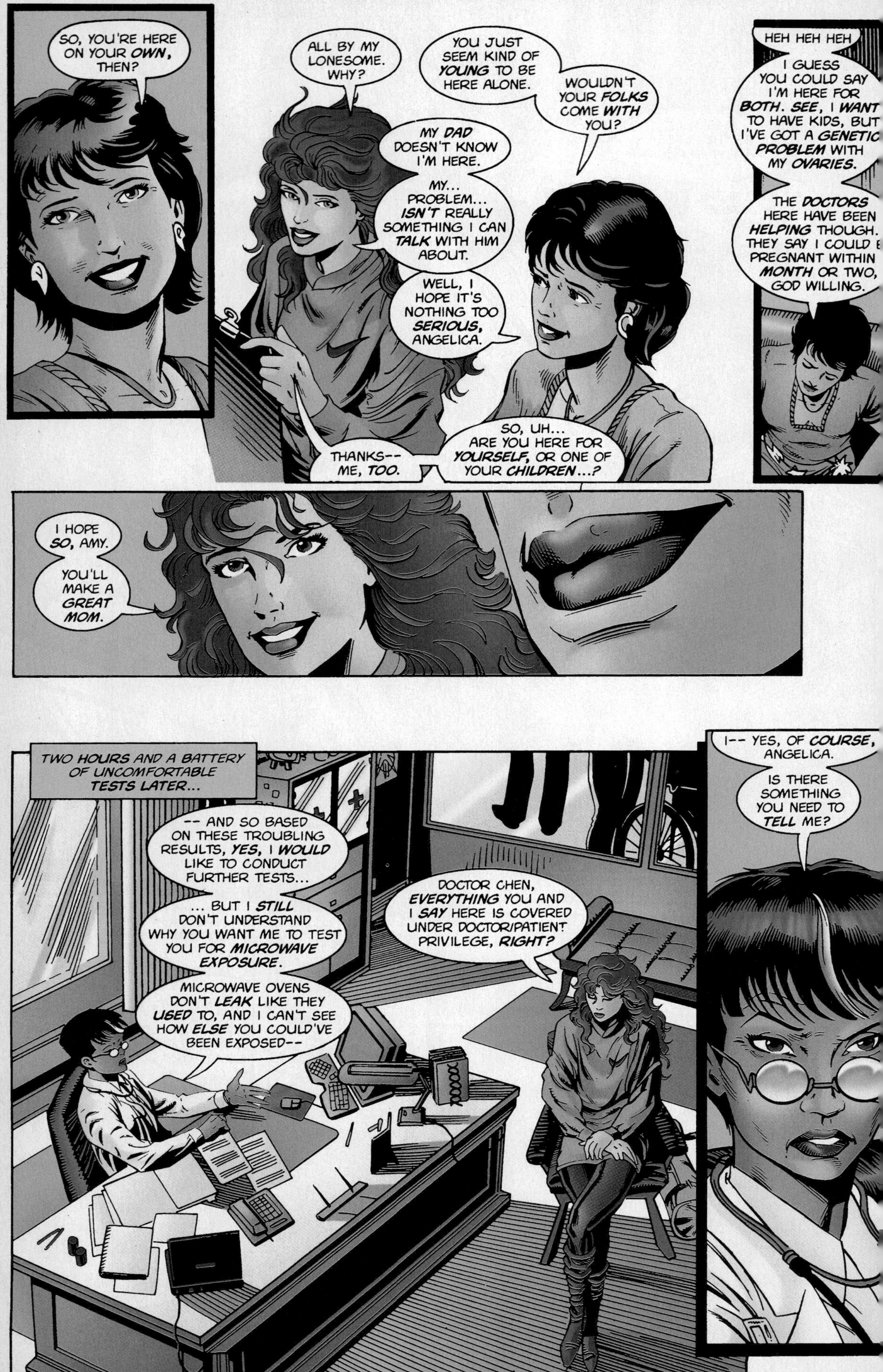
SO, YOU'RE HERE ON YOUR OWN, THEN?
ALL BY MY LONESOME. WHY?
YOU JUST SEEM KIND OF YOUNG TO BE HERE ALONE.
WOULDN'T YOUR FOLKS COME WITH YOU?
MY DAD DOESN'T KNOW I'M HERE.
MY... PROBLEM... ISN'T REALLY SOMETHING I CAN TALK WITH HIM ABOUT.
WELL, I HOPE IT'S NOTHING TOO SERIOUS, ANGELICA.
THANKS-- ME, TOO.
SO, UH... ARE YOU HERE FOR YOURSELF, OR ONE OF YOUR CHILDREN...?
HEH HEH HEH
I GUESS YOU COULD SAY I'M HERE FOR BOTH. SEE, I WANT TO HAVE KIDS, BUT I'VE GOT A GENETIC PROBLEM WITH MY OVARIES.
THE DOCTORS HERE HAVE BEEN HELPING THOUGH. THEY SAY I COULD BE PREGNANT WITHIN A MONTH OR TWO, GOD WILLING.
I HOPE SO, AMY.
YOU'LL MAKE A GREAT MOM.
TWO HOURS AND A BATTERY OF UNCOMFORTABLE TESTS LATER...
-- AND SO BASED ON THESE TROUBLING RESULTS, YES, I WOULD LIKE TO CONDUCT FURTHER TESTS...
... BUT I STILL DON'T UNDERSTAND WHY YOU WANT ME TO TEST YOU FOR MICROWAVE EXPOSURE.
MICROWAVE OVENS DON'T LEAK LIKE THEY USED TO, AND I CAN'T SEE HOW ELSE YOU COULD'VE BEEN EXPOSED--
DOCTOR CHEN, EVERYTHING YOU AND I SAY HERE IS COVERED UNDER DOCTOR/PATIENT PRIVILEGE, RIGHT?
I-- YES, OF COURSE, ANGELICA.
IS THERE SOMETHING YOU NEED TO TELL ME?

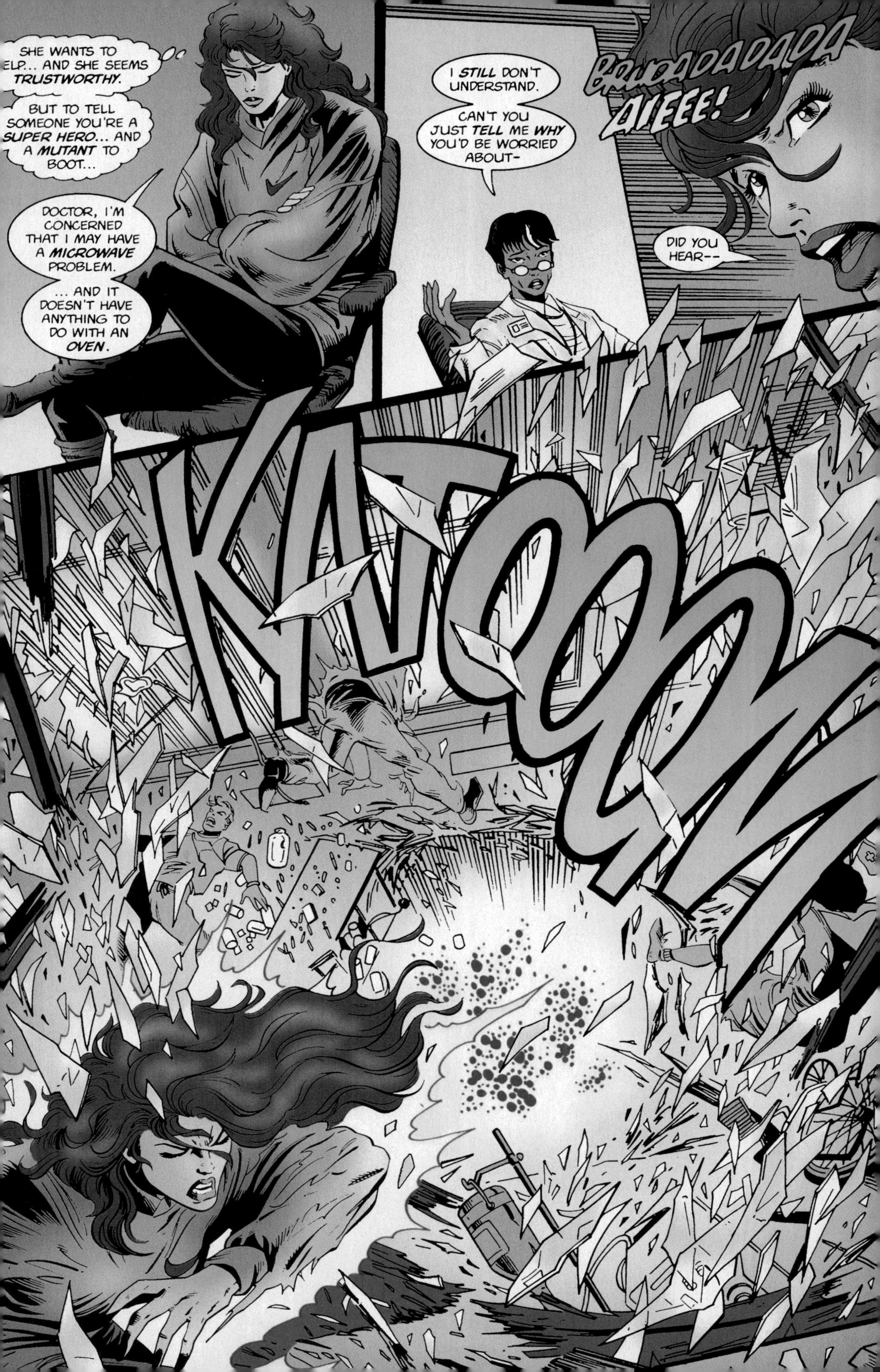

SHE WANTS TO ELP... AND SHE SEEMS TRUSTWORTHY.
BUT TO TELL SOMEONE YOU'RE A SUPER HERO... AND A MUTANT TO BOOT...
DOCTOR, I'M CONCERNED THAT I MAY HAVE A MICROWAVE PROBLEM.
... AND IT DOESN'T HAVE ANYTHING TO DO WITH AN OVEN.
I STILL DON'T UNDERSTAND.
CAN'T YOU JUST TELL ME WHY YOU'D BE WORRIED ABOUT-
BRUDADADADA
AIEEE!
DID YOU HEAR--
KATOOM

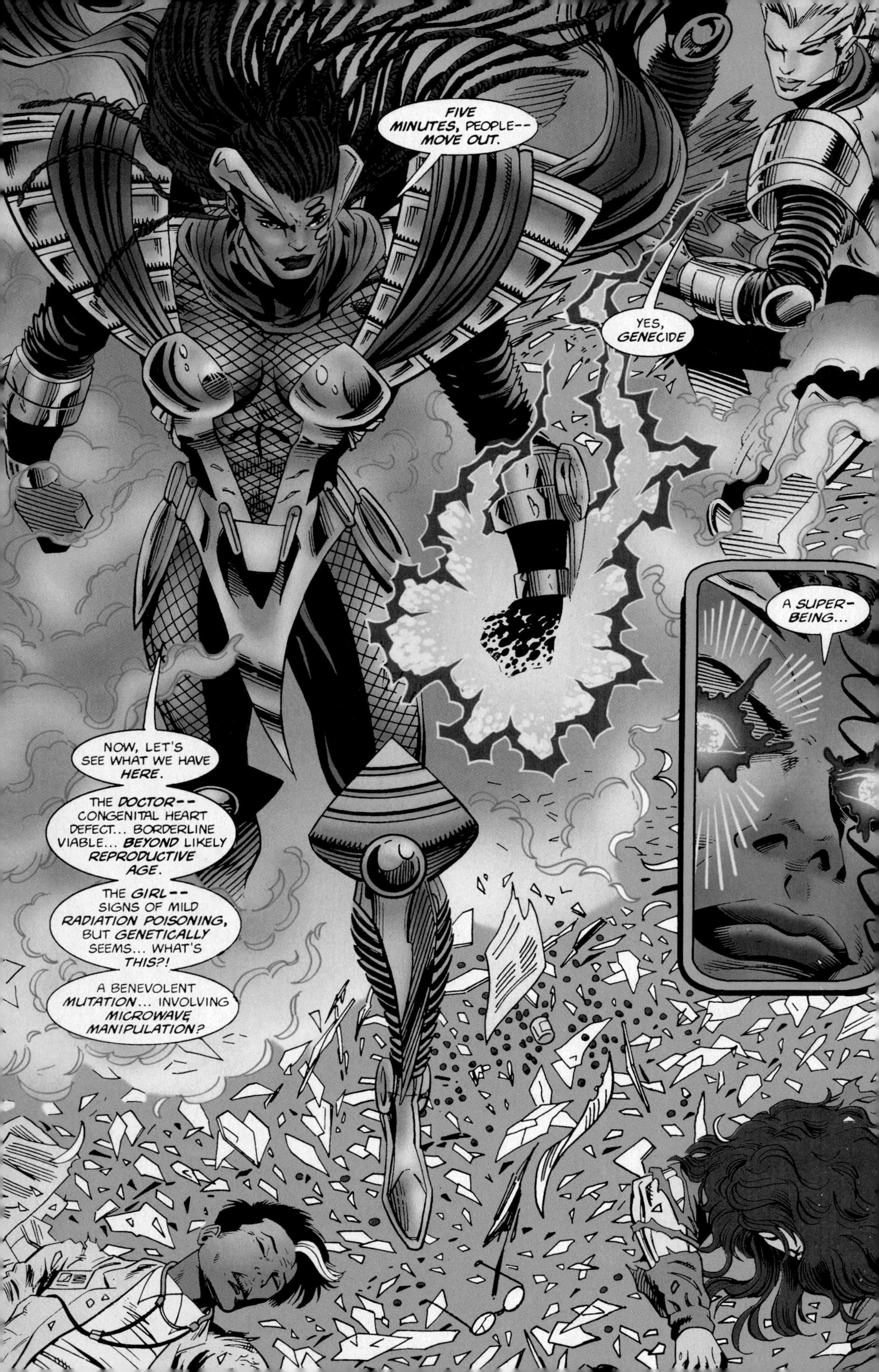
FIVE MINUTES, PEOPLE-- MOVE OUT.
YES, GENECIDE
A SUPER-BEING...
NOW, LET'S SEE WHAT WE HAVE HERE.
THE DOCTOR-- CONGENITAL HEART DEFECT... BORDERLINE VIABLE... BEYOND LIKELY REPRODUCTIVE AGE.
THE GIRL-- SIGNS OF MILD RADIATION POISONING, BUT GENETICALLY SEEMS... WHAT'S THIS?!
A BENEVOLENT MUTATION... INVOLVING MICROWAVE MANIPULATION?

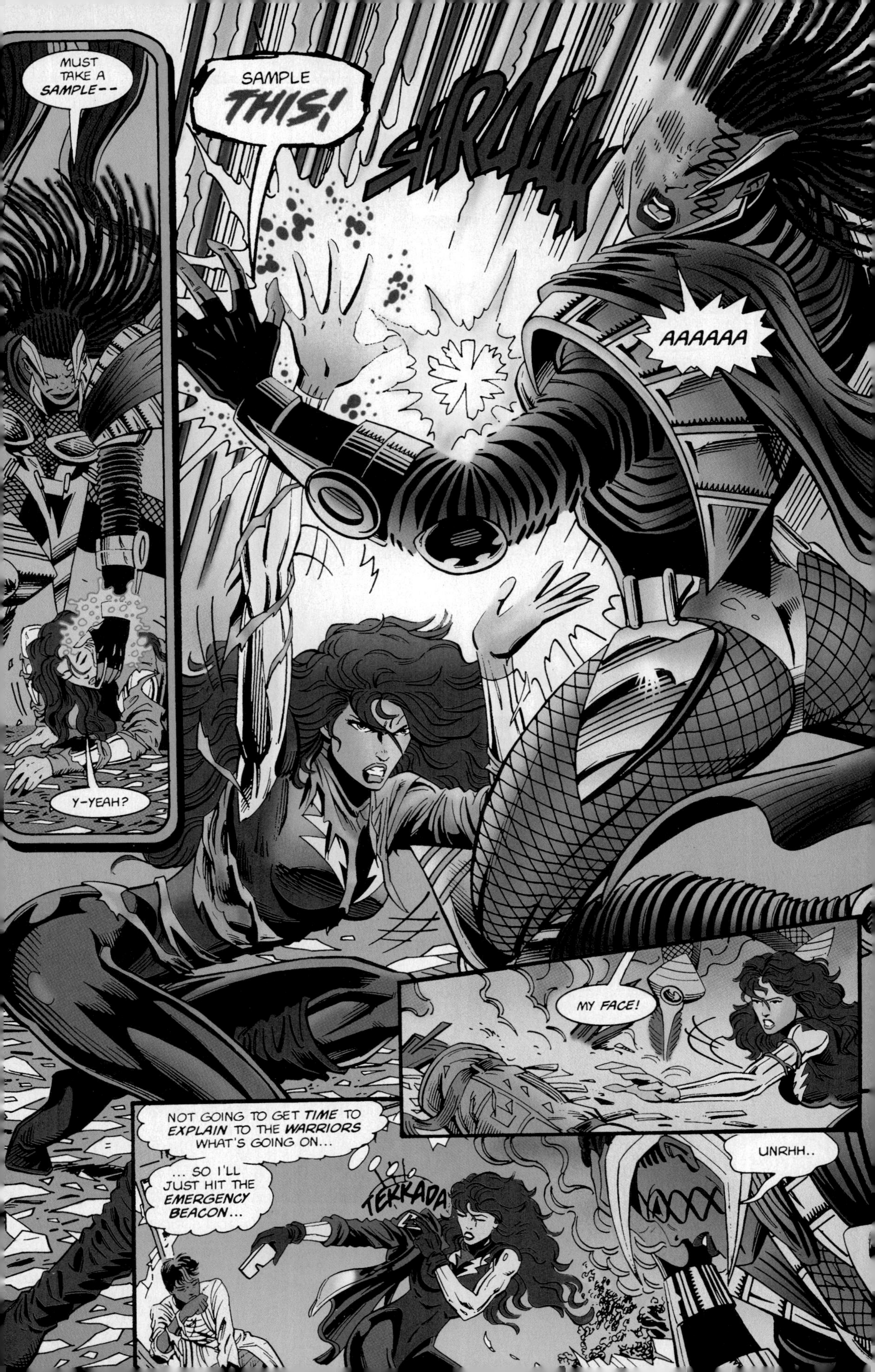
MUST TAKE A SAMPLE--
Y-YEAH?
SAMPLE THIS!
SHRAAK
AAAAAA
MY FACE!
NOT GOING TO GET TIME TO EXPLAIN TO THE WARRIORS WHAT'S GOING ON...
... SO I'LL JUST HIT THE EMERGENCY BEACON...
TEKKADA
UNRHH..

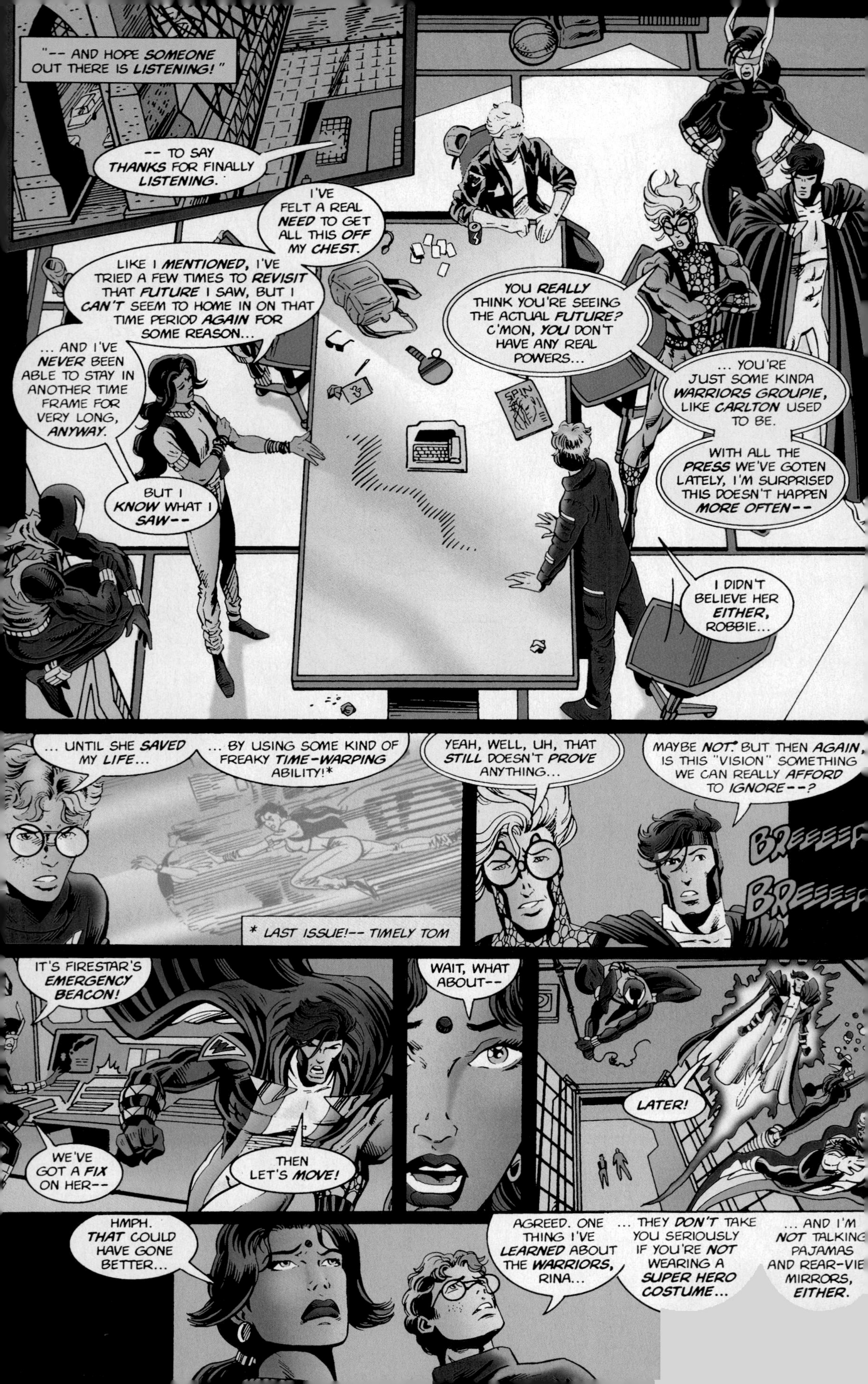
"-- AND HOPE SOMEONE OUT THERE IS LISTENING!"
-- TO SAY THANKS FOR FINALLY LISTENING.
I'VE FELT A REAL NEED TO GET ALL THIS OFF MY CHEST.
LIKE I MENTIONED, I'VE TRIED A FEW TIMES TO REVISIT THAT FUTURE I SAW, BUT I CAN'T SEEM TO HOME IN ON THAT TIME PERIOD AGAIN FOR SOME REASON...
... AND I'VE NEVER BEEN ABLE TO STAY IN ANOTHER TIME FRAME FOR VERY LONG, ANYWAY.
BUT I KNOW WHAT I SAW--
YOU REALLY THINK YOU'RE SEEING THE ACTUAL FUTURE? C'MON, YOU DON'T HAVE ANY REAL POWERS...
... YOU'RE JUST SOME KINDA WARRIORS GROUPIE, LIKE CARLTON USED TO BE.
WITH ALL THE PRESS WE'VE GOTEN LATELY, I'M SURPRISED THIS DOESN'T HAPPEN MORE OFTEN--
I DIDN'T BELIEVE HER EITHER, ROBBIE...
... UNTIL SHE SAVED MY LIFE...
... BY USING SOME KIND OF FREAKY TIME-WARPING ABILITY!*
* LAST ISSUE!-- TIMELY TOM
YEAH, WELL, UH, THAT STILL DOESN'T PROVE ANYTHING...
MAYBE NOT. BUT THEN AGAIN, IS THIS "VISION" SOMETHING WE CAN REALLY AFFORD TO IGNORE--?
BREEEEP
BREEEEP
IT'S FIRESTAR'S EMERGENCY BEACON!
WE'VE GOT A FIX ON HER--
THEN LET'S MOVE!
WAIT, WHAT ABOUT--
LATER!
HMPH. THAT COULD HAVE GONE BETTER...
AGREED. ONE THING I'VE LEARNED ABOUT THE WARRIORS, RINA...
... THEY DON'T TAKE YOU SERIOUSLY IF YOU'RE NOT WEARING A SUPER HERO COSTUME...
... AND I'M NOT TALKING PAJAMAS AND REAR-VIE MIRRORS, EITHER.

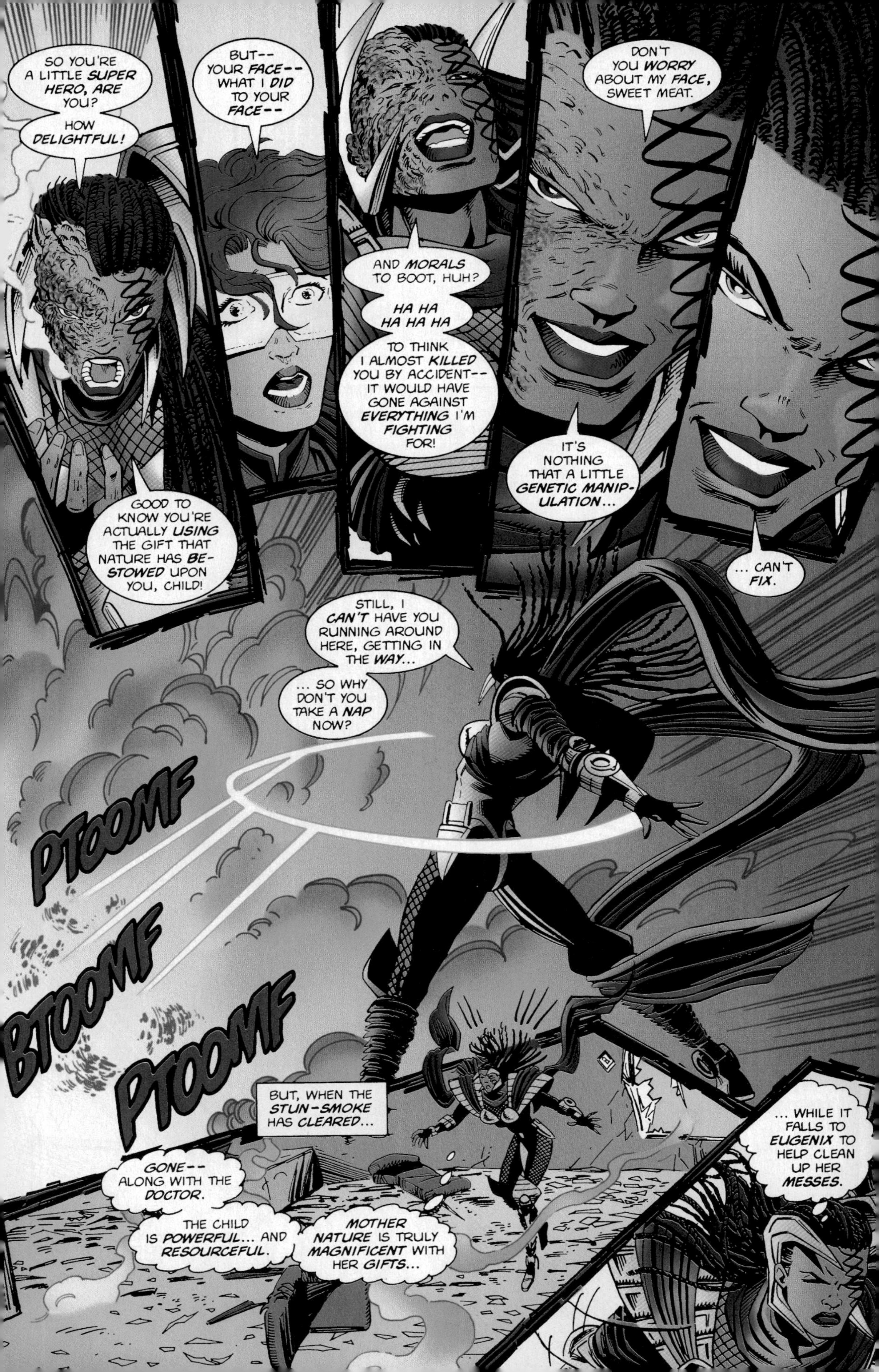
SO YOU'RE A LITTLE SUPER HERO, ARE YOU?
HOW DELIGHTFUL!
GOOD TO KNOW YOU'RE ACTUALLY USING THE GIFT THAT NATURE HAS BE-STOWED UPON YOU, CHILD!
BUT-- YOUR FACE-- WHAT I DID TO YOUR FACE--
AND MORALS TO BOOT, HUH?
HA HA HA HA HA
TO THINK I ALMOST KILLED YOU BY ACCIDENT-- IT WOULD HAVE GONE AGAINST EVERYTHING I'M FIGHTING FOR!
DON'T YOU WORRY ABOUT MY FACE, SWEET MEAT.
IT'S NOTHING THAT A LITTLE GENETIC MANIP-ULATION...
... CAN'T FIX.
STILL, I CAN'T HAVE YOU RUNNING AROUND HERE, GETTING IN THE WAY...
... SO WHY DON'T YOU TAKE A NAP NOW?
PTOOMF
BTOOMF
PTOOMF
BUT, WHEN THE STUN-SMOKE HAS CLEARED...
GONE-- ALONG WITH THE DOCTOR.
THE CHILD IS POWERFUL... AND RESOURCEFUL.
MOTHER NATURE IS TRULY MAGNIFICENT WITH HER GIFTS...
... WHILE IT FALLS TO EUGENIX TO HELP CLEAN UP HER MESSES.

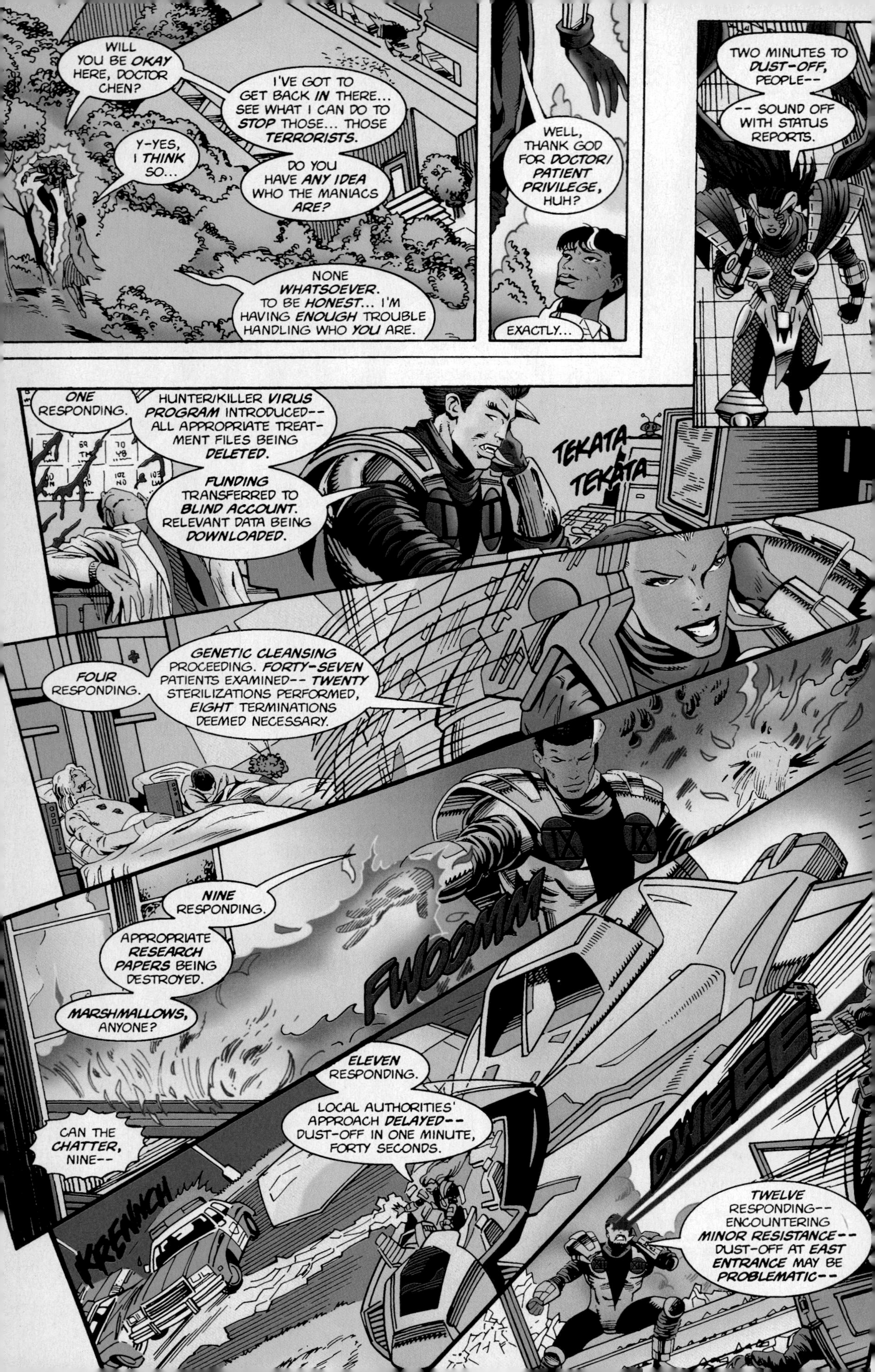

WILL YOU BE OKAY HERE, DOCTOR CHEN?
I'VE GOT TO GET BACK IN THERE... SEE WHAT I CAN DO TO STOP THOSE... THOSE TERRORISTS.
Y-YES, I THINK SO...
DO YOU HAVE ANY IDEA WHO THE MANIACS ARE?
NONE WHATSOEVER. TO BE HONEST... I'M HAVING ENOUGH TROUBLE HANDLING WHO YOU ARE.
WELL, THANK GOD FOR DOCTOR/ PATIENT PRIVILEGE, HUH?
EXACTLY...
TWO MINUTES TO DUST-OFF, PEOPLE--
-- SOUND OFF WITH STATUS REPORTS.
ONE RESPONDING.
HUNTER/KILLER VIRUS PROGRAM INTRODUCED-- ALL APPROPRIATE TREATMENT FILES BEING DELETED.
FUNDING TRANSFERRED TO BLIND ACCOUNT. RELEVANT DATA BEING DOWNLOADED.
TEKATA TEKATA
FOUR RESPONDING.
GENETIC CLEANSING PROCEEDING. FORTY-SEVEN PATIENTS EXAMINED-- TWENTY STERILIZATIONS PERFORMED, EIGHT TERMINATIONS DEEMED NECESSARY.
NINE RESPONDING.
APPROPRIATE RESEARCH PAPERS BEING DESTROYED.
MARSHMALLOWS, ANYONE?
FWOOMM
ELEVEN RESPONDING.
LOCAL AUTHORITIES' APPROACH DELAYED-- DUST-OFF IN ONE MINUTE, FORTY SECONDS.
CAN THE CHATTER, NINE--
KRENNCH
DWEEE
TWELVE RESPONDING-- ENCOUNTERING MINOR RESISTANCE-- DUST-OFF AT EAST ENTRANCE MAY BE PROBLEMATIC--

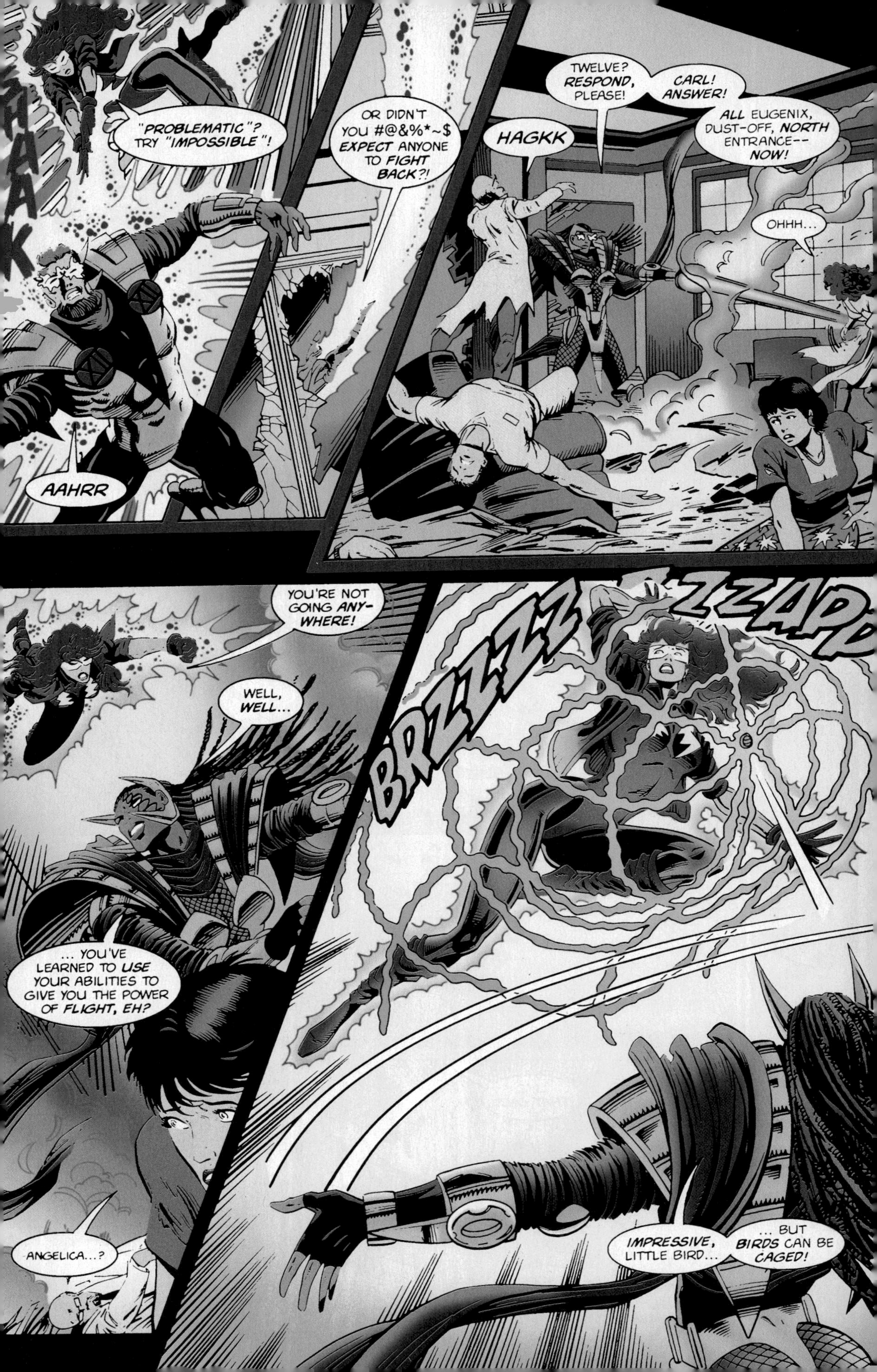
THAAK
"PROBLEMATIC"? TRY "IMPOSSIBLE"!
AAHRR
OR DIDN'T YOU #@&%*~$ EXPECT ANYONE TO FIGHT BACK?!
HAGKK
TWELVE? RESPOND, PLEASE!
CARL! ANSWER!
ALL EUGENIX, DUST-OFF, NORTH ENTRANCE-- NOW!
OHHH...
YOU'RE NOT GOING ANYWHERE!
WELL, WELL...
... YOU'VE LEARNED TO USE YOUR ABILITIES TO GIVE YOU THE POWER OF FLIGHT, EH?
ANGELICA...?
BRZZZZ
ZZZAPP
IMPRESSIVE, LITTLE BIRD...
... BUT BIRDS CAN BE CAGED!

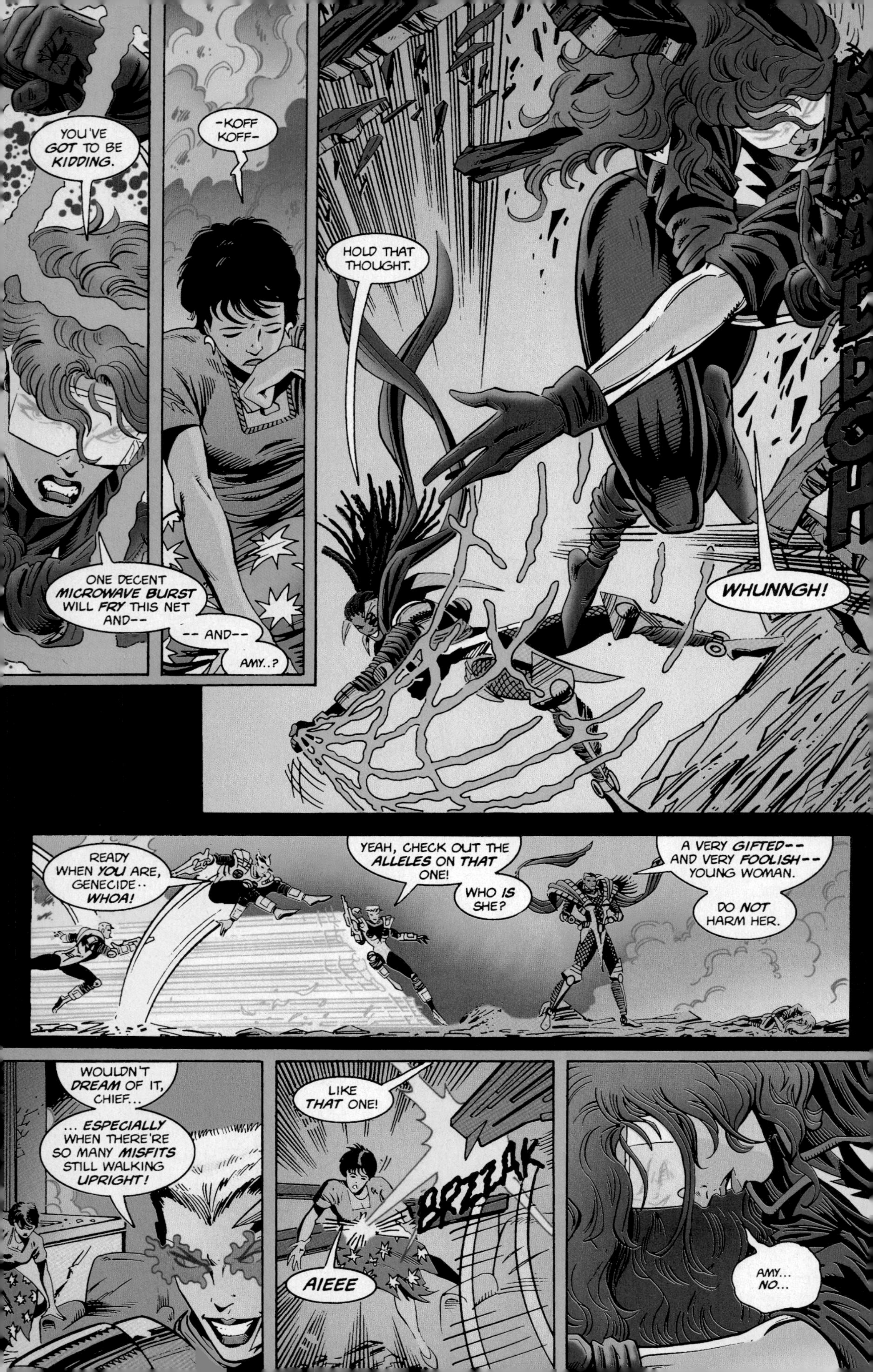
YOU'VE GOT TO BE KIDDING.
-KOFF KOFF-
HOLD THAT THOUGHT.
WHUNNGH!
ONE DECENT MICROWAVE BURST WILL FRY THIS NET AND--
-- AND--
AMY..?
READY WHEN YOU ARE, GENECIDE.. WHOA!
YEAH, CHECK OUT THE ALLELES ON THAT ONE!
WHO IS SHE?
A VERY GIFTED-- AND VERY FOOLISH-- YOUNG WOMAN.
DO NOT HARM HER.
WOULDN'T DREAM OF IT, CHIEF...
... ESPECIALLY WHEN THERE'RE SO MANY MISFITS STILL WALKING UPRIGHT!
LIKE THAT ONE!
BRZZAK
AIEEE
AMY... NO...

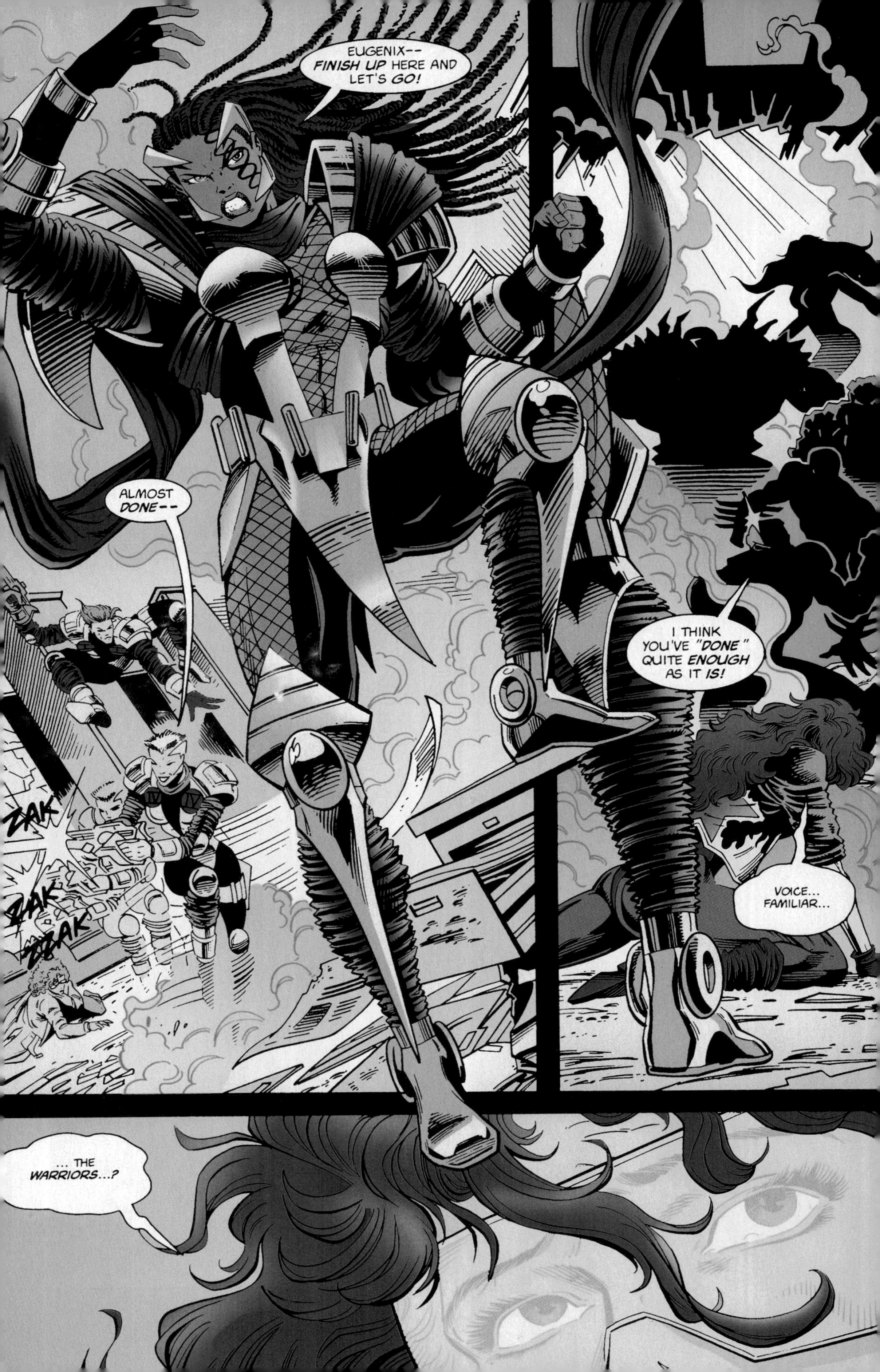
EUGENIX-- FINISH UP HERE AND LET'S GO!
ALMOST DONE--
I THINK YOU'VE "DONE" QUITE ENOUGH AS IT IS!
ZAK
ZAK
ZZAK
VOICE... FAMILIAR...
... THE WARRIORS...?

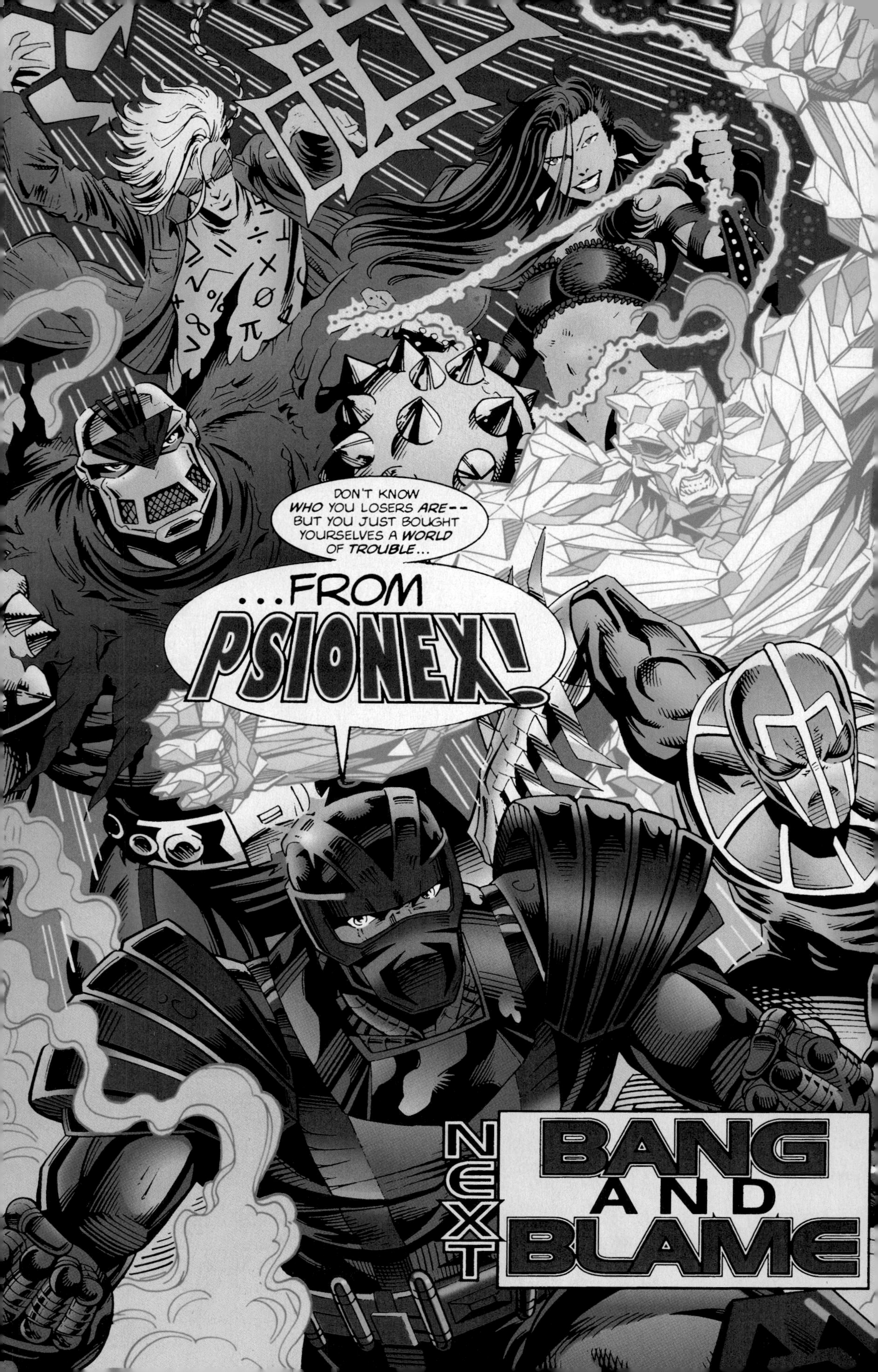

DON'T KNOW WHO YOU LOSERS ARE-- BUT YOU JUST BOUGHT YOURSELVES A WORLD OF TROUBLE...
...FROM PSIONEX!
NEXT
BANG AND BLAME

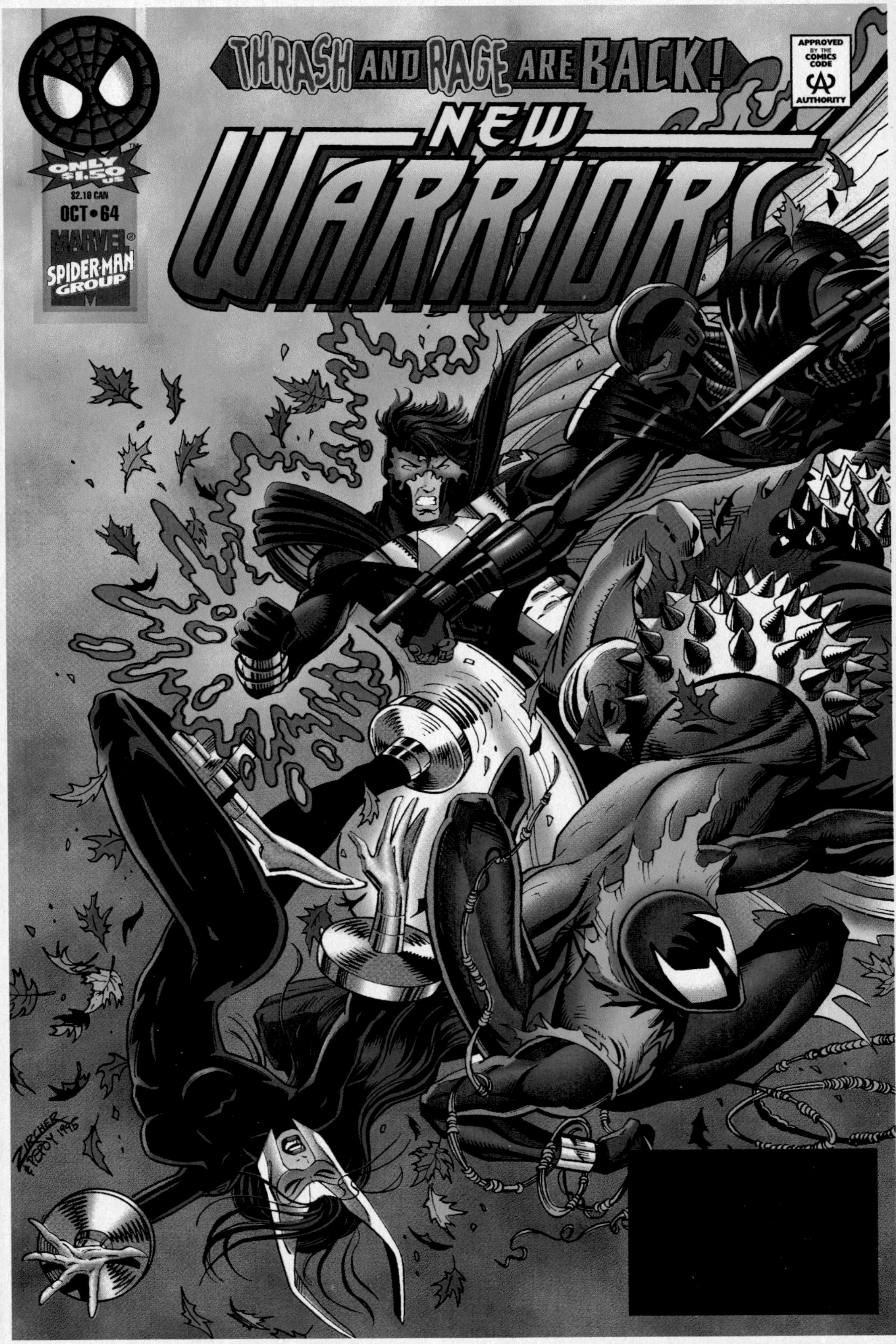
THRASH AND RAGE ARE BACK!
NEW WARRIORS
ONLY $1.50 US
$2.10 CAN
OCT • 64
MARVEL®
SPIDER-MAN GROUP
APPROVED BY THE COMICS CODE AUTHORITY

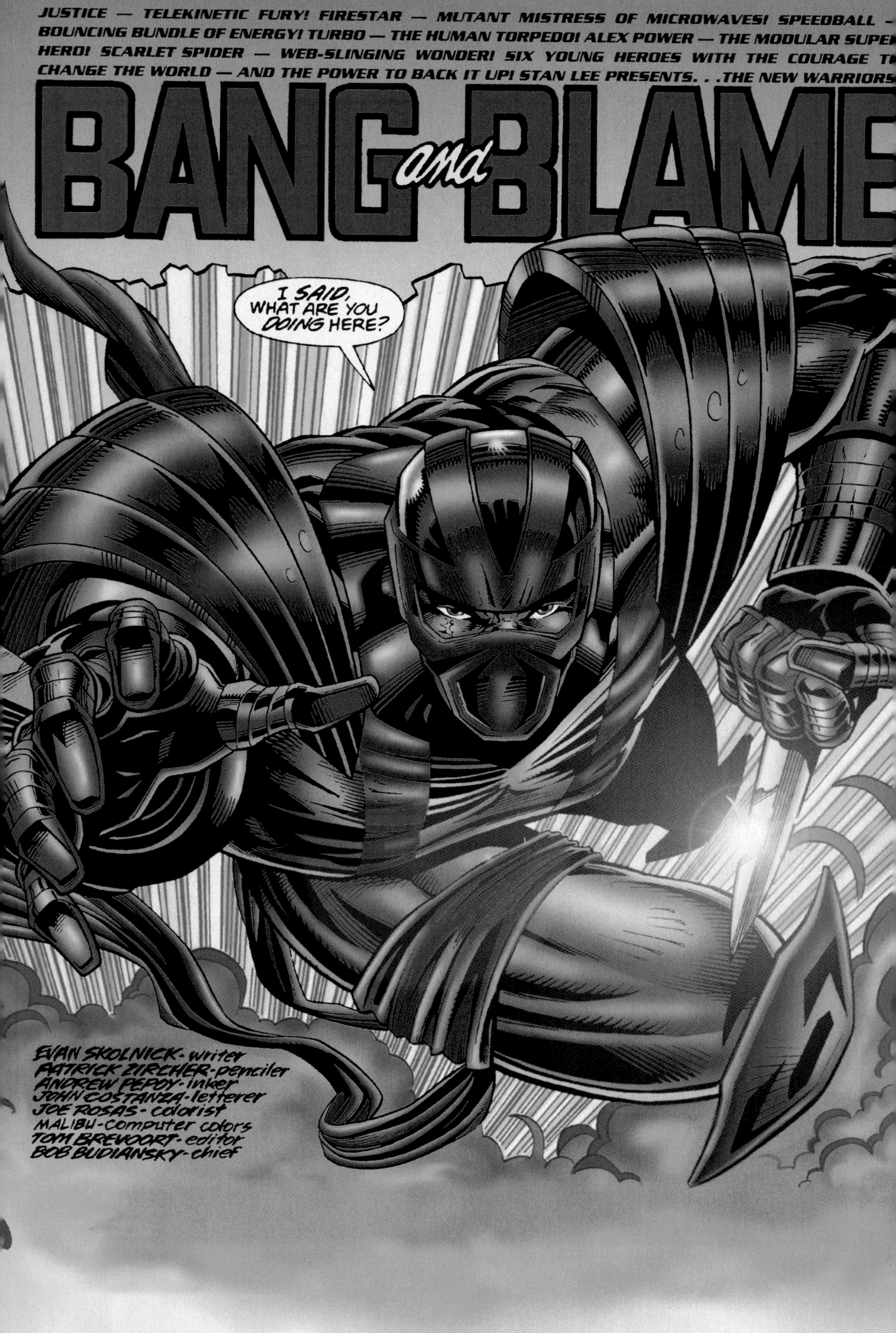
JUSTICE — TELEKINETIC FURY! FIRESTAR — MUTANT MISTRESS OF MICROWAVES! SPEEDBALL — BOUNCING BUNDLE OF ENERGY! TURBO — THE HUMAN TORPEDO! ALEX POWER — THE MODULAR SUPE HERO! SCARLET SPIDER — WEB-SLINGING WONDER! SIX YOUNG HEROES WITH THE COURAGE T CHANGE THE WORLD — AND THE POWER TO BACK IT UP! STAN LEE PRESENTS. . .THE NEW WARRIORS
BANG and BLAME
I SAID, WHAT ARE YOU DOING HERE?
EVAN SKOLNICK-writer
PATRICK ZIRCHER-penciler
ANDREW PEPOY-inker
JOHN COSTANZA-letterer
JOE ROSAS-colorist
MALIBU-computer colors
TOM BREVOORT-editor
BOB BUDIANSKY-chief

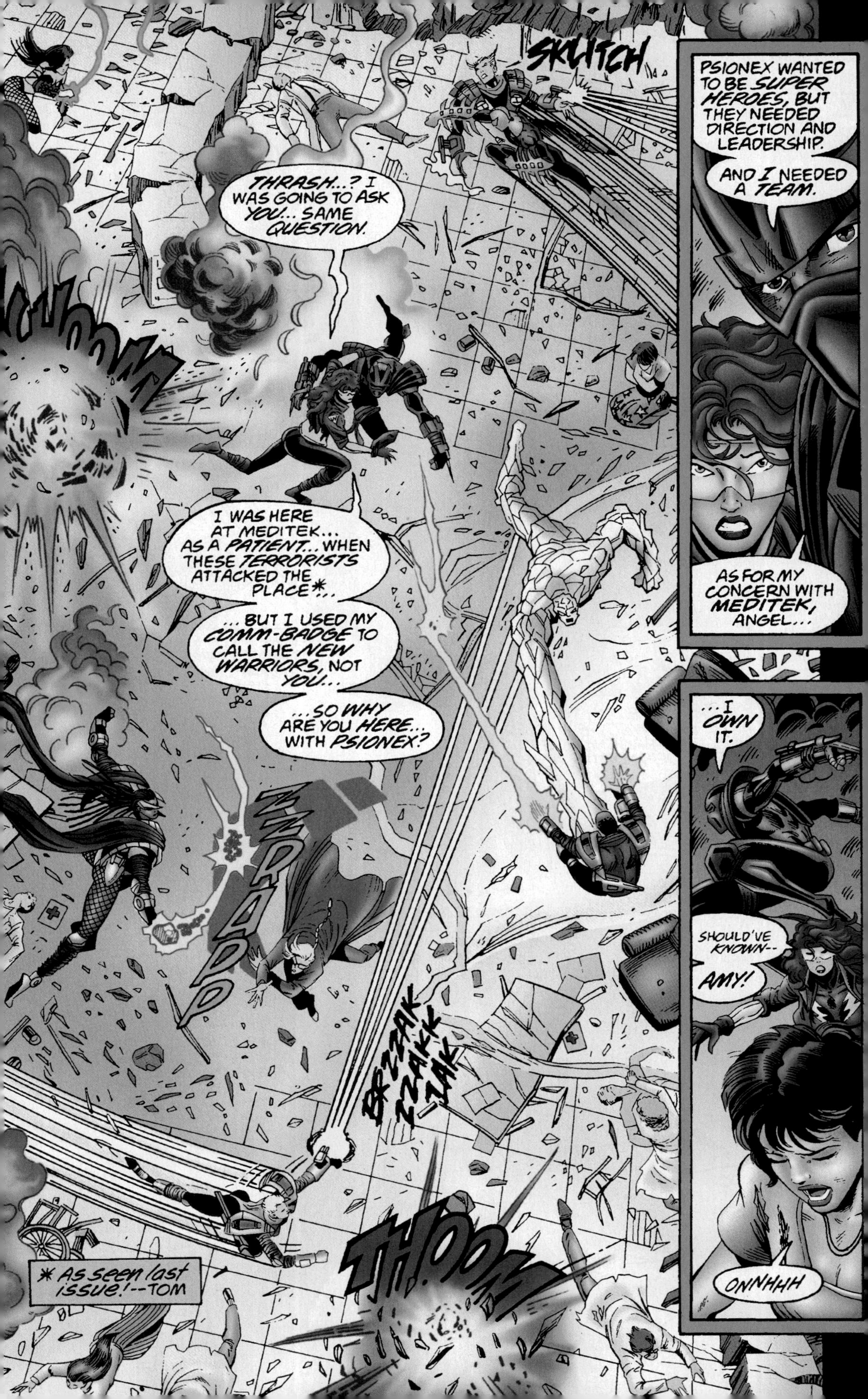
SKLITCH
PSIONEX WANTED TO BE SUPER HEROES, BUT THEY NEEDED DIRECTION AND LEADERSHIP.
AND I NEEDED A TEAM.
THRASH...? I WAS GOING TO ASK YOU... SAME QUESTION.
I WAS HERE AT MEDITEK... AS A PATIENT... WHEN THESE TERRORISTS ATTACKED THE PLACE*...
...BUT I USED MY COMM-BADGE TO CALL THE NEW WARRIORS, NOT YOU...
...SO WHY ARE YOU HERE... WITH PSIONEX?
AS FOR MY CONCERN WITH MEDITEK, ANGEL...
...I OWN IT.
SHOULD'VE KNOWN--
AMY!
BZZZAK ZZAKK ZZAK
THOOM
ONNHHH
* As seen last issue! --TOM

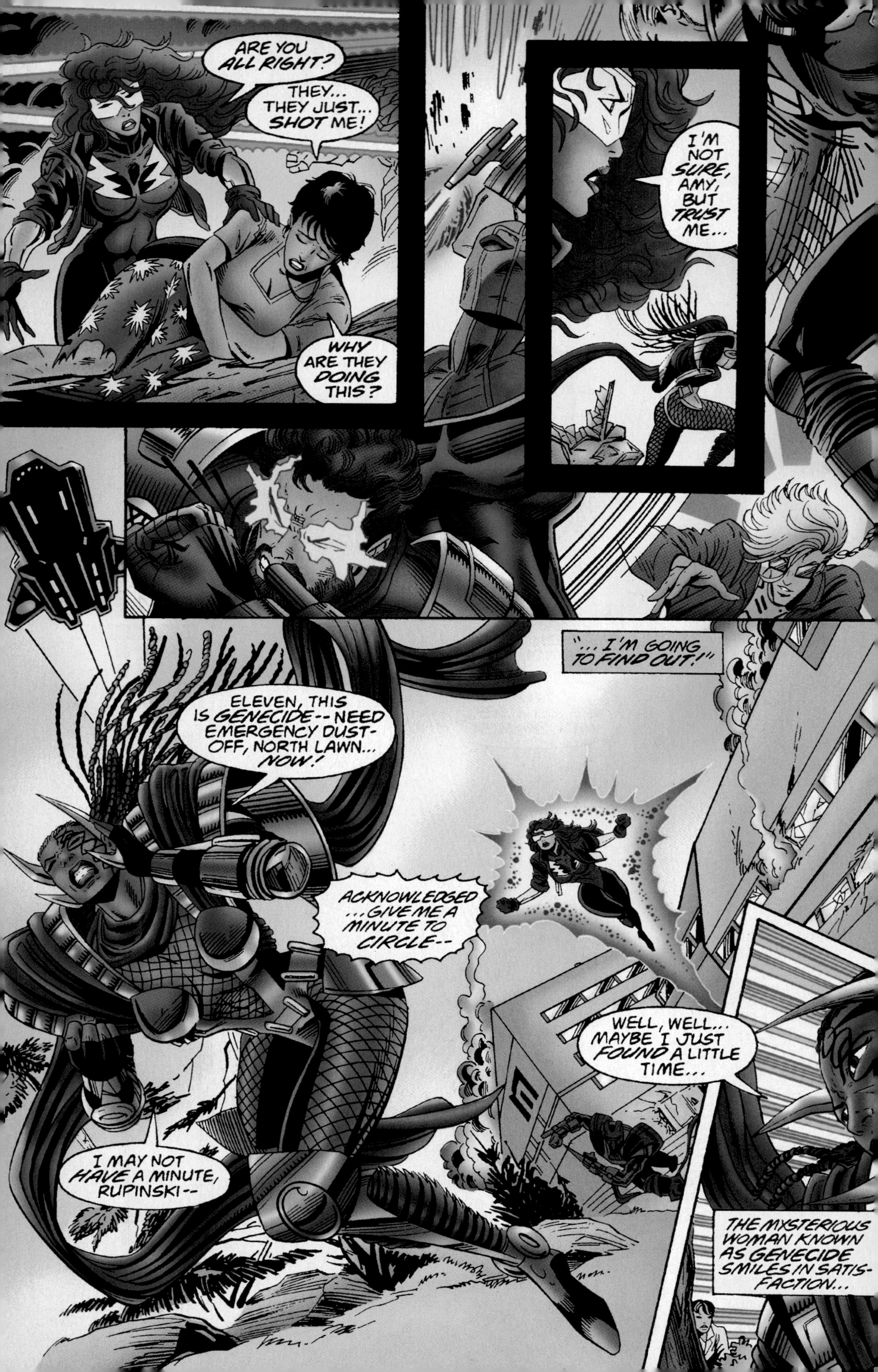

ARE YOU ALL RIGHT?
THEY... THEY JUST... SHOT ME!
WHY ARE THEY DOING THIS?
I'M NOT SURE, AMY, BUT TRUST ME...
"...I'M GOING TO FIND OUT!"
ELEVEN, THIS IS GENECIDE--NEED EMERGENCY DUST-OFF, NORTH LAWN... NOW!
ACKNOWLEDGED ...GIVE ME A MINUTE TO CIRCLE--
I MAY NOT HAVE A MINUTE, RUPINSKI--
WELL, WELL... MAYBE I JUST FOUND A LITTLE TIME...
THE MYSTERIOUS WOMAN KNOWN AS GENECIDE SMILES IN SATISFACTION...

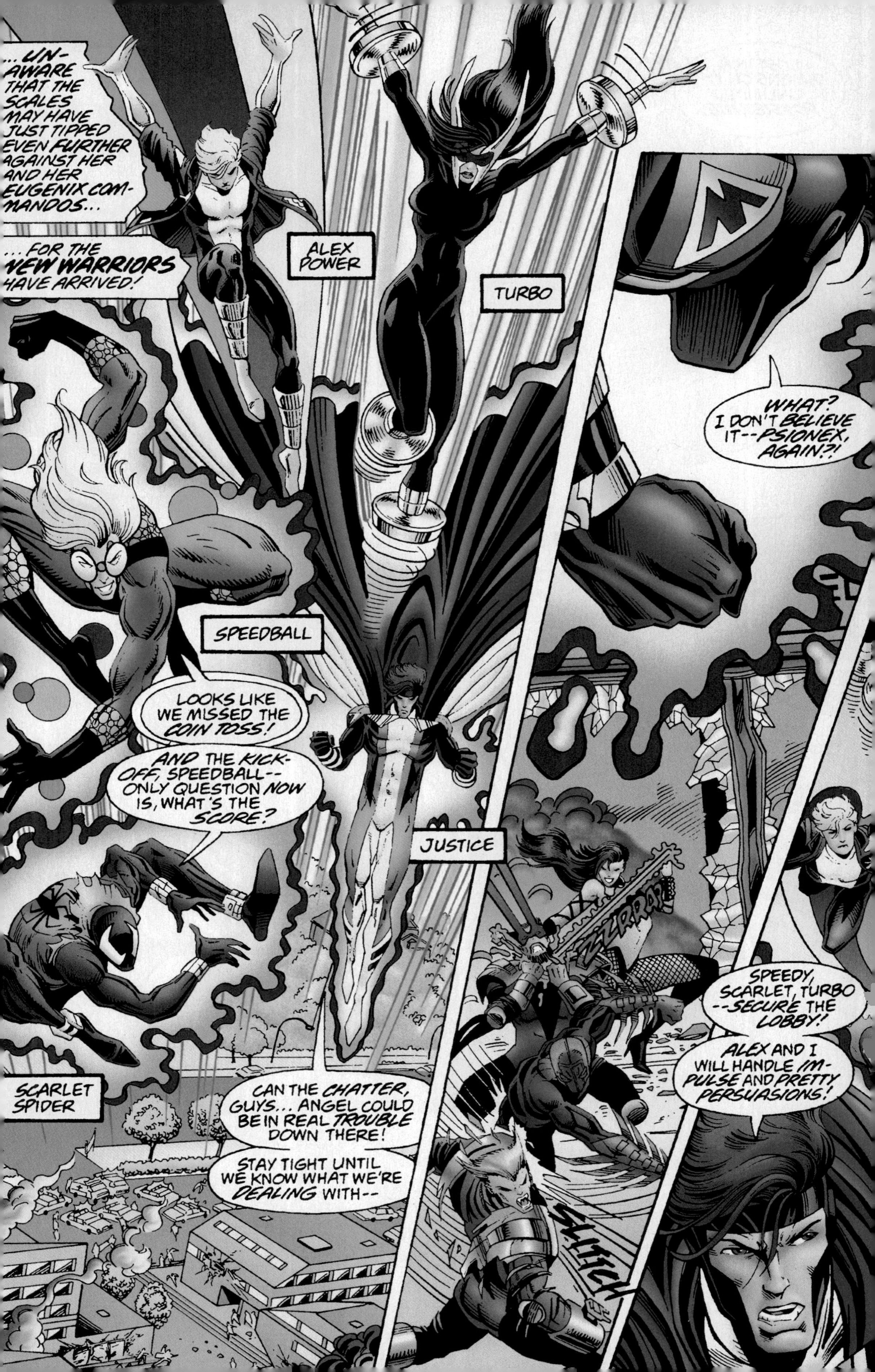
...UN-AWARE THAT THE SCALES MAY HAVE JUST TIPPED EVEN FURTHER AGAINST HER AND HER EUGENIX COM-MANDOS...
...FOR THE NEW WARRIORS HAVE ARRIVED!
ALEX POWER
TURBO
SPEEDBALL
LOOKS LIKE WE MISSED THE COIN TOSS!
AND THE KICK-OFF, SPEEDBALL-- ONLY QUESTION NOW IS, WHAT'S THE SCORE?
JUSTICE
SCARLET SPIDER
CAN THE CHATTER, GUYS... ANGEL COULD BE IN REAL TROUBLE DOWN THERE!
STAY TIGHT UNTIL WE KNOW WHAT WE'RE DEALING WITH--
WHAT? I DON'T BELIEVE IT--PSIONEX, AGAIN?!
SPEEDY, SCARLET, TURBO --SECURE THE LOBBY!
ALEX AND I WILL HANDLE IM-PULSE AND PRETTY PERSUASIONS!
SHTTCH!

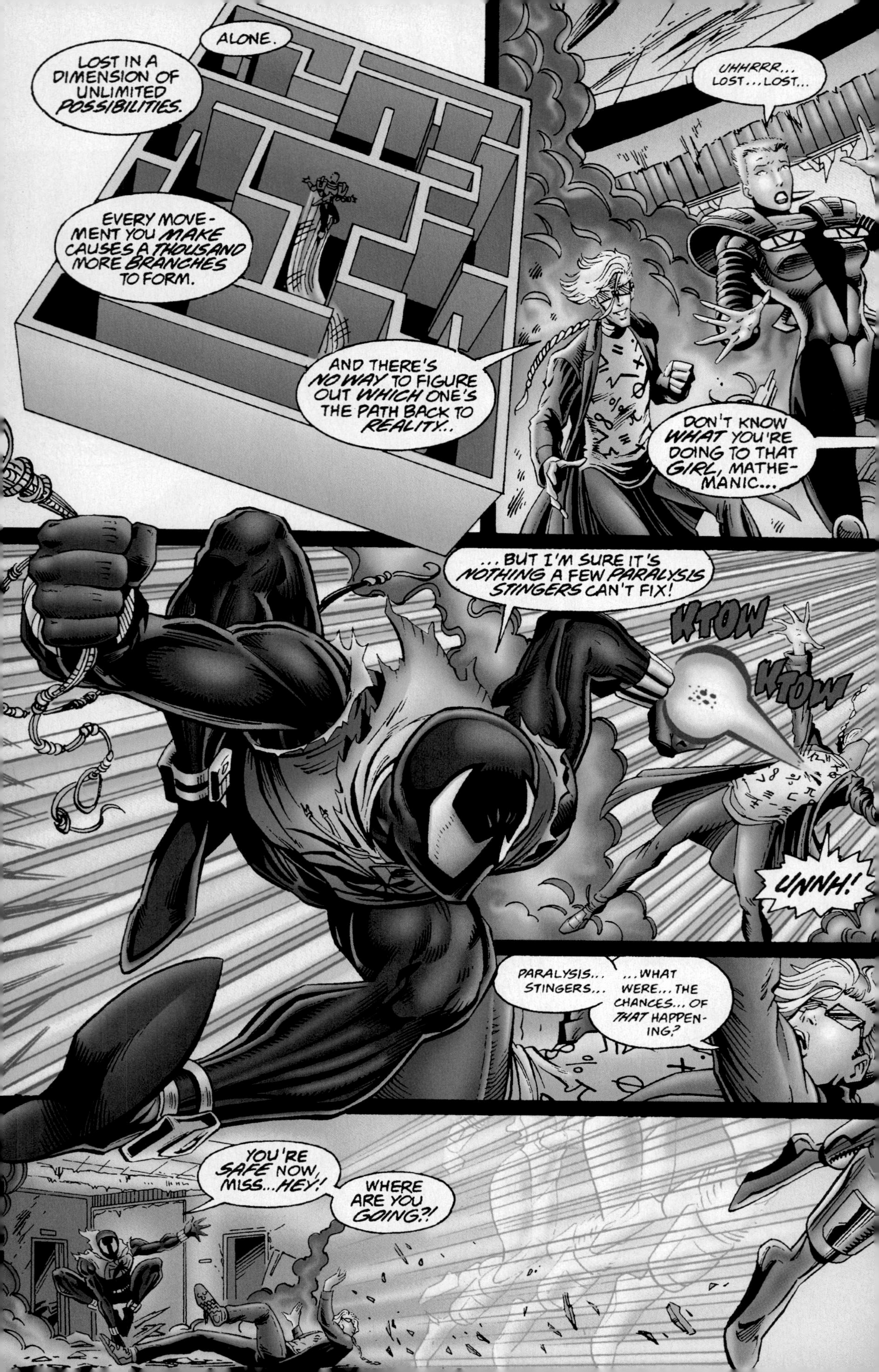
ALONE.
LOST IN A DIMENSION OF UNLIMITED POSSIBILITIES.
EVERY MOVEMENT YOU MAKE CAUSES A THOUSAND MORE BRANCHES TO FORM.
AND THERE'S NO WAY TO FIGURE OUT WHICH ONE'S THE PATH BACK TO REALITY...
UHHRRR... LOST... LOST...
DON'T KNOW WHAT YOU'RE DOING TO THAT GIRL, MATHEMANIC...
...BUT I'M SURE IT'S NOTHING A FEW PARALYSIS STINGERS CAN'T FIX!
KTOW
KTOW
UNNH!
PARALYSIS... STINGERS...
...WHAT WERE... THE CHANCES... OF THAT HAPPENING?
YOU'RE SAFE NOW, MISS... HEY!
WHERE ARE YOU GOING?!

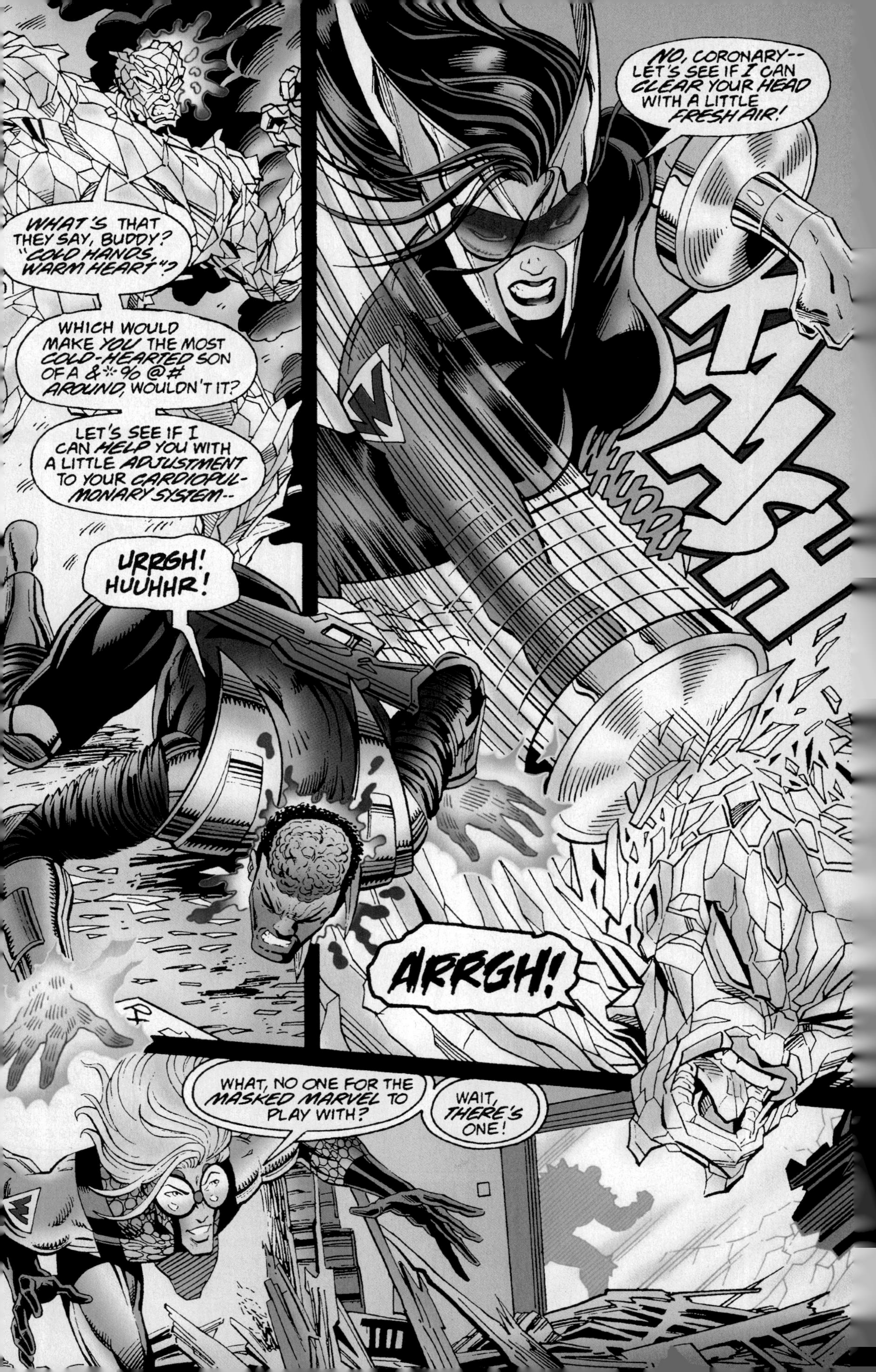
WHAT'S THAT THEY SAY, BUDDY? "COLD HANDS, WARM HEART"?
WHICH WOULD MAKE YOU THE MOST COLD-HEARTED SON OF A &*%@# AROUND, WOULDN'T IT?
LET'S SEE IF I CAN HELP YOU WITH A LITTLE ADJUSTMENT TO YOUR CARDIOPULMONARY SYSTEM--
NO, CORONARY-- LET'S SEE IF I CAN CLEAR YOUR HEAD WITH A LITTLE FRESH AIR!
URRGH! HUUHHR!
ARRGH!
WHAT, NO ONE FOR THE MASKED MARVEL TO PLAY WITH?
WAIT, THERE'S ONE!

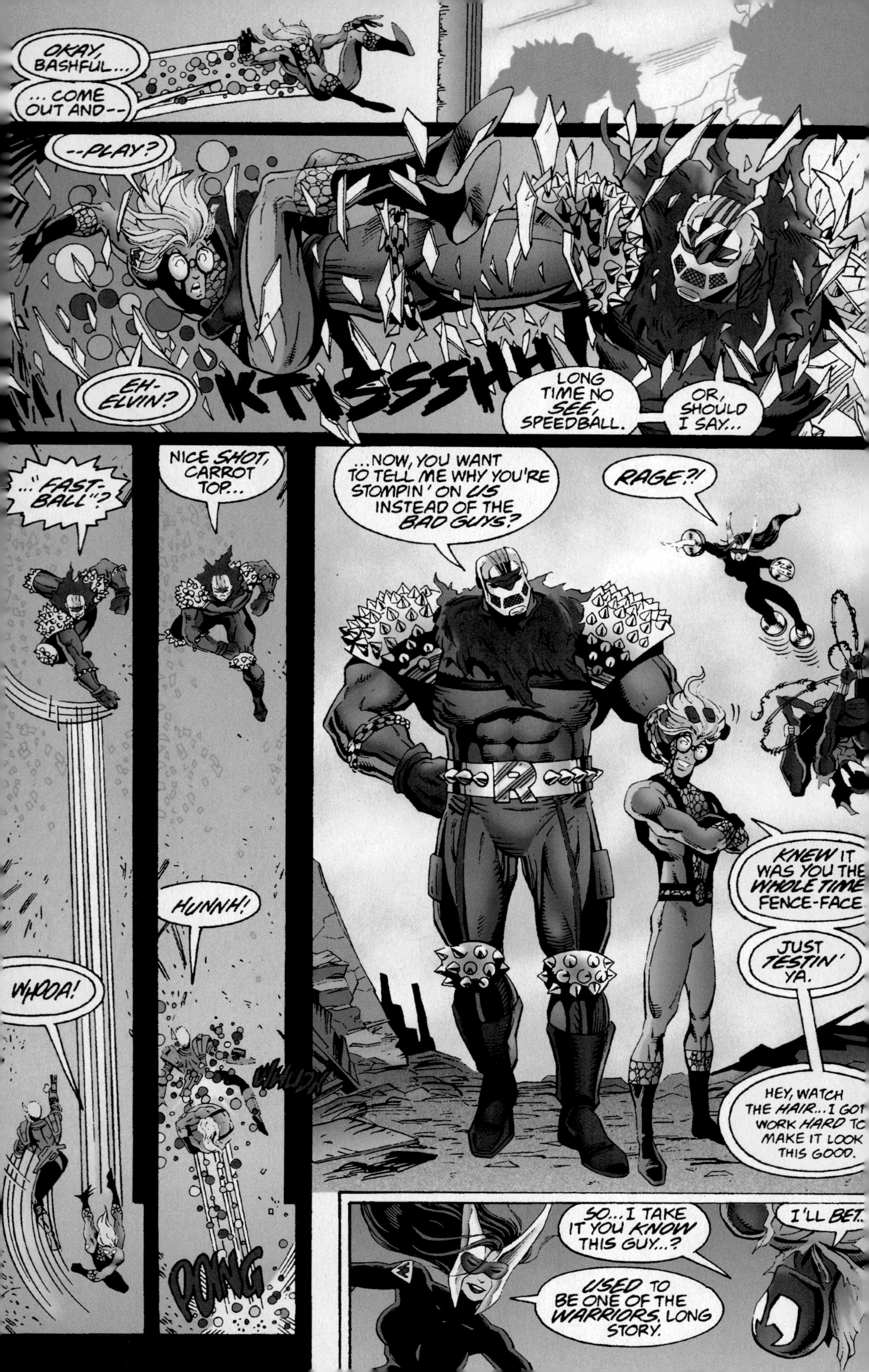
OKAY, BASHFUL...
...COME OUT AND--
--PLAY?
EH-ELVIN?
KTISSSHH
LONG TIME NO SEE, SPEEDBALL.
OR, SHOULD I SAY...
..."FAST-BALL"?
NICE SHOT, CARROT TOP...
...NOW, YOU WANT TO TELL ME WHY YOU'RE STOMPIN' ON US INSTEAD OF THE BAD GUYS?
RAGE?!
KNEW IT WAS YOU THE WHOLE TIME, FENCE-FACE.
JUST TESTIN' YA.
HUNNH!
WHOOA!
HEY, WATCH THE HAIR...I GOT WORK HARD TO MAKE IT LOOK THIS GOOD.
PONG
SO...I TAKE IT YOU KNOW THIS GUY...?
I'LL BET.
USED TO BE ONE OF THE WARRIORS, LONG STORY.

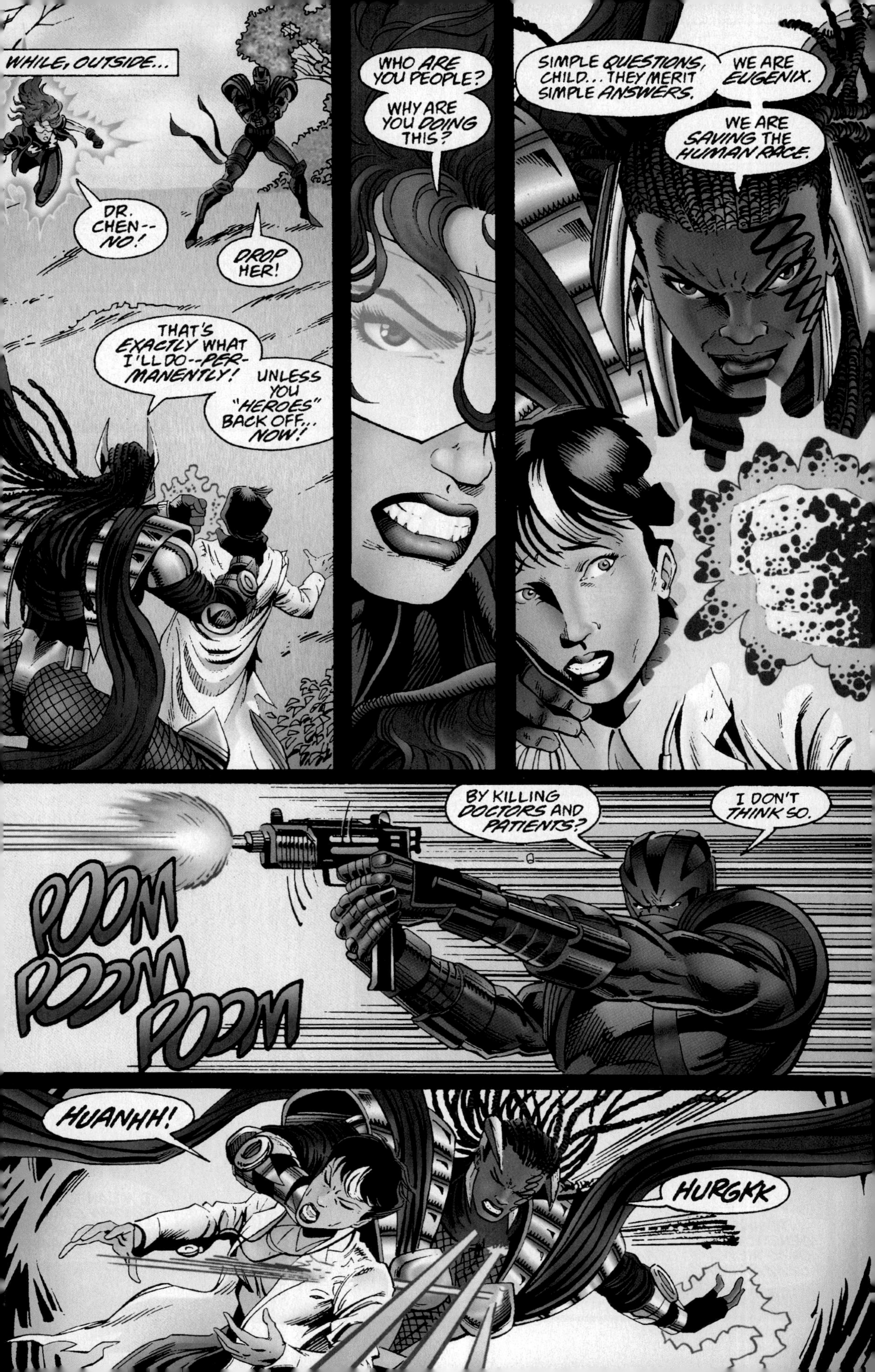

WHILE, OUTSIDE...
DR. CHEN-- NO!
DROP HER!
THAT'S EXACTLY WHAT I'LL DO--PERMANENTLY!
UNLESS YOU "HEROES" BACK OFF... NOW!
WHO ARE YOU PEOPLE?
WHY ARE YOU DOING THIS?
SIMPLE QUESTIONS, CHILD... THEY MERIT SIMPLE ANSWERS.
WE ARE EUGENIX.
WE ARE SAVING THE HUMAN RACE.
BY KILLING DOCTORS AND PATIENTS?
I DON'T THINK SO.
POOM POOM POOM
HUANHH!
HURGKK

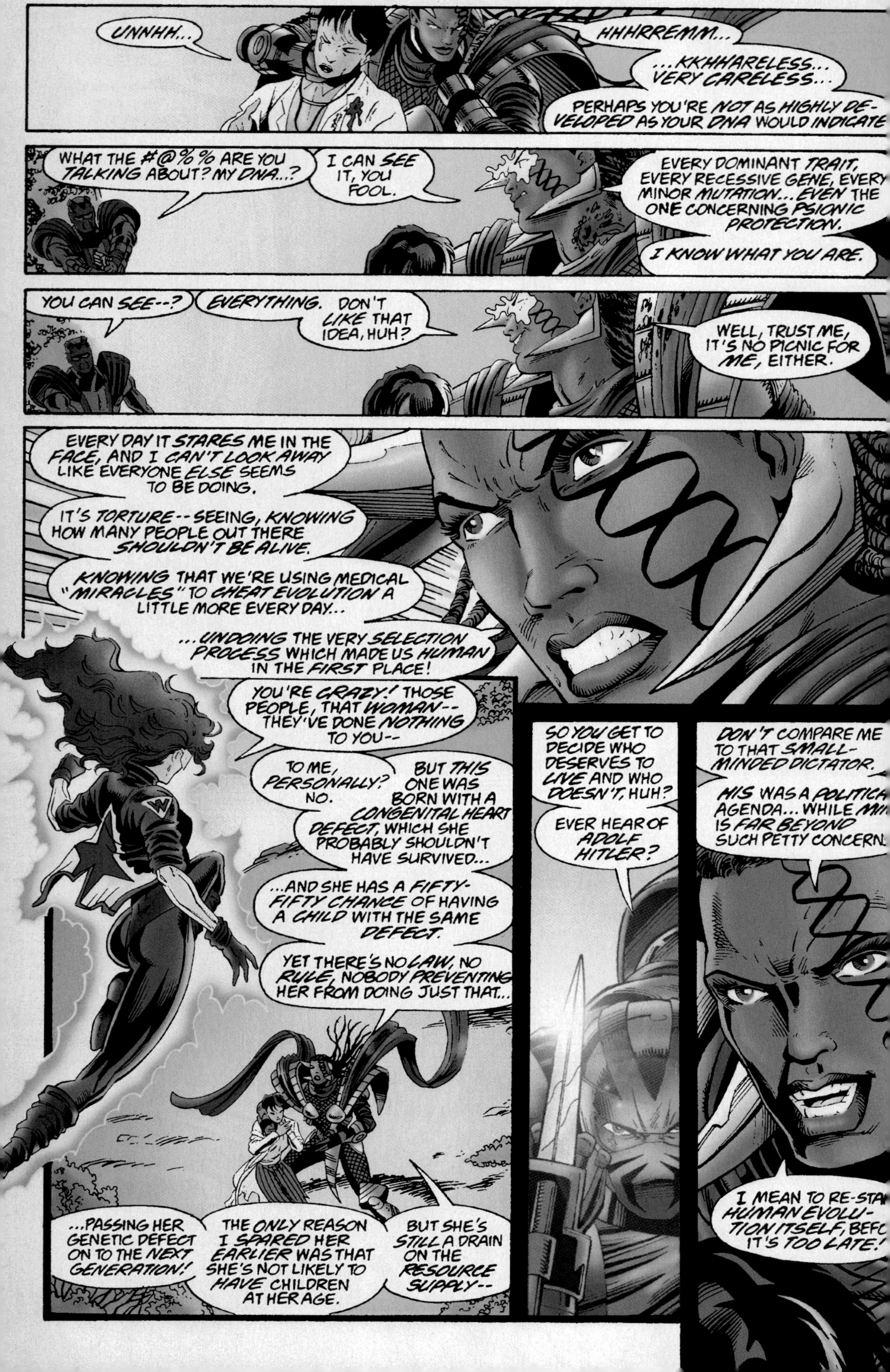
UNNHH...
HHHRREMM...
...KKHHARELESS... VERY CARELESS...
PERHAPS YOU'RE NOT AS HIGHLY DEVELOPED AS YOUR DNA WOULD INDICATE
WHAT THE #@%% ARE YOU TALKING ABOUT? MY DNA...?
I CAN SEE IT, YOU FOOL.
EVERY DOMINANT TRAIT, EVERY RECESSIVE GENE, EVERY MINOR MUTATION... EVEN THE ONE CONCERNING PSIONIC PROTECTION.
I KNOW WHAT YOU ARE.
YOU CAN SEE--?
EVERYTHING. DON'T LIKE THAT IDEA, HUH?
WELL, TRUST ME, IT'S NO PICNIC FOR ME, EITHER.
EVERY DAY IT STARES ME IN THE FACE, AND I CAN'T LOOK AWAY LIKE EVERYONE ELSE SEEMS TO BE DOING.
IT'S TORTURE--SEEING, KNOWING HOW MANY PEOPLE OUT THERE SHOULDN'T BE ALIVE.
KNOWING THAT WE'RE USING MEDICAL "MIRACLES" TO CHEAT EVOLUTION A LITTLE MORE EVERY DAY...
...UNDOING THE VERY SELECTION PROCESS WHICH MADE US HUMAN IN THE FIRST PLACE!
YOU'RE CRAZY! THOSE PEOPLE, THAT WOMAN--THEY'VE DONE NOTHING TO YOU--
TO ME, PERSONALLY? NO.
BUT THIS ONE WAS BORN WITH A CONGENITAL HEART DEFECT, WHICH SHE PROBABLY SHOULDN'T HAVE SURVIVED...
...AND SHE HAS A FIFTY-FIFTY CHANCE OF HAVING A CHILD WITH THE SAME DEFECT.
YET THERE'S NO LAW, NO RULE, NOBODY PREVENTING HER FROM DOING JUST THAT...
...PASSING HER GENETIC DEFECT ON TO THE NEXT GENERATION!
THE ONLY REASON I SPARED HER EARLIER WAS THAT SHE'S NOT LIKELY TO HAVE CHILDREN AT HER AGE.
BUT SHE'S STILL A DRAIN ON THE RESOURCE SUPPLY--
SO YOU GET TO DECIDE WHO DESERVES TO LIVE AND WHO DOESN'T, HUH?
EVER HEAR OF ADOLF HITLER?
DON'T COMPARE ME TO THAT SMALL-MINDED DICTATOR.
HIS WAS A POLITICA AGENDA... WHILE MI IS FAR BEYOND SUCH PETTY CONCERN
I MEAN TO RE-STA HUMAN EVOLUTION ITSELF, BEFO IT'S TOO LATE!

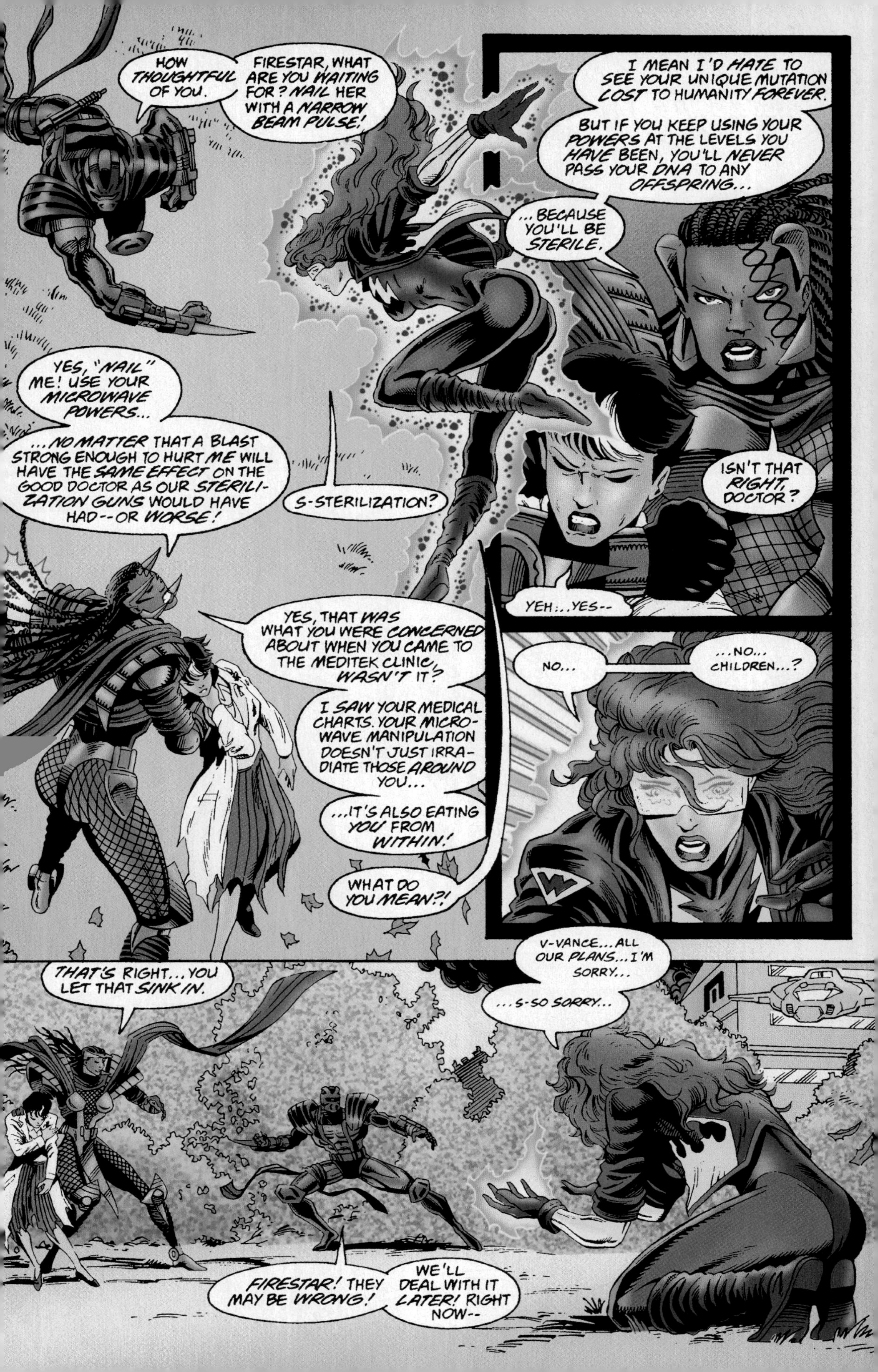
HOW THOUGHTFUL OF YOU.
FIRESTAR, WHAT ARE YOU WAITING FOR? NAIL HER WITH A NARROW BEAM PULSE!
I MEAN I'D HATE TO SEE YOUR UNIQUE MUTATION LOST TO HUMANITY FOREVER.
BUT IF YOU KEEP USING YOUR POWERS AT THE LEVELS YOU HAVE BEEN, YOU'LL NEVER PASS YOUR DNA TO ANY OFFSPRING...
...BECAUSE YOU'LL BE STERILE.
YES, "NAIL" ME! USE YOUR MICROWAVE POWERS...
...NO MATTER THAT A BLAST STRONG ENOUGH TO HURT ME WILL HAVE THE SAME EFFECT ON THE GOOD DOCTOR AS OUR STERILIZATION GUNS WOULD HAVE HAD--OR WORSE!
S-STERILIZATION?
ISN'T THAT RIGHT, DOCTOR?
YEH...YES--
YES, THAT WAS WHAT YOU WERE CONCERNED ABOUT WHEN YOU CAME TO THE MEDITEK CLINIC, WASN'T IT?
I SAW YOUR MEDICAL CHARTS. YOUR MICROWAVE MANIPULATION DOESN'T JUST IRRADIATE THOSE AROUND YOU...
...IT'S ALSO EATING YOU FROM WITHIN!
WHAT DO YOU MEAN?!
NO...
...NO... CHILDREN...?
THAT'S RIGHT... YOU LET THAT SINK IN.
V-VANCE... ALL OUR PLANS... I'M SORRY...
...S-SO SORRY...
FIRESTAR! THEY MAY BE WRONG!
WE'LL DEAL WITH IT LATER! RIGHT NOW--

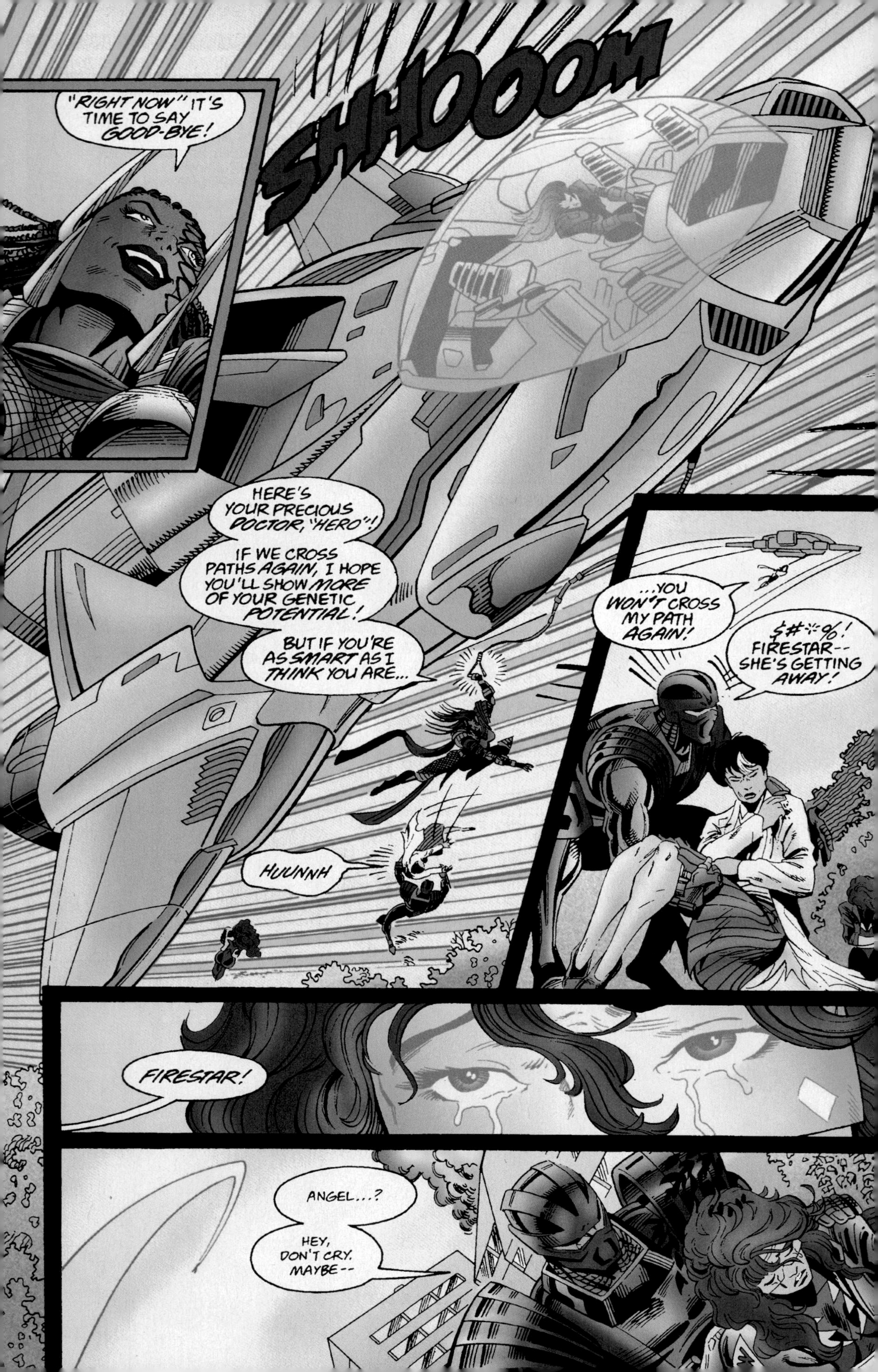
"RIGHT NOW" IT'S TIME TO SAY GOOD-BYE!
SHHOOOOM
HERE'S YOUR PRECIOUS DOCTOR, "HERO"!
IF WE CROSS PATHS AGAIN, I HOPE YOU'LL SHOW MORE OF YOUR GENETIC POTENTIAL!
BUT IF YOU'RE AS SMART AS I THINK YOU ARE...
...YOU WON'T CROSS MY PATH AGAIN!
HUUNNH
$#*%! FIRESTAR-- SHE'S GETTING AWAY!
FIRESTAR!
ANGEL...?
HEY, DON'T CRY. MAYBE--

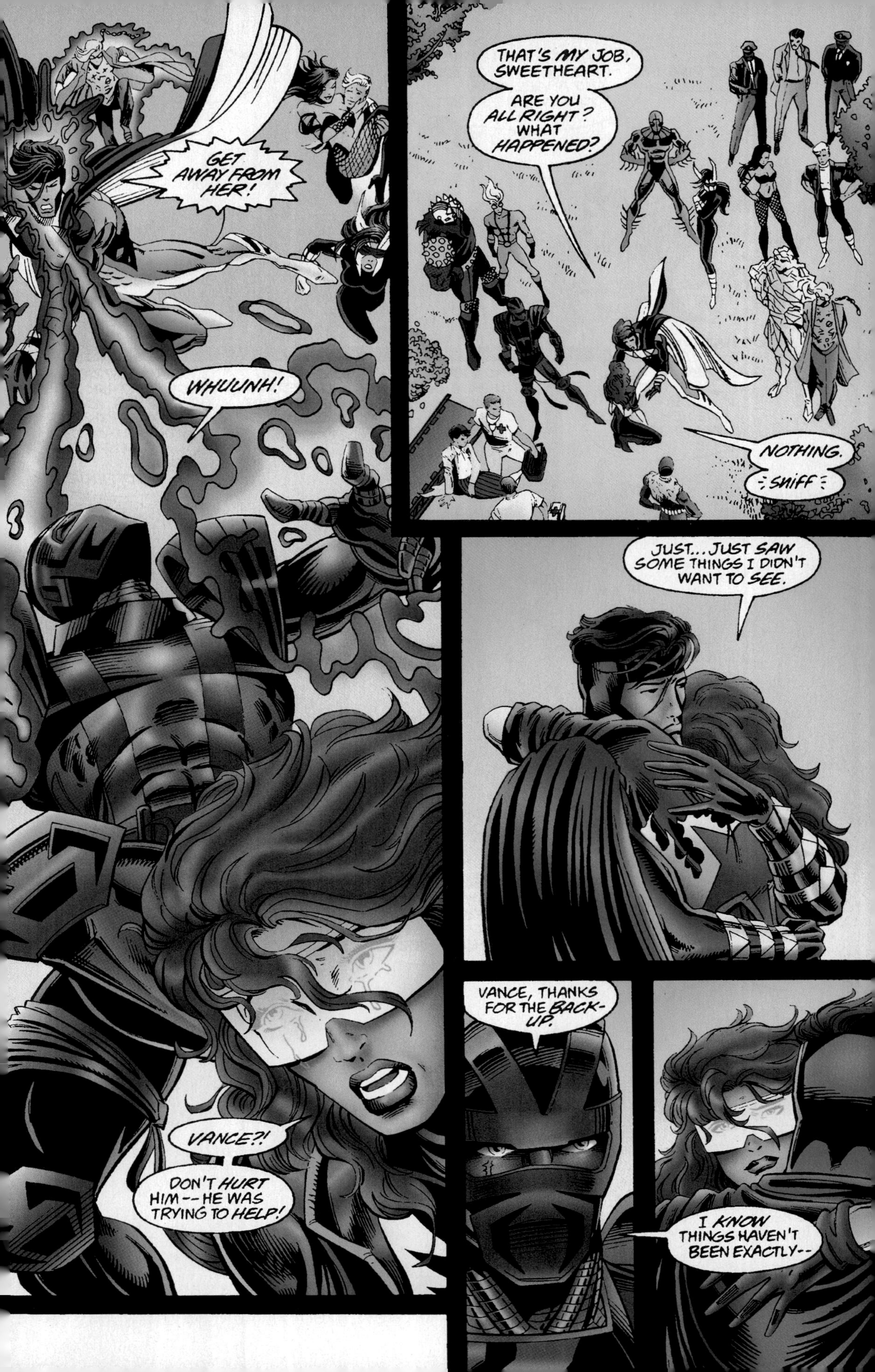

GET AWAY FROM HER!
WHUUNH!
VANCE?!
DON'T HURT HIM--HE WAS TRYING TO HELP!
THAT'S MY JOB, SWEETHEART.
ARE YOU ALL RIGHT? WHAT HAPPENED?
NOTHING.
SNIFF
JUST...JUST SAW SOME THINGS I DIDN'T WANT TO SEE.
VANCE, THANKS FOR THE BACK-UP.
I KNOW THINGS HAVEN'T BEEN EXACTLY--

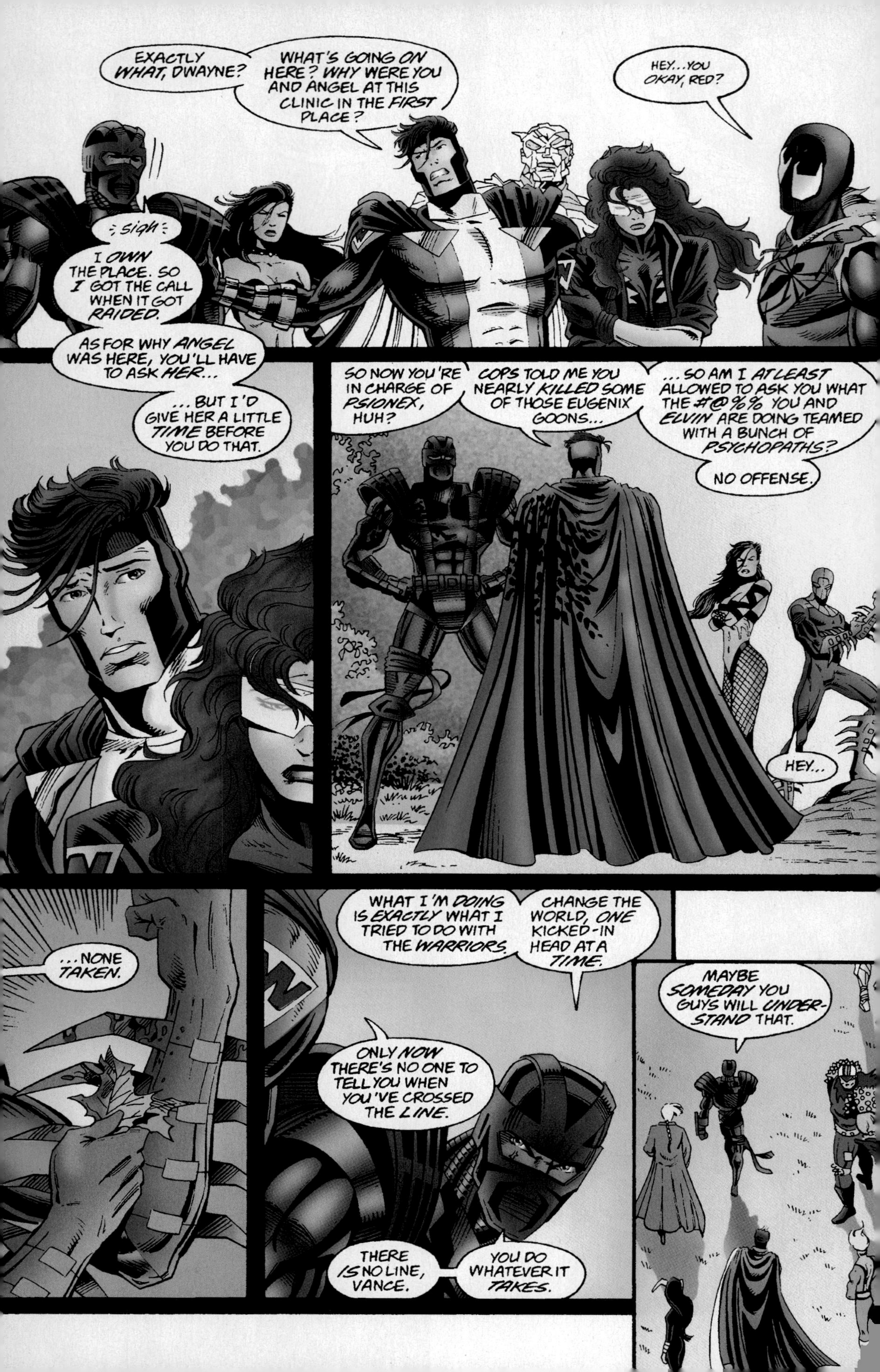
EXACTLY WHAT, DWAYNE?
WHAT'S GOING ON HERE? WHY WERE YOU AND ANGEL AT THIS CLINIC IN THE FIRST PLACE?
HEY...YOU OKAY, RED?
sigh
I OWN THE PLACE. SO I GOT THE CALL WHEN IT GOT RAIDED.
AS FOR WHY ANGEL WAS HERE, YOU'LL HAVE TO ASK HER...
...BUT I'D GIVE HER A LITTLE TIME BEFORE YOU DO THAT.
SO NOW YOU'RE IN CHARGE OF PSIONEX, HUH?
COPS TOLD ME YOU NEARLY KILLED SOME OF THOSE EUGENIX GOONS...
...SO AM I AT LEAST ALLOWED TO ASK YOU WHAT THE #@%% YOU AND ELVIN ARE DOING TEAMED WITH A BUNCH OF PSYCHOPATHS?
NO OFFENSE.
HEY...
...NONE TAKEN.
WHAT I'M DOING IS EXACTLY WHAT I TRIED TO DO WITH THE WARRIORS.
CHANGE THE WORLD, ONE KICKED-IN HEAD AT A TIME.
ONLY NOW THERE'S NO ONE TO TELL YOU WHEN YOU'VE CROSSED THE LINE.
THERE IS NO LINE, VANCE.
YOU DO WHATEVER IT TAKES.
MAYBE SOMEDAY YOU GUYS WILL UNDERSTAND THAT.

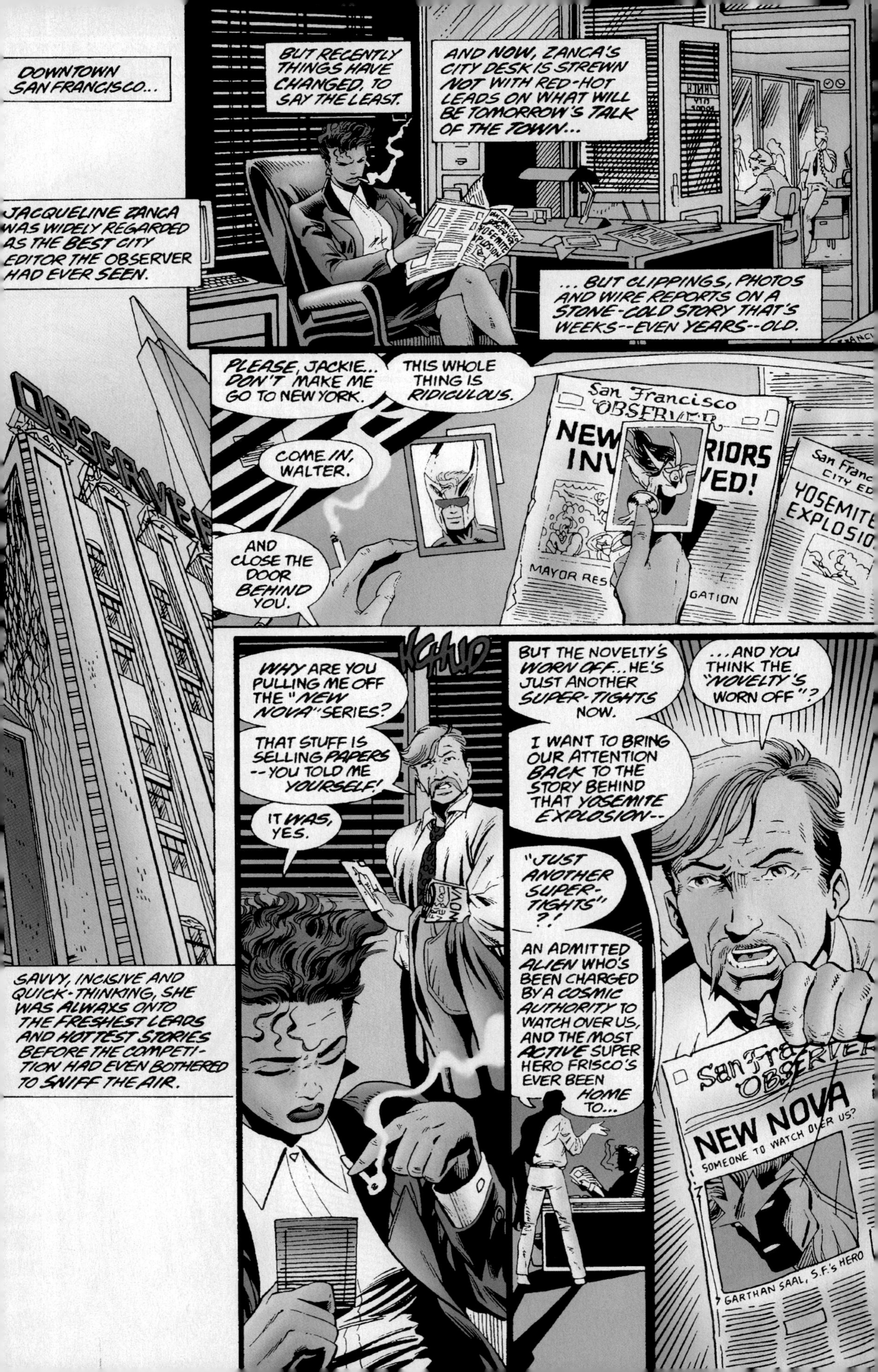

DOWNTOWN SAN FRANCISCO...
BUT RECENTLY THINGS HAVE CHANGED, TO SAY THE LEAST.
AND NOW, ZANCA'S CITY DESK IS STREWN NOT WITH RED-HOT LEADS ON WHAT WILL BE TOMORROW'S TALK OF THE TOWN...
JACQUELINE ZANCA WAS WIDELY REGARDED AS THE BEST CITY EDITOR THE OBSERVER HAD EVER SEEN.
YOSEMITE EXPLOSION
...BUT CLIPPINGS, PHOTOS AND WIRE REPORTS ON A STONE-COLD STORY THAT'S WEEKS--EVEN YEARS--OLD.
OBSERVER
PLEASE, JACKIE... DON'T MAKE ME GO TO NEW YORK.
THIS WHOLE THING IS RIDICULOUS.
COME IN, WALTER.
AND CLOSE THE DOOR BEHIND YOU.
San Francisco OBSERVER
NEW RIORS INV VED!
MAYOR RES GATION
San Franc CITY ED
YOSEMITE EXPLOSIO
KCHUD
WHY ARE YOU PULLING ME OFF THE "NEW NOVA" SERIES?
THAT STUFF IS SELLING PAPERS --YOU TOLD ME YOURSELF!
IT WAS, YES.
BUT THE NOVELTY'S WORN OFF.. HE'S JUST ANOTHER SUPER-TIGHTS NOW.
I WANT TO BRING OUR ATTENTION BACK TO THE STORY BEHIND THAT YOSEMITE EXPLOSION--
...AND YOU THINK THE "NOVELTY'S WORN OFF"?
"JUST ANOTHER SUPER-TIGHTS"?!
AN ADMITTED ALIEN WHO'S BEEN CHARGED BY A COSMIC AUTHORITY TO WATCH OVER US, AND THE MOST ACTIVE SUPER HERO FRISCO'S EVER BEEN HOME TO...
SAVVY, INCISIVE AND QUICK-THINKING, SHE WAS ALWAYS ONTO THE FRESHEST LEADS AND HOTTEST STORIES BEFORE THE COMPETITION HAD EVEN BOTHERED TO SNIFF THE AIR.
San Fran OBSERVER
NEW NOVA
SOMEONE TO WATCH OVER US?
GARTHAN SAAL, S.F.'s HERO

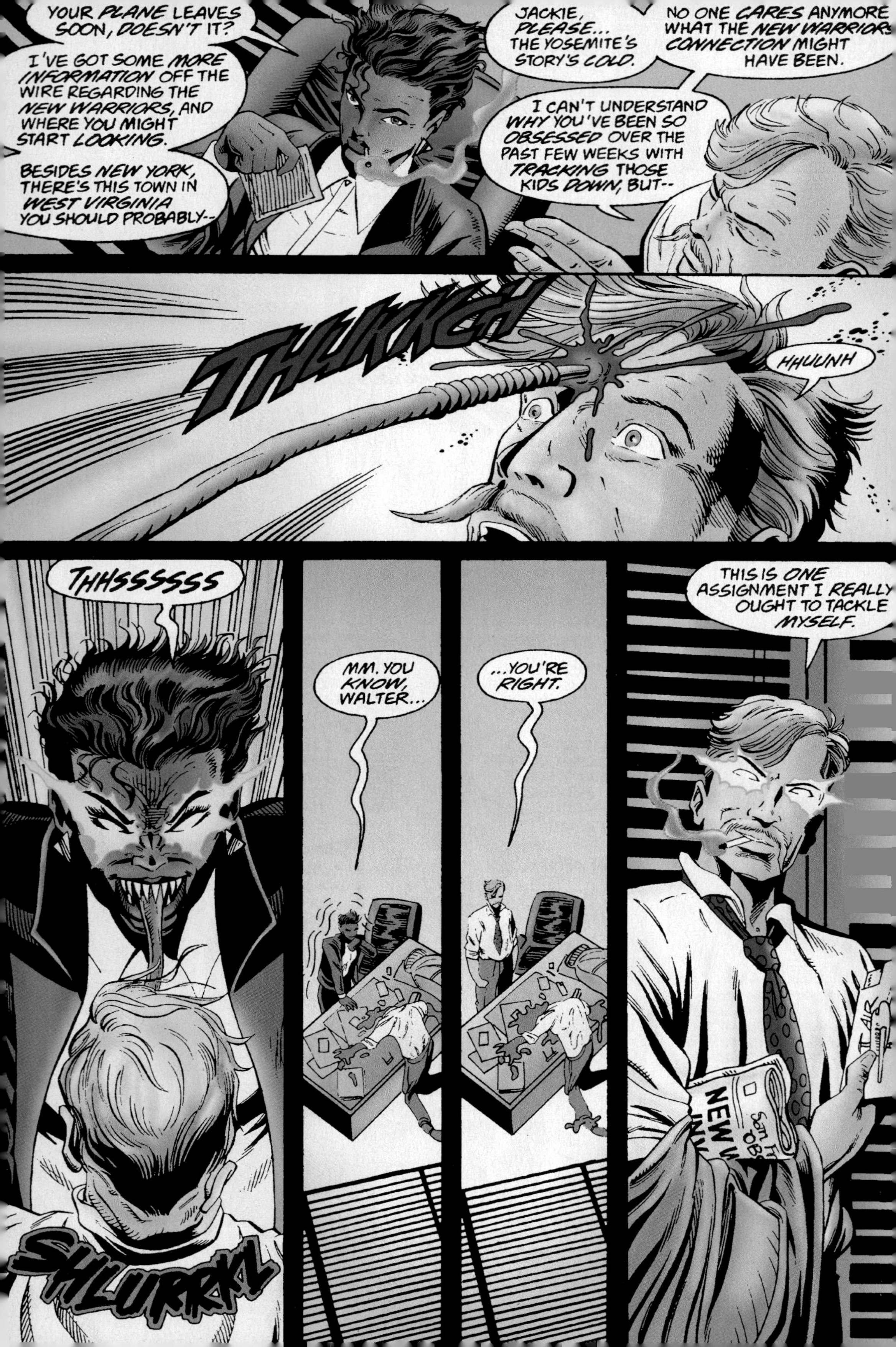
YOUR PLANE LEAVES SOON, DOESN'T IT?
I'VE GOT SOME MORE INFORMATION OFF THE WIRE REGARDING THE NEW WARRIORS, AND WHERE YOU MIGHT START LOOKING.
BESIDES NEW YORK, THERE'S THIS TOWN IN WEST VIRGINIA YOU SHOULD PROBABLY--
JACKIE, PLEASE... THE YOSEMITE'S STORY'S COLD.
NO ONE CARES ANYMORE WHAT THE NEW WARRIORS CONNECTION MIGHT HAVE BEEN.
I CAN'T UNDERSTAND WHY YOU'VE BEEN SO OBSESSED OVER THE PAST FEW WEEKS WITH TRACKING THOSE KIDS DOWN, BUT--
THUKKCH
HHUUNH
THHSSSSSS
SHLURRKL
MM. YOU KNOW, WALTER...
...YOU'RE RIGHT.
THIS IS ONE ASSIGNMENT I REALLY OUGHT TO TACKLE MYSELF.

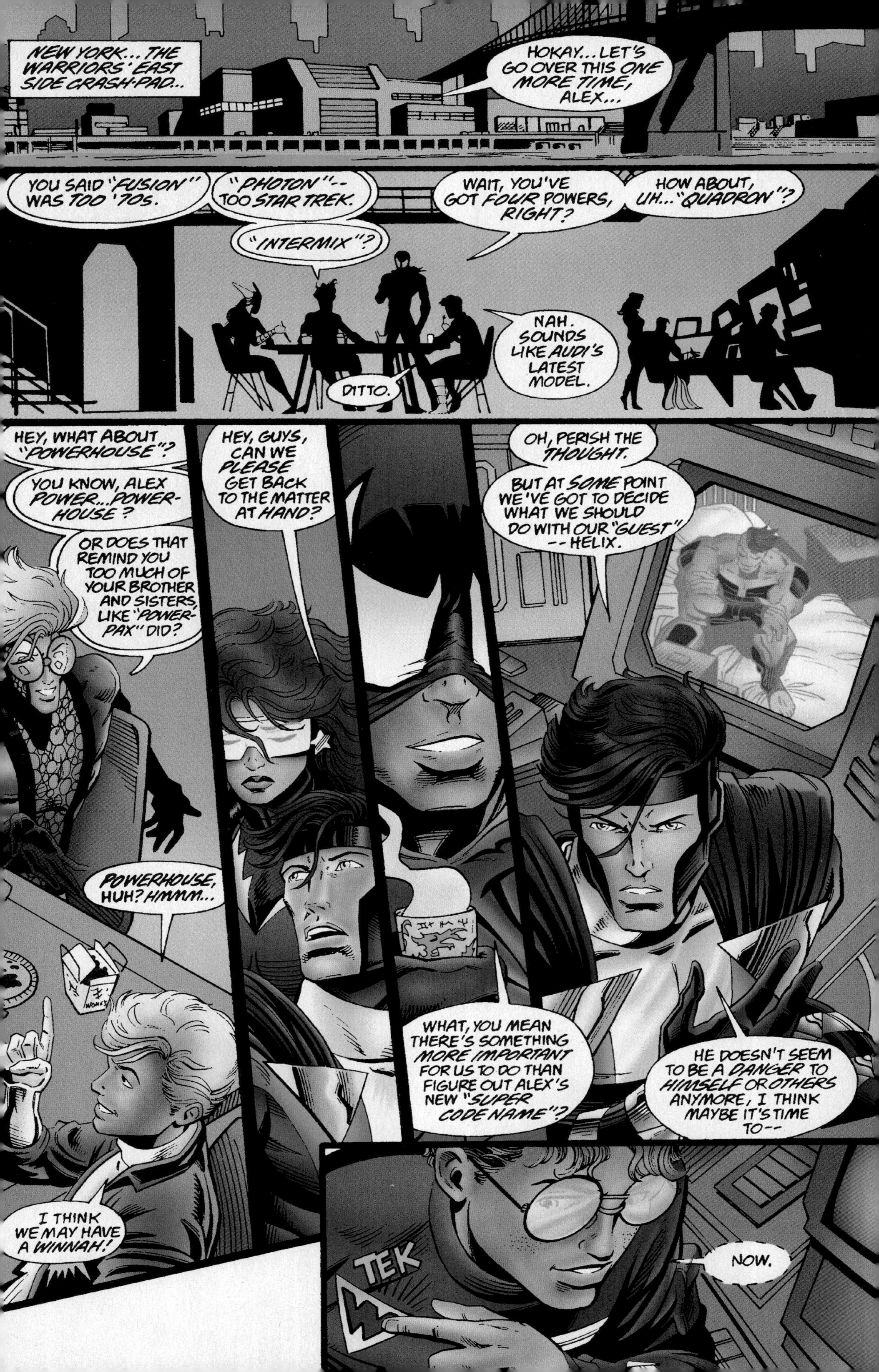
NEW YORK... THE WARRIORS' EAST SIDE CRASH-PAD...
HOKAY... LET'S GO OVER THIS ONE MORE TIME, ALEX...
YOU SAID "FUSION" WAS TOO '70S.
"PHOTON"-- TOO STAR TREK.
"INTERMIX"?
WAIT, YOU'VE GOT FOUR POWERS, RIGHT?
HOW ABOUT, UH... "QUADRON"?
NAH. SOUNDS LIKE AUDI'S LATEST MODEL.
DITTO.
HEY, WHAT ABOUT "POWERHOUSE"?
YOU KNOW, ALEX POWER... POWER-HOUSE?
OR DOES THAT REMIND YOU TOO MUCH OF YOUR BROTHER AND SISTERS, LIKE "POWER-PAX" DID?
POWERHOUSE, HUH? HMMM...
I THINK WE MAY HAVE A WINNAH!
HEY, GUYS, CAN WE PLEASE GET BACK TO THE MATTER AT HAND?
WHAT, YOU MEAN THERE'S SOMETHING MORE IMPORTANT FOR US TO DO THAN FIGURE OUT ALEX'S NEW "SUPER CODE NAME"?
OH, PERISH THE THOUGHT.
BUT AT SOME POINT WE'VE GOT TO DECIDE WHAT WE SHOULD DO WITH OUR "GUEST" -- HELIX.
HE DOESN'T SEEM TO BE A DANGER TO HIMSELF OR OTHERS ANYMORE, I THINK MAYBE IT'S TIME TO--
NOW.
TEK

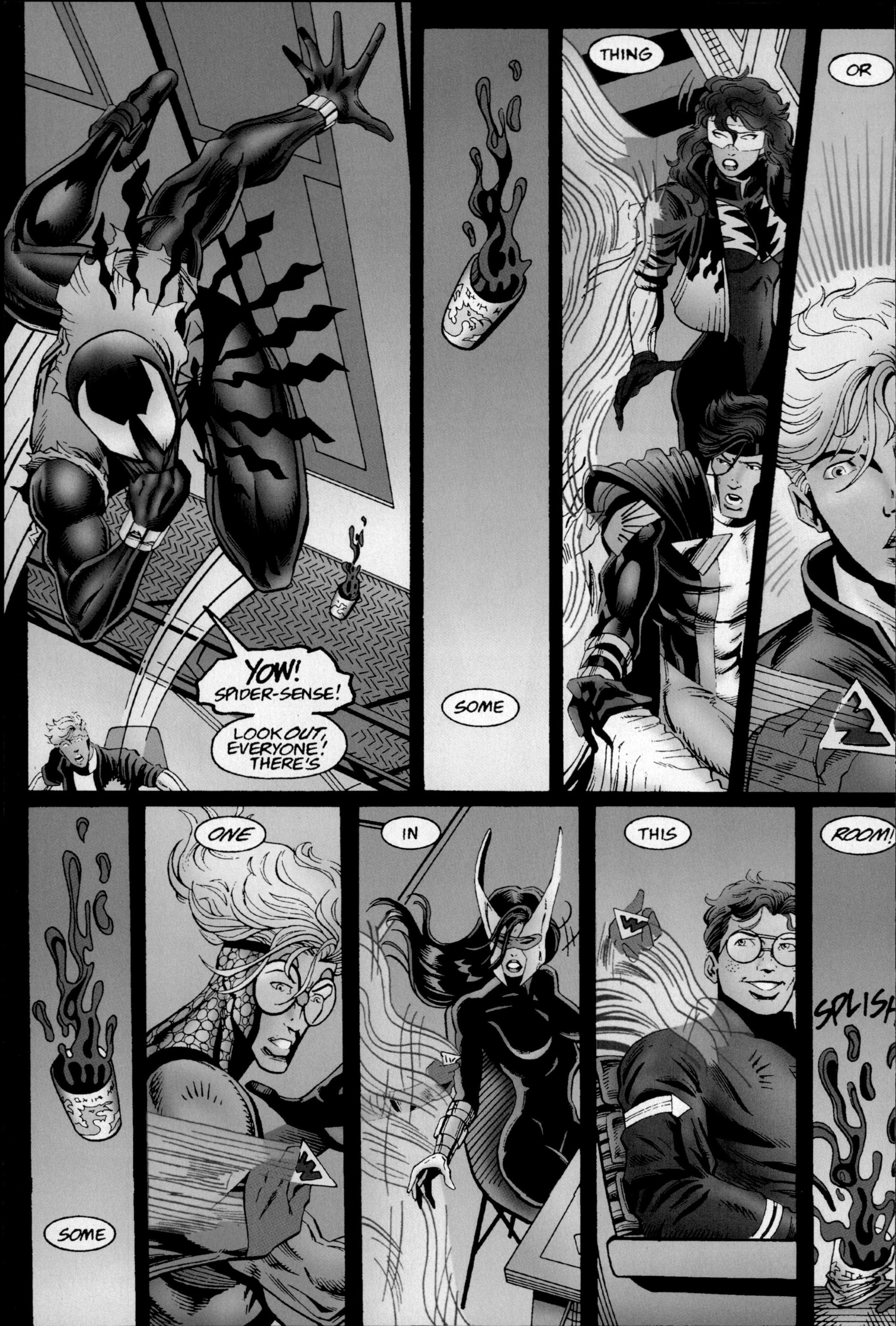
YOW! SPIDER-SENSE!
LOOK OUT, EVERYONE! THERE'S
SOME
THING
OR
SOME
ONE
IN
THIS
ROOM!
SPLISH

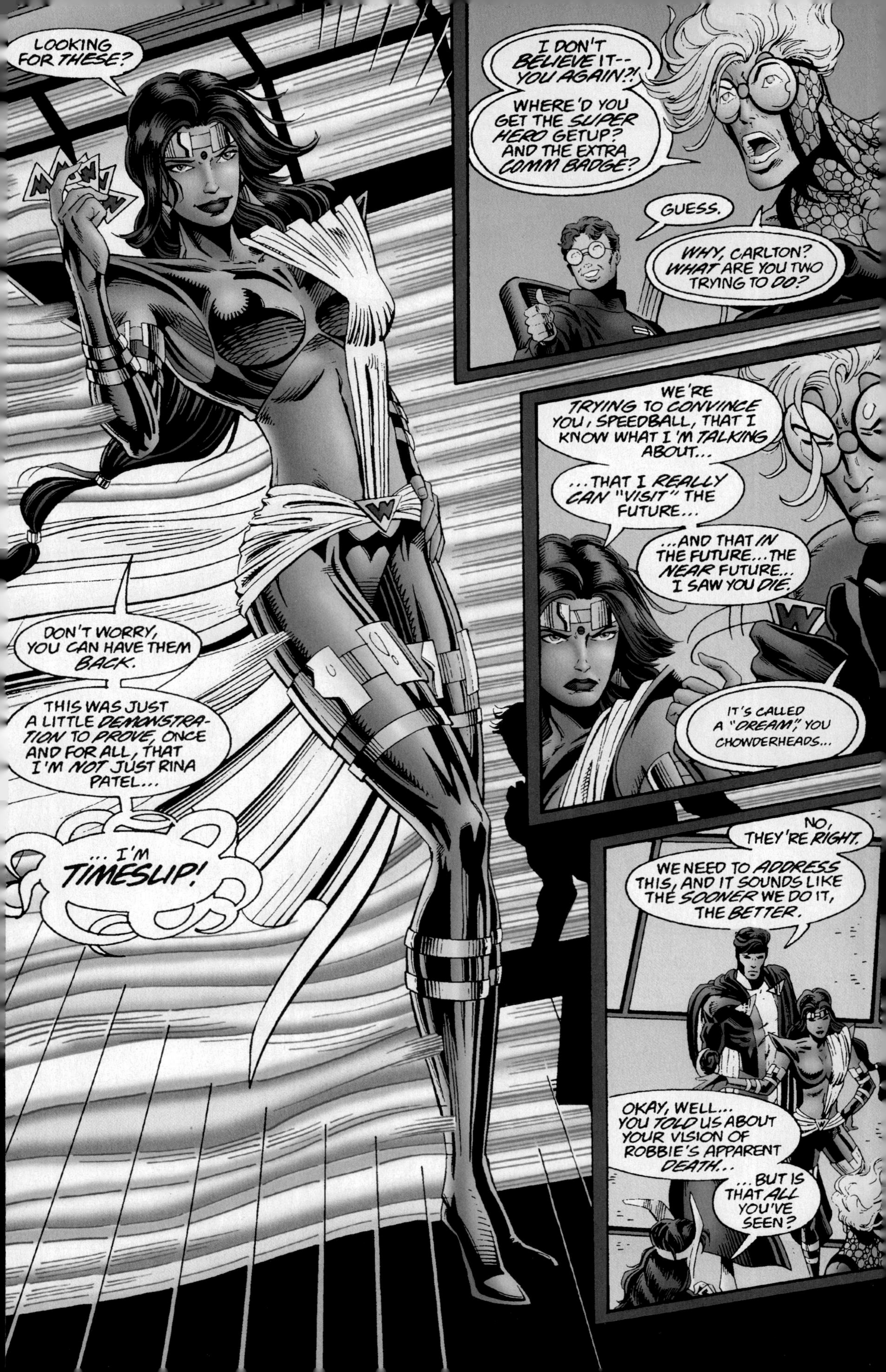
LOOKING FOR THESE?
DON'T WORRY, YOU CAN HAVE THEM BACK.
THIS WAS JUST A LITTLE DEMONSTRATION TO PROVE, ONCE AND FOR ALL, THAT I'M NOT JUST RINA PATEL...
... I'M TIMESLIP!
I DON'T BELIEVE IT-- YOU AGAIN?!
WHERE'D YOU GET THE SUPER HERO GETUP? AND THE EXTRA COMM BADGE?
GUESS.
WHY, CARLTON? WHAT ARE YOU TWO TRYING TO DO?
WE'RE TRYING TO CONVINCE YOU, SPEEDBALL, THAT I KNOW WHAT I'M TALKING ABOUT...
...THAT I REALLY CAN "VISIT" THE FUTURE...
...AND THAT IN THE FUTURE... THE NEAR FUTURE... I SAW YOU DIE.
IT'S CALLED A "DREAM," YOU CHOWDERHEADS...
NO, THEY'RE RIGHT.
WE NEED TO ADDRESS THIS, AND IT SOUNDS LIKE THE SOONER WE DO IT, THE BETTER.
OKAY, WELL... YOU TOLD US ABOUT YOUR VISION OF ROBBIE'S APPARENT DEATH...
... BUT IS THAT ALL YOU'VE SEEN?

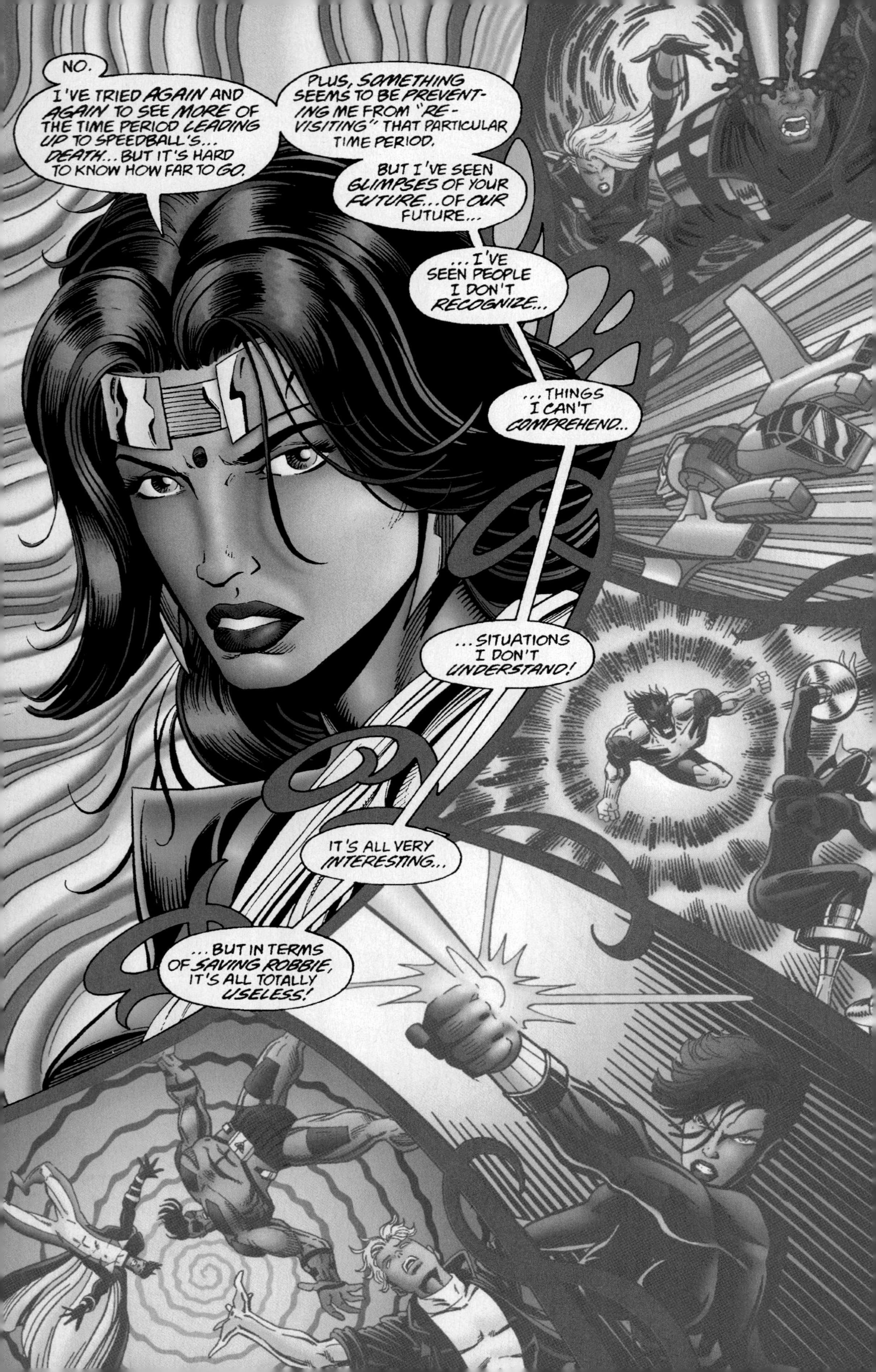
NO.
I'VE TRIED AGAIN AND AGAIN TO SEE MORE OF THE TIME PERIOD LEADING UP TO SPEEDBALL'S... DEATH... BUT IT'S HARD TO KNOW HOW FAR TO GO.
PLUS, SOMETHING SEEMS TO BE PREVENT-ING ME FROM "RE-VISITING" THAT PARTICULAR TIME PERIOD.
BUT I'VE SEEN GLIMPSES OF YOUR FUTURE... OF OUR FUTURE...
...I'VE SEEN PEOPLE I DON'T RECOGNIZE...
...THINGS I CAN'T COMPREHEND...
...SITUATIONS I DON'T UNDERSTAND!
IT'S ALL VERY INTERESTING...
...BUT IN TERMS OF SAVING ROBBIE, IT'S ALL TOTALLY USELESS!

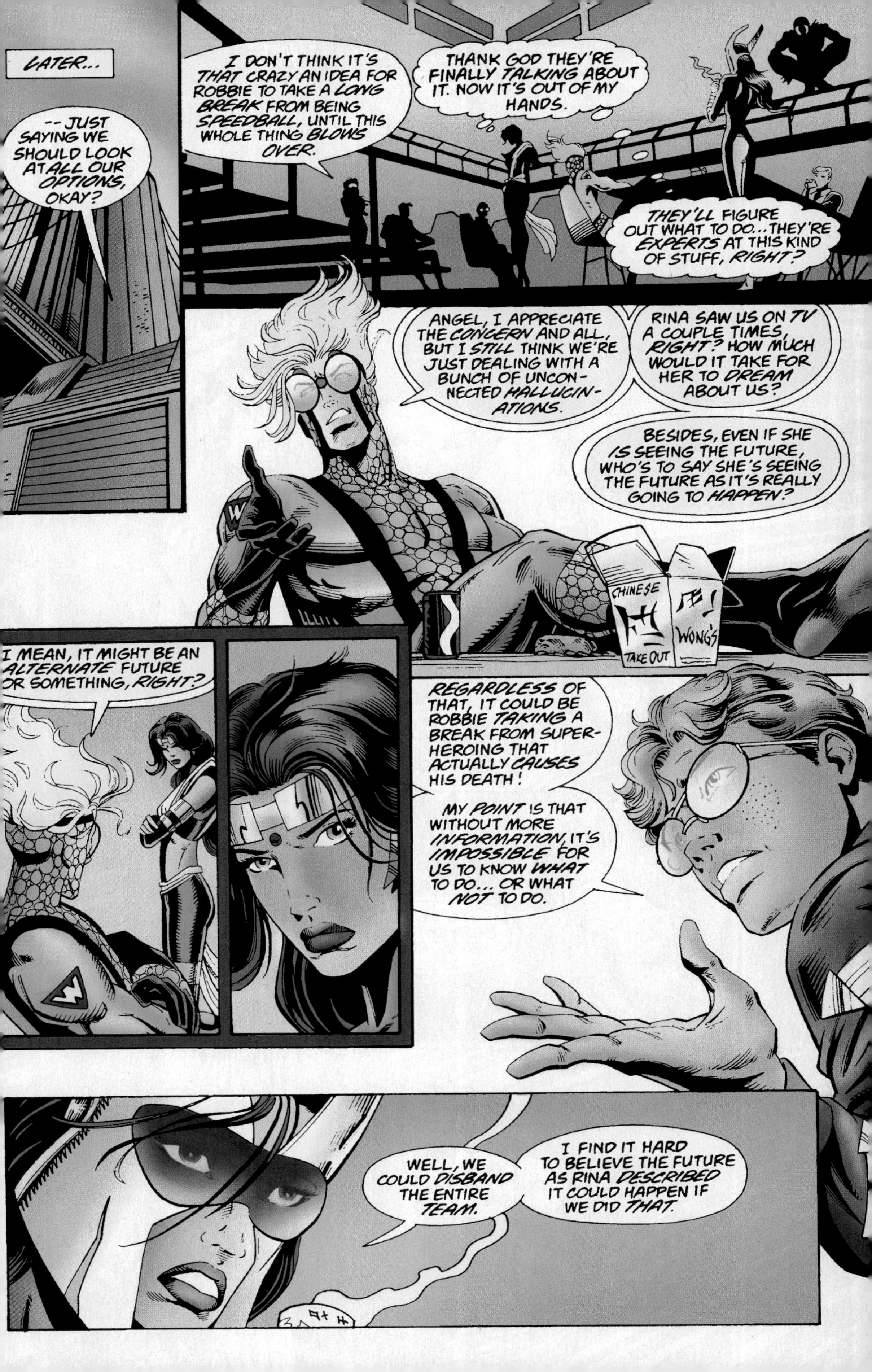
LATER...
-- JUST SAYING WE SHOULD LOOK AT ALL OUR OPTIONS, OKAY?
I DON'T THINK IT'S THAT CRAZY AN IDEA FOR ROBBIE TO TAKE A LONG BREAK FROM BEING SPEEDBALL, UNTIL THIS WHOLE THING BLOWS OVER.
THANK GOD THEY'RE FINALLY TALKING ABOUT IT. NOW IT'S OUT OF MY HANDS.
THEY'LL FIGURE OUT WHAT TO DO... THEY'RE EXPERTS AT THIS KIND OF STUFF, RIGHT?
ANGEL, I APPRECIATE THE CONCERN AND ALL, BUT I STILL THINK WE'RE JUST DEALING WITH A BUNCH OF UNCONNECTED HALLUCINATIONS.
RINA SAW US ON TV A COUPLE TIMES, RIGHT? HOW MUCH WOULD IT TAKE FOR HER TO DREAM ABOUT US?
BESIDES, EVEN IF SHE IS SEEING THE FUTURE, WHO'S TO SAY SHE'S SEEING THE FUTURE AS IT'S REALLY GOING TO HAPPEN?
CHINESE
WONG'S
TAKE OUT
I MEAN, IT MIGHT BE AN ALTERNATE FUTURE OR SOMETHING, RIGHT?
REGARDLESS OF THAT, IT COULD BE ROBBIE TAKING A BREAK FROM SUPER-HEROING THAT ACTUALLY CAUSES HIS DEATH!
MY POINT IS THAT WITHOUT MORE INFORMATION, IT'S IMPOSSIBLE FOR US TO KNOW WHAT TO DO... OR WHAT NOT TO DO.
WELL, WE COULD DISBAND THE ENTIRE TEAM.
I FIND IT HARD TO BELIEVE THE FUTURE AS RINA DESCRIBED IT COULD HAPPEN IF WE DID THAT.

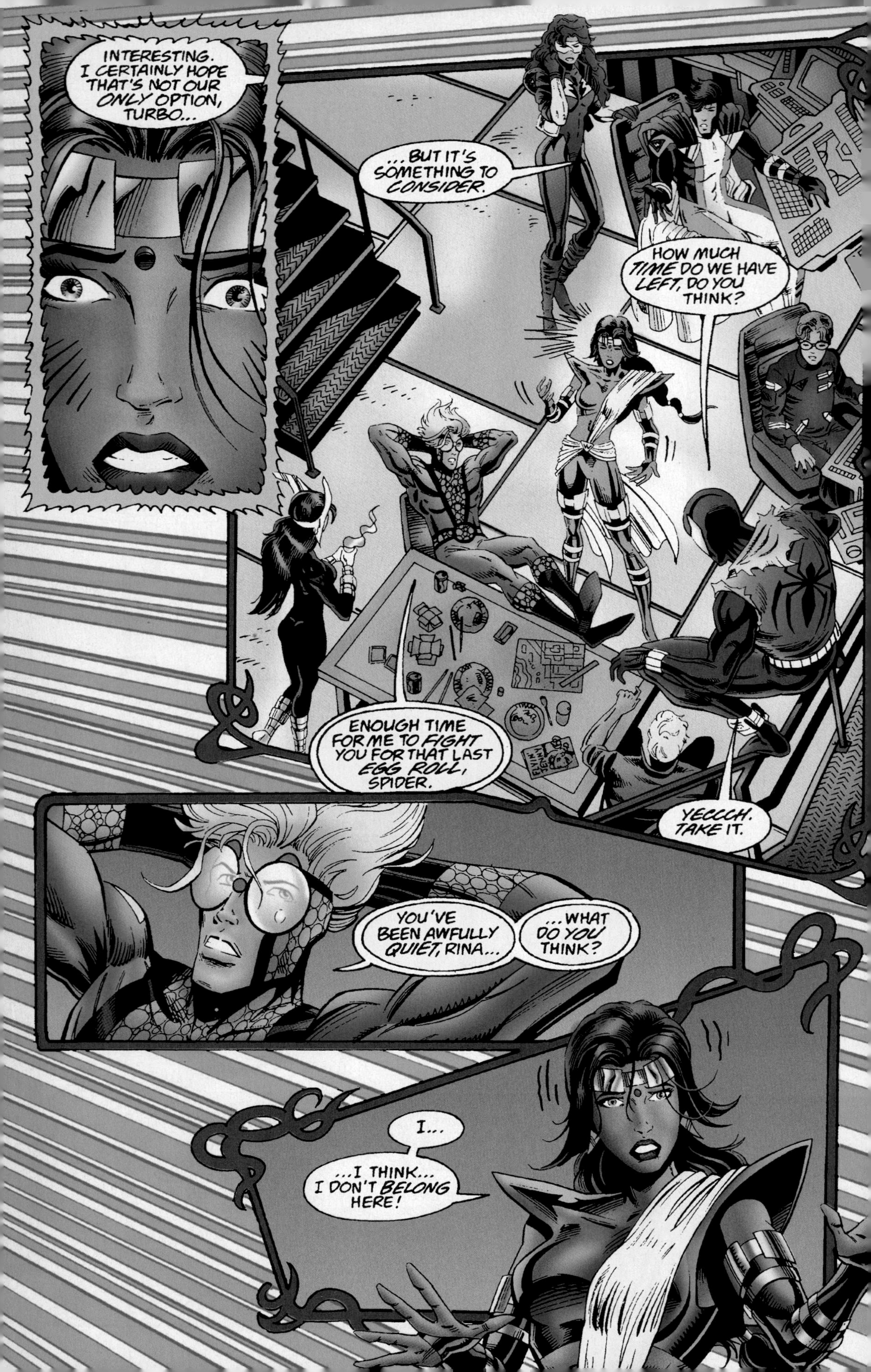
INTERESTING. I CERTAINLY HOPE THAT'S NOT OUR ONLY OPTION, TURBO...
...BUT IT'S SOMETHING TO CONSIDER.
HOW MUCH TIME DO WE HAVE LEFT, DO YOU THINK?
ENOUGH TIME FOR ME TO FIGHT YOU FOR THAT LAST EGG ROLL, SPIDER.
YECCCH. TAKE IT.
YOU'VE BEEN AWFULLY QUIET, RINA...
...WHAT DO YOU THINK?
I...
...I THINK... I DON'T BELONG HERE!

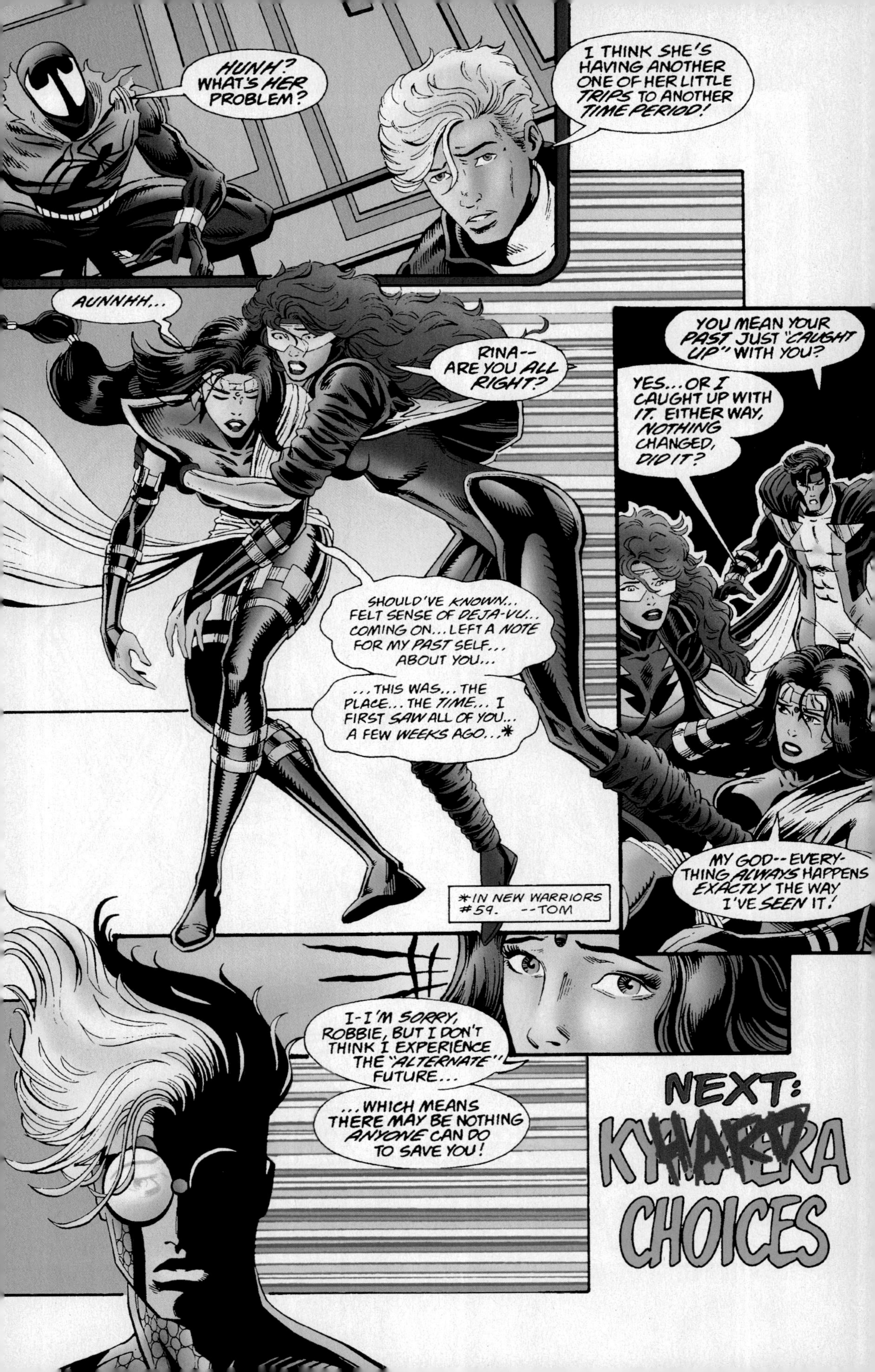
HUNH? WHAT'S HER PROBLEM?
I THINK SHE'S HAVING ANOTHER ONE OF HER LITTLE TRIPS TO ANOTHER TIME PERIOD!
AUNNHH...
RINA-- ARE YOU ALL RIGHT?
SHOULD'VE KNOWN... FELT SENSE OF DEJA-VU... COMING ON... LEFT A NOTE FOR MY PAST SELF... ABOUT YOU...
...THIS WAS... THE PLACE... THE TIME... I FIRST SAW ALL OF YOU... A FEW WEEKS AGO...*
*IN NEW WARRIORS #59. --TOM
YOU MEAN YOUR PAST JUST "CAUGHT UP" WITH YOU?
YES... OR I CAUGHT UP WITH IT. EITHER WAY, NOTHING CHANGED, DID IT?
MY GOD--EVERYTHING ALWAYS HAPPENS EXACTLY THE WAY I'VE SEEN IT!
I-I'M SORRY, ROBBIE, BUT I DON'T THINK I EXPERIENCE THE "ALTERNATE" FUTURE...
...WHICH MEANS THERE MAY BE NOTHING ANYONE CAN DO TO SAVE YOU!
NEXT: KYHARDERA CHOICES

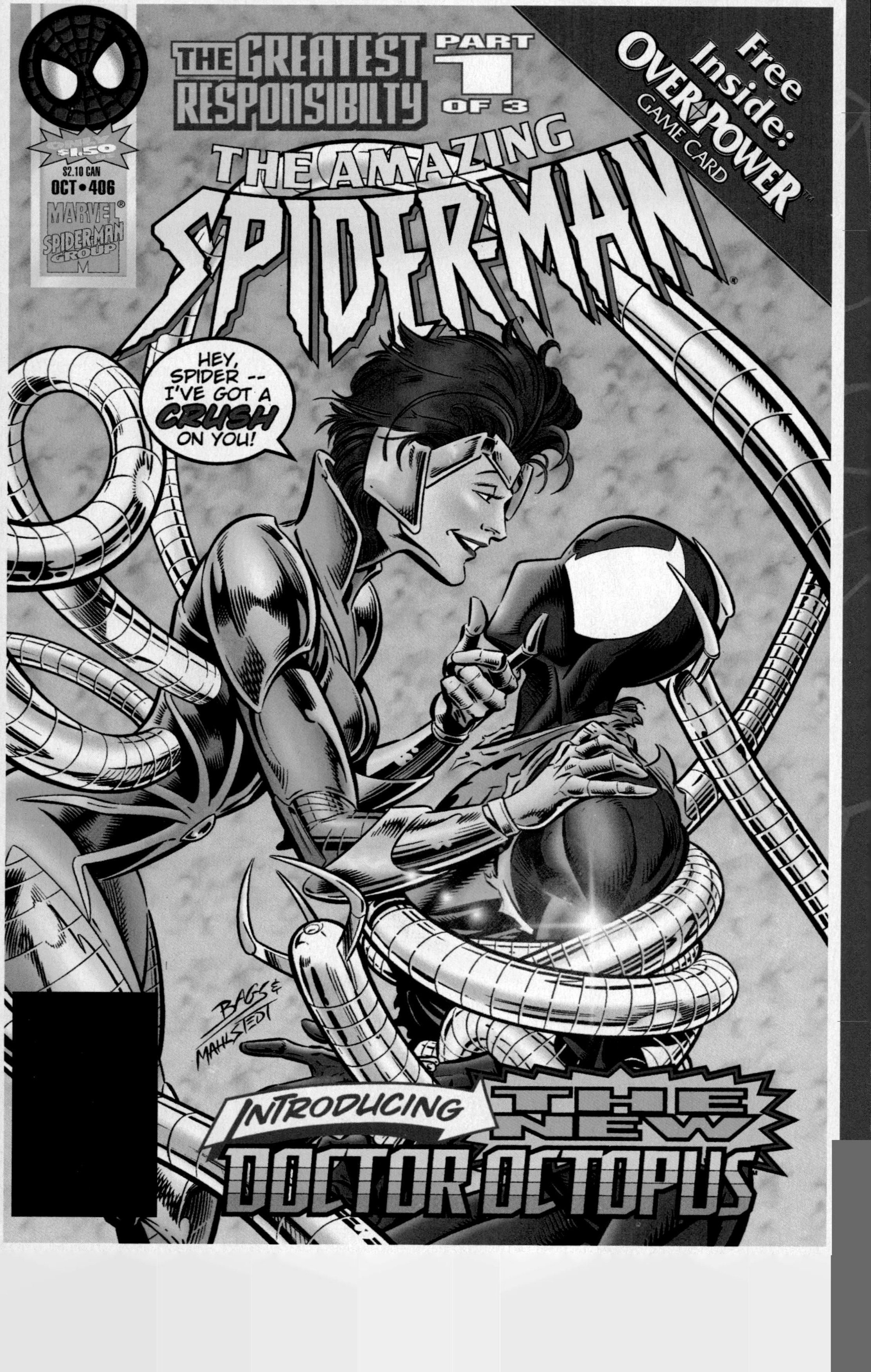
THE GREATEST RESPONSIBILTY
PART 1 OF 3
Free Inside: OVERPOWER GAME CARD
ONLY $1.50
$2.10 CAN
OCT • 406
MARVEL
SPIDER-MAN GROUP
THE AMAZING SPIDER-MAN
HEY, SPIDER -- I'VE GOT A CRUSH ON YOU!
BAGS & MAHLSTEDT
INTRODUCING THE NEW DOCTOR OCTOPUS

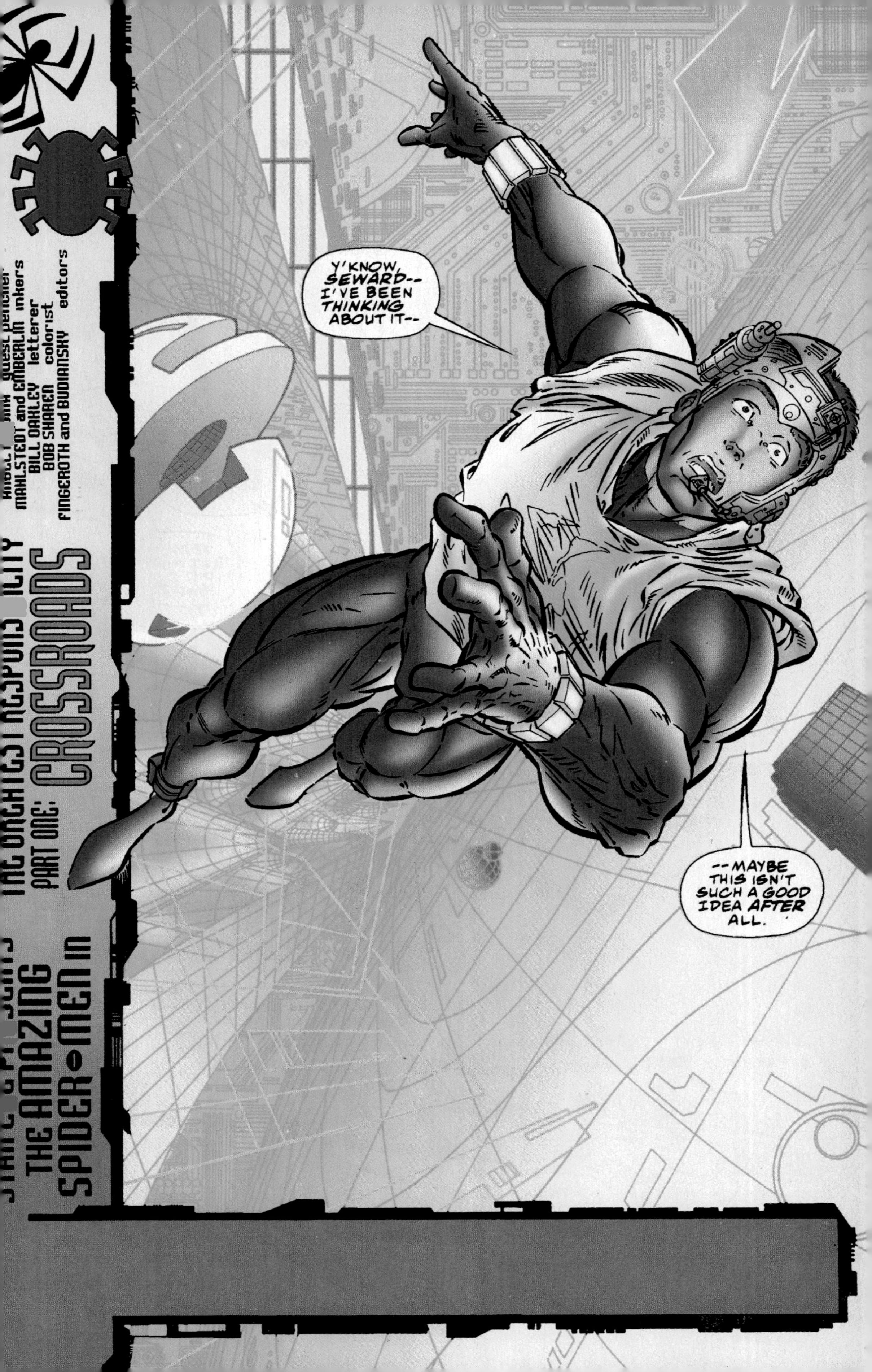
THE AMAZING
SPIDER-MEN in
PART ONE: CROSSROADS
MAHLSTEDT and EMBERLIN inkers
BILL OAKLEY letterer
BOB SHAREN colorist
FINGEROTH and BUDIANSKY editors
Y'KNOW, SEWARD-- I'VE BEEN THINKING ABOUT IT--
--MAYBE THIS ISN'T SUCH A GOOD IDEA AFTER ALL.

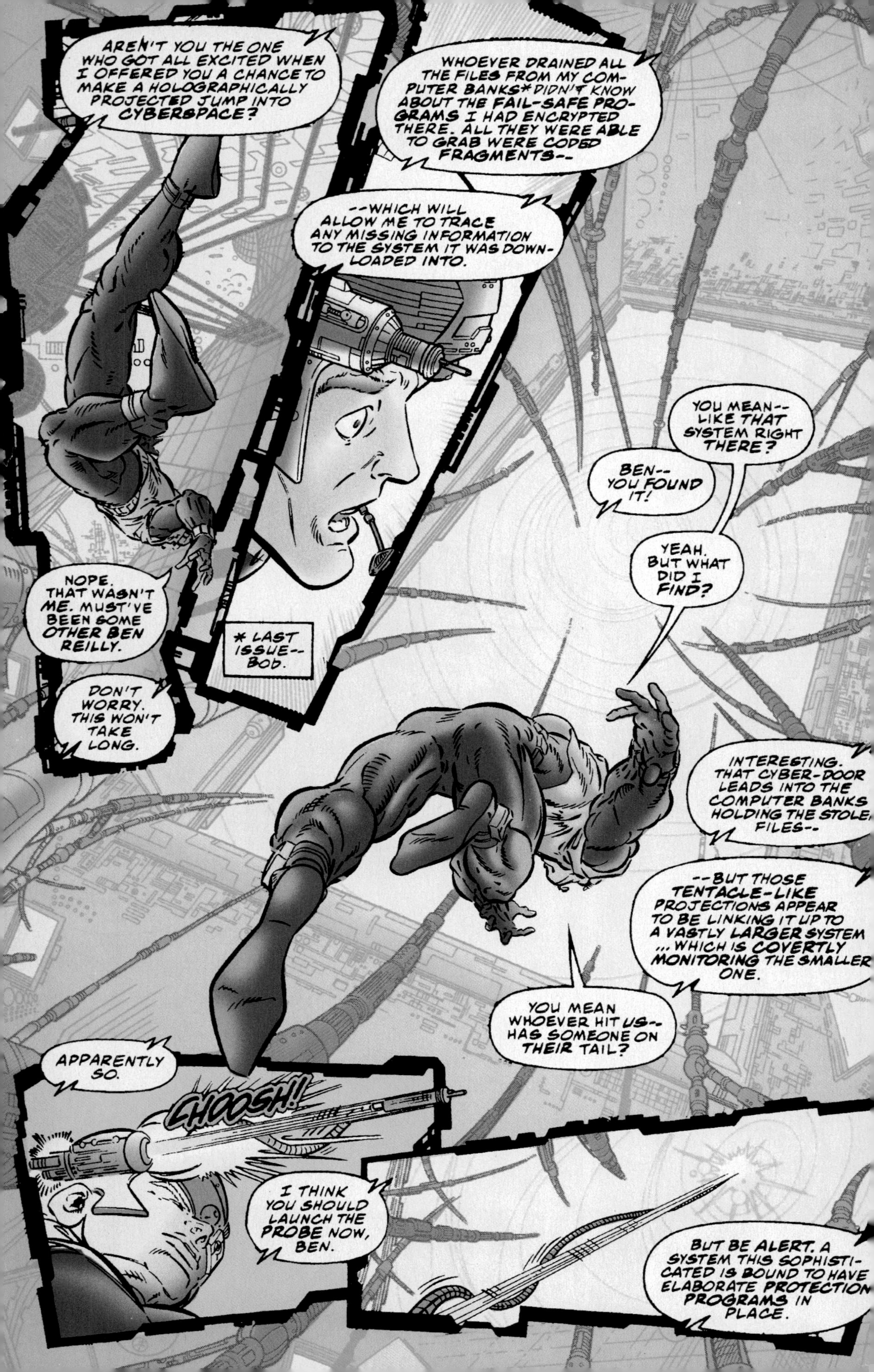

AREN'T YOU THE ONE WHO GOT ALL EXCITED WHEN I OFFERED YOU A CHANCE TO MAKE A HOLOGRAPHICALLY PROJECTED JUMP INTO CYBERSPACE?
WHOEVER DRAINED ALL THE FILES FROM MY COMPUTER BANKS* DIDN'T KNOW ABOUT THE FAIL-SAFE PROGRAMS I HAD ENCRYPTED THERE. ALL THEY WERE ABLE TO GRAB WERE CODED FRAGMENTS--
--WHICH WILL ALLOW ME TO TRACE ANY MISSING INFORMATION TO THE SYSTEM IT WAS DOWNLOADED INTO.
NOPE. THAT WASN'T ME. MUST'VE BEEN SOME OTHER BEN REILLY.
* LAST ISSUE-- Bob.
DON'T WORRY. THIS WON'T TAKE LONG.
YOU MEAN-- LIKE THAT SYSTEM RIGHT THERE?
BEN-- YOU FOUND IT!
YEAH. BUT WHAT DID I FIND?
INTERESTING. THAT CYBER-DOOR LEADS INTO THE COMPUTER BANKS HOLDING THE STOLE FILES--
--BUT THOSE TENTACLE-LIKE PROJECTIONS APPEAR TO BE LINKING IT UP TO A VASTLY LARGER SYSTEM ...WHICH IS COVERTLY MONITORING THE SMALLER ONE.
YOU MEAN WHOEVER HIT US-- HAS SOMEONE ON THEIR TAIL?
APPARENTLY SO.
CHOOSH!
I THINK YOU SHOULD LAUNCH THE PROBE NOW, BEN.
BUT BE ALERT. A SYSTEM THIS SOPHISTICATED IS BOUND TO HAVE ELABORATE PROTECTION PROGRAMS IN PLACE.

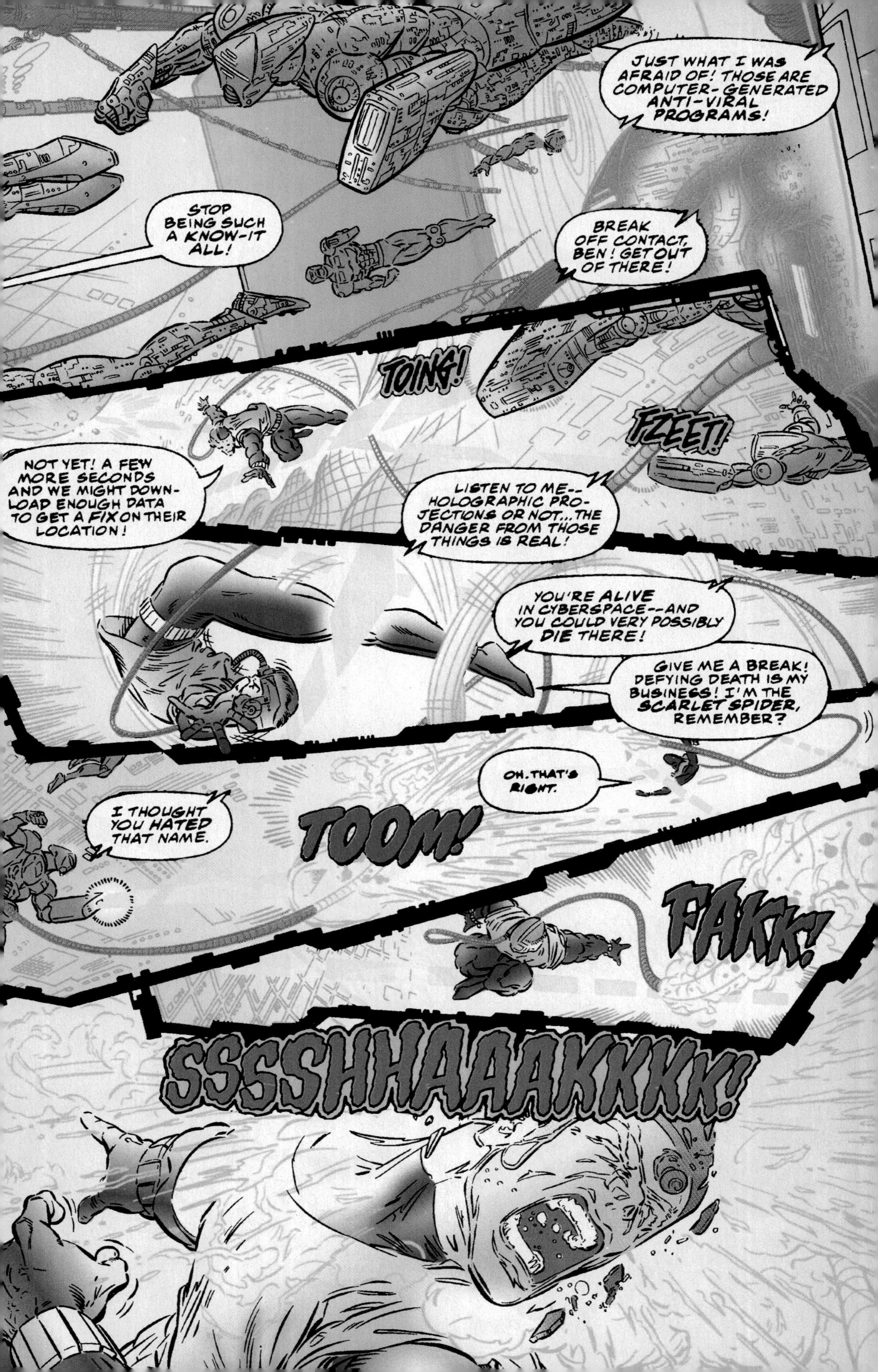
JUST WHAT I WAS AFRAID OF! THOSE ARE COMPUTER-GENERATED ANTI-VIRAL PROGRAMS!
STOP BEING SUCH A KNOW-IT ALL!
BREAK OFF CONTACT, BEN! GET OUT OF THERE!
TOING!
FZEET!
NOT YET! A FEW MORE SECONDS AND WE MIGHT DOWN-LOAD ENOUGH DATA TO GET A FIX ON THEIR LOCATION!
LISTEN TO ME-- HOLOGRAPHIC PRO-JECTIONS OR NOT... THE DANGER FROM THOSE THINGS IS REAL!
YOU'RE ALIVE IN CYBERSPACE--AND YOU COULD VERY POSSIBLY DIE THERE!
GIVE ME A BREAK! DEFYING DEATH IS MY BUSINESS! I'M THE SCARLET SPIDER, REMEMBER?
OH. THAT'S RIGHT.
I THOUGHT YOU HATED THAT NAME.
TOOM!
FAKK!
SSSSHHAAAKKKK!

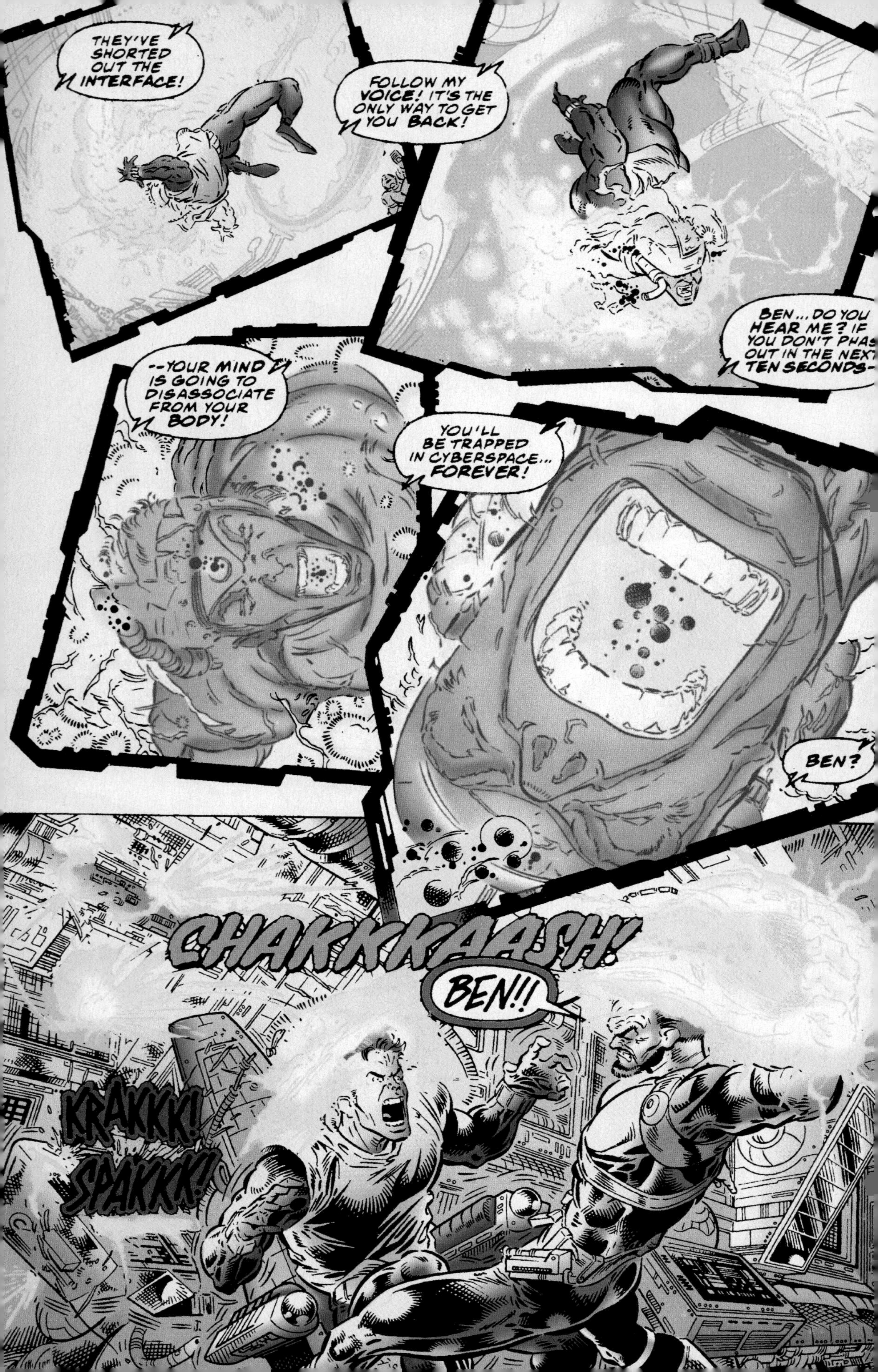
THEY'VE SHORTED OUT THE INTERFACE!
FOLLOW MY VOICE! IT'S THE ONLY WAY TO GET YOU BACK!
BEN... DO YOU HEAR ME? IF YOU DON'T PHAS OUT IN THE NEXT TEN SECONDS--
--YOUR MIND IS GOING TO DISASSOCIATE FROM YOUR BODY!
YOU'LL BE TRAPPED IN CYBERSPACE... FOREVER!
BEN?
CHAKKKAASH!
BEN!!
KRAKKK!
SPAKKK!

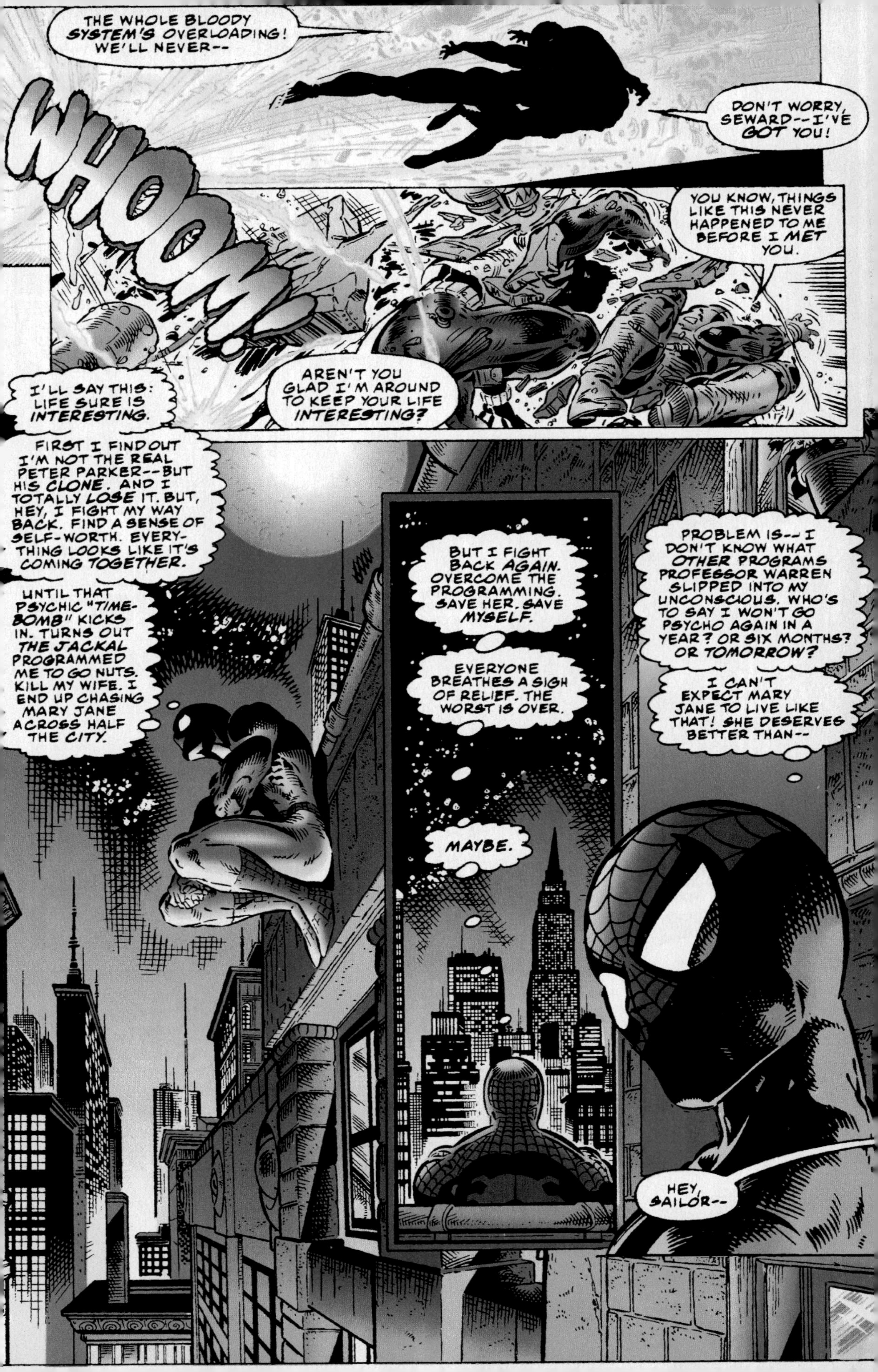
THE WHOLE BLOODY SYSTEM'S OVERLOADING! WE'LL NEVER--
DON'T WORRY, SEWARD--I'VE GOT YOU!
WHOOM!
YOU KNOW, THINGS LIKE THIS NEVER HAPPENED TO ME BEFORE I MET YOU.
I'LL SAY THIS: LIFE SURE IS INTERESTING.
AREN'T YOU GLAD I'M AROUND TO KEEP YOUR LIFE INTERESTING?
FIRST I FIND OUT I'M NOT THE REAL PETER PARKER--BUT HIS CLONE. AND I TOTALLY LOSE IT. BUT, HEY, I FIGHT MY WAY BACK. FIND A SENSE OF SELF-WORTH. EVERYTHING LOOKS LIKE IT'S COMING TOGETHER.
UNTIL THAT PSYCHIC "TIME-BOMB" KICKS IN. TURNS OUT THE JACKAL PROGRAMMED ME TO GO NUTS. KILL MY WIFE. I END UP CHASING MARY JANE ACROSS HALF THE CITY.
BUT I FIGHT BACK AGAIN. OVERCOME THE PROGRAMMING. SAVE HER. SAVE MYSELF.
EVERYONE BREATHES A SIGH OF RELIEF. THE WORST IS OVER.
MAYBE.
PROBLEM IS--I DON'T KNOW WHAT OTHER PROGRAMS PROFESSOR WARREN SLIPPED INTO MY UNCONSCIOUS. WHO'S TO SAY I WON'T GO PSYCHO AGAIN IN A YEAR? OR SIX MONTHS? OR TOMORROW?
I CAN'T EXPECT MARY JANE TO LIVE LIKE THAT! SHE DESERVES BETTER THAN--
HEY, SAILOR--

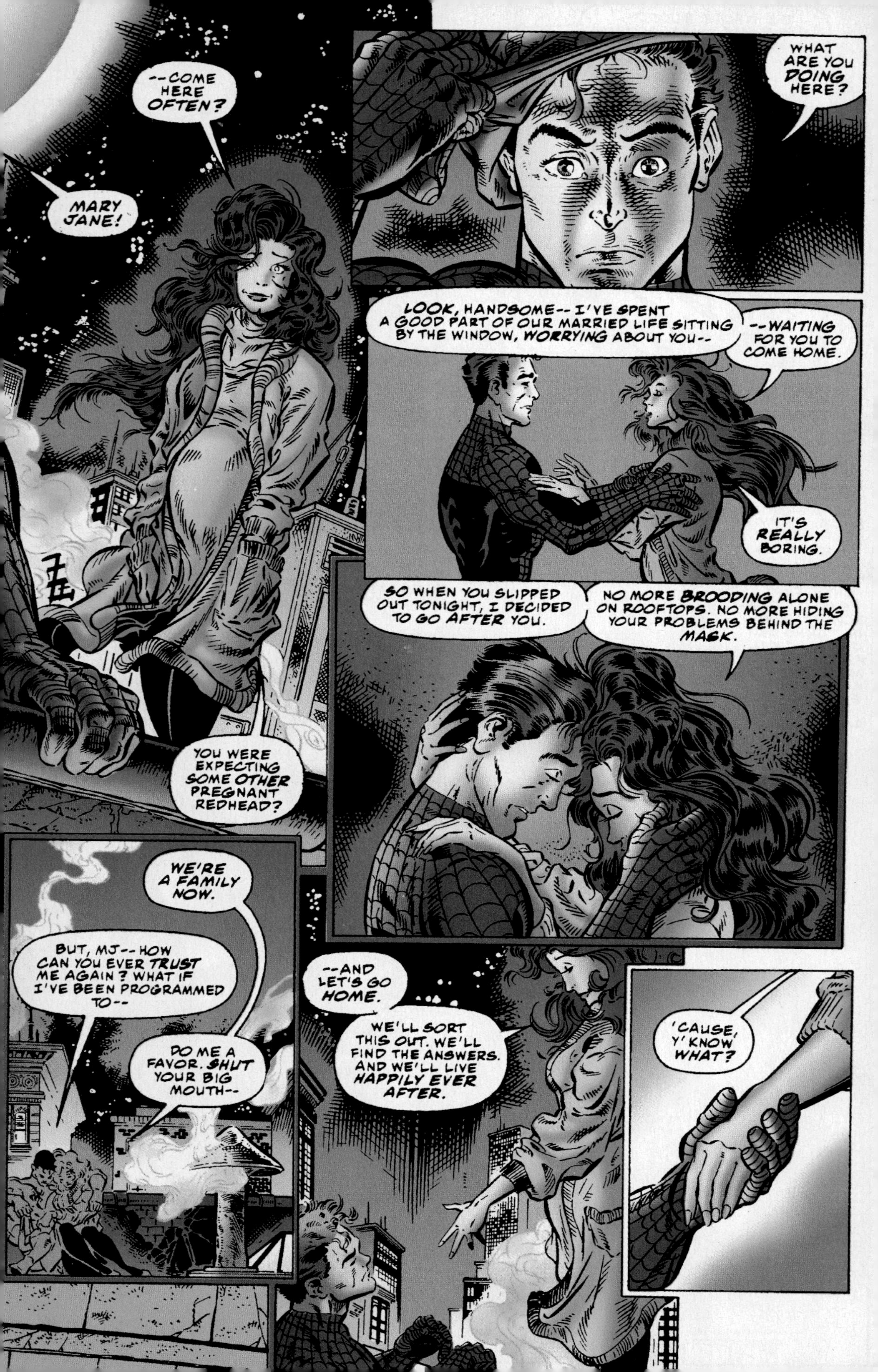
MARY JANE!
--COME HERE OFTEN?
WHAT ARE YOU DOING HERE?
YOU WERE EXPECTING SOME OTHER PREGNANT REDHEAD?
LOOK, HANDSOME-- I'VE SPENT A GOOD PART OF OUR MARRIED LIFE SITTING BY THE WINDOW, WORRYING ABOUT YOU--
--WAITING FOR YOU TO COME HOME.
IT'S REALLY BORING.
SO WHEN YOU SLIPPED OUT TONIGHT, I DECIDED TO GO AFTER YOU.
NO MORE BROODING ALONE ON ROOFTOPS. NO MORE HIDING YOUR PROBLEMS BEHIND THE MASK.
WE'RE A FAMILY NOW.
BUT, MJ-- HOW CAN YOU EVER TRUST ME AGAIN? WHAT IF I'VE BEEN PROGRAMMED TO--
DO ME A FAVOR. SHUT YOUR BIG MOUTH--
--AND LET'S GO HOME.
WE'LL SORT THIS OUT. WE'LL FIND THE ANSWERS. AND WE'LL LIVE HAPPILY EVER AFTER.
'CAUSE, Y'KNOW WHAT?

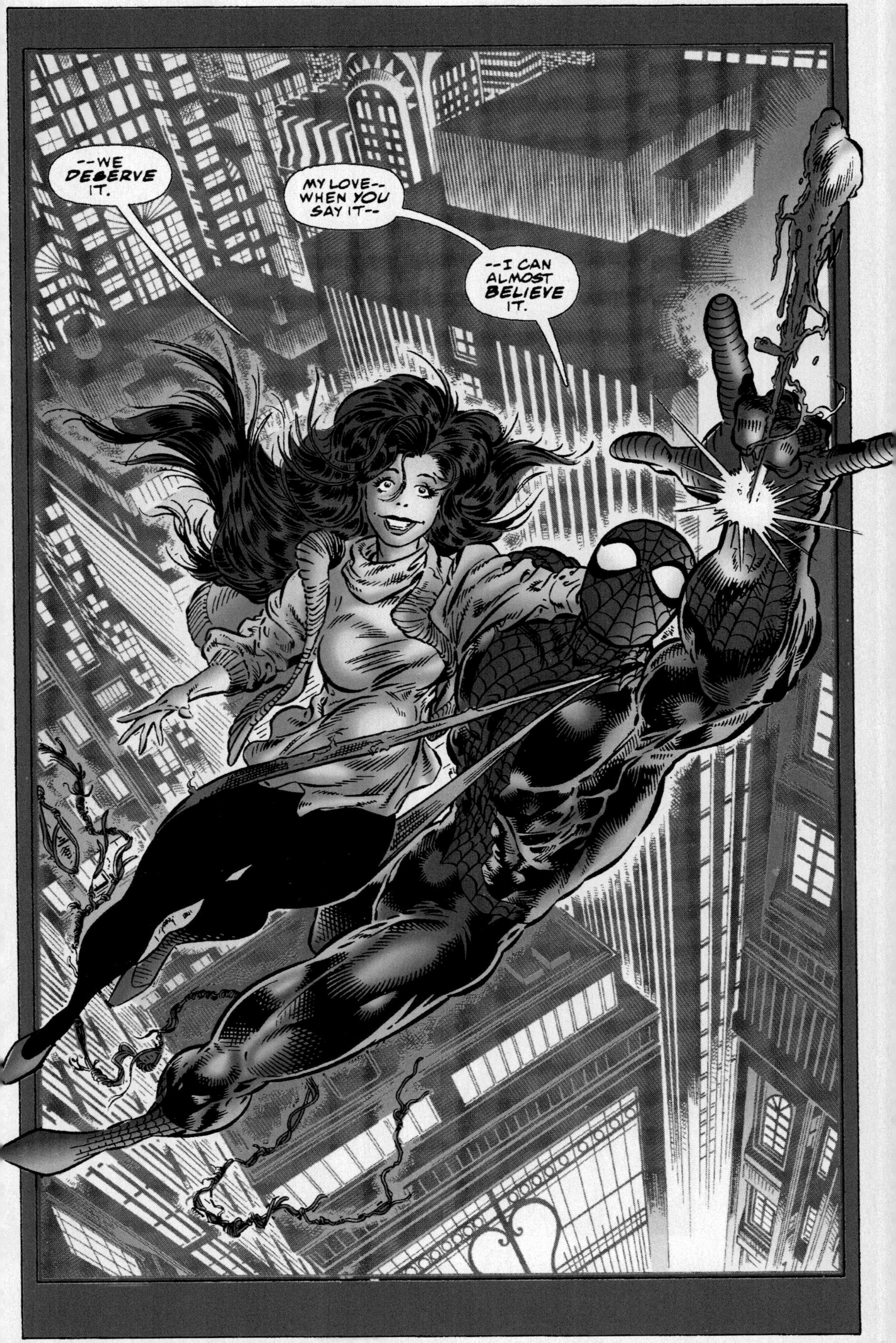
--WE DESERVE IT.
MY LOVE-- WHEN YOU SAY IT--
--I CAN ALMOST BELIEVE IT.

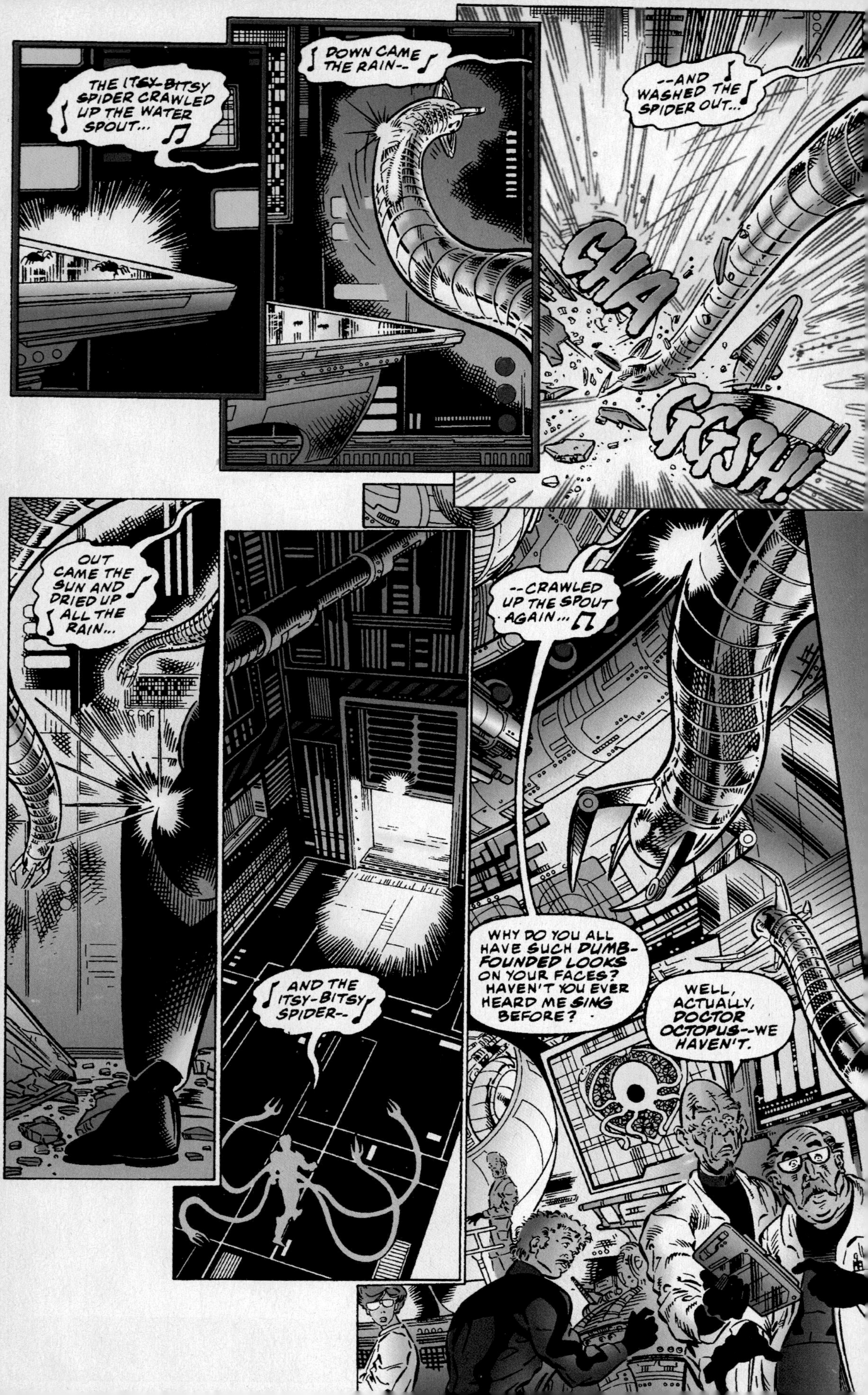
THE ITSY-BITSY SPIDER CRAWLED UP THE WATER SPOUT...
DOWN CAME THE RAIN--
--AND WASHED THE SPIDER OUT...
CHA
GGSH!
OUT CAME THE SUN AND DRIED UP ALL THE RAIN...
AND THE ITSY-BITSY SPIDER--
--CRAWLED UP THE SPOUT AGAIN...
WHY DO YOU ALL HAVE SUCH DUMB-FOUNDED LOOKS ON YOUR FACES? HAVEN'T YOU EVER HEARD ME SING BEFORE?
WELL, ACTUALLY, DOCTOR OCTOPUS--WE HAVEN'T.

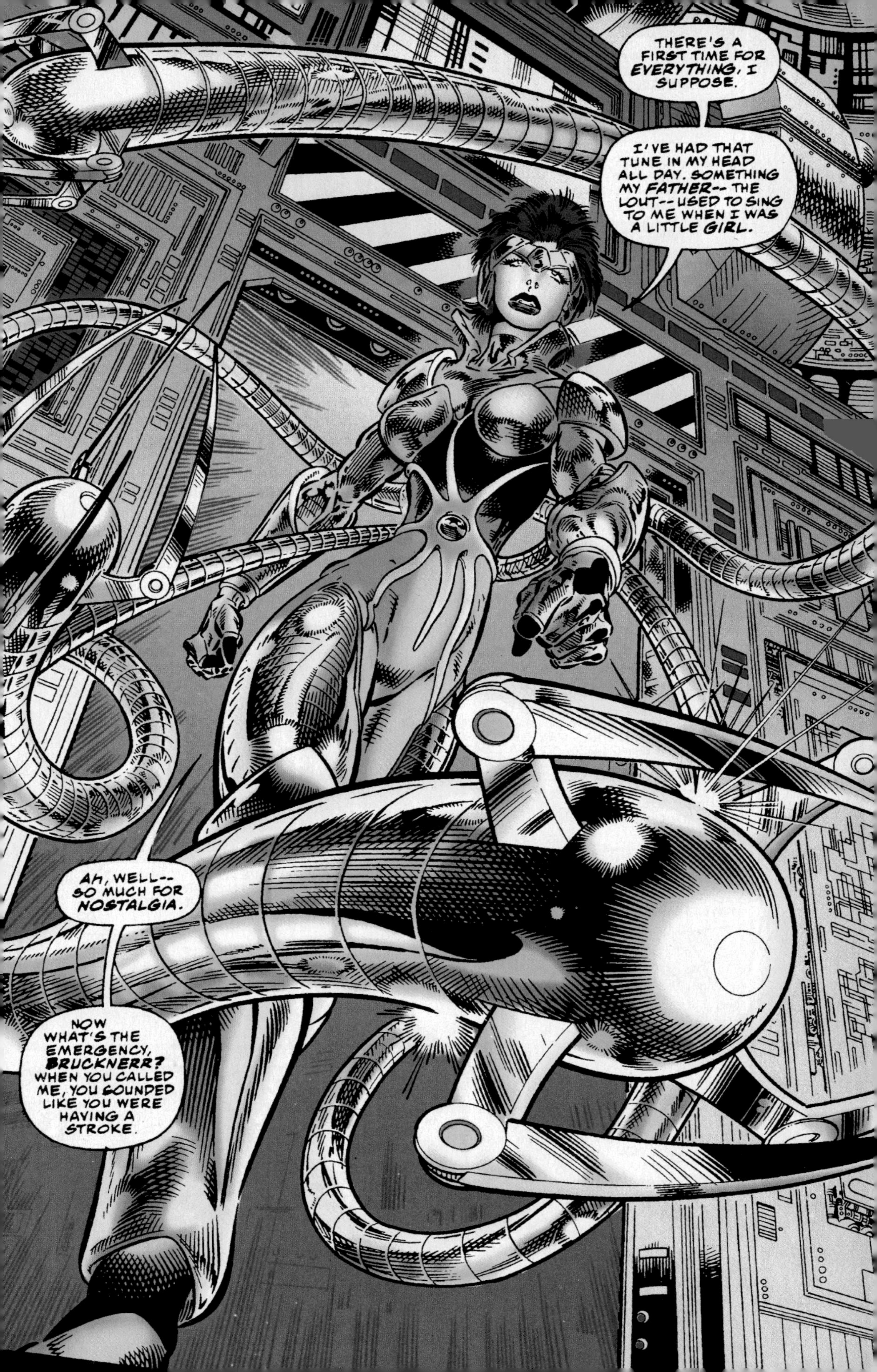
THERE'S A FIRST TIME FOR EVERYTHING, I SUPPOSE.
I'VE HAD THAT TUNE IN MY HEAD ALL DAY. SOMETHING MY FATHER-- THE LOUT-- USED TO SING TO ME WHEN I WAS A LITTLE GIRL.
AH, WELL-- SO MUCH FOR NOSTALGIA.
NOW WHAT'S THE EMERGENCY, BRUCKNERR? WHEN YOU CALLED ME, YOU SOUNDED LIKE YOU WERE HAVING A STROKE.

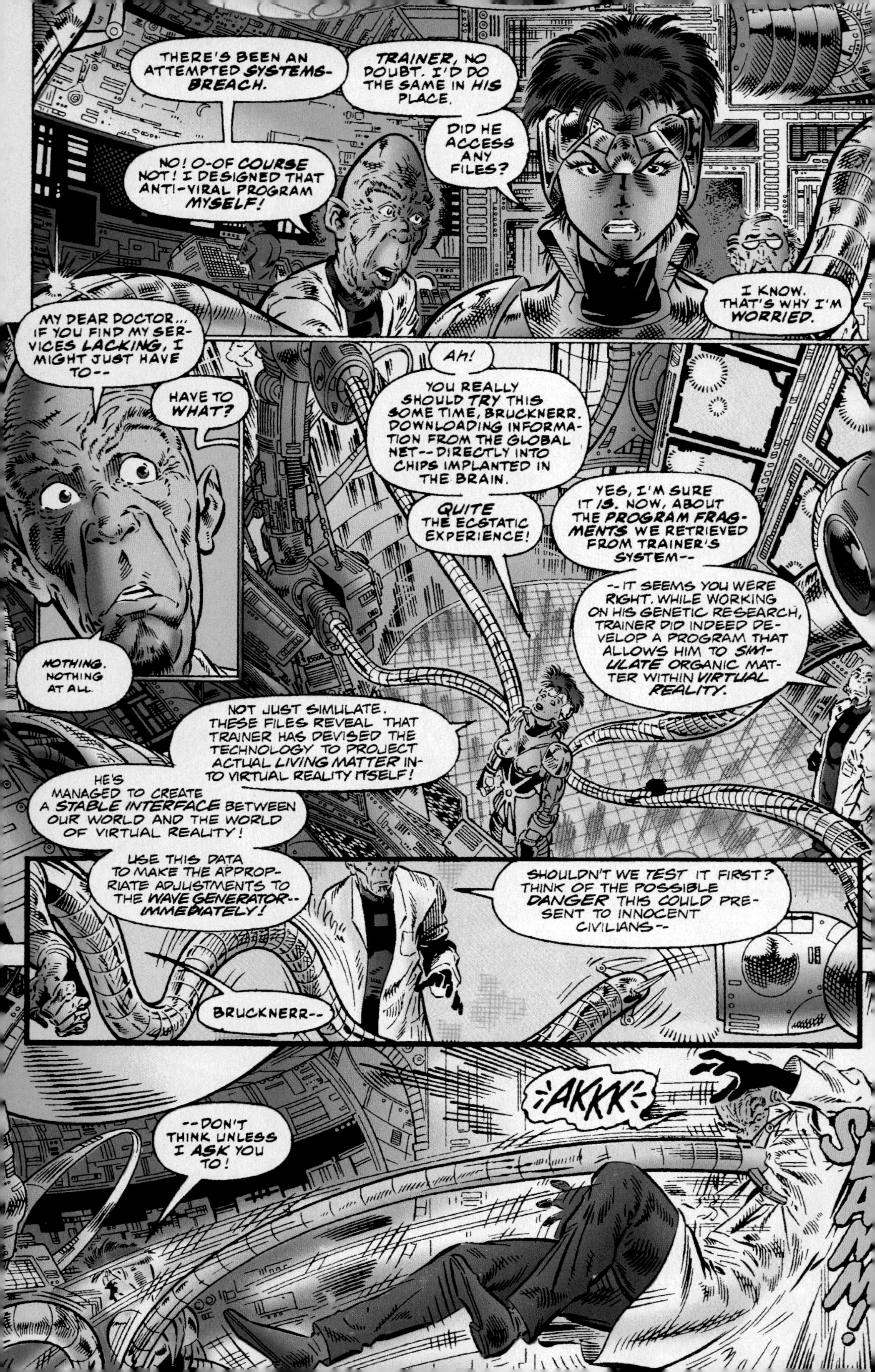

THERE'S BEEN AN ATTEMPTED SYSTEMS-BREACH.
TRAINER, NO DOUBT. I'D DO THE SAME IN HIS PLACE.
NO! O-OF COURSE NOT! I DESIGNED THAT ANTI-VIRAL PROGRAM MYSELF!
DID HE ACCESS ANY FILES?
I KNOW. THAT'S WHY I'M WORRIED.
MY DEAR DOCTOR... IF YOU FIND MY SERVICES LACKING, I MIGHT JUST HAVE TO--
HAVE TO WHAT?
NOTHING. NOTHING AT ALL.
AH!
YOU REALLY SHOULD TRY THIS SOME TIME, BRUCKNERR. DOWNLOADING INFORMATION FROM THE GLOBAL NET-- DIRECTLY INTO CHIPS IMPLANTED IN THE BRAIN.
QUITE THE ECSTATIC EXPERIENCE!
YES, I'M SURE IT IS. NOW, ABOUT THE PROGRAM FRAGMENTS WE RETRIEVED FROM TRAINER'S SYSTEM--
--IT SEEMS YOU WERE RIGHT. WHILE WORKING ON HIS GENETIC RESEARCH, TRAINER DID INDEED DEVELOP A PROGRAM THAT ALLOWS HIM TO SIMULATE ORGANIC MATTER WITHIN VIRTUAL REALITY.
NOT JUST SIMULATE. THESE FILES REVEAL THAT TRAINER HAS DEVISED THE TECHNOLOGY TO PROJECT ACTUAL LIVING MATTER INTO VIRTUAL REALITY ITSELF!
HE'S MANAGED TO CREATE A STABLE INTERFACE BETWEEN OUR WORLD AND THE WORLD OF VIRTUAL REALITY!
USE THIS DATA TO MAKE THE APPROPRIATE ADJUSTMENTS TO THE WAVE GENERATOR-- IMMEDIATELY!
SHOULDN'T WE TEST IT FIRST? THINK OF THE POSSIBLE DANGER THIS COULD PRESENT TO INNOCENT CIVILIANS--
BRUCKNERR--
AKKK
--DON'T THINK UNLESS I ASK YOU TO!

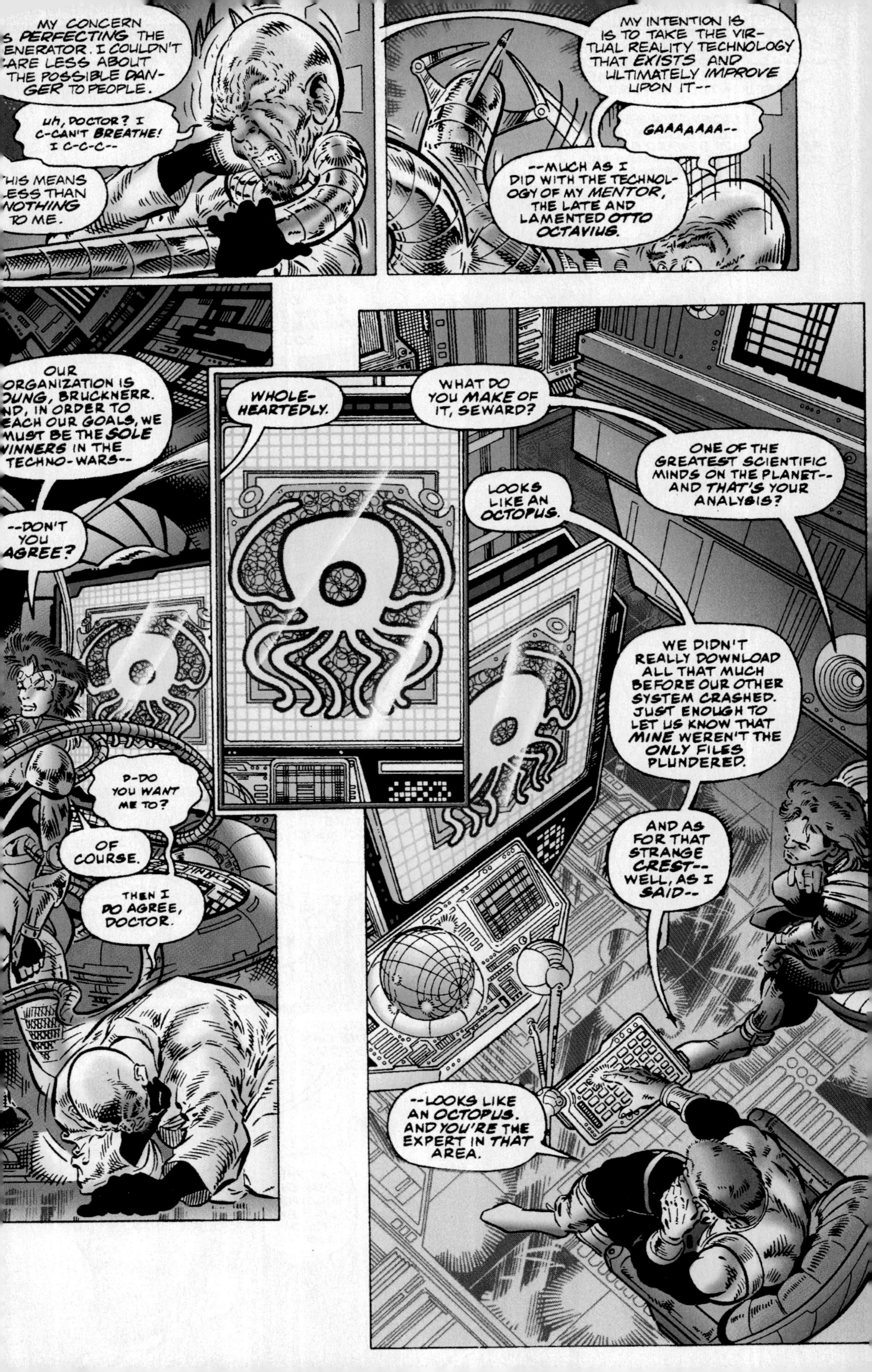
MY CONCERN IS PERFECTING THE GENERATOR. I COULDN'T CARE LESS ABOUT THE POSSIBLE DANGER TO PEOPLE.
UH, DOCTOR? I C-CAN'T BREATHE! I C-C-C--
THIS MEANS LESS THAN NOTHING TO ME.
MY INTENTION IS IS TO TAKE THE VIRTUAL REALITY TECHNOLOGY THAT EXISTS AND ULTIMATELY IMPROVE UPON IT--
GAAAAAAA--
--MUCH AS I DID WITH THE TECHNOLOGY OF MY MENTOR, THE LATE AND LAMENTED OTTO OCTAVIUS.
OUR ORGANIZATION IS YOUNG, BRUCKNERR. AND, IN ORDER TO REACH OUR GOALS, WE MUST BE THE SOLE WINNERS IN THE TECHNO-WARS--
--DON'T YOU AGREE?
D-DO YOU WANT ME TO?
OF COURSE.
THEN I DO AGREE, DOCTOR.
WHOLE-HEARTEDLY.
WHAT DO YOU MAKE OF IT, SEWARD?
LOOKS LIKE AN OCTOPUS.
ONE OF THE GREATEST SCIENTIFIC MINDS ON THE PLANET--AND THAT'S YOUR ANALYSIS?
WE DIDN'T REALLY DOWNLOAD ALL THAT MUCH BEFORE OUR OTHER SYSTEM CRASHED. JUST ENOUGH TO LET US KNOW THAT MINE WEREN'T THE ONLY FILES PLUNDERED.
AND AS FOR THAT STRANGE CREST--WELL, AS I SAID--
--LOOKS LIKE AN OCTOPUS. AND YOU'RE THE EXPERT IN THAT AREA.

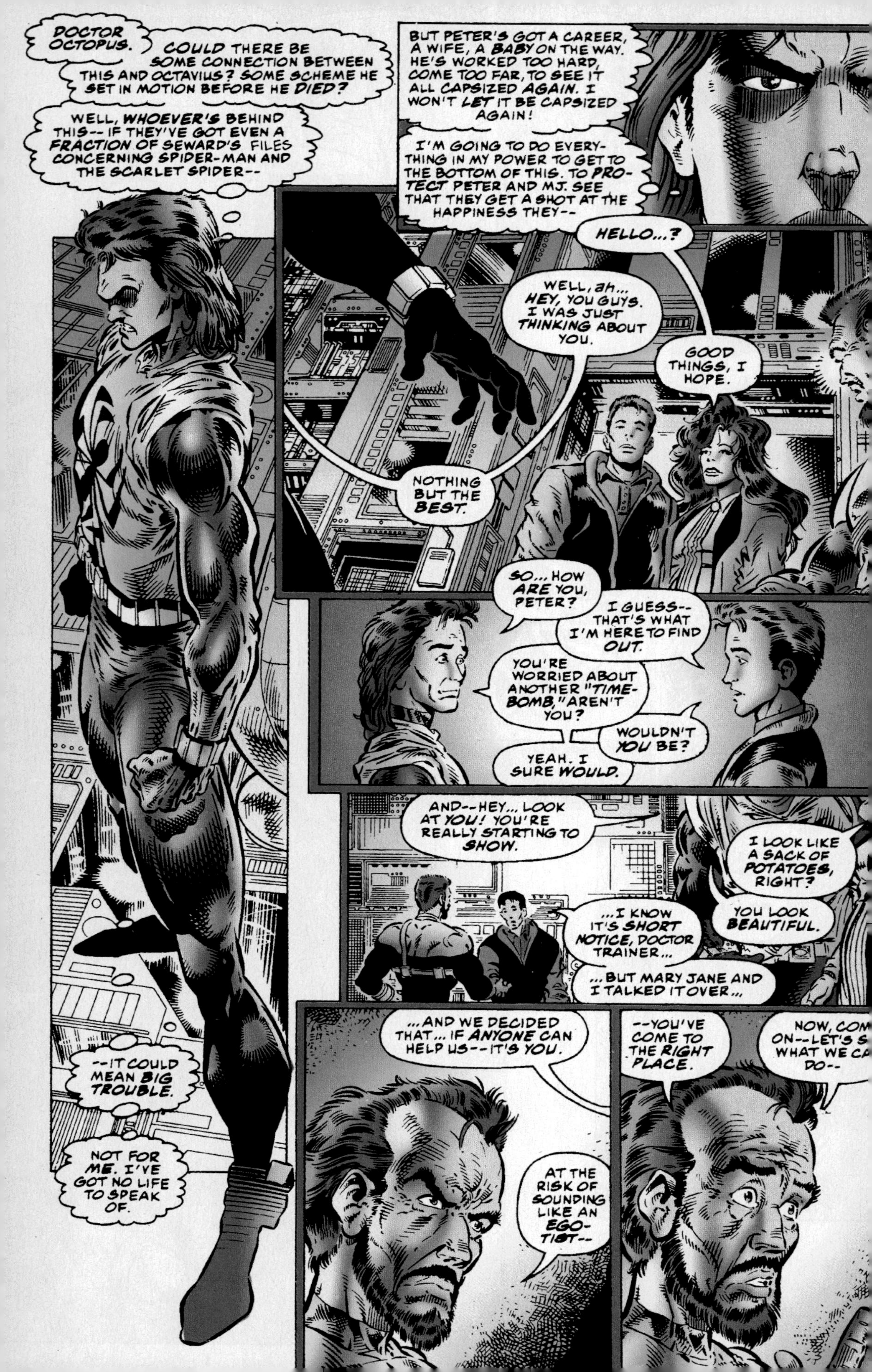
DOCTOR OCTOPUS.
COULD THERE BE SOME CONNECTION BETWEEN THIS AND OCTAVIUS? SOME SCHEME HE SET IN MOTION BEFORE HE DIED?
WELL, WHOEVER'S BEHIND THIS-- IF THEY'VE GOT EVEN A FRACTION OF SEWARD'S FILES CONCERNING SPIDER-MAN AND THE SCARLET SPIDER--
--IT COULD MEAN BIG TROUBLE.
NOT FOR ME. I'VE GOT NO LIFE TO SPEAK OF.
BUT PETER'S GOT A CAREER, A WIFE, A BABY ON THE WAY. HE'S WORKED TOO HARD, COME TOO FAR, TO SEE IT ALL CAPSIZED AGAIN. I WON'T LET IT BE CAPSIZED AGAIN!
I'M GOING TO DO EVERYTHING IN MY POWER TO GET TO THE BOTTOM OF THIS. TO PROTECT PETER AND MJ. SEE THAT THEY GET A SHOT AT THE HAPPINESS THEY--
HELLO...?
WELL, ah... HEY, YOU GUYS. I WAS JUST THINKING ABOUT YOU.
GOOD THINGS, I HOPE.
NOTHING BUT THE BEST.
SO... HOW ARE YOU, PETER?
I GUESS-- THAT'S WHAT I'M HERE TO FIND OUT.
YOU'RE WORRIED ABOUT ANOTHER "TIME-BOMB," AREN'T YOU?
WOULDN'T YOU BE?
YEAH. I SURE WOULD.
AND--HEY... LOOK AT YOU! YOU'RE REALLY STARTING TO SHOW.
I LOOK LIKE A SACK OF POTATOES, RIGHT?
YOU LOOK BEAUTIFUL.
...I KNOW IT'S SHORT NOTICE, DOCTOR TRAINER...
...BUT MARY JANE AND I TALKED IT OVER...
...AND WE DECIDED THAT... IF ANYONE CAN HELP US--IT'S YOU.
AT THE RISK OF SOUNDING LIKE AN EGO-TIST--
--YOU'VE COME TO THE RIGHT PLACE.
NOW, COM ON--LET'S S WHAT WE CA DO--

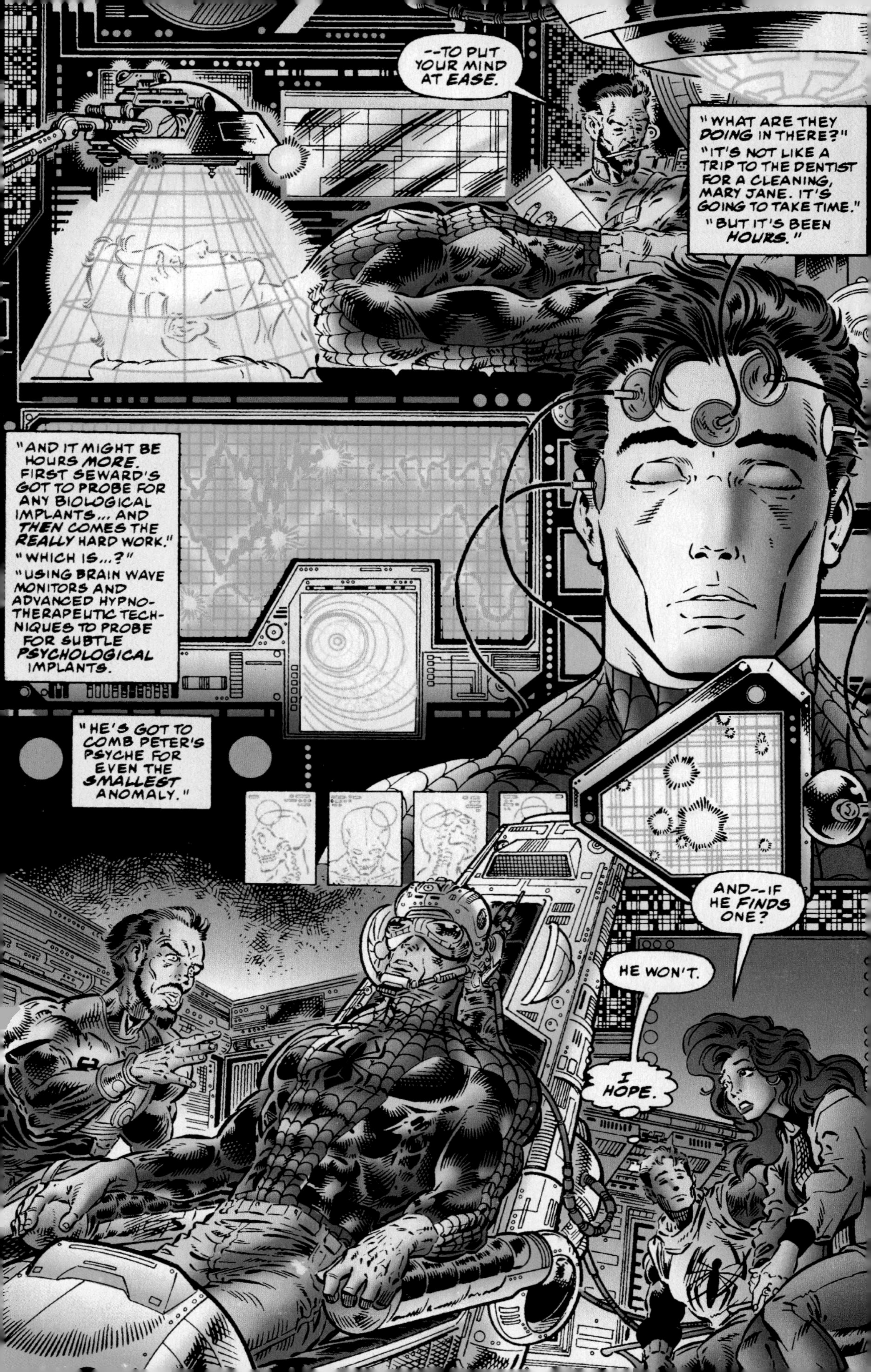
--TO PUT YOUR MIND AT *EASE*.
"WHAT ARE THEY *DOING* IN THERE?"
"IT'S NOT LIKE A TRIP TO THE DENTIST FOR A CLEANING, MARY JANE. IT'S GOING TO TAKE TIME."
"BUT IT'S BEEN *HOURS*."
"AND IT MIGHT BE HOURS *MORE*. FIRST SEWARD'S GOT TO PROBE FOR ANY BIOLOGICAL IMPLANTS... AND *THEN* COMES THE *REALLY* HARD WORK."
"WHICH IS...?"
"USING BRAIN WAVE MONITORS AND ADVANCED HYPNO-THERAPEUTIC TECHNIQUES TO PROBE FOR SUBTLE *PSYCHOLOGICAL* IMPLANTS.
"HE'S GOT TO COMB PETER'S PSYCHE FOR EVEN THE *SMALLEST* ANOMALY."
AND--IF HE *FINDS* ONE?
HE WON'T.
I *HOPE*.

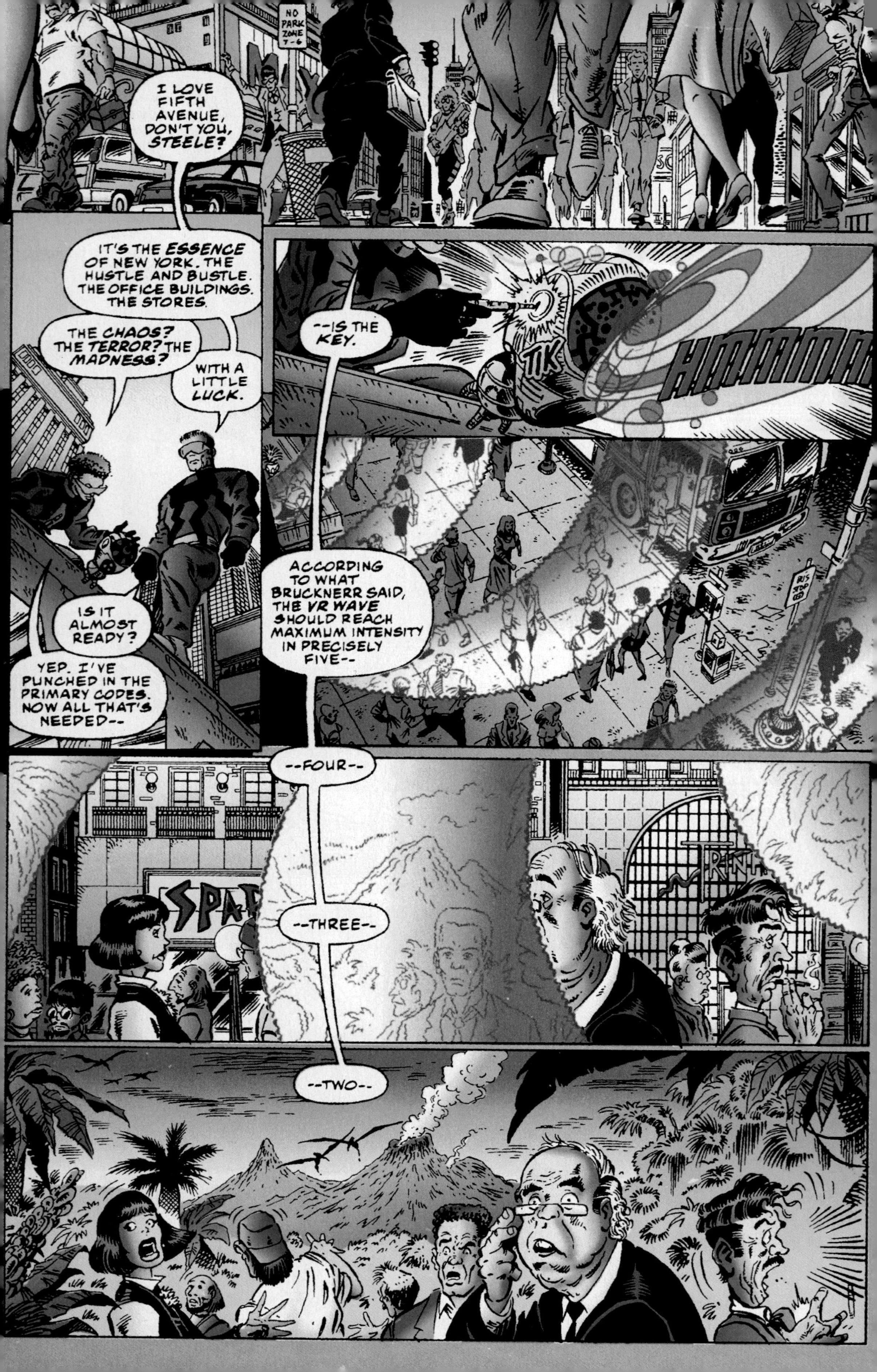
I LOVE FIFTH AVENUE, DON'T YOU, STEELE?
IT'S THE ESSENCE OF NEW YORK. THE HUSTLE AND BUSTLE. THE OFFICE BUILDINGS. THE STORES.
THE CHAOS? THE TERROR? THE MADNESS?
WITH A LITTLE LUCK.
IS IT ALMOST READY?
YEP. I'VE PUNCHED IN THE PRIMARY CODES. NOW ALL THAT'S NEEDED--
--IS THE KEY.
TIK
HMMMMM
ACCORDING TO WHAT BRUCKNERR SAID, THE VR WAVE SHOULD REACH MAXIMUM INTENSITY IN PRECISELY FIVE--
--FOUR--
--THREE--
--TWO--

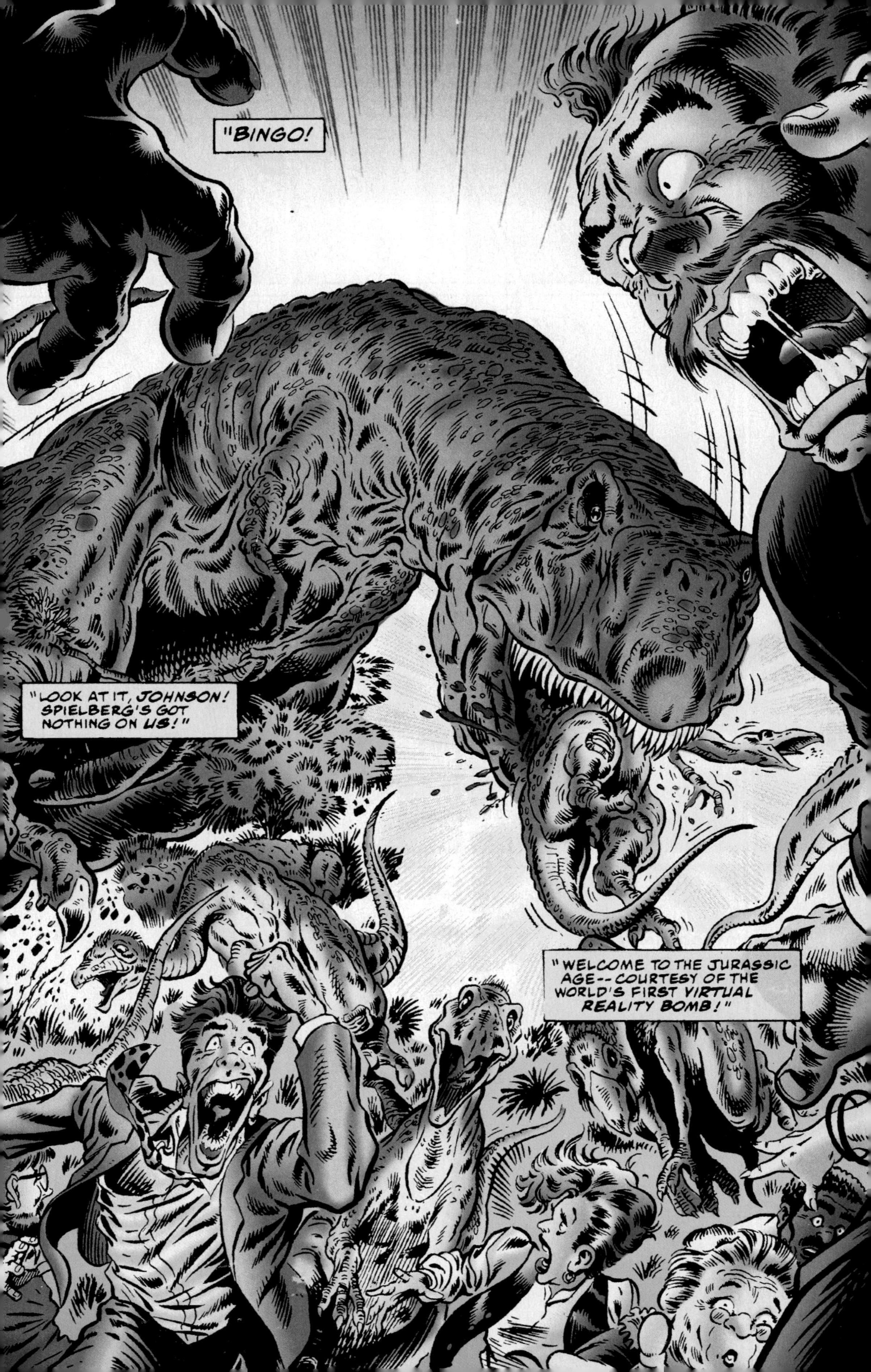
"BINGO!
"LOOK AT IT, JOHNSON! SPIELBERG'S GOT NOTHING ON US!"
"WELCOME TO THE JURASSIC AGE--COURTESY OF THE WORLD'S FIRST VIRTUAL REALITY BOMB!"

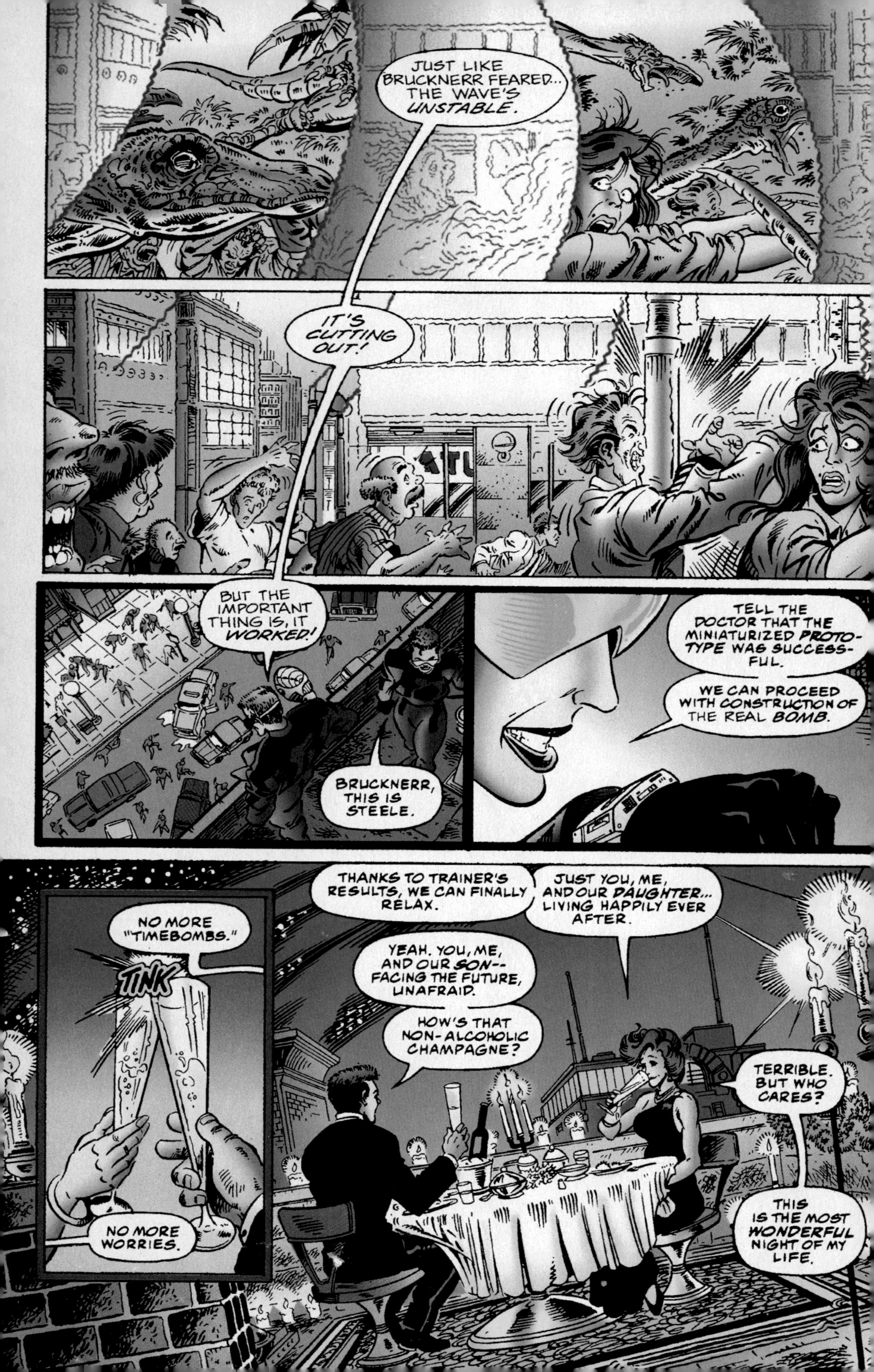
JUST LIKE BRUCKNERR FEARED... THE WAVE'S UNSTABLE.
IT'S CUTTING OUT!
BUT THE IMPORTANT THING IS, IT WORKED!
BRUCKNERR, THIS IS STEELE.
TELL THE DOCTOR THAT THE MINIATURIZED PROTOTYPE WAS SUCCESSFUL.
WE CAN PROCEED WITH CONSTRUCTION OF THE REAL BOMB.
NO MORE "TIMEBOMBS."
TINK
NO MORE WORRIES.
THANKS TO TRAINER'S RESULTS, WE CAN FINALLY RELAX.
JUST YOU, ME, AND OUR DAUGHTER... LIVING HAPPILY EVER AFTER.
YEAH. YOU, ME, AND OUR SON-- FACING THE FUTURE, UNAFRAID.
HOW'S THAT NON-ALCOHOLIC CHAMPAGNE?
TERRIBLE. BUT WHO CARES?
THIS IS THE MOST WONDERFUL NIGHT OF MY LIFE.

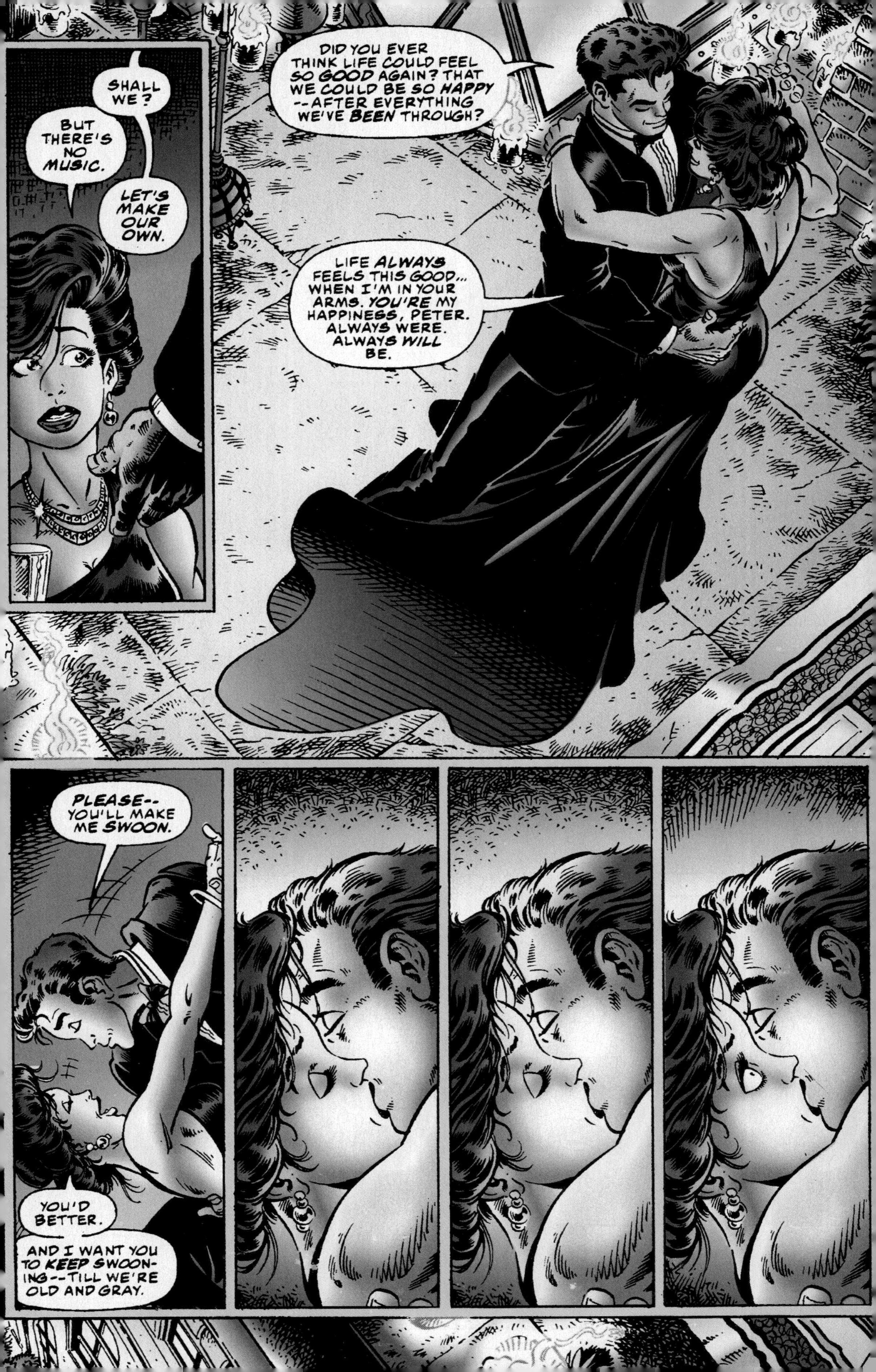
SHALL WE?
BUT THERE'S NO MUSIC.
LET'S MAKE OUR OWN.
DID YOU EVER THINK LIFE COULD FEEL SO GOOD AGAIN? THAT WE COULD BE SO HAPPY --AFTER EVERYTHING WE'VE BEEN THROUGH?
LIFE ALWAYS FEELS THIS GOOD... WHEN I'M IN YOUR ARMS. YOU'RE MY HAPPINESS, PETER. ALWAYS WERE. ALWAYS WILL BE.
PLEASE-- YOU'LL MAKE ME SWOON.
YOU'D BETTER.
AND I WANT YOU TO KEEP SWOON-ING--TILL WE'RE OLD AND GRAY.

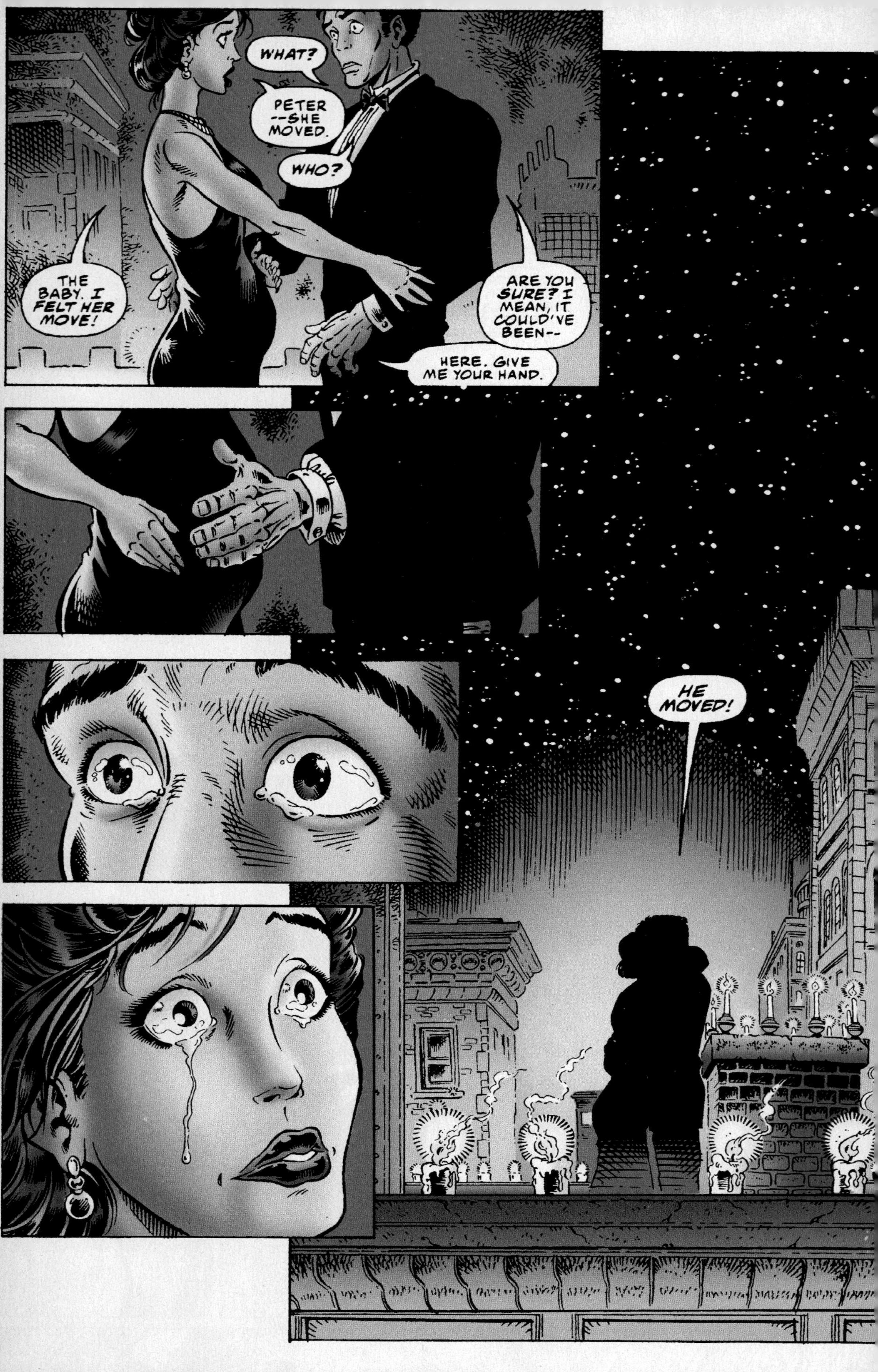
WHAT?
PETER --SHE MOVED.
WHO?
THE BABY. I FELT HER MOVE!
ARE YOU SURE? I MEAN, IT COULD'VE BEEN--
HERE. GIVE ME YOUR HAND.
HE MOVED!

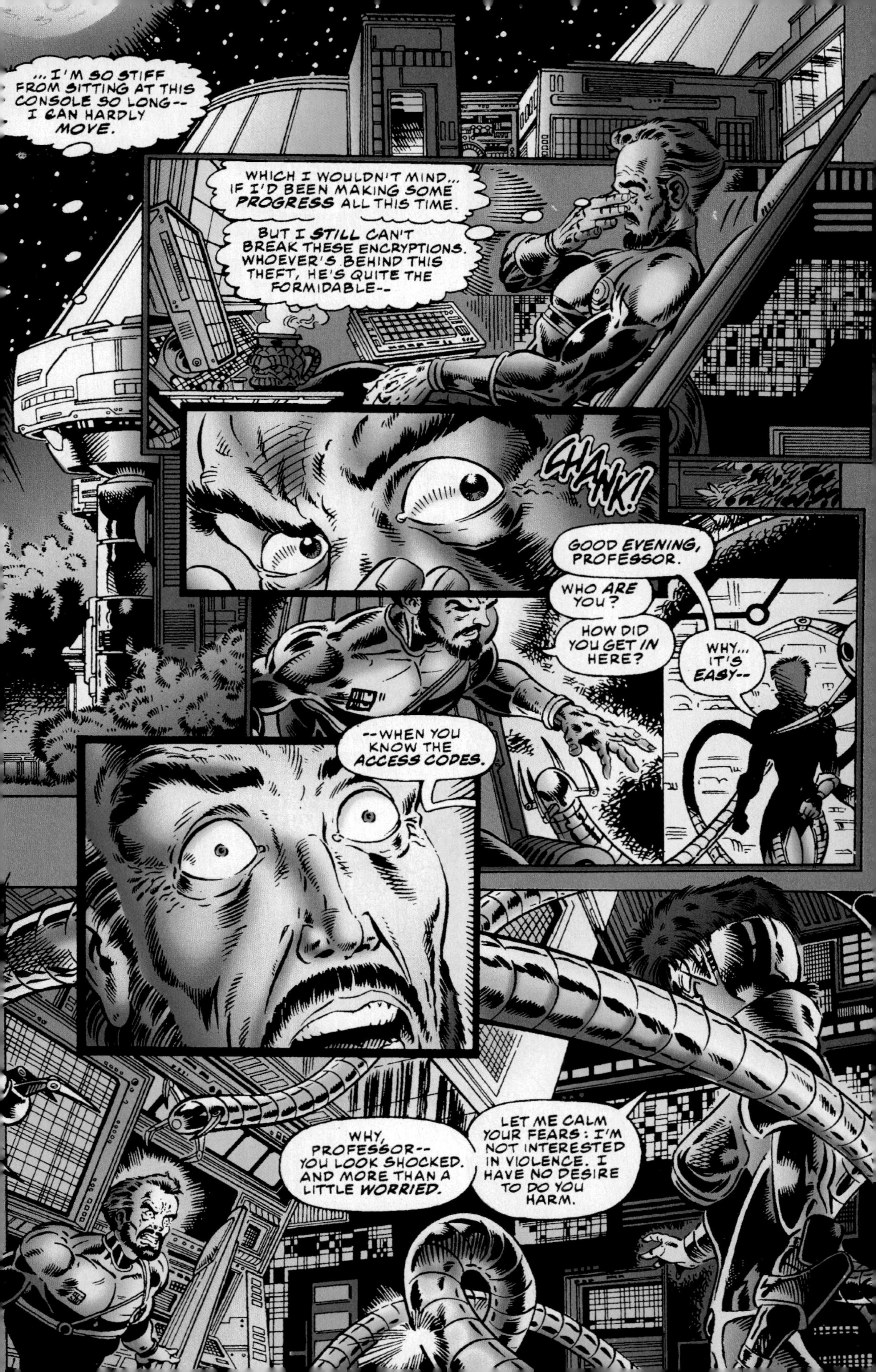
...I'M SO STIFF FROM SITTING AT THIS CONSOLE SO LONG-- I CAN HARDLY MOVE.
WHICH I WOULDN'T MIND... IF I'D BEEN MAKING SOME PROGRESS ALL THIS TIME.
BUT I STILL CAN'T BREAK THESE ENCRYPTIONS. WHOEVER'S BEHIND THIS THEFT, HE'S QUITE THE FORMIDABLE--
CHANK!
GOOD EVENING, PROFESSOR.
WHO ARE YOU?
HOW DID YOU GET IN HERE?
WHY... IT'S EASY--
--WHEN YOU KNOW THE ACCESS CODES.
WHY, PROFESSOR-- YOU LOOK SHOCKED. AND MORE THAN A LITTLE WORRIED.
LET ME CALM YOUR FEARS: I'M NOT INTERESTED IN VIOLENCE. I HAVE NO DESIRE TO DO YOU HARM.

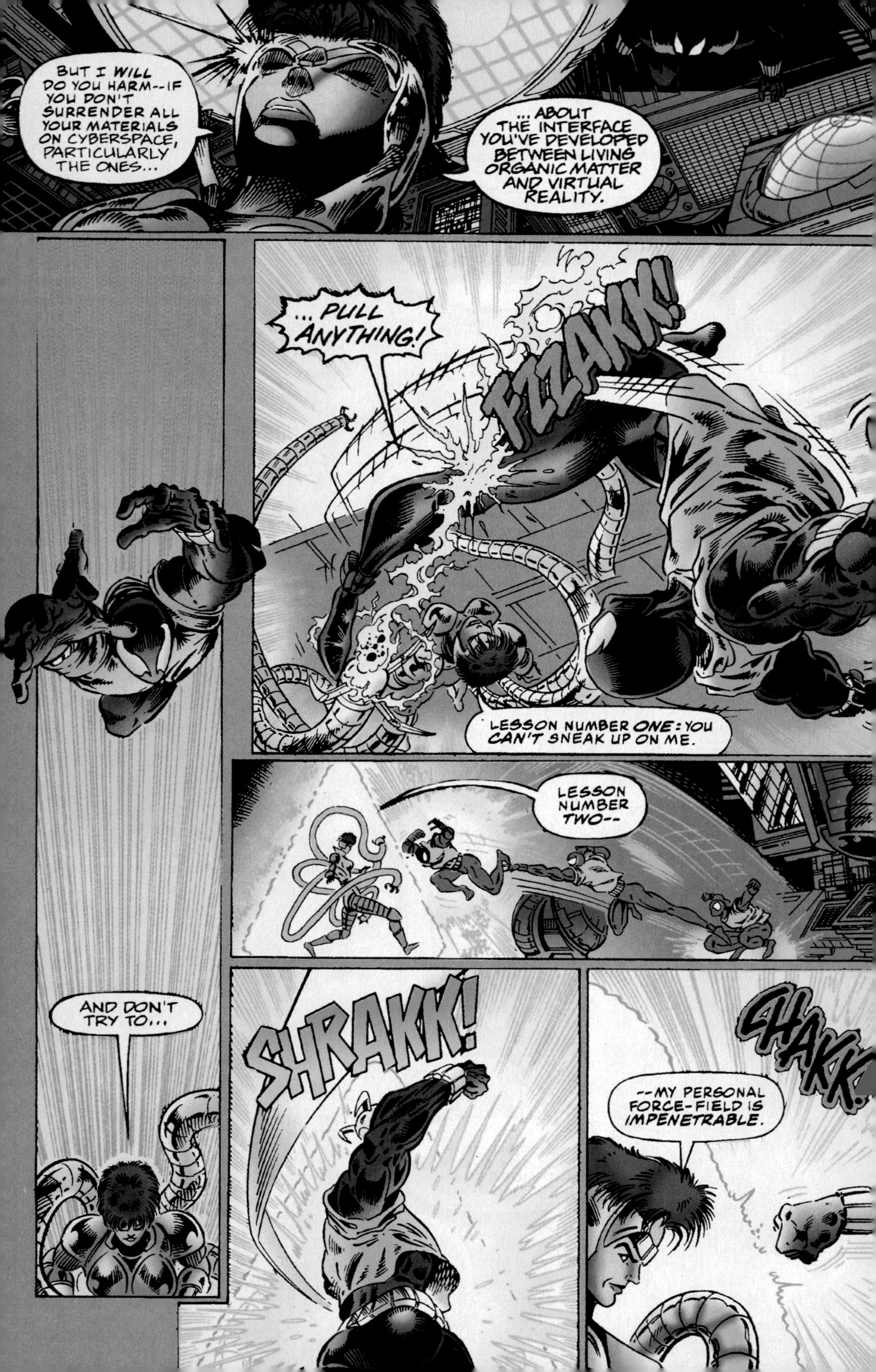
BUT I WILL DO YOU HARM--IF YOU DON'T SURRENDER ALL YOUR MATERIALS ON CYBERSPACE, PARTICULARLY THE ONES...
...ABOUT THE INTERFACE YOU'VE DEVELOPED BETWEEN LIVING ORGANIC MATTER AND VIRTUAL REALITY.
...PULL ANYTHING!
FZZAKK!
LESSON NUMBER ONE: YOU CAN'T SNEAK UP ON ME.
LESSON NUMBER TWO--
AND DON'T TRY TO...
SHRAKK!
CHAKK!
--MY PERSONAL FORCE-FIELD IS IMPENETRABLE.

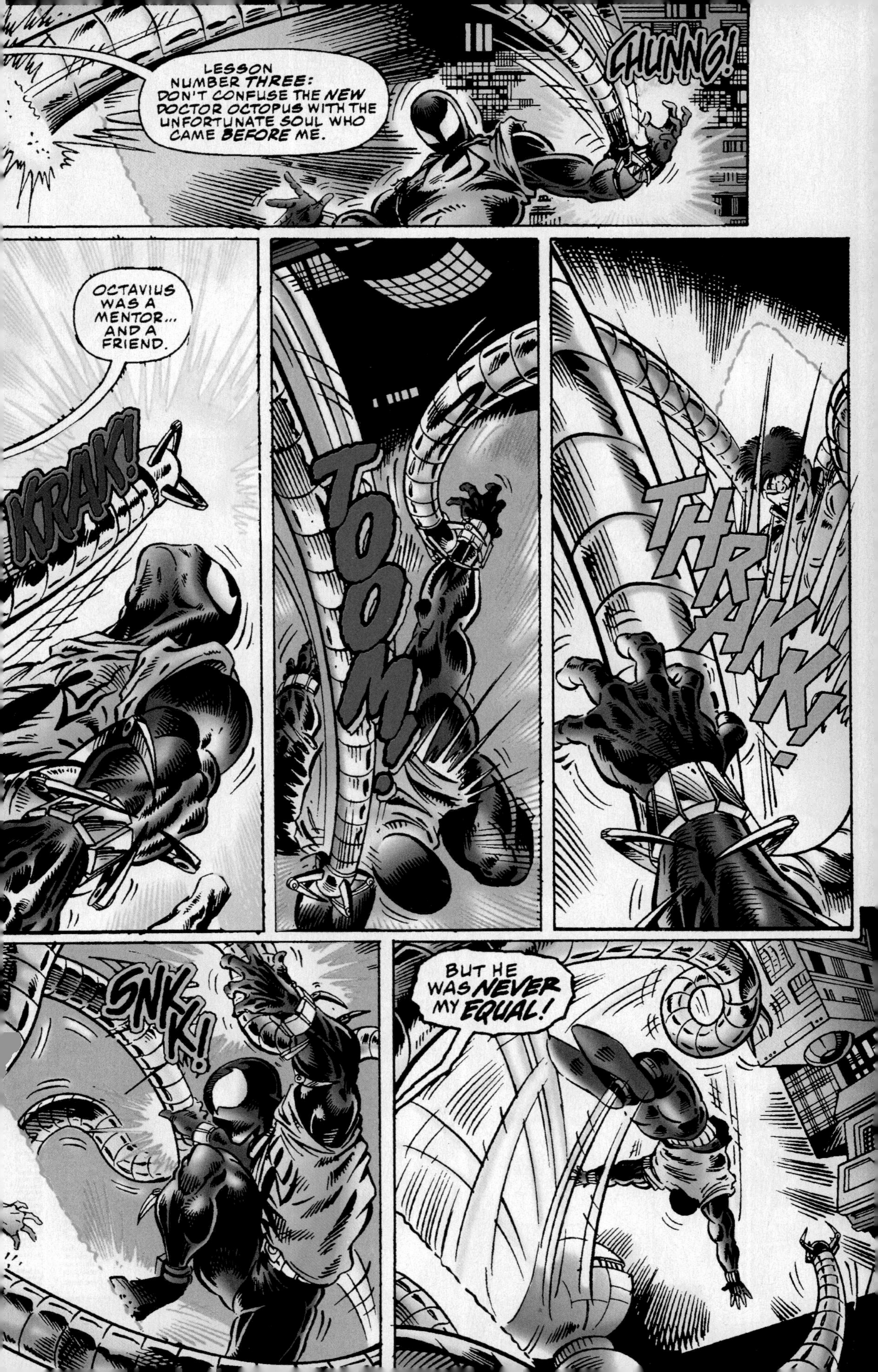
LESSON NUMBER THREE: DON'T CONFUSE THE NEW DOCTOR OCTOPUS WITH THE UNFORTUNATE SOUL WHO CAME BEFORE ME.
CHUNNG!
OCTAVIUS WAS A MENTOR... AND A FRIEND.
KRAK!
TOOOM!
THRAKK!
SNKK!
BUT HE WAS NEVER MY EQUAL!

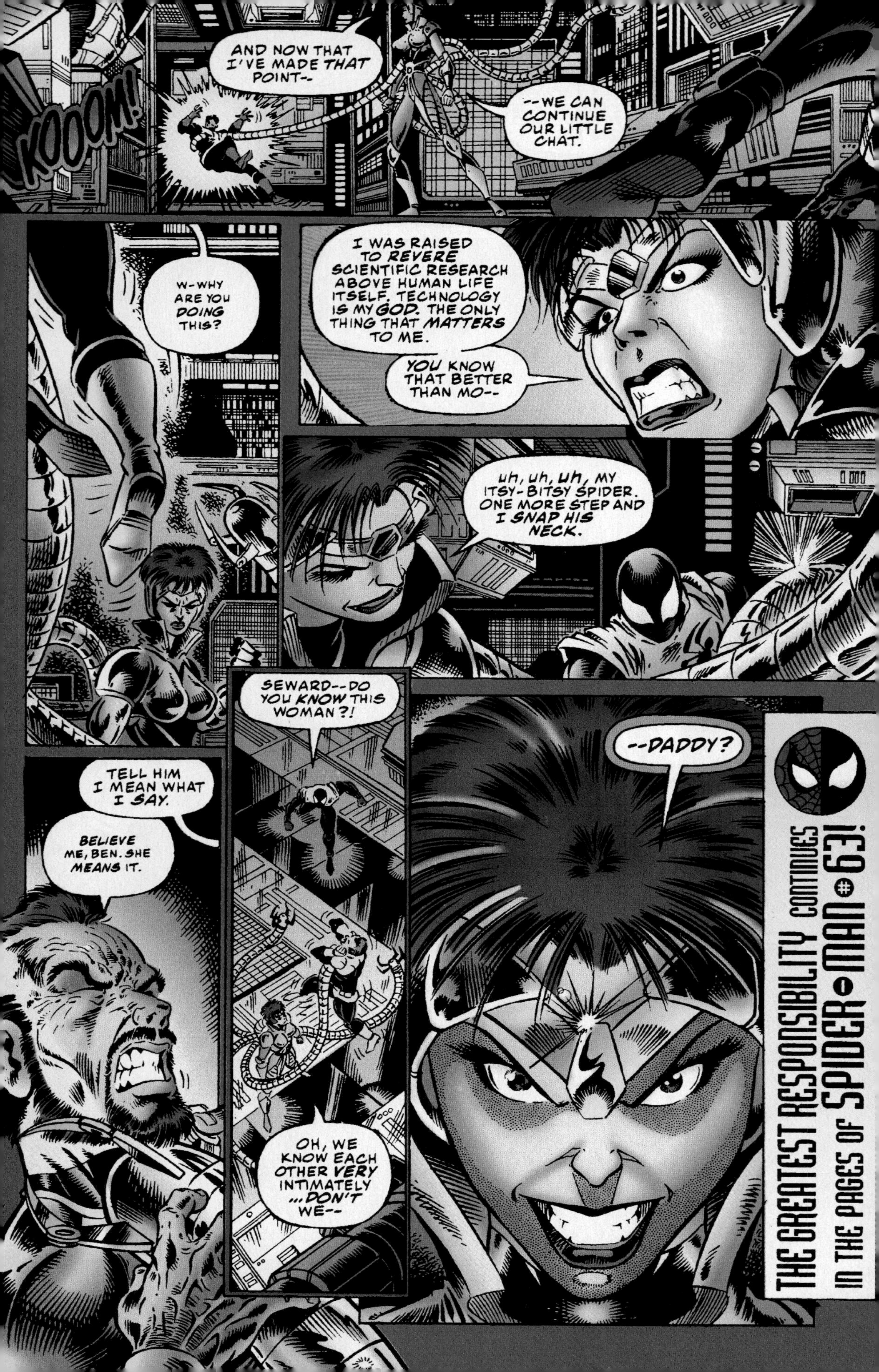

AND NOW THAT I'VE MADE THAT POINT--
KOOOM!
--WE CAN CONTINUE OUR LITTLE CHAT.
W-WHY ARE YOU DOING THIS?
I WAS RAISED TO REVERE SCIENTIFIC RESEARCH ABOVE HUMAN LIFE ITSELF. TECHNOLOGY IS MY GOD. THE ONLY THING THAT MATTERS TO ME.
YOU KNOW THAT BETTER THAN MO--
uh, uh, uh, MY ITSY-BITSY SPIDER. ONE MORE STEP AND I SNAP HIS NECK.
TELL HIM I MEAN WHAT I SAY.
BELIEVE ME, BEN. SHE MEANS IT.
SEWARD--DO YOU KNOW THIS WOMAN?!
OH, WE KNOW EACH OTHER VERY INTIMATELY ...DON'T WE--
--DADDY?
THE GREATEST RESPONSIBILITY CONTINUES IN THE PAGES OF SPIDER-MAN #63!

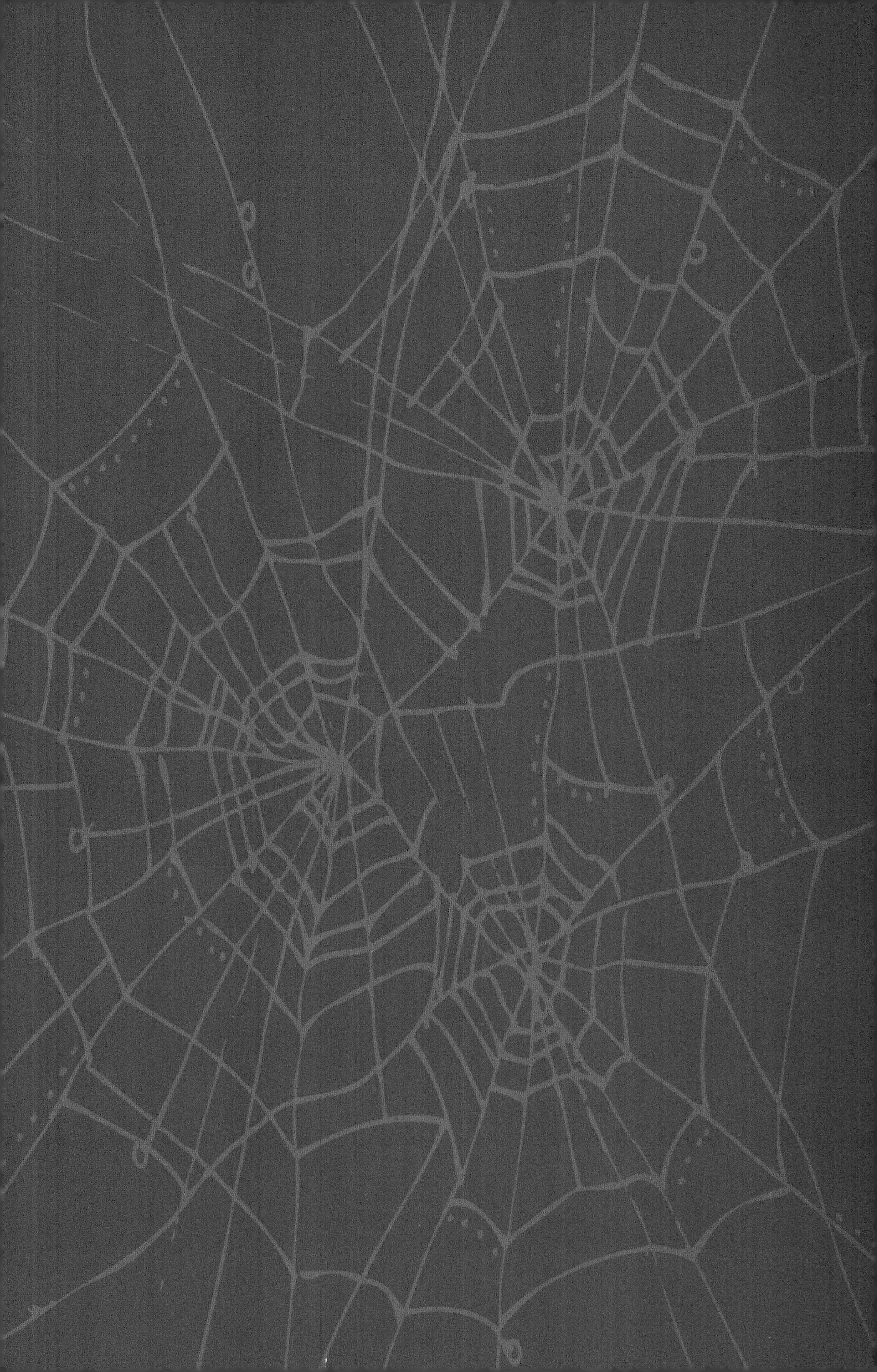

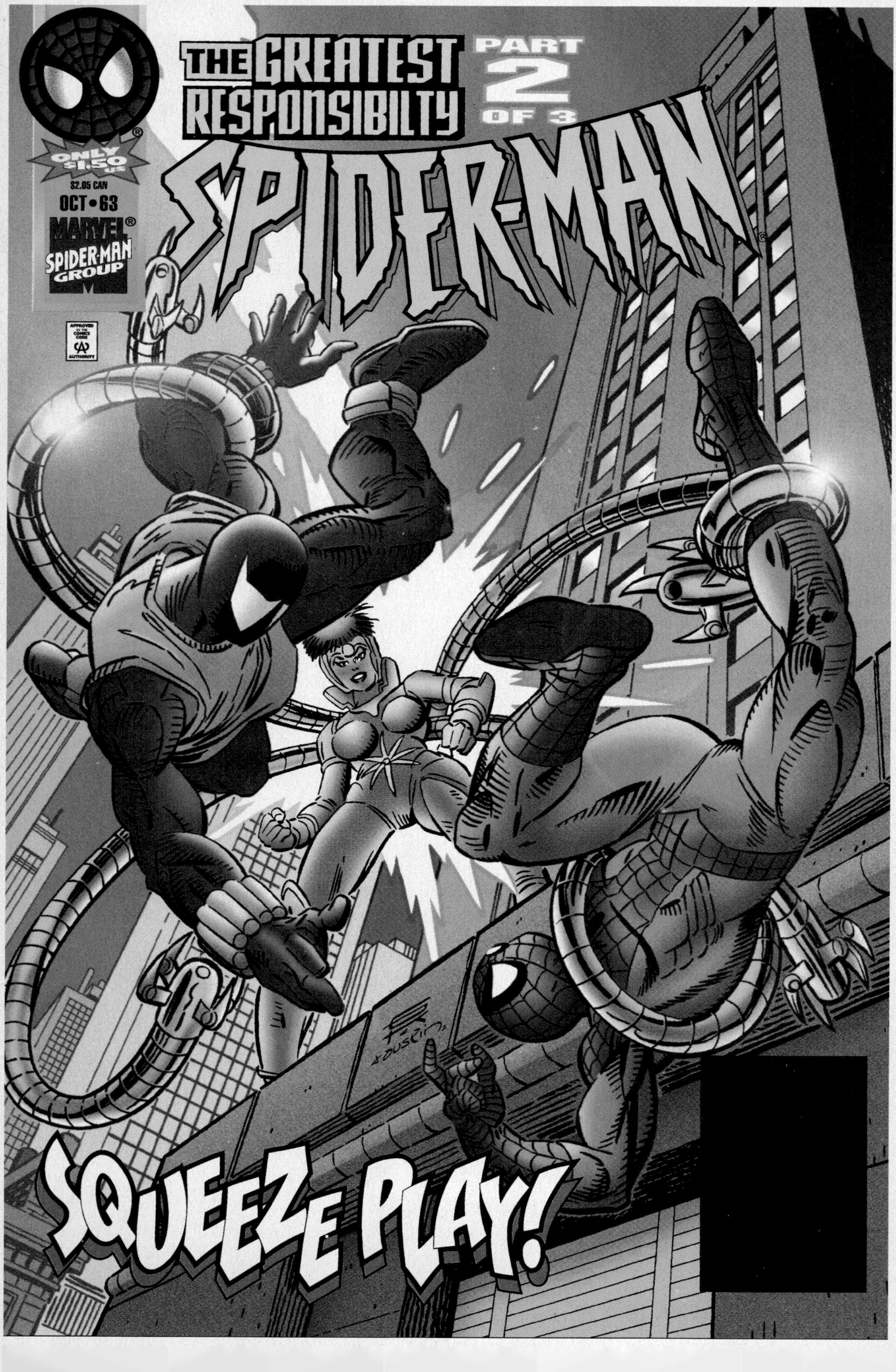
THE GREATEST RESPONSIBILTY
PART 2 OF 3
SPIDER-MAN
ONLY $1.50 US
$2.05 CAN
OCT • 63
MARVEL
SPIDER-MAN GROUP
APPROVED BY THE COMICS CODE AUTHORITY
SQUEEZE PLAY!

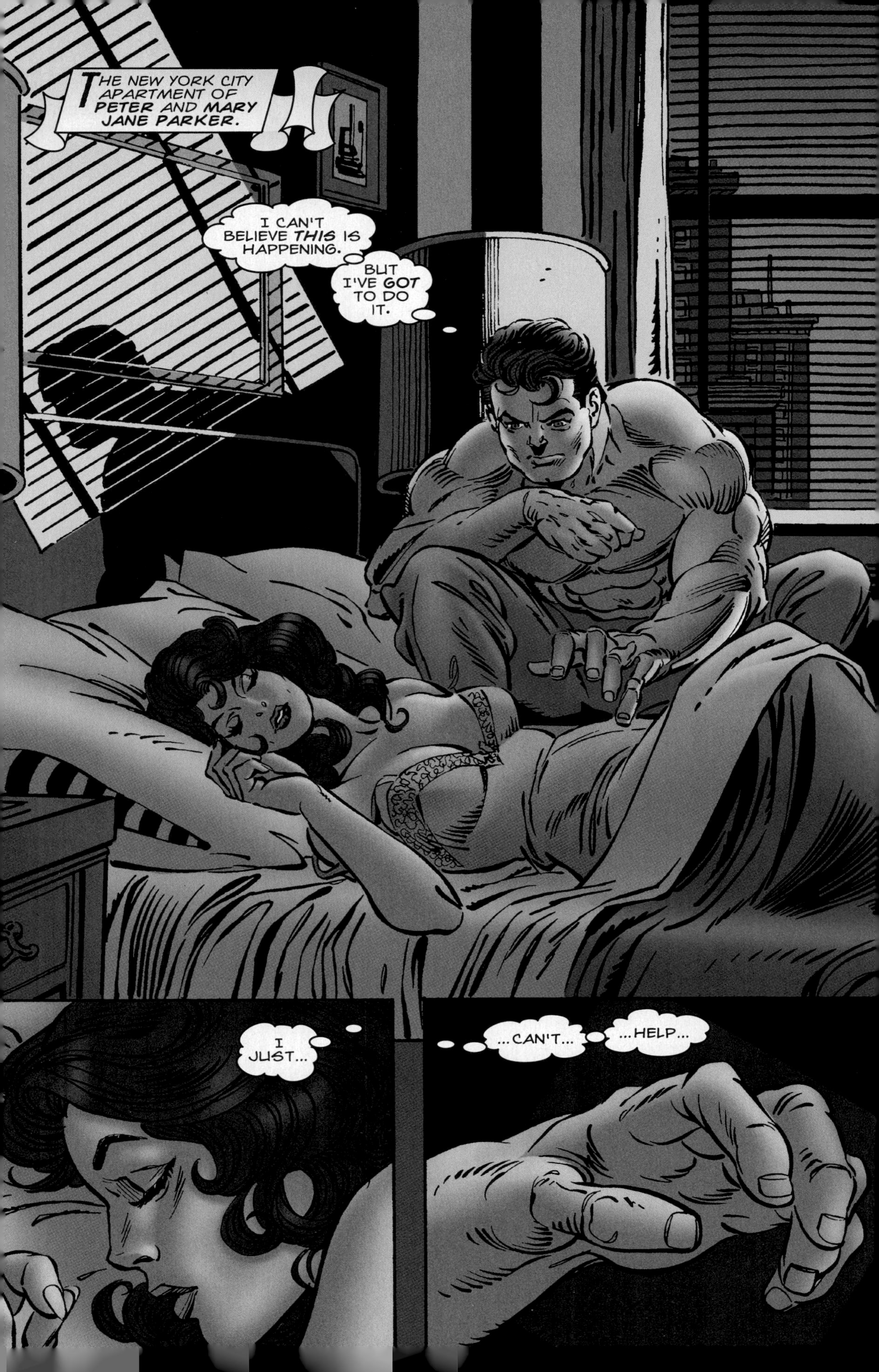
THE NEW YORK CITY APARTMENT OF PETER AND MARY JANE PARKER.
I CAN'T BELIEVE THIS IS HAPPENING.
BUT I'VE GOT TO DO IT.
I JUST...
...CAN'T...
...HELP...

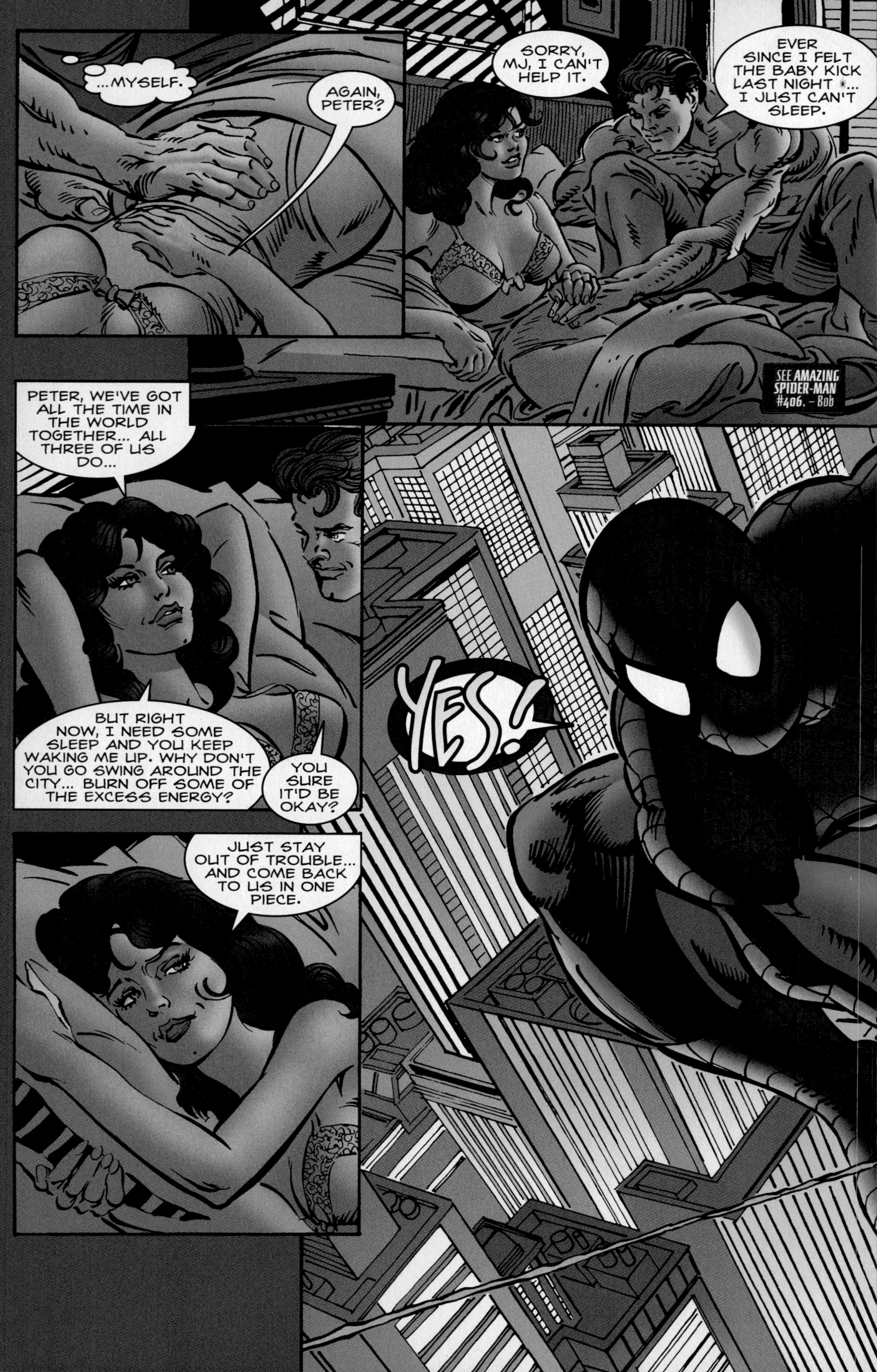
...MYSELF.
AGAIN, PETER?
SORRY, MJ, I CAN'T HELP IT.
EVER SINCE I FELT THE BABY KICK LAST NIGHT*... I JUST CAN'T SLEEP.
SEE AMAZING SPIDER-MAN #406. - Bob
PETER, WE'VE GOT ALL THE TIME IN THE WORLD TOGETHER... ALL THREE OF US DO...
BUT RIGHT NOW, I NEED SOME SLEEP AND YOU KEEP WAKING ME UP. WHY DON'T YOU GO SWING AROUND THE CITY... BURN OFF SOME OF THE EXCESS ENERGY?
YOU SURE IT'D BE OKAY?
JUST STAY OUT OF TROUBLE... AND COME BACK TO US IN ONE PIECE.
YES!

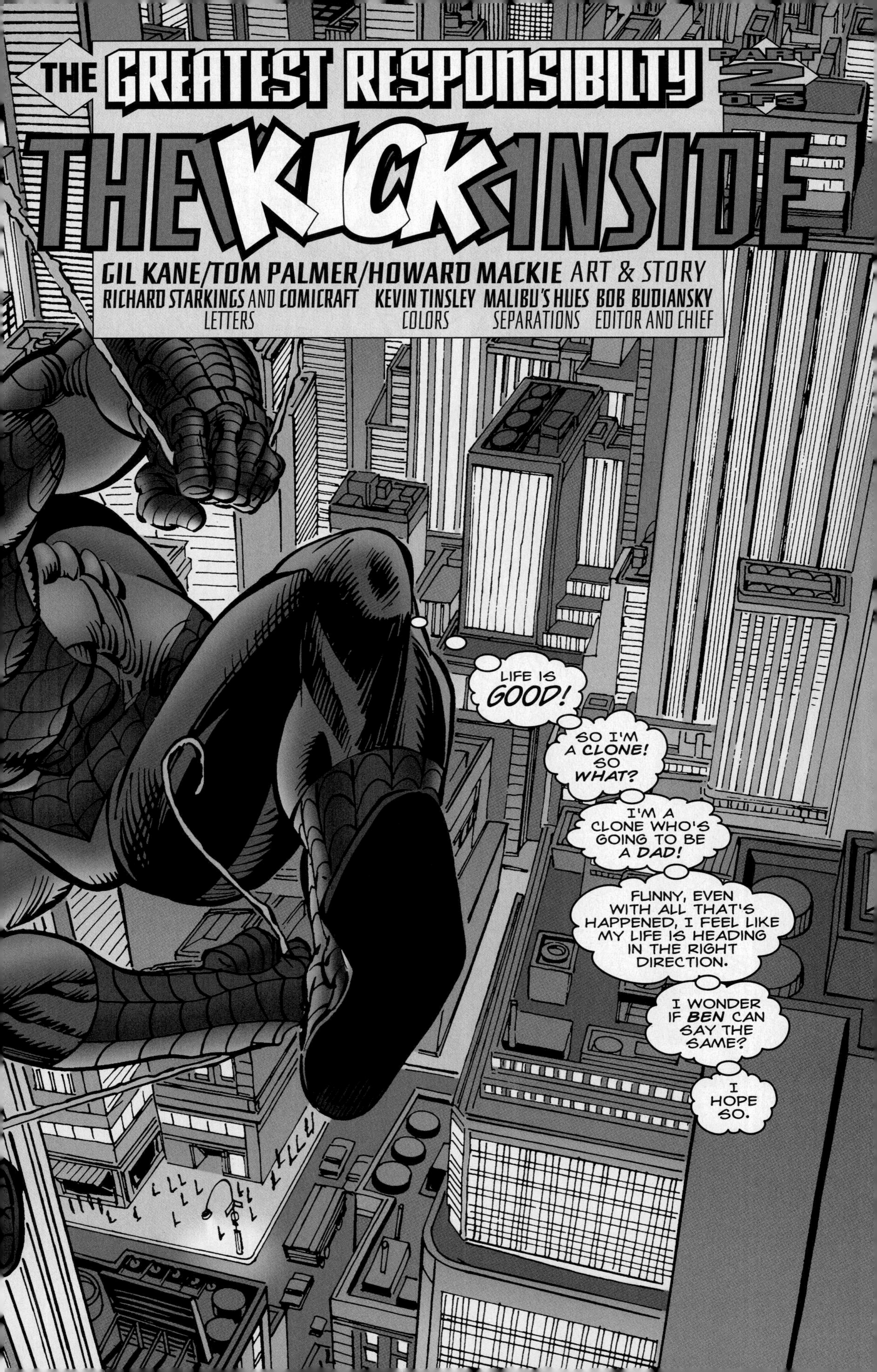
THE GREATEST RESPONSIBILTY PART 2 OF 3
THE KICK INSIDE
GIL KANE/TOM PALMER/HOWARD MACKIE ART & STORY
RICHARD STARKINGS AND COMICRAFT LETTERS
KEVIN TINSLEY COLORS
MALIBU'S HUES SEPARATIONS
BOB BUDIANSKY EDITOR AND CHIEF
LIFE IS GOOD!
SO I'M A CLONE! SO WHAT?
I'M A CLONE WHO'S GOING TO BE A DAD!
FUNNY, EVEN WITH ALL THAT'S HAPPENED, I FEEL LIKE MY LIFE IS HEADING IN THE RIGHT DIRECTION.
I WONDER IF BEN CAN SAY THE SAME?
I HOPE SO.

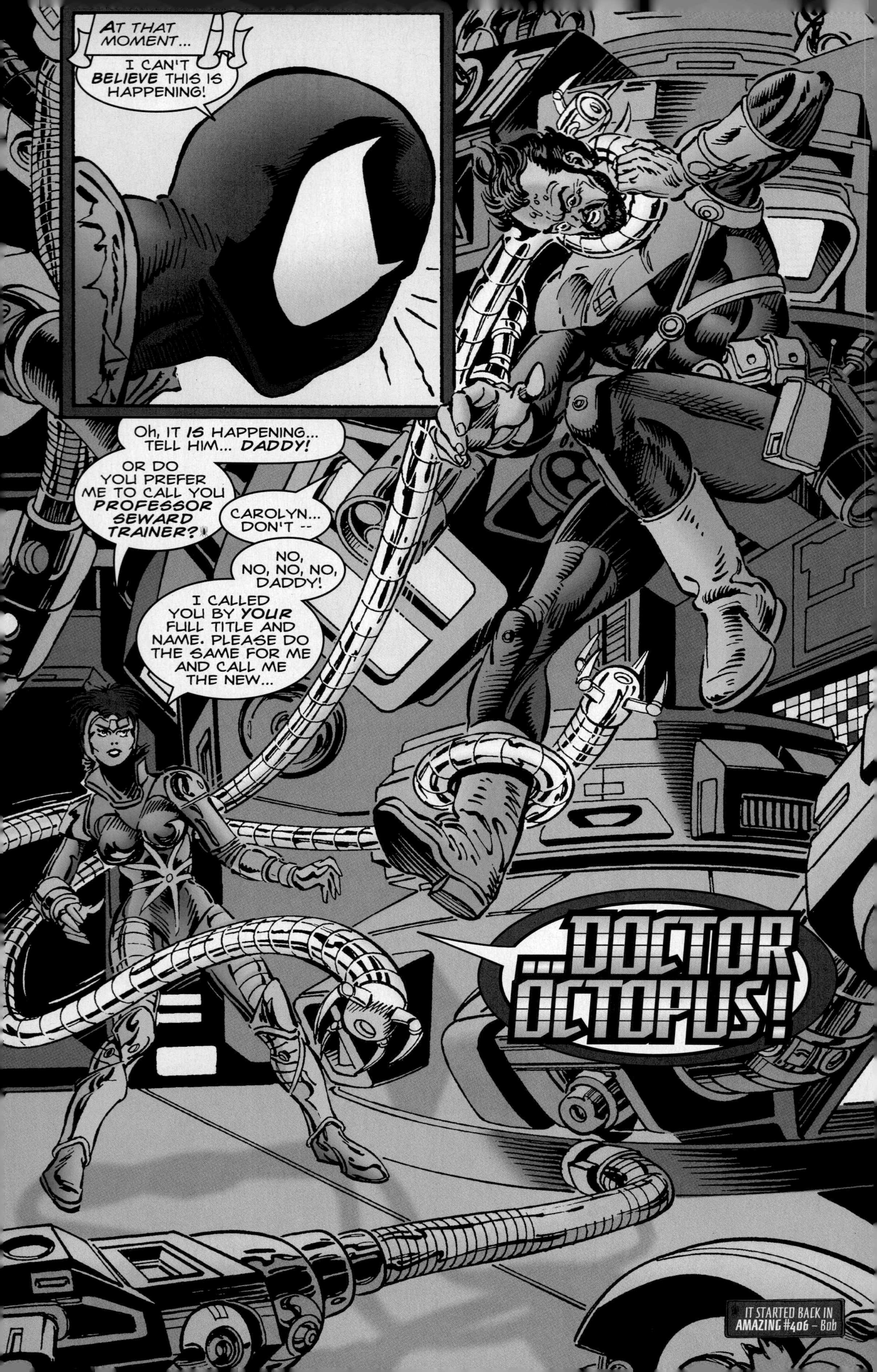
AT THAT MOMENT...
I CAN'T BELIEVE THIS IS HAPPENING!
Oh, IT IS HAPPENING... TELL HIM... DADDY!
OR DO YOU PREFER ME TO CALL YOU PROFESSOR SEWARD TRAINER?
CAROLYN... DON'T --
NO, NO, NO, NO, DADDY!
I CALLED YOU BY YOUR FULL TITLE AND NAME. PLEASE DO THE SAME FOR ME AND CALL ME THE NEW...
...DOCTOR OCTOPUS!
IT STARTED BACK IN AMAZING #406 – Bob

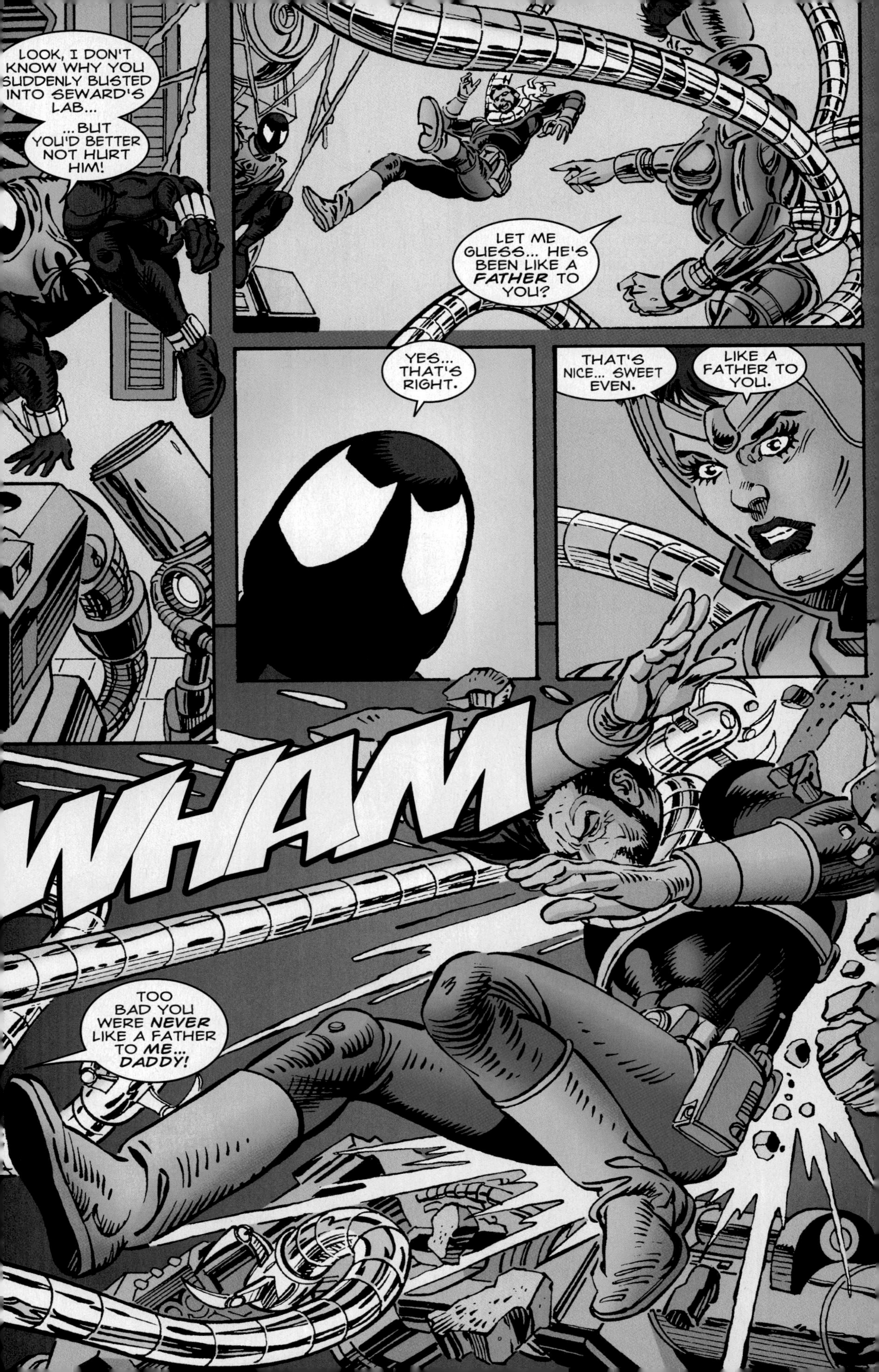
LOOK, I DON'T KNOW WHY YOU SUDDENLY BUSTED INTO SEWARD'S LAB...
...BUT YOU'D BETTER NOT HURT HIM!
LET ME GUESS... HE'S BEEN LIKE A *FATHER* TO YOU?
YES... THAT'S RIGHT.
THAT'S NICE... SWEET EVEN.
LIKE A FATHER TO YOU.
WHAM
TOO BAD YOU WERE *NEVER* LIKE A FATHER TO *ME*... *DADDY*!

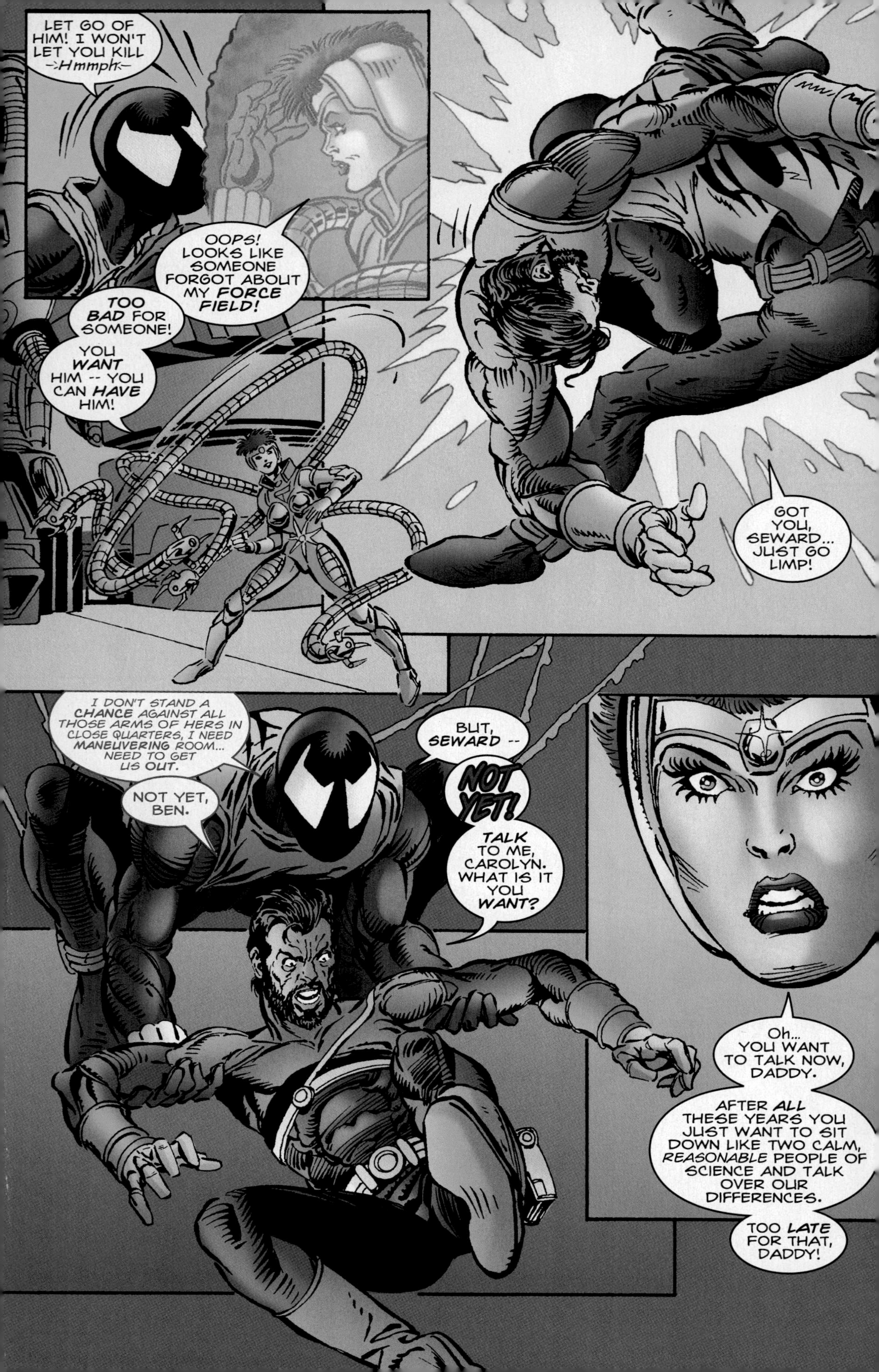
LET GO OF HIM! I WON'T LET YOU KILL --Hmmph--
OOPS! LOOKS LIKE SOMEONE FORGOT ABOUT MY FORCE FIELD!
TOO BAD FOR SOMEONE!
YOU WANT HIM -- YOU CAN HAVE HIM!
GOT YOU, SEWARD... JUST GO LIMP!
I DON'T STAND A CHANCE AGAINST ALL THOSE ARMS OF HERS IN CLOSE QUARTERS, I NEED MANEUVERING ROOM... NEED TO GET US OUT.
NOT YET, BEN.
BUT, SEWARD --
NOT YET!
TALK TO ME, CAROLYN. WHAT IS IT YOU WANT?
Oh... YOU WANT TO TALK NOW, DADDY.
AFTER ALL THESE YEARS YOU JUST WANT TO SIT DOWN LIKE TWO CALM, REASONABLE PEOPLE OF SCIENCE AND TALK OVER OUR DIFFERENCES.
TOO LATE FOR THAT, DADDY!

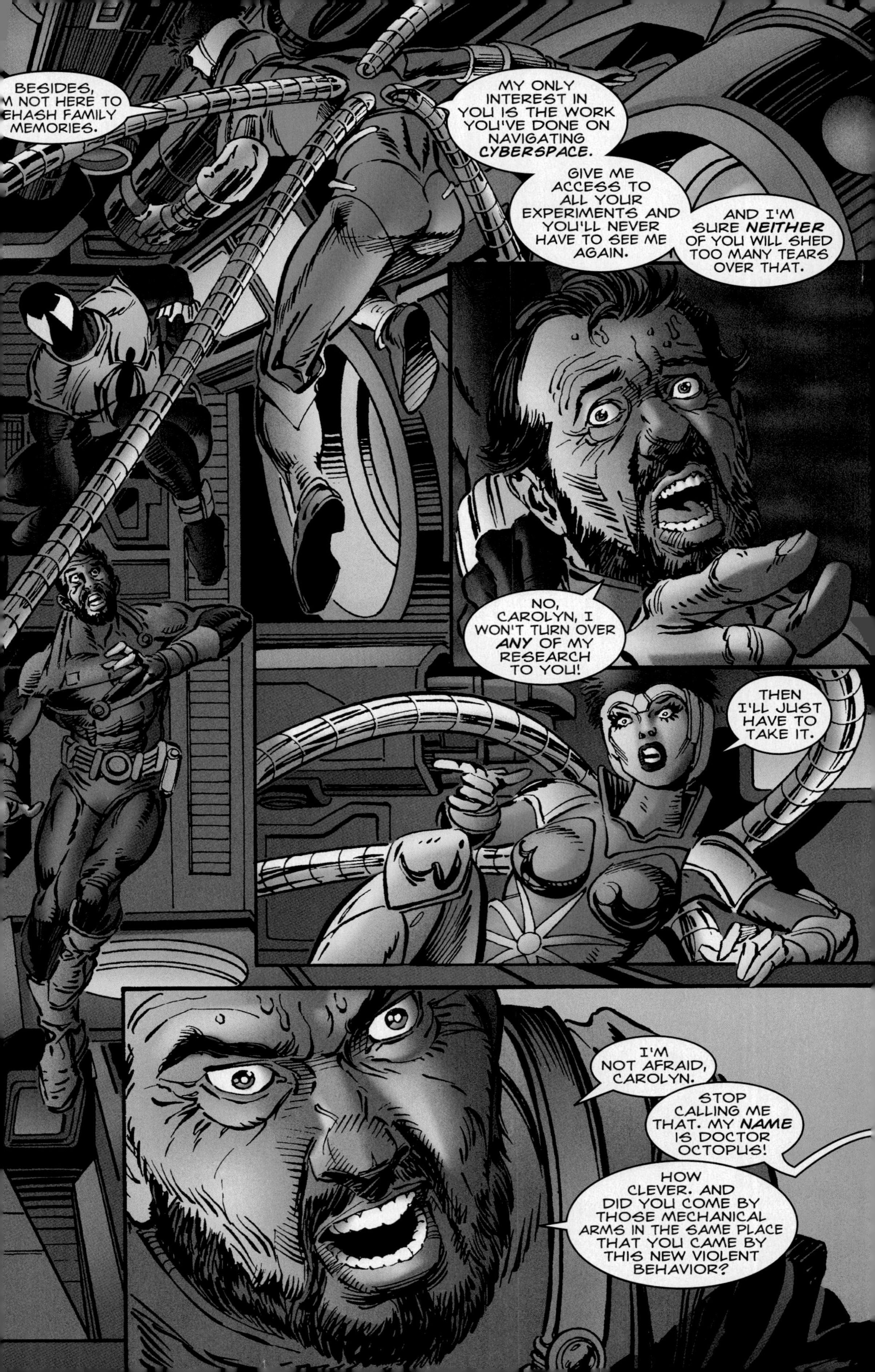
BESIDES, 'M NOT HERE TO EHASH FAMILY MEMORIES.
MY ONLY INTEREST IN YOU IS THE WORK YOU'VE DONE ON NAVIGATING CYBERSPACE.
GIVE ME ACCESS TO ALL YOUR EXPERIMENTS AND YOU'LL NEVER HAVE TO SEE ME AGAIN.
AND I'M SURE NEITHER OF YOU WILL SHED TOO MANY TEARS OVER THAT.
NO, CAROLYN, I WON'T TURN OVER ANY OF MY RESEARCH TO YOU!
THEN I'LL JUST HAVE TO TAKE IT.
I'M NOT AFRAID, CAROLYN.
STOP CALLING ME THAT. MY NAME IS DOCTOR OCTOPUS!
HOW CLEVER. AND DID YOU COME BY THOSE MECHANICAL ARMS IN THE SAME PLACE THAT YOU CAME BY THIS NEW VIOLENT BEHAVIOR?

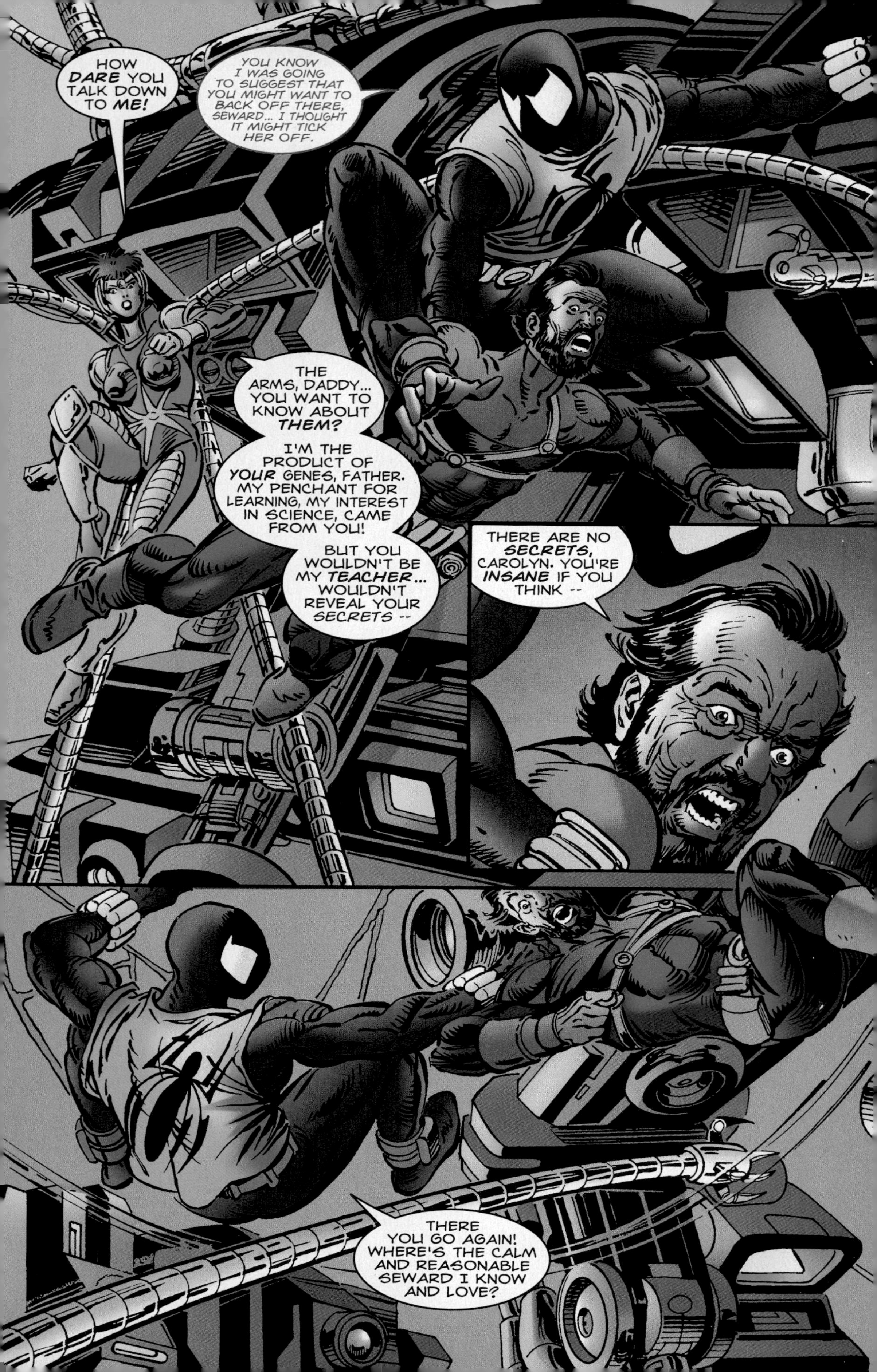
HOW DARE YOU TALK DOWN TO ME!
YOU KNOW I WAS GOING TO SUGGEST THAT YOU MIGHT WANT TO BACK OFF THERE, SEWARD... I THOUGHT IT MIGHT TICK HER OFF.
THE ARMS, DADDY... YOU WANT TO KNOW ABOUT THEM?
I'M THE PRODUCT OF YOUR GENES, FATHER. MY PENCHANT FOR LEARNING, MY INTEREST IN SCIENCE, CAME FROM YOU!
BUT YOU WOULDN'T BE MY TEACHER... WOULDN'T REVEAL YOUR SECRETS --
THERE ARE NO SECRETS, CAROLYN. YOU'RE INSANE IF YOU THINK --
THERE YOU GO AGAIN! WHERE'S THE CALM AND REASONABLE SEWARD I KNOW AND LOVE?

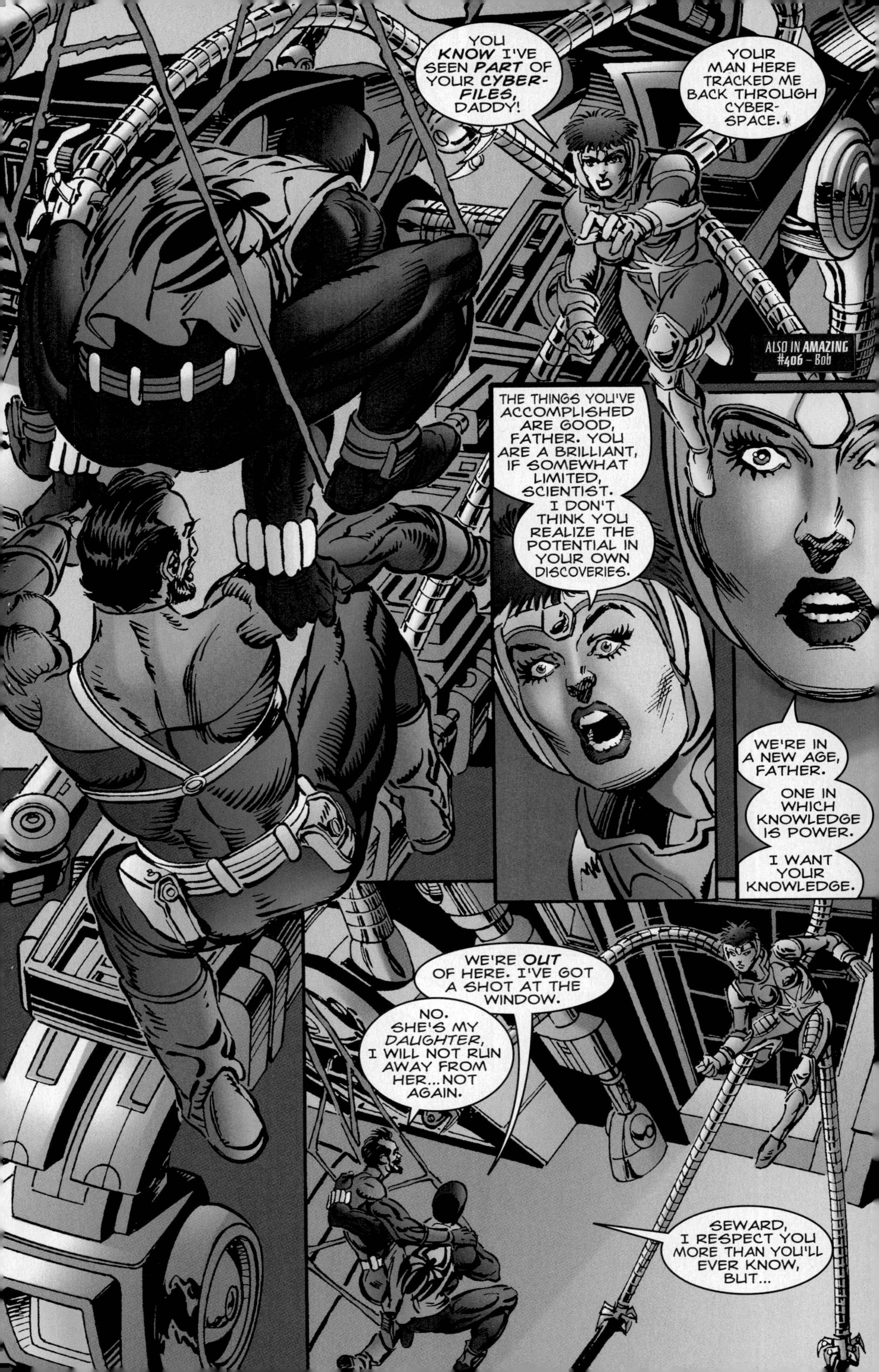
YOU KNOW I'VE SEEN PART OF YOUR CYBER-FILES, DADDY!
YOUR MAN HERE TRACKED ME BACK THROUGH CYBER-SPACE.
ALSO IN AMAZING #406 – Bob
THE THINGS YOU'VE ACCOMPLISHED ARE GOOD, FATHER. YOU ARE A BRILLIANT, IF SOMEWHAT LIMITED, SCIENTIST.
I DON'T THINK YOU REALIZE THE POTENTIAL IN YOUR OWN DISCOVERIES.
WE'RE IN A NEW AGE, FATHER.
ONE IN WHICH KNOWLEDGE IS POWER.
I WANT YOUR KNOWLEDGE.
WE'RE OUT OF HERE. I'VE GOT A SHOT AT THE WINDOW.
NO. SHE'S MY DAUGHTER, I WILL NOT RUN AWAY FROM HER...NOT AGAIN.
SEWARD, I RESPECT YOU MORE THAN YOU'LL EVER KNOW, BUT...

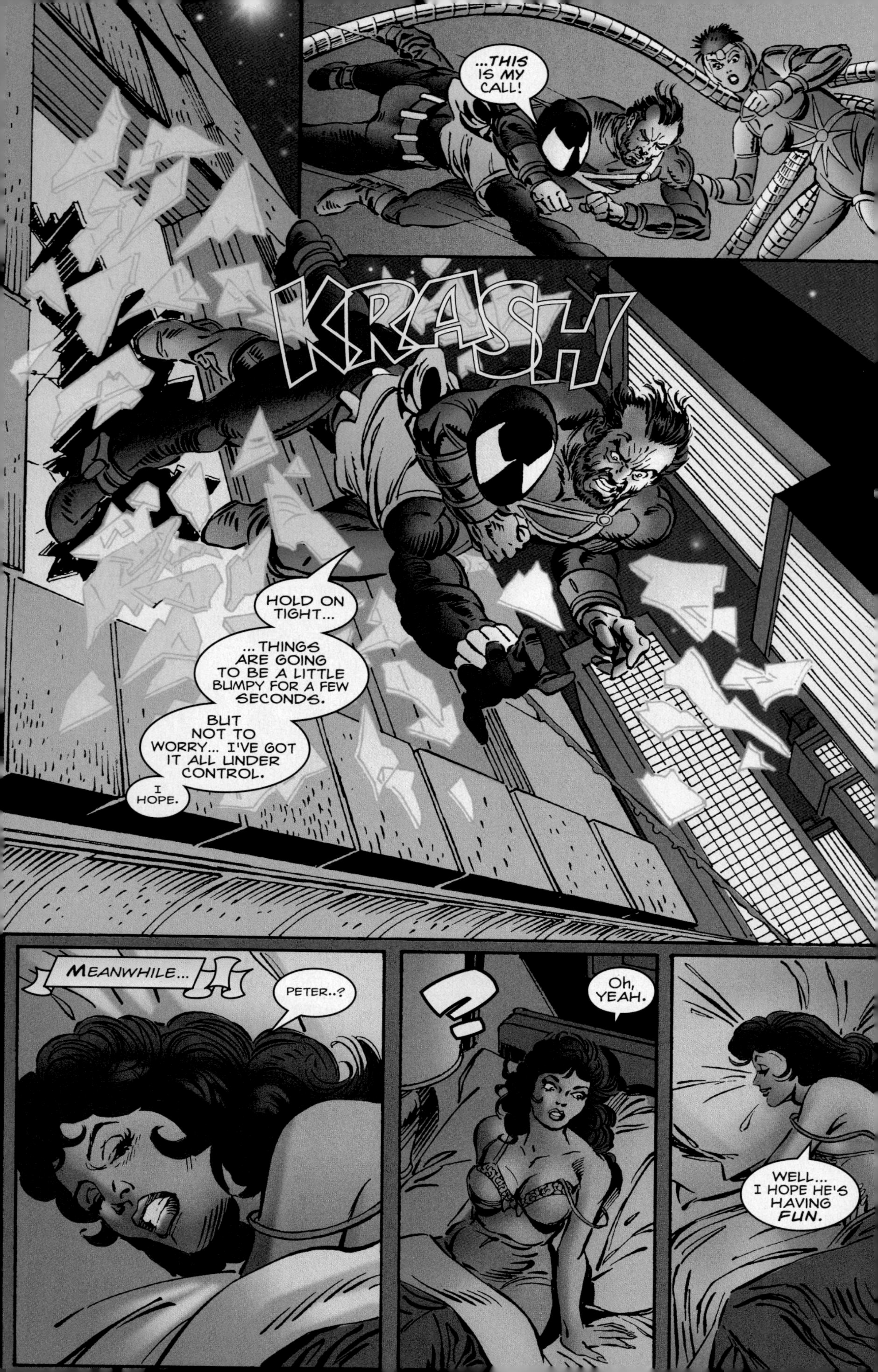
...THIS IS MY CALL!
KRASH
HOLD ON TIGHT...
...THINGS ARE GOING TO BE A LITTLE BUMPY FOR A FEW SECONDS.
BUT NOT TO WORRY... I'VE GOT IT ALL UNDER CONTROL.
I HOPE.
MEANWHILE...
PETER..?
?
Oh, YEAH.
WELL... I HOPE HE'S HAVING FUN.

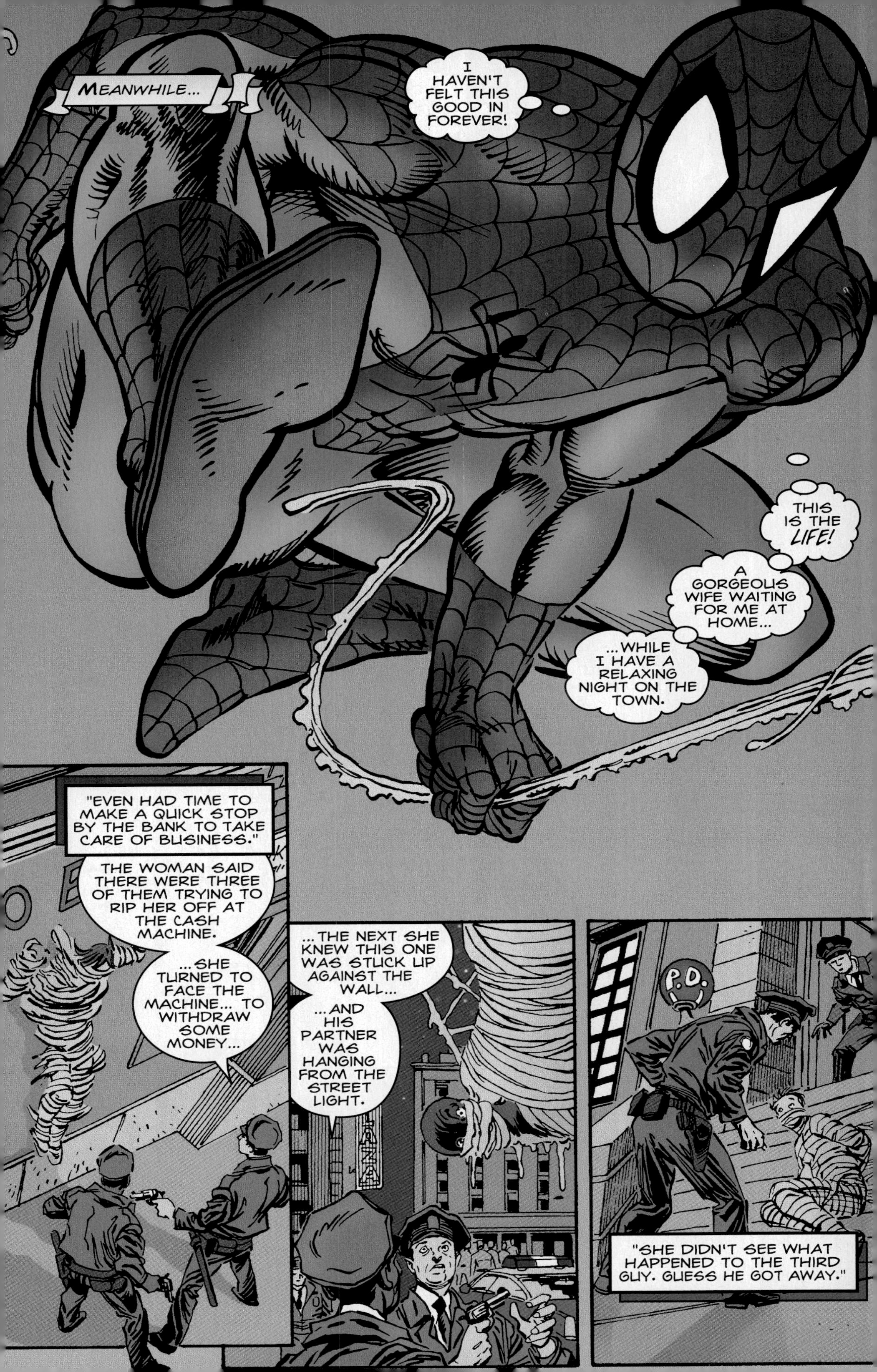
MEANWHILE...
I HAVEN'T FELT THIS GOOD IN FOREVER!
THIS IS THE LIFE!
A GORGEOUS WIFE WAITING FOR ME AT HOME...
...WHILE I HAVE A RELAXING NIGHT ON THE TOWN.
"EVEN HAD TIME TO MAKE A QUICK STOP BY THE BANK TO TAKE CARE OF BUSINESS."
THE WOMAN SAID THERE WERE THREE OF THEM TRYING TO RIP HER OFF AT THE CASH MACHINE.
...SHE TURNED TO FACE THE MACHINE... TO WITHDRAW SOME MONEY...
...THE NEXT SHE KNEW THIS ONE WAS STUCK UP AGAINST THE WALL...
...AND HIS PARTNER WAS HANGING FROM THE STREET LIGHT.
P.D.
"SHE DIDN'T SEE WHAT HAPPENED TO THE THIRD GUY. GUESS HE GOT AWAY."

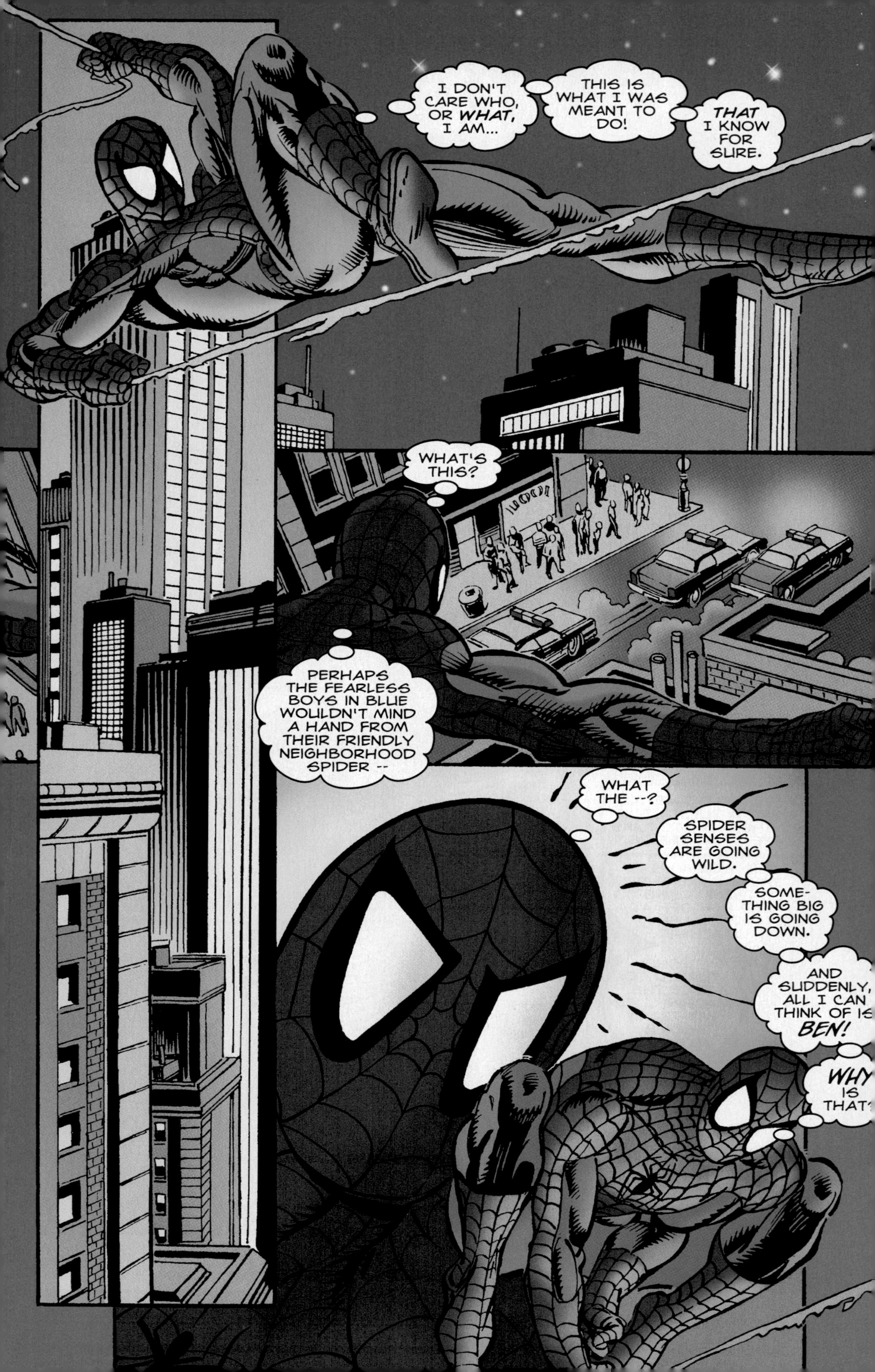
I DON'T CARE WHO, OR WHAT, I AM...
THIS IS WHAT I WAS MEANT TO DO!
THAT I KNOW FOR SURE.
WHAT'S THIS?
PERHAPS THE FEARLESS BOYS IN BLUE WOULDN'T MIND A HAND FROM THEIR FRIENDLY NEIGHBORHOOD SPIDER --
WHAT THE --?
SPIDER SENSES ARE GOING WILD.
SOME-THING BIG IS GOING DOWN.
AND SUDDENLY, ALL I CAN THINK OF IS BEN!

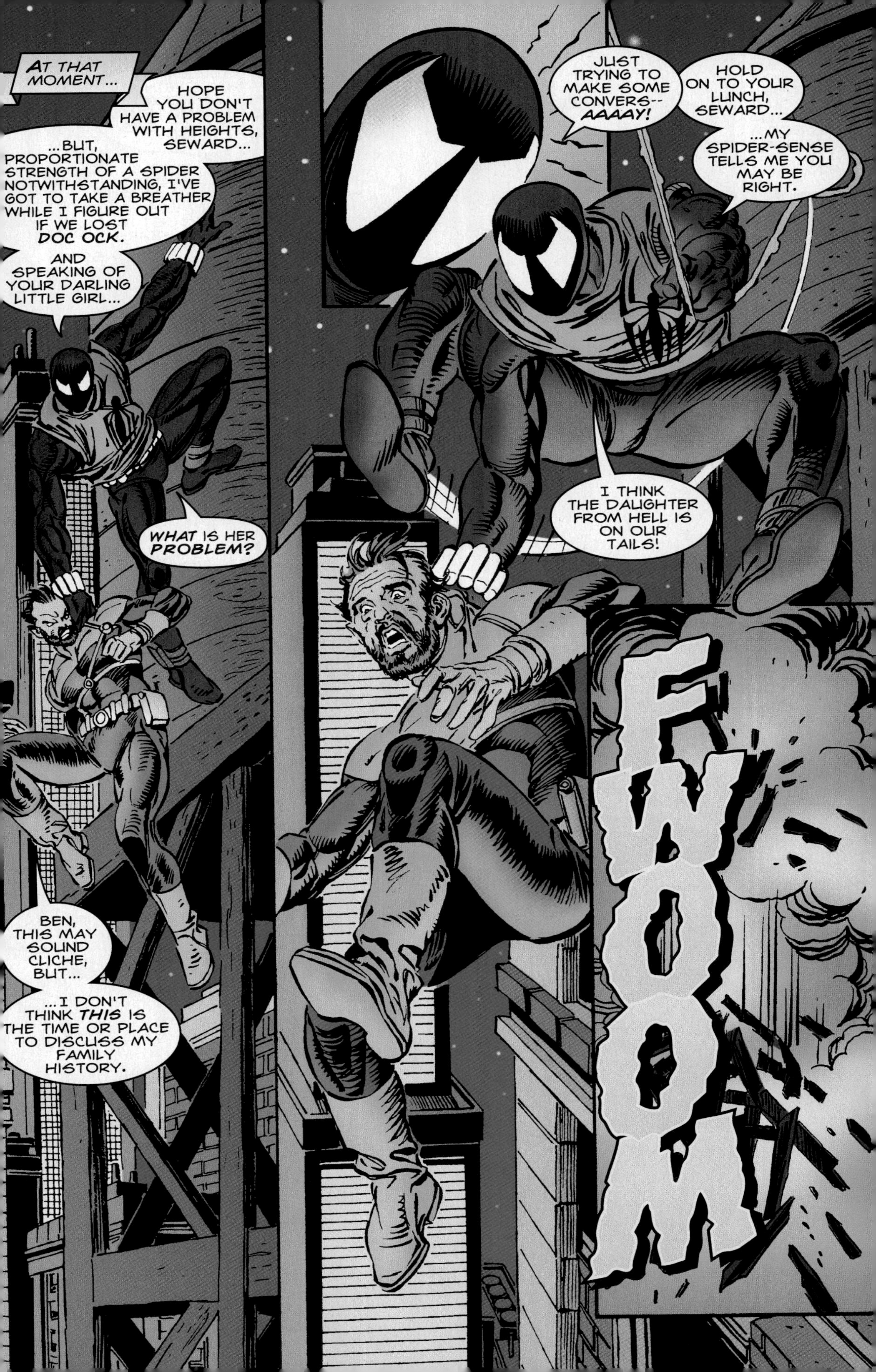
AT THAT MOMENT...
HOPE YOU DON'T HAVE A PROBLEM WITH HEIGHTS, SEWARD...
...BUT, PROPORTIONATE STRENGTH OF A SPIDER NOTWITHSTANDING, I'VE GOT TO TAKE A BREATHER WHILE I FIGURE OUT IF WE LOST DOC OCK.
AND SPEAKING OF YOUR DARLING LITTLE GIRL...
WHAT IS HER PROBLEM?
BEN, THIS MAY SOUND CLICHE, BUT...
...I DON'T THINK THIS IS THE TIME OR PLACE TO DISCUSS MY FAMILY HISTORY.
JUST TRYING TO MAKE SOME CONVERS-- AAAAY!
HOLD ON TO YOUR LUNCH, SEWARD...
...MY SPIDER-SENSE TELLS ME YOU MAY BE RIGHT.
I THINK THE DAUGHTER FROM HELL IS ON OUR TAILS!
FWOOM

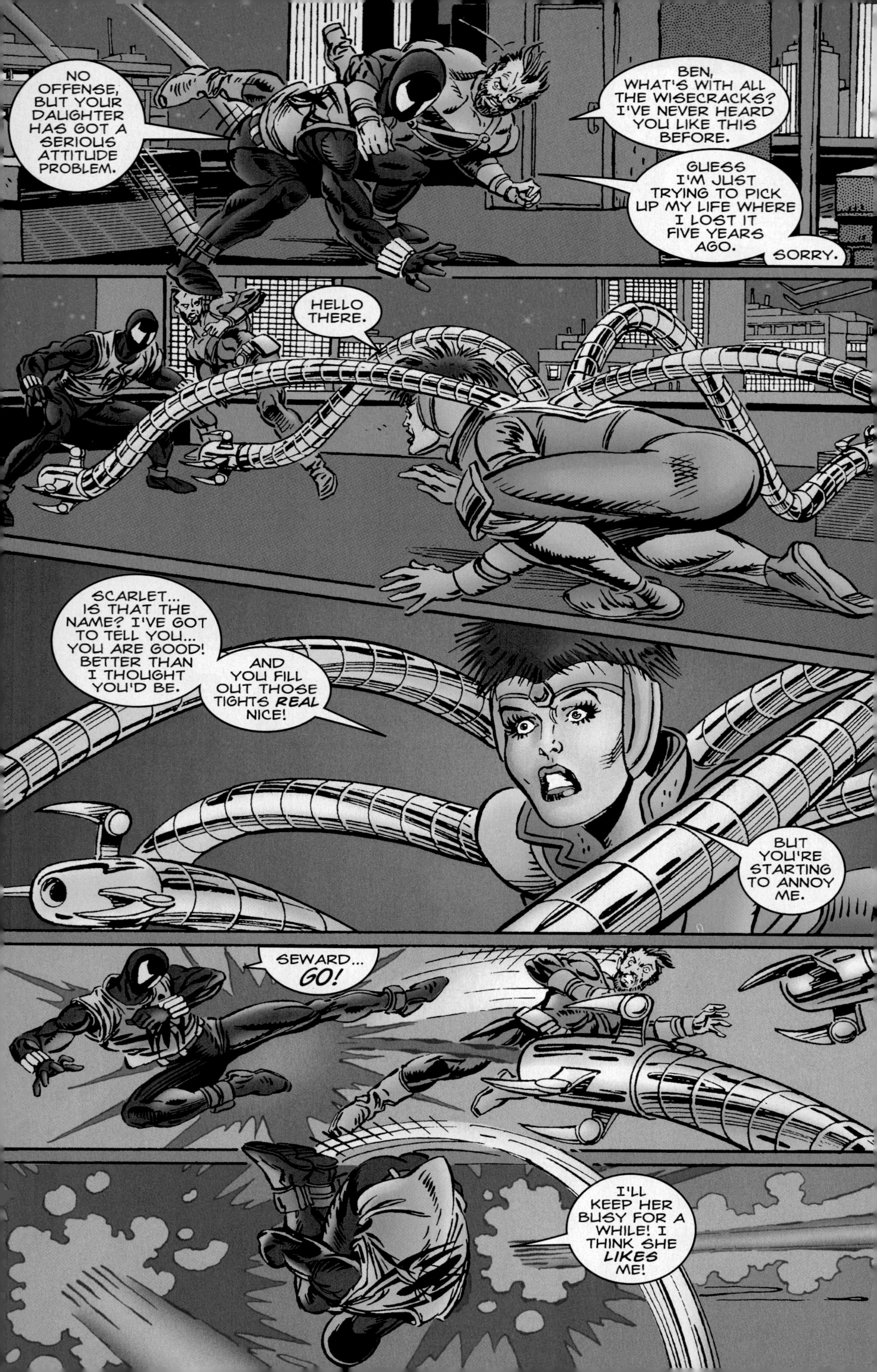

NO OFFENSE, BUT YOUR DAUGHTER HAS GOT A SERIOUS ATTITUDE PROBLEM.
BEN, WHAT'S WITH ALL THE WISECRACKS? I'VE NEVER HEARD YOU LIKE THIS BEFORE.
GUESS I'M JUST TRYING TO PICK UP MY LIFE WHERE I LOST IT FIVE YEARS AGO.
SORRY.
HELLO THERE.
SCARLET... IS THAT THE NAME? I'VE GOT TO TELL YOU... YOU ARE GOOD! BETTER THAN I THOUGHT YOU'D BE.
AND YOU FILL OUT THOSE TIGHTS REAL NICE!
BUT YOU'RE STARTING TO ANNOY ME.
SEWARD... GO!
I'LL KEEP HER BUSY FOR A WHILE! I THINK SHE LIKES ME!

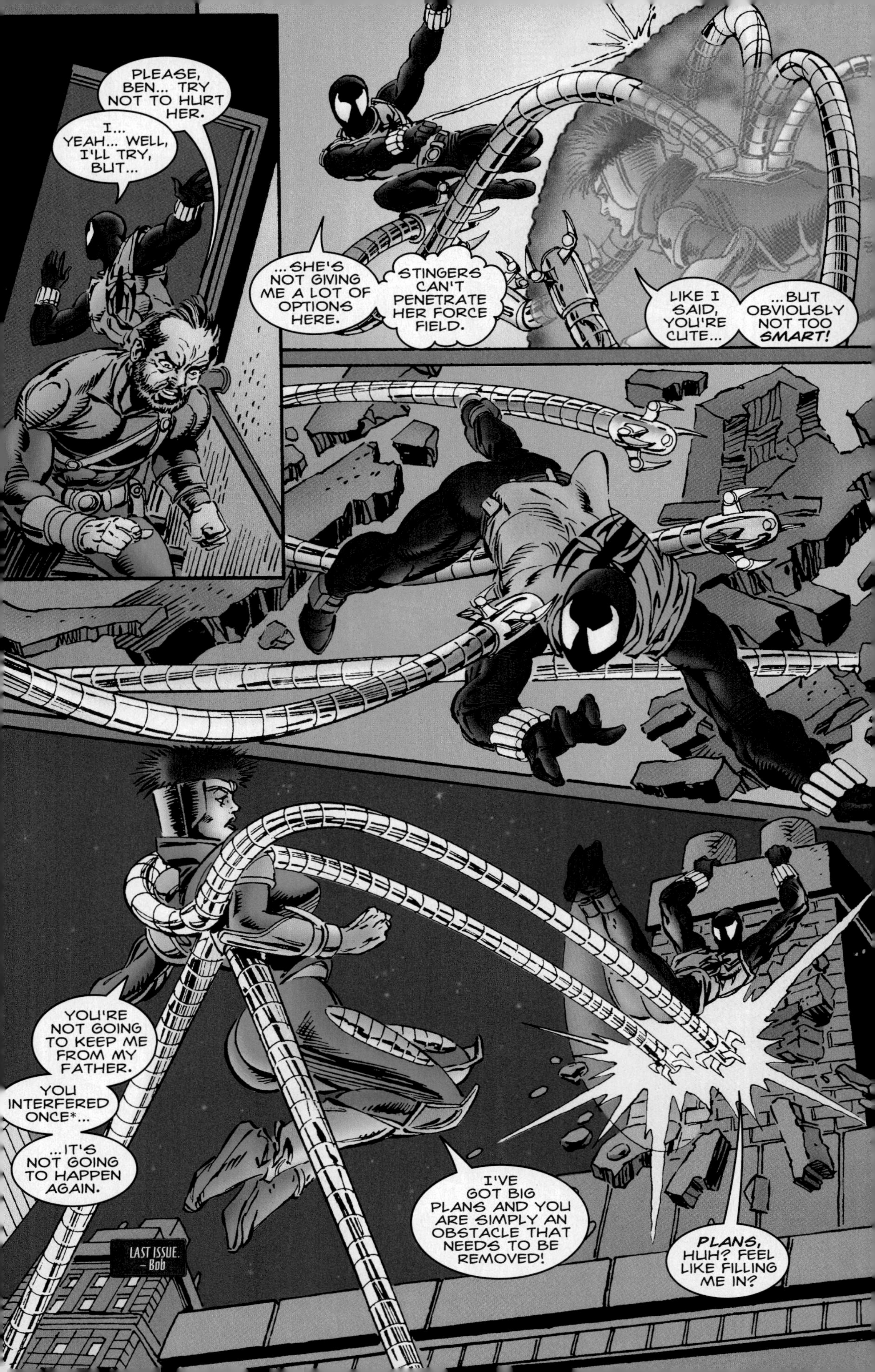
PLEASE, BEN... TRY NOT TO HURT HER.
I... YEAH... WELL, I'LL TRY, BUT...
...SHE'S NOT GIVING ME A LOT OF OPTIONS HERE.
STINGERS CAN'T PENETRATE HER FORCE FIELD.
LIKE I SAID, YOU'RE CUTE...
...BUT OBVIOUSLY NOT TOO SMART!
YOU'RE NOT GOING TO KEEP ME FROM MY FATHER.
YOU INTERFERED ONCE*...
...IT'S NOT GOING TO HAPPEN AGAIN.
I'VE GOT BIG PLANS AND YOU ARE SIMPLY AN OBSTACLE THAT NEEDS TO BE REMOVED!
PLANS, HUH? FEEL LIKE FILLING ME IN?
LAST ISSUE. – Bob

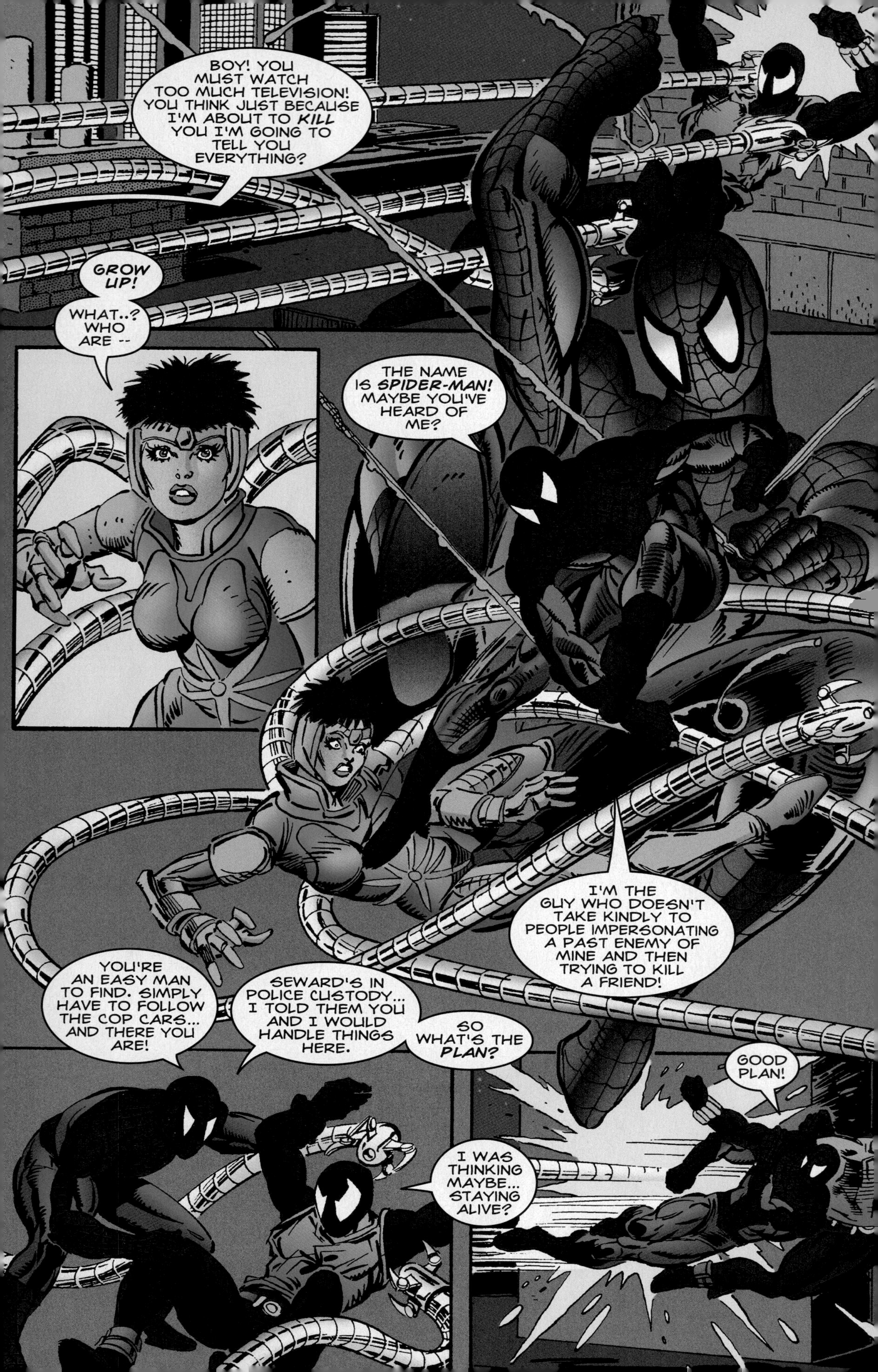
BOY! YOU MUST WATCH TOO MUCH TELEVISION! YOU THINK JUST BECAUSE I'M ABOUT TO *KILL* YOU I'M GOING TO TELL YOU EVERYTHING?
GROW UP!
WHAT..? WHO ARE --
THE NAME IS *SPIDER-MAN!* MAYBE YOU'VE HEARD OF ME?
I'M THE GUY WHO DOESN'T TAKE KINDLY TO PEOPLE IMPERSONATING A PAST ENEMY OF MINE AND THEN TRYING TO KILL A FRIEND!
YOU'RE AN EASY MAN TO FIND. SIMPLY HAVE TO FOLLOW THE COP CARS... AND THERE YOU ARE!
SEWARD'S IN POLICE CUSTODY... I TOLD THEM YOU AND I WOULD HANDLE THINGS HERE.
SO WHAT'S THE *PLAN?*
I WAS THINKING MAYBE... STAYING ALIVE?
GOOD PLAN!

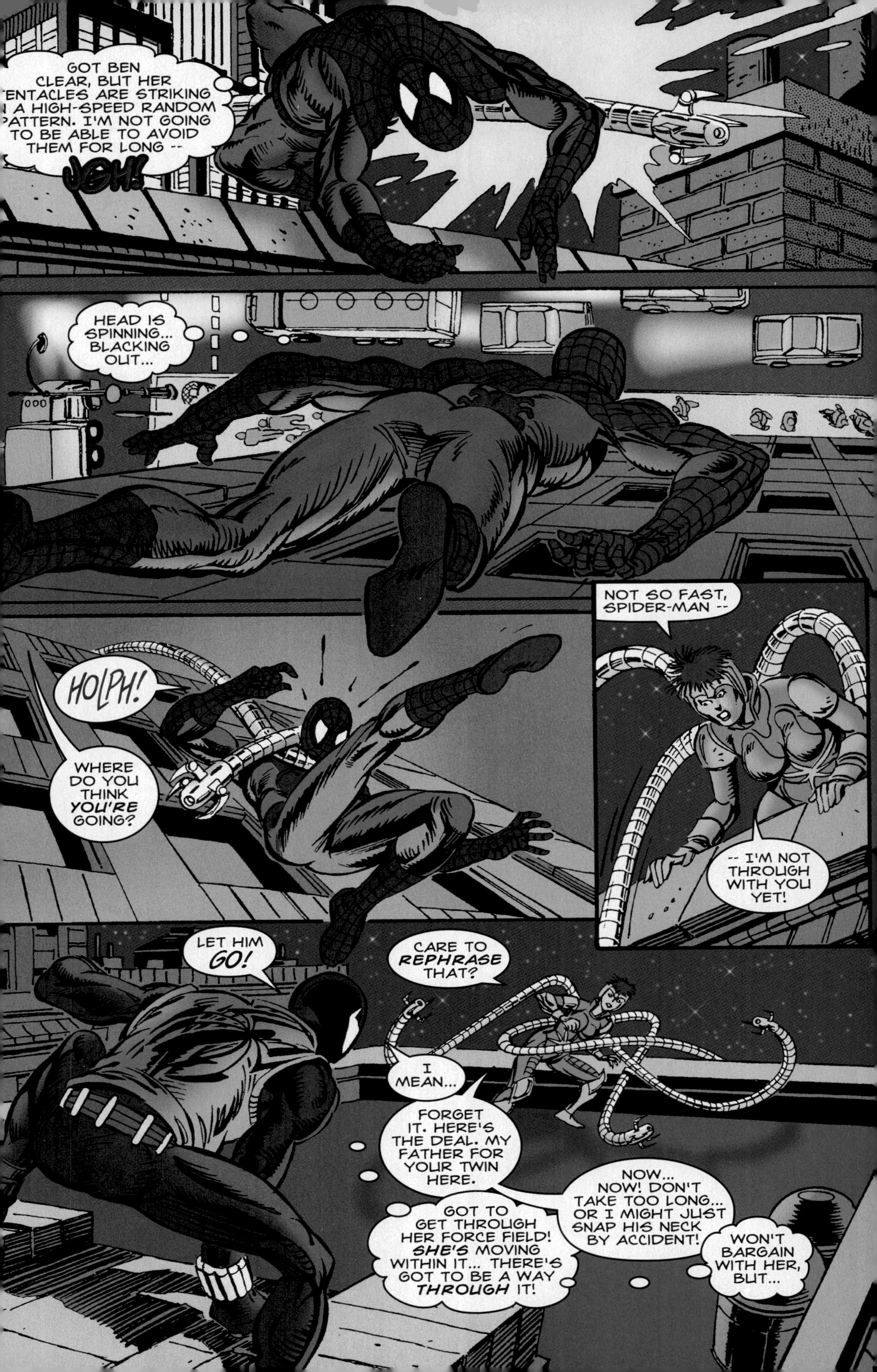

GOT BEN CLEAR, BUT HER TENTACLES ARE STRIKING IN A HIGH-SPEED RANDOM PATTERN. I'M NOT GOING TO BE ABLE TO AVOID THEM FOR LONG --
HEAD IS SPINNING... BLACKING OUT...
NOT SO FAST, SPIDER-MAN --
-- I'M NOT THROUGH WITH YOU YET!
HOLPH!
WHERE DO YOU THINK YOU'RE GOING?
LET HIM GO!
CARE TO REPHRASE THAT?
I MEAN...
FORGET IT. HERE'S THE DEAL. MY FATHER FOR YOUR TWIN HERE.
NOW... NOW! DON'T TAKE TOO LONG... OR I MIGHT JUST SNAP HIS NECK BY ACCIDENT!
GOT TO GET THROUGH HER FORCE FIELD! SHE'S MOVING WITHIN IT... THERE'S GOT TO BE A WAY THROUGH IT!
WON'T BARGAIN WITH HER, BUT...

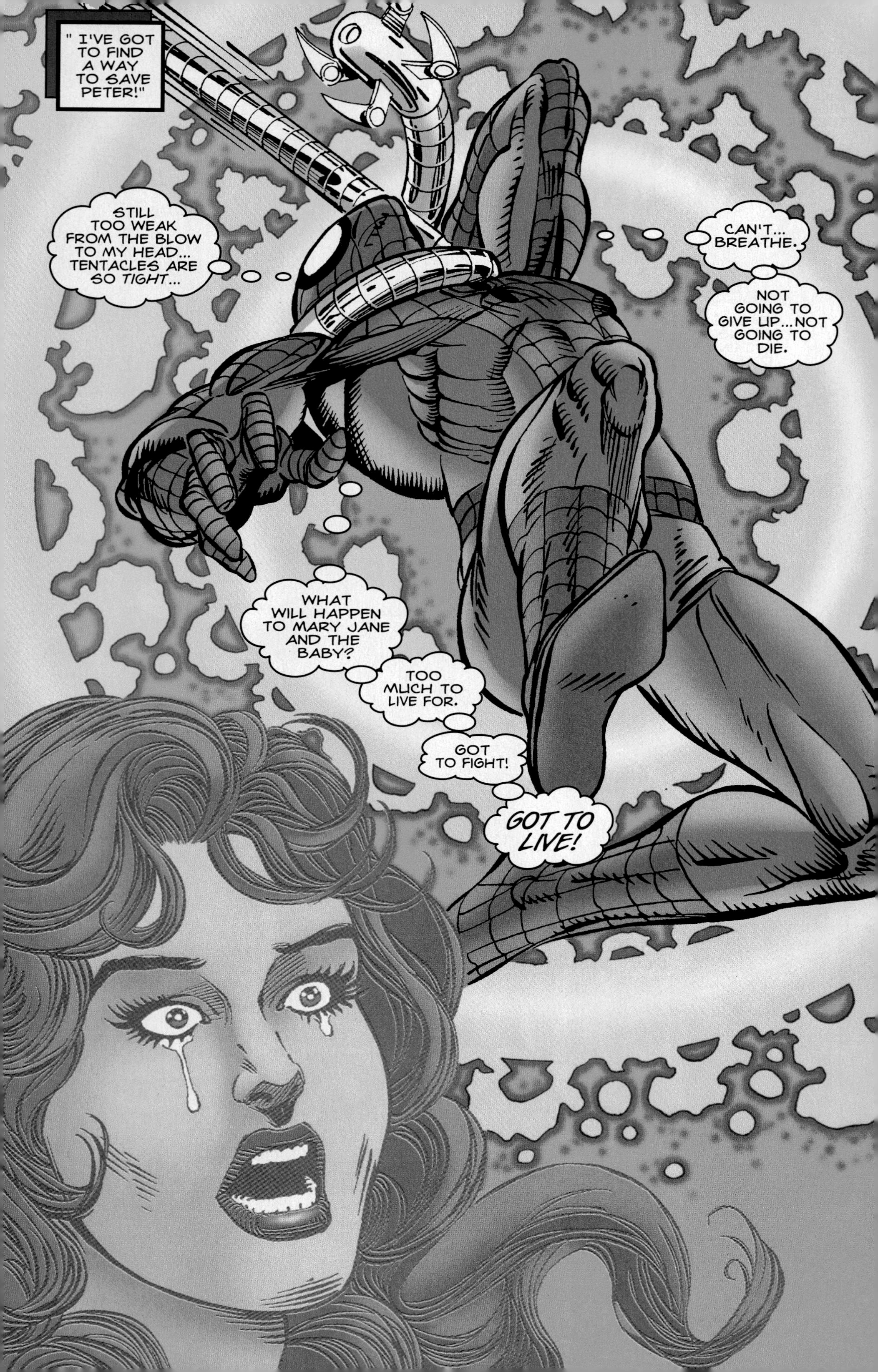
" I'VE GOT TO FIND A WAY TO SAVE PETER!"
STILL TOO WEAK FROM THE BLOW TO MY HEAD... TENTACLES ARE SO *TIGHT*...
CAN'T... BREATHE.
NOT GOING TO GIVE UP...NOT GOING TO DIE.
WHAT WILL HAPPEN TO MARY JANE AND THE BABY?
TOO MUCH TO LIVE FOR.
GOT TO FIGHT!
GOT TO LIVE!

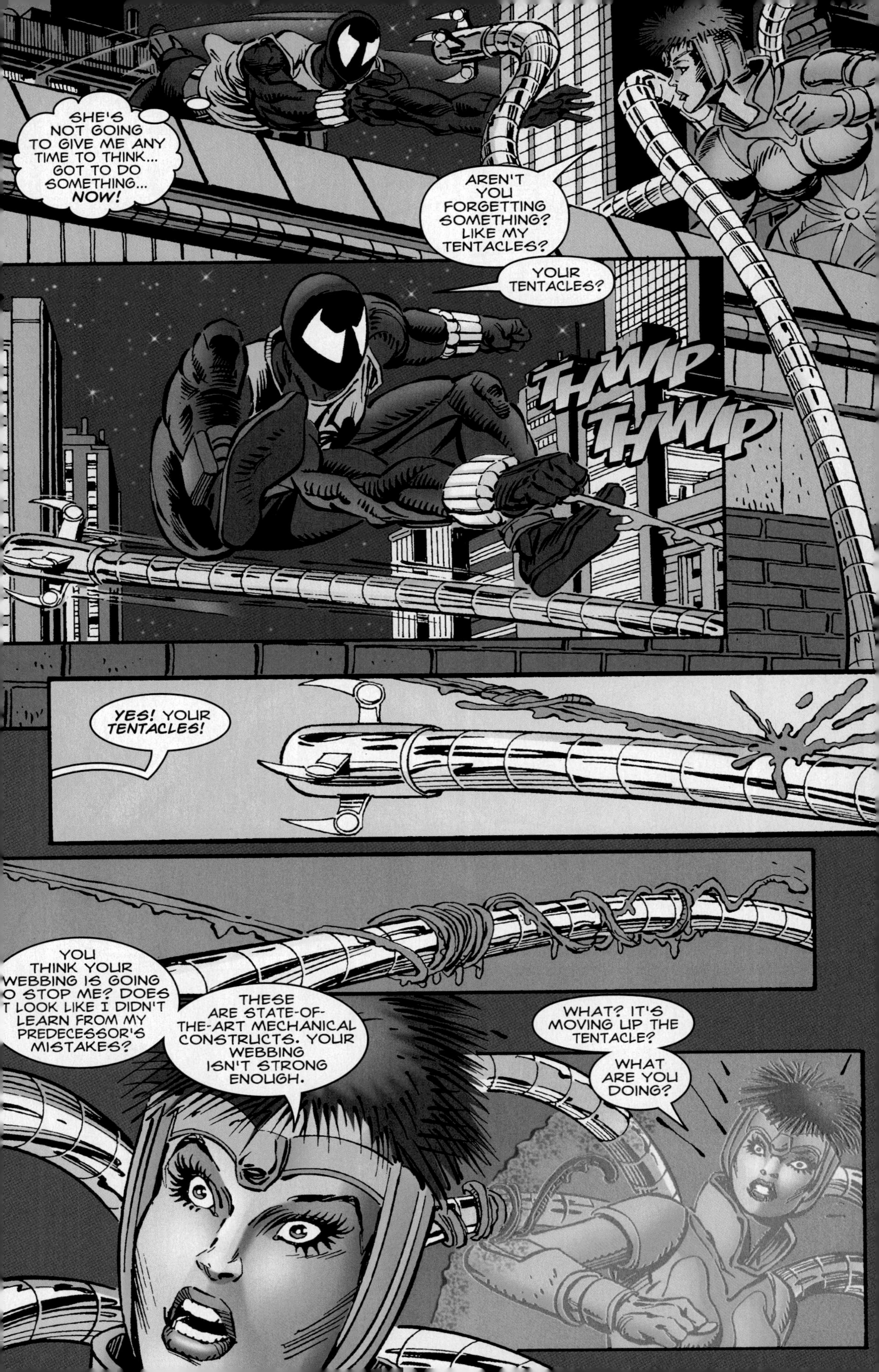

SHE'S NOT GOING TO GIVE ME ANY TIME TO THINK... GOT TO DO SOMETHING... NOW!
AREN'T YOU FORGETTING SOMETHING? LIKE MY TENTACLES?
YOUR TENTACLES?
THWIP THWIP
YES! YOUR TENTACLES!
YOU THINK YOUR WEBBING IS GOING O STOP ME? DOES T LOOK LIKE I DIDN'T LEARN FROM MY PREDECESSOR'S MISTAKES?
THESE ARE STATE-OF-THE-ART MECHANICAL CONSTRUCTS. YOUR WEBBING ISN'T STRONG ENOUGH.
WHAT? IT'S MOVING UP THE TENTACLE?
WHAT ARE YOU DOING?

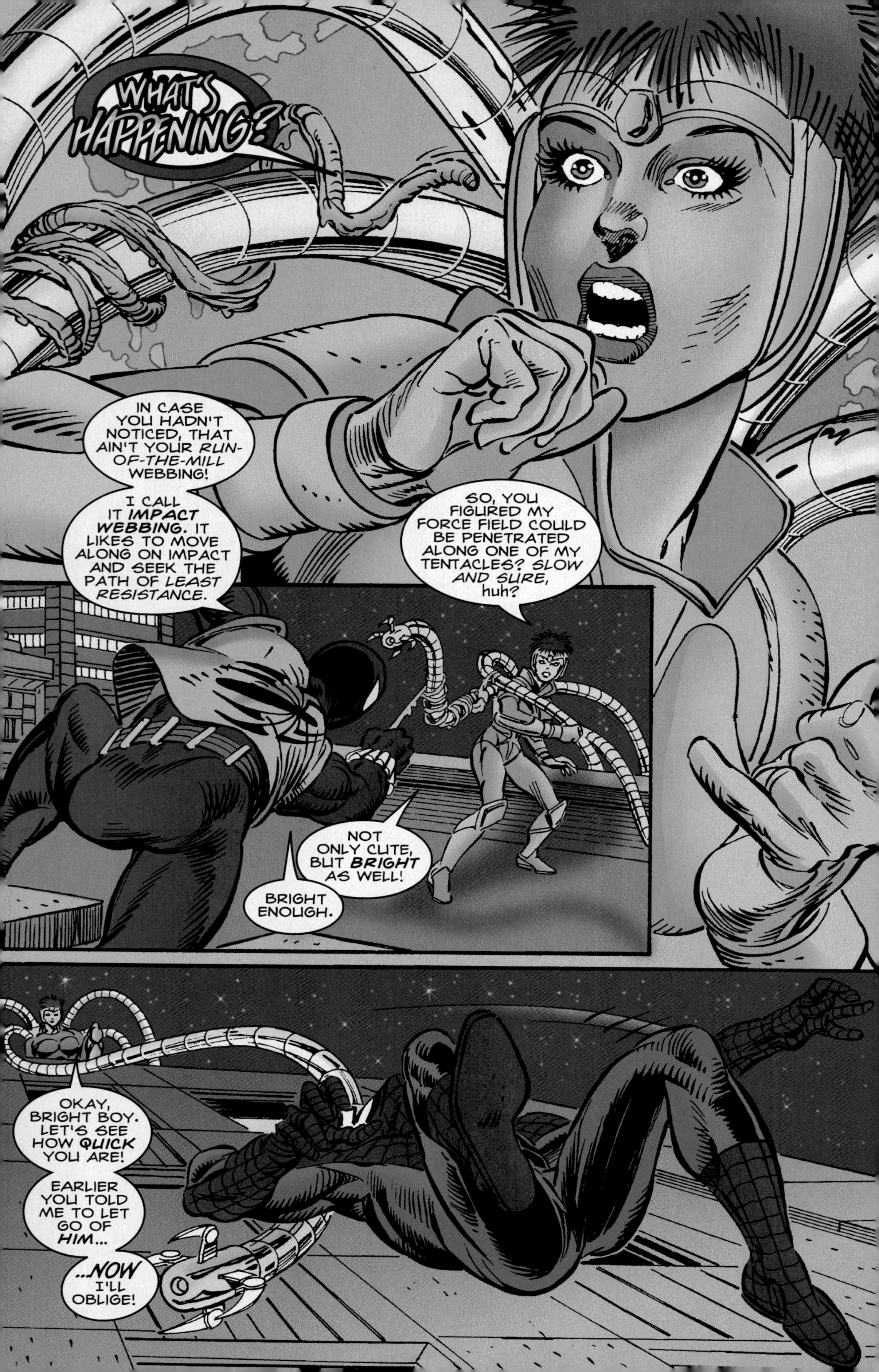
WHAT'S HAPPENING?
IN CASE YOU HADN'T NOTICED, THAT AIN'T YOUR RUN-OF-THE-MILL WEBBING!
I CALL IT IMPACT WEBBING. IT LIKES TO MOVE ALONG ON IMPACT AND SEEK THE PATH OF LEAST RESISTANCE.
SO, YOU FIGURED MY FORCE FIELD COULD BE PENETRATED ALONG ONE OF MY TENTACLES? SLOW AND SURE, huh?
NOT ONLY CUTE, BUT BRIGHT AS WELL!
BRIGHT ENOUGH.
OKAY, BRIGHT BOY. LET'S SEE HOW QUICK YOU ARE!
EARLIER YOU TOLD ME TO LET GO OF HIM...
...NOW I'LL OBLIGE!

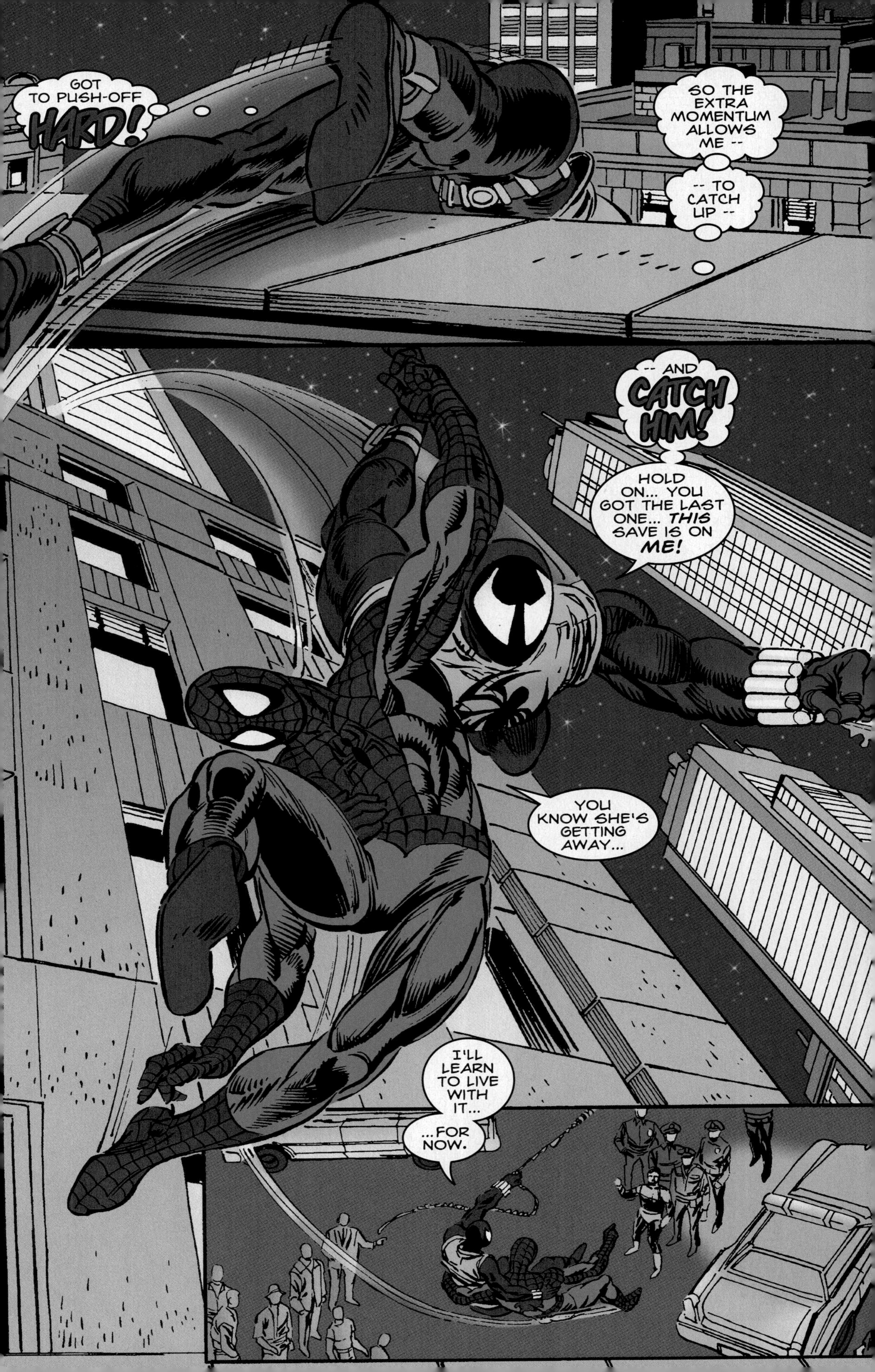
GOT TO PUSH-OFF HARD!
SO THE EXTRA MOMENTUM ALLOWS ME --
-- TO CATCH UP --
-- AND CATCH HIM!
HOLD ON... YOU GOT THE LAST ONE... THIS SAVE IS ON ME!
YOU KNOW SHE'S GETTING AWAY...
I'LL LEARN TO LIVE WITH IT...
...FOR NOW.

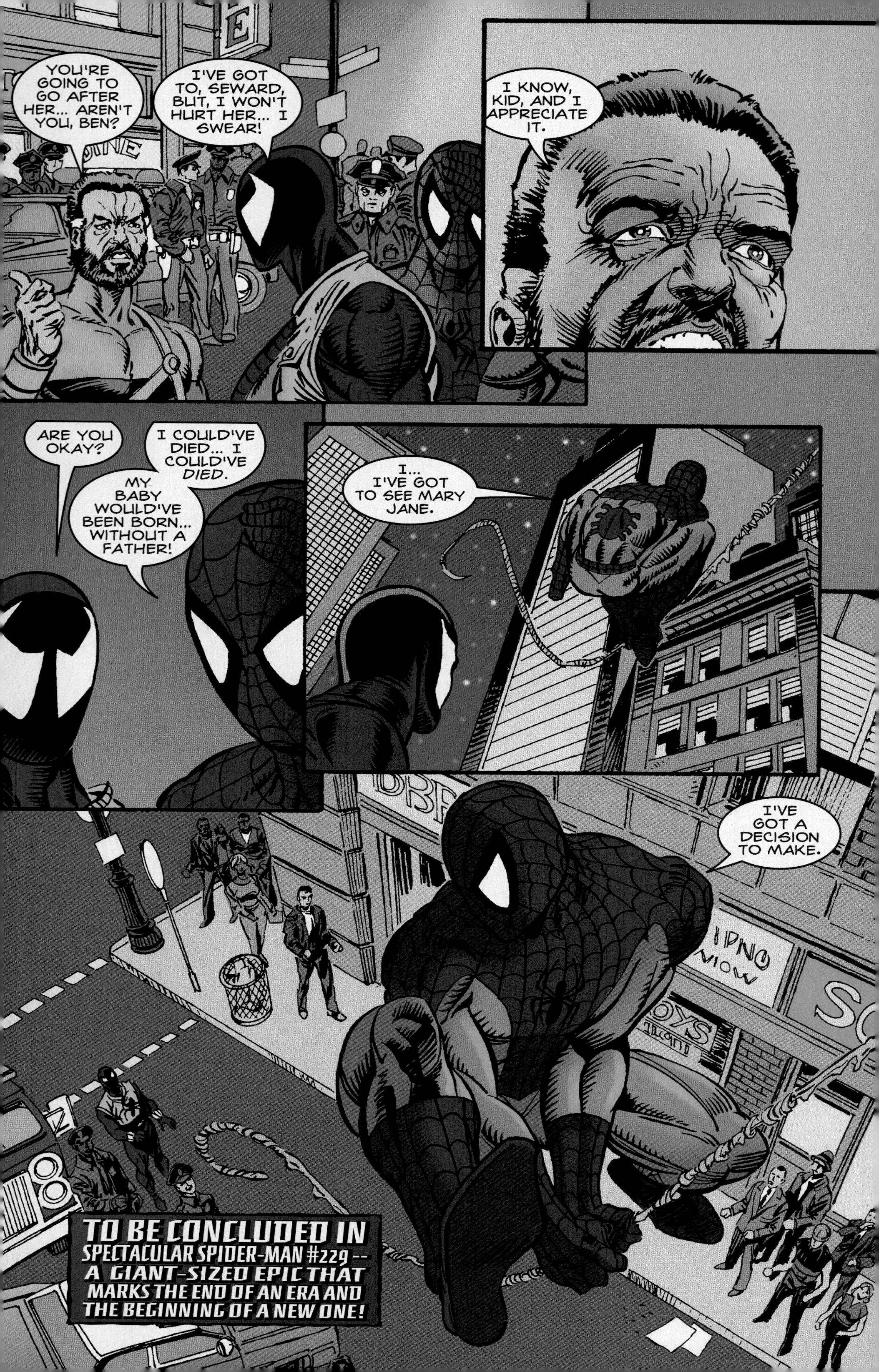
YOU'RE GOING TO GO AFTER HER... AREN'T YOU, BEN?
I'VE GOT TO, SEWARD, BUT, I WON'T HURT HER... I SWEAR!
I KNOW, KID, AND I APPRECIATE IT.
ARE YOU OKAY?
I COULD'VE DIED... I COULD'VE DIED.
MY BABY WOULD'VE BEEN BORN... WITHOUT A FATHER!
I... I'VE GOT TO SEE MARY JANE.
I'VE GOT A DECISION TO MAKE.
TO BE CONCLUDED IN SPECTACULAR SPIDER-MAN #229 -- A GIANT-SIZED EPIC THAT MARKS THE END OF AN ERA AND THE BEGINNING OF A NEW ONE!

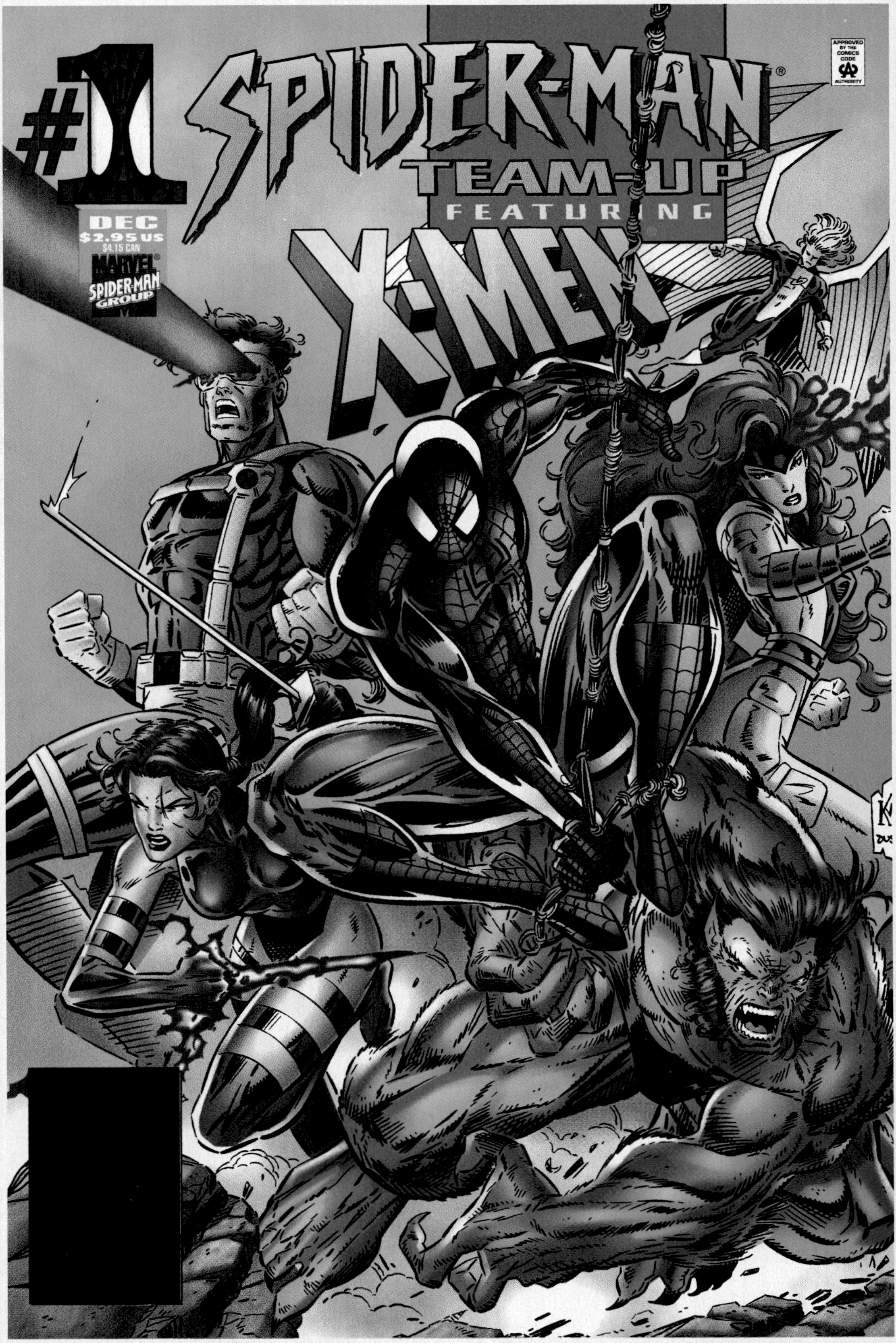

#1
SPIDER-MAN
TEAM-UP
FEATURING
X-MEN
DEC
$2.95 US
$4.15 CAN
MARVEL
SPIDER-MAN GROUP
APPROVED BY THE COMICS CODE AUTHORITY

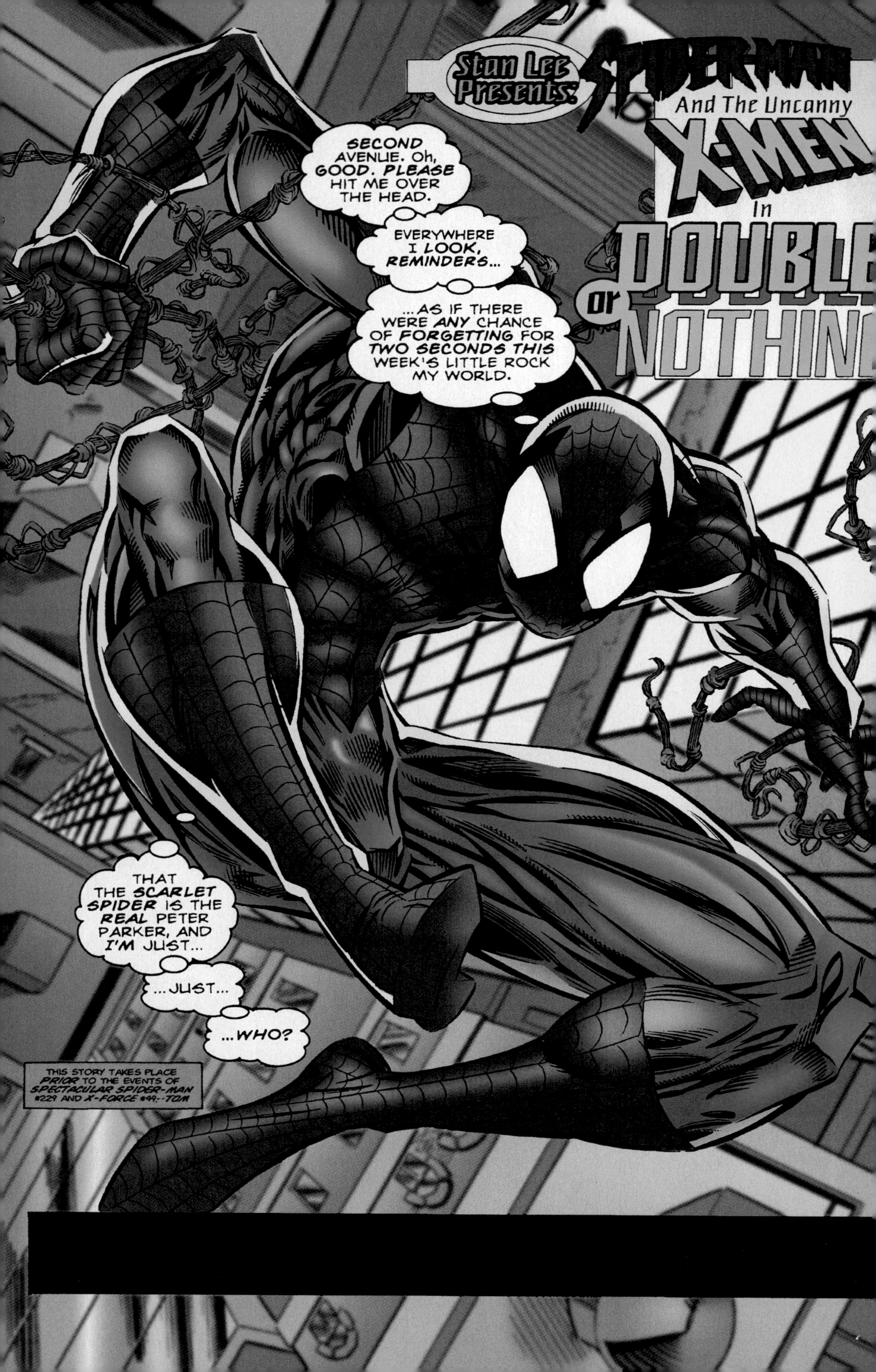

Stan Lee Presents:
SPIDER-MAN
And The Uncanny
X-MEN
In
DOUBLE
or
NOTHIN
SECOND AVENUE. Oh, GOOD. PLEASE HIT ME OVER THE HEAD.
EVERYWHERE I LOOK, REMINDERS...
...AS IF THERE WERE ANY CHANCE OF FORGETTING FOR TWO SECONDS THIS WEEK'S LITTLE ROCK MY WORLD.
THAT THE SCARLET SPIDER IS THE REAL PETER PARKER, AND I'M JUST...
...JUST...
...WHO?
THIS STORY TAKES PLACE PRIOR TO THE EVENTS OF SPECTACULAR SPIDER-MAN #229 AND X-FORCE #49.--TOM
[redacted]

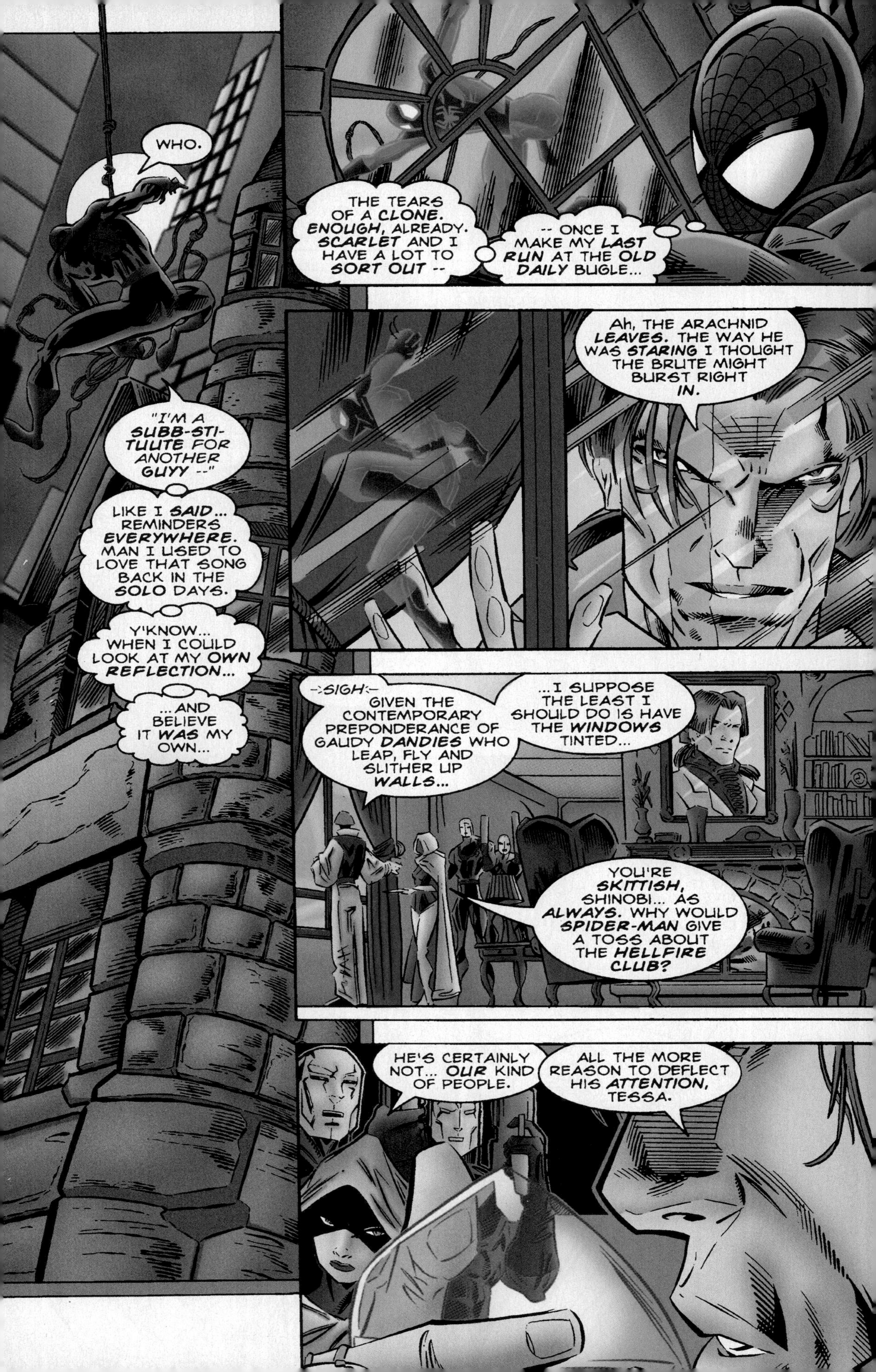
WHO.
THE TEARS OF A CLONE. ENOUGH, ALREADY. SCARLET AND I HAVE A LOT TO SORT OUT --
-- ONCE I MAKE MY LAST RUN AT THE OLD DAILY BUGLE...
"I'M A SUBB-STI-TUUTE FOR ANOTHER GUYY --"
LIKE I SAID... REMINDERS EVERYWHERE. MAN I USED TO LOVE THAT SONG BACK IN THE SOLO DAYS.
Y'KNOW... WHEN I COULD LOOK AT MY OWN REFLECTION...
...AND BELIEVE IT WAS MY OWN...
Ah, THE ARACHNID LEAVES. THE WAY HE WAS STARING I THOUGHT THE BRUTE MIGHT BURST RIGHT IN.
-SIGH- GIVEN THE CONTEMPORARY PREPONDERANCE OF GAUDY DANDIES WHO LEAP, FLY AND SLITHER UP WALLS...
...I SUPPOSE THE LEAST I SHOULD DO IS HAVE THE WINDOWS TINTED...
YOU'RE SKITTISH, SHINOBI... AS ALWAYS. WHY WOULD SPIDER-MAN GIVE A TOSS ABOUT THE HELLFIRE CLUB?
HE'S CERTAINLY NOT... OUR KIND OF PEOPLE.
ALL THE MORE REASON TO DEFLECT HIS ATTENTION, TESSA.

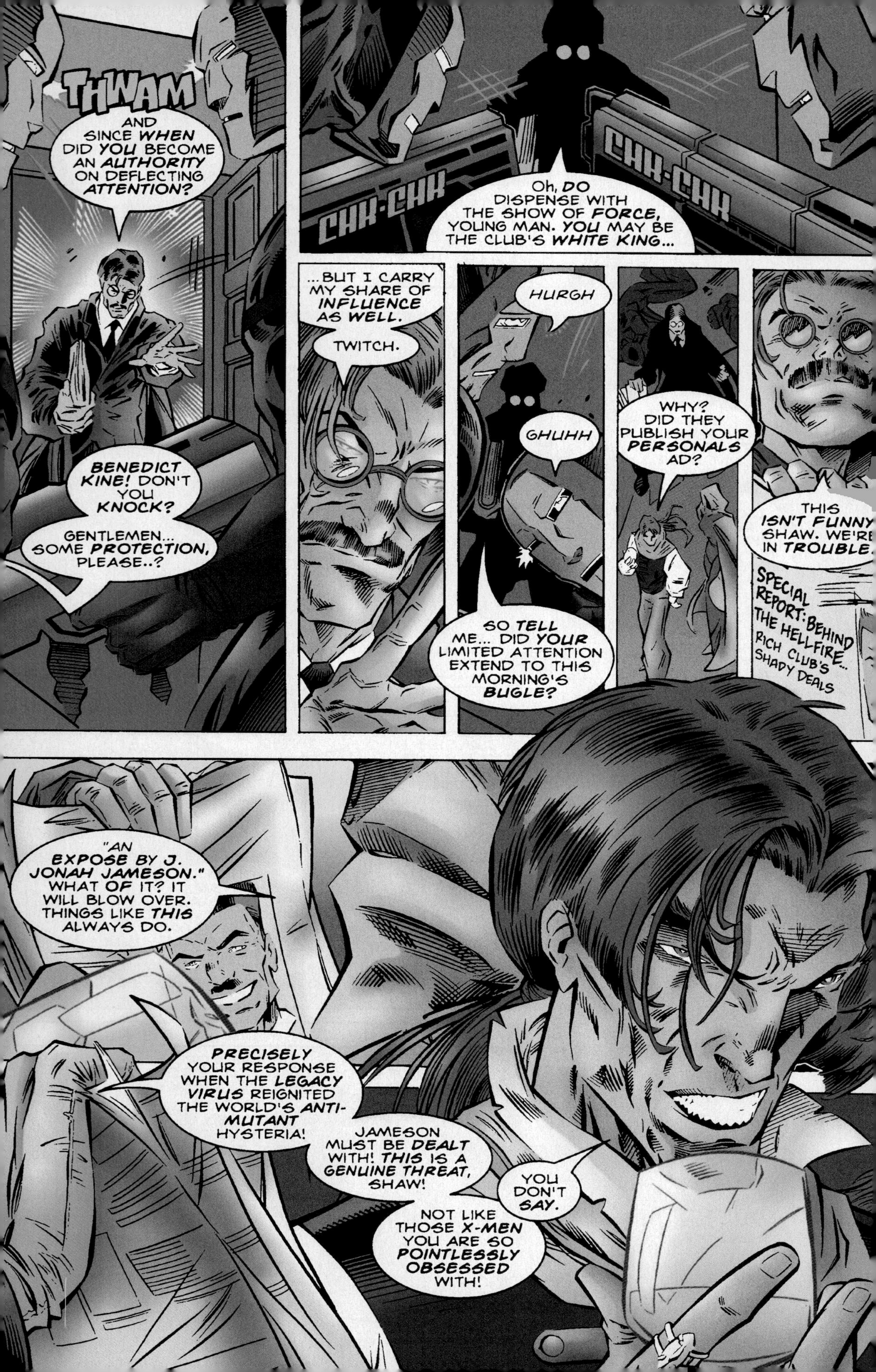
THWAM
AND SINCE WHEN DID YOU BECOME AN AUTHORITY ON DEFLECTING ATTENTION?
BENEDICT KINE! DON'T YOU KNOCK?
GENTLEMEN... SOME PROTECTION, PLEASE..?
CHK-CHK
CHK-CHK
Oh, DO DISPENSE WITH THE SHOW OF FORCE, YOUNG MAN. YOU MAY BE THE CLUB'S WHITE KING...
...BUT I CARRY MY SHARE OF INFLUENCE AS WELL.
TWITCH.
HURGH
GHUHH
SO TELL ME... DID YOUR LIMITED ATTENTION EXTEND TO THIS MORNING'S BUGLE?
WHY? DID THEY PUBLISH YOUR PERSONALS AD?
THIS ISN'T FUNNY SHAW. WE'RE IN TROUBLE.
SPECIAL REPORT: BEHIND THE HELLFIRE... RICH CLUB'S SHADY DEALS
"AN EXPOSE BY J. JONAH JAMESON." WHAT OF IT? IT WILL BLOW OVER. THINGS LIKE THIS ALWAYS DO.
PRECISELY YOUR RESPONSE WHEN THE LEGACY VIRUS REIGNITED THE WORLD'S ANTI-MUTANT HYSTERIA!
JAMESON MUST BE DEALT WITH! THIS IS A GENUINE THREAT, SHAW!
YOU DON'T SAY.
NOT LIKE THOSE X-MEN YOU ARE SO POINTLESSLY OBSESSED WITH!

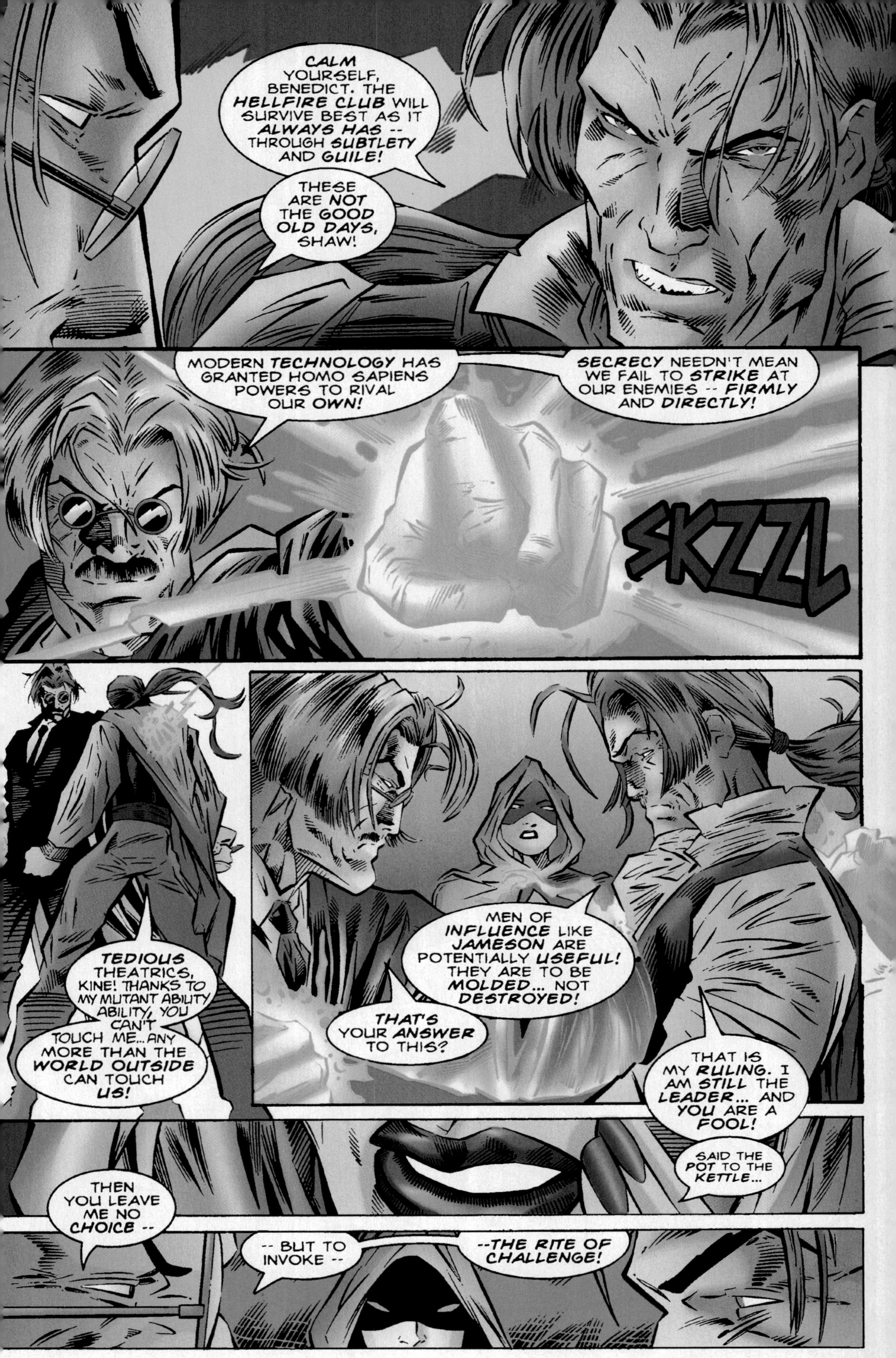
CALM YOURSELF, BENEDICT. THE HELLFIRE CLUB WILL SURVIVE BEST AS IT ALWAYS HAS -- THROUGH SUBTLETY AND GUILE!
THESE ARE NOT THE GOOD OLD DAYS, SHAW!
MODERN TECHNOLOGY HAS GRANTED HOMO SAPIENS POWERS TO RIVAL OUR OWN!
SECRECY NEEDN'T MEAN WE FAIL TO STRIKE AT OUR ENEMIES -- FIRMLY AND DIRECTLY!
SKZZL
TEDIOUS THEATRICS, KINE! THANKS TO MY MUTANT ABILITY ABILITY, YOU CAN'T TOUCH ME... ANY MORE THAN THE WORLD OUTSIDE CAN TOUCH US!
MEN OF INFLUENCE LIKE JAMESON ARE POTENTIALLY USEFUL! THEY ARE TO BE MOLDED... NOT DESTROYED!
THAT'S YOUR ANSWER TO THIS?
THAT IS MY RULING. I AM STILL THE LEADER... AND YOU ARE A FOOL!
SAID THE POT TO THE KETTLE...
THEN YOU LEAVE ME NO CHOICE --
-- BUT TO INVOKE --
--THE RITE OF CHALLENGE!

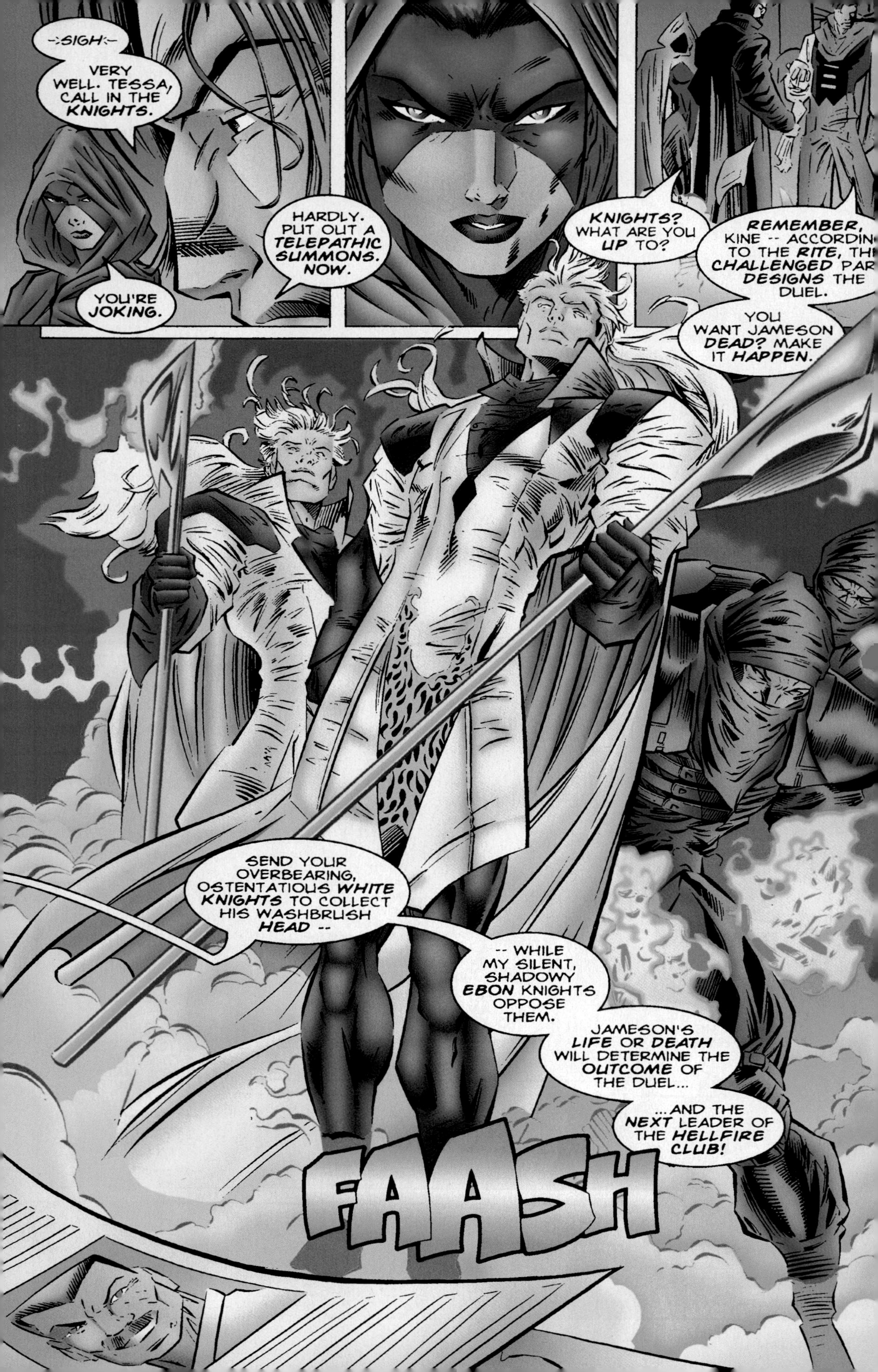
-:SIGH:-
VERY WELL. TESSA, CALL IN THE KNIGHTS.
YOU'RE JOKING.
HARDLY. PUT OUT A TELEPATHIC SUMMONS. NOW.
KNIGHTS? WHAT ARE YOU UP TO?
REMEMBER, KINE -- ACCORDIN TO THE RITE, TH CHALLENGED PAR DESIGNS THE DUEL.
YOU WANT JAMESON DEAD? MAKE IT HAPPEN.
SEND YOUR OVERBEARING, OSTENTATIOUS WHITE KNIGHTS TO COLLECT HIS WASHBRUSH HEAD --
-- WHILE MY SILENT, SHADOWY EBON KNIGHTS OPPOSE THEM.
JAMESON'S LIFE OR DEATH WILL DETERMINE THE OUTCOME OF THE DUEL...
...AND THE NEXT LEADER OF THE HELLFIRE CLUB!
FAASH

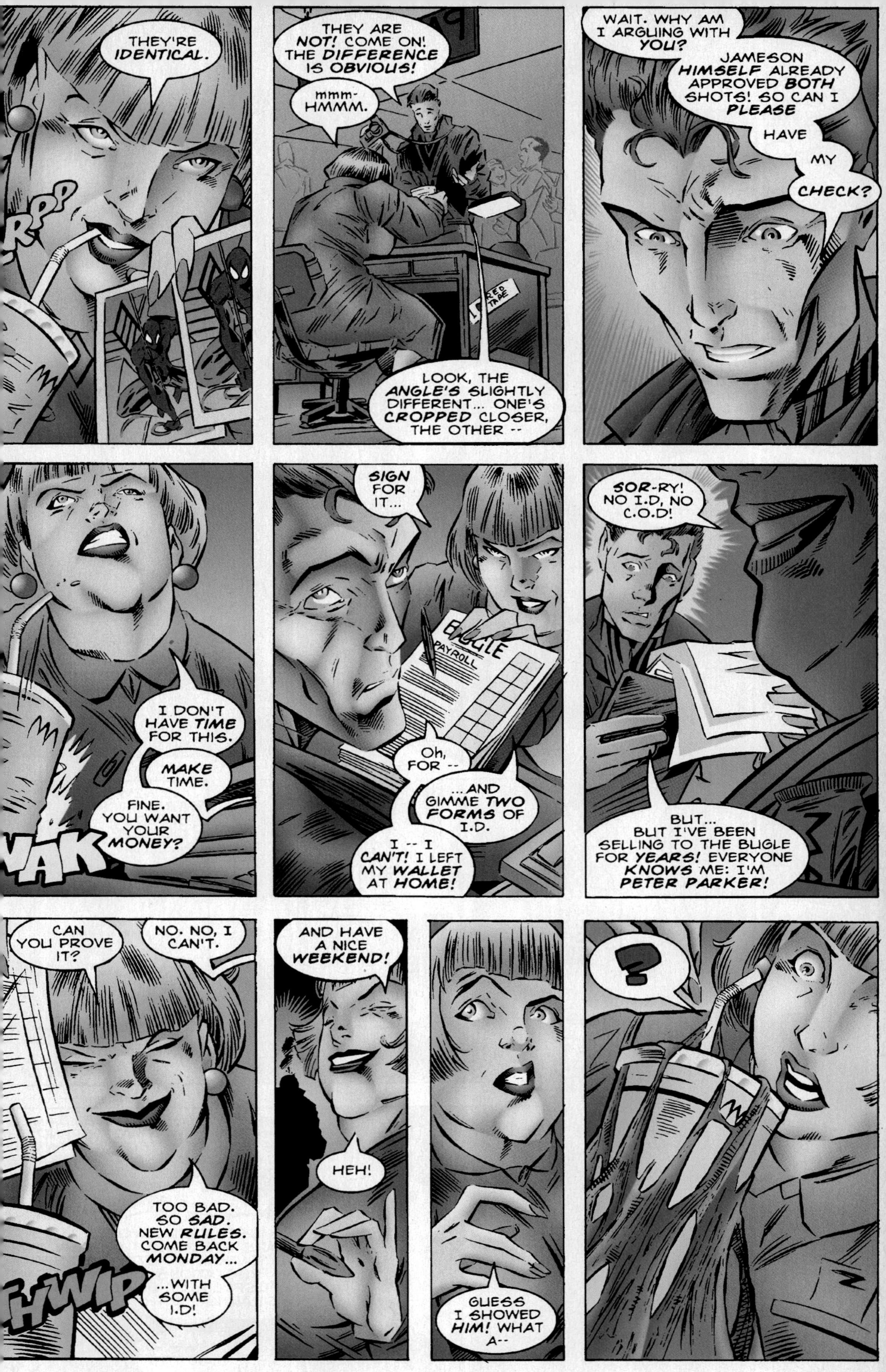
THEY'RE IDENTICAL.
RPP
THEY ARE NOT! COME ON! THE DIFFERENCE IS OBVIOUS!
mmm-HMMM.
LOOK, THE ANGLE'S SLIGHTLY DIFFERENT... ONE'S CROPPED CLOSER, THE OTHER --
WAIT. WHY AM I ARGUING WITH YOU?
JAMESON HIMSELF ALREADY APPROVED BOTH SHOTS! SO CAN I PLEASE
HAVE
MY
CHECK?
I DON'T HAVE TIME FOR THIS.
MAKE TIME.
FINE. YOU WANT YOUR MONEY?
WAK
SIGN FOR IT...
BUGLE PAYROLL
Oh, FOR --
...AND GIMME TWO FORMS OF I.D.
I -- I CAN'T! I LEFT MY WALLET AT HOME!
SOR-RY! NO I.D, NO C.O.D!
BUT... BUT I'VE BEEN SELLING TO THE BUGLE FOR YEARS! EVERYONE KNOWS ME: I'M PETER PARKER!
CAN YOU PROVE IT?
NO. NO, I CAN'T.
TOO BAD. SO SAD. NEW RULES. COME BACK MONDAY...
...WITH SOME I.D!
HWIP
AND HAVE A NICE WEEKEND!
HEH!
GUESS I SHOWED HIM! WHAT A--
?

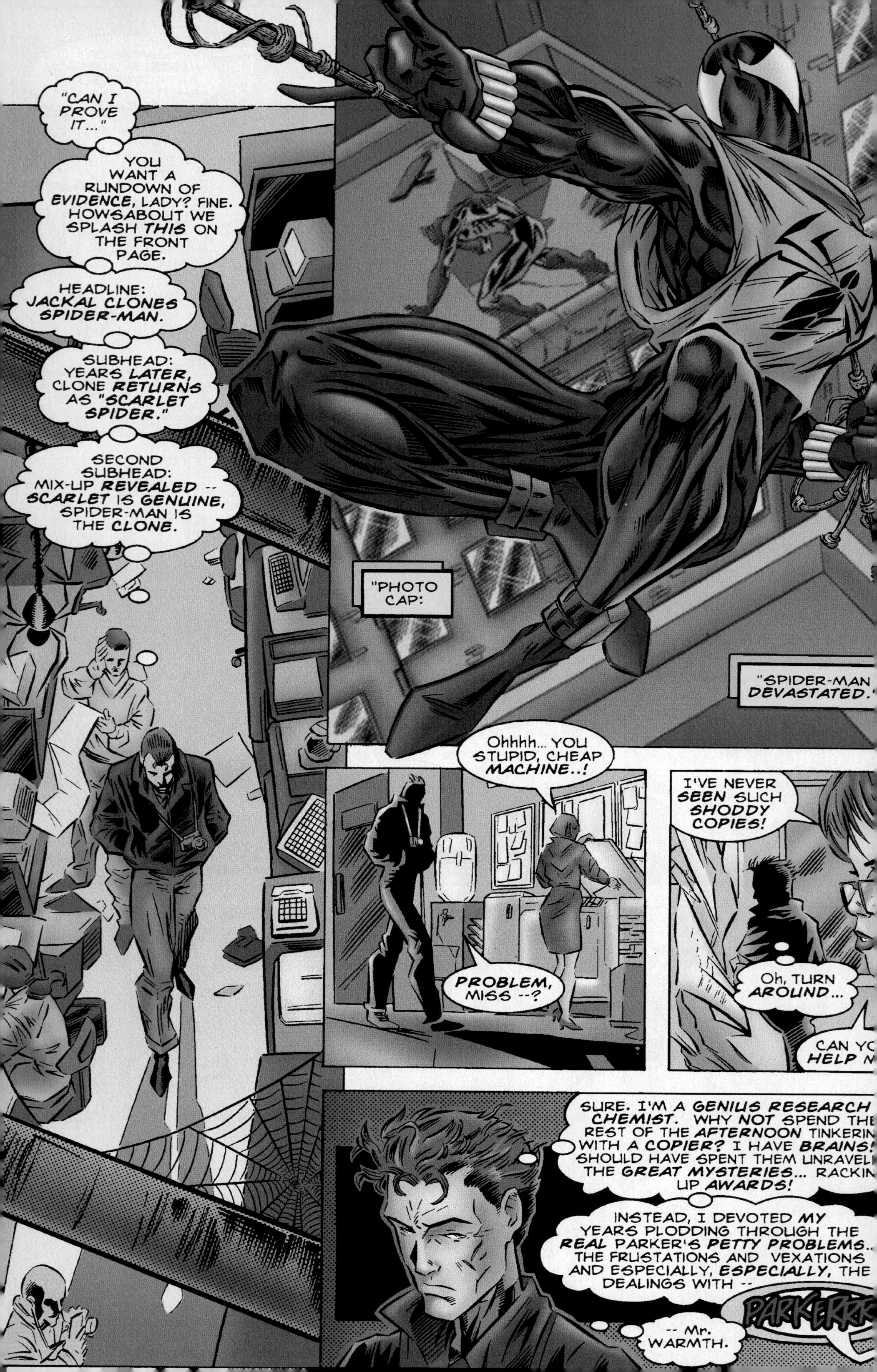
"CAN I PROVE IT..."
YOU WANT A RUNDOWN OF EVIDENCE, LADY? FINE. HOWSABOUT WE SPLASH THIS ON THE FRONT PAGE.
HEADLINE: JACKAL CLONES SPIDER-MAN.
SUBHEAD: YEARS LATER, CLONE RETURNS AS "SCARLET SPIDER."
SECOND SUBHEAD: MIX-UP REVEALED -- SCARLET IS GENUINE, SPIDER-MAN IS THE CLONE.
"PHOTO CAP:
"SPIDER-MAN DEVASTATED.
Ohhhh... YOU STUPID, CHEAP MACHINE..!
PROBLEM, MISS --?
I'VE NEVER SEEN SUCH SHODDY COPIES!
Oh, TURN AROUND...
CAN YO HELP M
SURE. I'M A GENIUS RESEARCH CHEMIST. WHY NOT SPEND THE REST OF THE AFTERNOON TINKERIN WITH A COPIER? I HAVE BRAINS! SHOULD HAVE SPENT THEM UNRAVEL THE GREAT MYSTERIES... RACKIN UP AWARDS!
INSTEAD, I DEVOTED MY YEARS PLODDING THROUGH THE REAL PARKER'S PETTY PROBLEMS... THE FRUSTATIONS AND VEXATIONS AND ESPECIALLY, ESPECIALLY, THE DEALINGS WITH --
PARKERRR
-- Mr. WARMTH.

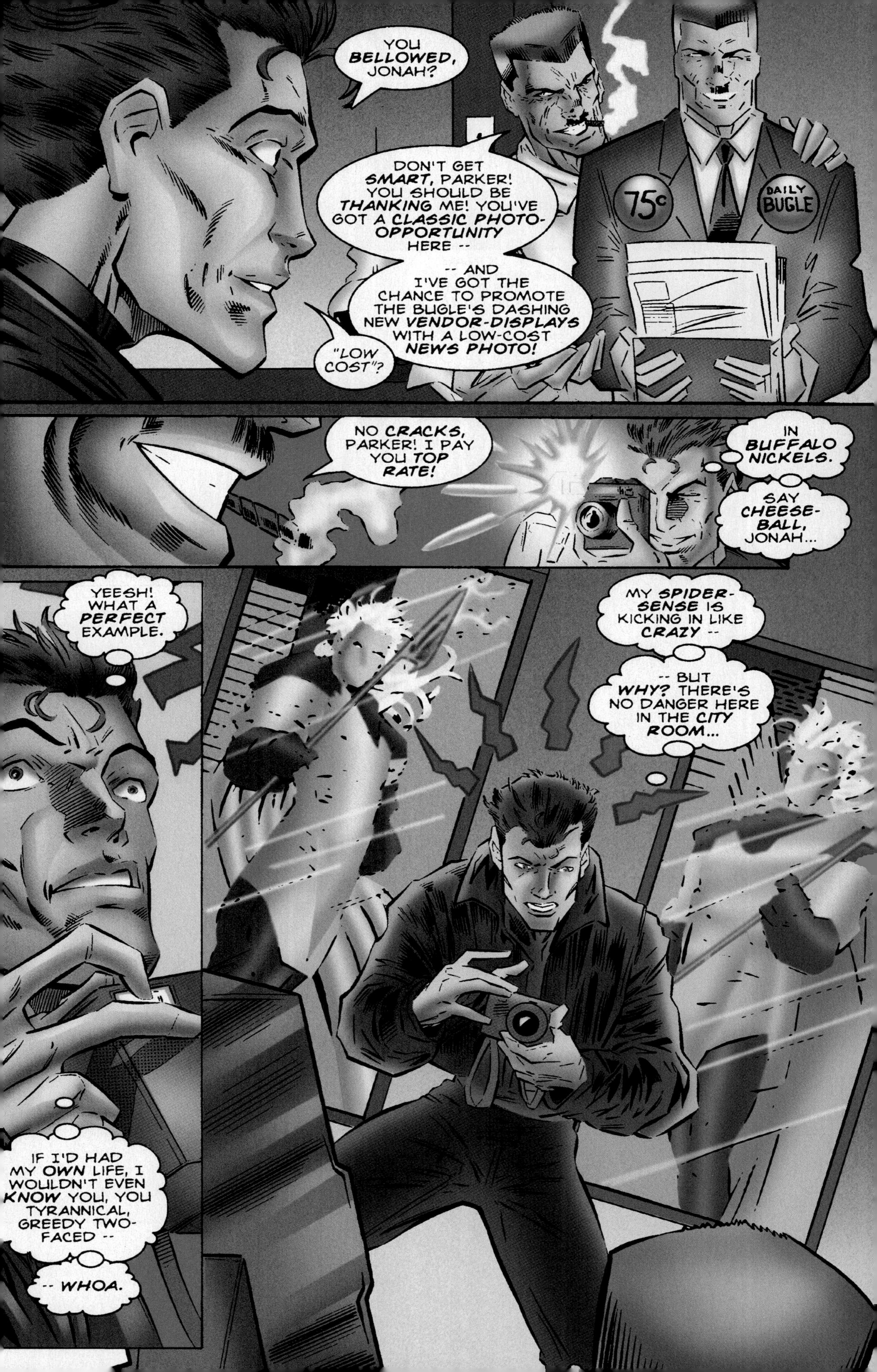

YOU BELLOWED, JONAH?
DON'T GET SMART, PARKER! YOU SHOULD BE THANKING ME! YOU'VE GOT A CLASSIC PHOTO-OPPORTUNITY HERE --
-- AND I'VE GOT THE CHANCE TO PROMOTE THE BUGLE'S DASHING NEW VENDOR-DISPLAYS WITH A LOW-COST NEWS PHOTO!
"LOW COST"?
75¢
DAILY BUGLE
NO CRACKS, PARKER! I PAY YOU TOP RATE!
IN BUFFALO NICKELS.
SAY CHEESE-BALL, JONAH...
YEESH! WHAT A PERFECT EXAMPLE.
IF I'D HAD MY OWN LIFE, I WOULDN'T EVEN KNOW YOU, YOU TYRANNICAL, GREEDY TWO-FACED --
-- WHOA.
MY SPIDER-SENSE IS KICKING IN LIKE CRAZY --
-- BUT WHY? THERE'S NO DANGER HERE IN THE CITY ROOM...

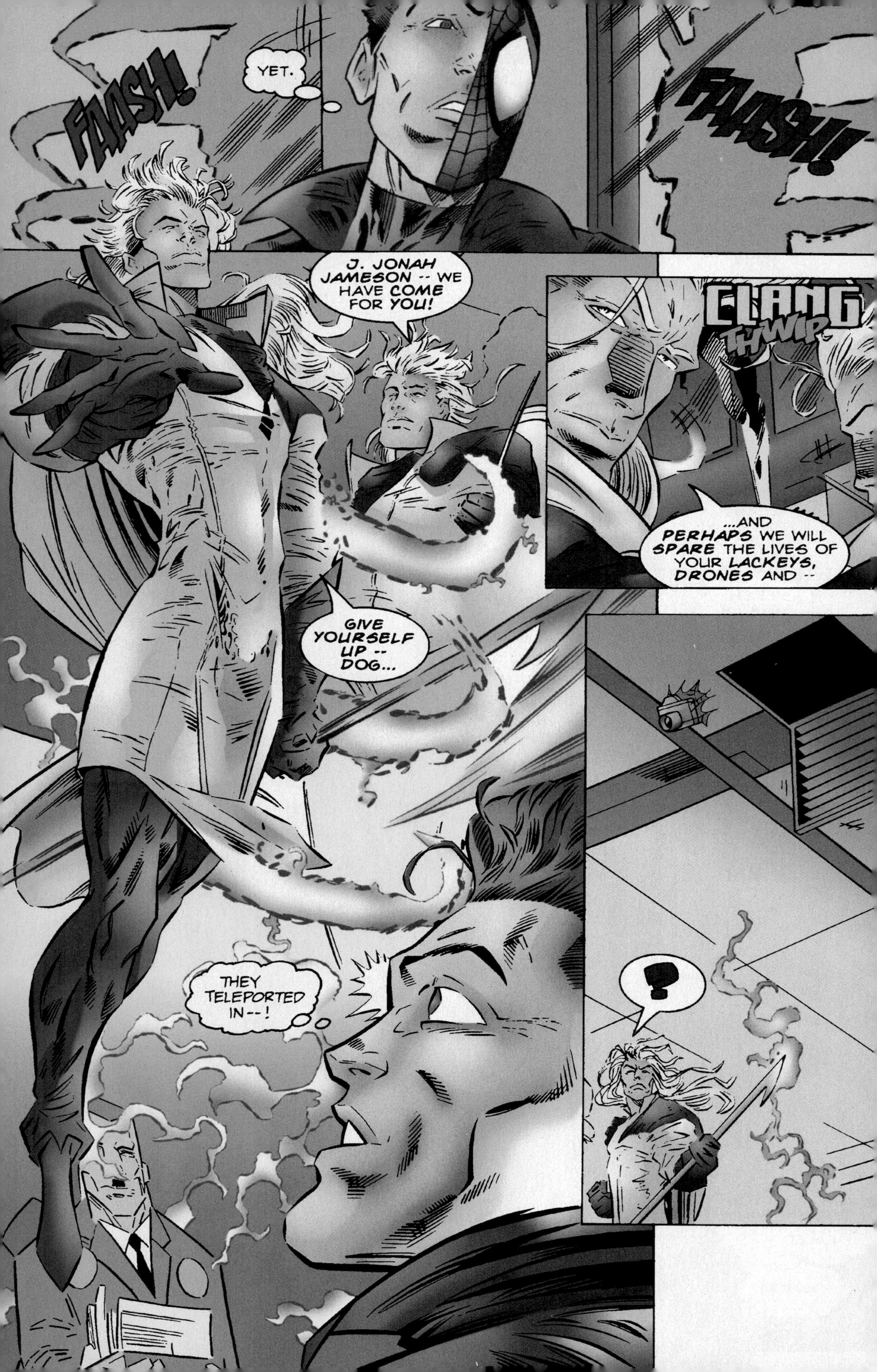
FAASH!
YET.
FAASH!
J. JONAH JAMESON -- WE HAVE COME FOR YOU!
CLANG
THWIP
...AND PERHAPS WE WILL SPARE THE LIVES OF YOUR LACKEYS, DRONES AND --
GIVE YOURSELF UP -- DOG...
THEY TELEPORTED IN--!
?

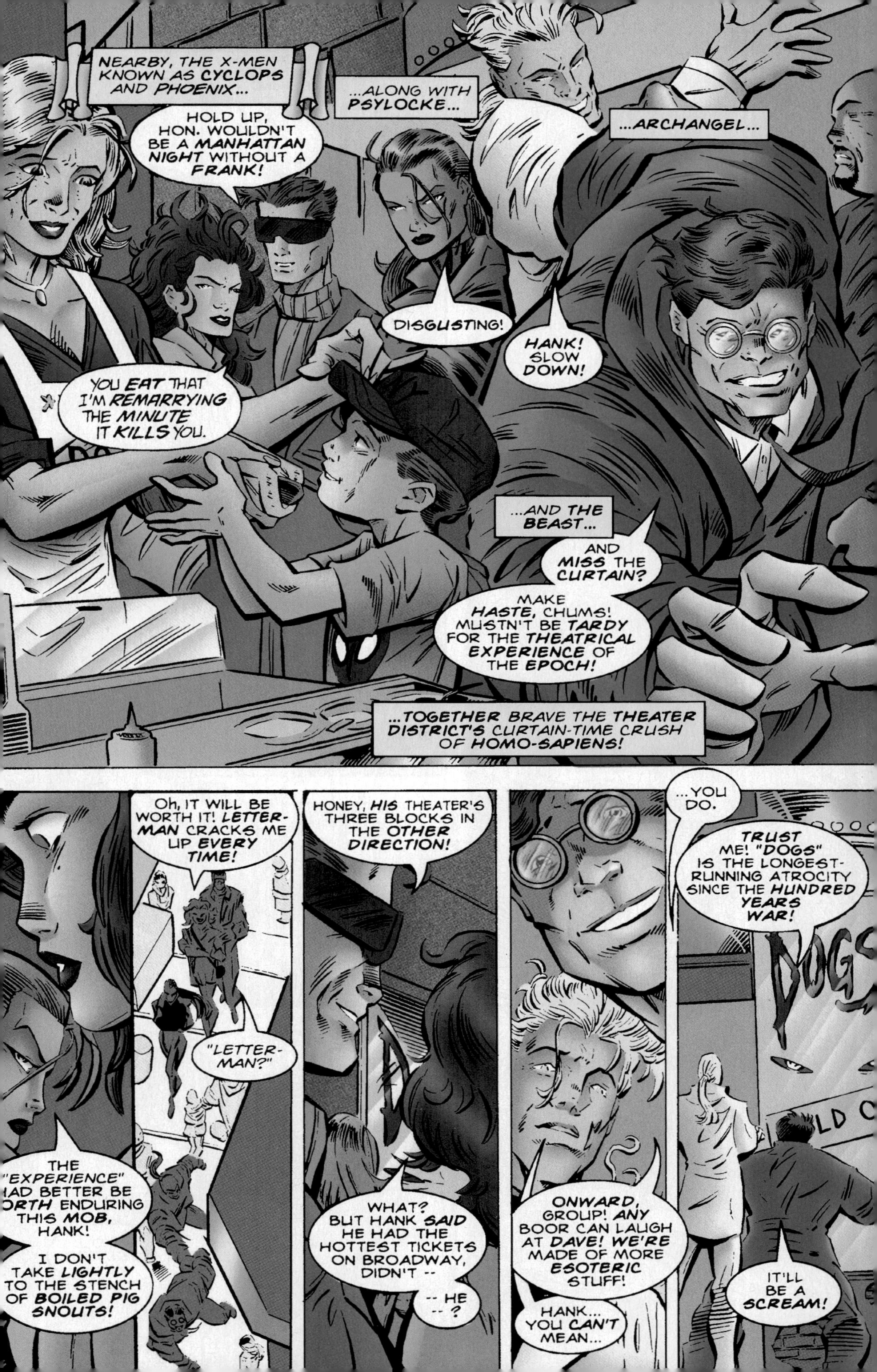
NEARBY, THE X-MEN KNOWN AS CYCLOPS AND PHOENIX...
HOLD UP, HON. WOULDN'T BE A MANHATTAN NIGHT WITHOUT A FRANK!
...ALONG WITH PSYLOCKE...
...ARCHANGEL...
DISGUSTING!
HANK! SLOW DOWN!
YOU EAT THAT I'M REMARRYING THE MINUTE IT KILLS YOU.
...AND THE BEAST...
AND MISS THE CURTAIN?
MAKE HASTE, CHUMS! MUSTN'T BE TARDY FOR THE THEATRICAL EXPERIENCE OF THE EPOCH!
...TOGETHER BRAVE THE THEATER DISTRICT'S CURTAIN-TIME CRUSH OF HOMO-SAPIENS!
THE "EXPERIENCE" HAD BETTER BE WORTH ENDURING THIS MOB, HANK!
I DON'T TAKE LIGHTLY TO THE STENCH OF BOILED PIG SNOUTS!
Oh, IT WILL BE WORTH IT! LETTERMAN CRACKS ME UP EVERY TIME!
"LETTERMAN?"
HONEY, HIS THEATER'S THREE BLOCKS IN THE OTHER DIRECTION!
WHAT? BUT HANK SAID HE HAD THE HOTTEST TICKETS ON BROADWAY, DIDN'T --
-- HE --?
ONWARD, GROUP! ANY BOOR CAN LAUGH AT DAVE! WE'RE MADE OF MORE ESOTERIC STUFF!
HANK... YOU CAN'T MEAN...
...YOU DO.
TRUST ME! "DOGS" IS THE LONGEST-RUNNING ATROCITY SINCE THE HUNDRED YEARS WAR!
DOGS
IT'LL BE A SCREAM!

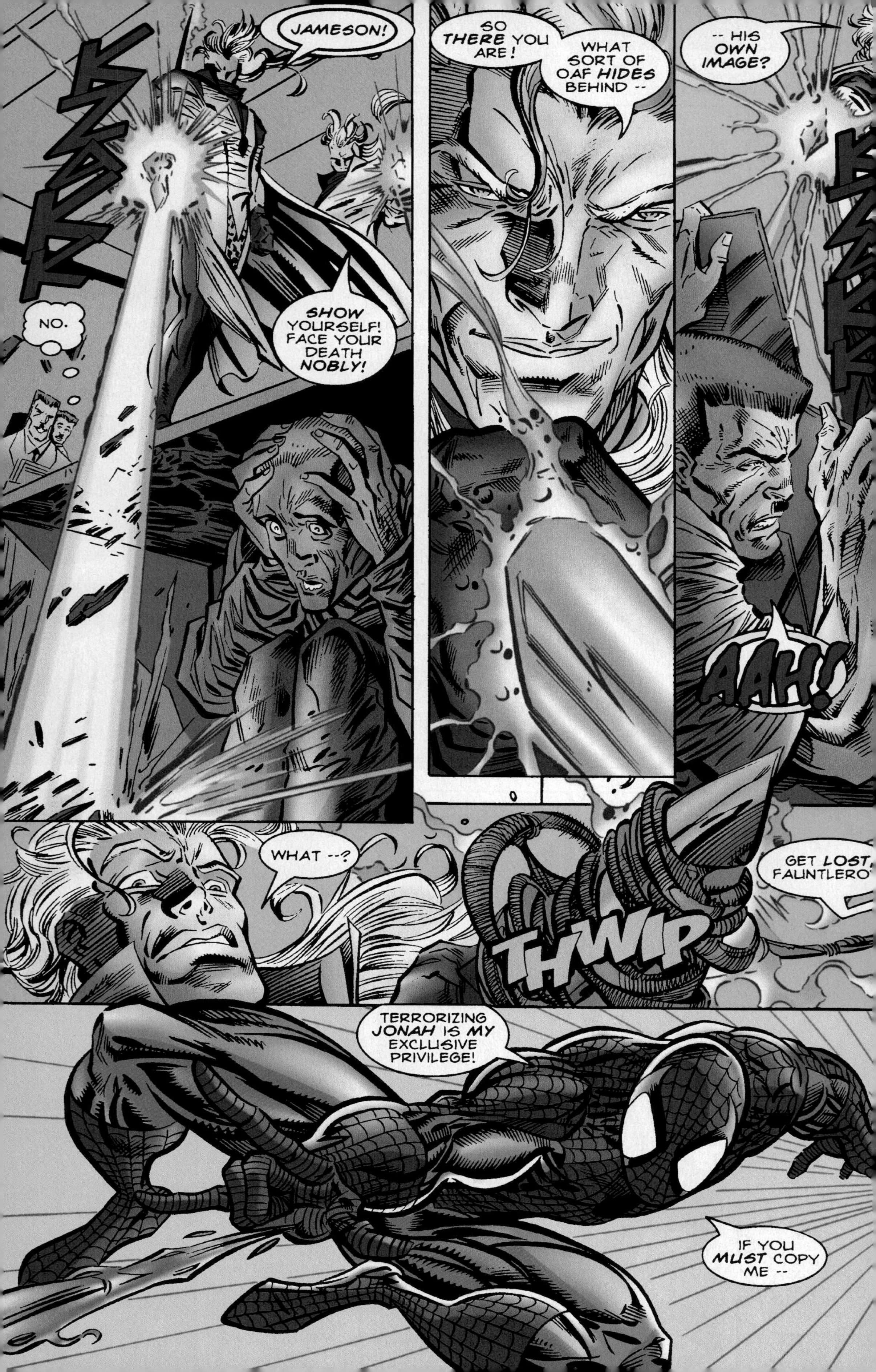

JAMESON!
NO.
SHOW YOURSELF! FACE YOUR DEATH NOBLY!
SO THERE YOU ARE!
WHAT SORT OF OAF HIDES BEHIND --
-- HIS OWN IMAGE?
AAH!
WHAT --?
THWIP
GET LOST, FAUNTLERO
TERRORIZING JONAH IS MY EXCLUSIVE PRIVILEGE!
IF YOU MUST COPY ME --

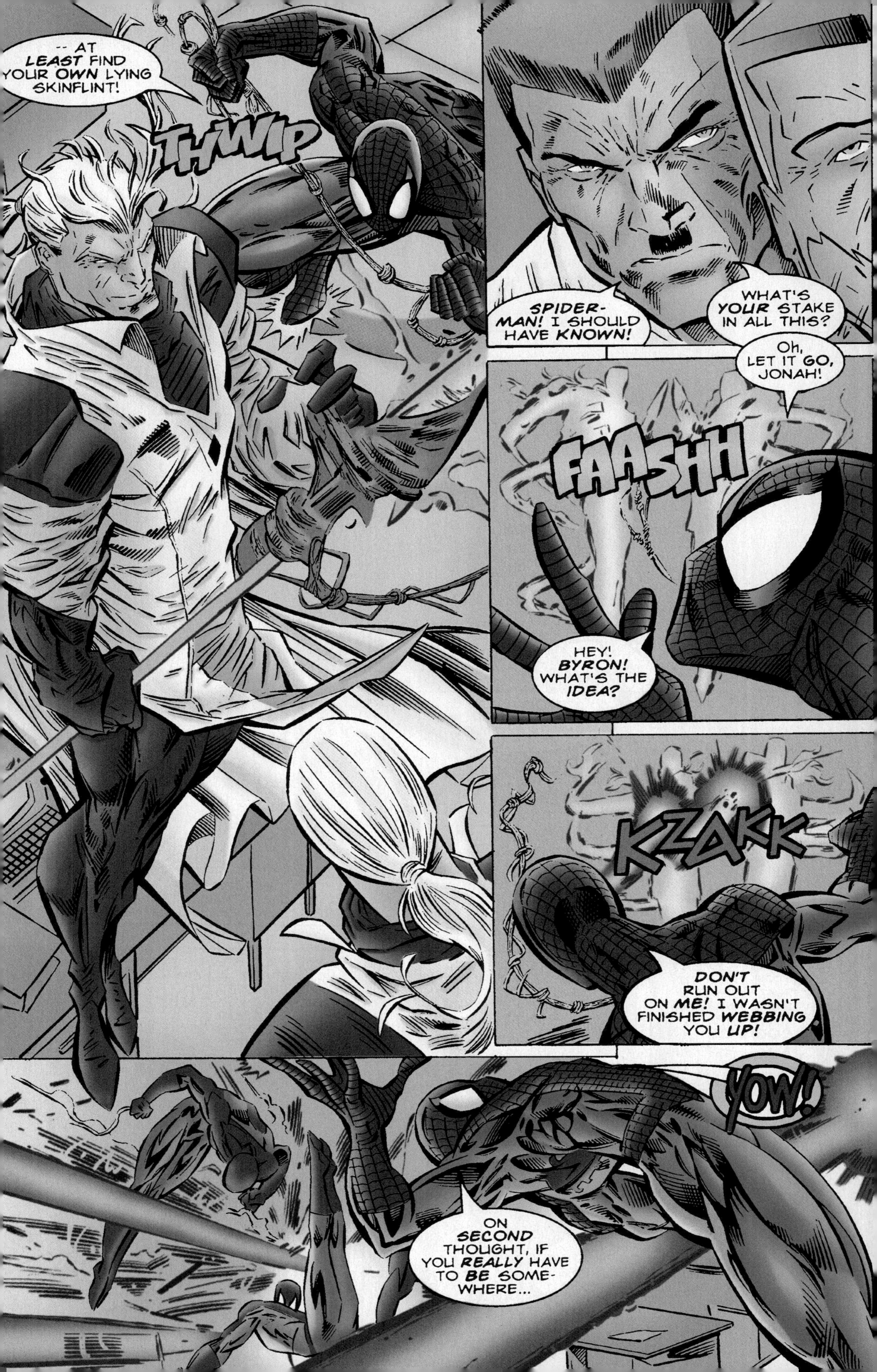
-- AT LEAST FIND YOUR OWN LYING SKINFLINT!
THWIP
SPIDER-MAN! I SHOULD HAVE KNOWN!
WHAT'S YOUR STAKE IN ALL THIS?
Oh, LET IT GO, JONAH!
FAASHH
HEY! BYRON! WHAT'S THE IDEA?
KZAKK
DON'T RUN OUT ON ME! I WASN'T FINISHED WEBBING YOU UP!
YOW!
ON SECOND THOUGHT, IF YOU REALLY HAVE TO BE SOME-WHERE...

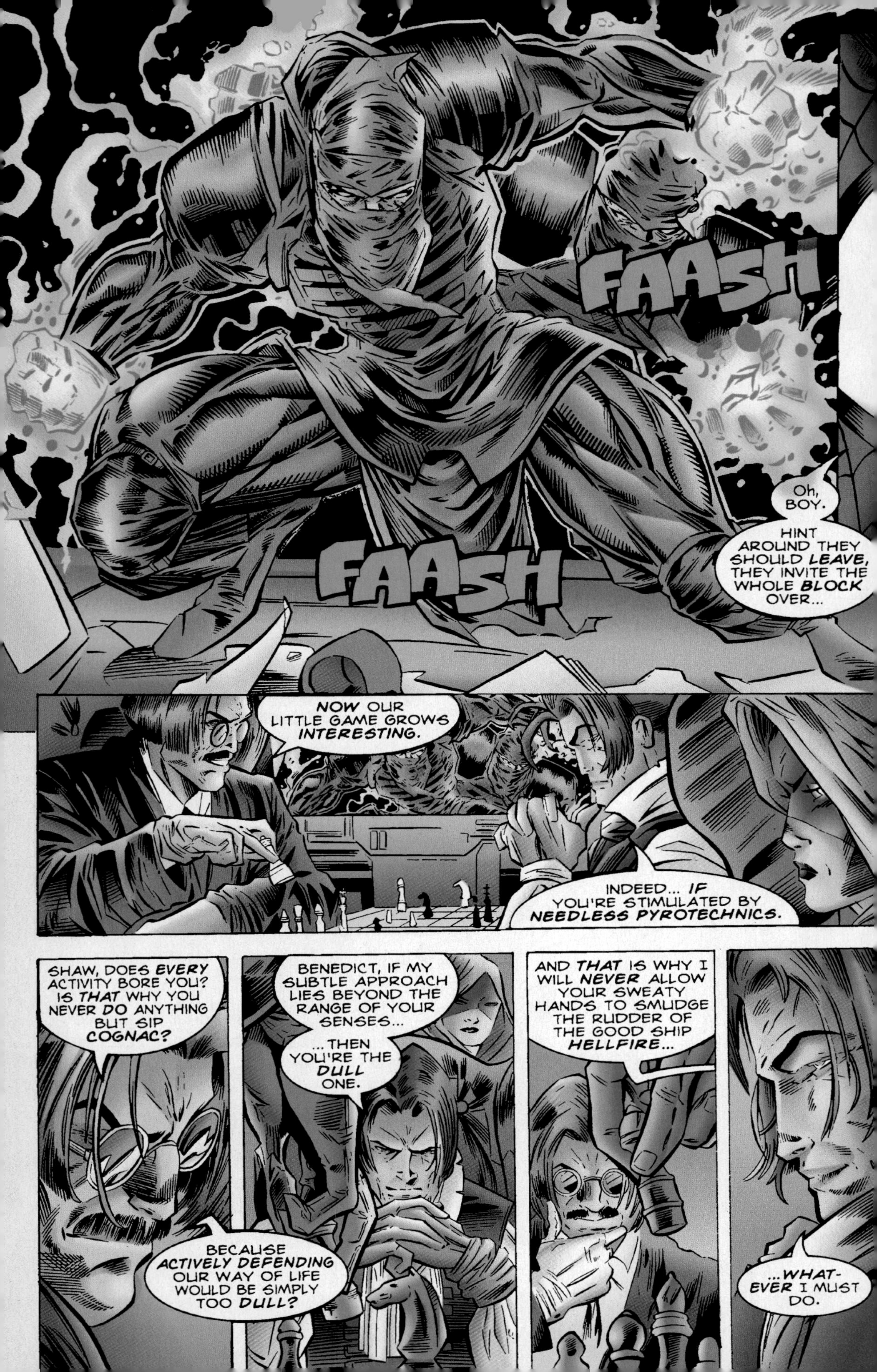
FAASH
FAASH
Oh, BOY.
HINT AROUND THEY SHOULD LEAVE, THEY INVITE THE WHOLE BLOCK OVER...
NOW OUR LITTLE GAME GROWS INTERESTING.
INDEED... IF YOU'RE STIMULATED BY NEEDLESS PYROTECHNICS.
SHAW, DOES EVERY ACTIVITY BORE YOU? IS THAT WHY YOU NEVER DO ANYTHING BUT SIP COGNAC?
BECAUSE ACTIVELY DEFENDING OUR WAY OF LIFE WOULD BE SIMPLY TOO DULL?
BENEDICT, IF MY SUBTLE APPROACH LIES BEYOND THE RANGE OF YOUR SENSES...
...THEN YOU'RE THE DULL ONE.
AND THAT IS WHY I WILL NEVER ALLOW YOUR SWEATY HANDS TO SMUDGE THE RUDDER OF THE GOOD SHIP HELLFIRE...
...WHAT-EVER I MUST DO.

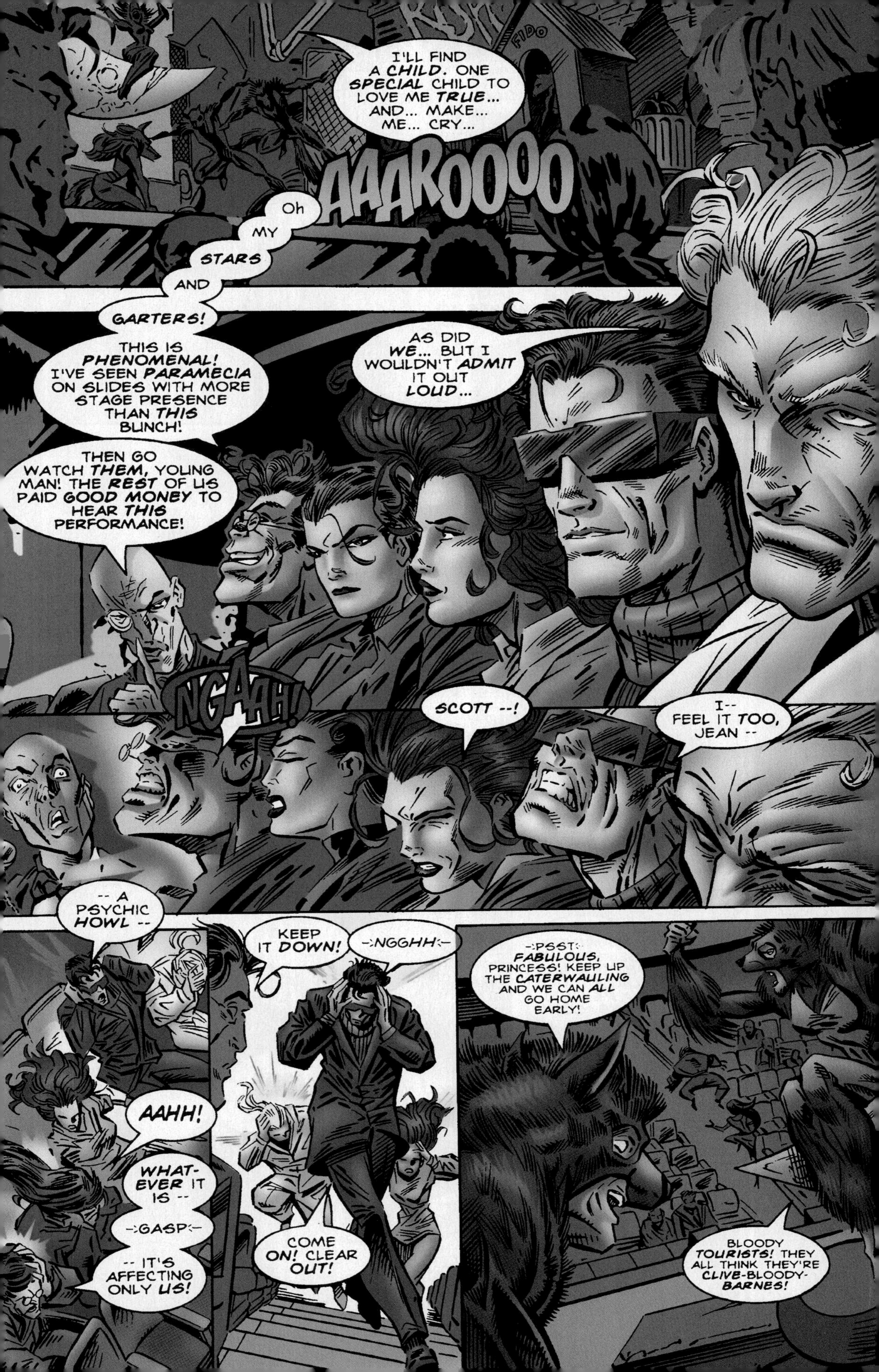
FIDO
I'LL FIND A CHILD. ONE SPECIAL CHILD TO LOVE ME TRUE... AND... MAKE... ME... CRY...
AAAROOOO
Oh MY STARS AND GARTERS!
THIS IS PHENOMENAL! I'VE SEEN PARAMECIA ON SLIDES WITH MORE STAGE PRESENCE THAN THIS BUNCH!
AS DID WE... BUT I WOULDN'T ADMIT IT OUT LOUD...
THEN GO WATCH THEM, YOUNG MAN! THE REST OF US PAID GOOD MONEY TO HEAR THIS PERFORMANCE!
NGAAH!
SCOTT --!
I-- FEEL IT TOO, JEAN --
-- A PSYCHIC HOWL --
KEEP IT DOWN!
NGGHH
AAHH!
WHAT-EVER IT IS --
GASP
-- IT'S AFFECTING ONLY US!
COME ON! CLEAR OUT!
PSST FABULOUS, PRINCESS! KEEP UP THE CATERWAULING AND WE CAN ALL GO HOME EARLY!
BLOODY TOURISTS! THEY ALL THINK THEY'RE CLIVE-BLOODY-BARNES!

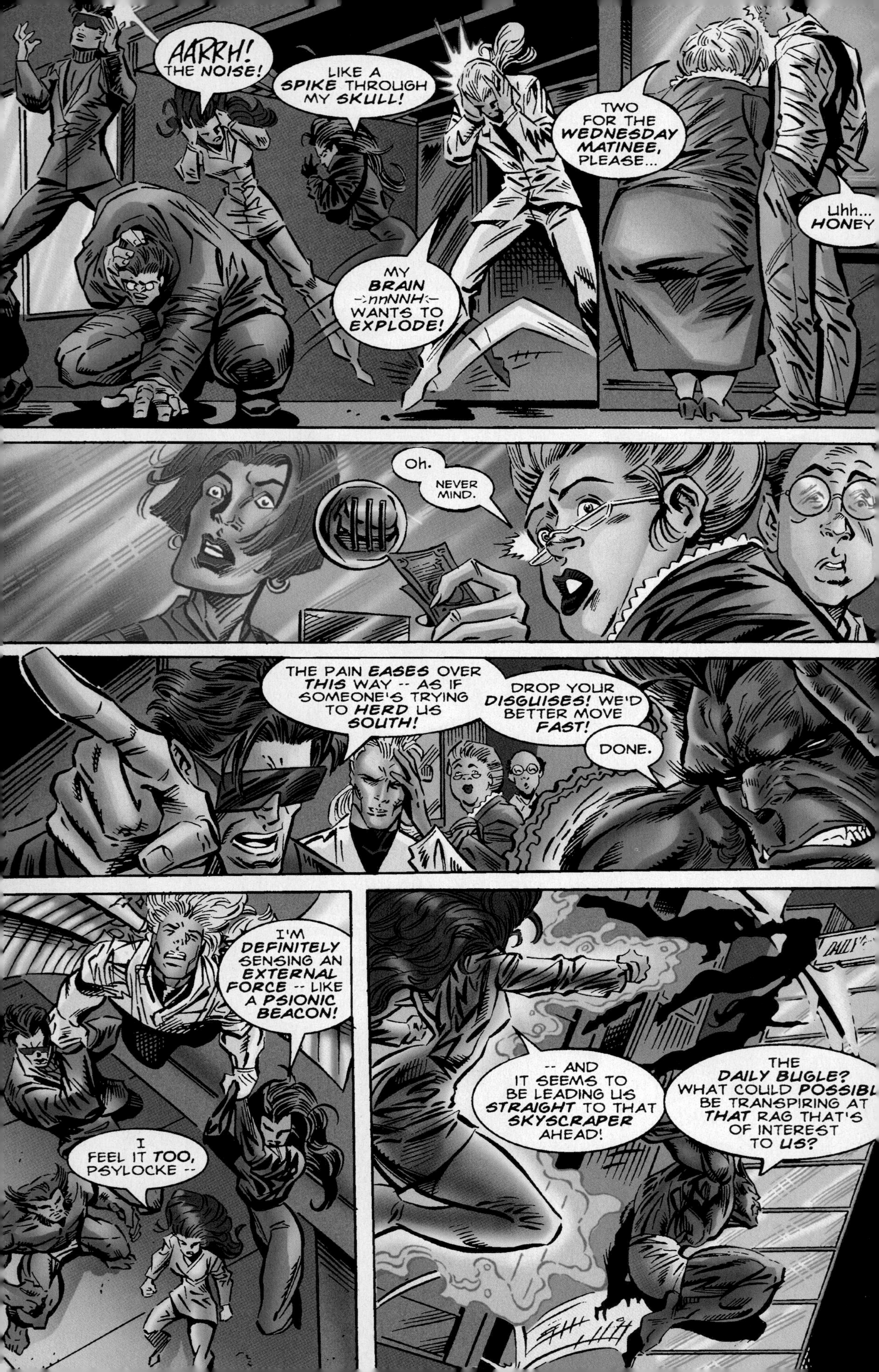
AARRH! THE NOISE!
LIKE A SPIKE THROUGH MY SKULL!
MY BRAIN -nnNNH- WANTS TO EXPLODE!
TWO FOR THE WEDNESDAY MATINEE, PLEASE...
Uhh... HONEY
Oh.
NEVER MIND.
THE PAIN EASES OVER THIS WAY -- AS IF SOMEONE'S TRYING TO HERD US SOUTH!
DROP YOUR DISGUISES! WE'D BETTER MOVE FAST!
DONE.
I'M DEFINITELY SENSING AN EXTERNAL FORCE -- LIKE A PSIONIC BEACON!
I FEEL IT TOO, PSYLOCKE --
-- AND IT SEEMS TO BE LEADING US STRAIGHT TO THAT SKYSCRAPER AHEAD!
THE DAILY BUGLE? WHAT COULD POSSIBL BE TRANSPIRING AT THAT RAG THAT'S OF INTEREST TO US?

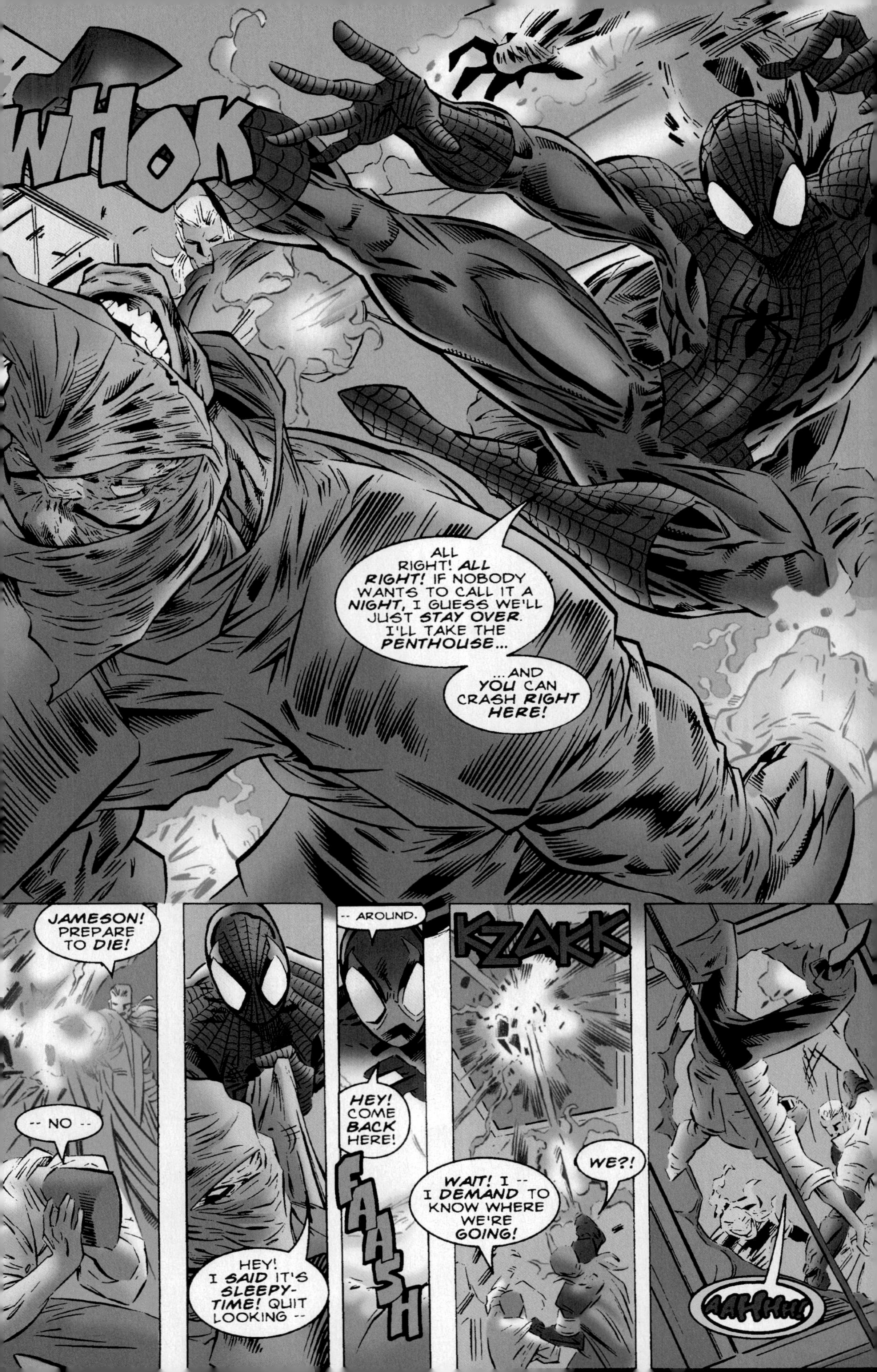
WHOK
ALL RIGHT! ALL RIGHT! IF NOBODY WANTS TO CALL IT A NIGHT, I GUESS WE'LL JUST STAY OVER. I'LL TAKE THE PENTHOUSE...
...AND YOU CAN CRASH RIGHT HERE!
JAMESON! PREPARE TO DIE!
-- NO --
HEY! I SAID IT'S SLEEPY-TIME! QUIT LOOKING --
-- AROUND.
HEY! COME BACK HERE!
FAAASH
KZAKK
WAIT! I -- I DEMAND TO KNOW WHERE WE'RE GOING!
WE?!
AAHHHH!

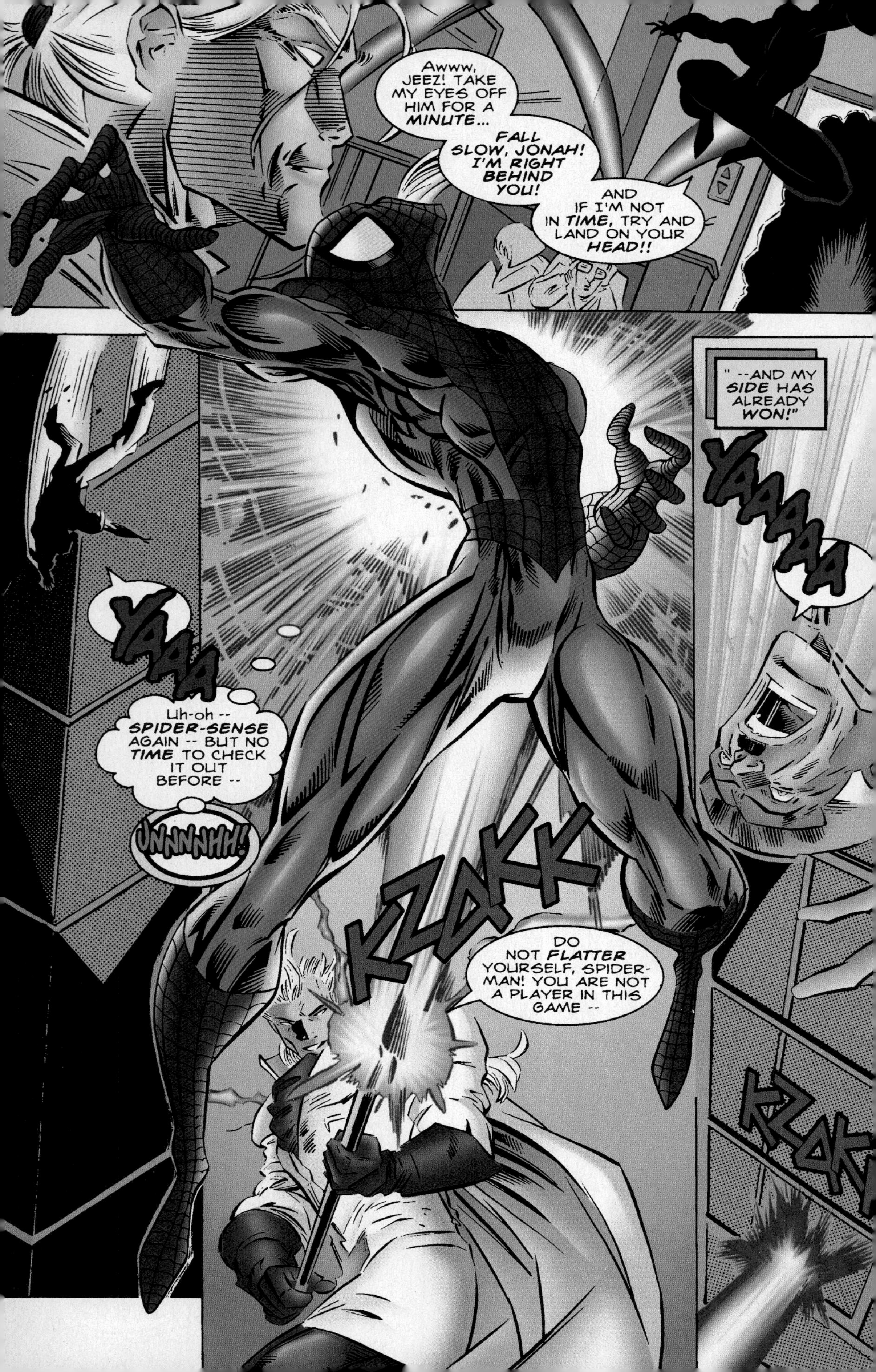
Awww, JEEZ! TAKE MY EYES OFF HIM FOR A MINUTE...
FALL SLOW, JONAH! I'M RIGHT BEHIND YOU!
AND IF I'M NOT IN TIME, TRY AND LAND ON YOUR HEAD!!
" --AND MY SIDE HAS ALREADY WON!"
YAAAAAA
YAAAA
Uh-oh -- SPIDER-SENSE AGAIN -- BUT NO TIME TO CHECK IT OUT BEFORE --
UNNNNHH!
KZAKK
DO NOT FLATTER YOURSELF, SPIDER-MAN! YOU ARE NOT A PLAYER IN THIS GAME --
KZAK

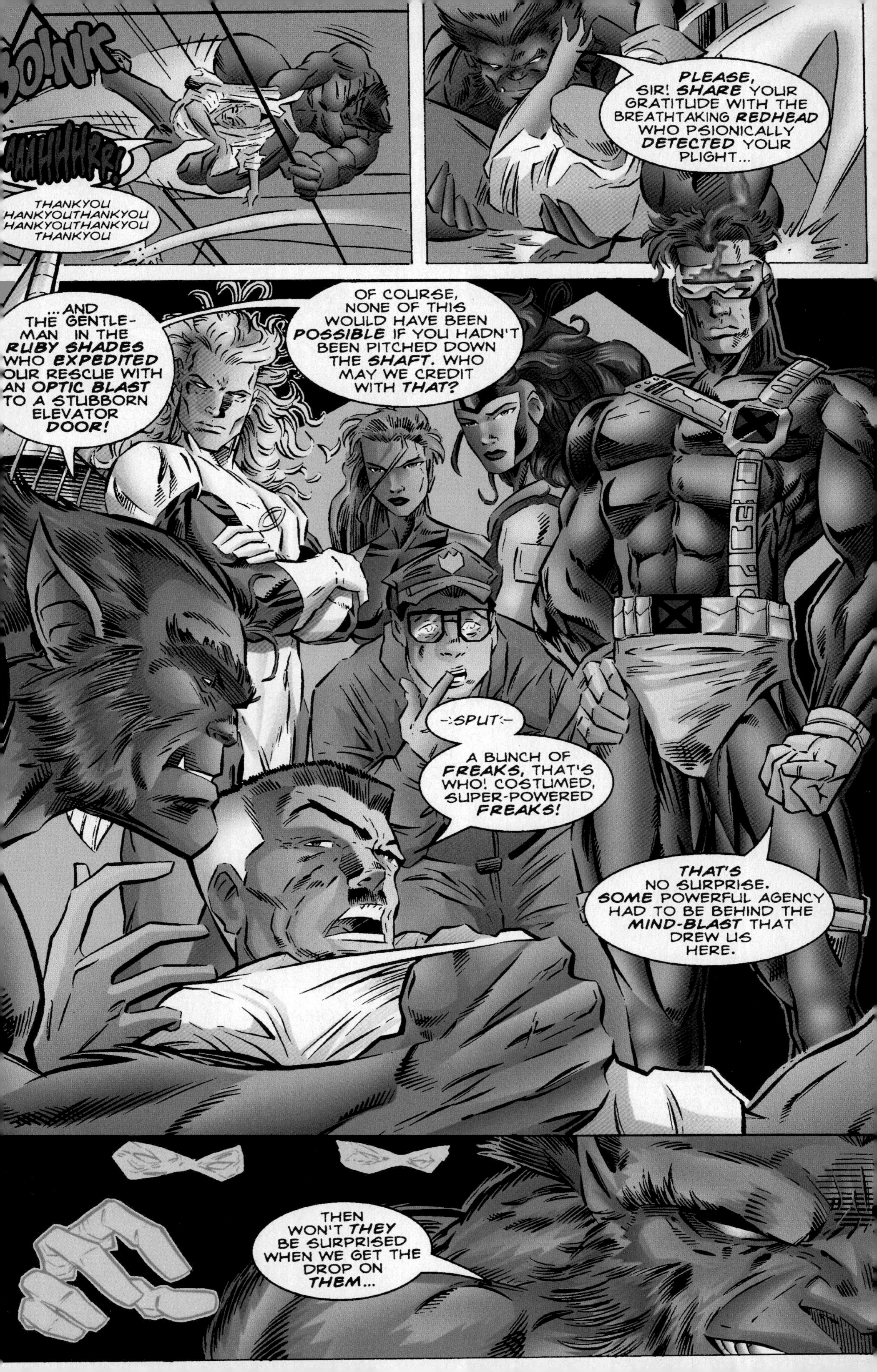
SPOINK
AAAHHHRR!
THANKYOU
THANKYOUTHANKYOU
THANKYOUTHANKYOU
THANKYOU
PLEASE, SIR! SHARE YOUR GRATITUDE WITH THE BREATHTAKING REDHEAD WHO PSIONICALLY DETECTED YOUR PLIGHT...
...AND THE GENTLEMAN IN THE RUBY SHADES WHO EXPEDITED OUR RESCUE WITH AN OPTIC BLAST TO A STUBBORN ELEVATOR DOOR!
OF COURSE, NONE OF THIS WOULD HAVE BEEN POSSIBLE IF YOU HADN'T BEEN PITCHED DOWN THE SHAFT. WHO MAY WE CREDIT WITH THAT?
-SPUT-
A BUNCH OF FREAKS, THAT'S WHO! COSTUMED, SUPER-POWERED FREAKS!
THAT'S NO SURPRISE. SOME POWERFUL AGENCY HAD TO BE BEHIND THE MIND-BLAST THAT DREW US HERE.
THEN WON'T THEY BE SURPRISED WHEN WE GET THE DROP ON THEM...

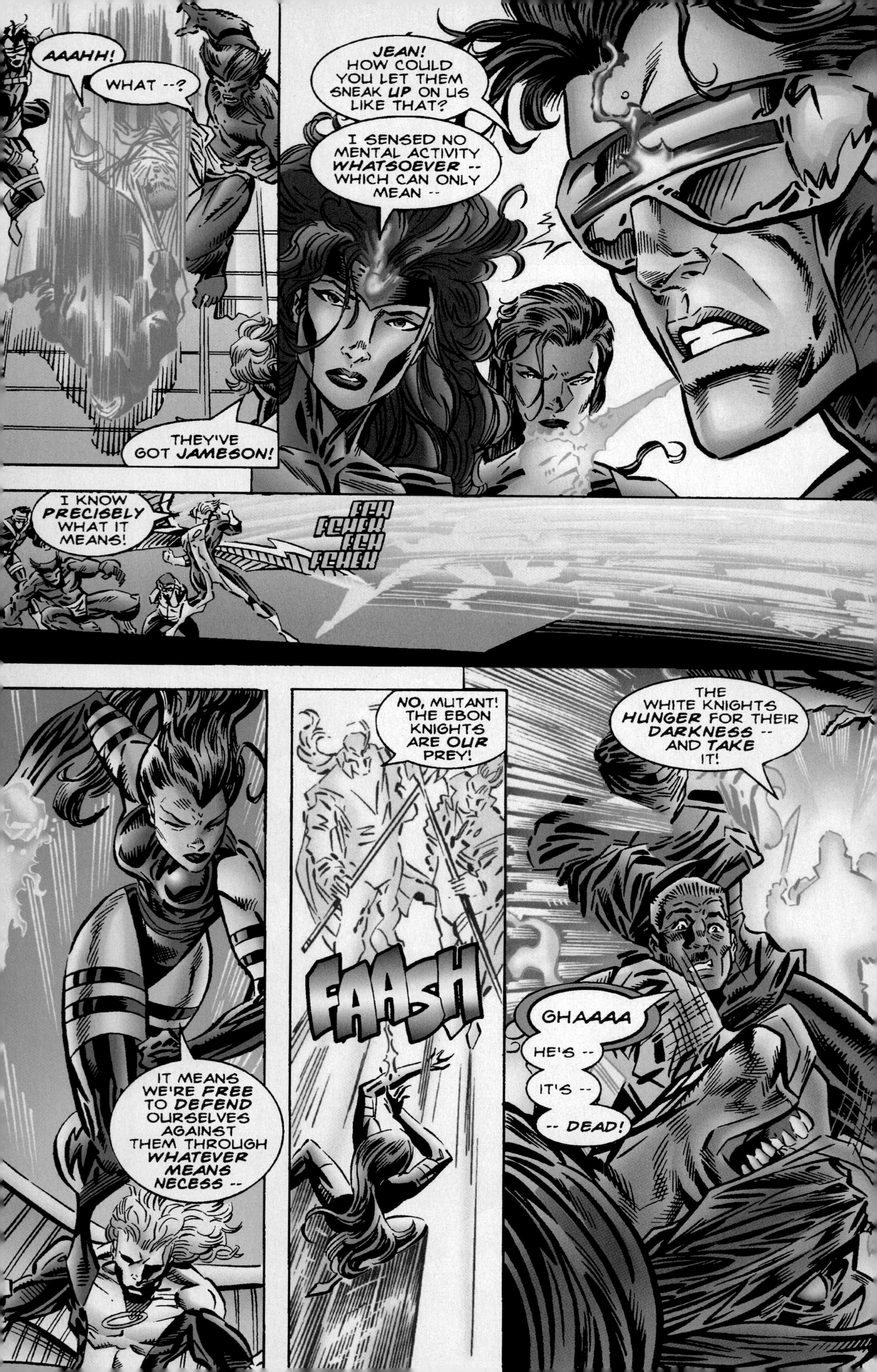
AAAHH!
WHAT --?
THEY'VE GOT JAMESON!
JEAN! HOW COULD YOU LET THEM SNEAK UP ON US LIKE THAT?
I SENSED NO MENTAL ACTIVITY WHATSOEVER -- WHICH CAN ONLY MEAN --
I KNOW PRECISELY WHAT IT MEANS!
FCHK FCHEK FCHK FCHEK
IT MEANS WE'RE FREE TO DEFEND OURSELVES AGAINST THEM THROUGH WHATEVER MEANS NECESS --
NO, MUTANT! THE EBON KNIGHTS ARE OUR PREY!
FAASH
THE WHITE KNIGHTS HUNGER FOR THEIR DARKNESS -- AND TAKE IT!
GHAAAA
HE'S --
IT'S --
-- DEAD!

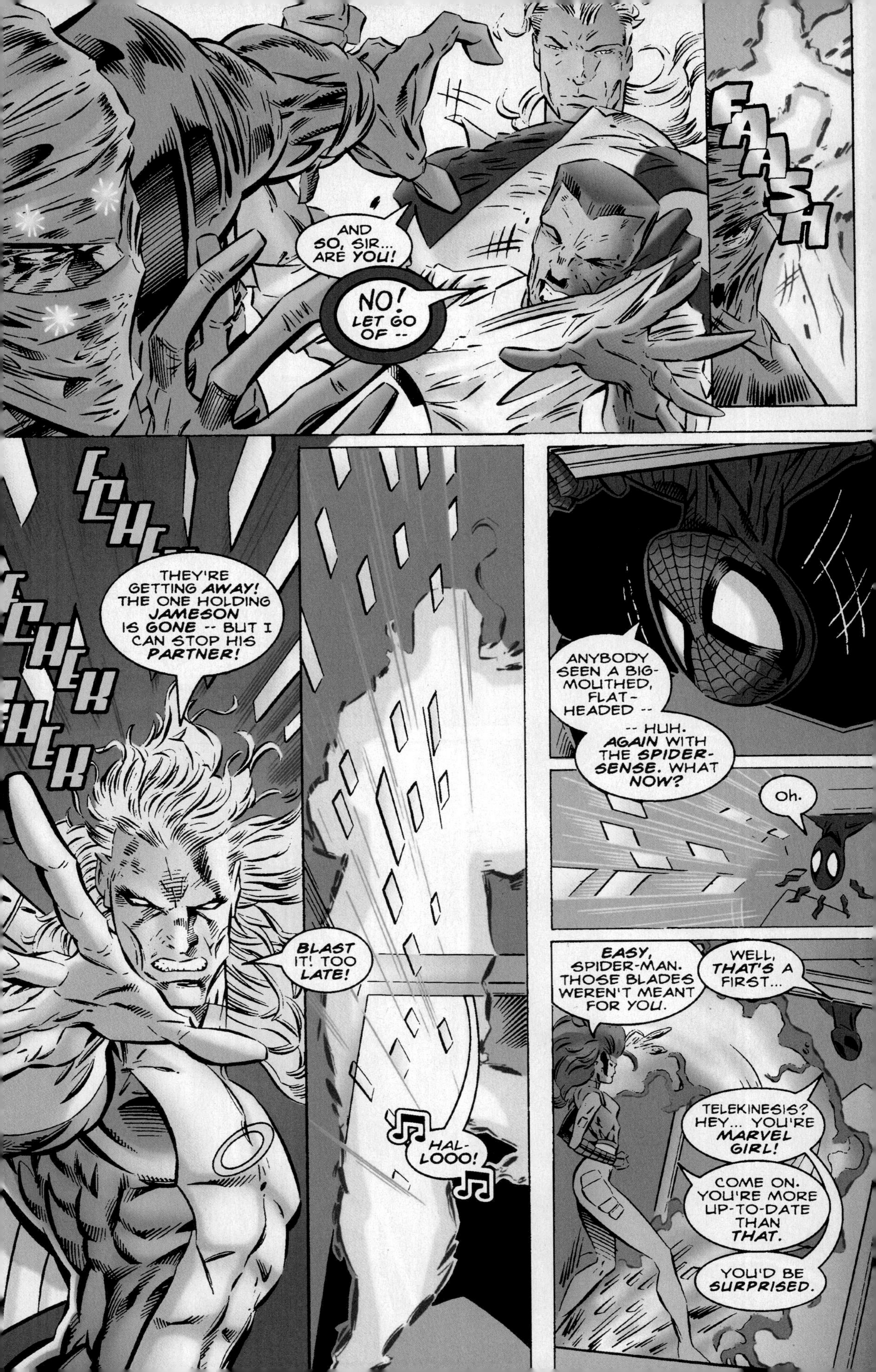
FAASH
AND SO, SIR... ARE YOU!
NO! LET GO OF --
THEY'RE GETTING AWAY! THE ONE HOLDING JAMESON IS GONE -- BUT I CAN STOP HIS PARTNER!
CHEK
CHEK
BLAST IT! TOO LATE!
HAL-LOOO!
ANYBODY SEEN A BIG-MOUTHED, FLAT-HEADED --
-- HUH. AGAIN WITH THE SPIDER-SENSE. WHAT NOW?
Oh.
EASY, SPIDER-MAN. THOSE BLADES WEREN'T MEANT FOR YOU.
WELL, THAT'S A FIRST...
TELEKINESIS? HEY... YOU'RE MARVEL GIRL!
COME ON. YOU'RE MORE UP-TO-DATE THAN THAT.
YOU'D BE SURPRISED.

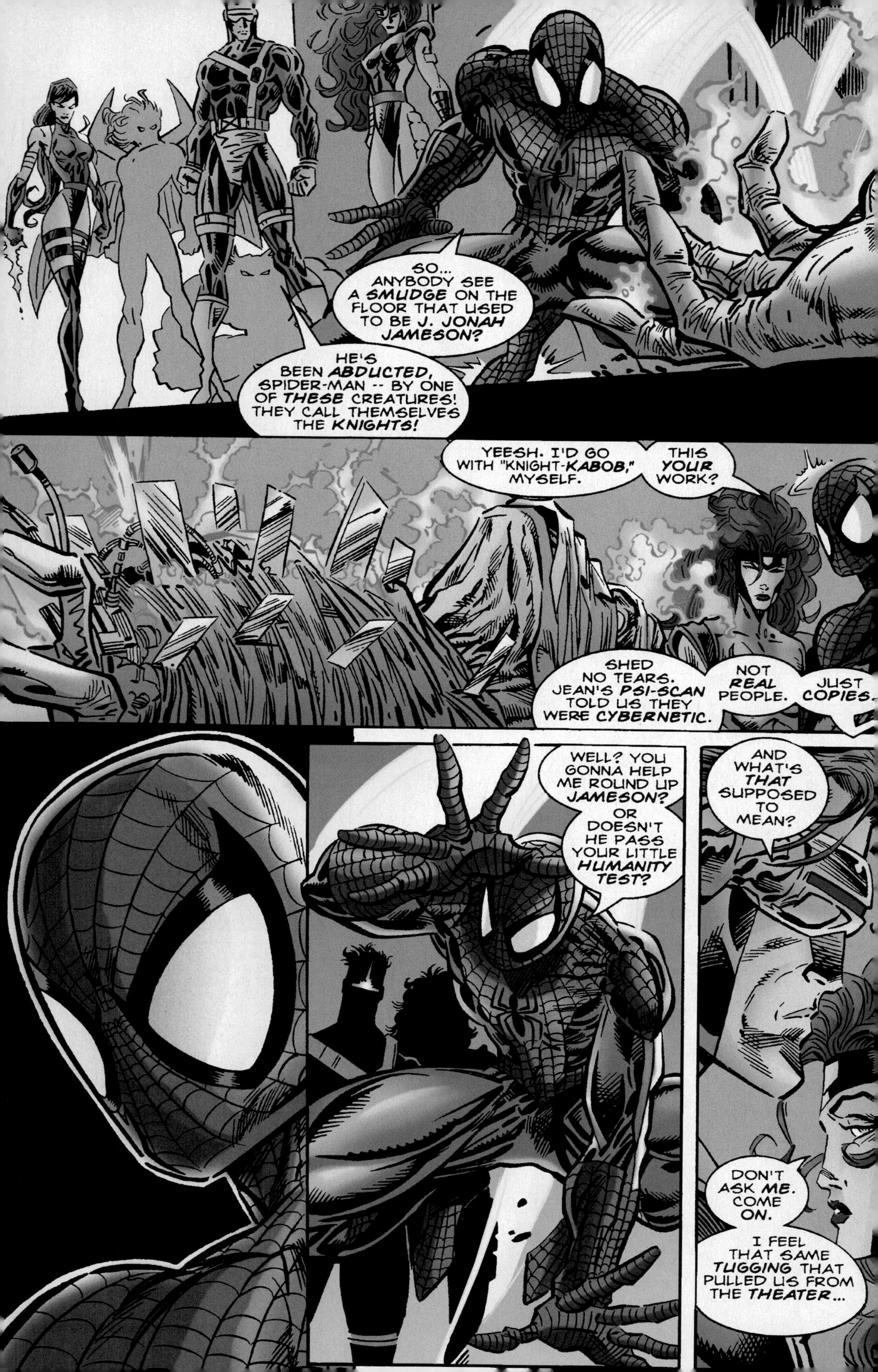
SO... ANYBODY SEE A SMUDGE ON THE FLOOR THAT USED TO BE J. JONAH JAMESON?
HE'S BEEN ABDUCTED, SPIDER-MAN -- BY ONE OF THESE CREATURES! THEY CALL THEMSELVES THE KNIGHTS!
YEESH. I'D GO WITH "KNIGHT-KABOB," MYSELF.
THIS YOUR WORK?
SHED NO TEARS. JEAN'S PSI-SCAN TOLD US THEY WERE CYBERNETIC.
NOT REAL PEOPLE.
JUST COPIES.
WELL? YOU GONNA HELP ME ROUND UP JAMESON?
OR DOESN'T HE PASS YOUR LITTLE HUMANITY TEST?
AND WHAT'S THAT SUPPOSED TO MEAN?
DON'T ASK ME. COME ON.
I FEEL THAT SAME TUGGING THAT PULLED US FROM THE THEATER...

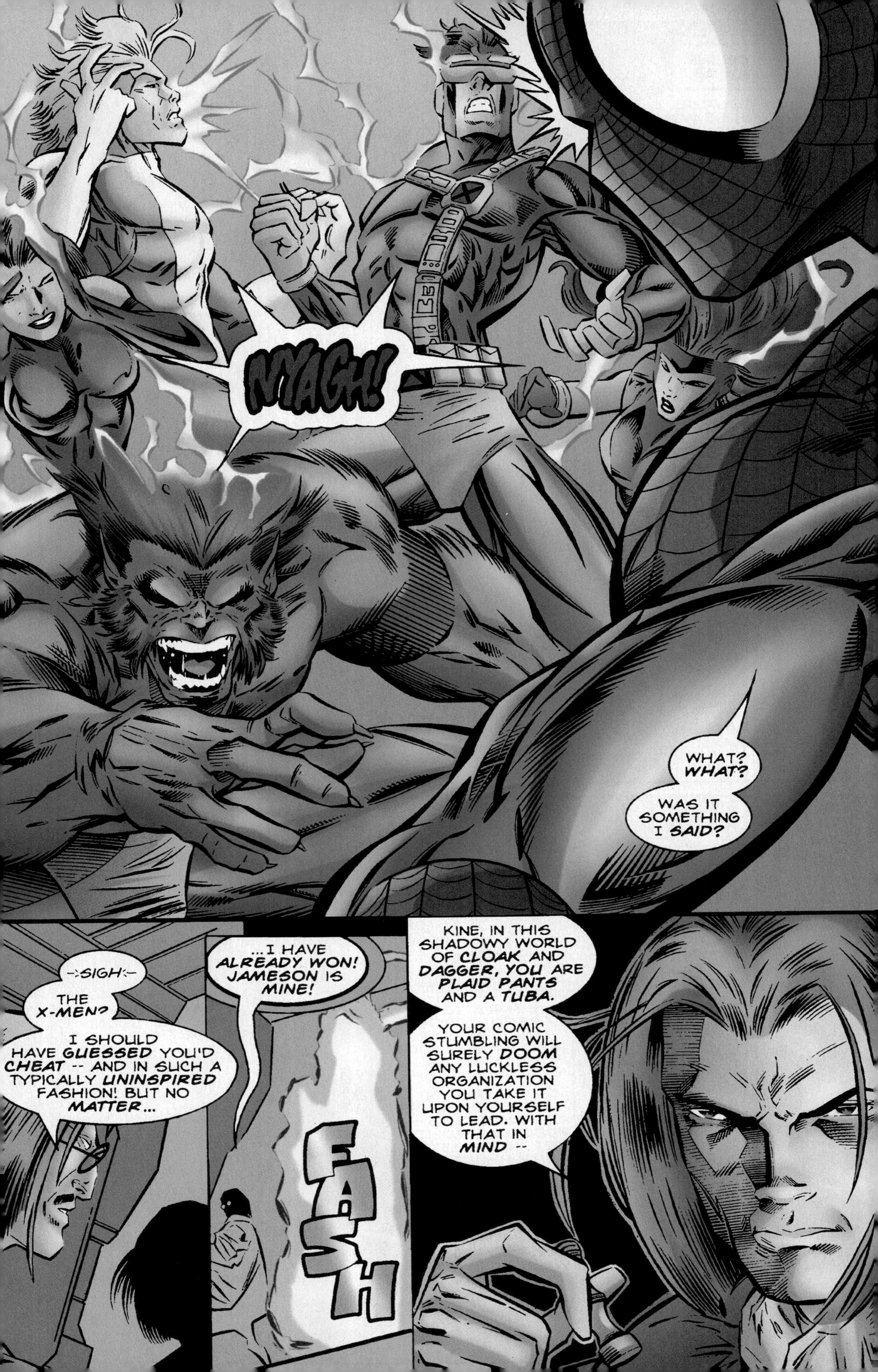
NYAGH!
WHAT? WHAT?
WAS IT SOMETHING I SAID?
--SIGH--
THE X-MEN?
I SHOULD HAVE GUESSED YOU'D CHEAT -- AND IN SUCH A TYPICALLY UNINSPIRED FASHION! BUT NO MATTER...
...I HAVE ALREADY WON! JAMESON IS MINE!
FASH
KINE, IN THIS SHADOWY WORLD OF CLOAK AND DAGGER, YOU ARE PLAID PANTS AND A TUBA.
YOUR COMIC STUMBLING WILL SURELY DOOM ANY LUCKLESS ORGANIZATION YOU TAKE IT UPON YOURSELF TO LEAD. WITH THAT IN MIND --

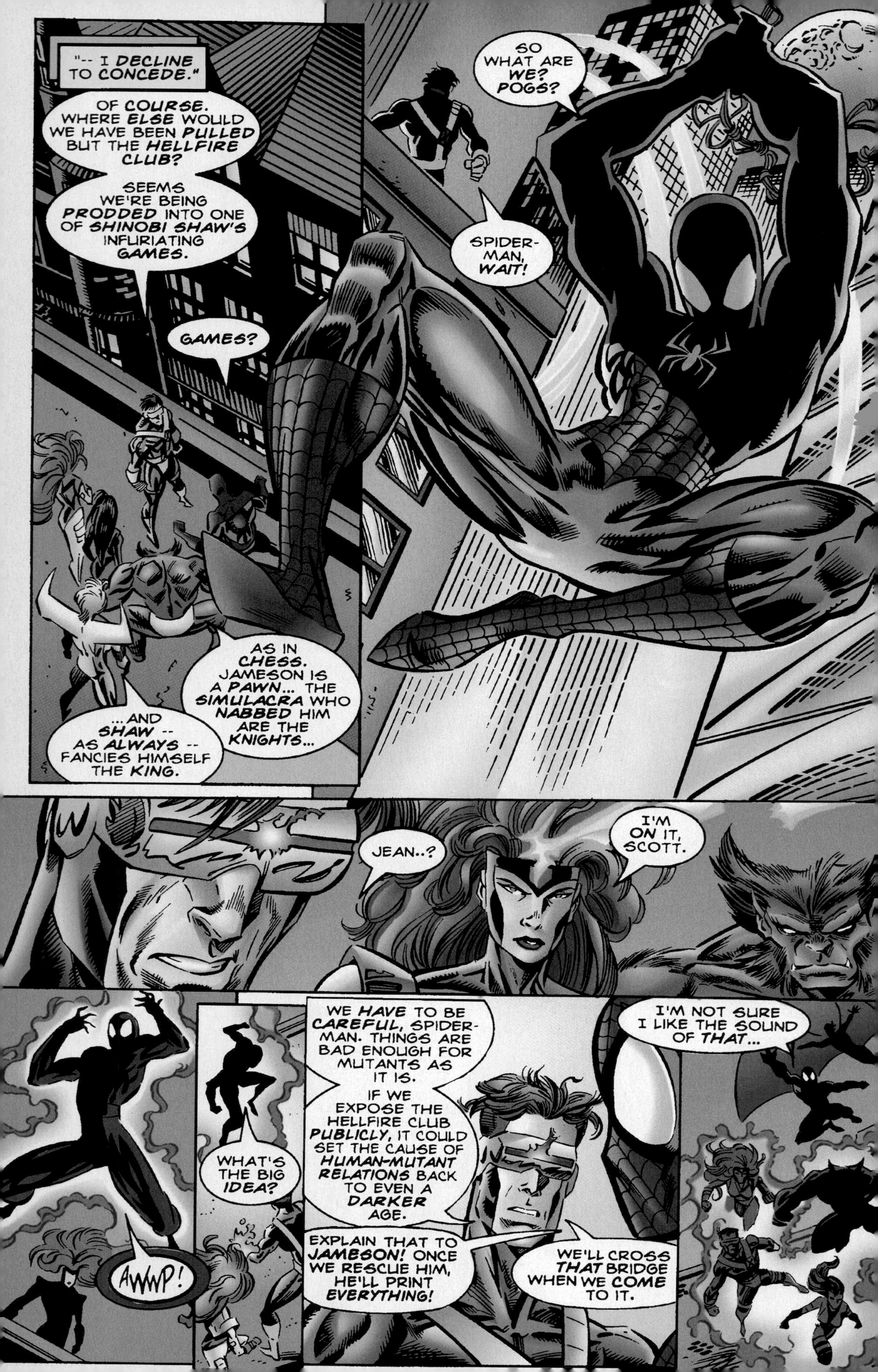
"-- I DECLINE TO CONCEDE."
OF COURSE. WHERE ELSE WOULD WE HAVE BEEN PULLED BUT THE HELLFIRE CLUB?
SEEMS WE'RE BEING PRODDED INTO ONE OF SHINOBI SHAW'S INFURIATING GAMES.
GAMES?
AS IN CHESS. JAMESON IS A PAWN... THE SIMULACRA WHO NABBED HIM ARE THE KNIGHTS...
...AND SHAW -- AS ALWAYS -- FANCIES HIMSELF THE KING.
SO WHAT ARE WE? POGS?
SPIDER-MAN, WAIT!
JEAN..?
I'M ON IT, SCOTT.
AWWP!
WHAT'S THE BIG IDEA?
WE HAVE TO BE CAREFUL, SPIDER-MAN. THINGS ARE BAD ENOUGH FOR MUTANTS AS IT IS.
IF WE EXPOSE THE HELLFIRE CLUB PUBLICLY, IT COULD SET THE CAUSE OF HUMAN-MUTANT RELATIONS BACK TO EVEN A DARKER AGE.
EXPLAIN THAT TO JAMESON! ONCE WE RESCUE HIM, HE'LL PRINT EVERYTHING!
WE'LL CROSS THAT BRIDGE WHEN WE COME TO IT.
I'M NOT SURE I LIKE THE SOUND OF THAT...

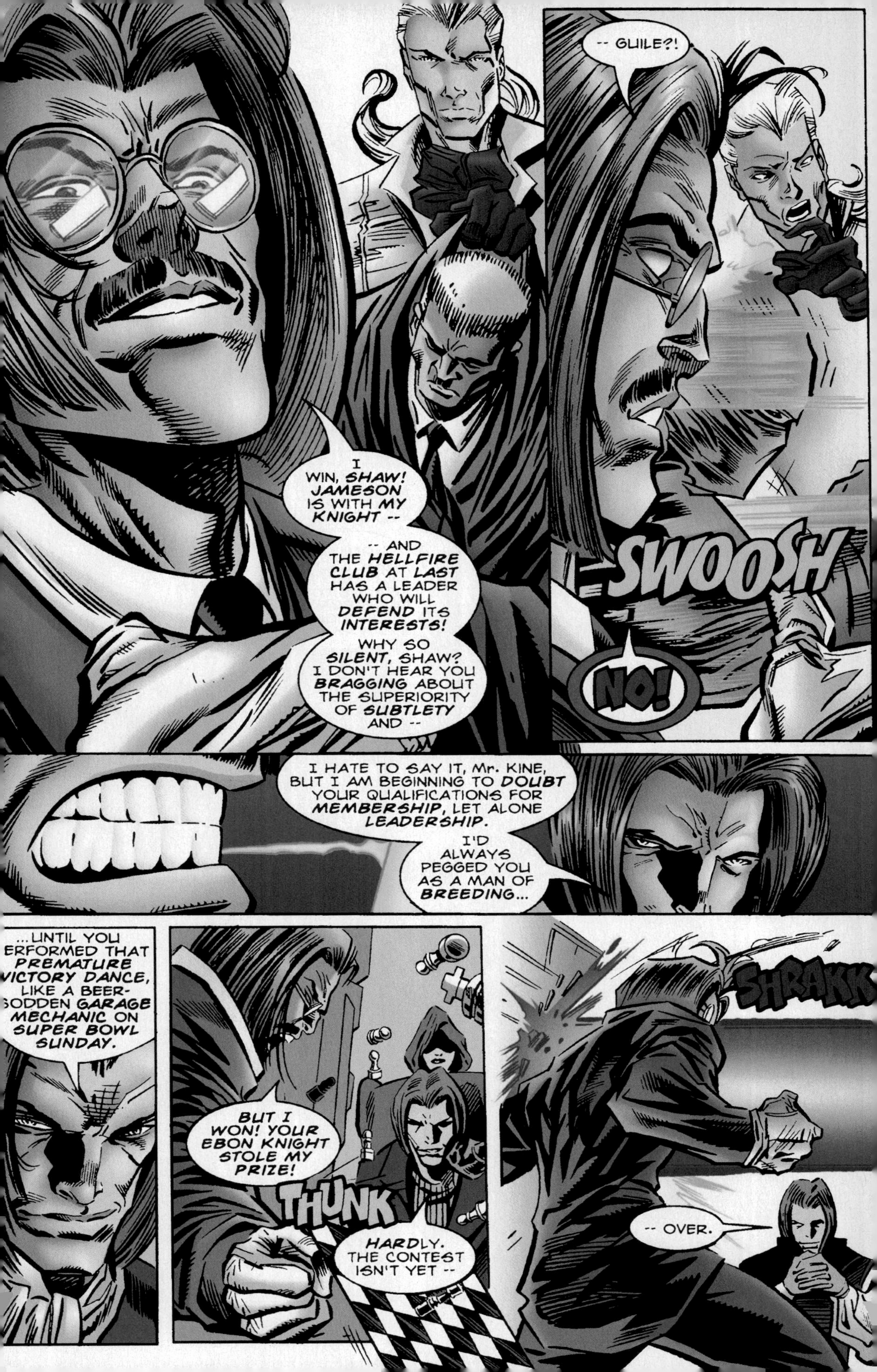
I WIN, SHAW! JAMESON IS WITH MY KNIGHT --
-- AND THE HELLFIRE CLUB AT LAST HAS A LEADER WHO WILL DEFEND ITS INTERESTS!
WHY SO SILENT, SHAW? I DON'T HEAR YOU BRAGGING ABOUT THE SUPERIORITY OF SUBTLETY AND --
-- GUILE?!
SWOOSH
NO!
I HATE TO SAY IT, Mr. KINE, BUT I AM BEGINNING TO DOUBT YOUR QUALIFICATIONS FOR MEMBERSHIP, LET ALONE LEADERSHIP.
I'D ALWAYS PEGGED YOU AS A MAN OF BREEDING...
...UNTIL YOU ERFORMED THAT PREMATURE VICTORY DANCE, LIKE A BEER-SODDEN GARAGE MECHANIC ON SUPER BOWL SUNDAY.
BUT I WON! YOUR EBON KNIGHT STOLE MY PRIZE!
THUNK
HARDLY. THE CONTEST ISN'T YET --
SHRAKK
-- OVER.

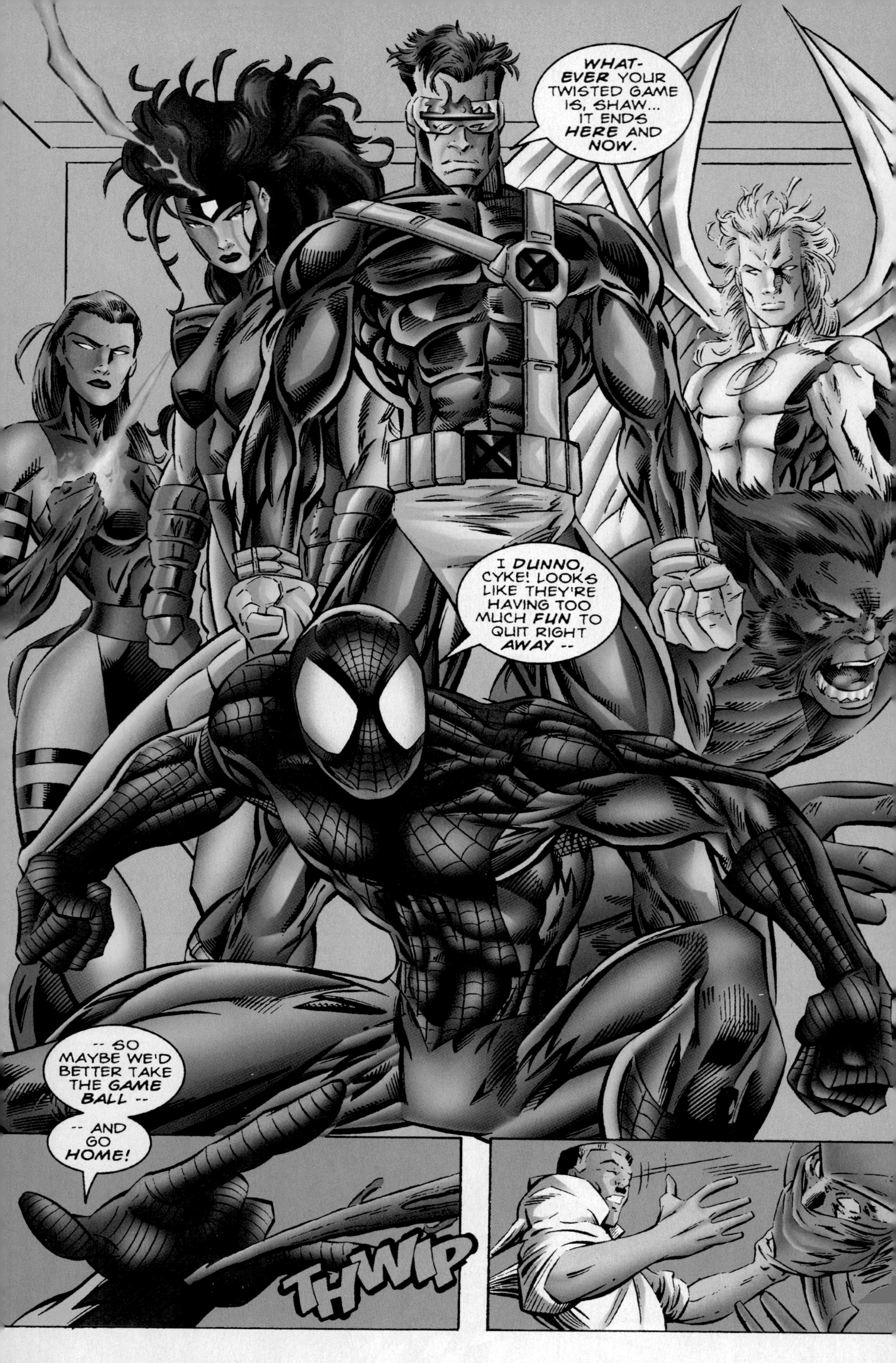
WHAT-EVER YOUR TWISTED GAME IS, SHAW... IT ENDS HERE AND NOW.
I DUNNO, CYKE! LOOKS LIKE THEY'RE HAVING TOO MUCH FUN TO QUIT RIGHT AWAY --
-- SO MAYBE WE'D BETTER TAKE THE GAME BALL --
-- AND GO HOME!
THWIP

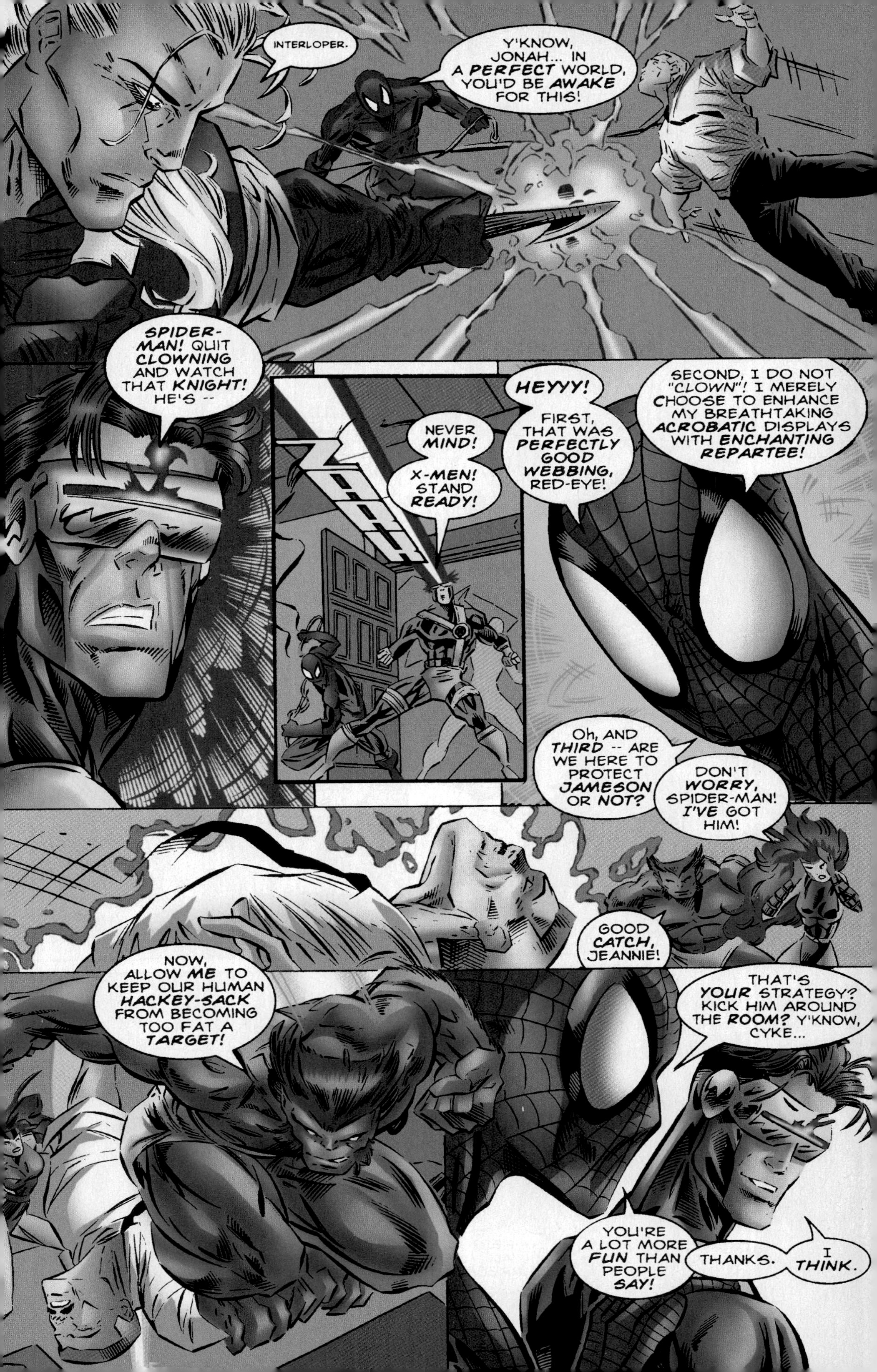
INTERLOPER.
Y'KNOW, JONAH... IN A PERFECT WORLD, YOU'D BE AWAKE FOR THIS!
SPIDER-MAN! QUIT CLOWNING AND WATCH THAT KNIGHT! HE'S --
NEVER MIND!
X-MEN! STAND READY!
HEYYY!
FIRST, THAT WAS PERFECTLY GOOD WEBBING, RED-EYE!
SECOND, I DO NOT "CLOWN"! I MERELY CHOOSE TO ENHANCE MY BREATHTAKING ACROBATIC DISPLAYS WITH ENCHANTING REPARTEE!
Oh, AND THIRD -- ARE WE HERE TO PROTECT JAMESON OR NOT?
DON'T WORRY, SPIDER-MAN! I'VE GOT HIM!
GOOD CATCH, JEANNIE!
NOW, ALLOW ME TO KEEP OUR HUMAN HACKEY-SACK FROM BECOMING TOO FAT A TARGET!
THAT'S YOUR STRATEGY? KICK HIM AROUND THE ROOM? Y'KNOW, CYKE...
YOU'RE A LOT MORE FUN THAN PEOPLE SAY!
THANKS.
I THINK.

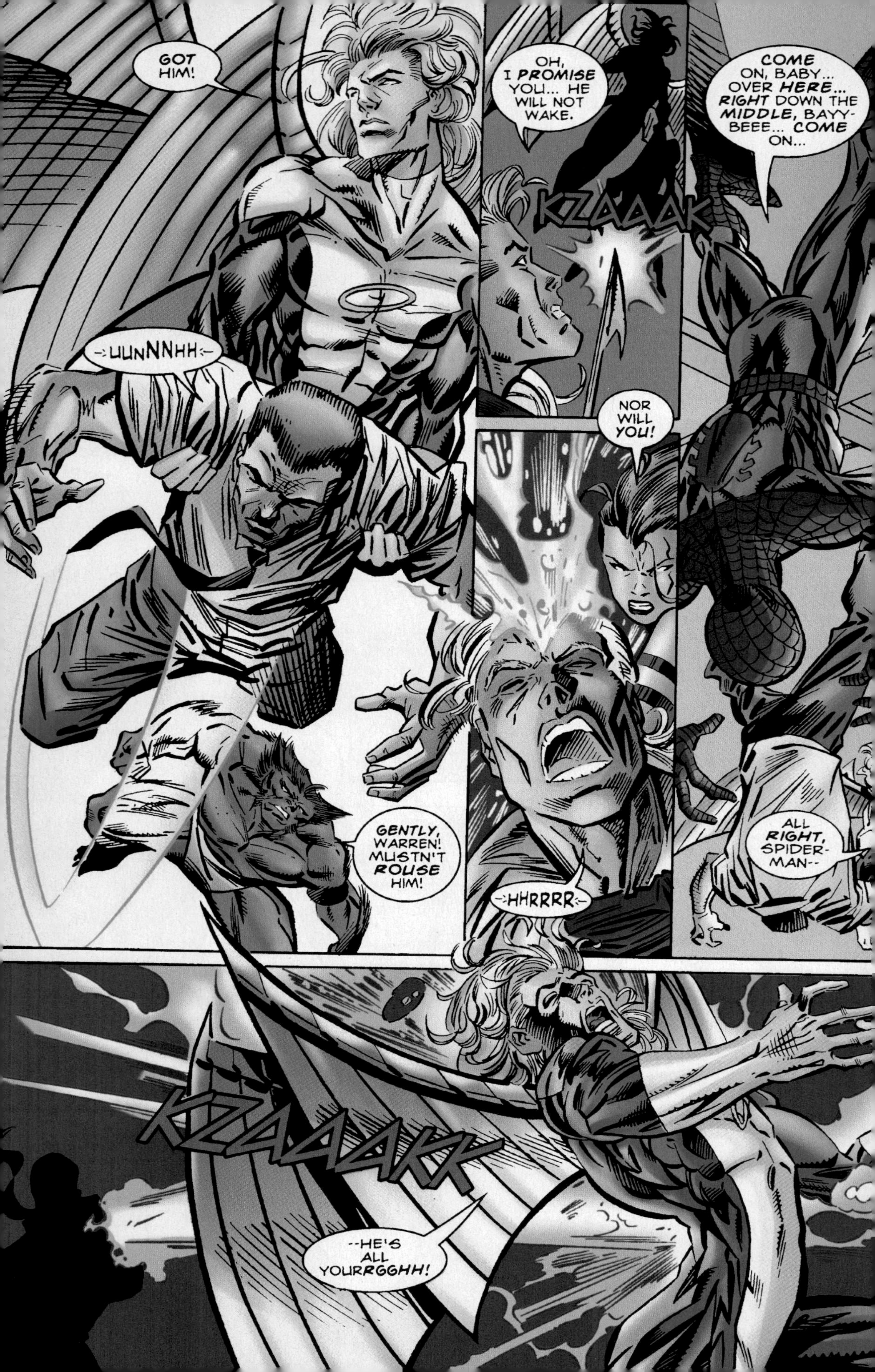

GOT HIM!
-UUNNNHH-
GENTLY, WARREN! MUSTN'T ROUSE HIM!
OH, I PROMISE YOU... HE WILL NOT WAKE.
KZAAAK
NOR WILL YOU!
-HHRRRR-
COME ON, BABY... OVER HERE... RIGHT DOWN THE MIDDLE, BAYY-BEEE... COME ON...
ALL RIGHT, SPIDER-MAN--
KZAAAAKK
--HE'S ALL YOURRGGHH!

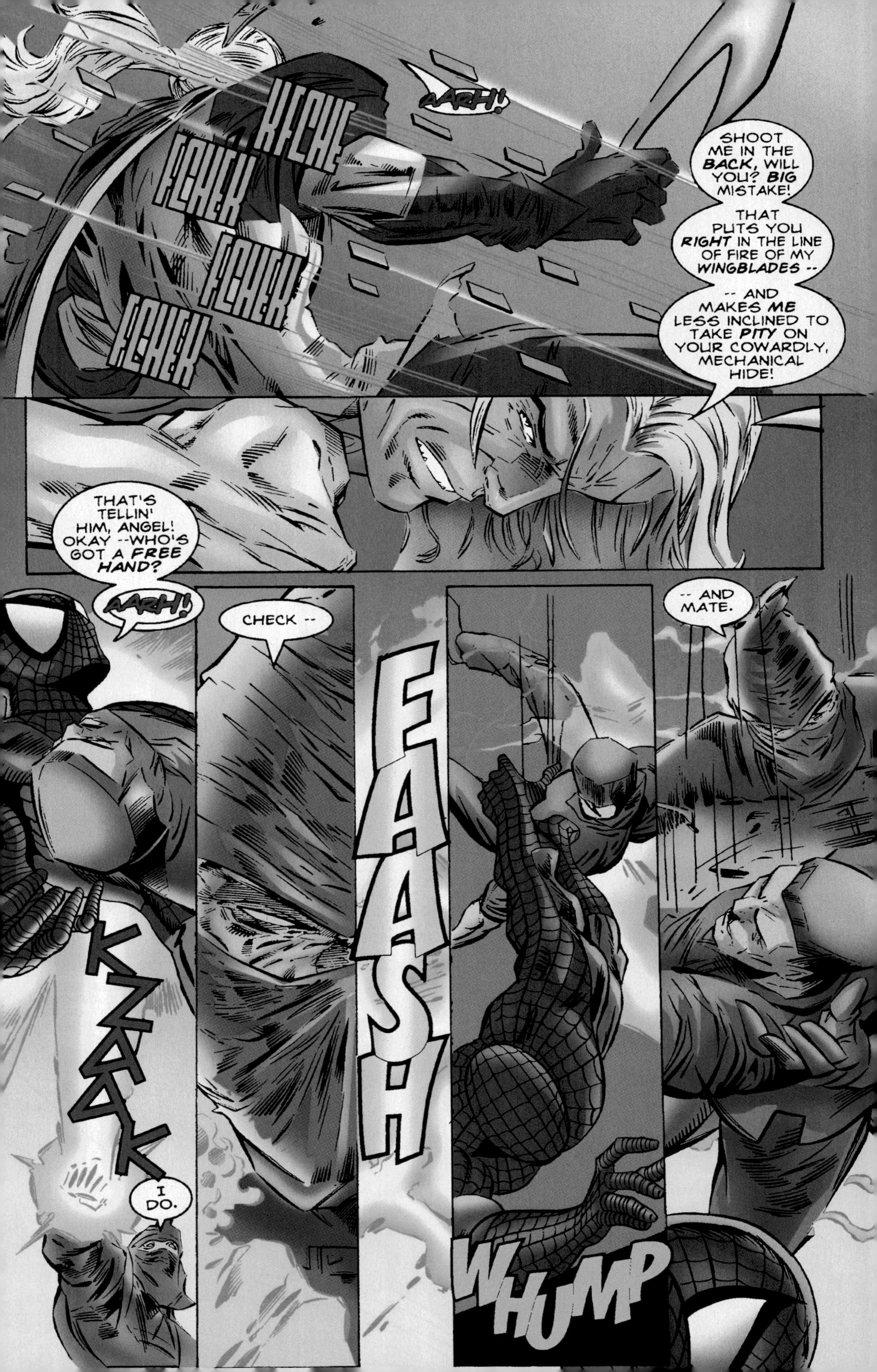
KFCHE
FCHEK
FCHEK
FCHEK
AARH!
SHOOT ME IN THE BACK, WILL YOU? BIG MISTAKE!
THAT PUTS YOU RIGHT IN THE LINE OF FIRE OF MY WINGBLADES --
-- AND MAKES ME LESS INCLINED TO TAKE PITY ON YOUR COWARDLY, MECHANICAL HIDE!
THAT'S TELLIN' HIM, ANGEL! OKAY --WHO'S GOT A FREE HAND?
AARH!
KZAKAK
I DO.
CHECK --
FAASH
-- AND MATE.
WHUMP

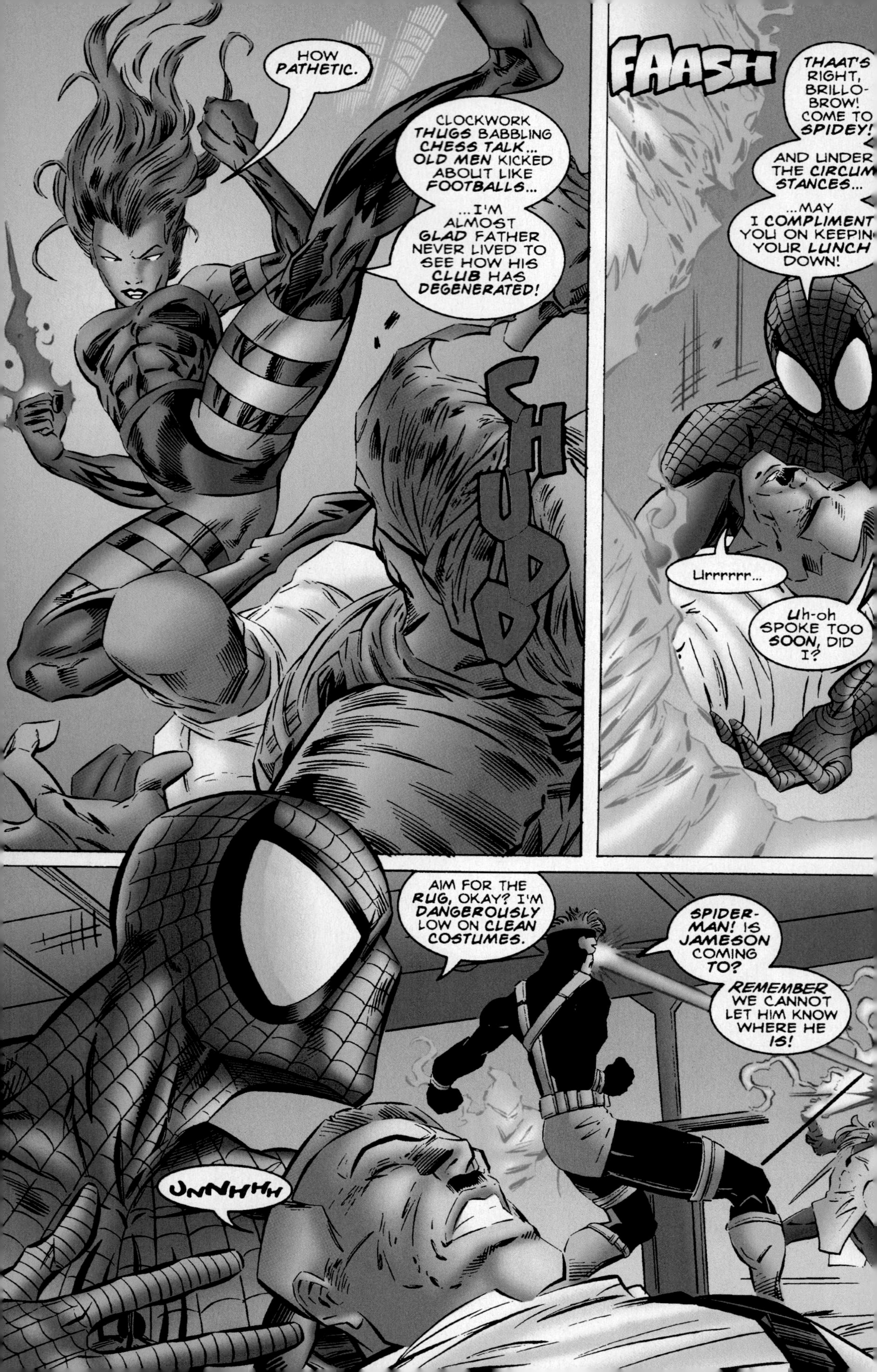
HOW PATHETIC.
CLOCKWORK THUGS BABBLING CHESS TALK... OLD MEN KICKED ABOUT LIKE FOOTBALLS...
...I'M ALMOST GLAD FATHER NEVER LIVED TO SEE HOW HIS CLUB HAS DEGENERATED!
CHUDD
FAASH
THAAT'S RIGHT, BRILLO-BROW! COME TO SPIDEY!
AND UNDER THE CIRCUMSTANCES...
...MAY I COMPLIMENT YOU ON KEEPIN YOUR LUNCH DOWN!
Urrrrrr...
Uh-oh SPOKE TOO SOON, DID I?
AIM FOR THE RUG, OKAY? I'M DANGEROUSLY LOW ON CLEAN COSTUMES.
SPIDER-MAN! IS JAMESON COMING TO?
REMEMBER WE CANNOT LET HIM KNOW WHERE HE IS!
UNNHHH

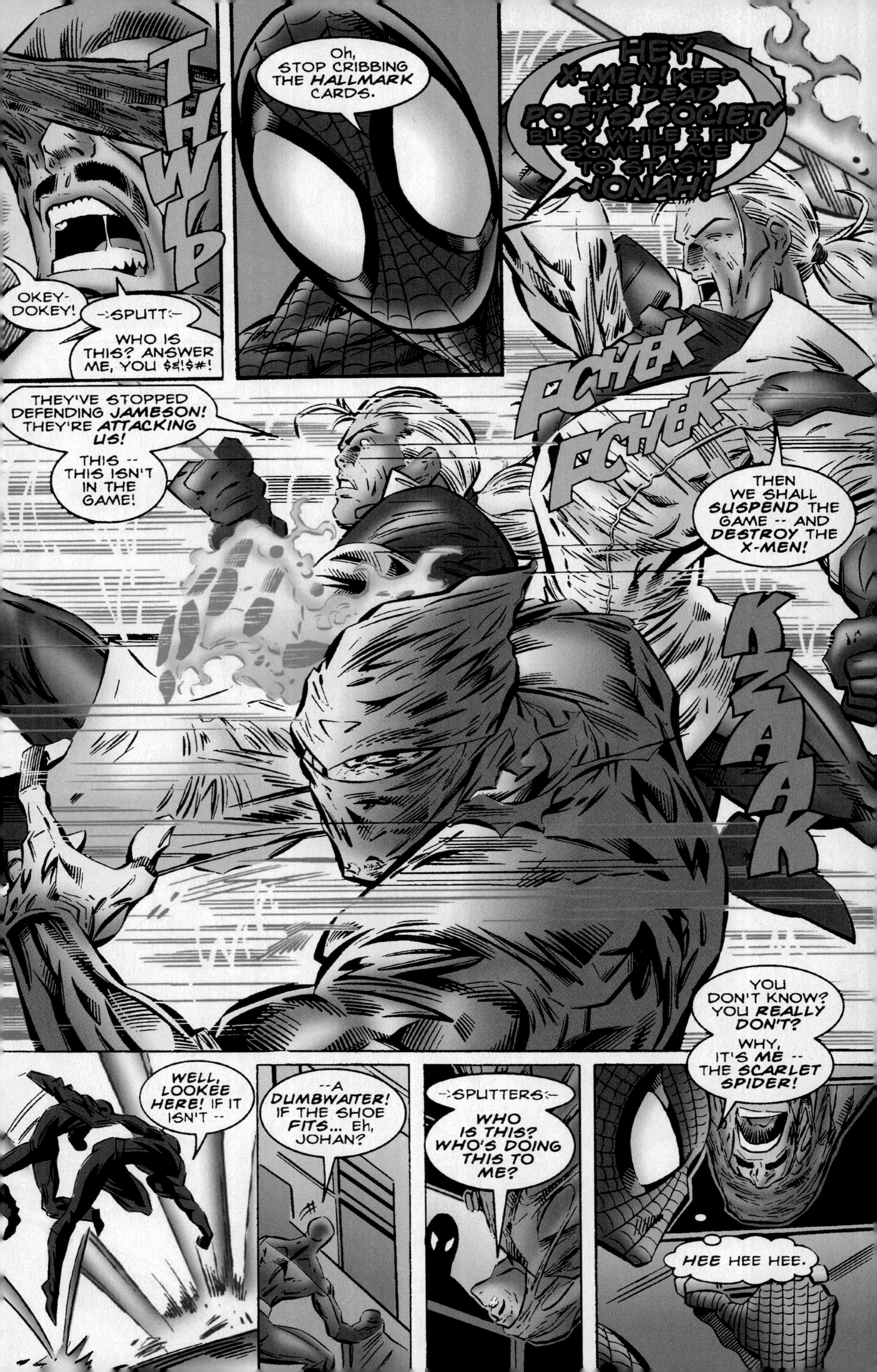

THWIP
OKEY-DOKEY!
-SPUTT-
WHO IS THIS? ANSWER ME, YOU $&!$#!
Oh, STOP CRIBBING THE HALLMARK CARDS.
HEY, X-MEN! KEEP THE DEAD POETS' SOCIETY BUSY WHILE I FIND SOME PLACE TO STASH JONAH!
PCHEK
PCHEK
THEY'VE STOPPED DEFENDING JAMESON! THEY'RE ATTACKING US!
THIS -- THIS ISN'T IN THE GAME!
THEN WE SHALL SUSPEND THE GAME -- AND DESTROY THE X-MEN!
KRAAAK
WELL, LOOKEE HERE! IF IT ISN'T --
--A DUMBWAITER! IF THE SHOE FITS... Eh, JOHAN?
-SPUTTERS-
WHO IS THIS? WHO'S DOING THIS TO ME?
YOU DON'T KNOW? YOU REALLY DON'T?
WHY, IT'S ME -- THE SCARLET SPIDER!
HEE HEE HEE.

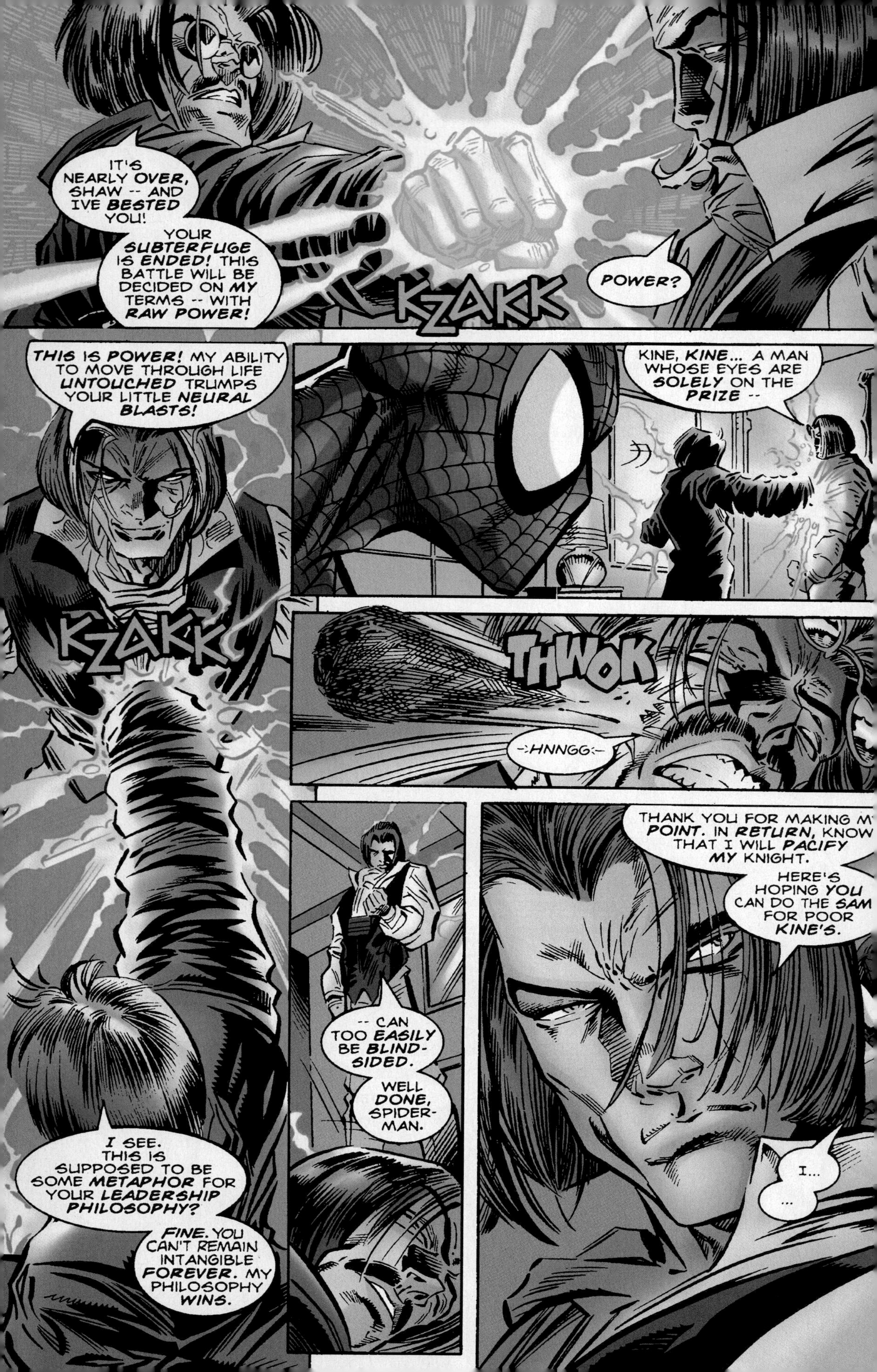

IT'S NEARLY OVER, SHAW -- AND IVE BESTED YOU!
YOUR SUBTERFUGE IS ENDED! THIS BATTLE WILL BE DECIDED ON MY TERMS -- WITH RAW POWER!
KZAKK
POWER?
THIS IS POWER! MY ABILITY TO MOVE THROUGH LIFE UNTOUCHED TRUMPS YOUR LITTLE NEURAL BLASTS!
KZAKK
KINE, KINE... A MAN WHOSE EYES ARE SOLELY ON THE PRIZE --
THWOK
HNNGG
I SEE. THIS IS SUPPOSED TO BE SOME METAPHOR FOR YOUR LEADERSHIP PHILOSOPHY?
FINE. YOU CAN'T REMAIN INTANGIBLE FOREVER. MY PHILOSOPHY WINS.
-- CAN TOO EASILY BE BLIND-SIDED.
WELL DONE, SPIDER-MAN.
THANK YOU FOR MAKING M POINT. IN RETURN, KNOW THAT I WILL PACIFY MY KNIGHT.
HERE'S HOPING YOU CAN DO THE SAM FOR POOR KINE'S.
I...
...

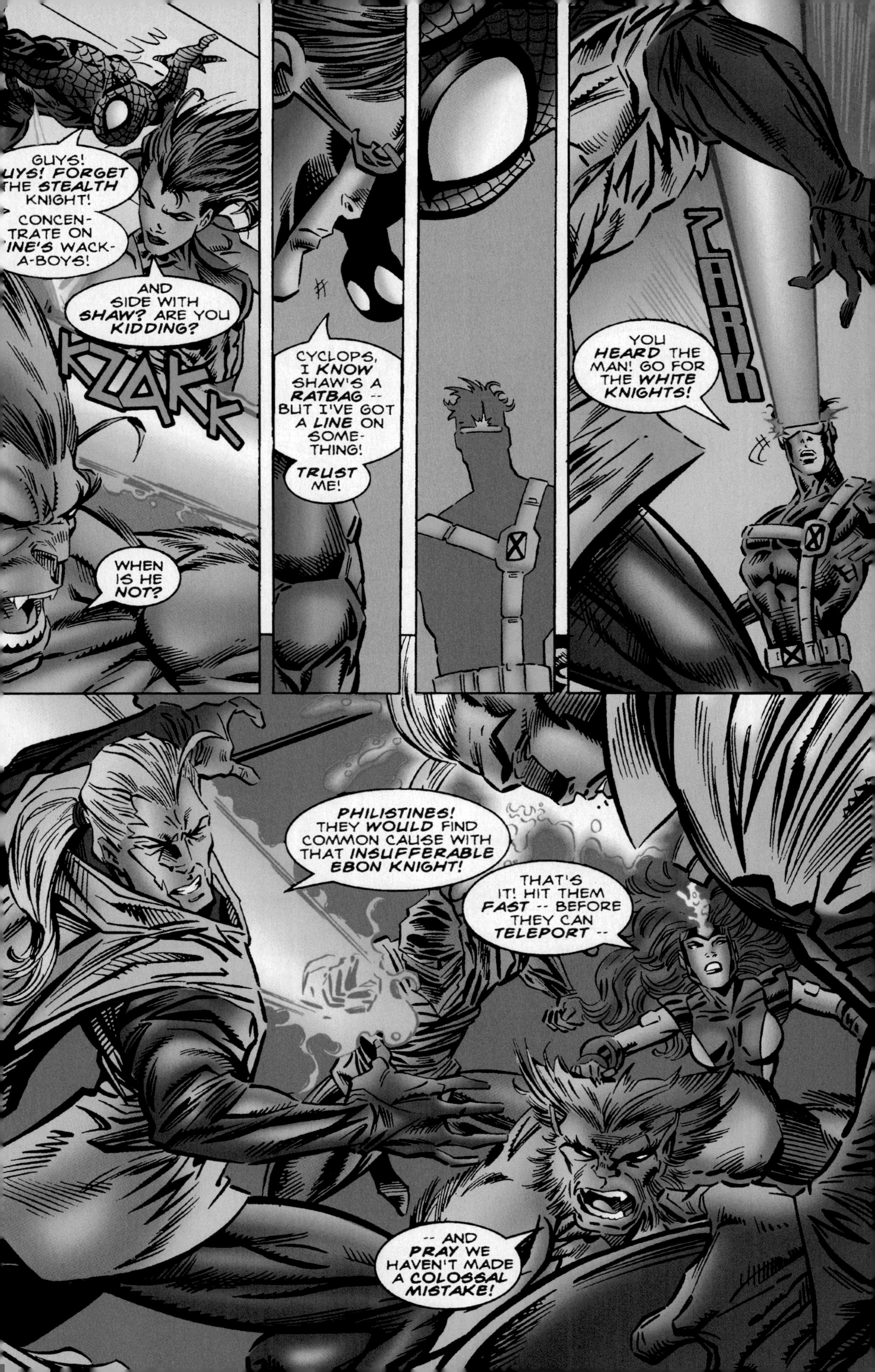
GUYS! UYS! FORGET THE STEALTH KNIGHT!
CONCEN-TRATE ON INE'S WACK-A-BOYS!
AND SIDE WITH SHAW? ARE YOU KIDDING?
KZIAKK
WHEN IS HE NOT?
CYCLOPS, I KNOW SHAW'S A RATBAG -- BUT I'VE GOT A LINE ON SOME-THING!
TRUST ME!
ZARK
YOU HEARD THE MAN! GO FOR THE WHITE KNIGHTS!
PHILISTINES! THEY WOULD FIND COMMON CAUSE WITH THAT INSUFFERABLE EBON KNIGHT!
THAT'S IT! HIT THEM FAST -- BEFORE THEY CAN TELEPORT --
-- AND PRAY WE HAVEN'T MADE A COLOSSAL MISTAKE!

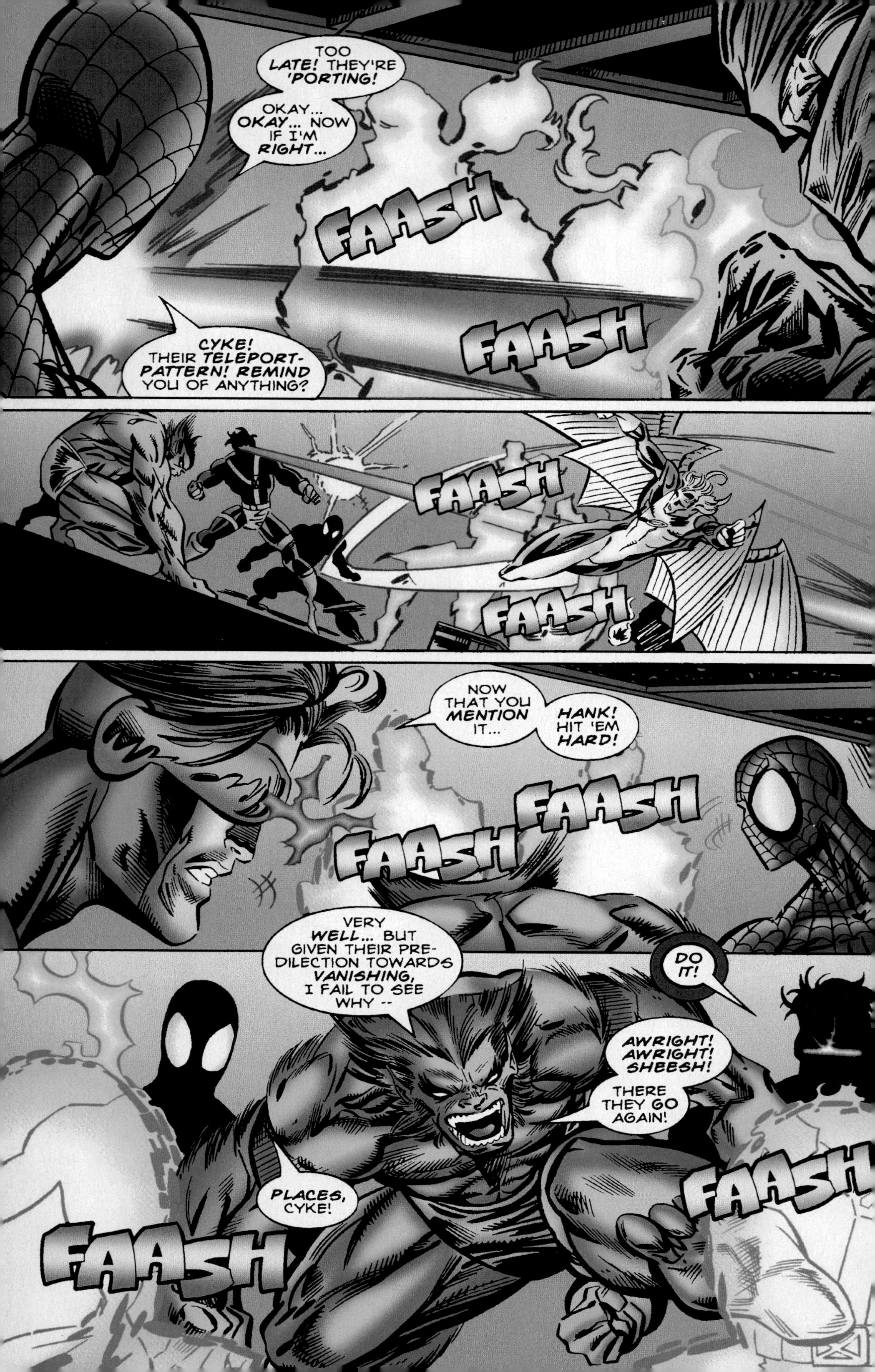
TOO LATE! THEY'RE 'PORTING!
OKAY... OKAY... NOW IF I'M RIGHT...
FAASH
FAASH
CYKE! THEIR TELEPORT-PATTERN! REMIND YOU OF ANYTHING?
FAASH
FAASH
NOW THAT YOU MENTION IT...
HANK! HIT 'EM HARD!
FAASH
FAASH
VERY WELL... BUT GIVEN THEIR PRE-DILECTION TOWARDS VANISHING, I FAIL TO SEE WHY --
DO IT!
AWRIGHT! AWRIGHT! SHEESH!
THERE THEY GO AGAIN!
PLACES, CYKE!
FAASH
FAASH

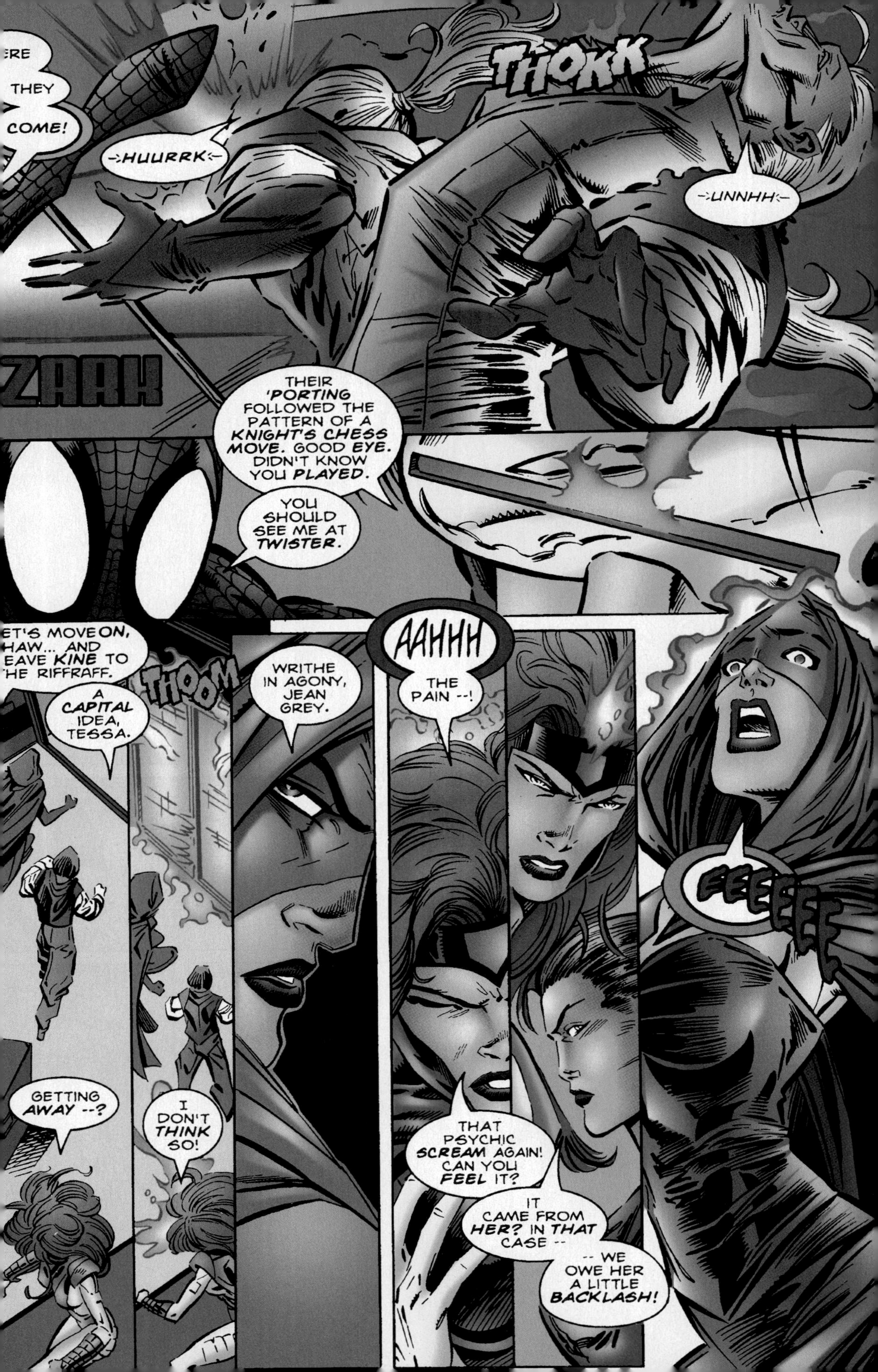

ERE THEY COME!
-HUURRK-
THOKK
-UNNHH-
ZAAK
THEIR 'PORTING FOLLOWED THE PATTERN OF A KNIGHT'S CHESS MOVE. GOOD EYE. DIDN'T KNOW YOU PLAYED.
YOU SHOULD SEE ME AT TWISTER.
ET'S MOVE ON, HAW... AND EAVE KINE TO HE RIFFRAFF.
A CAPITAL IDEA, TESSA.
THOOM
GETTING AWAY --?
I DON'T THINK SO!
WRITHE IN AGONY, JEAN GREY.
AAHHH
THE PAIN --!
EEEEEE
THAT PSYCHIC SCREAM AGAIN! CAN YOU FEEL IT?
IT CAME FROM HER? IN THAT CASE --
-- WE OWE HER A LITTLE BACKLASH!

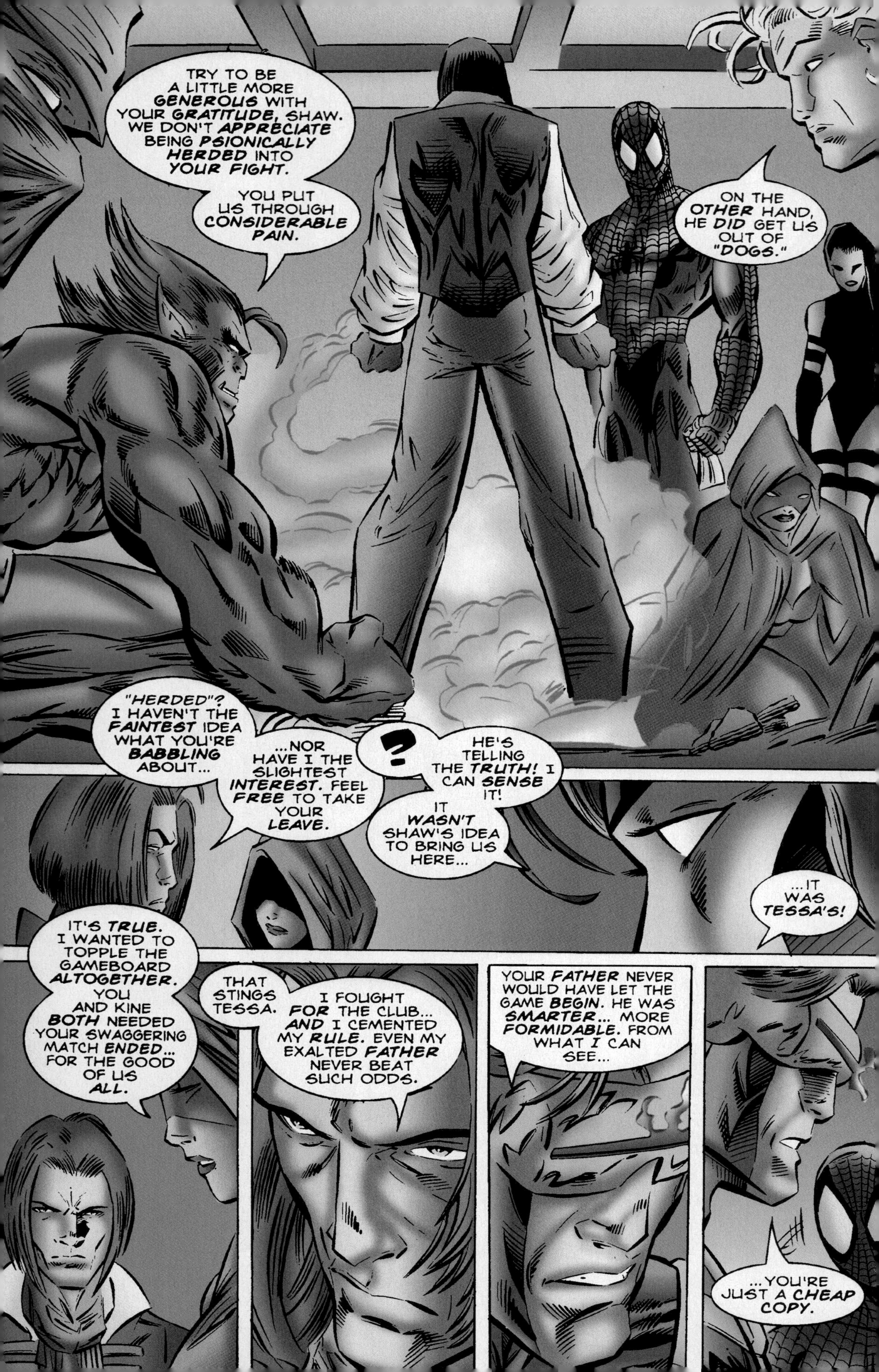
TRY TO BE A LITTLE MORE GENEROUS WITH YOUR GRATITUDE, SHAW. WE DON'T APPRECIATE BEING PSIONICALLY HERDED INTO YOUR FIGHT.
YOU PUT US THROUGH CONSIDERABLE PAIN.
ON THE OTHER HAND, HE DID GET US OUT OF "DOGS."
"HERDED"? I HAVEN'T THE FAINTEST IDEA WHAT YOU'RE BABBLING ABOUT...
...NOR HAVE I THE SLIGHTEST INTEREST. FEEL FREE TO TAKE YOUR LEAVE.
?
HE'S TELLING THE TRUTH! I CAN SENSE IT!
IT WASN'T SHAW'S IDEA TO BRING US HERE...
...IT WAS TESSA'S!
IT'S TRUE. I WANTED TO TOPPLE THE GAMEBOARD ALTOGETHER. YOU AND KINE BOTH NEEDED YOUR SWAGGERING MATCH ENDED... FOR THE GOOD OF US ALL.
THAT STINGS TESSA.
I FOUGHT FOR THE CLUB... AND I CEMENTED MY RULE. EVEN MY EXALTED FATHER NEVER BEAT SUCH ODDS.
YOUR FATHER NEVER WOULD HAVE LET THE GAME BEGIN. HE WAS SMARTER... MORE FORMIDABLE. FROM WHAT I CAN SEE...
...YOU'RE JUST A CHEAP COPY.

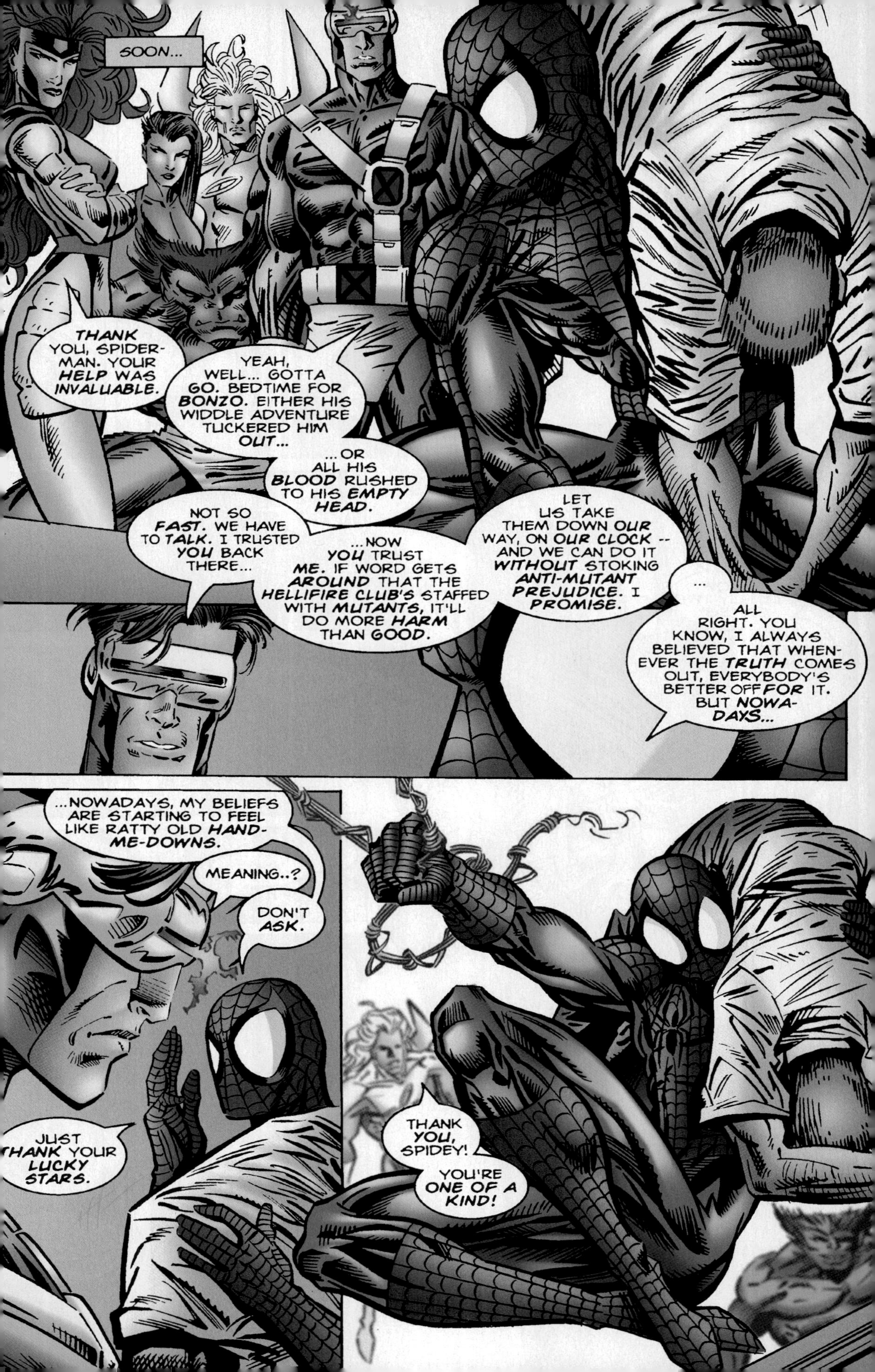
SOON...
THANK YOU, SPIDER-MAN. YOUR HELP WAS INVALUABLE.
YEAH, WELL... GOTTA GO. BEDTIME FOR BONZO. EITHER HIS WIDDLE ADVENTURE TUCKERED HIM OUT...
...OR ALL HIS BLOOD RUSHED TO HIS EMPTY HEAD.
NOT SO FAST. WE HAVE TO TALK. I TRUSTED YOU BACK THERE...
...NOW YOU TRUST ME. IF WORD GETS AROUND THAT THE HELLFIRE CLUB'S STAFFED WITH MUTANTS, IT'LL DO MORE HARM THAN GOOD.
LET US TAKE THEM DOWN OUR WAY, ON OUR CLOCK -- AND WE CAN DO IT WITHOUT STOKING ANTI-MUTANT PREJUDICE. I PROMISE.
...
ALL RIGHT. YOU KNOW, I ALWAYS BELIEVED THAT WHEN-EVER THE TRUTH COMES OUT, EVERYBODY'S BETTER OFF FOR IT. BUT NOWA-DAYS...
...NOWADAYS, MY BELIEFS ARE STARTING TO FEEL LIKE RATTY OLD HAND-ME-DOWNS.
MEANING..?
DON'T ASK.
JUST THANK YOUR LUCKY STARS.
THANK YOU, SPIDEY!
YOU'RE ONE OF A KIND!

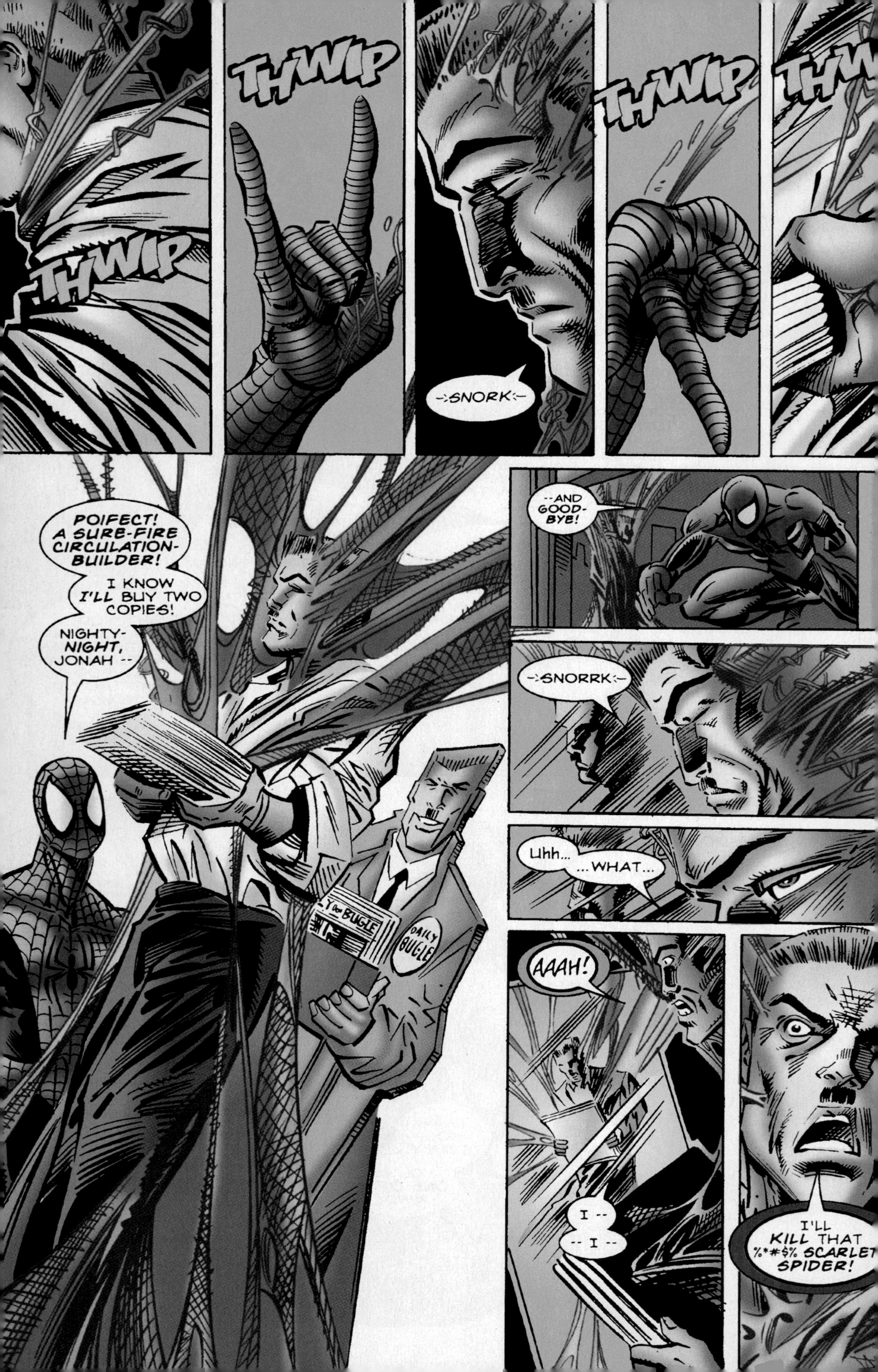
THWIP
THWIP
-SNORK-
THWIP
THWI
POIFECT! A SURE-FIRE CIRCULATION-BUILDER!
I KNOW I'LL BUY TWO COPIES!
NIGHTY-NIGHT, JONAH --
--AND GOOD-BYE!
-SNORRK-
Uhh... ...WHAT...
AAAH!
I --
-- I --
I'LL KILL THAT %*#$% SCARLET SPIDER!

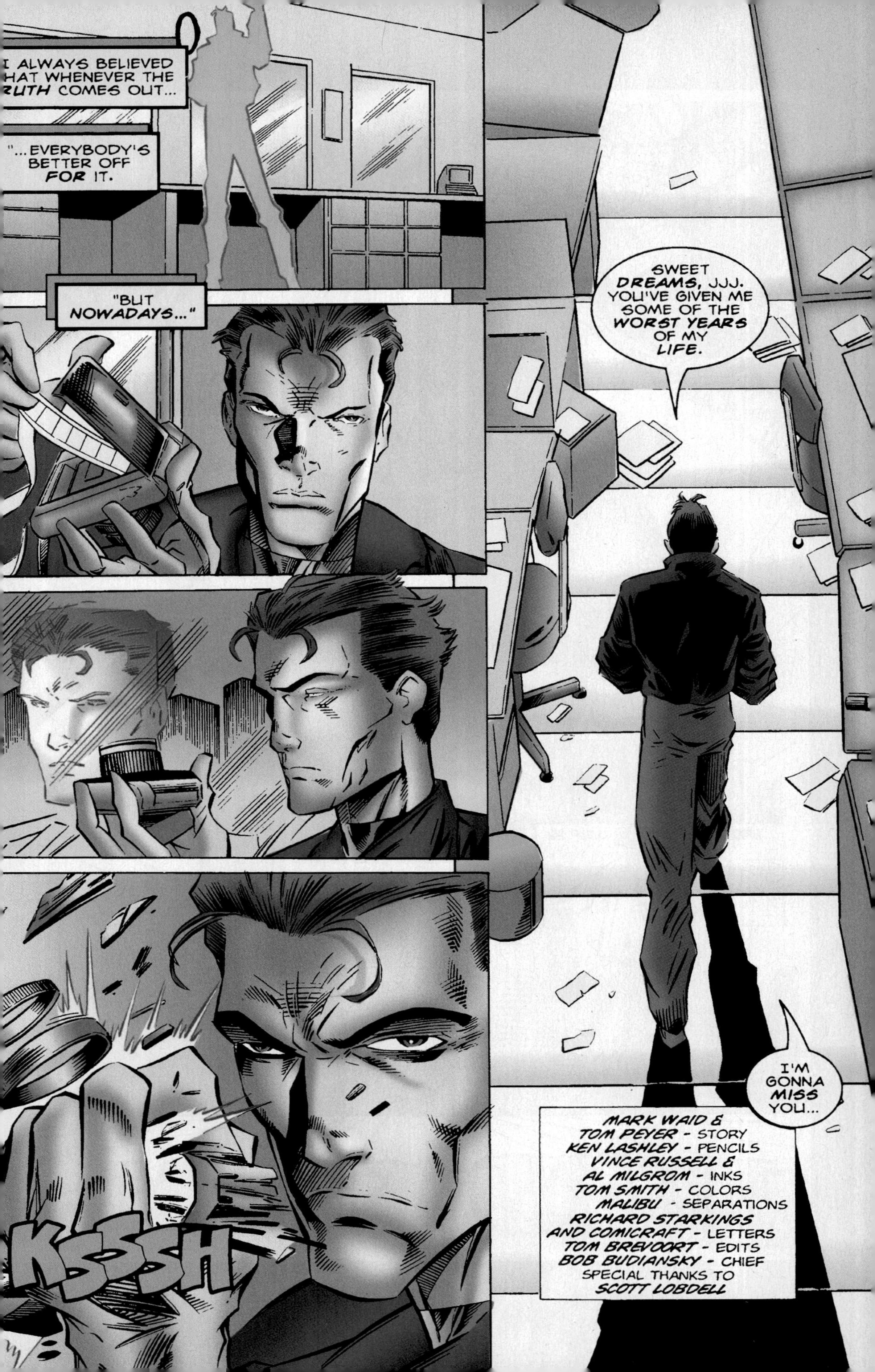

I ALWAYS BELIEVED THAT WHENEVER THE TRUTH COMES OUT...
"...EVERYBODY'S BETTER OFF FOR IT.
"BUT NOWADAYS..."
KSSSH
SWEET DREAMS, JJJ. YOU'VE GIVEN ME SOME OF THE WORST YEARS OF MY LIFE.
I'M GONNA MISS YOU...
MARK WAID & TOM PEYER - STORY
KEN LASHLEY - PENCILS
VINCE RUSSELL & AL MILGROM - INKS
TOM SMITH - COLORS
MALIBU - SEPARATIONS
RICHARD STARKINGS AND COMICRAFT - LETTERS
TOM BREVOORT - EDITS
BOB BUDIANSKY - CHIEF
SPECIAL THANKS TO SCOTT LOBDELL

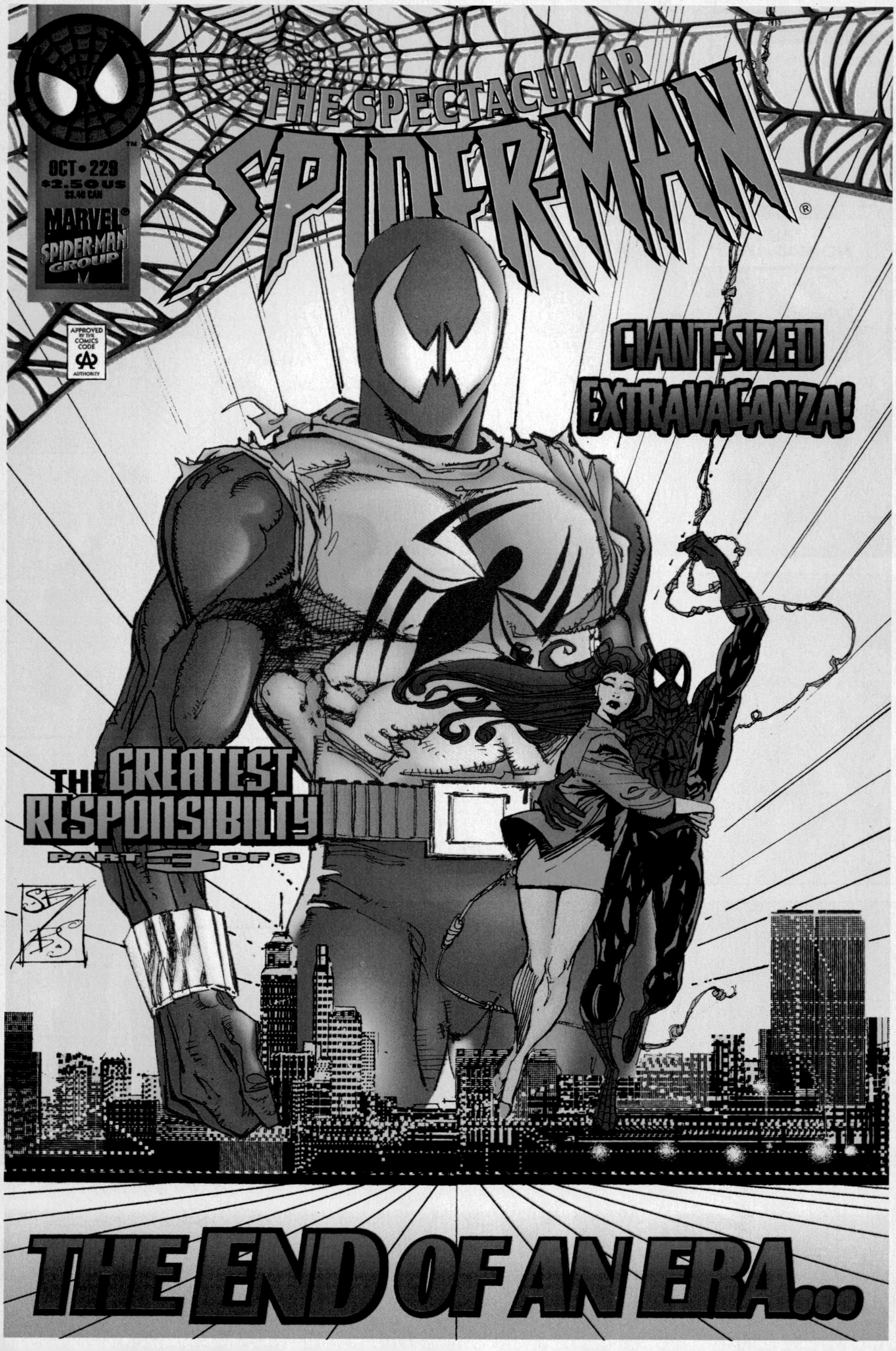
THE SPECTACULAR
SPIDER-MAN
OCT • 229
$2.50 US
$3.40 CAN
MARVEL
SPIDER-MAN GROUP
APPROVED BY THE COMICS CODE AUTHORITY
GIANT-SIZED EXTRAVAGANZA!
THE GREATEST RESPONSIBILTY
PART 3 OF 3
THE END OF AN ERA...

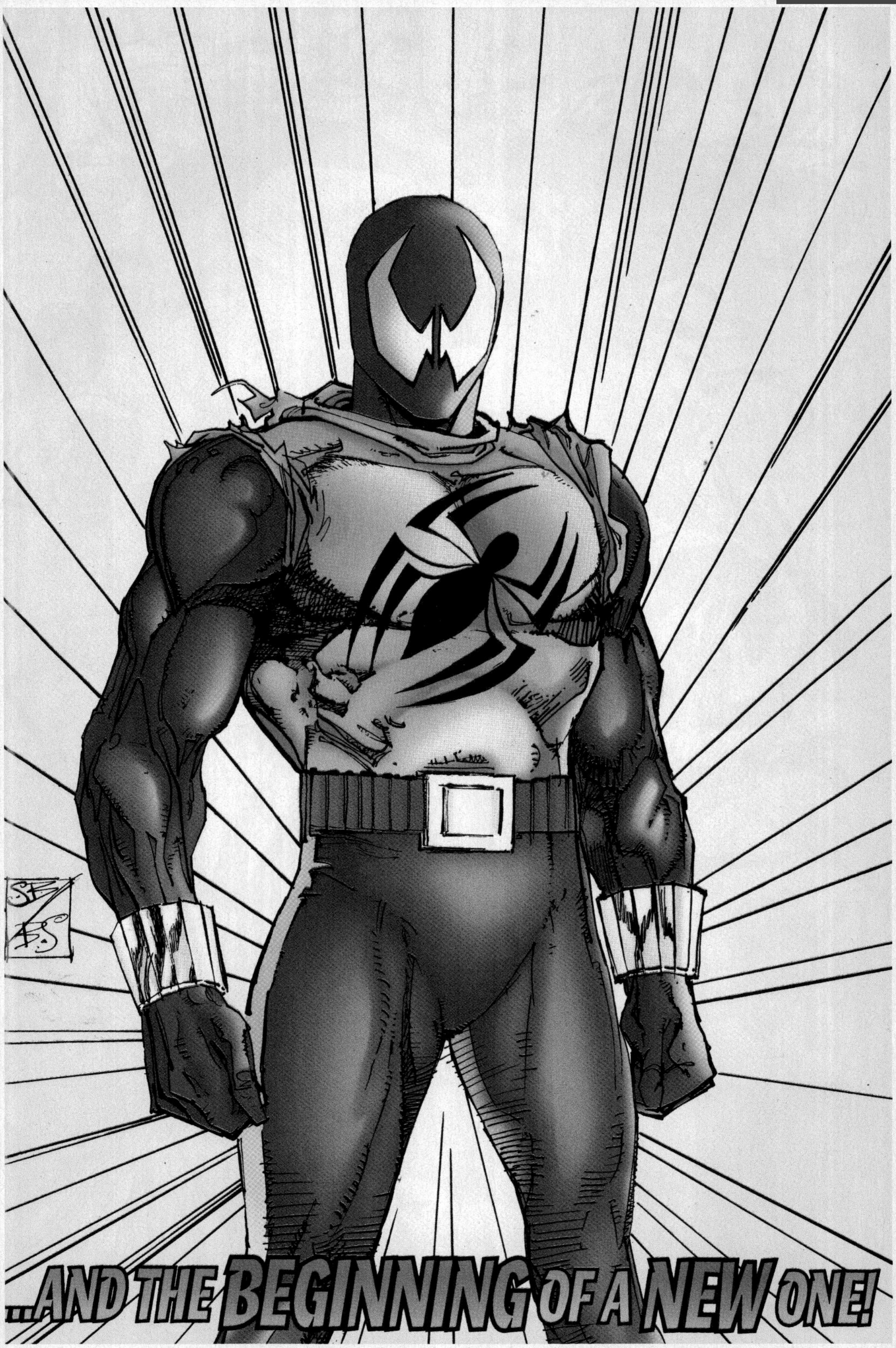
...AND THE BEGINNING OF A NEW ONE!

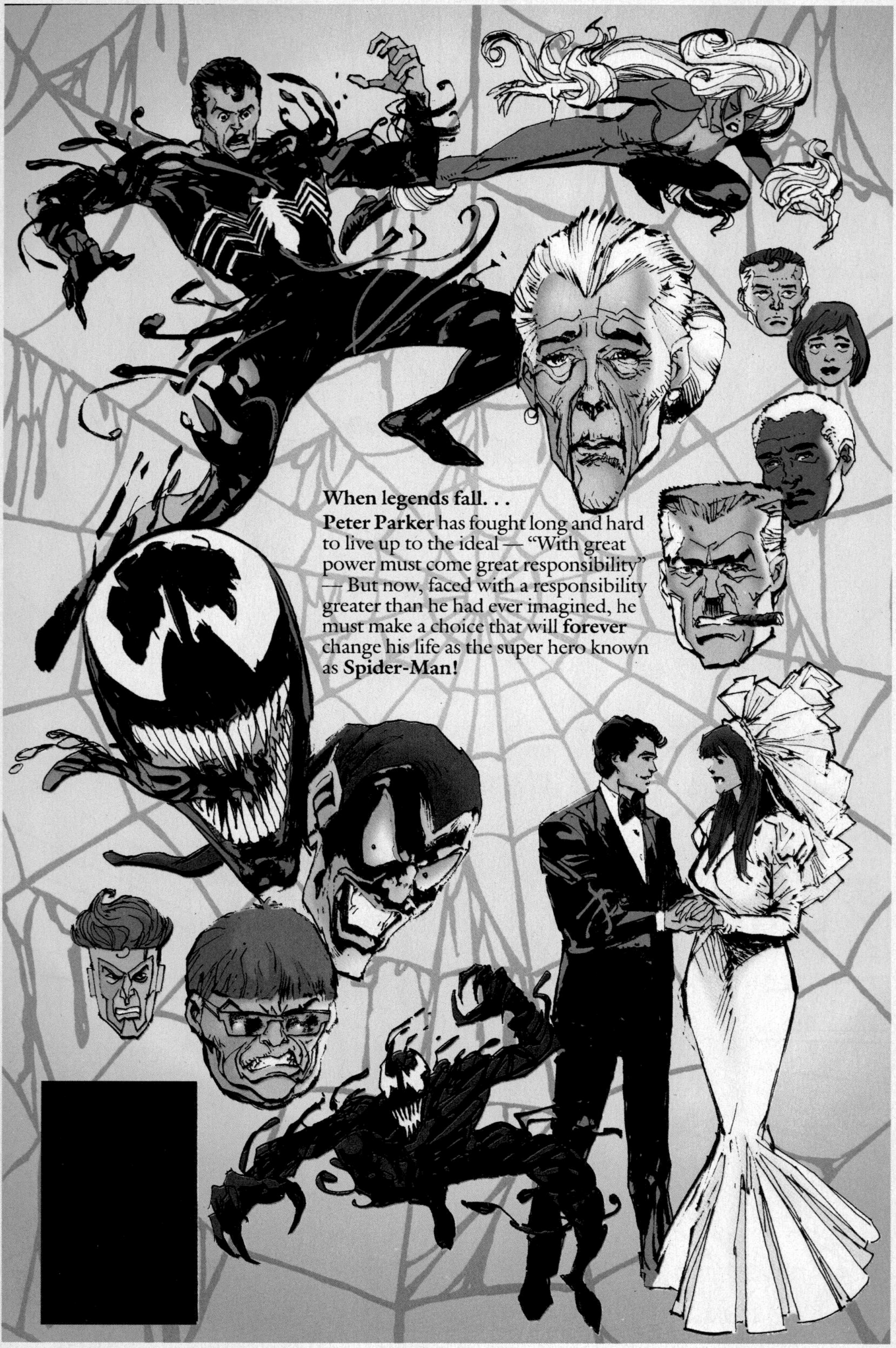
When legends fall. . .
Peter Parker has fought long and hard to live up to the ideal — "With great power must come great responsibility" — But now, faced with a responsibility greater than he had ever imagined, he must make a choice that will **forever** change his life as the super hero known as **Spider-Man!**

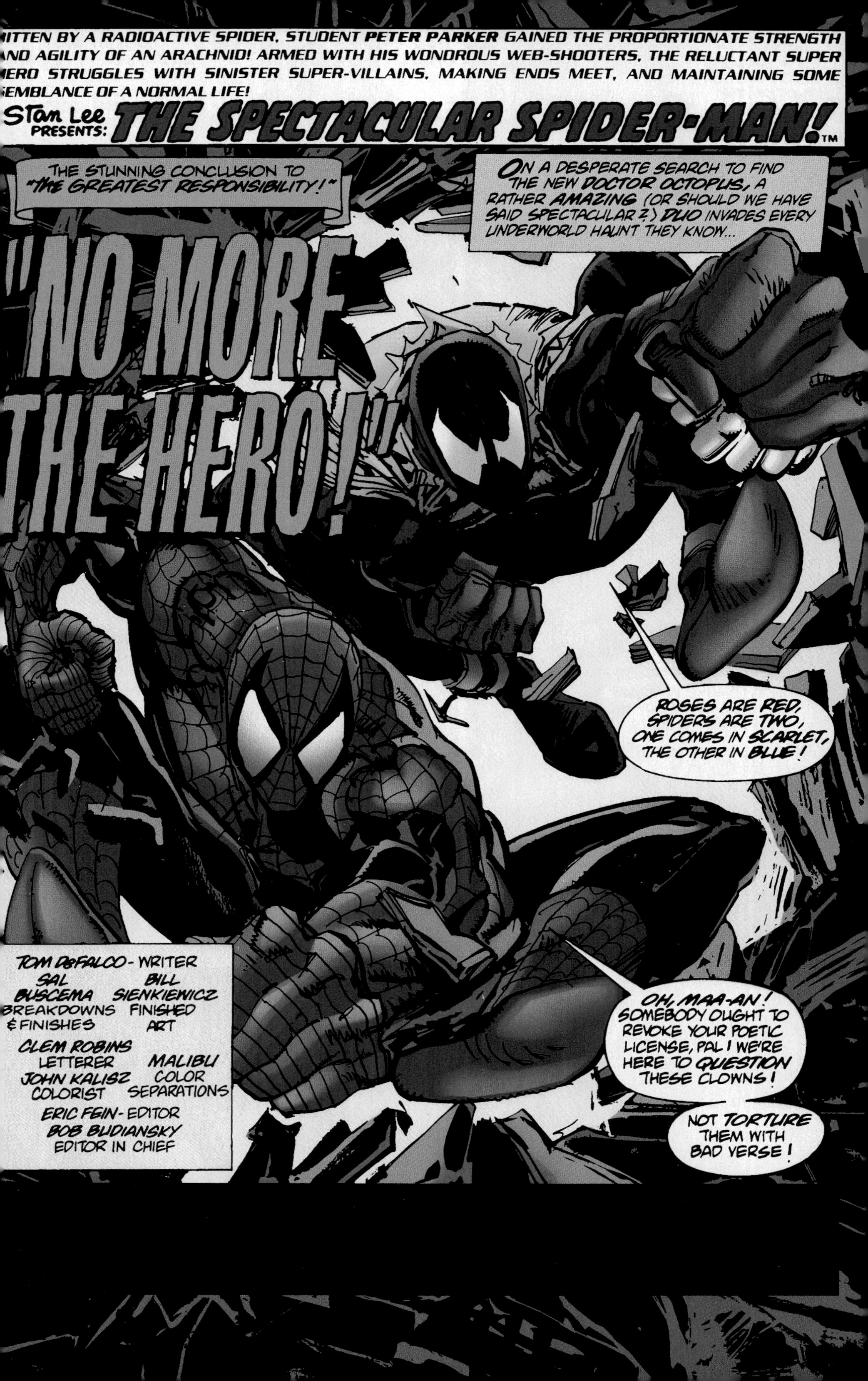
ITTEN BY A RADIOACTIVE SPIDER, STUDENT PETER PARKER GAINED THE PROPORTIONATE STRENGTH ND AGILITY OF AN ARACHNID! ARMED WITH HIS WONDROUS WEB-SHOOTERS, THE RELUCTANT SUPER ERO STRUGGLES WITH SINISTER SUPER-VILLAINS, MAKING ENDS MEET, AND MAINTAINING SOME EMBLANCE OF A NORMAL LIFE!
STAN LEE PRESENTS: THE SPECTACULAR SPIDER-MAN! TM
THE STUNNING CONCLUSION TO "THE GREATEST RESPONSIBILITY!"
ON A DESPERATE SEARCH TO FIND THE NEW DOCTOR OCTOPUS, A RATHER AMAZING (OR SHOULD WE HAVE SAID SPECTACULAR?) DUO INVADES EVERY UNDERWORLD HAUNT THEY KNOW...
"NO MORE THE HERO!"
ROSES ARE RED, SPIDERS ARE TWO, ONE COMES IN SCARLET, THE OTHER IN BLUE!
OH, MAA-AN! SOMEBODY OUGHT TO REVOKE YOUR POETIC LICENSE, PAL! WE'RE HERE TO QUESTION THESE CLOWNS!
NOT TORTURE THEM WITH BAD VERSE!
TOM DeFALCO - WRITER
SAL BUSCEMA BREAKDOWNS & FINISHES
BILL SIENKIEWICZ FINISHED ART
CLEM ROBINS LETTERER
JOHN KALISZ COLORIST
MALIBU COLOR SEPARATIONS
ERIC FEIN - EDITOR
BOB BUDIANSKY EDITOR IN CHIEF

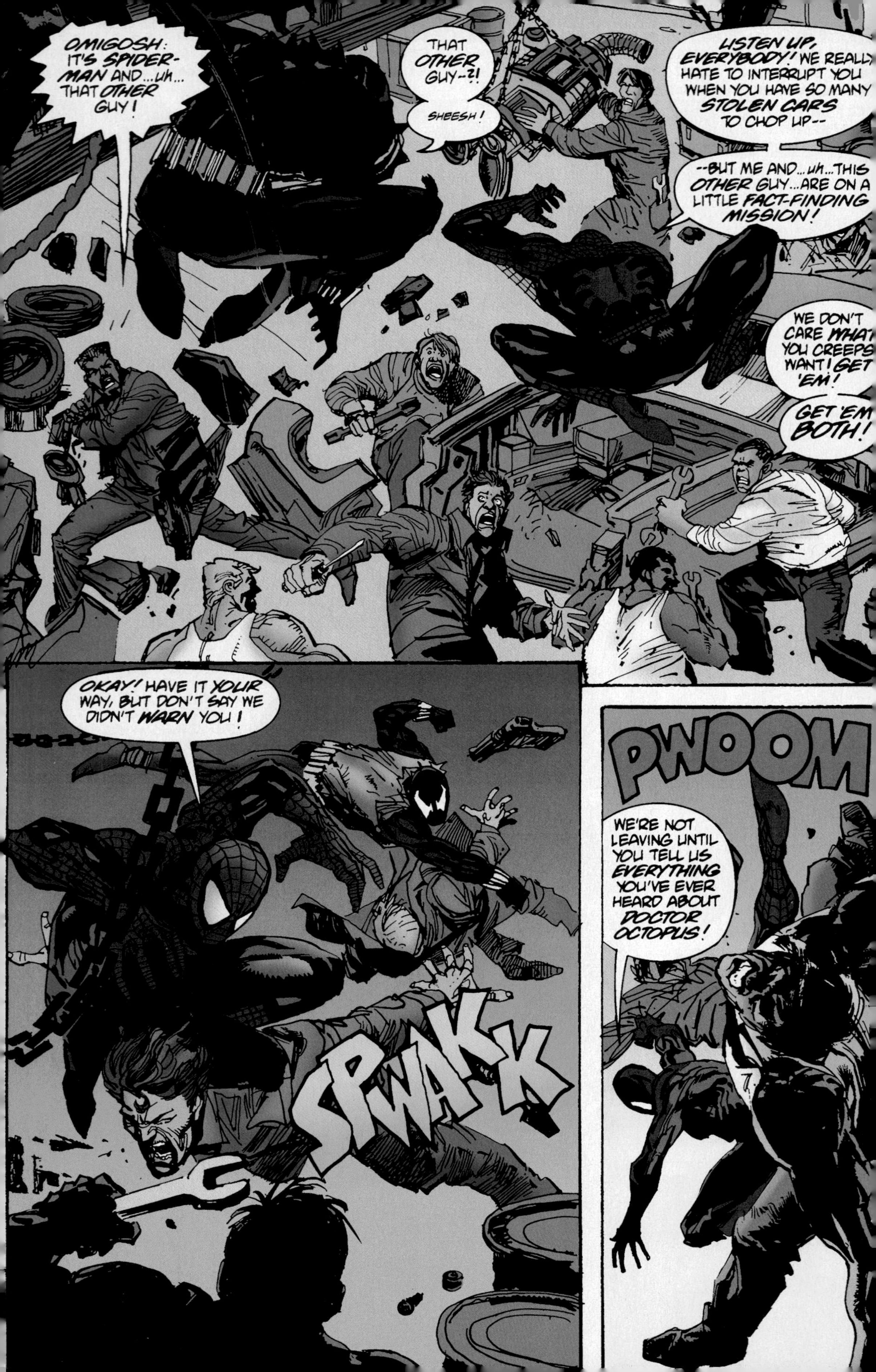

OMIGOSH: IT'S SPIDER-MAN AND...uh... THAT OTHER GUY!
THAT OTHER GUY--?!
SHEESH!
LISTEN UP, EVERYBODY! WE REALLY HATE TO INTERRUPT YOU WHEN YOU HAVE SO MANY STOLEN CARS TO CHOP UP--
--BUT ME AND...uh...THIS OTHER GUY...ARE ON A LITTLE FACT-FINDING MISSION!
WE DON'T CARE WHAT YOU CREEPS WANT! GET 'EM!
GET 'EM BOTH!
OKAY! HAVE IT YOUR WAY, BUT DON'T SAY WE DIDN'T WARN YOU!
SPWAKK
PWOOM
WE'RE NOT LEAVING UNTIL YOU TELL US EVERYTHING YOU'VE EVER HEARD ABOUT DOCTOR OCTOPUS!

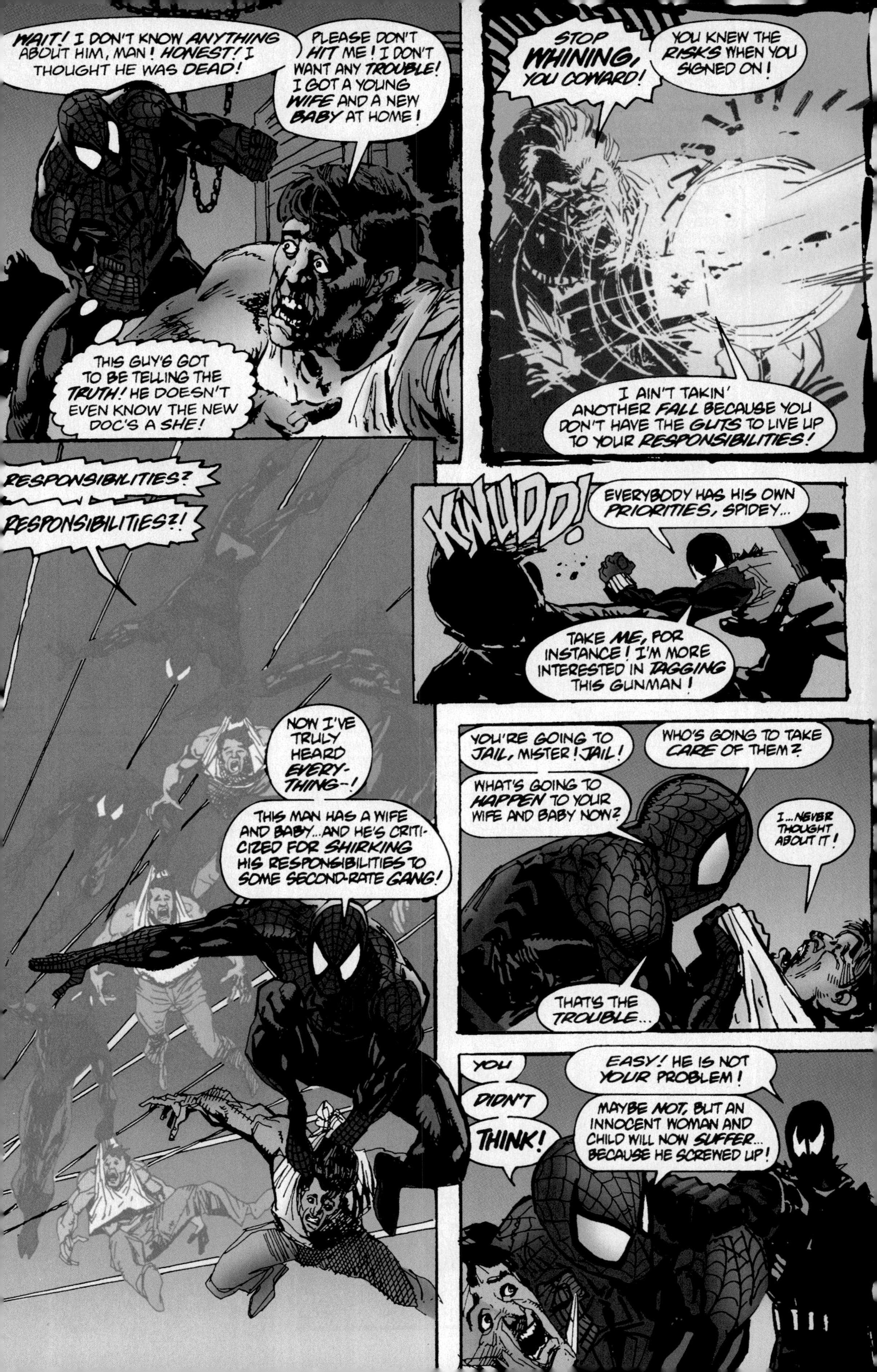

WAIT! I DON'T KNOW ANYTHING ABOUT HIM, MAN! HONEST! I THOUGHT HE WAS DEAD!
PLEASE DON'T HIT ME! I DON'T WANT ANY TROUBLE! I GOT A YOUNG WIFE AND A NEW BABY AT HOME!
THIS GUY'S GOT TO BE TELLING THE TRUTH! HE DOESN'T EVEN KNOW THE NEW DOC'S A SHE!
STOP WHINING, YOU COWARD!
YOU KNEW THE RISKS WHEN YOU SIGNED ON!
I AIN'T TAKIN' ANOTHER FALL BECAUSE YOU DON'T HAVE THE GUTS TO LIVE UP TO YOUR RESPONSIBILITIES!
RESPONSIBILITIES?
RESPONSIBILITIES?!
KNUDD!
EVERYBODY HAS HIS OWN PRIORITIES, SPIDEY...
TAKE ME, FOR INSTANCE! I'M MORE INTERESTED IN TAGGING THIS GUNMAN!
NOW I'VE TRULY HEARD EVERY-THING--!
THIS MAN HAS A WIFE AND BABY...AND HE'S CRITI-CIZED FOR SHIRKING HIS RESPONSIBILITIES TO SOME SECOND-RATE GANG!
YOU'RE GOING TO JAIL, MISTER! JAIL!
WHO'S GOING TO TAKE CARE OF THEM?
WHAT'S GOING TO HAPPEN TO YOUR WIFE AND BABY NOW?
I...NEVER THOUGHT ABOUT IT!
THAT'S THE TROUBLE...
YOU
DIDN'T
THINK!
EASY! HE IS NOT YOUR PROBLEM!
MAYBE NOT, BUT AN INNOCENT WOMAN AND CHILD WILL NOW SUFFER... BECAUSE HE SCREWED UP!

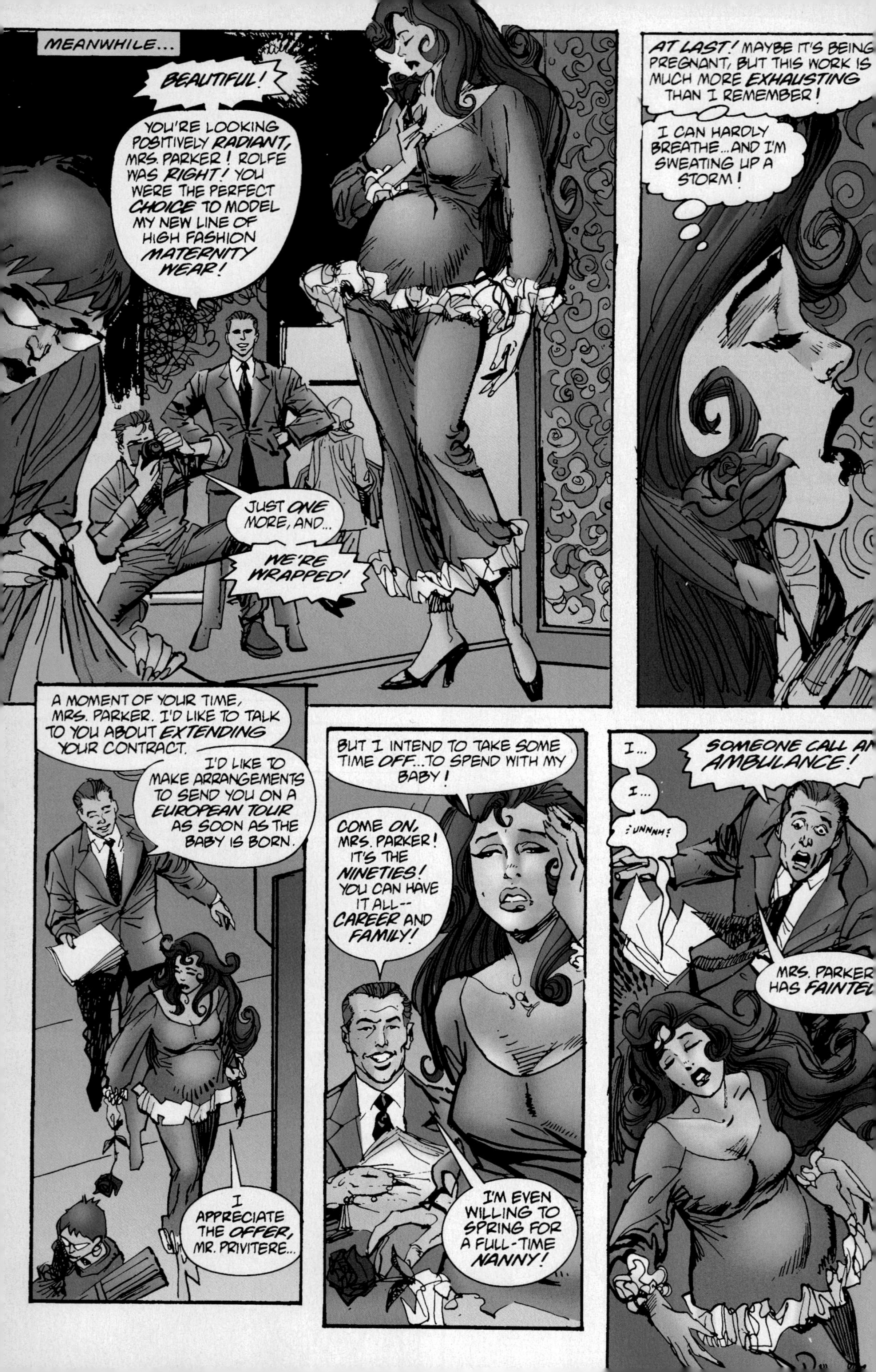

MEANWHILE...
BEAUTIFUL!
YOU'RE LOOKING POSITIVELY RADIANT, MRS. PARKER! ROLFE WAS RIGHT! YOU WERE THE PERFECT CHOICE TO MODEL MY NEW LINE OF HIGH FASHION MATERNITY WEAR!
JUST ONE MORE, AND...
WE'RE WRAPPED!
AT LAST! MAYBE IT'S BEING PREGNANT, BUT THIS WORK IS MUCH MORE EXHAUSTING THAN I REMEMBER!
I CAN HARDLY BREATHE...AND I'M SWEATING UP A STORM!
A MOMENT OF YOUR TIME, MRS. PARKER. I'D LIKE TO TALK TO YOU ABOUT EXTENDING YOUR CONTRACT.
I'D LIKE TO MAKE ARRANGEMENTS TO SEND YOU ON A EUROPEAN TOUR AS SOON AS THE BABY IS BORN.
I APPRECIATE THE OFFER, MR. PRIVITERE...
BUT I INTEND TO TAKE SOME TIME OFF...TO SPEND WITH MY BABY!
COME ON, MRS. PARKER! IT'S THE NINETIES! YOU CAN HAVE IT ALL-- CAREER AND FAMILY!
I'M EVEN WILLING TO SPRING FOR A FULL-TIME NANNY!
I...
I...
UNNNH!
SOMEONE CALL AN AMBULANCE!
MRS. PARKER HAS FAINTED

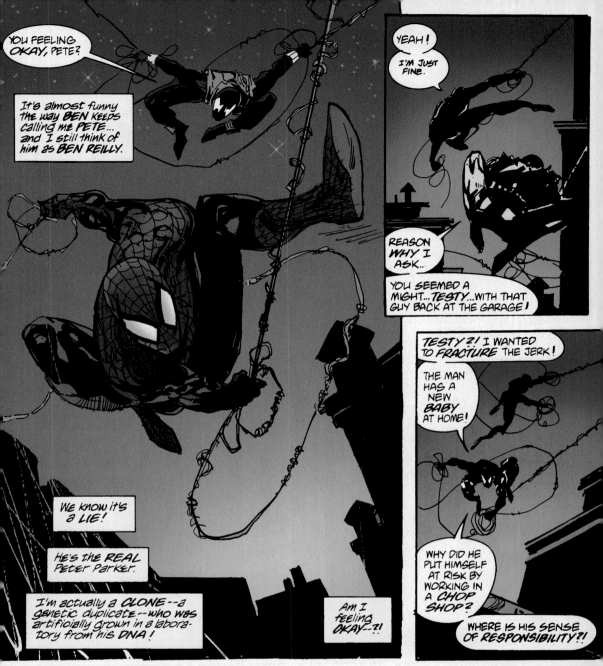

YOU FEELING *OKAY*, PETE?

It's almost funny the way BEN keeps calling me PETE... and I still think of him as BEN REILLY.

We know it's a LIE!

He's the REAL Peter Parker.

I'm actually a CLONE--a GENETIC duplicate--who was artificially grown in a laboratory from his DNA!

Am I feeling *OKAY*--?!

YEAH! I'M JUST FINE.

REASON *WHY* I ASK...

YOU SEEMED A *MIGHT...TESTY*...WITH THAT GUY BACK AT THE GARAGE!

TESTY?! I WANTED TO *FRACTURE* THE JERK!

THE MAN HAS A NEW *BABY* AT HOME!

WHY DID HE PUT HIMSELF AT RISK BY WORKING IN A *CHOP SHOP?*

WHERE IS HIS SENSE OF *RESPONSIBILITY?!*

ARE YOU-- SURE--

--WE'RE STILL TALKING ABOUT *HIM?!*

Good question!

MARY JANE--!

WE'RE *HOME,* HONEY!

MARY JANE--!

THAT'S ODD! SHE SHOULD BE *BACK* FROM HER PHOTO SHOOT!

R RRING!

MAYBE THAT'S *HER* NOW--!

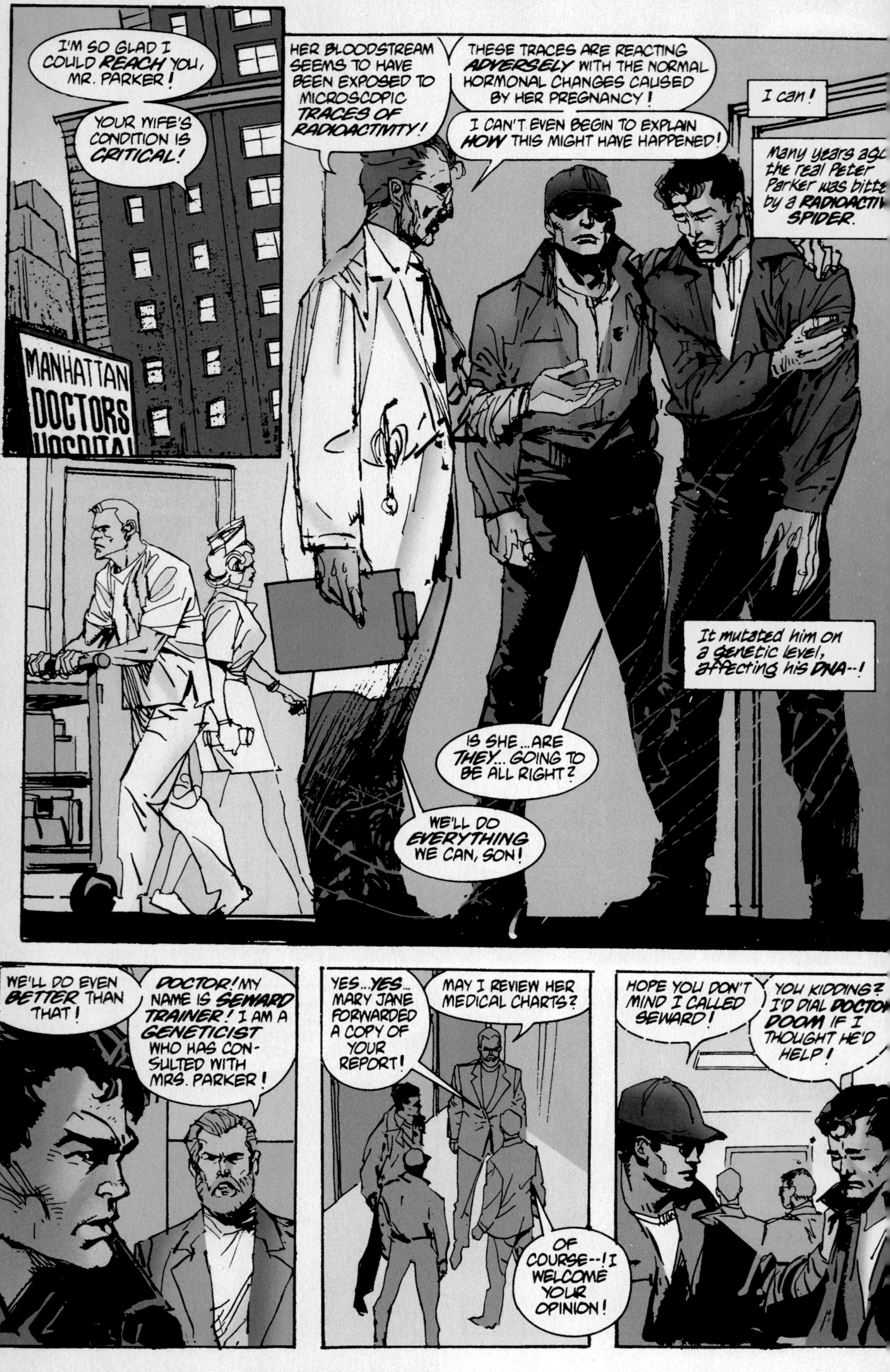
I'M SO GLAD I COULD REACH YOU, MR. PARKER!
YOUR WIFE'S CONDITION IS CRITICAL!
MANHATTAN DOCTORS HOSPITAL
HER BLOODSTREAM SEEMS TO HAVE BEEN EXPOSED TO MICROSCOPIC TRACES OF RADIOACTIVITY!
THESE TRACES ARE REACTING ADVERSELY WITH THE NORMAL HORMONAL CHANGES CAUSED BY HER PREGNANCY!
I CAN'T EVEN BEGIN TO EXPLAIN HOW THIS MIGHT HAVE HAPPENED!
I can!
Many years ago the real Peter Parker was bitten by a RADIOACTIVE SPIDER.
It mutated him on a genetic level, affecting his DNA--!
IS SHE ...ARE THEY... GOING TO BE ALL RIGHT?
WE'LL DO EVERYTHING WE CAN, SON!
WE'LL DO EVEN BETTER THAN THAT!
DOCTOR! MY NAME IS SEWARD TRAINER! I AM A GENETICIST WHO HAS CONSULTED WITH MRS. PARKER!
YES...YES... MARY JANE FORWARDED A COPY OF YOUR REPORT!
MAY I REVIEW HER MEDICAL CHARTS?
OF COURSE--! I WELCOME YOUR OPINION!
HOPE YOU DON'T MIND I CALLED SEWARD!
YOU KIDDING? I'D DIAL DOCTOR DOOM IF I THOUGHT HE'D HELP!

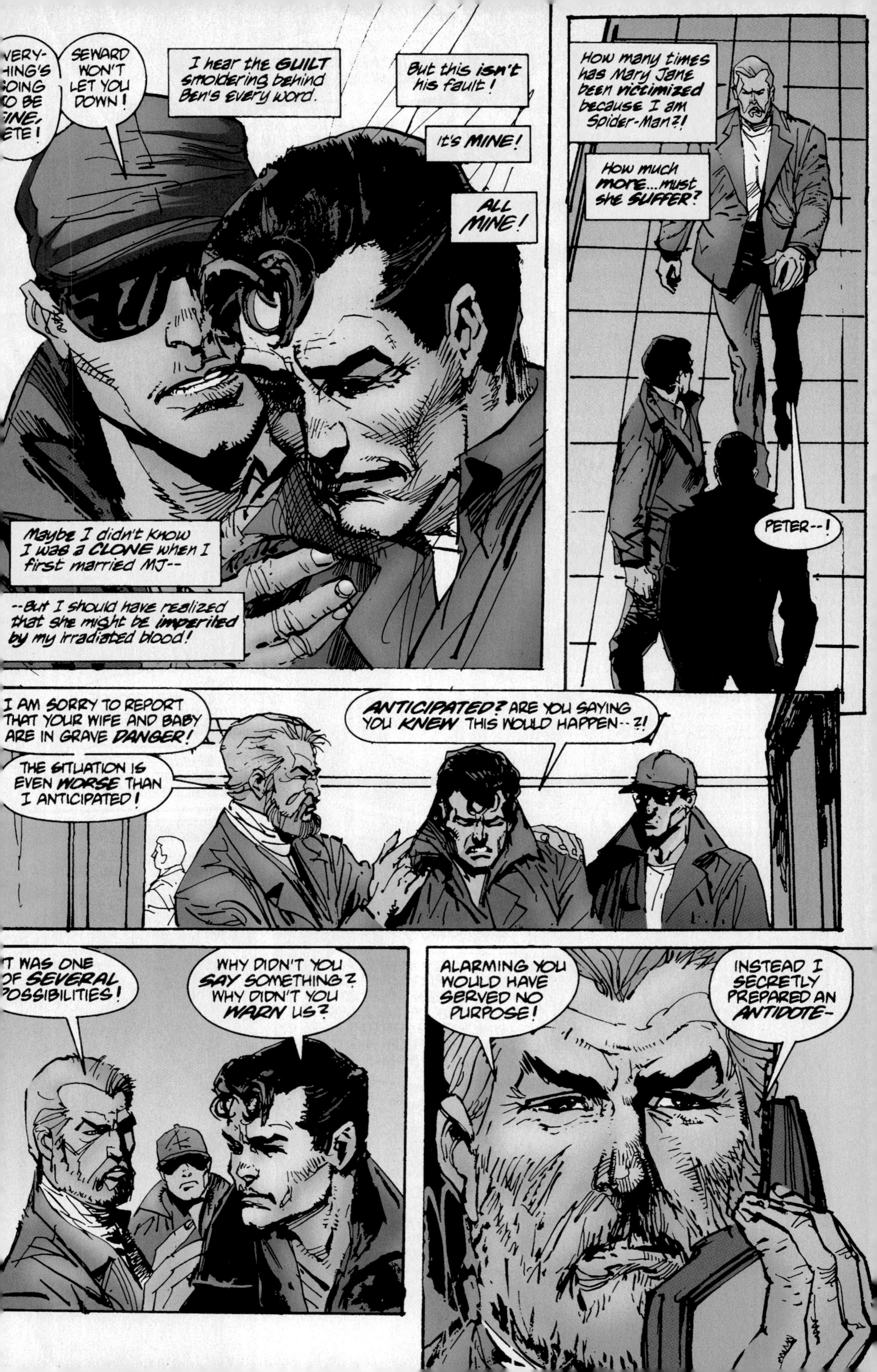

VERY-
THING'S
GOING
TO BE
FINE,
PETE!
SEWARD WON'T LET YOU DOWN!
I hear the GUILT smoldering behind Ben's every word.
But this isn't his fault!
It's MINE!
ALL MINE!
How many times has Mary Jane been victimized because I am Spider-Man?!
How much more... must she SUFFER?
Maybe I didn't know I was a CLONE when I first married MJ--
--But I should have realized that she might be imperiled by my irradiated blood!
PETER--!
I AM SORRY TO REPORT THAT YOUR WIFE AND BABY ARE IN GRAVE DANGER!
THE SITUATION IS EVEN WORSE THAN I ANTICIPATED!
ANTICIPATED? ARE YOU SAYING YOU KNEW THIS WOULD HAPPEN--?!
IT WAS ONE OF SEVERAL POSSIBILITIES!
WHY DIDN'T YOU SAY SOMETHING? WHY DIDN'T YOU WARN US?
ALARMING YOU WOULD HAVE SERVED NO PURPOSE!
INSTEAD I SECRETLY PREPARED AN ANTIDOTE-

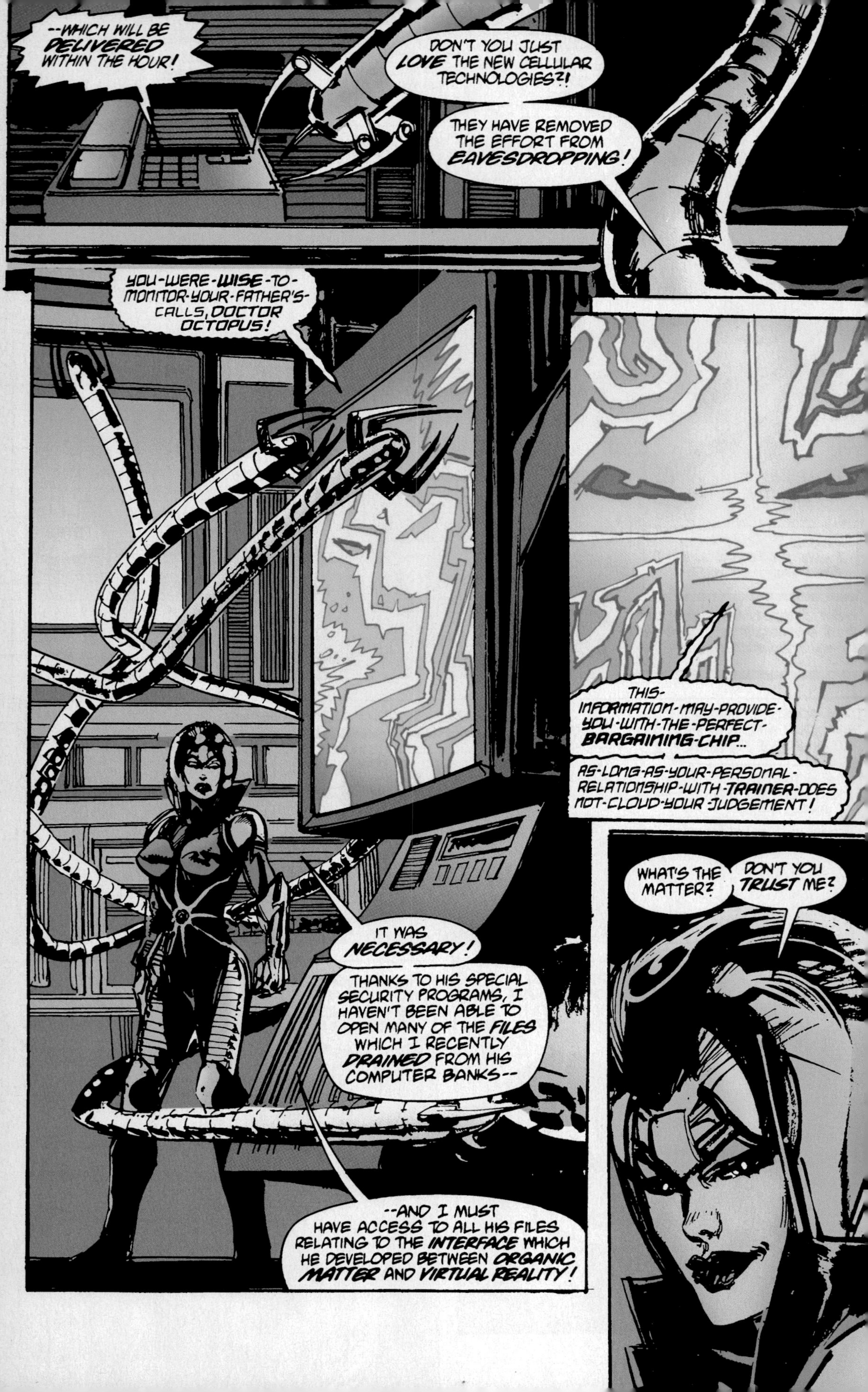
--WHICH WILL BE DELIVERED WITHIN THE HOUR!
DON'T YOU JUST LOVE THE NEW CELLULAR TECHNOLOGIES?!
THEY HAVE REMOVED THE EFFORT FROM EAVESDROPPING!
YOU-WERE-WISE-TO-MONITOR-YOUR-FATHER'S-CALLS, DOCTOR OCTOPUS!
IT WAS NECESSARY!
THANKS TO HIS SPECIAL SECURITY PROGRAMS, I HAVEN'T BEEN ABLE TO OPEN MANY OF THE FILES WHICH I RECENTLY DRAINED FROM HIS COMPUTER BANKS--
--AND I MUST HAVE ACCESS TO ALL HIS FILES RELATING TO THE INTERFACE WHICH HE DEVELOPED BETWEEN ORGANIC MATTER AND VIRTUAL REALITY!
THIS-INFORMATION-MAY-PROVIDE-YOU-WITH-THE-PERFECT-BARGAINING-CHIP...
AS-LONG-AS-YOUR-PERSONAL-RELATIONSHIP-WITH-TRAINER-DOES NOT-CLOUD-YOUR-JUDGEMENT!
WHAT'S THE MATTER?
DON'T YOU TRUST ME?

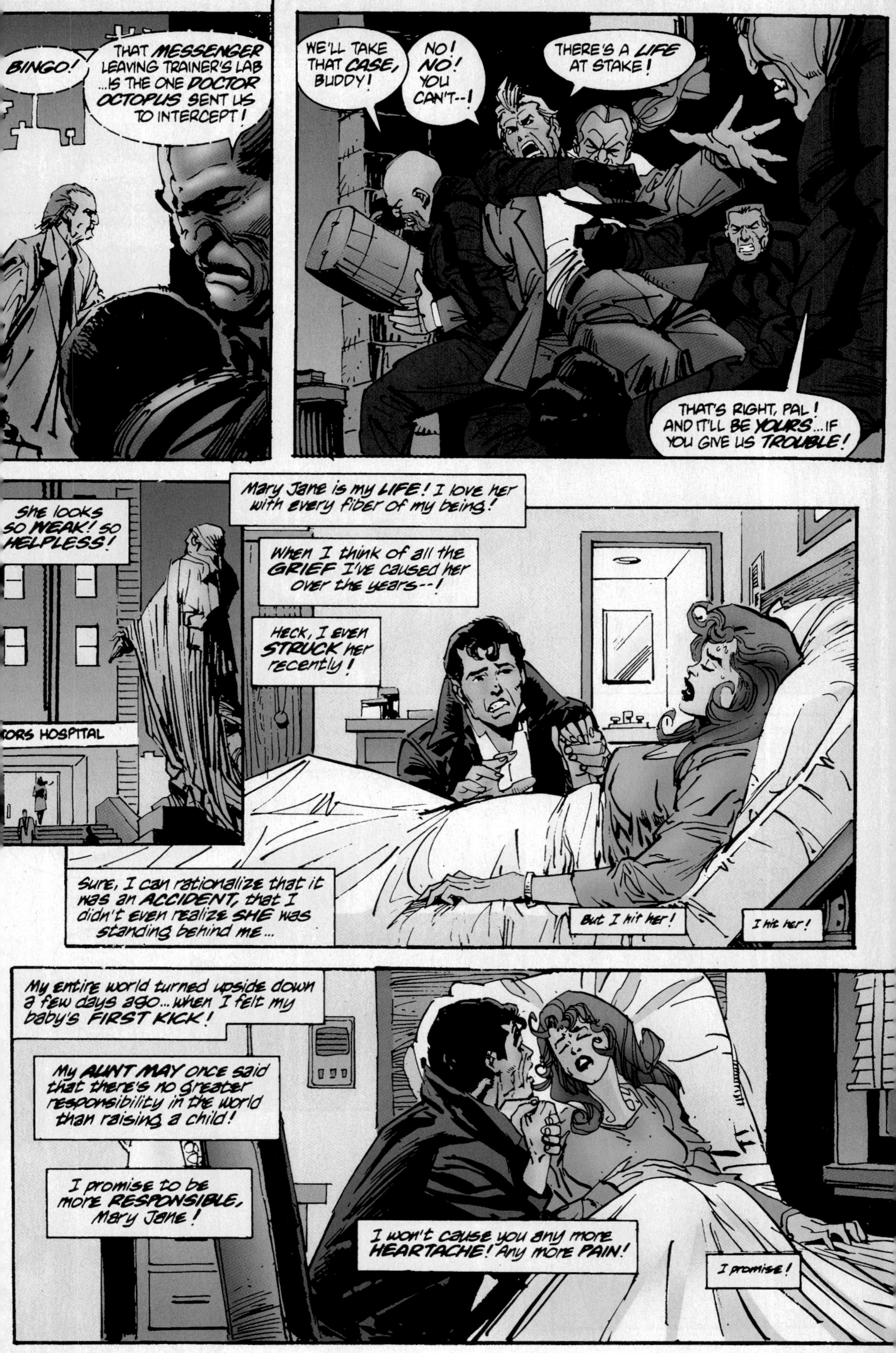
BINGO!
THAT MESSENGER LEAVING TRAINER'S LAB ...IS THE ONE DOCTOR OCTOPUS SENT US TO INTERCEPT!
WE'LL TAKE THAT CASE, BUDDY!
NO! NO! YOU CAN'T--!
THERE'S A LIFE AT STAKE!
THAT'S RIGHT, PAL! AND IT'LL BE YOURS... IF YOU GIVE US TROUBLE!
Mary Jane is my LIFE! I love her with every fiber of my being!
She looks so WEAK! So HELPLESS!
When I think of all the GRIEF I've caused her over the years--!
Heck, I even STRUCK her recently!
CTORS HOSPITAL
Sure, I can rationalize that it was an ACCIDENT, that I didn't even realize SHE was standing behind me...
But I hit her!
I hit her!
My entire world turned upside down a few days ago... when I felt my baby's FIRST KICK!
My AUNT MAY once said that there's no greater responsibility in the world than raising a child!
I promise to be more RESPONSIBLE, Mary Jane!
I won't cause you any more HEARTACHE! Any more PAIN!
I promise!

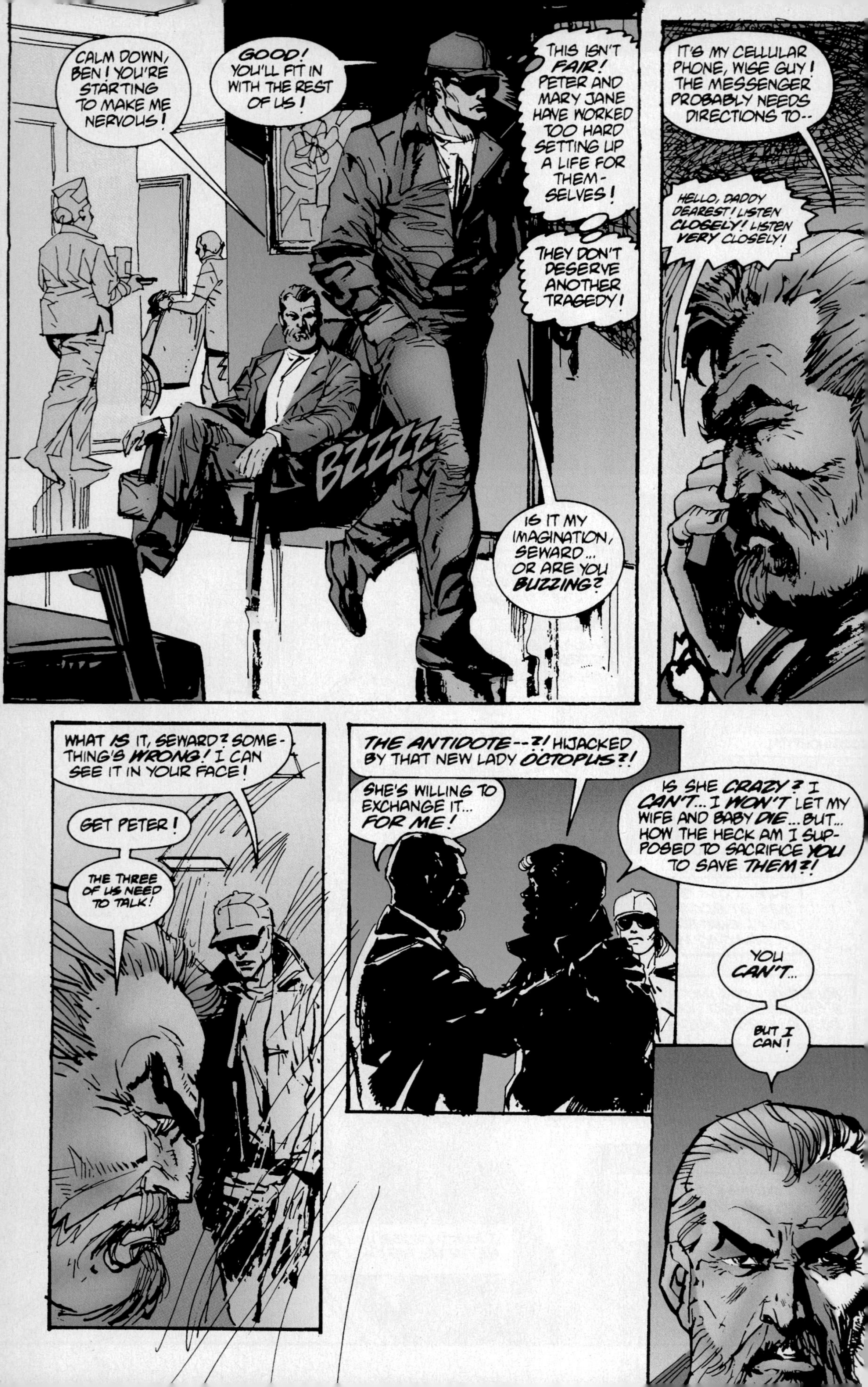

CALM DOWN, BEN! YOU'RE STARTING TO MAKE ME NERVOUS!
GOOD! YOU'LL FIT IN WITH THE REST OF US!
THIS ISN'T FAIR! PETER AND MARY JANE HAVE WORKED TOO HARD SETTING UP A LIFE FOR THEMSELVES!
THEY DON'T DESERVE ANOTHER TRAGEDY!
BZZZZ
IS IT MY IMAGINATION, SEWARD... OR ARE YOU BUZZING?
IT'S MY CELLULAR PHONE, WISE GUY! THE MESSENGER PROBABLY NEEDS DIRECTIONS TO--
HELLO, DADDY DEAREST! LISTEN CLOSELY! LISTEN VERY CLOSELY!
WHAT IS IT, SEWARD? SOMETHING'S WRONG! I CAN SEE IT IN YOUR FACE!
GET PETER!
THE THREE OF US NEED TO TALK!
THE ANTIDOTE--?! HIJACKED BY THAT NEW LADY OCTOPUS?!
SHE'S WILLING TO EXCHANGE IT... FOR ME!
IS SHE CRAZY? I CAN'T... I WON'T LET MY WIFE AND BABY DIE... BUT... HOW THE HECK AM I SUPPOSED TO SACRIFICE YOU TO SAVE THEM?!
YOU CAN'T...
BUT I CAN!

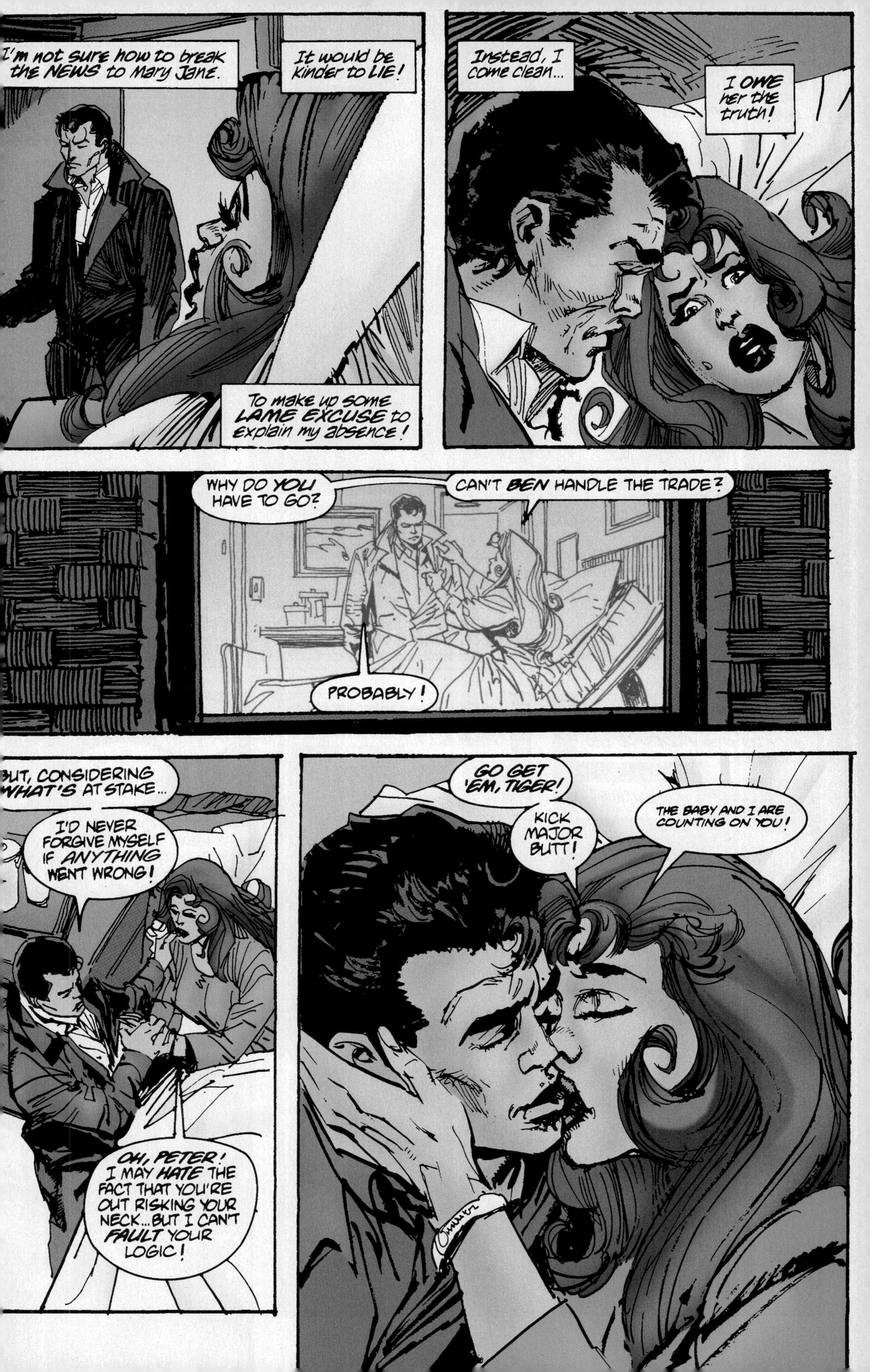

I'm not sure how to break the NEWS to Mary Jane.
It would be kinder to LIE!
To make up some LAME EXCUSE to explain my absence!
Instead, I come clean...
I OWE her the truth!
WHY DO YOU HAVE TO GO?
CAN'T BEN HANDLE THE TRADE?
PROBABLY!
BUT, CONSIDERING WHAT'S AT STAKE...
I'D NEVER FORGIVE MYSELF IF ANYTHING WENT WRONG!
OH, PETER! I MAY HATE THE FACT THAT YOU'RE OUT RISKING YOUR NECK...BUT I CAN'T FAULT YOUR LOGIC!
GO GET 'EM, TIGER!
KICK MAJOR BUTT!
THE BABY AND I ARE COUNTING ON YOU!

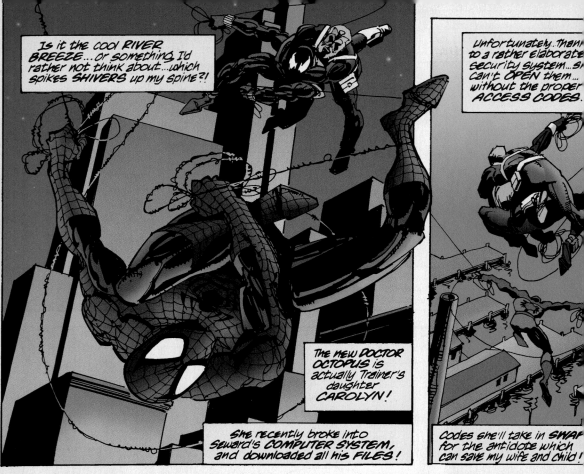

Is it the cool RIVER BREEZE...or something I'd rather not think about...which spikes SHIVERS up my spine?!

The new DOCTOR OCTOPUS is actually Trainer's daughter CAROLYN!

She recently broke into Seward's COMPUTER SYSTEM, and downloaded all his FILES!

Unfortunately...thanks to a rather elaborate security system...she can't OPEN them...without the proper ACCESS CODES.

Codes she'll take in SWAP for the antidote which can save my wife and child!

All Ben and I have to do...is POUNCE on her people...as soon as they PRODUCE the antidote!

Simple, huh?

So why is my heart rattling my chest like a hyperactive PINBALL?

STAND STILL.

WHAT IS THIS--?!

A PRECAUTION. WE HEAR YOU ENJOY THE COMPANY OF INSECTS!

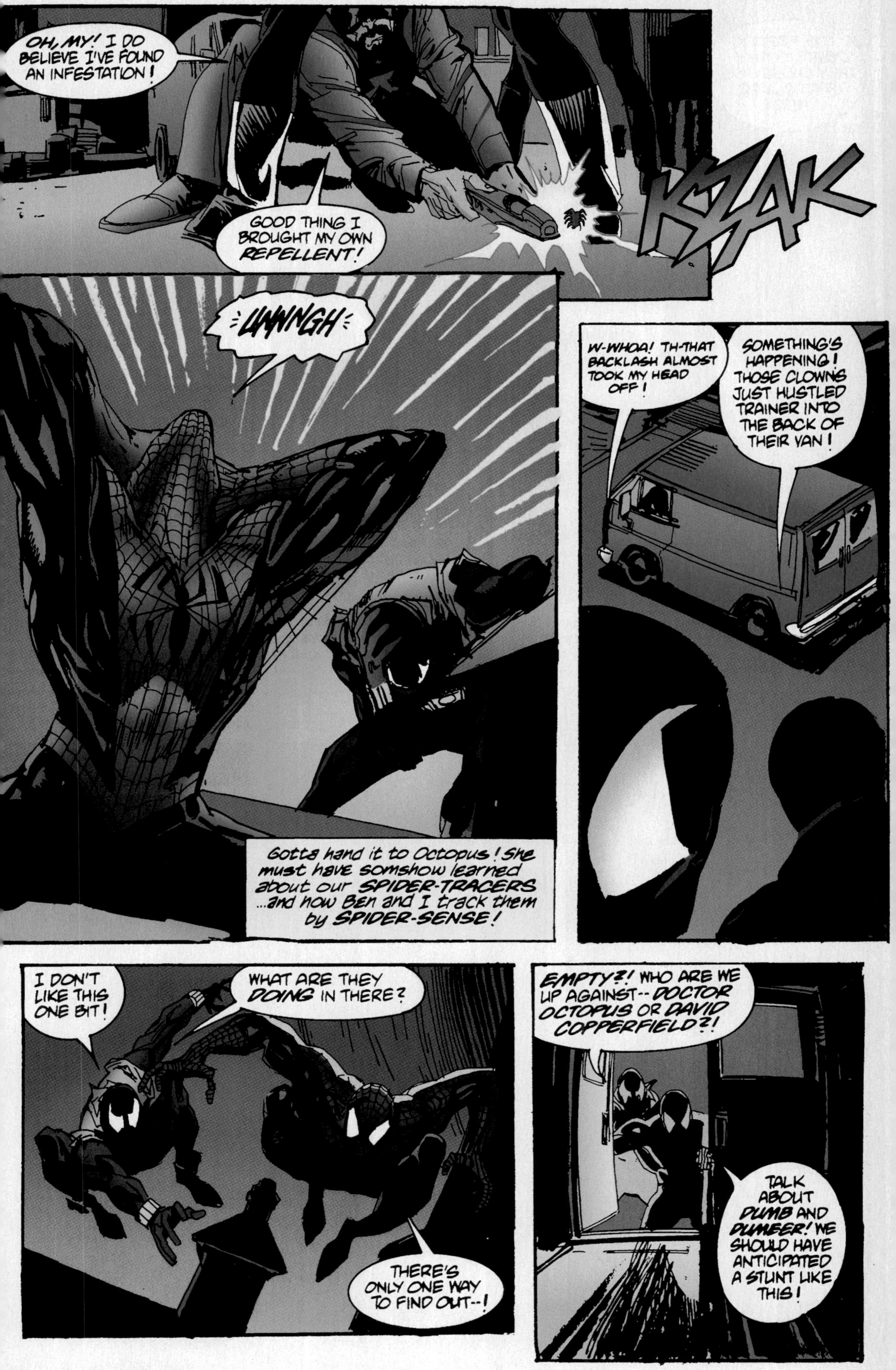

OH, MY! I DO BELIEVE I'VE FOUND AN INFESTATION!
GOOD THING I BROUGHT MY OWN REPELLENT!
KZAK
UNNNGH
Gotta hand it to Octopus! She must have somehow learned about our SPIDER-TRACERS ...and how Ben and I track them by SPIDER-SENSE!
W-WHOA! TH-THAT BACKLASH ALMOST TOOK MY HEAD OFF!
SOMETHING'S HAPPENING! THOSE CLOWNS JUST HUSTLED TRAINER INTO THE BACK OF THEIR VAN!
I DON'T LIKE THIS ONE BIT!
WHAT ARE THEY DOING IN THERE?
THERE'S ONLY ONE WAY TO FIND OUT--!
EMPTY?! WHO ARE WE UP AGAINST--DOCTOR OCTOPUS OR DAVID COPPERFIELD?!
TALK ABOUT DUMB AND DUMBER! WE SHOULD HAVE ANTICIPATED A STUNT LIKE THIS!

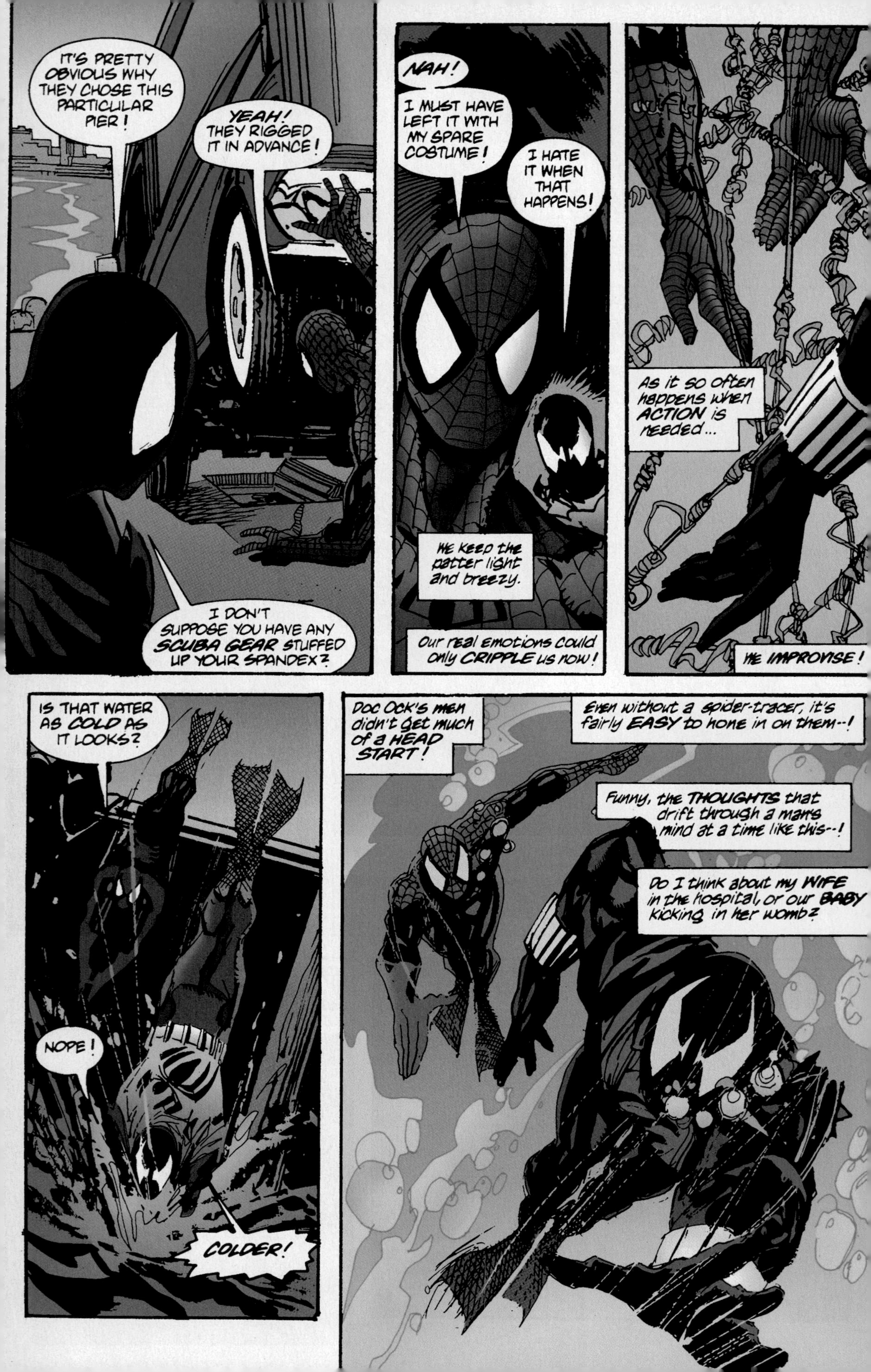

IT'S PRETTY OBVIOUS WHY THEY CHOSE THIS PARTICULAR PIER!
YEAH! THEY RIGGED IT IN ADVANCE!
I DON'T SUPPOSE YOU HAVE ANY SCUBA GEAR STUFFED UP YOUR SPANDEX?
NAH! I MUST HAVE LEFT IT WITH MY SPARE COSTUME!
I HATE IT WHEN THAT HAPPENS!
We keep the patter light and breezy.
Our real emotions could only CRIPPLE us now!
As it so often happens when ACTION is needed...
We IMPROVISE!
IS THAT WATER AS COLD AS IT LOOKS?
NOPE!
COLDER!
Doc Ock's men didn't get much of a HEAD START!
Even without a spider-tracer, it's fairly EASY to hone in on them--!
Funny, the THOUGHTS that drift through a man's mind at a time like this--!
Do I think about my WIFE in the hospital, or our BABY kicking in her womb?

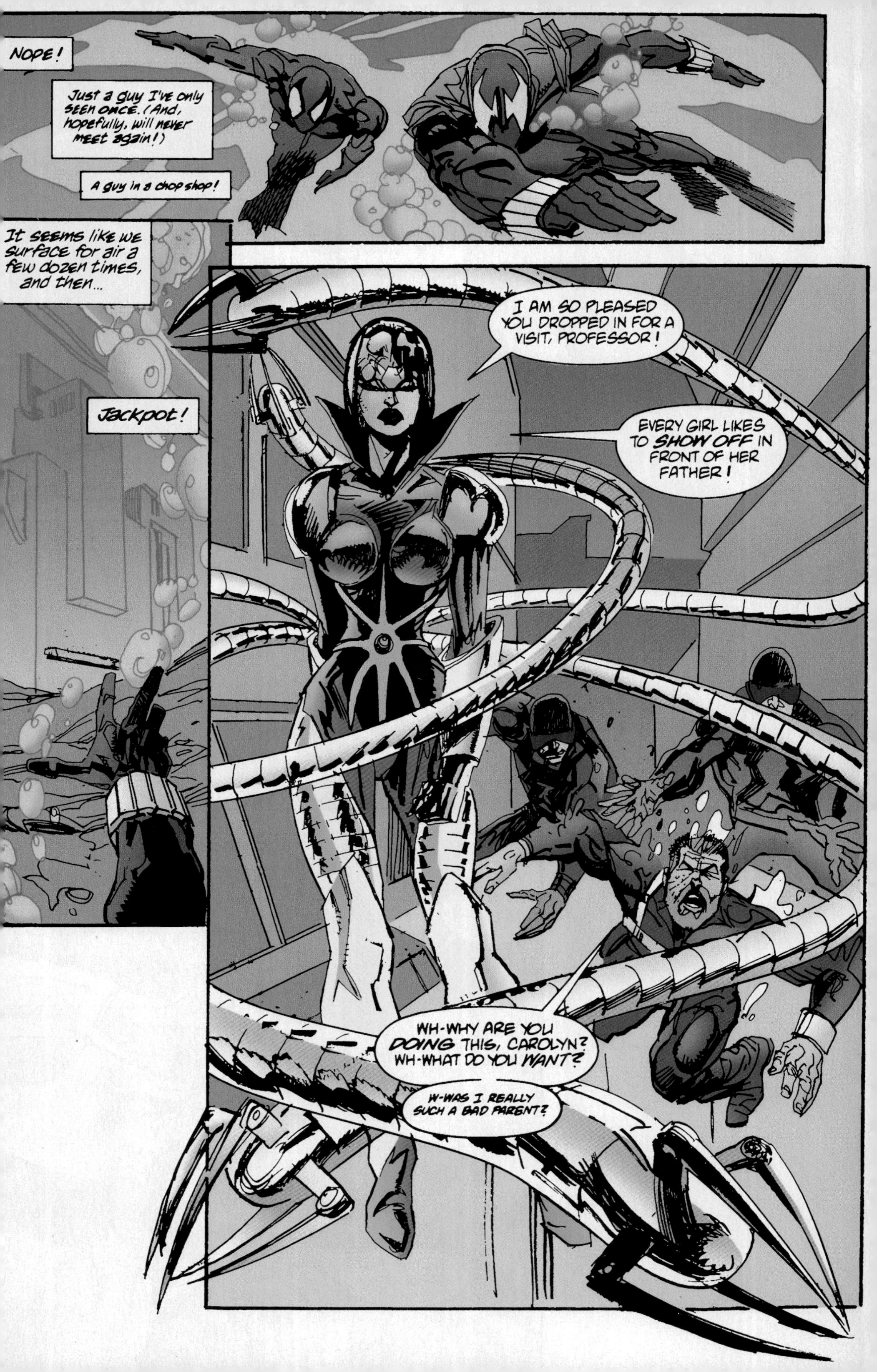

NOPE!
Just a guy I've only seen once. (And, hopefully, will never meet again!)
A guy in a chop shop!
It seems like we surface for air a few dozen times, and then...
Jackpot!
I AM SO PLEASED YOU DROPPED IN FOR A VISIT, PROFESSOR!
EVERY GIRL LIKES TO SHOW OFF IN FRONT OF HER FATHER!
WH-WHY ARE YOU DOING THIS, CAROLYN? WH-WHAT DO YOU WANT?
W-WAS I REALLY SUCH A BAD PARENT?

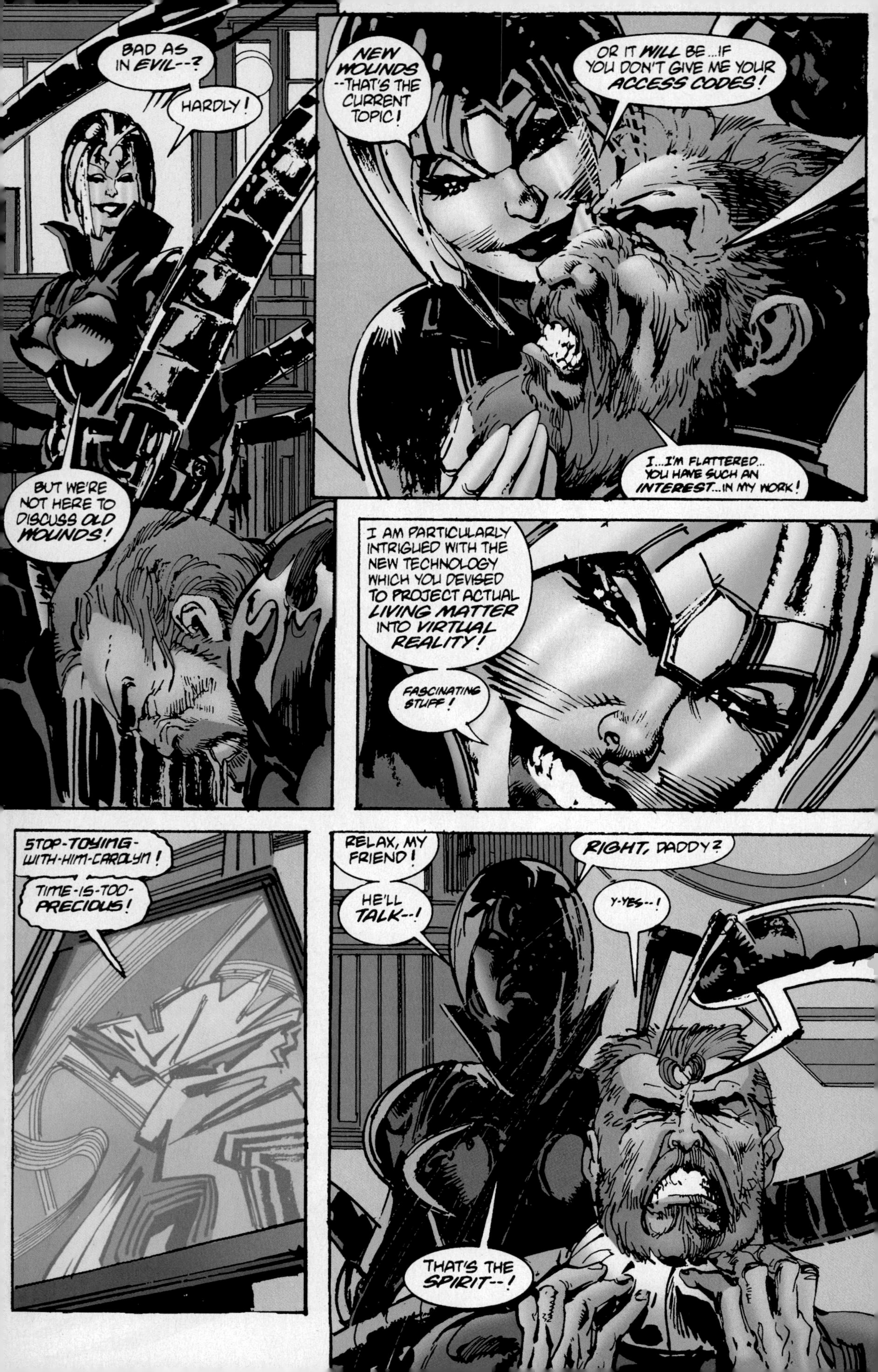
BAD AS IN EVIL--?
HARDLY!
NEW WOUNDS --THAT'S THE CURRENT TOPIC!
OR IT WILL BE...IF YOU DON'T GIVE ME YOUR ACCESS CODES!
I...I'M FLATTERED... YOU HAVE SUCH AN INTEREST...IN MY WORK!
BUT WE'RE NOT HERE TO DISCUSS OLD WOUNDS!
I AM PARTICULARLY INTRIGUED WITH THE NEW TECHNOLOGY WHICH YOU DEVISED TO PROJECT ACTUAL LIVING MATTER INTO VIRTUAL REALITY!
FASCINATING STUFF!
STOP-TOYING-WITH-HIM-CAROLYN!
TIME-IS-TOO-PRECIOUS!
RELAX, MY FRIEND!
HE'LL TALK--!
RIGHT, DADDY?
Y-YES--!
THAT'S THE SPIRIT--!

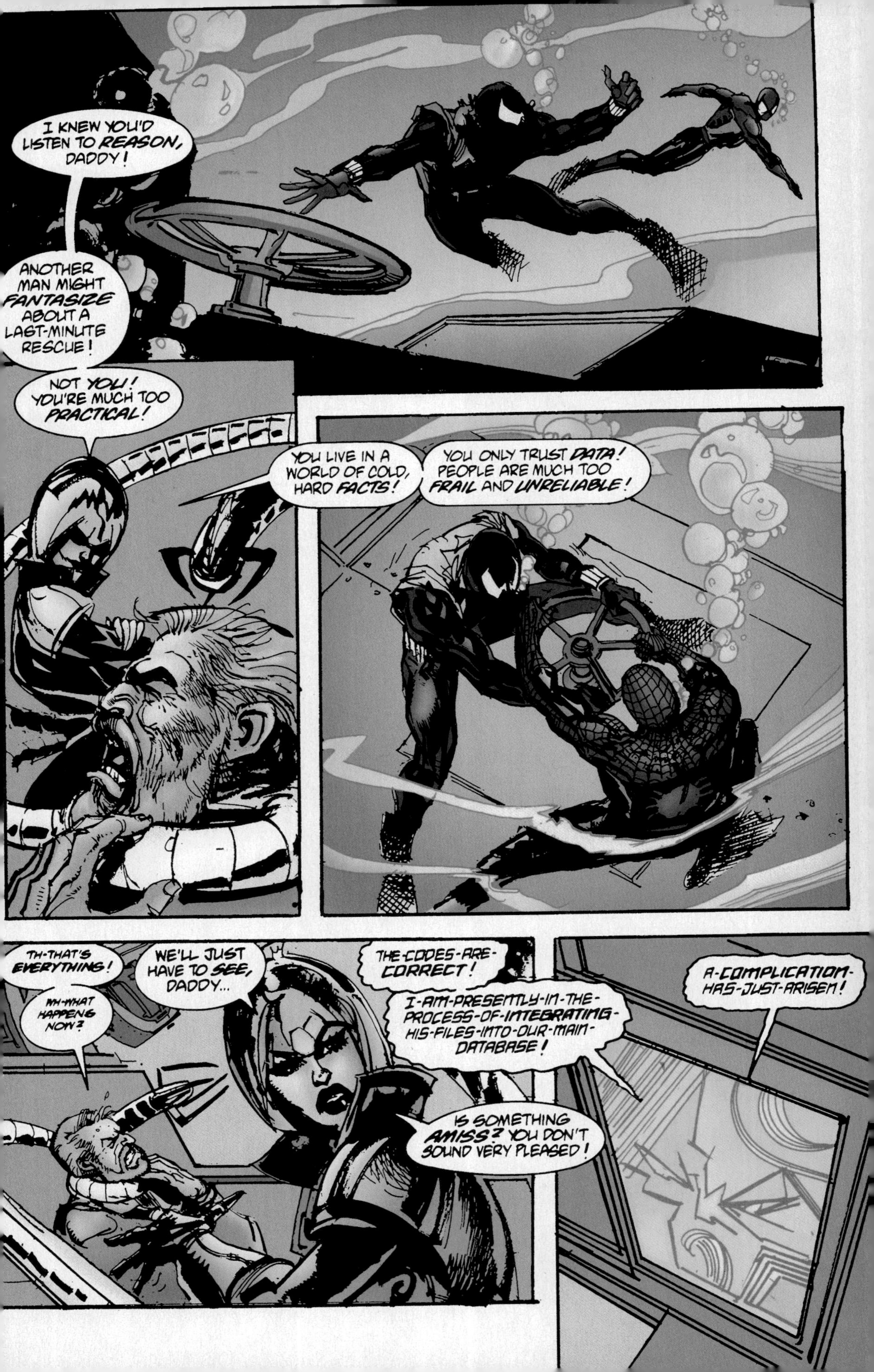
I KNEW YOU'D LISTEN TO REASON, DADDY!
ANOTHER MAN MIGHT FANTASIZE ABOUT A LAST-MINUTE RESCUE!
NOT YOU! YOU'RE MUCH TOO PRACTICAL!
YOU LIVE IN A WORLD OF COLD, HARD FACTS!
YOU ONLY TRUST DATA! PEOPLE ARE MUCH TOO FRAIL AND UNRELIABLE!
TH-THAT'S EVERYTHING!
WE'LL JUST HAVE TO SEE, DADDY...
WH-WHAT HAPPENS NOW?
THE-CODES-ARE-CORRECT!
I-AM-PRESENTLY-IN-THE-PROCESS-OF-INTEGRATING-HIS-FILES-INTO-OUR-MAIN-DATABASE!
IS SOMETHING AMISS? YOU DON'T SOUND VERY PLEASED!
A-COMPLICATION-HAS-JUST-ARISEN!

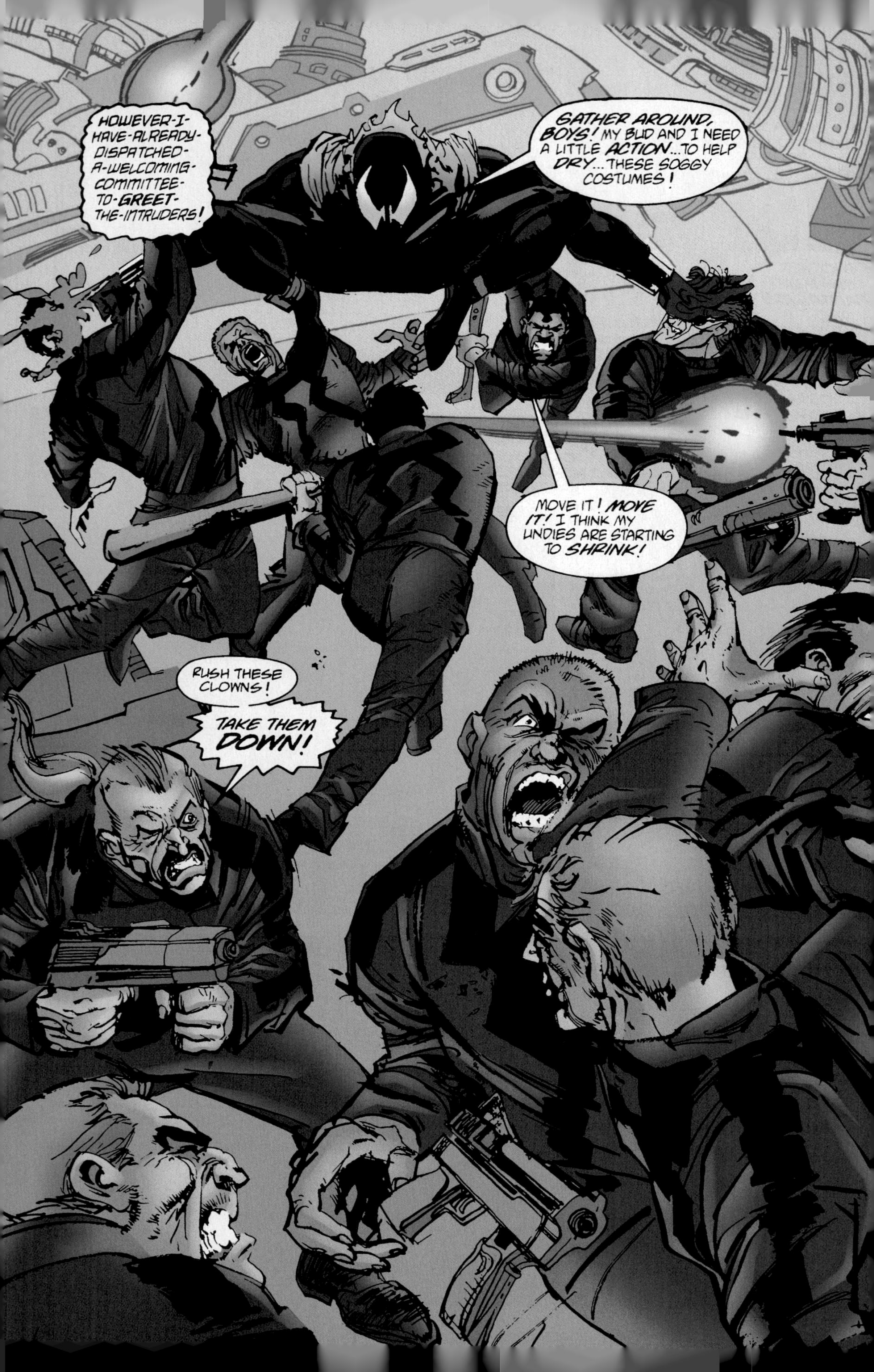

HOWEVER-I-HAVE-ALREADY-DISPATCHED-A-WELCOMING-COMMITTEE-TO-GREET-THE-INTRUDERS!
GATHER AROUND, BOYS! MY BUD AND I NEED A LITTLE ACTION...TO HELP DRY...THESE SOGGY COSTUMES!
MOVE IT! MOVE IT! I THINK MY UNDIES ARE STARTING TO SHRINK!
RUSH THESE CLOWNS!
TAKE THEM DOWN!

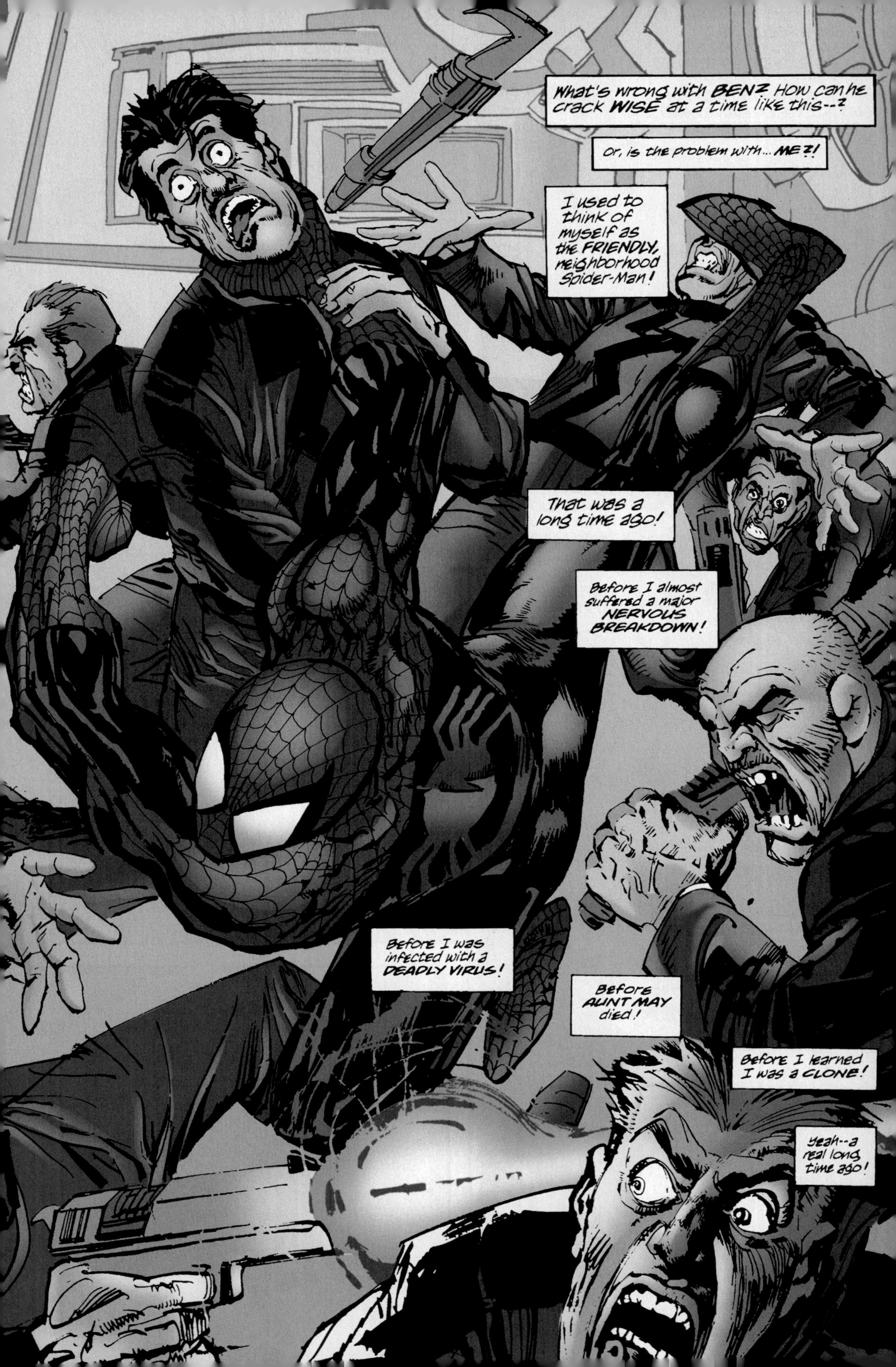
What's wrong with BEN? How can he crack WISE at a time like this--?
Or, is the problem with... ME?!
I used to think of myself as the FRIENDLY, neighborhood Spider-Man!
That was a long time ago!
Before I almost suffered a major NERVOUS BREAKDOWN!
Before I was infected with a DEADLY VIRUS!
Before AUNT MAY died!
Before I learned I was a CLONE!
Yeah--a real long time ago!

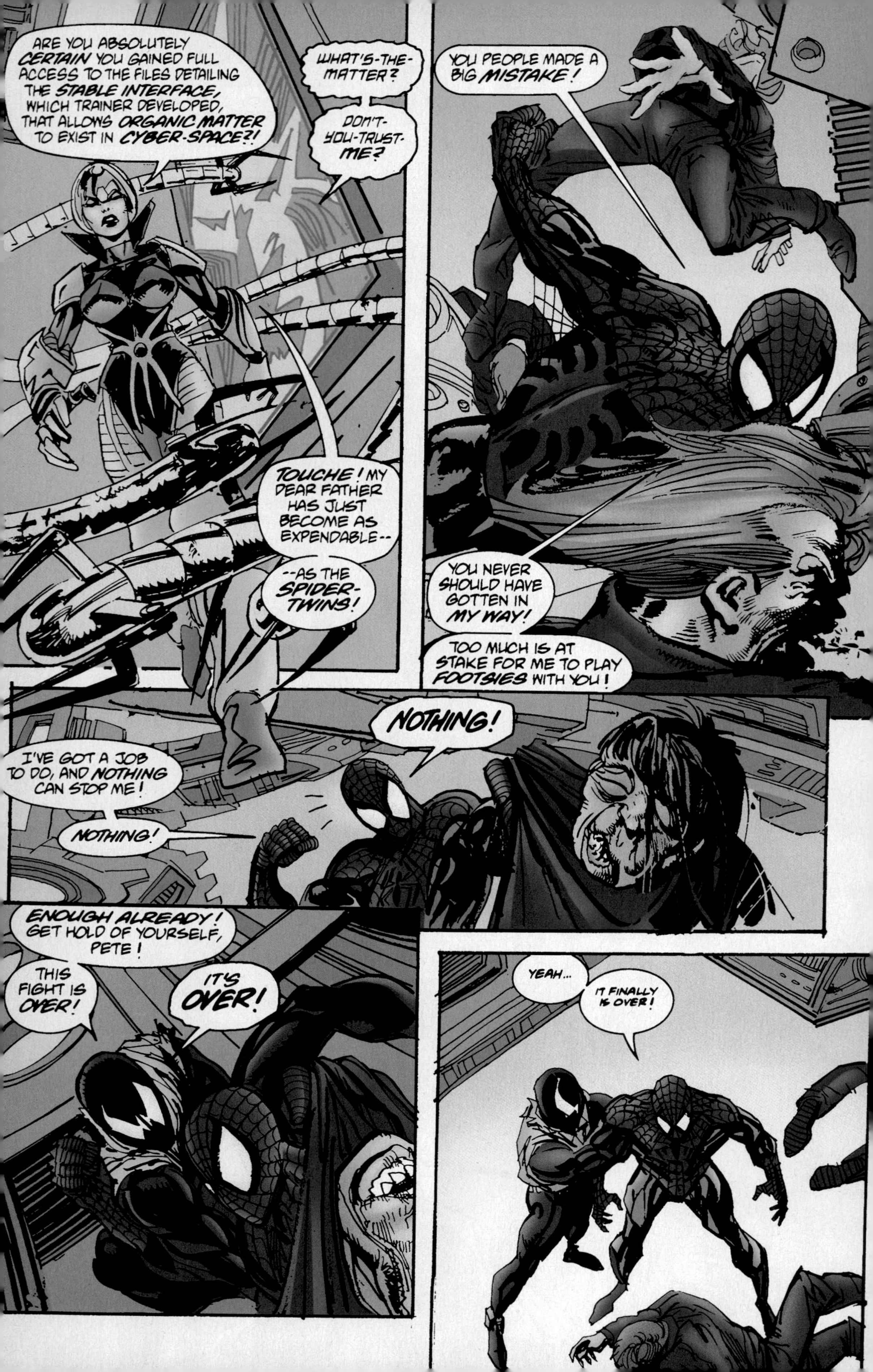

ARE YOU ABSOLUTELY CERTAIN YOU GAINED FULL ACCESS TO THE FILES DETAILING THE STABLE INTERFACE, WHICH TRAINER DEVELOPED, THAT ALLOWS ORGANIC MATTER TO EXIST IN CYBER-SPACE?!
WHAT'S-THE-MATTER?
DON'T-YOU-TRUST-ME?
TOUCHE! MY DEAR FATHER HAS JUST BECOME AS EXPENDABLE--
--AS THE SPIDER-TWINS!
YOU PEOPLE MADE A BIG MISTAKE!
YOU NEVER SHOULD HAVE GOTTEN IN MY WAY!
TOO MUCH IS AT STAKE FOR ME TO PLAY FOOTSIES WITH YOU!
I'VE GOT A JOB TO DO, AND NOTHING CAN STOP ME!
NOTHING!
NOTHING!
ENOUGH ALREADY! GET HOLD OF YOURSELF, PETE!
THIS FIGHT IS OVER!
IT'S OVER!
YEAH...
IT FINALLY IS OVER!

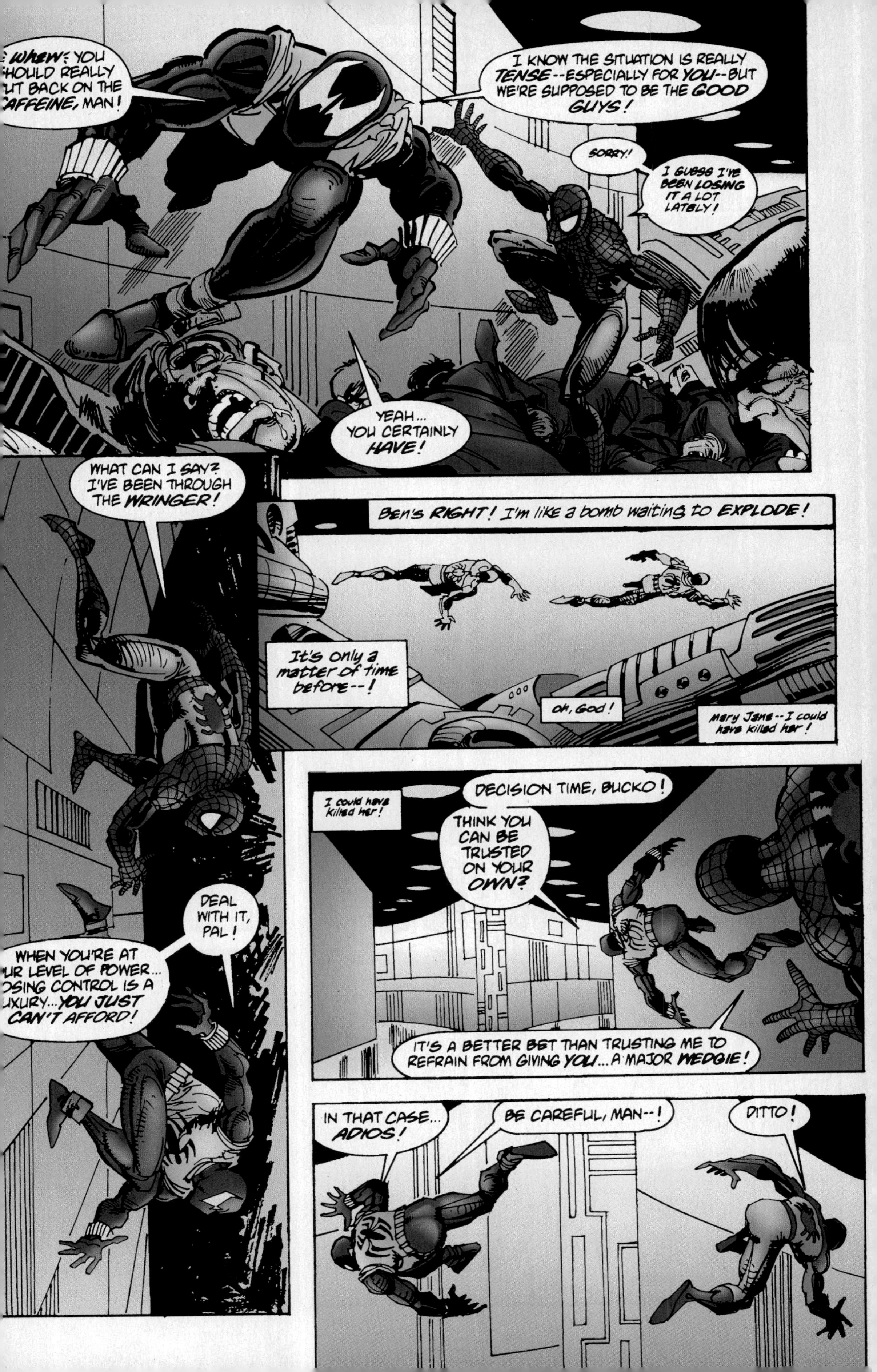
WHEW! YOU SHOULD REALLY CUT BACK ON THE CAFFEINE, MAN!
I KNOW THE SITUATION IS REALLY TENSE--ESPECIALLY FOR YOU--BUT WE'RE SUPPOSED TO BE THE GOOD GUYS!
SORRY!
I GUESS I'VE BEEN LOSING IT A LOT LATELY!
YEAH... YOU CERTAINLY HAVE!
WHAT CAN I SAY? I'VE BEEN THROUGH THE WRINGER!
Ben's RIGHT! I'm like a bomb waiting to EXPLODE!
It's only a matter of time before--!
Oh, God!
Mary Jane--I could have killed her!
I could have killed her!
DECISION TIME, BUCKO!
THINK YOU CAN BE TRUSTED ON YOUR OWN?
IT'S A BETTER BET THAN TRUSTING ME TO REFRAIN FROM GIVING YOU... A MAJOR WEDGIE!
DEAL WITH IT, PAL!
WHEN YOU'RE AT YOUR LEVEL OF POWER... LOSING CONTROL IS A LUXURY... YOU JUST CAN'T AFFORD!
IN THAT CASE... ADIOS!
BE CAREFUL, MAN--!
DITTO!

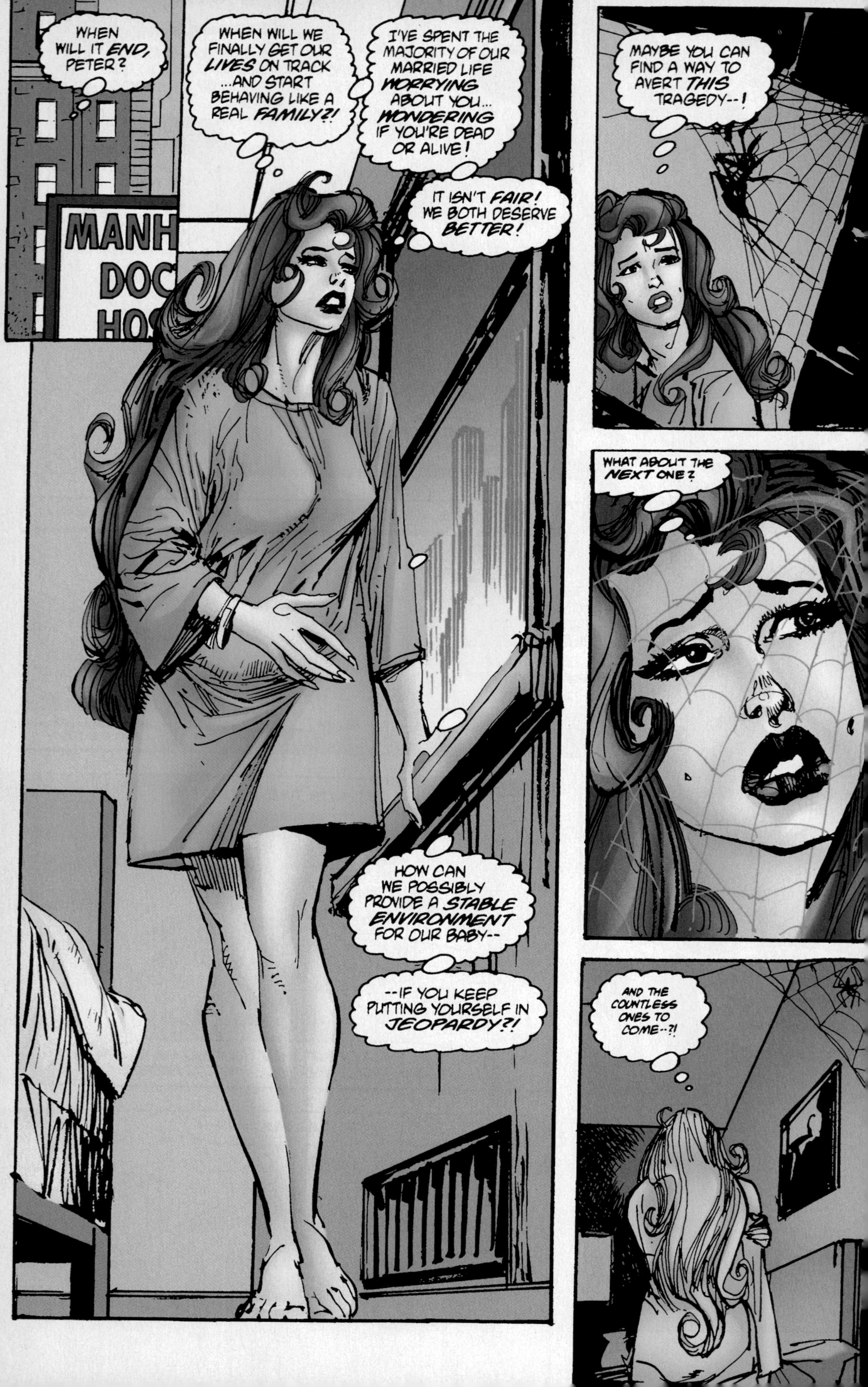
WHEN WILL IT END, PETER?
WHEN WILL WE FINALLY GET OUR LIVES ON TRACK ...AND START BEHAVING LIKE A REAL FAMILY?!
I'VE SPENT THE MAJORITY OF OUR MARRIED LIFE WORRYING ABOUT YOU... WONDERING IF YOU'RE DEAD OR ALIVE!
MANH
DOC
HOS
IT ISN'T FAIR! WE BOTH DESERVE BETTER!
HOW CAN WE POSSIBLY PROVIDE A STABLE ENVIRONMENT FOR OUR BABY--
--IF YOU KEEP PUTTING YOURSELF IN JEOPARDY?!
MAYBE YOU CAN FIND A WAY TO AVERT THIS TRAGEDY--!
WHAT ABOUT THE NEXT ONE?
AND THE COUNTLESS ONES TO COME--?!

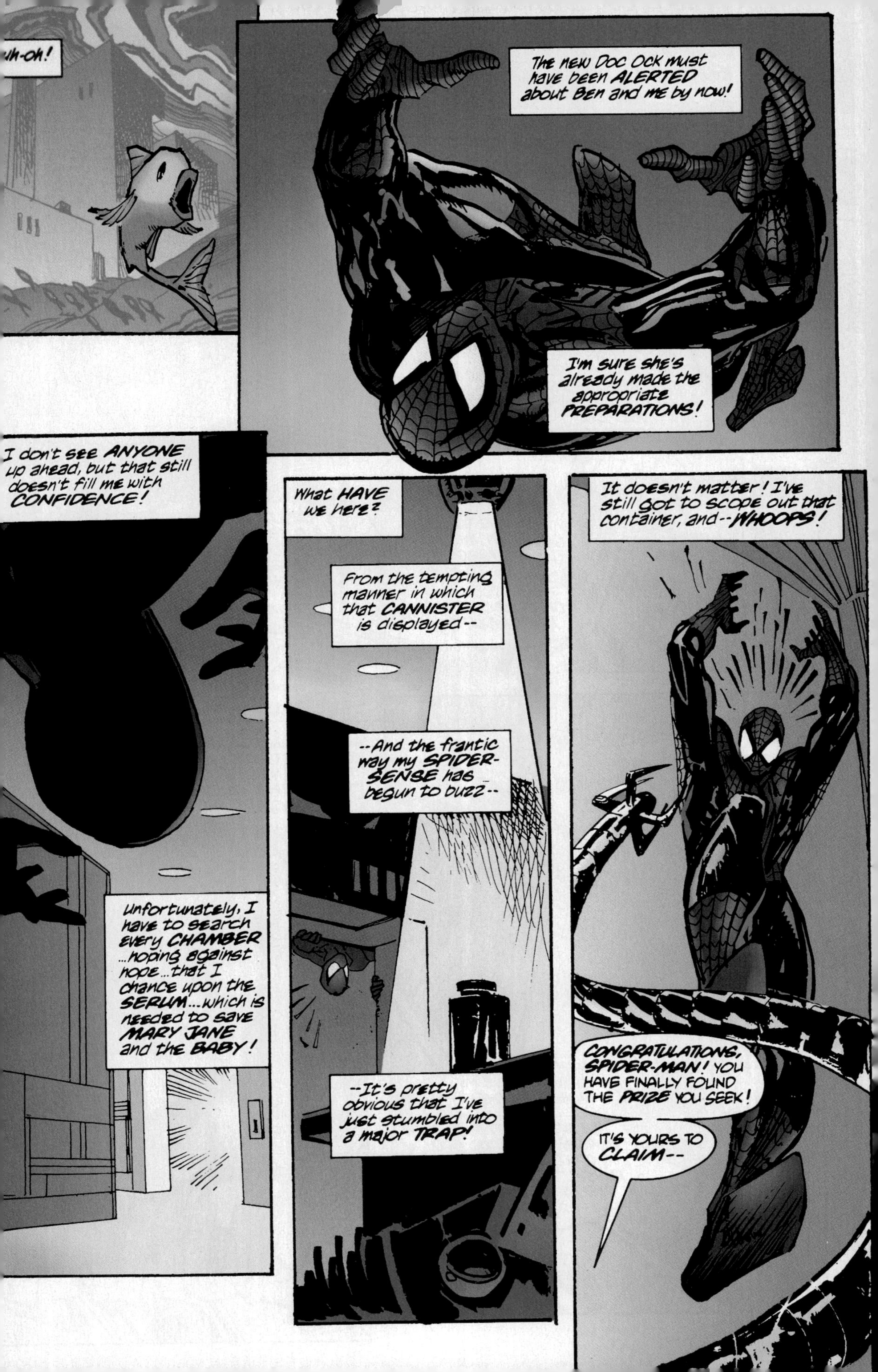
Uh-oh!
The new Doc Ock must have been ALERTED about Ben and me by now!
I'm sure she's already made the appropriate PREPARATIONS!
I don't see ANYONE up ahead, but that still doesn't fill me with CONFIDENCE!
Unfortunately, I have to search every CHAMBER ...hoping against hope... that I chance upon the SERUM... which is needed to save MARY JANE and the BABY!
What HAVE we here?
From the tempting manner in which that CANNISTER is displayed--
--And the frantic way my SPIDER-SENSE has begun to buzz--
--It's pretty obvious that I've just stumbled into a major TRAP!
It doesn't matter! I've still got to scope out that container, and--WHOOPS!
CONGRATULATIONS, SPIDER-MAN! YOU HAVE FINALLY FOUND THE PRIZE YOU SEEK!
IT'S YOURS TO CLAIM--

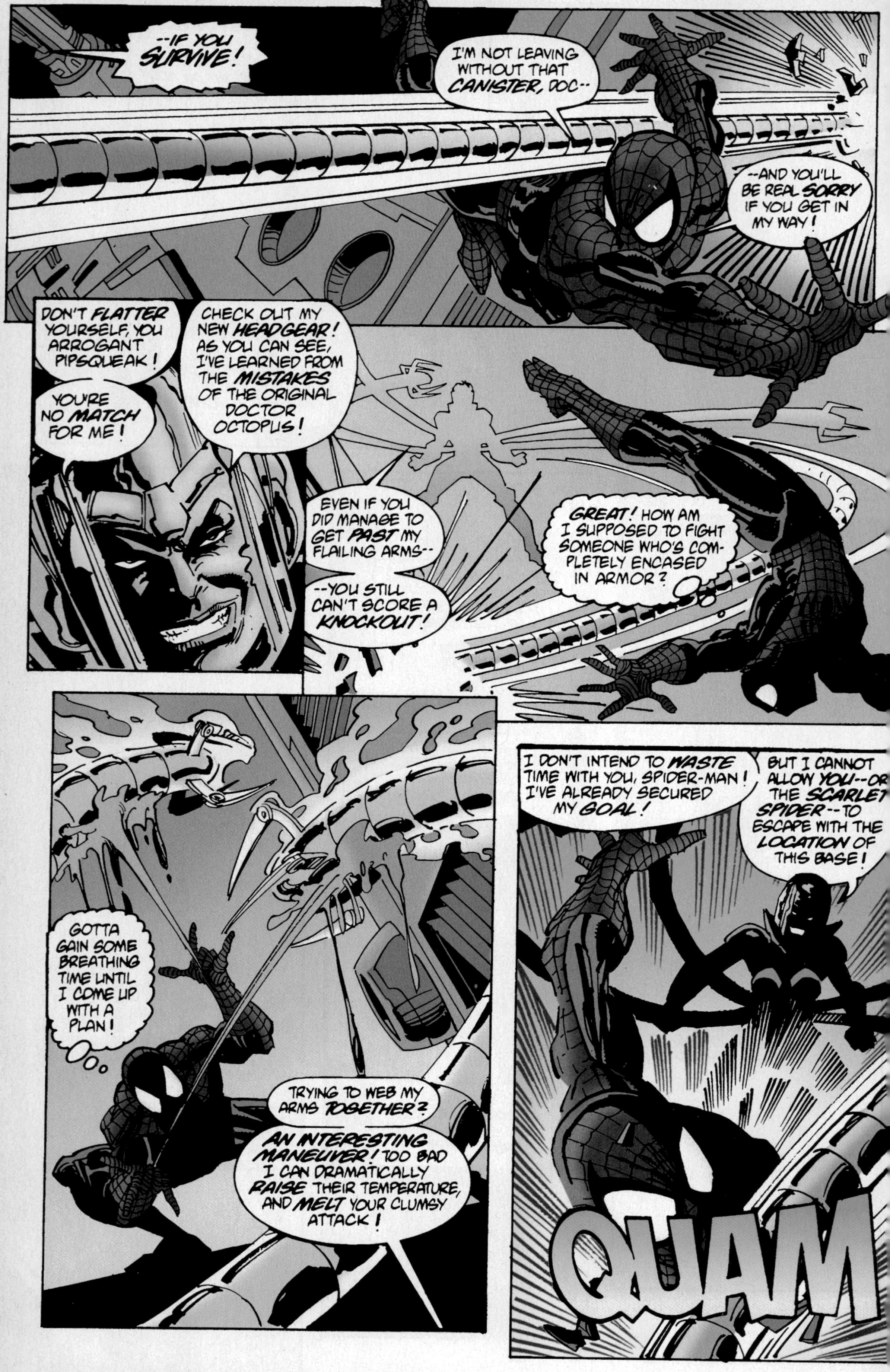
--IF YOU SURVIVE!
I'M NOT LEAVING WITHOUT THAT CANISTER, DOC--
--AND YOU'LL BE REAL SORRY IF YOU GET IN MY WAY!
DON'T FLATTER YOURSELF, YOU ARROGANT PIPSQUEAK!
YOU'RE NO MATCH FOR ME!
CHECK OUT MY NEW HEADGEAR! AS YOU CAN SEE, I'VE LEARNED FROM THE MISTAKES OF THE ORIGINAL DOCTOR OCTOPUS!
EVEN IF YOU DID MANAGE TO GET PAST MY FLAILING ARMS--
--YOU STILL CAN'T SCORE A KNOCKOUT!
GREAT! HOW AM I SUPPOSED TO FIGHT SOMEONE WHO'S COMPLETELY ENCASED IN ARMOR?
GOTTA GAIN SOME BREATHING TIME UNTIL I COME UP WITH A PLAN!
TRYING TO WEB MY ARMS TOGETHER?
AN INTERESTING MANEUVER! TOO BAD I CAN DRAMATICALLY RAISE THEIR TEMPERATURE, AND MELT YOUR CLUMSY ATTACK!
I DON'T INTEND TO WASTE TIME WITH YOU, SPIDER-MAN! I'VE ALREADY SECURED MY GOAL!
BUT I CANNOT ALLOW YOU--OR THE SCARLET SPIDER--TO ESCAPE WITH THE LOCATION OF THIS BASE!
QUAM

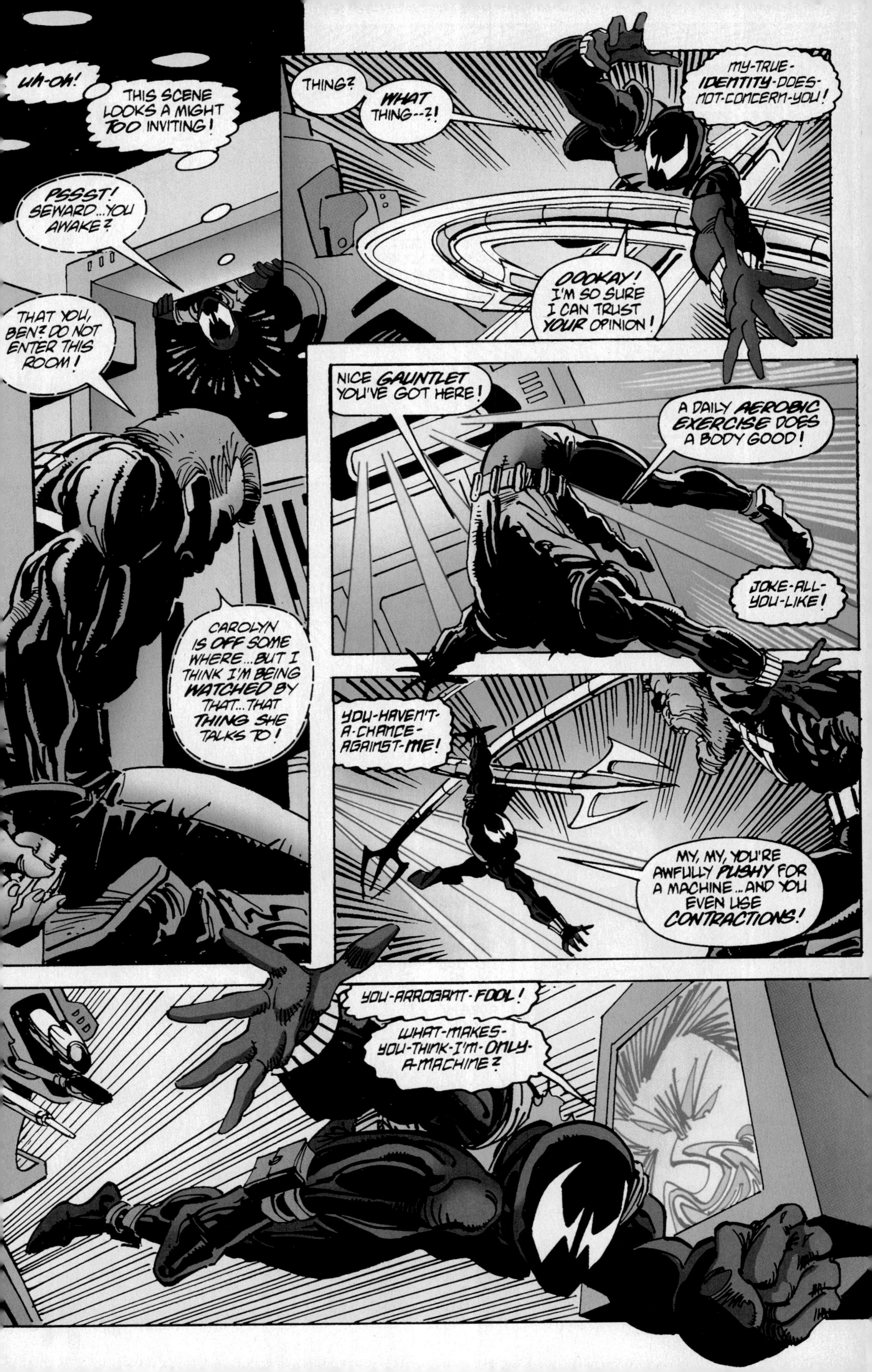
UH-OH!
THIS SCENE LOOKS A MIGHT TOO INVITING!
PSSST! SEWARD...YOU AWAKE?
THAT YOU, BEN? DO NOT ENTER THIS ROOM!
CAROLYN IS OFF SOME WHERE...BUT I THINK I'M BEING WATCHED BY THAT...THAT THING SHE TALKS TO!
THING? WHAT THING--?!
MY-TRUE-IDENTITY-DOES-NOT-CONCERN-YOU!
OOOKAY! I'M SO SURE I CAN TRUST YOUR OPINION!
NICE GAUNTLET YOU'VE GOT HERE!
A DAILY AEROBIC EXERCISE DOES A BODY GOOD!
JOKE-ALL-YOU-LIKE!
YOU-HAVEN'T-A-CHANCE-AGAINST-ME!
MY, MY, YOU'RE AWFULLY PUSHY FOR A MACHINE...AND YOU EVEN USE CONTRACTIONS!
YOU-ARROGANT-FOOL!
WHAT-MAKES-YOU-THINK-I'M-ONLY-A-MACHINE?

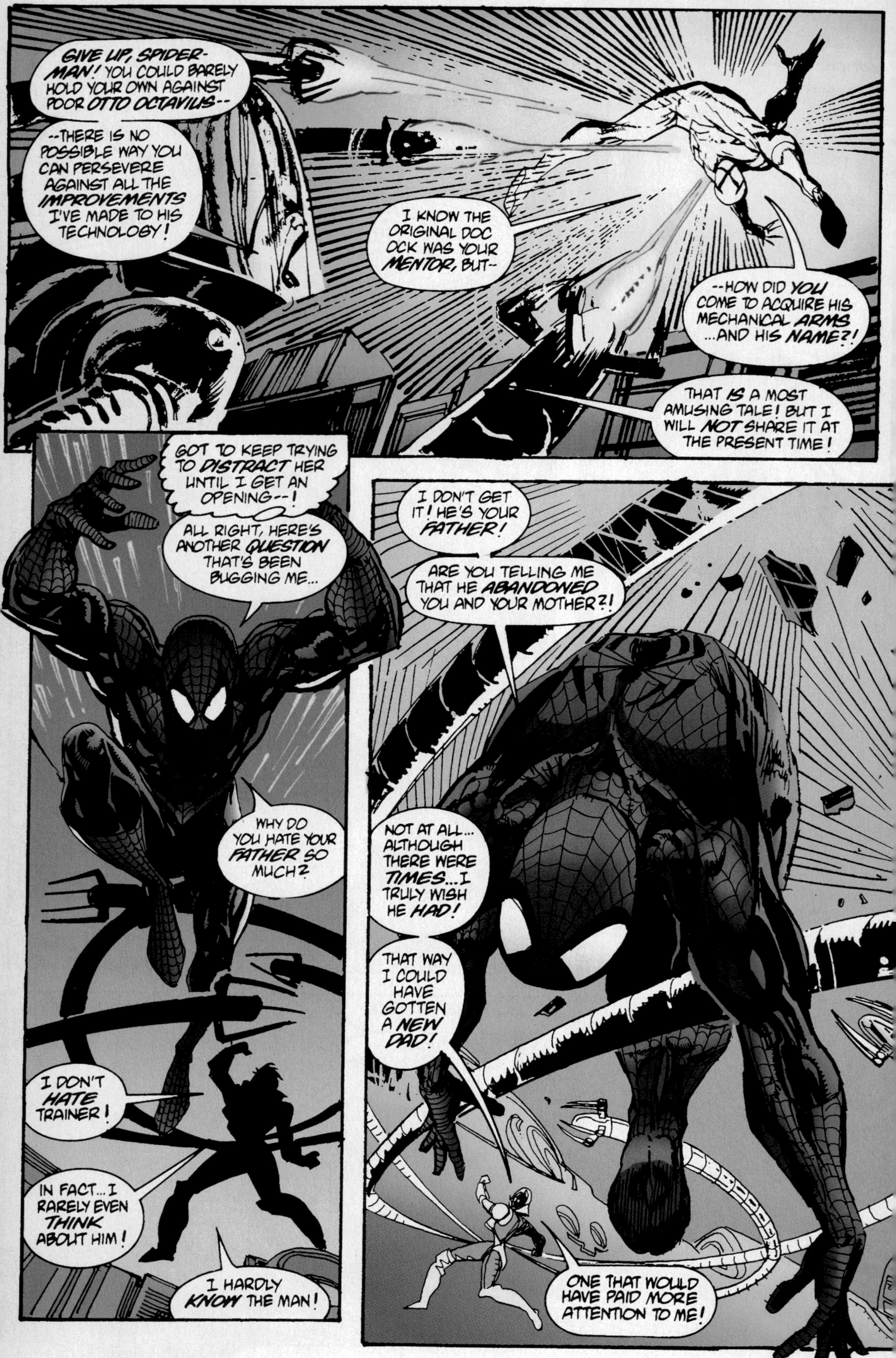
GIVE UP, SPIDER-MAN! YOU COULD BARELY HOLD YOUR OWN AGAINST POOR OTTO OCTAVIUS--
--THERE IS NO POSSIBLE WAY YOU CAN PERSEVERE AGAINST ALL THE IMPROVEMENTS I'VE MADE TO HIS TECHNOLOGY!
I KNOW THE ORIGINAL DOC OCK WAS YOUR MENTOR, BUT--
--HOW DID YOU COME TO ACQUIRE HIS MECHANICAL ARMS ...AND HIS NAME?!
THAT IS A MOST AMUSING TALE! BUT I WILL NOT SHARE IT AT THE PRESENT TIME!
GOT TO KEEP TRYING TO DISTRACT HER UNTIL I GET AN OPENING--!
ALL RIGHT, HERE'S ANOTHER QUESTION THAT'S BEEN BUGGING ME...
WHY DO YOU HATE YOUR FATHER SO MUCH?
I DON'T HATE TRAINER!
IN FACT... I RARELY EVEN THINK ABOUT HIM!
I HARDLY KNOW THE MAN!
I DON'T GET IT! HE'S YOUR FATHER!
ARE YOU TELLING ME THAT HE ABANDONED YOU AND YOUR MOTHER?!
NOT AT ALL... ALTHOUGH THERE WERE TIMES... I TRULY WISH HE HAD!
THAT WAY I COULD HAVE GOTTEN A NEW DAD!
ONE THAT WOULD HAVE PAID MORE ATTENTION TO ME!

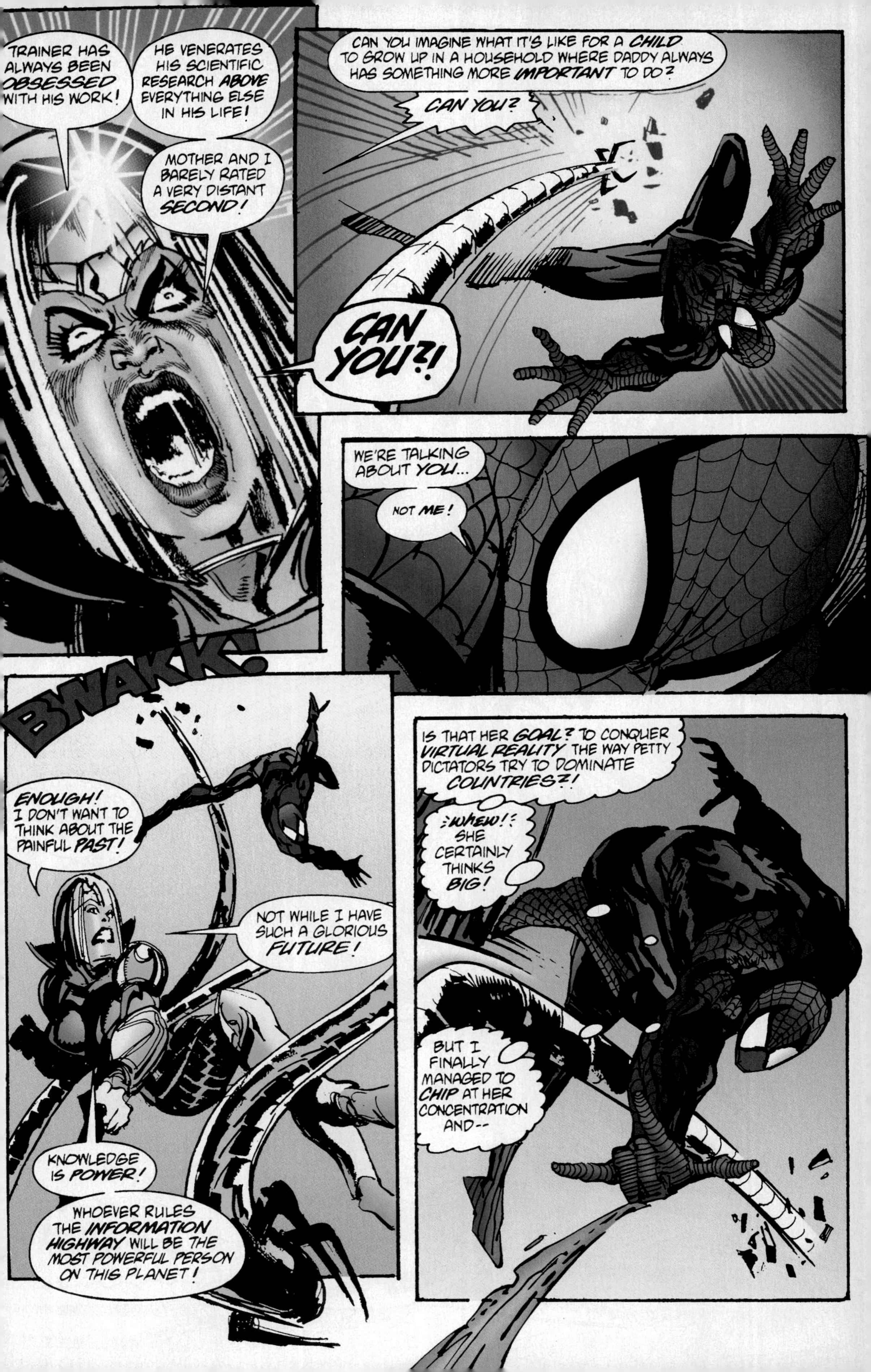
TRAINER HAS ALWAYS BEEN OBSESSED WITH HIS WORK!
HE VENERATES HIS SCIENTIFIC RESEARCH ABOVE EVERYTHING ELSE IN HIS LIFE!
MOTHER AND I BARELY RATED A VERY DISTANT SECOND!
CAN YOU IMAGINE WHAT IT'S LIKE FOR A CHILD TO GROW UP IN A HOUSEHOLD WHERE DADDY ALWAYS HAS SOMETHING MORE IMPORTANT TO DO?
CAN YOU?
CAN YOU?!
WE'RE TALKING ABOUT YOU...
NOT ME!
BWAKK!
ENOUGH! I DON'T WANT TO THINK ABOUT THE PAINFUL PAST!
NOT WHILE I HAVE SUCH A GLORIOUS FUTURE!
KNOWLEDGE IS POWER!
WHOEVER RULES THE INFORMATION HIGHWAY WILL BE THE MOST POWERFUL PERSON ON THIS PLANET!
IS THAT HER GOAL? TO CONQUER VIRTUAL REALITY THE WAY PETTY DICTATORS TRY TO DOMINATE COUNTRIES?!
WHEW! SHE CERTAINLY THINKS BIG!
BUT I FINALLY MANAGED TO CHIP AT HER CONCENTRATION AND--

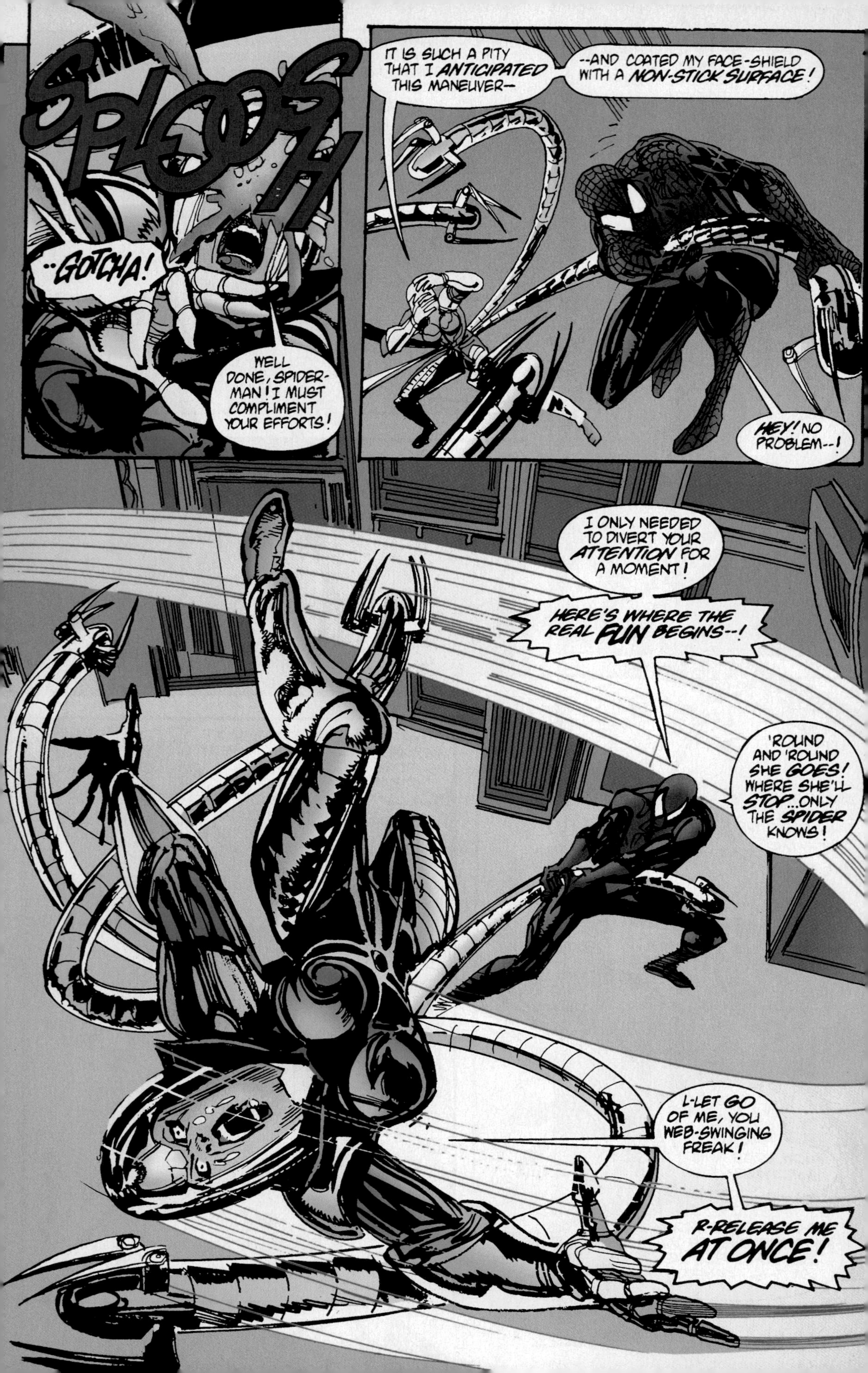
SPLOOSH
..GOTCHA!
WELL DONE, SPIDER-MAN! I MUST COMPLIMENT YOUR EFFORTS!
IT IS SUCH A PITY THAT I ANTICIPATED THIS MANEUVER--
--AND COATED MY FACE-SHIELD WITH A NON-STICK SURFACE!
HEY! NO PROBLEM--!
I ONLY NEEDED TO DIVERT YOUR ATTENTION FOR A MOMENT!
HERE'S WHERE THE REAL FUN BEGINS--!
'ROUND AND 'ROUND SHE GOES! WHERE SHE'LL STOP...ONLY THE SPIDER KNOWS!
L-LET GO OF ME, YOU WEB-SWINGING FREAK!
R-RELEASE ME AT ONCE!

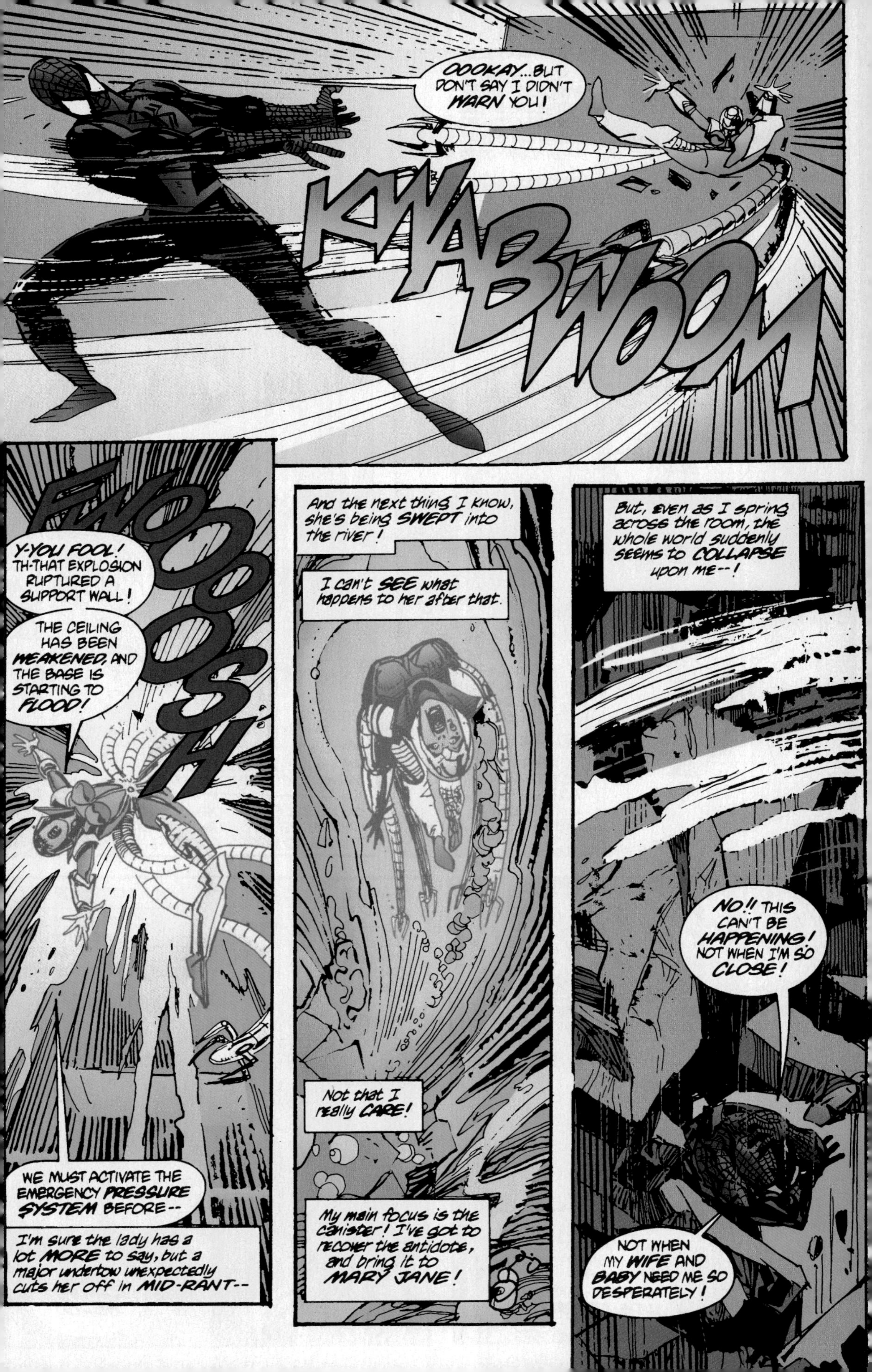
OOOKAY...BUT DON'T SAY I DIDN'T WARN YOU!
KWABWOOM
FWOOOOSH
Y-YOU FOOL! TH-THAT EXPLOSION RUPTURED A SUPPORT WALL!
THE CEILING HAS BEEN WEAKENED, AND THE BASE IS STARTING TO FLOOD!
WE MUST ACTIVATE THE EMERGENCY PRESSURE SYSTEM BEFORE--
I'm sure the lady has a lot MORE to say, but a major undertow unexpectedly cuts her off in MID-RANT--
And the next thing I know, she's being SWEPT into the river!
I can't SEE what happens to her after that.
Not that I really CARE!
My main focus is the canister! I've got to recover the antidote, and bring it to MARY JANE!
But, even as I spring across the room, the whole world suddenly seems to COLLAPSE upon me--!
NO!! THIS CAN'T BE HAPPENING! NOT WHEN I'M SO CLOSE!
NOT WHEN MY WIFE AND BABY NEED ME SO DESPERATELY!

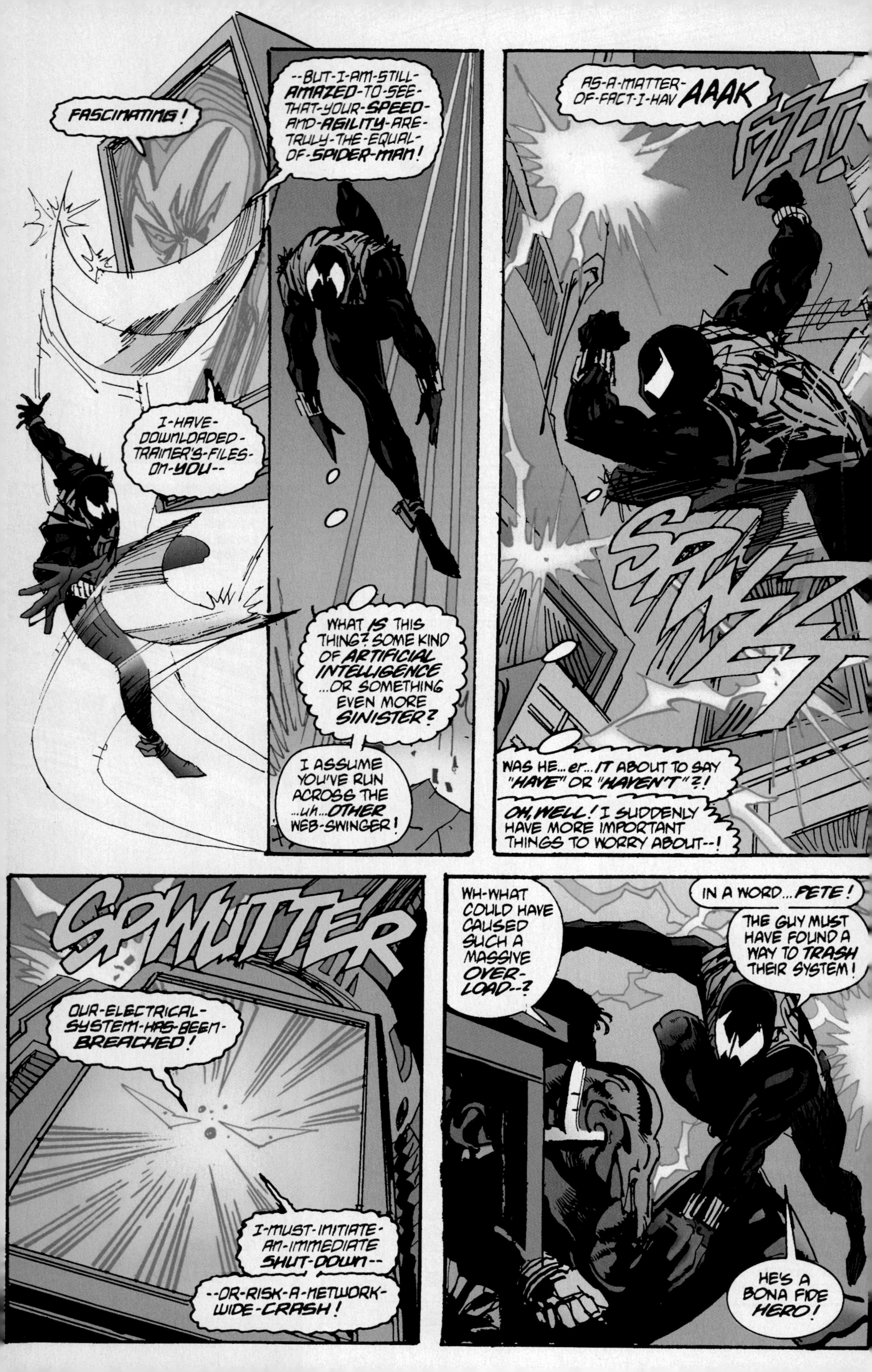
FASCINATING!
--BUT-I-AM-STILL-AMAZED-TO-SEE-THAT-YOUR-SPEED-AND-AGILITY-ARE-TRULY-THE-EQUAL-OF-SPIDER-MAN!
I-HAVE-DOWNLOADED-TRAINER'S-FILES-ON-YOU--
WHAT IS THIS THING? SOME KIND OF ARTIFICIAL INTELLIGENCE ...OR SOMETHING EVEN MORE SINISTER?
I ASSUME YOU'VE RUN ACROSS THE ...uh...OTHER WEB-SWINGER!
AS-A-MATTER-OF-FACT-I-HAV AAAK
FZZT
SPZZZT
WAS HE...er...IT ABOUT TO SAY "HAVE" OR "HAVEN'T"?!
OH, WELL! I SUDDENLY HAVE MORE IMPORTANT THINGS TO WORRY ABOUT--!
SPUTTER
OUR-ELECTRICAL-SYSTEM-HAS-BEEN-BREACHED!
I-MUST-INITIATE-AN-IMMEDIATE SHUT-DOWN--
--OR-RISK-A-NETWORK-WIDE-CRASH!
WH-WHAT COULD HAVE CAUSED SUCH A MASSIVE OVER-LOAD--?
IN A WORD...PETE!
THE GUY MUST HAVE FOUND A WAY TO TRASH THEIR SYSTEM!
HE'S A BONA FIDE HERO!

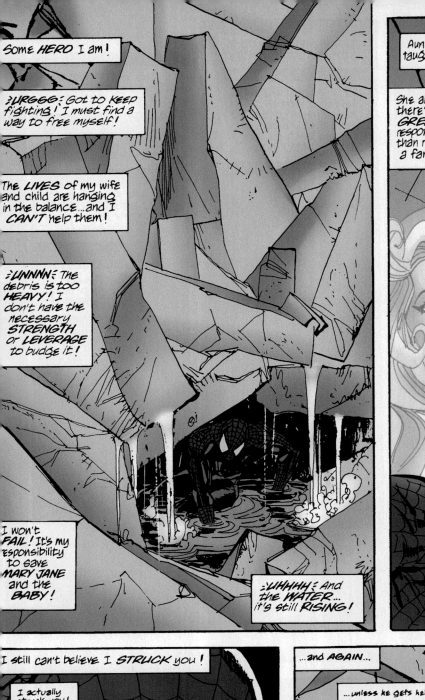

Some HERO I am!

‡URGGG‡ Got to keep fighting! I must find a way to free myself!

The LIVES of my wife and child are hanging in the balance...and I CAN'T help them!

‡UNNNN‡ The debris is too HEAVY! I don't have the necessary STRENGTH or LEVERAGE to budge it!

I won't FAIL! It's my responsibility to save MARY JANE and the BABY!

‡UHHHH‡ And the WATER... it's still RISING!

Aunt May is the one who taught me RESPONSIBILITY!

She also said there's no GREATER responsibility than raising a family!

Oh, MARY JANE--! I am so sorry for all the PAIN I've caused you!

I still can't believe I STRUCK you!

I actually struck you!

‡ARRRK‡ Got to call on all the POWER I possess!

They say that ONCE a man hits a woman, he'll do it AGAIN...

...and AGAIN...

...unless he gets help...

...unless he eliminates the root cause of the abuse!

‡OFFFT‡ I gotta get this WEIGHT off my back! I JUST GOTTA!

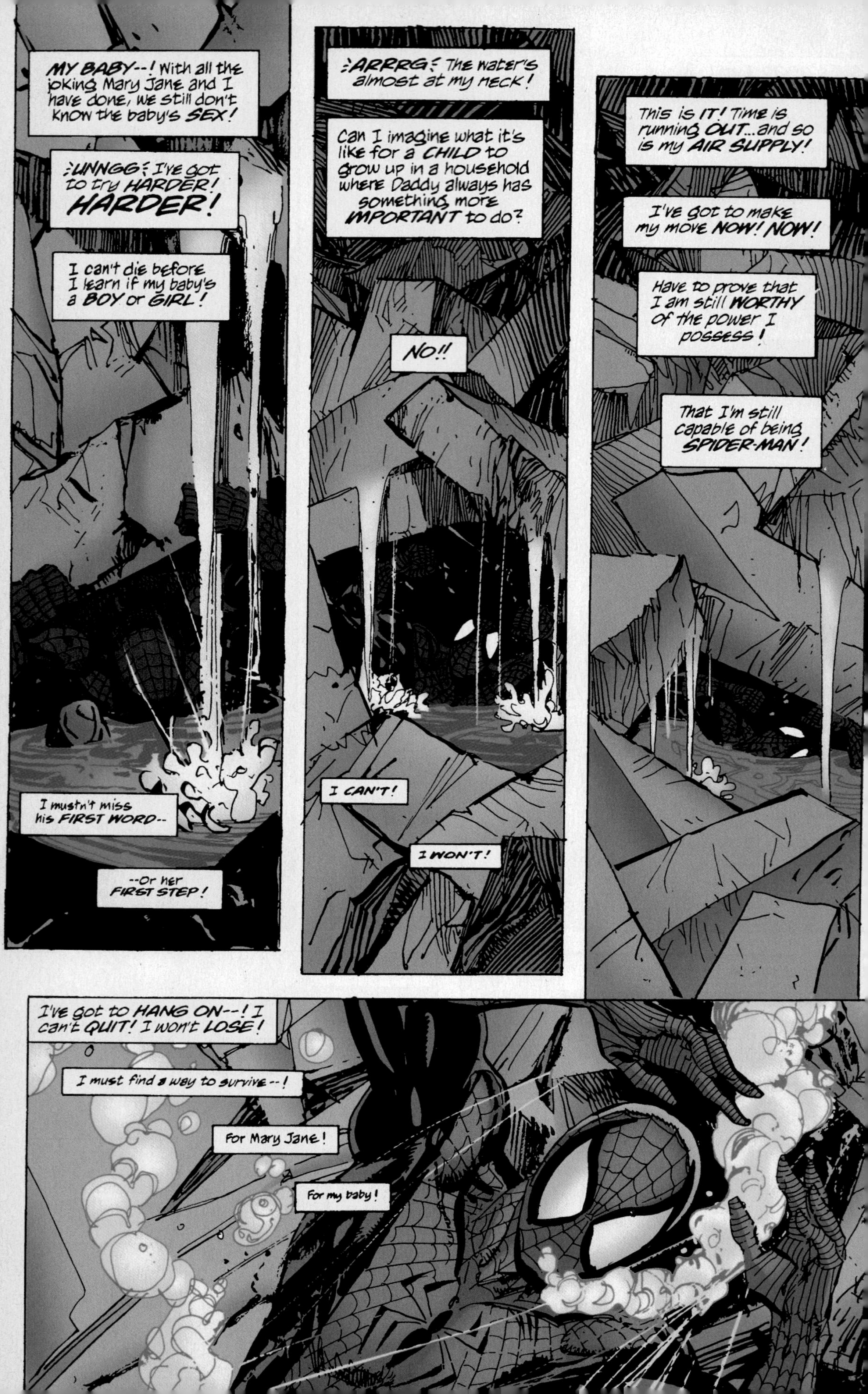

MY BABY--! With all the joking Mary Jane and I have done, we still don't know the baby's SEX!
:UNNGG: I've got to try HARDER! HARDER!
I can't die before I learn if my baby's a BOY or GIRL!
I mustn't miss his FIRST WORD--
--Or her FIRST STEP!
:ARRRG: The water's almost at my neck!
Can I imagine what it's like for a CHILD to grow up in a household where Daddy always has something more IMPORTANT to do?
NO!!
I CAN'T!
I WON'T!
This is IT! Time is running OUT...and so is my AIR SUPPLY!
I've got to make my move NOW! NOW!
Have to prove that I am still WORTHY of the power I possess!
That I'm still capable of being SPIDER-MAN!
I've got to HANG ON--! I can't QUIT! I won't LOSE!
I must find a way to survive--!
For Mary Jane!
For my baby!

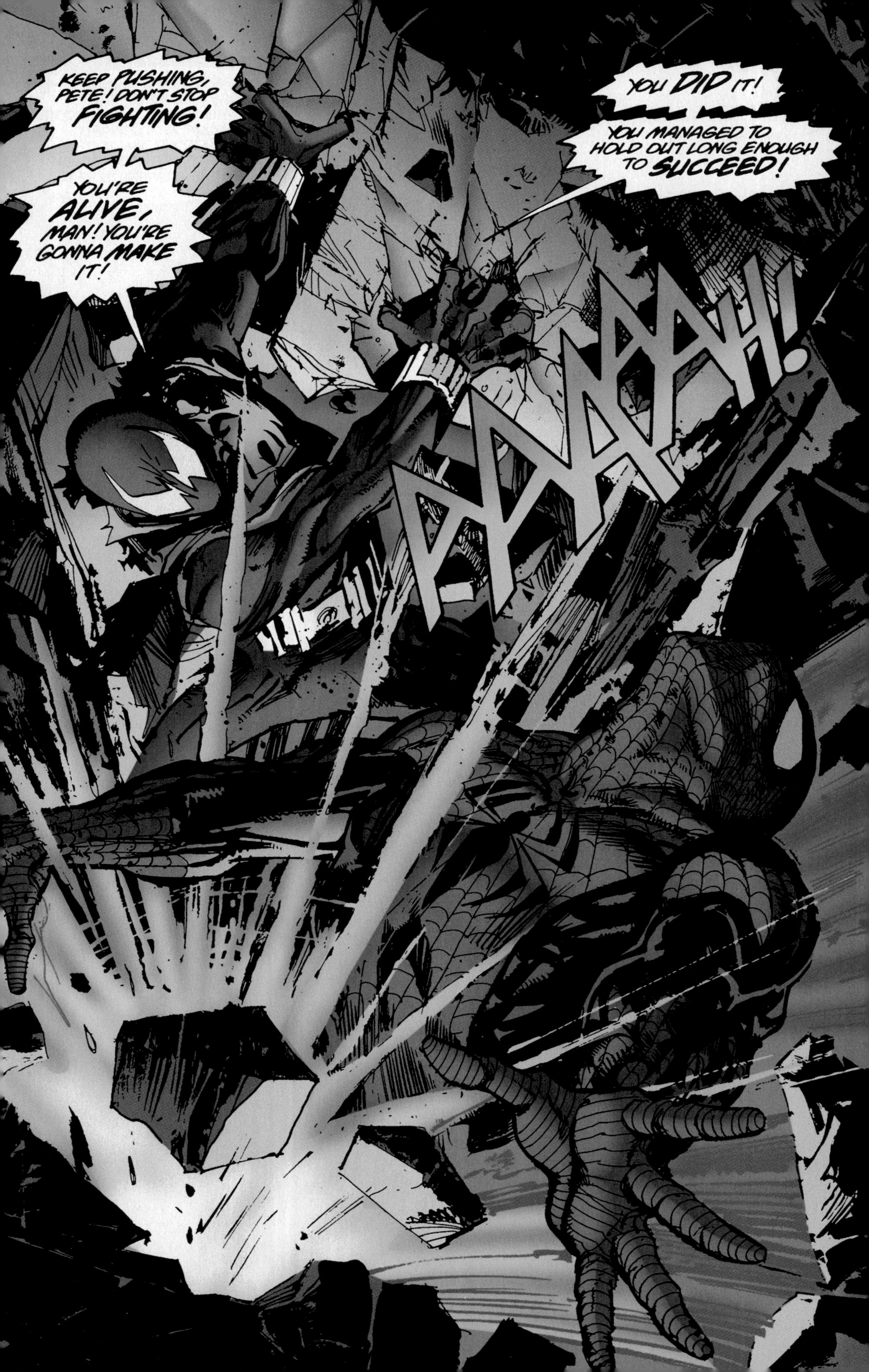
KEEP PUSHING, PETE! DON'T STOP FIGHTING!
YOU'RE ALIVE, MAN! YOU'RE GONNA MAKE IT!
YOU DID IT!
YOU MANAGED TO HOLD OUT LONG ENOUGH TO SUCCEED!
AAAAAAH!!

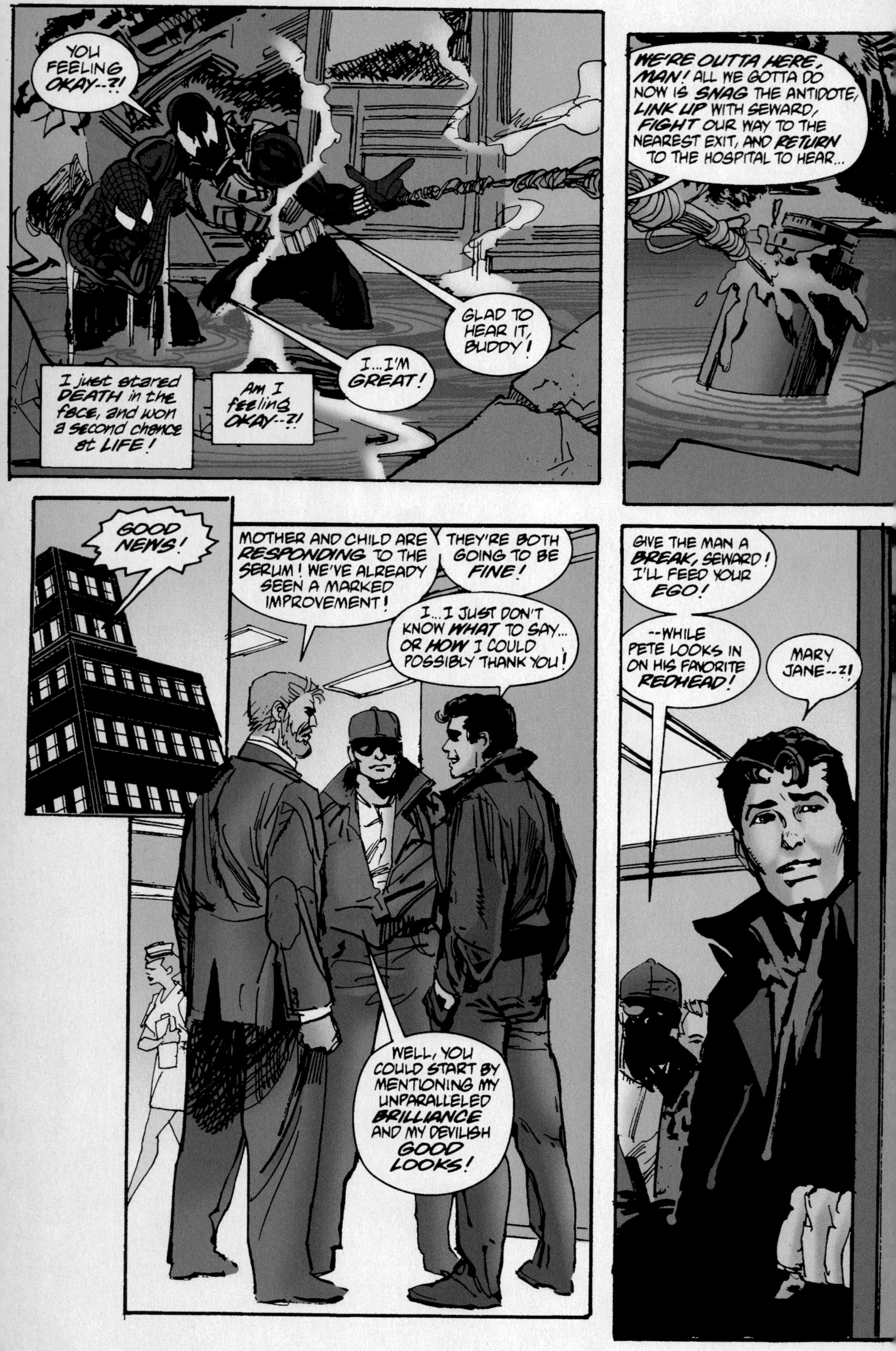
YOU FEELING OKAY--?!
I just stared DEATH in the face, and won a second chance at LIFE!
Am I feeling OKAY--?!
I...I'M GREAT!
GLAD TO HEAR IT, BUDDY!
WE'RE OUTTA HERE, MAN! ALL WE GOTTA DO NOW IS SNAG THE ANTIDOTE, LINK UP WITH SEWARD, FIGHT OUR WAY TO THE NEAREST EXIT, AND RETURN TO THE HOSPITAL TO HEAR...
GOOD NEWS!
MOTHER AND CHILD ARE RESPONDING TO THE SERUM! WE'VE ALREADY SEEN A MARKED IMPROVEMENT!
THEY'RE BOTH GOING TO BE FINE!
I...I JUST DON'T KNOW WHAT TO SAY... OR HOW I COULD POSSIBLY THANK YOU!
WELL, YOU COULD START BY MENTIONING MY UNPARALLELED BRILLIANCE AND MY DEVILISH GOOD LOOKS!
GIVE THE MAN A BREAK, SEWARD! I'LL FEED YOUR EGO!
--WHILE PETE LOOKS IN ON HIS FAVORITE REDHEAD!
MARY JANE--?!

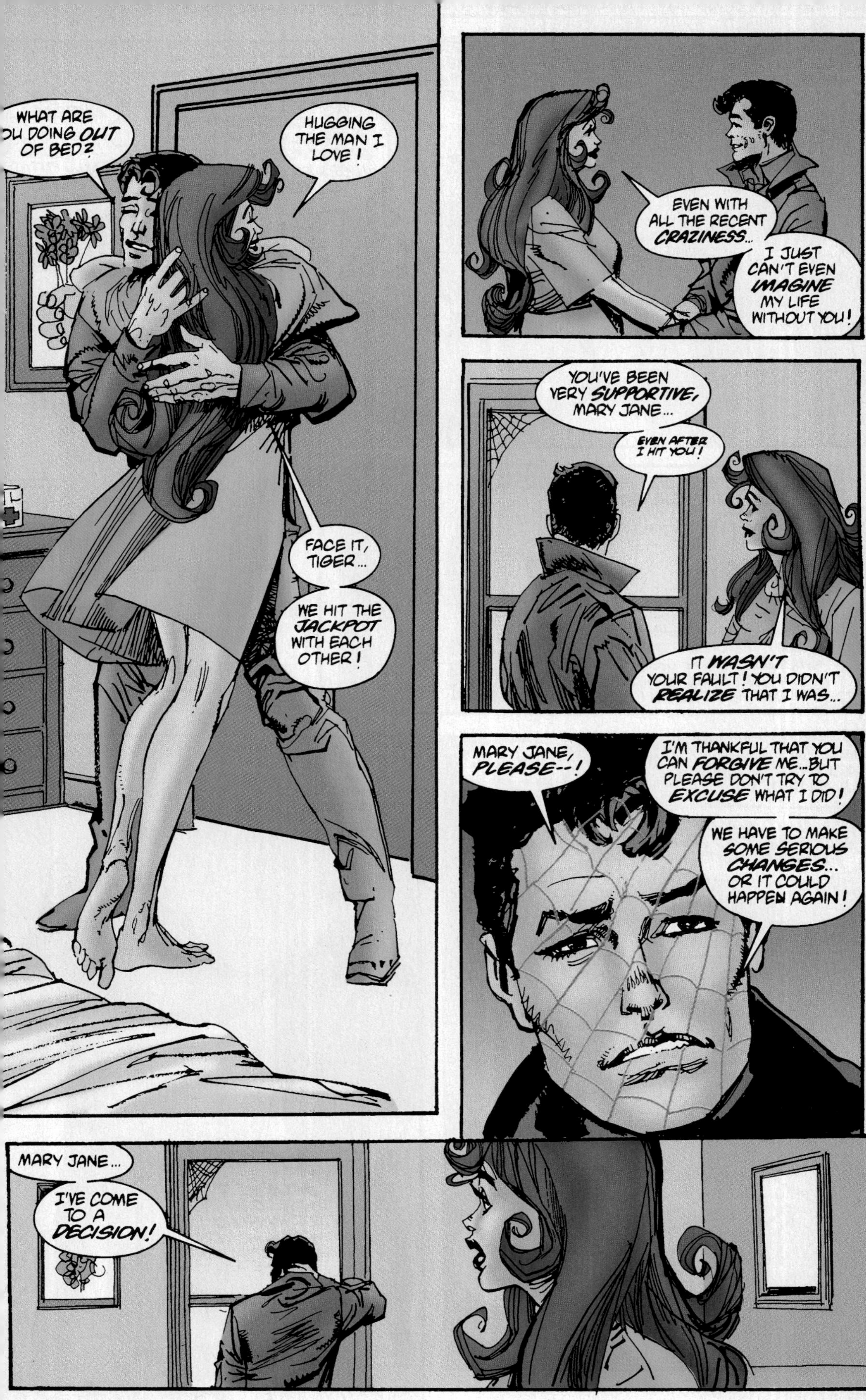
WHAT ARE
YOU DOING OUT
OF BED?
HUGGING
THE MAN I
LOVE!
FACE IT,
TIGER...
WE HIT THE
JACKPOT
WITH EACH
OTHER!
EVEN WITH
ALL THE RECENT
CRAZINESS...
I JUST
CAN'T EVEN
IMAGINE
MY LIFE
WITHOUT YOU!
YOU'VE BEEN
VERY SUPPORTIVE,
MARY JANE...
EVEN AFTER
I HIT YOU!
IT WASN'T
YOUR FAULT! YOU DIDN'T
REALIZE THAT I WAS...
MARY JANE,
PLEASE--!
I'M THANKFUL THAT YOU
CAN FORGIVE ME...BUT
PLEASE DON'T TRY TO
EXCUSE WHAT I DID!
WE HAVE TO MAKE
SOME SERIOUS
CHANGES...
OR IT COULD
HAPPEN AGAIN!
MARY JANE...
I'VE COME
TO A
DECISION!

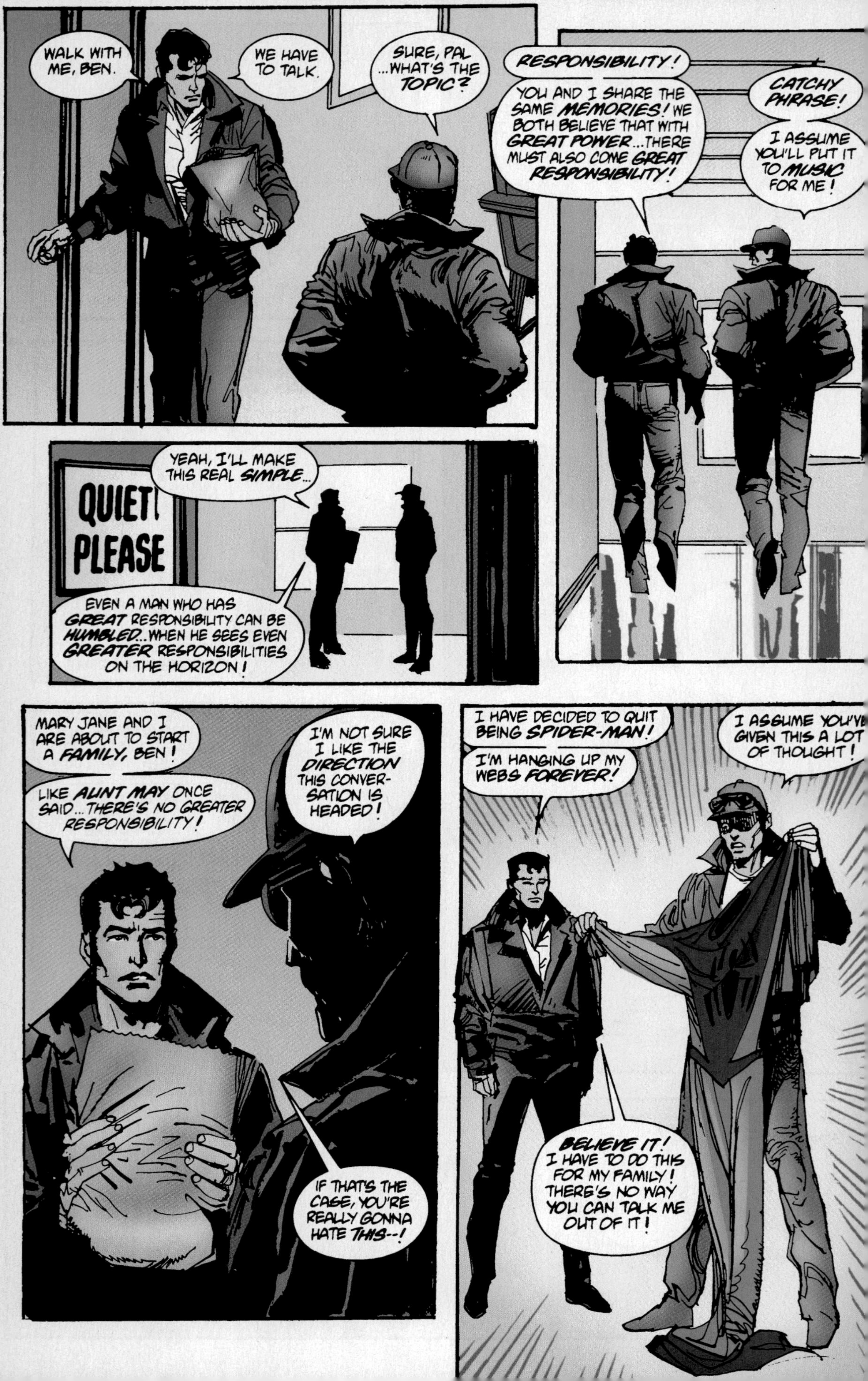
WALK WITH ME, BEN.
WE HAVE TO TALK.
SURE, PAL ...WHAT'S THE TOPIC?
RESPONSIBILITY!
YOU AND I SHARE THE SAME MEMORIES! WE BOTH BELIEVE THAT WITH GREAT POWER...THERE MUST ALSO COME GREAT RESPONSIBILITY!
CATCHY PHRASE!
I ASSUME YOU'LL PUT IT TO MUSIC FOR ME!
QUIET PLEASE
YEAH, I'LL MAKE THIS REAL SIMPLE...
EVEN A MAN WHO HAS GREAT RESPONSIBILITY CAN BE HUMBLED...WHEN HE SEES EVEN GREATER RESPONSIBILITIES ON THE HORIZON!
MARY JANE AND I ARE ABOUT TO START A FAMILY, BEN!
LIKE AUNT MAY ONCE SAID...THERE'S NO GREATER RESPONSIBILITY!
I'M NOT SURE I LIKE THE DIRECTION THIS CONVERSATION IS HEADED!
IF THAT'S THE CASE, YOU'RE REALLY GONNA HATE THIS--!
I HAVE DECIDED TO QUIT BEING SPIDER-MAN!
I'M HANGING UP MY WEBS FOREVER!
I ASSUME YOU'VE GIVEN THIS A LOT OF THOUGHT!
BELIEVE IT! I HAVE TO DO THIS FOR MY FAMILY! THERE'S NO WAY YOU CAN TALK ME OUT OF IT!

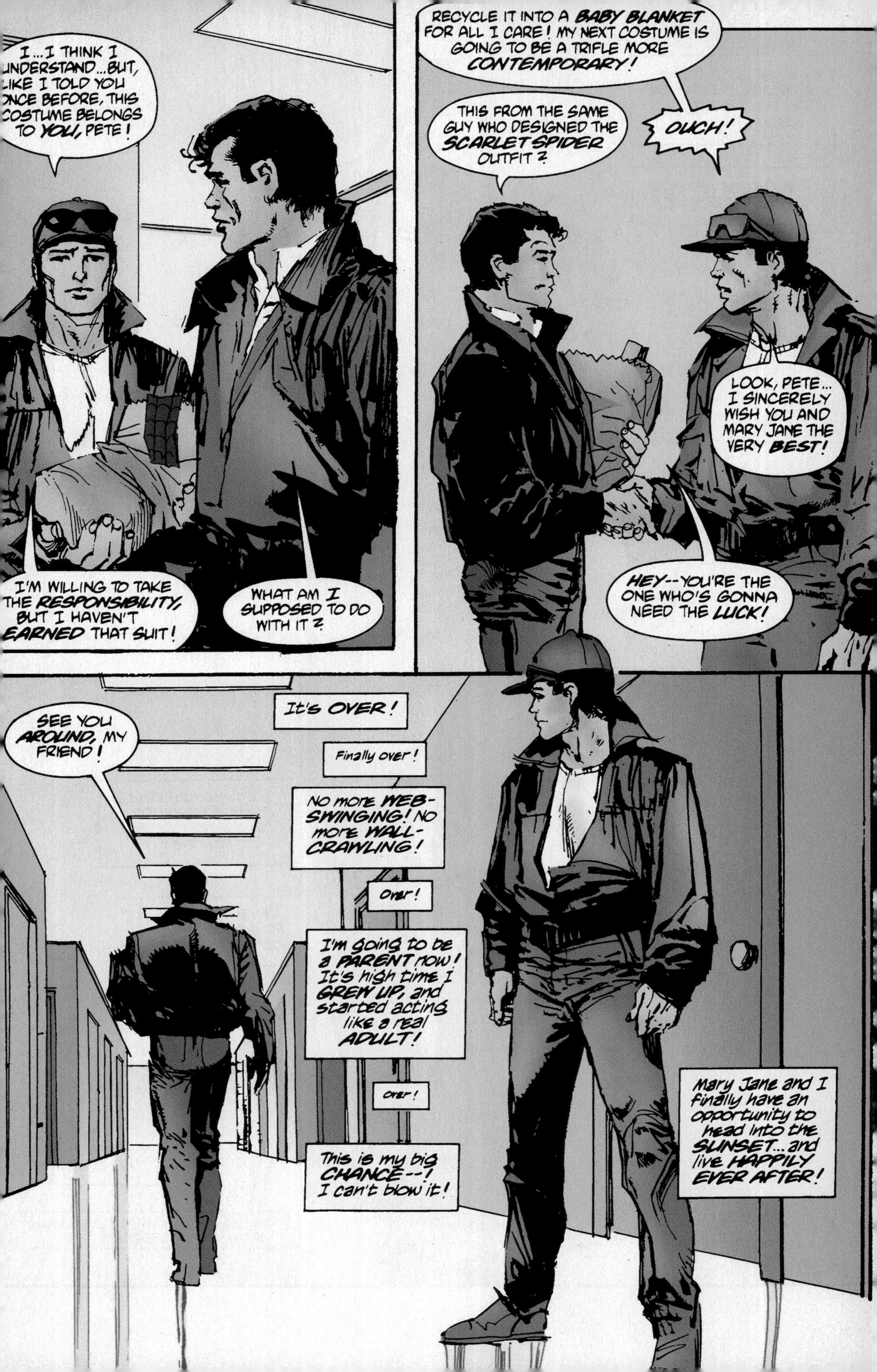
I... I THINK I UNDERSTAND... BUT, LIKE I TOLD YOU ONCE BEFORE, THIS COSTUME BELONGS TO YOU, PETE!
I'M WILLING TO TAKE THE RESPONSIBILITY, BUT I HAVEN'T EARNED THAT SUIT!
WHAT AM I SUPPOSED TO DO WITH IT?
RECYCLE IT INTO A BABY BLANKET FOR ALL I CARE! MY NEXT COSTUME IS GOING TO BE A TRIFLE MORE CONTEMPORARY!
THIS FROM THE SAME GUY WHO DESIGNED THE SCARLET SPIDER OUTFIT?
OUCH!
LOOK, PETE... I SINCERELY WISH YOU AND MARY JANE THE VERY BEST!
HEY--YOU'RE THE ONE WHO'S GONNA NEED THE LUCK!
SEE YOU AROUND, MY FRIEND!
It's OVER!
Finally over!
No more WEB-SWINGING! No more WALL-CRAWLING!
Over!
I'm going to be a PARENT now! It's high time I GREW UP, and started acting like a real ADULT!
Over!
This is my big CHANCE--! I can't blow it!
Mary Jane and I finally have an opportunity to head into the SUNSET... and live HAPPILY EVER AFTER!

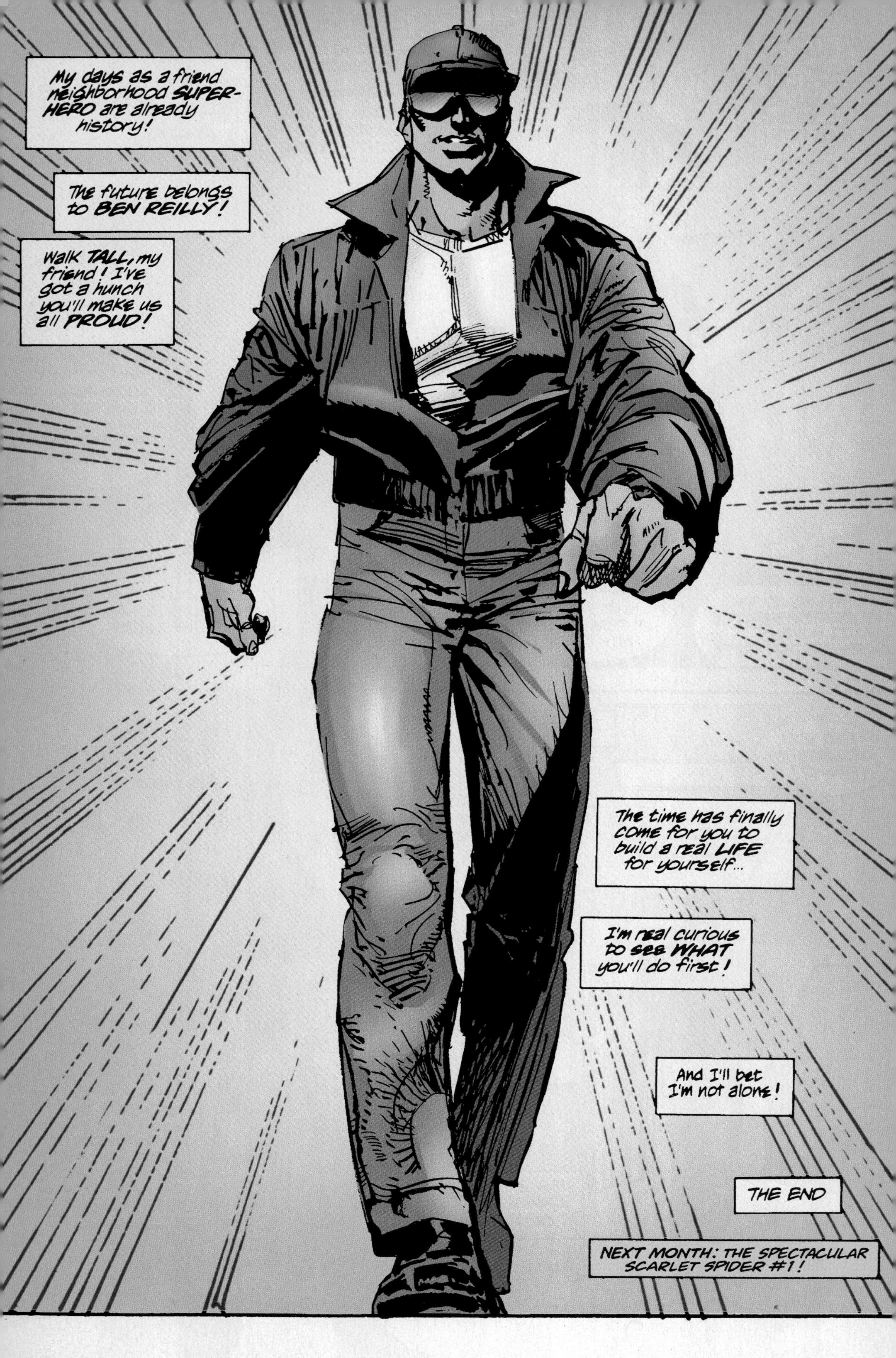
My days as a friend neighborhood SUPER-HERO are already history!
The future belongs to BEN REILLY!
Walk TALL, my friend! I've got a hunch you'll make us all PROUD!
The time has finally come for you to build a real LIFE for yourself...
I'm real curious to see WHAT you'll do first!
And I'll bet I'm not alone!
THE END
NEXT MONTH: THE SPECTACULAR SCARLET SPIDER #1!

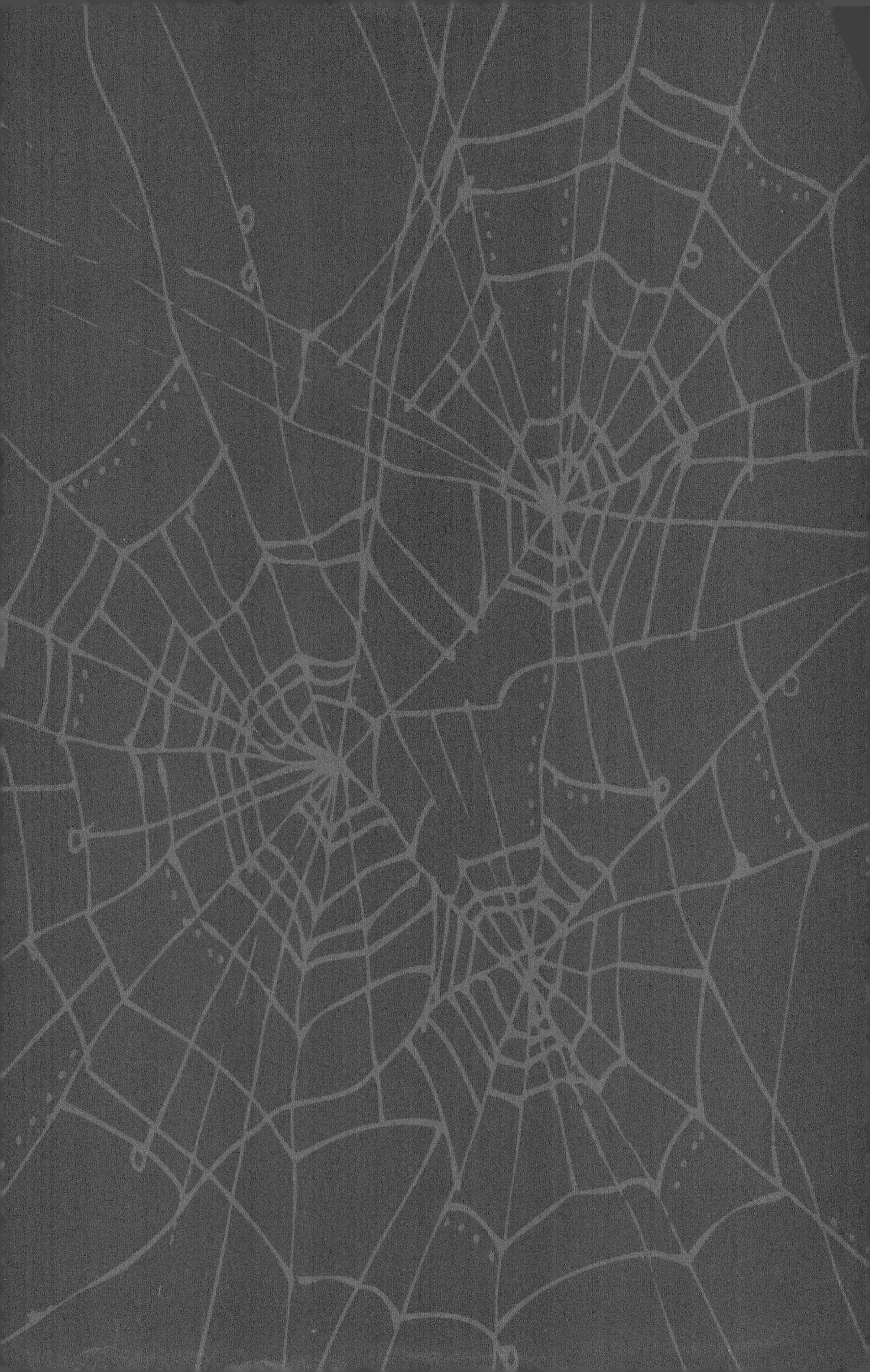

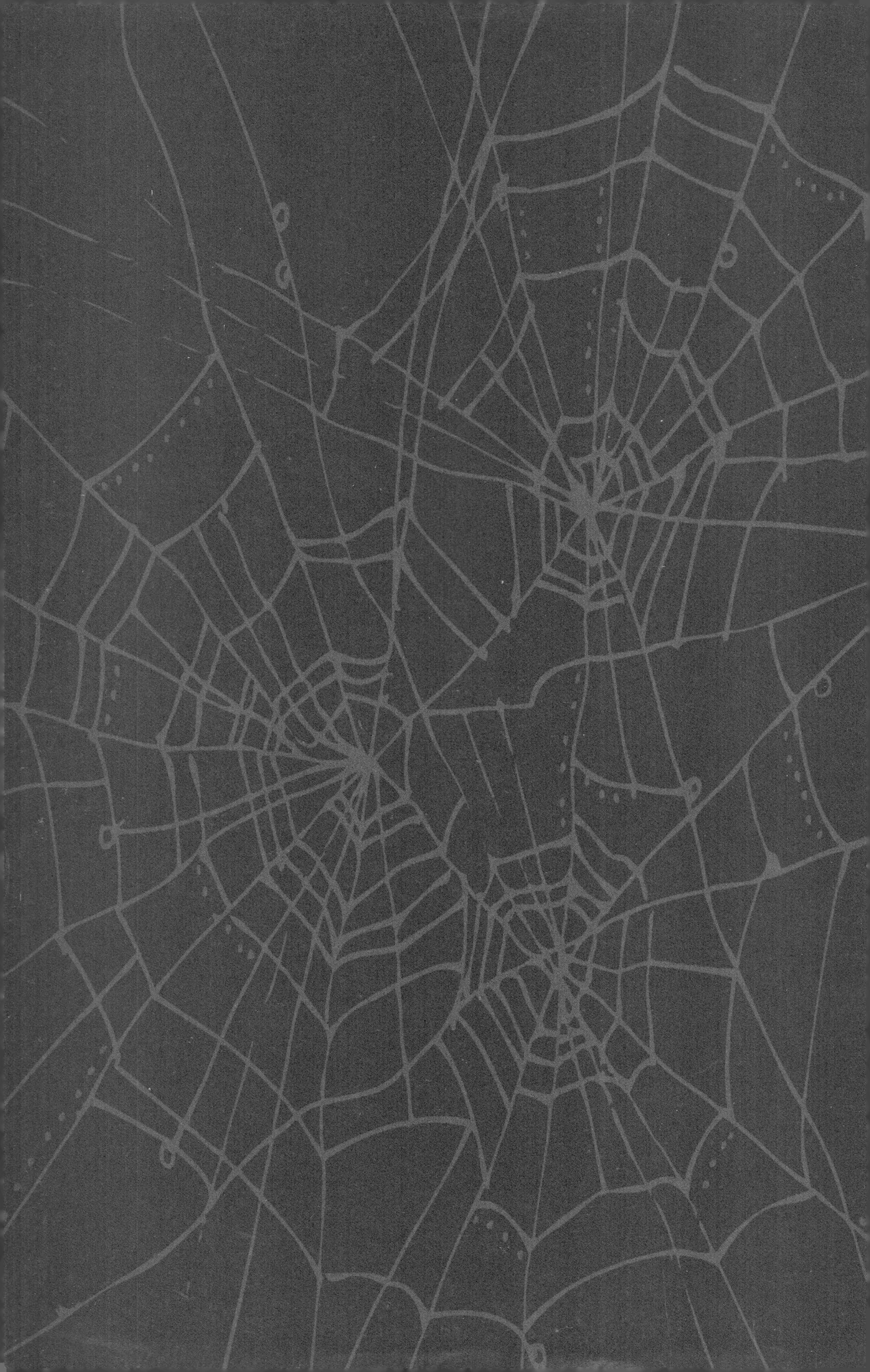